Professional Windows DNA

Christopher Blexrud
Matthew Bortniker
Jonathan Crossland
Dino Esposito
Jason Hales
Whitney Hankison
Vishwanath Honnaya
Tim Huckaby
Slava Kristich
Edward Lee
Rockford Lhotka
Brian Loesgen
Stephen Mohr
Simon Robinson
Ash Rofail
Brad Sherrell
Scott Short
Dan Wahlin

Wrox Press Ltd.

Professional Windows DNA

wrox

Published by Wrox Press Ltd,
Arden House, 1102 Warwick Road, Acocks Green,
Birmingham, B27 6BH, UK
Printed in Canada
ISBN 1-861004-45-1

Trademark Acknowledgements

Credits

Authors
Christopher Blexrud
Matthew Bortniker
Jonathan Crossland
Dino Esposito
Jason Hales
Whitney Hankison
Vishwanath Honnaya
Tim Huckaby
Slava Kristich
Edward Lee
Rockford Lhotka
Brian Loesgen
Stephen Mohr
Simon Robinson
Ash Rofail
Brad Sherrell
Scott Short
Dan Wahlin

Additional Material
Scott Case

Technical Architect
Dev Lunsford

Technical Editors
Catherine Alexander
Gary Evans
Peter Morgan
Dianne Parker
Lisa Stephenson

Category Manager
Dominic Lowe

Author Agents
Sarah Bowers
Sophie Edwards

Project Administrator
Charlotte Smith

Index
Michael Brinkman

Technical Reviewers
Sergey Blyashov
Stuart Brown
Michael Corning
Cristof Falk
James Foster
Mark Goedert
Tony Greening
Rob Howard
Greg Jackson
Stephen Kaufman
Brad Kingsley
Ajoy Krishnamoorthy
Rob MacDonald
Craig McQueen
Todd Meister
Ruth Nantais
J Boyd Nolan
Phil Powers
Simon Robinson
Steve Schofield
Ulrich Schwanitz
Steven A Smith
Kevin Spencer
Blair Taylor
Ruud Voight
Lee Whitney

Production Coordinators
Tom Bartlett
Mark Burdett

Figures
Tom Bartlett
Shabnam Hussain
Robert Stroud

Cover
Shelley Frasier

Proof Readers
Lisa Rutter
Christopher Smith

About the Authors

Christopher Blexrud

Christopher Blexrud, a Microsoft Certified Solution Developer, is a senior consultant from Minneapolis, Minnesota. His main area of expertise resides in the Windows DNA architecture and the components within it. Chris has worked with Wrox on several projects including co-authoring Professional ASP 3.0 as well as writing numerous articles on ASPToday.com. When Chris is not developing business solutions, he enjoys snowmobiling and hunting in northern Minnesota and spending time with family and friends. Chris can be reached at chris@blexonline.net.

Matthew Bortniker

Matthew Bortniker has been in the computer field since 1982. Currently he is an independent consultant for local businesses in the Washington D.C. area and for the U.S. Government. At the moment his main tasks include upgrading client-server applications to enterprise-wide, n-tier systems written entirely in Visual Basic using Microsoft technologies. His main specialty is working with n-tier applications incorporating MTS/COM+, database, and Internet technologies.

Matthew is the author of Professional VB6 MTS Programming, also by Wrox Press, and he has also been extensively involved with other Wrox publications as a technical reviewer. He can be reached at PC_Geek37@hotmail.com.

Acknowledgements

I want to thank all the people at Wrox who helped make this book possible. I want to give special thanks to Dev Lunsford who did an incredible job by keeping this book on track. I would like to thank Sarah Bowers for giving me a chance to work on this book. Thank you to two great editors, Dianne Parker and Gary Evans who provided me with much needed encouragement. Also I would like to thank all the authors who worked on this book. I am honored to be a part of such a great team.

Dedication

I would like to dedicate my work to my family, Ernest, Shirley, Dori, and Jeff (who is like a brother to me); and my loving wife Natalia who encouraged me to stop dreaming and to start writing.

Jonathan Crossland

Jonathan Crossland is a Systems Component Architect at Spotlight Interactive and specializes in distributed n-tier applications for business. Jonathan is currently involved with creating generic components for use within the fleet of business applications he is involved with as well as teaching developers the ways of enterprise development.

Jonathan was previously a musician/songwriter in his teenage years. Having started with writing musical notes he ended up enjoying writing bytes in Assembler instead. Now at the age of 24, he spends most of his time developing in and out of Visual Basic and C++.

Jonathan lives in Cape Town, South Africa with his wife and son, his two horses, three dogs, and three cats.

Acknowledgements

I would just like to thank Wrox for the opportunity to be a part of this book. I have gained valuable experience and enjoyed every minute. I would like to thank my wife, Zita, for her support, and I'd also like to say to Neil, come home buddy...

Dino Esposito

Dino Esposito is a trainer and consultant based in Rome, Italy. He specializes in XML and scripting, and worked for Andersen Consulting focusing on development of web-based applications. Dino is a contributing editor to MSDN Magazine for which he runs the Cutting Edge column. He also contributes regularly to MSDN News, Windows 2000 Magazine, and ASPToday. Get in touch with Dino at dinoe@wrox.com.

Jason Hales

Jason Hales, BSc, is a freelance consultant based in Cambridgeshire, England. He has over 10 years commercial experience in software development focusing primarily on Microsoft development tools with a touch of Oracle. Prior to VB he developed in PowerBuilder, C, and Sybase on UNIX and is a great supporter of OO-based development. He is also President of Digital Tier (www.digitaltier.com) a company formed in January 1995 to promote enterprise-wide scalable Windows and Internet development.

When he's not programming or writing articles, Jason can be found windsurfing (in the summer months only), studying New Scientist magazine, or in the company of his family. His hobbies include weightlifting, cycling, listening to music, and motor sports.

Jason can be contacted by e-mail at jason.hales@digitaltier.com or jason_hales@yahoo.com.

Acknowledgements

Without such an understanding wife this would not have been possible, so I thank her for the never-ending support.

I'd also like to thank Ian Stirk and Mark Greene for their valuable contributions to all things VB/COM.

Finally thanks to Enigma for 'MCMXC A.D.' and Moby for 'Play' – the only music that helped me through the early-morning hours.

Dedication

To my wife, Ann, and our wonderful daughters, Emma and Sophie.

Whitney Hankison

Whitney Hankison is an Financial Systems Analyst working with the County of Santa Barbara in California. She has been working on computer software and hardware since 1984. She holds MCP certification in NT Server and Workstation and is working toward the MCSD certification. She is experienced in system architecture, design, and implementation and also works developing and installing applications related to the accounting disciplines.

Whitney likes playing softball, mountain biking, and playing tennis. She can be reached by e-mail at whankison@earthlink.net.

Vishwanath Honnaya

Vishwanath Honnaya (vish@honnaya.com) is currently working as a Senior e-Commerce Architect for Mercedes-Benz and several other subsidiaries of Daimler Chrysler Corp. He has over eleven years of experience in all facets of project lifecycle development including hands-on development for many Fortune 500 and other large companies such as Microsoft Consulting Services, Digital Equipment Corp., Phillip Morris, Kraftfoods Inc, American Express, Andersen Consulting, and KPMG. He holds a Masters degree in Computer Science and Bachelor degree in Electronics Engineering. He is a Microsoft Certified Solution Developer and teaches Web development for e-Commerce and advanced Windows programming at Fairfield University, CT. He lives in Monroe, CT where he and his wife Raj are anxiously awaiting the arrival of their first child.

Tim Huckaby

Tim Huckaby is President of InterKnowlogy, a software engineering firm dedicated to Enterprise, e-Commerce, B2B, and Windows DNA consulting, application software design, and development on the Internet, extranet, and intranet. As Technical Architect, Software Development Lead, and Microsoft Regional Director and member of the Microsoft Commerce Advisory Council, Tim Huckaby brings over 20 years of industry experience. Tim has worked on web-based projects for such clients as Microsoft, Pacific Life Insurance Company, Gateway, Mobile Planet, SkyMall, Kingston Technology, Cooking.com, and the United States Navy as a Developer, Architect and Technical Lead. Tim continues to be involved in a number of books as an author for Wrox Press, continues to write for a number of magazines, and does many speaking events around the world for Microsoft and others.

Slava Khristich

Slava works as a Software Engineer at Stellcom Inc., one of the leading software consulting firms in San Diego. Slava is usually involved in the development of the most challenging projects at Stellcom, with most experience in the areas of n-tier application development and COM (Visual Basic 6.0). Slava teaches VB and VBScript classes at the Advanced Institute of Technology in San Diego, and enjoys playing soccer and surfing.

Acknowledgements

I would like to thank Ivo Stoyanoff and Sergey Blyashov at Stellcom and my family for supporting my long working hours.

elikinfo@consultant.com

Edward Lee

Ed Lee is the Vice President of Development at netEXE, Inc., where he oversees the development of wireless applications for hand-held devices. Prior to working with netEXE, Ed worked with a Fortune 100 financial services company, where he designed and developed systems to facilitate secure web-based storage and maintenance of highly sensitive financial information. Ed holds a BS and an MBA from Brigham Young University. He also holds MCSD, MCSE, and Sun Certified Java Programmer certifications.

Rockford Lhotka

Rockford Lhotka is the author of 'Visual Basic 6 Distributed Objects' and 'Visual Basic 6 Business Objects' published by Wrox Press and is a contributing author for Visual Basic Programmers Journal and DevX. He has presented at numerous conferences including Microsoft Tech Ed and VBITS. He has over 13 years experience in software development and has worked on many projects in various roles, including software architecture, design and development, network administration, and project management. Rockford is the Principal Technology Evangelist for Magenic Technologies, one of America's premiere Microsoft Certified Solution Providers dedicated to solving today's most challenging business problems using 100% Microsoft tools and technology.

Brian Loesgen

Brian Loesgen is a Principal Engineer at San Diego-based Stellcom Inc., a leader in end-to-end e-commerce, Internet, and wireless solutions. At Stellcom, Brian is involved in some of the most advanced web application development projects being built today. Brian has spoken at numerous technical conferences worldwide, and has been known to seize every opportunity possible to promote new technologies. He enjoys playing with 'bleeding edge' software and translating those new technologies into real-world benefits.

In his spare moments, Brian enjoys outdoor activities such as cycling, hiking in the mountains, camping in the desert, or going to the beach with his wife Miriam and children Steven and Melissa.

Brian can be reached at `bloesgen@msn.com`.

Stephen Mohr

Stephen Mohr is a software systems architect with Omicron Consulting, Philadelphia, USA. He has more than ten years' experience working with a variety of platforms and component technologies. His research interests include distributed computing and artificial intelligence. Stephen holds BS and MS degrees in computer science from Rensselaer Polytechnic Institute.

Simon Robinson

Simon Robinson lives in Lancaster, in the UK, where he shares a house with some students. He first encountered serious programming when he was doing his PhD in physics, modelling all sorts of weird things to do with superconductors and quantum mechanics. The experience of programming was nearly enough to put him off computers for life (though oddly, he seems to have survived all the quantum mechanics), and he tried for a while being a sports massage therapist instead. But then he realised how much money was in computers and wasn't in sports massage and rapidly got a job as a C++ programmer/researcher instead. (Simon is clearly the charitable, deep, spiritual type, who understands the true meaning of life.)

His programming work eventually lead him into writing, and he now makes a living mostly writing great books for programmers. He is also an honorary research associate at Lancaster University, where he does research in computational fluid dynamics with the environmental science department. You can visit Simon's web site at `http://www.SimonRobinson.com`.

Ash Rofail

Ash Rofail is Chief Technology Officer of UTA Group, an e-Services firm of over 1000 IT professionals located in Northern Virginia, focusing on delivering User-Centric e-Business Soltutions. Ash is a contributing author for VBPJ and Senior Technical Reviewer. He is the author several books on COM(+) and XML. When not writing articles, presenting at conferences, or heading UTA's technical direction he teaches at the George Washington University in Washington DC.

You can reach Ash at Rofaila@utanet.com.

Brad Sherrell

Brad is the Director of Information Technology for the Life Insurance Division of Pacific Life Insurance Company, the second leading seller of life insurance in the United States. In his current role, Brad is responsible for Enterprise Architecture and all IT planning and strategy. Brad specializes in application architecture using Microsoft technologies. Brad is also a lecturer at the University of California, Irvine where he teaches Visual Basic programming and application architecture to some of the brightest undergraduates in the country. Brad lives in San Clemente, California, with his wife Christy and their son Justin. He would like to thank his wife and son for putting up with him during another authoring adventure.

Scott Short

Scott Short is a consultant with Microsoft Consulting Services. He works mostly with dot-com and telecommunications companies helping them architect scalable, available, and maintainable component-based web applications. Before joining Microsoft, he was a software developer for JD Edwards and MCI. When not working with the latest beta software, writing, or presenting at developer conferences, Scott enjoys spending time in the Colorado Rocky Mountains skiing, backpacking, hiking, and rock climbing with his incredibly supportive wife, Suzanne.

Dan Wahlin

Dan Wahlin is Director of Internet/Wireless Application Development for netEXE, Inc. and also works as a corporate trainer for Global Knowledge. He has previously worked in the technology environment as an Enterprise Web Site Manager and Senior Consultant for a global systems integrator. Dan's current endeavors include working with several Microsoft technologies including SQL Server, ASP, Visual Basic, and COM/COM+. He also spends a lot of time syncing up a variety of distributed backend systems using XML, XSLT, and SOAP. Aside from his normal daily work routine, Dan enjoys experimenting with C# and ASP+ on Microsoft's new .NET platform.

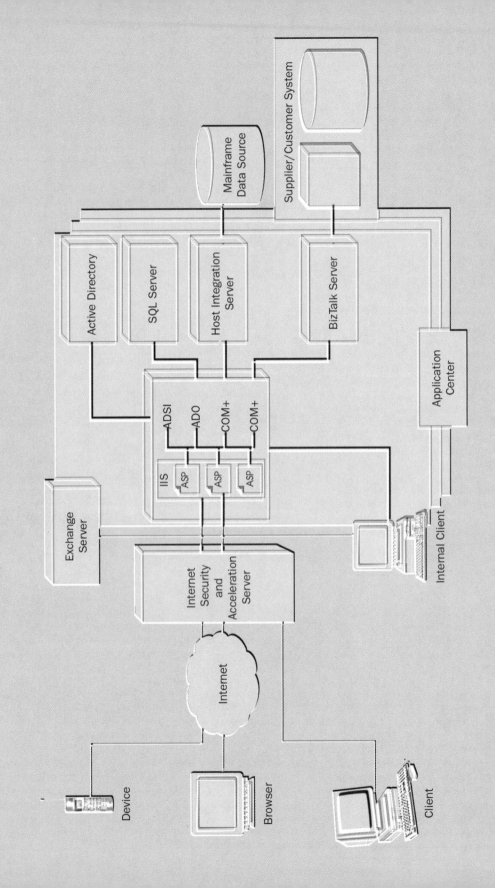

Table of Contents

Table of Contents

Table of Contents

Table of Contents

Table of Contents

Table of Contents

Table of Contents

Table of Contents

Table of Contents

xvi

Table of Contents

Table of Contents

Table of Contents

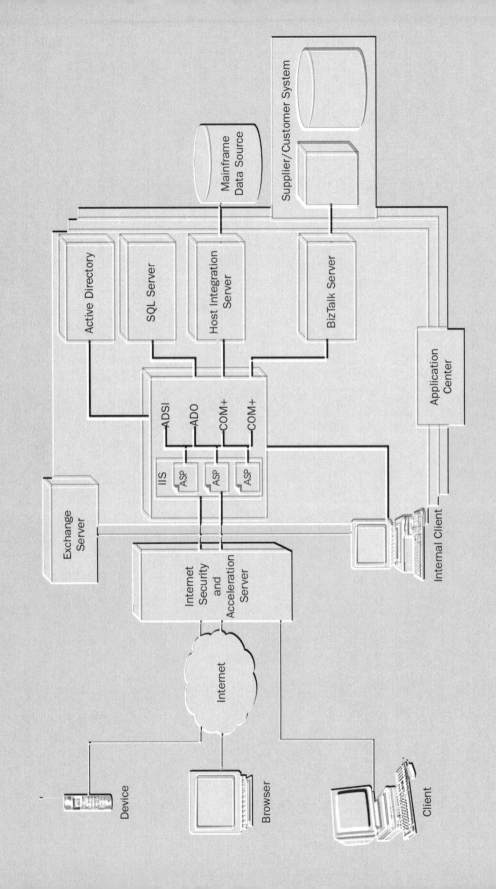

Introduction

The world of Windows-based distributed programming is one that's always in a state of flux. New technologies are always being released, and new ways of looking at the big picture are continually being introduced. While this book was being developed, the architecture formerly known as DNA 2000 was a fairly recent announcement. The original design aims of this book were to comprehensively overview the whole DNA 2000 structure, that is, Windows 2000 and all its inherent services. These include COM+ component-based business objects, universal data access, a range of clients, and the support of the new 2000-series Enterprise Server family.

In July 2000, the Microsoft Professional Developers Conference brought the announcement of a new architecture: .NET. All trace of the DNA 2000 name was eradicated. DNA still exists, since .NET is, at the time of writing, a long way away. Also, there may be a time gap after its release before you start using it. So you'll probably find yourself developing on the DNA architecture while you're waiting for .NET to kick off. Throughout this book, we'll continue to use the term DNA for what we're describing. We'll specifically be covering the more modern flavor of DNA, since the term's been around for a couple of years already.

That means that we'll be talking exclusively about DNA on the Windows 2000 operating system, which contains a great many services that enhance your programming capabilities. We won't, however, be talking about the Enterprise Servers (BizTalk, Exchange 2000, and so on) in any depth – that's another book. At the time of writing there was little or no concrete information to reveal. You'll see in Chapter 2 that they will sit nicely in your DNA architecture if you have need of them, but the plans are to integrate them fully into the .NET platform and not 'officially' call them part of DNA. Thus, we've left them out of this book. Here, we'll just discuss the things that make DNA what it is, and the issues you'll face when developing enterprise applications on the Windows 2000 platform.

As you'd imagine, DNA is an enormous topic, so rather than trying and failing to get into detail on all the component parts (if you'll excuse the pun) of DNA, we'll be concentrating on helping you to see where everything fits in the big picture, and whether you need to pursue each topic in greater depth. That way, if after reading a chapter on, say, COM+ Events, you decide that they wouldn't benefit you any further, you can leave the topic alone. Or you could decide that finding out what COM+ Events do was the single most significant event (sorry) of your development career, and you want to know all about them. Most likely, you'll be somewhere healthily in between those extremes, but you get the picture.

Who is This Book For?

This book is for professional developers who want to see the big picture of DNA development. DNA conceptually contains a lot of technologies that you can use to construct your applications. You may use all of them, or just a subset of them. We're aiming to give you an overview of these main technologies in DNA, in such a way as to enable you to make further decisions about whether each technology would benefit you.

We've assumed a decent level of programming knowledge, specifically in VB and ASP, because typically if you need to know about the DNA architecture you'll be a professional programmer. We aren't expecting you to necessarily know both, though. You should be able to follow what's going on in any case, and see how what you do know fits into the big picture. As such, we won't really be worrying about showing you how to do cool things with ASP and VB so much as letting you know how everything fits into the bigger picture of application development. Of the two, you'll also find a slant towards VB simply because of the amount of COM+ we cover.

What's Covered in This Book

This book is divided into five main sections, with the material split across the conceptual tiers of an application:

❑ **Introduction** – In this section, we first introduce the problems that the DNA architecture was designed to overcome, and then look at DNA to see how it solves these problems.

❑ **Business Layer** – Here we look into COM, distributed processing, and COM+, including transactions, events, and queuing. We'll also see how to create business objects and take a brief look at SOAP.

❑ **Data Layer** – This section introduces UDA and looks at the role of SQL Server 2000 (yes, I know we said no Enterprise Servers...). We also look at Directory Services.

❑ **Presentation Layer** – This section describes the DNA approach to the presentation layer, and then goes into detail about programming a Win32 front end and how to use Office in your presentation layer.

❑ **Application-Level Issues** – Now we turn our attention to some issues that affect the application as a whole: scalability, security, and debugging.

❑ **Case Studies** – We round off the book with a series of case studies that show DNA development in some real detail. As we've said, we've had to take a pretty high-level overview approach to DNA, so here's a chance to see more of how it can be applied to your actual applications.

The appendices include a listing of further reading references, since you'll almost certainly have discovered a number of things over the course of this book that you'll want to pursue in greater depth. We've included links to web articles and other books that you might like to look into (including the occasional non-Wrox publication). Understandably, with so many disparate subjects covered in the book, we'd need to include reference appendices on everything from HTML to C++. This would lead to a very fat and strange volume, so we've opted for the other extreme of not including any reference material.

There's also an appendix that describes how to get the most out of our support network, by sending feedback or questions either to our support group or to our p2p discussion forums. If you have any questions relating to this book, you should refer to this appendix to make yourself heard.

What You Need to Use This Book

Listed below is a summary of the main tools you'll need to try out the code examples:

- ❑ Windows 2000.
- ❑ Visual Studio 6.0. Most of the examples are based on Visual Basic, so you could get away with just having VB, but there are some C++ examples as well on occasion.

Also optionally for certain chapters, you may need:

- ❑ Site Server 3.0 with Service Pack 4.
- ❑ SQL Server 2000.
- ❑ Certificate Server.
- ❑ Microsoft Office.

All source code from the book is available for download from: `http://www.wrox.com`.

Conventions

To help you get the most from the text and keep track of what's happening, we've used a number of conventions throughout the book.

For instance:

> **These boxes hold important, not-to-be forgotten information that is directly relevant to the surrounding text.**

...while this background style is used for asides to the current discussion.

As for styles within the text:

- ❑ When we introduce them, we **highlight** important words.
- ❑ We show keyboard strokes like this: *Ctrl-A*.
- ❑ We show filenames and code within the text like so: `CalculatePrice()`
- ❑ Text on user interfaces is shown as: Menu.

We present code like this:

```
In our code examples, the code foreground style shows new, important,
    pertinent code...
...while code background shows code that's less important in the present
    context, or has been seen before.
```

3

Online discussion at http://p2p.wrox.com

1

Why Do We Need DNA?

Windows DNA is a platform for building distributed applications using the Microsoft Windows operating system and related software products. That statement leaves a considerable amount of room for confusion. What is a "platform"? What are "related products"? Even the term **distributed computing** has been given various definitions.

It's worth the effort to sort out the confusion because multi-tier architectures like DNA are widely regarded as the future of large-scale development. As we will see in this chapter, such architectures offer significant benefits in the construction of mission-critical and enterprise-scale systems. This book will introduce and overview, just about everything you want to know about building modern, forward-looking applications for Windows. The **Windows DNA** architecture is a blueprint and set of guidelines for doing this.

Before we can begin, however, we need to examine a few concepts. When we talk about **modern applications**, we are almost always talking about network applications. It's rare to develop an application today that does not either make use of distributed resources or incorporate technologies developed for the Web. Even standalone desktop applications make use of techniques and technologies influenced by distributed programming, such as data source abstraction and component development.

In this chapter, we'll look at:

❑　The nature of modern, networked applications, and a brief review of the history that brought us to the current state of software development

❑　What we want to get out of an application, and the inherent problems we need to overcome when designing distributed applications

❑　The goals that Windows DNA is designed to tackle over and above other architectures

Before we embark on our voyage through Windows DNA, let's examine the nature and needs of a modern application. Building such applications is what Windows DNA is about.

Internet Application Design

In case you haven't noticed, most of the new software development taking place today centers around delivering functionality via the Internet. What does the typical Internet-based application look like today?

There really is no single answer to that question. There are so many types of business solutions being built using Internet technology that there are probably thousands of different types of Internet-based applications. However, there is one question we can probably answer: what are the basic characteristics of these applications?

Internet Application Requirements

In general, an Internet-based application will:

❑ Present a unified view of data from multiple data sources

❑ Allow a user to update data

❑ Provide full e-commerce capabilities

❑ Be fast

❑ Be scalable to thousands of concurrent users

Now let's take a look at each of these characteristics in a little more detail.

Presenting a Unified View of Data From Multiple Data Sources

Presenting a unified view of data coming from multiple sources creates a number of problems. A lot of businesses have multiple types of data stores, ranging from mainframe-based VSAM applications, to SQL Server databases, to Oracle databases, to e-mail stores and directory services. There needs to be a way to "tie" all of this data together. So obviously we are going to need a robust data access mechanism, which allows us to access multiple types of data sources that might even reside on different platforms. In addition, we might need host, or mainframe, integration capability. Just getting data from a mainframe application to a web page is a huge technical feat.

Allowing a User to Update Data

If our application allows a user to purchase something, or initiate financial transactions, or update personal data, we're going to need transactional capability. By having transactional capability, we need to somehow make certain that either all parts of a piece of work, or transaction, complete successfully or none of the transaction is allowed to occur.

To make matters more complicated, we already know that the likelihood of having data in multiple sources is fairly high. The consequence is we will need the ability to define transactions that span multiple data sources, while still having full two-phase commit and rollback.

Full e-Commerce Capabilities

Providing full e-commerce capability is a must these days. If you're selling products over the Internet, you will need a framework that provides a shopping cart, and management tools to manage product catalogs, run promotions and sales, and present cross-selling opportunities to your users. Additionally, you will need this framework to be extensible so you can incorporate your own business logic, such as calculating taxes in foreign countries. It would also be really nice if this e-commerce framework used the same transactional capability described above when users commit their purchases.

Fast

You might get users to your web site the first time, but if your site is so slow that they have a bad user experience, they might never come back. So you're going to need to be able to architect a solution that solves your business problem, but is fast at the same time.

Being able to distribute requests among many machines is one way to help achieve a speedy solution. Other design characteristics, such as performing work asynchronously, can also help speed up things.

An example, albeit a crude one, might be an online purchasing application. When a user actually places an order, they probably don't need any kind of response other than "we received your order, here is your confirmation number". You could then place the order on a queue and process it later. The user doesn't know their order won't be processed until later, but they've got the result they wanted quickly.

The implication here is that you'll need a queuing or messaging mechanism at your disposal, so you can incorporate it into your application design.

Scalable to Thousands of Concurrent Users

Not only does your site need to be fast, it probably needs to support thousands of concurrent users. Again, load balancing across multiple machines will help solve this problem. Not only will load balancing help you handle more users, it will also improve your "uptime", and help ensure you are running 24x7x365 like all users expect these days.

Platform Capability Requirements

So now you have a better picture of some characteristics of applications being built today. There's obviously a lot of infrastructure needed to build these applications. What we can do now is take these characteristics, and from them create a list of the capabilities we're going to need from our platform. These include:

- ❑ A web server
- ❑ Transaction processing and object brokering
- ❑ Message queuing
- ❑ A data access mechanism
- ❑ Security
- ❑ Load balancing capabilities

We'll see later in the book that Windows 2000 provides these, but that's jumping the gun a little. We should probably turn our attention first to identifying the things that drive us when designing applications.

Application Design Goals

For most Internet-based applications you can usually identify two sets of goals:

- ❑ **Business Goals:**
  - ❑ Faster time to market
  - ❑ Low cost

❑ **Architecture Goals:**

    ❑   Interoperability

    ❑   Adaptability

Obviously, these are traits we would like for any type of application. You're probably thinking to yourself that these are common sense – so what's the big deal?

Look at the demands being placed on application developers today, and the software they write. These goals are no longer just *expected* – they are *demanded*. This fast-paced, Internet economy has turned loose a whole new group of users. These users are not just people in the cubes down the hall – they are your customers!

These folks don't understand, nor do they care, how hard it is to write Internet software that integrates with all of the other systems in your company. They don't care that we work 18 hours a day to meet our deadlines. They don't care that some of us have invested millions of dollars in developing mainframe-based software using 25+-year-old technology, and we need to make our web servers talk to it! These users want to be able to do everything with a click of the mouse instead of talking to a person on the telephone. They want all of the functionality currently available via phone and paper to be available on the company web site, and they want it now!

Whew! The world of the software application developer has changed drastically over the last 5 years. Once the Internet burst onto the scene, and we started developing applications that were being used by people outside the walls of our companies, the pressure was turned up substantially. Couple all of those demands with the fact that these people want all of this available to them all day, every day, and it appears that we as software developers are in big trouble.

Let's take a moment to look at some of the goals in more detail:

❑ **Faster time to market** – why build it if you can buy it? If you're a software developer in this Internet world, this should be the first question you ask yourself on a daily basis. Time is too precious to be spent building infrastructure or functionality you can buy off the shelf. You need to spend the majority of your time solving the business problem at hand, and not worrying about how to build infrastructure such as a transaction-processing monitor. Do you get the idea?

❑ **Low cost** – whether you're working at a newly formed dot-com company or a Fortune 500 corporation, cost will always be an issue. The question we asked earlier, "Why build it if you can buy it?" should have a cost element attached to it. The next question you probably need to ask is "How much will it cost to buy this infrastructure?" Wouldn't it be nice if you could get as much infrastructure as possible from the operating system? In other words, if you pay good money for an operating system, wouldn't it be nice to inherit a great deal of functionality without paying extra for it?

Not only is it cheaper to buy infrastructure, the people signing your paycheck are going to be happier if you spend your time solving business problems instead of unnecessarily building infrastructure.

❑ **Interoperability** – unless you're working at a brand new company with no computer systems at all, you're going to need to make more than one piece of software "talk" to another piece of software. As stated earlier, you're going to have to integrate systems that reside on multiple platforms, and present a unified view of data to an end user. From an architecture standpoint, we need to be able to produce a set of services that allow us to integrate disparate computer systems on disparate platforms, whether it be the mainframe, UNIX, AS400, etc.

Instead of reworking existing systems so they can be used on the Internet, we want to leverage existing investments in these existing systems. We can also take advantage of software that is created for a special purpose, such as accounting software or bill-processing software, and just build an interface to "talk" to it.

❑ **Adaptability** – the world is moving pretty fast these days and the pace of business is keeping up with it. Just when you think you have done a good job of gathering requirements and turning them into functional specifications, the situation changes. The software we write today has to be able to be changed quickly to meet rapidly changing requirements, and take advantage of opportunities when they arise. If you are reading this book, you probably agree with the concept of n-tier architecture or a component-based architecture. We need an architecture and a platform that allows us to take an application and separate it into tiers, or layers, of functionality. Where have you heard that before?

Now that we've looked at our own common application design goals, we're going to examine some of the problems inherent in designing network applications, and then go on to see how architecture has evolved to try to solve these problems.

Network Applications

If you had to pick a single concept to represent Windows DNA, "network applications" would be the one you'd pick. Any single technology in Windows DNA can be applied to specific problems or features, but taken together, the tools that make up the DNA architecture are all about applications that live on, use, or are accessed by networks.

> **Formally speaking, we'll define** network applications **as software applications that require or substantially benefit from the presence of networked computers.**

You could run a multi-user database (like SQL Server) or a directory service without a network, but what would be the point? Web-based applications effectively require a network.

Breaking applications into their functional pieces and deploying them across a network lets us make the best possible use of an organization's resources. Once you do this, however, you become reliant on the network for the full use of your applications. This implies requirements for reliability, scalability, and security, and soon you realize you need a well-planned architecture. In our case, that's Windows DNA. It's about adopting network applications as the future of general purpose computing, then developing an architecture that supports them.

The definition of network applications given above is rather vague. You probably know what is meant intuitively, but intuition doesn't go very far in programming. So let's look at the characteristic problems that network applications will need to deal with.

Network Application Characteristics

We've just said that network applications break their implementation into functional modules and rely on (or at least substantially benefit from) the presence of a network of computers. Some characteristics follow from that:

❑ Communications

❑ Concurrent usage

❑ State management

❑ Latency

❑ Rigorous encapsulation

Let's look at these in more detail.

Communications

The first point is essentially a given one – if my applications work through a network, they must have some means of communication. However, as we'll see in a little while, communications can become a deep topic. There are issues of protocols and data formats that arise in network applications. Simply running a cable between two computers and configuring them for the network is the easy part. Life for the application programmer can get very interesting.

While you may not actually have to worry about the detailed implementation of network communications, you must be concerned with the issues that arise when applications span multiple computers.

Concurrent Usage

You could deploy network applications in a single user manner. You might insist that every client be matched with an individual server, or you might have a multi-user server that forced clients to wait for service in series. This would simplify the programming task, but it would also negate many of the benefits of using networks in the first place. We want applications to dynamically access some bit of software on the network, obtain service, and go about the rest of their processing. Forcing them through the iron gates of single-use software would mean incurring all the overhead of distributed processing while also incurring the limitations of standalone software. You'd feel cheated, wouldn't you?

Even if you don't develop multi-user software, you rely on concurrent access to system services and network servers. I can write a web page with single-user client-side script, but I want the web server it accesses to be able to accommodate multiple users at the same time. Could you imagine a corporate database application denying a user service because one other user somewhere in the organization was already connected?

Some part of a network application, then, must handle the tough tasks of concurrent access. These include multithreading, concurrency, and integrity. **Multithreading** is what enables a single piece of software to have more than one task underway in a program at any given time. **Concurrency** is what keeps one task distinct from another. Most importantly, concurrency concerns itself with how to maintain the **integrity** of the data or process, when different users want to modify the same bit of information.

State Management

State management is closely related to concurrency. Technically, this is another facet of concurrency, but we'll consider it as a characteristic in its own right because this is a topic that almost all programmers will encounter when writing network applications.

If an application is using other applications or components on the network, it must keep track of where it is in the process – the **state** of the process. Single-user, standalone applications find it easy to maintain state. The value of the variables is the state of your data, while the line of code that is currently executing defines where you are in the overall process.

Multiuser, distributed applications have it harder. Suppose I have an e-commerce web site whose implementation involves sending a message to another application and receiving a reply. I have to maintain a set of data for each user. When I send a message, I have to record where that particular user is in the overall process, together with the current state of that user's data. When a reply comes in, I have to be able to determine which user is affected by the reply and retrieve the data I saved.

If you've worked with the `Session` and `Application` objects in Active Server Pages, you've programmed state management information. You've told the ASP component to keep track of something you'll need again later. The more widely distributed you make your application, the more state information needs to be coordinated. It's best to try to minimize state information on remote servers using a **stateless** server model, which we'll see a little more about later in the book.

Latency

How long does it take to communicate with other components on the network? The time attributed solely to the network is the **network latency** of the application.

This would seem to be too small to worry about at first glance. How fast are electrons in a wire? It turns out that for practical purposes, the speed of electrons in copper wire is slightly less than the speed of light. A good rule of thumb is 200 meters per microsecond.

Surely that's good enough, you might say. In a standalone application, though, the time to access a function might be a fraction of a millisecond. Now measure the path through your network – seldom a straight line on a LAN – and multiply by two. Add the time imposed by routers or switches, and you find that networks have latency that is significant compared to the time to execute instructions within a component.

Latency is especially important for Internet applications. The distance alone is significant. A round trip across the United States should take, in theory, 50 milliseconds. But that's a direct hop. When I send a packet from Philadelphia to a particular server in San Francisco, I find that it takes almost three times as long to get there and back. My packet is bouncing around my service provider, then heading south to the major interconnect MAE East in Virginia, then making its way across country. Each router or switch takes its toll along the way.

This is an extreme case, but even crossing the office is more expensive than moving between addresses in a single computer's memory. Programmers and architects need to consider how they can minimize the number of times their systems need to call on a remote server if they want to maintain acceptable performance. Latency changes the way we design applications.

Rigorous Encapsulation

Encapsulation is a technique in which you hide – or encapsulate – the details of some implementation from some software using that implementation. Object oriented programming is a classic example of encapsulation. An application using an object has no idea how the object maintains its data or implements its methods. Structured programming, the traditional function-by-function method of building an application, may also practice encapsulation by hiding the implementation details of a subroutine from the main program. A programming Application Programming Interface (API) is an encapsulation.

In a standalone application, encapsulation was a good idea. It helped programmers develop and maintain software effectively and efficiently. Network applications have no choice but to practice rigorous encapsulation – different programming teams may write the components of a network application. One team may not have any influence over another, or even know who wrote the component.

If I were to write a shipping application that relied on information from the Federal Express tracking application on the Web, for example, I would have no choice but to use their application using their HTTP-based API, as I have no other access to the application. Certainly, I cannot call Federal Express and ask them to make some internal modifications for me. Network applications live and die by clean interfaces, behind which implementation details are encapsulated.

We're now going to take a possibly familiar trip down memory lane, tracing the history of applications from monoliths to component-based distributed applications. You may have seen it before, but it's still necessary to discuss this because it's central to DNA's concept.

Evolution of Network Applications

The earliest computer applications – and many of the applications still in use – were **monolithic**. All the logic and resources needed to accomplish an entire programming task were found in one program executing on a single computer. There was neither need nor provision for a network.

As computer science evolved in its capabilities, the desirability of the **client-server** model became evident. Clients would obtain critical services, either data or computing, from server software that usually resided on another computer. As networks approach ubiquity, though, the advantages and challenges of distributed computing emerge. The basic model for addressing the challenges is variously called the **3-tier** or **n-tier** model. These models of computing did not spring out of a vacuum. Rather, each evolved from its predecessor as the challenges of the old model were solved, thereby uncovering new challenges.

Monolithic Applications

Monolithic applications are a bit like rocks. Everything you need to make a rock is found inside the rock, indivisible from all other parts and invisible to an outside observer. Similarly, a monolithic application is what you get when you write a program that does not rely on outside resources and cannot access or offer services to other applications in a dynamic and co-operative manner. Clearly, even a simple application has some I/O – keyboard input, reading and writing disk files – but basically, these applications rely strictly on local resources. They read and write data locally, and all logical operations are embedded in a single executable program.

In many ways, this simplifies the life of an application programmer. The program runs on one operating system, so the entire program has access to the same set of services. It executes wholly on one computer, so connectivity isn't an issue. The program runs or it doesn't; if it runs out of resources, it declares a failure and exits (gracefully, one hopes).

Security is simple, as well. There is one user at a time, and his identity is either known to the application or is unimportant to the execution of the program.

Finally, the program can use native formats, as the data never leaves home. Not only are the data structures consistent and known throughout the application, but also the underlying system representations – the size and bit ordering of primitives like integers – are consistent, because the program is only concerned with a single platform.

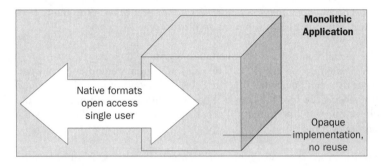

The very strength of a monolithic application – its unity – becomes a weakness as the scope of the programming task increases. Everything must be implemented within the single application. There is little or no reuse of clever and well-tested utilities. The program cannot defer a challenging task to a more powerful computer. All the data it needs must be local. Monolithic applications are ideal for simple tasks, but they simply are not up to handling complicated or mission-critical jobs.

Somewhere along the way, theorists began to address the reuse problem. This was to be the strong point of object oriented programming. Functions and features would be implemented and tested once in well-encapsulated entities, then reused whenever the same problem came up.

Unfortunately, the level of reuse was at the level of source code, or, in the case of precompiled object libraries, at the link level. A body of code could be reused, but once added to an application, it was not visible to outside applications. Within the big, opaque block of the monolithic application, the pieces of the application became co-operative. From the outside, however, the application looked the same. From a distributed perspective, programs built from objects were still monolithic.

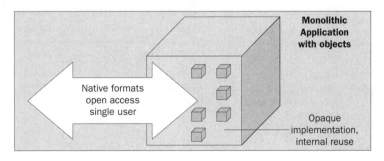

The Road to Client-Server

The relational database community made the advantages of the client-server model apparent. Any database is inherently a centralized resource. All users must have the same view of the data they are permitted to see, which implies that they are all reading from and writing to the same database. If multiple users have access to the same body of data, then the data must reside on a central server accessible via a network. Several advantages become apparent when moving to client-server:

- ❑ Comparatively expensive yet powerful hardware may be used on the server for reliability and availability

- ❑ Client resources may be minimized, as the implementation of transactions and queries resides on the server and is accessed through a relatively thin client interface library

- ❑ Rules for data integrity may be enforced on the server, avoiding the potential for differing rules being implemented in different applications

The last point is especially important. While data integrity is the major concern for relational databases, any sort of business rule may be enforced. The rules are implemented and enforced by the entity managing the data, so it can guarantee that the rules are always enforced and data remains secure or business rules are always observed. Because there is a single, central implementation, there is no chance for application developers to implement different rules that could conflict, and which will certainly lead to data corruption over time.

In the illustration below, we see how application architecture evolved from monolithic applications. The client, represented by the cube on the left, is granted access to data hosted by a server. Access is subject to permissions in the server's **access control list** (ACL) for the user, and access is made through a set of API calls that collectively define the interface to the database. Access is not entirely encapsulated, however. The interface is specific to the vendor of the server application, and native data formats are used:

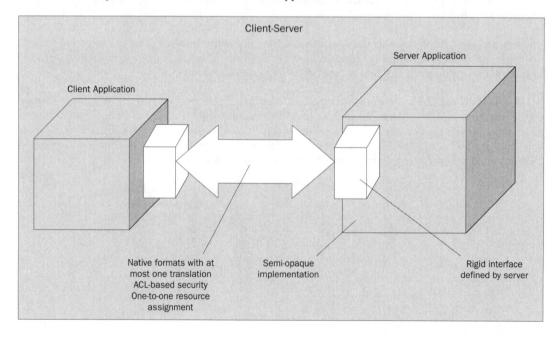

Now consider what changes result from moving from a monolithic model to a client-server model. The challenge of connectivity immediately arises (except, of course, where the client-server model is used for logical purposes only, and both client and server reside on the same machine).

It may not be obvious, but attention must be paid to differing data formats. It's not uncommon, for example, to host a large database on a Unix-based server, but access it from Windows clients. As a result, the interface libraries for clients and servers must provide for translation between different data representations. In practice, this is not so burdensome as might be imagined. The server software vendor typically writes both sides of the libraries. Even when a third party writes database drivers, they are writing to the server vendor's structures. Data translation, then, is restricted primarily to coping with platform differences.

Standards like SQL (Structured Query Language) muddy this distinction somewhat, as vendors may have internal structures that must be mapped to SQL structures and types. For our purposes, however, the abstraction between the standards layer and the vendor layer means that the application programmer is concerned with a single translation, from application-native formats to the server formats exposed at the interface.

Security and resource utilization are tightly bound to the number and identity of the clients. This is good for security, as very specific permissions may be granted for each user. The database can maintain very accurate audit trails of what user performed what transaction. For large numbers of users, of course, this means very long ACLs. This brings us to resource utilization. Each client actively using the server consumes resources: connections, session memory, transactions, etc. The database scales exactly as the client load scales. This is suitable for workgroup and department level applications, but not suitable for exposing a critical database to an entire enterprise. Some means of pooling resources must be devised.

From the standpoint of reuse, the client-server model makes only modest gains. Reuse is confined to a single service and the interface to that service. A client accessing more than one server must support as many interfaces (to include interface code and data formats) as there are servers. In practice, that means the client computer must have drivers installed and configured for each database it plans to access. The server is the smallest unit of reuse. If there is a smaller module that provides useful features, it is lost to networked clients.

n-Tier Architecture

The notion of separating clients from servers, though, provided programmers a great service. No longer were they tied to the resources of a single machine for the accomplishment of their tasks. Resources and implementations could be moved to the computer that best accomplished the task. In fact, as database applications grew in complexity, it became apparent that multiple classes of servers would be needed.

Relational databases implemented the ability to perform processing so that database administrators could implement data integrity rules. Triggers and stored procedures began to look like small programs in their own right. At some point, it became obvious that databases were implementing more processing than was strictly necessary for data integrity. They were implementing **business rules**: units of processing or algorithms that represent some concept of importance to the organization using the database. This might consist of how discounts are calculated, for example.

Because business rules are broadly applicable, it's desirable to implement them once, on a centrally managed server. Since they are not directly related to data integrity, however, it's not clear that they should be implemented on a relational database using data-oriented tools and languages. The **n-tier architecture model** resulted from this.

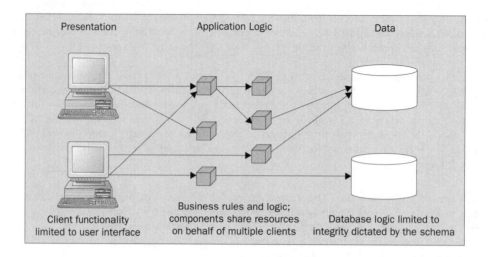

Presentation | Application Logic | Data

Client functionality limited to user interface | Business rules and logic; components share resources on behalf of multiple clients | Database logic limited to integrity dictated by the schema

In this model, sometimes also known as the **3-tier model**, clients remain focused on presenting information and receiving input from users. This is known as the **presentation tier**.

Data, meanwhile, is hosted on one or more data servers in the **data tier**. Only that processing required to access data and maintain its integrity gets implemented on this tier. This includes SQL query engines and transaction managers for commercial software, as well as triggers and stored procedures written by database administrators. Unlike the client-server model, however, these triggers and procedures are limited in scope to managing the integrity of the data residing on this tier.

Business rules are moved to the **application logic tier**, sometimes referred to as the **business services** or **middle tier**.

> *Stored procedures on the database are sometimes used to implement and to enforce business rules. While this can lead to performance gains, the approach does not go along with the purist concept of n-tier or DNA, where the data tier is kept strictly for data.*

> *The term n-tier comes from the fact that the application logic tier is often subdivided into further logical tiers dedicated to one task or another; the application tier is seldom homogeneous. Some programmers view the division as three tiers, while others view the different classes of application logic as individual tiers.*

Dividing a task into three or more tiers brings the following benefits:

❑ Separation of presentation from function

❑ Ability to optimize each tier in isolation for scaling and performance

❑ Limited parallelism during development

❑ Reuse of functional modules

❑ Ability to select the appropriate platform for each task

Separation of Presentation and Function

The separation of functional behavior – calculations and algorithms – from their visual presentation is important in two ways. First, it becomes easy to change visual presentation in isolation from tested functionality. You can change a display from a grid representation, for example, to a graph. You can support different classes of users with different views of the same data, providing each with a view appropriate to their needs. In fact some users will not need visual presentation – they might be other programs consuming the data.

Second, with the sort of separation we have been talking about, the client computer need only be powerful enough to perform the rendering tasks and make requests of the server. Perhaps you've seen an intranet application in which complex functionality was implemented on the server, allowing users to have rich visual access anywhere they have access to a web browser and the hosting server. In fact, this scenario is enjoying surging popularity right now, and Windows DNA supports it quite well.

It's not inconceivable that a PDA (personal data assistant) could be a **thin client** (where minimal processing is performed on the client itself), even while a very powerful workstation (a **fat** or **rich client**) connects to the same application logic layer to offer its user a different, richer view of the data. Regardless of the presentation, the code on the server that implements the application logic remains the same.

Optimization

Any programmer who has profiled and optimized an application has been surprised by the performance bottlenecks found. As each problem is resolved, new issues are uncovered. So it is with a distributed system. Each subsystem has its own unique challenges, each with an optimal solution.

These subsystems exist in monolithic and client-server applications, but there they are bound up with each other. With an n-tier architecture, it becomes possible to isolate each and make appropriate adjustments.

In the simplistic case, you can throw expensive hardware at the servers. The data tier needs high-powered servers with redundant disks. Redundant disks are important for high availability, but are quite expensive. There are ways to write application logic tier components, as we shall see elsewhere in this book, so that that tier, while it needs powerful machines, does not need to have redundant disks. Because the tiers are distinct, the machines that support the application logic may be less expensive than the computers hosting the data services tier. The client can be an inexpensive computer.

At a more sophisticated level, software can be adjusted for the needs of each tier. Servers are tuned for background processes, having little or no interaction with a foreground user. The exact opposite condition exists on the client. Relational databases involve complicated mixes of disk and memory performance, while the application logic tier operates largely in memory and prefers CPU and network I/O performance. If these functions were housed on the same machine, some compromise would have to be reached. Overall performance, in consequence, would be less than the ideal case for each subsystem.

Parallel Development

A monolithic application has few opportunities for parallel development. While multiple teams can be spun off for different parts of the application, there are so many dependencies that each progresses at the pace of the slowest.

Client-server improves the process somewhat. The client team can work, at least initially, in isolation from the server team, using a very limited stub application in lieu of the server. Unfortunately, the server possesses all the interesting logic. Recall that the functions of the application logic tier are generally implemented as stored procedures and triggers in a client-server application. The client quickly reaches an impasse, awaiting interesting results the stub cannot provide. The server software, in turn, will not be fully challenged until it is tested against the sort of interesting requests and conditions that arise only when multiple, fully-featured clients begin accessing it.

> *The situation is even worse if application logic is split between the client and the server. In such a case, each team can make limited progress without the other, and development resembles monolithic application programming.*

Things are a bit better in n-tier archtiectures. There is still the need for stubs at each level, but now the stubs are selectively removed as each tier makes progress. It is a more finely tuned sort of development. If the application tier progresses ahead of the data tier, clients can still resolve more difficult issues as they are going against the live component. The underlying data is still stub data, so the client cannot be fully tested, but the client team can work on more challenging issues than if they had stub logic and stub data.

In fact, as the world moves to n-tier architecture as the model for large and robust systems, development will be continuous and some programming teams will have no knowledge of one another. If the tiers communicate through open protocols like HTTP and open formats like XML, new client applications can be developed for existing servers without access to the server software programming team. Similarly, servers may be upgraded or data migrated without upsetting clients. The key is clean interfaces between the tiers.

> *An extended case is made for this form of development in Designing Distributed Applications (Wrox Press, 1999, ISBN 1-861002-27-0).*

Functional Reuse

Somewhat related to this is functional reuse. Because the key pieces of an application are broken out and integrated using clean interfaces, they are ready for reuse in other applications having need of the same functionality.

Object oriented programming made a bid for software reuse, but it required source code level reuse. With the source code available, it was too easy to modify software when the interfaces were insufficient. Since the software could be easily changed, less emphasis was placed on interface design.

Component software, such as the VBX controls of the early nineties and COM controls and components of today, advance the cause of reuse. Since they are reused at run-time, and the source is seldom available to the using program, greater effort must go into interface design. Interfaces must be clean and broadly useful. Designers must consider how another program will use these components.

Still, when these components are deployed on the same computer as the client application, which is the most typical case, the problems of optimizing a monolithic application recur. For the same reason, anyone who wants to reuse the functionality must acquire the software and host it themselves. This includes configuring and maintaining the component. When server code is deployed on multiple tiers, it can be deployed once and managed by an organization that understands the proper configuration and tuning of the software. More importantly, it is controlled by the organization that is responsible for the business function that the software represents. Since they control the software, clients can be assured they will keep it current.

Platform Selection

Windows is no longer a single platform. It spans a range from Windows CE on palmtop devices, through consumer and small business desktops running Windows 98, up to highly critical systems running Windows 2000. In fact, Windows 2000 itself is available in four variations (Professional and three grades of Server) depending on your needs.

As much as we would like you to use Microsoft Windows for your platform (and we will make a very strong case for it in this book), we have to concede that there is life apart from Windows. This diversity isn't some horrible accident caused by programmers' egos and the marketplace. The fact is that different platforms serve different needs. Different hardware is required to service different tasks. Choices and design tradeoffs are made throughout a job as difficult as bringing an operating system to market, and a wise software architect will select the platform that offers functionality closest to the requirements they have. Occasionally, the choice is as simple as sticking with a platform you know best – productivity matters.

This book, though, is specific to the Windows 2000 operating system and the services provided within it.

You may find that different layers of your application work best on different platforms. Monolithic applications had no choice – everything ran on the same platform. Client-server applications brought programmers their first choice of platform freedom, and it became quite common to use different platforms for the client and server. Still, some compromises had to be made.

n-Tier architecture lets you divide an application into pieces as small as you desire (within some practical limits, of course). You are free to use multiple platforms for each tier, and even multiple platforms *within* each tier. This exacerbates the problems of application integration, so it's important that your architecture provides for integration solutions.

As we shall see, Windows DNA takes a careful approach. There is ample provision for integration within the DNA infrastructure, as well as robust support for open protocols such as HTTP. If you stay with the Windows platform, you can take advantage of the tight integration enabled by the Windows infrastructure. If your requirements take you to a mixed environment, you can integrate the tiers using open protocols and data formats. You have more choice with Windows DNA.

DNA Design Objectives

Now that we have seen the benefits of a traditional architecture, we can look at the various other issues that DNA was designed to overcome. We'll see how the current DNA architecture succeeds in these areas in the next chapter.

Windows DNA had five major design objectives. These are common themes that run through the architecture, guiding the design decisions at each step. Without these, the architecture would be incoherent, and would not address the challenges of network applications. These design objectives are:

- ❏ Autonomy
- ❏ Reliability
- ❏ Availability
- ❏ Scalability
- ❏ Interoperability

We'll discuss each of these in turn.

Autonomy

Autonomy is the extension of encapsulation to include control of critical resources. When a program uses encapsulation, as with object oriented programming, each object protects the integrity of its data against intentional or accidental corruption by some other module. This is just common sense extended to programming: if something is important to you, you will take care of it. No one else will protect it as well as you will.

Unfortunately, client-server computing violates encapsulation when it comes to resources. A server, no matter how well written and robust, can only support a finite number of connections. System memory, threads, and other operating system objects limit it. Database programmers see this expressed in the number of concurrent connections an RDBMS (Relational Database Management System) can support.

Conservation of system resources was a sensitive topic in departmental level client-server applications. It becomes an essential issue as we build mission-critical systems at enterprise scale. The sheer multiplicty of components and applications in a distributed system puts pressure on any one server's resources. The dynamic nature of resource usage makes tracking and managing resources hard.

Extending encapsulation to resources should suggest that the server, which is critically interested in conserving its resources, is best positioned to manage those resources. It is also best suited to track their utilization. The server is the only entity that has a global view of the demands on it. Consequently, it will try to balance those demands. It must also manage secure access to its resources – access is a resource no less important than a physical entity like memory or database connections.

The addition of the application logic tier between presentation tier clients and data servers clouds the issue of resource management. The data server knows the demands presented to it by the components and servers on the application logic tier. It cannot know, however, what kind of load is coming into that tier from the clients on the presentation tier (or from other servers within the application logic tier, for that matter). Thus, application logic tier components must practice autonomy as well.

Just as a component is a client of data servers, it is also a server to presentation clients. It must pool and reuse critical resources it has obtained from other servers, as well as managing the resources that originate within it. A component managing access to a database, for example, will likely acquire a pool of connections based on its expected demand, then share them across clients that request its services.

Servers in any tier, then, practice autonomy in some form. They practice native autonomy on resources they originate, and they act as a sort of proxy for servers they encapsulate. In the latter case, they must not only share resources, but also ensure that access control is respected. In the case of a database, for example, the component acting as a proxy knows the identity (and by implication the access permissions) of the requesting client. Because the component acts as a proxy, using shared resources, the data server no longer has direct access to this information. Instead, the database typically establishes access based on roles. The proxy component is responsible for mapping a particular client's identity to a role within the system as it grants access to the resources it serves from its pool.

Reliability

Computers are reliable, aren't they? Surely if we submit the same set of inputs to the same software we'll obtain the same results every time. This is certainly true from the vantage point of application programmers (hardware engineers might have a few quibbles). As soon as we open an application to the network, however, the challenge of maintaining the integrity of the overall system – **reliability** – requires our involvement.

If you have ever programmed a database application, you have encountered the classic bank account example. When an application transfers funds from one account to another, it must debit the losing account and credit the gaining account. A system failure between the two operations must not corrupt the integrity of the bank.

Client-server applications only had to concern themselves with the failure of the server or loss of a single connection to ensure the integrity of the application. A three-tier distributed system introduces many more **points of failure**. The challenges we enumerated earlier for network applications, especially connectivity, resource collection, and availability, offer the possibility of failures that are harder to unravel.

Relational databases offer **transactions** within their bounds; a network application using multiple data stores requires a distributed transactional capability. If the system experiences a loss of connectivity, the transaction service must detect this and rollback the transaction. Distributed transactions are difficult to implement, but are critically important to the success of a network application. Their importance is such that distributed transactions must be viewed as critical resources requiring the protection and management we discussed under the goal of autonomy.

Availability

This goal is concerned with the ability of the network application to perform its functions. Such an application contains sufficiently many resources prone to failure that some failure must be expected during the course of operation. Optimal availability, then, requires that the network application take the possibility of failure into account and provide redundancy, either in terms of extra hardware or duplicate software resources, or in the provision for gracefully dealing with failure.

A network is inherently redundant in that it has multiple computers on the network. To achieve high availablity, a network application must be designed with the known points of failure in mind, and must provide redundancy at each point. Sometimes this is a matter of hardware, such as RAID disk drives and failover clusters, and other times it's a matter of software, as in web server farms. Software detects the loss of one resource and redirects a request to an identical software resource.

In the monolithic world, if we had our computer, we had our application. Network applications, however, give the illusion of availability to the user whenever their machine is available. The actual state of the network application's resources, however, may be very different. It's the goal of availability to ensure that the resources of the network are deployed in such a way that adequate resources are always available, and no single failure causes the failure – or loss of availability – of the entire application.

> *Availability is the goal behind such buzzwords as "five nines", that is 99.999%. If you are going to the expense of fielding a network and writing a distributed application, you expect the application to be available. A monolithic application running on commodity PC hardware is scarcely capable of hosting mission-critical functions. Windows DNA aspires to host such functions on networks of commodity computers. Availability is a make or break point for Windows DNA.*

Scalability

It would be close to pointless to deploy a network for a single-user application. One of the points of network application architecture is to efficiently share resources across a network on behalf of all users. Consequently, we should expect our network applications to handle large volumes of requests. Each of, say, 100 users should have a reasonable experience with the server, not 1/100th of the experience and performance provided to a single user of the application.

Scalability measures the ability of a network application to accommodate increasing loads. Ideally, **throughput** – the amount of work that can be completed in a given period of time – scales linearly with the addition of available resources. That is, if I increase system resources five times (by adding processors or disks or what have you), I should expect to increase throughput five times.

In practice, the overhead of the network prevents us from realizing this ideal, but the scalability of the application should be as close to linear as possible. If the performance of an application drops off suddenly above a certain level of load, the application has a scalability problem. If I, say, double resources but get only a 10% increase in throughput, I have a bottleneck somewhere in the application.

The challenges of network applications and the responses we make to them – distributed transactions, for example – work against scalability. Architects of network applications must continually balance the overhead of distributed systems against scalability. A scalable architecture provides options for growing the scalability of an application without tearing it down and redesigning it. An n-tier architecture like DNA helps. If you encounter a bottleneck on any single machine, such that adding additional resources to that machine does not alleviate the bottleneck, you are able to off-load processing to other machines or move processing between tiers until the bottleneck is broken.

Interoperability

The challenge of platform integration arises from the fact that organizations will end up possessing dissimilar hardware and software platforms over time. In the past, organizations sought to fight this through standardizing on one platform or another. The sad reality of practical computing, however, is that standardization is nearly impossible to maintain over time.

Sometimes there are sound technical reasons for introducing heterogeneous platforms – a given platform may not be sufficiently available or scalable for a particular need, for example. Other times, the problem arises from a desire to protect the investment in outdated hardware. Sometimes, it's simply a matter of the human tendency to independence and diversity. Whatever the cause, **interoperability** – the goal of being able to access resources across dissimilar platforms and cooperate on a solution – is the answer. Any architecture that claims to be suitable for network applications must address the problems of differing system services and data formats that we described under the challenge of platform integration.

Summary

We've used this chapter to set the scene for why we need to consider a specific architecture like Windows DNA.

We saw what requirements we're likely to have of our applications and of our platform – they should present a unified view of data from multiple data sources, allow a user to update data, possibly provide full e-commerce capabilities, be fast, and be scalable to thousands of concurrent users. We also saw some of the problems inherent in network applications (communications, concurrency, state, latency, and encapsulation). We then went on a sideline track to see how network applications have evolved from monoliths to distributed component-based n-tier architectures. Finally, we looked at what DNA professes to achieve for your applications (autonomy, reliability, availability, scalability, and interoperability).

Although we've not seen exactly what DNA is, we have seen what it's supposed to do for us. In the next chapter, we'll take a look at what's in DNA, and see how these things can solve the problems we've looked at here.

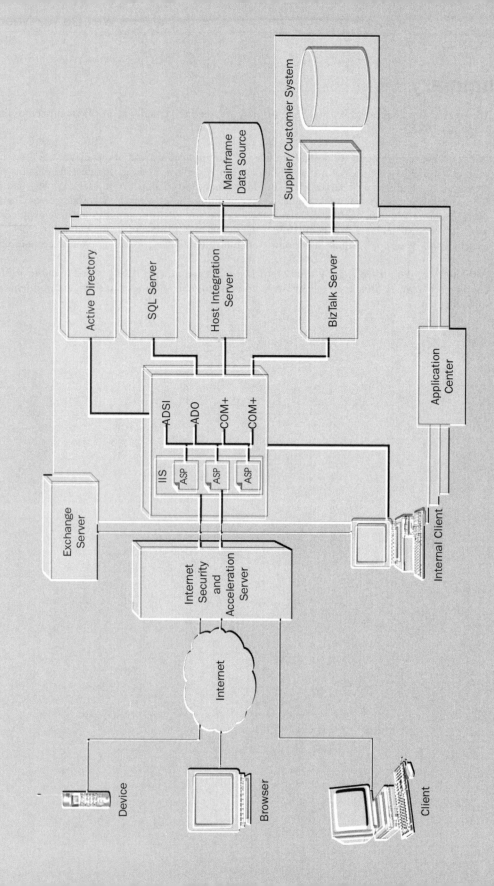

What Is Windows DNA, Anyway?

The last chapter presented a lot of the issues you face when you're looking to develop distributed web applications. You should hopefully understand the problems whatever architecture you choose should address. This chapter is designed to show what DNA is, and how it solves those problems.

You may see the term used in various contexts, with various meanings. You'll also likely see a lot of people developing DNA apps without even realizing. That's fine – we're not on some crusade to make everyone use the term.

> **Essentially, what we're calling DNA throughout this book is really just 'component-based distributed web programming on the Windows 2000 platform, using COM+ and the services inherent in Windows 2000'.**

We've decided that it's really just quicker to call it DNA.

This chapter is designed to see what makes up DNA, and how it can help us tackle the issues we raised in the first chapter. We'll see where DNA came from, and what it is now. You should begin to get a feel for how what you already do (and will do more of in the future) fits into this picture.

Here, we'll provide a high-level view of everything contained within DNA. Windows development is increasingly specialized, with programmers gravitating toward database, Web, or component development. Depending on your specialty, goals, and available time, you may wish to focus on certain threads rather than reading the entire contents, but you will hopefully find that the book provides a great way of putting your work into perspective within the bigger picture. Windows DNA is a very ambitious architecture that covers all forms of development on an entire general-purpose platform. A good software architect is careful to select the right tools for a particular project. After you read this chapter, you'll have a better idea of where you want to go next.

So what we are going to do in this chapter is describe the features of Windows DNA, with an emphasis on the new features of the Windows 2000 operating system. Along the way we'll state some of the goals of Windows DNA, and then look at the features of this platform and map those features back onto those stated goals. In addition, we'll take a short look at most of the technologies that make up Windows DNA, of which there are many, while at the same time trying not to make this a Microsoft commercial. Fortunately for you, most of these technologies are going to be covered in depth throughout the remainder of this book, so we can keep this chapter pretty short and get you on to writing some code.

Microsoft Windows DNA

If you've been keeping in touch with Microsoft strategy for a few years, you will know that there was a Windows DNA before now. DNA is not new, and we'll see later what the original DNA picture consisted of. We've come along an evolutionary progression from that architecture.

At the moment, though, we're really between acronyms, what with the announcement of .NET (which we'll look into in passing later on). We've decided, as we've said, to keep calling the platform Windows DNA until the real advent of .NET.

Since current Windows DNA shares a common core with its predecessor, introduced in 1997, it will be useful to see what was in the original version. Therefore, we'll start with a look at the structure behind DNA.

The Structure of DNA

Since Microsoft is in the business of developing software, not paper solutions, it provided the products to support Windows DNA in its original form. Of course, many of these products existed before Windows DNA was published. DNA is not, however, a cynical exercise in marketing. These products addressed real requirements, and these requirements did not vanish with the advent of a new architecture. Exactly the opposite is true. A realistic architecture arises to solve existing, real-world needs.

Among the improvements of Windows DNA over the original implementation were many low-level additions or modifications to bring previously independent products together under the Windows DNA umbrella.

DNA and n-Tier Architecture

We've looked at the evolution of the n-tier model, and have said that DNA is based on this very model. We're now going to look around at how DNA fits across all these tiers.

Presentation Services

Well before DNA was advanced as an architecture for building robust applications, Visual Studio offered presentation services through its Microsoft Foundation Classes (MFC) for C++ programmers. Visual Basic programmers sought productivity in the presentation tier with VB forms. These tools are still available, and remain viable tools for building presentation elements. Certainly they remain the best performing solutions in terms of speed. They are, however, tightly tied to the Windows platform. If you choose to take advantage of your freedom of choice between the tiers, you will want to opt for an open solution.

The popularity of the Web and intranet applications thrusts HTML into the forefront of the presentation services tier. Indeed, many Microsoft applications are adopting a browser approach to presentation. For any architecture that hopes to compete in the market for distributed applications, support of web tools for visual presentation is a virtual must.

The Windows operating system offers Internet Explorer as a starting point. Besides basic HTML presentation capability, Internet Explorer supports a rich Dynamic HTML programming model, as well as an implementation of open standards like cascading style sheets and XML. Certainly, Internet Explorer's implementation of these standards is imperfect (as are those of all the mainstream browsers). Nevertheless, Internet Explorer supports a broad array of standards to a very deep level of compliance. The result is a powerful arsenal of tools for crafting rich visual presentations.

> *The author of this chapter believes that a modern operating system requires a web browser and that Internet Explorer is legitimately part of the operating system. Many other talented programmers disagree – as, apparently, do the lawyers at the United States Department of Justice. However you feel about this contentious issue, the fact remains that Internet Explorer comes with the operating system, and is therefore widely available. It includes robust support for HTML presentation, and it is integrated with the various features of Windows' infrastructure. Consequently, it is a valuable presentation tier tool for intranet applications within the DNA platform.*

HTML is a great choice for presentation, because to some extent, it's cross-platform compatible – in other words, any browser on any platform can interpret HTML locally in a "uniform" fashion. The chief limitations are in the versions of these browsers, since HTML has evolved with time as well. However, most of these limitations can be overcome by using commonly supported HTML elements in your presentation layer.

The browser is only one half of the HTML picture. You also need something to serve HTML. If you are building applications rather than a marketing site, you need the capability to script dynamic HTML solutions as well. So while the HTTP server is a server, it properly belongs in the presentation services tier.

Windows includes Internet Information Server (IIS) as its HTTP server, and IIS includes Active Server Pages (ASP), the Windows solution to server-side HTML generation. ASP leverages the script interpreters built into the operating system. While Windows ships with interpreters for VBScript and JavaScript, the script engine in the operating system is designed to incorporate language-specific interpreters in a modular fashion. Third parties provide Perl interpreters, for example. You can write dynamic scripts in ASP using one of these scripting languages, and IIS will serve it up for you.

e-Commerce applications have certain tasks in common and are an important class of application. Each such application requires a shopping basket, for example, and must have a mechanism for handling the detailed logic of checkout and ordering. Site Server Commerce Edition is an extension of IIS that offers pre-built tools and frameworks for filling these needs.

Application Logic

The application logic tier in DNA is all about software components. These components have no visual representation, but they must be capable of communicating with the other tiers. The Windows platform component technology is COM (and its successor COM+), with its associated distributed capability, DCOM.

COM lets you write small bits of functionality that can be deployed on a server and used by any COM-enabled client, regardless of its implementation language. This is particularly attractive to DNA solutions, where you may have a variety of clients. The same component can be accessed from ASPs and HTML pages using VBScript or JavaScript, or from VB and C++ applications. Once configured, the component makes its capabilities available to any application (assuming the client has the appropriate security permissions) through the operating system. The application logic tier then consists of a cloud of COM components that interact with web servers, and that interact with clients on the presentation services tier through DCOM. Similarly, these COM components typically use COM components like ADO to access data services on the data services tier. We'll be looking specifically into COM later on.

Network applications, as we have seen, face more challenges than simply breaking functionality into little pieces. Scalability and availability require resource pooling, component management, and fault isolation. These are tasks traditionally solved in enterprise applications with **transaction processing coordinators** (**TPC**) in the mainframe and minicomputer world. TPCs also solve data integrity issues by providing distributed transactional capabilities.

In the original Windows DNA implementation, Microsoft Transaction Server (MTS) filled the TPC function. MTS allows an administrator to deploy and manage COM components. Security is specified through the use of functional roles, which is how security is scaled in network applications. MTS also includes facilities for resource pooling.

MTS introduces several COM interfaces. Some of these are used to support resource pooling, while others allow component developers to communicate with the MTS run-time. A component using the latter interfaces can indicate when it is safe to recycle a component, and MTS can provide signals to the component that let it manage its resources more efficiently.

> *We'll look at transactional programming in Windows 2000 in Chapter 8. Complete coverage of the MTS interfaces and details of programming components specifically for deployment under MTS are found in* Beginning Components for ASP *(Wrox Press, ISBN 1-861002-88-2). Language specific information about programming MTS is also the subject of Wrox's* Professional Visual Basic 6 MTS Programming, ISBN 1-861002-44-0, *and* Professional Visual C++ MTS Programming, ISBN 1-861002-39-4. *MTS is available with NT Option Pack 4.*

Data Services

When you think of data services in an enterprise system you think of **Relational Database Management Systems** (**RDBMS**). Windows DNA manages relational data through its RDBMS, SQL Server, and provides easy access to structured data through the **ActiveX Data Objects** (**ADO**), a family of COM components used to work with relational data. Windows, of course, has long supported the abstraction of relational data access. Shortly after the widespread adoption of the client-server model, Microsoft introduced **Open Database Connectivity** (**ODBC**) which largely isolated the programmer from the specific details of accessing a vendor's RDBMS.

> *Complete isolation is not possible with ODBC, ADO, or any other abstraction mechanism. The SQL standard specifies various levels of capability. The drivers for various vendors vary in their compliance, and programmers must be aware of the capabilities supported by the drivers.*

Relational data makes up only a small fraction of the entire universe of information recorded in electronic form. Admittedly, the vast majority of data is in unstructured form and will not be accessed via conventional data services. Object databases, spreadsheets, and other structured data, however, are amenable to search and management strategies such as we expect from the data services tier.

Windows DNA offers the beginning of an access strategy through the concept of **Universal Data Access** (**UDA**). In its current version, UDA specifies a family of cooperating components that work to abstract all sorts of structured data representations into a uniform view of data using a rows and columns model. A specification of this vision is OLE DB – a set of COM interfaces that vendors can write to that support a common interface to data, regardless of the underlying implementation. ADO participates in UDA and OLE DB as the primary implementation of this component model.

> *Complete coverage of UDA, OLE DB, and the relationship between the two is provided in Chapter 13.*

Much of this data exists in e-mail or on legacy systems. Exchange Server manages e-mail, and SNA Server provides a variety of gateway and access services to legacy hosts. Of course, these products offer more than just access. Exchange Server, in particular, includes workflow capabilities, and is something of an application solution platform through its **Collaborative Data Objects (CDO)** component family. In general, though, these products are about data – managing and maintaining it, moving it, and providing structured access to it.

The Original DNA Picture

The individual products that made up the first implementation Windows DNA were:

- Windows NT
- MSMQ, MTS, and IIS
- Site Server 3.0 Commerce Edition
- SNA Server 4.0
- SQL Server 6.5
- Exchange Server 5.5
- Visual Studio 6.0

This is a book about 'modern' Windows DNA, or what was originally to be called DNA before the .NET announcements in July 2000. You've seen what challenges face network applications, and how software architectures have evolved. You learned how the Windows DNA architecture started out, and even read some criticisms of it. Clearly there is room for improvement, which is where modern Windows DNA comes in.

Elements of Modern DNA

There were two key driving elements in the evolution of DNA: customer feedback and the normal evolutionary pressures coming from the product teams. You'll see that the new version is a mix of incremental changes to existing products, the introduction of some completely new products, and some revisions and schedule changes made in response to customer feedback.

The product list for supporting the Windows DNA vision is now:

- Windows 2000, including its native services:
  - IIS
  - COM+
  - MSMQ
  - Security features
  - Load balancing
  - XML Support
  - UDA
- Visual Studio 6.0
- SQL Server 7.0 (*or 2000*)

❑   Exchange Server 5.5 (*or 2000*)

❑   Site Server 3.0 (*or Commerce Server 2000*)

❑   SNA Server (*or Host Integration Server 2000*)

❑   *Optionally, BizTalk Server 2000, ISA Server 2000, ApplicationCenter Server 2000*

The heart of Windows DNA, like its predecessor, remains the Windows operating system, in this case Windows 2000. All the other products are integrated with it because it provides an extremely rich set of system services.

At the moment, Visual Studio 6.0 is still the vehicle for creating our components. The Microsoft servers that optionally make up the DNA picture include Exchange and SQL Server. We've put "(*or 2000)*" because once the new servers are out, you should have no problem in upgrading at your own discretion.

The point is that modern DNA is in between definitions: the original DNA as described above and the .NET vision, which we'll mention later on. As such, the exact makeup of your DNA solution can be very different from someone else's. The key is really Windows 2000 and its inherent services, which will be much of this book's emphasis.

Now that the situation has been framed up and the problems and goals have been exposed, what are we going to do about it? The simplest answer is use Windows DNA to build our applications. I'm certain that after this discussion you will be impressed with the amount of infrastructure and functionality you will have at your disposal. As we discuss the various technologies that make up this platform, we'll map them back to the problems we're trying to solve, and to the business and technology goals we stated in Chapter 1.

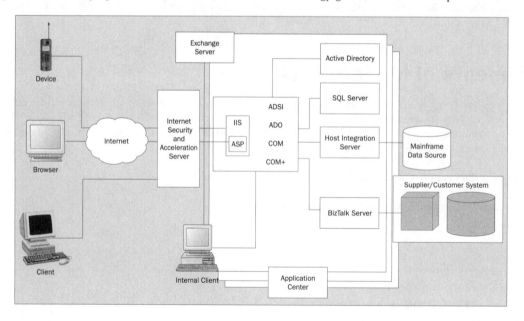

As you can see in the above picture, there are a lot of technologies at your disposal. Again, we are only going to give a very brief overview of these technologies here in this chapter and present them in the context of Windows DNA. The rest of this book is dedicated to "deeper dives" into these technologies, and Wrox Press has entire books dedicated to some of them.

You'll find that the Enterprise Servers themselves won't be covered extensively in this book, since at the time of publication limited concrete information was available. We decided it would be better not to discuss them in any depth, than to try and fail to guess correctly which features would make final release.

Windows 2000

The most significant advance to the Windows DNA platform is the introduction of an entirely new operating system: Windows 2000. Microsoft has spent billions of dollars to finally deliver a true enterprise-level operating system that can stand against the likes of big UNIX systems. Of particular interest to software developers will be the infrastructure services provided by Windows 2000. They are significant. Never before have we had a Microsoft operating system that provided this much functionality while at the same time providing a high level of stability. There is a lot of new functionality in Windows 2000 that directly supports the Windows DNA platform.

Remember that list of capabilities we derived last chapter? Web server, transaction processing and object brokering, message queuing, a data access mechanism, security, and load balancing... it's no coincidence that Windows 2000 provides all of those capabilities. You get all those services just by installing Windows 2000! Try getting these capabilities on the Sun platform or on Linux! Windows 2000 is the centerpiece, or hub, of Windows DNA. Moreover, all of the other server products that make up Windows DNA make use of these capabilities.

So let's take a look at these technologies provided by Windows 2000, paying particular attention to what's new with these technologies. Again, keep in mind that this is intended to be an overview and an identification of new features, and not a comprehensive look at any of these technologies.

Windows 2000 and Platform Integration

Windows-hosted products from Microsoft have long been closely integrated with the operating system and, consequently, with one another. The common support for COM and scripting, for example, gives the platform a unified programming model. All operating system services are available to any application that is COM-enabled. With the introduction of the new COM+ services, applications get access to important new capabilities.

Beyond having a common programming model, though, there are measures to allow network applications to work cooperatively. A prime example is use of object persistence through the `IPersistStream` and `IStream` COM interfaces. COM+ uses stream persistence to enable queued components. ADO uses this technique to implement writing recordsets as XML documents. Many components can be directly integrated through this technique.

For example, a programmer can save an ADO recordset directly to an instance of the XML parser component with one method call. ADO, the parser, and COM all engage in a sophisticated interface negotiation behind the scenes to make the right thing happen. The `Request` and `Response` objects in ASP, and MSMQ messages support similar behavior. You can retrieve an XML document passed in an HTTP request with one call and save it directly to an MSMQ message body, for example.

As a result of this seamless platform integration, the lines between active behavior – COM+ components – and persistent form (data) are usefully blurred for programmers. It's increasingly easy to work with data in components and transfer it where it needs to go with simple instructions. Windows takes care of the details, leaving programmers free to focus on the requirements of their applications.

Internet Information Services (IIS)

Until Windows 2000, IIS was an add-on product that shipped with the NT4 Option Pack. Now IIS has become a part of the operating system, and is installed as a network service on Windows 2000. You have undoubtedly heard of IIS, and know that it is the leading web server on the market today. IIS is easy enough to configure and use that a very small web site can take advantage of it immediately, while at the same time, some of the largest sites on the Internet use IIS.

COM+

COM has been the basis for delivering new features on Windows for some years now. It's therefore especially important to consider COM+ and how it differs from COM. In fact, several chapters of this book are devoted to exactly that task. To summarize for our immediate purposes, it's sufficient to say that COM+ swallowed MTS – you will not find MTS anywhere in a pure modern Windows DNA design.

We noted earlier that satisfying autonomy and reliability using COM components required a substantial amount of discipline and avoidance of stateful programming. The prohibition on stateful programming for maximum scalability remains in place – although you can write non-scalable COM+ components. Nevertheless, the tools to write components that support the design objectives are drawn under one roof – the core COM+ run-time system.

COM+ supports transactions natively – you designate a component as requiring a transaction. There is no need to deploy the component and then specify its transactional requirements. Instead, the transactional semantics are part of the component as defined by the programmer, thereby closing off an avenue for administrative error. In addition, COM+ adds some transactional semantics that MTS did not support, offering programmers a greater degree of control over their application's behavior. We'll see more of this in Chapter 8.

COM has long had an event model, but it required the direct cooperation of event publishers and subscribers. COM+ interposes an event database and operating system support for reconciling publishers and subscribers. Because the mechanism is tied into the operating system, various efficiencies, notably parallel delivery, can be obtained when publishing an event to large numbers of subscribers. This incremental improvement to an existing model will make event-driven programming more appealing to developers. In consequence, we should see fewer applications resorting to resource intensive pooling, and more using the more efficient event model.

Transaction Processing

As we mentioned above, MTS has been renamed and now falls under the COM+ umbrella. The functionality you were accustomed to with MTS has not really changed with COM+. The notion of taking physical units of work, like database updates, and grouping them together to form a logical transaction that is managed by a transaction-processing monitor has not changed at all.

The COM+ transaction-processing monitor allows the software developer to write COM objects and group them together into a transaction. If at any time an error condition occurs, in any of the objects, COM+ will take on the responsibility of rolling back all of the work that had been done to that point. This saves you the developer an enormous amount of time, since you do not have write any code that deals with the rollback of database updates, etc.

Loosely Coupled Events

One of the hardest problems to solve in this distributed computing paradigm is notifying someone when something changes. One reason this is so difficult is because, in the distributed computing world, you have no idea when those who are interested in being notified of changes will actually be around. Secondly, you might not even know who all of the interested parties are.

When we wrote client-server software we enjoyed enormous luxuries (even though that model has been proven to be obsolete) – we were always connected and most of the components in our client-server systems were tightly coupled. Always being connected allowed us to use RPC-style communication mechanisms like DCOM. By being tightly coupled, components had a lot of knowledge about each other.

We as developers have been using a notification system for years on the Windows platform. The problem was it usually only worked on a single machine, and the "publisher" (one who raises the event) and "subscriber" (one who receives and acts on the event) knew a lot about each other – they were tightly coupled.

With COM+ **Loosely Coupled Events** (**LCE**), we now have operating system level infrastructure that allows for publishing events and subscribing to them relatively easily. The phrase "loosely coupled" is used to describe this service, because the publisher and subscriber know nothing about each other. You as a developer register an event class (a COM interface) with COM+, and the publisher executes methods on that event class to raise an event. Those who wish to be notified when this event is raised subscribe with the COM+ Event Service. Also, those who are going to be notified have to implement the same interface that is being called by the publisher. When the event is fired, COM+ goes through all of the event subscriptions that have been registered, and calls the methods on those subscriber objects.

The possibilities for this infrastructure are limited only by your imagination. Applications that raise events when stock prices change, business events occur in your organization, errors in applications occur, etc. – the list is endless.

Queued Components

Another problem in distributed computing is unreliable networks. Using an RPC-style communication mechanism, like DCOM, works well when the object and the program calling it are always connected. What do we do when there are network problems? What do we do when a connection is not possible? The designers of COM+ solved this problem with COM+ **Queued Components** (**QC**).

The concept behind QC is quite simple, but very powerful. First, a COM object is registered with COM+ and marked as queued. When a client calls methods on that object, the method calls and all the associated parameters are actually recorded on the client; they are not sent directly to the object. Once the client has completed making method calls, the recording is stopped, an MSMQ message is created, and attached to it is a package containing all of the method call data that was just recorded. Then the MSMQ message is sent on its way to the server where the actual object lives. Now that we're using MSMQ, we get guaranteed delivery of the message; we just don't know when the message will arrive. Once the message does arrive at the destination, an instance of the object is created, the recording of all those method calls is "played back", and they are actually executed. In effect, we're now getting guaranteed delivery of method calls to a COM object.

One more thing – the programming model you're accustomed to using does not change. The client code to call a queued component is exactly the same as the traditional COM programming model.

There are design implications we should be aware of before using COM+ Queued Components. The caller, or client, cannot receive a response from any of the method calls it makes. Since we have no idea when the MSMQ message with the recorded method calls will actually arrive at the destination, the caller could wait an indefinite period of time for a response. The implication is that firstly, we cannot use functions that return values when using QC, and secondly, any parameters that are passed to a method must be marked [in] only. We cannot receive return values in parameters either.

MSMQ

The messaging product for Windows NT 4.0 and later is **Microsoft Message Queue** (**MSMQ**). MSMQ, in very simple terms, does for applications what Exchange Server does for people.

A sending application sends an arbitrary message to a known receiver. MSMQ provides a number of features that allow the system to attempt to route around network outages. When the message is received, it's placed into a queue. The receiving application removes messages from the queue as quickly as possible, but if it encounters a brief surge, messages may safely back up in the queue until they can be dealt with when the load drops below the average level of service.

MSMQ is an excellent answer to both scalability, through its queuing model, and availability, through its persistent queues. We have seen in brief how COM+ leverages its services to bring those benefits to the platform's component programming model. MSMQ will continue to evolve, and Windows DNA applications will increasingly embrace it as an asynchronous integration mechanism. The messaging story though, does not end there.

Over the next few years we're going to see the programming model for Internet applications change to a more message-based model. There are several benefits that messaging, or queueing, provides. Messaging allows for high-speed, asynchronous processing, and systems based on messaging scale very well and are typically highly available. To make a messaging-based system scale, we can simply add more processing power to process more messages. When unreliable networks become a part of the picture, messaging becomes very beneficial. Messages can be routed around unreliable portions of a network, or can be continually resent until they arrive at their destination.

Another benefit to messaging is in the area of application integration. If a system can just exchange messages with another system, the process of integrating the two systems can be made much easier. This really becomes the case when the systems reside on different computing platforms – it's much easier to make a Windows 2000 system talk to a UNIX system if they can just exchange messages.

Security

Let's face it, we as developers usually hate to deal with application security. However, if you were to ask any business executive at your company, they would probably place a high priority on application security. One of the reasons we hate to deal with security is that there has been little or no operating system level support for security. For most application scenarios, we have had to "roll our own" security, because there was very little infrastructure to leverage.

Security was hard before we starting writing Internet applications and distributed applications – once we did start writing them, security became a nightmare. Fortunately, with Windows 2000, we have more security infrastructure to leverage for application security, even for distributed applications.

We're going to devote a whole chapter of this book to the topic of security, so for a full discussion, go to Chapter 20.

Windows 2000 includes an entirely new authentication mechanism called **Kerberos**. The old Windows NT authentication mechanism, NTLM, is gone. Kerberos is a widely accepted industry standard and is much stronger than NTLM.

Another advance in security infrastructure is **Active Directory** (**AD**). Again, we have a whole chapter devoted to AD – Chapter 15 – and we'll come back to it briefly later in this chapter. All information about users and their permissions, and permissions on resources, is now stored in AD. By centralizing this information, it's much easier for application developers to query the AD, and get information about users and their permissions. It's also relatively easy to store application security data in the Active Directory.

COM+ also contains new security features.

First, COM+ allows us to secure objects down to the method level now. If you remember, with MTS, we could only apply security at the package level, which forced us to design our package structure around our security requirements. Now we can create our COM+ application structure independent of our security requirements.

With both COM+ and MTS, applying security for individual users of our domains is an administrative exercise – using the MMC. Now, with role-based security in COM+, we can design generic roles that can be "played" by users, and then factor those roles through our application design. Information about these roles is stored in COM+. Domain users are placed in one or more roles, and access to methods can be controlled using roles instead of individual users, which can be easier to manage.

COM+ role -based security integrates with Active Directory, so information about the users and their permissions is integrated with the role data stored in COM+ to create a very flexible security environment. COM+ also provides a set of security interfaces that allow the developer to implement even tighter security if their requirements call for it.

Clustering and Network Load Balancing

One of the biggest "knocks" against Windows NT was the lack of clustering capability to enable highly available applications. In this context, a cluster is defined as a set of computers that are working together to run a single application. If a problem arises on one of the machines in the cluster, the other machine(s) step in and take over, resulting in continuous availability.

For example, with Windows NT there was not a lot of support for creating a cluster for mission critical applications like SQL Server, thus creating a highly available data server. Now that we are running applications on the Internet and our users are located in every corner of the world, high availability is critical. With Windows 2000 Advanced Server and Windows 2000 DataCenter there is operating system support for clustering.

There are actually two types of clusters in Windows 2000. The first is the failover type of cluster described above. In Windows 2000, this is simply called the **Cluster Service** and clusters of this type are typically just referred to as **clusters**. The second type is called a **Network Load Balance** (**NLB**) cluster, and its purpose is to balance IP traffic, primarily to web servers. Clusters of this type are typically called **load-balanced clusters**. The NLB service is a software version of the popular hardware-based IP load balancing solutions, like the LocalDirector from Cisco.

We'll look at clusters and Network Load Balancing in Chapter 19 when we look at improving scalability and availability for our applications.

35

XML Support

XML is one of the under-appreciated success stories in the Windows platform. Many developers understand what tools Windows makes available for XML programming, but few realize how widely XML has spread through the platform. XML support in ADO, and native support in SQL Server, renders platform-specific relational data (binary recordsets) accessible to other computing platforms in the form of text-based markup.

The XML parser available with Internet Explorer is COM-based, so it's well integrated with the rest of the platform. As we'll see in a bit, XML is also well supported in several other products and services. In fact, Microsoft has firmly committed to XML as the Windows DNA data interoperability solution. Although native binary methods for representing data will always be more efficient, XML is usually just a method invocation away. When your application needs to cross platform boundaries, XML is an excellent and easily accessible solution. Even within the Windows platform, XML is frequently an integration solution.

> *For example, we'll see how XML can be used in a distributed messaging system in one of the case studies at the end of this book.*

Universal Data Access

One feature of software applications that is almost universal is that they access some sort of data source. There are a wide range of data sources that can exist in a typical enterprise today – mainframe databases and applications, directory services, spreadsheets, and even text files are all examples. Not only are there multiple types of data, but these different types of data reside on multiple computing platforms.

Universal Data Access has been Microsoft's data access strategy for a few years now. The goal of UDA is to provide a common way for the software developer to access all of these different types of data in the enterprise.

What's impressive about the UDA strategy is that, even as application development has evolved over the last several years, the UDA strategy has remained mostly intact. Now UDA is just part of the enormous Windows DNA platform – albeit an important one. The UDA strategy might have remained intact, but it has grown over the years as advances in technology have been developed. What we'll do in this section is identify the major portions of the Microsoft UDA strategy.

A Brief Look at Architecture

By now, you should be well aware of the concept of the architecture behind Windows DNA. What we are going to do here is put data access in context with the architectural principles of Windows DNA. We all know that we're partitioning our applications into at least three layers, or tiers:

- ❑ A presentation layer that acts as the interaction point for users of our application.

- ❑ A business services tier – often called the application logic or "middle tier" – that contains all of the business logic for our application. This business logic is typically encapsulated in components so that it can be reused in the context of other applications.

- ❑ A data services tier, where all of the data for our application should reside.

Another important aspect of the middle tier is that it acts as the "middle man" between the presentation and data services tiers. The implication is that the middle tier becomes responsible for delivering data to the presentation tier. The presentation tier should not be allowed to directly interact with the data services tier.

By introducing an indirection layer between displaying the data in the presentation tier and the actual data in the data services tier, we can easily do things like change, upgrade, and add data sources without impacting on the presentation tier. All the presentation tier knows is that it calls methods in the business services tier and it gets data. The same concept holds true for the storage of data.

As far as UDA is concerned, most of the work will be done in the business services and data services tiers.

So now let's start talking about some of the technologies being used in Microsoft's Universal Data Access strategy. Consider the following picture:

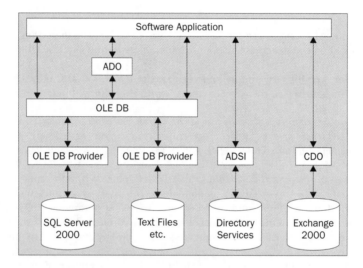

As you can see there are a lot of technologies involved here, although the two most frequently used are ADO and OLE DB. Since these are the technologies used to access and modify relational databases, such as SQL Server 2000, these will be used more than ADSI and CDO.

OLE DB

As you can see from the diagram above, OLE DB plays a pretty big role in the UDA strategy. OLE DB is a set of COM interfaces that a developer can use to access any type of data for which there is an OLE DB provider.

In this portion of the UDA strategy, for each different type of data source, there must be an OLE DB provider. An OLE DB provider knows how to deal with a specific type of data source, how to read from it, write to it, etc., and translate the results of those reads and writes into a row-based format.

This notion of a row-based format is what separates OLE DB from most other data access mechanisms. No matter what type of data we're accessing – be it SQL Server tables or text files – we treat the data in a row-based metaphor. This way, we as developers learn a common way to deal with data, no matter what the type. Furthermore, OLE DB is simply a set of COM interfaces for interacting with data. So not only do we learn a common way of dealing with data, we learn a common interface as well. Microsoft creates OLE DB providers for data sources it knows how to deal with, such as SQL Server. For other data sources, Microsoft provides a toolkit to create these OLE DB providers.

Our diagram shows a software application "talking" to OLE DB in two different ways: directly, and via ADO. The only drawback to using OLE DB directly is that it's fairly complicated and beyond the abilities of most VB developers. This is the reason ADO was created – to provide a simpler interface to OLE DB.

37

You might have noticed that ODBC is not present in the diagram – that's because we purposely didn't include it. Don't get the idea that ODBC is going away – ODBC was the preferred data access mechanism before COM really took off, and that goes back a few years! If you need to access data and are in an environment where COM is still not available (I hope this is not happening to you!) ODBC is just about your only option for accessing data.

However, the ODBC API is even harder to use than the native OLE DB interfaces. It's much easier if you can use OLE DB to access an ODBC data source – OLE DB simply makes calls to the native ODBC API, and translates the results into its own row-based format.

ADO

ActiveX Data Objects (ADO) provide a simpler mechanism to access data than using OLE DB directly. Most software developers who need to access a data source for which there is an OLE DB provider will use ADO.

The object model for ADO is very simple and very easy to use. Like OLE DB, the interface we learn is consistent across data sources, so the way we interact with the data will be consistent as well.

> *Since our focus in this chapter is to really provide an overview of these technologies, a detailed discussion on ADO would be out of scope. However, you really need to have a copy of* Professional ADO 2.5 Programming, ISBN 1-861002-75-0, *from Wrox Press if you are going to use ADO.*

ADO takes the notion of row-based data from OLE DB, and extends it to the concept of a recordset – a collection of data that can be traversed and manipulated. One interesting characteristic of recordsets is that they can be disconnected from their source, and actually passed as parameters to COM objects. These are called **disconnected recordsets**. Once a recordset has been disconnected from its source, we can perform the same functions on that recordset as we could if we were actually connected to the data source.

The advantage to using disconnected recordsets is that we don't need to maintain a costly database connection for the entire life of the recordset. For example, to create a recordset in ADO, we would establish a connection to a data source, then somehow fill the recordset with rows of data – perhaps we would run a SQL query. Once we've filled the recordset, we can disconnect it and release the resources required to maintain the connection to the data source.

In read-only situations, we would just pass this disconnected recordset to a display function. We can also make modifications to a disconnected recordset, re-create the connection to the data source, and have the updates committed to the original data source. What's more, we can persist ADO recordsets as XML, and pass the XML to any environment that can handle XML – for example we could pass it to Internet Explorer for display.

ADSI

The reach of UDA continues to expand. Windows 2000 offers a hierarchical directory service, the Active Directory. For a variety of reasons, directory services are very important to enterprise scale applications.

Active Directory is a non-relational store of essential data, and there's a non-relational object model for accessing it, called the **Active Directory Service Interfaces** (**ADSI**). ADSI is a non-UDA set of COM+ interfaces that provides full access to Active Directory. These are more effective, since they are tailored to the data source.

To simplify matters, however, ADO also brings directory data under the umbrella of UDA. You can query Active Directory through ADO, and receive the data contained in the directory as a standard recordset. UDA has collapsed the hierarchical model into UDA's rows-and-columns model. At present, however, you cannot use ADO to write to the directory as you can with ADSI.

CDO

Collaboration Data Objects (CDO) is now the primary access mechanism for Microsoft Exchange. CDO was introduced with Exchange 5.0, and was actually a simplified object model that sat on top of MAPI. This relationship was much like the current ADO and OLE DB relationship. When Exchange 5.5 was released, an additional version of CDO was introduced called **CDONTS** (**CDO for Windows NT**). CDONTS provides much the same functionality as CDO, but is based entirely on Internet standards, so you can access SMTP mail and Usenet news.

Now with the upcoming release of Exchange 2000, there is an entirely new family of CDO libraries:

❑ The first of these new libraries is called **CDOEX**. CDOEX has been entirely rewritten and divorced from MAPI. You can use CDOEX as a COM based mechanism to access all of the areas of Exchange 2000, such as the mail, calendaring, and contact stores.

❑ There's another library for managing Exchange 2000 resources called **CDOEXM**, which allows you to programmatically access management tasks such as adding and configuring mailboxes.

❑ Exchange 2000 will ship with a workflow engine for developing workflow applications. A CDO library called **CDOWF** allows you to interact with this new routing and workflow engine.

Open Communications

We've seen COM+ at a low level, and MSMQ at a moderate level, for communications between applications. These are native and platform-proprietary communications protocols. Windows DNA is adding open communications protocols at a low level, as well as adding a high-level communications product for performing cross-platform messaging with application semantics.

At present, you need to use HTTP and IIS, or SMTP and Exchange Server if you wish to have open standard communications, but a new, low-level open standard is rapidly gaining ground. It's called **SOAP**, the **Simple Object Access Protocol.** It uses XML to convey method invocations and their parameter stacks between platforms over one or another protocol, of which HTTP is expected to be the most common.

It's helpful to think of this like COM or RPCs for the Web. By remaining agnostic with respect to the transport protocol, SOAP paves the way to using whatever protocol suits your needs. By using XML, issues of data representation are smoothed out between platforms.

Since SOAP encapsulates the endpoints (client and server), each participant in a SOAP call can use whatever implementation technology suits their needs. A Windows client using COM and scripting on the client can access a CGI script written in Perl running on a Unix server. Microsoft is expected to release tools for connecting COM components to SOAP endpoints with Visual Studio.NET.

A product we shall see shortly, **BizTalk Server**, is a high-level communications tool. SOAP focuses on low-level communications issues, and leaves the semantics of a call to the application. Issues of application access, message routing for availability, and the meaning of a particular message are all the concern of the application, not SOAP. BizTalk Server, by contrast, will let programmers transmit data between applications over any one of a number of communications mechanisms, both open and proprietary. Its value is in adding robust security, redundancy, message tracking, and application integration semantics. Windows DNA continues the tradition of offering well-integrated tools with overlapping feature sets and allowing application designers to select the appropriate tool for the job.

Foreshadowing .NET

Before we round out the DNA picture, we need to take a short sideline to briefly introduce the future of distributed applications – the .NET vision. With the advent of the next version of Visual Studio, the next version of ASP, and the .NET Framework (which provides a large range of plumbing services and cross-language interoperability features, to keep it brief), the architecture we're calling DNA at the moment will evolve into .NET.

The new series of Enterprise Servers, replacing such things as Exchange 5.5, SQL Server 7.0, and SNA Server, will officially be part of the .NET platform, and aren't being heavily marketed as DNA servers. However, until the .NET platform is truly released, these products will sit perfectly in a DNA solution, and provide you with much of the infrastructure you'd ordinarily have to construct yourself. At the time of writing, not enough concrete information was available on these products to cover them fully, so we've just summarized them here. Keep an eye out for future developments in these products at `www.microsoft.com/servers`.

DNA isn't dead with the announcement of .NET. The term itself may not be used so frequently, but until the whole .NET vision is released, there's no other official term for the solutions you'll be developing. We're going to continue using DNA for simplicity.

Server Packages

The Enterprise Server family of products includes:

- ❑ Commerce Server 2000
- ❑ Host Integration Server 2000
- ❑ SQL Server 2000
- ❑ Exchange Server 2000
- ❑ BizTalk Server 2000
- ❑ Application Center 2000
- ❑ Internet Acceleration and Security Server 2000

You'll notice that some of these are direct descendants of previous DNA Server products. You should feel quite secure in using a newer Enterprise Server in place of an older one – our purpose in listing DNA as using the older variety was simply to emphasize that DNA is still DNA before the release of the next wave of servers. Again, we've unfortunately had to hold off on these topics until enough hardcore information is available – we didn't want to give you half-baked information...

Commerce Server 2000

Commerce Server 2000 leverages core services and products like IIS and ASP to deliver a platform for building e-commerce applications. As such, it is the vehicle for migrating from single server HTTP service and state maintenance, to web farms with central state storage. Although Commerce Server continues to rely on SQL Server for its state storage solution, it's expected to make increased use of the Active Directory as that product matures, and when the type of data is better suited to hierarchical storage rather than relational database storage.

Commerce Server uses the operating system services for COM and scripting to allow application developers to build chains of e-commerce functionality, termed **pipelines**, that are specific to their business needs. An example might be a customer checkout pipeline. Your local business rules might involve checking the availability of the product, putting through a credit card transaction, and updating your supply chain software to reflect the new transaction.

While some functions are common to all e-commerce sites, many are custom and tailored to a specific site. Site developers can use prepackaged COM components and scripts to implement the processing they need. The COM components use published interfaces that allow Commerce Server to call the components at the appropriate time, and pass common data into and out of the component. Some of the interfaces developed for Commerce Server see use again in BizTalk Server, making it easier to share components between automated and interactive e-commerce.

Host Integration Server 2000

Host Integration Server 2000 is the new name for the old SNA Server product. This new version expands the reach of the product into legacy and enterprise platforms previously excluded from the reach of the Windows platform.

The key to understanding Host Integration Server is in appreciating where organizations have traditionally placed their mission critical data, and how conservative people are about changing platforms. Mainframes and minicomputers possessed the properties needed for mission critical applications long before Windows did. As a result, a wealth of information important to businesses lives on mainframes, and is accessed through network architectures like IBM's SNA.

SNA Server has long allowed programmers to reach these hosts from PC platforms. Despite the advances of the Windows platform, businesses will not migrate the legacy data anytime soon – the cost is too high, it works well, and the platform is understood. Rather than try to pry the data free from its current host, Windows DNA seeks to make scalable and efficient access to legacy data available to Windows applications.

SNA Server offered gateways and terminal support to PCs. The COMTI bridge permitted legacy resources to participate in transactions with resources residing on Windows. Host Integration Server adds the following:

❑ Access to OS/390, OS/400, and selected Unix systems

❑ Bidirectional access, allowing legacy resources to participate in network applications on a more nearly equal footing with native Windows applications

❑ XML support for host interoperability

Increasingly, programmers accessing legacy systems will be able to use the same techniques for building network applications that they use when developing native Windows applications. Host Integration Server 2000 will provide the design time tools and run-time services to make XML, COM, and MSMQ work with non-Windows host platforms.

SQL Server 2000

SQL Server is Microsoft's Relational Database Management System (RDBMS) and has been their flagship data management product for approximately ten years. SQL Server 7.0 brought major performance gains, as the core relational engine was completely overhauled. SQL Server pioneered the Distributed Transaction Coordinator that underlay MTS and is used in COM+. Beyond performance and usability improvements, what remains for SQL Server 2000?

One avenue of interest is expanded support for enterprise-grade hardware. SQL Server was an early user of MSCS, because the SQL Server team took pains to make sure their product obeyed the "rules of the road" for Microsoft clusters. Enterprise applications required greater performance, and SQL Server 2000 is developing support for eight processor multiprocessing servers and the projected 64-bit version of Windows 2000. Even under 32 bit Windows 2000 (the currently shipping version), SQL Server 2000 leverages support for 64-bit memory addressing to make in-memory manipulation of result sets possible. This enables very powerful RDBMS servers crammed with large amounts of RAM for high performance.

Consistent with the cluster philosophy of Windows DNA, SQL Server 2000 is expected to offer support for partitioned databases. These databases share some subset of their data or their data schema across multiple servers. While the data tier is not stateless, clusters can be built that allow requests to be routed to the appropriate server. Multiple servers can manage high volumes of queries by sharing the work.

A second avenue is support for OLAP and data mining. If you aspire to manage enterprise data, you will acquire very large sets of data. Organizations will then expect you to derive value from these mass stores through data mining. Existing data mining support in SQL Server 7.0 will be extended in SQL Server 2000, with more scalable algorithms and tighter integration with the relational engine.

Moving in another direction, SQL Server 2000 will make its relational capabilities available in smaller packages, as well. An earlier version introduced a single set version designed for developers. This allowed programmers to have a cost effective, "right-sized" relational engine built on the same core as their deployment target.

The move to mobile computing and non-traditional clients produced further downward pressure. A suitably reduced set of SQL Server capabilities will be made available for Windows CE portable computers. This will allow DNA programmers to target the full range of data storage needs, from the mobile individual to the enterprise data center, with one platform-compatible RDBMS.

A final avenue of support for the DNA vision in SQL Server 2000 is native support for XML representations. ADO and the XML-SQL technology preview pioneered relational to XML translation on the Windows platform. That experience has been taken into the SQL Server engine for increased interoperability options. With SQL Server 2000, it will be possible for application developers to specify XML as the return data format when they issue a SQL query. Rather than receiving a recordset, the requesting application will receive an XML document representing the results of the SQL query. This puts the application one step closer to interoperability, by eliminating the need to walk a recordset and generate XML.

Exchange Server 2000

What can be said about an old product like Exchange? Surely a mail server is a rather pedestrian member of the Windows DNA platform. In actuality, this new version of an old product is important to DNA in two ways. First, it is tightly integrated with new features of Windows 2000. This makes it a first-class member of the product line. Second, it contains new or enhanced features that offer programmers new options when developing distributed applications.

First and foremost, Exchange is fully integrated with the Active Directory. All security and address information is stored in the directory. This makes Exchange easier to manage. It also means that Exchange becomes more reliable as Active Directory content is replicated between domain controllers. Loss of a single server does not mean loss of mail capabilities, provided that server is not also hosting Exchange.

To protect against that sort of loss, Exchange now supports two-node active-active clusters. When one server fails, the other takes over its functions. Because both servers in the cluster are active, Exchange can accommodate more traffic while both servers are functioning normally. The protocol and storage functions of Exchange can be split between servers, as well. This means that messages can be stored on servers with RAID disk arrays, while the actual transmission protocols execute on less expensive machines. This feature supports both availability and scalability.

Exchange is also well-integrated with Internet Information Server. HTML documents can be sent through Exchange, and MIME content is supported in Exchange. While web content poses obvious security concerns, it can, when properly controlled, permit programmers to create rich applications on top of messaging. Like IIS and Explorer, Exchange now supports XML. It even uses XML for its native representation of certain content when using the HTTP protocol for transmission. Exchange 2000 is blurring the line between mail protocols like MAPI and SMTP, and the web protocol HTTP. This may be difficult to grasp at first, but it ultimately offers system architects additional options for their applications.

Exchange, in concert with Windows 2000, also adds some new features. For a start, it fully supports WebDAV. This allows Office 2000 users to save their documents directly to Exchange.

It also supports another storage system, the **Web Storage System**. Despite the "Web" in its name, this storage system is a Microsoft creation. It is a database for documents, permitting properties describing documents to be saved together with the documents themselves. Since it is a database, the Web Storage System permits indexed searches for documents. If you're familiar with searching for e-mail messages in current versions of Outlook, you'll be ready to search for Office documents the same way. Tied as it is to both the operating system and to Exchange, the Web Storage System becomes an interesting intermediary between Exchange and other applications. Exchange can save messages to the Web Storage System and retrieve them. The operating system exposes the Web Storage System as a mapped disk drive to applications through the Win32 API.

Exchange continues to support an object-based interface through the Collaboration Data Objects. CDO was introduced in an earlier version of Exchange to permit programmers to build workflow applications using Exchange as a message passing mechanism. Documents could, for example, be routed through a series of users for comments or approval, with conditional logic along the way. Exchange 2000 introduces version 3.0 of CDO. CDO 3.0 is built on OLE DB, so Exchange content is readily accessible via database mechanisms. Perhaps more importantly for Windows DNA developers working with Internet technology, CDO 3.0 also supports LDAP and MIME, thereby opening Exchange to clients other than Outlook.

BizTalk Server 2000

This is the first of the products we've introduced that doesn't have a famous predecessor. One important Windows DNA scenario is application integration across platform boundaries. This might involve integrating applications hosted by different corporate departments with different infrastructures, or integrating trading partners and external suppliers via the Internet. Microsoft's entry in this marketplace is called **BizTalk Server 2000**.

BizTalk Server uses a message passing paradigm to integrate applications. The idea is to allow one application to pass a message – really some application-specified data in a structured format – to another application, with the implication that some agreed upon processing will take place as a result. This is very definitely a network application, so all the challenges we have seen apply. When we expand into the challenge of many-to-many communications, such as you would expect from Internet trading partners, what we would really prefer is some middleware server that takes configuration details like data formats, delivery points, and transmission protocols, then intercepts messages and performs the desired conversions. That is precisely the approach that BizTalk Server takes.

BizTalk Server is oriented toward XML as a data format, but is not limited to it. For interoperability with older applications, BizTalk Server supports conversions to and from flatfile formats. An originating application submits a message bound for another application to BizTalk Server. If it is a new application built with knowledge of the BizTalk Server API, it submits the message directly. Older applications submit the message to a known location, such as an HTTP URL or MSMQ queue, where BizTalk has been configured to listen for messages. In the latter case, the originating application need have no knowledge of BizTalk Server.

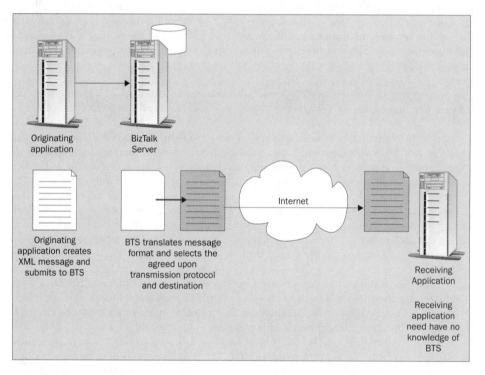

BizTalk Server compares the message source, message type, and message destination to locate an integration agreement in its database. The agreement specifies such details as the desired format at the destination, the translation specification for converting the format, and the desired communications protocol for transmitting the message to the recipient. BizTalk translates the message to the required format and retransmits it on the required protocol. In the process, BizTalk records fields in the message specified in the agreement for tracking purposes.

The result is a bit like package delivery through a commercial carrier like Federal Express or UPS. The sender and recipient do not care how the message gets there, but they care very much that it does, and that they are able to track its progress. Unlike package carriers, BizTalk Server is able to convert between message formats, so that each application can work with the format it prefers. Also unlike package carriers, applications do not have to conform to the carrier's delivery process – such as waiting for the deliveryman – but instead BizTalk conforms to their requirements for transmission. This may take the form of a platform-specific protocol like COM or MSMQ, or an open protocol like HTTP or FTP. BizTalk facilitates the development and integration of network applications by replacing custom integration code in applications with dynamic, run-time integration based on a configuration database.

Another very important aspect of BizTalk Server 2000 is **orchestration**. This is the term used to describe the part of the product that controls and manages business rules, allowing you to effectively execute a Visio-like business flow diagram as if it were COM+ -based code. In fact, it is just that. With links to your own components and message queues, the diagram can be the basis for your program's flow. If your business flow changes, you can alter the diagram to fit. Transactions are also supported, just by selecting a group of entities on the diagram and marking them as such. And any external (for example business-to-business) information transfer can be queued and treated as described above. This allows us to concentrate our efforts on writing components that perform specific actions, such as updating our databases, rather than having to write components to control business flow.

Application Center 2000

Originally, COM+ was going to support clustering services some time ago, but that feature was pulled from the final release version in Windows 2000. This was because potential customers demanded administration tools for managing clusters of COM+ servers, before such clusters would be viable for deployment in DNA applications. As a result, the ability to scale COM+ applications through clusters of stateless servers is packaged into the forthcoming **Application Center 2000** product.

The basic scheme for clustering COM+ components in the application services tier is this: an application that wishes to use a COM+ component sees a single image of the deployed component. That is, it believes there is a single component deployed on a single server, even though there are multiple, identically configured COM+ servers ready to service incoming requests. That way, the client is written and behaves just the way COM clients do today.

These features were initially tested as part of an early beta of Windows 2000. The problem that beta testers had was that deploying components and managing clusters was hard in the absence of specialized tools. This is the additional piece that Application Center 2000 offers. It provides a central management console so that system administrators can add and delete servers from the cluster, and it assists with component deployment to ensure all servers are properly configured for the COM+ application.

Clustering COM+ components requires that components are stateless, just as COM components had to be stateless to fully realize the benefits of MTS. The concept has been out in the development community for a few years, however, so this is no longer quite so novel. The improved integration of services formerly handled by MTS with the core operating system COM+ run-times also helps; as developers are better able to specify configuration requirements on the components themselves, where Application Center 2000 can read the information.

When Visual Studio.NET is released with full support for COM+, programmers will have the final piece for scaling the application services tier in Windows DNA network applications. It also contains tools for the Network Load Balancing and administration of web servers, to allow you to keep your application available full-time.

Internet Security and Acceleration Server 2000

This is an entirely new product and a comparative surprise. **Internet Security and Acceleration Server 2000** (ISA) was a late-breaking addition to the Enterprise Server product family. It is interesting less for the technology it introduces than for the customer needs it answers, and the fact that it combines two functions that have rarely, if ever, been seen together in a single product.

The first half of the product – Internet Security – is a firewall designed to protect LAN users from outside intrusion via a corporate Internet connection. It provides administrators the ability to set access policies and force authentication at the circuit (VPN and connections), packet, and application levels. It also performs Network Address Translation (NAT) – hiding the IP addresses of internal users from outside scrutiny, by translating the IP address of individual packets as they transit the server on their way to their destination.

Firewall technology is not new, nor does ISA offer new capabilities to application developers. Its security function, however, is a vital one in typical corporate environments. Organizations will not move to network applications involving external partners unless they can secure their Internet connection.

The second half of ISA – Acceleration – is a content caching server. Frequently accessed content is retained on the ISA server. Subsequent requests for this content from internal users will be satisfied much more quickly, because they don't have to travel to the originating server, but can instead be fulfilled by ISA without leaving the local network.

This will not help us with dynamic content such as is served up by web applications. However, a considerable amount of traffic is static, or nearly so (perhaps changing daily rather than with every request). This holds true even for intranet applications. One example of the latter might be a company's human relations handbook. Users will frequently access the section on benefits, say, to determine the codes for their health insurance. This content can be held on the ISA thereby taking some load from the originating server, which then has more capacity for its dynamic content.

As with the security function, caching is not a new technology, nor does it offer new features to DNA programmers. ISA is simply a part of the network infrastructure that makes the entire network work a little bit better. The fact that these two less than glamorous functions are bundled together is convenient for small and mid-sized organizations that might otherwise overlook them.

How Windows DNA Solves our Problems

So, all that said, now we know what DNA is. Are we convinced yet that our problems will be solved? Well, obviously, it's only an architecture, and you as a programmer will need to inject the DNA mold with your own exciting (?) mixture of solutions to your own problems. But we *can* see if the DNA architecture is capable of meeting its own design goals, and the problems with network applications we identified earlier. Throughout the book, you'll then be able to see where the DNA platform affords you services that are of some use to you when developing your own distributed applications, and maybe even where it doesn't.

Meeting the Design Objectives

In Chapter 1, we saw the objectives that the Microsoft DNA team has always tried to write to:

❑ Autonomy

❑ Reliability

❑ Scalability

❑ Availability

❑ Interoperability

Let's see how it tackles each issue in turn.

Autonomy

The principal tool for promoting autonomy in the original Windows DNA is MTS. In fact, IIS adopted MTS as infrastructure with version 4.0. This provided valuable isolation in addition to resource pooling. Properly configured, IIS allowed individual ASP applications to run in isolation from one another and the server process. This meant that in the event of a critical failure in an application, the server remained running and other applications remained available.

The **Distributed Transaction Coordinator** (**DTC**), originally introduced with SQL Server, is the mechanism in MTS for controlling transactions. It allows application designers a point from which to control transactions that span multiple resources.

Where RDBMSs managed transactions on their own resources in the client-server model, n-tier systems inherently have a problem with transactions. Any single product or application can control transactions involving its resources alone, but n-tier systems quickly develop a need for distributed transactions. MTS is the product that provides the central capability for coordinating the efforts of individual applications. It requires cooperation from participating applications and components, but it implements the system architect's intentions toward transactions.

Another feature of MTS, resource dispensers, is not so much a shipping software module as it is a set of design interfaces. Application developers can write components that implement these interfaces and use them to implement resource pooling on custom software resources. MTS comes with a resource dispenser for database connections.

COM+ integrates all the functions MTS provides with the operating system. COM+ applications also specify their own transactional requirements within the application itself. In that way, each COM+ app can take greater responsibility for itself.

Reliability

The DTC in MTS, as we just saw, provides transaction control for components. SQL Server, for its own part, implements the same properties for data under its management. The two provide substantial scope for building data reliability into an application. Under the original Windows DNA, however, it required considerable programming discipline to ensure this objective was met.

MTS appeared several years after COM had become widely adopted, so many existing COM components did not support its interfaces. The interfaces, to be most useful, require the design pattern called stateless programming. Briefly, a stateless component provides computing services, but does not hold data – the state of the application – across method invocations. Many existing components were stateful, so gaining full benefit from MTS required more than simply adding the new interfaces.

Many components, moreover, accessed data outside SQL Server, or were written to access SQL Server directly. Since MTS in general, and the DTC in particular, were add-ons to the COM programmer's toolkit, it was entirely too easy to breach data integrity and hence fail in the design objective of reliability. Making reliability central to COM-based programming is one of the most important enhancements leading to Windows DNA.

Again, COM+ improves this even more. The transaction support of COM+ and MSMQ is improved, and enhancements to the OS mean that things are more reliable. Active Directory replication improves reliability in other directions.

Scalability

Often, it's hard to tell where scalability ends and availability begins. A web server farm is a good example. Incoming requests for pages on a site are sent to HTTP servers on a round robin basis. This helps scalability in that the site can handle many more concurrent requests than if it had only a single server. On the other hand, this may be viewed as an availability measure, as well. A flood of incoming requests can overwhelm a single server. Because the load is distributed across multiple servers, the site remains available to users longer than it would have with a single server.

Windows 2000 greatly improves on Windows NT in this area. Pre-release testing has shown the basic operating system to have a higher mean time between failures than Windows NT. In addition, the basic product line, which formerly included a desktop client, a basic server, and an advanced server version, now adds Windows 2000 Datacenter Server. Four computer clusters are supported. In complex applications where a server farm hosts a large number of components and services, a single failover node might be insufficient to take over the load.

Moving to n-tier architecture lets us optimize each tier independently of the others. Each generation of the software enjoyed incremental improvements to performance. Is this the end of scalability in Windows DNA? Of course not.

The chief communications mechanism within the platform is COM. COM method calls are synchronous; a component blocks until the called component replies or times out. This tends to waste resources, as a lightly loaded server on one tier can become blocked waiting for a heavily loaded server on another tier. The same is true of web servers; an HTTP call forces the requesting client to wait for a reply or a timeout.

There are many times when an application doesn't need an immediate reply. We would simply like to know that the call went through. Such a call could involve the receiving server replying later. This is known as asynchronous behavior. The client and server components are not locked into the same pace or time.

MSMQ, which we've seen briefly before, makes good use of this. The IBM mainframe world also introduced MQSeries for messaging. This product is older than MSMQ, and is now available for a wide variety of platforms, so you can expect to find a lot of sites with MQSeries deployed.

> *MSMQ is available with Option Pack 4 for Windows NT. The client components for MSMQ may be deployed on Windows 95 and 98.*

MSMQ is a strong addition to the family of products supporting Windows DNA, but there is one glaring problem. The dominant tool for writing Windows applications is COM, but COM components cannot make asynchronous calls. While MSMQ uses COM components for its API, COM components themselves cannot be made asynchronous. It would be very nice if this could be changed.

COM+ also adds a great deal to the scalability story. To begin with, COM+ supports object pooling, making COM components one more resource that can be controlled and recycled. An application can maintain a pool of components on the server, decreasing the time to service a new request. Of far greater importance, though, are two entirely new services offered with COM+ that we saw earlier: **queued components** and **events**.

Queued components give a programmer the ability to make asynchronous method invocations. A queued component is capable of persisting itself to a stream. When a queued call is made, the component is persisted by a component provided by the COM+ system called a **recorder**. The stream is passed to MSMQ, giving the COM+ run-time messaging middleware behavior. On the receiving end, a component called a **player** restores the original component and performs a synchronous call on the server.

Buffering calls in a queue lets the system smooth out spikes in demand. Since MSMQ queues can be stored on disk, the overall system is far more fault tolerant. Any messages in the queue at the time of a failure are recovered from disk and transmitted upon recovery. All of MSMQ's availability features, such as alternative routing to bypass connectivity outages, are available seamlessly to COM+.

Availability

As we have seen, MTS goes a long way toward improving the availability of a web-based network application. Windows NT, additionally, has strong innate safety mechanisms to isolate one running process from another.

SQL Server is a mature RDBMS, which means, among other things, that it has robust transaction logs for replaying transactions in the event of a failure. With such logs, it's possible to either rollback a series of transactions, or to recover the state of a database by replaying transactions.

Exchange Server uses a store and forward messaging model. Messages are stored on a server until they can be delivered to the recipient server or mail client. In the event of a recovery, then, there is a high likelihood that undelivered messages are intact. It would seem that the server products supporting Windows DNA had this design objective well covered.

Recovery is nice, but remaining online is better. Running two servers in parallel using Microsoft Cluster Services (MSCS) can protect critical resources. Each server sends a periodic heartbeat signal to the other. Should a server fail, the other server takes over its functions. This is termed **failover redundancy**, and the two servers are known as a **failover cluster**.

MSCS supports two models:

❑ **Active-passive**, in which one server is actively managing the load while the other is dormant

❑ **Active-active**, in which each shares the ongoing load

SQL Server, in particular, is designed to take advantage of failover clustering. Typically, you use a RAID array of redundant disks in a failover cluster. That way, MSCS protects you against processor and memory failures, while your critical data is guarded against disk failure.

Unfortunately, getting full advantage from MSCS requires the applications running on the clustered servers have incorporated support for MSCS. Even when this is true, such as a cluster running SQL Server, a cluster can be difficult to configure. Active-active clusters, in particular, have proven to be very difficult to deploy with current applications and the shipping version of MSCS.

Failover clusters and redundant disk arrays are a very good option, but expensive. In the case of the data tier, we have no other choice – persistent data written to disk is irreplaceable. The application logic tier, though, should ideally be stateless. RAID is unnecessary in that case, but it would still take a failover cluster to completely guard against failure and ensure availability.

It would be better, though, if we could avoid the expense of a failover cluster, and simply spread the load over a number of identically configured servers. Since no state is involved, there would be no need for failover clusters; if a machine failed, the load would simply migrate to other boxes in this sort of cluster. Clients currently in-call to the failed server would receive an error, but all other calls would complete successfully.

As of Windows DNA, however, there was no simple solution. If you wanted high availability on the presentation services and application logic tiers, you had to use failover clusters or select a third party solution.

Interoperability

Windows DNA has interoperability well covered. SNA Server, for example, is wholly dedicated to interoperability with an entirely different operating environment. IIS and Exchange Server embrace interoperability through support for open networking protocols like HTTP, FTP, and SMTP. Together with the native IP networking support in the core operating system, the universe of open standards is well represented.

Windows DNA also comes at interoperability from a novel direction: data interoperability. As we've already mentioned, Windows was an early adopter of the **eXtensible Markup Language** (**XML**). XML permits application data to be converted to a structured representation entirely in text. Since XML is an open standard and widely popular, it's extremely useful for exchanging data with another platform. Text is universally supported, and an application designer may safely assume that tools for processing XML are available on nearly every platform and for most popular languages.

The XML support in Windows ships with Internet Explorer. Introduced with version 4.0, this support has evolved so that it is at the forefront of XML standards implementation. Microsoft is extremely active with the standards setting body for XML.

The interesting part about XML support in Windows DNA, though, is not the fact that Windows has a tool for processing XML. As we hinted at earlier, it is the fact that support for generating XML is rapidly being spread throughout the platform.

ADO 2.1 introduced the ability to save a recordset to a file as XML, and ADO 2.5 permits a recordset to be saved or read to and from any component supporting the Istream interface. This interface is the basis for supporting object persistence throughout the platform. With it in place, relational data can be read through ADO, then written as XML to a file, MSMQ message body, or directly to the XML processor for further manipulation.

In ASP, an XML document in the processor can be written to and from the Response and Request objects, simplifying XML-handling code for ASP programmers. ADO also has the ability to issue queries to the Active Directory, meaning that data stored there – the directory service built into the entire platform – may be written as XML.

> *The weak link in this interoperability is the presentation tier. If an XML document is to be presented using an XSL style sheet applied at the client, then the only suitable client is Internet Explorer. XML support in browsers varies widely. Counting on the browser for XML support is not a cross-platform option, and is viable within the platform only if Internet Explorer is the browser.*

Meeting Network Challenges

The characteristics of network applications that we looked at in the last chapter suggest some issues that do not arise in standalone applications. Most issues are related to the characteristics, but all arise from the very nature of networked computers. Here's a representative list of the challenges that network applications face:

❑ Loss of connectivity

❑ Resource collection

❑ Security

❑ Platform integration

❑ Management and configuration

Ultimately, it is up to architects and programmers to solve these problems in their own applications. As you read the chapters that follow, and study the implementation details of specific DNA technologies, remember these challenges, and consider how you might overcome them with the technology being presented. We will of course discuss some of the solutions to these problems, but there is always room for creativity on your part.

Connectivity

A standalone application has no worries about **connectivity**. Once you distribute functional resources across a network, though, you begin to care about connectivity a great deal. Individual machines hosting necessary resources may crash. Client applications may be terminated unexpectedly. The network path between the computers participating in a calculation may be cut.

Given enough participating computers, and a sufficiently complex network – for instance, the Internet – we have to expect losses of connectivity more frequently than on a LAN. Rather than treating them as isolated and exceptional occurrences, we must cope with them in the normal course of operations.

Connectivity is difficult to address outside specific applications and systems. One shared resource that the operating system can protect, however, is the Active Directory. If a computer were completely cut off from the directory service, applications running on it would not have access to configuration information stored therein. Active Directory, therefore, maintains copies of the directory on backup servers, and replicates changes between them. This is done primarily for reasons of performance, but it also has the effect of partially guarding against connectivity outages.

MSMQ takes similar measures for guarding its queue configuration information. In addition, MSMQ can route messages around an outage on the shortest path between the sender and recipient of a message.

Resource Collection

If you have lost an application in the middle of some work, you may leave resources dangling on a server.

Consider a web application. If a busy host is taking too long to process your request, you may quite reasonably go to another site or shut down your browser altogether. You do nothing to notify the server, you simply abandon the request. If the server didn't have a mechanism to detect that a given interaction has been abandoned, its resources would quickly be used up and the computer would have to be restarted.

Consumer Internet applications are notorious for this, but it's certainly not unknown in other distributed applications as well. Loss of connectivity, whether intentional or accidental, compels DNA programmers to plan for garbage collection and recycling.

DCOM introduced the concept of a periodic "ping", to let a server know that a DCOM client machine was still connected to the network. DCOM performed a simple form of resource collection, cleaning up COM DLLs that were no longer needed based on the loss of the "ping". Still, resource collection in DNA is less robust than in some languages, like SmallTalk and Java.

Recent announcements regarding the .NET initiative in general and the Common Language in particular seem to promise greatly improved resource collection at the operating system level. These are early pronouncements, of course, and such capabilities are well off in the future.

Security

Security is another topic that is less important on standalone applications, but is absolutely critical to the success of distributed applications.

A standalone application using local resources will have at best a simple password protection scheme. More likely, it will have no security. If you have physical access to the computer, you have access to the application and everything in it. An operating system with built-in security, such as Windows 2000, is inherently security aware, but too often resources are left unsecured. After all, if you have access to the machine, why enforce security?

Moving to network applications changes this. A remote resource needs to identify a requesting user. Who makes this information available? What protocols are used to implement security? How are priorities established? Without security for authentication and access control, the availability and integrity of valuable resources is left to chance. Abuse may not even be intentional; a perfectly harmless user might deny access to a more important user simply by being the first to connect and making large demands on the server. Clearly, a priority scheme is needed, and for that the identity of users – both applications and human users – is needed.

Within the DNA platform, the primary security enhancement with Windows 2000 is the introduction of the Kerberos protocol as the default security subsystem. Kerberos, developed at MIT on Unix systems, enjoys wide-spread popularity, although it's not, strictly speaking, an open standard. It uses a sophisticated system of encryption to ensure access to resources is well-guarded. An interesting facet of Kerberos is that a user's password need never be passed between the machine desiring a resource and the Kerberos server granting access to that resource.

A controversial extension to the Kerberos protocol in the Microsoft implementation makes it impossible for a Windows 2000 computer to act as a security client of a Unix-hosted Kerberos server, although Unix computers can be clients of a Windows 2000 Kerberos server.

Outside the platform, security remains a challenge, as it is for all operating systems. Security in this setting is a matter of standard protocols and methods. Windows has long supported measures like the Secure Sockets Layer (SSL) and digital certificates. Similarly, the CryptoAPI COM interface makes it easier for Windows DNA programmers to include public key encryption in their programs. Still, security across platforms is approximately as hard to implement within DNA as it is on any other platform.

Platform Integration

Platform integration is a major factor in the success of distributed applications. It seems like a little problem at first glance, but the scope of the effort quickly grows as you look into it, until it threatens the entire project.

A standalone application has no problem: it runs on one platform. The data formats to communicate between the parts of the application are those offered by the platform, and the core services are those of the platform. Any piece of code within the application has access to the services. A native type in one part of the application, say an integer, has the same size representation everywhere and may be freely passed between modules.

These advantages quickly disappear when we go to distributed applications. Even passing between two computers on the same platform causes problems. Modules within a standalone application can share a common memory space – this is what lets a C programmer pass a pointer to a structure, or a Java programmer pass an array. Data that is to be passed between computers must be copied.

The problems multiply when going between dissimilar operating systems or hardware architectures. An integer on a Windows computer may have a size different from that on a Sun Sparc station running Solaris. Even the order in which the bits of the integer are written can change. Application developers don't want to worry about these issues just to pass the number 105 from one computer to another. An entire layer of translation software becomes necessary.

Core services – system-wide utility functions and APIs – are a harder problem. Windows offers encryption support through the CryptoAPI and data access through OLE DB. Another platform may or may not have these features. If the services are available, the API may change, or the two implementations may have differing limitations. One encryption utility may have a different set of algorithms from another, while one set of data access routines offers distributed transactions when another does not. The designer of a distributed application has to worry about these issues, and make sure they are well encapsulated.

Windows DNA addresses platform integration largely by continuing its support for XML in various products and system services. SQL Server 2000 brings native XML support to the database engine, allowing developers to obtain the results of a query in the form of an XML document rather than a recordset. In addition, SQL Server can receive a request via HTTP, and return the information as XML. This greatly facilitates the exposure of a database through web browsers.

In addition to XML support in existing product lines, the new BizTalk Server 2000 product offers application integration through messaging. BizTalk Server is strongly oriented toward the use of XML for the body of its messages. At a lower level, SOAP is being supported in DNA development tools. Visual Studio.NET will almost certainly include tools for generating a SOAP interface to COM+ components.

Management and Configuration

Efficient use of network resources in accomplishing some task, to include the assignment of subtasks to the computer best able to accomplish them, is one of the primary goals of network applications. Close behind is free and dynamic access to computing resources. Network applications should be able to request the use of the resources they need, when they need them, for only as long as they need them. If the goal is met, the application can adapt to configuration changes made after design-time. If access isn't completely ad hoc, as is usually the case in today's systems, changes in resources are at least implemented through configuration, rather than causing a fresh build of the application.

Incremental improvements in the existing product lines make DNA slightly easier to manage than its predecessor. As we have seen, COM+ clustering was delayed until suitable management services could be developed for it. The administrative function for COM+, Component Services (found under Administrative Tools), makes it easier to deploy and support component-based systems and applications than was the case under MTS.

The Active Directory is integral to DNA and network management. It's a great improvement over the registry, as it provides a remotely accessible store for information regarding network resources. Most Microsoft products released under the DNA banner use Active Directory for their configuration. Active Directory, unlike the machine-specific registry, provides tools for replicating directory information. This makes it much more reliable than registry settings.

While DNA makes great strides in system management, this topic is likely to remain a challenge for DNA developers and administrators for the foreseeable future. While long-standing concerns have been answered to some extent, the trend toward distributed applications introduces new network management concerns.

A Word on Open Standards and Proprietary Systems

A real challenge is deciding when to use proprietary protocols and data formats, and when to go with open standards. Some people would have you believe that open standards are the only way to go, while others swear by the performance of native features. The fact is, you frequently need open standards to bridge the gaps between platforms, or to operate in a pure Internet environment, but you will seldom mix and match platforms within your local network.

Choose the feature that offers the right set of services and performance for the task at hand. This should be a pragmatic decision, not a matter of staunch loyalty to a particular platform and the associated stubbornness that comes with it. Windows DNA has overlapping support in most areas, offering either native and proprietary services or a related open protocol. ADO, for example, lets you use native binary representations within your operating environment, and then allows you to switch to XML for transport outside your organization. Choose where you want to draw the line between open and closed features, then test and profile rigorously.

Summary

We began our introduction to Windows DNA itself by briefly looking at the structure of DNA in terms of an n-tier architecture. Next, we looked at what was in the original version of Windows DNA, and then saw a concise overview of the system services and products that make up modern Windows DNA. We got an introduction to the new Enterprise Server products that can be combined into an existing DNA solution as desired. Finally, we saw how the problems we introduced in the last chapter can be solved with the tools DNA provides.

As we've seen, Windows DNA offers a bewildering array of products and infrastructure services. Hopefully, this chapter has helped orientate you to what pieces of the platform serve which functions. Remember, you don't need to use every product and embrace every buzzword to have a true Windows DNA solution. The feature set is rich precisely so that you have a choice, and can select the right piece or product for the job. Examine the feature set and requirements of each product and evaluate them against your application requirements. Use the challenges of network applications we have laid out as a basic set of criteria for your evaluation, then consider the Windows DNA design objectives and try to state how your selection meets the objectives.

As you work through this book, refer to the challenges and design objectives, and think how the technology at hand fits in. Ask yourself how you can use the technique and when it's appropriate. You are about to learn some very exciting programming techniques, but remember that you are seeking solutions, not entertainment. The right architecture for your needs is the one that uses the minimum set of appropriate technologies to satisfy your business requirements.

This book is going to provide you with the programming skills to tackle Windows DNA solutions. Despite the road map presented in this chapter, you may often feel lost. Remember, though, that Windows DNA is an architecture, and an architecture is intended to provide a conceptual framework and set of plans to guide construction. Consider the n-tier model and network applications when you feel lost. If in doubt, return to fundamentals.

For the Windows 2000 operating system, COM+ is the fundamental building block. Everything else is built on top of that. Let's begin our exploration of Windows DNA, then, with a look at COM, and the basic techniques of component programming on Windows.

The best place – other than this book – to get information on the Windows DNA platform is the Microsoft web site dedicated to this topic. This site acts as a portal to all of the other technologies of the Windows DNA platform. You can find it at: `http://www.microsoft.com/dna`.

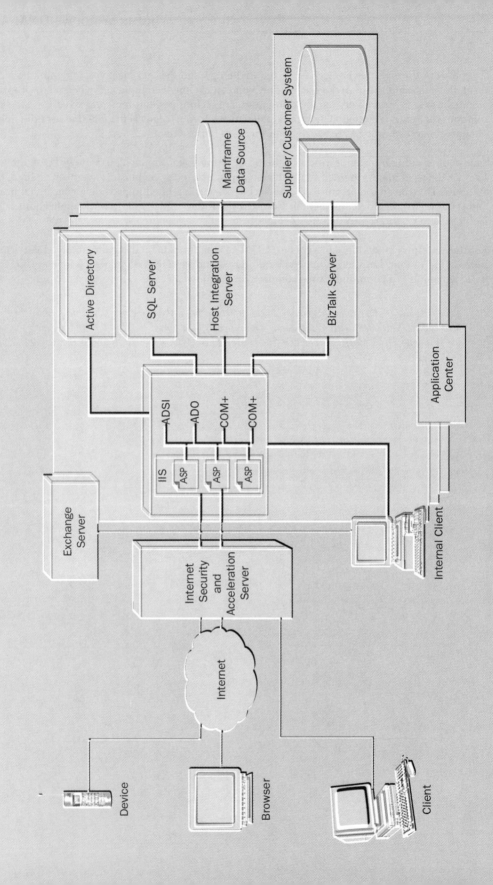

3

The Component Object Model

There is no doubt that the demand for businesses to deploy solutions across multiple servers will increase. With the growth and acceptance of the Internet, businesses have found that not only information, but also actual business applications, can be connected and distributed across multiple servers from remote locations. Additionally, data can be processed through the use of browsers as well as other desktop systems. This all sounds wonderful, but building and deploying such applications is much more difficult and costly than building simple desktop systems. Common problems include security authorization, and communication issues among different programming languages. These problems involve complex low-level programming.

Microsoft has introduced new technologies that address these programming problems. In this chapter, you will learn how the **Component Object Model** (**COM**) can be used to create high performance applications that are robust and scalable, eliminating programming nightmares while reducing cost. Furthermore, COM is the fundamental foundation for Microsoft's DNA model.

After completing this chapter, you will understand the following concepts:

❏   What COM is all about

❏   What the difference between a component, an object, and an instance is

❏   What COM interfaces are and how they work

❏   What IDL is and who needs to use it

❏   What GUIDs, UUIDs, and CLSIDs are and how they are used

❏   How objects are instantiated

❏   What the difference is between an in-process component and a component that is out-of-process

What is COM?

COM is the acronym for Component Object Model. Knowing the acronym is the easy part, as COM is possibly one of the most misunderstood concepts created by Microsoft. Go and ask your colleagues what COM is and I bet you will receive several different points of view, ranging from "COM allows software objects to talk to other software objects" to "Beats me, but I use it all the time". It's not because programmers cannot comprehend what COM is all about. On the contrary, the problem lies within Redmond. Although the COM specification itself has not changed, the description of COM has been redefined so often, the ink on the paper describing its specification hasn't had time to dry. Another major reason COM causes a lot of confusion is because the COM specification covers many areas, thus it is difficult to define COM within a single unified definition.

Incidentally, the COM specification is not an abstract theory. It is a detailed plan of how COM works and how it is implemented. As a matter of fact, you can go to Microsoft's web site and download COM's specification, comprising a few hundred pages:

http://www.microsoft.com/COM/resources/COM1598B.ZIP

As we'll see in this chapter, the component object model is an outgrowth of the object-oriented paradigm. COM is a specification that is based on a binary standard for reuse through interfaces. This means that components (pre-compiled blocks of code) written for COM can be reused without any dependencies on the language in which they were written. It does not matter if an application contains components written in Visual Basic, C++, Java, or even COBOL. What is important is that the components follow the COM specification.

The COM Library

OK, we have talked a little about COM's written specification. However, it is important to realize that the COM specification goes much further than the few hundred pages of its written version. COM actually involves system-level code that is implemented though what is known as the **COM library** in the form of **dynamic link libraries** (**DLLs**).

The COM library consists of several **application programming interface** (**API**) functions that are necessary for COM components to do their "magic". In more technical terms, the COM library is responsible for locating and activating server applications. For example, with client applications, COM APIs will bring about the necessary functions for instantiating objects that the client requests. Also, the COM library provides locator services through the use of the **System Control Manager** (**SCM**). The SCM is a mechanism that makes it possible for COM to find the location of a particular COM class as well as provide transparent remote procedure calls when an object is executing out-of-process in a local or remote server (remote procedure calls are covered further in Chapter 4). If this does not appear to make much sense at the moment, have no fear – all this will be clear by the time you complete this chapter. For now, the important thing to understand is that COM provides a system of low-level programming that provides the necessary functions for the creation of objects, regardless of where the COM classes reside.

Advantages of COM

Perhaps another way to help understand COM is to look at the major advantages COM offers:

❑ **COM promotes component-based development**: before component-based development hit the scene, programs tended to be written in a linear form that typically executed from the first line of code and completed when the last line of code was reached. This method of programming is referred to as **procedural programming**. Both C and many VB programs today are still written this way. Component-based development has numerous advantages over linear programming. One major benefit is the ability to use pre-packaged components and tools from other vendors. In other words, a component created by a third party source can easily be incorporated into an application. Another major benefit of component-based development is code reuse within an application. Once a class has been created, it can be reused in other locations in an application, thus reducing the need to write redundant code.

❑ **COM promotes code reuse**: even with the use of class-based development, using standard classes, classes tend not to be easily reused in other applications. In other words, classes tend to be compiled within a program and any code reuse in another program often involves the need to cut and paste portions of code to other projects. COM components, on the other hand, are designed to separate themselves from single applications. Instead, COM components can be accessed and shared by numerous different applications without any problems.

❑ **COM promotes object-oriented programming (OOP)**: COM was designed with OOP in mind. There are three major characteristics that OOP provides: **encapsulation**, which allows the implementation details of an object to be hidden; **polymorphism**, which is the ability to exhibit multiple behaviors; and **inheritance**, which allows for the reuse of existing classes in order to create new and more specialized objects. Among these three characteristics, perhaps encapsulation (often referred to as COM's black box) is one of COM's most important characteristics. Encapsulation provides the ability to hide details of an object, such as data and the implementation of logic. In other words, how an object implements a procedure internally is kept hidden (it's a secret!) An analogy is turning on a lamp. All you do is flip a switch and a light goes on. Nevertheless, there are a lot of processes going on in order for the light to shine, but we don't need to concern ourselves with the hidden details, such as voltage, alternating current, and closed circuits.

❑ **COM provides the necessary mechanics for COM components to communicate with each other**: software components (non COM) typically do not communicate well with components written in other programming languages. Think about this; would you be able to take Visual Basic source code and expect it to work within a program written in C++? You should have answered no, as the two languages don't understand each other. This is where COM provides a solution to the language problem. As previously mentioned, COM is language independent. As a result, COM components can be mixed and matched using different programming languages.

❑ **COM provides the means to access components across different machines on the network**: COM components are location independent. What this means is a COM component can reside anywhere on your computer, or even on another computer connected to a network. In other words, applications using COM can access and share COM components regardless of where the components reside. The important thing to realize is the client does not have to concern itself with the details of where the server component resides, as COM takes care of it. This is referred to as **location transparency**. You will learn more about distributed COM components in the next chapter.

Objects & Classes

Before we delve further into the aspects of COM, let's quickly take a look at two items that are essential to understanding the component object model: **classes** and **objects**.

Objects

Objects are code-based abstractions that represent real-world items or real word relationships. Each object has three basic characteristics: **identity, behavior,** and **state**. An identity is simply a unique name assigned to an object in order for it to be distinguished from other objects. The behavior of an object is based on the set of methods that can be called to query or manipulate an object's state. State is simply data that is correlated with a particular object.

Classes

A component may consist of one or more classes. Remember, objects are abstractions for real-world items and relationships. So for every object, there must be a class that defines the object. A class is simply a template, (call it a blueprint or a plan if you like) from which an object is created. Because a class is a template, it stands to reason that many objects based on a single class can be created. The classic analogy is a cookie cutter. The cookie cutter is like a template; thus it represents a class. We can make numerous cookie copies (objects) based on the cookie template. Back to classes and objects – when an object is created, it is said to be **instantiated** from a class. Simply put, an object is an **instance** of a class.

The word class is pretty descriptive, since we're basically classifying our objects. For instance, if we have a couple of objects, Invoice and SalesOrder, they could be instances of a Document class. Each actual invoice or sales order would have its own object, but all the objects would be created from the same template, the Document class.

In Visual Basic, we define classes using **class modules**. We can then create objects based on the class module, with each object being an instance of the class.

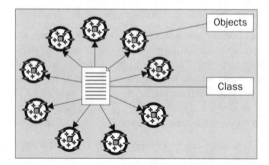

Class modules are like form or standard modules, in that they have a declaration section followed by a series of Sub, Function, and Property subroutines. The difference is that the variables and code in a class module can only be used by creating an instance of the class.

Let's see how this all fits together. Suppose we want to create a software model that represents customers who purchased books about DNA. First we could design a class called DNACustomers with a method called PurchaseDNABook. We could then use this class to create object instances for each customer who purchases a book about DNA. Thus we could instantiate an object for each of the customer names such as Natalia, Dori, and Jeff. In other words, each object would represent one customer. Each object also would have a method (behavior) called PurchaseDNABook and the state would keep track of the number of books purchased.

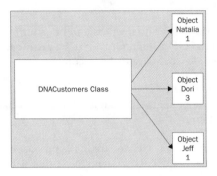

Objects exhibit identity, behavior, and state. The customer names for each object (Natalia, Dori, and Jeff) are examples of object identity. The behavior of each object is to purchase a book about DNA and the number of books purchased by each customer represents state. In this diagram, Natalia and Jeff purchased one book while the object Dori purchased three books.

So how would this appear in an executing program? When an object is instantiated during runtime from a class, a contiguous block of memory is assigned for the member variables (the number of books purchased by each customer in our example). The identity of the object is simply the address in memory. The behavior is controlled by the methods (PurchaseDNABook for this example) that can be called to query or manipulate an object's state. Finally, the state is the actual contents of the block of memory.

COM Components

Until recently, if we had the code for, say, a Customer object in one program, and we wanted to use that object in another application, we'd have to *copy* the code into our application. We got to reuse the code, but, if anything changed, we had to find and change each copy of the customer object in all the different applications where it could be in use.

The problem is that as soon as there are two or more different copies of the same code, there's no easy way to keep them all synchronized. In many ways, we're back where we started – with simple copy-paste code reuse. At best, we've simply come up with a new way to create source code libraries:

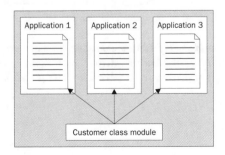

This is where **component-oriented design** comes in. Components build on object technologies to provide a better way of achieving reuse of our objects.

Just as the definition of COM is often confused, so are the terms for components and objects, so let's define them now and end any further confusion. The phrases COM component and COM object are frequently interchanged, and although this is technically not correct, it's unlikely that you will be misunderstood for what you mean. Nevertheless there is a difference, and using correct terminology only increases your credibility!

The term **component** is one of those over-used words and has a different meaning to just about anyone you'd care to ask. Even within the OO community, there's a great deal of disagreement about the meaning of the term. Many people would argue that a component is nothing more than a large or complex business object.

In fact, the terms 'object' and 'component' are often used interchangeably, but there's a distinct and important difference between them:

❑   Objects are created from classes. Classes are made up of source code that defines the object's data and the routines that are needed to manipulate that data.

❑   Components are precompiled *binary* code. Since components are precompiled, they are independent of the language in which they were created.

Since we're using a Microsoft development tool to create software for Microsoft operating systems, we'll stick with Microsoft's definition of a component. In its view, components are precompiled units of code that expose one or more interfaces for use by client programs components. Typically these are made available through ActiveX servers or ActiveX controls:

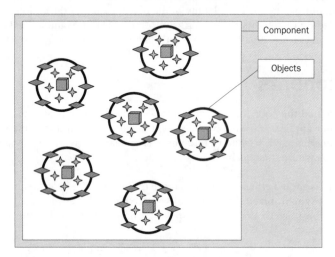

Even within the Microsoft world you'll find some confusion. To many people, ActiveX controls and components are synonymous. In reality, however, ActiveX controls are merely one type of component, along with various other types of ActiveX servers. We'll look at all these different types of components in the next section.

With binary components, we can achieve a whole new level of reuse in our applications. Going back to our `Customer` object, we can put the code into our component rather than into each individual application. The applications can then use the object directly from the component:

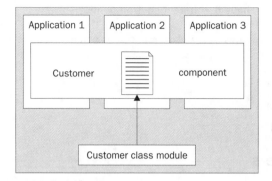

We get the same functionality as when we copied the source code into each application, but now we only need to maintain that code in a single place – the component.

Both classes and COM components provide some type of services. Classes provide services to *single* applications because they cannot communicate with other applications, while COM components provide services to *numerous* applications at the system level because they can communicate with other applications.

There are generally hundreds of components within the very Windows-based system you use at work and at home. These COM components can potentially be used among hundreds and even thousands of different applications. Furthermore, a different software vendor can create COM components using different programming languages without any integration problems. The sky really is the limit when it comes to COM components.

Client versus Server

Generally speaking, a client requests some type of services from a server. Thus the server's job is to perform some type of task on the client's behalf. On a large scale, this can be as simple as a common database application where the client represents the user's interface that makes requests to the database (server) for various tasks such as information storage, manipulation of data, and data retrieval.

Assuming the client-server database application just described is built with COM technology, we can break things down into smaller pieces – COM components. COM components themselves follow the same client-server principle just described. However, determining if a COM component is a client or server can become confusing because it can be both! When a client application makes a request to a COM component, the COM component acts as a server (to the client). When a COM component makes a request to another COM component, the calling COM component is considered the client while the COM component being requested is the server. In simpler terms, the reason a COM component can be both client and server is because each COM component exposes what are known as **interfaces**. These interfaces lead to a variety of functions that are available for a client to call upon.

Later in this chapter you will learn about interfaces and this will become more clear to you. For now, the thing to keep in mind is that a client makes requests and the server performs tasks based on client requests.

Server Components

Now that you can properly distinguish between COM components and COM objects, and know how COM components can act as both client and server, let's move on and look at COM components in general and see how they behave in different environments.

The COM environment provides us with several options when we create a component. These include:

❑ Out-of-process server

❑ In-process server

❑ ActiveX control

Out-of-process Servers

An out-of-process server is a component that is effectively a separate program containing objects. This type of server will always run in its own process space, and will thus be largely independent from any client programs.

Out-of-process servers are often standalone applications that happen to also provide access to their internal objects through COM, though they can be designed to only expose their objects to other applications.

These servers are often large applications in themselves, and provide access to their objects to make it easy for other programs to create macros or otherwise make use of existing functionality. Examples of out-of-process servers include Microsoft Word, Excel, SAP, and any other application that allows a COM programmer to access its objects.

A while back, Microsoft began licensing the VBA toolset to software vendors so they could use VBA as a macro language. For this to work, the software vendor has to expose their application's functionality via COM objects so a VBA programmer can write macros. The beneficial side-effect of this is that we can also use those COM objects from VB, VC or any other language that can be a COM client.

Another reason for creating out-of-process servers is because an out-of-process server runs within its own process – not within the process of the calling code. This is illustrated by the following diagram, which shows several clients interacting with objects running in the same out-of-process server:

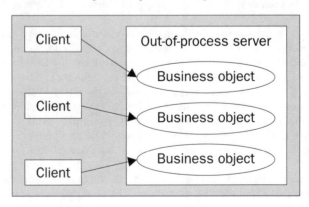

This can be very beneficial, because it means that we, as the component author, can choose our own threading models and do pretty much whatever we feel is required to make our component work.

The drawback to this is that we *have to* handle our own threading and do a lot of other work. As we'll see in the next few chapters, most of that work can be handled by COM+.

There is also a performance issue. Because our client application is communicating with objects in an entirely different process there is quite a bit of overhead. COM steps in between the client and the server in this case, and handles all the communication between them. While this is nice, because it keeps things simple and easy to program, it tends to slow things down since there is extra work involved in cross-process communication.

In general, out-of-process servers are useful if we need to do something truly out of the ordinary, or if we are trying to make use of the objects in a pre-existing application. Otherwise more mainstream in-process servers are the way to go.

In-process Servers

An in-process server is a component where our objects run inside the *client's* process. Each client essentially gets its own private copy of our component – and therefore a copy of all our objects.

> **In-process servers are often called COM DLLs or ActiveX DLLs.**

When people talk about COM servers or COM components, they are probably talking about an in-process server.

In-process servers don't have a process of their own – they always run within the context of another process. Often this other process is the client application itself, but may be run within the context of a different process entirely.

> *As we'll see in later chapters, if the component is part of a COM+ application, it is typically hosted by the COM+ environment – running in a separate process from the client application and allowing COM+ to create a process to host the DLL.*

In the case where a component is directly hosted by the client application, we get a performance boost. There is very little overhead involved when having client code interact with an object that is running in the same process:

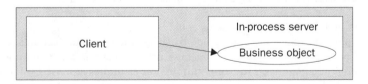

When the 'in-process' component is hosted by some other process, such as a COM+ application, things are a bit different. In this case, the client has to communicate across processes to interact with the object. In fact, this is quite similar to the out-of-process server scenario:

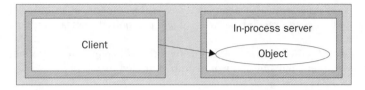

The advantages to running such a component in a COM+ application include stability and increased manageability.

We gain some theoretical stability because if a COM object crashes its process it won't bring down the client application (for example, ASP in Windows DNA). It would bring down the COM+ host process however, including all the other objects running in that host process.

We also gain some manageability. When ASP hosts an in-process server directly in its own process, that DLL will be locked until the IIS server is shut down and restarted. This can be impractical in a 24x7 environment.

If we run the in-process server in another process, such as a COM+ application, we can unlock the DLL by shutting down and restarting the COM+ application – leaving IIS running. While this still means that we have to shut down our application to update a DLL, we do avoid shutting down the entire web server.

ActiveX Controls

The final form of component is the ActiveX control. ActiveX controls are typically used to create visual objects as part of an interface design.

When we look at Windows DNA applications, ActiveX controls play a somewhat limited role. They can be used on the client if we know that the user is running Windows 9x, NT or 2000, and that they are using Internet Explorer. In most Windows DNA applications we are concerned with being browser and platform neutral on the client, so ActiveX controls are not very useful.

On the web server itself, ActiveX controls have no real place. There's no physical presentation on the web server, and that is what ActiveX controls are all about. Anything that we'd like to encapsulate in an ActiveX control on the web server can (and should) be handled through the use of an in-process server.

Interfaces – COM's Binary Standard

The advantages that COM provides for distributed application development are provided through the use of **interfaces**. COM interfaces are the mechanisms by which a client or consumer interacts with a component.

I previously mentioned that COM components could be written in any language. If all COM components were written exclusively in only one language, then communication among objects would not be difficult. However, when we use components written in various programming languages, we need a way for these different components to communicate. For example, suppose I want to talk to my wife about how my day at work was. Because she speaks the same language as I do, there is no language problem. Communication between my wife and me is easy. But what if I wanted to address my day's events to everyone at the United Nations? Certainly I would encounter numerous language barriers. I would need someone to intervene in the middle who could communicate for me. This is similar to what an interface does. It's true that unless everyone at the United Nations knew how to program using COM, interfaces would not help me communicate my day's events to the UN. But when it comes to communication with different programming languages, COM's interfaces provide a universal mechanism so each COM component can communicate in a language understood by all.

COM interfaces are nothing more than a group or collection of public functions that allows COM components to interact with each other. In other words, an interface is simply a list of methods a COM component supports. Furthermore, it's important to understand that an interface is neither a class nor an object. While a class can be instantiated to create a COM object, a COM interface cannot.

COM's Binary Contract

Every interface constitutes a binding contract between a COM object and an object offering an interface. Interfaces must never be changed. In other words, COM interfaces are said to be **immutable** as they are never versioned (although see the next section entitled *Version Control* to see what happens in real life). This means that once an interface has been published, it must never be modified. By published, I mean a COM component has been released into the production environment.

However, don't misunderstand this rule; this does not mean you cannot make any changes to a COM component. On the contrary, you can change business logic as long as you don't interfere with the original properties and methods. For example, in a growing business, it is normal for business rules (business logic) to change. Being able to change business logic such as mathematical and accounting formulae in a single COM component is an important advantage to COM and DNA applications. It is much easier to change business logic within a few COM components as opposed to having to recompile every client in a monolithic environment.

In addition, COM makes life easier by being able to support more than one interface at a time. New interfaces can be added to support new features while keeping the original interfaces intact. This means older applications will continue to work by using the original interfaces of the component while updated applications can take advantage by working with the new interfaces.

Version Control

As previously mentioned, once a COM interface is published, it is considered immutable. Altering an existing interface is likely to cause the application to fail. If you want to extend the functionality of a COM component by adding new methods, the correct procedure is to introduce a new interface and append it with a version number. In other words, because COM interfaces are immutable, they must not be altered in any way. When you version a COM component, you create a new interface while leaving the original interfaces intact. For example, suppose I have a COM component that can add the sum of two numbers. Now I have a need to be able to add more than two numbers. Instead of altering the original interface, a new interface should be added. You should increment a version number for the new interface such as ICanAdd2. A class module then would need to be implemented for both interfaces (ICanAdd and ICanAdd2) in order to support both old clients that rely on the interface ICanAdd and new clients that can take advantage of the new interface (ICanAdd2) functionality for adding more than two numbers.

IDL/MIDL

You may be wondering how it is possible to create a component in different languages and still be able to define an interface that can be called from any other programming language. After all, if we are programming in one language such as VB, how is it possible for an interface that is a part of one component to be able to communicate with an interface on another component that is written in C++? The answer lies with **Interface Definition Language** (IDL). The syntax for IDL looks very similar to C++ yet IDL goes beyond what C++ can offer by being able to define functions that extend process boundaries. IDL provides numerous extensions that allow attributes such as type libraries, coclasses, interfaces, methods, and parameters to be specified; again something C++ is not able to adequately do. However, it is important to understand that IDL is not an actual programming language. Instead, IDL is used specifically for defining interfaces and nothing more.

Do you have to use IDL to define your interfaces? The answer is no. Interfaces are essential to COM yet it does not matter how they are implemented as long as there is there is an agreement between the caller and the implementer regarding the interface definition.

Let's take a look at a simple method from a COM component written in VB:

```
Public Function SumOfNumbers(lngSum1 As Long, lngSum2 As Long) As Long

   SumOfNumbers = (lngSum1 + lngSum2)

End Function
```

If you use Visual Basic to program, the interfaces are generated for you during compilation. Indeed VB does take care of a lot of low-level programming for the developer. If you are a C++ programmer, you have to define your own interfaces.

Regardless of what language you use to program it is always to the programmers' benefit to understand how interfaces are defined. Furthermore, even with Visual Basic, you do have the option to create your own interfaces and it is often beneficial to do so. Because VB tries to take matters into its own hands, version control (see previous section) can become a real headache.

Let's take a look at an interface definition for the component we just looked at:

Note: the following IDL is for a component written in C++. Although this is an example of how IDL looks, this example will not work with Visual Basic.

```
[ object,
    uuid ( 05897BF4F-9D17-11D2-B7A3-9E6F29000000 )
]
interface ICalcSum : IUnknown

{
    import "unknown.idl"
      HRESULT SumOfNumbers ([in] long lsum1,
                            [in] long lsum2,
                            [out, retval]long* total);
}
```

If you are familiar with C++ you will see that IDL does indeed look similar to C and C++. However, you should be able to immediately identify attributes such as `[in]` and `[out]` that are not a part of the C or C++ languages. Let's take a look at this interface in more detail.

The beginning of an interface definition begins with an `object` attribute. The `object` attribute is used to identify a COM interface. Directly following the object attribute is a **UUID** (**universally unique identifier**). The UUID provides a unique number that is used to identify a particular interface. We will return to UUIDs later in this chapter.

The `interface` keyword is followed by the name of the interface. In this example, the interface is named `ICalcSum` to reflect the logic of adding numbers. Note that the interface name is described in a readable format, that is, humans can make sense of it. Following `ICalcSum` is a colon and then the interface name `IUnknown`. You will learn about `IUnknown` shortly. For now you just need to understand that `IUnknown` is the most fundamental interface and it is required with every object.

The next line down is `"import unknown.idl"`. This statement is used to locate the definition for the IUnknown interface.

Continuing to the next line, we have the interface method for SumOfNumbers. This interface method is designed to return an HRESULT value (see the *HRESULT* section later in this chapter). Briefly, an HRESULT is used with COM to indicate whether a method call is successfully accomplished or not.

Immediately following the HRESULT are three parameters for the interface method SumOfNumbers:

```
SumOfNumbers    ([in] long lsum1,
                [in] long lsum2,
                [out, retval]long* total);
```

The `[in]` found in the first two parameters specifies that these parameters are to be passed to the interface method SumOfNumbers. If you work with Visual Basic, you can correlate the `[in]` parameter with VB's ByRef.

The `[out, retval]` indicates that this parameter returns a value that will ultimately be passed to back to the client. Again, if you use Visual Basic, you can correlate the `[out]` parameter with VB's ByVal.

If you are a Visual Basic programmer you will discover that VB eliminates the need to write interface definitions for components. Although, you do have the ability to deal with interfaces by working with IDL and Microsoft's IDL compiler (midl.exe) that comes with C++. The IDL compiler translates the interface into C language source files. I will not go into IDL any further but if you are a VB developer and are curious, you can use OleView.exe to view IDL:

❑   Fire up the OLE Object Viewer (type **OLEVIEW** at the command line or choose **Tools OLE/COM Viewer**)

❑   Open the **Type Libraries** folder in the left hand pane and select the required COM object

❑   Right-click an object and select **View Type Information** to display the **ITypeLib Viewer**, where you can see the IDL file

By convention, interface names begin with the letter "I". By looking at the name ICalcSum, you can identify that this is an interface.

As you can see, Visual Basic saves a lot of time and trouble by eliminating the need to deal directly with component interfaces by automatically creating component interface definitions into a binary form called type libraries. On the other hand, C++ gives you much greater control over your interfaces. Also, by using C++ ATL (Active Template Library), the job of creating interfaces has been greatly reduced.

HRESULT

Almost all COM interfaces return a special 32-bit code from their methods. This 32-bit code is called an HRESULT. Although this code is basically just a mechanism to return status information, it is actually the method COM utilizes to return errors to the caller of the method. The reason COM needs an HRESULT to return errors is because COM objects are not capable of transmitting error messages back to the client using standard exception mechanisms, because standard exception mechanisms cannot cross process boundaries. Furthermore, COM components are often written in different languages, and different languages handle exceptions differently.

We can divide an HRESULT into four divisions:

❑ **Severity** uses a single bit. It returns a value indicating how successful the method call was. Thus a bit of 0 indicates the method call was a success while a bit of 1 indicates an error.

❑ **Reserved** comprises two bits that may be used in the future but are currently not used and must remain set to zero values.

❑ **Facility** provides information to the client as to where the error occurred.

❑ **Code** is used to describe the error that occurred. COM defines its own error codes that range from 0x00 through 0x01FF. Additionally, COM allows the range of 0x200 through 0xFFF that COM uses for `FACILITY_ITF`. It is here that application developers can define their own HRESULTs.

IUnknown

Due to COM's specifications, every COM object must have an interface called `IUnknown`. This is the most fundamental interface a COM object has. What makes `IUnknown` so special is it can be used to hold a pointer to any other interface. As a matter of fact, `IUnknown` enables interfaces to be used without actually knowing anything about them.

`IUnknown` has three methods that a client can invoke: `QueryInterface`, `AddRef`, and `Release`. However, realize if you are using Visual Basic, VB does all this behind the scenes. In other words, with VB you cannot directly invoke these three methods.

AddRef and Release

The methods `AddRef` and `Release` manage reference counting. This reference count is an internal count of the number of clients using a particular COM object. It is possible that several clients will invoke the services of an object at the same time. When a client actually begins a session with an object, it calls the `AddRef` method. Once `AddRef` is called, a count of one is added to the tally. As soon as the session is over, the `Release` method is invoked thus removing a count of one from the tally. As long as a client holds a single reference to the object, the object will remain in existence. However, when the reference count reaches zero, the object destroys itself.

QueryInterface

The `QueryInterface` method is the mechanism that a client uses to discover and navigate the interfaces of a component dynamically. `QueryInterface` is probably the most significant method of all COM interfaces because it allows run-time inspection of all the interfaces that a component supports. When the `QueryInterface` method provides an interface pointer to a consumer, the `QueryInterface` calls `AddRef`. As we have previously seen, `AddRef` will increment a count by one.

Virtual Function Tables

The only way to access a COM object is through a pointer to an interface. Now that you think you have a good understanding of interface pointers, let me make things a little more confusing by saying: an interface pointer is really a pointer to a pointer in a **virtual table** (**v-table**) that is implemented in memory! Perhaps in more clear terms, for every class that contains public methods, a v-table will be created and placed in memory at runtime. Each v-table contains an array of function pointers whose elements contain the address of each specific function that an object can implement. Sitting at the very top of every v-table array will be three fundamental methods that make up perhaps the most important COM interface, discussed above, `IUnknown`. Virtual tables are only created for each class and not for each instance of the class.

Let's see how this all works. Suppose we have a business object that has an interface called `IPurchaseMyBook`. The client sends an interface pointer to `IUnknown` and requests a pointer to the function called `OrderTwoCopies`. The `QueryInterface` will return a pointer to the v-table where `AddRef` increments the reference count by one. As soon as the object is finished with the function `OrderTwoCopies`, the method `Release` kicks in and decreases the reference count by one. When the reference count reaches zero, the object `PurchaseMyBook` will release itself, thus being destroyed.

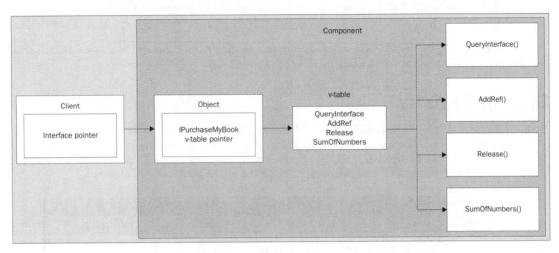

UUIDs, GUIDs, and the Windows Registry

Historically, UUIDs were first designated to identify interfaces regarding Distributed Computing Environment Remote Procedure Calls (DCE RPC). If you recall the example in this chapter for defining an interface using IDL, the `object` attribute was identified with a UUID. The reason for this is that COM IDL is based on the Open Software Foundation's Distributed Computing Environment. However, Microsoft likes to change things. As a result Microsoft has renamed UUIDs to GUIDs when referring to COM.

Pronounced *Goo-id*, a **globally unique identifier** (**GUID**) is a unique 128-bit value that uniquely identifies every exposed COM component and every COM interface without duplication anywhere in the world – guaranteed. This guarantee is beneficial and mandatory to the application developer as well as the application user because it ensures that COM components will never connect to a wrong component due to duplicate GUIDs.

Take a close look at the GUID shown below. You should notice that they are typically seen as a string of hexadecimal digits. Hyphens are used to make these strings more readable.

```
{00000010-0000-0010-8000-00AA006D2EA4}
```

Have you ever wondered how a GUID is generated? An algorithm is used to generate GUID numbers by taking the unique value from the network card on the programmer's PC and the current system date and time. If the programmer's machine does not have a network card, then a random number is used with the system date and time. The chances against two GUIDs ever being the same are astronomical.

You will come across strings of numbers that look like GUIDs but that are referred to as CLSIDs and IIDs. Actually CLSIDs and IIDs are all GUIDs. When referring to GUIDs that identify COM classes, we refer to them as **Class IDs** (**CLSIDs**). However, GUIDs that are used to name an interface are called **interface identifiers** (**IIDs**).

> **Object instances of COM classes are not identified by GUIDs or CLSIDs.**

Now that you know what a GUID is, let's continue with the next section and learn why GUIDs play such an important role within COM.

System Registry

Earlier in this chapter I mentioned that COM was location-independent, which means that a COM component can reside anywhere on your computer or even another computer connected to a network. Before an object can be created, the COM runtime must first locate the COM components. The COM runtime is able to locate COM components through the use of the Windows registry.

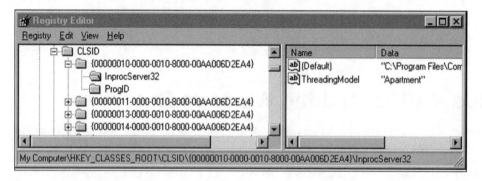

This screenshot of the registry provides a lot of information. We can see that we are looking at a CLSID, so we know that it is a COM class from which a COM object can be instantiated. Underneath the CLSID we can tell that this COM class is an in-process server (a DLL). Jumping to the right-hand pane, we can see the location path where this object is installed. The type of threading model is also identified. In this case, the object is using Apartment threading.

Back to the left-hand pane, a folder called ProgID can be opened. To further identify the object, the programmer can provide a text string that is easily read by humans. Usually, a company name and the name of the class is used for easy identification, such as:

```
MyCompanyName.CalcSUM
```

Creating a COM Object

OK, you have now learned the different aspects of COM. Let's put everything together and create a COM object. As you may have gathered by now, there is a lot of communication that must occur behind the scenes in order for a COM object to be created. I warn you if you are new to COM, the process for creating an object can at first seem overwhelming. To help present you with a clear picture, take a look at the following diagram, based on an in-process server, and then reference it as I continue this discussion:

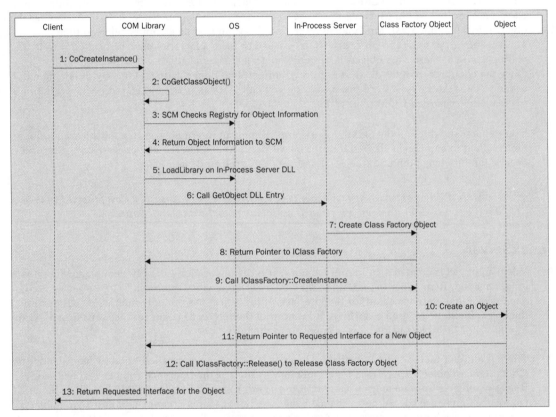

In order for an object to be instantiated, a client must first make a call to an API function called `CoCreateInstance` (step 1).

C++ programmers can simply make a call to `CoCreateInstance`, however with Visual Basic much of the work is done behind the scenes for you. VB programmers can use the `New` operator followed by a coclass name. In other words, with VB, the `New` operator translates a call to `CoCreateInstance`. The prefix `Co`, such as in `CoCreateInstance` and `CoGetClassObject`, is a typical naming convention for COM runtime API functions.

`CoCreateInstance` calls another API function called `CoGetClassObject` (step 2). This is part of COM's specification and it is designed to create objects from a desired class as well as define a special interface called `IClassFactory`. At this point, you just need to know that the job of the `IClassFactory` interface is to talk to other class objects. We will return to `IClassFactory` shortly. In simpler terms, `CoGetClassObject` is a COM class object whose sole purpose is to create a new instance of a different class. Because this COM class (`CoGetClassObject`) creates class objects by implementing the `IClassFactory` interface, `CoGetClassObject` is often referred to as a **class factory**.

In case you are curious, `CoCreateInstance` *asks the SCM (Service Control Manager) to search the registry location:* `HKEY_CLASSES_ROOT\CLSID`.

OK, back to creating a COM object. When a client makes a call to `CoCreateInstance`, the CLSID for the class is also specified. In this case CLISD is used to identify the particular class the client wants an object for. Deep within COM's runtime lies what is known as the Service Control Manager (SCM pronounced as *scum*). The SCM's job is to locate the requested class object by using the specified CLSID. The first place the SCM looks to locate the class object is within its own internal database. If the class is not located within its database, the SCM turns to the system registry (step 3). As soon as the class object is located, the SCM immediately returns to COM an interface pointer referred to as `IClassFactory` (steps 4 to 8). Every COM class must have a factory object associated with it. The main purpose of these class objects is to implement the `IClassFactory` interface.
Once the client receives the `IClassFactory` pointer, two things happen. One, by obtaining a pointer to the `IClassFactory`, `CoCreateInstance` can call `IClassFactory::CreateInstance` in order to create the requested COM object (steps 9 and 10).

You can actually think of the SCM's job as simply being an intermediary. In a nutshell, all it does is bind a client to an object and then it drops out of sight. As soon as the object is created, a second step occurs: the interface pointer to the `IClassFactory` is released (step 12).

If you are a VB programmer, you will have to be a believer, as you cannot see a class factory. I guess this is a fair trade as if you use VB you will never have to deal with class factories.

LockServer

When an object is created it resides in memory. It is the client's job to notify the object when it is no longer needed. Remember the `Release` method associated with `IUnknown`? The `Release` method decrements the reference count for the interface. If the object has multiple interfaces, it is possible that the object is still being used elsewhere. It is not until the reference count reaches zero for all existing interfaces for the object before it is released from memory.

There is another method that is available through `IClassFactory` called `LockServer`. Under normal circumstances, objects are released from memory as soon as the reference counter reaches zero. Releasing objects from memory usually improves performance. Note that I said "usually". Some complex clients have special performance issues where constantly creating and destroying objects actually causes a hindrance to the application's performance. The `LockServer` method allows components to remain in memory by incrementing the reference count by one. Because `LockServer` keeps a count of one in the reference counter, the object will stay in memory even if it is not currently being accessed. Having the component reside in memory has the advantage of allowing the object to be called without having to go through the process of recreating it. The cost is memory. If objects are not destroyed when they are no longer used, the application runs the risk of reducing system memory resources, thus reducing overall performance.

There you have it! Now that you have toured the internals of COM and you have learned how an object is instantiated, let's try a hands-on COM project.

Try It!

Let's visit a fictitious company called MyCompany, who have decided to write a program that will take two numbers and add them together. Off the record, I think the owners of the company plan to use this calculator to add bonuses to their regular paychecks. This company only has two programmers: one knows only Visual Basic and the other knows only Visual C++. It would not be in the best interests of this or any company to have programmers who can't work together. Without COM, only one of the programmers would write the program.

Let's write our client in Visual Basic. For fun, we will write a very simple server component using Visual C++. Don't worry if you are not a C++ programmer. C++ is not the scope of this chapter, however I am going to present a tiny amount for learning and demonstration purposes only. I will point out a few interesting things that Visual Basic automatically hides from the developer.

Let's start with C++, as it is more difficult than Visual Basic. After completing the C++ portion, I think you will realize how powerful and easy Visual Basic makes things for COM developers. Nevertheless, you cannot argue with the fact that C++ is much more powerful and provides the application programmer complete control over each circumstance. It's lucky for us application developers that COM allows us to program in either language.

1. Start Visual C++. Create a new project by choosing New from the File menu. Be sure the Projects tab has been selected. To speed us along, we will use the ATL COM AppWizard. This should already be highlighted by default. Enter the project name SumCalculator and a path location. In this example I have used C:\MTSProjects\SumCalculator, as shown. Then click OK to start the ATL COM AppWizard:

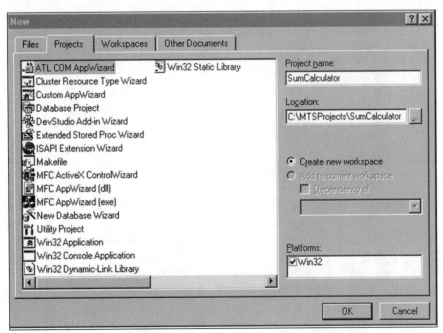

2. Leave the default for the Server Type set to Dynamic Link Library (DLL) and click Finish:

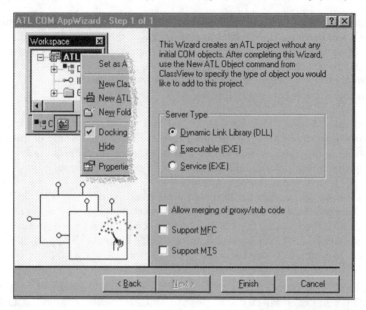

3. The dialog for New Project Information is displayed with the information you previously provided. If you entered everything correctly, click OK. By clicking Cancel, the wizard will take you back to the previous screen.

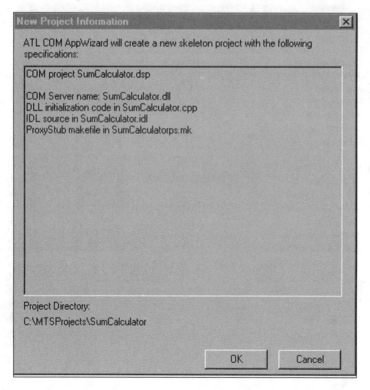

4. In the left pane, you should notice the name of this project followed by the word classes:

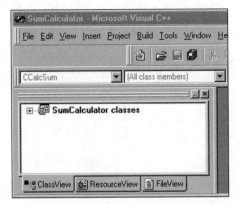

5. So far so good! We are now going to add a new ATL object to our project by choosing Insert from the main menu bar and then choosing New ATL Object. From the ATL Object Wizard dialog, we will use the default icon Simple Object and then click Next:

6. Type CalcSum in the edit box labeled Short Name. Notice that, as you type, all the other boxes will change to reflect relevant values based on the short name you provide. This is how the edit boxes should look:

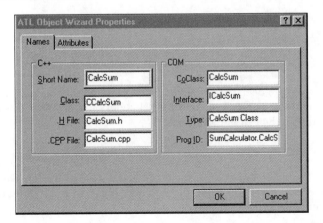

7. Stop and take a closer look at the different names. You should be familiar with many of the items being created. Do not click OK; we first need to look at the attributes. Click the **Attributes** tab. Again look at the different attributes that can be selected. We will learn about many of these later in this book. For now, accept the defaults by clicking OK:

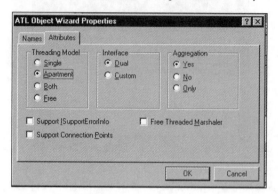

8. If you haven't already, expand the SumCalculator classes in the left pane by clicking the "+" icon. Notice that we have an interface named ICalcSum. Remember our discussion about interface naming? Highlight **ICalcSum** and then right-click with your mouse. From the pop-up menu, select **Add Method.**

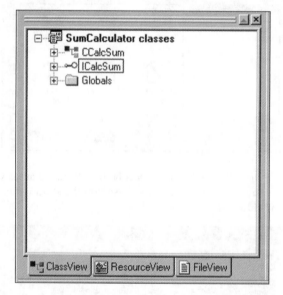

9. We are now going to declare the method SumOfNumbers to the interface using the **Add Method to Interface** dialog. Type in SumOfNumbers for the **Method Name** and then type the following string in the **Parameters** box:

```
[in]long lsum1, [in]long lsum2, [out,retval]long* total
```

The string of parameters you have just typed is IDL. Visual Basic makes all this invisible to the developer. However, C++ developers tend to work with interfaces directly. Click the OK button to continue to the next step:

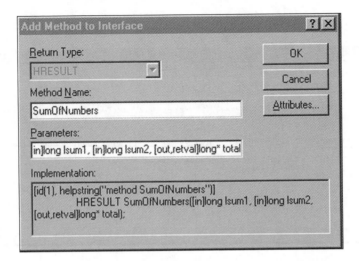

10. Make sure that ICalcSum in the left pane is completely expanded. Locate the first SumOfNumbers(long lsum1, long lsum2, long *total). It has a small cube-shaped icon. Double-click it. This will open up the source code window.

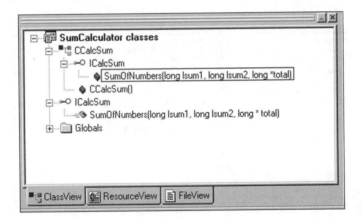

11. We are going to enter our logic for adding two numbers. Locate the line:

```
STDMETHODIMP CCalcSum::SumOfNumbers(long lsum1, long lsum2, long * total)
```

Directly under this line is a curly bracket { and directly underneath is a comment line:

```
// TODO: Add your implementation code here
```

Add this line of code under the comment:

```
*total=(lsum1 + lsum2);
```

Your source code should match the screenshot below:

```
CalcSum.cpp
// CalcSum.cpp : Implementation of CCalcSum
#include "stdafx.h"
#include "SumCalculator.h"
#include "CalcSum.h"

/////////////////////////////////////////////////////////////////////////////
// CCalcSum

STDMETHODIMP CCalcSum::SumOfNumbers(long lsum1, long lsum2, long *total)
{
    // TODO: Add your implementation code here
    *total=(lsum1 + lsum2);
    return S_OK;
}
```

12. You have come to the final step of this C++ project! On the main menu, click Build then select Build SumCalculator.dll from the drop down menu. Look at the bottom of the screen. The Build tab should be selected by default. It may take a few moments but if you have followed all of these instructions exactly as they have been presented, you should receive zero warnings and zero errors:

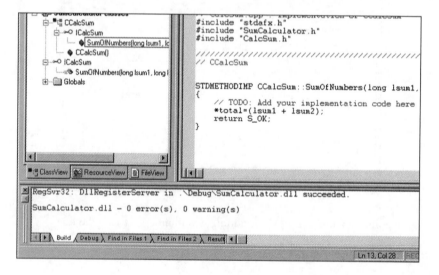

Congratulations – you have just built a COM component using Visual C++. Be sure to save your project! We still need to build the client component using Visual Basic. Because Visual Basic is much more intuitive, I will not present you with as many screenshots as for the COM component just built using C++.

1. Open Visual Basic and select Standard EXE from the New Project box. Before we go any further, click Project from the main menu and select References from the drop down menu. Locate SumCalculator 1.0 Type Library and select it.

You should recognize the name SumCalculator. This reference was created when we successfully built the SumCalculator.dll in Visual C++. This reference is known as a type library. Type libraries are the mechanisms by which components within a COM server are described to the consumers of that server. A type library is a catalog that lists what components, interfaces, enumerations, and structures are available inside a COM server.

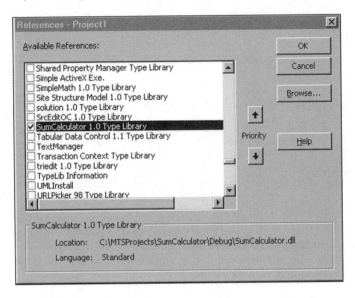

2. Let's name the project SumCalcClient. Name the form frmCalc and set the caption to I Can Add!

3. Add two command buttons to the form. Make one button larger than the other. Name the large command button cmdCalcSum with the caption CalcSum and name the small command button cmdExit with the caption Exit:

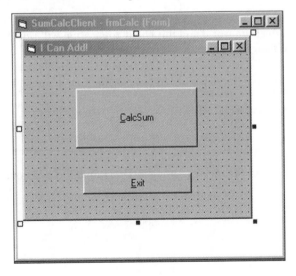

4. Open the code window by double-clicking the command button **CalcSum** and enter the following code:

```
Private Sub cmdCalcSum_Click()

   Dim sReturnString1 as String
   Dim sReturnString2 as String
   Dim objCalcSum as CalcSum

   Set objCalcSum = New CalcSum

   sReturnString1 =  InputBox$ ("Enter a number:")
   sReturnString2 =  InputBox$ ("Enter another number:")

   MsgBox "The total =" & objCalcSum.SumOfNumbers (sReturnString1, _
                sReturnString2)

   Set objCalcSum=Nothing
End Sub
```

Pay close attention to the code you just entered. We can deduce that the total is derived from two numbers entered by the user. However, we don't know how these numbers are being added as the formula has been encapsulated into our C++ component. Although this demonstration is not a distributed (n-tier) application, you can get an idea of how business logic can be separated from the client.

Again, think in terms of a distributed client-server application. This client application is not coded in a monolithic manner. If we decided that we want to change the business rule from adding two numbers to adding two numbers and then multiplying the total by two, all we need to do is adjust the formula on the server component. The client(s) accessing this component do not need to be changed or updated. You will be able to appreciate this more after you complete the next chapter on DCOM.

There you have it – COM in action. We can encapsulate, separate, and distribute COM components all over the world and this client application will run just as if everything was installed on the same machine.

5. Let's go ahead and put the following code in for the **Exit** command button:

```
Private Sub cmdExit_Click()
   Unload Me
End Sub
```

6. Save your project and then try executing it. Don't forget to add your bonus to your paycheck!

Summary

This chapter covered one of the most fundamental building blocks for Microsoft's DNA model, namely the Component Object Model (COM). This chapter started off by explaining COM's written specification as well as introducing you to COM's system-level code called the COM library.

Next you learned about the advantages of COM. You learned how COM:

❑ Promotes component-based development and OOP

❑ Promotes code reuse

❑ Provides the necessary mechanics for COM components to communicate with each other

You also learned the differences between COM components and COM objects. After this we moved on to learning about how COM components behave in different environments. More specifically you learned about different types of server components.

Next you toured COM's interfaces. You learned about COM's binary standard and you even took a short tour of COM's Interface Definition Language (IDL). You learned about COM's most fundamental interface, IUnknown, and its three fundamental methods, QueryInterface, AddRef, and Release.

You also learned about UUIDs, GUIDs, and CLSIDs and how they relate to COM.

Finally, you had the opportunity to bring together all the concepts covered in this chapter and saw how an object is instantiated from a COM component. To wrap things up, you had a hands-on exercise where you built a simple COM application using both VB and C++ components.

Now that you have a good understanding of COM, you are ready to learn about the Distributed Component Object Model (DCOM) coming up in the next chapter.

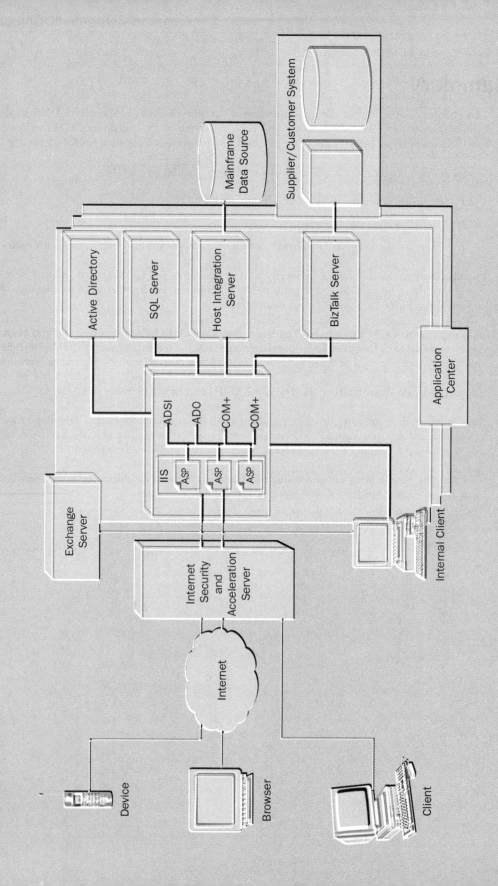

4

Distributed Processing

In Chapter 1 you were introduced to the n-tier logical model. You may recall the arrows between the components on the various tiers. The overall application was composed of all the components and the communication between them. In a monolithic application, the parts of an application communicate through the transfer of control from one function or routine to another.

In the last chapter, you had a look at creating COM components that would serve as building blocks for larger applications. In Windows DNA, we need some way of communicating between components and even between computers. This is where the challenges of network applications come in – this communication, even in a modern, well-constructed network, is far less certain than that between the routines in a single executable.

Just as the advantages of the n-tier model outweigh the challenges, so too can we turn communications to our advantage. In overcoming latency and connectivity outages, we build infrastructure that improves availability and scalability. Asynchronous techniques that overcome latency also let us cope with spikes in demand, letting us use hardware scaled to the average case rather than the worst case. When we store data to overcome network outages, we also protect against a lost server. Implementing these features is difficult, but Windows DNA gives us a variety of tools for the job.

In this chapter, you will be exposed to the basic problems of distributed processing. We'll take a very brief look at the history of distributed technology, by way of seeing how challenges have been met in the past and how DNA improves on them. We'll have an extended look at distributed COM+, the core infrastructure technology for distributing processing between machines in DNA. We'll take a sample COM component developed with the techniques you learned in the last chapter and distribute it to a remote server using COM+.

> *A detailed overview at COM+ will be saved for the next chapter, but we'll have to introduce some aspects of it here as and when they become integral to our discussion.*

There are also tools on the near horizon for doing distributed processing between Windows and non-Windows platforms. We'll describe those and show you the "when" and the "why" of using those technologies.

Distributed Processing

What is **distributed computing** (also known as distributed processing)? As you saw in Chapter 1, distributed computing is at the heart of network applications. It is the notion of distributing the parts of an application or system across various computers on a network. To rely on distributed computing, you need communications to physically connect the computers, and some technology built on top of the communications layer to plug applications software into the communications layer. This technology is what we are generally concerned with when we are talking about distributed computing. The technology provides a metaphor or model for applications programming. That metaphor affects how you look at and interact with remote resources, so it necessarily has an effect on how you build applications that use the technology. The last chapter introduced you to COM, which provides an object-based metaphor for distributed computing.

There are distributed computing technologies that do not use an object-oriented metaphor, of course, including some of the earliest. In fact, depending on where you draw the line between the communications infrastructure and distributed computing technology, you will find that some of the earliest distributed technologies are still around underneath later arrivals. In fact, distributed COM, or DCOM, relies on remote procedure calls, which in turn are built on sockets in Windows. Socket programming goes back quite far, so it is interesting to see some of the newest technologies relying on some of the oldest. Peeling back the layers to the simplest methods will help you to understand where distributed processing in Windows DNA came from, and even where it is going as it reaches out to non-Windows platforms.

Implementations

The most common distributed technologies fall into three categories, though these categories do not exhaust the list of distributed technologies:

❑   Sockets

❑   Remote Procedure Calls (RPC)

❑   Components

Each category provides a programming metaphor, and each addresses the common challenges of network applications. These techniques are all available to DNA programmers, although in some cases they are more interesting from a theoretical standpoint.

Sockets

The earliest mainstream technology for distributed processing is **sockets**. It is closely tied to the IP protocol that underlies virtually all networks today. Sockets look at distributed communications through the metaphor of an electrical line. At each end of the line, an application plugs into a socket. Data is passed back and forth over the wire, and the applications on either end respond according to an agreed protocol.

However, the matter is a bit more complicated. Multiple sockets must be permitted per machine in order for socket programming to be useful. You may need only a single connection, but you would hardly want to be restricted to one. You might, after all, want to run more than one distributed application concurrently. If we were limited to one socket per computer, you'd have to shut down one distributed application to run another. Both web browsers and e-mail use sockets – you wouldn't be able to click on a mailto link in a web page and send the e-mail if we couldn't have more than one socket per machine. A socket, therefore, is the combination of the machine's IP address and a port number. A port is a numerical identifier that allows the socket software to sort out different connections. HTTP, for example, uses a well-known port, 80, by default so that all web browsers know how to connect to web servers. Occasionally you will see a URL that begins with http: but includes a number following the hostname, for example http://hostname:2000. This is how HTTP communicates the fact that the web server hosting the URL's target wishes to use a port other than 80.

In the diagram below, application A and application B are connected using sockets to communicate through the network. The computer running application A also has another socket-based application running that is connected, through the network, to a computer that is not shown in the diagram:

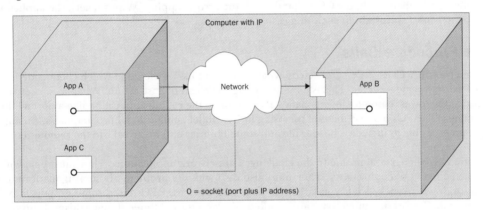

All that is very interesting, but we are application programmers and we want to know *how* the applications are communicating. In highly simplified terms, the applications take turns reading and writing byte streams to and from their sockets. Upon reading some bytes, a computer interprets the results according to a protocol. HTTP is such a protocol. Web browsers and web servers implement the same protocol. An HTTP GET request, for example, is simply a stream of characters. For example GET index.html. The page served up in response arrives as a stream of characters, in this case the HTML that describes the page. The popularity of Internet applications depends on how widely known the protocol is. I could configure my proprietary application to use sockets and TCP/IP on port 80, but a web browser on the other end will not be able to make sense of what I am sending, and I will not be able to make sense of the browser's requests.

> *You can take advantage of this by using a telnet client to communicate with a web server over port 80. You (blindly) type in the GET command – say GET index.html – and the web server replies with the requested page in raw text form. This mimicry is useful when debugging an ASP or CGI script that is badly misbehaving and when you cannot connect to the server with debugging tools.*

In Chapter 1 we indicated that you have to worry about the binary representation of some primitive types when connecting two computers with dissimilar hardware or operating systems. TCP/IP uses a common scheme for representing integers called **network byte order**. Socket programmers who wish to use integers in their byte streams must avail themselves of several low-level functions provided by their sockets implementation to convert integers to and from network byte order.

How are sockets important to distributed computing? To begin with, they are unquestionably the most successful form of distributed processing. The entire Internet relies on sockets. They illustrate the fact that you can only pass data between applications, not running code loaded in memory. You must have a running program on the other end of your socket. Some experimental technologies for transferring programmatic agents between computers rely on streaming some code to the other machine, where the receiving socket application activates it.

Sockets also illustrate the problem of isolating machine-specific data formats. The socket code offers rudimentary conversion routines, but it is completely the responsibility of the application programmer to ensure they are called. If the application fails to do so, the results will be unintelligible on dissimilar machines.

The final problem of sockets is that they offer only the most rudimentary programming metaphor. Sockets offer byte streams; what happens on either end is up to the application. You could build an object-based metaphor (as DCOM does), or a state machine (the most common technique). Designing real-world protocols and implementing them is hard work. Contrast what a web server must do – error handling and all – with the COM interfaces you saw in the last chapter. You created components, set properties, and called methods. COM handled all the error trapping. With sockets, the application programmer must worry about such things.

Remote Procedure Calls

Remote Procedure Calls (**RPC**) are exactly what they sound like: a model in which client code invokes a procedure on a remote server. This is a bit further up the chain of abstraction. Whereas sockets are trapped at the lowest common level – data – RPCs look to the calling application like a normal function or subroutine call. RPCs put distributed processing into a model familiar to all programmers. An application programmer is able to include a header file and some libraries and make calls to the remote resource.

RPCs are not, of course, immune to the challenges of network applications. They must deal with unexpected losses of connectivity. They must also deal with the problem of differing platform data formats. But where sockets left you largely to your own devices, RPCs build some support into the RPC runtime code. Losses of connectivity are handled with an internal timeout mechanism. If no reply is received in a specified interval, an error is propagated up into the application making the call. This is novel for a programmer new to distributed computing, of course. When was the last time you called a well-tested function in a monolithic program only to have it suddenly fail for reasons outside your control? Almost never, if it is truly well tested. Almost everything in a monolithic application is within your control. Still, programmers trying to move to distributed processing have to get used to some new ideas, no matter how great the support provided by the implementing technology.

Rather than map from each supported platform to every other supported platform, RPCs support a **wire format** common to all platforms. It specifies all the basic data types including their size and byte order. It is an arbitrary format designed to provide common ground for all platforms which use it. It becomes the responsibility of each client and each server to translate from their binary format into the common format and vice versa. Each RPC call, then, involves four translations:

❑ client to wire format

❑ wire to server format

❑ server back to wire (for the return value)

❑ wire format back to client format

Unlike socket programming, RPC programming tools give programmers a bit more support. Function interfaces – the parameter list and the return type – are specified in an **interface definition language**. IDL is a text-based description of interfaces, their methods, parameters, and return values. At build time, an IDL compiler generates **proxies** and **stubs**. The client application compiles and links one of these into its executable image to handle client-side translations, and the server application that implements the body of the RPC compiles and links the other.

RPCs are a good model for programmers in as much as every programmer is intimately familiar with the concept of functions and subroutines. The protocol for RPCs is implied by the functional interface: call the routine synchronously with a given parameter list and wait until a known return type is sent back from the server. Although synchronous calls have problems in terms of scalability, this is much simpler than having to develop a protocol and implement a state machine. Where good RPC development tools are available for a platform, RPCs are one of the more accessible technologies for doing distributed processing.

There is one area in which RPCs are somewhat lacking, though, and this is the matter of maintaining state. State is essential to a traditional, top-down structured application that is handled through global data. Obviously, though, when you have a central server supporting multiple clients, the server has to maintain state information for each client, or each client has to maintain state information for itself. In the latter case, the state information must be provided to the server every time an RPC is invoked. If the server is stateful, something in the functional interface must suggest this. The function call metaphor does not cover the idea of holding information from one call to another, so you typically end up with calls along the lines of SetSomeValue(). It works, but there should be a more intuitive way of handling this.

Another factor that has diminished the popularity of RPCs is the rise of object oriented programming and its close cousin, component software. RPCs hark back to the heyday of structured programming – the 1970s. The fashion for nearly twenty years has been objects, so it should not be surprising that we should desire an object metaphor for distributed computing. Happily, there are several such technologies, and they address the state issue.

Components

Object-oriented programming began at the level of source code. A programmer would write a class and compile and link it into a program. Reuse consisted of source-code inheritance, or the static linkage of a binary library into a program. These are poor models for distributed processing. If you have the source, you are less likely to need the server. The whole idea is to use the resources of the server without having to reimplement them. If the client and server machines are of different types, you are right back to the problem of dissimilar data formats that we saw in sockets and RPCs.

The next step in object programming, then, was **component** software. Components look and act like objects. They have properties and methods. Although you can't generally inherit from a component the way you can from an object, reuse is greater because you aren't sharing source code or implementation libraries.

There is major controversy in component software as to whether certain technologies truly support inheritance and whether inheritance between components is even desirable. We do not need to enter that battle here. Suffice to say, if you wish to compare some of the technologies listed here you must be prepared for spirited discussions.

All distributed component technologies have a few things in common. They must include timeout and wire format facilities like RPCs. They must have a central, well-known mechanism, to allow a client program to locate component implementations of the desired type. There must be some facility at the operating system level to locate components orphaned due to losses of connectivity and clean up their resources.

The Smalltalk programming language gave rise to several distributed implementations, but that technology never really took off due to the fact that Smalltalk never caught on as a mainstream langauge. A number of vendors of distributed technology joined together to produce the consortium-standard **Common Object Request Broker Architecture** (**CORBA**). CORBA is one of the most popular distributed technologies. It was designed from the start as an object-based distributed processing technology. Like RPCs, it handles lost connections with timeouts and dissimilar data formats through generating stubs and proxies.

> *The home for "all things CORBA" is the Object Management Group, which maintains the definitive web site at http://www.omg.org.*

CORBA suffered from the usual practical pitfalls experienced by multi-vendor consortia, but survived to become widely supported. It is not well suited for use on a single machine. Since it was designed to be distributed, all the mechanisms for distributed calls must be present and used in all cases, even if the call never leaves the local machine. Each machine using CORBA has an **Object Request Broker** (**ORB**) that performs the component location and housekeeping functions for the system. The fact that CORBA is implemented by multiple vendors is a double-edged sword. On the one hand, multiple vendors protect customers from the risk of a single vendor going out of business. They spur competition leading to improved features. On the other hand, each vendor has an incentive to include extensions to the CORBA standard. If you use those extensions, interoperability between ORBs becomes problematic. Despite these handicaps, though, CORBA is widely supported and is the primary means of doing distributed processing in Java for enterprise-scale systems.

> *The other Java technology for distributed processing is **Remote Method Invocations** (**RMI**). Sun's early statements about distributed technology were mixed and caused some confusion as to which technology to use. Java RMI requires Java on both ends of the exchange – client and server – and application servers are generally supporting CORBA for their distributed technology.*

No book on Windows DNA can get away without discussing the Component Object Model (COM). That friendly little technology popped up in the context of local programming in the last chapter. You had an application that wanted to distribute its implementation across resources hosted on the same machine. This proved to be a very popular technique, particularly when Visual Basic added support for COM. When Windows NT 4.0 came along, **Distributed COM** (**DCOM**) was introduced. The Microsoft team behind DCOM introduced the famous – or notorious – slogan "DCOM is COM with a longer wire". To a programmer, that was largely true. The COM runtime services handled the challenges of network applications as quietly as possible. As we shall see shortly, the addition of various scalability features changes the equation a bit. Still, for a Windows DNA programmer, COM, or the enhanced version COM+ that is native to Windows 2000, is the cleanest solution for component-based distributed processing.

Distributed Processing and Windows DNA

Windows DNA offers a wealth of solutions for doing distributed processing. Under the original Windows DNA, these were largely confined to the Windows platform. One of the most exciting enhancements to the architecture is the introduction of distributed solutions for crossing platform boundaries. Technologies like XML coupled with Web communications protocols like HTTP help you take data from a program on one operating system and send it to another program on a completely different platform. These solutions are built on top of open standards for communications protocols and data transfer.

This addition to the architecture is critically important for the next generation of Internet-enabled business-to-business and business-to-consumer solutions. Such solutions cannot demand a single platform and operating system. Disparate systems will increasingly have to work together using a common denominator of open standards. Open methods have the advantage of facilitating cross-platform integration. The price you pay is less integration with the various software pieces on a single platform. Consequently, a good software architect has to know when to specify a proprietary method and when open standards are demanded. There is no single choice; proprietary solutions will generally have better performance and tighter integration, but fail to make the grade when trying to cross platforms. We'll begin our look at distributed technologies in Windows DNA with the platform-specific methods, then follow the architecture's evolution to open standards.

Native Methods

As noted previously, distributed processing on Windows DNA is centered on COM+. Its predecessor, COM, was entirely synchronous. The calling program waited for the serving component to complete processing the method before it could continue. For asynchronous processing, you had to leave the component model for Microsoft Message Queue. That is, while you used MSMQ's COM components, your code was oriented to passing messages, not making method calls on components. With the advent of COM+, the boundary is blurred. COM+ enables queued components. These are asynchronous method invocations. These are implemented by arranging a marriage of COM over MSMQ. To some extent, then, you could proceed on the assumption that native distributed processing could be limited to COM+. In practice, the semantics of MSMQ are similar to those used in one of the open methods, so it is still worthwhile to consider MSMQ as a separate topic.

> *At the risk of being completely pedantic, sockets and RPCs are part of the platform as well. Obviously, to support open methods Windows must support sockets. RPCs have never gone away, either. In practice, however, these technologies are relegated to the infrastructure. If you are building or designing distributed systems for Windows DNA, you will either be using high-level, proprietary solutions like COM+ or proprietary implementations of open methods. There is no practical need to drop down to the low-level, detailed programming inherent in sockets or RPCs on Windows.*

COM+

COM+, like its predecessor COM, is an object-based component system supported by the Windows 2000 operating system. There are third-party ports of the COM infrastructure for other platforms, but they have not entered the mainstream of development for those operating systems. Its runtime components manage object creation and reclamation, as well as providing a central registry of information used by applications seeking COM+ interfaces. A typical COM+ component is a DLL known as an **in-process server**, so called because it executes within the **process space** of the calling application. A COM+ method invocation, then, is not that much different from a function call within an application. Values passed back and forth exist within the memory space of the application, so there is no need to marshal information to and from the memory spaces of different applications and components. In-process servers are comparatively fast, too. Without marshalling across process boundaries, the COM+ runtimes impose little extra overhead. An in-process server, however, doesn't by itself help us in distributed processing – where the component and the application are in inherently different processes because they are hosted by completely separate machines.

In the original implementation of DCOM, in-process server components could not be used for distributed calls. This restriction was lifted for the average programmer when MTS came along. MTS acted as a proxy for the application. COM components executed in the MTS process space, and applications called across to MTS, which handled calls off to the components. In this situation, all calls involve marshalling. Any data that involves a pointer must be copied and transferred to the other machine's memory space, where the pointers can be meaningfully reconstituted. This can be more complicated than you might think. Suppose you wish to pass a value by reference so that the called method can act on it. In C++, you would do this by passing a pointer.

This works for a monolithic application, because the caller and callee are in the same process space and share the same range of memory. If I am calling your component on another machine, unfortunately, I cannot give you access to the memory owned by my application. Such calls, so efficient in monolithic applications, involve copying the data or parameter to the memory space of the called component, and then handing the component a pointer to the bit of memory into which the value was copied. On return, the changed value is copied back to the calling application's process by the COM+ runtimes, where it is copied back to the original spot in memory from which the parameter came. As you might imagine, all this copying incurs substantial overhead.

Because MTS acts as a proxy for COM components, it can provide other valuable services such as pooling of valuable resources like database connections. In COM+, the functions provided by MTS vanish into the component services of the operating system. An application programmer thinks that he is dealing directly with components, albeit components with rich support from the operating system. You can specify the need for transactions and specify which users can launch and access the component.

We indicated earlier that the classic view of components – objects with properties as well as methods – built state information into the programming metaphor. This is great for local applications, but not very good for servers supporting large numbers of users. All that state information ties a component to the application that called for its creation. As long as an application is idle, waiting for user input for example, the resources consumed by the component are wasted as far as the server is concerned. MTS introduced a set of interfaces designed to let MTS communicate with the component regarding the context in which it was operating, and for the component to indicate to the runtime system when it was safe to reclaim resources. This **stateless server** model is continued in COM+. While COM+ can handle stateful components, it scales best when stateless components are used. The goal is not to hold state across method invocations, instead holding state on the client, where it matters most. This takes us part way back to the RPC model – components provide functionality, but little state. Unlike RPCs, however, COM+ keeps the possibility of state in the programming metaphor, even if it discourages its use.

Everything in Windows DNA comes down to COM+ at some point. The application services offered by the operating system are almost always exposed as COM+ interfaces, although a C/C++ API is sometimes offered as well. The server products that bolster DNA support object models in the form of COM+ interfaces. With the introduction of queued components, even the asynchronous behavior previously available only to MSMQ applications is available in a form component programmers will recognize. If you are remaining within the boundaries of the Windows platform, COM+ is far and away your best bet for an efficient and well-integrated distributed technology.

Microsoft Message Queue

What is this interesting thing called MSMQ? Let's examine it more closely and see how it supports scalability and availability through asynchronous calls and how such calls work. MSMQ operates on a message-passing model in which applications place **messages** – arbitrary blocks of data – into **queues**, which are simply ordered sequences of messages. Other applications retrieve messages from the queues and act on the data they find. In certain respects, MSMQ uses a programming metaphor reminiscent of socket programming. Unlike sockets, though, queues can be *reliable*, in which cases messages added to queues are written to disk. In the event of a crash, messages waiting in the queue are recovered from disk. Also unlike sockets, and central to our discussion, queues introduce asynchronous behavior. That is, applications place messages into queues and retrieve them independently of the behavior of the server application with which they are corresponding.

This is the chief virtue of MSMQ (and indeed, all other messaging middleware applications like it). Imagine if you could submit a URL (your message) to your browser and go about your business. At some later time, when you connected to the Internet, the URL request would be forwarded to the server and the requested page would be placed in a queue on your machine. At some time after that, when you reopened your browser, it would retrieve the page from the queue and display it. Your browser is no longer operating in lock time-step with the server. Your requests and the server's responses are asynchronous and neither application is blocking, waiting for the other.

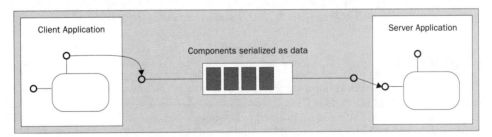

Now, let's go a step further. Suppose you submit a flurry of URLs to your hypothetical MSMQ-enabled browser, resulting in a long list of URLs to be processed. Your browser dequeues them and sends them to their respective servers as fast as it is able to process them, but not as fast as you are submitting them (it's a very slow link). One of the sites to which you are making a request is extremely busy; requests are arriving at its intake queue faster than it can process them. When the rush slows down, the server catches up. This strange little queue-based web illustrated a couple of points. First, you continue to have asynchronous behavior. Your browser was able to accept requests even as it waited for responses to earlier messages. Second, both your browser and the overloaded server were able to remain active and accept new messages while processing old ones. If you received more requests than the server could handle, the overflow remained in the queue until server resources became available. In the real world of synchronous, socket-based browsers, your browser would timeout waiting for a reply from the server. The server, assuming it was sufficiently busy, would probably drop the request. Queues allow applications on both ends of the distributed transaction to be sized for the average load while still allowing them to safely accept surges in demand above that level.

93

MSMQ, as a participant in Windows DNA, has a twist that helps integrate it with the rest of the Windows platform. It implicitly understands COM+ objects. Any component that implements the `IPersistStream` interface, such as the ADO recordset or the Microsoft XML parser, can be assigned to a message body. For example, I could have an XML document in an instance of the XML parser component, MSXML, and make the following call:

```
msg.Body = parsedDoc;
```

In this case, `msg` is a component of the type `MSMQMessage` and `parsedDoc` is my parser containing the XML document. Behind the scenes, the message component negotiates with the parser component for its `IPersistStream` interface and causes the document to be written to the message body. The first few bytes will be a binary header indicating the type of component, in this case MSXML. The remainder of the message body consists of whatever the component writes. In our case, it will be the text of the XML document. On the receiving end, the application that dequeues the message can perform the reverse operation and load the document directly into another instance of the parser component, simply by assigning the data in the message body to an instance of the parser.

MSMQ takes us back to the practice of passing data. Although MSMQ sports a COM+ based object model as its API, applications using it still have to implement an implicit protocol with the applications with which they communicate. Each party must understand the structure of the messages passed and implement a protocol for performing actions in response to the arrival of messages. We are back to passing the simplest programming construction – data. This opens the way to interoperability with different messaging middleware products. Host Integration Server, formerly known as SNA Server, for example, includes a bridge to MQSeries, the IBM counterpart to MSMQ. Bridges, though, are rare, so MSMQ remains primarily a proprietary technology for doing distributed processing within the Windows platform.

We'll take a closer look at the details of MSMQ later in this chapter. In particular, we'll discuss the types of configurations available and how MSMQ is used in conjunction with COM+.

Open Methods

COM+ does not, for all practical purposes, carry us beyond the Windows platform. Although there are implementations of COM for various Unix operating systems, they are not in common use and COM+ has not yet been ported. MSMQ can be bridged to MQSeries, but that is still a limited subset of the entire computing world. Under Windows DNA, that would have been the end of the story. Windows DNA has to do better. The world is increasingly integrating applications and distributing services via open networking technologies, so Windows DNA must have a link to that wider arena.

The open standards support in Windows DNA is still unfolding. It heavily favors XML for the wire format of data, and relies on open communications protocols like SMTP and HTTP for transmission. Microsoft's support divides into two areas: an implementation of the Simple Object Access Protocol (SOAP) and Microsoft BizTalk Server. SOAP is being introduced as part of the operating system and supporting development tools, while BizTalk Server is a product. Despite their close connections to Windows, both .NET and BizTalk Server will enable DNA programmers to connect the closed world of Windows to the open world of the Internet.

At the time of writing, .NET had just been announced. The description that follows is based on prior announcements in the press and the newly released SOAP Toolkit.

SOAP and .NET

Sometimes you need a low level protocol like sockets. In the case of the Web, that is all that is needed. In other cases, when you need a richer protocol, it is convenient to have a well-tested communications layer on which to build. The **Simple Object Access Protocol** (**SOAP**), discussed in Chapter 12, is the open standards answer to this need.

SOAP began as a joint effort between Microsoft and its partners, DevelopMentor and UserLand. It was strongly influenced by the prior XML-RPC effort, which sought to bring the RPC metaphor to the Web with XML as the wire format. IBM, Lotus, and, more recently, Sun, subsequently joined the SOAP effort, and talks are underway with the W3C to make SOAP a Recommendation. While SOAP does not have the open standards pedigree of, say, HTTP, it is heading for that status.

The core idea is simple. A client application makes calls by submitting an XML document describing the method to be called and the parameters to be passed. The return type and any error messages are also represented by XML documents. On the server, some component receives the message and implements the desired interface. This implementation is termed a web service because it offers an interface to some useful service via web protocols. Note there is no absolute requirement to have a component technology on the other end. Early prototypes connected SOAP receivers to both Java servlets and CGI scripts written in Perl. There is nothing to say that a SOAP implementation could not be connected to an ASP implementation. Since the Windows component technology of choice is COM+, however, the Microsoft prototype implementation of SOAP connects SOAP requests to COM components.

> *The SOAP Toolkit for VisualStudio 6.0 was released on 5 June 2000 and is available at* http://msdn.microsoft.com/xml/general/toolkit_intro.asp.

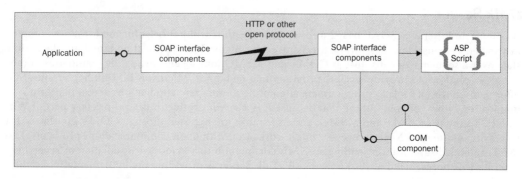

The SOAP Toolkit provides the following tools for implementing web services using SOAP on Windows DNA:

❑   ROPE

❑   ISAPI and ASP SOAP listeners

❑   SOAP Wizard

ROPE implements the communications aspect of SOAP. It is not a protocol itself, but rather a utility for working with the low-level XML issues in SOAP. It handles the formating and parsing of SOAP messages. It is not strictly necessary to use ROPE. Indeed, if you are interoperating with a SOAP implementation on another platform, the other platform's implementation will not be using ROPE.

A web server hosting a web service needs to listen for incoming requests. The SOAP Toolkit offers two types of listeners: an ASP implementation and an ISAPI extension. If you chose to use ASP, you will be including the page `listener.asp` (provided in the toolkit) in a page generated for your service. This approach gives you total control over the way .NET accesses your components. The ISAPI extension, by contrast, is a high performance way to access COM components (recall that ASP is itself an interpreter implemented as an ISAPI extension – you are bypassing a layer by using the ISAPI listener). Another crucial distinction is that the ASP listener lets you implement your web service as an ASP page – indeed, the sample that is included in the toolkit is an ASP implementation. The ISAPI listener, though, is best for high volume web services that access a COM implementation.

How do you wire everything together? That is the function of the SOAP Wizard. The Wizard is a free-standing utility executable that solicits information from the programmer and generates two files. The first is a file describing your service. This is an XML document written in a vocabulary called **SOAP Definition Language** (**SDL**), which is SOAP's counterpart to COM's IDL. The other file generated depends on whether you chose ASP or ISAPI for your listener, but it serves to connect the listener provided by SOAP to your service implementation. If you chose ASP, you get an ASP that includes calls to your object. If you chose the other option, you get an ISAPI DLL that does the same thing.

SOAP in general, and the Toolkit in particular, are extremely new. SOAP implementations on every platform are also largely in the prototype stage. Not surprisingly, there is a high level of controversy regarding interoperability between different implementations. Since SOAP is intended to be interoperable, this will be worked out in time. Early adopters, however, should note that web services built with the Toolkit may not be interoperable with other SOAP implementations. The use and syntax of SDL, in particular, are a matter of some debate in SOAP circles.

BizTalk Server

As simple and useful as SOAP-based web services are, they will not be sufficient for more complex distributed systems. They lack formal mechanisms for higher-level application functions like maintaining state over a sequence of calls. Just as COM+ and MSMQ join sockets inside the boundaries of the Windows platform to provide a richer programming metaphor, Microsoft BizTalk Server joins SOAP to offer more powerful tools to programmers attempting to integrate applications across platform boundaries. Now, you might think that because it is a server product it is a proprietary part of Windows. In fact, it supports COM+ and MSMQ, and its features are exposed through COM+ interfaces. It is heavily biased toward XML, however, and it works well with open communications protocols. Like .NET, an outside application sending an XML document into a Windows installation or receiving one from BizTalk Server need never know that BizTalk Server is providing the implementation of the programming metaphor.

BizTalk Server can be integrated into the DNA platform quite easily, although nominally it's actually part of the .NET platform. You'll find a lot of overlap between current DNA thinking and the new .NET ideas – a lot of things are equally at home in both.

BizTalk Server's metaphor takes us back to message passing. Unlike sockets, it is generally asynchronous. It is helpful to think of it as the open equivalent of MSMQ with translation tools added into it. BizTalk Server sits between applications and provides the interface needed to connect two or more dissimilar applications. Each application may be using related but different message formats, and each may be using a different communications protocol. For example, consider the situation depicted below. An application running under Windows generates a message in XML format and sends it via MSMQ. The application that is to receive it is older and requires a CSV format and FTP communications. We could simply write the translation routines into both applications, but that would require access to the source code for both. Of greater concern is the fact that we would have to add new translation routines for every application we add.

Suppose that our organization switches suppliers. To support the switch, we have to replace the CSV-reading application with a new application belonging to the new supplier. This one reads XML, but its vocabulary is slightly different from ours. Moreover, this application is designed to accept documents via HTTP. This is where BizTalk comes in. It listens to various protocols and receives messages. Upon receiving a message, BizTalk finds a matching pipeline. A **BizTalk pipeline** is a pair of agreements that specify the details of how messages come into and depart BizTalk Server. Based upon the requirements of the pipeline, BizTalk Server may perform a message translation and send the new version over a different protocol. In our hypothetical case, switching suppliers becomes a matter of altering pipelines. Since BizTalk agreements and pipelines are stored in a database, changing application integration details becomes a matter of configuring BizTalk rather than modifying a running software application.

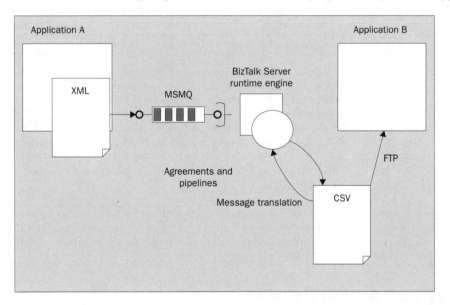

BizTalk inherits the simplicity of the message passing metaphor, but it also picks up the richer features of the communications protocols on which it rides. If you need more reliability than HTTP provides, you can switch to MSMQ. If you want a component interface, you can integrate with COM+ components. If you need a simple, asynchronous exchange, you can send a message via SMTP. The flexibility is there in BizTalk Server.

If that were all there was to it, that wouldn't be much of a product. The target audience for BizTalk Server is corporations implementing e-commerce. A higher level of management, auditing, and reliability is needed. BizTalk includes an orchestration tool. Using this tool, you are able to outline your workflow, in other words, the sequence and type of messages needed to implement a complex e-commerce exchange, and have the tool assist in the creation of the required pipelines. These robust services are what distinguish BizTalk from the communications protocols it uses. It is a layer on top of, say, HTTP, document tracking and the orchestration of multiple messages. The messages orchestrated may be sent over different protocols. It is not inconceivable that BizTalk might also support SOAP as a communications protocol at some future date.

DCOM: COM with a Longer Wire

Let's take a closer look at what happens when you use COM in its distributed form. Issues that aren't apparent in the local case appear when method calls are made to a remote server. DCOM may be "COM with a longer wire", but that wire has a few twists in it.

Marshalling

Once you cross machine, process, or even apartment boundaries you run into the issue of marshalling. DCOM with in-process servers looks like out of process servers did in the local case in terms of marshalling. Parameters to be passed are in a different memory space from that of the called component. The parameters have to be copied in a block for transmission, the block is copied to the remote machine, and the values are copied, or marshaled, into the process space of the server component.

On the server, the COM+ runtime libraries in the operating system handle this marshalling for you. The client machine, however, must have information about the called component's interface and must have a component to perform the marshalling. In the case of the IDispatch interface, which you might use from a scripted client, the operating system again comes to your rescue. Dispatch interfaces require no early knowledge of the interface. The names of methods and the names and types of method parameters are not checked until the method invocation occurs. So far, this is pretty easy; you point the client machine to the server and everything works.

If you are using a compiled client, for example a C++ application for performance, you need a proxy for the component, as well as a type library on the client. The proxy may be provied by the Universal Marshaller in the presence of a standalone type library. The type library describes the interface to the client machine, while the proxy handles marshalling on the client.

Security and Authentication

When you are making calls to a local component, the local security subsystem checks your permissions when you attempt to instantiate the component. In Windows 2000, this involves checking Active Directory. Once you have a running copy, you can be presumed to be permitted access to its methods and properties.

The distributed case is a bit different. Your local machine checks to see if you have access to the proxy, but the server must check to see if you have access to instantiate the component and call its methods. Since your calls are traversing a network (potentially the Internet), checking should be more meticulous. The component services in COM+ can be configured to check security rights at various levels. First, the identity of the caller can be the caller's user ID or the caller can impersonate the interactive user on the server. Security will be enforced when the component is launched. When it comes to using the component, you may configure the component to check access at each method call or even down to the level of individual packets. Whereas a local call can assume all the packets of a method call come from the same client, in the distributed case you have to worry about attacks in which a malicious user might spoof valid packets and attempt to take control of the component.

Resource Collection

Resource collection for a locally hosted in-process server was easy. If you forgot to clean up instantiated components (or if your application crashed), resources vanished along with the process. (Of course, we don't crash applications – it's those other programmers!) We're careful, so resource collection came down to calling the component's `Release` method (part of the `IUnknown` interface common to all COM+ components) in C++, or releasing the component in Visual Basic or a scripting language by setting the object variable's value to nothing. In the latter case, the langauge's support for COM/COM+ causes the `Release` method to be called. In either case, when the count of clients using the component drops to zero, the DLL can be unloaded from memory. If you are careful, resources are reclaimed in the local case.

Despite the best intentions and programming skill, though, resources can become orphaned when making distributed calls. Both the client machine and the server can be up and running with all software intact, but the server-side component will become orphaned if the network path between them is broken. DCOM uses a **machine-level ping**. That is, so long as a client has any components instantiated on a given remote server, it will periodically send a small message to the COM+ system on that server to indicate that it is still interested in the components. If the server does not detect this message for some configurable interval, it reclaims any components held on behalf of the client computer. This conserves resources and helps prevent memory leaks.

Application Issues

So far there has been little to specifically interest architects and programmers. COM+ is managing things behind the scenes. The fact that DCOM is a "longer wire" should cause you to reconsider the nature of your COM+ interfaces, however. There are two issues to consider: network round-trips and scalability.

When an in-process component is executing locally, the overhead of COM+ calls is small. You can make as many property sets and gets as you wish, and call methods as often as you wish without undue penalty. In that case, it makes sense to expose a lot of properties and set them individually before calling a method. This keeps the parameter list for methods simple. Anything that can be considered to be the state of the component as a whole should be exposed as a property. Only those bits of information that are specific to the method to be invoked should be passed as parameters of the method.

In the remote case, the "longer wire" reaches out to trip you. Now, in addition to making calls through the COM+ layer, you have the considerable overhead of marshalling and network latency. You are copying memory and passing it across your network. Instead of accessing memory that is physically inches from the processor via the bus, you are accessing another machine that is no closer than a few feet and may be across the globe via the network. In this case, it makes sense to compromise the logical purity of the interface and pack as much as we can into each method call. All those property calls in the local case should generally become part of the parameter list or a user defined type passed in the parameter list. If multiple methods are related, combine them into one method you can call via DCOM. The idea is to limit the number of times the client application has to call the remote component.

This guideline fits neatly with our other concern, scalability. Recall that we said MTS, and by succession, COM+, works best with stateless components. Ideally, state is not held across method invocations. You send everything you need to the component as part of the method call. Once the call completes, COM+ is free to release or reuse the component, depending on what the component communicates to COM+ and how the component is configured. This allows scarce resources like database connections to be recycled. If you use an interface that was designed for local use, then you are unlikely to be able to achieve this ideal. You will make multiple round trips to the server, and the state established by a call must be maintained until all the calls are complete. For example, if you are used to setting a number of properties that affect the behavior of a method call, you cannot allow COM+ to reclaim the resource until the properties are set and the method call completes. A component instance on the server is largely idle until the client application has made all these calls and released the component. If the component is holding a database connection or has allocated large amounts of memory, the server will not scale well. If you have compressed the interface to a single round trip, you will be able to allow COM+ to reclaim the resources as soon as the method completes.

Julian Dates Example

Let's see an example of this in practice. We're going to dust off an old COM in-process component and try to install it under Windows 2000 as a DCOM component. This will test the backward compatibility of COM+: can it recognize and make use of something that was never designed for the COM+ runtimes? More importantly, it will let us examine whether DCOM really is "COM with a longer wire".

The component in question allows you to calculate calendar dates using the Julian numbering system. This component can take a date and return the Julian number, as well as tell you what day of the week this date represents. The Julian number is a real number whose integral part is a count of days since a start date and whose fractional part denotes the time as a fraction of a whole day. It is particularly robust in that it also handles dates before the Gregorian reform and can handle the difference between the astronomical calendar and the civil calendar, that is, the calendar you are using right now (assuming you aren't an astronomer). The Gregorian reform wasn't adopted all at once. Most countries in Europe made the switch in 1582, while Great Britain and her colonies held out until 1752. There are even nations, like Greece and Russia, that waited until the twentieth century. The component supports properties that let you tell it when you want to make the Gregorian switch, as well as some other technical details of calendar conversions. If you supply a Julian number, the component will helpfully tell you the day, month, and year of the date.

> *The business of calendars and date computations in the Western nations is deeper than you might think at first glance. Full details are given at http://www.voicenet.com/~smohr /activex_demo.htm#JNum. You can also check the Explanatory Supplement to the Astronomical Almanac (1992, University Science Books, ISBN 1-93570-268-7) which provides another algorithm and explains several non-Western calendars. The algorithm implemented in this component is a substantial extension of the one provided for astronomical calculations in Practical Astronomy with Your Calculator (Cambridge University Press, 1988, ISBN 0-521-35699-7).*

Active Template Library

The component is an in-process server, in other words a DLL, created with the **Active Template Library** (**ATL**). This is a set of comparatively thin C++ templates designed to facilitate the creation of COM components. Using the wizards in Visual Studio, you specify the public interface – properties and methods – and the wizard uses the template library to generate the needed macros and class definitions for supporting COM. This relieves programmers of the tedium of implementing the basic COM plumbing, such as the IUnknown interface and class factories, allowing them to focus on the implementation of the component.

IJulianDate Interface

Visual Studio generates an interface definition language (IDL) file that the various build tools use to create a type library that describes the COM interface to the COM (and COM+) runtimes. This file is a useful shorthand look at what the interface entails. Here's the one generated for our sample component. You won't need all the details provided in the IDL file to follow the rest of the sample, so just skim over it to get an idea of what IDL provides. Note that we've defined a dual interface so we can use the component from scripts as well as compiled applications:

```
interface IJulianDate : IDispatch
{
    import "oaidl.idl";
    [propget, id(1), helpstring("New Year's month prior to reform")]
        HRESULT OldNewYearMonth([out, retval] long *retval);
    [propput, id(1)]
        HRESULT OldNewYearMonth([in] long rhs);
    [id(2), propget, helpstring("New Year's day prior to reform")]
        HRESULT OldNewYearDay([out, retval] long *retval);
    [id(2), propput]
        HRESULT OldNewYearDay([in] long rhs);
    [id(3), propget, helpstring("Year in which Gregorian calendar was
            adopted")]
        HRESULT ReformYear([out, retval] long *retval);
    [id(3), propput]
        HRESULT ReformYear([in] long rhs);
    [id(4), propget, helpstring("Day on which Gregorian calendar was
            adopted")]
        HRESULT ReformDay([out, retval] long *retval);
    [id(4), propput]
        HRESULT ReformDay([in] long rhs);
    [id(5), propget, helpstring("Month in which Gregorian calendar was
            adopted")]
        HRESULT ReformMonth([out, retval] long *retval);
    [id(5), propput]
        HRESULT ReformMonth([in] long rhs);
    [id(6), propget, helpstring("Gregorian reform date in YYYYMMDD
            format")]
        HRESULT FirstGregorianDate([out, retval] double *retval);
    [id(6), propput]
        HRESULT FirstGregorianDate([in] double rhs);
    [id(7), propget, helpstring("Julian date of the Gregorian reform")]
        HRESULT FirstGregorianJNumber([out, retval] double *retval);
    [id(7), propput]
        HRESULT FirstGregorianJNumber([in] double rhs);
    [id(8), propget, helpstring("True for civil calendar, False for
            astronomical")]
        HRESULT IsCivil([out, retval] BOOL *retval);
```

```
        [id(8), propput]
          HRESULT IsCivil([in] BOOL rhs);
        [id(9), helpstring("Compute a Julian number for the given date and
            time")]
          HRESULT MakeJulianNumber([in] long year, [in] long month, [in]
            double day, [out, retval] double *JulianDate);
        [id(10), helpstring("Recover the date and time from the given Julian
            number")]
          HRESULT DateFromJulian([in] double JulianDate, [out] long *year,
            [out] long *month, [out] double *day,
            [out, retval] short int *Success);
        [id(11), helpstring("Calculate the day of the week 1 (Monday) to 7
            (Sunday) for the given Julian number")]
          HRESULT DayOfWeek([in] double JulianDate,
            [out, retval] long *day);
    };
```

We'd like to make a plea for COM programmers to remember to include help strings within the IDL. This information is exposed through Visual Basic and other application environments and is very useful to client programmers. Far too many talented programmers forget to provide this information, leaving their customers to guess at the interface.

There are three main properties to worry about. Since the component defaults to the civil calendar in use in the UK and the United States, you can forget about most of the properties. If you are dealing with modern dates and don't use the component for astronomical calculations, you can forget about the properties entirely. We are mainly interested in three methods:

❑   `MakeJulianNumber` – compute the Julian number given the year, month, and day

❑   `DateFromJulian` – compute the year, month, and day for a given Julian number

❑   `DayOfWeek` – determine the number of the day of the week for a given Julian number

If you download the code for this chapter, you will receive an Excel spreadsheet that uses this component and provides a friendly interface to the user. The component itself provides no conversion from the human-friendly form of a date, such as 20 July 1969, and the parameters passed to and from the component. The spreadsheet fills that function for us; we used Excel to throw together a rough user interface, then took advantage of VBA to match the interface to the component. Here's what it looks like:

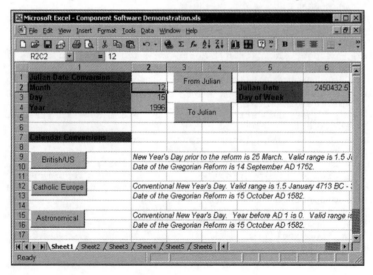

Here's a sample of the VBA code that illustrates how the component is used to compute Julian numbers:

```
Sub ToJulian_OnClick()
    'Button click handler for the To Julian Button
    Dim month As Long
    Dim year As Long
    Dim day As Double
    Dim jnum As Double
    Dim index As Long
    Dim week As String

    ' Set error handler

    On Error GoTo ErrorHandlerToJulian

    month = CLng(form.Cells(2, 2).Value)
    year = CLng(form.Cells(4, 2).Value)
    day = CDbl(form.Cells(3, 2).Value)
```

At this point, the subroutine has done some housekeeping. It establishes an error handler and retrieves the month, year, and day from known cells in the spreadsheet. The user would have input 6, 6, 1944 in three different cells to represent the date 6 June 1944, for example. The cell at R2C2 holds the number of the month, while R4C2 holds the year and R3C2 holds the day. Elsewhere in the VBA script code we've instantiated an instance of the component in a variable named dtg (for "date-time group"). Let's put it to work:

```
    jnum = dtg.MakeJulianNumber(year, month, day)
    index = dtg.DayOfWeek(jnum)
```

In two lines we've got the Julian number and the number $(0 - 6)$ of the day of the week for good measure. Now it is up to Excel and VBA to stuff the values back into the spreadsheet for the user to see.

```
    form.Cells(2, 6).Value = jnum
    form.Cells(3, 6).Value = WeekDay(index)
    Exit Sub
```

The subroutine WeekDay is a VBA utility that turns the index returned from the component into a string, such as Sunday, Monday, etc., for the user.

The error handler needs a bit of explanation:

```
ErrorHandlerToJulian:
    week = Error(Err)
    If Err = 91 Then
        Auto_Open
        Resume Next
    Else
        MsgBox ("Error: " & week)
    End If

End Sub
```

Error 91 indicates that the component has not been instantiated. The `Auto_Open` routine, invoked when the page is opened, instantiates the component. We call that routine in an attempt to fix things, then call the VBA `Resume Next` instruction to keep processing the script. For any other error, we convert the error to string format and display it to the user.

Hopefully, you can see this is a fairly simple way to offer a programmer a robust capability to handle dates in the Western calendar. Since the implementation is centralized in a well-tested COM component, all applications that use it can be assured of proper date calculations. Application programmers don't have to worry about calendar algorithms, which is a bigger benefit than you might think.

C++ Implementation

That's all well and good, but the real meat of this example is in the component implementation. This component was built with C++ and the ATL to keep the component small and to maximize performance.

"Small" is relative. When this component was originally built, with an early version of ATL, it was 17K in size for the release build. The last time it was built (1996) prior to writing this book, it had grown to 19K with a later version of ATL. Rebuilding this component today (also in release configuration) with the latest version of ATL, took the component size up to approximately 36K.

Most of the work is done for us by the ATL and the ATL component wizard in Visual Studio. Having specified a dual interface (automation as well as a custom interface), the wizard generated a number of files. Dual interfaces and automation will be covered in later chapters – what automation does is to allow an application to programmatically manipulate another, through a set of well-defined interfaces. The following fragment invokes templates that implement the dual interface, an error handling interface, and the root of COM support in ATL:

```
class CJulianDateObject :
    public CComDualImpl<IJulianDate, &IID_IJulianDate, &LIBID_DTGXLib>,
    public ISupportErrorInfo,
    public CComObjectRoot,
    public CComCoClass<CJulianDateObject, &CLSID_JulianDate>
{
```

This class declaration gives us a C++ class, `CJulianDateObject`, that offers a dual COM interface, `IJulianDate`. The identifiers for the interface and the associated type library are designated in `IID_IJulianDate` and `LIBID_DTGXLib`. The class ID for the component is given in `CLSID_JulianDate`. `CComCoClass` is a C++ template into which we pass the class itself and the CLSID to initiate the proper COM support from the ATL standard classes.

The following lines, also generated by the Wizard, declare the entry points for the various interfaces:

```
class CJulianDateObject :
    public CComDualImpl<IJulianDate, &IID_IJulianDate, &LIBID_DTGXLib>,
    public ISupportErrorInfo,
    public CComObjectRoot,
    public CComCoClass<CJulianDateObject, &CLSID_JulianDate>
{
```

```
public:
   CJulianDateObject();
BEGIN_COM_MAP(CJulianDateObject)
   COM_INTERFACE_ENTRY(IDispatch)
   COM_INTERFACE_ENTRY(IJulianDate)
   COM_INTERFACE_ENTRY(ISupportErrorInfo)
END_COM_MAP()
```

The wizard also generates the proper registry information:

```
DECLARE_REGISTRY (CJulianDateObject, _T("JulianDateObject.1.1"),
   _T("JulianDateObject"), IDS_JULIANDATE_DESC, THREADFLAGS_BOTH)

DECLARE_AGGREGATABLE(CJulianDateObject)
// ISupportsErrorInfo
   STDMETHOD(InterfaceSupportsErrorInfo)(REFIID riid);
```

Next, the methods and property accessors are declared. The following lines declare the long integer property OldNewYearMonth, which is set and read by the accessor methods get_OldNewYearMonth and put_OldNewYearMonth. Note that client programmers don't see the accessors –they simply call the property:

```
// IJulianDate
public:
   // Accessor functions for properties
   STDMETHOD(get_OldNewYearMonth)(long *retval);
   STDMETHOD(put_OldNewYearMonth)(long rhs);
```

Turning from the declarations to the implementation source code, here is the implementation that goes with the property declarations you just saw. The wizard generates the shell of the method, leaving us to fill in the body with our algorithms. Note that the method that sets the property checks to ensure a valid month number has been passed in and returns the standard COM error HRESULT if the parameter is invalid:

```
STDMETHODIMP CJulianDateObject::get_OldNewYearMonth(long *retval)
{
   *retval = m_lOldNewYearMonth;
   return S_OK;
}

STDMETHODIMP CJulianDateObject::put_OldNewYearMonth(long rhs)
{
   if (rhs <= 12 && rhs >= 1)
   {
    m_lOldNewYearMonth = rhs;
    return S_OK;
   }
   else
    return E_INVALIDARG;
}
```

The remainder of the component source is similar to this. Our immediate purpose is to discuss the issues that arise when a local component is made distributed, so there is little value in wading through the algorithms for implementing Julian date calculations. The interested reader can download the entire source from the Wrox web site at http://www.wrox.com.

Deploying Components with COM+

Remember that one of our goals was to show how an existing component could integrate with COM+. Further consider that in a distributed setting we will need to install and configure support for our server component on multiple client machines. It is therefore desirable to see how to configure our sample component on the server using COM+ management tools. We'll also show how to create a file that will let you configure client computers with minimal fuss.

There are three steps to be performed:

❑   First, you must create a COM+ application on your server and add the sample component to it

❑   Next, you export a proxy to that application to a Windows install file

❑   Finally, you use the install file to configure client computers

When you are done, you can use the sample spreadsheet to invoke the component on the server computer from a client.

Configuring a COM+ Application

The first thing to do is create a COM+ application on the server. The tool we will be using throughout is the **Component Services snapin** for the Windows MMC. It is accessed from the **Administrative Tools** menu or the folder of the same name under **Settings | Control Panel**.

Before configuring the server component, you must create a new application. This is done by expanding the desired server computer under the **Component Services** branch, right-clicking on the **COM+ Applications** node, and selecting **New | Application**. You will see the first window of the COM Application Install Wizard. Clicking the next button brings you to a window asking you to make the choice between installing a pre-built application or creating an empty application. Select the latter choice. This brings you to a window in which you need to provide a name for the application and indicate how the application will run:

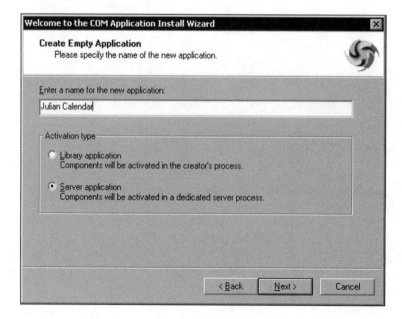

A library application is like an in-process server. It is faster to load but does not provide process isolation, hence a fault in the application or the component will cause both to fail. Since we intend to call this component from a remote client, we need to create a server application.

The next window prompts you to indicate the application identity for the COM+ application. This is the account under which the application executes. You may select the interactive user, in which case the component will run with whatever permissions are accorded the user currently logged into the server. If you intend to run the server unattended, create a user account for the application (or designate an existing one with suitable permissions) and specify that account here. After finishing with the application identity information, click the button labelled Finish on the final window. The Wizard will then create a new application. A node for the application will appear under the COM+ Applications branch in the Component Services tool. You may wish to fine-tune the security settings here, including when authentication is performed. For the purposes of our demonstration, we'll stick with the default.

Now that we have an application, we need to add the component and its proxy. This is done through the COM Component Installation wizard. This tool is invoked by expanding the application node added in the previous step, right-clicking on the Components node, and selecting New | Component.

The first choice you have to make in the Component Installation Wizard is where you will be getting the component. You have three choices, two of which apply to our example (the top two shown in the screenshot).

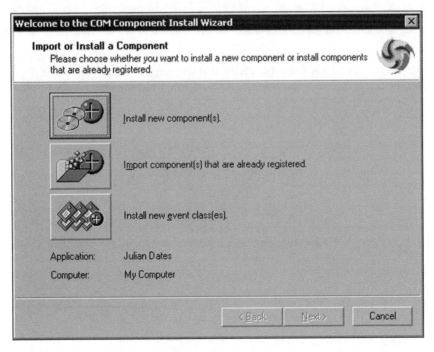

If you have built the component by building the Visual C++ project, the component will be registered on the build machine. If you separately run nmake with the external makefile ps.mak, the proxy stub DLL will have been built and registered. In this case, select the Import component(s) that are already registered option. You will see a list of progids registered on your machine:

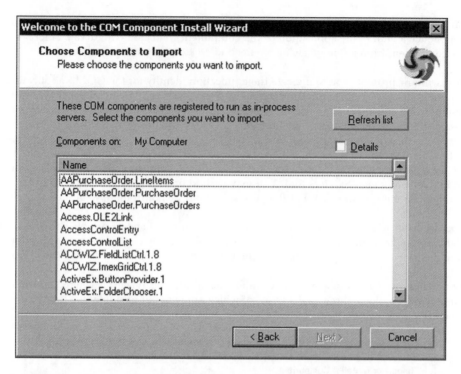

Otherwise, if you merely copied the binary images to the server machine, select Install new component(s).You will find a familiar file dialog that lets you browse the server for the files you wish to install. Select the files DTGX.DLL and DTGXPS.DLL. If you forget one, the window following the file dialog displays what you have selected and allows you to add more components.

> **Due to a known problem with the COM+ Components Services tool which we will discuss later, do not select the type library file DTGX.TLB.**

Once you have finished with the Component Installation Wizard, you will see a node for the new component. You can right-click and inspect its properties, or expand the node and view its interfaces and methods. For the purposes of this demonstration, you are finished configuring the server.

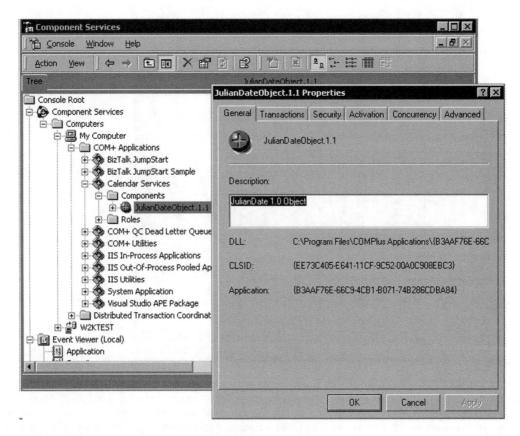

Packaging a Component for Export

The simplest way to get the required files to the client is to package the COM+ application for export using the COM Application Export Wizard. This is similar to the package export feature of MTS which it replaces. The end result from the Export Wizard is a Windows installation file (.MSI extension) and a CAB file containing the same installation file and the INF file needed to install it. You invoke this Wizard by selecting the application node in the Component Services tool, right-clicking, and selecting Export.

If the machine on which you are performing the export operation is not the intended server, select the export computer's node in the Component Services tool prior to invoking the Wizard, right-click, and select Properties. On the Options tab of the resulting dialog, enter the name of the server machine in the edit field labelled Export Application proxy RSN. This causes the export package to configure the client for the desired machine.

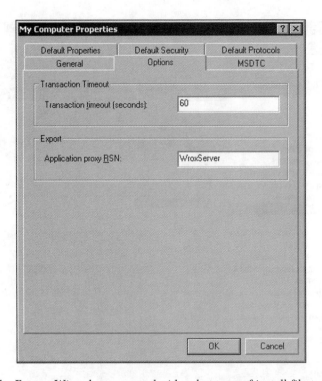

Once you invoke the Export Wizard, you must decide what type of install file to create. If you simply want to install copies of the component on other machines for local use, you can select the Server Application option. This option generates an install file that would result in copying the component to the client and registering it for local use. The second option, Application Proxy, is intended to install the type library and the proxy stub DLL and configure the client to invoke the component on the server from which the export package was created. This is the option to select for our example:

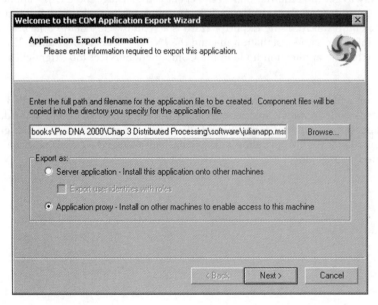

There is a known issue with this Wizard involving components that include the type library with the component. ATL-based components such as ours fall into this category. Attempting to export an application that includes such a component and a separate type library file will result in an inability to create the installation file. This is why we omitted the file DTGX.TLB during the installation process. Ideally, we want an installation file that would install only the type library and the proxy stub. This is all that is needed for remote invocation. Due to the known issue, our installation file will install the component itself and the proxy stub. The issue is documented in the Microsoft Knowledge Base under a topic accessible from http://support.microsoft.com/support/kb/articles/Q255/9/73.ASP.

When the Wizard completes, you are ready to install the application on the client computer.

Configuring the Remote Client

The installation file you created in the preceding step makes configuring the client very easy. Prior to COM+ and MTS, you had to register the proper DLLs manually, then invoke the configuration utility DCOMCNFG to specify the remote server. This still works, but the installation file is much simpler.

The easiest way to install the application is to double-click on the installation file from Windows Explorer. You may also drag and drop the file into the Component Services tool when the COM+ Applications node is expanded. Once the installer completes, you will see a new COM+ application that is indistinguishable from the server except that the configuration options are disabled. If you use a tool like OLE View (from Visual Studio), you will not see the component under the All Objects node. Instead, look under AppIds. At this point, you may run the Excel spreadsheet or any other client that invokes this component and it will run on the server.

The suspicious programmer will wonder whether DCOM is really being used since the known issue in the Export Wizard forced us to install the entire component on the client. To test this, open the Excel spreadsheet, then shut down the server or unplug either the server or the client from the network. Click on one of the buttons and you will receive an error indicating that the remote server is unavailable.

Implications for a DNA Application

By now you may be getting the feeling that this example was contrived solely to show you what *not* to do. There is a lot of effort involved in getting a proxy stub DLL, and the interface we presented makes a lot of roundtrips to configure and use the component. That is indeed the case. There are some problems here that show that DCOM is not simply "COM with a longer wire". The component runs effectively in the distributed case, but it will not scale well and there are concerns regarding multiple users. The problems are these:

❑ The component maintains state across method calls

❑ The interface requires too many round trips between the client and the server

❑ The component requires a proxy stub DLL and type library on the client machine

Let's dissect these problems in turn and see what you might do about them to improve the performance of this component and make it a better candidate for distributed processing. Logically, it makes sense to distribute this component. We'd like everyone in our organization to use the same calendar. Practically, though, this component would need some work.

Stateful Components and Network Round Trips

At first glance, the IJulianDate interface looks like a good candidate for distribution. The principal methods are basically functions: we pass some parameters and receive values in return. So long as we can accept the default values established upon the creation of the component, this is the case.

The properties are the problem. Simply selecting the civil over the astronomical calendar takes a round trip, assuming you are not simply staying with the default value. If you wish to change from the default British Gregorian changeover date, you may need to set as many as seven properties. Not only do these entail expensive round trips to the server, but the state of the component is being held until you finish with your method calls. A French user wishing to calculate the Julian date for some day falling within the period between the time France accepted the Gregorian calendar reform and the time Britain accepted the reform would need to instantiate the component, make those seven round trips, and then – only then – call the method that gives the value that is really wanted.

A better solution would be to incorporate the reform-related values in the parameter list for each method. Another alternative would be to incorporate all the reform values into a single method, say, SetReformDate, that would configure the component. Assuming the user wishes to make multiple calls for multiple dates, they would only have to pass the reform date parameters once. State would still be held, but at least the number of round trips would be reduced.

Proxies and Stubs

Unlike the local case, we had to worry about proxy stub components. For the purposes of our example, we simply deployed the component itself and redirected the COM+ application to the remote server. Of course, this defeats much of the purpose of resorting to distributed computing. In production we would want to build a separate type library and proxy stub DLL for the component. Without some sort of marshalling assistance, we cannot use DCOM. The problem is especially acute with early binding, in other words a library reference in a Visual Basic project, or any use of COM+ in a C++ application. At that point we can no longer rely on dispatch marshalling and we absolutely have to have a type library local to the client machine. In production, we must be careful to keep the proxy stub and type library up to date with the server-side component.

An interesting comparision can be drawn with SOAP. SOAP is inherently late-bound insofar as the client has to discover the available methods of a server. The server may or may not use late binding. While the equivalent of the type library must still exist, it is downloaded from the hosting server when needed.

Microsoft Message Queue

While COM+ is far and away the most widely used distributed technology within the platform's boundaries, it is worth looking over some of the capabilities of MSMQ in terms of network applications. Besides supporting the simple, asynchronous data passing metaphor for programming, MSMQ offers capabilities that differ from COM+. Even as queued components bridge this gap, it is worth knowing what technology underlies the component model so that we can appreciate the capabilities of the overall system.

Scalability and Availability

The chief advantage of MSMQ is supporting scalability and availability for distributed applications. Because a queue exists to hold a backlog of traffic, the capacity of the receiving application to process incoming messages need only be that of the average expected load. Spikes in load are accommodated when incoming traffic drops below the average level or sufficient new resources become available to handle the load. This allows us to build an application with lesser server resources than we would have to have in the synchronous case. Synchronous communications require servers that can handle the maximum expected load. Queued COM+ components participate fully in this aspect of scalability.

Another aspect of message queues is availability. If you break the network between the client and server in our Julian calendar COM sample during a method call, the call fails. Unless the client application has custom retry logic built into it, the request will never be serviced. As we shall see when we take up the nature of MSMQ queues in a little while, message queues may or may not survive this outage and forward the request when it is corrected. It depends on how the clients are set up and what sort of message was sent. Generally speaking, though, queues are reliable programming tools.

The final aspect of availability is the ability of a queuing system to detect network outages and route around them. This is what we'd like to have happen in the ideal case. Rather than wait for connectivity to resume, we'd like MSMQ to try another path. This, too, is possible. This time, though, it depends on how the MSMQ servers in a network are configured.

Servers

MSMQ networks are organized around the concepts of **enterprise** and **site**. The enterprise is the entire business organization. A site is a bit more abstract, but corresponds with the general idea of a single physical site or LAN. These concepts are important to MSMQ in terms of the messaging servers it supports. Each enterprise has a single **Primary Enterpise Controller** (**PEC**). Each site has a **Primary Site Controller** (**PSC**) and a **Backup Site Controller** (**BSC**) that takes the place of the PSC should it fail. The site hosting the PEC also has a BSC.

The main point of having PECs, PSCs, and BSCs – indeed, the reason we have messaging servers at all – is to host the **Message Queue Information Store** (**MQIS**). This is a database that MSMQ uses to record information describing the network. It includes information on the structure of the network, the names of the servers, and queue information. Clients query the MQIS to learn about queues. Servers use the MQIS to perform **smart routing**. Smart routing allows servers to forward messages along the shortest path under normal circumstances, and to route around outages when the network is degraded. Primary controllers – the PEC and PSCs – hold read/write copies of the MQIS and replicate changes between themselves. BSCs hold read-only copies of the MQIS. The MQIS is an important addition to the data passing metaphor where architecture is considered. It helps maintain system availability in the face of outages.

Clients

Any computer that has the software for accessing the MSMQ COM API is considered a client. MSMQ provides for two forms of clients: **independent** and **dependent**. Independent clients are capable of managing local queues for the storage of messages awaiting transmission. This is what lets an application send messages even while the client is disconnected from the network. An independent client is used for mobile users, for example. When connectivity is restored, the local queue is cleared and the messages sent.

Dependent clients, in contrast, require access to a server at all times. This is useful for thin clients with minimal resources, but it requires more storage capacity on the server. Dependent clients are good for users – fewer local resources – but bad for availability. They can even impact on scalability as there is a four gigabyte limit on the amount of queue storage on servers. All dependent clients assigned to a particular server for queue storage purposes must share this capacity.

Queues and Messages

You might be under the impression that queues are first-in, first-out in terms of message delivery. That is certainly the impression the data passing metaphor would give you, and it is the nature of common queues as they are known and accepted in the literature of computer programming. MSMQ, however, allows priorities to be assigned to messages. Messages are sorted by priority within a queue, ensuring high priority messages are delivered first.

Messages may also be declared *public* or *private*. Private messages are encrypted for the user by MSMQ when they are sent, and decrypted upon reciept. This is of some interest to the developers of network applications. It does not help with the usual challenges of network applications. If anything, it impedes performance slightly. However, if delivery is across network segments not under the physical control of the organization, for example a virtual private network over the Internet, privacy is very important. Of course, such links are usually encrypted at the packet level. Nevertheless, it is one more tool in an architect's kit for developing network applications.

Component Streaming in DNA

The MSMQ team shrewdly built `IPersistStream` capability into their COM/COM+ interfaces. This allows application programmers to rapidly pass component state to another application. The hard work of serializing the component to a data message and reconstituting it on the receiving end is performed within the MSMQ object model and COM+. MSMQ calls on the IPersistStream implementation to serialize itself. This extends the data passing metaphor slightly so that we have an object passing model. The applications on both ends of the exchange are able to use component software, while the communications between application tiers benefit from asynchronous communications and the simplicity of the data passing metaphor.

Queued COM+ Components and MSMQ

We'll be discussing queued components in detail in later chapters, but you might like to compare the basic architecture of queued components and MSMQ in terms of the basic concepts of distributed processing. COM+ interposes a pair of components between a queued COM+ server component and a client invoking methods on it:

❑   When a client makes a call to a queued component, the COM+ **Recorder** component accepts the call and writes the parameters to an MSMQ queue along with the security context of the client.

❑   This message is taken off the queue by the COM+ **Listener** component on the server. The listener acts as a proxy for the client, making the call using the client security context.

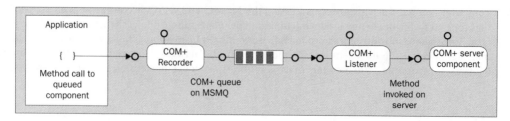

The method invocation is one-way. This is important and is a direct consequence of the fact that method invocations on queued components are aysnchronous. You cannot have methods with return values of pass parameters by reference as the calling process might not be around when the server gets around to servicing the method call. The COM+ component may not be active at the same time the client application calls the method. This greatly helps with scalability and availability, which is the main reason the asynchronous data passing model was joined to the component model in the first place. It represents a departure for component programmers, however. A method call may be acknowledged, indicating successful acceptance and commitment to the queue, but the exchange is one way. If you wish to receive information from the server component, you must set up another queued component on the client and have the server call it in another queued method call.

Queued COM+ components are an interesting merger of the component and data-passing programming metaphors. The logical integrity of the component model is joined to the scalability and availability benefits of the data-passing, messaging model. The implementation of COM+ queued components in Windows DNA is another example of the benefits of an integrated platform. The existing features of MSMQ were brought into the service of COM+ by using COM+ components to write to queues.

Summary

The challenges of network applications discussed in Chapter 1 became apparent as we considered the technologies available for implementing communication between the tiers of a distributed, n-tier application. We examined some early distributed technolgies as a way of shedding light on the various programming metaphors implemented to accomplish distributed processing. The simple data-passing model of sockets recurred in slightly more complex form in MSMQ and BizTalk. The familiar function call metaphor seen in RPCs came back into vogue with SOAP. The component-based model is firmly entrenched in Windows DNA through COM+.

Windows DNA offered rich tools for distributed processing, but they were proprietary to the Windows operating system. Programmers who had to cross platform boundaries and communicate with other operating systems had to resort to low-level socket programming. Windows DNA forever altered that with the introduction of Windows implementations of open protocols for distributed computing. SOAP is a cross-platform protocol that is increasingly gaining acceptance as an open standard. It follows the function call model of RPCs, but allows programmers to use functional or component-based technologies for the implementation. Its implementation on Windows, .NET, promises to allow programmers to extend the benefits of their internal systems, notably COM+ components, to outside users through web services. BizTalk Server builds on proprietary and open protocols to offer robust capabilities and system management to e-commerce applications. Although .NET is still unfolding, it is arguably one of the most important developments in the platform in recent years. Assuming SOAP gains mainstream acceptance and .NET is interoperable with other popular SOAP implementations, it could provide a strong refutation of the charge that Windows is a closed system, forever condemned to remain a proprietary island of functionality. The features enjoyed by Windows programmers for years will now be available to rapidly construct web applications and services.

You next saw how to take an existing COM component, developed for local use, and use it in a distributed setting. COM+ takes the best parts of MTS and utilities like DCOMCNFG and pulls them into the operating system. Looking at the example, we saw how the act of distributing resources should force changes in the interface of a component.

Finally, we considered the refinements MSMQ brings to the data-passing metaphor. The simplicity of sockets is joined to the reliability and scalability of message queuing middleware. In Windows DNA, COM+ joins MSMQ with components to offer the best of both. Programmers enjoy the component interface metaphor, while also gaining the benefits of queuing. The integration of `IStream`-based component persistence in MSMQ is seldom noted, but is an excellent example of the productivity gained by subscribing to a single platform's architecture.

Distributed processing is integral to the applications of the future. The advent of the Web and business-to-business integration has irretrievably brought distributed technologies into the mainstream of application development. Windows DNA fully embraces distributed processing to the extent that distributed technologies are available throughout the architecture. Programmers, particularly those who design application architectures, must understand both the challenges of network applications and the ramifications of the technologies used to meet those challenges.

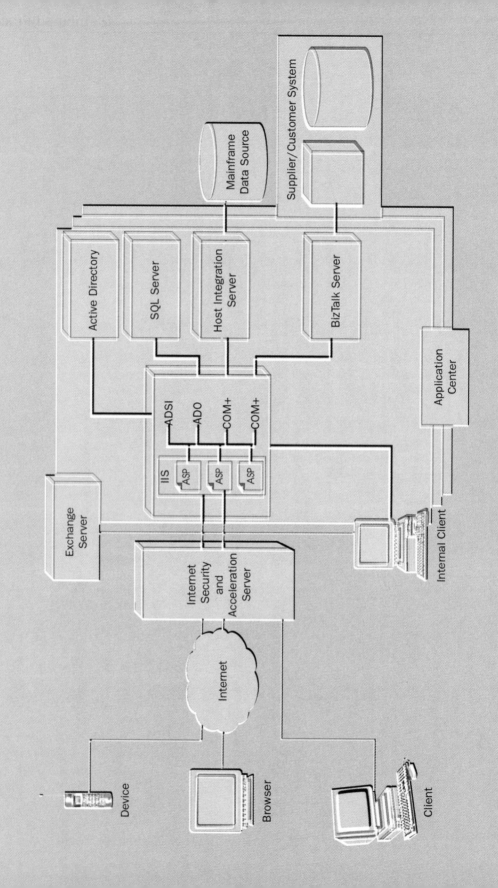

Business Objects

Windows DNA defines an n-tier architecture for application development. It does not specifically address *how* each tier will be developed. This chapter will focus on the middle, or business, tier. While we may choose to implement our business logic in ASP pages, we can increase our application's performance and maintainability by making use of business objects written in Visual Basic or Visual C++.

In this chapter we'll explore the concepts behind the use of objects in more detail. In particular, we'll be looking at the use of **business objects**. Just looking at the words, you might decide that these are *objects* that reflect or represent your *business*. And you'd pretty much be right – at a high level, it really is that simple. Business objects allow us to create programs to simulate parts of the world around us – to record what's happening or to make predictions about what might happen.

In this chapter we'll discuss the nature of business logic and why we might choose to put our business logic in objects. There are also some things to watch out for when using COM objects in a Windows DNA application, and we'll discuss those to make sure that we use objects to increase, rather than decrease, our application's performance and scalability.

Introduction to Business Objects

Before we get too deep into those details though, let's quickly recap, from Chapter 3, what we learned about the nature of objects at a high level.

> An object is a code-based abstraction of a real-world entity or relationship.
> Objects are software constructs that encapsulate both data and behaviors behind
> a defined interface.

We can represent the object as something like the following diagram:

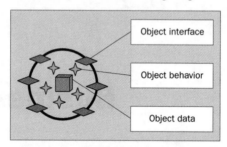

For instance, an ADO `Recordset` is an object. The `Recordset` object encapsulates (or contains like a black box) a lot of data, and provides us with access to behaviors that act on that data. A `Recordset`'s data includes the data from our database, but also includes a lot of parameters and metadata – such as our current row in the data set, the data types of each field, and so on. The behaviors include moving through the data set, retrieving data from a database and updating data back into the database. To get at the data and behaviors we use the `Recordset` object's interface – the set of properties and methods it makes available for our use.

On the other hand, a `Recordset` is not a business object. There are many kinds of objects in the world – and not all of them model a concept or entity that is part of our business. The `Recordset` object is a computer construct that has little to do with any particular business. Instead it provides an abstraction for virtually any data. Business objects are much more focused, providing abstractions for things like customers, products, or invoices.

The idea behind using business objects is that we can create an abstract model of our business entities and concepts within the computer. If our business objects enforce the rules and behaviors of our business processes, then we will have created a software model of our business. Having such a model makes it very easy to build applications, since our applications can simply interact with these objects – with complete assurance that the objects will only allow us to perform valid processes or behaviors.

Composition of a Business Object

Business objects are composed of three main parts:

- ❑ State (or data)
- ❑ Implementation
- ❑ Interface

It is important to understand these three parts of an object before we move on.

State

When we say **state**, we are talking about whatever set of variables or other information is required by our code. An object's state is the data contained within the object itself. This data is not typically available directly to any code outside the object, relying on the object's interface to provide access to the data.

> **Good object design dictates that an object's state should *never* be made directly available to any external code.**

All objects contain data about themselves. For instance, an object representing a customer might have data including the customer's name, address, city, state, and postal code. Furthermore, we might have many customer objects, each with its own set of state data.

Implementation

Implementation is the code in a class module. This is the code that implements an object's behaviors – performing any business logic or processing.

Like state data, our implementation code is not directly available to any code outside of our object. This is critical to the concept of objects, since it means that any code using our object can have no idea *how* any given behavior is implemented.

For instance, a `Person` object may provide information such as the person's age. As a user of the `Person` object, all we know is that we can retrieve the age:

```
intAge = objPerson.Age
```

This behavior could be implemented in VB by providing a static value:

```
Public Property Get Age() As Integer
   Age = mintAge
End Property
```

The great thing about object-oriented programming is that we can entirely replace this implementation with more sophisticated code – with absolutely no change to the calling code:

```
Public Property Get Age() As Integer
   Age = CalculateAge(mdtBirthDate)
End Property
```

What isn't clear from these bits of code is that what we're looking at is both *implementation* and *interface* code.

Interface

The **interface** is a set of methods and properties the object provides to the rest of the world – allowing other code to interact with the object as needed:

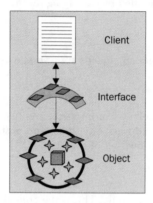

If we look at the Age property from our previous example, only part of the code is implementation. The highlighted code is actually part of our object's interface:

```
Public Property Get Age() As Integer
    Age = CalculateAge(mdtBirthDate)
End Property
```

An object's interface is perhaps the most critical part of the object, since it is the interface that determines how the object can be used.

> **The interface can be viewed as a 'contract' between the object and the rest of the world.**

Any code that wants to interact with our object will do so through the interface. As long as the interface never changes, that code will continue to operate. This allows us to change our implementation code, the data being used, or anything else behind the scenes – but *not* the interface.

As soon as we change our object's interface, we can expect that any code written to use our object will cease working until that client code is updated to reflect the changes.

> *The original COM specification allowed no changes to an interface. Over time that requirement has been relaxed a bit – allowing an interface to be extended by adding new properties and methods. However, any existing properties, methods or parameters must remain constant, or the contract with the object's clients will be broken. Refer back to Chapter 3 for more information.*

In Visual Basic, an object's interface is defined by the properties and methods that are declared Public in scope.

Why Use Objects?

Object-oriented analysis, design, and programming have become increasingly popular over the past few years. Where OO was a somewhat arcane concept just a decade ago, today it's quite commonplace, and is used (to one degree or another) in a great many business development efforts. This rise in popularity is due to many factors, not least of which are the benefits it brings to an organization and the developers who are building systems.

Objects are defined by the fact that they encapsulate related business data and behaviors – essentially providing a 'black box' that contains a set of useful functionality. This leads to a powerful set of benefits for our applications. In particular, objects offer us:

- ❑ Maintainability
- ❑ Reusability
- ❑ Abstraction

We'll look at each of these in turn.

Maintainability

Because the data and logic in an object are hidden from the client, we can change the data and logic without requiring changes to the client. This is because the client only ever interacts with the object's interface. This provides a huge benefit in terms of the maintainability of our applications, since we can maintain and enhance our objects over time without substantial impact on the rest of our application logic.

Reusability

Not only do we increase the maintainability of the application, but we also increase our ability to re-use code. This has been an elusive goal of software developers for time untold. It would be ideal to write a segment of code once, then be able to use it whenever appropriate. Unfortunately this goal is almost never achieved.

In the past we used modular programming techniques to gain reuse – the idea being that we could write a module of code and then reuse it where appropriate. The downfall of this approach is that only the code is stored in the module – the data on which the code would act isdifferent each time, leading to a lot of complexity to gain the reuse.

This is where objects come into play. They encapsulate both the code *and* the data. This means that the odds of us being able to reuse the code is much higher, since the code already has complete control over the data with which it will interact.

Obviously code reuse is an ideal. Sometimes objects provide us with huge opportunities for reuse – other times the benefit is lessened due to other factors. However, object-oriented programming provides substantial benefits in this area as compared to previous techniques such as modular design.

Abstraction

Our objects not only encapsulate code and data, but they embody another important attribute that leads to reuse – **abstraction**. Well-designed business objects provide an abstract model of our business concepts and entities. This means that our objects can be used to create a 'simulation' of our business processes within the computer.

In the following diagram we have a series of objects that clearly abstract some key business components of a sales order system. While this diagram shows business entities, it is also describing key objects that will exist within our application:

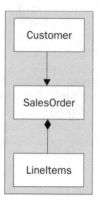

If we have an object that accurately models a key aspect of our business, it will likely be involved in many parts of our applications as well. Typically our applications are modeling various business processes – enabling our users to perform valuable tasks. Each time a business process utilizes a pre-existing business object, we have a huge opportunity for reuse.

In reality this typically means that our objects will continue to be enhanced with new data and behaviors as we continue to model more and more business processes. Through this process our objects become more and more comprehensive in terms of modeling our business entities – continually increasing the chance of being able to reuse them for subsequent application enhancements.

Business Logic

If business objects encapsulate **business logic** (and related data), then it makes sense that we should have a good grasp of the concept of business logic itself.

Types of Business Logic

Business logic is a fairly broad term, and it is not always clear just what is or is not business logic within an application. Unfortunately, if we don't encapsulate all the right business logic into our objects we will largely defeat the purpose of using objects at all.

Another risk is that we could start overloading our objects with logic that *isn't* business logic – often this will be UI or presentation logic that accidentally slips into our objects.

> **The single biggest mistake made when using business objects is to blur the line between business logic and user interface (UI) logic.**

Calculations

Some business logic is pretty obvious:

- ❑ Calculating tax
- ❑ Averaging a set of values
- ❑ Sorting a set of data by some priority criteria

Many, if not most, calculations performed in an application are business logic. Typically the calculations are required by the business, and the way in which they are performed is dictated by the rules of our business.

However, it's important to keep in mind that *some* calculations exist solely for the benefit of the user's presentation. We may choose to sort a list of values to make them appear nicely for the user – even though the business itself doesn't dictate such a sort. In other cases a sort might be part of the business rules – such as choosing the correct inventory bucket from which to sell some parts.

Rules

Rules are another fairly obvious type of business logic. Many of these will appear as conditional checks within our code, for example:

- ❑ If the customer's debt rating is below x then don't issue the loan
- ❑ If the product weight exceeds y then ship it by ground transport

In some cases rules and calculations will blur, since the results of calculations are often used as the basis for conditional rules checks. For instance, we may need to calculate the total amount on a sales order before that amount can be verified against the customer's credit limit. A complex calculation is required before we can perform the rule check.

Rules often dictate relationships or requirements of data. A sales order line item can't exist without an actual sales order. A sales order can't exist without a customer. When we talk about business objects, this type of business logic almost always describes relationships between objects – a topic that we'll cover in the second business objects chapter later in this book.

Validation

One type of business logic that's often overlooked is validation of data. The following are all examples of validation:

- ❑ A specified field must be a date – or perhaps it must specifically be a date in the past
- ❑ Another field must be numeric and greater than zero
- ❑ The field containing the product description is required

For whatever reason, validation is often considered to be a user interface artifact rather than 'real' business logic. Yet this logic is as 'real' as any other. Consider for a moment what would happen if the validation rules *weren't enforced*. Our application would either cease to function, or more likely would allow the user to perform actions that are invalid for our business.

That's the real litmus test – does non-compliance mean that the application could do something that is invalid for our business? If so, then we're dealing with business logic.

UI Logic versus Business Logic

Now, that's not the same thing as non-compliance being inconvenient. Just being inconvenient or lacking aesthetics is *not* a requirement to put something into business logic.

For instance, let's take the formatting of data. Our business logic may calculate a currency value for a sales order by summing up all the line items and applying tax. That process is governed by a set of business rules – and so it's pretty obviously business logic. However, the result is just a numeric value with no specific display format.

Before displaying the value to the user, we need to change its format so it appears aesthetically pleasing. The logic to handle this formatting is *not* business logic – it's UI logic. A different UI might need a different format; another UI might not want it formatted at all. In short, the display format of a value is meaningless from a business rules perspective.

There are other common examples, such as the code to format a list as an HTML table, sorting some values alphabetically for user convenience, or code to populate an ActiveX grid control in a certain way.

> In the final analysis, business logic includes all calculations, rules, and validation that must occur to ensure our application behaves properly and prohibits any actions that would be invalid for our business. Any such logic should be contained within our business objects. Everything outside of that sphere is not business logic, and doesn't belong in business objects – belonging instead in other parts of our application.

Component-Oriented Design

Components are an extension of objects. A component contains one or more objects, and often makes those objects available for use by client code.

Because components themselves are black boxes, however, we have some interesting design options available to us that aren't available in simpler object-oriented environments. This is because components provide us with some new **scoping** capabilities that go beyond the simple Public/Private/Protected scoping of objects.

With object-oriented design we have three types of scope:

- ❑ **Public scope** indicates methods or properties that are part of our object's interface. This means that these methods or properties can be called by code outside our object.

- ❑ **Private scope** indicates methods or properties that are only available within our object. These are very useful for adding structure and readability to our classes, but are totally invisible and unavailable to any code outside our objects. These types of functions are often utility functions, used to support the overall functionality of the class.

- ❑ **Protected scope** exists to support inheritance (something C++ programmers are used to, and Visual Basic programmers will get in VB7, according to Microsoft). A method or property scoped as protected is very much like one that is private in scope – it is only available to code within the object. However, it is also available to any code in a class that is subclassed from the original class. So if we create a new class that inherits from a class that has a protected method, we can use that method.

In Visual Basic we can use the `Friend` keyword to declare a property or method to be `Public` – but only within our component. Outside the component, a `Friend` property or method is effectively `Private`.

While these are powerful, they don't provide all the options that we might like. For instance, object-oriented design views all objects in a model as being available for use by all other objects. There's no concept of a component, or objects that may only be available *within* that component. Fortunately, component-oriented design within the COM environment does support this.

When we create a COM component, be it in-process or out-of-process, we get to choose which objects – and in fact which methods of those objects – will be available to external clients. This means that we can create an object that exposes some of its methods to clients, exposes others only to objects within the component, and keeps others totally private to itself.

Likewise, we can create objects that expose their entire interface to external clients, and have other objects be totally invisible to outside code.

What we are dealing with here is an extra layer of encapsulation. One of the key benefits of using objects is that we are able to encapsulate data and implementation code within a class – making it invisible to the user of our object. Components offer us a layer of encapsulation *on top of* our objects.

Now we can not only encapsulate things inside our objects, but we can choose to encapsulate our objects themselves within a component.

Developing with Components

There are some important considerations when developing COM components. They are somewhat less important when creating components for scripting languages, but it pays to be aware of them.

Interfaces and GUID Values

As discussed in Chapter 3, all components are identified by a unique numeric value. In fact, the value is unique within time and space – it is a type of value known as **GUID**, or **globally unique identifier**.

A GUID is a 128-bit structure generated by the Win32 API. When expressed as text, they appear like this: {73A4C9C1-D68D-11D0-98BF-00A0C90DC8D9}. The value is created by combining the current date and time with either the ID number from the computer's ethernet card or a randomly-generated value. The GUID was developed to provide identification values that are unique in time and space.

GUID values are used extensively within the COM environment. Each interface our component exposes has an **interface ID** (**IID**), which is also a GUID. Each public class in a component has a **class ID** (**CLSID**).

All these unique identifiers are critical when compiled languages such as Visual Basic or C++ go to use a component. Typically, when applications are built using these languages, the unique identifiers (and other critical interface information) are compiled right into the client applications. This allows those applications to access components very quickly and efficiently.

The drawback is that these applications are counting on those GUID values and component interface information to never change.

If we ever change an IID value or a CLSID, then all those programs will cease to function. If we ever change an interface on a public object – by removing a method, changing a parameter, changing the name of a method, etc. – then these programs will cease to function.

> *When programming in Visual C++ we have quite a lot of control over our ID values and the various interface information. However, most components are created using Visual Basic, and VB hides almost all of these details from the developer – making it somewhat challenging to ensure that no IID, CLSID, or interface definitions change over time.*

When building components in Visual Basic, the version compatibility option should typically be set to Binary Compatibility – aimed at a copy of the compiled DLL with which to remain compatible. This option is found on the Component tab after selecting the Project | Properties menu option:

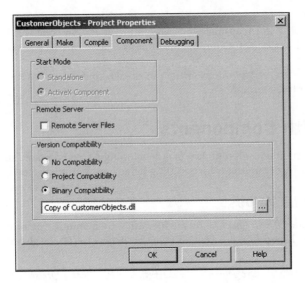

The screenshot illustrates a DLL named CustomerObjects, with binary compatibility set so the server will remain compatible with a copy. The steps we need to follow are:

❑ Create the component, including all required classes

❑ Compile the DLL

❑ Make a copy of the DLL

❑ Use the Project Properties dialog to set binary compatibility to the copy

If we set compatibility to the actual DLL rather than to a copy there's no guarantee that our component will remain compatible with anything we've deployed to clients. If we accidentally become incompatible with the deployed DLLs, then next time we deploy our DLL we'll get a lot of upset users as they find their application no longer works.

Components and ASP

The impact of all these issues is quite minimal for the typical ASP developer. This is because ASP relies on scripting languages, and they always use `IDispatch` to communicate with components. `IDispatch` is dynamic rather than static, so (while it is slower) it is quite tolerant of changes to object interfaces, IID, and CLSID values.

In fact, assuming that our ASP code doesn't attempt to interact with an object that has been removed, or a method expecting different parameters, changes to a component or an object will have pretty much no impact on our application from the client's perspective.

This doesn't mean that we shouldn't use good component programming practices – maintaining consistent interfaces for our components and ensuring that the IID and CLSID values don't change. One reason for using components is that they are not only useful to an ASP application, but also may be used by other applications within our organization – and those may be written using something other than scripting languages.

Fitting This into Windows DNA

Windows DNA is interesting in that, based on the typical diagrams and descriptions, we might debate whether it is a logical architecture or a physical architecture.

❑ Logical n-tier architectures define layers, or tiers, of an application in the abstract sense. Often these tiers include presentation, user interface, business logic, and data services. The logical architecture doesn't specify whether all the tiers will run on a single computer, whether they'll be spread out across many computers, or something in between.

❑ A physical architecture takes the abstract logical architecture and physically places the various tiers on specific hardware. The presentation and UI tiers may go on a client workstation, with the business logic in an application server, and the data services being provided by a database server.

This is illustrated by the following diagram, where the logical tiers of an application are shown on the left, and the corresponding physical tiers are shown on the right:

Presentation	Client workstation
User interface	
Business	Application server
Data	Database

There are many variations on this theme, the idea being that if we can design our applications in a logical sense, then we can adapt them to various physical environments as needed later. The drawback to this approach is that there is a lot of complexity involved in coming up with a solid logical design, then translating it into a workable physical architecture against which software can be developed.

Separation of UI, Business, and Data

At its heart, Windows DNA is an n-tier client-server architecture extended to the Web. One of the primary requirements of n-tier client-server design is that the business logic remains separate from both the presentation logic and the data services. This doesn't necessarily mean this logic is physically somewhere else, rather our concern is that it is separate in a *logical* sense.

Separation of UI and Business

Maintaining separation between the UI and business logic is very important for flexibility and maintainability of our application. If there's any part of an application that is constantly changing, it is the UI. Every time we turn around it seems that someone has come up with a new or more interesting way to interact with the user.

More often than not, a change to the UI doesn't really mean that our business policies, rules, or validations have changed. If our UI and business code are intermixed, then any time we adapt our application to a new UI we will end up impacting on our business logic – even if it should have remained constant.

The flip side is that applications today rarely have only one interface. In many cases they'll have a couple of user interfaces, and one or more other applications with which they interface. If we've written our UI code in script within ASP pages, it may be very difficult to reuse that logic from another application, or to reuse that logic when we need to support a Microsoft Excel-based user interface.

Separation of Data and Business

Likewise, maintaining separation between data processing and business logic is very important. This comes into play in two different ways.

Firstly, it's best to keep our application relatively database-independent. How many applications started out talking to JET (Access) databases and then had to be rewritten to work well with SQL Server or Oracle? In many cases these applications were written with data access code spread throughout the application – meaning that changing databases affected virtually every part of the program.

Secondly, it's preferable to shield our application from *data access* technology. It seems that every couple of years Microsoft comes out with a new, better, way for us to access data. First we had dblib, then DAO, then DAO with ODBC, then RDO, now ADO.

Each time a new data access technology comes out we end up going through our entire application, changing the code to accommodate, and hopefully take advantage of, the new services. In some cases this type of change can be even more difficult to implement than simply changing the type of database with which we're interacting.

> *This is one reason why I tend to shy away from the use of disconnected ADO* Recordset *objects when possible. Given that any given data access technology has only ever remained in favor for 2-3 years, I wouldn't want to bet my application's future on any technology matching* '*DO'.

Business objects can help in this regard by encapsulating the code that accesses the database. This way we limit the amount of code that utilizes data access technology or relies on a specific database. Our UI and presentation code doesn't use any data access at all – relying on the objects to handle that.

To make this truly successful we need to design our objects to restrict the use of data access technology there as well. Rather than spreading data access logic through all the routines within our objects, we should create two methods – one to retrieve data and one to save it.

All other routines within the object should avoid any subsequent data access – and minimize the use of data access technologies such as ADO in general. By taking these steps we severely restrict the amount of code that would need to be changed if the database was changed or if ADO became replaced by something newer and better.

We'll come back to this topic later in the book, when we examine a more complex application design that further shields our application from changes in databases, data structure and data access technologies.

Objects and Windows DNA

Microsoft designed the Windows DNA architecture with objects in mind. Windows DNA defines a general **application logic tier**, generally allowing us to write our application logic using the tool and technique of our choice. However, the recommendation is to place our business logic and processing within a set of COM objects – using those objects to encapsulate the data and logic:

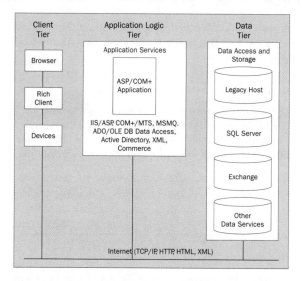

By putting our business logic in COM objects instead of ASP script we gain some serious advantages.

Firstly, COM objects are typically created using compiled languages such as Visual Basic or C++. When compared to interpreted script code, compiled components are almost always many times faster.

This is compounded by the different ways script code interacts with objects as compared to compiled languages. Script code uses a very slow technique for object interaction, while Visual Basic and Visual C++ use highly optimized techniques. To drive this point home, consider that the ADO `Recordset` is an object – a highly used object. Each time our code interacts with a `Recordset` via script we are losing performance – in fact VB or VC will interact with the object about 60 times faster!

Interestingly enough, there's typically no difference between the performance of VB and VC code in this setting. Both languages use the same optimizing compiler and tend to have quite comparable performance.

Additionally we gain substantial design flexibility by moving business logic into COM objects. If the logic is all contained in our ASP pages, then we are pretty much stuck running that code on the web server. By moving it into a well-designed set of COM objects we can choose to run the objects on a separate machine – allowing the web server to focus on providing UI support, while a whole other machine handles business processing.

Unfortunately there's a complimentary set of drawbacks that are important. Because ASP code is interpreted, it can be updated without compilation – while COM components must be recompiled before they can be used. Worse yet, IIS locks any DLLs that are run in-process by ASP – meaning that the IIS server needs to be restarted any time a COM component needs to be updated.

Also, many third-party Application Service Providers are reluctant to install COM components on their servers. They frequently restrict applications such that they can only rely on ASP script pages for application development.

As with most techniques available to us as developers, COM components and business objects have strengths and weaknesses. While COM components can make deployment to the web server more complex, and may be problematic with Application Service Providers, the use of business objects is typically highly beneficial due to improved performance, maintainability, and reuse.

In this chapter we'll work with COM objects designed to run on the web server along with the ASP code. Later in the book we'll explore the architectural changes required to efficiently move some or all of that processing onto separate machines.

Business Objects on the Web Server

The next diagram drills down a bit, showing that the client interacts with a set of ASP pages, which in turn interact with COM objects. In this model, the ASP pages handle all user interface tasks – formatting data for display, retrieving user input, and so forth. The COM business objects are responsible for all business processing, including validation, business rule enforcement, and calculations.

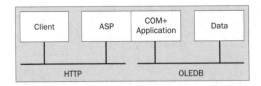

Another interesting side-effect of this approach is that the ASP code doesn't interact directly with data services – that task is handled by the business objects as well. In many ways this is very nice, since it simplifies the task of the ASP developers – allowing them to focus on the many issues surrounding building a high quality user interface. In the meantime, the business developers can avoid most UI issues, remaining largely focused on implementing code to handle business logic and interact with data as needed.

While it might be ideal to suggest that business logic should only exist in a set of business objects, and that the UI code will reside entirely in ASP, this is typically not a realistic expectation.

Why? There are very sound reasons why some business processing, often validation, should happen in the presentation or UI tiers. In other cases there may be very sound reasons for pushing some business processing into the data tier itself.

> Windows DNA is all about putting logic in the optimal location, while at the same time achieving a level of balance for maintainability. This is why software development is often more of an art than a science, since the 'right' answer will vary from application to application.

We'll get into this subject in substantial depth in the advanced business objects chapter later on. For now, we'll stick with the recommended Windows DNA approach of encapsulating our business logic within a set of COM objects in the middle tier. Such an approach is very appropriate for many Windows DNA applications being constructed.

Things to Watch For

When we look at using COM objects within a Windows DNA application, there are a few issues that we need to be aware of. Some of these, if ignored, can cause serious problems with our applications – fortunately most are easily dealt with once understood.

Though there are many factors that go into building a successful application based on COM objects, there are some common areas of concern. These fall into three main areas – **usability**, **performance/scalability** and **maintainability**.

Object and Component Usability

COM and COM+ are very powerful technologies. While they are key to the Windows DNA architecture, they extend into other types of applications as well. Because of this, they provide some capabilities that don't fit well (or at all) into the Windows DNA environment.

Multiple Interfaces

COM objects can be accessed in two main ways – via `IDispatch` (late binding) or via a v-table (early binding) – as we discussed in Chapter 3.

`IDispatch` is a general technique for accessing COM objects by which the calling code asks the object a series of questions to determine whether it has a specific method, how to call that method, and finally to actually invoke that method.

`IDispatch` is powerful in that it allows the calling code to know very little about the object with which it is interacting. It is also the technique used by scripting languages such as VBscript and JavaScript – hence it's critical to ASP programmers.

> To be used from ASP, an object *must* implement an `IDispatch` interface.

The problem with `IDispatch` is that it is quite slow, and doesn't provide access to all the features provided by COM. Most objects implement a v-table interface, which allows calling code to directly call the methods exposed through the object's interface.

Even more powerful is the ability of an object to expose more than one interface. This allows us to create, say, a `SalesOrder` object, and have that object also expose a more generic `Document` interface. If our `Invoice` objects also expose the `Document` interface, we can write code that treats both types of object just as generic documents:

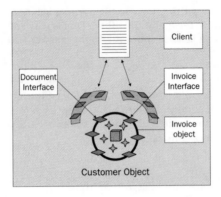

This capability is not available to ASP coders – so it's very important that our COM objects always provide any needed functionality via the default IDispatch interface.

In Visual Basic the default IDispatch interface is composed of all properties and methods that are declared with Public scope in our class module.

There are two solutions to allow ASP developers to use objects with multiple interfaces:

❑   The easiest is to simply add all the methods and properties from any secondary interfaces to the object's main interface. This is not always good object design, since the object's main interface can become quite large and complex, but it does make the object very easy to work with from an ASP perspective.

❑   The second approach is to create a set of façade objects that expose the alternative interfaces as their native interfaces. The only code behind each method in such an object will be code that delegates the method call to the actual business object – using the appropriate interface on that object:

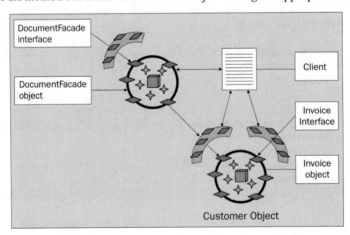

Now our client code can interact with the Invoice object through its regular interface, or if we need the Document interface, it can interact with a DocumentFacade object. The DocumentFacade object merely relays each method call to the same method on the Invoice object's Document interface.

This second approach is more complex, but is particularly useful when dealing with pre-existing objects that already implement multiple interfaces.

Events

A COM object can raise events to the code that holds a reference to the object. As will be discussed in Chapter 10, this is handled through a type of callback mechanism, so when the object raises the event a method is called within the original code:

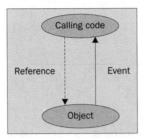

The exception is error events, since they are handled via HRESULT, not via COM callbacks.

This technology originated with ActiveX controls, since controls are constantly raising events into the dialog in which they are contained. Subsequently it has been extended throughout COM, so it works between objects and most calling code.

However, it is not a universal capability. In particular, this capability is useless for scripting languages such as those available within ASP pages.

> **This means that, while a COM object can raise an event, code in an ASP page can't receive it.**

This is an important usability concern as we design our objects. While raising events is a powerful and useful technique, we need to provide alternative means for the script coder to get the functionality if our objects will be used by scripting languages. In short, if our object will be used by scripting languages, avoid the use of events.

Parameter Data Types

COM objects support many data types – some quite complex. Scripting languages, on the other hand, are typeless – only supporting the concept of a `Variant`.

The `Variant` 'data type' is powerful, since it can hold many different types of data:

Byte	Date
Integer	String
Long	Boolean
Single	Empty
Double	Null
Currency	Object
Decimal	Nothing

Notice the `Object` entry in the list. A variable of type `Variant` (such as all those in a scripting language) can hold a reference to an object. The unfortunate thing is that this is a reference to the object's default `IDispatch` interface rather than any specific interface.

This means that script code can't pass an object reference to a method that expects a specific type of object. For instance, suppose that we have a `Customer` object that accepts a `Contact` object as a parameter to one of its methods. This code might be written like this:

```
Public Sub PrimaryContact(NewContact As Contact)
   Set mobjPrimaryContact = NewContact
End Sub
```

Such a method is common when designing objects for use by other objects. Unfortunately this method can't be called from script code because the script code would provide merely a generic object reference – even if it were actually trying to pass a valid `Contact` object.

When programming such a method for use by script code we need to change it to accept a `Variant`, then do our own type checking to ensure the object is valid:

```
Private mobjPrimaryContact As Contact

Public Sub PrimaryContact(NewContact As Variant)

  Dim objContact As Contact

  ' cast the object into the correct type
  ' this will error if parameter is the wrong type
  Set objContact = NewContact

  ' now do our normal business code
  Set mobjPrimaryContact = objContact

End Sub
```

This is obviously a bit more work, and thus is more prone to error. It also makes our object less readable or programmer friendly, since object browsers and other similar technologies can no longer show a developer the expected data type for our parameters. On the other hand, this allows ASP developers to interact with our objects – a key requirement when building Windows DNA applications.

An alternative approach is to create a façade object, which exposes a method that accepts a Variant parameter, then delegates the call to the actual business object using the real data type. Such a façade method may look something like this:

```
Public Sub SetPrimaryContact(Cust As Variant, Cont As Variant)

  Dim objContact As Contact

  Set objContact = Cont
  Cust.PrimaryContact objContact

End Sub
```

Notice how we cast the `Variant` object reference to be of type `Contact`, then pass it as a parameter to the `Customer` object's method.

This second approach is more complex, but is particularly useful when dealing with pre-existing objects that already have strongly typed parameters.

Performance/Scalability

Performance and scalability are two different, though closely related, concepts. Performance is typically viewed as the speed of an application for one user. Scalability is what happens to performance as we add more load to the system – typically by adding more users.

In many cases, things that increase performance will increase scalability. This is not always the case, however, so it's worth considering the larger ramifications of any change made to increase performance.

The two main areas of concern when using business objects in a Windows DNA application affect both scalability and performance.

COM Objects, ASP, and Binding

ASP makes it very easy to interact with COM objects. We can simply create an object and begin working with it with very little code:

```
<%
   Dim objObject
   Set objObject = Server.CreateObject("MyDLL.MyClass")
   objObject.DoSomething
   Set objObject = Nothing
%>
```

What isn't obvious from this code is that there is a performance issue lurking under the surface. COM allows us to interact with objects in various ways – some more efficient, others more flexible.

ASP uses a technique known as **late binding** to interact with COM objects. This is the most flexible approach, allowing languages (such as VBScript and JavaScript) that have no formal concept of data types to interact with objects. Unfortunately, it is also the slowest mechanism available for communicating with objects.

> *Late binding is handled via the `IDispatch` COM interface implemented by many objects. Not all COM objects implement this interface – and those that don't are unavailable for use by ASP. However, most COM objects for Windows DNA applications are written using Visual Basic, and it always provides the `IDispatch` interface for our use.*

What this means to us is that we need to design our business objects with efficient, easily used interfaces. The fewer properties and methods called by ASP code, the faster our application will run.

This is one major benefit of handling data access within a COM object rather than directly from ASP. ASP communicates with ADO `Recordset` objects via late binding as well, while C++ and Visual Basic use the very fast v-table binding approach – thus often providing substantial performance benefits over ASP.

Direct Access or COM+ App – Performance versus Reliability

Another important issue is the question of whether to run our business objects in the same process as ASP, or to have the objects run in their own process.

Code running within a single process tends to be quite fast. All method and property calls, though late-bound, happen within the same memory and context – making them pretty efficient:

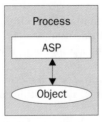

If our objects are running in their own process, separate from ASP, then things get a bit more complex. In order to ensure safe and proper interaction between the code in two processes, COM steps in the middle and provides a set of services for us. On the upside, this makes communicating between processes very easy, but the downside is that the extra processing tends to slow things down.

The performance hit means that it is at least 60 times slower to go across processes as opposed to working within the same process. For a single method call this doesn't matter much, but if our ASP code is making dozens of property and method calls to our objects, this can become a serious issue for performance:

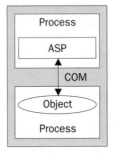

However, there are a couple of benefits to running our objects in their own process that may offset the performance impact. By running the objects in their own process, we may increase the overall stability of our application. Additionally, if the objects are running in a COM+ application, we will gain some important management capabilities. (We'll discuss COM+ applications more completely later in this book.)

Our application's overall stability may be improved by running the business objects in a separate process from ASP. The primary scenario where this comes into play is if our objects are unstable and crash. When they crash they'll bring down the process in which they are running. By being in a separate process from ASP, we can avoid crashing the ASP process itself – minimizing the impact.

In reality, most COM business objects tend to be quite stable. It's relatively unlikely that such objects will destabilize our process – especially if we apply some decent testing to the components before running them live on the server. Additionally, if our application makes heavy use of business objects (which it should), then there would still be substantial impact on users were our objects to crash – regardless of whether they are in the ASP process or a separate process.

The management benefits are more tangible. If our COM components are running in the same process as ASP, the only way to update them is to restart the entire IIS process. This is because IIS loads the DLL into memory and never releases it – increasing performance, but making it very difficult to update the site with changes.

If we choose to run our DLL in some other process (using COM+ applications or other techniques), we can leave IIS running and just restart the process hosting our DLL when we need to apply an update.

In the end, running our component in the ASP process is *much* faster, but has potential stability and management drawbacks. Running our component outside of ASP increases stability and management, but the price tag comes in the form of much slower performance and reduced scalability.

COM Objects and ASP Objects

Windows DNA applications often get very complex. In many cases we need to collect data from one page and then have that data available to our code in subsequent ASP pages as they are processed.

If we have a set of business objects encapsulating our data, it certainly seems to make a lot of sense that we should simply keep those objects around from page to page – thus making the data (and related business logic) available to all the ASP pages of our application.

Unfortunately even such a seemingly simple concept is rife with problems. To understand why, we need to have a basic understanding of how COM and ASP handle threads.

The term **thread** is short for 'thread of execution'. Any time a computer is doing some work, that work is done in a certain sequence – one line of code at a time. If we imagine all this code strung out in order, it might appear as a long thread of events – or a thread of execution.

A Windows 2000 server is typically running many, many threads. In reality, a CPU can only be doing one thing at a time, so in a single processor machine only one thread is really running at a time. However, the operating system keeps track of all the possible threads on the system and schedules them to run in an efficient manner – giving us the illusion that the computer is doing many tasks at once.

> *In a multi-processor machine the computer really **is** doing many tasks at once – as many tasks as there are CPUs.*

Creating and destroying threads takes time, and to minimize this, ASP manages a **thread pool**. This means that it provides an environment where there is a pool of threads available for use by pages and COM components. The idea is that any time a request comes in for an ASP page, the system can grab a free thread from the pool, have it do the work, then release it back into the pool for reuse later. This is powerful, and critical to the high scalability possible though ASP.

Many COM objects cause trouble in this free-wheeling environment of promiscuous threads. All Visual Basic 6 objects, and many created in C++ or other languages, have a thing called **thread affinity**. This means that these objects can only run on the thread that created them.

Such a concept flies directly in the face of a thread pool, where any random thread should be able to run the code of any ASP page, any object, etc. If we say instead that we need to use exactly the same thread each time for a given object, then we've created a scenario of possible bottlenecks. If the thread needed for my object is busy – my object will just have to wait until that thread is free.

So what does this have to do with ASP? Well, ASP provides us with a couple of objects that allow us to maintain data from one page to another, or across an entire ASP application. These are the `Application` and `Session` objects.

The `Application` and `Session` objects, like ASP itself, are not permanently associated with any thread – meaning that they take full advantage of thread pooling. Both the `Application` and `Session` objects can be used to store arbitrary values as we see fit – providing us with a very convenient technology for storing data for the life of a user's session or as long as our application is running.

Interestingly, the `Application` and `Session` objects also allow us to store objects. This is where things get dicey. Though the ASP objects are thread-neutral, remember that most COM objects have thread affinity. As soon as an object with thread affinity is stored in an ASP object, that object and the entire ASP processing for that application or session become trapped on that thread. No more thread pooling.

> *Technically we don't get to store objects. Instead we're storing **object references** in the* `Application` *or* `Session` *object. The objects themselves exist in memory – just a pointer, or reference, is maintained from the ASP objects.*

In fact, this problem is so severe that the ASP `Application` object will prohibit us from storing a reference to an inappropriate object (that is, one with thread affinity). Were we to do such a thing, the entire application – for *all users* – would be locked onto a single thread. Talk about an application killer!

The `Session` object is not so restrictive – we can, in fact, store a reference to an object with thread affinity into a `Session` object. The result is that the session for that user will be serialized onto a single thread. This can be a substantial performance problem as we noted earlier, though it does mean that we can store our application's state in our business objects – providing a very nice programming model.

> **If we know that the application will be used by a very small number of users we may be able to get away with storing object references in the `Session` object. However, it is strongly recommended that no object references be maintained in this manner.**

One powerful solution to this problem is to store the object's *state* in the ASP `Session` object, rather than storing a reference to the object itself. If we construct our business objects properly, we can easily extract the state data into a simple String variable, which can be stored in the `Session` object. Then on subsequent ASP pages we can create new, empty, business objects and simply put the state data back into them – essentially cloning the objects from page to page.

The process of converting an object's complex state into a single data element is called **serialization**. The complimentary process of converting the data element back into complex state is called **deserialization**.

> *Various techniques for handling this in Visual Basic are discussed in* Visual Basic 6 Distributed Objects, ISBN 1-861001-07-X, from Wrox Press. *Similar techniques exist for other programming languages that we might use when building COM objects.*

The simplest approach available in Visual Basic is to use the `PropertyBag` object to store our object's data, then simply export the resulting data as a single `String` variable. We can do this by writing a `GetState` method similar to the following:

```
Public Function GetState() As String

   Dim pb As PropertyBag

   Set pb = New PropertyBag
   With pb
     .WriteProperty "Name", mstrName
     .WriteProperty "BirthDate", mdtBirthDate
     GetState = .Contents
   End With
   Set pb = Nothing

End Function
```

This method simply creates an instance of the PropertyBag object and then uses its WriteProperty method to store each data value from our object into the PropertyBag. Once all the important values are stored, we can simply call the PropertyBag object's Contents property to retrieve all its data as a single variable.

The value returned is actually a Byte array, but Visual Basic will automatically convert it to a String as it's returned from the function. This is important, because scripting languages such as VBScript do not support the concept of a Byte array – but they do support the String data type.

Having added a GetState method to our business object, we can then write some simple ASP script at the end of our page to store that state in the ASP Session object:

```
<%
   Session("ObjectState") = objObject.GetState
%>
```

At this point ASP has stored the *data* from our object, so we can allow the object itself to be destroyed. On subsequent ASP pages, the data will continue to be available, meaning we can create a new instance of our object and put that data into it – effectively cloning our business objects from page to page.

Putting the data back into the object requires a method that does the reverse of GetState. For instance, in Visual Basic we could create a complimentary SetState method as follows:

```
Public Sub SetState(ByVal Buffer As String)

   Dim pb As PropertyBag
   Dim arBuffer() As Byte

   Set pb = New PropertyBag
   arBuffer = Buffer
   With pb
     .Contents = arBuffer
     mstrName = .ReadProperty("Name")
     mdtBirthDate = .ReadProperty("BirthDate")
   End With
   Set pb = Nothing

End Function
```

This method is very similar to GetState, except that instead of putting values into the PropertyBag object, it takes them out and puts them into the object's instance variables.

The only bit of magic in this code is where we copy the `String` variable `Buffer` into a `Byte` array variable, `arBuffer`. This is required to force Visual Basic to convert the `String` value stored by ASP into an array so we can put it into the `PropertyBag` object.

With this routine added to a business object, we can now write ASP code at the top of a page to restore an object's data:

```
<%
   Set objObject = Server.CreateObject("MyDLL.MyClass")
   objObject.SetState CStr(Session("ObjectState"))
%>
```

As soon as this code has run, our ASP page has full access to our business object – essentially exactly the same object we had in the previous page.

This technique allows us to use objects from ASP, without storing a reference to an object. By doing this, we enable the use of objects without the huge performance and scalability impact that would result from tying our entire ASP session to a single thread. Even so, storing any data in the ASP `Session` object is not recommended for high volume sites.

State in Web Farms

Whether we use the ASP `Session` object to store our object's data or even direct references to our business objects, there is an important side effect to be aware of. This data, critical to our application, is stored on a *specific* web server.

For small to mid-sized Windows DNA applications this is not a problem. However, for larger applications – those supporting more users – a single web server machine may not be sufficient. In such a case we'll need to deploy a **web farm**.

A web farm is nothing more than a group of identical web servers that share the load of many requests. When a user comes to a simple web site, they always interact with that site's server. If we have a web farm, the user will interact with any one of the servers in our farm – each of them able to provide exactly the same content on demand:

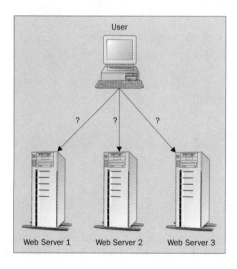

The idea behind a web farm is that we can support a lot more users if we can spread their requests across a number of machines. And in fact this is a very powerful and important technique used in most large web applications.

Our challenge is that this environment makes storing state in a web server's memory problematic. For instance, consider this example:

❑ On page 1, the user interacts with server 1. At the end of the page, we store our object's state data in the ASP `Session` object – on server 1.

❑ On page 2, the user is routed to server 3. At the top of our page we attempt to restore the business object's state from the data in the ASP `Session` object – except that the data isn't *there.* The data doesn't exist on server 3 – only on server 1. Oops.

There are two general solutions to this problem. The easiest is to set up the web farm such that a user will continue to interact with the same web server throughout their entire session. A more complex, but perhaps better solution is to provide a mechanism by which an ASP page can store data values and make them available to all servers in the web farm.

Most web farm technologies provide direct support for the concept of keeping a user on the same server for their entire session. In this scenario the user is assigned to an arbitrary server on their *first* request for a page, but on subsequent requests they are always routed to that same server. This means that our use of the ASP `Session` object to store object data will work just fine.

Unfortunately, this approach somewhat defeats the purpose behind implementing a web farm. Web farms typically implement a load balancing algorithm, to make sure that the load of all user requests is spread evenly across all the servers. As soon as we tie a user to a specific server, this load balancing becomes less effective – though not totally useless.

Perhaps more importantly, web farms provide a level of fault tolerance for our application. If a web server crashes, all further user requests will be handled by the remaining servers. Unfortunately, if our user started on a particular server, and that server crashed, then that user is out of luck, because their state data is also gone. So much for fault tolerance...

A more complex, but thorough, approach to this issue of state management in a web farm is to make the state available equally to all the web servers in the farm. This is not the easiest thing to do – at least not while avoiding performance costs. Essentially what we're saying is that an ASP page on one server can change some data, and that data should be instantly available to all other servers in the web farm.

There are various technologies and techniques that address this type of solution, the two most common being to store the data on a centrally available machine (perhaps in a database), or to replicate the data across all the machines in the farm.

This topic is too complex to delve into in this chapter, but suffice it to say that this type of solution preserves the benefits of a web farm – scalability and fault tolerance – while also enabling ASP developers to store state data as needed. This includes the ability to store the data from our business objects and make it available to all web servers in the farm.

Maintainability

One of the major goals behind the use of objects is to increase the maintainability of our applications. It sounds nice – encapsulate business data and logic in objects, then use those objects from any user interface as needed, reusing the logic over and over.

And, with care, use of objects can dramatically increase the maintainability of our applications. Unfortunately, there are some key areas where many object-based projects fall short, leading to serious maintenance problems over time. As we said earlier, the most common mistake is to blur the line between the user interface logic and business logic.

Another challenging area is deciding what logic to put in objects and what logic to put into the database, using stored procedures and triggers. Let's cover the use of stored procedures and triggers first.

Stored Procedures

Stored procedures are perhaps the easiest topic to cover. Stored procedures allow us to write part of our application's logic directly within the database itself.

This is powerful, since we can set up our database security such that users *must* use our stored procedures to interact with the data. Essentially we can ensure that there's no way to bypass our logic and interact directly with the data. On the surface this seems like the perfect place to put all our business logic – centralized and inescapable.

There are a couple of drawbacks, however. Firstly, this means we'd be writing our business logic in SQL rather than in a conventional programming language. As compared to Visual C++ or Visual Basic, SQL and its related debugging environments are pretty primitive and limiting.

Heavy use of PL-SQL in Oracle or Transact-SQL for SQL Server will limit portability of our application as well. Given the continual mergers and acquisitions in business today, we can't assume our application will always use the same database forever.

Perhaps more importantly, putting logic in the database means that we can't find out if any business rules or validation rules have been broken until we are physically trying to store the data. This means we can't tell the user if they've entered good data until long after they've clicked the Save button. This is the ultimate in terms of providing the user with a batch-oriented experience!

Finally, if we put business logic into the database when we're constructing an application based around business objects, there will be substantial complexity introduced – leading to complicated design and maintenance difficulties.

The primary reason for putting business logic (not data manipulation, but *business* logic) in stored procedures is to centralize all the business logic to control and protect both it and the data. The primary reason for using business objects is exactly the same! Having two tiers in our architecture with exactly the same goal is problematic.

How do we decide which logic goes where? By moving any logic out of the database we've negated the benefit of totally protecting our data, so then why put *any* logic there? The reason is performance.

Stored procedures can utilize services within the database to interact with data much faster than our business objects can. Using stored procedures to retrieve data – especially when joins are involved, and to insert or update data, will often improve an application's performance substantially.

Rather than moving *business logic* into stored procedures, we should look at stored procedures as places to store *data logic*. Data logic is entirely concerned with highly efficient access to data for retrieval or update:

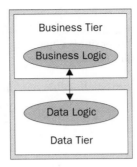

This is exactly where stored procedures shine – increasing our application's performance while retaining the clarity of our architecture.

Referential Integrity in the Database

Most, if not all, databases provide built-in capabilities to manage **referential integrity**. Typically these mechanisms get involved when we insert, update data, or remove data. They ensure that we don't create invalid keys or foreign keys, remove parent records while child records exist, etc.

For instance, if a row in the parent table of a one-to-many relationship is deleted, referential integrity mechanisms will kick in to delete all the related child rows.

The challenge with referential integrity enforcement is that referential integrity is basically a form of business logic. The relationship between a sales order and its line items is dictated by business rules – and reflected in the database as referential integrity rules. Such a relationship will also be reflected in our objects (we'll discuss object relationships later in the book).

Fortunately relational logic is a pretty focused type of business logic. Given the performance gains of handling referential integrity within the database, it's typically worth the added complexity of moving this business logic from our business objects into the database. We can design our objects to rely on the database to handle those aspects of our business processing.

Separation of UI and Business Logic

Earlier in this chapter we discussed business logic and how it is different from UI logic, such as formatting values for presentation. It is important to keep this separation at the forefront of our design and coding.

It's incredibly tempting for a UI developer to just add a bit of logic to validate a value, rather than requesting that the change be made in a business object. This leads to problems later though, since we're likely to reuse our objects in more than one ASP page (or from Office, or from a VB UI). The odds of forgetting to replicate the validation logic from page to page are quite high – leading to inconsistently enforced validation (otherwise known as bugs).

There's also the temptation to put UI logic into our business objects. For instance, it might seem quite attractive to have our sales order business object generate an HTML table to display its line items. Of course the next requirement will be to display on a cell phone or some other non-HTML device, so what do we do then? The obvious solution is to add a new method to generate the new display.

Following this approach, eventually our object will have code to support myriad displays – very likely containing more UI code than actual business logic. This will end up defeating the purpose behind creating business objects – which is to encapsulate business logic and separate it from the UI.

If we want to use objects to encapsulate generation of HTML for the UI, we need to treat these as UI utility objects – not business objects. Our business objects can then remain focused on implementing business logic, while the UI objects build the display.

In Chapter 16 we'll explore the issues surrounding thin and intelligent clients in more detail.

Summary

In this chapter we have defined business objects and business logic. We explored the key benefits of business objects:

- ❑ Encapsulation

- ❑ Abstraction

- ❑ Maintainability

- ❑ Code reuse

We moved beyond object-oriented design and covered component-oriented design. Component-oriented design builds on object-oriented design, but provides us with another layer of abstraction – allowing us to create very useful building blocks for our applications.

We also discussed the recommended use for business objects within the Windows DNA architecture, which is to encapsulate business logic and data. When using objects in this scenario, our ASP code should handle all user interface and presentation logic, relying entirely on our business objects to handle business processing and data access.

This approach maximizes our flexibility, as well as increasing the performance and scalability of our application.

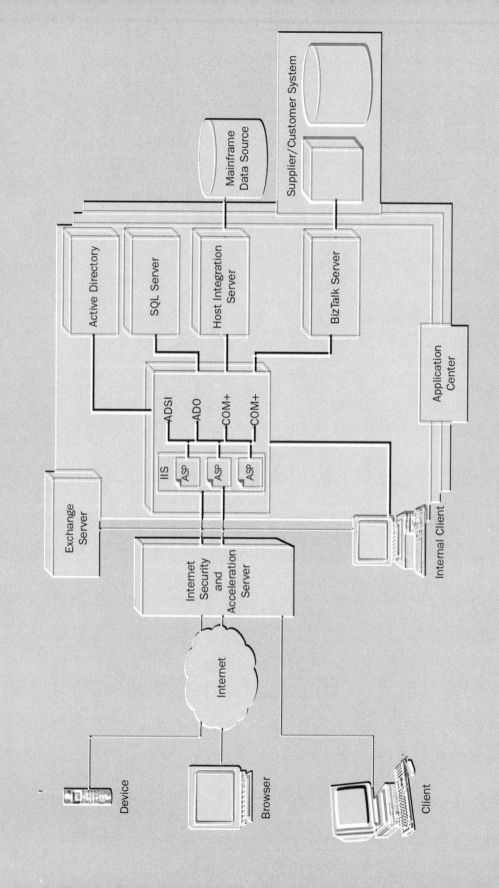

6

COM+ Architecture

Since its first introduction as Object Linking and Embedding (OLE), Microsoft's first try at object development, COM, has come a long way; and the jump to COM+ is just as significant. One of the most impressive capabilities for developers that has accompanied these technologies (versions) is backward compatibility. Without backward compatibility, developers would be forced to rewrite their code every time Microsoft released a new version. Luckily, the latest release of this technology, COM+, is really the next logical version of COM and Microsoft Transaction Server (MTS) rolled into one bundle.

This chapter will start with a quick recap of Microsoft Transaction Server and the services it provides. As the chapter moves on it will get into the changes COM+ brings and will set up an introduction for the chapters to come. We will look at:

- ❑ A review of MTS
- ❑ MTS Services
- ❑ What is COM+
- ❑ COM+ Services
- ❑ Components of COM+

COM and MTS Join Forces

What do we mean by 'COM and MTS join forces'? Essentially, COM+ takes baseline COM and integrates the services from MTS into it, instead of on top of it. When Microsoft developed MTS it really built a layer that sat on top of COM; however, with COM+ the two have been built together to form a single seamless product. This not only makes things run faster, but as you will see later, it also simplifies many of the tasks that seemed cumbersome in MTS. We've already looked into basic COM, but we've not looked at what MTS is for, so before we dive into COM+ and what it does, let's take a step back and look at MTS and the services it provides.

Microsoft Transaction Server

MTS was Microsoft's first product/suite of services in the component middleware arena. MTS provides a large set of services that sit on top of COM and DCOM. Most of the services have a common theme throughout them – they are all 'plumbing' services. What I mean by this is that they are not a solution in themselves, but they provide a strong foundation onto which a solution can be built.

MTS is really a host, or a place to store COM components. However, this host not only lets COM components live there, it also provides them with a set of services to work with. See, as you've heard before, COM is all about love!

MTS Services

As noted above, MTS provides a set of services that sit on top of COM; but what are these services and what do they do? The following is a list of services available from MTS, followed by a quick recap of what each services is and the benefits it provides:

- ❏   Transactions
- ❏   Connection Pooling
- ❏   Security
- ❏   Thread Pooling
- ❏   Synchronization
- ❏   Administration features

Transactions

MTS stands for Microsoft Transaction Server, so you'd be forgiven for thinking that transactions came into the picture somewhere. You'd be right, by the way. So what are transactions? Transactions are a way to group several tasks into one single unit of work that either fails or succeeds as a whole. If a transaction encounters an error while in process, it fails as a whole, and any changes are undone or **rolled back**. This is useful in a whole range of cases, for example in an e-commerce site. Here you'd want to check the validity of the credit card number, and if successful, log a shipping request, decrease the inventory, and send a confirmation e-mail, among other things. You'd obviously either want all of these things to happen, or none of them, so you'd group them into a single transaction. In MTS, and also therefore in COM+, a grouping of work into a single unit is also often referred to as an **activity**.

Just like its name suggests, transactions form one of the most widely used services within MTS. However, MTS actually gets its transaction capabilities from a Microsoft service called MSDTC or Microsoft Distributed Transaction Coordinator, which was first introduced with SQL Server.

MSDTC is a very powerful service that enables developers to produce components that can interact with one another across various resources, such as SQL Server and Microsoft's Message Queuing Service (MSMQ). The downside of MSDTC is that it is a difficult service to program to. This is where MTS comes in to save the day for developers. MTS provides an easy-to-use COM API that developers can code to.

Security

MTS provides security to COM components through roles. This system is known as **role-based** security. This is done by defining various roles or groups that can access components. An example of a role would be a teller or a loan officer for a banking application.

MTS provides a very easy-to-use COM API to check on the incoming caller, get their username, and determine if they are part of a defined role. MTS roles are very similar to user groups in Windows NT and Windows 2000. They both can be assigned various rights, and contain a list of members and users.

Role-based security also provides security settings that will automatically deny or grant users access to the component, based upon these same roles. Roles can also be established at the interface level of a COM component.

Thread Pooling

MTS provides another resource called thread pooling, which it utilizes to maintain a pool of threads for itself. Even though most of us probably develop a lot of our COM object for MTS in VB, MTS will still be utilizing multiple threads to work with the objects when there are multiple requests sent to it.

Although this is done automatically behind the scenes, it is a noteworthy feature of MTS, especially since the creation and destruction of threads is rather expensive.

Synchronization

Synchronization is a huge benefit for developers. It allows them to forget the fact that there is more than one concurrent user on the system, so they can focus on the business logic instead.

Synchronization isolates all of the tasks carried out by an MTS *activity* and places locks on them. Although this may seem like it would be a performance bottleneck, it actually works quite well.

Synchronization also promotes the development of stateless components since resources are locked. It is best to lock the resources as late as possible and free them up as soon as possible. Note that the locking and unlocking of resources is done at a lower level than most developers code at, so to minimize the time the resources are locked, updates should be kept close together and the database connection should be closed as soon as possible (which actually returns it to a pool of connections).

Administration

Although the administration features that MTS provides are not something to build applications upon, they are appreciated by most developers and administrators. The MTS administrator is integrated into the Microsoft Management Console (MMC). The MMC is a framework that allows utilities to be snapped into it, hence the name MMC "snap-in".

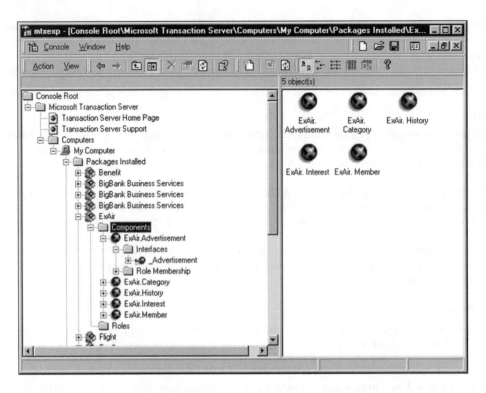

The MMC snap-in for MTS allows the creation of packages (groups of COM Components), the registration of COM classes, and the management of roles for security. The MTS administrator also provides a way to view the components installed within it and the status associated to them.

All of the functionality provided through the snap-in can also be controlled programmatically through a COM API knows as the MTS Administration Object. Here are a couple more resources for more information:

```
http://msdn.microsoft.com/library/psdk/mts20sp1/adminref_506b.htm
http://msdn.microsoft.com/library/psdk/mts20sp1/adminref_3fqr.htm
```

Other Features?

Aside from core services and features already mentioned above, MTS also provides a few more features that developers can build upon and utilize. One popular feature is a resource dispenser. A resource dispenser provides a mechanism for accessing shared information. This provides an excellent way for components to persist information while still remaining stateless.

MTS also provides hooks for clients to receive notifications from MTS; these are known as MTS event sinks. This is a great feature that is often used to create monitor and logging utilities for MTS.

As you can see, MTS provided a lot of plumbing work for developers. This not only aids development, it also provides a more stable solution, as opposed to developing all of the services by hand, which costs time and money.

Now let's get ready to look into COM+ and the additional features it provides.

Introducing COM+

As noted earlier, COM+ is the next logical progression of COM and MTS, fused into one seamless suite of services integrated into the Windows 2000 operating system.

The last section reviewed the major services that are provided with MTS and the advantages they bring with them. Now for a brief introduction to COM+, and the improvements and new features it brings with it to improve the development of COM-enabled applications.

Improvements to Features from COM and MTS

COM+ has not only added new features and services to COM and MTS, it has also enhanced some of its existing services. Let's see how.

Automatic Transactions

COM+ has improved on its ability to perform transactions by providing a setting to allow the automatic committal or rollback of a transaction based on whether the code encounters an error or not. If the routine throws an exception, COM+ will automatically rollback the transaction; otherwise the transaction is allowed to continue as normal.

Role-based Security

Roles now have the ability to be used down to the method level, in addition to the interface level, which MTS allowed. This enables developers to design their interfaces around the business requirements instead of the security requirements, which leads to a better structured and easier-to-follow object model.

Synchronization

Synchronization within COM+ is greatly improved when compared to MTS. Where MTS simply places locks on resources that the components are utilizing, COM+ will also lock the component to stop other users from using the same instance at the same time. However, this is not very useful in components with the apartment-threading model (thread affinity), like the ones built in VB. It is very useful for free-threaded components that have the potential to be accessed by two threads at the same time.

Instantiating Objects

Once of the biggest improvements when programming with COM+, as opposed to MTS, is not having to use a special syntax when calling between objects. In MTS, a developer had to make a call to MTS and ask it to create an instance of the component for it. Now with COM+ all we have to do is simply create an object just like any other object, and COM+ will look up its requirements for us and provide it with the proper runtime. This improvement is the result of COM and MTS being rolled into a single package. This way COM+ will know what the requirements of the component are. Exactly how COM+ is able to find out the requirements is described later in this chapter in the COM+ Catalog section.

We will cover this topic again throughout the book.

New Services to COM+

What would a new release be without any additional features? There are three new major features that have been integrated into COM+. These three features are the most common topics developers discuss about COM+: object pooling, queued components, and COM+ events.

Object Pooling

Object pooling has been a long desired feature for many developers, especially those from the C++ world. Object pooling enables developers of free-threaded COM components to develop objects that can be recycled and used again by other consumers (clients), instead of immediately being destroyed.

Although it may seem that all objects in COM+ should be pooled, it is not very efficient. Maintaining a pool of objects consumes resources that are otherwise free to be used on other tasks. The best place to utilize COM+'s object pooling functionality is when the initialization of an object is expensive (processor intensive). For instance, look at database connection pooling. ODBC and OLE DB both provide the ability to *pool* connections, but why? They pool connections because they are expensive to make. If you had to establish a database connection every time you needed a new one the application would drastically degrade in performance. For exatly the same reason Microsoft has built in the ability to pool your business objects.

When a request is made to COM+ for a component that is enabled for object pooling, COM+ will first look at its pool and determine if it has one to give to the consumer. If it does the server passes a reference to the consumer. This is what typically happens. If all of the objects in the pool are currently in use, COM+ will check its maximum pool size configuration and if it has not reached it, COM+ will create a new object and pass a reference of it to the consumer. This typically only happens when the server goes from low utilization to high utilization. As consumers release their reference to the object, COM+ will take the objects and place them back into the pool, instead of destroying them.

Currently at the time of this writing, poolable objects can only be built in VC++, because of the threading requirements. Objects that are going to be pooled must be built with the multi-threaded neutral apartment-threading model.

Queued Components

COM+ Queued Components (QC) is a very exciting and useful feature of COM+ that allows developers to build COM components that asynchronously communicate with each other. Behind the scenes QC sits on top of Microsoft Message Queue (MSMQ). This not only allows asynchronous communication, but it also provides the ability to make a call on a component that is not even available due to network communication issues or restrictions.

The best way to visualize QC is to think of it as COM components e-mailing each other instead of opening a direct synchronous connection (RPC) to one another. This style of communication is also known as loosely coupled; the interaction between the client and the server is not direct or tight. In fact when the client creates an instance of the server object, it actually has a reference to an object within QC that is imitating the server component.

Within the architecture of QC there are four sections; the recorder, MSMQ, the listener, and the player. The recorder resides on the client and logs all of the method calls invoked by the consumer. The recorder is the piece of QC that has the ability to imitate the requested server component; this way the consumer thinks they are working with the server component, when actually they haven't even communicated with the server. Once the consumer releases the reference to what it thinks is the server object, the listener builds an MSMQ message holding all of the log information from the consumer's interaction and sends it off to MSMQ.

With the utilization of MSMQ, QC inherits a lot of attributes, such as the ability to utilize server components even if the server is unavailable. MSMQ also provides the breaking point between the server and the client. MSMQ gives QC the ability to utilize loosely coupled communications as opposed to tightly coupled, which we have in the traditional COM/DCOM environment.

The listener section of QC resides on the server and responds to the messages sent to MSMQ from the recorder. As the listener responds to a new message, it forwards it to the last section of the QC, the player. The player is the part of QC that actually invokes the real server object. The player analyzes the log information from the recorder and invokes the methods in the same order that the client invoked them on the recorder.

More information on the background and implementation of Queued Components can be located in Chapter 9, Building Asynchronous Applications.

COM+ Events

COM+ Event services provide a mechanism for COM components to publish events and/or subscribe to events. The biggest benefit of COM+ Events is that the COM classes are not directly tied to one another – everything is configured through the COM+ components manager (MMC snap-in) or at runtime depending on the type of subscription.

Within COM+ Events there are three parts – the publisher, the event system, and the subscriber. Before we can talk about the publisher, we need to discuss the parts it calls upon in the event class. The event class resides within the event system and is really just an interface. For VC++ developers it is just an interface defined in MIDL and packaged into a type library file (.tbl). For VB developers this is a normal class within an ActiveX DLL with the methods defined with no code in them, just the declaration. The event class just provides a way to define and group events and make them available for the subscribers.

Now with an understanding of an event class and its role within COM+ events we can get into the publisher. The publisher can be a consumer that understands COM; VBScript, VB, and VC++, just to name a few. The publisher creates an instance of the event class and invokes the desired methods on it. As the publisher invokes a method, COM+ notices that the class is actually an event class and looks up all of its subscribers to the event class. Once it has the list, COM+ will invoke the same method on all of its subscribers, raising events on them. You may be wondering how COM+ can invoke the method on the client. One requirement of all subscribers is that they must implement the same interface they are subscribing to. As the subscriber implements an interface it defines a routine for them to place code into.

The greatest part of COM+ Events is that once the interface is defined and configured as an event class, multiple consumers of the event class can publish events to multiple subscribers without any of them knowing about one another. Since this interaction between the publisher and the subscribers is not direct, COM+ Events are often referred to as a loosely coupled event system.

More information on the background and implementation of the event service in COM+ can be located in Chapter 10, COM+ Events.

COM+

Now that we have a high-level understanding of COM+ and the services it brings to the COM developer, let's take it another step further to see what else COM+ has to offer and how it accomplishes these things. The following is a list of the areas of COM+ that will be covered:

- ❑ Component Activation
- ❑ COM+ Applications
- ❑ COM+ Components, Interfaces, and Methods
- ❑ COM+ Contexts
- ❑ COM+ Catalog

We'll start out by discussing the hierarchy of the various parts within COM+ and how our components fit into it. Then we'll talk about the steps that COM+ takes when a component is called upon from a consumer, and the how the types of COM+ applications affect the process. Next we'll talk about the Context object within COM+ and how it provides us with information about our surroundings in the COM+ runtime environment. Then we will discuss COM+ security and how it integrates with the security of Windows 2000. Lastly we will discuss the various apartment and threading models available in Windows 2000 and how they interact in COM+.

The configuration settings for COM classes are stored in COM+ beneath a structured hierarchy. At the top of the hierarchy is the computer (usually a server) running Windows 2000. Within each computer, COM+ will have multiple *applications*. These applications group multiple COM classes together and are synonymous with packages in MTS. Besides holding COM classes, COM+ applications also hold security settings known as **roles**. These are closely related to the roles from MTS and security groups in Windows NT and 2000.

The following screen shot displays the Component Services MMC snap-in. This tool is the central point for administrating COM+ and the components registered within it. To open this tool select the **Component Services** shortcut under the **Administrative Tools** folder located in the **Control Panel** or under the **Programs** folder from the **Start** menu.

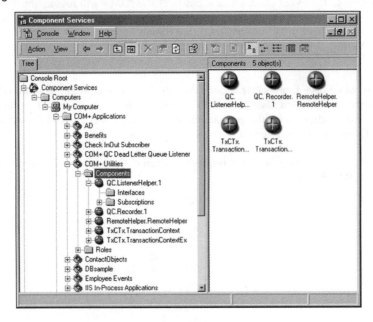

Within COM+ and Windows 2000, just like in MTS and Windows NT 4.0, there are two types of COM components, ones that are registered in COM+ (or MTS in Windows NT), and those that are not. Components that are registered are often referred to as configured components.

As noted above, configured COM classes are stored within COM+ applications. Each class has a set of properties that informs COM+ how to accommodate the class and the requirements. COM+ settings can actually be assigned down to the interfaces and the methods on each interface. This allows COM+ administrators to have a fairly granular level of control of the components.

Component Activation

The most common way to instantiate COM objects is through the `CreateObject` function for VB and ASP (VBScript) developers, or `CoCreateInstance` for the VC++ developer. If you have programmed with MTS you may be wondering about the `CreateInstance` function. Well I have great news; it's not needed! Since COM and MTS are now one product, COM+ can determine the runtime requirements of the requested class.

As requests are made for objects, COM+ uses a technique called **interception** to step in between the consumer of the component and the component itself. As COM+ intercepts the requests for instances of COM classes, it can take a brief moment to determine the requirements of the class and create the proper runtime environment.

MTS Object Communication

The following diagram displays the communication between the COM consumer and the server object configured within MTS. Notice the client side is the same as a normal DCOM call. DCOM creates a **proxy** for marshalling the method calls across the network through a normal remote procedure call (RPC) channel.

On the server side, things start off the same with the stub that communicates with the client's proxy. After the stub, things on the server side differ from a normal DCOM call. The stub interacts with a **Context Wrapper**. The Context Wrapper provides an environment (security, transaction, and activity) within MTS for the component to run in. Since the Context Wrapper sits between the DCOM layers and the actual component, MTS is also able to destroy the component when it's not needed, to conserve memory.

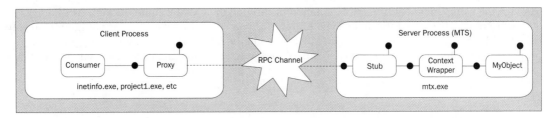

The above diagram also displays the communication for a Server MTS package, as opposed to a Library package. The difference between these types of packages is discussed in the Activation Type section below.

COM+ has also altered the Context Wrappers from MTS and created a new form of them called **Contexts**. Contexts are actually the objects that sit between the consumer and the object and perform the interception. We will be discussing these in more detail later on in the chapter, but for now note that the context object sits in front of the COM object and also acts as the stub for communication with the client's proxy.

COM+ Object Communication

Now let's compare MTS's object communication to COM+'s. In the following diagram you will notice that the client –side is the same. The DCOM on the consumer makes a proxy call to the server via an RPC channel. This is a very important feature of COM+ to note. Since the client side remains the same, moving to COM+ is that much easier.

On the server side things have changed. The stub has been moved into the COM+ runtime and is now processed with the same object as the interceptor and the COM+ context. This is one of the impacts that we can easily see from the unification of MTS and COM into one single product. Microsoft has combined the two products and therefore was able to combine some of the layers.

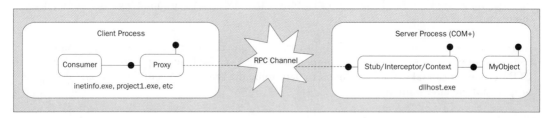

COM+ Applications

As mentioned many times throughout this chapter, COM+ applications provide a way to group multiple configured COM components together. So why do we have COM+ applications, and what is the need to group them together? One of the main reasons is to improve the performance of cross component calls, because components that are in the same application can communicate with one another without introducing DCOM. Conversely, components that are in separate applications must utilize marshaling to safely communicate with each other. Each COM+ application can be associated with an instance of the dllhost.exe.

Let's take a look at some of the other reasons that configured COM components are grouped into COM+ applications and the settings they can be assigned. All of the settings below can be configured though the Component Services MMC Snap-in or through the COM+ administration API library, comadmin.dll (COM+ 1.0 Admin Type Library). If you wish to set these settings programmatically, the COM API resides in the comadmin.dll located in the COM directory under the system32 directory. For more information on configuring these settings programmatically, consult Microsoft's online documentation at http://msdn.microsoft.com/library/psdk/cossdk/pgcreatingapplications_automatingadmin_9a26.htm.

Security

Security in applications really comes in two forms: **authentication** and **authorization**. Authentication is the process of identifying whether or not a user is really who they say they are. This is usually done by the operating system, as in Windows 2000. This process is either done by a user logging into their workstation, or by a web site requiring the user to enter a valid network username and password.

Within some applications, the process of authentication is done through code instead of relying on the operating system. Whichever process is used to verify users, it is usually done by a username and password.

Within COM+ applications, authentication can be configured at various levels. The most common is packet level. At the packet level COM+ will analyze the user of the COM object on every packet that is sent back from the user to the server. This level provides a fair amount of security without dramatically degrading performance. COM+ has five other settings for authentication. It can weaken security until it does not verify the client (None), it can also go to the other extreme and inspect each packet to make sure that no one has tampered with it while at the same time encrypting the packets as they are sent back and forth across the network.

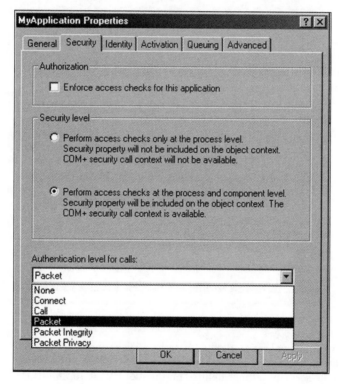

As you can imagine, the higher the security setting for authentication, the slower the applications will run. This only makes sense as the level of checking moves from none to per connection to per packet.

Once a user has been authenticated, they then have to be authorized to perform certain tasks throughout the system. Most of the time this is done through custom code within the application, however COM+ provides an infrastructure that developers can leverage and use to possibly eliminate some of the development costs, by instead relying on the operating system. This is where COM+'s role-based security comes in. Role-based security is configured at the component level down to a specific method on an interface, therefore we will talk more about role-based security later in the chapter.

New to COM+ is the ability for components to utilize **impersonation**. Impersonation allows the server to take on the security attributes (identity) of the caller. For example, the server will utilize a resource on the client's behalf. To this resource it will appear as if the client actually made the call. Impersonation in COM+ can be tailored for each application at four different levels: **anonymous**, **identity**, **impersonate**, and **delegate**.

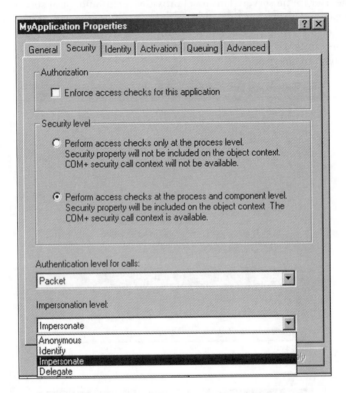

Anonymous

With the impersonation level set at anonymous, the server cannot see and does not care who the caller is. This is basically a way to disable impersonation, which will cause COM+ to run all of the components with the security settings defined on the Identity tab on the COM+ application settings.

Identity

The Identify level setting allows the server to access the access control list (ACL) from the client, and perform checks against it. However, the server is not able to make calls on behalf of the client. Remember, in a web-based solution, the client to the COM+ configured components is IIS and not the browser.

> The ACL is a list defining what permissions various user accounts have on a given object. An object can be anything from a file to a mailbox, or anything else that supports NT authentication (Windows-based security). In this case the object is a component.

Impersonate

The Impersonate level allows the server to not only have the rights to identify the user, but also to make calls on the client's behalf. Even though this setting provides a great deal of functionality, there are still restrictions. The component can only access resources that are local on the server or local to the client. For example, a component could access a printer or files that are local to the web server on behalf of the client.

Delegate

Delegate is the highest level of impersonation available. It provides the same rights as the impersonate level without all the restrictions. The server is able to call upon resources acting as the client. It's basically as if the user were sitting directly at the application server.

Considerations

When working with impersonation there are a few things to keep in mind. One show-stopper that stumps some developers is that it is not supported in Queued Components. Another consideration to be aware of is the reason for all four different settings: performance. The stronger the impersonation level the more processing that needs to be done, and therefore will have a negative impact on performance. However, relying on the operating system to perform these tasks is usually faster and more cost efficient than developing the functionality by hand.

The process of authorization is not performed at the COM+ application, instead it is carried out at the component, interface, and method levels. Therefore it will be discussed in the section below entitled *Configuring COM+ Components, Interfaces, and Methods.*

Roles

Another type of security, which is configured at the application level, is the use of roles. Roles, which are similar to groups in Windows 2000 and Windows NT security, are a way to define sets of users with various rights to the component, its interfaces, and the methods within its interfaces. Roles can be very useful to grant and deny access to various parts of the business logic. The following screen shot displays a COM+ application that has a number of roles defined below it. Also note that each of these roles has a series of users (or members) within them.

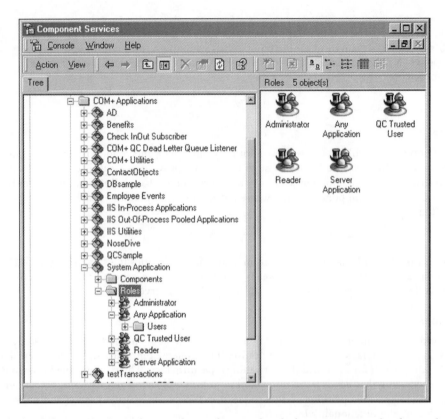

Although the defining of roles is done at the application level, the assignment of rights to these roles is done at the component, interface, and method levels, which will be discussed in the security section of the Configuring COM+ Components, Interfaces, and Methods area below.

Activation Types

Within COM+ there are two activation types for applications: **library** and **server**. Library applications run within the process space of the client, which can really speed up communications between the consumer and the components. A good example of where a lot of developers utilize library web applications is with IIS front-ends.

One drawback to configuring a COM+ application as a library is that since the consumer of the components and the components themselves are in the same process space, process isolation is lost. If a COM object were to encounter an error and spin out of control, it would bring down the IIS process, since this is really where the object resides.

Another drawback of utilizing library packages is security. When a package is set to library package, COM+ will run the components under the caller's identity. In the case of web applications in IIS this is usually the IUSR_<ComputerName>, if anonymous access was permitted. Within COM+ and Windows 2000, there is one way to get around this, called cloaking. Although cloaking is not very easy to implement, it does provide the ability for components to run under a different user identity from the consumer's. For more information on cloaking and how to implement it reference Microsoft's documentation at http://msdn.microsoft.com/library/psdk/com/security_711z.htm.

The following screenshot displays the **Activation** type setting within COM+. The setting is located on the **Activation** tab with the properties of a COM+ application.

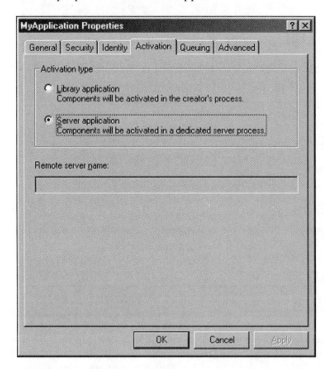

Usually, though, COM+ applications are configured as server applications. This provides process isolation for the consumer and also allows the processing to reside on a different machine from the client. The server where the COM objects reside for this type of configuration is known as an application server. The drawback to using a **server application** in COM+ is performance. Since each method call has to be marshaled across processes (sometimes to another machine depending on the architecture), performance can be affected. However, as the number of users within a system increases, this loss in performance is usually regained since the load is being distributed across various processes and computers.

Identity

The identity of the package determines what user account the components within the COM+ application will run under. This enables the developer to consistently rely on a set of permissions to code with.

The following screenshot displays the tab for setting the identity attribute for a COM+ application. It is located on the **Identity** tab with the properties of a COM+ application.

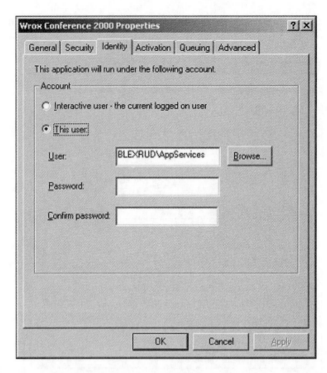

Notice in the above screenshot there are two options, Interactive user and This user. Within a normal production environment it is always better to specify a user with the This user setting. This enables the components within the COM+ application to be available even when no one is logged into the active console (at the actual computer).

The Interactive user setting is great within a development environment; it enables developers to interact with the component for debugging.

Queuing

The queuing configurations in the COM+ application settings enable the components within the application to utilize COM+ queued component services, which were discussed earlier in the chapter. The following screenshot displays the queuing configurations that can be set on a COM+ application. This screen, like the others within this section, is available within the Components Service MMC snap-in and is available within the properties of a COM+ application on the Queuing tab.

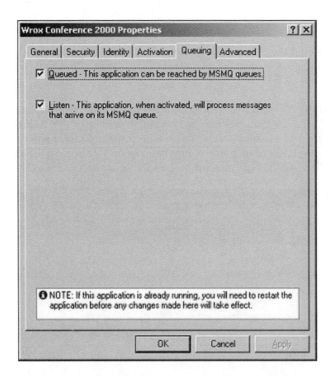

As you can see above, there are two settings within the Queuing section; Queued and Listen. The Queued setting enables the components within the application to utilize the services provided by queued components. The Listen setting informs COM+ to automatically watch MSMQ for incoming messages to be processed.

There are two important things to note when setting these configuration values. The first one is the note that Microsoft placed on the bottom of the tab. It basically says that the application must be restarted before any changes will be seen. The other important note is that this is not the only setting that must be made to utilize COM+ Queued Components. There are other settings that must be set within the Interface properties in each Component. This setting will be discussed in the Configuration Class Requirements below.

Now with an understanding of the settings and resources available at the COM+ application level, let's take a look into the classes within these applications and the settings available.

COM+ Components, Interfaces, and Methods

The runtime requirements for a COM class, its interfaces, and the methods on those interfaces, can all be configured one of two ways, just like the COM+ applications settings above; either through the Component Services MMC snap-in, or programmatically using the COM API. This chapter will cover setting the requirements or properties through the MMC snap-in.

Let's take a look the configuration option within the class level and the layers below it (interface and method). To access any of the following screenshots, open the properties dialog box on the specified level (component, interface, or method).

Transactions

We have already covered the definition of a transaction while discussing the service provided by MTS and COM+; now let's take a look at the various configuration settings that can be applied at the component level within COM+.

First of all, recall from earlier that a transaction is a group of tasks that either succeed or fail as a whole. With MTS and COM+, these tasks can span from a single method within a single component to multiple methods from multiple components, which can even be configured from different COM+ applications. In many situations, developers need all of the components to be in a single transaction together, but sometimes they don't. The following screenshot shows how to configure a COM+ component.

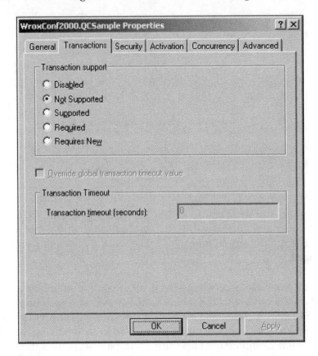

Let's start out by defining the various levels of Transaction Support that COM+ offers us. As you can see in the screenshot above there are five different levels of transaction support that are offered by COM+, ranging from disabling transactions to always requiring a new one. The following section explains the various settings and the impacts they have when one configured COM+ component (component A) is calling upon another (component B).

Disabled

When a component is configured with the Disabled setting, it is equivalent to a non-configured component. This means that COM+ may or may not include the component within a transaction, because it depends on whether a configured COM+ component is calling it and whether it is in a transaction or not. For instance, if component A is configured to require transactions and component B is disabled, component B would join the context of component A if a method in component A calls upon a method in component B, because component B would also be taking part in the transaction.

Not Supported

Although Not Supported may sound similar to Disabled, they are different. An object with the Not Supported setting will never enter a transaction, no matter what the call is in. For example, when component A calls on component B, component B is not in a transaction with component A, in fact, in this case component B is not in a transaction at all.

Supported

The Supported setting is most 'easy-going' setting. It doesn't matter what the consumer of the object is doing. If the call is within a transaction it will join it, if it isn't it won't. In our component A and component B example, when component A (requiring transaction) calls on component B (supported), B will join the same transaction (and context) as A. If component A were not in a transaction, neither would component B be.

Required

The Required setting is the most frequently used setting because it provides the most desired affects for most situations. With a required setting a component will always be in a transaction whether or not the consumer is. For example, if component A calls upon component B when A requires a transaction, B will not only be in a transaction, but it will be in the same transaction as A. Whereas, if component A does not require a transaction component B will enter its own transaction.

Requires New

The Requires New setting along with the Not Supported setting above is a setting that will always take the same action whether the consumer is in a transaction or not. With the Requires New setting the component will always receive its own transaction. Although this setting is not used often, it is useful when a component needs a transaction, but does not want its outcome to affect the consumer's transaction. As you can easily guess, in the component A and component B example component B will always be started in its own transaction regardless of what component A is up to.

Since this is such a major part of COM+ and the Windows DNA architecture, we have devoted a whole chapter to this very topic – Chapter 8, Introduction to Transactions.

Security

As discussed from above, COM+ utilizes roles to grant or deny access to functionality provided from a component, down to the method level. Let's take a look into securing a component at its various levels, and how the impacts of other security settings at the application level affect it.

The following screen shot displays the options that COM+ provides at the component level. Since the component level is the highest level at which roles can be assigned, you will notice some differences compared to the role settings that are set at the interface and method levels.

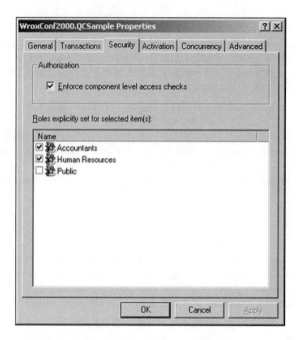

Notice above that two of the three roles (**Accountants** and **Human Resources**) have been assigned access at the component level. Any users that are not members of these roles will receive an access denied error when trying to utilize the component, unless other settings at the interface or method level override these settings. Actually this overriding of the security setting at the component level is displayed in the following screenshot, which is at the method level (under the interface, which is under the component):

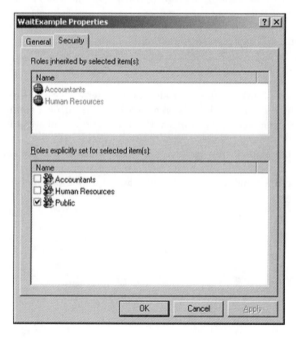

At the top of the Security tab are the settings that are inherited from the levels above. In this case they are inherited from the setting at the component level. Next, notice the overriding of these settings at the bottom of the screenshot where the public role is granted access. Since this property box is for the WaitExample method, any members of the Public role will only be able to utilize the functionality provided by the method and nothing else throughout this component.

COM+ security provides the ability for developers to write code that interacts with its security model. This can be very useful when a more granular control is needed to solve a business need. For instance, you may want to grant two or more roles access to a method, however, you may need the method to behave differently depending on the role the user is in. Checking security through code is easily done by checking the IsCallerInRole function from the ISecurityCallContext interface.

```
Dim objContextSecurity as COMSVCLib.SecurityCallContext
Set objContextSecurity = GetSecurityCallContext

If objContextSecurity.IsCallerInRole("Teller") Then
...
Else
...
End If
```

Activation

The Activation tab provides the ability to change the runtime behavior that a component takes when it is initialized. The first part of the Activation tab allows for the enabling of object pooling, if the object utilizes a multi-threaded apartment or the neutral apartment, is stateless, and implements the IObjectControl interface. The following screen shot displays how the Activation tab looks for most developers. Notice that the object pooling settings are disabled; this is due to the fact that the WroxConf2000.QCSample component was built in VB 6.0, which does not utilize multi-threaded or neutral apartments.

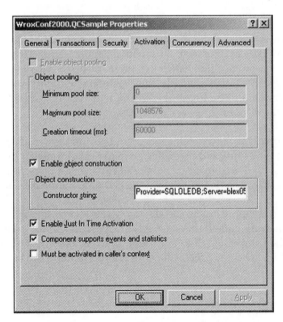

Another group of settings located on the **Activation** tab is the **Constructor String**. The **Constructor String** provides an administrative location to place information to be used at runtime by a method within the component. A connection string is a common value that is assigned to the constructor string, although if there are components within the application the registry is a much better place for the connection string.

The following code displays how to access the constructor string from VB. Notice that we first implement the `IObjectConstruct` interface and then wait for the `Construct` routine to fire from COM+. Once the routine is called the value is cached to a private string where it can be called upon from other routines in the class module.

```
Option Explicit

Implements COMSVCSLib.IObjectConstruct

Private m_strMyConstructorString As String

Private Sub IObjectConstruct_Construct(ByVal pCtorObj As Object)
    m_strMyConstructorString = pCtorObj.ConstructString
End Sub
```

Another configuration setting on the **Activation** tab is **Enable Just In Time (JIT) Activation**. JIT allows the server to conserve system resources. Instead of creating an instance of the class when the client requests it, COM+ waits for the client to invoke the method. Once this happens COM+ creates an instance of the COM class, invokes the method call from the client, returns any result to the client, and then destroys the object.

COM+ will not always utilize JIT with all COM classes. The only time it does is if the component is configured to utilize it or if the component utilizes transactions. If a component is in a COM+ transaction, JIT is always used.

JIT also promotes the utilization of stateless components. However, just because it promotes stateless programming doesn't mean that stateful classes cannot be installed. COM+ will work happily with almost any type of COM class as long as it is contained within a DLL. However, if components are built stateless, it only makes sense to use JIT, which can dramatically increase the scalability of an application. The idea behind it is fairly simple; why maintain an object when the consumer is not utilizing it? This may not seem like a big deal with 10 to 100 clients, but move this to a system with thousands of users and the difference is very noticeable.

There are two other setting that are available when configuring the activation setting within a component; the support for events and the caller's context requirements. By enabling the component to support events and statistics, the component services MMC snap-in will provide information about it such as how many objects are active and the average call time in milliseconds, just to name a couple.

The last setting, caller's context, instructs COM+ to only let the component be activated within the context of the initial caller. By default this setting is unchecked, and for good reason, since it normally is not used. However, if the component does not support cross-context marshalling, or performance requirements are very high, checking this will cause the call to fail if the consumer is not the initial caller (ASP for example).

Concurrency

COM+ has added another service that works very closely with the neutral apartment type, **call concurrency**. These new services provide developers who write components that can be accessed by multiple threads concurrently (neutral and multi-threaded components) with the ability to forget about the dangers of multiple threads stepping on one another, allowing them to concentrate on the task of solving business needs. The concurrency service provides this by implementing an idea called **activity-based synchronization**. Activity-based synchronization does just what it says, it stops threads from interfering with each other by blocking ones that are trying to access an object that is currently participating in another activity.

As you might guess, activity-based synchronization is not really needed for apartment-threaded components because the apartment enforces this, but you might be wondering what is the point of multi-threaded and neutral threaded components? One reason is for object pooling and the ability for different threads to access the same component at different times. If you recall, single threaded components can only run on one thread. This isn't always bad, because you can rely on resources like thread-local storage. However, it is sometimes unacceptable to limit each object to a single thread. This is known as thread affinity. When a call is made to a component that requires synchronization and is currently involved in an activity, any new call will be blocked until the first activity is complete.

COM+ provides five settings for synchronization that can be configured through the MMC snap-in. Each one of these settings provides a different level of synchronization support from COM+ and Windows 2000. The following screen shot displays the settings available for synchronization support on the Concurrency tab. Notice that most of the options are unavailable. This is because the component WroxConf2000.QCSample was built in VB 6 and uses the single-threaded apartment model.

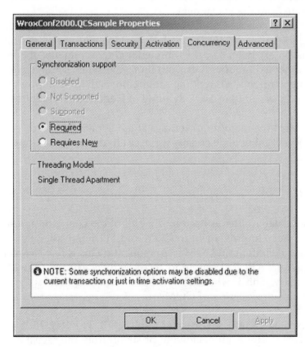

Let's step through the various settings COM+ provides for synchronization and see how they differ from one another.

Disabled

The Disabled level will inform COM+ that the component does not require synchronization support. A disabled setting is comparable to an un-configured component that does not reside in COM+. This does not mean that the component will never utilize COM+ synchronization support, since its caller may require it.

Not Supported

Not Supported is different from Disabled in the sense that it will never utilize the synchronization support, regardless of what the caller requires. This setting can only be used when components are configured as non-transactional and do not utilize JIT.

Supported

Components that have the Supported setting are the most friendly components. They will only utilize COM+'s synchronization support if the caller requires them to. This setting's usually used to provide the flexibility to adapt to the consumer's requirements, while at the same time conserving resources when synchronization support is not needed.

Required

The Required setting is also a very friendly setting because it too will join within the consumer's activity and take advantage of the synchronization support. If the consumer is not taking advantage of the support, it will start its own.

Requires New

The Requires New setting is similar to the Required, however it will always enter its own activity and therefore will be separate from the consumer.

There are a few considerations to be aware of when working with the synchronization support in COM+. First of all it is closely related to the transactional requirements of components. In fact, depending on the transactional requirements, certain concurrency settings are not available. These settings are also dependent upon the threading requirements of the components. For example an apartment threaded object must either have a setting of Required or Requires New.

Now that we have analyzed the majority of settings at the application level, component level, and lower, let's look into the COM+ Catalog and see how it stores all of the settings, and how it differs from MTS and Windows NT.

COM+ Catalog

The COM+ catalog is a database that is used to store all of the configuration settings discussed above. The COM+ catalog is a huge improvement to COM and MTS and still enables a smooth integration of standard COM classes and configured COM+ components. This is due to the simple fact that the COM+ Catalog is really one API that is used to access two data stores. One of these data stores you can probably guess, the registry. This is what allows all of the existing standard COM components to work in Windows 2000 with the introduction of COM+.

The other data store used by COM+ is known as the RegDB. The RegDB is a new data store to Windows 2000 and COM+. Microsoft decided to break off from the registry and go with a different data store. This was probably a wise decision, otherwise the registry would become even more cluttered.

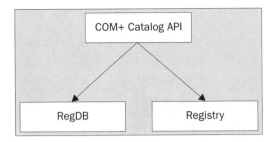

Since all COM+ requests are looked up through this single API, there is no more need to utilize the `CreateInstance` routine through the `IObjectContext` interface, even if one COM+ configured object is calling another. All requests for COM components in Windows 2000 can just be made through the common ways like `CreateObject` or `New` for VB developers and `CoCreateInstance` for VC++ developers.

The COM+ catalog is utilized when setting normal properties like JIT and various security settings through the MMC or by programming settings through the `COMAdmin` API.

Now that we have a grasp on a majority of the configuration setting available in COM+ and where they are stored, let's take a look into COM+'s Context and how it is used to provide a source of information for developers on the runtime COM+ environment that's surrounding their components.

COM+ Context

The context object is where most developers interact with COM+. The context object provides anything and everything a developer needs to know about the current object and the runtime environment surrounding it that COM+ provides. Although most of the information within the context object is read-only, it does expose various interfaces and methods on these interfaces to interact with the COM+ runtime.

Every instance of a COM class (object) has its context around it. One is created every time an object is *activated*. The exact time an object is activated depends on the JIT requirement that was discussed earlier. Also, as noted earlier, these context objects relate very closely to MTS's context wrappers, however, COM+ context objects are tied into the Windows 2000 operating system, serve as the stub for marshalling, and provide much more information via various interfaces.

Context Interfaces

The context object that accompanies every request object in MTS has a variety of interfaces that allow developers to gain access to it. Each one of these interfaces provides the developers with different information from the same context object. Most of these interfaces will be used through the remaining chapters in this book, so for now let's take a quick look at the different interfaces available, and a summary of the functionality they provide.

IObjectContext

The `IObjectContext` interface is the most common interface and was also available in MTS. This provides a single interface that will provide developers with the most common properties from the other interfaces. The information available from the `IObjectContext` interface can be broken down into three categories: object creation, transaction, and security.

To obtain a reference to the `IObjectContext` simply make a call to the `GetObjectContext` method.

The `GetObjectContext` function is global to the `COMSVCSLib` library and is available once a reference is made to `comsvcs.dll`.

```
Dim objContext As COMSVCSLib.ObjectContext
Set objContext = GetObjectContext()

If objContext.IsCallerInRole("User") Then
   '...
End If

objContext.SetComplete
```

IObjectContextInfo

`IObjectContextInfo` is one of the interfaces new to COM+. It provides various IDs that surround the current object, such as the transaction ID, the context ID, and the activity ID. The transaction ID is a unique identifier that ties all of the participating objects of a single transaction together. The context ID provides an ID that identifies the context that is associated with the current COM+ object. Remember, since each instance of a COM class has its own context this ID will always be unique. The activity ID is used by COM+ to tie together all of the objects that have been invoked from the same task. COM+ uses this ID to know whether to block another call or to allow it to pass through when synchronization support is required.

The `IObjectContextInfo` can be referenced by accessing the `ContextInfo` object from the `GetObjectContext` method mentioned above.

```
Dim objContextInfo As COMSVCSLib.ContextInfo
Dim strActivityID As String

Set objContextInfo = GetObjectContext.ContextInfo
strActivityID = objContextInfo.GetTransaction
```

IContextState

This interface is used by COM+ to allow the developer to vote (play a role in determining the outcome) on the current transaction and set the done bit (flag stating that their part is completed) to inform COM+ that the transaction is complete. This is the same functionality that is accessed when utilizing the `SetAbort`, `SetCommit`, `DisableCommit`, and `EnableCommit` methods from the `IObjectContext` interface.

The `IContextState` allows developers to set the done bit by invoking `SetDeactivateOnReturn`, and set the transaction vote (also known as the happy bit) by invoking `SetMyTransactionVote`. There are also two methods that allow the developer to look up the current status of these bits, `GetDeactivateOnReturn` and `GetMyTransactionVote`.

A pointer to this interface can be obtained by querying the return value of the `GetObjectContext` function for the `IContextState` interface.

```
Dim objContextState As COMSVCSLib.IContextState
Set objContextState = GetObjectContext()

SetMyTransactionVote TxCommit
objContextState.SetDeactivateOnReturn True
```

ISecurityCallContext

This interface provides the developer with a mechanism to retrieve security for the current call. This can be very useful when the basic role-based security checks don't give developers enough flexibility. With this interface the developer can check the roles of the caller making the current call at runtime and take appropriate action.

Most of the functionality exposed through this interface can be accessed through the `IObjectContext` interface via the `IsSecurityEnabled` and `IsCallerInRole` methods. However, `ISecurityCallContext` exposes a collection of roles the caller is a part of.

Getting a reference to the `ISecurityCallContext` interface is a little different from the others. It is the return value of the `GetSecurityCallContext` method, which is available when making a reference to the `COMSVCSLib` library, just like the `GetObjectContext` routine. The `GetSecurityCallContext` method will return `Nothing` if the current object does not utilize COM+'s role-based security.

```
Dim objContextSecurity As COMSVCSLib.SecurityCallContext
Set objContextSecurity = GetSecurityCallContext

If objContextSecurity.IsSecurityEnabled Then
  If objContextSecurity.IsCallerInRole("Accounting") Then
    '...
  End If
End If
```

IObjectControl

This is not an interface used to provide information or functionality like the others. Instead the `IObjectControl` interface provides an interface for developers to implement within their classes. By implementing this interface, developers can respond to various events that COM+ will invoke during the activation and deactivation of a configured COM+ object.

The `IObjectControl` interface comprises three methods: `Activate`, `Deactivate`, and `CanBePooled`. This interface is mostly used by objects that support object pooling. Since a single object (class instance) can be utilized by more than one consumer, developers sometimes need an event to respond to, to clean up the object and make it ready for the next user. The `Activate` and `Deactivate` methods on the `IObjectControl` interface provide this functionality. The `Activate` event fires just before COM+ passes a reference to the object to the requester. The `deactivate` event is fired off when the COM+ consumer is done with the object, just before the object is placed back into the pool.

The last part of the interface is really COM+ asking a question; `CanBePooled`. By returning the appropriate value to COM+ (`True` or `False`) COM+ will know whether or not to place the current object into a pool or to destroy it.

Summary

With the merger of COM and MTS, COM+ has really risen and made dramatic improvements, both by providing developers with more services to develop to and by providing more control and information about components and the environment that surrounds them.

Throughout this chapter we have delved into COM+, the services it provides, the various settings at the application level, component level, and deeper. We have looked into how COM+ stores these configuration settings within its catalog. Lastly we looked at how developers can communicate with COM+ to fully take advantage of the runtime environment it provides.

The following chapter will now build upon the service and features of COM+ and guide you into developing your own COM+ components that use these services.

Online diagramming at MSN.com Corp.

Building COM+ Components

We discussed in Chapter 3 that components are discrete, reusable blocks of code, which expose an interface to allow developers to incorporate such code into their applications. In Chapters 4 and 6 we covered how COM+ is the latest Microsoft technology for designing and managing components, and we learned about the principles behind it. We also saw how to deploy a COM+ component. In this chapter we're going to build a component, which Chapter 23 will use in an n-tier application. While building the component, we will take a look at some of the issues that need to be considered when designing and creating a COM+ component. These include:

❑   Choosing a language

❑   Design Issues

❑   COM+ Transactions and State

❑   JIT

Choosing a Language for COM+ Components

From the way that DNA is described in its documentation, and indeed within the chapters of this book, you would be forgiven for thinking that it is a large, complex set of technologies, aimed at giving you more than your fair share of late nights. In fact you can probably bet that it will!

Most of that time is likely to be spent just familiarizing yourself with all those large, complex-sounding buzzwords. If that doesn't do the trick, coding for them will. The point that you should be most aware of though, as you design, develop, and release applications built on these technologies, is how much *complexity* they actually hide from you.

COM+ is language-independent, therefore the tools that you choose to create COM+ components in are up to you. These tools include Java, Delphi, VC++, VB as well as newer languages such as C#, among others. All of these languages support most of the services that COM+ provides. Choosing a language for your development will probably depend on many things, including your knowledge of a particular language as well as what language suits the occasion. Many of your goals may be suited to a language like Visual Basic as it hides a lot of the complexity involved with coding for COM+.

Complexity is not always a bad thing, as is the case with a language like C++. When implementing with C++, you will find many areas of the process challenging, but eventually satisfying, as you begin to discover that what it provides you with grants you more power. There is a negative side to this, and one obvious pitfall of the power of implementation is that such power has to be used wisely, or it becomes a liability. The move from complex code to simpler code has been ushered in by a wave of tools that offer high productivity levels. Sometimes, however, in order to use a simpler method, you must understand more.

Creating simple interfaces and methods in C++ is not a difficult thing to do, as was described in Chapter 3 of this book. Rather, it is when faced with the *advanced* features that you will find coding a little harder and more time consuming, as you are left with more to write and more to understand about COM+.

The C++ language gives you access to more functionality by presenting you with the IDL for interfaces and the ability to alter them. C++ also grants you the ability to create objects for object pooling, because all threading models are supported and can be coded for. Visual Basic objects cannot be pooled because it lacks some of the power that C++ offers when dealing with threads. The ability in C++ to create the threading models of your choice brings in all kinds of complexities that a developer using VB would not have to endure.

Specifically, coding for COM+ in C++ has been made easier by the fact that, among other things, you do not have to code your own transaction manager to manage data transactions. Instead, just like in VB, you can use COM+ transactional services. So COM+ hides a lot of complexity, even from the C++ developer. Complexity in C++ can be a good thing, but only in situations when that extra complexity is required.

Visual Basic

Now, Visual Basic is a language that is well known for hiding complexities. In fact, many have felt that it hides too much, although some complexities may hinder our progress when designing applications that do not need them. So, how well does VB hide the complexities of COM+?

Building COM+ components in Visual Basic is by no means difficult, but do not be complacent – COM+ is an intelligent system that needs intelligent understanding. VB *does* hide many complexities, but as a consequence, as mentioned above, it also loses a bit of the power that C++ would grant you.

But Windows DNA is about *business*; it is about servers and clients, multiple workstations all effectively utilizing services for a business task. Regarding those goals, Visual Basic is by far a better way of quickly creating scalable systems that grant businesses the platform from which they can run and ultimately succeed. Also, for our purposes, showing COM+ in VB is a quicker way of demonstrating the use of terminologies that you may have picked up by now, hopefully filling in some of the pieces of the puzzle along the way.

In fact, if there were a moral to this chapter it would be 'Simplicity over Complexity – a better choice!' The word 'Simplicity' here does not mean that you will *not* write complex code, or shouldn't have to, it means that the developer using your components should *feel* that it is a simplistic component, which most of the time means that you have to *encapsulate* more, and code even harder. There is proof when you look at how VB has grown into one of the most used languages today, by being simpler than most other languages. This does not mean that VB itself was simple to code.

Unfortunately, keeping things too simple sometimes leads to huge tradeoffs. That is why the range of languages that support COM+ is a good thing as we can all benefit from COM+ by using the languages that best suit our needs.

Simplicity is a powerful aspect of VB that suits many implementations. VB grants us power by the fact that we can keep our code simple and clean. It can also provide more time; its simplicity can lead to shorter development time as less time is wasted on the complexities, which grants us the ability to enhance our applications rather than iron out technicalities of implementation.

In summary, there is always a compromise when developing in different languages for a particular technology. Specifically choosing between VB and C++ for COM+ component development is a compromise between complexity and power. C++ is more powerful (for example developers can benefit from the IDL for working with interfaces, and can use object pooling). However, C++ is more complex, although some of the complexity is hidden (for example COM+ transactional services can be used). VB is less complex, and therefore it is an easier and quicker language for developing COM+ components, especially useful in the business sector as a lot of business needs are ever changing and VB offers benefits to this kind of development. In this chapter we're going to use VB because it is simple, quick, and sufficiently powerful for our needs.

Creating a COM+ Component in VB

In this chapter we'll be looking at a variety of issues, which need to be considered when designing, and building a COM+ component. Since the two-tier approach to developing applications, many advances in the way that applications are developed have been made. These advances have helped both the design process and the implementation of the next generation of scaleable applications. The two-tier approach with its business logic, presentation code, and data accessing code all compiled into one executable offered little towards easy maintenance. The 3-tier or n-tier approach has been offered as a better alternative, which has brought in a new wave of application design issues together with the new technologies that have been developed for it. As one of these new technologies, COM+ has brought tremendous services for coding this n-tier approach.

The component that you build in this chapter will be used in Chapter 23 to access a SQL Server database. The database, and the UI code which uses the contact, will be discussed in detail there. All of the code in this chapter, and Chapter 23, is available to download from the Wrox website at www.wrox.com. The design issues section later in this section will begin to try to explain various topics relating to the creation of a COM+ component. It will look at issues such as performance, when to use a particular COM+ service, and generally overview a component building technique. Keep in mind that although particular COM+ services, like COM+ Transactional support and COM+ Events, are beyond the scope of this chapter, we will still look at them briefly to introduce you to some of the key points surrounding the services from a 'When to Implement' point of view.

The Contacts Sample

Most of our business logic and data access will be taken care of by business logic created in Visual Basic. This code is compiled, so it's a bit more difficult to update than simple script code. On the other hand, VB code has access to a wide range of data types, is compiled for better performance, and employs v-table binding for talking to COM objects – all contributing to fast, scalable, and easily maintained applications.

Because our sample application's scope is small, we'll be only creating two business objects:

❑ Contact, which will provide an abstract representation of a contact, allowing us to add, edit, and remove a contact

❑ ContactList, which will provide access to a list of contacts for display and selection

The Contact Object

This object will encapsulate all the business logic and data access code for a Contact – meaning that the UI code in ASP can rely entirely on this object for all business validation, rules, and processing. The following UML class diagram illustrates the makeup of this class (Universal Modeling Language – a way of analyzing and describing objects):

This object appears to be 'stateful' since it has properties as well as methods. However, as we pointed out earlier, such objects are no more stateful than an ADO Recordset object that might be used to hold data for the duration of a page. While it is certainly recommended that objects in Windows DNA applications be stateless, there is absolutely nothing wrong with creating objects that are designed to maintain state for the duration of a single ASP page.

The Contact object is a fine-grained object, meaning that it has many properties and methods rather than a few that do a lot of work each. This type of object provides a powerful set of services to the UI developer, since it's pretty obvious how to set or retrieve data from the object, and there is a great deal of flexibility in how it can be used.

There are two data types worth mentioning – PhoneType and EMailType. These will be implemented as Enums – user-defined numeric types. This object will allow us to maintain a list of phone numbers and e-mail addresses for each contact. The index into each of these lists is a numeric value – made more readable by creating a human-readable data type via an Enum.

Notice that the object also has two private methods, Fetch and Update. Not only will the Contact object encapsulate data access, hiding those details from the ASP code, but these two methods further encapsulate the data access code from the rest of the Contact object itself.

This model gives us two benefits. First, it shields as much code as possible from the underlying database and data access technology. If either SQL Server or ADO has to be replaced at some point, we've severely limited the amount of code affected. Secondly, this model makes it very easy to scale our solution up to the next level. In Chapter 11, we'll see how we can increase our application's scalability by moving this data access code out of the object and onto a separate physical machine. By keeping this code separate from the rest of the Contact object now, we make that process much simpler.

> **Applications should be designed, whenever possible, to make it easy to adapt to future scalability requirements.**

The ContactList Object

The second object will follow a different model, simply providing a set of data to the ASP developer via an ADO Recordset. This object's job is to allow the UI developer to retrieve a list of contact data for display to the user. The object provides read-only data, and basically encapsulates the underlying data access from the ASP code, so the UI developer can focus entirely on building a presentation based on the supplied data. The object's design is illustrated by the following UML diagram:

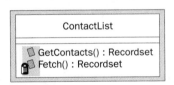

This object is much simpler, since it merely encapsulates the process of retrieving an ADO Recordset object for use within ASP. However, we still have the public GetContacts method separate from the Fetch method where we'll implement the actual data access. This provides much of the same abstraction from the database as we had with the Contact object – and makes it very easy for the application to be enhanced to be more scalable later.

There is a tradeoff between scalability and complexity, as well as between scalability and performance. The model we're using in this chapter is quite simple and easy to implement. To increase scalability, we may choose to move the Fetch and Update methods to another object running on an application server separate from the web server. This is obviously more complex, and is covered in Chapter 11.

This model has very high *performance*, even if it sacrifices some scalability. Performance is the measure of response time for a user. Scalability is a measure of response time as we add load to the system – either more users or more transactions per user. In many cases we sacrifice a single user's performance to gain scalability. This is almost always true when we add extra physical tiers to an architecture.

For example, old-fashioned single-tier Foxpro applications are much faster than n-tier SQL Server-based applications – for a small number of users. This is because of the minimal overhead involved in dealing with xBase databases as compared to something more complex like SQL Server. However, as we scale up by adding more and more users, the Foxpro application would rapidly increase in response time, while the SQL Server solution keeps a decent response time.

The Database

The database was created in SQL-Server 7.0 and can be installed onto your server by executing the script provided. The script must be executed inside of the **Query Analyzer**. With SQL-Server 2000 installed you can run the **Query Analyzer** by selecting **Microsoft SQL Server | Query Analyzer** from the **Start** menu. Inside the **Query Analyzer**, select **File | Open** on the toolbar and point the dialog to the SQL script.

> *The SQL Script, and all the code in this chapter, can be downloaded from the Wrox website at http://www.wrox.com. We'll be creating the rest of the app in Chapter 23.*

The diagram of the database shows the layout of the tables and the relationships between the tables that the script will create inside SQL-Server.

Design Issues

Designing what methods, properties and events should appear on which interface is important in creating a great finished product. As you will see in the next section, COM+ offers services that will make certain tasks easier when writing scalable applications, but you must understand the basic concepts first. This section will discuss what considerations you will want to keep in mind as you develop you COM+ components.

Designing in Layers

The n-tier approach to servers allows us to split our application so that it resides in a number of different tiers, comprising the presentation tier, business logic tier, and data tier. The contacts sample was created to sit on the business tier, but it could have been split further, into two more separate layer.

The Contacts component is split into a data access layer and a business logic layer. Building the component in two separate layers does have a number of advantages. The contacts sample lends itself easily to the fact that we could have two different servers, one holding the data access layer (contactList) and the database and the other holding the middle layer, which could distribute resource usage over two machines rather than one.This is often necessary and COM+ offers us the service of Load Balancing which greatly enhances this capability without exposing the details to you.

It is good practice to design in three or more layers:

❑ Data Layer – concerned with data. Creates easier debugging of data as it provides you with one entry point for all other objects accessing the data, which means that no other object needs to access the database directly, which in turn is important for database efficiency as well as licensing issues with certain databases. If you had to put a breakpoint on the `Fetch` method on the `ContactList` object you would receive all of the data accessing code from the object, which can make debugging simpler. This layer encapsulates the functionality of actually speaking to the database.

❑ Business Layer – concerned with applying business logic. When componentized into its own layer, it makes for easier replacement of business rules without touching the presentation UI or how it accesses the data. In other words, inserting business flow and logic in this layer provides you with the knowledge that if later the database or user-interface changes, your business rules will not, or if your business rules change, your other layers will be minimally effected.

❑ Presentation Layer – concerned with presenting information and accepting input from the user. Separating this from all the other layers is what makes this powerful. It is easier to snap on a new interface to your application. In other words, in today's fast paced web development, which sometimes requires a lot of changes to keep the look and feel up to date and modern, the business rules behind it will not change.

All in all the separation of the layers allows for easier maintenance from all angles, from data access, to presentation layer and so on.

Designing an n-tier system requires that you compile different components for each of the layers. Since they are separate, you have to pass information from one component to another. Passing information sounds easy enough, but what is the best method for transporting this data?

Transport Data

Creating a component that passes data from one layer to another requires some form of container, a carrier if you will, like the ADO recordset object. I do not want to confuse the VB Collection object and the fact that a recordset is also a kind of collection, so let us use the term *carrier* for this section. An ADO recordset is a common carrier used by many developers to pass information from one piece of code to another. The recordset is passed from methods to other methods, sometimes across objects and sometimes even across components on different machines. Other types of *carriers* include arrays, collections, and delimited strings, as well as newer technologies such as XML. What is the best choice for transporting data across these layers? – Not an easy question to answer.

I have used the recordset in the `contactList` component for various reasons, one of which is to have less complicated sample code, by not dealing with some other abstract solution (even if it is better). Arrays are probably the fastest of all the transport *carriers,* but leave a lot to be desired when you need to sort the data or delete entries within the array. Sorting algorithms, such as the bubble sort, are not as speedy in VB as they are in C++. Also, data received from the client with missing or added records needs to be handled by you as well, as in the case of a batch update. The recordset has facilities for this and is far more compatible as it hides these things from you. The collection in VB is a little friendlier, but unfortunately is a lot slower when you access items and move them around within it. Which brings us to XML. The Extensible Markup Language (XML) is more powerful than a traditional string or array as it comes with engines that can be used to query the data within the XML document. Also, the fact that SQL-Server 2000 and Visual Studio 7 (soon to be released) will support a lot of XML capabilities will make XML a better option. As Microsoft aligns our development with more of the open standards like XML and SOAP (Simple Object Access Protocol), XML will probably become the standard data transport mechanism for the next generation of applications.

However, even though data access technologies change from year to year, which is a tremendous drawback when you think of the changes that have to be made to existing code, the ADO recordset is by far a more versatile mechanism when you think of the services that it provides. Another interesting fact is that most objects that are passed across boundaries travel by reference (ByRef), which causes a lot of activity between the client and the server component. However, the ADO recordset has been designed to be marshaled by value (ByVal) which is basically the same as passing a string data type ByVal. This means that it is not as expensive as many people believe.

The passing of objects brings us to another point. In MTS, objects could only be passed from one component to another by use of the `SafeRef` function in Visual Basic. This is now not the case with COM+. Although you can pass objects safely now, it does not mean that it is a good choice. Passing objects can be extremely inefficient as mentioned above, as it causes more activity between the caller and server component. Therefore do not use ByRef parameters either, rather pass values ByVal.

In Visual Basic you can also have collections of objects. Since a function that returns an object is defaulted to passing it ByRef, it is something that you should try and avoid. A collection of objects is a tremendously resource-heavy method. Instead pass a single object at a time if need be or better yet pass a recordset object, which is passed ByVal.

Within this section, objects and methods have been mentioned within the context of a data transport mechanism, but there has been no discussion on how these methods should look or where they should be found. In the next section let us look at this in more detail.

Factoring

The questions of *'how many parameters and methods should an object expose?'* or *'should an object have properties rather than methods?'* are not issues that would render your object completely useless although it may be ineffective. There are though, some things to consider.

Imagine a component that contains over forty methods and properties on each of its twenty or so objects. Also imagine that each of the object's methods contains at least fifteen parameters. Would you not agree that this component might be a little daunting? In fact, a component should *never* wield such statistics.

Instead, when designing your objects, try to follow the golden rule – *simplicity*. Simplicity has been mentioned many times, and is probably the most crucial element that I could instill into building components, so I make no apologies for repeating it. I am not saying that creating an extremely large component is an incredibly bad thing, but a few components aided by a few smaller components is by far a better solution.

When dealing with a large complex set of business rules for a large system, the code within the component could be extremely complex, which can cause debugging and maintanance nightmares. In many situations, getting around the fact that many objects would need to be created is a difficult task, especially in certain circumstances. The point that needs to come across, though, is that there are many situations that lend themselves to a reusable nature. The more reusable the components or objects, the smaller the end product will be.

Every developer who uses your component should be able to do so successfully without major effort or a tremendous amount of reading on his or her part. You can achieve this in many ways:

❑ Try to keep your methods to a five or six parameter *maximum,* unless completely necessary. This will make for easier coding.

❑ Make sure that all of those parameters and methods have meaningful names. Try to spell the function out rather than keeping it short. As an example, it is not as easy to identify the name 'GetCnts' as it is to identify the name 'GetContacts'.

❑ Do not over-exert yourself by adding every conceivable method and functional enhancement that it can have, rather think ahead, but code later. You can easily complicate matters for your developers by granting them too much choice, and at the same time you may be adding functionality that may not ever be used.

❑ Try to keep objects within your components down to a minimum. Better reuse comes from keeping your components smaller.

❑ Properties are extremely useful in a component, and enable it to be used more easily, but there is a tradeoff when it comes to efficiency as well as maintaining object instance state. (Read on for more on this issue.)

Multi-Use Objects

With Windows DNA, the web client is an extremely valuable part of the entire architecture, and designing objects for use over the web as well as for the traditional form-based client creates all kinds of problems. Today, the web client does not support all the features supported by your form-based client. Therefore the term 'Multi-Use' in this case means creating objects that can be used from both languages and scripts.

As an example, *events* within an object can be extremely useful from a form-based client, but ASP cannot receive these events. So building objects with events proves useless when deploying for the Web. Callbacks and events should rather be replaced with methods, which could be called from the client to interrogate the status of a routine. In other words, let the object handle any callbacks or events that are raised and make the result available via a property or a method on the interface. The client can interrogate the interface you expose for results.

Early binding is another feature that only works with a form-based (compiled executable) client, but cannot be implemented by scripts. The reason behind this goes all the way down to what makes an object a COM object. COM objects have to inherit from an interface known as IUnknown and optionally also inherit from IDispatch. These two interfaces are responsible for how the objects are used and called. When a COM object supports both IUnknown and IDispatch is it is known as having a **dual interface**. Visual Basic objects only support dual interfaces and cannot inherit from only IUnknown. The reason behind this is probably largely due to the fact that scripts can only create an instance of a class that supports IDispatch, which is known as late binding and Visual Basic, to save on complexity opted to support both. In Visual Basic you can create an instance of a class by means of early binding as well as late binding.

The two forms of binding can best be described in Visual Basic as follows:

Early Binding

- ❑ Explicitly referencing a COM Server by selecting it in the **References** window (**Project | References** menu item).

- ❑ By explicitly declaring a variable (placeholder) as the appropriate type:

```
Dim MyObj as Recordset
```

- ❑ By creating an instance of the class with the New keyword:

```
Set MyObj = New Recordset
```

Late Binding

- ❑ With no reference made to the COM Server.

- ❑ Declaring a variable (placeholder) as Object (Object is the fundamental interface for all objects):

```
Dim MyObj as Object
```

- ❑ Using the CreateObject method to create an instance of the desired class:

```
Set MyObj = CreateObject("ADODB.Recordset")
```

ASP only supports the latter – Late binding by use of the CreateObject() or Server.CreateObject() method.

Also, scripts such as ASP do not support **typecasting**, and thus depend on the variant data-type for everything. This means that passing parameters as references of any other type than variants will not work. This plays a role in how you code your objects. In the blWorker component you will see that a recordset is passed ByRef to the GetRecordset function, This means that a call to this object from an ASP script will not work.

> **MTS programmers will remember the need for using the GetObjectContext.CreateInstance method. Later, as you learn more about transactional objects in COM+, you will see that you now do not have to use this method. A call to the CreateObject method is now perfectly fine and will allow transactional support to flow to the created object just as GetObjectContect.CreateInstance did.**

The Business Objects

In a Windows DNA environment, business objects are typically contained in COM components, or ActiveX DLLs. These can be created using any language that has the ability to create a COM DLL. In this chapter we'll use Visual Basic, as it's the most widely used COM development tool in the world.

Now we will code the component, and examine the topics that you have to bear in mind when creating components.

Unattended Execution

It is good practice for you to never use message boxes or other UI functions within a DLL. For this reason make sure that Unattended Execution is checked and the Retained In Memory option is checked as well. Both can be seen on the Properties window as shown in the screenshot below. When you add a form or other user-interface objects, this setting is disabled.

When the unattended execution property is set to True, Visual Basic logs any user interface calls to the event log. Therefore the MsgBox function writes to the log and does not appear on screen. This is a necessary and important option, as you do not want anything stopping the execution of your object and its methods. Remember that a message box is modal and will not let anything else in the object occur until the message box has been dealt with. If you wish to create, as an example, a progress notification by showing a form with a progressbar, be sure not to make the form modal as doing so will stop the execution of the process that is being executed. Any modal user-interactive forms should be avoided.

The Retained In Memory option will cause our DLL to be retained in memory even if there are no objects currently in use. Loading a DLL into memory takes precious time, and if this operation had to happen each time a user came to our site that could be a problem. Turning on this option will help improve performance by keeping the DLL loaded in memory and ready for use.

Open Visual Basic and create a new ActiveX DLL project. Choose the Project | Properties menu option, and change the project's name to ContactObjects. Also make sure to check the Unattended Execution and Retained In Memory boxes:

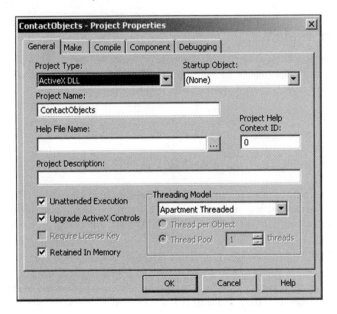

Click OK to accept these settings.

We'll also need to set some references in our project, in order to be able to use ADO in our code. Set references to Microsoft ActiveX Data Objects 2.5 Library and Microsoft ActiveX Data Objects Recordset 2.5 Library as shown:

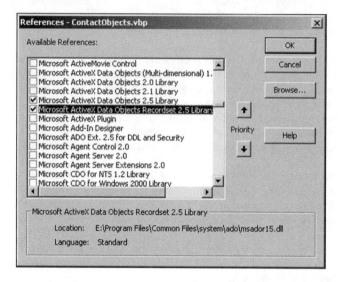

Now we are ready to create some code.

The ContactMain Module

In this component we'll end up with two class modules: ContactList and Contact. Both of these will contain code to access the database – meaning both will need a database connection string for use with ADO. This connection string is just a simple string value:

```
Provider=SQLOLEDB.1;Password=contact;User ID=contactapp;Initial
Catalog=contact;Data Source=dbserver
```

The Provider entry specifies the type of database – in this case a SQL Server database.

The User ID and Password entries contain the database login information. This contains the login name and password that are added in the SQL Server script we mentioned earlier. By always using the same login name throughout our application, we will take full advantage of database connection pooling.

> *Database connections are pooled by connection string. If we need a new connection, the pooling mechanism will look for connections with the same connection string as ours. The more connections based on the same connection string, the more efficient the pooling will be.*

The Initial Catalog specifies the name of the database to be used – in our case the Contact database.

Finally the Data Source specifies the name of the database server. In this example, it's set to *dbserver*, and that will need to be changed to reflect the real server name in any given environment.

There are many ways of making a connection string available to our code. It may be stored in the registry, be provided to our component via the COM+ constructor string, be stored in an INI file, or be coded directly into the component.

For simplicity, we'll code it directly into the component by storing it in a globally available constant. This can easily be adapted to one of the other techniques if that's more appropriate for a given environment.

In Visual Basic, choose the **Project | Add Module** menu option to add a code module. In the **Properties** window (typically on the right-hand side) change the **(Name)** property to ContactMain.

Add the following code:

```
Option Explicit

Public Const DB_CONN = "Provider=SQLOLEDB.1;Password=contact;" & _
    "User ID=contactapp;Initial Catalog=Contact;Data Source=dbserver"
```

Remember to change *dbserver* to reflect the real database server name.

The constant DB_CONN is now available throughout our component – centralizing the management of the database connection string.

The ContactList Class

When we opened the new project, Visual Basic started us out with the default Class1 module. Double-click on this entry in the **Project** window to bring up the code window. In the **Properties** window change the **(Name)** property to ContactList.

This class will be fairly simple, since we'll use it primarily to encapsulate the process of retrieving an ADO Recordset object and converting it to a Variant array. The Variant array containing the data will then be provided directly to the ASP code, so it can create whatever display is appropriate for the data.

The use of a Variant array is a nod toward the capabilities of scripting languages. Scripting languages deal with data types like a Variant array much faster than they do with objects such as a Recordset. One of the key performance tips for ASP developers is to use the GetRows method to convert a Recordset to a Variant array before working with the data. In our case, we'll bypass this step by simply providing a Variant array right up front – the ASP code will never see a Recordset.

The Fetch Method

We'll see the rest of our app in Chapter 23, but there are a few things we need to know about it to write our component. In our SQL Server database, there's a getContacts stored procedure. This stored procedure returns all the basic contact information for all contacts in the database, and it was designed to support the ContactList object. The Fetch method will invoke that stored procedure and will return the resulting Recordset containing the data.

Add the following code to the module:

```
Option Explicit

Private Function Fetch() As ADOR.Recordset
   Dim cn As ADODB.Connection
   Dim cm As ADODB.Command
   Dim rs As ADODB.Recordset

   Set cn = New Connection
   cn.CursorLocation = adUseClient
   cn.Open DB_CONN

   Set cm = New Command
   With cm
       .ActiveConnection = cn
       .CommandText = "getContacts"
       .CommandType = adCmdStoredProc
       Set rs = .Execute
   End With
   Set rs.ActiveConnection = Nothing
   Set Fetch = rs

   Set rs = Nothing
   Set cm = Nothing
   cn.Close
   Set cn = Nothing
End Function
```

This code opens an ADO Connection object to gain access to the database, using the DB_CONN constant we declared earlier. It's also set to use a client-side cursor. This is important, as we want to retrieve the data from the database and provide it to the ADO code as a disconnected Recordset to minimize the impact on the database:

```
Set cn = New Connection
cn.CursorLocation = adUseClient
cn.Open DB_CONN
```

We then create a Command object that will be used to call the stored procedure. The Command object is set to use the Connection object we just opened, and it then calls the getContacts stored procedure, returning a Recordset object containing the data.

```
Set cm = New Command

With cm
    .ActiveConnection = cn
    .CommandText = "getContacts"
    .CommandType = adCmdStoredProc
    Set rs = .Execute
End With
```

The next line is important, as it disconnects the `Recordset` object from the database – meaning that the `Recordset` can be used without tying up valuable database server resources.

```
Set rs.ActiveConnection = Nothing
```

Then the `Fetch` function is set to return the `Recordset`, and all the various objects are closed and dereferenced to clean up.

```
Set Fetch = rs
```

The `Fetch` method is now set up to retrieve all the data returned by the `getContacts` stored procedure.

The GetContacts Method

Unlike the `Fetch` method, the `GetContacts` method will be `Public` in scope – making it available to be called from outside the class module itself. It's the `GetContacts` method that will be called by the ASP code when we build the user interface.

In this case, all the hard work is being done in the `Fetch` method, so the `GetContacts` method is pretty straightforward. It merely converts the `Recordset` into a `Variant` array by calling the `GetRows` method, and then returns the array as a result.

Add the following code:

```
Public Function GetContacts() As Variant
   GetContacts = Fetch.GetRows
End Function
```

In both the `ContactList` and `Contact` objects we will keep all the code that interacts with the database contained in `Private` methods. The reason for doing this is to make it as easy as possible to alter our code in the future if we need more scalability. By keeping the data access code separate from the bulk of the other code in our class modules, we make it relatively easy to move that data access code out to other objects – possibly running on an application server instead of the web server.

Though this leads to a bit more coding now, it is worth the effort since it keeps our options open in the future.

We'll discuss building a separate data access tier in Chapter 11.

That wraps up the `ContactList` class. It can now be used to retrieve a `Variant` array with a simple method call like this:

```
Dim objContactList
Dim arData
Set objContactList = Server.CreateObject("ContactObjects.ContactList")
arData = objContactList.GetContacts
```

All the ADO code, database connection strings, and other details are nicely encapsulated within the object itself, making the ASP code very streamlined and focused on UI creation.

The Contact Class

The Contact class will be quite a bit more sophisticated than the class we just created. This class will do more than simply provide data to the UI – it will actually encapsulate business logic as well as data access.

In Visual Basic, choose the Project | Add Class Module menu option, and change the (Name) property of the new module to Contact.

Declarations

To get started, let's declare the variables and types that will be used within the class. First off, to make our code as readable as possible, let's create a couple of enumerated types to indicate the type of phone and e-mail values we're dealing with:

```
Option Explicit

Public Enum PhoneType
    HomePhone
    WorkPhone
    CellPhone
End Enum

Public Enum EMailType
    HomeEMail
    WorkEMail
End Enum
```

Each entry corresponds to a numeric value (starting with zero and counting up). Enums work much like constant values, but they have the advantage of being clearly related to each other, and they work with Visual Basic's IntelliSense technology where appropriate.

Next we'll declare a set of variables to store the contact data itself. While it is possible to keep this data in a Recordset object, it's faster and easier to work with the data if it is stored in a set of local variables within the object:

```
Private mstrID As String
Private mstrLastName As String
Private mstrFirstName As String
Private mstrAddress1 As String
Private mstrAddress2 As String
Private mstrCity As String
Private mstrState As String
Private mstrZipCode As String
Private mstrPhoneWork As String
Private mstrPhoneHome As String
Private mstrPhoneCell As String
Private mstrEMailWork As String
Private mstrEMailHome As String
```

As we'll see in the code, storing the data in local variables means that only two methods within the entire class will need to interact with ADO. By minimizing the amount of code that deals with data access technologies, we shield ourselves from future changes in technology – after all, we may change to XML instead of ADO at some point.

Finally we'll need some variables to keep track of our object's status. In particular we need to keep track of whether the user wants to delete our object, whether any data in the object has been changed, and whether our object is new:

```
Private mblnIsDeleted As Boolean
Private mblnIsDirty As Boolean
Private mblnIsNew As Boolean
```

These are all the module-level variables we'll need for the class.

We'll also need a `Class_Initialize()` method:

```
Private Sub Class_Initialize()
    mblnIsNew = True
End Sub
```

Next let's build the basic set of properties that will allow client code to view or change the data for a contact.

Basic Properties

Visual Basic allows us to expose properties to client code through the use of `Public Property Get` methods. We can also allow the client code to change property values by implementing `Public Property Let` methods. Of course, neither of these methods needs to actually allow direct access to a private attribute value – we write code to control the access.

For instance, the `ID` attribute is read-only, since it reflects the primary key for the contact in the database. In this case we'll implement only a `Property Get` method for read-only access. Add the following code:

```
Public Property Get ID() As String
    ID = mstrID
End Property
```

The `LastName` property will be read/write, so it will have both a `Get` and a `Let` property. Add the following code:

```
Public Property Get LastName() As String
    LastName = mstrLastName
End Property

Public Property Let LastName(ByVal Value As String)

    If Len(Value) <= 50 Then
        mstrLastName = Value
    Else
        Err.Raise vbObjectError + 1001, , "String too long"
    End If
    mblnIsDirty = True

End Property
```

The `Property Let` is a bit more complex, since this is a primary location for the enforcement of business rules. In this case, we're simply checking to make sure that the new value doesn't exceed the maximum length of 50 characters. However, we could implement more complex business logic and validation code here if needed.

Also note that we set the `mblnIsDirty` variable to `True` if the value is changed. This variable is used to identify whether the object's internal data has been changed.

The property routines for the remainder of the basic contact information are very similar:

```
Public Property Get FirstName() As String
    FirstName = mstrFirstName
End Property

Public Property Let FirstName(ByVal Value As String)

    If Len(Value) <= 50 Then
        mstrFirstName = Value
    Else
        Err.Raise vbObjectError + 1001, , "String too long"
    End If
    mblnIsDirty = True

End Property

Public Property Get Address1() As String
    Address1 = mstrAddress1
End Property

Public Property Let Address1(ByVal Value As String)

    If Len(Value) <= 50 Then
        mstrAddress1 = Value
    Else
        Err.Raise vbObjectError + 1001, , "String too long"
    End If
    mblnIsDirty = True

End Property

Public Property Get Address2() As String
    Address2 = mstrAddress2
End Property

Public Property Let Address2(ByVal Value As String)

    If Len(Value) <= 50 Then
        mstrAddress2 = Value
    Else
        Err.Raise vbObjectError + 1001, , "String too long"
    End If
    mblnIsDirty = True

End Property
```

```
Public Property Get City() As String
   City = mstrCity
End Property

Public Property Let City(ByVal Value As String)

   If Len(Value) <= 30 Then
      mstrCity = Value
   Else
      Err.Raise vbObjectError + 1001, , "String too long"
   End If
   mblnIsDirty = True

End Property

Public Property Get State() As String
   State = mstrState
End Property

Public Property Let State(ByVal Value As String)

   If Len(Value) <= 20 Then
      mstrState = Value
   Else
      Err.Raise vbObjectError + 1001, , "String too long"
   End If
   mblnIsDirty = True

End Property

Public Property Get ZipCode() As String
   ZipCode = mstrZipCode
End Property

Public Property Let ZipCode(ByVal Value As String)

   If Len(Value) <= 20 Then
      mstrZipCode = Value
   Else
      Err.Raise vbObjectError + 1001, , "String too long"
   End If
   mblnIsDirty = True

End Property
```

The basic properties for this class are fairly simplistic, but it should be pretty obvious that we could implement substantially more complex logic as needed. The advantage to this is that the logic is encapsulated in an object that will be compiled into a COM component. This resulting component can be used across many different ASP pages, as well as by other possible clients of our application such as Microsoft Office applications.

The Phone and EMail Properties

The `Phone` and `EMail` properties are a bit different from the properties we've seen so far. This is because our `Contact` object will allow the user to provide a number of different phone numbers and e-mail addresses.

The type of property we'll use in this case is called a **named property**. A named property has more than one value – each value being differentiated by a parameter value. A named property is essentially an array of property values.

Add the following code to implement the `Property Get` for the phone numbers:

```
Public Property Get Phone(ByVal PhoneType As PhoneType) As String

    If PhoneType = WorkPhone Then
        Phone = mstrPhoneWork
    ElseIf PhoneType = HomePhone Then
        Phone = mstrPhoneHome
    ElseIf PhoneType = CellPhone Then
        Phone = mstrPhoneCell
    Else
        Phone = ""
    End If

End Property
```

Notice that the method accepts a parameter. This parameter is used to determine which phone number is to be returned – based on the `PhoneType` enumerated value. To call this property we'd use code similar to the following:

```
Debug.Print objContact.Phone(WorkPhone)
```

Note that we will not have `Debug.Print` statements in our real code: this just illustrates how the property would be called.

The `Property Let` is similar, in that it also uses the `PhoneType` enumerated type to determine which phone number to update. Enter the following code:

```
Public Property Let Phone(ByVal PhoneType As PhoneType, _
                         ByVal Value As String)

    If Len(Value) > 20 Then
        Err.Raise vbObjectError + 1001, , "String too long"
    Else
        If PhoneType = WorkPhone Then
            mstrPhoneWork = Value
        ElseIf PhoneType = HomePhone Then
            mstrPhoneHome = Value
        ElseIf PhoneType = CellPhone Then
            mstrPhoneCell = Value
        End If
        mblnIsDirty = True
    End If

End Property
```

Before the object's internal variable is updated, the business rules are checked – in this case to make sure that we don't exceed the maximum length.

> *Note that when we raise an error we're using the* vbObjectError *constant. This constant is provided for our convenience to ensure that the error numbers raised by our program don't conflict with those raised by Microsoft-supplied components. Any error numbers raised by our VB code should start at* vbObjectError *and climb from there.*

The methods to handle the e-mail addresses work in the same manner. Enter the following code:

```
Public Property Get EMail(ByVal EMailType As EMailType) As String

    If EMailType = WorkEMail Then
        EMail = mstrEMailWork
    ElseIf EMailType = HomeEMail Then
        EMail = mstrEMailHome
    Else
        EMail = ""
    End If

End Property
```

```
Public Property Let EMail(ByVal EMailType As EMailType, _
                        ByVal Value As String)

    If Len(Value) > 100 Then
        Err.Raise vbObjectError + 1001, , "String too long"
    Else
        If EMailType = WorkEMail Then
            mstrEMailWork = Value
        ElseIf EMailType = HomeEMail Then
            mstrEMailHome = Value
        End If
        mblnIsDirty = True
    End If

End Property
```

At this point we've added properties to handle all the basic contact data, as well as the phone and e-mail addresses. Of course our object isn't set up to interact with the database yet. Let's add code to retrieve data first.

Retrieving Data

Following the practice of keeping the data access code isolated from the rest of the class – including the public interface used to request data from the database – we'll first implement a Fetch method that contains all the code needed to read our data.

The Fetch method will make use of a stored procedure, getContact, that is stored in the contact database. That stored procedure is interesting, in that it returns three data sets as a result – the basic contact data, the phone numbers, and the e-mail addresses. Fortunately, ADO supports this concept, making it quite easy to work with this set of results.

Enter the following code:

```
Private Sub Fetch(ByVal ID As String)

    Dim objCN As ADODB.Connection
    Dim objCM As ADODB.Command
    Dim objRS As ADODB.Recordset

    Set objCN = New Connection
    objCN.Open DB_CONN

    Set objCM = New Command
    With objCM
        .ActiveConnection = objCN
        .CommandText = "getContact"
        .CommandType = adCmdStoredProc
        .Parameters.Append .CreateParameter("id", adGUID, _
                             adParamInput, -1, ID)
        Set objRS = .Execute
    End With

    With objRS
        mstrID = objRS("ID")
        mstrLastName = objRS("LastName")
        mstrFirstName = objRS("FirstName")
        mstrAddress1 = objRS("Address1")
        mstrAddress2 = objRS("Address2")
        mstrCity = objRS("City")
        mstrState = objRS("State")
        mstrZipCode = objRS("ZipCode")
    End With

    Set objRS = objRS.NextRecordset
    With objRS
        Do While Not .EOF
            If objRS("PhoneType") = PhoneType.WorkPhone Then
                mstrPhoneWork = objRS("Phone")
            ElseIf objRS("PhoneType") = PhoneType.HomePhone Then
                mstrPhoneHome = objRS("Phone")
            ElseIf objRS("PhoneType") = PhoneType.CellPhone Then
                mstrPhoneCell = objRS("Phone")
            End If
            .MoveNext
        Loop
    End With

    Set objRS = objRS.NextRecordset
    With objRS
        Do While Not .EOF
            If objRS("EMailType") = EMailType.WorkEMail Then
                mstrEMailWork = objRS("EMail")
            ElseIf objRS("EMailType") = EMailType.HomeEMail Then
                mstrEMailHome = objRS("EMail")
            End If
            .MoveNext
        Loop
    End With
```

```
    Set objRS = Nothing
    Set objCM = Nothing
    objCN.Close
    Set objCN = Nothing

    mblnIsNew = False
    mblnIsDeleted = False
    mblnIsDirty = False

End Sub
```

This routine opens a `Connection` object to the database. That connection is then used when running a `Command` object to execute the `getContact` stored procedure:

```
Set objCM = New Command
With objCM
    .ActiveConnection = objCN
    .CommandText = "getContact"
    .CommandType = adCmdStoredProc
    .Parameters.Append .CreateParameter("id", adGUID, _
                        adParamInput, -1, ID)
    Set objRS = .Execute
End With
```

This stored procedure accepts a single parameter – the primary key value of the contact to be retrieved. This is provided to the stored procedure via the `Parameters` collection of the `Command` object. The `CreateParameter` method creates the parameter, setting the value to the `Fetch` method's parameter – `ID`. As we'll see shortly, the `Fetch` method is called from the `Load` method. The client code is expected to have already retrieved the contact's unique `ID` number – presumably through the use of the `ContactList` object.

Once the procedure has been executed we'll have a `Recordset` object that contains three data sets. ADO handles this by having the `Recordset` object start out by reflecting the first data set returned – in this case, the data from the `Contact` table. Later, we'll use the `NextRecordset` method to move through the remaining data sets.

For now we can use the data from the `Contact` table to load our object's variables:

```
With objRS
    mstrID = objRS("ID")
    mstrLastName = objRS("LastName")
    mstrFirstName = objRS("FirstName")
    mstrAddress1 = objRS("Address1")
    mstrAddress2 = objRS("Address2")
    mstrCity = objRS("City")
    mstrState = objRS("State")
    mstrZipCode = objRS("ZipCode")
End With
```

With that done, we're ready to move on to the Phone table's data. This is as simple as calling the NextRecordset method of the Recordset object. This method can be used to set either a new Recordset variable, or the one we already have. Since we no longer need the Contact table's data, we can simply reuse the same variable:

```
Set objRS = objRS.NextRecordset
With objRS
    Do While Not .EOF
        If objRS("PhoneType") = PhoneType.WorkPhone Then
            mstrPhoneWork = objRS("Phone")
        ElseIf objRS("PhoneType") = PhoneType.HomePhone Then
            mstrPhoneHome = objRS("Phone")
        ElseIf objRS("PhoneType") = PhoneType.CellPhone Then
            mstrPhoneCell = objRS("Phone")
        End If
        .MoveNext
    Loop
End With
```

From there, we simply work with the Recordset object, which now reflects the data from the Phone table. The process is repeated to get the EMail table's data.

The Fetch method is Private in scope. To allow our object's client code to request that a contact be retrieved from the database, we'll need to add a Public method – Load. Enter the following code:

```
Public Sub Load(ByVal ID As String)
    Fetch ID
End Sub
```

This simple method accepts the ID value from the client code, and uses it to call the Fetch method we built earlier. That Fetch method retrieves the data from the database and places it in our object's local variables for use by the rest of our object's code.

At this point, we've built routines to retrieve the data for the contact that's required to set up the object's internal variables. Now our object's client code can view, print, or edit the data as needed. Next the object needs to be able to store those changed values into the database.

Adding and Updating Data

Adding a contact to the database is handled through the addContact stored procedure, while updating the data is handled via the updateContact procedure.

With the exception of the ID parameter (the first one), the parameter lists of each stored procedure are identical. This makes it very easy to write the code for an Update method in the class, since we can reuse most of the code that sets up the call to each stored procedure.

To keep our object's functionality as simple as possible, the Update method will also take care of deleting the object. We'll know if the object is to be deleted because the mblnIsDeleted variable will be set to True. We'll cover the code to manage this flag shortly.

For now, enter the following code to create the Update method itself:

```
Private Sub Update()

    Dim objCN As ADODB.Connection
    Dim objCM As ADODB.Command

    Set objCN = New Connection
    objCN.Open DB_CONN

    Set objCM = New Command
    With objCM
        .ActiveConnection = objCN
        .CommandType = adCmdStoredProc
    End With

    If mblnIsDeleted Then
        With objCM
            .CommandText = "deleteContact"
            .Parameters.Append .CreateParameter("id", adGUID, adParamInput, _
                4, mstrID)
            .Execute
        End With
        mblnIsNew = True
    Else
        If mblnIsNew Then
            With objCM
                .CommandText = "addContact"
                .Parameters.Append .CreateParameter("@id", adGUID, _
                                            adParamOutput)
            End With
        Else
            With objCM
                .CommandText = "updateContact"
                .Parameters.Append .CreateParameter("@id", adGUID, _
                                            adParamInput, 4, mstrID)
            End With
        End If
        With objCM
            .Parameters.Append .CreateParameter("@lname", adVarChar, _
                                        adParamInput, 50, mstrLastName)
            .Parameters.Append .CreateParameter("@fname", adVarChar, _
                                        adParamInput, 50, mstrFirstName)
            .Parameters.Append .CreateParameter("@add1", adVarChar, _
                                        adParamInput, 50, mstrAddress1)
            .Parameters.Append .CreateParameter("@add2", adVarChar, _
                                        adParamInput, _ 50, mstrAddress2)
            .Parameters.Append .CreateParameter("@city", adVarChar, _
                                        adParamInput, 30, mstrCity)
            .Parameters.Append .CreateParameter("@state", adVarChar, _
                    adParamInput, 20, mstrState)
            .Parameters.Append .CreateParameter("@zip", adVarChar, _
                                        adParamInput, 20, mstrZipCode)
            .Parameters.Append .CreateParameter("@phome", adVarChar, _
                                        adParamInput, 30, mstrPhoneHome)
```

```
            .Parameters.Append .CreateParameter("@pwork", adVarChar, _
                                    adParamInput, 30, mstrPhoneWork)
            .Parameters.Append .CreateParameter("@pcell", adVarChar, _
                                    adParamInput, 30, mstrPhoneCell)
            .Parameters.Append .CreateParameter("@emhome", adVarChar, _
                                    adParamInput, 100, mstrEMailHome)
            .Parameters.Append .CreateParameter("@emwork", adVarChar, _
                                    adParamInput, 100, mstrEMailWork)
            .Execute
            .ActiveConnection = Nothing
            If mblnIsNew Then
                mstrID = objCM.Parameters("@id").Value
                mblnIsNew = False
            End If
        End With
    End If

    Set objCM = Nothing
    Set objCN = Nothing
    mblnIsDeleted = False
    mblnIsDirty = False

End Sub
```

As with our other database methods, this routine opens a `Connection` object to access the database, and then uses it to initialize a `Command` object. In this case, we'll choose the particular stored procedure to invoke, based on the state of the object. To begin with, if the `mblnIsDeleted` variable is `True` then the object is to be deleted, so we'll call the `deleteContact` procedure:

```
If mblnIsDeleted Then
    With objCM
        .CommandText = "deleteContact"
        .Parameters.Append .CreateParameter("id", adGUID, adParamInput, _
            4, mstrID)
        .Execute
    End With
    mblnIsNew = True
```

If, on the other hand, the object is not marked for deletion then it will either be a new object that we're adding, or an existing object that needs to be updated. The `mblnIsNew` variable designates whether the object is new. If this value is `True` then the `addContact` procedure will be called:

```
If mblnIsNew Then
    With objCM
        .CommandText = "addContact"
        .Parameters.Append .CreateParameter("@id", adGUID, _
                                    adParamOutput)
    End With
```

If the object isn't marked as new then the `updateContact` procedure will be called:

```
With objCM
    .CommandText = "updateContact"
    .Parameters.Append .CreateParameter("@id", adGUID, _
                                    adParamInput, 4, mstrID)
End With
```

Again, the first `Parameter` object is created, though this time it is marked as an input parameter – it is being passed from our VB code into the procedure.

Once the stored procedure and first parameter have been set up, the code to call either stored procedure is identical. In both cases we simply set up all the remaining parameters and call the `Command` object's `Execute` method:

```
.Execute
.ActiveConnection = Nothing
If mblnIsNew Then
    mstrID = objCM.Parameters("@id").Value
    mblnIsNew = False
End If
```

Once the `Execute` method has been called, the `Command` object is disconnected from the database by setting the `ActiveConnection` property to `Nothing`. If the object was marked as being new, we get the new primary key value from the `@id` parameter, and mark the object as no longer being new. After all, now that it's stored in the database it is no longer new.

Note that the `ActiveConnection` property must be set to `Nothing` before the `@id` parameter value can be retrieved. This is because the stored procedure doesn't return a `Recordset` object as a result, and this step is required to force ADO to update the local values. This behavior doesn't occur with client-side cursors, but is the case with server-side cursors like this one.

To wrap things up we set a couple variables:

```
mblnIsDeleted = False
mblnIsDirty = False
```

Since we've now updated the database, the data we have in the object is no longer considered marked for deletion. Likewise, since we now know that the data in our object exactly matches the database (since we just updated it), the data is no longer considered to be dirty, so the `mblnIsDirty` flag can be set to `False`.

The `Update` method is `Private` in scope. To allow client code to request that the `Contact` object be saved, we'll add a `Public` method:

```
Public Sub Save()

    If Not mblnIsDeleted Then
        If Len(mstrLastName) = 0 Then
            Err.Raise vbObjectError + 1002, , "Last name required"
        End If
        If Len(mstrFirstName) = 0 Then
            Err.Raise vbObjectError + 1003, , "First name required"
        End If
        If Len(mstrCity) = 0 Then
            Err.Raise vbObjectError + 1004, , "City required"
        End If
        If Len(mstrState) = 0 Then
            Err.Raise vbObjectError + 1005, , "State required"
        End If
    End If

    If mblnIsDirty Then Update

End Sub
```

This method is interesting. It first checks some business rules – in this case to make sure some required fields are filled in. The Save method is the final check point before the database is updated, so it's an ideal location for this type of validation.

Assuming the business rules are met, the database can be updated. The Update method itself is only called if the data in the Contact object has been changed – a condition marked by the mblnIsDirty variable being set to True.

Deleting Data

The Contact object is marked for deletion by setting the mblnIsDeleted variable to True. This is handled by the Delete method. Enter the following code:

```
Public Sub Delete()

    mblnIsDirty = True
    mblnIsDeleted = True
    Save

End Sub
```

To keep the object's behavior simple, this method not only sets the flag to mark the object as deleted, but it also calls the Save method to cause an immediate database update.

Since we know that a primary client of the Contact object will be ASP pages, it would also be nice to allow a client to directly remove a contact from the database without first having to load the Contact object. This makes sense for performance – it's a waste to load the data from the database if all we're going to do is turn around and delete it.

Enter the following code to support this functionality:

```
Public Sub DeleteContact(ByVal ID As String)

    mstrID = ID
    Delete

End Sub
```

Instead of marking an already loaded Contact object for deletion, this method accepts the primary key value as a parameter, sets it into the object's internal state, and then calls the Delete method. This will cause the specified contact to be removed cleanly and simply.

Building the Component

At this point our ContactList and Contact objects are complete. However, before we can use them we need to compile the ActiveX DLL, by choosing File | Make ContactObjects.dll and confirming the path in the subsequent dialog. We can't build the component straight away – there are a few setting which we will want to discuss and then make.

Compiling a COM Object Under VB

When compiling a Visual Basic project that uses COM+ services and/or runs on a server, or indeed, only runs locally, you should be aware of the property options available to you. Some are self-explanatory, others you can find more on from your MSDN or from other resources, and we will be discussing the following main Project Properties options:

- ❏ Unattended Execution
- ❏ Retained In Memory
- ❏ Threading Model
- ❏ Base Address
- ❏ Compatibility Issues

Compatibility Issues

Since OOP, COM, and all related technologies aim for reusability, scalability, and performance, it is very important to maintain **compatibility**. Compatibility is important for deployment, and it is not always necessarily done successfully on your behalf. When you deploy an application and later want to enhance a feature, COM components are meant to make that process easier by allowing you to simply change a DLL and 'upgrade' your existing installation by only supplying the new DLL.

This is all fine, provided that the existing application can see your new DLL, and can use it successfully. When you compile an EXE that references a DLL, the EXE is bound to the interfaces of the DLL. Changes to the DLL's interfaces, or more importantly the GUIDs that represent them, will result in errors from the EXE. Compatibility will then be broken.

COM objects consist of interfaces that are defined in IDL. Within the declaration language, each interface and method is assigned a valid GUID, a CLSID (Class Identifier) or an IID (Interface Identifier). The type library also has a GUID associated with it known as LIBID.

These assignments are for the purpose of distinguishing the interfaces from one another and provide uniqueness where textual naming cannot. When your component is compiled, the type library that has been generated for it is compiled into the DLL as well, thus embedding these GUIDs.

Any changes to this type library will make your component incompatible with previous compilations of it, that is if these GUIDs change. The trick is to make sure that the interfaces of the DLL do not change.

Visual Basic does provide some assistance by providing you with the Compatibility settings in the Options dialog. Visual Basic offers three types of settings for the quest of remaining compatible between builds. These settings are used when VB negotiates the IDL declarations for you:

- ❏ No Compatibility – Visual Basic will recompile the type library and will not care about the GUIDs involved, thus generating new GUIDs for the LIBID, CLSID as well as IIDs.

- ❏ Project Compatibility – for when you are designing your application and have not yet compiled or released it. Visual Basic will then preserve the LIBID and CLSIDs but will not reserve the IIDs, as it generated new GUIDs for them.

- ❏ Binary Compatibility – a little closer to the desire of making our DLLs compatible with previous builds. Setting this option will inform VB that you wish to keep compatibility for your DLL against a particular interface. When you set the option, you must also specify with which DLL you wish to be compatible. Usually this is a copy of the DLL you have just compiled. VB will then make sure that builds have the same LIBID, CLSID, and IIDs.

We will concentrate on the binary compatibility, as it is the most relevant to our concerns.

As mentioned above, when the binary compatibility option in Visual Basic is set, Visual Basic makes sure that all GUIDs are the same as the type library it has been made to try and be compatible with. What happens though if you had to change a method name or parameter, or even add something new?

If you do change anything in the declarations, that is the Get, Let, Set, the Sub or Function lines as well as any User-Defined Types, VB will then be forced to break compatibility as the interface is not the same as the interface it is trying to be compatible with. When this occurs Visual Basic prompts you with a form asking for permission to do one or the other actions. It is strongly recommended though, that you never get this far. Keeping compatibility is important for versioning, upgrading, and keeping older systems in good working order.

In conclusion, be aware of these issues and try to never change an interface after it is released into the world. With saying that, there are ways to better your situation when it comes to compatibility, ways that involve implementing interfaces and perhaps even building your interfaces in IDL rather than with just VB. All of these should not be ruled out depending on the type of component that you are developing.

Now that we have discussed compatibility, we are free to make the setting in the dialog.

In the project | properties window click on the **Component** tab. Change the **Version Compatibility** setting to **Binary Compatibility**. Then click on the ellipsis (...) button to bring up a file dialog.

Click on the ContactObjects.dll file, press *Ctrl-C* and *Ctrl-V*. This will make a copy of the DLL in the same directory as the original. Click on the copy, then click **Open** and **OK**.

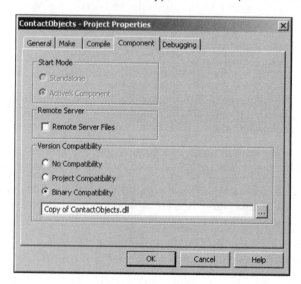

I am often asked why set compatibility to a copy of the DLL rather than the DLL itself. I have three reasons. The first reason is that this is recommended by Microsoft. The second is that experience has shown that this approach is more stable – meaning it decreases the chances of having to reinstall the operating system to fix registry problems. The third is that it protects us against 'accidental' changes to the component, in that we'll be constantly reminded that we've broken an interface until we take the extra step of updating the copy of the DLL with the new (changed) version.

The Threading Model

In order to better understand this section let us briefly define some threading terms:

❑ Firstly a **process** (to keep it simple) is a combination of data and code.

❑ An **apartment** is where instances of classes (objects) are created.

❑ A **thread** is a block of code to be executed.

These terms are all low-level abstractions and are not physical elements, but an analogy to a building could be beneficial. The Building is the Process; the Apartments are the apartments within the building, which are of different types just like in the physical world where a Penthouse is different from another one-bedroom apartment on the first floor.

There are two different apartment **threaded models** that are supported by Visual Basic, these are:

❑ Single threaded

❑ Apartment threaded

Single-Threaded Apartments (STA)

In C++ the **Single-Threaded Apartment** is created by calling `CoInitialize` and is the simplest of the threading models. `CoInitialize` creates a primary thread that takes care of all the needs of its processes. It is the only thread that has access to the apartment. In Visual Basic we simply use the option on the Threading model section of the General tab and you do not need the lower API for managing this.

When an object is associated with a single-threaded apartment, only that particular thread may execute calls on the object. When another thread wishes to execute a call on the single-threaded object, the call is marshaled to the apartment that contains the object and that thread executes the call. If a result is required, it is then marshaled back to the original caller.

Marshaling in COM+ requires that two additional objects be created, the proxy and the stub. These objects are responsible for getting data back and forth between apartments. This affects performance as two objects lie between the caller and the server code. The second figure below shows the proxy/stub pair and how it fits between apartments for marshalling.

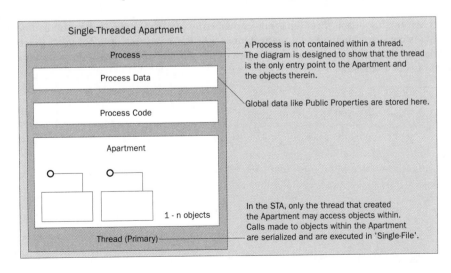

Since there is only one thread, calls made to the object all execute in 'single-file'. This is not a particularly useful scenario when you consider this model with a large number of clients.

Below, the diagram shows the marshaling scenario across apartments using the proxy/stub combination. This marshaling also occurs across processes and machine boundaries.

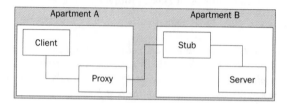

The above figure shows two apartments and the proxy/stub combination that marshals calls across apartment boundaries.

> **The term marshalling does not *only* occur across apartment boundaries, but also across machine boundaries and thread boundaries.**

Apartment-Threaded

The Apartment Threaded option is basically the same as the Single Threaded option except for the fact that there are many threads involved. An apartment can have many threads of executable code, which can all execute simultaneously. This makes it a better option for a server component, as clients do not have to wait for calls to complete while it waits in a queue as in the single threaded option.

Although this is a better option, there is the fact of global data. Public variables declared in BAS modules in Visual Basic are considered to be global data.

When a public variable is declared, each class instance instantiates a copy of the data on its own thread. This is the way that Visual Basic deals with the potential conflicts that could occur if multiple objects were to read and write randomly to the same global data.

The negative though, of each thread having its own copy of global data, is that you can never be sure that the data is consistent between all the instances. For these reasons, it is not good practice to use public variables. Also, due to the fact that copies of the global data are made for every instance, there are also resources to consider.

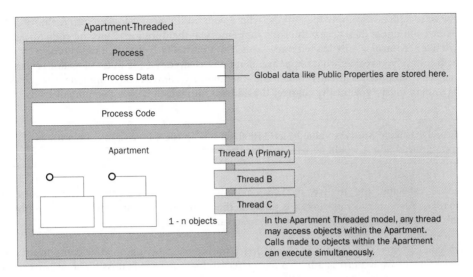

The threading models within Visual Basic are limited – other models such as neutral apartment are not supported, which means that it cannot take part in object pooling.

When compiling your project make sure that your component has the threading model of Apartment. Using Single Threaded will make your object serialized, which means all calls on the object will be dealt with one at a time, no matter which instance of the object called it.

Base Address

Too many developers ignore the **base address** on their components, much to their own downfall. Managing the base address of your component is a good thing and doesn't require much effort on your part. The following screen shot shows the Visual basic Project Properties window with the DLL Base Address with its default value:

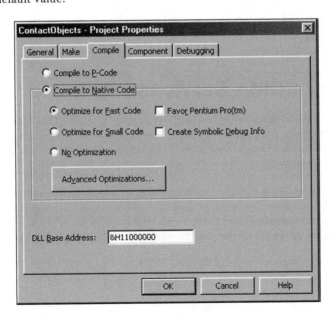

Firstly, the base address is simply the address where your component is loaded into memory. All who require your component then access the code in memory at that location. Thus the code for an ActiveX DLL or ActiveX control is only loaded once. This is not particularly useful in explaining why you should bother with it until you realize what happens when there is already code in that location. If it is found that another active component is already loaded into the memory address your component requires, the operating system must dynamically changes the address into which it your component loads.

> **If the DLL Base Address value is &H11000000 like in the above figure, then it has been ignored and it would be wise to alter the value.**

This is called **rebasing**, and involves the recalculating of the memory locations where your component can be loaded. Also, due to rebasing, it is possible that your component's code could then be loaded more than once and this too involves more resources.

Although you can never be certain as to whether rebasing is occurring on your component and perhaps also never know to what address other components are loading to, it is possible to at least make sure that all of your own components do not fall over each other.

A good many developers compile without changing the address, so many components out there are configured to load at the default address of &H11000000.

In order to change this value you must keep to the requirements that values must be a multiple of 64k (65536), starting at the address &H10000000 (16,777,216 [16MB]) to &H80000000 (2,147,483,648[2MB]).

Therefore good values are &H10000000, &H10100000, &H10200000 etc.

The way to get the base address of your next component is to add the size of your DLL or OCX to the base address of that component and round that number to the nearest multiple of 64k (65536).

It is good practice to keep track of your components and their base addresses in a database or specification document.

Designing for COM+ Services

This next section will deal with some issues specifically surrounding COM+. Other COM+ services, such as making your component transactional, will be described in later chapters. COM+, as described again and again, is in essence the encapsulation of COM and MTS (Microsoft Transaction Server) with extended services such as security.

If you are familiar with coding for MTS, you will remember a reference to a DLL named mtxas.dll that had to be made with each and every MTS project. The file might have changed but the principle is the same. This time, a file by the name of comsvcs.dll (COM Services DLL) is responsible for providing you with COM+ functionality. The following screenshot shows the file in the References window.

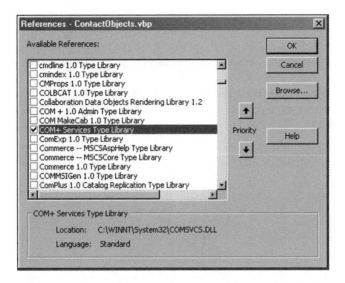

As opposed to the relatively simple model of the MTS version, the COM Services model is packed with COM+ niceties. The COM services DLL is by default provided by all the Windows 2000 operating systems, so with one installed you will have no problem in referencing it from VB. Once referenced, you can gain a peek at its contents by viewing the type library information in your Object Browser.

Supporting Transactions

Components are often linked to a database of some form or another and when doing so, risk the chance of being affected by an inadequate database design. A good design involves a great number of variables that can be discussed in volumes of books, so it would be foolish to think that it could be conveyed in its entirety here, although we can mention some factors that may be useful. As an example, querying data on primary keys and using stored procedures are all important to help speed up queries. It is important that you make sure that you are aware of the best SQL practices. Tips and tricks on database design can be found from many resources, including on-line web sites as well as books and magazines. See the Further Reading section at the end of this chapter for some resources to get you started.

> **To get more information on how the COM+ Transactional Services work, see Chapter 8.**

Coding: Properties, Objects, Parameters, and more

When creating a Windows COM+ component you will be faced with issues regarding the actual building of the interfaces and will need to decide what the interface will look like. Traditonally, a developer would go straight ahead and start creating properties on a class, which would represent certain fields in the database. But properties under COM+ are actually very inefficient, as they require more 'trips over the wire'.

Although the contacts sample makes use of properties (*a.* to show you the normal property approach and *b.* to get you as an informal exercise to change it so it uses a method instead), the 'no properties' approach is a speedier option. The larger the number of parameters required, generally, the greater the increase in speed achieved by using a method, as it will decrease the number of trips that the same number of properties would incur. Sometimes, though, dealing with properties is far more appealing than long-winded parameters on methods.

For similar reasons, in order to also reduce trips across boundaries, you should not use object hierarchies in your objects or objects that return other objects. Objects that are returned to the client are not tremendously efficient, as it requires many trips from the client to the server and then back again. Each call has to be marshaled back and forth between process and thread boundaries.

A recordset should be disconnected when given to the client. Another aspect, in terms of efficient coding for COM+, is making sure that objects are released from memory as soon as possible, as is the case with the following code snippet:

```
Dim myObj As Object
'Other code

Set myObj = New Object 'Acquire Late
MyObj.SomeMethod       'Just before this method
Set myObj = Nothing    'Release Early

'Other code
```

> **It is good practice to release your objects once you are finished with them. In other words, acquire late, release early.**

The issues described in this section all have two aims in common, to save resources and to make COM+ objects more efficient. Though the techniques to accomplish this often require you to code against a term known as *instance state*. Each instance of a class is required to know its purpose and the data it requires at any given time. Unfortunately, issuing property values in quick succession is not foolproof. Consider the following:

```
MyObj.Gallons = 10 ' a call is made to the COM+ SetComplete() method
                     in this property.
MyObj.Pump = 1     ' can you be sure that the Gallons property is still 10
MyObj.BuyGallons   ' if network traffic delayed the execution of this line?
```

For this reason, your objects cannot expect to know the values that were being held after they were recreated. If you think of this as not having state, then you are on track. You handle state, and COM+ does not care either way.

The issues described here continue with a slightly different angle as we look at the next related COM+ service.

Just-In-Time (JIT) Activation

Just-In-Time Activation is a service that COM+ provides you with, that achieves a high level of resource-efficient objects on the server. The objects that you create with Visual Basic will automatically inherit these benefits provided that they support transactions one-way or the other. JIT takes care of your objects' activation and deactivation for you.

Resource Friendly

Resources are extremely valuable to a server, as they affect the performance of applications or server components running on it, and the purpose of JIT is to make the server more efficient with those resources. Usually, the client application would have to control the resource of objects created on the server by keeping track of instances and setting them back to nothing when complete. Making a public variable in Visual Basic and setting it when the form loads will require resources of the server until it is set back to nothing.

This is an expensive method of coding, and scaling the example up 100-fold could have disastrous results on your server.

There is also a performance decrease when many objects are consistently loaded and reloaded into memory, considering the fact that initializing your object can often take longer than your average method's execution time. To help this situation, COM+ activates your object and deactivates your object when it is needed and not needed respectively.

Leaving a Trace

When you call a method or property on your transactional object and COM+ is told that it can deactivate your object, it releases the object from memory on your behalf. When you access another property on that object, COM+ creates the object once again on your behalf and executes it, releasing it again when done.

So COM+ activates and deactivates instances of your objects for you. But isn't that what you are told to do?

As you have seen, the registry is important to COM+. It manages the GUIDs associated with your components' objects and this is what COM+ uses for instantiating those objects. COM+ searches the registry for the GUID and creates a proxy on the client. The proxy is created based on the type library information and when a method is called it sends the call to the stub on the server. The stub also has to be created based on the GUID provided, and is responsible for actually executing the called method on the server. This involves time-consuming searching within the registry, time for proxy-stub creation, the creation of additional structures like context, and then the time for the called method to execute. When you release the object, all of these activities are then made void and the reference freed when released from memory.

In the case of JIT activation the server knows the connection is valid and although it releases the object from memory, it caches the information about the object. The proxy, stub, and context structures are left intact, leaving a trace of itself.

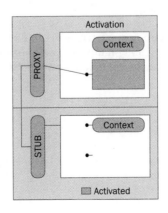

Therefore registry lookups are not needed, proxy-stub and context structures do not have to be recreated and thus the recreation of the object is much simpler and faster.

JIT activation occurs when you access another method on the cached object as it activates the object just in time. As it gets the new call, it recreates the object and calls the method. This is a faster solution than any "instantiating and releasing" code you may use.

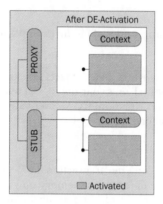

As was said before, JIT works hand-in-hand with transactions. If your object supports transactions, then it also supports JIT.

Although COM+ documentation advises you to take advantage of JIT within COM+ and not care about when and why you release your objects, I must urge you to still maintain your coding practice by acquiring late and releasing early. The reason is clear. Not all of your objects are going to be transactional, thus not all of your objects are going to be JIT-enabled. To simply keep track of which objects are benefiting from JIT and those which are not is not good enough for me. Also, many web clients are written in server-side ASP and, since it is usually on the same server as the objects, the proxy-stub situation overhead is decreased due to the fact that no network travel is needed.

By no means am I excluding its benefits and to show that, let's look at JIT a little more.

Hooking into JIT

The activation and deactivation features of JIT on your object can be hooked into by means of **interface inheritance**. Inheriting interfaces is not a new thing and is a powerful method of inheriting interfaces of other COM objects.

In order to hook into JIT, you must implement `IObjectControl`, an interface provided by the COM+ Services object model. When implementing interfaces you must implement all methods on the interface. The `IObjectControl` interface contains the following methods:

-   `Activate()`
-   `CanBePooled()`
-   `Deactivate()`

To implement the `IObjectControl` interface, a reference to `comsvcs.dll` must be made and the following code inserted:

```
Option Explicit

    Implements ObjectControl

Private Sub ObjectControl_Activate()

End Sub

Private Function ObjectControl_CanBePooled() As Boolean

End Function

Private Sub ObjectControl_Deactivate()

End Sub
```

The methods seen here have to be implemented, as those are the methods that `IObjectControl` exposes.

`Activate()` and `Deactivate()` correspond to the activities that the JIT service provides and fires for you to write code behind that activity. Object initialization code and deactivation code can be inserted into these methods. Remember, though, to carefully assess why you would need such a thing, as your object should not care about state in this way.

AVOID coding in the `Class_Initialize` event, especially when hooking into `IObjectControl`. The `Class_Initialize` event occurs before the `Activate` event and could cause problems for your object.

Consider the following code within a transactional object implementing the `IObjectControl` interface:

```
Dim myObject As Class1

Private Sub Class_Initialize()
    Set myObject = New Class1
End Sub
```

A COM+ transactional object is an object that has a context. In this case the word context is a COM+ structure that stores information on the object. The information that the context structure contains is encapsulated inside properties, some of which you can `Get` and `Set`. (See `IContextState`, `IObjectContextInfo` in your COM+ documentation.)

Since the class initialize event fires before the `Activate` method on `IObjectControl`, objects created within the class' event will not be included in the context of the object. Also do not use `SetComplete` or `SetAbort` within any of the `IObjectControl` methods.

With our coding complete and the DLL compiled, the component is ready to be used by the user interface in Chapter 23. The chapter will build the contacts database, and also a user interface which will use our component.

Summary

In summary there are three incredibly important factors to pay attention to when designing and developing a COM+ component in VB. Firstly you must take special care in how you design your interfaces, in terms of naming conventions, instance state, trips over the wire as well as what techniques you use for carrying data across layers and more. Secondly, when applying COM+ services like transactions, you must be aware of how JIT works and how to utilize it, which will give you better performance. Lastly, develop in tiers so that you create a climate for better scalability.

A last point to leave you with is regarding testing. Always test performance and design issues. Never accept the first solution as law; there just may be a better way. When you test be on the lookout for bottlenecks, most used methods, and queries.

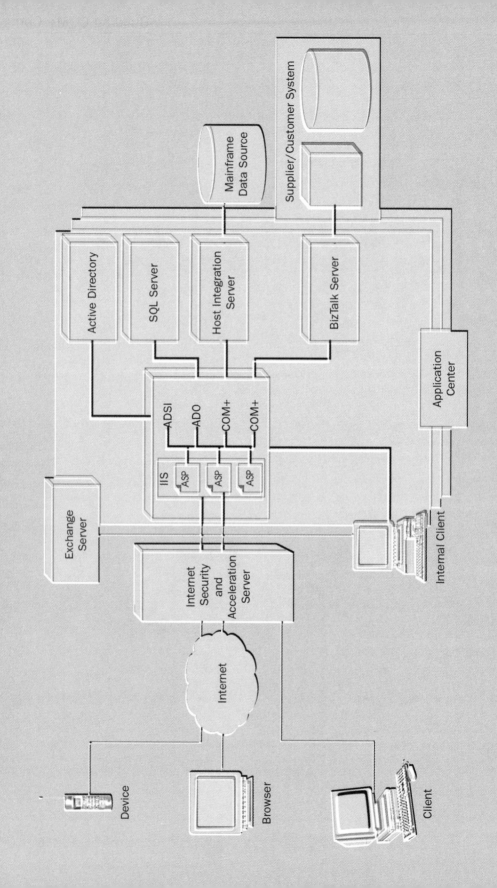

Introduction to Transactions

8

In December 1996, Microsoft released **Microsoft Transaction Server** (**MTS**) **1.0**, introducing a declarative model for providing transactional support for components. MTS gave the developer the ability to declare the transactional support required for individual components within an application.

As we've seen in previous chapters, COM+ brought a unification of COM and MTS, and also extended the declarative model beyond transactions to other services, such as object pooling.

In this chapter, we're going to concentrate on the concepts behind transactional programming, and see how COM+ makes our job easier. In particular, this chapter includes:

❑　A basic introduction to transactions

❑　How resource managers and transaction managers work

❑　Transactional support in COM+

❑　How to build transactional components, and in particular, how to create a Compensating Resource Manager

So let's start by recapping exactly what a transaction is.

Basics of Transactions

Even though there was considerably more to MTS, transactional support for components was definitely one of its core offerings.

> **A transaction is a discreet unit of work that represents a particular activity or function within a system. The activity is often composed of a series of steps that must be treated as a single unit of work. In other words, it's all or nothing – either all of the steps successfully complete, or none of them do.**

Transactions in programming terms are pretty similar in concept to the transactions we come across every day in the business world, for example when you transfer money to your bank account or purchase goods from a supplier.

Providing transactional support within your applications may sound deceptively easy. However, transactional programming is very difficult to implement without a supporting infrastructure, especially across heterogeneous data sources.

It's time to be more specific about what we mean when we talk about transactions.

ACID Properties

A transaction within the context of a transaction processing system must meet four requirements. It must be:

❑ **Atomic** – a transaction will either commit or abort. If a transaction **commits**, all of the steps of the transaction successfully complete. If a transaction **aborts**, then all of the effects of the steps that have completed up to the point of failure will be undone (or **rolled back**). For example, say you ask to transfer one hundred dollars out of your checking account to your savings account. If the transaction is atomic, either the money is transferred, or the request is denied.

❑ **Consistent** – a transaction is a *correct* transformation of the state of a system. Individual steps within a transaction often alter the state of the system so that it is temporarily invalid. Before a transaction completes, it must ensure that the system is returned to a valid state. For example, one of the steps to transfer funds is to deduct one hundred dollars from your checking account. But if those funds are not deposited into your savings account, the system state is invalid. Regardless of the outcome, you should not be one hundred dollars poorer: your account balance should be reset or one hundred dollars should be added to your savings account.

❑ **Isolated** – uncommitted changes are hidden from other concurrent transactions. This is often accomplished by serializing access to the data that is used within a transaction by applying locks. For example, say the step to withdraw money out of your checking account has completed, but the step to deposit money into your savings account has not. If a transaction responsible for creating your monthly statement is executed concurrently, the withdrawal should not appear on your statement until the transaction has been committed.

❑ **Durable** – once a transaction commits, changes made to the system state will persist even if there are system failures. For example, say I deposit my paycheck into my account. If a power outage occurs just after the transaction commits, my deposit should still be on record after the system comes back on line.

These requirements are often referred to by their acronym, the **ACID** properties.

All participants in a transaction must abide by the ACID rules.

Why Do We Need Transactions?

So what's the big deal about support for transactions?

First and foremost it makes the programmer's life much easier. Writing transactional logic within your applications, and ensuring that the ACID properties of a transaction are maintained, can be very difficult.

For example, say we write an accounting component that implements a transactional Withdraw method:

```
Private Sub Withdraw (lAcctID as Long, curAmount as Currency)

    Dim objCN As New ADODB.Connection
    Dim objRS As New ADODB.RecordSet
    Dim strSQL As String
    Dim strConnection As String

    ' Initialize.
    strConnection = "Provider=SQLOLEDB;server=ServerName;" & _
                    "Database=DBName;User ID=sa;Password=;"

    ' Open the database connection.
    objCN.Open strConnection

    ' ***BEGINNING OF TRANSACTION***

    ' Step 1:  Account balances can never fall below 0.
    '          Therefore, we will check to see if we have sufficient funds.
    strSQL = "SELECT sum(DebitCredit) Balance from Ledger where " & _
             "AccountID = " & lAcctID
    objRS.Open strSQL, objCN, adOpenKeyset, adLockOptimistic, adCmdText
    curBalance = objRS("Balance")
    If (objRS("Balance") < curAmount) Then _
        Err.Raise vbObjectError + 1, "TransferFunds", "Insufficient funds."
    objRS.Close

    ' Step 2:  Deduct the amount from the account.
    strSQL = "SELECT DebitCredit from Ledger where AccountID = " & lAcctID
    objRS.Open strSQL, objCN, adOpenKeyset, adLockOptimistic, adCmdText
    objRS.AddNew
    objRS("AccountID") = lAcctID
    objRS("DebitCredit") = curAmount * (-1)
    objRS.Update
```

```
      ' Ignore errors once change has been committed to DB.
      On Error Resume Next

      objRS.Close
      ' ***END OF TRANSACTION***

      ' Close the database connection.
      objCN.Close
      Set objRS = Nothing
      Set objCN = Nothing

End Sub
```

This simple method obtains the account balance from the database and checks to see if there are sufficient funds to make the withdrawal. If there are sufficient funds, the amount withdrawn is added to the account's ledger. However, even code as simple as this violates the ACID properties. Care to guess which one?

Since the above transaction is only performing one action that modifies system state, all steps within the transaction will either fully commit or abort. Therefore, the transaction is *atomic*. Since the modification to the database will only be visible to concurrent transactions once the transaction completes, it is *isolated*. Finally, since the new ledger entry is recorded persistently in the database, the transaction is *durable*.

The ACID property that the code sample above violates is the *consistency* property. In order to understand why, let's look at the following scenario. Say the starting balance is one hundred dollars, and we call the Withdraw method to withdraw all one hundred dollars. If the account balance was modified by another concurrent Withdraw transaction in between steps 2 and 3 of our transaction, the one hundred dollar deduction in step 3 will drop our account balance below zero, violating our rule imposed by step 2.

We can correct this by having the Withdraw method call a stored procedure, which performs the validation and withdrawal all within the context of a transaction. The stored procedure checks to see if the account has sufficient funds. If it does, then we insert a record to withdraw the requested amount:

```
CREATE PROCEDURE sp_withdraw @nAcctID AS INT, @curAmount AS MONEY AS

BEGIN TRANSACTION

IF (SELECT SUM(DebitCredit) Balance FROM Ledger
    WHERE AccountID = @nAcctID) > @curAmount
BEGIN
    INSERT INTO Ledger (AccountID, DebitCredit)
              values(@nAcctID, @curAmount * (-1))
    COMMIT TRANSACTION
END
ELSE
BEGIN
    RAISERROR ('Insufficient funds.', 16, 1)
    ROLLBACK TRANSACTION
END
```

SQL Server ensures that the range of rows in the Ledger table is locked for the specified account. Therefore, concurrent transactions would not be allowed to add, modify, or delete records containing the account ID. As we'll see later in the chapter, COM+ handles these details (and many more) for you!

What if the Withdraw method was just one of a series of steps within a transaction? What if the transaction spanned multiple method calls? What if those multiple method calls were contained in many different objects? What if, over the course of the transaction, multiple persistent resources were modified? What if those resources existed on multiple servers? Obviously, writing transactional code can get very complicated, very quickly. That's the beauty of a transactional processing system – it provides an infrastructure for managing the transaction for you.

Transaction Processing Systems

A **transaction processing system** is one that provides an infrastructure for handling the coordination of transactions. A transaction processing system consists of:

❑ An application

❑ Transaction managers

❑ Resource managers

The application contains business logic. If the implementation of the business logic requires transactional support from the transaction processing system, the transaction manager is enlisted. The transaction manager is responsible for coordinating with the resource managers enlisted in the transaction on the local machine. The resource managers are responsible for coordinating updates to persistent data.

A typical transaction processing architecture is shown in the following figure:

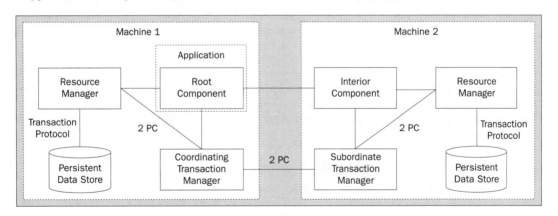

2PC stands for two-phase commit. We'll cover this in more detail later in the chapter, but essentially, this is a protocol that helps ensure the ACID properties for a transaction are not violated.

In this figure, the root component enlists another component located on another machine (an "interior" component – we'll see why shortly) to perform some work on its behalf. The interior object must perform its work within the root component's transaction. Therefore, the transaction manager on machine 1 enlists the transaction manager on machine 2 to coordinate the resource managers enlisted in the transaction on machine 2.

Let's clarify this by discussing the three major constituents of a transaction processing system in more detail.

Resource Managers

> Resource managers **are responsible for ensuring that modifications made to persistent resources in a transaction are made in a consistent, isolated, and durable manner.**

The resource manager assists the transaction manager by ensuring that the changes made are either fully committed upon successful completion of the transaction, or are completely rolled back in the event the transaction is aborted. The resource manager is also responsible for notifying the persistent resource of the required isolation level that needs to be maintained throughout the life of the transaction, and whether or not to abort or commit the changes.

A persistent resource must have an associated resource manager (or a Compensating Resource Manager for COM+ initiated transactions) in order for it to participate in a distributed transaction. (We'll discuss Compensating Resource Managers later in the chapter.)

For example, the Windows 2000 Active Directory does not have a resource manager. AD operations are transactional only within the scope of an LDAP connection, and since the AD does not have an RM, it cannot participate in distributed transactions. Any changes made to Active Directory within the context of the transaction will be persisted to the Active Directory whether the transaction commits or aborts. Therefore, it's important to ensure that all persistent resources modified during the course of a transaction have an associated resource manager.

The most commonly used resource managers are those that ship with relational databases, such as SQL Server and Oracle. Additional resource managers are available via third party vendors. If a resource manager is unavailable for a particular persistent resource, you have the option of writing your own. However, writing a resource manager is not trivial and is beyond the scope of this book. See the MSDN Library for more information.

Compensating Resource Managers

The **Compensating Resource Manager** (**CRM**) provides an alternative way to integrate a persistent resource with a DTC coordinated transaction. A CRM should be created when a persistent resource needs to be updated within the context of a COM+ transaction, and a resource manager is not available from either the vendor of the persistent resource or a third party.

The CRM is able to vote on the outcome of a transaction, and will receive notification as to whether or not the transaction was committed or aborted. The CRM also provides a durable log – if the system crashes, the CRM will automatically recover from the log when the system restarts.

In order to create a CRM, we must write two components – the **CRM Worker** and the **CRM Compensator** – both of which support standard interfaces:

❑ The CRM Worker is responsible for accessing and manipulating resources

❑ The CRM Compensator is responsible for voting on the outcome of the transaction, and for committing or aborting the operations performed against the resource by the CRM Worker

Compensating Transactions

A **compensating transaction** is one that violates the *isolated* property. During the course of a compensating transaction, changes made to a persistent resource are visible to other transactions. This is usually done for the sake of better concurrency, or when the persistent resource lacks support for locking mechanisms necessary to implement a fully ACID-compliant transaction. However, compensating transactions can wreak havoc if used within transaction processing systems.

For example, say a compensating transaction to create a new employee involves creating a record in the employee table, then creating a record in the address table, and then creating records in various other tables, including creating a record in the contact information table for each phone number. In the midst of creating the employee record, another transaction to set up the employee's payroll completes successfully. However, the original transaction fails because an invalid phone number was given. Since the setting up of the payroll record was in a separate transaction, even though the employee record is deleted, the individual will start receiving paychecks. Obviously this is not the most ideal situation!

The CRM ensures consistency and durability, and the transaction manager ensures atomicity. However, the CRM does not inherently ensure isolation – hence the name. It is up to the developer of the CRM to ensure that changes made during the course of a transaction are not visible to any other transaction until it is complete. In a later section, we'll examine an example implementation of a CRM that ensures isolation.

Transaction Managers

When multiple resource managers are deployed for a given transaction, something has to be responsible for the overall transaction.

> **The** transaction manager **is responsible for coordinating resource managers located on the local machine, and enlisting other transaction managers in the transaction.**

When a local transaction manager enlists another transaction manager located on a different machine, the local transaction manager is referred to as the **coordinating transaction manager**, and the remote transaction manager is referred to as a **subordinate transaction manager**. If the application fails, the coordinating transaction manager is responsible for informing each enlisted resource manager and any subordinate transaction manager to rollback any changes that were made.

DTC

The Microsoft **Distributed Transaction Coordinator** (**DTC**) is Microsoft's transaction manager. The DTC runs as a multi-threaded service, and guarantees atomicity when transactions span across multiple resource managers.

The DTC was first introduced with SQL Server 6.5, and then in December 1996 the DTC was distributed as a part of MTS 1.0. The DTC is now installed by default with Windows 2000.

The DTC is employed to ensure that distributed transactions do not violate the ACID properties. It accomplishes this by enlisting the resource managers for each machine involved in the transaction, and communicates through the use of a two-phase commit protocol.

Two-Phase Commit Protocol

The **two-phase commit protocol** is used when managing distributed transactions. The transaction manager communicates with the resource managers enlisted in a transaction via the two-phase commit protocol. This communication usually occurs over a separate communication channel and, as the name implies, is composed of two phases: the **prepare** phase and the **commit/abort** phase.

The prepare phase is entered when the root and its interior objects have all voted to commit the transaction. In the prepare phase, the transaction manager asks each of the enlisted resource managers to prepare to commit the transaction. Each resource manager attempts to save its state to a durable store without actually committing the changes, and votes on whether or not to commit the transaction. Once the resource manager completes the prepare phase, it must honor the outcome of the transaction.

In the commit/abort phase, a commit or abort is sent to each resource manager. If the transaction manager receives a vote to commit the transaction from every enlisted resource manager within the transaction timeout period, a commit is sent to each resource manager. If the transaction manager receives a vote to abort the transaction by the root object, its interior components, or the enlisted resource manager, or does not receive all of the votes within the transaction timeout period, an abort is sent to each of the resource managers.

The transactional communication between the resource manager and the persistent resource usually occurs over a separate communication channel using any one of a number of transaction protocols. Typical transactional protocols utilized within Windows DNA applications include:

- ❏ OLE Transactions – the native protocol used by the DTC to communicate with the resource managers.

- ❏ X/Open XA – a standard transaction protocol defined by the X/Open Distributed Transaction Processing (X/Open DTP) group, which defines the API used by the resource manager to communicate with the transaction manager. For relational databases that support the XA protocol, the ODBC driver typically acts as a bridge between the DTC and the XA compliant resource manager.

- ❏ Transaction Internet Protocol (TIP) – a standard transaction protocol defined by the Internet Engineering Task Force (IETF). The DTC provides direct support for communicating with resource managers via TIP.

Application

The **application** is responsible for enlisting the resource manager to coordinate its distributed transactions, and each of the resource managers needed. On the Microsoft platform, the application must:

- ❏ Establish a connection with the coordinating DTC by calling the `DtcGetTransactionManager()` function to receive a reference to the `ITransactionDispenser` interface

❏ Create a new transaction by calling the `BeginTransaction` member function, which returns a reference to the new transaction's `ITransaction` interface

❏ Obtain connections to persistent resources, and then manually enlist their transaction managers to participate in the transaction

Obviously there are quite a few error prone details that must be followed in order to write transactional applications. Wouldn't it be nice if these details could be taken care of for you?

That's exactly what COM+ does for us. COM+ Component Services are responsible for enlisting the DTC, creating the root component, enlisting the root component within the transaction, and finally enlisting the resource managers for persistent resources on behalf of the application.

As we'll see in the next section, COM+ provides a rich declarative environment that greatly simplifies the creation and control of transactional component-based applications.

Transactional Support in COM+

COM+ provides a declarative environment for managing transactions within your component-based application. Very minor changes, if any, are required within your component in order to support transactions.

COM+ lets us declare which components require transactional support via an administrative interface (the Component Services GUI). When a component requiring transactional support is created, it's automatically enlisted in the transaction. When the transactional component acquires a connection to a persistent resource, COM+ automatically enlists the resource manager in the component's transaction.

Root and Interior Objects

Because of the declarative model, you can combine various methods exposed by many different objects to compose a transaction.

The **root object** is the first COM+ object that is included in the context of a new transaction. The root object may instantiate additional COM+ objects in order to accomplish its tasks – these objects are referred to as **interior objects**. Depending on its configurations, an interior object may or may not participate in the transaction.

The diagram below shows two transactions. The first transaction contains a root object and two interior objects. The object created by the second interior object requires its own transaction: therefore, it becomes the root of a new transaction and creates its own interior object:

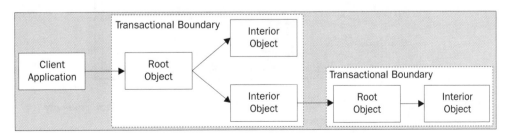

The root object and each of the interior objects participating in its transaction gets an opportunity to vote on the outcome of the transaction. When the root object is deactivated, the transaction completes, at which point the votes of the root and all of its participating interior objects are tallied, and the transaction is either committed or aborted. For a transaction to be committed, all objects must vote to commit the transaction. If any object participating in the transaction votes to abort, the transaction is aborted, and all changes made to persistent resources managed by resource managers are rolled back to their original state.

So how do we specify whether the interior objects we create will enlist in the current transaction or become the root object of a new transaction? And how can we ensure that a particular object will always be the root of a new transaction? We can specify the transactional behavior of any component using the transactional support property.

The Transactional Support Property

Each class has its own transactional support property, allowing us to declare the type of transactional support objects of this class require.

As we saw in Chapter 6, we can view the transactional support property for a particular class by selecting that class in the Component Services MMC, and opening the Transactions tab of the Properties dialog box:

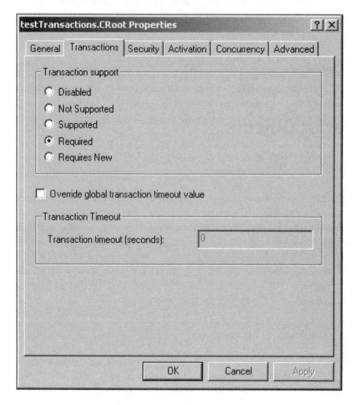

These properties can be manipulated both using the MMC, and programmatically from within our components. We'll see more about the programmatic methods later in this chapter.

To recap, the properties for transaction support are:

❑ **Disabled** – if the transaction support attribute is set to disabled, the object still exists within a context and is a part of an activity stream. However, COM+ will simulate the transactional behavior of an un-configured COM component. In general, this option is selected if the object does not manipulate any persistent resources managed by a resource manager, and is not required to be the root of a transaction. We can use this if we don't want to incur transaction-related overheads.

❑ **Not Supported** – this is the default setting for all COM+ components. The object will not participate in a transaction regardless of the transactional state of its caller. The object will not be able to vote within the caller's transaction, or start a transaction of its own. Any changes made to persistent resources managed by resource managers will be committed, regardless of the outcome of the caller's transaction.

❑ **Supported** – objects created from this class can participate in a transaction, but don't require one. The object will participate in the caller's transaction, if one exists. However, the object will not be allowed to initiate its own transaction. This setting is frequently used when an object updates a single persistent resource that is managed by a resource manager. In order to leave the system in a valid state, the component may be required to participate in a larger transaction.

❑ **Required** – objects created from this class require a transaction. If the caller is enlisted in a transaction, the object will participate in the caller's transaction. Otherwise, COM+ will create a new transaction with the object serving as the root. This is the most common setting for objects that must update, either directly or indirectly, multiple persistent resources in a consistent manner, because it guarantees COM+ will provide transactional support for the object.

❑ **Requires New** – an object created from this class will always serve as the root object of a transaction, regardless of whether or not the object was created within the context of a transaction. Since a new transaction is created for the object, the outcome of the caller's transaction will not affect the outcome of the new transaction, and vice versa. Objects that need to update persistent data managed by resource managers, independent of the outcome of other existing transactions, require a new transaction. For example, an audit of all attempted transactions may be desired, regardless of whether the transaction was committed or aborted. In this scenario, an auditing component that needs to ensure that the auditing database is left in a valid state may require a new transaction.

So we can specify the level of transactional support our components have. The next thing we need to understand is how COM+ helps to ensure that the ACID properties are not violated. The Object Context is fundamental to how COM+ does its job.

Object Context

In a well-written component-based application, COM+ provides every COM+ object with its own **Object Context**. The Object Context serves a variety of functions, but the following are the most important to transaction processing:

❑ Transaction management

❑ Concurrency

❑ Just-In-Time (JIT) activation

We've already come across these in previous chapters, but let's take a closer look at each of these in terms of transactional applications.

The IObjectContext Interface

COM+ provides an interface to some of the Object Context's properties and methods via the appropriately named `ObjectContext` object.

A reference to the `ObjectContext` can be obtained via the `GetObjectContext` function in VB and the `CoGetObjectContext` function in C++. Both functions return the default interface for the `ObjectContext`, in other words `IObjectContext`.

The `IObjectContext` interface was first introduced with MTS 1.0 and is still supported in COM+. This interface includes four methods that allow us to programmatically control the outcome of a transaction.

The following table lists its properties:

Property	Description
Count	Returns the number of properties available to the object.
Item	Retrieves a particular property.
Security	Returns the security object.
ContextInfo	Returns a reference to the `ContextInfo` object, and hence to the transaction, activity, and context information on the current context object.

And the available methods are:

Method	Description
CreateInstance	Deprecated method that is used for creating an instance of an object. Now simply use `CoCreateInstance` or the equivalent (such as `CreateObject` in VB). Included for backward compatibility with MTS.
DisableCommit	Called just before an object is about to modify state in an inconsistent manner.
EnableCommit	Called when an object has modified state in a consistent manner, but the object should not be deactivated unless the transaction has completed.
SetAbort	Called when an object can be deactivated and has modified its state in an inconsistent manner, or an unrecoverable error has occurred.
SetComplete	Called when an object has modified state in a consistent manner and the object can be deactivated.
IsCallerInRoll	Returns whether or not the object's direct caller is in a specified role (either directly or as part of a group).
IsInTransaction	Returns whether or not the object is participating in a transaction.
IsSecurityEnabled	Returns whether or not security is enabled for the object.

There is very little overhead involved in obtaining a reference to the Object Context, therefore the performance gains for retaining a reference for later use are minimal.

For example, the following code snippet shows a completely acceptable way to call the `SetComplete` method in VB:

```
GetObjectContext.SetComplete
```

Casting Your Vote

Each object that participates within a transaction gets an opportunity to vote on its outcome.

Participants in a transaction cast their vote on the outcome of a transaction through its `ObjectContext`. There are two bits that control the outcome of a transaction: `DeactivateOnReturn` and `MyTransactionVote`. These bits are often referred to as the **Done** and **Consistency** bits:

❑ The `DeactivateOnReturn` or Done bit is used by COM+ to determine whether or not to deactivate the object once the method call completes

❑ The `MyTransactionVote` or Consistency bit is used by COM+ to determine whether to commit or abort the transaction

The state of these bits is exposed via the `ObjectContext`'s `IContextState` interface, specifically the `GetDeactivateOnReturn` and `GetMyTransactionVote` methods. The following is a complete list of methods for this interface:

Method	Description
SetDeactivateOnReturn	Sets the value of the `DeactivateOnReturn` or Done bit.
GetDeactivateOnReturn	Returns the value of the `DeactivateOnReturn` or Done bit.
SetMyTransactionVote	Sets the value of the `MyTransactionVote` or Consistency bit.
GetMyTransactionVote	Returns the value of the `MyTransactionVote` or Consistency bit.

We might use these methods something like this. The following VB code will display the state of the two transactional bits in the Immediate Window:

```
Dim objCS              As COMSVCSLib.IContextState
Dim bDeactivateOnReturn As Boolean
Dim myTransactionVote  As COMSVCSLib.tagTransactionVote

' Obtain a reference to the IContextState interface of the ObjectContext.
Set objCS = GetObjectContext()

' Obtain the state of the transaction bits.
objCS.GetDeactivateOnReturn bDeactivateOnReturn
objCS.GetMyTransactionVote myTransactionVote

' Display the current state of the transaction bits.
Debug.Print "DeactivateOnReturn = " & bDeactivateOnReturn

If (myTransactionVote = TxCommit) Then
    Debug.Print "MyTransactionVote = TxCommit"
ElseIf (myTransactionVote = TxAbort) Then
    Debug.Print "MyTransactionVote = TxAbort"
End If
```

In this example, we set up a couple of variables that will tell us the current state of our transaction bits:

❑   MyTransactionVote contains the state of the object's vote to either commit or abort the transaction – the Consistency bit

❑   bDeactivateOnReturn contains the value of the DeactivateOnReturn or Done bit

And we retrieve the values of these variables using the GetDeactivateOnReturn and GetMyTransactionVote methods respectively.

Setting the Transaction Bits

COM+ uses the DeactivateOnReturn bit to determine whether or not to deactivate the object once the method call has completed: if DeactivateOnReturn is set to True, then COM+ will deactivate the object. Unless the object supports pooling (which we discussed in Chapter 6, COM+ Architecture), the object is deactivated by destroying it. We can use the SetDeactivateOnReturn method to change the value of this bit. The initial state of the DeactivateOnReturn bit is False.

MyTransactionVote contains the state of the object's vote to either commit or abort the transaction, and we can use the SetMyTransactionVote method to change the value of this bit. This method accepts one of two values in the tagTransactionVote enumeration – TxAbort and TxCommit – where the initial state of the MyTransactionVote bit is TxCommit. When the transaction completes, COM+ will tally all of the votes, and either commit or abort the transactions based upon all of the votes received.

We can also use the methods provided by the IObjectContext interface to set the MyTransactionVote and DeactivateOnReturn bits. The methods we're most interested in are SetAbort, SetComplete, EnableCommit, and DisableCommit. These methods allow us to alter both bits with a single method call.

The following table shows how the methods for modifying the transactional bits relate to the IObjectContext and IContextState interfaces:

	DisableCommit	EnableCommit	SetAbort	SetComplete
MyTransactionVote	TxAbort	TxCommit	TxAbort	TxCommit
DeactivateOnReturn	False	False	True	True

For example, in its initial state an object has MyTransactionVote set to TxCommit and DeactivateOnReturn set to False – which is equivalent to calling the EnableCommit method. Calling SetAbort indicates that something has gone wrong, so we want COM+ to deactivate the object and abort the transaction, and so forth.

Using Transaction Bits to Ensure the ACID Properties

It's important to realize that if the transaction bits are not altered from the initial state through the course of a method call, and no other step in the transaction voted to abort the transaction, any changes made during the course of the method call will be committed. This could be a problem if your error handling has a code path where the MyTransactionVote bit is not changed to TxAbort. Therefore, it's good practice to call DisableCommit or its equivalent at the beginning of the method call, alter persistent state, and then call SetAbort or EnableCommit when complete.

At the very least, you should call `DisableCommit` or its equivalent before updating persistent data in such a way as to leave the system in an invalid state. For example, say a particular method call is responsible for creating a customer record. When a customer record is created, it must be added to both the sales force automation (SFA) system and the billing system. `DisableCommit` or its equivalent should be called before attempting to add the new customer record to the SFA application and billing system. Doing so would help ensure that the transaction was properly aborted in the event that an error occurred updating one of the two systems. Say `DisableCommit` was not called, and the SFA application was successfully updated, but there was an error updating the billing system. If a code path exists in the error handling code where the `MyTransactionVote` bit is not set to `TxAbort`, then the transaction may commit, leaving the system in an invalid state.

Concurrency

In a multi-user, component-based COM+ application there is going to be concurrent processing on behalf of your users. If it's not managed, concurrency can be the death of transaction processing systems.

As we've already seen, resource managers often use locks to ensure that transactions are isolated (the I in ACID). Two potential side-effects of locking are reduced throughput of the system, and a condition known as deadlock. In this section, we'll see how COM+ manages concurrency issues through an abstraction called activities and the just-in-time (JIT) activation feature.

Activities

> **An** activity **is a single logical thread of execution that flows through a collection of distributed COM+ objects.**

A **single** thread of execution implies that only one object in an activity is running at a time. A collection of **distributed** COM+ objects implies that an activity can flow across machine or process boundaries. The activity starts when a client creates a COM+ object that requires synchronization and then flows through any child objects created by the original object.

To demonstrate activities, we'll use the following VB code to implement the class `testTransactions.CTest`. We'll write a couple of clients that utilize the `CTest` class to illustrate an activity, and we'll modify CTest's transaction support property to test the resulting behavior.

The code for our `CTest` module is as follows:

```
Option Explicit

'**********************************************
'* Class: CTest
'**********************************************

Private m_objChild As CTest


Public Property Get contextID() As String
    contextID = GetObjectContext().ContextInfo.GetContextId
End Property


Public Property Get activityID() As String
    activityID = GetObjectContext().ContextInfo.GetActivityId
End Property
```

```
Public Property Get transactionID() As String
    If (GetObjectContext().isInTransaction) Then
        transactionID = GetObjectContext().ContextInfo.GetTransactionId
    Else
        transactionID = "Object not in transaction."
    End If
End Property
```

```
Public Sub CreateChild(Optional strMachineName As String = "")
    If (strMachineName <> "") Then
        Set m_objChild = CreateObject ("testTransactions.CTest", _
                                    strMachineName)
    Else
        Set m_objChild = CreateObject("testTransactions.CTest")
    End If
End Sub
```

```
Public Property Get child() As CTest
    Set child = m_objChild
End Property
```

This code just uses methods of the `ContextInfo` object to get identifiers for the current object's context, activity and transaction. It also contains the functionality to create a child object of the root object (we'll come back to the various ways we can create interior objects later in this chapter).

Next, we'll create our client application, which creates a root object and an interior object, and displays each object's context information:

```
Dim objTest As Object

Set objTest = CreateObject("testTransactions.CTest")

Debug.Print "Root Object:"
Debug.Print vbTab & "Context ID     = " & objTest.contextID
Debug.Print vbTab & "Activity ID    = " & objTest.activityID
Debug.Print vbTab & "Transaction ID = " & objTest.transactionID
Debug.Print

objTest.CreateChild
Debug.Print "Child Object:"
Debug.Print vbTab & "Context ID     = " & objTest.child.contextID
Debug.Print vbTab & "Activity ID    = " & objTest.child.activityID
Debug.Print vbTab & "Transaction ID = " & objTest.child.transactionID
```

With `CTest`'s transaction support property set to **Required**, the client code produces something like the following output in the Immediate Window:

```
Root Object:
    Context ID     = {A54C4BBE-8361-479E-AE86-99D65F294E98}
    Activity ID    = {156882FC-7B54-414E-8EE7-90E1A8FDB89A}
    Transaction ID = {7A535BE1-E3A4-41AB-ADCB-48129F80948B}

Child Object:
    Context ID     = {12D4F591-C436-4564-BCE7-F75308A624EA}
    Activity ID    = {156882FC-7B54-414E-8EE7-90E1A8FDB89A}
    Transaction ID = {7A535BE1-E3A4-41AB-ADCB-48129F80948B}
```

As you might have expected, the root and the child objects reside within their own context, and they both reside within the same activity and transaction.

Now if we adjust the transaction property to **Requires New**, and rerun the client code, we'll produce something similar to the following output in the Immediate Window:

```
Root Object:
    Context ID    = {A7488D30-D0BA-439D-B8ED-3E25098819C0}
    Activity ID   = {1267FFEF-493D-4FFF-BBD4-48226D0C817F}
    Transaction ID = {59955773-C75D-4412-A002-AA83075D0E71}

Child Object:
    Context ID    = {71C027F1-448A-4DA7-A5ED-703180517C6D}
    Activity ID   = {1267FFEF-493D-4FFF-BBD4-48226D0C817F}
    Transaction ID = {3C643012-A7AA-4C54-926E-577E3F713183}
```

Notice that each object not only has its own context, but also has its own transaction. However, both objects still reside in the same activity.

Next we'll modify the transaction property back to **Required**, and then modify the line in the client code so that the child object is created on another machine:

```
Dim objTest As Object

Set objTest = CreateObject("testTransactions.CTest")

Debug.Print "Root Object:"
Debug.Print vbTab & "Context ID    = " & objTest.contextID
Debug.Print vbTab & "Activity ID   = " & objTest.activityID
Debug.Print vbTab & "Transaction ID = " & objTest.transactionID
Debug.Print

ObjTest.CreateChild "LABSERVER2"
Debug.Print "Child Object:"
Debug.Print vbTab & "Context ID    = " & objTest.child.contextID
Debug.Print vbTab & "Activity ID   = " & objTest.child.activityID
Debug.Print vbTab & "Transaction ID = " & objTest.child.transactionID
```

The modified client code produces the following output in the Immediate Window:

```
Root Object:
    Context ID    = {289C0A45-3499-4C76-ADAF-AD56E1CFED04}
    Activity ID   = {A3C79A20-5C03-41D5-9BE6-2FB87C7108DB}
    Transaction ID = {B171FCA3-1661-4EDF-8585-3110F7684990}

Child Object:
    Context ID    = {67C334A7-3D26-4448-AA48-5492A98F0DE6}
    Activity ID   = {A3C79A20-5C03-41D5-9BE6-2FB87C7108DB}
    Transaction ID = {B171FCA3-1661-4EDF-8585-3110F7684990}
```

Notice that both the transaction and the activity flowed to the second machine, LABSERVER2. This is evident from the fact that the root and the child share the same activity and transaction ID. The logical thread of execution and the transaction boundaries now span across two machines.

Deadlocking

Deadlocking can occur when a single thread of execution attempts to acquire a resource that it already has locked. Recall that most resource managers utilize locking as a means to achieve isolation. Let's take a look at a potential single thread deadlocking scenario, shown in the figure below:

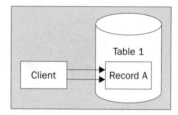

A transactional thread of execution modifies Record A in Table 1, and places a read/write lock on that record until the transaction completes, to enforce the isolation property. It then attempts to obtain all of the records in Table 1: but the thread cannot obtain all of the records in Table 1, since it must wait until the read/write lock is released for the modified record. This lock will not be released until the transaction completes, and since the transaction won't complete until all of the records are obtained, the thread deadlocks as a result.

Most modern databases can recognize and resolve deadlock situations that occur within the context of a single database connection (most databases will rollback one transaction after a certain period of time has passed in a deadlock situation). However, what if the root object modifies the record in Table 1, and an interior object attempts to obtain all of the records in Table 1 using a separate database connection?

Activities play an important role in avoiding this type of deadlock. The DTC is responsible for recognizing when the same activity tries to acquire resources from the same resource manager, and will request that the resource manager compensate accordingly, usually by allowing one of the connections to override the locks established by the other connection. Note that this doesn't violate the isolated property, since both connections are within the context of the same transaction.

A second type of deadlock occurs when two transactional threads of execution stall because they are competing for the same resources. An example of this is shown in the figure below. Client 1 creates a lock on Table 1, and Client 2 creates a lock on Table 2. Then they both try to obtain resources that the other already has locked:

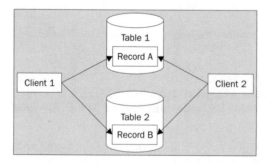

These types of deadlock situation are usually resolved with at least one transaction timing out, and therefore aborting.

The default timeout for a transaction is 60 seconds, but this value can be altered in the Component Services MMC. Right-click on the computer icon, select Properties, and then select the Options tab. The timeout value can also be overridden at the class level by right-clicking on a particular class, and then selecting the Transactions tab.

Isolation

As we have learned, the isolation property of a transaction ensures that uncommitted changes to the state of a system are hidden from other concurrent transactions. Isolation is typically achieved by using locks to serialize access to the data.

Serialization guarantees data integrity within the system, but on the down side, serialization can reduce the overall throughput of the system. For example, as the number of concurrent transactions requiring serialized access the same data increases, the throughput of the system decreases.

The ANSI SQL 2 standard published by the ANSI SQL Committee defines four isolation levels, and each of these levels is defined according to which of three violations of serialization they permit. The three phenomena in which serialization can be violated are:

❑ **P1 – Dirty Read** – Say transaction 1 (T1) modifies a row. Transaction 2 (T2) then reads the row before T1 completes. If T1 performs a rollback, then T2 has seen a row that never really existed.

❑ **P2 – Non-repeatable Read** – Say T1 retrieves a row, and then T2 updates that row. If T1 retrieves the same row again, then T1 has retrieved the same row twice, but has seen two different values for it.

❑ **P3 – Phantoms** – Say T1 reads a set of rows that satisfy certain search conditions. T2 then inserts one or more rows that satisfy the same search conditions. If T1 repeats the read, it will see rows that did not exist previously – "phantoms".

The four isolation levels are then defined as follows:

❑ **READ_UNCOMMITTED** – Permits P1, P2, and P3: the lowest level of isolation, where transactions are isolated just enough to ensure that physically corrupt data is not read. Transactions of this type are typically read-only.

❑ **READ_COMMITTED** – Permits P2 and P3, but does not permit P1. This is usually the default isolation level for databases like SQL Server.

❑ **REPEATABLE_READ** – Permits P3, but does not permit P1 and P2.

❑ **SERIALIZABLE** – Does not permit P1, P2, or P3: the highest level of isolation, where transactions are completely isolated from one another. This is the default isolation level for COM+ 1.0.

OLE Transactions, the default transaction protocol of the DTC, has always supported different isolation levels. However, COM+ 1.0 only supports serializable, the most conservative isolation level. The next version of COM+, scheduled to ship with Whistler, will allow us to configure the lowest level of isolation supported by the component. The root object will determine the isolation level required for the transaction, and interior objects must support the same isolation level or lower. COM+ will deny requests to create interior objects that require a higher isolation level than the root object.

Allowing certain transactions to run under a lower isolation level can help improve the overall scalability of the application. However, the lower the isolation level, the higher the potential is for incorrect data. When determining the isolation level of a transaction, it's better to err on the safe side, and select a high level of isolation. Setting the isolation level to anything other than serializable should be a very deliberate and conscientious decision.

You should also avoid modifying the isolation level within the implementation of the COM+ object. For example, avoid modifying the isolation level for a SQL Server connection by calling the T-SQL command SET TRANSACTION ISOLATION LEVEL. Instead, place the code that requires different isolation levels in separate classes, and configure the isolation level in COM+ for each class. If you need to create a class where its methods support various isolation levels, consider creating an interface class. The interface class itself would be configured to not support transactions: the actual implementation of the methods would be deferred to classes configured for the required isolation level.

Just-In-Time Activation

Since the root object has ultimate control over the lifetime of the transaction, it is important that COM+ deactivates the root object as soon and as often as possible throughout the object's lifetime, ideally at the end of each method call. Otherwise, the transaction may live longer than intended, potentially decreasing the throughput of your application and increasing the probability of deadlock situations. This is the reasoning behind Just-In-Time (JIT) Activation.

We met JIT activation in our earlier COM+ chapters.

Building Transactional Applications Using VB 6.0

In this section, we'll explore how to build transactional component-based applications using Visual Basic 6.0. Specifically, we'll learn how to set the default transactional attribute for a VB class. We'll also examine one of the idiosyncrasies of VB, and its potential effect on the outcome of a transaction. Finally, we'll learn how to create a Compensating Resource Manager component.

Transactional Support for VB 6.0 Classes

VB 6.0 introduced integrated support for building transactional MTS/COM+ components. In addition, it implemented one of the new properties associated with classes created in ActiveX DLL projects: MTSTransactionMode. This property allows us to declare whether the component is COM+ aware and, if it is, whether or not the component requires transactional support.

We can set the `MTSTransactionMode` property by selecting a particular class, and then modifying the `MTSTransactionMode` property in the Properties window, as shown:

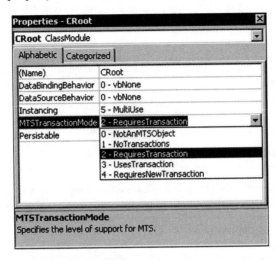

The `MTSTransactionMode` property can be set to one of five values, which correspond to the transaction support properties we saw earlier:

MTSTransactionMode	COM+ Transaction Support
0 – NotAnMTSObject	Not Supported
1 – NoTransactions	Disabled
2 – RequiresTransaction	Required
3 – UsesTransaction	Supported
4 – RequiresNewTransaction	Requires New

The `MTSTransactionMode` property is used to determine the initial COM+ transaction support property setting for a particular VB class.

This property is stored in the component's type library, and is only referenced by COM+ to set the transaction support property when the component is installed into a COM+ application. Below is the IDL – the textual representation of the type library– for the `CRoot` class that was reverse-engineered using the OLE/COM Object Viewer (see Chapter 3 for more information on the type library and IDL):

```
[
  uuid(2993189E-98AE-4B54-B46A-2312C174D325),
  version(1.0),
    custom({17093CC5-9BD2-11CF-AA4F-304BF89C0001}, "0")
]
coclass CRoot {
    [default] interface _CRoot;
};
```

As you can see, there is a custom property associated with the class. When a new COM+ component is being installed, COM+ will read the type library and set the transactional support property based on the custom property. We can then look up the transactional support type for the specified custom property in MTXATTR.H, or use the following table:

IDL Transactional Support Type Definition	Custom IDL Property
TRANSACTION_REQUIRED	17093CC5-9BD2-11CF-AA4F-304BF89C0001
TRANSACTION_NOT_SUPPORTED	17093CC6-9BD2-11CF-AA4F-304BF89C0001
TRANSACTION_REQUIRES_NEW	17093CC7-9BD2-11CF-AA4F-304BF89C0001
TRANSACTION_SUPPORTED	17093CC8-9BD2-11CF-AA4F-304BF89C0001

When the component is installed, COM+ will examine the component's type library and set the initial transaction setting accordingly. Note that in order for COM+ to act upon the transactional support properties defined in a component's type library, you must choose the Install new component(s) button in the COM Component Install Wizard:

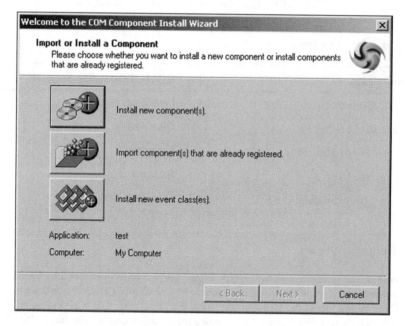

Creating Interior COM+ Objects in VB

VB programmers have the ability to create interior COM+ objects in a variety of different ways:

❑ Using the CreateObject method

❑ Using the New operator

❑ Using the ObjectContext.CreateInstance method

Prior to COM+, the preferred method for creating interior MTS objects was via the `ObjectContext.CreateInstance` method. This was the only way to create objects within the same activity as the root object. Now that MTS and COM have been integrated into COM+ that's no longer the case, and `CreateObject` is the preferred method.

The VB `New` operator reacts differently depending on how it is used. When the `New` operator is used to create an object from another DLL, it instantiates the object in a similar fashion to `CreateObject`. However, if the class for the requested object resides within the same DLL as the client, the implementation of the `New` operator bypasses COM+ altogether. The problem is that the child object resides within the same Object Context as the parent object.

To demonstrate this, we'll add a new method to the `CTest` class we used earlier in the Activities section. The `CreateChildUsingNew` method creates a child using the `New` keyword instead of `CreateObject`. Let's take a look at the changes to the code (the highlighted text):

```
Option Explicit

'*******************************************
'* Class: CTest
'*******************************************

Private m_objChild As CTest

Public Property Get contextID() As String
    contextID = GetObjectContext().ContextInfo.GetContextId
End Property

Public Property Get activityID() As String
    activityID = GetObjectContext().ContextInfo.GetActivityId
End Property

Public Property Get transactionID() As String
    If (GetObjectContext().IsInTransaction) Then
        transactionID = GetObjectContext().ContextInfo.GetTransactionId
    Else
        transactionID = "Object not in transaction."
    End If
End Property

Public Sub CreateChild(Optional strMachineName As String = "")
    If (strMachineName <> "") Then
        Set m_objChild = CreateObject("testTransactions.CTest", _
                                      strMachineName)
    Else
        Set m_objChild = CreateObject("testTransactions.CTest")
    End If
End Sub

Public Sub CreateChildUsingNew()
    Set m_objChild = New CTest
End Sub

Public Property Get child() As CTest
    Set child = m_objChild
End Property
```

We'll now create a client to test the difference between using the New operator and calling CreateObject. The following code generates two message boxes that display the context ID for the root object and its interior object:

```
Dim objTest As Object

' Initialize
Set objTest = CreateObject("testTransactions.CTest")

' Create child using CreateObject.
objTest.CreateChild
MsgBox "Root object context ID = " & objTest.contextID & vbCrLf _
    & "Interior object context ID = " & objTest.child.contextID, vbOKOnly, _
        "CreateObject"

' Create child using the New operator.
objTest.CreateChildUsingNew
MsgBox "Root object context ID = " & objTest.contextID & vbCrLf _
    & "Interior object context ID = " & objTest.child.contextID, vbOKOnly, _
        "CreateObject"
```

The first message box displays the context ID for an interior object created with CreateObject, and the second message box displays the context ID for an interior object created with the New operator.

The code above will produce a first message box similar to the one shown below:

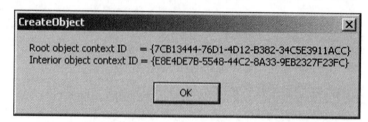

Notice that root and its interior object each have their own Object Context, as shown by the context IDs.

The second message box will be similar to this:

As you can see, the context IDs are the same for both the root and child object. So why is this a problem? Since the root and interior object share the same Object Context, they also share the same transaction bits. This is a problem because one object has the ability to override the other's vote without their knowledge.

Take a look at the following VB code:

```
'*****************************************
'* Client Code
'*****************************************
Dim objRoot As New CRoot

objRoot.DoSomething
```

```
'*****************************************
'* Class: CRoot
'*****************************************
Public Function DoSomething()
    Dim objInterior As New CInterior

    objInterior.DoSomethingElse

    GetObjectContext.SetComplete
End Function
```

```
'*****************************************
'* Class: CInterior
'*****************************************
Public Function DoSomethingElse()
    GetObjectContext.SetAbort
End Function
```

Here, the problem is that even though the DoSomethingElse method voted to abort the transaction, the transaction will still commit – objInterior voted to abort the transaction, but objRoot overrode the vote since they share the same Object Context. It's the equivalent of having a voting booth with one ballot and a pencil. The last person to vote determines the outcome of the election … not what you want to have happen.

The solution is to rewrite CRoot so that it creates objInterior by using either IObjectContext.CreateInstance or CreateObject. For example:

```
'*****************************************
'* Class: CRoot
'*****************************************
Public Function DoSomething()
    Dim objInterior as CInterior

    Set objInterior = CreateObject("testTransactions.CInterior")


    objInterior.DoSomethingElse

    GetObjectContext.SetComplete
End Function
```

Remember, since IObjectContext.CreateInstance is deprecated, CreateObject is the preferred method.

The Compensating Resource Manager

As we mentioned earlier, the Compensating Resource Manager (CRM) provides a framework that allows us to integrate a persistent resource within the context of a transaction. We're going to walk through the steps required to create a CRM in VB. Our sample CRM will be used to create and delete directories within the context of a transaction.

Recall that in order to implement a CRM, we need to create two classes:

❑ The **CRM Worker** is responsible for performing the actual work on behalf of the user

❑ The **CRM Compensator** is responsible for ensuring that the changes made to the persistent resource were properly committed or aborted

CRM Worker

Our Worker is responsible for creating and deleting the directories within the file system. We'll need to create a VB class with two methods: `Create` and `Delete`.

In a moment, we'll step through the implementation of the `Create` method on the `CDirectory` class. But first, lets take a look at the complete code for this method:

```
Public Sub Create(ByVal strDirPath As String)

    On Error GoTo ErrorHandler

    Dim objFS               As Scripting.FileSystemObject
    Dim strDirName          As String
    Dim objCRMLogCtl        As COMSVCSLib.ICrmLogControl
    Dim aRecord(2)          As Variant
    Dim lErrNumber          As Long
    Dim strMyActivityID     As String
    Dim strLocksActivityID  As String
    Dim bAquiredLock        As Boolean
    Dim strCompProgID       As String
    Dim strCompDesc         As String

    ' Initialize.
    Set objFS = New Scripting.FileSystemObject
    Set objCRMLogCtl = New COMSVCSLib.CRMClerk
    strDirName = objFS.GetFolder(strDirPath).Name
    strCompProgID = "FileSystemCRM.CDirectoryCompensator"
    strCompDesc = "The compensator for CDirectory."
    strMyActivityID = GetObjectContext().ContextInfo.GetActivityId
    bAquiredLock = False

    ' Strip the trailing backslash off of the directory path.
    If (Right(strDirPath, 1) = "\") Then _
        strDirPath = Left(strDirPath, Len(strDirPath) - 1)

    ' Register compensator
    On Error Resume Next
    Do
```

```
            objCRMLogCtl.RegisterCompensator strCompProgID, strCompDesc,_
                    COMSVCSLib.CRMREGFLAG_ALLPHASES
        lErrNumber = Err.Number
    Loop While (lErrNumber = XACT_E_RECOVERYINPROGRESS)

    On Error GoTo ErrorHandler

    If (lErrNumber <> 0) Then _
        Err.Raise vbObjectError + 1, "RegisterCompensator", _
        "Could not register the compensator component " & _
        "(err=" & lErrNumber & ")."

    ' Obtain lock for folder.
    On Error Resume Next
    Do While (bAquiredLock)
        ' Loop until lock is freed.
        Do
            If (objFS.FileExists(strDirPath & "\..\" & strDirName & _
            "_lock.txt")) Then _
                strLocksActivityID = objFS.GetFile(strDirPath & "\..\" & _
                strDirName & "_lock.txt").OpenAsTextStream.ReadLine
        Loop While (strLocksActivityID = "" Or _
                strMyActivityID <> Trim(strLocksActivityID))

        ' If not locked by my activity, attempt to obtain lock.
        If (strLocksActivityID = "") Then
            objFS.CreateTextFile(strDirPath & "\..\" & strDirName & _
                "_lock.txt", False)._
                WriteLine GetObjectContext.ContextInfo.GetActivityId
            If (Err = 0) Then bAquiredLock = True
        Else
            bAquiredLock = True
        End If
    Loop

    ' Write event information to the CRM log.
    aRecord(0) = tagDirCommands.DIRDELETE
    aRecord(1) = strDirPath
    objCRMLogCtl.WriteLogRecordVariants aRecord
    objCRMLogCtl.ForceLog

    ' Perform the action in and attempt to isolate the new directory from
    ' other clients.
    objFS.CreateFolder strDirPath
    objFS.GetFolder(strDirPath).Attributes = _
        objFS.GetFolder(strDirPath).Attributes + Hidden

    ' Clean up.
    Set objFS = Nothing
    Set objCRMLogCtl = Nothing

    Exit Sub

ErrorHandler:
    Err.Raise vbObjectError + 1, "Delete", "Error deleting directory: " & _
            Err.Source & " (err=" & Err.Number & "): " & Err.Description

End Sub
```

After performing some initialization, the first thing we must do is to register the Compensator that will be used during the two-phase commit portion of the transaction. We can register the Compensator via the `RegisterCompensator` method of the `ICrmLogControl` interface for the `CRMClerk` object.

In our initialize section, we obtain a `CRMClerk` object and cast it to the `ICrmLogControl` interface:

```
Dim objCRMLogCtl          As COMSVCSLib.ICrmLogControl
...
    ' Initialize.
    Set objFS = New Scripting.FileSystemObject
    Set objCRMLogCtl = New COMSVCSLib.CRMClerk
```

The `RegisterCompensator` method will return an error if there is a recovery currently in progress. When this occurs, the SDK documentation advises you to retry until the Compensator is registered. Unfortunately, the CRM framework does not provide a way for the method call to block while the recovery is in progress, so we have little choice but to enter into a spin lock instead:

```
    ' Register compensator
    On Error Resume Next
    Do
        objCRMLogCtl.RegisterCompensator strCompProgID, strCompDesc, _
                    COMSVCSLib.CRMREGFLAG_ALLPHASES
        lErrNumber = Err.Number
    Loop While (lErrNumber = XACT_E_RECOVERYINPROGRESS)

    On Error GoTo ErrorHandler
    If (lErrNumber <> 0) Then _
        Err.Raise vbObjectError + 1, "RegisterCompensator", _
        "Could not register the compensator component " & _
        "(err=" & lErrNumber & ")."
```

Note that we need to define the error number `XACT_E_RECOVERYINPROGRESS` in the declarations section of our class:

```
    Private Const XACT_E_RECOVERYINPROGRESS = -2147799170#
```

Next, we need to enforce serialized access to resources participating in a transaction. We do this by implementing a lock file for the directory – a text file that resides within the subdirectory's parent directory. The naming convention we use for the file is the name of the subdirectory followed by `_lock.txt`.

The file contains one line of text, which stores the activity ID that owns the lock. It's important to note that the lock is owned by the activity, and not by any one process. This is to help avoid an activity deadlocking on itself. In order to obtain the lock, we implement a simple spin lock, and we'll remain in the spin lock until our activity acquires the lock or the transaction times out:

```
    ' Obtain lock for folder.
    On Error Resume Next
    Do While (bAquiredLock)
        ' Loop until lock is freed.
        Do
```

```
        If (objFS.FileExists(strDirPath & "\..\" & strDirName & _
            "_lock.txt")) Then _
                strLocksActivityID = objFS.GetFile(strDirPath & "\..\" & _
                strDirName & "_lock.txt").OpenAsTextStream.ReadLine
    Loop While (strLocksActivityID = "" Or _
                strMyActivityID <> Trim(strLocksActivityID))

    ' If not locked by my activity, attempt to obtain lock.
    If (strLocksActivityID = "") Then
        objFS.CreateTextFile(strDirPath & "\..\" & strDirName & _
            "_lock.txt", False)._
            WriteLine GetObjectContext.ContextInfo.GetActivityId
        If (Err = 0) Then bAquiredLock = True
    Else
        bAquiredLock = True
    End If
Loop
```

One important point is that our locking mechanism is only valid for clients manipulating directories via our CRM. Clients accessing the directory directly can easily bypass our locking mechanism. One solution would be to secure the directory and its contents by modifying the permissions on the directory.

Once we've registered the Compensator and have obtained a lock on the required resource, we can write records to the CRM persistent log by calling the `WriteLogRecordVariants` method. The persistent log is used to document what actions were performed over the course of a transaction, and the Worker must write to the logs before performing an action. This is necessary in case a crash occurs while the action is being performed, because the Compensator would require this information to bring the system back to a consistent state.

We must represent the record as a variant array of simple variant data types. In our case, the first element represents the command being executed, and the second element contains the path for the final destination of the directory. Finally, we call the `ForceLog` method to force the record to be written to disk. For efficiency, the `WriteLogRecordVariants` method performs a lazy write to the log, and is not flushed to disk until the `ForceLog` method is called:

```
' Write event information to the CRM log.
aRecord(0) = tagDirCommands.DIRDELETE
aRecord(1) = strDirPath
objCRMLogCtl.WriteLogRecordVariants aRecord
objCRMLogCtl.ForceLog
```

Finally, we perform the action on the persistent resource. In this case, we add the requested directory:

```
' Perform the action in and attempt to isolate the new directory from
' other clients.
objFS.CreateFolder strDirPath
objFS.GetFolder(strDirPath).Attributes = _
    objFS.GetFolder(strDirPath).Attributes + Hidden
```

Note that we lock the directory before we create it to prevent a potential race condition. We also hide the directory after it has been created in an attempt to isolate this change from other clients.

The `Delete` method of our class is similar to the `Create` method. The first major differences is that we need an extra section of initialization, to ensure that the directory we're trying to delete actually exists:

```
Public Sub Delete(ByVal strDirPath As String)

    On Error GoTo ErrorHandler

    Dim objFS              As Scripting.FileSystemObject

...

    Dim strCompDesc        As String

        ' Initial validation.
        If (Not objFS.FolderExists(strDirPath)) Then _
            Err.Raise vbObjectError + 1, "FolderExists", _
            "Directory does not exist."
```

And we also don't need any code to perform the action, as we're going to defer the actual delete to the Compensator:

```
' Write event information to the CRM log.
    aRecord(0) = tagDirCommands.DIRDELETE
    aRecord(1) = strDirPath
    objCRMLogCtl.WriteLogRecordVariants aRecord
    objCRMLogCtl.ForceLog

        ' Perform the action.
        ' Nothing to do.

        ' Clean up.
    Set objFS = Nothing
    Set objCRMLogCtl = Nothing
```

The complete code for this class is available for download from the Wrox web site at `http://www.wrox.com`.

CRM Compensator

The compensator for `CDirectory` is `CDirectoryCompensator`. It's responsible for committing or aborting the actions performed by the `CDirectory` methods, `Create` and `Delete`. We will step through the implementation of the `CDirectoryCompensator` class. But first, let's take a look at the complete code:

```
Option Explicit

' Class:     CDirectoryCompensator

Implements COMSVCSLib.ICrmCompensatorVariants

Public Enum tagDirCommands
    DIRCREATE = 0
    DIRDELETE = 1
```

```
End Enum

Private m_bCommitTX            As Boolean
Private m_objDirsToBeUnlocked  As Scripting.Dictionary

Private Sub ICrmCompensatorVariants_SetLogControlVariants _
        (ByVal pLogControl As COMSVCSLib.ICrmLogControl)

    ' First method called when compensator is created.
    ' Used to obtain the ICrmLogControl interface, if needed.

End Sub

Private Sub ICrmCompensatorVariants_BeginPrepareVariants()

    ' Used to receive notification when prepare phase is beginnng.
    ' Note that prepare phase is skipped during recovery.
    m_bCommitTX = True

End Sub

Private Function ICrmCompensatorVariants_PrepareRecordVariants _
            (pLogRecord As Variant) As Boolean

    Dim lCommand      As Long
    Dim strDirPath  As String

    ' Initialize.
    lCommand = pLogRecord(0)
    strDirPath = pLogRecord(1)

    ' If in debug mode, display the CRM flags and sequence number
    ' appended to the end of the array.
    #If DEBUGGING Then
        Debug.Print "CRM flags  = " & pLogRecord(UBound(pLogRecord) - 1)
        Debug.Print "Sequence # = " & pLogRecord(UBound(pLogRecord))
    #End If

    ' See if we received a valid record.
    If (m_bCommitTX = False) Then
        ' Do nothing.  No need to continue validating if we are not going
        ' to commit the transaction.
    ElseIf (lCommand = tagDirCommands.DIRCREATE And strDirPath <> "") Then
        ' Do nothing.
    ElseIf (lCommand = tagDirCommands.DIRDELETE And strDirPath <> "") Then
        ' Do nothing.
    Else
        m_bCommitTX = False
    End If

    ' We don't want to forget this record.
    ICrmCompensatorVariants_PrepareRecordVariants = False

End Function
```

```
Private Function ICrmCompensatorVariants_EndPrepareVariants() As Boolean

    ' Return whether or not prepare phase completed successfully
    ' and it is OK to commit transaction.
    ICrmCompensatorVariants_EndPrepareVariants = m_bCommitTX

End Function
```

```
Private Sub ICrmCompensatorVariants_BeginCommitVariants _
        (ByVal bRecovery As Boolean)

    ' Don't need to perform any initialization nor care whether this
    ' is a recovery.

End Sub
```

```
Private Function ICrmCompensatorVariants_CommitRecordVariants _
            (pLogRecord As Variant) As Boolean

    Dim objFS          As Scripting.FileSystemObject
    Dim lCommand       As Long
    Dim strDirPath     As String

    ' Initialize.
    Set objFS = New Scripting.FileSystemObject
    lCommand = pLogRecord(0)
    strDirPath = pLogRecord(1)

    Select Case lCommand
        Case tagDirCommands.DIRCREATE

            ' Unhide directory and then add it to the list of locks
            ' to be removed.
            If (objFS.FolderExists(strDirPath)) Then
                objFS.GetFolder(strDirPath).Attributes = _
                    objFS.GetFolder(strDirPath).Attributes - Hidden
                If (Not m_objDirsToBeUnlocked.Exists(strDirPath)) Then _
                    m_objDirsToBeUnlocked.Add strDirPath, "unlock"
            End If
        Case tagDirCommands.DIRDELETE
            If (objFS.FolderExists(strDirPath)) Then
                ' Delete folder and then add it to the list of locks
                ' to be removed.
                objFS.DeleteFolder strDirPath
                If (Not m_objDirsToBeUnlocked.Exists(strDirPath)) Then _
                    m_objDirsToBeUnlocked.Add strDirPath, "unlock"
            End If
    End Select

    ' We don't want to forget this record.
    ICrmCompensatorVariants_CommitRecordVariants = False

End Function
```

```
Private Sub ICrmCompensatorVariants_EndCommitVariants()

    Dim varLock     As Variant
    Dim objFS       As Scripting.FileSystemObject
    Dim strDirName  As String

    ' Remove lock(s) from directory(s).
    For Each varLock In m_objDirsToBeUnlocked
        strDirName = objFS.GetFolder(varLock).Name
        objFS.DeleteFile varLock & "\..\" & strDirName & "_lock.txt"
    Next

End Sub
```

```
Private Sub ICrmCompensatorVariants_BeginAbortVariants(ByVal bRecovery As Boolean)

    ' Don't need to perform any initialization nor care whether
    ' this is a recovery.

End Sub
```

```
Private Function ICrmCompensatorVariants_AbortRecordVariants _
            (pLogRecord As Variant) As Boolean

    Dim objFS           As Scripting.FileSystemObject
    Dim lCommand        As Long
    Dim strDirPath      As String

    ' Initialize.
    Set objFS = New Scripting.FileSystemObject
    lCommand = pLogRecord(0)
    strDirPath = pLogRecord(1)

    Select Case lCommand
        Case tagDirCommands.DIRCREATE
            If (objFS.FolderExists(strDirPath)) Then
                ' Delete folder and then add it to the list of locks
                ' to be removed.
                objFS.DeleteFolder strDirPath
                If (Not m_objDirsToBeUnlocked.Exists(strDirPath)) Then _
                    m_objDirsToBeUnlocked.Add strDirPath, "unlock"
            End If
        Case tagDirCommands.DIRDELETE
            If (objFS.FolderExists(strDirPath)) Then
                ' Add directory to the list of locks to be removed.
                objFS.DeleteFolder strDirPath
                If (Not m_objDirsToBeUnlocked.Exists(strDirPath)) Then _
                    m_objDirsToBeUnlocked.Add strDirPath, "unlock"
            End If
    End Select

End Function
```

```
Private Sub ICrmCompensatorVariants_EndAbortVariants()

    Dim varLock       As Variant
    Dim objFS         As Scripting.FileSystemObject
    Dim strDirName    As String

    ' Remove lock(s) from directory(s).
    For Each varLock In m_objDirsToBeUnlocked
        strDirName = objFS.GetFolder(varLock).Name
        objFS.DeleteFile varLock & "\..\" & strDirName & "_lock.txt"
    Next

End Sub
```

During the prepare phase, the Compensator is responsible for ensuring that changes made to the persistent store can be committed. In order to facilitate this, the compensator is passed each log entry written by the Worker. The Compensator's `PrepareRecordVariants` method is called for each of these log entries. Our implementation validates each record to ensure that we can commit the transaction. Also notice that the CRM framework appends the CRM flags and the sequence number at the end of the array. The CRM flags provide information about when the record was written and whether this record was forgotten at some point. Finally, we indicate that we don't want this record to be forgotten and effectively removed from the log, by setting the return parameter to `True`:

```
Private Function ICrmCompensatorVariants_PrepareRecordVariants _
            (pLogRecord As Variant) As Boolean

    Dim lCommand       As Long
    Dim strDirPath    As String

    ' Initialize.
    lCommand = pLogRecord(0)
    strDirPath = pLogRecord(1)

    ' If in debug mode, display the CRM flags and sequence number
    ' appended to the end of the array.
    #If DEBUGGING Then
        Debug.Print "CRM flags  = " & pLogRecord(UBound(pLogRecord) - 1)
        Debug.Print "Sequence # = " & pLogRecord(UBound(pLogRecord))
    #End If

    ' See if we received a valid record.
    If (m_bCommitTX = False) Then
        ' Do nothing.  No need to continue validating if we are not going
        ' to commit the transaction.
    ElseIf (lCommand = tagDirCommands.DIRCREATE And strDirPath <> "") Then
        ' Do nothing.
    ElseIf (lCommand = tagDirCommands.DIRDELETE And strDirPath <> "") Then
        ' Do nothing.
    Else
        m_bCommitTX = False
    End If

    ' We don't want to forget this record.
    ICrmCompensatorVariants_PrepareRecordVariants = False

End Function
```

The Compensator informs the DTC as to whether or not it is prepared to commit the transaction via the return value of its EndPrepare method. In our case, we'll return the value of m_bCommitTX. If the Compensator returns True, it is obligated to commit the changes made by the Worker when asked to do so:

```
Private Function ICrmCompensatorVariants_EndPrepareVariants() As Boolean

    ' Return whether or not prepare phase completed successfully
    ' and it is OK to commit transaction.
    ICrmCompensatorVariants_EndPrepareVariants = m_bCommitTX

End Function
```

The commit phase starts when the BeginCommit method is called. The method is passed the bRecovery parameter, which indicates whether or not a recovery is in progress. Next, the CommitRecordVariants method is called to commit each action logged by the Worker or the Compensator itself. Notice that once the action is performed, we don't immediately release the lock on the resource. The reason is that we don't want to release any locks until all actions are performed, since more than one action in the activity may have required a lock on the resource:

```
Private Function ICrmCompensatorVariants_CommitRecordVariants _
            (pLogRecord As Variant) As Boolean

    Dim objFS           As Scripting.FileSystemObject
    Dim lCommand        As Long
    Dim strDirPath      As String

    ' Initialize.
    Set objFS = New Scripting.FileSystemObject
    lCommand = pLogRecord(0)
    strDirPath = pLogRecord(1)

    Select Case lCommand
        Case tagDirCommands.DIRCREATE

            ' Unhide directory and then add it to the list of locks
            ' to be removed.
            If (objFS.FolderExists(strDirPath)) Then
                objFS.GetFolder(strDirPath).Attributes = _
                    objFS.GetFolder(strDirPath).Attributes - Hidden
                If (Not m_objDirsToBeUnlocked.Exists(strDirPath)) Then _
                    m_objDirsToBeUnlocked.Add strDirPath, "unlock"
            End If
        Case tagDirCommands.DIRDELETE
            If (objFS.FolderExists(strDirPath)) Then
                ' Delete folder and then add it to the list of locks
                ' to be removed.
                objFS.DeleteFolder strDirPath
                If (Not m_objDirsToBeUnlocked.Exists(strDirPath)) Then _
                    m_objDirsToBeUnlocked.Add strDirPath, "unlock"
            End If
    End Select

    ' We don't want to forget this record.
    ICrmCompensatorVariants_CommitRecordVariants = False

End Function
```

255

Once all actions are performed by the resource manager, `EndCommitVariants` is called signaling the end of the commit phase. Since all updates on the persistent resource in the context of the transaction have been completed, we then release all of the open locks:

```
Private Sub ICrmCompensatorVariants_EndCommitVariants()

    Dim varLock     As Variant
    Dim objFS       As Scripting.FileSystemObject
    Dim strDirName  As String

    ' Remove lock(s) from directory(s).
    For Each varLock In m_objDirsToBeUnlocked
        strDirName = objFS.GetFolder(varLock).Name
        objFS.DeleteFile varLock & "\..\" & strDirName & "_lock.txt"
    Next

End Sub
```

The implementation for the abort phase is similar to the commit phase. `BeginAbortVariants` is called when the abort phase starts. Then `AbortRecordVariants` is called for each log where each action is rolled back. Finally, `EndAbortVariants` is called at the end of the abort phase, where all locks are released.

Configuring and Using the FileSystemCRM

A CRM can only be used within a COM+ Server application. If the CRM will only be used by one COM+ application, then you can install it in the application where it will be used. However, the CRM will only be available for use within that application. If the CRM will be used by more than one application, you may install it within its own COM+ Library application and call it from a Server application. However, the Worker and Compensator should always be installed in the same application.

The Worker and Compensator class settings should be configured as follows:

Class	Transaction Support	JIT	Threading Model
Worker	Required	Checked	Apartment or Both
Compensator	Disabled	Unchecked	Apartment or Both

In order to use a CRM, the server application must have the **Enable Compensating Resource Managers** option checked. To do so, open the Component Services MMC and navigate to the COM+ application that will use the CRM. Open the application properties dialog box by right-clicking on the COM+ application, and select **Properties**. Finally, check the **Enable Compensating Resource Managers** checkbox:

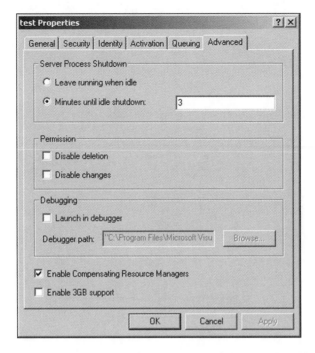

Once the CRM is configured, components within the application can use the CRM by creating a worker object, and then calling its methods to manipulate a persistent resource.

Summary

In this chapter we learned the fundamental properties of a transaction:

❑   **A**tomic

❑   **C**onsistent

❑   **I**solated

❑   **D**urable

We also learned about the major components within a transaction processing system, and the role they play in ensuring that the ACID properties are met throughout the lifetime of a transaction. Resource managers are deployed to ensure that a transaction is consistent, isolated, and durable, whereas the transaction manager ensures atomicity for distributed transactions.

COM+ provides a robust infrastructure that provides transactional support for component-based applications. We learned how to create and configure transactional COM+ components, and how to use the Object Context to vote on the outcome of a transaction.

COM+ uses a declarative model and leverages auto-enlisting resource managers to make transactional programming as easy for the developer as possible. However, we have also learned that a good solid understanding of the underlying architecture is important to ensure that the application behaves as expected. For example, we learned that any persistent resources modified within the context of a transaction should have a corresponding resource manager or should be modified through a correctly written CRM.

257

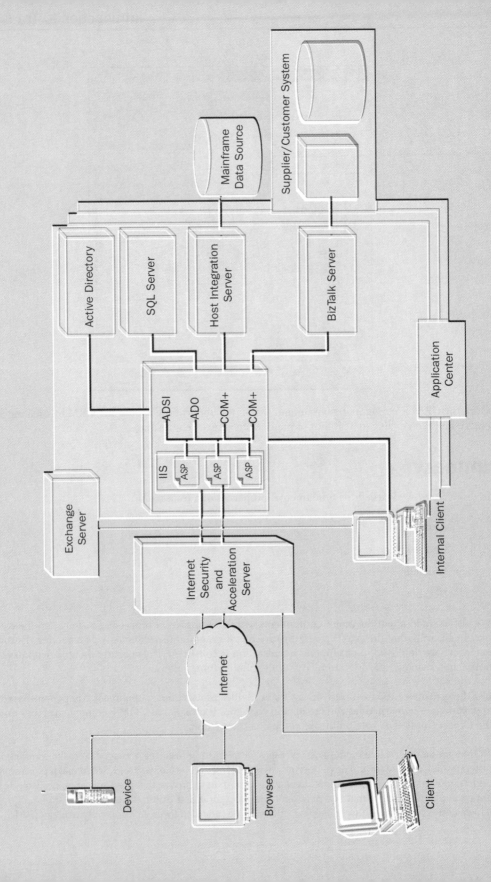

9

Building Asynchronous Applications

The demand and expectation for Internet applications to scale up and perform actions as fast as possible is at an all time high, and it doesn't appear as if it will stop any time soon. If an e-commerce site doesn't perform fast enough, users may feel that it is unreliable and will more than likely go to a different site. The competition is fierce and your site must be able to at least keep up with (but preferably exceed) the others. But what about those tasks that inevitably take a while to process? For example, when a large process must start after some interaction with a user, do you want the user to sit there looking at a spinning IE icon, waiting for the page to finally load? Probably not. The user will most likely give up, hit **Refresh** ten times causing ten more instances of this long process to kick off, or worst of all, leave the site.

So how do we solve this issue? Do we just not process the task? If we don't process the task the job will not be completed – for example, the user will not receive their order (and we won't collect their money). One solution is to have another process (and/or thread) carry out the task while the user is free to move around and perform other tasks. This type of processing is known as **asynchronous processing**.

In the following sections, this chapter will further define what asynchronous processing is and how it differs from synchronous processing. Next, the chapter will demonstrate various ways to counteract the problem described above. In summary you will learn:

❑ What asynchronous processing is

❑ Where to implement asynchronous processing

❑ Ways to implement asynchronous processing

Now that we have a plan of what we are going to cover in this chapter, let's get started. We'll begin with a detailed explanation of asynchronous processing by building on the quick definition from above.

What is Asynchronous Processing?

Asynchronous processing is an application design pattern that allows non-linear execution of code, whereas synchronous processing is linear-based, and can only complete a single task at a time. In a Windows-based system tasks within a process are carried out by one or more threads.

Threads

A **thread** is the entity to which the operating system allocates CPU time, and is responsible for executing the application code (instructions). All threads within a given process share the same virtual address space, global variables, and operating-system resources.

An example of when a thread is utilized is when a user requests an ASP page on a web server. When the request is received, a thread is assigned within the `inetinfo.exe`'s process space (IIS) to process the ASP page. No matter what the ASP page does, whether it's accessing a database, analyzing the `Request` object, or calling upon other resources, the thread will be busy processing all of the tasks or waiting for other processes to finish. (That is, unless asynchronous processing is utilized.)

Synchronous or Asynchronous Processing?

During this entire time the user is waiting for the ASP page to be processed and the resulting HTML to be sent to the browser. This is *usually* accomplished in an acceptable time frame, so synchronous processing is the logical choice. However, let's revisit the issue of a task taking too much time to process.

What if the page performs a huge task like billing a user and publishing their reports? This could take a long time depending on how large their account is and the type and number of reports that need to be generated. Does the user really need immediate feedback, or is it acceptable to simply let them know that their reports will soon be available? If your business requirements permit this, it's a great place to implement asynchronous processing.

> *Sometimes the processing of certain tasks can also be done in a batch style. This is widely used in billing and accounting solutions that require large processing times and perform large table locks with data sources. Batch style processing is very similar to asynchronous processing, in fact a great number of people view them as one and the same because they both allow processing to be off loaded to another thread and/or process.*

Types of Asynchronous Processing

Since the user is free to continue on their way while an asynchronous process is carried out, there has to be a mechanism to break apart this task and push it to another thread or even another process space. This is usually done by utilizing queues or events (also knows as callbacks). Let's take a quick look into queues and events.

Queues

Queues can take on a wide variety of forms. They can be as simple as a database table or as sophisticated as a queue within Microsoft's **Message Queuing** (**MSMQ**) service. Queues allow a place for requests to sit and wait for another process to handle them. Note that the queue does not *process* anything; its sole purpose is to *store* requests.

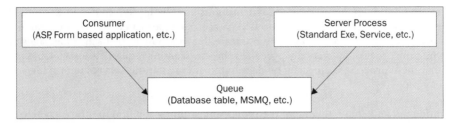

This approach is often taken with orders that are placed within a system. Normally a user does not wait for an order to be placed, fulfilled, billed, and shipped. Instead, an order table of some sort is utilized to hold the order at various steps through the process while the user is free to leave and check on the order at a later time, or even place more orders!

This same style of thinking about queues and tables is used when processing application tasks asynchronously.

Events

Events (or callbacks) provide a hook for another process to call upon to inform the client that something has happened. This type of processing is utilized heavily within Windows, but can be difficult to use within the web paradigm.

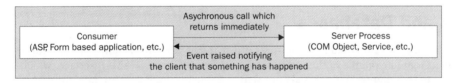

Events can be very useful when processing is taking place on the client, either in the browser or in traditional form-based applications. When utilizing this style of processing, the client code usually interacts with a COM API by invoking an asynchronous method that also takes a reference to the client. While the server is processing the method the client is able to continue and process other tasks. This enables the server to callback (or raise an event back on) the client, informing them when processing is completed.

Within Windows 2000 a service exists for handling events, and this is the subject of the next chapter.

Why Implement Asynchronous Processing?

As has just been suggested, asynchronous processing provides a great way to break up a task by letting some of it process in the background; but where are the best places to utilize it?

The most obvious place where asynchronous processing can be used is when the task takes too long, causing the user to become frustrated and lose faith in your application. A good example of this would be running a complex pricing stored procedure on a database, or generating monthly billing invoices. However, before converting all of your bottlenecks to utilize asynchronous processing, you first need to assess the situation.

Another reason to off-load the processing asynchronously in the background is to decouple the components. By decoupling the process into two pieces, each part can operate independently from the other. For instance, an ASP page could communicate to a component that sends messages or requests to a queue, while the process that actually processes the messages or requests is unavailable. Another benefit is that these processes can easily be distributed among various servers to provide scalability and process isolation.

Before running out and converting all of the processing within a solution to utilize asynchronous processing, there are a couple questions to ask. The first question to ask is if the task can be broken up or off-loaded somewhere else. Often this cannot be done, simply because of the business requirements. The second question to ask is whether the process requires immediate feedback. If this is needed, asynchronous processing may not be the best alternative. However, this alone is not always a reason to completely disregard using asynchronous processing.

Ways to Implement Asynchronous Processing

As mentioned above, the communication involved in asynchronous processing can usually be broken into two types: queues and events. The following section explores these areas and demonstrates various ways to implement asynchronous processing. The code for all of the sample projects presented here is available in the download file from the Wrox web site.

Queues and Databases

A great number of asynchronous frameworks utilize queues and/or databases to provide asynchronous processing. A good example of this is Microsoft's Message Queue (MSMQ) service, which is talked about later in this chapter. Jobs or tasks are sent to a queue where they are held until another process carries out the desired work.

Custom Database Solution

In this solution we are going to address the issue of a SQL statement that is taking far too long to process. Keep in mind that this is just a sample solution and therefore is very basic, with much room for improvement. However, it will provide you with an understanding of the concepts and a starting point when implementing your own solution.

This solution comprises three main parts:

- ❑ The component to submit requests to
- ❑ The database to serve as a queue and hold the requests
- ❑ The processing component

The submit component is a Visual Basic ActiveX DLL, with one single class and a method to send SQL requests to. The database is located in a SQL Server database. The final piece is a simple Visual Basic executable that is used to process the request located in the database table.

Queue

Let's start by building the database table (or queue) for holding these requests. This is easily done through the Enterprise Manager MMC snap-in. First create a new database called AsyncSample. Then create a table called Requests within the database, to hold the requests.

The following screenshot displays the structure of the table. Notice the Status field, which should be given a default value of 1. This is used as a flag notifying the processor of the request whether or not to process the request. The other fields within the Requests table may differ for each system and its needs. However, the more flexible the solution, the more applications and systems it can be used on. This example will simply hold a SQL statement (SQL) that needs to be executed on a given connection string (ConnectionString).

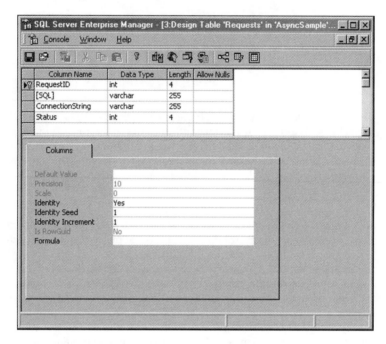

API to Queue

Now that we have a table to hold the request, we'll build a simple API to shield the underlying functionality from the consumer. For this example we will build the API in a standard COM DLL in Visual Basic.

Start by firing up VB, select an ActiveX DLL, rename the project DBSample and change Class1 to Request. Set a reference to **ActiveX Data Objects**. Now we'll add some code to log the request from the user to the database. The following code builds this functionality into a single routine called SubmitRequest:

```
Public Sub SubmitRequest(ByVal strConnectionString As String, _
                    ByVal strSQL As String, ByRef strError As Variant)

    Dim objConn As ADODB.Connection

    On Error GoTo Error_Handler
```

```
'connect to the db and execute the string
'change server name for your system

Set objConn = New ADODB.Connection
objConn.Open "Provider=SQLOLEDB;Server=blex05;" & _
             "DATABASE=AsyncSample;UID=sa;PWD="
objConn.Execute "INSERT INTO Requests VALUES ('" & strSQL & _
                "', '" & strConnectionString & "', 1)"

Exit_Handler:
 If objConn.State = adStateOpen Then objConn.Close
 Exit Sub

Error_Handler:
 strError = Err.Description & " (" & Err.Number & " - " & _
            Err.Source & " )"
 Resume Exit_Handler

End Sub
```

As you can see above, the code is fairly simple. It connects to the database and inserts a record (request) into the `Requests` table with a status of 1, which indicates the request is waiting to be processed by the Visual Basic application, as will be explained below. The main point to remember from this part of the solution is that it shields the client code (ASP for example) from knowing the underlying structure. It simply provides a mechanism for the client to call upon.

Request Processor

The next section that needs to be built is a process that can watch the table and process the request within it. This process is the heart of this solution since it is the piece actually carrying out the task. In this example, we will simply build a standard VB EXE called `DBProcessor.exe`, which occasionally queries the `Requests` table looking for records with a status of 1. If it finds records that fit this criterion, it calls upon a private routine called `ProcessRequest`. Start by creating a standard VB EXE and place a textbox named `txtInfo` and a timer called `tmrProcess` on the form. Add a reference to ActiveX Data Objects.

Next, add the following code to the form, which will provide the functionality to watch the database table process the request:

```
Private Sub tmrProcess_Timer()

Dim objRS As ADODB.Recordset

On Error GoTo Error_Handler

 'connect to the db and execute the string
 Set objRS = New ADODB.Recordset
 objRS.CursorType = adOpenKeyset

 objRS.ActiveConnection = _
 "Provider=SQLOLEDB;Server=blex05;DATABASE=AsyncSample;UID=sa;PWD="
 objRS.Open "SELECT * FROM Requests WHERE Status = 1"
```

```
Do Until objRS.EOF
 If ProcessRequest(objRS("ConnectionString"), objRS("SQL")) = 0 Then
  'worked
  objRS("Status") = 2
  txtInfo = "Processed: " & objRS("SQL")
 Else
  'failed
  objRS("Status") = 3
  txtInfo = "Failed: " & objRS("SQL")
 End If
 objRS.Update
 objRS.MoveNext
Loop

Exit_Handler:
 If objRS.State = adStateOpen Then objRS.Close
 Set objRS = Nothing
 Exit Sub

Error_Handler:
 txtInfo = Err.Description
 Resume Exit_Handler

End Sub
```

Again, this code is very straightforward. After making a connection to the database, a recordset is obtained containing all records with a status of 1 (to be processed). The ProcessRequest method (discussed below) is called for each and the status is set according to whether the processing succeeded or failed.

The ProcessRequest function takes the connection string and the SQL statement from the database table, connects to the requested database and executes the SQL statement:

```
Private Function ProcessRequest(ByVal strConnectionString As String, _
                                strSQL As String) As Long

Dim objConn As ADODB.Connection

On Error GoTo Error_Handler

 'connect to the db and execute the string
 Set objConn = New ADODB.Connection
 objConn.Open strConnectionString
 objConn.Execute strSQL, , adExecuteNoRecords

 'everything worked
 ProcessRequest = 0

Exit_Handler:
 If objConn.State = adStateOpen Then objConn.Close
 Set objConn = Nothing
 Exit Function

Error_Handler:
 ProcessRequest = Err.Number
 Resume Exit_Handler

End Function
```

Client

Now that the functionality is there for clients to send requests, let's build two ASP pages to test it out. The first ASP page, `AsyncSample1.asp`, is nothing more than a form to fill out. It gathers the connection string and SQL statement from the user and posts the values to the `AsyncSample2.asp` page. (This first page could actually be a simple HTML file, but with IIS 5.0 there is no overhead in using an ASP page instead.)

The following screenshot displays what the end result of the first ASP page, `AsyncSample1.asp`, should look like. Keep in mind that this is just a sample solution and not something to implement in a production environment. That said, this example accepts two input values from the client: a connection string and a SQL statement. This provides the most flexibility for you when testing the application for yourself.

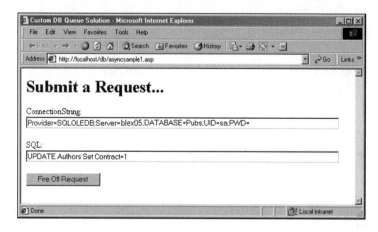

The following HTML code is used to build the page:

```
<%@ Language=VBScript %>
<HTML>
<HEAD>
<TITLE>Custom DB Queue Solution</TITLE>
</HEAD>
<BODY>

<FORM
    ACTION="AsyncSample2.asp"
    ID="frmTest"
    NAME="frmTest"
    METHOD="POST">

    <H1>Submit a Request...</H1>

    ConnectionString:<BR>
    <INPUT
        TYPE="TEXT"
        STYLE="WIDTH:600px"
        NAME="txtConnectionString"
        VALUE="Provider=SQLOLEDB;Server=blex05;DATABASE=Pubs;UID=sa;PWD=">
<BR><BR>SQL:<BR>
    <INPUT
        TYPE="TEXT"
        STYLE="WIDTH:600px"
        NAME="txtSQL"
        VALUE="UPDATE Authors Set Contract=1">
```

```
    <BR><BR>
    <INPUT
        TYPE="Submit"
        VALUE="Fire Off Request"
        NAME="btnGo">

</FORM>

</BODY>
</HTML>
```

The second ASP page, `AsyncSample2.asp`, is used to receive the information from `AsyncSample1.asp` and send the request to the COM object built earlier:

```
<%@ Language=VBScript %>
<% Option Explicit %>

<HTML>
<HEAD>
<TITLE>DB Sample</TITLE>
</HEAD>
<BODY>

<%

    Dim objRequest
    Dim strError

    Set objRequest = Server.CreateObject("DBSample.Request")
    objRequest.SubmitRequest Request.Form("txtConnectionString"), _
        Request.Form("txtSQL"), strError

    If len(strError & "") = 0 then
        Response.Write "Request was successfully sent."
    Else
        Response.Write "Error sending request: " & strError
    End If

    Set objRequest = Nothing

%>

<BR>
<BR>

<A href="javascript:history.back(1)">Back</A>

</BODY>
</HTML>
```

After making COM call the page, it checks the result of the call. If the error string's length is zero, the submission of the request succeeded, otherwise it failed. An alternative option to passing the errors back out to the consumer is to let COM "bubble" the error back. However, this option is not the cleanest to track on the client side with VBScript, so this example simply places the error in a string value.

Putting it All Together

Next let's configure and try out the solution. Once the database is built, the COM DLL (`DBSample.dll`) must be registered. This can be done in one of two ways: either by registering the DLL with `regsvr32.exe` (`regsvr32 C:\SomeFolder\DBSample.dll`), or by placing it within a COM+ application under the Component Services MMC snap-in. (For more information on registering a COM DLL refer back to Chapter 3, and for more information on COM+ applications in general see Chapter 6.)

If you haven't already done so, place the two ASP pages together within an IIS directory of some kind. For example, I placed the files in a virtual web called DB off the root level.

The last piece of this example, the VB executable DBProcessor.exe, doesn't require any setting. It just needs to be up and running in order for it to respond to the request from the clients.

The following diagram displays the communication of the various pieces (layers) within this solution. Notice how multiple clients can call upon the DBSample.Request component, but all requests are still handled by the single VB executable.

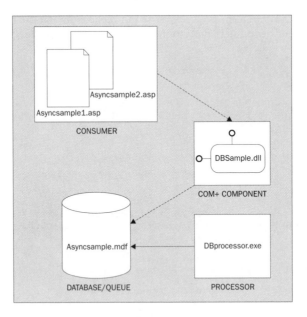

As requests are submitted to the table (queue) they should be picked up from the DBProcessor executable as long as it is running. The following screenshot displays what the Requests table looks like after a few tasks are submitted to it:

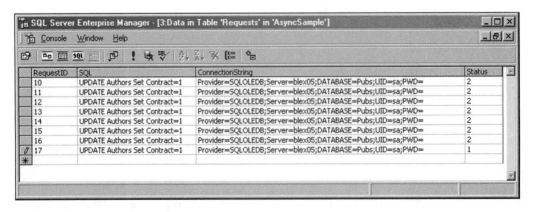

As you can see all the requests have been successfully processed except for the last one, which is waiting to be processed. (Remember, the Status field is used to determine which files still need to be processed.)

The following shows the VB executable that is actually processing the request:

As you can see, utilizing asynchronous processing promotes the distribution of a task across multiple processes. This can greatly improve the performance of tasks, and also provide process isolation (communicating asynchronously while the end users continue other processing).

Other Possibilities

Now that we have gone through a basic example of implementing our own asynchronous framework using a custom database, let's go over some areas where this can be built upon and improved.

First of all, this is an example of an application that can only process SQL statements that don't have any special characters that would mess up the SQL statement string, such as single quotes. Another way to utilize this framework is to send a SQL statement that will execute a **job** within SQL Server. Jobs in SQL Server can be very powerful. They can execute SQL commands, batch files, or even VBScript or JavaScript. SQL Server jobs can easily be executed by utilizing the extended stored procedure called `sp_start_job 'MyJob'`. For more information on executing SQL Server jobs see the section at the end of this chapter, or consult the SQL Server Books Online within the Enterprise Manager.

Some other ways to improve this sample would be to add more information columns to the `Requests` table and to also add a lookup table, related to the `Status` field. For example, you could add a request type on the table, which would hold a 1 for SQL statements, a 2 for COM calls, etc. Then you could also rework the `SQL` statement and `ConnectionString` columns to hold a more generic meaning, for example, possibly rename them to `Data1` and `Data2`, or combine them together and utilize delimiters to hold multiple values. The variations and permutations are limitless.

Regardless of how the database structure is designed and how flexible it becomes, there are still a few drawbacks. The first and major one is that you must build it. Although it is sometimes enjoyable to build your own infrastructure, an infrastructure does not directly solve your business needs; it provides a base to build your solution upon, and can add unnecessary development time. The other drawback with the database solution is that you must know COM to utilize it or you have to go behind the COM API we built and hack the database table – not the type of thing you want consumers of your infrastructure to do.

Well, I have good news: Microsoft has developed a server that enables us to do the same thing we did with the database example and more, without the drawback we mentioned above. It's called Microsoft Message Queue (MSMQ) and is discussed in the next section.

What is MSMQ

MSMQ, a key part of the DNA architecture, is a service that runs on Windows NT 4.0 Server and Windows 2000 Server, which provides loosely coupled, asynchronous communication between applications (the consumer and the provider of the service do not communicate directly and do not have to be online at the same time). MSMQ 1.0 is available for Windows NT 4.0 Server in the NT 4.0 Option Pack. MSMQ 2.0, which this chapter will focus on, is available in the Windows 2000 Server installation.

The basic concept of MSMQ is simple: it's a message forwarding system. It allows messages (that can contain almost anything) to be bundled up and sent to a destination across the network for another application or service to process. Think of it as two or more applications talking together over their own messaging system, an "e-mail for applications". Let's look into MSMQ in more detail and see how we can use it in the same scenario for which we previously used the database solution.

A message in MSMQ is a package or container, which is sent to a destination, where it is persisted in a queue until a recipient is ready to read or process it. These queues provide MSMQ with the ability to guarantee delivery of messages (**store-and-forward** messaging), regardless of the state and reliability of a network connection. MSMQ 2.0 accomplishes this through Microsoft's Active Directory, while MSMQ 1.0 does this through a two-phased commit (see Chapter 8 for an explanation of this protocol), because it utilizes SQL Server.

Just like e-mail messages, MSMQ messages have a **sender** and **receiver**. The receiver, however, is a little different. The receiver of a message in MSMQ is defined as who has "receive access" to the queue. This enables multiple receivers to respond to a single message in a single queue. For example, in most web applications that use MSMQ, the sender of the message is the web server (either through ASP or a COM component) and the receiver (responder) to the message is a custom application that resides on a different machine. The custom application doesn't have to be on a different machine, but it allows for greater scalability and flexibility.

Similar to most BackOffice products, MSMQ is administered via the Microsoft Management Console (MMC) snap-in called Computer Management. This console link is located under the Administrative Tools folder within the Control Panel. The following screenshot displays the new MSMQ administrator in Windows 2000. Notice that it is located under the Services and Applications node.

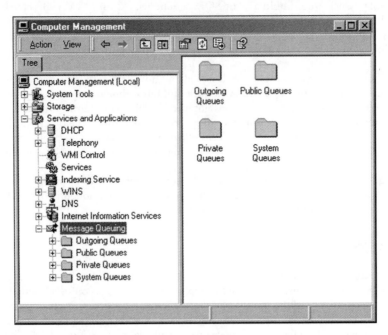

Now that we have a basic understanding of MSMQ, let's take a closer look at its queues and messages before we start converting our database solution from above.

MSMQ Queues

As noted above, queues are designed as places to persist or hold messages. In a way they are similar to e-mail – queues are closely related to the various boxes, such as the inbox. A message will stay in a queue until it expires, it is read, or the queue is purged (cleaned out). Each queue belongs to a single server, but one server can have multiple queues.

The main attributes of a queue are a **unique name** and two **global unique identifiers** (**GUIDs**). The unique name is nothing more than a simple string that is commonly used to define the queue. The first GUID, known as the ID, also defines the queue uniquely. The second GUID is a TypeID, which defines a group or type of queues. The TypeID can and will most likely be duplicated across multiple queues that perform a common task to group them together.

The following screenshot displays what an MSMQ message looks like from the MMC snap-in administrator. This can be accessed by selecting to view the properties of any message in a queue. Notice the GUIDs and other attributes of the message which were discussed above:

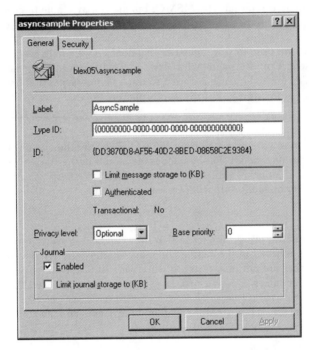

There are four types of queues within MSMQ 2.0 – each type and the queues beneath it can be accessed through the Computer Management MMC snap-in, under the Message Queues node:

- ❑ Outgoing
- ❑ System
- ❑ Public
- ❑ Private

Outgoing Queues

Outgoing queues are used to persist messages when a remote MSMQ server is unavailable. Outgoing queues are what provide MSMQ with the flexibility to operate even when another server is down. Applications cannot be programmed to use outgoing queues; they are only used internally by MSMQ when a queue is opened, by specifying the `FormatName` with the `DirectOS` identifier.

When the `FormatName` name is utilized, MSMQ will not directly communicate with the destination server, instead it allows the code to send a message to a queue that could be offline. The message is placed in an outgoing queue until the destination server is available or the message expires.

If a queue is opened by specifying the `PathName` property, it will only work when all resources are available. Unlike when the `FormatName` name is utilized, using the `PathName` requires that the destination server be available. If not, the opening of the queue will fail.

System Queues

System queues are also used internally by MSMQ, but are not available to custom applications. Examples of system queues are dead-letter queues, report queues and journal queues.

The dead-letter queues are used to store message that could not be delivered. Report queues are used when tracing is enabled. A report queue will receive messages as a message is moved from the sender to its final destination. The journal queues are used to track the messages that have been read from a queue. Journaling is great for storing historical information.

Public Queues

Public queues are the most common queues in MSMQ. They are the queues that can be used by custom applications to fulfill business needs. Public queues are stored in the Active Directory service, and therefore are known to all other MSMQ servers throughout the enterprise. An example of a public queue would be an order queue for an order processing system.

Private Queues

Private queues are similar to public queues in that they can be accessed from custom applications, however they are not published in the Active Directory, so they are not available to applications outside the local computer. These are not only faster to work with, but they are very secure, since they are not available from other computers.

Now let's look into the messages that are stored within these queues and the attributes associated with them.

MSMQ Messages

Messages in MSMQ are similar to e-mail messages; however, they are not sent to a single user or even a group of users. Instead they are sent from one single application to a single queue on a single computer. However, a message may be sent through a series of servers before it reaches its destination queue.

MSMQ messages are mainly composed of three parts:

- ❏ The label
- ❏ The body
- ❏ The destination queue

The **label** is similar to the subject of an e-mail message. Most of the time a label is used to group various types of messages together, so a custom server-side application can distinguish what the message contains.

The **body** of an MSMQ message is very extensible. It is designed to hold anything from a string, to an array, to a COM object that supports the `IPersist` interface. For example, it is possible to create an instance of an ADO recordset, retrieve a resultset, disconnect it from the data source and set it to the body of an MSMQ message. Then when the message is read, the instance of the ADO recordset object is pulled out of it!

The **destination queue** property of a message can be compared to the recipient of an e-mail message. One difference between an e-mail and an MSMQ message is that e-mail messages can be sent to multiple recipients whereas an MSMQ message can only be sent to a single queue. However, when the message reaches its destination, it can have multiple readers.

Let's take a look at an MSMQ message from the administrator point of view, through the MMC snap-in. The component for controlling MSMQ is within the Computer Management snap-in under the Services and Applications node. The following screenshot displays what the properties of an MSMQ message look like through the administrator. This dialog box can be displayed by right-clicking on a message and selecting Properties.

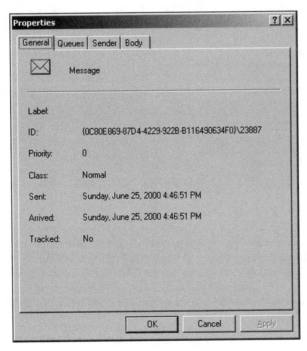

Now that we have a general overview of MSMQ and the high level parts it is composed of, let's take a look into the object model within it and see what each of these objects provides.

MSMQ Object Model

Like most services, MSMQ has a COM API, which provides an interface for developers to code against. MSMQ's object model is composed of a series of objects; however, most applications only need to utilize four of them:

- ❑ MSMQQueueInfo
- ❑ MSMQQueue
- ❑ MSMQMessage
- ❑ MSMQEvent

The following diagram shows all of the MSMQ objects and how they relate to one another. Although we will give an overview of all of the objects and their purpose, we will only concentrate on the four objects mentioned above.

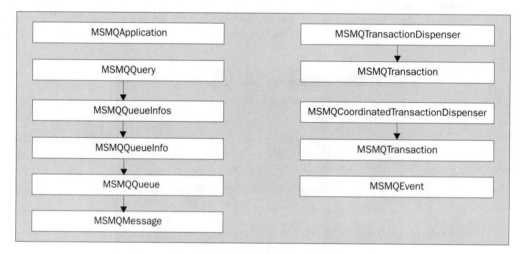

MSMQApplication

MSMQApplication is a small object that is normally not used when developing solutions with MSMQ. It has two methods: MachineIdOfMachineName and RegisterCertificate. MachineIdOfMachineName is used to look up the GUID (unique identifier) for the server name passed to it. This GUID can be used to specify the server instead of coding to the common NETBIOS name. The RegisterCertificate method is used by the clients to register a certificate to verify the identity of themselves and the server.

MSMQQueueInfo

The MSMQQueueInfo object provides the functionality to add, delete and open queues within MSMQ on a given server. This object is often the starting point when working with the MSMQ object model.

In order to work with a queue the PathName or the FormatName is usually set. The PathName and FormatName properties inform MSMQ what queue is desired and also tell it which machine the queue is located on. The PathName is used when the server where the queue resides is known to be available. An example of this, although it is not recommended, is when the code is running on the MSMQ server itself. The FormatName is more commonly used, because it does not require the server to be available.

The following code is an example of opening a queue named `MyQueue` located on the local computer:

```
<%
Dim objQueueInfo
Dim objQueue

Set objQueueInfo = Server.CreateObject("MSMQ.MSMQQueueInfo")
objQueueInfo.FormatName = "DIRECT=OS:MyServer\MyQueue"

Set objQueue = objQueueInfo.Open(MQ_SEND_ACCESS, MQ_DENY_NONE)
%>
```

First, we dimension a variable (optional, but good practice). Next, we create an instance of the `MSMQQueueInfo` object. The next line sets the name and location of a queue and the last line opens the queue. When opening a queue, two parameters must be specified: `Access` and `ShareMode`. `Access` determines what can be done with the queue. The possible values for this parameter can be found within the `MQACCESS` enumerator, which has three values:

❑ `MQ_RECEIVE_ACCESS` (1) – Messages within the queue can be removed as they are read

❑ `MQ_SEND_ACCESS` (2) – Used when sending messages to the queue

❑ `MQ_PEEK_ACCESS` (32) – Used to look (peek) at messages, but does not remove them

The `Open` routine returns a reference to an `MSMQQueue` object that is to send and receive messages. The `MSMQQueue` object is discussed below.

Creating and deleting message queues is performed much like opening a queue, by setting the `PathName` and then calling the `Create` or `Delete` method. Although this is usually done through the MMC snap-in, the following shows how it can be done through code:

```
<%
  Dim objQueue
  Set objQueue = Server.CreateObject("MSMQ.MSMQQueueInfo")
  objQueue.PathName = ".\MyQueue"
  objQueue.Create
%>
```

```
<%
  Dim objQueue
  Set objQueue = Server.CreateObject("MSMQ.MSMQQueueInfo")
  objQueue.PathName = ".\MyQueue"
  objQueue.Delete
%>
```

MSMQQueue

The `MSMQQueue` object provides the functionality to work with a queue that has been opened through the `MSMQQueueInfo` object. Although most web applications that use MSMQ are usually *sending* messages, there are times when web applications need to open a queue and *display* the messages, such as administrative pages. Also, all MSMQ-enabled applications need a server-side service or application to respond to the messages as they are received.

MSMQ messages can be read asynchronously or synchronously from a queue. Reading messages asynchronously allows a process to respond to a message though the use of events. MSMQ will get a reference to the code within the process and raise an event when a message arrives. Reading messages synchronously requires a process to occasionally open the queue and look for messages on its own. This can not only take up unnecessary system resources, but can be much more difficult to program. An example of responding to messages asynchronously is covered below. The following code shows how to open a queue synchronously and display the messages within the queue in a standard message box:

```
Public Sub DisplayMessages()

    Dim objQueueInfo As MSMQQueueInfo
    Dim objQueue As MSMQQueue
    Dim objMessage As MSMQMessage

' Create the queue, ignoring the error if it's already there
    Set objQueueInfo = New MSMQQueueInfo
    objQueueInfo.PathName = ".\MyQueue"
    objQueueInfo.Label = "My Sample Queue"

' If queue already exists ignore it
    On Error Resume Next

    objQueueInfo.Create
    On Error GoTo 0

' Open the queue
    Set objQueue = objQueueInfo.Open(MQ_RECEIVE_ACCESS, MQ_DENY_NONE)

' Loop through all the messages in the queue
    Do While True
        Set objMessage = objQueue.Peek(, , 1000)
        If objMessage Is Nothing Then Exit Do
        MsgBox "Message: " & objMessage.Label
    Loop
    MsgBox "No more new messages."

' Clean up
    objQueue.Close
    Set objMessage = Nothing
    Set objQueue = Nothing
    Set objQueueInfo = Nothing

End Sub
```

The above code starts off by using the MSMQQueue object and enters a Do While ... Loop until the Peek routine returns Nothing. When this routine returns Nothing, it means that the time-out expires. In this case the time-out is set to 1000 milliseconds. Although we have not covered the MSMQMessage object yet (below), the main part to note is that the code is setting a reference to an MSMQ message through the use of the Peek method on the queue.

MSMQMessage

The MSMQMessage object is the heart of MSMQ and provides a piece of functionality that all MSMQ-enabled applications take advantage of – sending and reading messages. An MSMQMessage object is very extensible because it is designed to hold a wide variety of information. For example, the Body of the message can hold a string, byte array, any numeric types, or even an instance of a persistable COM object! The Label of a message is a string that simply describes what the message is. It is comparable to the title of an e-mail message.

Messages can be retrieved in one of two ways, by opening or peeking. When a message is opened, it is removed from the queue once it is read and placed in the journal folder, if journaling is enabled. When a message is peeked, it remains in the queue until the message expires or until it is read by another process. The opening and peeking of a message are performed in the MSMQQueue object through the Open and Peek routines, which then return back a reference to the instance of an MSMQMessage object.

The following code displays how to open a message and display the Body and Label:

```
Private Sub LookForMessage()

    Dim objQInfo As MSMQQueueInfo
    Dim objQReceive As MSMQQueue
    Dim objMessage As MSMQMessage

' Open the queue
    Set objQInfo = New MSMQQueueInfo
    objQInfo.PathName = ".\MyQueue"
    Set objQReceive = objQInfo.Open(MQ_RECEIVE_ACCESS, MQ_DENY_NONE)

' Look for a message with a time-out of 100 ms
    Set objMessage = objQReceive.Receive(, , , 100)

' Was there a message?
    If Not objMessage Is Nothing Then
      'Display the contents of the message
       MsgBox objMessage.Label & " - " & objMessage.Body
    Else
      'No message
       Msgbox "Nothing in the queue"
    End If

' Clean up
    objQReceive.Close
    Set objQInfo = Nothing
    Set objQReceive = Nothing
    Set objMessage = Nothing

End Sub
```

The code sample above starts by opening a queue, then looks for a message within the queue, by invoking the Receive routine with a time-out of 100 milliseconds. A time-out is used to tell MSMQ when to stop waiting for a message. To see if there was a message, we test the MSMQMessage object returned by the Receive function to see if it is Nothing. If the Receive method returned a valid message the code then displays the Label and the Body properties.

Sending a message is the most common task performed with MSMQ in web applications. To send a message, a queue is opened with send access (MQ_SEND_ACCESS), a message is built, and the Send routine on an MSMQMessage object is invoked:

```
<%
'Dim some variables
Dim objQInfo
Dim objQSend
Dim objMessage

'Open the queue
```

```
Set objQInfo = Server.CreateObject("MSMQ.MSMQQueueInfo")
objQInfo.PathName = ".\test"

Set objQSend = objQInfo.Open(MQ_SEND_ACCESS, MQ_DENY_NONE)

'Build/send the message
Set objMessage = Server.CreateObject("MSMQ.MSMQMessage")
objMessage.Label = "This is the label."
objMessage.Body = "This is the body."
objMessage.Send objQSend
objQSend.Close

'Clean up
Set objQInfo = Nothing
Set objQSend = Nothing
Set objMessage = Nothing
%>
```

The code example above starts out like the other sample and opens a queue, however this queue is opened with send access. Next a message is built by creating an instance of the MSMQMessage class and setting the Label and Body properties. Finally, the message is sent by calling the Send method on the message, passing a reference to the queue as a parameter.

MSMQQuery

The MSMQQuery object is used to provide a way to search for a queue given a wide variety of information. This object has just a single method, LookupQueue, which returns a collection of MSMQQueueInfo objects within a single MSMQQueueInfos object.

MSMQQueueInfos

MSMQQueueInfos is returned from the LookupQueue method on the MSMQQuery object. This object is a limited collection of MSMQQueueInfo objects (missing Add, Remove, Count, and so on) that only has two methods.

MSMQEvent

The MSMQEvent object is a very useful class when building server-side applications in languages like VB and VC++, because it provides a mechanism for MSMQ to call into the code and fire events when messages are received in a queue (asynchronously). The MSMQEvent object is a small object, in fact, it has no properties or methods; it only consists of two events, Arrived and ArrivedError.

The following code example shows how to open a local queue and respond to messages asynchronously through the use of the MSMQQueue and MSMQEvent objects:

```
Option Explicit

Private m_objQueueInfo As MSMQQueueInfo
Private m_objQueue As MSMQQueue
Private WithEvents m_objMSMQEvent As MSMQEvent

Private Sub Form_Load()
```

```
' Create the queue, ignoring the error if it's already there
  Set m_objQueueInfo = New MSMQQueueInfo
  m_objQueueInfo.PathName = ".\MyQueue"
  m_objQueueInfo.Label = "My Sample Queue"

' If queue already exists ignore it
  On Error Resume Next
  m_objQueueInfo.Create
  On Error GoTo 0

' Open the queue
  Set m_objQueue = m_objQueueInfo.Open(MQ_RECEIVE_ACCESS, MQ_DENY_NONE)

' Link the events
  Set m_objMSMQEvent = New MSMQEvent
  m_objQueue.EnableNotification m_objMSMQEvent, MQMSG_CURRENT, 1000

End Sub

Private Sub m_objMSMQEvent_Arrived(ByVal Queue As Object, _
                                   ByVal Cursor As Long)

' Process the message
  Dim objMessage As MSMQMessage
  Set objMessage = Queue.PeekCurrent

  MsgBox "Message Received: " & m_objMessage.Label

' Link the event for the next message
  m_objQueue.EnableNotification m_objMSMQEvent, MQMSG_NEXT, 10000

End Sub

Private Sub m_objMSMQEvent_ArrivedError(ByVal Queue As Object, _
                                        ByVal ErrorCode As Long, _
                                        ByVal Cursor As Long)
' Something went wrong!
  MsgBox "Error recorded: " & ErrorCode

End Sub
```

The above code starts with the `Form_Load` event and opens a queue named `MyQueue`. Then the `m_objMSMQEvent` object is linked to the queue. This is done by calling the `EnableNotification` method on the `MSMQQueue` object and passing a reference to the `m_objMSMQEvent` object. Once the `MSMQEvent` object is linked, the only thing left to do is fulfill the `Arrived` and `Arrived_Error` (optional) events. The `Arrived` event fires every time a new message is received in the queue. However, any time a notification is received of a message arrival or error, the `EnableNotification` method must be called again to tell MSMQ to inform the code when the next message is received. If the code fails to call `EnableNotification`, the next message will never be seen. When the `Arrived` event is raised by MSMQ it returns a reference to the queue where the message can be read from and also returns a reference to the cursor. If an error occurs, the `ArrivedError` event will fire with a reference to the `Queue` object, a long variable holding the error number, and a reference to the cursor.

MSMQTransaction

The MSMQTransaction object is used to tell MSMQ to abort or commit a transaction that has been started by either the MSMQTransactionDispenser or the MSMQCoordinatedTransactionDispenser object. An instance of the MSMQTransaction object cannot not created by using the New keyword or CreateObject function. It can only be created through the use of the BeginTransaction method on the MSMQTransactionDispenser and MSMQCoordinatedTransactionDispenser objects.

MSMQCoordinatedTransactionDispenser

The MSMQCoordinatedTransactionDispenser object provides one way to hook into the power of the DTC within MSMQ. This object is quite small and only contains a single method called BeginTransaction. By using the Distributed Transaction Coordinator (DTC), transactions are not only able to encompass reading from and writing to message queues, but they are also able to contain any other service that supports DTC. This enables developers to write routines that modify data in databases like SQL Server (6.5 or 7.0) and send/read messages to/from a queue, all within one single transaction.

Transactions that span across multiple DTC-compliant services can also be held within a transaction under COM+ (or MTS in Windows NT). This enables developers to encapsulate code into COM DLLs and place them under the control of COM+.

MSMQTransactionDispenser

The MSMQTransactionDispenser object provides the functionality to wrap multiple message sends and receives to multiple queues in MSMQ in a transaction. Using this object is very useful for internal MSMQ transactions, but it cannot contain anything else like SQL Server database updates or inserts. When a transaction is needed and will only contain operations with MSMQ, use the MSMQTransactionDispenser object transaction. It is much faster than the MSMQCoordinatedTransactionDispenser transaction because it does not have to deal with the overhead of the DTC.

MSMQ Sample Solution

Now it's time to utilize what we've learned about MSMQ and develop an application that uses MSMQ to implement asynchronous communication. In fact, this sample solution will accomplish the same task as the custom database solution earlier, but it will use MSMQ instead of a database table.

Queue

Like the previous example, let's start out by defining the queue where the requests will be sent. To do this, open the **Computer Management MMC** snap-in located in the **Administrative Tools** folder in the **Control Panel**. Within the **Computer Management** snap-in, expand the **Message Queuing** node under **Services and Applications**. Within the **Public Queue** node, add a **New** queue called AsyncSample:

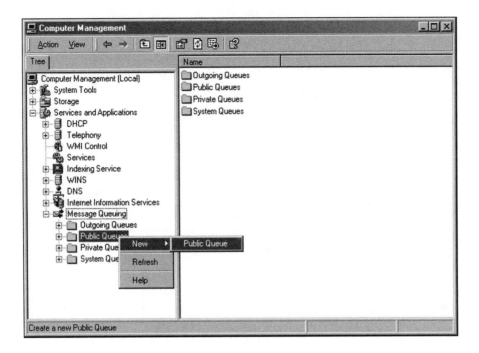

Note that you must be using a domain machine, not a workgroup machine, in order to get this code to work. For more information on this read either of the following two articles:

http://msdn.microsoft.com/library/psdk/msmq/msmq_guide_8778.htm

http://support.microsoft.com/support/kb/articles/q248/5/00.asp

API to Queue

Now that we have a queue to send requests or messages to, we can alter the code from the database sample above. Start by opening the DBSample project that we created earlier and renaming it MSMQSample. You may also want to save the project files to a different location. Next remove the reference to **ActiveX Data Objects** and make a new one to the **MSMQ 2.0 Object Library**. Now we can rewrite the code that used ADO to use MSMQ. This can easily be done by first creating an instance of the MSMQQueueInfo object. The MSMQQueueInfo object provides the necessary functionality to create, delete, and open various queues. Since we have already created the queue in the MMC snap-in, we can simply open the queue with send rights, as shown in the code below:

```
Public Sub SubmitRequest(ByVal strConnectionString As String, _
                ByVal strSQL As String, ByRef strError As Variant)

   Dim objQueueInfo As MSMQ.MSMQQueueInfo
   Dim objQueue As MSMQ.MSMQQueue
   Dim objMessage As MSMQ.MSMQMessage

   On Error GoTo Error_Handler

   'open the queue with send access
   Set objQueueInfo = New MSMQ.MSMQQueueInfo
```

```
objQueueInfo.FormatName = "DIRECT=OS:blex05\AsyncSample"
Set objQueue = objQueueInfo.Open(MQACCESS.MQ_SEND_ACCESS, _
              MQSHARE.MQ_DENY_NONE)


'set the message
Set objMessage = New MSMQ.MSMQMessage
With objMessage
 .Label = strConnectionString
 .Body = strSQL
 .Send objQueue
End With

Exit_Handler:
 Set objMessage = Nothing
 If Not objQueue Is Nothing Then If objQueue.IsOpen = 1 Then _
        objQueue.Close
 Set objQueue = Nothing
 Set objQueueInfo = Nothing
 Exit Sub

Error_Handler:
 strError = Err.Description & " (" & Err.Number & " - " & _
        Err.Source & " )"
 Resume Exit_Handler
```

```
End Sub
```

The code above starts off with the same interface from the database example, but instead utilizes MSMQ. Note how it first attaches to the queue by using the `FormatName` and invoking the `Open` routine on the `objQueueInfo` object. Next the code creates a message and stores the connection string in the label of the message, and the SQL string in the body. It sends the message by invoking the `Send` routine on the message itself and passes a reference to the queue. Lastly the code cleans up by setting all of the object references to `Nothing`, and closes the queue.

Let's take a more detailed look at how we opened the queue. A call is made to the `Open` method on the `MSMQQueueInfo` object once the desired queue is specified. Notice that the example above sets the desired queue by specifying the `FormatName` property with `DIRECT=OS:`. Queues can also be opened by specifying the machine and queue name through the `PathName` property, `objQueueInfo.PathName = "MyComputer\MyQueue"`. When using the `PathName` property, the opening of the queue is very fast, however, if the desired queue is unavailable then the `Open` routine will fail. With the `FormatName` property, the opening of the queue takes a little longer, but it will not fail when the queue is opened, even if the specified queue is unavailable. Unless you can guarantee the queue will always be available it is best to use the `FormatName` with `Direct=OS:`.

Request Processor

Next, let's rework the `DBProcessor` executable developed in the database solution earlier, and have it listen for the messages we send to the queue. Open the `DBProcessor` project and rename it to `MSMQProcessor` (you may also want to save it to a different location).

One aspect of the `DBProcessor` solution that was not very effective was that it faked the asynchronous process style by using the timer control. In this solution we will actually be listening for messages to be sent to the queue. This not only stops the program from checking the queue when there are no requests, it also enables the program to respond to the requests almost immediately.

Start by adding a reference to the **MSMQ Object Library 2.0**. The reference to ADO cannot be removed in this section since it needs to execute the SQL statement sent from the client. Next declare two private objects at form level, one called m_objQueue, which will be a reference to the desired queue, and the other m_objMsmqEvents which is declared with WithEvents and is of type MSMQEvent. The instance of the MSMQEvent class declared with WithEvents provides an event sink in which MSMQ can raise events informing us when a new message has arrived in the queue (m_objQueue).

```
Dim m_objQueue As MSMQ.MSMQQueue
Dim WithEvents m_objMsmqEvents As MSMQ.MSMQEvent
```

Declaring an object with WithEvents *provides the object a mechanism to inform the consumer of notifications by raising events in code. Responding to these events is very similar to responding to the* Click *event of a button; the only difference is the action which prompted the event.*

Next, on form load we need to open the AsyncSample queue for read access, and hook up the m_objMsmqEvents object. This is done by opening the queue, as in the MSMQSample project, but with the MQ_RECEIVE_ACCESS flag instead of the MQ_SEND_ACCESS flag. Once the queue is opened the code creates a new instance of the MSMQEvent class and passes a reference of it to MSMQ through the EnableNotification method on the m_objQueue object:

```
Private Sub Form_Load()

Dim objQueueInfo As MSMQ.MSMQQueueInfo

On Error GoTo Error_Handler

  'open the queue
  Set objQueueInfo = New MSMQ.MSMQQueueInfo
  objQueueInfo.FormatName = "DIRECT=OS:blex05\AsyncSample"
  Set m_objQueue = objQueueInfo.Open(MQACCESS.MQ_RECEIVE_ACCESS, _
              MQSHARE.MQ_DENY_NONE)

  'hook in the events
  Set m_objMsmqEvents = New MSMQ.MSMQEvent
  m_objQueue.EnableNotification m_objMsmqEvents, , 1000

Exit_Handler:
  'clean up
  Set objQueueInfo = Nothing
  Exit Sub

Error_Handler:
  MsgBox Err.Description & " (" & Err.Number & ")", vbCritical, Err.Source
  Resume Exit_Handler

End Sub
```

Now the only code left to write is to respond to the events from the m_objMsmqEvents and execute the SQL statement request from the client:

```
Private Sub m_objMsmqEvents_Arrived(ByVal Queue As Object, _
            ByVal Cursor As Long)

 Dim objConn As ADODB.Connection
 Dim objMessage As MSMQ.MSMQMessage

On Error GoTo Error_Handler

 'get the current message
 Set objMessage = Queue.ReceiveCurrent

 'connect to the db and execute the string
 Set objConn = New ADODB.Connection
 objConn.Open objMessage.Label
 objConn.Execute CStr(objMessage.Body), , adExecuteNoRecords

 'everything worked!
 txtInfo.Text = "Processed: " & objMessage.Body

Exit_Handler:
 'hook in the next event
 Set m_objMsmqEvents = New MSMQ.MSMQEvent
 m_objQueue.EnableNotification m_objMsmqEvents

 'clean up
 Set objMessage = Nothing
 If objConn.State = adStateOpen Then objConn.Close
 Set objConn = Nothing
 Exit Sub

Error_Handler:
 txtInfo.Text = Err.Description & " (" & Err.Number & ")"
 Resume Exit_Handler

End Sub
```

The code above will be fired every time a message is received by MSMQ within the AsyncSample queue. The code starts off by reading the current message. Once it has the message, the code reads the Label that contains the connection string and the Body that contains the SQL statement and performs the desired execution on the desired database.

Notice that as the method is finishing it reconnects the m_objMsmqEvents object. This needs to be done every time a message is read from MSMQ; in fact it is even needed in the other event that can be raised by MSMQ, the ArrivedError event.

Depending on the requirements of each application, different things can be done when MSMQ raises the ArrivedError event. This example displays a message box stating the message label. In a production environment you wouldn't want to display a message box, but for testing it is useful.

```
Private Sub m_objMsmqEvents_ArrivedError(ByVal Queue As Object, _
                        ByVal ErrorCode As Long, ByVal Cursor As Long)

 Dim objMessage As MSMQ.MSMQMessage

On Error GoTo Error_Handler

 'see what happened
 Set objMessage = Queue.ReceiveCurrent
 MsgBox "Investigating message: " + objMessage.Label
 m_objQueue.EnableNotification m_objMsmqEvents, , 10000

Exit_Handler:
 Set objMessage = Nothing
 Exit Sub

Error_Handler:
 MsgBox Err.Description + " in Arrived event"

End Sub
```

Client

Now that all of the pieces to submit a request and process the request through MSMQ have been developed, let's revisit the ASP code for the UI and make one small modification. Since the class name, `Request`, and the method signature have remained unchanged, the only code that needs to be modified is the `ProdID` within the `AsyncSample2.asp` page:

```
<%@ Language=VBScript %>
<HTML>
<HEAD>
<META NAME="GENERATOR" Content="Microsoft Visual Studio 6.0">
</HEAD>
<BODY>

<%

    Dim objRequest
    Dim strError

    Set objRequest = Server.CreateObject("MSMQSample.Request")
    objRequest.SubmitRequest Request.Form("txtConnectionString"), _
        Request.Form("txtSQL"), strError

    If len(strError & "") = 0 then
        Response.Write "Request was successfully sent."
    Else
        Response.Write "Error sending request: " & strError
    End If

    Set objRequest = Nothing

%>

<BR>
<BR>

<A href="javascript:history.back(1)">Back</A>

</BODY>
</HTML>
```

Let's try it out! Open the `AsyncSample1.asp` page in a browser and submit a request:

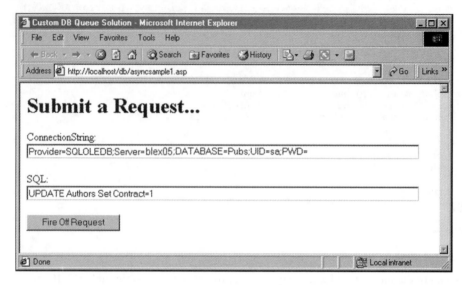

As requests are made to the `MSMQSample` COM component, messages are sent to the `AsyncSample` queue within MSMQ. If the `MSMQProcessor` executable is not running, you can open the MSMQ administrator (Computer Management MMC snap-in) and view the messages (the messages are not processed until the `MSMQProcessor` is running).

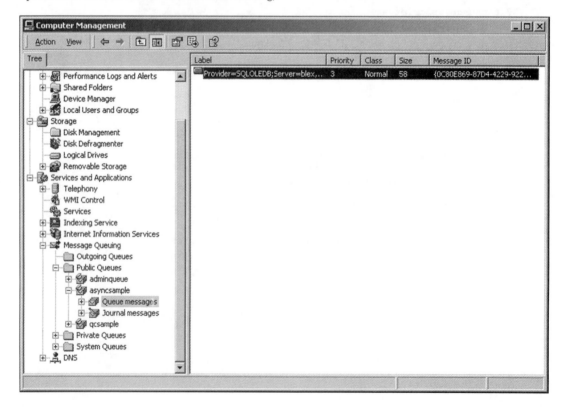

You can also open up the properties of the message (right click on the message and select **Properties**) and view a wide variety of attributes, and even take a look at the body of the message and see how it is stored:

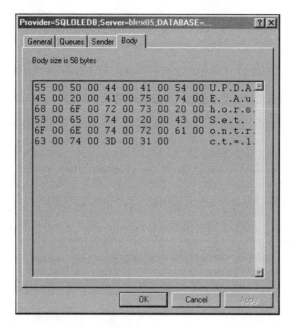

Now, if you haven't already fired up the `MSMQProcessor` executable, do so and it will process any messages within the queue. Also, as noted above, the messages will be processed right away as long as the `MSMQProcessor` executable is running:

Other Possibilities

As you can see, MSMQ provides a very powerful and flexible way to implement asynchronous communication. Since the body of a message is a variant, it can hold a wide variety of information, including objects, as long as they support the `IPersist` interface. Another great benefit of MSMQ is that the communication is loosely coupled and you can easily add more servers into the mix to counteract an increase in users.

Another possible way to use MSMQ is for an ordering system. There can be various queues for each step within the order process, from placing an order to its fulfillment. As each message is processed, within each step a new message is created and placed in the next queue, with the required information. The information or state for each message can even be stored within a COM object that supports `IPersist` and can be placed in the body of the message.

Another possibility is a dispatching system that invokes a COM object on behalf of the client. This can be very useful when web clients need to invoke a routine that is very processor intensive. Instead of the client invoking the method directly, a request can be made through MSMQ where a listener of the queue can invoke the process. This type of architecture is very useful; in fact it is so useful Microsoft developed a service within COM+ called Queued Components, which is the subject of the next section in this chapter.

COM+ Queued Components

Queued Components (QC) is a service within COM+ that is built upon MSMQ. QC provides an advanced architecture for the interaction with a component (method calls) to be recorded and packed into an MSMQ message, and then read by another process where the actual method call performed by the client is carried out.

Queued Components Architecture

Even though it may sound like a lot of magic is happening here, the architecture behind QC is actually quite straightforward and closely relates to the MSMQ sample developed above.

QC can really be broken up into three sections: the **recorder**, **listener**, and **player**. The recorder is similar to our `MSMQSample` component in the fact that it hides all of the underlying MSMQ instructions inside it. However, the recorder section of QC is quite flexible. Instead of simply taking a connection string and a SQL string, the recorder records or logs the interaction (method calls) between the consumer (ASP in this case) and the object. Once the consumer is finished with the object and the reference is dropped, the recorder takes all of the interaction it logged and sends it to a queue within MSMQ where it sits and waits for the listener to pick it up.

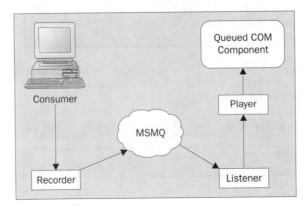

If you think about it, the recorder within QC is actually a very powerful component. It has to be very intelligent to understand how each method performs and to condense all of that information into a single MSMQ message. However, there are a few restrictions with QC that you should be aware of while developing components. The two main restrictions are very similar: there can be no parameters passed in `ByRef` (pointers) and there can be no return values. These restrictions are not dependent upon a language – they are a limitation of QC and COM. This makes sense because the caller (ASP in this case) is not actually interacting with the component, it's really talking to the recorder object within COM+'s QC.

The next piece of the QC architecture is the listener. The listener does just what its name suggests; it listens for MSMQ messages and passes them on to the player. When a component is registered in COM+ as a queued component, a series of queues are made, one public and five private. The main queue is the public queue and it is given the same name as the COM+ application in which the component resides. QC uses the five other queues in case it encounters communication issues processing the MSMQ message and sending the message to its final destination.

To make a COM+ application available through QC all that is needed is to check the **Queued** selection on the **Queuing** tab of the **Properties** page of the desired COM+ application:

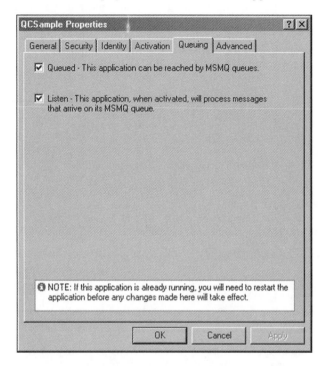

The Properties page of a COM+ application can be located by right-clicking on the application, under the Computers/COM+ Applications node within the Component Services MMC Snap-in.

Notice the **Listen** section on this tab; this specifies how to inform COM+ to watch the queue and inform the next section of QC, the player, to carry out the interaction recorded from the client.

The player is the section of QC that takes the message from the listener section, creates an instance of the desired class, and invokes the method calls the recorder logged from the user's interaction.

One important note within this whole process of QC is that is it broken up into three transactions. The first is the recording of the message. This is all done within the process of the client and can easily be transactional with other tasks the client is performing. The next transaction is solely within MSMQ and that is the sending of the message from the client to the server. There is nothing that we need to do; it is a benefit of MSMQ's guaranteed delivery of messages. The last transaction is the reading of the message. Since the listener and player components of QC are contained within a COM+ application and are configured to require a transaction, they and the component that is queued will all be contained within the same transaction. For example, if a class called `MyQC.Test` required or supported a transaction it would be brought into the same transaction as the listener and player components.

QC Sample Solution

Let's again take the same sample we have been working with and rework it to utilize the asynchronous aspects of COM+ Queued Components. As we convert the code you will notice that most of the layers we wrote in the database and MSMQ samples above will be ripped out. This is because we are simply building upon the architecture of QC instead of writing it ourselves.

Start by opening the MSMQSample or DBSample project and renaming it QCSample. Now it's time to rework the SubmitRequest method. Since we can now rely on QC to package the interaction from the client into an MSMQ message, the code within this routine can simply execute the SQL statement on the connection string that is passed from the client. There are a couple of other changes to this routine. First the error string parameter has been taken out. Since the code within this routine will actually be run by the player component within QC, there is no benefit from passing an error string. In fact, since it was passed by reference, it would violate one of QC's restrictions.

```
Public Sub SubmitRequest(ByVal strConnectionString As String, _
                         ByVal strSQL As String)

  Dim objConn As ADODB.Connection

  On Error GoTo Error_Handler

    'connect to the db and execute the string
    Set objConn = New ADODB.Connection
    objConn.Open strConnectionString
    objConn.Execute strSQL, , adExecuteNoRecords

  Exit_Handler:
    'clean up
    If Not objConn Is Nothing Then If objConn.State Then objConn.Close
    Set objConn = Nothing
    Exit Sub

  Error_Handler:
    'log to the event log
    App.LogEvent Err.Description & " (" & Err.Number & ")", _
                    LogEventTypeConstants.vbLogEventTypeError
  End Sub
```

The other change is within the error handler, which is changed because of the loss of the error string. Since a BackOffice process is actually invoking the method, an entry is logged to the event viewer. Another possibility here would be to submit an e-mail message to an administrator and submit an MSMQ message to an error queue.

Since the code above provides an interface for the client to call upon and QC will execute the code within it back on the server, the MSMQProcessor and DBProcessor sections are not needed in this example. We will instead pull the functionality from QC.

The last change to the code is for the user interface. The ASP code within the AsyncSample2.asp page needs to create an instance of the QCSample.Request class instead of the DBSample.Request or the MSMQSample.Request classes. However, the simple CreateObject method on the Server object cannot be used. This is because of QC and the way that the record is instantiated. Notice in the code shown opposite that the GetObject routine is used with the queue: and new: monikers. By creating the object with GetObject instead of the normal CreateObject the recorder within QC is able to step in and act as the ProgID specified. This is very similar to the proxy within normal DCOM calls.

A moniker is nothing more than another COM object that knows how to create other COM objects based on a string provided from the consumer. Monikers have actually been around since the early days of OLE when they were used for compound document linking.

This change in creating objects is the only change that is required on the client. Also note that the error string is also removed from this page and now relies on QC to raise an error if the listener object were to fail.

```
<%@ Language=VBScript %>
<HTML>
<HEAD>
<META NAME="GENERATOR" Content="Microsoft Visual Studio 6.0">
</HEAD>
<BODY>

<%
    Dim objRequest

    Set objRequest = GetObject("queue:/new:QCSample.Request")
    objRequest.SubmitRequest Request.Form("txtConnectionString"), _
                             Request.Form("txtSQL")

    Response.Write "Request was successfully sent."

    Set objRequest = Nothing
%>

<BR>
<BR>

<A href="javascript:history.back(1)">Back</A>

</BODY>
</HTML>
```

The last part to make this work is it to configure the QCSample.Request component as a configured COM+ queued component:

❑ First compile the new component.

❑ Next open the **Component Services** MMC snap-in located within the **Administrative Tools** folder. Drill down in the **COM+ Applications** folder and create a new application called **QCSample** (right-click on the COM+ application node and select **New**).

❑ Now expand the node for the new application and add the **QCSample.Request** component.

❑ Next configure the new COM+ application as a queued application. This is done by selecting the **Queuing** tab within the application's **Properties** and checking the **Queued** and **Listen** boxes.

❑ The last step is to specify the interface or interfaces that are queued within the COM+ application. This is done by selecting the **Properties** on the desired interface and marking the **Queued** checkbox on the **Queuing** tab. In this case select the interface called **_Request**, located under the **Interfaces** folder, which can be found in the **QCSample** COM+ application.

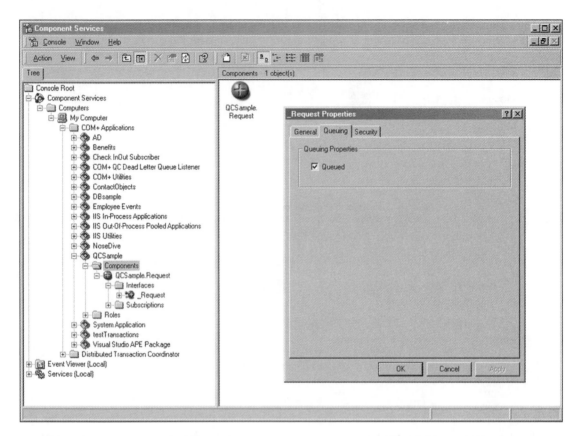

Since this example uses a web client with anonymous access turned on, the COM+ application must also be configured to ignore authentication level security, since all requests will be assigned to the IUSR_<Computer Name> account. To disable authentication within COM+, open the **Properties** window on a COM+ application and select the **Security** tab. Next set the **Authentication level for calls** to **None**. Just to make sure that the change takes place immediately, shut down the application, by right-clicking on the COM+ application and selecting **Shut down**. Although this type of security setting may be useful in some circumstances (as it is for this demonstration), remember that it opens a security hole. A better solution for a production environment would be to leave the authentication level at **Packet** and require the browser users to authenticate themselves.

Now fire up the browser to the AsyncSample1.asp page and submit a request. Instead of our code comprising MSMQ messages, COM+'s Queued Components architecture is building the message on our behalf, while another process (the listener and player) will carry out the execute on the database for us. The best part about the whole process is that the client is not waiting for the processing of the SQL statement to complete, instead the interaction from the ASP page has been queued and will process somewhere else. Another great benefit of QC is that the actual processing of the MSMQ messages can be postponed and queued until more server resources are available. This can be very useful for accounting and billing tasks. To find out more about starting up a COM+ application at a desired time, see the support article Q11111 from Microsoft at http://support.Microsoft.com/.

As you can see, there is a wide variety of asynchronous processing that can be done by utilizing queues in one form or another. Now, let's take a look at another way to implement asynchronous processing by using events and callbacks.

Events and Callbacks

Events and callbacks provide a way for another process to hook in and notify the consumer (client) that something has happened. One example of this that was used earlier is the MSMQEvent object. This object was declared with events and was passed by reference (a pointer) to MSMQ, which raised events within the code when a message arrived or an error occurred. Utilizing events and callbacks eliminates a lot of unnecessary code that sits in a loop or a timer, periodically checking the status of something.

How Do Events and Callbacks Work?

So how does an event or callback really work? Well, it starts when the client invokes a method on the object. Within this method call or a previous method call, the consumer must pass a reference to itself or an object it is using. This provides a hook for the process to call back to the client, and invokes a method that actually fires on the client. Although you may not be aware of it, this is the same type of communication as happens when a user client clicks on a button in a normal form-based application; Windows and the VB runtime capture the user's interaction and raising the On_Click event in your code. Events are also known as connection points in the VC++ developer community.

Events, callbacks and connection points are discussed further in the next chapter.

There are a wide variety of object models that support asynchronous processing by implementing events and callbacks and you can also utilize events in your own objects. For example, many technologies and tools developed by Microsoft, such as ActiveX Data Objects (ADO), Remote Scripting, and XMLDOM, support events and callbacks. We'll look at each of these next.

ActiveX Data Objects

Many of the objects within **ActiveX Data Objects (ADO)** support asynchronous processing by providing events for the consumer to listen to. One of most widely used ones is the Connection object. For example, instead of waiting for a connection to be made to the data source, a flag can be set on the Open routine stating to make this call asynchronous. This call would look like the following statement:

```
m_objMyConn.Open txtMyConnectionString, , adAsyncConnect
```

Now that ADO knows to make the call asynchronous, it will need an event to respond to and raise once the connection is made, ConnectionComplete. This is done by declaring the objMyConn at the form, module, or class level and using the WithEvents keyword:

```
Dim WithEvents m_objMyConn As ADODB.Connection
```

Once a variable is declared using WithEvents, a series of methods are available to code to. This list is available by looking at the **Object Browser** within VB, or by selecting the variable in the combo box at the top left of the code panel and then looking at the list of events in the combo box to the right. Once the event is defined, all that is left is to place code within it:

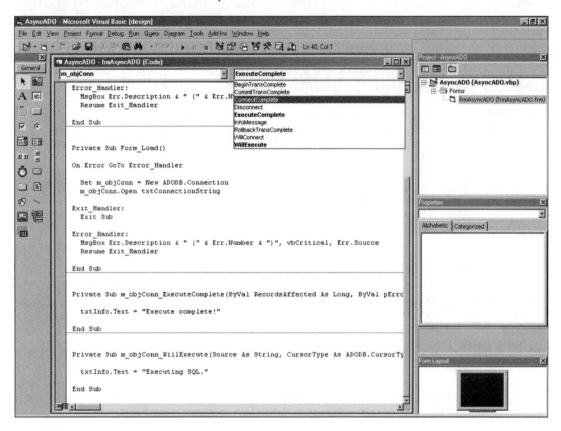

ADO Sample Solution

Let's build a sample VB application that executes a SQL statement asynchronously, just like our other example did, but instead using the asynchronous ability of ADO.

First start out by opening a new standard EXE VB project (AsyncADO). Next add a reference to Microsoft **ActiveX Data Objects** and place three textboxes and one button on the form. Within the code below, one textbox is named txtInfo, another is named txtConnectionString, and the last one is named txtSQL. The command button on the form has been named cmdExecute.

Now that the form is set up, we can add the code to asynchronously execute the SQL statement input by the user. First declare a variable called m_objConn at the form level using WithEvents:

```
Dim WithEvents m_objConn As ADODB.Connection
```

Next add the code to connect to the data source defined in the `txtConnectionString` textbox on loading of the form:

```
Private Sub Form_Load()

On Error GoTo Error_Handler

  Set m_objConn = New ADODB.Connection
  m_objConn.Open txtConnectionString

Exit_Handler:
  Exit Sub

Error_Handler:
  MsgBox Err.Description & " (" & Err.Number & ")", vbCritical, Err.Source
  Resume Exit_Handler

End Sub
```

Now that a connection has been made to the data source, it is time to make the asynchronous call to ADO. This is done on the `Click` event of the `cmdExecute` button, which makes a call to the `Execute` routine on the `m_objConn` object:

```
Private Sub cmdExecute_Click()

On Error GoTo Error_Handler

  m_objConn.Execute txtSQL.Text, , ExecuteOptionEnum.adAsyncExecute

Exit_Handler:
  Exit Sub

Error_Handler:
  MsgBox Err.Description & " (" & Err.Number & ")", vbCritical, Err.Source
  Resume Exit_Handler

End Sub
```

Notice that with the method call to execute the SQL statement, the flag `adAsyncExecute` from the `ExecuteOptionEnum` enumeration is specified. This is a flag that informs ADO to create another thread behind the scenes and execute the SQL statement on that, letting the client's thread continue processing other tasks such as painting the VB form.

The last piece of code that needs to be implemented is to respond to ADO when the execution of the SQL statement completes. Once this happens ADO will raise an event by calling the `ExecuteComplete` routine:

```
Private Sub m_objConn_ExecuteComplete(ByVal RecordsAffected As Long, _
    ByVal pError As ADODB.Error, _
    adStatus As ADODB.EventStatusEnum, _
    ByVal pCommand As ADODB.Command, _
    ByVal pRecordset As ADODB.Recordset, _
    ByVal pConnection As ADODB.Connection)

  txtInfo.Text = "Execute complete!"

End Sub
```

As you can see, for this example we will simply inform the user that the SQL statement has been executed. This example also has added code to respond to another event from ADO, the `WillExecute` event. This way the user can see that something is happening while the SQL statement is executed:

```
Private Sub m_objConn_WillExecute(Source As String, _
    CursorType As ADODB.CursorTypeEnum, _
    LockType As ADODB.LockTypeEnum, _
    Options As Long, _
    adStatus As ADODB.EventStatusEnum, _
    ByVal pCommand As ADODB.Command, _
    ByVal pRecordset As ADODB.Recordset, _
    ByVal pConnection As ADODB.Connection)

  txtInfo.Text = "Executing SQL."

End Sub
```

Try it out! Fire up the VB application and enter a valid connection string and SQL statement. Notice that the `txtInfo` textbox displays **Executing SQL** when the button is clicked and then **Execute complete** when it finishes:

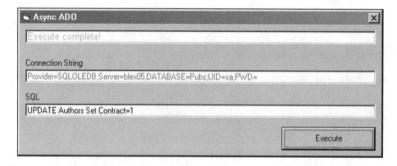

If the execute completed too quickly and you're using SQL Server, copy and paste the SQL statement a few times, placing semicolons between each statement. If you add enough to the SQL statement to slow it down sufficiently, you will notice that the form can be moved around while the SQL statement is still executing and the VB form still paints. Normally if this was done without asynchronous processing, the VB form would not paint until the SQL statement completed executing.

This example of asynchronous processing with ADO, is just one of many events that ADO supports. For a list of other events to code to, reference the object browser within VB, by pressing *F2* after referencing the Microsoft **ActiveX Data Object** library. Another common utility that developers use (especially VC++ developers) is the OLE View, which can be found in the **Visual Studio 6 Tools** in the **Start** menu.

Let's now take a look at an object that is getting more and more popular to use every day, especially with all of the B2B processing that is happening, the XMLDOM.

XMLDOM

Since the primary function of the **XMLDOM** is parsing, viewing, and editing strings, the processing it does can sometimes take a while. Because of this the XMLDOM supports events much like ADO does. By calling certain methods and passing the proper flags, XML can do a lot of processing in the background while the consumer of the XMLDOM is free to perform other tasks.

DOMDocument

One example of using the XMLDOM in this way is by calling the Load method on the DOMDocument object. The following code loads an XML file into the DOMDocument object, but first informs it to load the files asynchronously, by setting the async property to True:

```
Private Sub Form_Load()
 Set m_objXMLDoc = New DOMDocument
 m_objXMLDoc.async = True
 m_objXMLDoc.Load "http://localhost/Test.xml"
End Sub

Private Sub m_objXMLDoc_onreadystatechange()
 If m_objXMLDoc.readyState = 4 Then
  If Not m_objXMLDoc.parseError.errorCode = 0 Then
   MsgBox "Error processing XML : " & m_objXMLDoc.parseError.reason
  Else
   MsgBox "Finished loading XML successfuly. "
  End If
 End If
End Sub
```

Just like in the ADO example above, the client is able to continue processing while the object is carrying out the task in a different thread in the background. Once the XML document is completely loaded the onreadystatechange event will fire and the readyState value will be equal to 4. Then the code checks the parseError collection and informs the user of the outcome of the operation.

XMLHTTPRequest

The XMLHTTPRequest object with the XMLDOM provides the ability to process asynchronously. XMLHTTPRequest is a great object that is used for communicating with a web server through code.

The following code demonstrates how to use the XMLHTTPRequest object by posting an XML file to a web server for processing. The code is fairly simple to follow. The important part to note is the Boolean flag at the end of the Open routine. This is the flag that tells the object to post the files asynchronously, which will return the process back to the client immediately.

```
Public Sub SendXML()
 Dim objDocument As MSXML.DOMDocument
 Dim objHTTPRequest As MSXML.XMLHTTPRequest
On Error GoTo Error_Handler

 'load the XML file
 Set objDocument = New MSXML.DOMDocument
 objDocument.Load "C:\Orders.xml"

 'send the xml to the web server
 Set objHTTPRequest = New MSXML.XMLHTTPRequest
 objHTTPRequest.open "POST", _
   "Http://www.MyServer.com/ProcessOrders.asp", True
 objHTTPRequest.send objDocument

Exit_Handler:
 'clean up
 Set objHTTPRequest = Nothing
 Set objDocument = Nothing
 Exit Sub

Error_Handler:
 MsgBox Err.Description & " (" & Err.Number & ")", vbCritical, Err.Source

End Sub
```

This example shows how to send the file off asynchronously, but what if you want to know when the send has completed? Well, Microsoft has added an extension to the XMLHTTPRequest object to provide this functionality. However, since the Microsoft developers could not change the signature of the open or send routines, nor could they add Microsoft-style events to the object model, they implemented another way to inform the consumer of the object that the send has completed. This functionality is achieved by utilizing callbacks.

To get the XMLHTTPRequest object to callback to the client code it must be passed the location (or address) of a method to call once the send is complete. The following code shows how to implement this. Notice that a new line has been added to the SendXML routine and a new routine has been added below. The address of this new routine is what is sent to the object through the onreadystatechange property. Back on the XMLDOM side another thread is created and assigned to carry out the requested task of loading and parsing the XML document, while the original thread immediately returns back to the client. Once the newly created thread finishes processing, it looks at the address of the method passed to it through the onreadystatechange property, in this case HandleStateChange, and calls upon it, raising an event:

```
Public Sub SendXML()
 Dim objDocument As MSXML.DOMDocument
 Dim objHTTPRequest As MSXML.XMLHTTPRequest
 On Error GoTo Error_Handler

 'load the XML file
 Set objDocument = New MSXML.DOMDocument
 objDocument.Load "C:\Orders.xml"

 'send the xml to the web server
 Set objHTTPRequest = New MSXML.XMLHTTPRequest
 objHTTPRequest.open "POST", _
```

```
                          "Http://www.MyServer.com/ProcessOrders.asp", True
    objHTTPRequest.onreadystatechange = HandleStateChange
    objHTTPRequest.send objDocument

  Exit_Handler:
   'clean up
   Set objHTTPRequest = Nothing
   Set objDocument = Nothing
   Exit Sub

  Error_Handler:
    MsgBox Err.Description & " (" & Err.Number & ")", vbCritical, Err.Source
  End Sub

  Sub HandleStateChange()
    MsgBox "XML has been sent!"
  End Sub
```

As you can see, the XMLDOM has some very useful asynchronous processing capabilities, but this is just the beginning. For a complete list of object within the XMLDOM and the asynchronous possibilities, refer to Microsoft's XMLDOM area located at http://msdn.Microsoft.com/xml.

SAX2

SAX2, which stands for **Simple API for XML version 2**, has just been released at the time of writing this book. It provides a new alternative to XMLDOM that is event-based. This can and will be helpful to a great deal of GUI developers who are accustomed to event-based programming. This also proves to be very beneficial when processing large XML files.

Events within SAX2 are handled in a very similar way to the ones with the MSMQEvents object, however, instead of declaring an object with events, SAX2 requires the consumer to implement a predefined interface and pass a reference of itself (Me keyword in VB, this in VC++) to a method within one of the objects in the SAX2 library.

This style of asynchronous processing produces more code since all methods must be defined on the implemented interface. However, it can be much faster, because early binding is when the object queries your reference for the predefined interface.

At this time SAX2 is in a premature stage. However, if you have the need to process XML in an event-based fashion, it is definitely worth checking out.

Next, let's take a look into another useful resource that supports asynchronous processing via callbacks and events: Remote Scripting.

Remote Scripting

Remote Scripting is similar to the callback which the XMLDOM utilized on the open routine in the XMLHTTPRequest object. However, Remote Scripting provides a mechanism to do this over the web between the client's browser and the web server, and the best part is that it is supported in both Internet Explorer and Netscape.

Remote Scripting allows client-side script in the browser to invoke routines located on ASP pages on the web server. The possibilities that are available through this are limitless, especially when the ability to invoke these routines asynchronously is added.

We won't be covering Remote Scripting in this chapter, but the setup and implementation of Remote Scripting is covered very nicely in an article written by Dino Esposito, located on Wrox's ASPToday site (http://www.asptoday.com/articles/19990930.htm).

Other Ways to Utilize Asynchronous Processing

Asynchronous processing can also be accomplished in a few other ways besides the traditional queues and events. Although some of the following are not truly asynchronous processing they do allow a way to obtain some of the same advantages. Depending on your situation, time, and experience the following solutions can sometimes be a better alternative.

Windows Scheduler

Windows 2000 has a scheduling utility called Scheduled Tasks, which can be used to define jobs or tasks to be run at certain times. Although this in itself is not asynchronous processing, it can be used to check a queue or database and process any requests that have been made.

The Windows scheduler can be accessed by opening the Scheduled Tasks folder within the Control Panel, or it can be accessed through the command prompt by using the AT command.

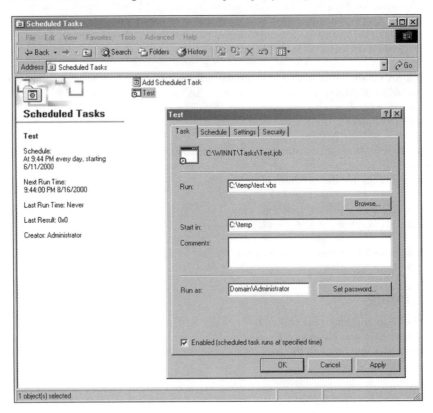

This utility is also very useful for kicking off maintenance routines and other BackOffice tasks.

SQL Server Jobs

SQL Server 6.5 and 7.0 both come with a very powerful scheduling service called the **SQL Server Agent**. This service is like the scheduler mentioned above, but much more powerful.

Within SQL Server, various tasks can be bundled up into a single unit of work. Within SQL Server 6.5 these were called **tasks**, within SQL Server 7.0 they are called **jobs**. For the remainder of this section these units of work will simply be referred to as jobs.

SQL Server jobs can take on a wide variety of roles and operations. They are often utilized to perform database maintenance tasks during off peak hours. These same jobs can be built to perform day-to-day operations like processing orders or exporting data to another system. They can run stored procedures, batch files, or even run VBScript or JavaScript that interacts with other objects.

The following is a screenshot of a job within SQL Server 7. When run it calls upon a stored procedure. Next it executes a batch file and then finishes up by executing a VBScript file. The main point to note here is how versatile SQL Server jobs are.

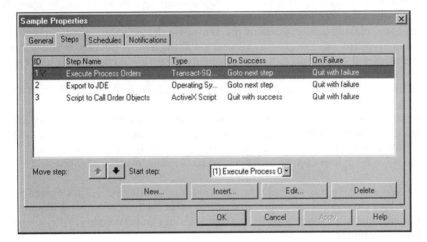

SQL Server also provides a very easy way to fire off a job by issuing a single SQL statement. The best part about this is that the execute call returns back right away, while the job is processing in the background on the server. This enables developers to kick off large SQL jobs through interaction from the end users without making them wait, instead of having the jobs process at set times.

The following code connects to a SQL Server database and fires off a job:

```
Sub FireSQLJob()
 Dim objConn As ADODB.Connection

On Error GoTo Error_Handler

 Set objConn = New ADODB.Connection

 objConn.Open _
        "Provider=SQLOLEDB;Server=MyServer;DATABASE=MyDB;UID=sa;PWD="
 objConn.Execute "sp_start_job 'Sample'"
```

```
Exit_Handler:
  If Not objConn Is Nothing Then If objConn.State = adStateOpen Then _
          objConn.Close
  Set objConn = Nothing
  Exit Sub

Error_Handler:
  MsgBox Err.Description & " (" & Err.Source & ")", vbCritical, Err.Source

End Sub
```

More detailed coverage of this topic can be found in *Professional SQL Server 7.0* by Rob Viera (Wrox Press, ISBN 1-861002-31-9).

Summary

Throughout this chapter we looked at asynchronous processing and how it can be used. We saw the advantages of distributing the processing of a task among various threads of execution, or even across various computers, making our applications much more scaleable. Also, when implemented correctly, we noticed that asynchronous processing can provide a much more interactive user interface. We then looked into queues and events and how they can be used provide asynchronous processing between parts of a solution. We first looked into the different types of queues such as database tables and MSMQ and finished up by talking about events and callbacks, which are used in tools like ADO and XML.

Whether you implement your own queued solution, use MSMQ, or build Queued Components, remember to keep in mind the pros and cons of asynchronous processing when deciding how or if to utilize it. If you do not require immediate feedback, a queued solution is a great choice; however, if you need the immediate feedback, and still want to break up the processing, consider using events and callbacks.

Although this chapter dove into the basic ways asynchronous processing is implemented, it has just touched on various tools and technologies that utilize asynchronous processing. There are many third-party components that implement asynchronous processing; and remember, you can even build it into your own business objects.

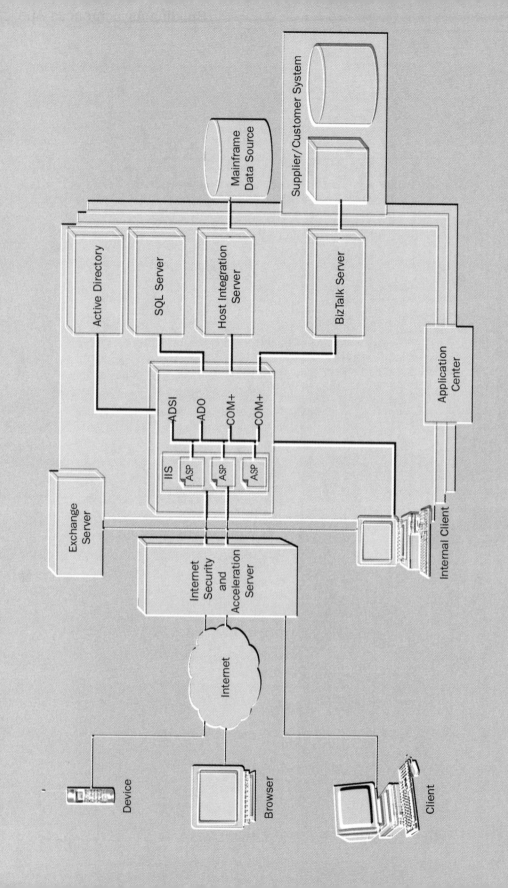

Mainframe
Data Source

Supplier/Customer System

Active Directory

SQL Server

Host Integration
Server

BizTalk Server

Application
Center

ADSI

ADO

COM+

COM+

IIS

ASP

ASP

ASP

Exchange
Server

Internet Security
and
Acceleration
Server

Internal Client

Internet

Device

Browser

Client

10

COM+ Events

As VB developers already know, **events** are one of the fundamental concepts behind the Windows operating system. A VB program will want to receive notification when a user interacts with the program's user interface. For example, when a user presses a button in a dialog box, Windows fires an event. The VB runtime captures that event and calls the function or method associated with that action. For example, say a VB developer creates a standard EXE project and drags a command button, named "Command1" by default, onto the VB form. The command button receives numerous events, one of those being the `Click` event. The developer can provide implementation when the event is received:

```
Private Sub Command1_Click()
    MsgBox "Received the Click event."
End Sub
```

In this case, the Windows operating system is the **publisher** and the VB program is the **subscriber**. The publisher provides notification of events, such as a user clicking the command button on the form. The subscriber receives notification when a particular event occurs and can choose to act upon it. In this example, a message box is displayed, notifying the user that the event was received.

Windows events are quite effective for notifying an application when a user clicks a button. But what if more than one application wishes to receive notification when an event occurs? One of the classic programming problems is how to deliver information to one or more interested parties without prior knowledge of their identity. In this scenario, there are two types of programs: those that *have* information (publishers) and those that *need* information (subscribers). The **COM+ Events** service addresses this problem by acting as the "middle man" between the publishers and subscribers. COM+ Events provides Windows DNA applications with a flexible and scaleable service for supporting events. The COM+ Events service is also tightly integrated with other COM+ services such as transactions and Queued Components.

In this chapter, we'll start by looking at different ways to implement events within your applications, including a brief overview of the design pattern upon which the COM+ Events service is based. We will then discuss how to make the most of COM+ Events within Windows DNA applications. We will learn how to subscribe to existing events and publish our own events. This will involve looking at a sample application, the full code for which is available in the download file from the Wrox web site.

Implementing Events in DNA Applications

There are a variety of techniques for implementing events within applications. In this section, we will review three of them: brute force, callbacks, and the loosely coupled events design pattern. We will also discuss why the loosely coupled events design pattern is usually the preferred choice for implementing events in enterprise applications.

Brute Force

One way to implement events is through brute force. We could have the COM subscriber continually poll the COM publisher to find out if the event has occurred. As you can imagine, this is very inefficient. There is considerable overhead associated with constantly making round trip calls between the subscriber and the publisher. In addition, latency is introduced that could be as high as the polling interval. In other words, if an event occurred just after the subscriber polled the publisher, we would have to wait until the next poll before the event notification would be received.

Callbacks

Another solution is to implement **callbacks**. The subscriber calls a method on the publisher, passing the publisher a reference to itself. When an event occurs, the publisher will notify the subscriber of the event, by calling a method on the subscriber via the reference it was previously passed. The following example code implements an event using a callback:

```
' Component:  SimplePublisher
' Object:     CPublisher

Private m_colSubscribers As Collection

Private Sub Class_Initialize()
  m_colSubscribers = New Collection
End Sub

Public Function Register(objSubscriber As Object)
  m_colSubscribers.Add objSubscriber
End Function

Public Function Unregister(objSubscriber As Object)
  m_colSubscribers.Remove objSubscriber
End Function

Public Function DoSomethingThatFiresAnEvent()
  ' Fire event on each subscriber.
  For i = 1 To m_colSubscribers.Count
    m_colSubscribers(i).FireEvent
```

```
    Next
End Function


' A form that creates a publisher and registers itself as a subscriber.

Private Sub Form_Load()
   Dim objPublisher As SimplePublisher.CPublisher

   ' Initialization.
   Set objPublisher = New SimplePublisher.CPublisher

   ' Register ourselves with the publisher.
   objPublisher.Register Me

   ' Use publisher.
   objPublisher.DoSomethingThatFiresAnEvent

   ' Unregister ourselves from the publisher.
   objPublisher.Unregister Me
End Sub

' Implement the function that will receive an event.
Public Function FireEvent()
   ' Do something as a result of receiving an event.
End Function
```

In this example, the subscriber is responsible for creating an instance of CPublisher and calls its Register method, passing a reference to itself. The publisher is responsible for storing the object reference it receives in the list of its subscribers. When the DoSomethingThatFiresAnEvent method is called, the publisher then iterates through its list of subscribers and notifies each one that a particular event has occurred. Finally, the subscriber calls Unregister when it is no longer interested in receiving events.

Connection Points – Tight Coupling

COM **connection points** provide a standard method for implementing events using callbacks. Connection points merely provide a well-defined interface between the publisher and subscriber. The subscriber must formally register itself with the publisher at runtime. The publisher is responsible for maintaining a list of subscribers and is responsible for notifying each subscriber. The publisher is also responsible for providing the implementation for notifying its subscribers when an event is fired.

Connection points have been around for quite some time. So why do we need yet another system for firing and receiving events? One of the limitations of the existing method is that connection points' use of callbacks provides **tight coupling** between the publisher and subscriber. VB's implementation of connection points notifies its subscribers serially, which limits its usefulness within enterprise applications. For example, the fiftieth subscriber will receive notification only after the first forty-nine subscribers received notification. If some of the first forty-nine subscribers are located on different machines, network latency can quickly bring the application to its knees.

Loosely Coupled Events

In contrast, the COM+ Events service is based on the **loosely coupled events** design pattern. This provides a mechanism to advertise and deliver information to one or more interested parties and have interested parties subscribe to events published by one or more publishers, without prior knowledge of their identity. One or more publishers can publish events to one or more subscribers. Unlike connection points, a subscriber does not know anything about its publisher(s) and a publisher does not know anything about its subscriber(s). The Events system serves as a cross-reference between its publisher(s) and subscribers(s). The publishers publish an event by calling a method on an **event object**, the Events system then notifies any subscribers that have registered to receive notification of that event:

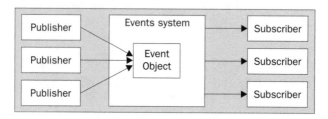

COM+ Events provides a standard implementation of the loosely coupled events design pattern for the Windows platform. One of the benefits of a standard events system is that publishers and subscribers can be combined in ways the developer could never have anticipated. For example, in an enterprise application, one system may be interested in receiving notification from another system. Imagine a Human Resources (HR) system that publishes an event when a new employee gets hired. Other systems within the enterprise may choose to be notified when this event occurs. The HR system does not need to have prior knowledge of the subscribers.

As you might expect, COM+ Events is built on top of COM+. The event object is a COM+ object created by COM+ Events. The publisher (itself a COM+ component registered with COM+ Events) fires an event by calling a method on the event object. COM+ Events is then responsible for notifying all of the event's subscribers. The subscribers are also COM+ components, implemented by the developer and registered with COM+ Events. Let's explore these concepts further by looking at an example.

Simple COM+ Events Example

One applicable use for the COM+ Events service is for integrating disparate applications within the enterprise. Our simple example will introduce a scenario that we will follow and expand upon throughout the chapter. A complete copy of the sample code may be found in the download file available from the Wrox web site.

Suppose that we have a Human Resource Information System (HRIS) that fires an event when a new employee is added to the database. One of the events that we would like to have happen is for a welcome e-mail to be sent to the employee, inviting them to join the health insurance scheme.

Event Class

The first thing we need to do is create an **event class**. The event class serves as the cross-reference between the publisher and subscriber. It is a COM+ class with an interface that is known by both the publisher and subscriber. It is responsible for retrieving/caching subscriptions and multicasting event calls. However, as we will see in the simple example, it is the COM+ Events service and not the developer that provides the implementation details. The developer is only responsible for defining the interface, ProgID, CLSID, and IID (the latter two are automatically generated by VB). All methods on the event class interface are events that may be subscribed to.

Our sample event class encapsulates all of the information that we wish to publish to our subscribers (in this case there is only one method, representing the onCreateNewEmployee event). We will create a standard VB ActiveX DLL project. The project is named EmployeeEvents and the class is named CEmployee:

```
' Component:   EmployeeEvents
' Class:       CEmployee

Option Explicit

Public Sub onCreateNewEmployee(ByVal strEmployeeID As String, _
                               ByVal strEmployeeType As String)

    ' No implementation.
End Sub
```

Subscribers are not allowed to return information back to the publisher, hence the method is a subroutine and not a function. Also notice that each of the parameters is passed by value instead of by reference. COM+ provides no mechanism for passing return parameters or error codes back to the publisher. If the publisher wishes to receive error information, it needs to do this out-of-band. For example, the publisher could also be a subscriber to an error event.

The subroutine does not have any implementation, because the Events service will never execute the methods implemented in the event class. Since we provide no implementation in our methods, it is tempting to set the Instancing property to PublicNotCreateable. Doing so would result in the class module being treated like an interface definition instead of a full-blown COM class. Since we are defining the interface to the event class and not providing the implementation, this sounds like what we want. However, COM+ Events provides the implementation for an event class but relies on the component to register its own event class. Therefore, the component needs to be able to register its event class in such a way that the publisher can create a new instance of the event class. In summary, ensure that your event class has its Instancing property set to MultiUse, the default setting.

Registering the Event Class

After compiling the DLL, now we are going to register our event class with the event service. First we need to create an empty COM+ application called Employee Events using the Component Services MMC. (The Component Services MMC for Windows 2000 Server can be found under Start, Programs, Administrative Tools, Component Services.) Run the COM Application Install Wizard by highlighting the COM+ Applications folder, right-clicking on the folder, and then selecting New Application. When creating your COM+ application, create a Library application, as shown in the screenshot overleaf:

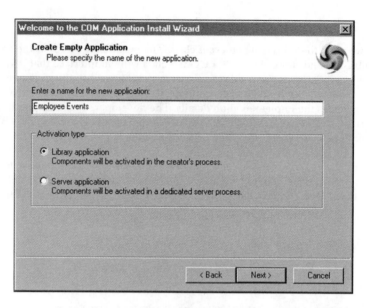

Generally, your event class will not contain any implementation, since COM+ provides the implementation for event classes. Even if your event class did contain an implementation, the Events service would never execute it. Therefore there is no need for process isolation, which is the primary advantage of a server application, and a library application is sufficient.

Next we will add the `EmployeeEvents` component to our **Employee Events** application. We'll use the COM Component Install Wizard to install the event class. To launch the wizard, expand the **Employee Events** application, highlight and right-click on **Components**, and then select **New Component**. When adding the component, be sure to select the "Install new event class(es)" button:

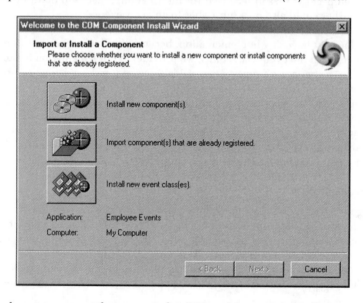

Note that whenever you recompile your event class DLL and do not maintain binary compatibility, you will have to re-install your component and re-register your subscribers. (For additional information on binary compatibility, see Chapter 7.)

Event Subscriber

A **subscriber** is a COM component responsible for receiving and processing notifications from the Events service. To receive event notification, the subscriber must implement the appropriate interface(s) for the events that the subscriber wishes to receive notification of.

Our event subscriber is responsible for sending a welcome e-mail to every new employee. The first thing we need to do is to create a class that provides the required implementation for the onCreateNewEmployee event. We will create a standard VB ActiveX DLL project. The project will be named Benefits and the class will be named CHealthInsurance. The code is shown below:

```
' Component:      Benefits
' Class:          CHealthInsurance
' References:     EmployeeEvents (EmployeeEvents.dll)
'                 Microsoft CDO for Windows 2000 Library
'                 (c:\windows\system32\cdosys.dll)

Option Explicit

Implements EmployeeEvents.CEmployee

' Sign up the new employee for benefits.
Private Sub CEmployee_onCreateNewEmployee(ByVal strEmployeeID As String, _
                                ByVal strEmployeeType As String)

    Dim objMessage      As CDO.Message
    Dim strBody         As String
    Dim strName         As String
    Dim strEmail        As String

    ' Initialize.
    Set objMessage = New CDO.Message

    'Obtain strName and strEmail address from the HRIS database ...

    strBody = "Welcome aboard " & strName & "!" & vbCrLf & vbCrLf _
        & "We are very excited that you are" & vbCrLf _
        & "joining our team. Please contact" & vbCrLf _
        & "us within the next two weeks " & vbCrLf _
        & "to enroll in your" & vbCrLf _
        & "health insurance. " & vbCrLf & vbCrLf _
        & "Sincerely," & vbCrLf & vbCrLf _
        & "The Benefits Staff"

    objMessage.To = strEmail
    objMessage.From = "benefits@company.com"
    objMessage.Subject = "Welcome Aboard!"
    objMessage.TextBody = strBody
    objMessage.Send

    Set objMessage = Nothing

End Sub
```

The first thing we did was to implement the EmployeeEvents.CEmployee interface. We then provided the implementation for the onCreateNewEmployee method. The onCreateNewEmployee method call sends an e-mail to the new employee asking them to enroll in health insurance.

Registering the Subscriber

After compiling the subscriber component, we need to register it within COM+ so that we can create a **subscription** to the onCreateNewEmployee event in the next section. A subscription is the relationship between a subscriber, an event, and possibly a specific publisher. A subscription object is the entity that encapsulates this relationship and, like any other entity, is stored in the COM+ catalog.

First we need to create an empty COM+ server application called Benefits using the Component Services MMC and add the component. This can be done by following similar steps as outlined in the *Registering the Event Class* section above. However, this time create a Server application and Install New Component. This will ensure that if your Benefits component crashes, it does not affect the publisher's process.

Subscribe to the Event

Now that our component is registered, we need to create a new subscription to the onCreateNewEmployee event. In the Component Services MMC, expand the Benefits.CHealthInsurance component to display the Subscriptions folder. Launch the COM New Subscriptions Wizard by selecting and right-clicking on the Subscriptions folder and then selecting New Subscription. After clicking the Next button on the welcome screen, select the event or events the subscriber is interested in receiving.

If a class *interface*, such as _CEmployee is selected, the subscriber will receive notification for every event supported by that class. If a *method* of a class is selected, the subscriber will receive notification for only the selected event. The final option is to select "Use all interfaces for this component". If this checkbox is selected, the subscriber will receive notification for events supported by all implemented event class interfaces. In our case, we will select the onCreateNewEmployee method exposed by the _CEmployee interface and then click the Next button. COM+ Events will notify the Benefits.CHealthInsurance component whenever a publisher fires the _CEmployee.onCreateNewEmployee event.

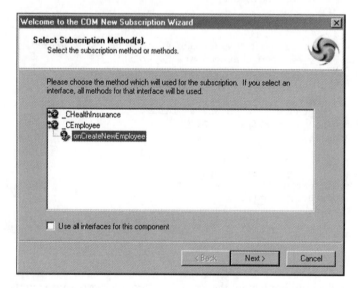

After COM+ Events obtains a list of event classes that support the CEmployee.onCreateNewEmployee event, select the event class the subscriber is interested in receiving events from. You may also select the "Use all event classes that implement the specified interface" option. If this checkbox is selected, the subscriber will receive notification when the onCreateNewEmployee method is called on any event object that supports the CEmployee interface. In our case, we'll select the EmployeeEvents.CEmployee event class and then click the Next button:

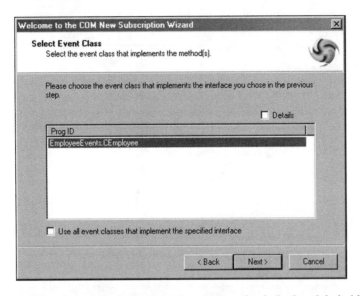

Enter New Employee for the name of the new subscription, check the box labeled "Enable this subscription immediately", and click the Next button. The checkbox tells the Events service to immediately start notifying the Benefits.CHealthInsurance component when the onCreateNewEmployee event is fired:

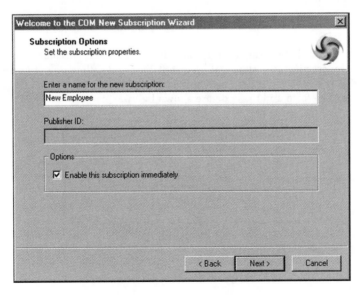

Click the Finish button to complete the subscription process. You have now created a subscription that allows the Benefits component to receive events from the onCreateNewEmployee event class. You can access the subscription from the Component Services MMC:

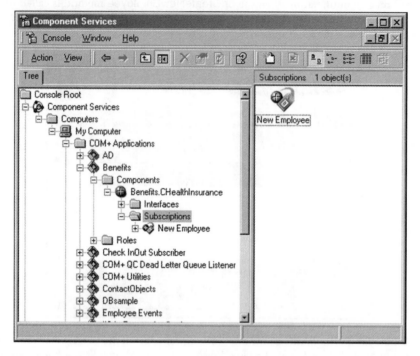

Each time the event is fired, COM+ Events will create an instance of the component, call its onCreateNewEmployee method, and then destroy the component. We'll discuss subscriptions in more detail later in the chapter.

Publisher

The publisher is responsible for firing events that will be received by its subscribers. The publisher accomplishes this by creating an instance of the event class and calling one of its methods. We will create a simple dialog-based application as a standard VB EXE project named HRIS with a form named frmNewEmployee. The form and the code are shown below:

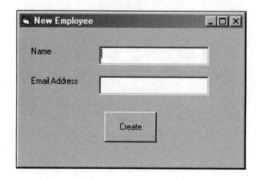

```
' Project:    HRIS
' Form:       NewEmployee
' References: EmployeeEvents (EmployeeEvents.dll)

Option Explicit

Private Sub btnCreateNewEmployee_Click()
    Dim objEmployeeEvent As EmployeeEvents.CEmployee

    ' Initialize.
    Set objEmployeeEvent = New EmployeeEvents.CEmployee

    ' Create the new employee and then fire the onCreateNewEmployee event.
    'Implementation for creating new employee ...
    objEmployeeEvent.onCreateNewEmployee tbName.Text, tbEmailAddress.Text

    Set objEmployeeEvent = Nothing
End Sub
```

The `HRIS` application is responsible for creating a new employee and then notifying its subscribers. As you can see, the publisher is very straightforward to implement. We simply create a new instance of the event class and call the appropriate method. COM+ Events will then notify the components that have subscribed to this event class.

Simple Example Summary

The following is a summary of the steps we took to create our simple example:

- ❑ Create the event class

- ❑ Register the event class with the Events service using the Component Services MMC

- ❑ Create a subscriber class that implements the event class's interface

- ❑ Add the subscriber class to a COM+ application using the Component Services MMC

- ❑ Subscribe the subscriber class to the event class

- ❑ Create a publisher application that instantiates the event class and then fires an event by calling one of its methods

Having seen a simple example that illustrated the basic principles behind COM+ Events, let's now look in more detail at the event class, subscriber, and publisher.

Event Class

As we saw earlier, the event class provides an interface known to both the publisher and subscriber. When a publisher creates an instance of the event class (using `CreateObject`, `CoCreateObject`, `New`, etc.) and invokes one of its methods, COM+ Events is responsible for making an identical call on all components that have subscribed to the event, by querying the Events service store. The Events service can fire events on the subscriber classes serially or in parallel. This can be set for persistent subscribers by using the MMC (more on persistent subscribers later, in the *Subscriber* section). Right-click on the event class and select **Properties**. In the loosely coupled events (LCE) pane of the **Advanced** tab, either check **Fire in parallel** or uncheck it to have your subscribers notified serially:

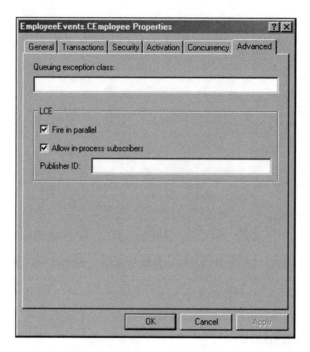

The **Publisher ID** can be optionally set in the **Advanced** tab. When the publisher ID is set, the event class will only accept events from the publisher with the corresponding GUID. If left blank, the event class will accept events from *any* publisher.

You may also programmatically alter the "fire in parallel" and the "publisher ID" settings at runtime. Every event object obtained from COM+ supports both the `IEventClass` and `IEventClass2` interfaces defined by the EventSystem 1.0 Type Library (`.\system32\es.dll`). The more recent interface, `IEventClass2`, allows the developer to alter the `FireInParallel` and `PublisherID` properties at runtime. However, any changes made will not be persistently stored. To permanently change the `FireInParallel` property for a particular event class, use the COM+ Administrative Components. The following code demonstrates how to alter the `FireInParallel` property:

```
Dim objES As EventSystemLib.IEventSystem
Dim objEvent As EventSystemLib.IEventClass2

Set objES = CreateObject("EventSystem.EventSystem")
Set objEvent = objES.Query(PROGID_EventClass, _
                "EventClassName = 'EmployeeEvents.CEmployee'", lErrorIndex)

objEvent.FireInParallel = True
objEvent.PublisherID = "{F02B2617-B268-4D7D-AF1E-D6A50D8EC166}"

objES.Store "EventSystem.EventClass", objEvent
```

Additional properties supported by the `IEventClass2` interface are listed in the table below:

Property	Description
EventClassID	The unique identifier (CLSID) for the event class within the Events service.
EventClassName	The ProgID name for this subscription.
Description	A comment field related to the event.
FiringInterfaceID	Deprecated property that contains the unique identifier (IID) for the interface method to which calls should be made. If the property contains an empty string, the default interface for the class will be used.
OwnerSID	Deprecated property that contains the security identifier of the owner of the event.
TypeLib	The full path to the file containing the TypeLib for the event class.
AllowInProcActivation	Allows the publisher to override the in-process activation setting at runtime.
FireInParallel	Specifies whether subscriber method calls will be serial or in parallel.
MultiInterface PublisherFilterCLSID	The unique identifier (CLSID) of the publisher filter class that supports the `IMultipleInterfaceEventControl` interface that is to be used when this event is fired.
PublisherID	Unique identifier of publisher required by the subscription. If the string is empty, the subscriber will accept events from any publisher.
CustomConfigCLSID	Deprecated property that returns `E_NOTIMPL` error code. Once used for accessing the CLSID of a component that can assist in adding properties to a subscription object's property bag.

The event object also exposes additional interfaces – these will be covered a little later in this chapter.

Subscriber

As discussed earlier, the subscriber is a COM component that receives information from the Events service. The subscriber can take many forms including, but not limited to, a queued component a transactional component, both of which will be discussed later in the chapter. The subscriber will not receive events until a subscription is made to the appropriate events. We will cover the details of subscriptions next.

Subscription

A subscription object encapsulates the relationship between a subscriber, an event, and possibly a specific publisher. Having a subscription as an independent entity, separate from the subscriber, allows a subscriber to create subscriptions to multiple events. For example, a subscriber component responsible for logging different error events to a common log file may need to subscribe to multiple error event classes. A subscription also has the ability to reference a specific publisher, allowing the subscriber to only receive events from a given publisher. The table below shows the list of properties and methods available for the `IEventSubscription2` interface:

Property	Description
SubscriptionID	The unique identifier (GUID) for the subscription within the Events system.
SubscriptionName	Human-readable name for this subscription.
Description	A comment field related to the subscriber.
SubscriberCLSID	The unique identifier (GUID) of the subscriber's class. Used by the event class to create the subscriber object.
SubscriberInterface	An `IUnknown` pointer to the interface to use to submit events to the subscriber. Used for transient subscriptions (which are discussed later).
Enabled	Allows the delivery of events to be turned on or off at runtime.
PublisherID	Unique identifier of publisher required by the subscription. If the string is empty, the subscriber will accept events from any publisher.
EventClassID	The unique identifier (GUID) for the required event class. Deprecated but supported for backward compatibility; `InterfaceID` generally used instead.
InterfaceID	The unique identifier (GUID) for the interface the subscriber wants to receive event notifications from.
MachineName	Name of the machine where the subscription resides.
MethodName	Name of the method the subscriber wants to receive event calls from. Method is relative to the `InterfaceID`.
OwnerSID	Security identifier of the owner of the subscription.
PerUser	Whether or not the `OwnerSID` is used to determine whether or not an event is received by the subscriber. When set to `True`, subscription only receives events when the `OwnerSID` is logged in.
FilterCriteria	The subscriber filter string used to determine whether or not to notify the subscriber.
SubscriberMoniker	The moniker used to instantiate the subscriber.

Method	Description
GetPublisherProperty	Retrieves a particular publisher property.
PutPublisherProperty	Stores a particular publisher property.
RemovePublisherProperty	Deletes a particular publisher property.
GetPublisher PropertyCollection	Retrieves a collection of publisher properties (IEventObjectCollection). Can be used by a publisher filter to determine whether or not to fire an event to the particular subscriber or to customize the event for the subscriber.
GetSubscriberProperty	Retrieves a particular subscriber property.
PutSubscriberProperty	Stores a particular subscriber property.
RemoveSubscriberProperty	Deletes a particular subscriber property.
GetSubscriber PropertyCollection	Retrieves a collection of subscriber properties (IEventObjectCollection).

A subscriber can either be **persistent** or **transient**. A persistent subscriber can survive system shutdown whereas a transient subscriber cannot. A transient subscription is only valid while the subscriber component is available to receive event notifications. Let's look at each of these in more detail.

Persistent Subscriptions

In our simple example, the Benefits.CHealthInsurance is a persistent subscriber. Every time a publisher fires an event, COM+ Events creates the COM object associated with the subscription and fires the appropriate method. One of the primary benefits of a persistent subscriber is that the lifetime issues of a component are abstracted away. Since COM+ Events will create an instance of the subscriber class(es) and then call the appropriate method, the Events service does not have to concern itself about whether or not the subscriber object will be available to accept the event.

Transient Subscriptions

A persistent subscription associates an event to a particular COM *class*. In contrast, a transient subscription associates an event to a particular COM *object* (instance of a class). Transient subscriptions are only valid during the lifetime of the particular object and therefore do not survive system shutdowns.

An example of where you might want to consider creating a transient subscription, as opposed to a persistent subscription, is an in/out message board application. Let's suppose we want to create an application that would notify the receptionists when employees check in and out of the office. This would allow the receptionists to determine whether or not to transfer incoming calls to the employee's extension or send the call to voice mail. The receptionists are only interested in receiving events when the application is running. The following diagram depicts how such an application could be created:

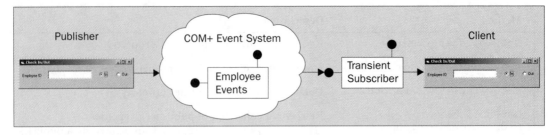

The first thing we need to do is expand the `EmployeeEvents.CEmployee` class. If the `EmployeeEvents` component were already released into production, then we would have created a new class in the `EmployeeEvents` component called `CEmployee2`. The `CEmployee` class would have remained unchanged for backward compatibility. We would have also had to ensure backward compatibility for events fired on the `CEmployee2` interface that are also supported by the `CEmployee` interface. A simpler alternative is to create a new class that only supports the `onCheckIn` and `onCheckOut` methods, say `CEmployeeInOut`. However, in this demonstration we will modify the existing `CEmployee` class. Since we are modifying the interface including the IID, we will have to re-register the event class with the Events service. (Refer to the instructions listed in the previous simple example.) Note that re-registering invalidates the `Benefits` subscription. This demonstrates the importance of creating immutable event interfaces.

```
' Component:  EmployeeEvents
' Class:      CEmployee

Option Explicit

Public Sub onCreateNewEmployee(ByVal strEmployeeID As String, _
    ByVal strEmployeeType As String)

    ' No implementation.
End Sub

Public Sub onCheckIn(ByVal strEmployeeID As String)
    ' No implementation.
End Sub

Public Sub onCheckOut(ByVal strEmployeeID As String)
    ' No implementation.
End Sub
```

Next we will create a simple dialog-based application as above. The publisher will send notification to its subscribers via the `EmployeeEvents.CEmployee` class. The subscriber will register a persistent subscription with the Events service for both the `onCheckIn` and `onCheckOut` events. The client dialog-based application will create an instance of the subscriber object and listen for events it receives from the subscriber object.

The publisher will be a dialog-based application (`CheckInOut.exe`) that employees will use to check themselves in and out, as shown in the previous diagram. Notice that the application simply creates an instance of the `EmployeeEvents.CEmployee` class and calls the new `onCheckIn` and `onCheckOut` methods:

```
' Form:          CheckInOutForm
' References:     EmployeeEvents (EmployeeEvents.dll)

Option Explicit

Private m_objEmployee As New EmployeeEvents.CEmployee

Private Sub optEmployeeIn_Click()
    Dim objEmployee As EmployeeEvents.CEmployee

    ' Initialize.
    Set objEmployee = New EmployeeEvents.CEmployee

    If (tbEmployeeID.Text <> "") Then
        objEmployee.onCheckIn tbEmployeeID.Text
    Else
        MsgBox "Please enter a valid employee ID first.", vbExclamation
    End If
End Sub

Private Sub optEmployeeOut_Click()
    Dim objEmployee As EmployeeEvents.CEmployee

    ' Initialize.
    Set objEmployee = New EmployeeEvents.CEmployee

    If (tbEmployeeID.Text <> "") Then
        objEmployee.onCheckOut tbEmployeeID.Text
    Else
        MsgBox "Please enter a valid employee ID first.", vbExclamation
    End If
End Sub
```

The original purpose of the Check In/Out application was to provide a means of notifying the receptionists, to help them function more effectively. However, the in/out message board application isn't the only subscriber. A group of clever employees decided to create a web application that notifies them when the boss checks in or out!

They created an ActiveX control hosted in a web page on the corporate intranet that provides notification whenever their *boss* checks in or out. The ActiveX control project is called BossInOutSubscriber. This implements the Employee.CEmployee interface and declares two member variables to hold the subscription IDs:

```
' Component:      BossInOutSubscriber
' Control:        BossInOut
' References:     EmployeeEvents (EmployeeEvents.dll)
'                 EventSystem 1.0 Type Library
'                 (c:windows\system32\es.dll)

Option Explicit

Implements EmployeeEvents.CEmployee

' Declare member variables.
Private m_strInSubscriptionID   As String
Private m_strOutSubscriptionID  As String
```

Next the control's constructor is implemented. The `UserControl_Initializate` method is responsible for creating two transient subscriptions, one to the `onCheckIn` event and the other to the `onCheckOut` event:

```
Private Sub UserControl_Initialize()
    On Error GoTo ErrorHandler

    Dim lErrorIndex         As Long
    Dim objES               As EventSystemLib.IEventSystem
    Dim objEvent            As EventSystemLib.IEventClass
    Dim objInSubscription   As EventSystemLib.IEventSubscription
    Dim objOutSubscription  As EventSystemLib.IEventSubscription

    ' Initialize objects.
    Set objES = CreateObject("EventSystem.EventSystem")
    Set objInSubscription = CreateObject("EventSystem.EventSubscription")
    Set objOutSubscription = CreateObject("EventSystem.EventSubscription")
```

The subscription IDs are then saved so that they can be found and removed when they are no longer needed:

```
    ' Store the subscription ID so that we can locate the object later.
    m_strInSubscriptionID = objInSubscription.SubscriptionID
    m_strOutSubscriptionID = objOutSubscription.SubscriptionID
```

We then query COM+ Events to obtain a reference to the event object we wish to subscribe to, in this case the `CEmployee` event object:

```
    ' Query for the event.
    Set objEvent = objES.Query("EventSystem.EventClass", _
        "EventClassName='EmployeeEvents.CEmployee'", lErrorIndex)
```

We then set the appropriate properties on the subscription object. We set the `SubscriptionName` and `Description` properties to help identify the object and its usage:

```
    ' Create a transient subscription to boss' onCheckIn event.
    objInSubscription.SubscriptionName = "BossInOutSubscriber"
    objInSubscription.Description = "Transient subscription to" _
                                    & " CEmployee's In/Out events."
```

We then create an association between the subscriber and the event by setting the `SubscriberInterface` to our subscriber object's `IUnknown` interface and set the `EventClassID` of the event we received as a result of our previous query. Finally, we set the name of the method of which we are interested in receiving notification:

```
    objInSubscription.SubscriberInterface = Me
    objInSubscription.EventClassID = objEvent.EventClassID
    objInSubscription.MethodName = "onCheckIn"
```

We then set the `Enabled` property so that the object can start receiving events once the subscription is stored:

```
objInSubscription.Enabled = True
```

Finally, we store the subscription in the Events service:

```
objES.Store "EventSystem.EventSubscription", objInSubscription
```

These steps are then repeated for the `onCheckOut` event:

```
    ' Create a transient subscription to onCheckOut event.
    objOutSubscription.SubscriptionName = "BossInOutSubscriber"
    objOutSubscription.Description = "Transient subscription to CEmployee's" _
                                & " In/Out events."
    objOutSubscription.SubscriberInterface = Me
    objOutSubscription.EventClassID = objEvent.EventClassID
    objOutSubscription.methodName = "onCheckOut"
    objOutSubscription.Enabled = True
    objES.Store "EventSystem.EventSubscription", objOutSubscription

    Exit Sub

ErrorHandler:
    MsgBox Err.Source & ":  " & Err.Description
End Sub
```

Next we implement the control's destructor. The `UserControl_Terminate` method is responsible for unregistering the transient subscription since we are no longer interested in receiving events:

```
Private Sub UserControl_Terminate()
    On Error GoTo ErrorHandler

    Dim objES          As EventSystemLib.IEventSystem
    Dim lErrorIndex    As Long

    Set objES = CreateObject("EventSystem.EventSystem")

    ' Remove the transient subscriptions.
    objES.Remove "EventSystem.EventSubscription", _
        "SubscriptionID = '" & m_strInSubscriptionID & "'", lErrorIndex
    objES.Remove "EventSystem.EventSubscription", _
        "SubscriptionID = '" & m_strOutSubscriptionID & "'", lErrorIndex

    Exit Sub

ErrorHandler:
    MsgBox Err.Source & ":  Error Index (" & lErrorIndex & "):  " _
                    & Err.Description
End Sub
```

The implementation of the onCheckIn and onCheckOut methods simply updates the radio buttons to reflect the status of the boss. These are the VB events that will be captured by our subscriber dialog-based application. Notice that we receive every IsIn and IsOut event and only pass the results of the event when the employee ID is Boss. We will be taking a look at more efficient ways of filtering events in a later section.

```
Private Sub CEmployee_onCheckIn(ByVal strEmployeeID As String)
    ' Inefficient way to filter for events where strEmployeeID = "Boss"
    If (strEmployeeID = "Boss") Then
        optBossOut.Value = False
        optBossIn.Value = True
    End If
End Sub

Private Sub CEmployee_onCheckOut(ByVal strEmployeeID As String)
    ' Inefficient way to filter for events where strEmployeeID = "Boss"
    If (strEmployeeID = "Boss") Then
        optBossIn.Value = False
        optBossOut.Value = True
    End If
End Sub
```

We are not interested in receiving the onCreateNewEmployee event, therefore we do not register for that event nor do we provide implementation for the method call:

```
Private Sub CEmployee_onCreateNewEmployee(ByVal strEmployeeID As String, _
    ByVal strEmployeeType As String)

    ' No implementation needed for events that the subscriber does
    ' not subscribe to.
End Sub
```

After registering the component we finally create our web page (BossInOutSubscriber.htm) that will display the events to the end user. The HTML below creates and displays our subscriber control (note you can obtain the classid using OLE/COM Object Viewer):

```
<HTML>
    <BODY>
        <OBJECT classid="clsid:DBFD33F9-0FB1-42BA-8840-2C3145CCA398">
        </OBJECT>
    </BODY>
</HTML>
```

Publisher

As we have seen, the publisher is responsible for firing the events. As we have also seen, firing an event is as easy as instantiating the appropriate event class and calling one of its methods.

Calls made to an event object are synchronous. The publisher will block until the event has been propagated to all of the subscribers. Specifically, a method call on an event object will not return until the following have occurred:

- ❑ The method calls on all subscribing components with transient subscriptions have returned
- ❑ All persistently subscribed objects have been created, their method calls have returned, and the objects have been destroyed
- ❑ The method call has been recorded for all queued components
- ❑ The recorded method call has been queued for all queued components persistently stored in the Events service

As we shall see, this is important when we enlist the event method call in a transaction to ensure that every component has an opportunity to vote to commit the transaction. However, the publisher may suffer if a subscriber takes an excessive amount of time to process the event. One potential solution to this problem is to use queued components, which will be discussed in a later section.

Registering a Publisher

Publishers may be optionally registered with COM+ Events. One advantage to registering the publisher is that subscribers can choose to subscribe to events submitted by a given publisher. A publisher must be implemented as a COM component in order to be stored within the Events service. The following code demonstrates how to register a publisher within COM+ Events using the Events service administrative components. First, the `EventSystem` and `EventPublisher` objects are created:

```
Dim objES        As EventSystemLib.IEventSystem
Dim objPublisher  As EventSystemLib.IEventPublisher

Set objES = CreateObject("EventSystem.EventSystem")
Set objPublisher = CreateObject("EventSystem.EventPublisher")
```

The properties of the publisher object are set. Note that the `PublisherID` is set to the IID for `CInOutPublisher`:

```
objPublisher.PublisherName = "TheBoss.CInOutPublisher"
objPublisher.Description = "Publishes when the boss enters and" &_
                           " leaves the office building."
objPublisher.PublisherID = _
  "{FB7FDAE2-89B8-11CF-9BE8-00A0C90A632C}"
```

The publisher is then stored in the Events service:

```
objES.Store "EventSystem.EventPublisher", objPublisher
```

The properties and methods supported by the `IEventPublisher` interface are listed below:

Property	Description
PublisherID	The unique identifier (GUID) for the publisher's interface
PublisherName	Human-readable name for this subscription
Description	A comment field related to the event
PublisherType	Optional administrative group of which the event publisher is a member
OwnerSID	Optional security identifier of the owner of the subscription

Filtering

The COM+ Events service provides the ability to perform both subscriber and publisher **filtering**. A *subscriber* may only be interested in receiving a subset of a particular event. For example, the `Benefits` subscriber may not wish to receive notification if a new employee is a contractor or temporary employee. The *publisher* may need to provide filtering so that only a certain subset of its subscribers receives notification. For example, the boss may not wish to notify every subscriber when he checks in and out. Let's take a closer look at subscriber and publisher filtering.

Subscriber Filtering

A subscriber to an event may not want to receive every single event that is fired. For example, a client may wish to subscribe to an event that notifies them when an employee checks in and out. However, as in the previous section on transient subscribers, the subscriber may only be interested in `IsIn` and `IsOut` events that relate to a specific employee, such as their boss.

Recall that our modified transient subscriber received all `IsIn` and `IsOut` events and then only passed them along to the client if the employee ID was equal to `Boss`. While this method of filtering works, it is not very efficient. Chances are that the subscriber and publisher will reside on different machines. In addition, there could be many subscribers to these events. Therefore, there would be many events sent to subscribers across the network that would simply be ignored. The subscribers would also be consuming CPU cycles performing client-side filtering. As the number of employees in the organization increases, you may reach a point where the client may not be able to keep up with the flood of incoming events. Finally, performing filtering within the client requires that the logic be coded into the subscriber. It would be more efficient to have the Events service perform filtering on the subscriber's behalf.

COM+ allows the client to specify the filtering criteria and let the event service handle the filtering on behalf of the client. The filtering criteria is a string that specifies which events the subscriber is interested in receiving based on the value of the event's parameters. The filter criteria string can contain standard relational operators, nested parentheses, and/or logical key words. Standard relational operators include:

- ❑ Greater than (<)
- ❑ Less than (>)
- ❑ Equal to (=)
- ❑ Less than or equal to (<=)
- ❑ Greater than or equal to (>=)
- ❑ Not equal to (!=)

Valid logical key words are AND, OR, and NOT.

Some example strings that apply to our sample application include:

StrEmployeeID = "Boss"	Only receive an event when the boss checks into the office
StrEmployeeID = "Boss" OR strEmployeeID = "BossOfBoss"	Only receive an event when the boss or his boss checks into or out of of the office
StrEmployeeID != "Employee1"	Do not receive events from Employee1

Persistent Subscribers

Persistent subscribers can set a filtering string within the Events service using the Component Services MMC. The filtering string can be set within the event class's Properties dialog box under the Options tab:

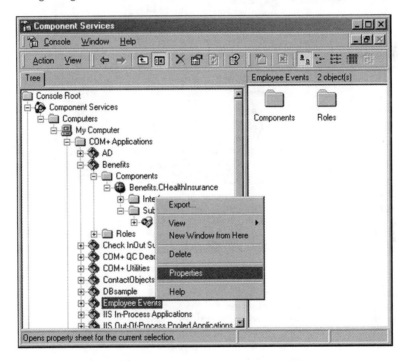

Recall the Benefits.CHealthInsurance subscriber created ealier. Say we only wanted to send an e-mail to full-time employees asking them to enroll in benefits. Full-time employees are of type FULLTIME. Therefore, we would set the filtering criteria for the component's subscription to strEmployeeType="FULLTIME":

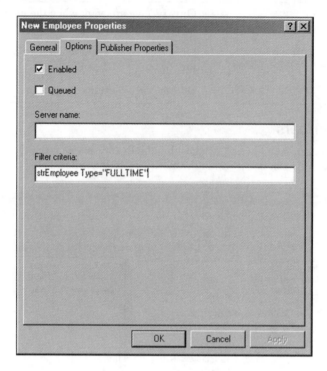

Transient Subscribers

Transient subscribers can set the filtering string when creating a subscription. The following code shows how we can alter our previous transient subscriber example to allow the event service to handle filtering on our behalf:

```
' Create a transient subscription to boss's onCheckIn event.
objInSubscription.SubscriptionName = "BossInOutSubscriber"
objInSubscription.Description = "Transient subscription to" &_
                                " CEmployee's In/Out events."
objInSubscription.SubscriberInterface = Me
objInSubscription.EventClassID = objEvent.EventClassID
objInSubscription.MethodName = "onCheckIn"
objInSubscription.FilterCriteria = "strEmployeeID = 'Boss'"
objInSubscription.Enabled = True
objES.Store "EventSystem.EventSubscription", objInSubscription
```

Publisher Filtering

Sometimes the publisher needs to exercise control over the event firing process. For example, the publisher may refuse to send an event to a particular set of subscribers or may want to control the order in which the subscribers are notified of the event. The publisher filter accomplishes this by taking control of the firing loop from the COM+ Events service.

The publisher filter is a COM component that can be instantiated and initialized at runtime by the publisher. We'll look at how to create a publisher filter later in the chapter, but first let's discuss how a publisher utilizes a publisher filter. At runtime, the publisher is responsible for creating an instance of the publisher filter COM component, initializing the filter, then registering it with COM+ Events.

The publisher filter is a COM component that is installed downstream of the event object and implements the interface(s) of the targeted event class(es). The publisher filter is also responsible for supporting either the IPublisherFilter interface, if one event class interface is supported, or the IMultiInterfacePublisherFilter interface, if more than one event class interface is supported. Both of these interfaces expose an Initialize method that the publisher calls to tell the filter which methods should be filtered and to pass the collection of subscriptions that the filter will iterate through when an event is fired.

The publisher is responsible for querying the Events service for an event object or a set of event objects and then accessing the IEventControl interface of an event object. The publisher can then call the interface's GetSubscriptions method to obtain a collection of all subscriptions. This brute force technique for performing publisher filtering has its drawbacks. First, the IEventControl interface is unsupported for event objects that are implemented as queued components, since it has methods that contain output parameters. Second, this method of accessing IEventControl tightly couples the publisher with the filter business logic.

COM+ Events allows the developer to decouple the publisher filter from the publisher. The developer can write a COM object that supports the IPublisherFilter interface or, if the event class supports multiple interfaces, the IMultiInterfacePublisher interface, and register it with the Events service.

The following table lists the methods of the IPublisherFilter interface:

Methods for IPublisherFilter	Description
Initialize	Used to initialize the publisher filter object
PrepareToFire	Called by the Events service when a publisher has fired the event – it tells the filter object to fire the event to the required subscribers

The methods of the IMultiInterfacePublisherFilter interface are shown in the next table:

Methods for IMultiInterface PublisherFilter	Description
Initialize	Used to initialize the publisher filter object
PrepareToFire	Called by the Events service when a publisher has fired the event – it prepares the filter to fire subscriptions through the event class object

Both the publisher and the publisher filter use the event object's IEventControl interface. The publisher is responsible for calling the SetPublisherFilter method, passing it a reference to the publisher filter object. The publisher filter calls the GetSubscriptions interface to obtain a collection of subscriptions that are registered to receive an event. The following tables show the methods and property of the IEventControl interface:

Method	Description
GetSubscriptions	Returns a self-updating collection of subscriptions that matched the specified query criteria
SetPublisherFilter	Accepts an IpublisherFilter interface to use at runtime
SetDefaultQuery	Sets the default filter criteria to use on a particular method when a publisher filter is not specified

Property	Description
AllowInProcActivation	Allows the publisher to override the in-process activation setting at runtime

Boss In/Out Publisher Filter

Recall from the *Transient Subscriber* section that a few employees created a web page on the corporate intranet that allows them to receive notification when their boss checks in or out. Unfortunately, the boss discovered the web page and has asked his IT department to ensure that events only get published to the *receptionists'* application. To correct this problem, a publisher filter needs to be created to ensure that only the receptionists' in/out board application receives notification. Let's take a look at the code. This is a new ActiveX DLL project called BossInOutFilter.

The publisher filter implements the publisher filter interface, IPublisherFilter, and the interface of the event class, CEmployee. We also create two dictionary objects that will be used to store subscription and firing control objects:

```
' Component:     BossInOutFilter
' Class:         CPublisherFilter
' References:    EmployeeEvents (EmployeeEvents.dll)
'                EventSystem 1.0 Type Library
'                (c:\windows\system32\es.dll)
'                Microsoft Scripting Runtime
'                (c:\windows\system32\scrrun.dll)

Option Explicit

Implements EventSystemLib.IPublisherFilter
Implements EmployeeEvents.CEmployee

Private m_dictSubscriptions     As New Scripting.Dictionary
Private m_dictFiringControls     As New Scripting.Dictionary
```

Next, we implement the class's constructor and destructor. We create two dictionary objects in the `Class_Initialize` method and release all object references maintained by the dictionary objects in the `Class_Terminate` method:

```
Private Sub Class_Initialize()
    Set m_dictSubscriptions = New Scripting.Dictionary
    Set m_dictFiringControls = New Scripting.Dictionary
End Sub

Private Sub Class_Terminate()
    On Error Resume Next
    Dim varObject As Variant

    ' Release all references to the dictionary objects.
    For Each varObject In m_dictSubscriptions
        Set varObject = Nothing
    Next
    Set m_dictSubscriptions = Nothing

    For Each varObject In m_dictFiringControls
        Set varObject = Nothing
    Next
    Set m_dictFiringControls = Nothing
End Sub
```

The publisher is responsible for calling the `IPublisherFilter.Initialize` method for each event to be filtered. The `Initialize` method expects the method name of the event to be filtered, accompanied by a reference to the event object. We obtain a collection of subscription objects for the specified method by casting the event object to obtain a reference to the `IEventControl` interface and calling its `GetSubscription` method. The collection of subscriptions is self-updating. For example, if a new subscriber is registered between the time the publisher is initialized and the time an event is fired, the new subscriber is added to the collection of subscriptions. This helps ensure that the filter always has a complete list of subscriptions. Finally, we clean up after ourselves by releasing the reference to the `IEventControl` interface:

```
Private Sub IPublisherFilter_Initialize(ByVal strMethodName As String, _
                                        ByVal dispUserDefined As Object)
    Dim objEventControl As EventSystemLib.IEventControl
    Dim lErrorIndex     As Long

    ' Obtain the self-updating collection of subscriptions for
    ' a particular method.
    Set objEventControl = dispUserDefined
    Set m_dictSubscriptions(strMethodName) = _
        objEventControl.GetSubscriptions(strMethodName, "", lErrorIndex)

    Set objEventControl = Nothing
End Sub
```

When a method on the event object is called, it makes two calls to the publisher filter. It first calls `IPublisherFilter.PrepareToFire` and passes it the name of the method being called and the firing interface. It then calls the method on the event class interface of the publisher filter.

The `PrepareToFire` method is responsible for receiving the firing control at the time the event is fired. Our implementation of the method stores a reference to the firing control in the firing control dictionary object indexed by the method string. The firing control will be used in our implementation of the event class method to inform the COM+ Events service which subscriber should receive notification:

```
Private Sub IPublisherFilter_PrepareToFire(ByVal strMethodName As String, _
    ByVal objFiringControl As EventSystemLib.IFiringControl)

    ' Optionally, do something before the actual method call is
    ' fired (logging, etc.) ...

    ' Store the firing control object for use within the method call.
    Set m_dictFiringControls(strMethodName) = objFiringControl
End Sub
```

Finally, we provide the implementation for the actual events. First, we obtain the firing control interface for the targeted event. We then iterate through the subscribers and only notify the ones with a class ID associated with the in/out board application. Since the method receives the same set of parameters the publisher passed to the event object, they can also be used to help determine who receives the event. As we iterate through the collection of subscribers, we call the `IFiringControl.FireSubscription` method for the subscribers that should receive the event. COM+ is then responsible for actually notifying the subscribers. Notice that we do not need to provide implementation for the `onNewEmployee` event since the publisher will never fire the event:

```
Private Sub CEmployee_onCheckIn(ByVal strEmployeeID As String)
    Dim objSubscription      As IEventSubscription
    Dim strEmployeeType      As String
    Dim objFiringControl     As EventSystemLib.IFiringControl
    Dim strInOutBoardCLSID   As String

    ' Initialize.
    Set objFiringControl = m_dictFiringControls("onCheckIn")
    strInOutBoardCLSID = "{7879F798-27A8-424F-A90B-766A05812A27}"

    ' Only notify the in/out board application.
    For Each objSubscription In m_dictSubscriptions("onCheckIn")
        ' Fire event only if subscriber CLSID matches the in/out board app.
        If (objSubscription.SubscriberCLSID = strInOutBoardCLSID) Then _
            objFiringControl.FireSubscription objSubscription
    Next

    Set objFiringControl = Nothing
    Set m_dictFiringControls("onCheckIn") = Nothing
End Sub

Private Sub CEmployee_onCheckOut(ByVal strEmployeeID As String)
    Dim objSubscription      As IEventSubscription
    Dim strEmployeeType      As String
    Dim objFiringControl     As EventSystemLib.IFiringControl
    Dim strInOutBoardCLSID   As String
```

```
      ' Initialize.
      Set objFiringControl = m_dictFiringControls("onCheckOut")
      strInOutBoardCLSID = "{7879F798-27A8-424F-A90B-766A05812A27}"

      ' Only notify the in/out board application.
      For Each objSubscription In m_dictSubscriptions("onCheckOut")
          ' Fire event only if subscriber CLSID matches the in/out board app.
          If (objSubscription.SubscriberCLSID = strInOutBoardCLSID) Then _
              objFiringControl.FireSubscription objSubscription
      Next

      Set objFiringControl = Nothing
      Set m_dictFiringControls("onCheckOut") = Nothing
  End Sub

  Private Sub CEmployee_onCreateNewEmployee(ByVal strEmployeeID As String, _
                                            ByVal strEmployeeType As String)
      ' No implementation needed for events that the publisher will not fire.
  End Sub
```

This component needs to be registered before moving on to the next task – modifying the publisher code.

Modified Publisher

We now need to modify our publisher, CheckInOut, so that it utilizes the publisher filter we created in the previous section whenever the boss checks in or out. This is available as the CheckInOutFiltered project. First we create an instance of the publisher filter class. Next we obtain a reference to the event class's IEventControl interface by casting our event object to the objEventControl variable. We then initialize the filter by passing it the method name and its corresponding event object's IEventControl interface. Finally, we fire the event. The event object will now defer the firing loop to the publisher filter object when either the event object's onCheckIn or onCheckOut method is called:

```
' Form:         CheckInOutForm
' References:   EmployeeEvents (EmployeeEvents.dll)
'               BossInOutFilter (BossInOutFilter.dll)
'               EventSystem 1.0 Type Library
'               (c:\windows\system32\es.dll)

Option Explicit

Private m_objEmployee As New EmployeeEvents.CEmployee

Private Sub optEmployeeIn_Click()
    Dim objEmployee As EmployeeEvents.CEmployee

    ' Initialize.
    Set objEmployee = New EmployeeEvents.CEmployee

    If (tbEmployeeID.Text = "Boss") Then
        ' Publish filtered event.
        Dim objEventControl     As EventSystemLib.IEventControl
        Dim objFilter           As EventSystemLib.IPublisherFilter

        Set objFilter = New BossInOutFilter.CPublisherFilter
```

```
            ' Obtain the IEventControl interface for the event object.
            Set objEventControl = objEmployee

            ' Initialize the publisher filter.
            objFilter.Initialize "onCheckIn", objEventControl

            ' Pass a reference to the publisher filter to the event object.
            objEventControl.SetPublisherFilter "onCheckIn", objFilter

            ' Fire event.
            objEmployee.onCheckIn tbEmployeeID.Text
        ElseIf (tbEmployeeID.Text <> "") Then
            m_objEmployee.onCheckIn tbEmployeeID.Text
        Else
            MsgBox "Please enter a valid employee ID first.", vbExclamation
        End If
    End Sub

    Private Sub optEmployeeOut_Click()
        Dim objEmployee As EmployeeEvents.CEmployee

        ' Initialize.
        Set objEmployee = New EmployeeEvents.CEmployee

        If (tbEmployeeID.Text = "Boss") Then
            ' Publish filtered event.
            Dim objEventControl      As EventSystemLib.IEventControl
            Dim objFilter            As EventSystemLib.IPublisherFilter

            Set objFilter = New BossInOutFilter.CPublisherFilter

            ' Obtain the IEventControl interface for the event object.
            Set objEventControl = objEmployee

            ' Initialize the publisher filter.
            objFilter.Initialize "onCheckIn", objEventControl

            ' Pass a reference to the publisher filter to the event object.
            objEventControl.SetPublisherFilter "onCheckIn", objFilter

            ' Fire event.
            objEmployee.onCheckIn tbEmployeeID.Text
        ElseIf (tbEmployeeID.Text <> "") Then
            m_objEmployee.onCheckOut tbEmployeeID.Text
        Else
            MsgBox "Please enter a valid employee ID first.", vbExclamation
        End If
    End Sub
```

Now when you run the BossInOutSubscriber web page, you can compare what happens when using the CheckInOut publisher with and without the filter.

Queued Components

COM+ Events is integrated with the **Queued Components service**. Basically, this is a COM+ service built upon Microsoft Message Queue service (MSMQ), which collates information from a client's method calls into a queue, then passes them on to be processed. (For more information on queued components, see Chapters 4 and 9.) A developer can use queued components in tandem with COM+ Events to provide asynchronous notification of events to its subscribers.

For an events-based application to run effectively, its subscribers must return in a timely fashion. The developer usually will not have control over every subscriber. Unfortunately, since the publisher blocks on method calls to event objects until all subscribers have returned, the performance of a publisher application can be severely affected by one misbehaving subscriber. However, if the action of firing an event were asynchronous from receiving and processing the event, then subscribers that take a long time to process the event would not adversely affect the performance of the publisher. Since the action of calling a method on a queued component is asynchronous from the activity, queued components can fill this role and can be used to improve the responsiveness of your publisher application.

Queued components can also be used to *guarantee delivery* of the event to the subscribed system. Sometimes a system that subscribes to an event must guarantee that the appropriate action was taken on a received event. For example, if an employee leaves the company then HR is responsible for updating the employee's record in its HRIS system. One of the subscribers to this event might be the payroll application. The subscribing payroll component must successfully remove the employee from the payroll system, otherwise the ex-employee might still be receiving their paychecks long after they have left the company. The subscriber (the payroll system) needs some mechanism to guarantee that each event of this type gets acted upon.

There are many circumstances that would cause the payroll application to not receive or react to the event. The payroll system could be down, the network could be down, the subscriber component could fail or be missing all together, etc. The subscribing system needs a way to ensure that the received event has been handled. The developer can use transactions on the receiving end of the application to ensure that the payroll component will not be removed from the queue unless the resulting action from the event completed successfully, which we'll discuss later.

The developer may configure an event component to be queued by marking the Queued check box in the Options tab of the property box for the event class. The Events service also allows a subscriber object to be queued. As opposed to marking the event object as a queued component, marking the individual subscriber object as a queued component allows a mixture of synchronous and asynchronous subscribers. For example, our `Benefits.CHealthInsurance` class referenced in the simple example creates a new mail message whenever a new employee is added to the company's HRIS database. If we discover that our SMTP e-mail server is slow and is therefore causing the publisher to block for an unacceptable period of time, we could choose to make an asynchronous call to the `CHealthInsurance` subscriber class. Instead of marking the event class as a queued component, we could mark the offending subscription to be queued, as shown in the screenshot overleaf:

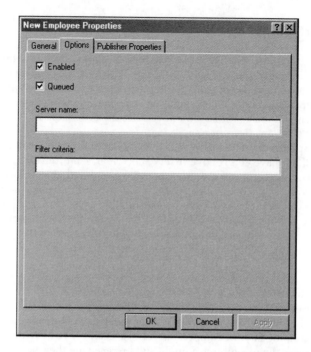

If we chose instead to mark the event class as a queued component, then the lifetime of *all* subscribers would be decoupled from the publisher. As we shall see in the *Transactions* section, this would not be desirable for subscribers who need to be enlisted in the publisher's transaction.

In summary, the tight integration between COM+ Events and Queued Components allows the developer the ability to decouple the lifetime of the publisher and one or more of its subscribers. Since the developer uses a declarative model to determine whether or not the subscriber is a queued component, the publisher uses one model to publish events regardless of whether the delivery or receipt of the event is queued or not.

Transactions

Sometimes the success of a publisher's activity is dependent on subscribers that support transactions having successfully received and acted upon the fired event. COM+ Events accomplishes this by supporting distributed transactions. Recall that a method call made on an event object will block until the given method is called on all subscriber objects and has returned. This is necessary for the publisher's subscribers to participate in its transactions. A subscriber can participate in a publisher's transactions by declaring that it supports transactions in COM+ and calling either the SetComplete or SetAbort methods on its ObjectContext. (For more information about writing and registering COM+ components that support transactions, see Chapter 8.)

An event object can be declared as either supporting or requiring transactions:

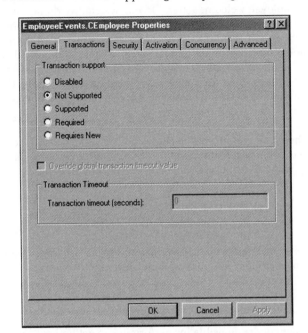

The event's subscribers that support transactions will automatically be enlisted within the context of the publisher's transaction. Therefore, any subscriber can call SetAbort and cause the publisher's transaction to be rolled back.

One of the more powerful uses for transacted events is for providing loose coupling between an activity and the business rules that dictate whether or not that activity should occur. For example in our sample, a new employee can only be hired if the employer has proof that the person is either a US citizen or has the appropriate government papers. Therefore a "create new employee" event could have one subscriber who will commit the transaction only if the company has the appropriate paperwork on file.

Since the business rules are loosely coupled for subscribers, if business rules change then the business rule subscriptions can be administratively altered at runtime. For example, let's assume that now a new hire also has to sign a non-disclosure contract with the employer before they can be officially listed as an employee. We would simply need to create a new subscriber whose responsibility is to ensure that the company has a signed disclosure agreement on file for the new hire. Once we subscribe the new subscriber to the "create new employee" event, then the business rule will be enforced for all subsequent attempts to create an employee.

Be cautious when subscribing non-transactional subscribers, or subscribers that make changes to persistent state that is not managed by a Resource Manager, to events that may be fired within the context of a transaction. As with any distributed transaction, using non-transactional components or making modifications to persistent state not managed by a Resource Manager within the context of a transaction should be a deliberate and conscious decision. (For more information on Resource Managers, see Chapter 8.)

For example, let's say we create a new subscriber to the "create new employee" event that is responsible for sending out a new employee welcome letter. On our system, we do not have a Resource Manager to manage the process of generating and sending out a welcome letter. Therefore, a welcome letter will be sent out to the individual even if the transaction failed, for example because the company didn't have the proper documentation to prove the individual's right to work within the United States. This situation could be avoided by subscribing our new welcome letter subscriber to an event that is fired once a new employee is added to the system. For this instance, we could write a COM+ Compensating Resource Manager that will ensure that the e-mail will only get sent if the transaction completes. (Compensating Resource Managers are also discussed in Chapter 8.)

There are situations where you would want to subscribe a non-transactional component to receive events from a transacted publisher. For example, you may wish to write a logging component that is responsible for logging all fired events regardless of whether the transaction succeeded or failed.

Summary

COM+ Events provides developers with a powerful and easy-to-use implementation of the loosely coupled events design pattern, that can be used within your applications. The major components within COM+ Events are:

- ❑ Publisher – the entity responsible for firing events
- ❑ Subscriber – the entity responsible for performing an action based upon receiving an event
- ❑ Event class – the entity that represents the contract between the publisher and subscriber
- ❑ Subscription – the entity that defines the relationship between a subscriber, an event class, and possibly a particular publisher

We learned that there are two different types of subscriptions, transient and persistent. A transient subscription is one where its lifetime is defined within the context of its subscriber. A persistent subscription can survive system failures and its subscriber has a lifetime defined within the context of a particular event.

We also looked at how filtering can be used, at both the subscriber (using filter criteria) and publisher (using a publisher filter object) levels.

COM+ Events is well integrated with other COM+ services such as queued components and support for distributed transactions. COM+ Events uses queued components to provide support for asynchronous events. Since a method call on an event object blocks until every subscriber has received notification, asynchronous events can dramatically improve the responsiveness of the publisher. Transacted events allow subscribers to participate in the publisher's transaction. Transacted events also provide an infrastructure so that you can easily add and remove atomic business rules within your application.

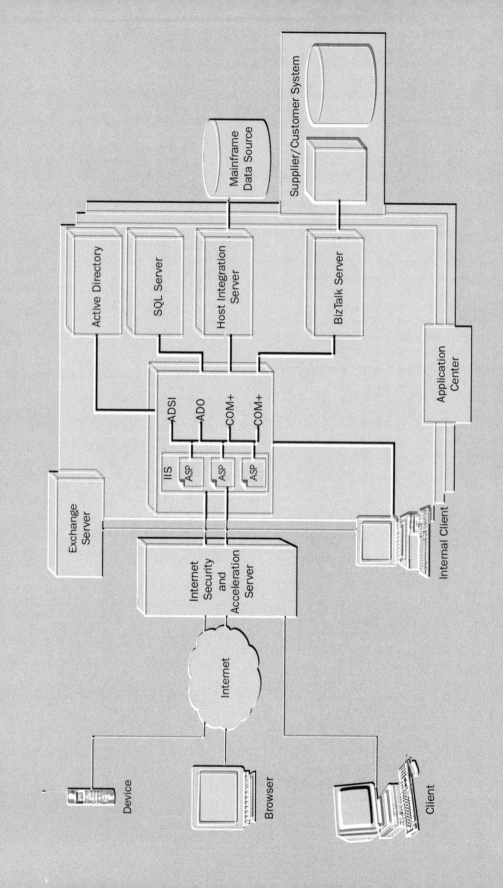

11

More Business Object Issues

In Chapter 5, we began discussing business objects, and why they are important and useful. We covered some basic object-oriented terminology, defined business logic, and saw how business objects can encapsulate that logic to increase the maintainability of our code. Business objects help ensure that our business logic and UI logic are kept separate – a key success factor when building n-tier solutions.

We also put this business object theory into practice when we built the component in Chapter 7, to be used in our simple DNA application case study in Chapter 23. You might also find it useful to refer to this case study before reading the present chapter.

Our discussion so far has been pretty basic – covering some basic object concepts and how they relate to Windows DNA and to COM components. In this chapter, we're going to expand on our discussion by introducing the concept of the **service** object, which is something slightly different from a traditional fine-grained object.

> *The* ContactList *'object' in our case study is an example of a service object.*

In the Windows DNA architecture, the concept of services is very important. While business objects and object-oriented concepts can play a vital role in the design of an application, it's important to take into account the differences between objects and services – leveraging the strengths of each.

The first topic we'll cover in this chapter is the relationship between services and objects. Then we'll focus on relationships between objects.

Creating a single object is relatively easy. However, it's rare that any meaningful business concept can be modeled by a single object, so we typically develop a set of related class modules that allow us to instantiate a group of objects within our application. The relationships between these classes are not random, they fall into some defined groups – typically is-a (generalization), has-a (aggregation and containment), uses, and association. We'll explore these types of relationship and see how to code them in Visual Basic.

Object-oriented (OO) technology doesn't always adapt well to a physical n-tier architecture. Classic OO design is focused around the idea that objects will maintain state data – enabling powerful modeling of business entities and processes. Unfortunately, management of state is a tricky issue in an n-tier environment.

In Chapter 5 we discussed the importance of keeping business logic separate from UI logic, and showed how business objects facilitate this separation. There are also substantial benefits to be gained by keeping data access technology and code separate from our business logic (and UI code). In this chapter we'll explore this issue, and see how we can construct our objects to shield the bulk of an application's code from changes in the underlying database, data structures, or data access technologies.

Services versus Objects

Traditional object-oriented design approaches typically view an application as a cohesive entity – where any object within the application can easily and directly interact with any other object. Essentially, all objects are considered equal – each as accessible as the next. Most object designs tend to involve fine-grained objects that act as a model for the real world. This works well in the abstract, but doesn't apply all that well to the physical realities of an n-tier environment.

In fact, a paramount design consideration in an n-tier environment is to minimize communication between any parts of our application that will be running on different machines. The networking overhead required to communicate between machines is so high that any such communication will always be a detriment to scalability and performance.

Classic objects contain state and provide a rich set of properties and methods against which we can program. These are **fine-grained** objects. As users of such an object, we can expect that it will allow us to set a property, then later we can retrieve that property value and it will contain the data we'd expect. For instance, a Customer object may have many properties – name, address, city, state, last year's sales, etc. If we write an application to use that object, we will have a great deal of communication back and forth between our code and the object:

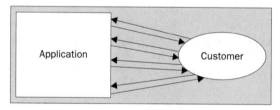

Each time we set or retrieve a property value we are communicating with the object. As long as the object is running in the same process as our application, this is just fine.

However, suppose there's a network between the application and the object. Now things get ugly real fast, since each time we set or retrieve a property we're sending the request and response across the network – relying on many layers of network transports and protocols, and competing with all the other traffic on the network to get the message across.

This problem is even evident in the case where the application and object are running on the same machine, but in different processes. For instance, if the application is written in ASP, and the object is running in a COM+ application (in its own process), the communications between the application and the object will be quite slow. This is because COM is very good about shielding us from the complexity of cross-process communication – keeping things simple, but adding enough overhead that performance will suffer.

Service-Based Architecture

The solution to this issue is to minimize communication between components of our application that run in separate processes or on separate machines. One common design technique is to use a **service-based** architecture, rather than a classic object-oriented architecture, wherever cross-process or cross-network communication is required.

This type of architecture is less concerned with the creation of objects than with the creation of a set of useful services.

> **A service can be thought of as a procedure or method that can be called from our application code.**

There are a couple key criteria that enter into the design of a service:

❑ Services are stateless

❑ Services are atomic

Services maintain no state or data – they just perform work. This means that when the service is done with its work, it won't remember any data. Each time we interact with the service, we need to provide it with all the information it needs to do its job.

This relates to the fact that services are atomic. Being atomic means that each service stands alone. It doesn't require that some other service be called first, nor does it rely on us calling another service once it's done. Each service is responsible for setting up, doing the work, and cleaning up afterwards.

This is the direct opposite of a traditional object-oriented approach. Objects typically rely on the calling code to set a few properties, call a method, and then retrieve various other property values later, whereas a service would be designed to handle all those activities in a single step.

This means that in a single call to a service we can accomplish a great deal of work. Another way to look at it is that with a single call across the network we can provide the service with the data it needs, it can do the work, and it can return any results. When compared to all the network calls required to do the same thing with a classic OO object, performance will be much better.

The drawback to services is that they don't provide all the benefits of objects. Where an object provides an abstract model of a business entity, a service is much closer to an old-fashioned modular programming paradigm, where we're just calling a procedure to get some work done.

Data-Centric Programming

In fact, many services simply provide access to raw data in the form of an XML document or a disconnected ADO `Recordset` – leaving the calling code to deal with the data as it sees fit. This is a far cry from providing the encapsulation and abstraction offered by an object-oriented approach.

This is illustrated by the following diagram, where our application calls the `GetData` service to get a set of customer data:

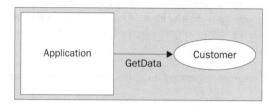

Typically such a call will return an ADO `Recordset` object or an XML document containing the customer data, allowing our application code to do with it as we please. This can be described as a **data-centric** programming model, since our services provide access to sets of data against which we write our applications.

> *At a basic level, data-centric programming is the type of thing we've been doing since DAO was introduced through Visual Basic 3.0. Whether we are programming against a recordset, rowset, array of data, or XML document, in the end we are programming directly against raw data.*

A side-effect of this model is that a service that *accepts* data from a client – perhaps via a `SaveData` call – must never assume that the data it receives is valid. In other words, it's the responsibility of a service to perform all business validation, rule checks, and processing on that data. In fact, a service should be written with the assumption that the client providing the data got it all wrong, and that everything must be checked in great detail.

> **Services that provide raw data to arbitrary client code must always perform all business validation, rules checks, and business processing on the data – never assuming that the appropriate checks were done somewhere else.**

When we're talking about enforcing business logic here, we're talking about several things. This includes validation of each piece of data to ensure it is the right data type and fits within any required ranges. There are also business rule checks – which often involve conditional checks across various pieces of data. Additionally, our service needs to perform any processing – calculations, manipulation of data, or any other work.

Service and Object Confusion

Service-based architectures are often confused with object-oriented architectures – especially in the COM and COM+ environments. This is because COM+ applications (and Microsoft Transaction Server packages) provide services via 'objects'.

Though COM+ applications (and MTS) can be used to host fine-grained stateful objects, this is not the typical approach. Most COM+ applications are either running on a server, in a separate process or on a separate machine from the client, or they are transactional in nature. Either way, when designing objects for these scenarios, each method is atomic and the object maintains no state data at all.

The result is that each method is a service. Thus the object isn't really an object at all – at least in the classic sense. Instead it is a container for a set of methods – or services.

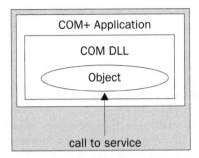

To be clear – traditional object-oriented design calls for objects to encapsulate behaviors *and* data – providing a model of some real-world concept or entity. Service objects encapsulate behavior, but not data – the data is always passed into the object as a parameter. Thus the data is most definitely *not* encapsulated, since the object's client has direct and unrestricted access to the raw data.

In COM+ applications, the application contains one or more components, and each component provides access to one or more objects. Given the isolated, atomic nature of a service, we can view a call to a service as merely penetrating all those containers – from the COM+ application, through the component, through the object, to get at the method that implements the service.

This gets confusing, because our code is calling a method on an object, when in reality we are calling a service. The thing to keep in mind is that in this context, what we're calling an *object* is merely a somewhat arbitrary collection of methods – each method being a service that can be called independently from the others.

In a broader sense, ignoring the way COM+ handles things, there is absolutely no requirement that a service be implemented as a method of an object. ASP pages are a good case in point. Each ASP page provides a service by running code and returning a result in a stateless, atomic manner. The client calls the service via an HTTP request, causing a specific ASP page (service) to be run. The resulting data is returned to the client for its use.

While the typical client of an ASP page is a browser, with the results being an HTML document, this is certainly not required. The client *could* be another application, with the results returned from ASP being an XML document. This is, fundamentally, the core concept behind the Simple Object Access Protocol (**SOAP**). Many people have used this technique to create ASP pages that simply return XML documents instead of HTML – thus creating a general service that returns data upon request.

Merging Objects and Services

On the surface, it appears than any relationship between services and objects is quite superficial – simply an artifact of the way that COM+ is being used to implement the services. However, there can be some very beneficial relationships between objects and services – ways in which we can merge these two concepts directly into the Windows DNA architecture. By doing this we can retain the performance and scalability benefits of a service-based architecture, while still leveraging the maintainability and reusability of an object-oriented architecture.

If we look at the use of services in Windows DNA, they appear in three general areas. This is illustrated by the following diagram:

In this diagram, each arrow is a call to a service. Services are provided to the browser (or other client) from ASP pages. They are provided to the ASP code by the business logic tier, and they are provided to the business tier by the database – typically via stored procedures.

The use of a service-based model between each of these parts of our application makes a great deal of sense. These parts of a Windows DNA application are very often separated by a network, and thus our application design should minimize communication between these major sections.

The one area that may vary in this regard is the ASP and business logic components of our application. In a simple application, or one where high scalability is not a requirement, these two components of our application may very well be running on the web server machine – in many cases, within the same process.

Nevertheless, it's a good idea to design any solution by assuming a service-based architecture between these components. It can be difficult to predict future growth and scalability requirements – and it can also be very nice to have the flexibility of running the business logic in a COM+ application in a separate process from ASP. Either way, a service-based model is important to success.

Given this model, where do business objects fit into the picture? They can fit into the model in two main areas:

❑ We can construct our services themselves to be based on object-oriented designs. This is rarely done due to performance ramifications, but is a valid approach.

❑ We can construct a set of objects that reside *between* the ASP UI code and the business services. These objects can provide the ASP developer with a very nice object-oriented interface, while still retaining the benefits of a service-based model for some tasks.

Let's take a look at these two approaches.

Object-Oriented Services

The business logic component, even though it appears as a set of services to the ASP code, can be constructed *internally* to use object-oriented designs:

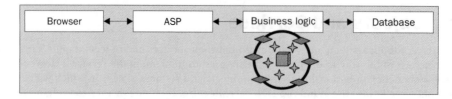

This doesn't change the view of our services from the perspective of an ASP developer. Our services are still a set of atomic, stateless methods that can be invoked to do some useful work.

Service Outside, Object Inside

What changes is *inside* our services. We can write them to rely on a set of business objects to do the actual work.

> *This follows a well-known object-oriented pattern known as the* Façade. *This pattern illustrates the concept of creating a set of high-level objects with broad-reaching methods. Those methods, in turn, interact with a set of lower-level, more complex objects. This is exactly what we are doing here by creating a set of high-level services that provide comprehensive behaviors by using our more complex business objects behind the scenes.*

For example, suppose we have a `SalesOrder` object. It would also have some `LineItem` objects associated with it, since most sales orders have multiple line items.

We can implement an `UpdateData` method on the `SalesOrder` object using a service-based model. This means that the `UpdateData` method will really be a service – an atomic method that does everything it needs to get done in a single call. In this case, our ASP code would merely see a single `UpdateData` method – accepting all the sales order and line item data via parameters.

Of course accepting all this data as a set of independent parameters could add up to a *lot* of parameters – probably an unrealistic number actually. The typical solution is to provide all this data via an ADO `Recordset`, an XML document, a VB `PropertyBag` object, or some other container for complex sets of data.

It is on the *inside* of the `UpdateData` method that things get interesting. In the method's implementation, we can make use of a set of objects designed following object-oriented principles.

In the diagram we see a UML representation of our `SalesOrder` object with its `UpdateData` method. The `SalesOrder` object and its methods are *not* object-oriented, they are service-based. However, behind this simple façade there are quite a number of objects designed based on object-oriented concepts – each of them working together to accomplish the requested task:

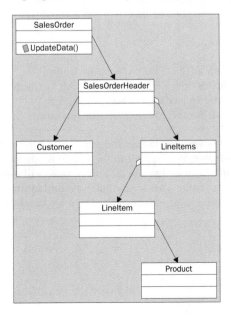

This approach provides a tradeoff. We may lose some performance by having a comprehensive object model, but we gain substantial maintainability and readability of code. These costs and benefits need to be weighed in terms of the requirements of each specific application, to decide whether the use of business objects makes sense.

Object Lifetime

Keeping in mind that the service layer of any application should be stateless, with atomic methods, it stands to reason that our business objects will only exist for the duration of a single method call. When the method is complete, all the objects will be destroyed – thus keeping everything nice and stateless.

In our `SalesOrder` example, the `UpdateData` method utilizes a set of objects. Because the method is stateless, these objects had to come into being at the beginning of the method, and will be destroyed when the method is complete.

This is an important concept, since it means that our business objects need to be quickly and easily instantiated and cleaned up. If our objects take a long time to create or destroy then this approach will not scale well at all.

One way to help this somewhat is through the use of object pooling. Object pooling is a feature of COM+ that will keep a set of objects in memory – instantiated and ready for use. However, the most time-consuming part of creating any object is typically *not* instantiation, but is rather the process of loading data into the object. Object pooling doesn't help this at all – so we need to ensure our objects can load their data as efficiently as possible to get good scalability.

Data-Oriented Design

One major challenge when building ASP pages to interact with a set of business services is that the ASP code tends to get direct access to raw data from the business tier. This means that the ASP code is typically implemented following a data-centric design model. Such a model is quite familiar to the typical ASP developer, since it's the model used when data is retrieved directly from the database via ADO. The code in the ASP pages interacts directly with a set of data.

There are two implications here.

First, the services we write (such as the `UpdateData` method of the `SalesOrder` object) must assume that any data coming from the ASP page may be invalid. All business rules, validation, and processing must be applied against that data to ensure it is acceptable. The only guarantee that any data is valid or calculations are correct comes from the code within our services.

Secondly, on a related point, it's very likely that some business logic will be implemented in the ASP code, or possibly even the browser. It's simply too inefficient to always send the data to the middle tier for simple validation or calculations, and so the ASP developer will undoubtedly implement at least some business logic in the script code. This is obviously redundant logic, since the business service ultimately implements all business logic – meaning that we are creating a potential maintenance problem in our application.

Objects for Use by ASP

Another place we may choose to use objects within the Windows DNA architecture is in the web server itself. The code that we write in an ASP page is written in scripting languages rather than more comprehensive languages such as Visual Basic or C++.

Script languages are interpreted and typeless – in other words they are slow and hard to maintain – not an ideal environment in which to write business logic that should be fast and easily maintained over time.

We can use business objects to improve this model as we discussed in Chapter 5. Business logic (validation, rules, and processing) can be encapsulated in a set of COM objects – written in compiled, advanced languages and tools. The ASP script code can then use these objects to generate the UI for the user.

Business Logic on the Web Server

In the simplest incarnation of this idea, we can simply move the business logic directly onto the web server, running in the same process as the ASP code. Then instead of implementing the business logic as a set of services, we can implement the logic in a set of objects:

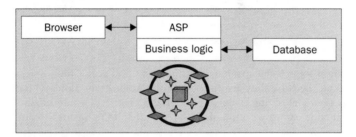

Since the objects will be running in the same process as the ASP code, we don't have to worry about minimizing communication due to network (or cross-process) performance problems. This means that the objects can be designed using OO concepts – including having lots of properties and methods, and providing a robust model of our business entities.

If we look at the `SalesOrder` object example from earlier, its `UpdateData` method (a service) relies on a set of objects to do its work. What we're talking about here is basically discarding the `SalesOrder` object, and allowing the ASP code to directly interact with the `SalesOrderHeader`, `LineItem`, and other objects in the model.

This is an improvement, because the ASP code will no longer be provided with raw data. Instead the ASP code will always interact with the objects to take care of any validation or business processing. The ASP code no longer needs to implement redundant validation logic or calculations because the objects are right there – accessible at any time.

One catch with this model is in the lifetime of the objects. Since they are being used by an ASP page – which is essentially a service – they will be frequently created and destroyed. The objects will only exist for the time it takes a given ASP page to run. Thus, the objects need to be easily created and destroyed with minimal effort. We'll discuss this issue in more detail later in the chapter when we discuss objects and state.

Another catch with this model is that of scalability. The advantage of having the business logic in services on a separate machine from the web server is increased scalability. In the service model, if the web server gets overloaded we can just add another web server – and it too will rely on the services for business processing. If our business application server gets overloaded, we can add another application server – distributing the load easily and effectively.

Distributed Business Logic

When we put the business logic directly on the web server things become a bit less fluid. If our business processing gets overloaded we have to add another web server – even if the web server wasn't the bottleneck. Likewise, if the web server gets overloaded, we'll end up with two servers running business logic, even though the business processing may not have been the issue.

What would be nice is to blend the two approaches: encapsulate some business processing behind services on an application server, but also shield the ASP code from directly interacting with data by having some objects running on the web server.

In the diagram we can see that the business logic has been broken into two parts – UI-centric and data-centric. This goes a long way towards enabling us to take advantage of both business objects and services:

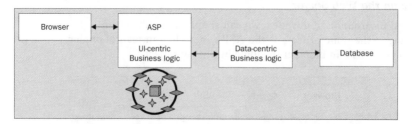

The UI-centric business logic is encapsulated within a set of objects. These objects can be designed following OO concepts, because they are running on the web server along with the ASP code. They provide a nice, logical model of our business entities and processes – minimizing the complexity of the ASP code, since that code can rely on the objects to handle all the business issues.

> **The UI-centric objects exist primarily to increase the maintainability of the application.**

To keep scalability as high as possible, some of the business logic should be implemented to run on a separate application server. In particular, the business logic and code that interacts with the database should be kept separate from the more object-oriented UI-centric business logic.

There are two reasons for this. First, by consolidating all the data access code onto a single application server we can maximize the effectiveness of database connection pooling. Second, data access code tends to be highly transactional – it's dealing with data updates after all. By running this code in a COM+ application we gain maximum control over the transactional nature of the services we'll be implementing.

Notice that the data-centric business logic in the diagram is *not* shown as using business objects. In many cases it's better to implement the data-centric code using procedural or modular designs than with object-oriented designs. This is because this code is typically running through a set of data to generate calls to stored procedures or to update ADO recordsets. The nature of the code itself tends to be quite linear and lends itself well to a modular design.

However, if the business logic being implemented to retrieve or update the data from the database is very complex we may choose to implement it using business objects. In such a case the data-centric services would be a façade that relies on the set of objects – as we discussed in the previous section.

Object Relationships

In earlier chapters we covered some basic object-oriented terms and concepts:

❑ Classes

❑ Objects

❑ Instancing

❑ Properties

❑ Methods

❑ Multiple interfaces

All of those are pretty basic concepts, and they can all be illustrated with a single object. When we start working with multiple objects that interact with each other, we need to expand the set of terms and concepts.

Already in this chapter we've seen some examples of objects working together. The SalesOrder object interacted with a SalesOrderHeader, which in turn interacted with an entire set of other objects:

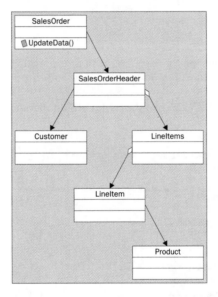

At the time we took it on trust that this all made sense. Now let's take a closer look at relationships between classes, including those in the SalesOrder diagram. In the process, we'll explain a little about the Universal Modeling Language (UML) notation used in the SalesOrder diagram.

There are many in-depth sources of information about UML, see the Further Resources appendix for some ideas.

Class Relationships

In UML, the most basic and common type of diagram is the **class diagram**. The primary intent of a static class diagram is to show the relationships between the classes in our application.

We'll go through the common relationships, and show the notations used for each.

Association

Association relationships cover a lot of ground, including:

❑ One object using another

❑ One object knowing about another

❑ One object creating another

In UML, a general relationship between classes is expressed using the following notation:

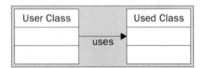

This diagram shows two classes: the User Class is in a relationship where it uses the Used Class. Any word could be substituted for uses in the diagram to indicate a different type of relationship.

For instance, in the SalesOrder example, the UpdateData method creates an instance of the SalesOrderHeader object:

```
Public Sub UpdateData(ByVal NewData As String)
   Dim objSOH As SalesOrderHeader

   Set objSOH = New SalesOrderHeader

   ' remainder of the code ...
End Sub
```

This code implements an association where the SalesOrder object *creates* a SalesOrderHeader object.

Aggregation and Containment

Aggregation occurs when one object is composed of one or more other objects. There are actually a couple variations on the aggregation theme. Simple aggregation indicates that one object is composed of other objects, but doesn't *own* those objects. **Containment** indicates not only composition, but ownership.

When we talk about ownership in this context, what we're really talking about is control over an object's lifetime. In an aggregate relationship between two objects, neither object controls the other object's existence. With a containment relationship, however, the contained object comes and goes based on the implementation of the containing object.

Unfortunately the Visual Modeler tool that ships with Microsoft Visual Studio doesn't support the notation for containment. The closest we can get is to use the aggregation relationship – which can lead to some ambiguity in class diagrams created with VM.

UML provides a special notation to denote aggregation:

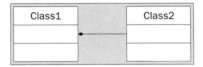

In this case, Class1 is *composed* of Class2. Another way to say this is that Class2 is *aggregated* into Class1. The classic example used to illustrate this relationship is that of a car. A car is an aggregate object, made up of wheels, doors, an engine, and so forth.

The containment relationship is very similar in its notation – the only difference being that the diamond is solid black:

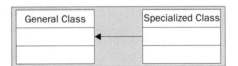

Containment is different from simple aggregation. In the case of containment, Class1 controls the lifetime of Class2. If Class1 ceases to exist, then Class2 must also cease to exist.

The containment relationship is commonly used in business applications, since it represents a common transactional relationship – parent-child. For example, a sales order contains line items. The line items cannot exist without the sales order itself, so the sales order controls the lifetimes of the line item objects.

Generalization (Inheritance)

Generalization is an analysis technique by which we identify a general class that can be used to create other, more specialized, classes. In UML we can show this relationship as:

```
General Class          Specialized Class
          ◀──────
```

Implementation Inheritance

The easiest and most common way to implement the generalization relationship is **implementation inheritance**.

In the previous, diagram the Specialized Class is created by inheriting the General Class. This means that the Specialized Class starts with the same interface (methods and properties) as the General Class, along with all its behaviors (implementation of those methods and properties). The Specialized Class can then add new methods and properties, as well as replacing or enhancing the implementation of the existing interface elements.

Multiple Interfaces

COM doesn't support the concept of inheritance like this, so COM components cannot implement generalization through the use of implementation inheritance.

> *This is not an issue of language (VB, C++, etc.), but a limitation of COM. For instance, C++ can use inheritance within a COM component, but not between one COM component and another. This is because inheritance is a source-code level concept (the compiler actually needs the code from the general class to build the specialized class), while COM is a binary standard that deals in pre-compiled modules – no source code is available.*

There is an alternative way to implement the generalization relationship in the COM environment – implementing COM interfaces. This is not the same as implementation inheritance, but provides similar results.

Within COM, an object can implement more than one interface. In fact COM interfaces can be viewed as being separate from COM objects – they are related, but separate. A COM object implements at least one interface that can be used by clients to interact with the object. This is illustrated in the following diagram:

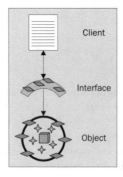

However, an object can implement more than one interface. Clients always interact with an object through an interface, but if an object has more than one interface, a client can choose *which* interface should be used. In a sense, this means that one object can appear to be different things at different times depending on the interface that's being used.

Take a `Customer` object for instance. It seems logical that this object would have a `Customer` interface. It might also have a more general interface – `Person`. Other objects may also implement the `Person` interface, for example `Employee` and `Vendor`. A client can then choose whether to interact with the `Customer` object as a customer, or as the more general person. This is illustrated by the following diagram:

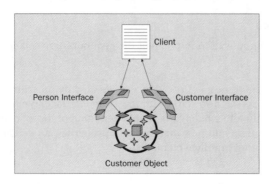

Delegation

Of course we probably don't want to re-implement all the common behaviors that might be behind the `Person` interface. Ideally, we'd have a `Person` object somewhere that implements all the behaviors common to any person – whether customer, vendor, or employee. If we employed implementation inheritance, we'd then not only get the `Person` interface, but we'd also get the implementation – the code behind the interface.

When implementing multiple interfaces, an object merely exposes the new interface – it doesn't get any additional behaviors. To overcome this limitation, we can employ **delegation** – having one object delegate work to another.

In the `Customer` object example, the `Customer` object now exposes a `Person` interface. To take advantage of `Person` behaviors, the `Customer` object might create its own `Person` object and delegate any calls from the client to the `Person` interface down to that internal `Person` object:

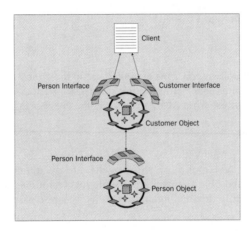

The client wouldn't even know that there was a `Person` object involved, but the `Customer` object can avoid reimplementing those common behaviors. The VB code within the `Customer` object might look something like this:

```
Private mobjPerson As Person

Private Sub Class_Initialize()
   Set mobjPerson = New Person
End Sub
```

```
Private Property Get Person_LastName() As String
   Person_LastName = mobjPerson.LastName
End Property
```

```
Private Property Get Person_FirstName() As String
   Person_FirstName = mobjPerson.FirstName
End Property
```

Notice how the `Customer` object creates a private `Person` object as it initializes. Then, rather than implementing its own code to handle the first and last names, the `Customer` object delegates those responsibilities to that `Person` object.

The `Person` object itself would just implement the properties normally – including enforcing business rules and so forth. In the following code, assume there's a `BusinessCheck` method that enforces those business rules:

```
Public Property Get LastName() As String
   If BusinessCheck Then
      LastName = mstrLastName
   Else
      LastName = "<unavailable>"
   End If
End Property
```

```
Public Property Get FirstName() As String
   If BusinessCheck Then
      FirstName = mstrFirstName
   Else
      FirstName = "<unavailable>"
   End If
End Property
```

Unfortunately, the use of multiple interfaces is of limited use in the typical Windows DNA application. It is difficult to make use of these interfaces from scripting languages – such as those used within ASP pages. This means that objects designed for use from ASP can't rely on the client being able to use those interfaces.

IDispatch

Scripting languages always interact with objects using late binding. In other words, they always interact with objects using IDispatch. IDispatch allows a client to dynamically invoke methods without specific prior knowledge of the objects interfaces. While this technique is comparatively slow (due to its dynamic nature), it is incredibly flexible (again, due to its dynamic nature).

> **Any objects that will be used from ASP should provide all functionality via the late-bound `IDispatch` interface – something automatically handled by Visual Basic, but which may take some extra work in other languages.**

The following diagram illustrates how a 'regular' client can use the `Customer` or `Person` interfaces, but an ASP client will interact with the object via the `IDispatch` interface:

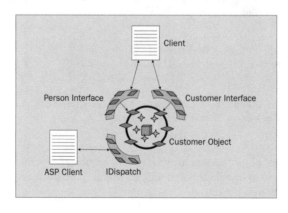

While multiple interfaces and the use of IDispatch don't replace implementation inheritance, these techniques can be used to provide similar functionality to clients. Unfortunately, these techniques are often of limited use for ASP clients, since they can only communicate with an object via its default IDispatch interface – making it virtually impossible to interact with any secondary interfaces on the object.

> *Technically, it is possible to build objects such that ASP can work with their secondary IDispatch interfaces. This is quite an arcane process, and is not widely practiced due to its complexity and the fact that it isn't supported by Visual Basic.*

Enforcing Business Rules

The question remains – *why* implement these different object relationships? We could just implement all our various objects independently, then glue them together with script code in ASP – after all, ASP is commonly described as the glue that ties objects together.

Unfortunately this is a poor description of ASP, and a non-optimal use of objects.

As we discussed in Chapter 5, ASP is best thought of as the place where UI code resides. From the perspective of a traditional Windows developer, ASP is the replacement for a VB form or a C++ dialog. While this UI code interacts with objects, the purpose of the code is to generate a quality UI, not to act as glue.

Another important concept we covered in Chapter 5 is that objects should enforce all business rules. It's pretty obvious how to do this *within* an object, since we can just write code to validate incoming data values, provide calculations, and so forth. Most business environments aren't that simple, however – meaning that some business rules or behaviors will span objects.

For example, in our SalesOrder example, there are many possible cases where rules span objects. One obvious one is in the relationship between the SalesOrderHeader and LineItem objects. The header object undoubtedly has a method returning the total amount of the sales order – but that amount is a calculation performed by asking all the LineItem objects for their individual subtotals – a clear and direct interaction between objects.

Unless we design these objects properly, a rogue bit of ASP code could cause problems. Suppose, for instance, that we *don't* enforce a containment relationship between the header and line item objects. In such a case, there would be no guarantee that the header and line items would remain properly in sync. For example, the ASP code might destroy a line item, or create a new one, without telling the header object. The end result would be an inaccurate representation of the sales order.

Instead, objects should always be constructed with proper relationships – and they should enforce those relationships. It should not be possible for client code to create or destroy a line item object without going through the header object. This way the header object can employ any required business processing during the creation or destruction process – ensuring that our business rules will be followed in all cases.

Separating Data Access from Objects

If there's one truism in Windows programming, it is that databases and data access technologies are always changing. Every time this happens it becomes a maintenance issue for any existing applications – often causing rewrites, or at least reworking. This is not only expensive, it is typically incredibly boring work to go painstakingly through an entire application changing the code.

Changes in the database are often outside our control. Companies are purchased or merged continually, and technology is continually being updated. While we might start with a JET database, our application may be converted to work with Oracle, then SQL Server, then – well, who knows. Even with ODBC or OLE DB buffering our code from the underlying database there are typically some changes that come with any new database – changes requiring reworking in our code.

Even if the type of database doesn't change, it's quite likely that database *structure* will change over time. As new features are added to our application, or other applications are created to use the same data, we'll find that the tables and relationships that existed in the application's initial design need to be altered. Each change requires updates to our application – sometimes substantial, complex changes.

It seems that any given data access offering only lasts about 3 years before it becomes obsolete. Not that DAO or RDO are *gone*, but they are obsolete. Each one had a few years in the light, and was then replaced. Each time the new technology came along, we rewrote our applications to utilize the newer, more powerful options. Today we use ADO and OLE DB, and while there's no hint of ADO going by the wayside, history has shown that there's always something new coming.

Ideally we'd adopt an application architecture that shields the bulk of our code from changes to the database, data structure, and data access technology. Given the fluidity of these elements, we can dramatically increase the maintainability and reduce reworking given such an architecture.

So far, both in Chapter 5 and in this chapter, we've focused much of our conversation on the benefits to be gained by separating UI code from business logic by encapsulating the business logic in objects. Earlier in this chapter we also discussed where, in a Windows DNA architecture, business objects can fit.

Properly architected, objects can be used to largely shield both our UI code and the bulk of our business logic from underlying database, data structure, and data access changes. That's what we're going to look at here.

Distributed Architecture

The general architecture will follow the distributed structure we discussed earlier:

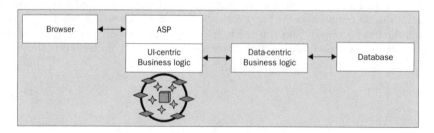

In this model, the ASP code handles all UI functions and interacts with the user via the browser. The ASP code also relies on our business objects to encapsulate all business logic. The data-centric business logic in this case will totally encapsulate data access – providing a single section of the application that deals with the database, data structure, and data access technology.

What we're going to explore is how to actually implement this distributed architecture – specifically focusing on the business objects on the web server and the data-centric services that support them.

UI-centric Business Objects

Much of our business logic will be encapsulated within objects running on the web server. By having a rich, powerful object model for use by our UI developers, we can keep the ASP code focused purely on user interaction, and the business objects can be designed following object-oriented principles.

This means that the UI-centric business objects will tend to be object-oriented in the traditional sense. They'll be fine-grained, with properties and methods that make the objects easy to understand and interact with. All the objects we've been working with so far in this chapter and in Chapter 5 have fit these criteria.

> *It's worth noting that this approach can take more work – more design and thought is required to build the solution – as compared to direct ASP programming. However, the long-term payoff is tremendous, since we'll have a faster, more maintainable application when we're done.*

However, so far we've been concentrating on business objects containing code that interacts with the database, and that relies on a data access technology such as ADO. As we just discussed, this intermingling of data access and business logic can become a maintenance problem over time.

So what does it mean to build a business object that doesn't interact with the database, and preferably doesn't rely on any specific data access technology?

It means that the object won't contain any code that establishes a connection to the database. No ADO `Connection` or `Command` objects, and no creation of `Recordset` objects by calling stored procedures or issuing SQL statements. In fact, it means that these objects will contain no SQL statements of any sort.

Instead, we'll design the objects to rely on the data-centric services that *do* interact with the database.

Basic Properties

A simple business object might look something like this:

```
Option Explicit

Private mlngID As Long
Private mstrName As String
Private mblnIsDirty As Boolean
Private mblnIsNew As Boolean
Private mblnIsDeleted As Boolean


Public Property Get ID() As Long
    ID = mlngID
End Property
```

```
Public Property Get Name() As String
   Name = mstrName
End Property
```

```
Public Property Let Name(Value As String)
 ' enforce business validation here
   mstrName = Value
   mblnIsDirty = True
End Property
```

```
Public Sub Delete()
   mblnIsDeleted = True
End Sub
```

Loading and Saving

As shown, the code implements a simple object that has a read-only ID property and a read-write Name property. Of course we'll also want to implement methods so the client code can cause the object to load or save data from a database:

```
Public Sub Load(ByVal ID As Long)
   Fetch ID
End Sub
```

```
Public Sub Save()
   Update
End Sub
```

Notice how the Load and Save methods don't directly work with the database. Instead they rely on Fetch and Update methods to contain that code. These last two methods aren't shown in detail here, as they are fairly long:

```
Private Sub Fetch(ByVal ID As Long)
 ' retrieve data from the database
End Sub
```

```
Private Sub Update()

   If mblnIsDeleted Then
      ' delete data
      Exit Sub
   Else
      If mblnIsNew
         ' add data
      Else
         ' update data
      End If
   End If

End Sub
```

We talk more about how these can be implemented in the sample application in Chapter 23. The Fetch and Update methods call stored procedures to retrieve, delete, insert, and update data. They are Private methods within the object – designed to offer some level of isolation between the general code within the object and the methods that interact with the database.

Serializing data

As discussed in Chapter 5, our object is also likely to implement `SetState` and `GetState` methods so it can be serialized:

```
Public Sub SetState(ByVal Buffer As String)

    Dim pb As PropertyBag
    Dim arBuffer() As Byte

    Set pb = New PropertyBag
    arBuffer = Buffer
    With pb
       .Contents = arBuffer
       mlngID = .ReadProperty("ID")
       mstrName = .ReadProperty("Name")
       mblnIsDirty = .ReadProperty("IsDirty")
       mblnIsNew = .ReadProperty("IsNew")
       mblnIsDeleted = .ReadProperty("IsDeleted")
    End With

End Sub
```

```
Public Function GetState() As String

    Dim pb As PropertyBag

    Set pb = New PropertyBag
    With pb
       .WriteProperty "ID", mlngID
       .WriteProperty "Name", mstrName
       .WriteProperty "IsDirty", mblnIsDirty
       .WriteProperty "IsNew", mblnIsNew
       .WriteProperty "IsDeleted", mblnIsDeleted
       GetState = .Contents
    End With

End Function
```

Serialization is particularly useful for objects that will be used from ASP, since we can easily convert the object's internal data into a simple `String`. A `String` can be safely stored in an ASP `Session` variable.

However, serialization is also very useful for sending object data across the network – something we'll need to do momentarily.

> *Visual Basic supports the concept of a Persistable object – which allows us to implement*
> *`Class_ReadProperties` and `Class_WriteProperties` methods. The code to implement*
> *these routines is essentially identical to that we've just seen, since they are also based on the*
> *`PropertyBag` object. Unfortunately making an object persistable in this manner is essentially*
> *useless in an ASP setting, since there's no direct or easy way to get ASP to invoke that capability.*

Interacting With Data-Centric Services

As they stand, the Fetch and Update methods assume they have access to the object's instance variables, or private module variables. If we move these methods out of the object, so they are running on an application server, they obviously won't continue to be able to interact with the UI-centric object's member variables.

This is where serialization comes into play. We can change the Load method to accept the object's data as a result of calling the Fetch method. This means that the Fetch method can retrieve the data from the database and return it to the Load method as a serialized set of data:

```
Public Sub Load(ByVal ID As Long)
    SetState Fetch(ID)
End Sub
```

The call to the Fetch method has been changed. It now expects Fetch to return a String value – which can be passed into the SetState method to deserialize the data.

Likewise, instead of having the Update method rely on access to local data, we'll alter the Save method to pass the UI-centric object's serialized data as a parameter:

```
Public Sub Save()
    SetState Update(GetState)
End Sub
```

Notice that the Update method will now not only accept the data as a parameter, but it will also be expected to return the data back to the UI-centric object. This is critically important, since the object's data might change during the update process. In the case of a new object, for instance, a new ID value will be generated during the process of adding the data to the database – and that new value needs to be returned to the UI-centric object for its use.

Given these changes, there's no longer any requirement that the Fetch and Update methods be contained within the UI-centric object itself. In fact, these two methods could be not only in another object, but running on some other machine – exactly what we needed. We might choose to invoke them using DCOM if the application server is on the same LAN as the web server, or SOAP if the server is across the Internet.

Were we to invoke them via DCOM, the Fetch and Update methods would be placed into a separate object in a separate DLL. That DLL would be installed on a remote server machine, but registered on the web server. In such a case, the Load and Save methods would appear as follows:

```
Public Sub Load(ByVal ID As Long)

    Dim objPersist As ObjectPersist

    Set objPersist = New ObjectPersist
    SetState objPersist.Fetch(ID)
    Set objPersist = Nothing

End Sub

Public Sub Save()
```

```
    Dim objPersist As ObjectPersist

    Set objPersist = New ObjectPersist
    SetState objPersist.Update(GetState)
    Set objPersist = Nothing

  End Sub
```

The code has now been enhanced such that it creates an instance of a remote object named `ObjectPersist`. This remote object will contain the `Fetch` and `Update` methods, so we can call them to retrieve and update the UI-centric object's data.

The UI-centric object that we've just walked through has no direct interaction with the database or its data structures and no reliance on data access technology. All that complexity will be encapsulated in a separate part of our application – limiting our exposure to underlying changes.

Data-Centric Services

Now that we've seen how a UI-centric object can be designed to avoid any SQL or data access technology, let's see how we can build a set of services to support such an object. These services will be designed to run on an application server separate from the web server where the ASP code for the UI and our UI-centric business objects will be running.

We already have a basic understanding of the services that need to be built. They are based on the code from the `Fetch` and `Update` methods that we constructed in our objects in Chapter 7, and that we referred to as we constructed the UI-centric object in the last section.

Constructing services in the COM+ environment is as simple as creating a COM DLL (or ActiveX DLL in VB 6 parlance). Any `Public` methods will be accessible by client code – they are our services.

Given the code we've already looked at for the UI-centric object's `Load` method, we can infer that the `Fetch` method we need to create will have the following declaration:

```
    Public Function Fetch(ByVal ID As Long) As String
    End Function
```

Likewise we know that the `Update` method will be declared as:

```
    Public Function Update(ByVal Buffer As String) As String
    End Function
```

Serializing Data

We also know that the `Fetch` function will be returning a serialized version of the object's state, and that the `Update` function will accept a serialized state as a parameter. This implies that we'll have `GetState` and `SetState` methods available to the code in both routines. These two methods will be identical to those in the UI-centric object – they need to be mirror images to ensure both the UI-centric and data-centric code can interoperate.

This means that our server-side code will appear as follows:

```
Option Explicit

Private mlngID As Long
Private mstrName As String
Private mblnIsDirty As Boolean
Private mblnIsNew As Boolean
Private mblnIsDeleted As Boolean

Public Sub SetState(ByVal Buffer As String)

    Dim pb As PropertyBag
    Dim arBuffer() As Byte

    Set pb = New PropertyBag
    arBuffer = Buffer
    With pb
      .Contents = arBuffer
      mlngID = .ReadProperty("ID")
      mstrName = .ReadProperty("Name")
      mblnIsDirty = .ReadProperty("IsDirty")
      mblnIsNew = .ReadProperty("IsNew")
      mblnIsDeleted = .ReadProperty("IsDeleted")
    End With

End Sub

Public Function GetState() As String

    Dim pb As PropertyBag

    Set pb = New PropertyBag
    With pb
      .WriteProperty "ID", mlngID
      .WriteProperty "Name", mstrName
      .WriteProperty "IsDirty", mblnIsDirty
      .WriteProperty "IsNew", mblnIsNew
      .WriteProperty "IsDeleted", mblnIsDeleted
      GetState = .Contents
    End With

End Function

Public Function Fetch(ByVal ID As Long) As String
End Function

Public Function Update(ByVal Buffer As String) As String
End Function
```

With that basic framework laid down, we can focus on implementation of the Fetch and Update methods themselves. Let's take the Fetch method first.

Fetch Method

We'll have to make some assumptions here – based on our work from other chapters. We'll assume a set of stored procedures for interacting with the database:

❑ getData

❑ insertData

❑ updateData

❑ deleteData

The Fetch method will make use of the getData procedure to retrieve the appropriate data based on the ID parameter. Given this stored procedure, the Fetch method will simply call the stored procedure to retrieve the data from the database, then copy that data into variables and return the serialized data by calling the GetState method:

```
Public Function Fetch(ByVal ID As Long) As String

    Dim objcn As Connection
    Dim objcm As Command
    Dim objrs As Recordset

    Set objcn = New Connection
    objcn.Open DB_CONN

    Set objcm = New Command
    With objcm
        .ActiveConnection = objcn
        .CommandText = "getData"
        .CommandType = adCmdStoredProc
        .Parameters.Append .CreateParameter("id", adGUID, adParamInput, 4, ID)
        Set objrs = .Execute
    End With

    With objrs
        mlngID = objrs("ID")
        mstrName = objrs("Name") & ""
    End With

    Set objrs = Nothing
    Set objcm = Nothing
    objcn.Close
    Set objcn = Nothing

    mblnIsNew = False
    mblnIsDeleted = False
    mblnIsDirty = False

    Fetch = GetState

End Function
```

The code is fairly straightforward. It uses the ID parameter as a parameter to the stored procedure call. Upon receiving the data from the database, the values are loaded into the object's variables. The Fetch method's result is generated through the call to GetState – which generates a serialized set of data that is returned to the UI-centric client code.

You might notice the use of an anti-NULL shortcut in the code – concatenating rs ("Name") *with an empty string. This is a fast, but somewhat obscure technique for avoiding problems with* NULL *values coming from the database – a technique that may not be supported in future versions of Visual Basic.*

Update Method

The Update method also relies on the stored procedures to do its work. It is a bit more complex than the Fetch method, but is essentially the same code model as used in the component in Chapter 7.

Obviously the code needs to be enhanced to work with the serialized data that is passed in as a parameter, and to return a set of serialized data as a result. The deserialization is handled by calling SetState right away at the top of the method, and the serialized return data is created through a call to GetState at the end:

```
Public Function Update(ByVal Buffer As String) As String

    Dim objcn As Connection
    Dim objcm As Command

    SetState Buffer

    Set objcn = New Connection
    objcn.Open DB_CONN

    Set objcm = New Command
    With objcm
        .ActiveConnection = objcn
        .CommandType = adCmdStoredProc
    End With

    If mblnIsDeleted Then
        With objcm
            .CommandText = "deleteData"
            .Parameters.Append .CreateParameter("id", adGUID, adParamInput, _
                4, mlngID)
            .Execute
        End With
        mblnIsNew = True
    Else
        If mblnIsNew Then
            With objcm
                .CommandText = "addData"
                .Parameters.Append .CreateParameter("@id", adGUID, adParamOutput)
            End With
        Else
            With objcm
                .CommandText = "updateData"
                .Parameters.Append .CreateParameter("@id", adGUID, _
                                                    adParamInput, 4, mlngID)
            End With
        End If
        With objcm
            .Parameters.Append .CreateParameter("@name", adVarChar, adParamInput, _
                50, mstrName)
```

```
            .Execute
            .ActiveConnection = Nothing
        If mblnIsNew Then
            mlngID = objcm.Parameters("@id").Value
            mblnIsNew = False
        End If
    End With
End If

Set objcm = Nothing
Set objcn = Nothing
mblnIsDeleted = False
mblnIsDirty = False

Update = GetState

End Function
```

In the case of a delete operation, the ID parameter is used to call the `deleteData` stored procedure.

Otherwise we know we're either inserting or updating data. In the case of an insert (`mblnIsNew` is `True`) we'll call the `insertData` stored procedure – passing the ID parameter so it can be returned from the stored procedure. The assumption here is that the database will generate an ID value for the new record – and that value will be the new ID value for our object.

If `mblnIsNew` is `False` then all we need to do is update the data. This causes a call to the `updateData` stored procedure, passing all the pertinent data as parameters to the stored procedure.

In all three cases, at the end of the method we call the `GetState` method to serialize the object's data and return it to the UI-centric object's `Save` method.

At this point we've seen how to build a UI-centric business object that is totally independent of any database, data structure, or data access technology. All of that code – vulnerable to change – is encapsulated in a set of services that can run on an application server separate from the web server. This application server may be on the local LAN, or across the Internet – callable via SOAP.

> It is important to note that SOAP is XML-based, and so it doesn't deal well with binary data streams such as the `PropertyBag` stream we've generated in this chapter. To transfer such a data stream via SOAP we'll need to employ a simple encoding mechanism to convert the binary data into printable ASCI characters.

Summary

In Chapter 5, we were introduced to objects, components, and related concepts. In this chapter we expanded that discussion, exploring a variety of more advanced concepts.

We explored the differences between service-based design and object-oriented design. While services and objects are different, we can use objects within services to create maintainable, powerful code. Additionally, due to the way services are implemented in the Windows environment, we are virtually always creating 'objects' to house services within COM+ or SOAP.

The object-oriented concepts in Chapter 5 were largely limited to a single object. In this chapter we added to that knowledge by looking at some basic relationships between objects. The basic uses relationship connects objects together in many ways, while aggregation and containment enable us to create complex object hierarchies to model business concepts. Generalization can be problematic in the COM environment, but we can employ multiple interfaces and delegation to implement generalization where needed. Of course this is a transitory problem, since the .NET technologies and VS.NET will provide not merely generalization, but cross-language inheritance.

Most of our discussions around objects have dealt with how objects can be used to separate business logic from UI code. Encapsulating business logic in objects helps ensure that business logic doesn't creep into our UI code – reducing maintainability in the long term. Likewise, in this chapter we saw how business objects can be architected to separate business logic from data access. By shielding the bulk of our application code from changes in the database, data structure, and data access technology, we increase our application's maintainability and reduce reworking.

Outline diagram of .NET (1x)

12

Interoperability for the Web – SOAP

Connectivity is definitely a key point today. And along with that, two other issues stand out more and more clearly. They are **programmability** and **interoperability**. The Web has made all of us and all of our applications interconnected, thanks to the HTTP protocol. The extreme simplicity and effectiveness of this protocol made it possible over the years to build a densely populated network – the Internet – that is now about to enter its third age.

In this chapter, we'll be looking at what this third age is. In particular, we'll be looking at the **Simple Object Access Protocol** (**SOAP**). SOAP is a network protocol designed to increase the interoperability of your existing applications by using existing technologies, thus making your applications accessible to a wider array of platforms and users. The existing technologies that SOAP uses to do this are HTTP and XML.

When it comes to communication, the **Extensible Markup Language** (**XML**) is one of the most pervasive technologies to emerge in recent years. XML is the key to data exchange across platforms. You can model any data through XML, being sure it will be recognized and properly processed wherever it is sent to.

At the time of writing, SOAP is still in development, but this chapter aims to prepare you for when the technology is finalized. In addition, we'll be looking at some similar technologies that you can start using right now, as well as some that will be available in the future.

We'll be discussing:

❑   Why we need SOAP

❑   How SOAP uses HTTP and XML for interoperability

❑   The basics of using SOAP

❑   SOAP of today – `XmlHttpRequest`

❑   SOAP of tomorrow – web services

❑   Alternatives to SOAP

Let's start by defining how the Web has evolved to reach this "third age".

The Third Age of the Web – Programmability and Interoperability

The first age of the Web coincided with raw connectivity, mostly achieved through TCP/IP and the higher-level HTTP protocol. A proliferation of HTML pages became available for download, giving people the capability to access and provide information across the globe, wherever an HTTP web server was up and running. e-Mail was the most advanced frontier of such communication, and its most interactive aspect.

The second age came along after a few years, and lasted from approximately 1997 to 1999. At this stage, HTML was standardized as the universal language of the Web. It was enriched with new features, and a number of side technologies blossomed around it. During this time, Microsoft built its own foundation of today and tomorrow's Web. The **Windows Distributed Internet Architecture** (**DNA**) provides the underpinnings of modern distributed applications, and has been broadly adopted as one of the most productive web architectures.

The more that web applications evolve and increase their basic set of functionality, the greater the need for interactivity, better performance, and programmability. In a single word, you need **interoperability** – between client pages, server pages, and any other category of software application.

> **Any software program, running on any platform and written in any language, should be able to access the information contained in any web page, exposed by any web server, running on any hardware/software platform.**

However, both Windows DNA and Java-based architectures are, perhaps, victims of HTML's limitations, and of misconceptions about what HTML actually is. HTML is only a presentation language – good, if not excellent, at providing graphic page layout, but not so good at providing the actual information as a completely separate component. Within HTML, data and graphical elements are mixed together.

However, there are cases where we just want the data, and don't need any of the additional formatting that HTML provides. For example, say we want to get up-to-date stock values – we could navigate to a URL, type in the stock symbols, submit the request, and wait to see a slightly modified version of the same page with the information we need. However, if we just want the data so that we can use it in another application, this might be unacceptable, even in more sophisticated cases where we can automate the research process and get the results page directly. What we'd expect to get in a non-web scenario is a procedure that takes in the stock symbols, and returns a data structure with the stock values alone – in other words, a raw, skeletal, maybe inelegant structure, with only data and without any graphical embellishment. HTML is simply inadequate to do this. Finding the solution to this problem moved us towards the third age of the Web: **programmability**.

Programming the Web

A programmable web site is made of programmable pages, no matter whether they are Active Server Pages, Java Server Pages produced through ISAPI modules, or servlets. By the expression "programming the Web", we mean "being able to interrogate existing pages or URLs, and have them understand the question and return the requested information".

On the surface, this might seem to be a rather straightforward objective, but it involves at least two classes of problems:

❑ Platform incompatibilities

❑ Component interoperability

Plus there's a third, even more subtle problem: what are we going to use as the format of the data that caller and data provider should exchange?

The global software community has found a valid answer to these problems, which relies heavily on HTTP and XML.

> *We'll assume in this chapter that you already have some idea of how XML works. If you want to know more about XML, try* Professional XML, *ISBN 1-861003-11-0, from Wrox Press.*

Let's consider our two main problems in more detail: first, platform incompatibilities.

Platform Incompatibilities

The key to the success of the Web is **ubiquity**. You can connect to the Internet from anywhere using any browser available. So far as connectivity goes, all the physical differences between the various hardware and software platforms disappeared with the HTTP protocol. The whole industry embraced it as the standard protocol for connecting machines, and companies developed their platform-specific code on *top* of it.

Today when you connect to a web site, you don't know – and more importantly, you don't care – what the web server and the underlying platform are. As a *user*, you only care about the *content* the page actually delivers. As a *programmer*, you only care about the *functions* the page actually exposes. When it comes to connecting, the characteristics of the platform are simply a non-issue, as long as you choose HTTP as the networking protocol.

If you decide to go for other approaches – including **Distributed COM (DCOM)** or **Internet InterORB Protocol (IIOP)** – it's not long before the platform hardware/software configuration once again becomes a serious issue. Both of these protocols seem to be great for server-to-server communications, but they're not so effective for a client-to-server interaction. The reason is that in server-to-server situations, you usually have more control over the environment and the products involved. Both protocols, in fact, perform best when used within a single vendor's implementation.

DCOM, for example, is mostly a Windows NT/2000 protocol (even though DCOM implementations do exist for other platforms). If you want to get the best out of DCOM, you should definitely choose a configuration based on Windows NT/2000. As for IIOP and CORBA, to get the most out of them you should consider working with a single Object Request Broker (ORB) to make sure you get a really interoperable environment.

In a client-to-server scenario – especially when the Internet is in the middle – both protocols have to comply with the possible presence of firewalls or proxy servers that usually block all but a few ports. The HTTP port 80 is one of the few exceptions.

In summary, the best available solution to our platform compatibility issues for client-server Internet applications is to use HTTP as our standard protocol.

Component Interoperability

While HTTP qualifies as a necessary element in the overall connectivity puzzle, we're still missing a component technology that makes it easier for developers to build cross-platform applications with the same ease as for Internet applications. But one question arises quite naturally – since we already have HTTP and the Internet to provide a basic, simple but effective connectivity service, why are we still looking for a way to have distributed and platform neutral components? What's wrong with HTTP and HTML?

Actually, there's nothing wrong with HTTP as the underlying transportation protocol – it's *exactly* what we need. The problem lies with HTML. HTML, in fact, is not at all what we need. HTML was fine and effective as long as the Web was a self-contained world *per se* – the second age of the Web. Then, the Web was a sort of meta-application, with HTML as its presentation language and its user interface. When you enter that world you can have read-only data, updateable data, client-server interaction, made-to-measure pages, and more.

However, the third age of the Web pushes and requires programmability, and HTML turns out to be the wrong language on top of the right protocol. HTML is a great language to *present* data, but not to *describe* it. If instead you want to be able to manipulate data as-is from the client, HTML is not the proper tool. We now want our data to be available as a separate entity from the page layout – and that's exactly what XML allows us to do.

> **What the third generation of web applications require is a component technology that allows URLs to be queried for data. The access to the URL takes place over HTTP, while the data exchanged is based on XML. HTML is confined to the role of displaying the content of the XML stream.**

Towards a New "Component Technology"

XML is a key element towards building a new web-oriented component technology. XML is much more than just a powerful language for data description. Mostly due to the all-encompassing meaning of the word 'data', XML is about to become a sort of component technology for distributed data. This technology is set to revolutionize the way we deal with data.

XML is text-based and, as such, human friendly – it's easier for us to author and read text-based documents. As text, it is portable to any platform, especially once you've encoded it properly. (Any XML 1.0 parser is required to support at least two encoding schemas (UTF-8 and UTF-16) that include ASCII as a special case.)

Furthermore, XML is about data description – and we can model *any* data through XML. That means we can define an XML data schema to describe a remote function call. Once we do that, we're close to the ultimate goal of obtaining a distributed, platform and language independent component technology. No special run-time or API is needed. All of the necessary infrastructure to process the method invocation could be buried into the web server, the operating system, the ORB, or even elsewhere.

Putting XML and HTTP Together

So it seems that we can't do without XML in this new millennium. Behind XML, though, there's much more substance than hype – the widespread acceptance it's gaining these days is indirect proof of its importance. XML is successful because it is simple, effective, easy to author, and more general than HTML. It is a data description language that can describe everything – and what's important in the case we're looking at here, "everything" includes a method call. What's more, it's supported on almost any platform – which is just what we need to overcome our compatibility issues.

> **While HTTP is the key to reach any platform, XML is the basic language to use to talk to components running on that platform.**

HTTP is good for transporting the call from point to point, regardless of the platform. XML is suited to transporting the method call from client to server, once again regardless of the platform and the component technology used to write the server. Once the server has understood and processed the request, the return data will be packed in XML and transported back to the client through the same mechanism.

To make this pattern a universal schema to do remote procedure invocation, we just need two additional steps:

❑ Formalizing the XML schema to describe a method call

❑ Arranging a run-time to process it

The XML schema – namely, the structure of the XML protocol to identify the method and parameters to call – is the **Simple Object Access Protocol** (**SOAP**).

At the time of writing, the run-time to process this, and the SOAP specification document, are nearing completion. See Appendix A for more information on resources. Visual Studio 7 (VS.NET) is expected to ship with significant functionality based on SOAP.

SOAP Breaks In

The following is the official definition of SOAP:

> **SOAP is a protocol specification for invoking methods on servers, services, components, and objects.**

SOAP is also a **minimal** protocol that allows functions to be invoked on remote components. This means, however, more simplicity rather than a lack of important features. SOAP is minimal and simple by design. It's targeted to provide developers with the most frequently used set of functionality, rather than with a powerful general-purpose protocol meant to replace and extend more or less seamlessly today's Internet protocols.

SOAP is not just another Internet protocol, even though it makes extensive use of HTTP and XML – two key players in the Internet arena. It's the first serious attempt to define a universal protocol capable of talking to virtually any component written with any language, and running on any platform.

SOAP does not propose new rules or a new programming paradigm. It limits itself to formalizing, in terms of HTTP headers and an XML vocabulary, what today appears to be the simplest, most portable, and efficient way to invoke methods on remote components.

Even though SOAP is mostly associated with HTTP as the underlying transportation protocol, it could be bound also to asynchronous protocols such as SMTP and MSMQ.

> *SOAP is a specification submitted to the **Internet Engineering Task Force (IETF)** whose draft can be viewed at* `http://www.ietf.org/internet-drafts/`.

SOAP and DCOM

As we're discussing a protocol to invoke methods on remote components, you might wonder how SOAP compares to DCOM. In a certain sense, SOAP was born due to the difficulty that both DCOM and CORBA's IIOP encountered in becoming a *de facto* standard for Internet-based communications. Both DCOM and IIOP, in fact, have yet to demonstrate that they can be adapted to the Internet.

While SOAP and DCOM share the same basic idea, they are opposite in terms of practical implementation. In particular, DCOM turns out to be rather complex in its configuration and administrative aspects. More importantly, it relies on dynamically assigned ports that make it pretty difficult for it to jump over firewalls.

DCOM has a far richer and extensible object model that provides some features that SOAP doesn't. In particular, SOAP doesn't manage and require object identity – it uses only URLs to identify objects, and needs stateless objects. With DCOM, on the other hand, CLSIDs and progIDs allow you to identify precisely the object to call. The DCOM object's lifetime is manipulated by the client through IUnknown interface methods, whereas no particular measure is mandated by SOAP, other than timing out the call or requiring stateless components.

There's also a performance aspect – since XML is a relatively verbose way of describing data, SOAP is not as efficient as DCOM.

All of these disadvantages, though, are partly a result of the way that SOAP has been designed – the principle aim is simplicity and platform independence, in place of non-essential features and slightly enhanced performance.

In summary, SOAP and DCOM have the following respective benefits– and bear in mind that what is a pro for one is a con for the other:

SOAP pros include:

❑   Platform and language neutrality

❑   Simplicity and ease of use

❑   Jumps through firewalls

And DCOM pros include:

❑   Object identification

❑   Object lifetime

❑   Transmission of binary data

❑   Performance

Today, we design client applications to communicate with specific server applications, taking into careful account the target platform. In most cases, especially when different hardware and software platforms are involved, we end up using proprietary text-based protocols. Sometimes we use XML to get more flexibility and ease of description. If you've already done this in the past, then you have implemented your own SOAP protocol – SOAP simply codifies existing practices.

> *There's one more benefit of SOAP that's frequently overlooked – the load balancing implementation that's immediately solved for you once you implement SOAP. Technology for load balancing the HTTP protocol has already been successfully implemented in several different ways: for example, Microsoft offers Network Load Balancing Services. This still works with various backend implementations of component based software, and eliminates the need to use Microsoft's Component Load Balancing Service (CLBS), which forces you to use COM-based implementation of component development.*

COM Internet Services

Firewalls and proxy servers are a common presence between corporate networks and the Internet. Firewalls usually block all ports but a few, one of those few being the HTTP port 80. This means that if we want to run applications that reside outside the firewall, we should obtain an additional range of ports from the system administrator, in order for a client and a server to talk to each other. However, since SOAP is based on HTTP, we can solve this big issue without lifting a finger.

If you can't avoid using some of the DCOM typical services that SOAP doesn't provide as of the current stage of the specification, then **COM Internet Services** (**CIS**) might help to force DCOM to operate over TCP port 80. CIS introduces support for a new DCOM transport protocol known as **Tunneling Transmission Control Protocol** (**TTCP**). TTCP works around firewall limitations by introducing a special HTTP handshake at the beginning of each DCOM connection. After this, the wire protocol is simply DCOM over TCP. Using CIS, neither the client code nor the server code needs updating, and you have all of the DCOM advantages, including DCOM security and lifetime management.

TTCP, though, is a platform-specific solution. In fact, it requires IIS 4.0 or higher to be on the server machine, since most of the CIS functionality is implemented through an ISAPI filter. While this is not the only limitation of CIS, it is enough to highlight that it can't help to get *real* interoperability over the Internet.

SOAP and BizTalk

BizTalk is an initiative meant to facilitate document exchange over the Internet. At its heart, a BizTalk client works in much the same way as a SOAP client. Both rely on HTTP as the favorite transportation protocol, and both use a request-response message pattern. However, SOAP is more general than BizTalk or other business-to-business (B2B) initiatives like OASIS.

As a general-purpose mechanism to allow remote method invocation, certainly SOAP can be used to transport BizTalk information. Actually, asking a BizTalk remote server to translate from one XML schema to another is an example of a remote method invocation on a server object that exposes a well-known and predefined interface.

> *SOAP is not limited to the request-response message pattern. If it happens to use an asynchronous protocol like SMTP or MSMQ, then the message pattern must necessarily be different. In this case, it would be a one-way method, also known as the 'fire-and-forget' message pattern.*

The SOAP Status Quo

The latest version of SOAP available at the time of writing is version 1.1. With this version, the group of companies that actively support and develop SOAP increased significantly. IBM and Lotus joined Microsoft, IONA Technologies, DevelopMentor, Rogue Wave Software, and UserLand, to name but a few.

To date, there's no released implementation of SOAP. Two trial engines are available from the DevelopMentor's web site (http://www.develop.com/soap) for both Perl and Java. Microsoft is using a SOAP implementation in the next edition of Visual Studio.

SOAP Programming Interface

While SOAP doesn't mandate or recommend any API or run-time engine, it actually needs one or the other to become easily usable. Sending a SOAP request is as easy as preparing a string of text, structurally similar to HTTP requests. Such a string will be received by a module listening to port 80, and be processed accordingly. Custom headers help to distinguish SOAP payloads from other packets.

It's reasonable to expect that, in the land of Windows, sooner or later someone – maybe Microsoft – will come up with an object model to simplify the creation of SOAP-based traffic. On other platforms, other vendors are free to provide the tools they want to manipulate SOAP. The overall situation is not that different from what happened to HTTP. In theory, you can use HTTP without any API or run-time engine: in practice, you often use ASP, whose object model mimics some of the HTTP features.

SOAP Security

SOAP is a sort of XML dialect spoken on top of HTTP. As such, it's simply another payload that can be carried via HTTP.

Lack of built-in security is sometimes listed as one of the disadvantages of SOAP, although from a security point of view, SOAP is certainly no more dangerous than HTTP itself. The same potential vulnerability you face with plain HTTP packets, you'll have to cope with using SOAP. On the other hand, any security feature you can activate with HTTP can be activated with SOAP. The specification, however, doesn't define any technology-specific features as regards security.

Notice that in order to send your SOAP payloads, you are completely free to employ SSL and HTTPS. You can also take advantage of any HTTP authentication mechanisms such as the basic, digest, or Windows Integrated authentication available under Windows NT/2000.

SOAP Requests and Responses

To put SOAP to work, we need two types of modules:

❑   A client-side proxy that builds up the SOAP request

❑   A server-side stub that receives, unpacks, and processes the request

As mentioned earlier, there's no mandated API or specification about how these two types of code should be written and/or exposed. Furthermore, there's also complete freedom to decide where such code should be located. In general, SOAP can be implemented on the web server, in the operating system, and needs some sort of support from either the browser or a client-side component like a Java applet, an ActiveX control, or a library of script functions.

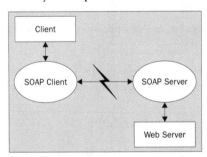

A minimal, but working, SOAP request looks like this:

```
POST http://expoware/soap/demo1.asp  HTTP/1.1
Content-Type: text/xml
Content-Length: 122
SOAPMethodName: urn:My-SOAP-Interface#DoSomething

<Envelope>
  <Body>
    <DoThis xmlns="My-SOAP-Interface">
      <arg1>First</arg1>
      <arg2>23</arg2>
    </DoThis>
  </Body>
</Envelope>
```

The first line specifies the HTTP command and the URL of the resource that's being requested. The next two lines indicate the content type and length of the packet. The SOAPMethodName header contains information about the object, the interface, and the method name to invoke.

What follows is the body of the SOAP payload. Its overall layout is depicted below:

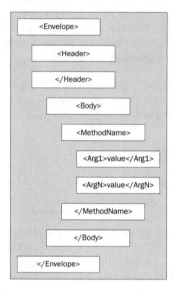

The <Envelope> and the <Body> tags belong to the standard SOAP URN:

    urn:schemas-xmlsoap-org:soap.v1

Within the <Envelope> tag you can find an optional <Header> tag containing custom protocol header extensions.

The method to call is described within the <Body> tag through a subtree rooted into a node with the method's name. Child nodes describe the arguments to pass. Each child node has the name of the formal parameter.

Uniform Resource Identifiers

To be accurate, the SOAP endpoint is a **URI** – a **Uniform Resource Identifier**. A URI can be one of two types:

❑   Uniform Resource **Locator** (URL)

❑   Uniform Resource **Name** (URN)

In general, a URI is a string that unequivocally identifies a resource over the network. According to the format of this string, you can distinguish between the two flavors above.

As you probably know, a URL is given by the protocol prefix, the host name or IP address, optionally the port, and the path. In addition, you can add as many parameters as you need at the end of it. For example:

    http://127.0.0.1:80/soap/demo1.asp

380

A URN is simply a unique descriptive string. For example, the human-readable form of a CLSID is a URN.

In the listing above, we could replace the URN `My-SOAP-Interface` with the CLSID of the COM object exposing the `DoThis` method:

```
POST http://expoware/soap/demo1.asp  HTTP/1.1
Content-Type: text/xml
Content-Length: 122
SOAPMethodName: urn:uuid:C0C0DADA-0000-BABA-AA00-C0C000000000:IFoo#DoThis

<Envelope>
  <Body>
    <DoThis xmlns="urn:uuid:C0C0DADA-0000-BABA-AA00-C0C000000000">
       <arg1>First</arg1>
       <arg2>23</arg2>
    </DoThis>
  </Body>
</Envelope>
```

Now the method `DoThis` comes from the `IFoo` interface of the object whose CLSID is the one specified. Using URNs demonstrates the extreme generality of SOAP – that it's not bound at all to Microsoft-related technologies. The method name is not necessarily the name of a method of a COM object.

The M-POST Command

Any SOAP request is based on an HTTP's `POST` verb. The **HTTP Extensions Framework** defines a mechanism to introduce new HTTP headers, and SOAP supports, but does not mandate, the use of such extensions.

> *For more information about the HTTP Extensions Framework, check out*
> `http://www.w3.org/Protocols/HTTP/ietf-http-ext.`

Using an HTTP verb in the form `M-POST` means that the HTTP server must recognize and understand any extended header specified as mandatory. For example:

```
M-POST http://expoware/soap/demo1.asp  HTTP/1.1
Man: "urn:schemas-xmlsoap-org:soap.v1"; ns=42
42-SOAPMethodName: urn:My-SOAP-Interface#DoSomething
Content-Type: text/xml
Content-Length: 122
```

The `Man` header establishes a mapping between the URI and the prefix number. All the headers prefixed with the specified number (`SOAPMethodName` in the example above) must be checked and processed.

Using `M-POST` instead of `POST`, a SOAP client can distinguish SOAP mandatory headers from optional headers. This also offers firewalls an opportunity to filter SOAP calls based on these custom header extensions.

Component Activation

What happens when the SOAP server-side stub processes the specified URL? Actually, the specification says nothing about particular procedures to be taken to activate the component and call the method. Everything is left to the code behind the URL, whatever that is – a CGI, an ASP, or JSP page, an ISAPI module, or a servlet. It could happen that what is described as a method ends up being a script function, or simply a key to select a piece of code in a switch statement within an ASP page.

> *Despite the extensive use of words like object, method, and interface, you should try to consider them in as general a way as possible. Disregard any thoughts of COM that might cross your mind at this time. Not because COM has nothing to do with this, but because COM is just one possible way of exploiting SOAP.*

The SOAP Response

Once the specified method has been executed, the SOAP server stub must prepare a string of text to send back to the caller. Once again, this string has the form of an HTTP packet and utilizes XML to put information together. A possible SOAP response looks like this:

```
HTTP/1.1 200 OK
Connection: Close
Content-Type: text/xml
Content-Length: 149

<Envelope>
  <Body>
    <DoThisResponse xmlns="My-SOAP-Interface">
      <return>1</return>
      <myRetVal>Hello</myRetVal>
    </DoThisResponse>
  </Body>
</Envelope>
```

The first line is a typical HTTP response substring indicating the status code. The content-type remains `text/xml`.

The structure of the message is not unlike the request case, but there are two differences:

❑ The name of the method's tag

❑ The list of the method's arguments

The tag name identifying the method is now suffixed by the word `Response`, so it becomes `DoThisResponse` instead of `DoThis`. The child nodes of this tag are now given by all the `out` and `retval` parameters of the method. In particular, the `<return>` tag contains the return value of the method. Any other internal tag evaluates to the name of the formal parameter passed by reference. Its content is the content of that variable.

With this overview, we just scratched the surface of the SOAP specification. For one reason or another, SOAP is still in development today, and is still an open specification that can be shaped by any programmers and companies. Why? Because it's been created to help developers and companies.

The key point of SOAP is that it is not reinventing anything, but it codifies today's best practices for remote method invocation over the Internet. In the sections to come, we'll cover alternative approaches and technologies that can obtain the same effect as SOAP, without achieving the same simplicity and platform independence. Nevertheless, the technologies we'll start describing in a moment are something you can use *today* and test while reading this book, without downloading anything, and without installing anything that Windows 2000 doesn't provide you with already.

SOAP of Today: XmlHttpRequest

Bundled with Internet Explorer 5.0 and the Microsoft XML parser toolkit, you already have a COM object called XmlHttpRequest. It's not a front-cover object, and its potential is often underestimated. The main purpose of this object is to enable you to issue HTTP commands to any sort of object that can live behind a URL. But why should you send a POST or a GET command to a URL, if not for requesting data or for asking the URL to execute a method?

From this point of view, XmlHttpRequest looks like the SOAP of today. There are a number of points that differentiate XmlHttpRequest from the SOAP specification. Let's summarize the main ones:

❑ XmlHttpRequest is a COM object, not a specification, which makes it much more useful for the WinDNA application designer

❑ It is mainly targeted to ASP and IIS

❑ It exposes an object model for you to program

❑ It cannot provide platform-independency, at least on the client side

In addition to all this, it turns out to suffer from a serious design flaw that makes it rather unusable in a server-to-server scenario. This problem is explained in the KB article Q237906 and will be fixed in the upcoming version 3.0 of MSXML – Microsoft's XML parser that includes the XmlHttpRequest object.

Compared to SOAP, XmlHttpRequest looks like a run-time engine that implements an XML-based protocol on the Win32 platform. This object is living proof that SOAP is mostly the formalization of existing good programming practices – you can create your own SOAP-like mechanism perfectly tailored to your needs.

XmlHttpRequest can be seen as a sort of implemented and Win32-specific version of what the SOAP specification promotes. Functionally speaking, XmlHttpRequest exposes a COM object model to send generic HTTP requests to a URL. SOAP only generalizes in terms of method invocation and interfaces the exchange of HTTP request-response packets. Under the hood of XmlHttpRequest there's no XML-based protocol for standardizing a method invocation. But this is only because the object, for the sake of simplicity, is limited to activating the object the URL points to.

Using XmlHttpRequest can be as powerful as using SOAP, provided that your clients are Win32 and COM-aware applications.

I don't know what Microsoft will be doing in the near future, but in principle there's nothing to prevent a new version of XmlHttpRequest from being internally based on SOAP.

Using XmlHttpRequest

`XmlHttpRequest` is part of the Internet Explorer 5.0 XML infrastructure. It's a COM object with a progID of `Microsoft.XmlHttp`. To make use of it, we need to do the following:

❏ Create an instance of the object

❏ Open the channel with the specified URL

❏ Execute the command

❏ Deal with the data we receive

`XmlHttpRequest` can be used to send back and forth mostly text, but it's also possible to make the client and the server exchange a whole XML document object model (XMLDOM). In other words, if you're making extensive use of the XMLDOM on the client, and need to exchange information with the server, you can ask the object to marshal the entire XMLDOM back and forth.

Code-wise, we use `XmlHttpRequest` like this:

```
Set xmlhttp = CreateObject("Microsoft.XmlHttp")
xmlhttp.Open "POST", "http://expoware/xmlhttp/test.asp", false
xmlhttp.Send ""
MsgBox xmlhttp.responseText
```

As we mentioned earlier, `XmlHttpRequest` has been designed mostly for a client-to-server usage so the use of `MsgBox` here makes sense.

The `Open` method serves the purpose of setting up the conversation by specifying the URL and the HTTP command to execute. The third parameter is a Boolean value denoting whether you want the operation to take place synchronously or asynchronously. By default, the operation is asynchronous. A value of `false` makes it synchronous.

The `Send` method actually starts the conversation – it's used to specify the body of the HTTP request. If you need to set request headers you can use the `setRequestHeader` method. The response you get from the URL is exposed to the caller in a number of different ways:

❏ Raw text

❏ XMLDOM

❏ An array of bytes

❏ `IStream` interface

There's a special property for each data type: `responseText`, `responseXML`, `responseBody` and `responseStream` respectively.

The response you get is determined by the behavior of the specified URL – the ASP page in the example above. A very simple page might look like this:

```
<%
Response.Write "Hello to everyone!"
%>
```

To exchange an XMLDOM, you just have to pass it to the Send method:

```
Set xmlhttp = CreateObject("Microsoft.XmlHttp")
xmlhttp.Open "POST", "http://expoware/xmlhttp/test.asp", false

' Create a XMLDOM
Set xmldom = CreateObject("Microsoft.XMLDOM")
xmldom.loadXML "<book>Pro WinDNA</book>"

xmlhttp.Send xmldom
Set xmldom = xmlhttp.responseXML
MsgBox xmldom.xml
```

In this case, the ASP page should be able to get and process the XMLDOM. You can do that through the ASP's Request object:

```
<%
   ' Get the XMLDOM from the HTTP request
   Set xmldom = CreateObject("Microsoft.XMLDOM")
   xmldom.load Request

   ' Make some changes
   Set node = xmldom.selectSingleNode("book")
   node.text = "Pro Windows DNA"

   ' Send the XML text back
   Response.ContentType = "text/xml"
   Response.Write xmldom.xml
%>
```

The ASP page can change the status and the content of the XMLDOM, and send it back as plain XML text. Such text is received by the XmlHttpRequest client proxy and properly cached. As soon as the caller invokes the responseXML property, the component attempts to convert the XML text into an XMLDOM. To enable such a conversion, the content type must be explicitly set to text/xml. In case of errors, responseXML returns the null string.

> *Full documentation for this object can be found on the MSDN Web Workshop:*
> *http://msdn.microsoft.com/xml/reference/scriptref/*
> *XMLHttpRequest_object.asp.*

SOAP of the Future: Web Services

A wire protocol like SOAP is the key element to program the Web. Basically, it enables remote access to internal business systems over the Internet. Any URL can be seen and perceived as a service publicly available over the Internet. To give it a fancy and evocative name, this is a **web service**. A web service, therefore, is a middle-tier business component exposed via standard web protocols.

A web service is a new type of component in the sense that it is reachable by anyone and from anywhere. Organizations can get incredible value from this. Integrating existing applications is suddenly easier and sometimes even trivial. Better yet, integrating with other vendors' services is possible– no matter what platform and technology is used to build the various services. A web service is a component for just about everyone.

Web Service Design

Web services is a terminology that Microsoft started pushing with the first previews of Visual Studio.NET. To fulfill all the wonders it promises, web services must rely on standard and broadly accepted technologies. HTTP and XML are two of them, and SOAP, which fuses them together, provides the internal plumbing for web services within the next generation of Visual Studio products.

SOAP, and a practical application of it such as web services, clearly represents an evolution in the use of the Internet. This shifts the perception of the Internet from browsing to programming, and from HTML to XML. In both cases, HTTP remains as the basic transportation protocol.

Creating a Web Service

To create a web service, we should figure out a way to describe the capabilities (most notably, methods) of the service. We do this through XML. The XML document must contain the signature of the method, including any input parameter and the return type. The web server uses this information to locate and execute the functionality, and return an XML document with the result. Nothing new, if you grabbed the essence of SOAP so far!

While trying to understand the role of SOAP and the evolution of the web, never forget that SOAP is just a protocol, and that you'll soon get a more powerful tool to work with it without needing to know the nitty-gritty details. Visual Studio.NET – and in particular Visual Basic.NET – will provide advanced user interface tools to make creating a web service no more difficult than creating a WebClass or a COM component.

Alternatives to SOAP

As cross-platform techniques to invoke methods on remote objects, there are a number of alternatives to SOAP, capable of providing the same functionality to some extent. Aside from the aforementioned XmlHttpRequest object, two of the technologies of interest are:

- ❏ Remote Scripting
- ❏ Remote Data Services

The former is a script-based library of functions that you can invoke from within HTML or ASP pages. Based on the ECMAScript standard (http://www.ecma.org) for script languages, **Remote Scripting** (**RS**) can be used with a number of different browsers on a number of different client platforms. Netscape Navigator 3.x for both Win32 and Linux, HotJava on Solaris, and Internet Explorer 3.0+ on Win32 are the main browsers that support RS.

On the other hand, **Remote Data Services** (**RDS**) is a COM-based toolkit that, while providing better performance due to its compiled code, poses a significant limitation in portability, being based on COM.

Remote Scripting

Remote Scripting (RS) allows you to invoke a function declared in an ASP page from a client page. As such, RS needs a web server that provides support for ASP. The ASP page should expose its externally callable functions through a JavaScript object with a conventional name: `public_description`. All the functions that such an object makes public could be called from a client page.

The RS proxy-stub layer takes care of marshaling data back and forth across the network. Notice that since the request to the remote URL arrives through an HTTP GET command, it has an inherent limitation of 2 KB of data that can be sent. No limit at all exists for communications going from the server back to the client.

In addition, remote methods can send back primitive data types (numbers, strings, dates, arrays) or JavaScript objects. They cannot handle – for security reasons – COM objects, including ADO recordsets.

Compared to a SOAP implementation, RS utilizes a Java applet to send HTTP packets from client to server and an ASP procedure to analyze the data and pass the control to the right function along the page. The final effect is akin to what you can get with SOAP, but considering the heterogeneous technologies involved you can't help but welcome the unified approach of SOAP.

Remote Data Services

RDS is a set of COM-based technologies to work with data, and in particular, with ADO recordsets. RDS is a collection of three objects:

❑   RDS.DataControl

❑   RDS.DataSpace

❑   RDSServer.DataFactory

DataControl provides data-binding functionality – in other words the ability to establish a run-time link between an HTML tag and a data field. DHTML data-binding is the HTML counterpart of Visual Basic data-aware controls.

DataSpace is the real SOAP-like component, as it allows you to invoke methods on remote COM automation objects. Through a pretty standard proxy-stub mechanism, DataSpace allows you to specify the progID of a COM object and the HTTP server where it resides. The proxy takes care of marshaling information towards the stub, which does the job and returns the requested information. On the server side, in order to get the data, you can use the system-provided DataFactory component or you can employ your own custom business objects. DataFactory is a simple query executor that takes a connection string and a command text and returns an ADO recordset.

More information and programming details about RDS can be found in Professional ADO 2.5 RDS Programming with ASP 3.0, ISBN 1-861003-24-2, *from Wrox Press.*

Getting Ready for SOAP

It's hard to predict how soon you'll be using SOAP in real-world projects with the same nonchalance with which you employ a COM or a DCOM call today. However, as far as we can currently foresee, SOAP appears to be the technology of the near future, so thinking about the steps to take to get ready for it shouldn't be considered a waste of time. Here are a few quick pieces of advice to plan your SOAP involvement.

Basically, there are three things to do:

❑ Study XML – XML is the key to SOAP – not so much because SOAP packets are written in XML, but because XML is a pervasive technology when it comes to communication.

❑ Keep on thinking in terms of components – if SOAP ultimately does fulfill all of today's promises, you'll be able to rely on a universal model of components. New generation components will expose services through the Web using HTTP as the transport method and XML to communicate. COM, CORBA and JavaBeans will all become particular instances of such a universal family of interoperable objects.

❑ Continue to write stateless COM components – loyal to the basic web principles, and for the sake of simplicity, SOAP doesn't take into account the notion of state. It does not prohibit it, but it does not provide any specific facility. Be aware of this, and continue on the MTS/COM+ mainstream route: stateless is cool!

Summary

In this chapter, we aimed to explain the "whys" of SOAP, not the "whats". You can find the whats fully described in the SOAP specification, and you can help to orient the technology too, by participating in the online forums. SOAP is on the way, and even if you don't intend to use it, understanding it is helpful anyway.

If SOAP does take root, however, you'll have higher-level interfaces to work with, and it's likely that you won't have to care about the nitty-gritty details of the payloads. Just like HTTP, chances are that you'll end up being mostly unaware of using it. Since SOAP is intended to be the fuel of a new generation of components – the Web Services – a basic understanding of its principles is in order.

In this chapter, you've learned about:

❑ What brought about SOAP

❑ The basic principles of SOAP

❑ The SOAP status quo

❑ Alternatives to SOAP

Online discussion at http://p2p.wrox.com

13

Universal Data Access

Throughout this book you have been learning about n-tier architectures by following Microsoft's DNA model. This chapter deals with the data services tier, which is responsible for the retrieval, manipulation, and storage of data. It will show you how to use Microsoft's **Universal Data Access** (**UDA**) architecture to provide an easy-to-use programming interface by implementing OLE DB and ADO. UDA offers high performance data connectivity, capable of accessing both relational and non-relational data sources.

After completing this chapter, you should understand the following concepts:

- ❏ Why new data access methods are necessary – why developers need UDA

- ❏ What UDA is and how it works

- ❏ Why Open Database Connectivity (ODBC) is not a total solution for UDA

- ❏ How Object Linking and Embedding Database (OLE DB) and ActiveX Data Objects (ADO) relate to UDA

- ❏ What data providers are and how they are used

- ❏ Why Remote Data Services (RDS) is important to UDA

So let's start with the first item on this list.

The Need for New Data Access Methods

Open Database Connectivity (**ODBC**) has been a tried and trusted technology among database developers for a long time. ODBC makes use of **Structured Query Language** (**SQL**) in order to query and manipulate data. However, as you'll soon learn, ODBC is limited to only accessing **relational** databases.

In the last few years, Microsoft has offered other solutions to access data, including the use of **Data Access Objects** (**DAO**) and **Remote Data Objects** (**RDO**).

❑ DAO was introduced mainly for desktop applications that utilized **ISAM** (**Indexed Sequential Access Method**) data sources, typically using the Microsoft Jet data engine. Examples include Microsoft Access, FoxPro and Dbase. DAO did work, but its performance was far from satisfactory – mainly due to the extra layer referred to as the **Jet Database Engine**:

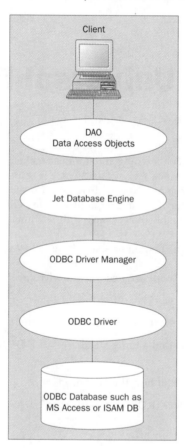

❑ RDO was released later and was designed to work with **ODBC**. By using RDO, it's possible to bypass Microsoft's Jet data engine, thus eliminating an extra "layer" or processing step. In other words, we can connect directly to ODBC, which results in faster data connections:

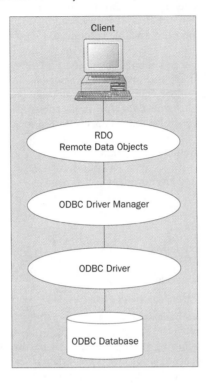

The important thing to keep in mind is that older technologies such as DAO, RDO, and ODBC all worked – and worked well. However, new data types have slowly been evolving, which take standard relational databases to new levels. And with the introduction of the Internet, more and more new data types are appearing that require new data access methods.

More specifically, many of today's databases are now storing non-relational data, such as e-mail, text files, and even multimedia data, including graphic, audio, and video files. Developers increasingly need new methods for accessing these different types of data stores.

Data Access – Two Philosophies

So, we've determined the need for an easy way to access relational data, as well as different types of non-relational data. But how should an application developer approach this?

Currently there are two major philosophies:

❑ Storing all types of data in a single database management system

❑ Storing data in diverse locations, and accessing it via some common data access method

Examples of this first philosophy – storing all types of data in a single database management system – are Oracle 8i and IBM DB2, which store both relational and non-relational data in one data storage system.

Perhaps the biggest drawback to this method is that it can be a costly process to convert old legacy systems by moving data into a new, centralized storage system. Moving data into a centralized data store often requires new software (such as Oracle 8i and DB2 database systems). And furthermore, older legacy servers are likely to be inadequate for handling the high demands of a centralized data system, so new equipment will be needed. Nevertheless, it's important to realize that this approach works very well, and the centralized data scenario is a viable solution to today's data access demands.

However, Microsoft believes data access should be approached differently. Instead of using centralized data management, it proposes that application developers need a "universal" way to programmatically access data, regardless of the type of data store or the location of that store. Instead of creating new technologies to handle accessing each new data type, it has come up with a strategy that provides easy data access to any type of data, wherever its location. This is referred to as **Universal Data Access** (**UDA**).

As we'll see shortly, UDA is an architecture designed to:

❑   Access data in a distributed environment

❑   Access relational data

❑   Access non-relational data

❑   Access data in disconnected environments

❑   Extend the influence of COM versus other competing technologies, such as CORBA

❑   Reduce development time

❑   Reduce application maintenance and application maintenance costs

UDA eliminates the need for purchasing and upgrading new hardware and software, because it's designed to programmatically access data for any type of data store. This makes UDA an excellent alternative for accessing legacy and proprietary data sources – and that includes relational as well as non-relational data.

So are there any drawbacks to Microsoft's UDA strategy? Well, as with anything in life, nothing is perfect. If you want to convert your legacy applications to take advantage of UDA technologies, you'll probably have to re-write some code. How much rewriting is required depends totally on the methods the application currently uses for accessing data.

For example, if you have an application that relies on some of Microsoft's previous technologies, such as DAO or RDO, you'll have some work to do. That's because UDA relies heavily on **ActiveX Data Objects** (**ADO** – covered later in this chapter), and neither DAO nor RDO will automatically convert to ADO. However, generally speaking, RDO applications will not need as much code conversion as applications using DAO.

Nevertheless, UDA provides methods that allow developers to customize data providers (discussed later) for accessing any type of data, so UDA is as viable as data-centric storage.

UDA – An Overview

Before we delve into the specifics of UDA, let's summarize UDA's grand scheme.

UDA allows us to access both relational and non-relational data from any data source, making use of OLE DB data providers. To implement UDA, we just leave the data where it resides, regardless of the type of data source or operating system.

We'll learn later in this chapter that OLE DB data providers are made up of COM components. Microsoft has supplied many of these data providers, and others are available from third-party sources. What makes UDA so powerful is that if there's no OLE DB provider available for a particular source, we can write our own.

Once we have chosen the OLE DB data provider we wish to utilize, we use ADO to call these drivers and hence access the desired data source. UDA with ADO also allows us to create something called disconnected recordsets, which allow us to retrieve data from a data source and bring it to a local machine, where it can be manipulated before returning the changes back to the original data source. This is a very powerful feature that is particularly suited web applications.

If all this sounds exciting to you, then you've come to the right place. But before we get into the nitty-gritty of UDA, let's continue with the next section, where we'll learn about the important advantages we gain when using UDA.

UDA Architecture

As previously mentioned, Microsoft has been listening to the needs of application developers for a better solution to deal with modern data-centric applications. UDA is its latest approach (introduced in 1996). However, it's important to realize that UDA is not a new *technology*, like ODBC or ADO. Instead, UDA is an *architecture* that incorporates many different data access technologies (including ODBC and ADO) to provide access to any type of data source.

> *Although ODBC is a part of UDA it's only for relational data and is not capable of properly handling non-relational data such as multimedia, e-mail, etc.*

Microsoft's UDA architecture is founded upon numerous open industry guidelines and specifications, so UDA does not revolve around a particular vendor's product. That's why UDA provides the application developer with access to most database platforms available today.

Some of the advantages that UDA has to offer are:

- Simplicity
- Maintainability
- Reliability
- Interoperability
- Scalability
- Reusability
- Extensibility

Let's take a look at each of these in more detail.

Simplicity

Certainly one of our first concerns is how easy it is to implement UDA methodologies. Put your mind at ease – following the UDA architecture does in fact simplify development, compared to using other data access techniques.

That's because it provides a direct means to access data sources, regardless of how or where they are located on a network. There's no need for time-consuming and costly resources for moving data from various databases into a single data store.

> When thinking of UDA, try to think of it as a language-independent tool designed to provide an easy to use programming interface for developing high-performance solutions to data access.

And because UDA is based on the Component Object Model (COM), we don't need to rely on specialized APIs written specifically for a particular data store. Instead, UDA provides the application developer with simplified COM components. This also means that UDA is language-independent.

We will return to UDA and COM later in this chapter.

Maintainability

Simplified development is not limited to reducing the amount of code required. On the contrary, UDA also provides an architecture that allows applications to be easily maintained.

As with many of the benefits we're looking at here, this can be attributed to UDA's reliance on COM. Just like with any other COM components, new interfaces can be added for new data sources, as well as for providing new enhancements.

Reliability

Web-based applications generally need to rely on data access 24 hours a day, seven days a week. This means that data access needs to be more reliable then ever – so we must be using technology that's reliable. UDA offers exactly this: building upon tried and proven technologies in order to enhance data access reliability.

Interoperability

UDA technologies can interoperate by using what's already available. This can be an old legacy data store, or a new modern database management system, such as MS SQL Server or an Oracle database management system.

UDA can access both legacy and new types of data stores so easily because it is not vendor specific – UDA follows an open industry architecture that's based on numerous industry standards. This has resulted in UDA receiving a lot of industry support, and it currently works with all major database platforms. If it was not able to provide interoperability with legacy data stores, in addition to modern database management systems, UDA would not be a satisfactory option.

Scalability

UDA technologies provide scalability and performance equal to native APIs and ODBC.

Reusability

In addition to being scalable, UDA technologies must provide an architecture that supports reusability. Because UDA is based on the Component Object Model, components used for data access can be reused without any dependencies on the language in which they were written. It's important to understand that components for data access can be shared with other applications.

Furthermore, components for data access can be developed in-house, or be obtained from third-party sources. We'll learn later in this chapter how OLE DB components rely on reusable COM components.

Extensibility

Extensible means open architecture. When dealing with distributed applications, extensibility begins with well-defined COM interfaces. By modeling an application that follows Microsoft's DNA strategy, the application will be built upon an open architecture, which allows for easy integration with existing data sources.

UDA: a Collection of Technologies

UDA is implemented through four types of run-time components:

❑ ODBC (Open Database Connectivity)

❑ OLE DB (Object Linking and Embedding Database)

❑ ADO (ActiveX Data Objects)

❑ RDS (Remote Data Services)

Throughout the rest of this chapter, we will cover each of these four run-time components in detail.

Together these components operate as a collective team and are the core technologies that make up what Microsoft refers to as **Microsoft Data Access Components** (**MDAC**).

Chances are, if you have Visual Studio or any of its components (such as VB, C++, or J++, with the latest service packs), you have the major MDAC components already. However, if you want to make sure you have the latest versions of all the MDAC components available, you can download them from the Microsoft web site at `http://www.microsoft.com/data/download2.htm`.

It's important to realize that these four technologies all interoperate. For instance, OLE DB relies on the appropriate ODBC drivers when accessing ODBC compliant data sources, while ADO and RDS both utilize OLE DB's functionality. Let's take a look at each in more detail.

ODBC

Open Database Connectivity (**ODBC**) has been a tried and true friend to the application developer for some time. It's been popular for so long because it's based on international standards, and as a result, ODBC has been widely accepted among most database vendors. As a matter of fact, ODBC can be used to access almost every type of relational database management system in use today.

The question you may be asking yourself is, "If ODBC can access *most* databases, why is there a need for a more unified architecture to access data?" In order to answer this, let's take a look at ODBC in detail.

The best way to understand ODBC's architecture is to break it down into four separate (yet related) parts:

❏   The ODBC Application Programming Interface

❏   The ODBC driver

❏   The ODBC driver manager

❏   The data source

The ODBC Application Programming Interface

An **Application Programming Interface** (**API**) is a set of functions or methods that a program can employ in order to direct the performance of procedures by the computer's operating system. In order for ODBC to connect to a data source, ODBC must call a standardized ODBC API. In addition to connecting to and disconnecting from data sources, ODBC utilizes API calls in order to retrieve and manipulate data from the data source.

ODBC Driver

The **ODBC driver** is used to translate SQL statements into a dialect of SQL that the database management system understands. This is where many problems arise when using ODBC, because each major database vendor has its own extended version of SQL that is proprietary to each database management system. Even when following standard SQL, subtle differences in syntax occur among database venders.

This means that for every type of database you intend to access, you also must have an ODBC driver in order to access it. This is one of the major drawbacks of using ODBC. For example, if you want to access MS SQL Server, Oracle, and Sybase, you will require three different ODBC drivers on each machine in order to do so.

ODBC Driver Manager

The **ODBC driver manager** is a library that manages communication between applications and ODBC drivers. Through the use of the **Data Source Administrator** you can configure new ODBC connections by selecting the ODBC driver manager to be used for accessing new data sources. The Data Source Administrator is a GUI tool provided in Windows operating systems, and it's found in the Control Panel under Administrative Tools.

The ODBC driver manager is also responsible for sending commands, as well as receiving data from the ODBC driver.

Data Source

When speaking of a **data source**, we really need to consider two things:

- ❏ The data store
- ❏ The database engine

The **data store** is simply where the data is located on disk, while a **database engine** is a program that manages how data is stored and retrieved.

Typically a database engine will not allow data to be directly accessed. This makes sense, particularly when thinking in terms of security. Aside from correct validation, the database engine also needs to protect the integrity of its data. This means that the only way to access the data is to first go through the database engine, which is where the ODBC drivers come into play.

A system based on ODBC can be represented as follows:

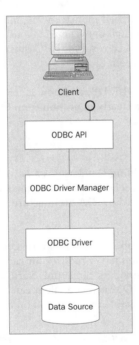

When an application connects to a data source via ODBC, an API call to the ODBC driver manager is invoked. The ODBC driver manager is also responsible for sending commands to and receiving data from the ODBC driver. It is the ODBC driver that's responsible for translating SQL statements to the dialect of SQL that the database understands.

Let's go back to our previous question of why we don't universally use ODBC. Previously, we've hinted about ODBC's relational characteristics, so the first part of our answer should be becoming apparent. ODBC provides access to relational databases that understand SQL. However, the new trend for data storage is non-relational – e-mail, images, video, audio files, and even complete web pages. Because ODBC only understands SQL processing, it must treat all data as relational, and this is where the problem arises. Because many databases now support unstructured and non-relational data, ODBC is going to struggle in the future.

Another problem with ODBC is that its API functions are complex and often difficult to work with – particularly if you use Visual Basic to directly call ODBC functions. One of the aims of UDA is to make things easy.

For example, VB programmers (more so than C++ programmers) who write code to directly utilize ODBC must write flawless code, otherwise they run the risk of fatally crashing the application. Furthermore, if you produce errors when using VB's IDE while working with ODBC, it will typically take the entire IDE down. If you follow safe programming practices, you shouldn't have to worry about losing development code if VB's IDE aborts with a fatal error, because you'll have saved your work before testing it!

Having said that, and although UDA embraces OLE DB as its native provider, it's not time to completely abandon ODBC. ODBC is still a very important player when it comes to relational databases. As a matter of fact ODBC is so important that it's a part of the UDA architecture, because many legacy applications can be accessed through ODBC. It's essential not to overlook the fact that ODBC can still serve as a backward-compatible solution for data access.

Furthermore, because ODBC is recognized industry-wide, most developers and third-party vendors are not going to be willing to make the switch between tried and true technologies (such as ODBC) and new (and perhaps untested) technologies. As a result, ODBC must be incorporated into the UDA architecture in order for UDA to succeed.

In the next section we'll learn about OLE DB, and how it can make any ODBC connection appear as an OLE DB source. This will allow for a steady migration from ODBC to OLE DB.

OLE DB

OLE DB (Object Linking and Embedding Database) is a key player in Microsoft's latest technology in an attempt to provide universal data access to most relational and non-relational data stores. OLE DB is often referred to as the glue that binds the UDA architecture together. Perhaps in more simple terms, OLE DB is the foundation of UDA.

OLE DB is actually a set of COM components that expose certain interfaces. These permit data access in such a way that the client application never realizes (or cares) what type of data source it's connected to. Through COM interfaces, data providers can supply various levels of support for data stores. What's cool about OLE DB being a part of COM is that a client can query the `QueryInterface` method in order to see if a specific feature is available or supported on a machine or data store.

> *OLE DB is considered a low-level or system-level data access technology because it utilizes COM interfaces.*

In order to understand OLE DB we need to divide it up into three separate entities, each comprising a set of COM components:

❑   Data consumers

❑   Service components

❑   Data providers

Data Consumers

Data consumers can be thought of as being any applications or components that use OLE DB data through OLE DB or ADO.

We'll cover ADO in depth later in this chapter. For now, all you need to understand is that ADO can be described as a high-level interface used to access all types of data.

When referring to OLE DB data consumers, we're really referring to an application, development tool, or component that accesses data through ADO or OLE DB. For example, a data consumer can be as simple as a class or component that binds itself to a data source. On a larger scale, a data consumer can be any application that accesses any type of data store. Even the Visual Basic IDE and the C++ IDE are considered data consumers, because each provides Data Link and Data Environment Designers that utilize ADO and OLE DB.

Service Components

OLE DB **service components** are probably the most important entities in the OLE DB architecture. Service components can be thought of as components that allow the standard functionality for data providers to be extended or enhanced. OLE DB service components are nothing more than components that consume and produce OLE DB data.

The *cursor service* is an example of a service component. The cursor service allows OLE DB consumers to search and manipulate data without being connected to a data provider.

Although service components play a central role, it's important to realize that service components are not mandatory. In other words, their use is entirely optional. However, in typical uses, several service components are often used in conjunction with each other.

Currently, under the existing MDAC, there are six types of OLE DB service components:

❑ **Cursor Service**: the cursor service allows OLE DB consumers to search and manipulate data without being connected to a data provider.

❑ **Session Pooling**: with the session pooling service component, OLE DB sessions can automatically be pooled.

❑ **Transaction Enlistment**: this service component is used for distributed transactions. It allows MTS/COM+ to automatically register or bring in an instance of a transactional component.

❑ **Data Shape Provider**: with the data shape provider, applications can create hierarchical models of data based on how it relates to other data.

❑ **Persistence Provider**: by using the persistence provider, you can save data to a stream where it can be placed in a file. Also, by saving data to a stream, it can be moved across the network.

❑ **Remote Data Provider**: as the name of this provider suggests, you can take advantage of an OLE DB provider that resides on another machine (as long as it is connected to the network!).

What makes these six components so attractive is that they can be utilized individually, or they can be mixed and matched as the occasion arises.

Data Providers

Data providers can be thought of as components that represent data sources. OLE DB data providers expose all types of data through the same standard OLE DB interfaces, allowing consumers access in a standard way. The OLE DB provider provides abstraction from all of the details about the data source, such as indexing and the storage mechanism. Just as in component development, this allows the implementation of data retrieval and data manipulation to change, due to new algorithms, bug fixes, etc., without affecting consumers of the data.

There are three required objects for each OLE DB provider:

❑ **Data Source Object**: this simply contains the necessary internal mechanisms needed in order to connect to a data source. Because a single Data Source object is capable of creating numerous (more than one) sessions, it is said to be a **factory** for sessions.

❑ **Session Object**: as previously mentioned, the Data Source object can create more than one Session object. Session objects are important because they are necessary for the creation of commands, transactions, and rowsets. Furthermore, Session objects are capable of incorporating numerous operations against a database into a single operation.

❑ **Rowset Object**: Rowsets can be created from either a Session or Command object (see the optional objects below.) The purpose of the Rowset object is to expose data in the format of a database table.

In addition to the three required objects, there are four optional objects that can be used:

❑ **Enumerator Object**: this can be used to search for available data sources. Enumerators can come in handy with consumers that do not have a customized data source. Enumerator objects are optional because OLE DB provides what is known as a **data links component**. This is used to manage connections between consumers and data providers. Normally, OLE DB consumers would use the data links component to select a data source as well as set its initialization properties. However, Enumerator objects can be a viable alternative to using the data links component.

❑ **Transaction Object**: if you use nested transactions (transactions within other transactions) other than at the lowest level, you should consider using the Transaction object for committing and aborting transactions.

❑ **Command Object**: if you need to use SQL statements or other text queries, you use the Command object for their execution. (Note: if you are using transaction handling via COM+, you would not want to use this functionality directly.)

❑ **Error Object**: this allows the developer to create custom error messages that can be generated from any interface on any OLE DB object.

Connecting to Data Sources using OLE DB

We have been talking a lot about OLE DB data providers, yet we've not talked about what providers are in use today. Currently Microsoft has several data providers for both relational and non-relational data, such as those for use with MS Jet, SQL Server, ODBC, and Oracle. Furthermore, there are OLE DB providers for the following types of non-relational data:

❑ MS Exchange

❑ OLAP

❑ Publishing to the Internet

❑ Active Directory

Although not totally exhaustive, the following chart lists many of the OLE DB data providers available. The important thing to keep in mind is that even if MS has not (yet) distributed an OLE DB provider for a particular data source, they can be developed for almost any type of data source in existence today.

OLE DATA PROVIDER	DESCRIPTION
MSDASQL	Used for connecting to data sources via ODBC
SQLOLEDB	Used for connecting to SQL Server versions 6.5 and above
MSIDXS	Used for connecting to MS Index Server
MSDAIPP	Used for Internet publishing
MSDAORA	Used for connecting to Oracle databases for versions 7.3 and above
MSOLAP	Used for connecting OLAP servers in order to access multidimensional data
ADSDSOObject	Used for connecting to Active Directory Services
MSDAIIP	Used to allow applications to access and manipulate files and folders across the HTTP protocol
EXOLEDB	Recently out of beta, EXOLEDB is used to connect to Web Stores in order to access and manipulate files in Exchange 2000
MSDAOSP	This can be used for creating custom providers when simple text data is involved

Let's take a look at a selection of the more common OLE DB providers: ODBC, SQL Server, Internet publishing, and Oracle.

OLE DB Provider for ODBC

Microsoft first provided **MSDASQL** to application developers back in 1996 when UDA was first introduced. As a matter of fact, MSDASQL was the first and only data provider Microsoft offered. MSDASQL makes use of OLE DB interfaces in order to access ODBC APIs. It's very powerful because it allows you to access any database that's exposed through an ODBC driver.

Take a look at the following diagram to see how this works:

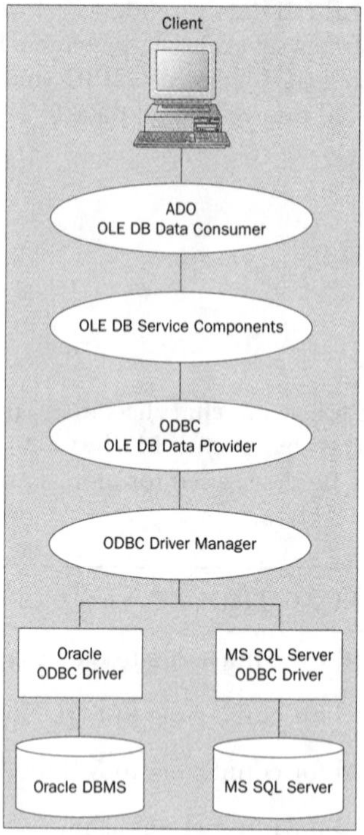

In this case, we're accessing MS SQL Server and Oracle databases. However remember that MSDASQL will work for any database that supports an ODBC driver.

We specify the provider in our code in a **connection string**. A connection string is simply a character string that provides the necessary information required to connect to a data source. A typical connection string will contain some or all of the following:

- ❑ **Provider**: this is the type of OLE DB provider we want to use for accessing a data source.

- ❑ **Driver**: the driver that is used when utilizing ODBC.

- ❑ **Data Source or Initial File Name**: this is the physical database path, including a file name.

- ❑ **Initial Catalog**: the initial catalog is simply the name of the database.

- ❑ **User ID**: this is the user name required to connect to the database. For example, MS SQL Server by default provides an administrator User ID designated as sa (for system administrator). Note that in a connection string, User ID is often abbreviated as UID, such as UID=sa.

- ❑ **Password**: this is the password associated with the User ID. Note that in a connection string, Password is often abbreviated as PWD, such as PWD=*password goes here*.

OK, so let's take a look at a sample connection string implementing MSDASQL for MS Access:

```
rstConnection.ConnectionString = "Provider=MSDASQL;" & _
            "Driver={Microsoft Access Driver (*.mdb)}" & _
            "DBQ=C:\Data\TestAccessData.mdb"
```

Notice that the next example does not list a provider. This is because the OLE DB provider for ODBC is automatically used by default. Nevertheless, it's recommended that you always include the provider to ensure you are actually getting what you want, as well as making your intentions more readable in code.

```
rstConnection.ConnectionString = "Driver={SQL Server};" & _
                                 "Server=MySQLServer;" & _
                                 "Database=Norwind; uid=sa; pwd="
```

Although the previous connection string works fine, the following example makes it clear that you want to use MSDASQL as opposed to SQLOLEDB (see next section), which may be a more efficient option:

```
rstConnection.ConnectionString = "Provider=MSDASQL;" & _
                                 "Driver={SQL Server};" & _
                                 "Server=MySQLServer;" & _
                                 "Database=Norwind; uid=sa; pwd="
```

OLE DB Provider for MS SQL Server

One problem with using MSDASQL is that it requires an additional layer, which can cause performance loss. As an alternative way to access SQL Server data via ODBC, Microsoft has provided an OLE DB provider called **SQLOLEDB**, which can be used to access data for SQL Server 6.5 and above.

We previously learned that MSDASQL maps out OLE DB interfaces to the ODBC API. The primary difference between using SQLOLEDB and MSDASQL is that SQL Server directly implements OLE DB on top of the client network libraries used.

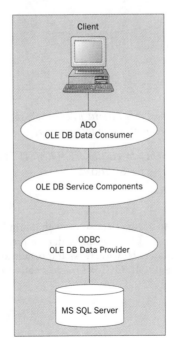

OLE DB Provider for Internet Publishing

MSDAIPP is a provider used for Internet publishing. This provider permits applications to access as well as manipulate files and folders using the HTTP protocol. What makes this provider so important is that files and folders can be accessed from web servers that support Microsoft's **FrontPage Web Extender (WEC)** or the protocol extensions for **WebDAV (Web Distributed Authoring and Versioning)** as if they were any common data source. That means that MSDAIPP gives access to non-relational data:

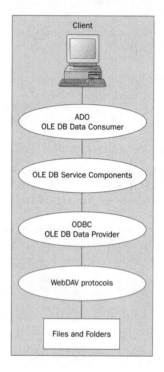

> *WebDAV extends the HTTP protocol that permits us to search, copy, edit, move, and even delete web files and web Folders (that are located at a web server.)*

> *You can find out more about WebDAV by visiting the WEBDAV Working Group at* `http://www.ics.uci.edu/~ejw/authoring`.

OLE DB Provider for Oracle

With Microsoft's MDAC, it's easy to access data sources that aren't Microsoft-specific (such as Oracle databases). Included with MDAC is an OLE DB provider referred to as **MSDAORA**, for accessing Oracle databases versions 7.3 and later. However, it's important to realize that MSDAORA sits as a layer above Oracle's Call Interface (OCI). OCI is Oracle's native API:

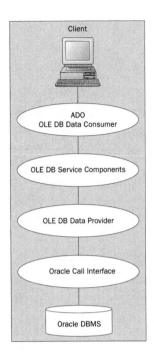

ADO

You may be familiar with some of Microsoft's previous attempts to support data access, such as Data Access Objects (DAO) and Remote Data Objects (RDO). Basically DAO was designed to work on desktop solutions, such as with MS Access. RDO was designed to access data over a network. Both of these technologies have been around for a while, and have proven to be relatively reliable in nature.

However, Microsoft felt that in order to provide universal access to data, it would be more efficient to create a unified method for accessing data by combining the functionality of DAO and RDO into one single technology – **ActiveX Data Objects** (**ADO**). Although DAO and RDO will be supported for some time to come, ADO actually supersedes DAO and RDO. In other words, if ADO and OLE are not yet considered by application developers to be the standard method for data access, they soon will be.

Because ADO builds upon DAO and RDO fundamentals, ADO's syntax is similar. If you know DAO or RDO, this makes ADO easier to learn – there's no need to start all over by learning an entirely new way to program. However, it's not necessary to know anything about DAO or RDO – ADO is actually easier to master.

What makes ADO so attractive is that it provides a consistent interface that allows high-performance data access to virtually any type of data source. Because ADO can be used as a single interface for data access, ADO can be used regardless of whether you're designing a front-end solution for a desktop data source, a middle tier component that contains business logic, a remote data source across the world, or even through an Internet browser.

If you've worked with DAO and RDO, you should realize that developers had to navigate various complex hierarchies. ADO does not follow a typical hierarchy: instead it follows more of a circular mode – ADO objects can be used independently of each other.

The following diagram represents ADO 2.5 objects as a circular layout:

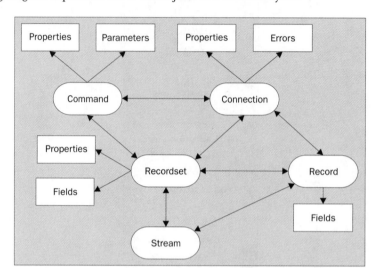

Although you don't have to explicitly create many of these objects, they are still automatically created behind the scenes as needed. However, not having to explicitly create objects reduces code complexity. This is a part of UDA's characteristics for simplified development – the developer doesn't have to navigate a complex hierarchy in order to use certain objects.

We'll see an example of explicit and implicit object creation shortly: but first, let's briefly examine each of these ADO objects.

ADO Objects

ADO provides us with several objects that help eliminate complex code.

The Connection Object

This object is used to establish a session connection with a data source. In other words, you use the Connection object to establish a physical connection to a data source. With ADO, the data source can be any type, such as ODBC or a database management system that supports some kind of OLE DB provider. Because OLE DB providers can be made to custom specifications, ADO can connect to any data source in existence.

The Error Object and Errors Collection

The Error object is exposed through the Connection object, and contains details of an error returned from the data provider. The Errors collection is the set of all the Error objects resulting from a failed data source connection. Whenever there is an error regarding a connection, it's placed into the Errors collection.

Connection errors can be traced through the Errors collection to provide valuable information, such as where the error occurred. However, it's important to understand that the Errors collection does not record ADO errors. This is because ADO errors are considered standard VB/C++ errors, which should be trapped using traditional error handling. Note that Errors is optional (not required).

The Command Object

The Command object is used to issue commands intended to execute against a data source. For example, a command can be any type of SQL statement, such as INSERT or UPDATE. Note that the Command object is optional.

The Parameter Object and Parameters Collection

The Parameter object contains details of a single parameter for a stored procedure or stored query associated with a Command object. The Parameters collection is nothing more than a collection of individual parameters that are used to represent the values passed into and out from a command. Note that the Parameter object is optional.

The Recordset Object

The Recordset object simply contains all the data retrieved from a data source, as well as any additional data you want to write back to the data source. In simple terms, a recordset contains rows and columns of data.

ADO recordsets can be very versatile, because ADO provides the ability create **disconnected recordsets**. This means that a recordset containing data can be retrieved from a data source, and then actually disconnected from the data source by literally dropping the connection. The client application retrieves a block of data, and is able to scroll through each record, and even add or modify data. In the event that the data is changed, we can re-establish a connection to the data source when we're finished working with the disconnected recordset, and execute batch updates to permanently modify the source.

We'll learn more about this in the section about Remote Data Sources (RDS) later in this chapter. For now, all you need to know is that disconnected recordsets with ADO play a very large part in the DNA model. This is because they provide great benefits when it comes to application scalability, by reducing demand on data source connections and server resources. Disconnected recordsets decrease the need for constant connections to the data source, as well as allowing much of the processing work to be performed on the client machine.

The Field Object and Fields Collection

A Field object is created for each field in a recordset, to contain details about that field. The Fields collection is a collection of all the Field objects for a recordset.

The Property Object and Properties Collection

All the previous objects for ADO, as well as the new objects that come with ADO 2.5 (see next section) and later versions, expose various Property objects and a Properties collection.

A Properties collection will typically contain one or more Property objects. Property objects contain information about a property of an object, such as its Name, Value, Type, and Attributes. The value of Name is a read-only value used to identify the property in question. The Value, Type, and Attributes properties are used to set or return the value, data type, or characteristics of that property for the appropriate object.

New Objects with ADO 2.5

ADO 2.5 introduced two new objects: Record and Stream. These objects also deal with non-relational data. Let's look at them in more detail.

The Record Object

Suppose you need to manage data that resides in semi-structured areas, such as folders and files in a directory? With the new Record object, these folders and files can be treated as if they were ordinary records in a database.

It's important to understand that the new Record object represents a file or directory within a **Document Source Provider**. A Document Source Provider simply manages resources. For example, the OLE DB provider for Internet Publishing (discussed earlier) is also a Document Source Provider, because it's designed to manage resources such as files and directories on a web site.

The Stream Object

The Stream object allows us to manipulate data that is held in web resources such as HTML files.

The Stream object is used to denote a stream of binary data or a stream of text, so we can use it when we want to view the contents of a file. Streams are not new, as they have been a part of OLE and Windows for several years. However, with version 2.5, ADO has incorporated Stream objects that can be used to open files directly from an existing Record object, or even directly from a URL.

Creating a Recordset Object

We were talking earlier about the circularity of the ADO object model. Let's look at an example to illustrate this. Suppose I wanted to create a recordset by instantiating a Recordset object. There are two different ways we can do this.

Explicit Creation of the Connection Object

This first example is more of a traditional method. First we create a Connection object, and then we create a Command object:

```
Dim conConnection     As ADODB.Connection
Dim rstRecordset      As ADODB.Recordset
Dim connectionString As String

Set conConnection = New ADODB.Connection
Set rstRecordset  = New ADODB.Recordset

ConnectionString =   "Provider=SQLOLEDB; Data Source=SampleADOConn;" & _
                     "User Id=sa; Password=secret; Initial Catalog=Pubs"

rstRecordset.Open "titles", conConnection

rstRecordSet.Execute "Select pubdate FROM titles", conConnection

rstRecordset.Close
conConnection.Close
Set conConnection = Nothing
```

Implicit Creation of the Connection Object

Although we need to connect to a data source in order to retrieve data, we don't necessarily need to explicitly create a Connection object first. Instead we can supply the necessary details for connecting directly to a Command or Recordset object. In other words, although we're still creating a Connection object, we're doing it implicitly, without having to follow a required hierarchy as with other data access technologies. Thus we can eliminate extra complex code.

The following code snippet shows how we can retrieve the same recordset as in the previous example, but without having to specify a `Connection` object first. Instead, ADO creates a `Connection` object through the use of the connection information that is provided in the `ActiveConnection` parameter:

```
Dim rstRecordset AS ADODB.Recordset

Set rstRecordset = New ADODB.Recordset

rstRecordset.Open Source:='Select pubdate FROM titles', _
                  ActiveConnection: = "Provider=SQLOLEDB;" & _
                  "Data Source=SampleADOConn;" & _
                  "User Id=sa; Password=secret; Initial Catalog=Pubs"

rstRecordset.ActiveConnection.Close
Set rstRecordset = Nothing
```

VB vs. C++

It seems as if ADO was designed with Visual Basic in mind. As a matter of fact, if you're using Visual Basic for your application programming, you cannot directly utilize OLE DB's interfaces, because OLE DB COM interfaces are not **automation compatible**. In other words, VB programmers (along with those using some other languages including J++) must utilize ADO.

For the most part, this is of no concern, because ADO simply acts as an intermediary – or a wrapper to be more specific – that's capable of calling the necessary OLE DB interfaces. Note we said "For the most part". Because we have to rely on ADO as another layer for data access, as opposed to calling OLE DB interfaces directly, there is some performance loss. However, under most circumstances this performance loss is ever so slight.

In the rare situation that this negligible performance hit makes a difference to your application, programming your data providers in C++ is probably your best option. With C++, you have the option of using ADO, or bypassing ADO entirely by calling OLE DB interfaces directly.

> **Regardless of what programming language is being used, clients that rely on scripting (such as VBScript or JavaScript) for data access must use ADO.**

In order to access ADO's COM classes through VB, you simply add a reference to ADO's type library through VB's **References** dialog.

C++ programmers need to access ADO COM classes through two header files plus an IDL file, provided by Microsoft. The two required header files are `Adoid.h` and `Adoit.h`. `Adoid.h` is responsible for providing the GUIDs to the various interfaces and coclasses, while `Adoint.h` is responsible for providing the necessary class definitions to the interfaces. The IDL file is called `MSADO15.IDL`, and it's responsible for providing (in a readable form) all the interface definitions and constant definitions required for working with ADO.

Note: although ADO has been upgraded numerous times since it was first introduced, the IDL file `MSADO15.IDL` has never been changed or altered, thus the name has remained the same.

RDS

We have reached our final component in UDA's architecture – **Remote Data Services** (**RDS**). Although we're covering this last, RDS is perhaps the most important feature of UDA.

RDS is capable of delivering a disconnected recordset from the server and sending it to a client, such as a web browser. This means that large amounts of data, such as recordsets retrieved from a database, can be cached at the client machine. Performance is increased because multiple records can be pulled from cached information without having to send out new requests to the server and have the information re-posted at the client's browser. Additionally, multiple recordsets can be manipulated while still on the client machine and then sent for processing as one batch, again providing the user with immediate responses.

How does RDS work? When a user enters a request for database information through a client web browser, client-side RDS components send a request to the web server. RDS components located at the server process the client's database request, and then direct it to the database management system (DBMS). The DBMS processes the data request, and sends the results back to the RDS components at the server. Now, RDS converts the data from the DBMS into an ADO `Recordset` object, which is returned to the client browser where the request originated. The recordset can also be cached into the client's memory and displayed through a datagrid, listbox, textbox, or other visual control:

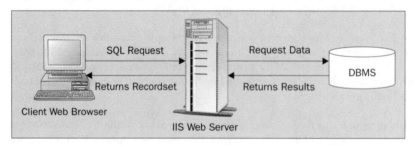

The key feature of RDS comes down to ADO's ability to provide a disconnected `Recordset` object. Remember, a disconnected `Recordset` object is nothing more than a recordset that has been detached from its `Connection` object. Because a recordset can be cached into a client's memory, all the data rows for the requested recordset are retrieved. An interesting thing about these cached recordsets (disconnected recordsets) is that they do not exhibit **locks**. As a result, two things happen when changes are made to the disconnected recordset:

❑ First, changes will not be permanent until they are returned back to the data store where new changes will be saved

❑ Second, because there are no locks being held on data that is being altered, it's possible that someone else may also make alterations to the same data

This is where OLE DB comes into play. It's the responsibility of OLE DB to check each modified row for any updates that may conflict at the data source. More specifically, OLE DB keeps a record of the original data for each disconnected recordset. When data is modified for a particular recordset, OLE DB checks to see if data has already been modified since the last time the disconnected recordset was cached. If there is a conflict, an error condition is reported to the client application.

Although RDS does exhibit complex communication, having a disconnected recordset at a user's machine can greatly improve performance and save processing time when working with databases across the Web. RDS is very efficient when it comes to marshalling recordsets across networks, including the Internet.

Summary

We started this chapter learning about the reasons why application developers need a more unified way of accessing the various types of data stores. We also discussed how they need a way to access various data sources regardless of where they are located on a network, including the Internet.

Next we looked at two different philosophies for accessing data. While some companies, such as Oracle and IBM, believe it's more practical to create one large data store for all types of data, others, such as Microsoft, believe it makes more sense to access data at the original locations, regardless of where they are located, without needing to transfer data to a single store.

That's what Microsoft's Universal Data Access architecture is all about. We took a look at the important characteristics of UDA, such as simplified development, and why UDA needs to be reliable, easily maintainable, and scalable. We looked at UDA's collection of technologies – referred to as Microsoft Data Access Components (MDAC) – and looked at a few of the common MDACs available.

We learned about ODBC: how it works, why ODBC is still a major player when it comes to accessing relational data, and why ODBC is an important part of UDA.

We also took a look at OLE DB – Microsoft's attempt to provide universal data access to most relational and non-relational data stores through the use of COM components. We divided OLE DB into three separate entities:

❑ Data Consumers

❑ Service Providers

❑ Data Providers

and we saw how these entities work and interact with each other.

After OLE DB, we moved on to ActiveX Data Objects (ADO). ADO follows more of a circular model, as opposed to the rigid hierarchical model followed by older data technologies, such as DAO and RDO. We briefly looked at the different ADO objects, and ended our discussion with programming language choices, primarily with views regarding Visual Basic and C++.

Last, but certainly not least, we learned about Remote Data Services. RDS is capable of delivering a disconnected recordset from a server to a client application, or even a web browser. We saw how OLE DB plays an important role by keeping track of each modified row, in case there are conflicts regarding updates and other data manipulation while a recordset is in a disconnected state.

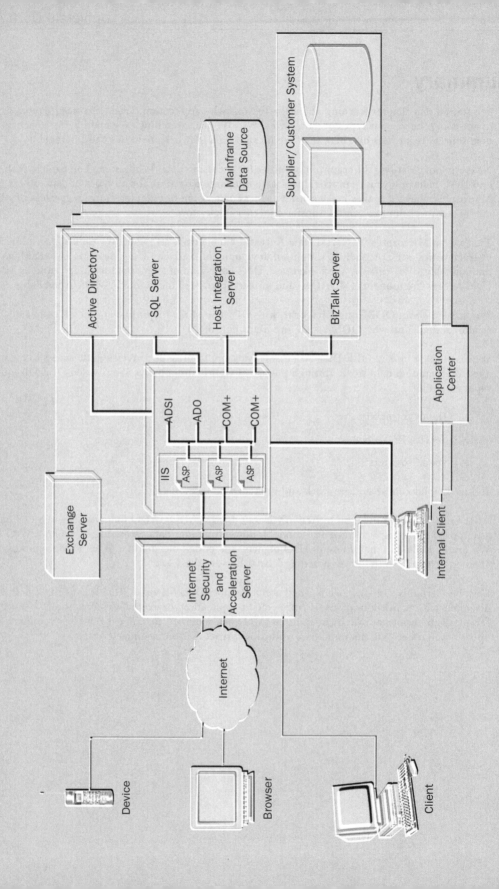

14

SQL Server 2000

As was introduced in Chapter 1, the Windows DNA architecture is comprised of various tiers. The **data tier** provides the back-end data storage and retrieval system. It is typically an enterprise-level relational database accessed using the standard SQL data query and manipulation language. It can be queried and updated by multiple applications while maintaining a consistent, logical view of the data. SQL Server 2000 is Microsoft's implementation of the data tier in the Windows DNA architecture, as shown in the diagram below:

Client Tier	Web Server Tier	Application Tier	Data Tier
Browser or Device	IIS or Acceleration Server 2000	Application Center 2000 Commerce Server 2000 or custom business logic	**SQL Server 2000** gateway to Oracle or mainframe

The data tier is separated from other tiers for several reasons:

❑ To ensure data reliability and availability, by preventing application failures in other tiers from affecting the data tier. If one application fails, a second application that relies on the same data is not affected.

❑ For performance, since the CPU and I/O needs of application logic and data retrieval are different and therefore are often better optimized by separate tiers.

❑ The administration of shared data is simpler and more convenient when it is localized to a dedicated server. Database administrators like to have control over this tier, where they can use their specialist knowledge of SQL and database systems.

SQL Server 2000 is Microsoft's SQL relational database. While non-Microsoft data tiers such as mainframes can be accessed through gateways in Windows DNA, SQL Server 2000 is native to the Windows DNA environment, and is therefore a logical choice for such applications.

SQL Server 2000 plays a very critical role in the development of Windows DNA applications. Not only as a data storage database, but because it contains new features and enhancements that have in mind some of the capabilities needed to build large-scale distributed applications without sacrificing performance. In this chapter we'll discuss these enhancements and new features. We will only cover, at a high level, the features that are *new* to SQL Server 2000. If you are completely new to SQL Server we strongly encourage you to dig deeper into it first.

Introduction to SQL Server 2000

SQL Server 2000 is actually a family of related components:

❑ The SQL Server 2000 **database engine** is the core data storage and retrieval component. As a relational database it stores data in tables, organizing each table in a row and column format, and using columns shared by multiple tables to relate those tables to each other. This means of organizing data is relatively simple for users to understand and manipulate, and has become a standard in the business world. The **SQL** language (**Structured Query Language**) used by SQL Server 2000 is also an official standard for accessing data in relational databases.

❑ Windows DNA application programmers query and update data from within applications by using one of the standard Microsoft data access application programming interfaces (**APIs**) within Windows applications. These APIs provide a set of programming functions that allow a program to send a SQL command to SQL Server and retrieve the resulting data. SQL Server 2000 directly supports the **ODBC** (**Open Data Base Connectivity**) and **OLE DB** SQL APIs, both of which are standard in Windows applications. Most new applications use **ADO** (**ActiveX Data Objects**), which is an abstraction layer on top of OLE DB. (All of these data access methods were discussed in Chapter 13.)

❑ The SQL Server 2000 engine also has direct support for **XML** (**Extensible Markup Language**), an emerging standard for data exchange on the Internet. XML is of great importance in the Windows DNA architecture as a means of communicating data between tiers. Microsoft also provides support for the XML language in the latest version of ADO and in other Microsoft programming interfaces, which makes XML especially convenient for application programs to process. More detail about XML and the new features of SQL Server 2000 that support it will be presented later in this chapter.

❑ SQL Server 2000 **Analysis Services** is a component designed to enable detailed analysis of data, especially data stored in **data warehouses**, which summarize data gathered from many sources within a business. SQL Server 2000 Analysis Services provides tools for viewing this multidimensional data and discovering trends within it for planning purposes. This process is termed **OLAP** (**OnLine Analytical Processing**), as opposed to the core engine's mission which is known as **OLTP** (**OnLine Transactional Processing**). OLAP concentrates on analysis of relatively static data, while OLTP is useful for quick updates and queries while many users access the system simultaneously.

❑ SQL Server 2000 **replication** allows duplicate copies of data to be easily created and synchronized on multiple servers and workstations. This facilitates offline access to the data, for example when a salesman using a laptop PC is on a trip, as well as offering another way to keep a backup server updated if a main server becomes unavailable.

- ❏ SQL Server 2000 **Data Transformation Services** (**DTS**) provide a set of tools for importing data into SQL Server from other data sources, exporting to other data formats, and also transforming data between SQL Server databases, for example by changing the character format.

- ❏ SQL Server 2000 **English Query** enables users to query databases with English-like questions, which are analyzed and transformed into standard SQL or OLAP queries. Instead of users having to understand the database structure and the SQL syntax, they can ask more intuitive questions which will be translated behind the scenes into SQL queries by English Query.

- ❏ SQL Server 2000 **Meta Data Services** provides a repository for storing and querying the schema or high-level description of the structure of the database. This feature of SQL Server was known as the Repository component in previous versions.

While each of these components has a potential role in Windows DNA applications, the key components within DNA are the database engine itself, replication, and DTS. Replication and DTS both transfer data between or across tiers, and so are useful in automating transfer tasks that would require custom application code. Other significant enhancements that are directed towards improving its role within the DNA architecture include the new direct support for XML in SQL Server 2000, and the performance and scalability enhancements to allow SQL Server 2000 to make use of multiple servers.

SQL Server and Windows DNA

It is easy to think of SQL Server 2000 as just a repository, and focus on the middle tier as the core tier of a Windows DNA application. However, you will find that SQL Server can play a very critical role in your DNA design and development. Applying the rules learned for programming the middle tier will certainly bring you closer to the perfect application architecture. Additionally, understanding how SQL Server works will help you better optimize and tune your application's performance.

When developing Windows DNA applications you must decide what is your primary architectural goal for your application. In most cases the answer is either scalability or performance. There is an important distinction between these two goals. First, scalability is the measure of how your application will run when additional users are using its services. Performance is the measure of how long a single task takes.

The middle tier is all about **scalability**. Scalability can be achieved in two ways:

- ❏ **Scaling up**, which means using a more powerful computer to increase the processing power.

- ❏ **Scaling out**, which means increasing the processing power by adding additional machines, with each machine having an identical set of components, and using Windows 2000 to balance the processing load. You must ensure that your middle tier components scale out – COM+ services helps you with that goal once you understand how to use these services and follow the rules.

What about **performance** – how do we achieve it? This is where focusing on the database comes in to play. You have a lot of flexibility when working with the database engine to fine-tune it to give the maximum performance.

SQL Server 2000 focuses heavily on performance, as well as scalability, through additional technologies that it uses, which we will discuss later. You have many choices with when dealing with SQL Server – some of these options you will need to consider *before* you begin your application development and others become important after you are finished. Let's explore these options.

Design Issues Prior to Development

Prior to designing your application architecture you need to determine what role SQL Server will play, in addition to being the repository for data. You may choose to distribute your business logic across the tiers by placing some logic in SQL Server as stored procedures. This may be an excellent choice if you plan to stay with SQL Server as your back-end database. However, if there is a chance that you might be using other databases in the future then this option will not be the ideal one. You also need to decide if you are going to place any rules or triggers on the tables and how these rules may impact on your business logic.

You will also need to understand how the SQL Server engine works when it comes to executing your SQL statements. For example, the SQL Query Analyzer will examine your SQL queries and create an **execution plan**, and cache this execution plan for later reuse. Many developers think that execution plans are specific to stored procedures – the fact that they are created for queries too should not negate the use of stored procedures but rather, allow you to architect your design accordingly.

Another issue to consider when developing web application is *state* – and whether you intend to use SQL Server to maintain state. We discuss this topic throughout the book, but it is important to note that SQL Server can provide several state management facilities; which is used depends on the size of the data that needs to be temporarily maintained. You can also use the SQL Server **pin table** capability to load a table and keep it in memory to provide quick read-only data access on the server. This can be a viable solution and a reasonable replacement for In-Memory Databases (IMDB).

Design Issues After Development

Once your application is developed, you will find that you have a team dedicated to the performance optimization of your application as well as general SQL Server administrative tasks. This is where the ease of use of SQL Server and the added wizards will come in very handy. You will spend numerous hours, based on the size of your application of course, running execution plans to see how your queries are performing. The **Index Tuning wizard** will make some indexing recommendations that you can evaluate. You will also spend time putting security to work and ensuring that your data is secure, especially since, as you will learn later, users can access your server from a web browser. And finally, you will need to set up failover support and replication.

The work performed at the server level pre, during and post development is an ongoing task. Performance is not a development item that has a scheduled start and end date. Performance tuning is a task that sometimes outlives the code lifetime. You may have fixed every bug in your code and, years after the application began to be used, you might still be tweaking performance. SQL Server provides great assistance with this endless task.

SQL Server 2000 Enhancements and Additions

As we mentioned earlier, the changes to SQL Server 2000 are to support the development of large-scale applications in a distributed environment, by combining scalability and reliability with ease of use. These three areas are actually the themes for SQL Server 2000, with the addition of enhanced Data Mining support and open programmability. SQL Server provides a set of tools, COM interfaces, open standards such as Open Information Model (OIM), and XML to allow you to exploit the services that SQL Server 2000 offers, such as Meta Data Services and Analysis Services.

To support the above themes several enhancements have been made. To better understand what these features are and the value they provide we need to explore the themes and goals for SQL Server 2000.

In Windows DNA, performance issues rest mostly with the database engine. SQL Server 2000 enhances performance by changes to the core engine, as well as added index enhancements, and tools and wizards that let you make better indexing decisions, as well as collation enhancements which we will discuss later.

For scalability SQL Server 2000 supports Federated Database Servers – a very important feature in supporting Windows DNA application development needs. Federated Servers allow the databases to be spread across a group of servers to support increasing workloads such as a sudden increase in web application traffic. SQL Server 2000 supports a different type of scalability from the one we discussed above; with Federated Servers you can partition your data across multiple servers that co-operate to process your workload.

SQL Server 2000's reliability theme is expressed in the failover clustering enhancements. Failover is used to provide high availability for your database. You must first set up and configure a failover cluster then, when your database is not available, applications can use any other node in the failover cluster. The enhancements to this feature have made it easier to configure and administer failover clusters.

Among the most exciting changes from a developer's point of view are the programmability enhancements. SQL Server 2000 now supports XML and a new SQL syntax; it also includes user defined functions as well as several COM interfaces and services that can you can use to customize the services offered by SQL Server.

And lastly, there are enhancements to the Data Mining support and general ease of use. SQL Server 2000 is ensuring that the developer experience, either by code or through the user interface, is easy and effective.

The following table summarizes how these themes are being supported:

SQL Server Theme	Theme Support Feature
Scalability	Federated Database Server
Reliability	Cascading referential integrity constraints
	Failover clustering enhancements
Programmability	XML support
	User-defined functions
	Full Text Search enhancements
Data Mining support	Meta Data Browser enhancements
	Repository Engine enhancements
	Repository Engine Modeling enhancements
Ease of Use	SQL Profiler enhancements
	SQL Query Analyzer enhancements

In the next few pages we will dig deeper into these enhancements and new features, and explore how to get the most value from what SQL Server 2000 has to offer.

Exploring Performance Enhancements

In the following section we will explore some of the enhancements to SQL Server, mostly those that relate to indexes, and how these enhancements can help tune your database performance.

Index Enhancements

With SQL Server 2000 you can now create indexes on computed columns. This was not available in prior versions of SQL Server, and allows for greater performance improvements when attempting to query a calculated column field.

Optimizing indexes is a very tricky task – you have to understand how the tables are used and which indexes provide the best value for your query. You can take a first stab at indexing your tables, however, you might also want to consider the Index Tuning Wizard (see the figure below). This allows you to select a Server, a Database and specify a workload (where the workload can either be a SQL table, a SQL query, or a trace file). The wizard will run the queries and stress test the table. Based on the tests, the wizard will recommend actions for indexing.

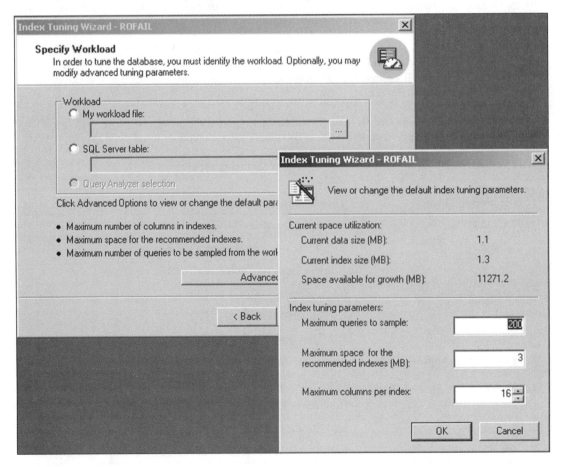

Indexed Views

This is probably one of the most requested features. If you use **views** a lot you certainly can identify with that need. With SQL Server 2000 you can now create indexes on a view. The cool thing about this feature is that if you already have existing code that uses views, by simply migrating to SQL Server 2000 you can take immediate advantage of this feature. However, there is one catch to creating indexes on views and that is, when you create a view you must check the "Bind to Schema" checkbox in the view's property dialog in order to be able to create an index on that view. You can also use the Index Tuning Wizard we discussed above to enhance index selection on a view, by selecting the checkbox "Include Views". The figure below shows you how to create a view and an index on that view through the SQL Query Analyzer. If you don't see the view as shown in the figure, hit *F8* to get to the object browser, navigate to the database and then to the view. After you select the view, select "Manage Indexes" to use the Index Wizard to create an index on that view:

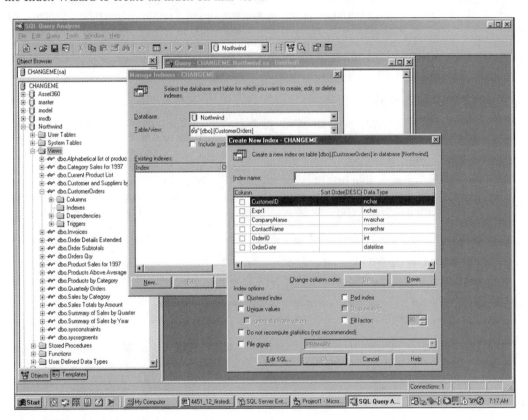

Collation Enhancements

Collation is the process and the rules that dictate how character strings are physically stored. This is a very detailed topic and almost transparent to the developer. However, it is important to note an enhancement to this process. In previous versions of SQL Server these rules could only be specified at the server instance level and applied to every database in that instance. Also, changing the setting required a database rebuild. With SQL Server 2000, you can specify collation at the database level as well as the column level without requiring a database rebuild as in previous versions. If you do a lot of international application development and need to control how you would like to specify the storage of characters and double byte characters, then this enhancement will give you extra flexibility and specificity.

Exploring Scalability Enhancements

One of the major values of adopting a Windows DNA architecture is the potential for scalability. SQL Server 2000, being a core part of the Windows DNA Server family, fulfills this promise by providing enhancements in SQL Server 2000.

Multiple SQL Server Instances

SQL Server 2000 supports multiple SQL Server **instances** on a single machine, which means that you can have multiple applications using different database engines connecting to different instances of the server on the same machine, in much the same way you would have multiple applications connecting to multiple databases in the same server. With every instance you will have your own set of users, and resources that will not be available across instances. This solves several problems for application hosting needs. You don't need to have multiple servers to support different applications, thereby reducing the number of servers you need in your physical environment – giving you the opportunity to consolidate your servers. Since SQL Server manages this by running each instance on a different port this configuration is used internally in the implementation of a shared disk failover. SQL Server 2000 currently supports 16 database engine instances.

Types of SQL Server Instances

There are two types of instances you can have with SQL Server. It is important to note that you can manage all instances from a single SQL Server Enterprise Manager and Network Manager.

❑ **Default instance** – you can only have one default instance. So you will need to select the SQL Server configuration that best fits your needs and make that your default instance. It is important to note that unless you explicitly provide the instance name when you connect to a machine using just the computer name, it is assumed that you will be using the default instance. You can switch between instances using the **vswitch** utility, which allows you to switch versions of SQL Server when you run it on the server.

❑ **Named instances** – you can identify any instance by its name when you are connecting to SQL Server, by providing the computer name, a "\" then the instance name, as follows:

```
SConn = "Provider=SQLOLEDB.1;Server=Corporate\Instance1;" &_
        "Database=Northwind;UID=sa;pwd=;"
```

The only catch to using named instances is that only SQL Server 2000 database engines can support them.

Federated Server

Federated Server in SQL Server 2000 provides an enhancement to the query processor to optimize the performance of what used to be known in previous versions as Distributed Partitioned Views. It does this by building dynamic plans to makes efficient use of the queries. In order to create a federation of servers, you must partition the tables that you want to distribute horizontally, meaning that you must split your tables to hold ranges of values. For example, if you want to create a distributed partition for your Orders tables, you must split the orders by ID where the first partition will hold OrderID 1-50000 and the second partition will hold OrderID 50001-10000, without overlapping, and so on for the rest of the table and for each table you want to partition. You would use a check constraint such as, on Server 1:

```
CREATE TABLE ORDER_1
(ORDERID INTEGER PRIMARY KEY)
      CHECK(ORDERID BETWEEN 1 AND 50000),

CREATE TABLE ORDER_2
(ORDERID INTEGER PRIMARY KEY)
      CHECK(ORDERID BETWEEN 50001 AND 100000),
```

This functionality allows you to spread your database processing based on payload and stress loads of tables. You can partition your tables across servers. This process is referred to as scaling out. Scaling out allows you to spread your processing across multiple units, which fits the Windows DNA and COM+ design model.

Exploring Reliability Enhancements

.A critical behavior of an application is how reliable it is. When putting together your code and architecture, you can make sure that your components are stable and available, that the web server is running 24/7; however, ensuring data reliability and integrity is also very important. A portion of this task can be left to the developer to ensure that he or she is implementing good design patterns and following good database modeling techniques. However, there has to be some reliability responsibility on the database itself. SQL Server 2000 contributes to ensuring reliability by supporting two new enhancements: cascading referential integrity constraints and failover clustering enhancements.

Cascading Referential Integrity Constraints

Referential integrity is the guard that prevents you from deleting parent data and leaving orphan data in your database. In SQL Server this is controlled by **foreign key relationships**. By creating a **constraint** you enforce the integrity of the database. Although in SQL Server rules can be enforced via **triggers**, it is recommended to enforce referential integrity rules via constraints and the reason is that the SQL Query Optimizer uses constraints to come up with the optimization plan. SQL Server enhances constraints by adding two new clauses called ON DELETE and ON UPDATE to the references clauses in the CREATE and ALTER TABLE statements. You can specify the action to be taken on a delete or an update to a row if the row has a referential relationship.

Failover Clustering Enhancements

The enhancements are primarily related to the configuration and maintenance of these clusters. **Failover clustering** is the ability to create and configure backup nodes should the primary node fail for any reason. This architecture allows us to maintain the integrity of the operation. The failover clustering architecture and setup relies on Windows NT Enterprise Edition, Windows 2000 Advanced Server, or Windows 2000 Datacenter Server, and the Microsoft Cluster Service, before you can install SQL Server 2000 failover clustering.

Data Transformation Services Enhancements

Data Transformation Services (DTS) is a tool that allows you to automate the manipulation and management of data from different sources. For example, you can use DTS to move data from an Access database to SQL Server and apply rules and conditions to this transformation process. Additionally, you can save the DTS as a package that you can later distribute to your customers so that they can run this process on their machines.

423

DTS adds the ability to create DTS Packages in SQL Server using the **DTS Designer** and to then save the packages as Visual Basic code (shown in the figure below).

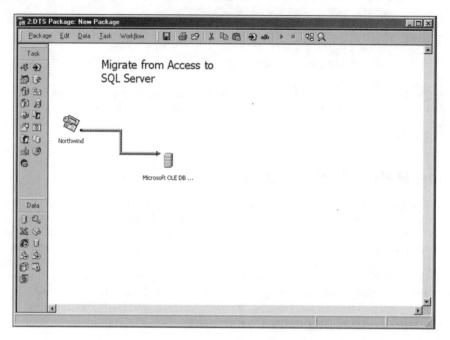

For this example, we have created a very simple DTS package using the DTS Designer. The package we created will assist in the migration of an Access database into a SQL Server database. The package will take care of all the required processes and conversions need to create and move the data from Access to a new SQL Server database. We will be able to save the package and send it to our user where they can run it and perform the migration. With the new DTS enhancements, we can save the package as VB code where a standard VB module will be created and we can just add it to a VB project where we could manipulate it. To generate the standard VB code module select the Package | Save As menu option in the DTS Designer – this will invoke the Save DTS Package dialog box:

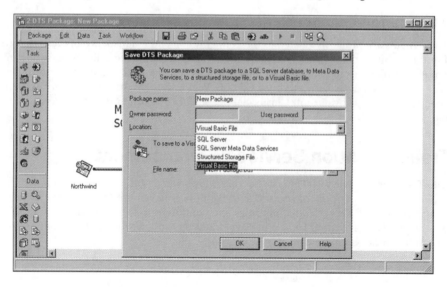

Here we have the option to specify a name for the package as well as passwords to be used to restrict the viewing of the package to certain users. In addition, we can also specify the location for the DTS Package to be saved to. There are four possible locations:

❑ A SQL Server msdb database

❑ Meta Data Services

❑ A structured storage file

❑ A Visual Basic file

The additional saving options vary depending on which location is selected. Select Visual Basic File, enter the file name and click the OK command button.

This results in the creation of a Visual Basic code module or **BAS file** that contains all of the code needed to create and execute the DTS Package from scratch. As mentioned earlier, this BAS file can be used to create a new Visual Basic application or added to an existing application or ActiveX DLL. Writing code with the DTS object model can be difficult and, historically, very little documentation has been available. The ability to generate Visual Basic code from the DTS Designer eliminates some of the headaches caused by writing code from scratch. It allows you to create a package using a graphical user interface, which can be done quicker and more easily, especially programmers who may be new to DTS or Visual Basic.

I have integrated my newly created BAS file into a new Visual Basic project (`NewPackage.vbp`) in order to review the code in VB. To do this, first open a new VB project and add the DTS module to the project by selecting Add File from the Project menu. You also need to add a reference to the DTS object library before you can run the project. Do this by selecting References from the Project menu and checking the Microsoft DTSPackage Object Library box on the Reference dialog window. The DTSPackage Object Library is installed when you install SQL Server 2000. If you still have a version of SQL Server 7.0 on your machine, be sure that you are selecting the most recent version of the DTSPackage Object Model. Once you have done this it's a good idea to review the DTS object library using the object browser in VB. This will help familiarize you with all of the properties and methods that are available in the object model, including the new items that have been added to the object model for DTS.

This is the code generated for the BAS file:

```
'******************************************************************
'Microsoft SQL Server 2000
'Visual Basic file generated for DTS Package
'File Name: C:\SQL Code\New Package.bas
'Package Name: New Package
'Package Description:
'Generated Date: 8/8/00
'Generated Time: 6:31:20 AM
'******************************************************************

Option Explicit
Public goPackageOld As New DTS.Package
Public goPackage As DTS.Package2
Private Sub Main()
        Set goPackage = goPackageOld
```

```
            goPackage.Name = "New Package"
            goPackage.WriteCompletionStatusToNTEventLog = False
            goPackage.FailOnError = False
            goPackage.PackagePriorityClass = 2
            goPackage.MaxConcurrentSteps = 4
            goPackage.LineageOptions = 0
            goPackage.UseTransaction = True
            goPackage.TransactionIsolationLevel = 4096
            goPackage.AutoCommitTransaction = True
            goPackage.RepositoryMetadataOptions = 0
            goPackage.UseOLEDBServiceComponents = True
            goPackage.LogToSQLServer = False
            goPackage.LogServerFlags = 0
            goPackage.FailPackageOnLogFailure = False
            goPackage.ExplicitGlobalVariables = False
            goPackage.PackageType = 0


'-----------------------------------------------------------------------
' create package connection information
'-----------------------------------------------------------------------

Dim oConnection As DTS.Connection2

'------------- a new connection defined below.
'For security purposes, the password is never scripted

Set oConnection = goPackage.Connections.New("Microsoft.Jet.OLEDB.4.0")

            oConnection.ConnectionProperties("User ID") = "Admin"
            oConnection.ConnectionProperties("Data Source") = "C:\Program " &_
                        "Files\Microsoft Visual Studio\VB98\Nwind.mdb"

            oConnection.Name = "Northwind"
            oConnection.ID = 1
            oConnection.Reusable = True
            oConnection.ConnectImmediate = False
            oConnection.DataSource = "C:\Program Files\Microsoft Visual" _&
                              " Studio\VB98\Nwind.mdb"
            oConnection.UserID = "Admin"
            oConnection.ConnectionTimeout = 60
            oConnection.UseTrustedConnection = False
            oConnection.UseDSL = False

            'If you have a password for this connection, uncomment and add
            'your password below.
            'oConnection.Password = "<put the password here>"

goPackage.Connections.Add oConnection
Set oConnection = Nothing

'------------- a new connection defined below.
'For security purposes, the password is never scripted

Set oConnection = goPackage.Connections.New("SQLOLEDB.1")
```

```
        oConnection.ConnectionProperties("Persist Security Info") = True
        oConnection.ConnectionProperties("User ID") = "sa"
        oConnection.ConnectionProperties("Initial Catalog") = "NewNorthwind"
        oConnection.ConnectionProperties("Data Source") = "(local)"
        oConnection.ConnectionProperties("Application Name") = "DTS Designer"

        oConnection.Name = "Microsoft OLE DB Provider for SQL Server"
        oConnection.ID = 2
        oConnection.Reusable = True
        oConnection.ConnectImmediate = False
        oConnection.DataSource = "(local)"
        oConnection.UserID = "sa"
        oConnection.ConnectionTimeout = 60
        oConnection.Catalog = "NewNorthwind"
        oConnection.UseTrustedConnection = False
        oConnection.UseDSL = False

        'If you have a password for this connection, uncomment and add
        'your password below.
        'oConnection.Password = "<put the password here>"

goPackage.Connections.Add oConnection
Set oConnection = Nothing

'-------------------------------------------------------------------------
' create package steps information
'-------------------------------------------------------------------------

Dim oStep As DTS.Step2
Dim oPrecConstraint As DTS.PrecedenceConstraint

'------------- a new step defined below

Set oStep = goPackage.Steps.New

        oStep.Name = "DTSStep_DTSDataPumpTask_1"
        oStep.Description = "Transform Data Task: undefined"
        oStep.ExecutionStatus = 1
        oStep.TaskName = "DTSTask_DTSDataPumpTask_1"
        oStep.CommitSuccess = False
        oStep.RollbackFailure = False
        oStep.ScriptLanguage = "VBScript"
        oStep.AddGlobalVariables = True
        oStep.RelativePriority = 3
        oStep.CloseConnection = False
        oStep.ExecuteInMainThread = False
        oStep.IsPackageDSORowset = False
        oStep.JoinTransactionIfPresent = False
        oStep.DisableStep = False
        oStep.FailPackageOnError = False

goPackage.Steps.Add oStep
Set oStep = Nothing
```

427

```
'-------------------------------------------------------------------------
' create package tasks information
'-------------------------------------------------------------------------


'------------- call Task_Sub1 for task DTSTask_DTSDataPumpTask_1 (Transform
'Data Task: undefined)
Call Task_Sub1(goPackage)


'-------------------------------------------------------------------------
' Save or execute package
'-------------------------------------------------------------------------

'goPackage.SaveToSQLServer "(local)", "sa", ""
goPackage.Execute
goPackage.Uninitialize
'to save a package instead of executing it, comment out the executing package
'line above and uncomment the saving package line
Set goPackage = Nothing

Set goPackageOld = Nothing


End Sub

'------------- define Task_Sub1 for task DTSTask_DTSDataPumpTask_1 (Transform
'Data Task: undefined)
Public Sub Task_Sub1(ByVal goPackage As Object)

Dim oTask As DTS.Task
Dim oLookup As DTS.Lookup

Dim oCustomTask1 As DTS.DataPumpTask2
Set oTask = goPackage.Tasks.New("DTSDataPumpTask")
Set oCustomTask1 = oTask.CustomTask

        oCustomTask1.Name = "DTSTask_DTSDataPumpTask_1"
        oCustomTask1.Description = "Transform Data Task: undefined"
        oCustomTask1.SourceConnectionID = 1
        oCustomTask1.DestinationConnectionID = 2
        oCustomTask1.ProgressRowCount = 1000
        oCustomTask1.MaximumErrorCount = 0
        oCustomTask1.FetchBufferSize = 1
        oCustomTask1.UseFastLoad = True
        oCustomTask1.InsertCommitSize = 0
        oCustomTask1.ExceptionFileColumnDelimiter = "|"
        oCustomTask1.ExceptionFileRowDelimiter = vbCrLf
        oCustomTask1.AllowIdentityInserts = False
        oCustomTask1.FirstRow = 0
        oCustomTask1.LastRow = 0
        oCustomTask1.FastLoadOptions = 2
        oCustomTask1.ExceptionFileOptions = 1
        oCustomTask1.DataPumpOptions = 0

goPackage.Tasks.Add oTask
Set oCustomTask1 = Nothing
Set oTask = Nothing

End Sub
```

```
Public Sub Task_Sub1(ByVal goPackage As Object)

Dim oTask As DTS.Task
Dim oLookup As DTS.Lookup

Dim oCustomTask1 As DTS.DataPumpTask2
Set oTask = goPackage.Tasks.New("DTSDataPumpTask")
Set oCustomTask1 = oTask.CustomTask

        oCustomTask1.Name = "DTSTask_DTSDataPumpTask_1"
        oCustomTask1.Description = "Transform Data Task: undefined"
        oCustomTask1.SourceConnectionID = 1
        oCustomTask1.DestinationConnectionID = 2
        oCustomTask1.ProgressRowCount = 1000
        oCustomTask1.MaximumErrorCount = 0
        oCustomTask1.FetchBufferSize = 1
        oCustomTask1.UseFastLoad = True
        oCustomTask1.InsertCommitSize = 0
        oCustomTask1.ExceptionFileColumnDelimiter = "|"
        oCustomTask1.ExceptionFileRowDelimiter = vbCrLf
        oCustomTask1.AllowIdentityInserts = False
        oCustomTask1.FirstRow = 0
        oCustomTask1.LastRow = 0
        oCustomTask1.FastLoadOptions = 2
        oCustomTask1.ExceptionFileOptions = 1
        oCustomTask1.DataPumpOptions = 0

goPackage.Tasks.Add oTask
Set oCustomTask1 = Nothing
Set oTask = Nothing

End Sub
```

Exploring the DTS Code

Even though the DTS package being used for this example is relatively simple, it still generates a module that contains quite a few lines of code. The code is relatively easy to understand. The code module created by the DTS Designer follows this logic.

The logic used to programmatically create and run DTS packages using the SQL Server 2000 DTS object model is the same as the logic used to do the same using the DTS object model that shipped with SQL Server 7.0. In fact, the object models for the two versions of DTS are very similar. However, the new DTS object model has enhanced several of the objects within it and provided them with additional functionality. The enhanced objects in DTS are denoted by the number 2, which follows the object name (Package2, Connection2, Step2, etc.). The original objects (Package, Connection, Step, etc.) still exist in the object model for backwards compatibility. You must use the original objects if you are building an application that will be run against SQL Server version 7.0 or earlier. If you attempt to run a DTS application that uses any of the extended objects against an earlier version of SQL Server, you will receive a "type mismatch" error. The code generated by the DTS Designer uses the new, extended objects.

The first step towards programming a DTS package is to create a new version of the package object and set its properties. One of the reasons that the code created by the DTS Designer is so lengthy is because it explicitly and individually sets every property for an object. One way to shorten the code is to remove some of the lines of code that set property values and use the default values that are assigned when the object is created. The side effect of doing this is that you will have to investigate, through reading the documentation, what the default values of the properties are. You will have to determine which properties should be explicitly set and which properties can be left to the default values on a case-by-case basis. For example, you can eliminate thirteen lines of code for the Connection object by using a single line connection string where all you need to provide in the string is the provider name, Data Source Name, user name, and password. For our example DTS, two connections are created: one to represent the SQL Server destination database and one to represent the Access data sources.

Once the connections have been created and appended to the package object, the steps and tasks for the package need to be created and appended to the package's Steps and Tasks collections. In the DTS object model, a step can be thought of as an operation that will be performed by the package, such as migrating data from Access to SQL Server, migrating data from Excel to SQL Server and sending an automatic e-mail notification. A task is an object that actually performs a portion of the total operation. The code generated by the DTS Designer for this example placed the code responsible for the creation of the tasks in separate subroutines. There are three separate subroutines, one for each task, entitled Task_Sub1, Task_Sub2 and Task_Sub3. If a task involves migrating data from a source to a destination, such as the tasks that import data from Access and Excel into SQL Server, additional code is generated to set up the transformations for each task. The transformations map each of the data columns in the source object to the appropriate data column in the destination object. Transformations are set up by creating a new instance of a Transformation object, setting its properties and appending it to the Transformations collection of a task. For this example, the DTS Designer has placed the code that creates each transformation associated with a task in its own separate subroutine. For our transformation from Access to SQL Server this generated one task subroutine.

After this code has been written, the package is ready to be executed by calling the package object's Execute method. The steps for programmatically creating a DTS package outlined in this chapter may vary depending on the functionality of your specific package, as will the code generated by the DTS Designer. The purpose of this example has been to provide you with a basic template for understanding how DTS Packages are programmatically represented by the DTS Designer. Once you have this knowledge, using the DTS Designer to create VB code and then customizing and integrating that code into your own custom VB applications is simple.

SQL Server Meta Data Services

Meta Data Services is an object store that holds any type of meta data. In previous versions of SQL Server this feature was called the Microsoft Repository. For example, the DTS Package that we just created can be versioned and stored in the Meta Data Services. There are several enhancements to the Meta Data Services, such as XML encoding support which provides a way to generate XML based on information stored in an information model. There is also an XML COM interface that is part of the Meta Data Services object model that allows you to import and export from an information model. At the engine level there are several enhancements that allow you to add ActiveX scripts to validate properties or invoke methods. There are also several programmatic enhancements to the object model that allow you to program information models more easily. SQL Server Meta Data Services is worthy of its own chapter in a SQL Server book, however this brief description should give you an overview of its capabilities and whether it fits within your DNA design.

SQL Server 2000 and the Web

Perhaps the most significant update to SQL Server 2000 is the increased support for XML and web-based access. SQL Server 2000 has taken several steps towards closing the gap between client-server based development and web application development. It now provides built in support that tightly integrates with IIS and web access, while taking advantage of XML and incorporating it into its core operations. In the following sections we will explore the new features and additions to SQL Server 2000 that relate to web technology.

Accessing SQL Server from the Web

SQL Server 2000 uses an ISAPI DLL (SQLISAPI.DLL) that is used by IIS to reference a SQL Server instance, and that gives you access to the databases available in that instance. This allows you to use a URL to invoke SQL commands and get data results back. The results are returned as XML files. Before we learn the syntax for using SQL Server over the Web we need to understand the architecture behind this implementation, then explore how to configure SQL Server to enable it to work on the Web. Then we can study the various ways that we can use SQL Server on the Web.

IIS Integration with SQL Server Architecture

As we stated above, you can now submit URL-based SQL queries that will retrieve data from a specific SQL Server instance. Well, how does this work? The figure shows a basic architecture:

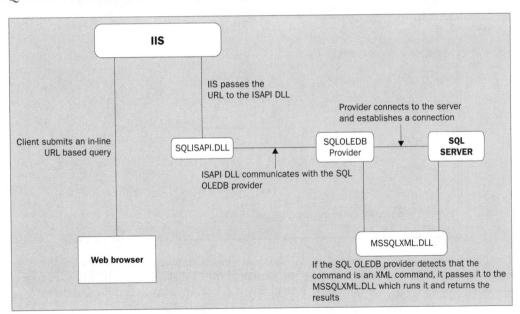

It is all done via SQLISAPI.DLL to which IIS passes the URL received from the client. The ISAPI DLL contacts the SQL OLEDB provider and passes it the SQL request. The provider then establishes a connection with the specified SQL Server. If, when parsing the SQL request, the provider establishes that the SQL command is an XML command (indicated by the presence of the FOR XML keywords), it passes the request to a DLL called MSSQLXML. This handles the XML portion of the request and passes it to the SQL Server instance.

From a browser a client will issue a command such as the following:

```
http://rofaila/Northwind?sql=SELECT+*+FROM+customers+FOR+XML+RAW
```

This shows the server name `http://rofaila` followed by the virtual directory name `Northwind` (that you will need to setup as we will show you later), then a "?" followed by the SQL statement, which should be separated by a "+" sign between each word.

Although the architecture is simple and straightforward, it is not the type of implementation or approach you would use to develop web applications that submit queries to SQL Server via IIS, due to performance and security issues related to this approach. However, it provides a very useful way to debug your applications without requiring an elaborate client-server setup.

IIS Virtual Directory Management

New with SQL Server 2000, to enable many of the web-related features, is a utility called "IIS Virtual Directory Management for SQL Server" that you can invoke from the SQL Server program group called **Microsoft SQL Server / Configure SQL XML Support in IIS**. This allows you to configure web access for SQL Server:

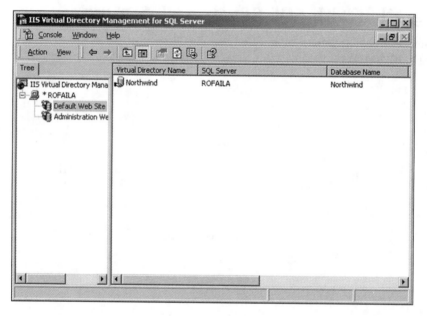

The utility is very simple, for every database that you would like to make available from the Web you need to create a **virtual directory**. You will be presented with a dialog where you will need to set some parameters, such as the Virtual Directory Name, the SQL Server instance and the Database:

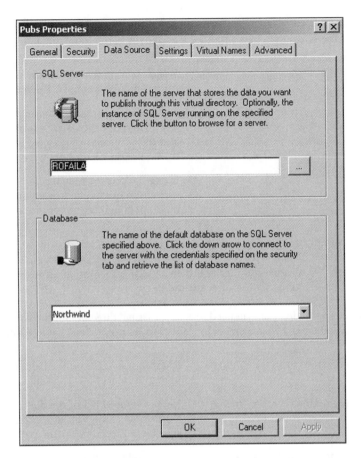

Additionally, you can enable or disable features such as allowing URL queries, or template queries, which we will discuss later, or even XPath queries. Once you set up the virtual directory, you can invoke a URL command similar to the one shown earlier and you will be able to retrieve the data straight into the browser. We'll be setting up a virtual directory for the sample application in the next section.

Creating XML

SQL Server 2000 has enhancements to the query processor to support a new SQL syntax. This enables the retrieval of data from SQL Server as XML. This is a major enhancement to SQL Server as it now eliminates the need for having a component dedicated to converting recordsets to XML. If you use XML as the data format of choice between tiers, you will appreciate the performance gain you get with obtaining XML straight out of the database. Benchmarks typically show performance gains of 50-fold over manually converting recordsets to XML.

The syntax for extracting XML from a table is simple. By using the new "FOR XML" clause you can get data out of any SQL Server table as XML using only the "SELECT" statement. Let's look at the following syntax (you can run the SQL query in the Query Analyzer to view the results):

```
SELECT * FROM Authors FOR XML Auto
```

433

You will notice that in this SQL statement we appended the "Auto" keyword. There are three options to use for the **mode** of the XML data being returned, as shown in the following table:

For XML Raw	When data returns, each row in the dataset is represented as an XML element.
For XML Auto	When data returns, it is represented as a nested tree, where the tables are represented as elements and the columns are mapped as the attribute to that element. That's how we get a nested tree.
For XML Explicit	Using Explicit specifies the shape of the XML tree and requires the first column of the data to hold positive integers representing XML tag IDs.

In the XMLSyntax sample application provided with this chapter, which also requires the template files in the XMLDom folder, we display each of the first two modes in a tree control to show how the data is different in each case. We also use another argument, ELEMENTS (only used with the Auto mode) which returns columns as sub-elements, rather than attributes.

Before trying out this application you will need to set up a virtual directory for the Northwind database. Invoke the IIS Virtual Directory Management for SQL Server, as mentioned above, and follow these steps:

Step 1	Create a new virtual directory	Right mouse click on the Default Web Site tree item and select New | Virtual Directory
Step 2	Configure the directory name	In the General tab of the dialog, type in Northwind as the Virtual Directory Name and select any directory for the path
Step 3	Configure the data source	In the Data Source tab select the SQL Server and select "Northwind" as the Database
Step 4	Configure security	In the Security tab select Windows Integrated Security or supply the user name and password for SQL Server security
Step 5	Configure settings	Make sure that Allow Template Queries is checked in the Settings tab
Step 6	Configure virtual names	In the Virtual Names tab add a New Virtual Name called "DOM" and select "template" for the type
		For the Path, navigate to the directory where the templates provided with this chapter are located ...\XMLDOM (there should be three template files)

When you run the application you can choose to view the data in one of three ways:

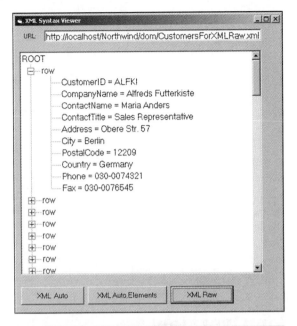

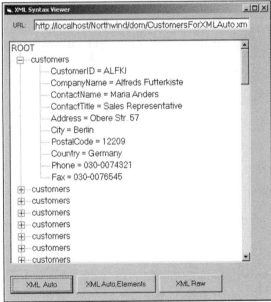

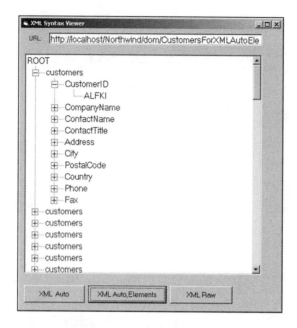

XML Application Overview

In the following section we will be building an XML-based application that displays in a framed browser the list of customers in our Northwind SQL Server database, and a listing of the orders for each customer, as well as the order details for each order. This is a simple application. However, what makes its architecture interesting is that we will:

- ❑ Access SQL Server from a URL
- ❑ Return resultsets as XML
- ❑ Explore a new feature called "XML templates"
- ❑ Pass SQL parameters from one query to another using XML
- ❑ Display the results in the browser

In order to build this application let's explore all the individual pieces that make this happen, starting with XML templates.

XML Templates

Templates are also a new feature introduced with SQL Server 2000. Templates are basically XML documents that contain one or possibly more SQL queries. Templates are used to encapsulate large SQL queries that you wouldn't necessarily put into a URL command. Because templates encapsulate the SQL query, they are considered a better approach to invoking SQL queries from a URL from a security point of view, by hiding the details of the query.

Setting Up Templates

So how do you set up a template? Once you put a template together, as we will discuss later, you can follow the above steps using the IIS Virtual Directory Manager. This is similar to setting up SQL Server on the Web to register the templates. All we need to do for this application is to add another virtual name to our existing Northwind virtual directory.

In the Virtual Names tab add a New Virtual Name called "Templates" and select "template" for the type. For the Path, navigate to the directory where the templates provided with this chapter are located ...\XML SQL Templates (there should be three template files and three XSL files).

Running Templates

Now that we have seen how to configure the templates, let's walk through how these templates are put together and how they work. Before you explore the templates, let's look at the HTML code that will invoke the first template example. The following code is a simple HTML page (Northwind.htm) with multiple frames. The first frame will display a list of customers. This list is returned when we invoke the Customer.XML file, which is the first template. When we select a customer, we will see the orders for that customer in the second frame and when we select orders we will see the order details in the last frame.

```
<html>
<head>
<title>Northwind Order System</title>
<meta name="GENERATOR" content="Microsoft FrontPage 4.0">
<meta name="ProgId" content="FrontPage.Editor.Document">
</head>
<frameset rows="100,*" framespacing="0" border="1">
<frame name="Header" scrolling="no" noresize target="Customersw" src="header.htm"
border = "1">
<frameset cols="370,*">
  <frame name="Customer" scrolling="auto" noresize target="Orders"
src="http://Rofaila/Northwind/Templates/Customer.xml" >
  <frameset rows="50%,*">
    <frame name="Orders" target="OrderDetails" scrolling="auto">
    <frame name="OrderDetails" scrolling="auto">
  </frameset>
</frameset>
</frameset>
</html>
```

The result is shown:

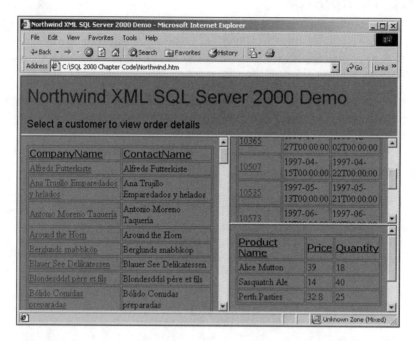

The Customer Template

This is the first template that was invoked from the master HTML page. As you can see, the first line references an XSL sheet that defines the format and color of the data. Next is the SQL query that retrieves `CustomerID`, `CompanyName` and `ContactName` and returns the result as XML:

```
<?xml-stylesheet type="text/xsl" href="customer.xsl"?>
<ROOT xmlns:sql="urn:schemas-microsoft-com:xml-sql">

<sql:query>select CustomerID, CompanyName, ContactName, Phone from Customers for
XML AUTO, elements</sql:query>
</ROOT>
```

The Orders Template

The `Orders` template receives the `CustomerID` from the first template embedded in the `header` tag `<sql:header>`. This contains the parameter called `name`, which represents the value used to invoke a second query to return all the orders for this customer. We again use an XSL sheet to format the contents:

```
<?xml-stylesheet type="text/xsl" href="Orders.xsl"?>
<ROOT xmlns:sql="urn:schemas-microsoft-com:xml-sql">
<sql:header>
<sql:param name="CustomerID">AAAA</sql:param>
</sql:header>
<sql:query>select OrderID, CustomerID, OrderDate, ShippedDate from Orders where
CustomerID=@CustomerID order by OrderDate for XML auto, elements
</sql:query>
</ROOT>
```

The Order Details Template

The final template is for the order details, which receives the `OrderID` in the `header` tag and runs a query to return all the order details for that specific `OrderID`:

```
<?xml-stylesheet type="text/xsl" href="OrderDetails.xsl"?>
<ROOT xmlns:sql="urn:schemas-microsoft-com:xml-sql">
<sql:header>
<sql:param name="OrderID">AAAA</sql:param>
</sql:header>
<sql:query>Select ProductName, UnitPrice, Quantity from [OrderDetailsView] where
OrderId=@OrderID for XML Auto, elements</sql:query>

<sql:query>Select Total from [OrderDetailsTotals] where OrderId=@OrderID for XML
Auto, elements</sql:query>
</ROOT>
```

As you can see, templates are a great way to run, return and display formatted, elegant results. With the added security of having them run under IIS virtual directory, they provide a viable commercial solution because they hide the details of the SQL query and share the security setting of any document that is running under IIS. If you don't have rights to the document you will not be able to invoke it nor will you have access to view it.

Writing XML Data

Now that we feel comfortable *reading* XML data from SQL Server, the question that is remaining is how do we *write* XML? SQL Server 2000 provides a new rowset function called `OpenXML` which can be used as a table reference, where we would use the XML data in the document and perform updates and inserts.

`OpenXML` is used to expose data in an XML document as a relational rowset that can be used as if it were a standard relational rowset, that is you can perform inserts and updates. Before we use the `OpenXML` syntax, there is some preparation work we need to do to the XML data in the document that we are about to update. There is a helper stored procedure that allows us to perform that task, called `sp_xml_preparedocument` (shown overleaf). This system stored procedure prepares the XML document for us.

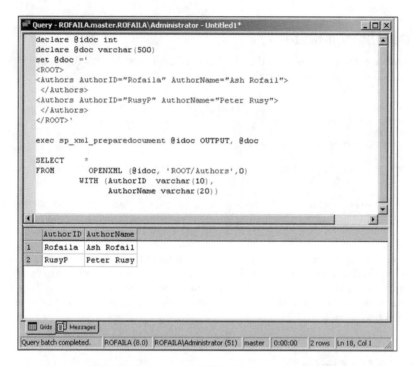

In the above example we explicitly included the XML document in our query to show how the rowset will be created and what the returned value will be. However, in normal use you would replace the explicit XML text with a text reference.

This system stored procedure has only two required parameters, the document handle (`idoc`) and the XPath pattern (`rowpattern`). This identifies, using XPath syntax, a precise point in the XML document, in this case `ROOT/authors`. Once you use `OpenXML`, you will get a rowset of data, where you can manipulate the XML data elements and update them as you wish. One precaution when using `OpenXML` is that every time you use the `sp_xml_preparedocument` procedure you have to use the `sp_xml_removedocument` procedure, passing it the handle to the newly created document, so that it will be released from memory.

Summary

As you can imagine, it is impossible to cover every aspect of SQL Server 2000 in just one chapter. Even an entire book dedicated to SQL Server might not be enough. However, the aim of this chapter was to highlight some of the most important improvements to SQL Server 2000 that will assist you in building your Windows DNA solutions. There are several enhancements to the OLAP capabilities in SQL Server 2000, now called Analysis Services, as well enhancements to the Meta Data Services (previously called the Repository). We did not cover these new features as they are filled with many details that could distract from the Windows DNA focus that we took with this chapter.

SQL Server 2000 is by far considered the most important release to come in a long time. What is encouraging about this release is that it focused on providing features that give immediate value to large-scale applications, while not ignoring some of the subtle enhancements in ease of use.

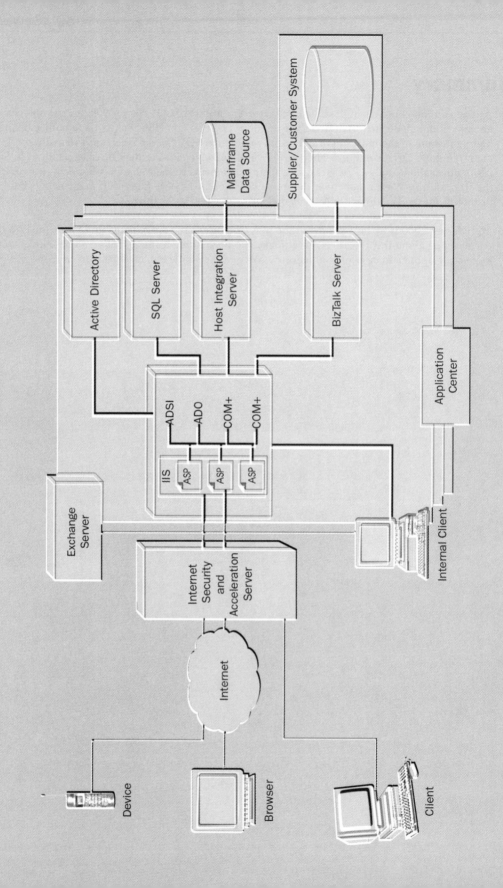

15

Windows 2000 Directory Services

I remember vividly when I got my first taste of Directory Services. It was in September of 1997 in building 25 on the Microsoft Campus in Redmond, Washington. The project was "Olympus", the Microsoft internal code name for Site Server Version 3.0. I was tasked with taking over for a developer lead who'd "had enough". I stepped into a "bug triage" meeting that was already in progress and very heated. I was introduced as the "dev lead taking over in architecture" and got some unfriendly stares. It's always uncomfortable taking over a lead position in the middle of a project, but it's especially difficult when it's the architecture team. The arguing continued immediately after I sat down. Acronyms, abbreviations, and code names dominated the conversation and I was lost: U2, Membership Server, Membership Directory, DS, LDAP, ADSI. These people communicated quickly and efficiently, but I had no idea what they were talking about. I wrote down as much as I could, hoping to get a translation after the meeting.

Here's what I learned:

- ❏ U2 – Microsoft internal code name for Site Server 3.0 Personalization and Membership. This is the Directory Service included in the Site Server 3.0 Product.

- ❏ Membership Server – A collection of software elements that manage Site Server 3.0's personalization and membership information.

- ❏ Membership Directory – The central repository of user data for Microsoft Site Server version 3.0

- ❏ DS – Directory Service

- ❏ LDAP – Lightweight Directory Access Protocol

- ❏ ADSI – Active Directory™ Services Interface

But, I still had no idea what they were, what they meant and what their purpose was.

I spent six months in Redmond working on Olympus, and by the time we shipped in March of 1998 I was infatuated with "Membership", the Directory Service of Microsoft Site Server version 3.0. And to the very day I write this, my love of the Directory Service has not faded.

Overview

In this chapter I am going to teach you about directory services – why you need them and what their purpose is. I'll show you some standard coding techniques to access directory services and I'll show you the tools you need to help you with programmatic access to the directory services. By the time you have completed this chapter, we will have worked through the encapsulation of directory service access in middle tier COM+ components.

The software development community has been talking about encapsulating Directory Server Access into the middle tier for a long time, but we haven't been doing it. I can remember a Windows DNA diagram from the Microsoft Developer Days Conference in 1998 – it had a Directory Service moniker in the drawing of the data tier. We have seen quite a few examples in documentation, which contain inline ASP script to access the directory service. Since most software developers writing web applications are "bought into" the idea of a set of standard data access COM components that all our page programmers are mandated to use for data access, it makes sense to encapsulate all directory service access in the very same way.

The majority of this chapter will cover the Windows 2000 Active Directory, the directory service of Windows 2000, but I will cover other Microsoft Directory Services also. Because, thankfully, there are standards for ADSI, and LDAP does the low-level translation for Directory Service access, I will show you how easy it is to access other directory services like the offerings from Netscape, Novell, and IBM, with the very same code. I will cover ADSI and LDAP heavily in this chapter because you will need to understand these fundamental services before effectively programming Directory Services.

Before digging into code, I'll show you the tools you need to help you with software development in Directory Services. Just as the Enterprise Manager is so valuable when programming data access to Microsoft SQL Server, the Windows 2000 Active Directory has its own set of tools – some are popular and well documented, like the Active Directory Users and Computers MMC tool. Some are not so popular and hidden by design, like the Active Directory Schema Editor.

You will need access to a Windows 2000 Active Directory to execute the code in this chapter. I will not go through the details of installing the Active Directory nor will I outline the prerequisites of installation. That is well documented in the Windows 2000 Server or Advanced Server documentation and well beyond the scope of my mission here. Even if you do not have an Active Directory available on your network, you will still get quite a bit out of this chapter. If you are an enterprise or web developer, sooner or later you are going to run into a directory service. This chapter will give you the head start you need to be effective.

Active Directory Defined

By definition, the directory service stores information about entities on a network. Software developers make this information available to users and network administrators. The Microsoft Windows 2000 Active Directory provides user access to permitted resources anywhere on the network using a single logon process. It provides network administrators with an intuitive hierarchical view of the network and a single point of administration for all network objects.

What this boils down to for the software developer is two issues:

❑ **Authentication** – the Windows 2000 Active Directory is the place to *authenticate* securely within the Operating System.

❑ **Attributes** – it also provides an enterprise available data store to persist data, called *attributes*. By design, Directory Services are made to store information about your users. The Windows 2000 Active Directory has taken a number of steps further by storing application and enterprise data. Every entity in the Active Directory is an instance of a class, and every entity is defined by (and consists of) a set of attributes. The class of these entities determine what attributes these entities can have, and all possible attributes are defined in the Active Directory schema. The attribute definition includes its syntax, which specifies the type of value it can have.

With those two concepts stated (authentication and attributes) you may ask yourself: "Why do I need another data storage mechanism and API when I have SQL Server and ADO?" And you may ask yourself: "Why do I need another authentication mechanism when I already have the Operating System to do that?" The answers to those two questions and more are covered in the subsequent sections.

The Authentication Features of the Active Directory

The Windows 2000 Active Directory supplies flexible and secure authentication and authorization services, which provide protection for data while minimizing barriers to doing business over the Internet, intranet, or extranet. Active Directory supports multiple authentication protocols including Kerboros V5 protocol (details can be found at `http://www.mit.edu/kerberos/www`), Secure Sockets Layer v3, and Transport Layer Security using X.509v3 certificates. Active Directory also supports security groups that span domains efficiently. Directory Services (and Active Directory in particular) overcome the domain authentication restrictions (generally around 2000 users) of Windows NT 4.0. Technically, you can have millions+ of authenticated users. User authentication in Windows 2000 Active Directory gives users the ability to log on to a system to access network resources, whether the access is from the local LAN, intranet, extranet, or Internet. Within this authentication model, the security system provides two types of authentication:

❑ **Interactive logon** – confirms the user's identification to the user's local computer or Active Directory account

❑ **Network authentication** – confirms the user's identification to any network service that the user is attempting to access

In addition to authentication, Active Directory provides a mechanism for **access control**. This allows software developers to write tools that allow administrators to control access to resources, or objects, on the network. Windows 2000 implements access control by allowing administrators to assign **security descriptors** to objects stored in Active Directory. A security descriptor lists the users and groups that are granted access to an object, and the specific permissions assigned to those users and groups. A security descriptor also specifies the various access events to be audited for an object. Examples of Active Directory objects are files, printers, and services. By managing properties on objects, administrators can set permissions, assign ownership, and monitor user access. Not only can software developers write tools for administrators to control access to a specific object, but we can also control access to a specific *attribute* of that object. For example, through proper configuration of an object's security descriptor, a user could be programmatically allowed to access a subset of information, such as an employee's e-mail address, but not their social security number.

Active Directory allows administrators to create **group accounts** so that they can more efficiently manage system security. For example, by adjusting a file's security properties, an administrator can permit all users in a group to have read access to that file. Groups also let us control access to resources in the directory. In this way, access to objects in Active Directory is based on group membership and thereby much easier to manage than by individual user.

The Attribute Features of the Active Directory

Attributes describe objects within the Active Directory. The types of object stored within the Active Directory fall into three main categories:

❑ User information

❑ Application information

❑ Enterprise information

Attributes in a directory service are analogous to columns in a database table, but organized much more rigidly. Attributes are organized into classes. The User Class in the Active Directory, for instance, contains attributes specific to a user, like name and address. Attributes are stored in the directory service as name/value pairs. For instance, if the value of a user's e-mail address is persisted in the Active Directory, the attribute name, "mail" and the value of the attribute, "TimHuck@InterKnowlogy.com" are persisted together. Unlike a relational database like Microsoft SQL Server, where table columns exist whether or not they are null, if an attribute in a directory service is not persisted, then the space for the attributes name is not persisted either, bypassing the wasted space. Also, the attributes in a directory service can be single-valued *or* multi-valued. An example of a multi-valued attribute is "userGroups". The userGroups attribute is multi-valued because it contains several values – the names of the multiple groups that a user belongs to.

As with a relational database like Microsoft SQL Server, all attributes have a **syntax** that determines the kind of data that the attribute can store. There are a fixed number of syntaxes allowed in the Active Directory Schema. You cannot add additional or "custom-made" syntaxes to the Active Directory. This is beneficial because, as a software developer, we don't have to worry about casting to user defined types. Some examples of attribute syntaxes are:

❑ Boolean: True or False

❑ Integer: a number between 0 (zero) and 4,294,967,295

❑ NumericString: a character string that contains only numbers

Similarly, attributes can have length or range **constraints**. For attributes with numeric syntax the range specifies the minimum and maximum value. For attributes with string syntax the range specifies the minimum and maximum length.

Again, like a relational database, Active Directory attributes can be **indexed**. Indexing attributes helps queries more quickly find objects having data persisted in that attribute.

Attributes can also be included in the **global catalog**. The Active Directory global catalog contains a subset of attributes for every object in the Active Directory. Applications can use the global catalog to locate objects within the Active Directory. The global catalog holds a replica of every object in Active Directory but with only a small number of their attributes. The attributes that exist in the global catalog are those most frequently used in search operations (such as a user's first and last names, e-mail address, login names, and so on). The global catalog facilitates quickly locating Active Directory objects without having to know what domain they live in. Attributes that may be appropriate to include in the global catalog have the following characteristics:

❑ Globally useful: the attribute is needed for locating objects that may occur anywhere on the network that the active directory is available to, or read access to the attribute is valuable even when the object itself is not accessible.

❑ Not volatile, in order words it doesn't change often: attributes in a global catalog are replicated to all other global catalogs in the enterprise. If an attribute changes often, significant replication traffic on the network will result.

❑ Small persisted footprint: For attributes which do change, the smaller the attribute the lower the network traffic impact of that replication. This is a tough scenario to pin down: if the attribute is large but very seldom changes, it will have a smaller replication impact than a small attribute that changes frequently.

Attributes that are frequently queried and referenced by users across the enterprise, such as employee names, e-mail addresses, and phone numbers, are good candidates for inclusion in the Active Directory global catalog. Attributes that are rarely queried, like home addresses, are not good candidates for inclusion in the Active Directory Global Catalog.

Directory Service Structure

The biggest difference between a database and a directory service is that a directory service is not relational. Directory Services, like the Active Directory are hierarchical and support **object inheritance**. Every object in Active Directory is an instance of a particular class. A class defines the attributes available to an instance of that particular class. A class, such as user, defines properties such as first and last name. An instance of a class, such as TimHuck, has Active Directory properties called attributes: firstname=Tim lastname=Huckaby. In the Active Directory, classes follow a simple inheritance model. When defining a class, you must declare a parent class. This class defines what attributes are *implicitly* inherited from the parent class. The figure to the right shows an example of the class hierarchy for the User Class. Notice that the class at the peak of the hierarchy tree is an object called *Top*, and that this class is the only one without a parent class.

The Active Directory **Schema** is a description of the object classes and attributes stored in the Active Directory. For each object class, the schema defines the attributes an object class must have, the additional attributes it may have, and the object class that can be its parent. For instance, the "Person" Class has one attribute that is mandatory (must have). It is cn. The Person Class has 4 attributes that are optional (may have): seeAlso, sn, telephoneNumber, userPassword. And as you saw in the Active Directory User Class Inheritance Diagram above, the "Parent" for the Person class is the Top class.

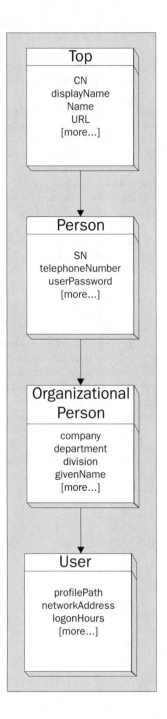

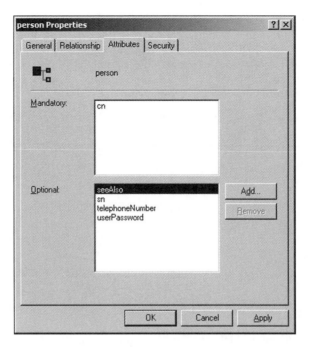

The Active Directory Schema is extensible and can be updated dynamically. For example, software developers can write applications that extend the schema with new attributes and classes, and use the extensions immediately in their applications. Schema updates are accomplished by creating or modifying the schema objects stored in the Active Directory. Like every object in the Active Directory, schema objects have an **access control list** (**ACL**), so only authorized users may alter the schema. Of course, this doesn't mean you are limited to modifications when accessing the schema programmatically. You can write code to read which attributes a particular class instance should have without making modifications.

Each class definition within the Active Directory specifies the following:

❑ The structure rules that determine the class's super-class or parent class. This is necessary to determine where to implicitly inherit from.

❑ The list of attributes that can be present in an instance of that class. For instance, the "User class" where domain users exist, has attributes available that are specific to a user, like an e-mail address. An attribute that determines the color printing capabilities of a printer would not be applicable in the User class.

❑ Which of the attributes are mandatory (*mustContain*). Examples of "Must Contain" attributes in the User class are Username and Password. Those two attributes are mandatory (there are others) for each instance of a user. A user cannot be created without persisting "Must Contain" attributes.

❑ Which of the attributes are optional (*mayContain*). Examples of "May Contain" attributes in the User class are attributes relating to the home address of the user. Attributes like the home address are not mandatory, and hence it's optional whether they are persisted or not.

Active Directory uses entities, often called objects (which should not be confused with COM Objects) to represent network resources such as users, groups, machines, devices, and application settings. Like all directory services, the Active Directory uses **containers** to represent organizations, such as the marketing department, or collections of related objects, such as printers. It organizes information in a hierarchical, tree-like structure made up of these objects and containers; similar to the way you use folders and files to organize information on your computer.

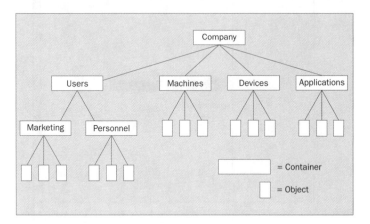

The Active Directory hierarchy is flexible and configurable, supporting the organization of resources in a way that optimizes usability and manageability. In the picture above, containers are used to represent collections of users, machines, devices, and applications. Containers can be nested (as in the case of the Marketing and Personnel containers being nested within the Users container) to reflect accurately a company's organizational structure. Nesting objects in the Active Directory facilitates the manageability of objects on a macro-level (as collections) rather than one-by-one. This, of course, increases Active Directory management efficiency because you can manage in organized groups and can leverage those objects' availability.

Directory services have object oriented properties. In Active Directory, all classes in the schema are ultimately derived from the special class called "Top". With the exception of "Top", which is often called "the top-level container", all classes are subclasses of some other class. Inheritance enables you to build new classes from existing classes. The original class becomes a super-class or "parent" of the new class. A subclass inherits the attributes of the parent, including structure rules and content rules. A class can inherit attributes from more than one parent. Structure rules define the possible hierarchical relationships between objects in the Active Directory. The structure rules are completely expressed by each Class Schema object's Poss Superiors (Possible Superiors) attribute. This attribute lists all of the possible super-class (parent) objects from which that particular object can inherit attributes.

For example, you could create a new Extranet User class that defines information about the domain users in your company, which don't specifically work in the home office or corporate headquarters. Attributes specific to these extranet users might include the location where they work, any network specific information regarding how they connect to the corporate LAN, etc. You could specify that the Extranet User class is a subclass of the User class. Because the Extranet User class would inherit all the Must Contain and May Contain attributes of the User class as well as the attributes of all of the super-classes (parent classes) of the User class, you would not have to define these attributes for the Extranet User class. The only attributes you would need to define would be the attributes specific to location and network connectivity, which would be unique for all instances of the Extranet User class.

Directory Services scale horizontally through partitioning over machines and multi-node replication. Availability in this case doesn't mean 24/7, which of course is a feature of Windows 2000. What is meant by availability is an enterprise available data store for user and application data. The Active Directory is completely integrated in Windows 2000 which means you get the security for free – no longer is a user database and security coding necessary for your enterprise applications.

What Goes in SQL Server and What Goes in the DS?

Determining what data goes into the relational database and what data goes into the directory service is a frequent source for heated debate. There is no clear-cut formula for making the distinction, but there are some concepts that can make it easier for you to decide. Relational databases like SQL Server are designed to spread performance evenly over the process of writing and reading data. For sake of explanation let's call this the "relational database 50-50 rule". Enormous amounts of engineering are done to ensure that writes to the database are accomplished just as quickly as reads. The SQL Server team at Microsoft has done this very well. Those of us in the Software Development community have been programming relational databases for so long that we have taken the "50-50 rule" for granted. I know I had, until I started programming directory services.

A directory service like the Windows 2000 Active Directory is designed quite differently. The hierarchical structure isn't simply architected to attain object-oriented properties. Hierarchical structures are designed for "lightning-quick" reads. The Windows 2000 Internet Information Server (IIS) metabase and the Windows 2000 registry are good examples of structures that were designed hierarchically to support fast access through reads. The drawback (or in this case, it might be explained as "by-product") is that the lightning fast reads accomplished with the hierarchical structure of a directory service is accomplished at the expense of some latency in the writes. For the sake of explanation, let's call this the "Directory Service 80-20 rule", which implies that reads are 4 times faster than writes, although the actual performance ratios between reads and writes is going to depend on a number of things, like the type of Directory Service, the resources available, the format of the hierarchical structure, etc. Additionally, LDAP servers have features that facilitate hosting directory services completely in memory – similar, if not identical, to the concept of "in-memory" databases. Obviously, you will see dramatic speed in reads and writes from directory services that are hosted completely in memory. I'll explore LDAP in detail later in the chapter.

So that sheds a little more light on what type of data is persisted as an *attribute* in the Directory Service and what type of data is persisted as a *field* in SQL Server:

❏ Data that is not frequently changed, and benefits from being "enterprise available", such as data specific to the user (username, password, e-mail address, home address, etc.) is more aptly placed in the directory service.

❏ Data like network resources (printers, computers, etc.) is more aptly placed in the directory service.

❏ Data like software application settings (language settings, look and feel settings, etc.) is more aptly placed in the directory service.

❏ Data that changes very frequently and does not gain benefit from being available to all software applications in the enterprise is more aptly placed in a table in a relational database like SQL Server.

Let's consider the example of designing a B2C (business-to-consumer) electronic commerce web application. As the software developer or software architect, you will want to profile your users when possible by authentication. You will *explicitly* force the users to persist data about themselves when they register on the web site: name, address, gender, favorite hobbies, age, etc. This type of data, which is entered once and is rarely ever changed, is perfect for the directory service. Additionally, and quite differently, you will want to *implicitly* profile your users also. Behind the scenes in the web application you will want to track the URLs and other resources on your web site that the user touches. You may also want to track the frequency with which a user on your web site looks at particular products. Additionally you may want to implicitly track referrals – where a visitor, or user on your web site comes from or where they leave to. Since the frequency of this type of implicitly profiled data is not controllable and has the potential for a massive amount of writes, it is perfect for a relational database like SQL Server.

So, in summary, I am not advocating an either/or scenario. You would rarely write a web application that only uses a directory service like Active Directory, without additionally using a relational database like SQL Server. Most likely, you would use them both, and persist data where it seems most suitable.

The Microsoft Commerce 2000 team figured this concept out early in their design. The Commerce 2000 User Profile System allows you, the software developer and/or software architect, to distribute data over the Active Directory and SQL Server in a fashion that makes most sense. The User Profile System contains a set of COM components that isolates you from what source the data actually lives in (Active Directory or SQL Server) so that you code to one simple interface and it handles the complexity of where the data actually lives. Additionally, you can write providers for other disparate data sources like Oracle or other directory services. At the time of writing, Commerce Server 2000 does not even have a beta version of the software yet, but industry experts are predicting that the User Profile System alone will drive enterprises to using Commerce Server 2000 whether they need the capabilities of electronic commerce or not!

The Types of Windows 2000 Directory Services

Now that you understand the purpose of directory services and why we need them, let's look at some of the different types of directory services.

Site Server 3.0 Membership

The Site Server 3.0 Membership Server provides the basic functionality to interface with an application server such as a Microsoft Internet Information Server (IIS) web site. Unlike the Windows 2000 Active Directory, multiple Membership Server instances can be configured on a given computer or on separate computers if needed. A separate Membership Server instance is required for each computer that runs an application server and/or a Lightweight Directory Access Protocol (LDAP) service. Multiple application servers on the same Windows 2000 Server can share a Membership Server if they are using the same Membership Directory Service. If they use different Membership Directory Services, then separate Membership Server instances are required. You can also implement multiple Membership Servers on the same Windows 2000 Server for applications that use the same Membership Directory. The primary features of the Site Server 3.0 Membership Directory Service are:

❑ Authentication Service – like the Active Directory, IIS 5.0 web site users can be authenticated against the Site Server 3.0 Membership Server

❏ AUO – the Active User Object, a COM component that which makes Membership Directory Service access easy, presents a convenient, unified set of user attributes across all data sources. The AUO can integrate data from one or more Membership Directories and from additional sources such as your pre-existing databases, creating a virtual user attribute schema that can be accessed from any script or program. An application can access the properties of the current user without having to worry about how to identify the user, where and how the user's properties are stored, or whether the user's properties need to be shared with another server or client. The AUO object has a simple programming interface and is extremely robust with features, but because it is simply a wrapper on ADSI, it has performance issues that prevent it from scaling under large membership community scenarios.

❏ LDAP Service – this service provides a Lightweight Directory Access Protocol (LDAP) version 3.0 interface for industry standard, platform-independent access to the Membership Directory by Microsoft Site Server version 3.0 and by other LDAP-capable software.

❏ Site Server Message Builder Service – a service that is responsible for building Direct Mail messages and sending them to a Simple Mail Transfer Protocol (SMTP) server for delivery.

The installation of Site Server 3.0 Membership is simple through a custom install on the Knowledge Management portion of Site Server. A simple patch, downloadable from the Microsoft site, (http://www.Microsoft.com/siteserver) facilitates an easy installation of the product on Windows 2000. Site Server Service Pack 3 (or SP4) is required for proper operation. Site Server 3.0 Membership (even multiple instances) can coexist peacefully on the same Windows 2000 Server hosting the Active Directory as long as they are not installed on the same LDAP port (Active Directory lives on port 389 and cannot be changed).

The Windows 2000 Active Directory

Active Directory is the directory service used in Windows 2000 Server and is the foundation of Windows 2000 distributed networks. It's an enterprise-available data store for the management of security and resources. Active Directory is a Directory Service that is much more robust than simply a place to persist information about your users.

Active Directory stores information about objects on the network and makes this information easy for administrators and users to find and use. The Active Directory directory service uses a structured data store as the basis for a logical, hierarchical organization of directory information.

Security is integrated with Active Directory through logon authentication and access control to objects in the directory. With a single network logon, administrators can manage directory data and organization throughout their network, and authorized network users can access resources anywhere on the network. Policy-based administration eases the management of even the most complex network.

The primary features of the Windows 2000 Active Directory are:

❏ **Security** – is fully integrated with Active Directory. Access control can be defined not only on each object in the directory but also on each property of each object. Active Directory provides both the store and the scope of the application for security policies. A security policy can include account information, such as domain-wide password restrictions or rights to particular domain resources. Security policies are implemented through Group Policy settings in Windows 2000.

453

❑ **Policy-based administration** – Active Directory includes both a data store and a logical, hierarchical structure. As a logical structure, it provides a hierarchy of contexts for the application of policy. As a directory service, it stores the policies (called Group Policy objects) that are assigned to a particular context. A Group Policy object expresses a set of business rules containing settings that, for the context to which it is applied, can determine:

   ❑ Access to directory service objects and domain resources

   ❑ What domain resources (such as applications) are available to users

   ❑ How these domain resources are configured for use

❑ **Extensibility** – Active Directory is extensible, which means that administrators can add new classes of objects to the schema and can add new attributes to existing classes of objects through tools, and software developers can accomplish the same tasks with code.

❑ **Scalability** – Active Directory includes one or more domains, each with one or more **domain controllers**, enabling you to scale the directory to meet any network requirements. Multiple domains can be combined into a domain **tree** and multiple domain trees can be combined into a **forest**. The directory distributes its schema and configuration information to all domain controllers in the directory. This information is stored in the initial domain controller for a domain and replicated to any additional domain controllers in the domain. When the directory is configured as a single domain, adding domain controllers scales the directory without the administrative overhead involved with additional domains. Adding domains to the directory enables you to partition the directory for different policy contexts and scale the directory to accommodate a large number of resources and objects.

❑ **Replication** – provides information availability, fault tolerance, load balancing, and performance benefits for the directory. Active Directory uses "multimaster" replication, enabling you to update the directory at any domain controller, rather than at a single, primary domain controller. The multimaster model has the benefit of greater fault tolerance since, with multiple domain controllers, replication continues, even if any single domain controller stops working.

❑ **Integration with DNS** – Active Directory uses the **Domain Name System** (**DNS**). DNS is an Internet standard service that translates easily readable host names, such as `TimHuck.InterKnowlogy.com`, to numeric IP addresses. This enables identification and connection to processes running on computers on TCP/IP networks. Domain names for DNS are based on the DNS hierarchical naming structure, which is an inverted tree structure: a single root domain, underneath which can be parent and child domains (branches and leaves). For example, a Windows 2000 domain name such as `child.parent.InterKnowlogy.com` identifies a domain named "`child`," that is a child domain of the domain named "`parent`," itself a child of the root domain "`InterKnowlogy.com`".

❑ **Interoperability with other directory services** – Because Active Directory is based on standard directory access protocols, such as Lightweight Directory Access Protocol (LDAP) version 3, and the Name Service Provider Interface (NSPI), it can interoperate with other directory services employing these protocols, like Site Server 3.0 Membership, or the Netscape Directory Service, and others.

The Windows 2000 Site Server ILS Service

If there's one technology in Windows 2000 that I really want to dig into, it's the **Internet Locator Service** (**ILS**) service. But, at the time of writing it's barely documented and unfortunately there's no SDK available. The Windows 2000 Site Server ILS is a special instance of the Site Server 3.0 Membership directory service that is persisted dynamically in RAM. Be careful, because if you install and run the SiteServer ILS service it will service its LDAP requests on port 1002, which is where, by default, the Site Server Default Membership Server lives. The programmatic interface for ILS is standard ADSI. As you can see from the screen shot below, there is a command line interface to configure the Site Server ILS. With this tool you can change it's default port of 1002 to another available port.

```
Command Prompt                                                    _ □ x

D:\WINNT\system32>ilscfg

    ILS Configuration Utility
    Copyright 1997, 1998 - Microsoft Corporation

    Commands for server configuration:
        ilscfg [<server>] /port       <port number>
        ilscfg [<server>] /sslport    <port number>
        ilscfg [<server>] /timeout    <timeout length in seconds>
        ilscfg [<server>] /maxresults < size of largest allowable search
                                       result set, or 0 for no limit>
    Commands for publishing of ILS servers in the NTDS:
        ilscfg            /listpub
        ilscfg <server>   /publish   [<port>]
        ilscfg <server>   /unpublish [<port>]
    Commands for listing conferences or users from an ILS server:
        ilscfg <server>   /listconf  [<port>]
        ilscfg <server>   /listuser  [<port>]

D:\WINNT\system32>ilscfg /listpub
ILS server: timhucknotebook.TimHuck.com, Port:1002
Found 1 service(s).
D:\WINNT\system32>_
```

Active Directory Service Interfaces (ADSI)

Active Directory Service Interfaces (**ADSI**) are the programming interfaces we have available to access directory services. ADSI is the "language" of the directory service. ADSI provides a simple, powerful, object-oriented interface to Active Directory and other directory services. ADSI makes it easy for programmers and administrators to create software that accesses directory services like the Active Directory by using high-level tools such as Microsoft Visual Basic, Java, C, Visual C++, and scripting languages without having to worry about the underlying differences between the different namespaces (Active Directory, Site Server 3.0 Membership, Netscape Directory Server, and so on). ADSI is a set of COM interfaces used to access the capabilities of directory services from different network providers in a distributed computing environment. ADSI delivers a single set of directory service interfaces for managing network resources. Administrators and software developers can use ADSI services to enumerate and manage the resources in a directory service, no matter which network environment contains the resource.

ADSI makes it easier to perform common administrative tasks, such as adding new users, managing printers, and locating resources throughout an enterprise environment.

x.500, the Origins of the DS

The origins of the ADSI standards we have today come from **x.500,** which is a messaging standard designed to provide a global directory that defines the global directory structure and directory access. Many software developers and network administrators who see ADSI in code for the first time are intimidated by its strange syntax which you will see later in this section. Thankfully, as discussed earlier, Active Directory and DNS are tightly integrated so access to containers in the Active Directory has a fairly straightforward look. The sample code below is a simple active server page that uses ADSI to retrieve attributes from the Active Directory, or from any LDAP 3.0 compatible directory service, for that matter.

Examine the line of code below closely. Pay special attention to the page-level ADSI – especially where the string strObject is assigned a value.

```
strObject = "LDAP://CN=Tim Huckaby,CN=Users,DC=timhuck,DC=com"
```

Historically, ADSI programmers have not had the luxury of tight DNS integration in directory services. Without DNS integration, Directory Service NameSpaces had to be specifically referenced by server name and port number. For instance, the same line of an ASP to access the Site Server 3.0 Membership Directory Service would look like:

```
strObject = "LDAP://InterKnowlogyDC:1003/o=InterKnowlogy/ou=Members/" & _
                "cn=Tim_Huckaby"
```

First an object reference is made to the ADSI IADs interface. Then the groups that a user belongs to are enumerated. Finally the "displayName" and "givenName" attributes are retrieved from the Active Directory and rendered to the browser.

```
<%@ Language=VBScript %>
<HTML>
<HEAD>
<META NAME="GENERATOR" Content="Microsoft Visual Studio 6.0">
</HEAD>
<BODY>

<P> </P>

<%
   Option Explicit
   Dim objADs
   Dim varAttribute, varElement
   Dim strObject

   'use the Get method on the IADs interface to retrieve attributes from AD
   'AD Users Container
   strObject = "LDAP://CN=Tim Huckaby,CN=Users,DC=timhuck,DC=com"
   Response.Write("Active Directory Object: <STRONG>" & _
      strObject & "</STRONG><BR><BR>")

   Set objADs = GetObject(strObject)

   Response.Write("<STRONG>Active Directory memberOf: </STRONG><BR>")
   'groups attribute in AD is "memberOf"
   varAttribute = objADs.Get("memberOf")
```

The **TypeName** function returns a string that provides the Variant subtype information about a variable. I use this function in debugging because, as you can see, from the the code snippet below, a multi-valued attribute is returned as a **Variant()**. At the page level, you can iterate through a variant array with **For Each**.

```
Response.Write("Type: " & TypeName (varAttribute) & "<BR>")

For Each varElement in varAttribute
  Response.Write(varElement) & "<BR>"
Next

Response.Write("<BR>Type: " & TypeName(objADs.Get ("displayName")) _
  & "<BR>")
Response.Write("givenName: " & objADs.Get("givenName"))

Set objADs = Nothing

%>
</BODY>
</HTML>
```

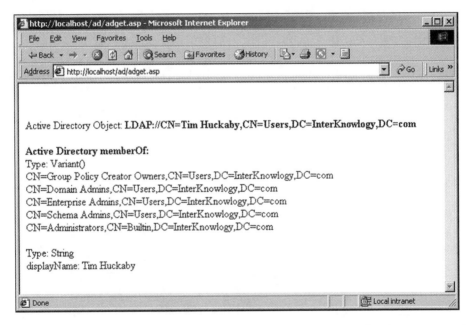

ADSI uses an LDAP provider to communicate with the Active Directory and is the recommended API for programming to directory services. LDAP is the high-level protocol that handles Directory Service requests and ADSI is the programming interface for Directory Service.

Lightweight Directory Access Protocol (LDAP)

Lightweight Directory Access Protocol (LDAP) is a communication protocol designed for use on TCP/IP networks. LDAP defines how a directory client can access a directory server and how the client can perform directory operations and share directory data. LDAP standards are established by working groups of the **Internet Engineering Task Force** (**IETF**). Active Directory implements the LDAP attribute draft specifications and the IETF standards for LDAP versions 2 and 3. In this light, LDAP can be considered the "Universal Translator". It doesn't matter what directory service you are programming to, the same ADSI code is translated for you by LDAP so that we have a common interface to all LDAP version 3.0 compliant directory services like Active Directory, Site Server 3.0 Membership, Windows 2000 ILS or other non Microsoft Directory Services like the ones provided by Novell, Netscape and IBM. This concept is similar to the ANSI standard SQL dialect – the very same SQL statement that works on Microsoft SQL Server works on Oracle.

As its name implies, LDAP is designed as an efficient method for accessing directory services without the complexity of other directory service protocols. Because LDAP defines what operations can be performed to query and modify information in a directory and how information in a directory can be securely accessed, you can use LDAP to find or enumerate directory objects and to query or administer Active Directory, Site Server 3.0 Membership, Windows 2000 ILS or other non Microsoft Directory Services like the ones provided by Novell, Netscape and IBM.

You are, of course, familiar with Microsoft Internet Explorer's ability to facilitate HTTP requests (such as `http://www.InterKnowlogy.com`). You may also be familiar with Microsoft Internet Explorer's ability to service FTP requests (`ftp://ftp.Microsoft.com`). But did you know that the Microsoft Internet Explorer browser is able to service LDAP requests? I have a Site Server 3.0 Membership Directory Service running on my notebook. If I type "ldap://timhucknotebook:1003/", Internet Explorer will prompt a search dialog like in the screen below:

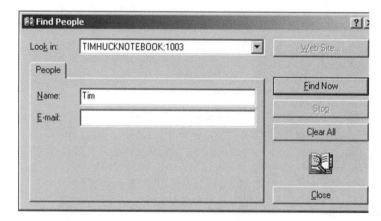

If I type Tim into the Name field and click Find Now, Internet Explorer will do a search of the Directory Service for me and return the results:

Now, if I click the Properties button, Internet Explorer will actually enumerate the attributes persisted in the Directory Service!

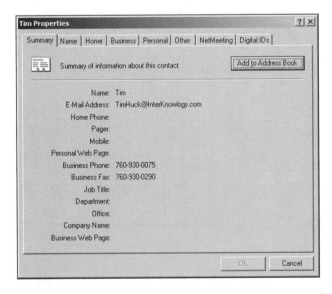

That is pretty cool functionality! Did you ever wonder why Microsoft Internet Explorer is 85+ MB? Well, it's because it has tons of functionality, like the ability to search a directory service. Now, it's important to note that a Membership Server created with Microsoft Site Server 3.0 has anonymous access enabled by default. Anonymous access facilitates the ability to successfully search within a Directory Service. The Active Directory comes "locked down" by default, so you wouldn't be able to search it without specifically configuring it for anonymous access.

Typically, LDAP functionality is provided by the LDAP Service feature of the directory service. The LDAP Service can be located physically on the same computer as the application server, on a standalone computer, or on the same computer as the Directory Service data. In the case of Site Server 3.0 Membership, sites can deploy one or more LDAP Services, as performance requirements dictate.

Any authorized LDAP-capable application, tool, or script running with appropriate credentials on any operating system platform can log on to an LDAP Service and access Directory Service information. The LDAP Service provides standard operations to search the Directory Service and retrieve, edit, add, and delete attributes. Both persistent and dynamic data in the Directory Service are read and written using LDAP. The LDAP Service also works with the Authentication Service to provide authentication and access control for the contents of the Directory Service.

Directory Service Tools

There are several tools that will aid you in your programming of directory services. I have chosen to highlight the most popular (hence the most powerful) ones here. As you get more adept with directory services, you will almost undoubtedly write your own tools. For instance, the Active Directory Users and Computers tool is an MMC snap-in that is used to manage data in the Active Directory, but it is extremely cumbersome to use for data entry. At InterKnowlogy we have written a web-based application (which uses the middle tier components explained later in the chapter) to manage the process of data entry more efficiently and more effectively for our clients.

Active Directory Users and Computers Tool

The **Active Directory Users and Computers** tool is an MMC snap-in that enables you to add, modify, delete, and organize the Windows 2000 user accounts, computer accounts, security and distribution groups, and published resources in your organization's Active Directory directory service.

Active Directory Users and Computers is a directory administration tool installed on computers configured as domain controllers. It is also available for installation with the optional Administration Tools package. This package can be installed on Windows 2000 Professional computers to enable you to administer Active Directory from a computer that is not a domain controller.

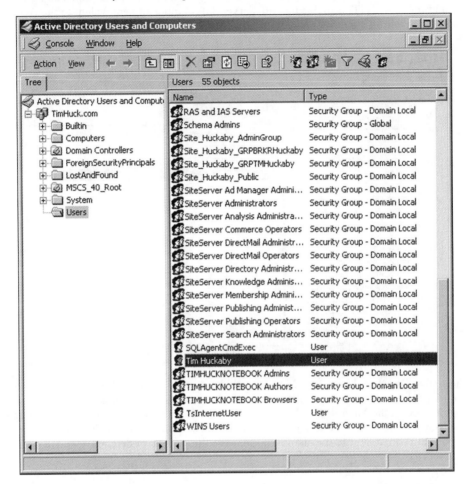

To use Active Directory Users and Computers you must be logged on to a Windows 2000 domain (not the local computer) and have sufficient privileges to perform the particular operation you are attempting. Members of the Users group have some privileges by default, while members of other groups may have additional privileges. Members of the Account Operators group, for example, can create and delete user accounts. Members of the Administrators group have additional privileges.

Membership Directory Manager

The Site Server 3.0 **Membership Directory Manager** (**MDM**) is an administrative tool (MMC snap-in) that manages all aspects of the Membership Directory Service, including accounts and groups, access control, and the schema. This tool is the Site Server 3.0 Membership equivalent to the Active Directory Users and Computers Tool described above.

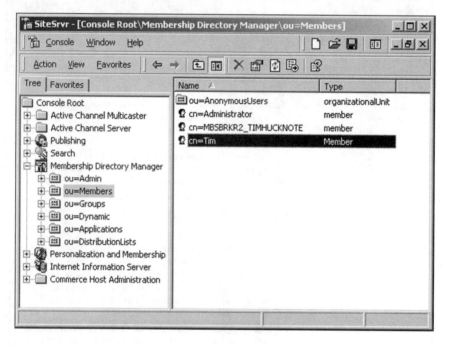

Like the Active Directory Users and Computers tool, which is also an MMC snap-in that enables you to add, modify, delete, and organize the Windows 2000 user accounts, computer accounts, security and distribution groups, the Membership Directory Manager is cumbersome to use for Data Entry. Just as we have, you will most likely choose to write a web-based application (which uses the middle tier components explained later in the chapter) to manage the process of data entry efficiently in your directory service.

Personalization and Membership MMC

The Site Server 3.0 **Personalization and Membership** MMC snap-in is an administrative tool that manages the LDAP server.

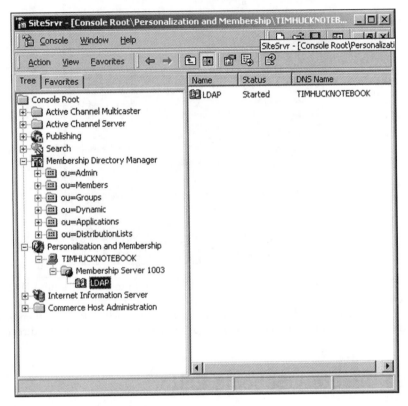

The LDAP Service element of a Membership Server provides the link between the Membership Server and the Membership Directory. Any client that accesses the Membership Directory must do so by logging on to an LDAP Service connected to that directory.

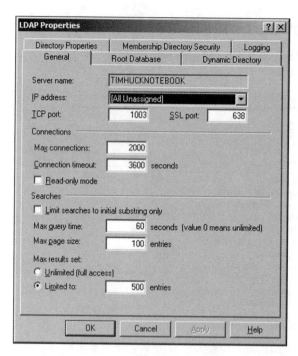

You can use the Personalization and Membership MMC snap-in to configure the LDAP Service. These settings include the service's physical location, limitations on search queries, the identity and location of the service's target database, and the internal Membership Directory security (authentication method and access defaults). You can also specify whether or not there will be a dynamic directory and if so, how it will be set up.

The Active Directory Schema Editor

For development and testing purposes, the Active Directory Schema Editor will allow you to view the Active Directory Schema without having to make modifications. The recommended way to extend the Active Directory schema is programmatically, through the Active Directory Service Interfaces (ADSI).

Adding attributes to the Active Directory Schema is non-reversible. Take caution in what you do on production systems. Schema Attributes can be marked as "non-useable", but they cannot be removed once they are added. It's best to have an Active Directory available in a test environment (ideally on a different network wire) so that you can test your changes before putting them into production.

There are two types of definitions in the Active Directory schema: **attributes** and **classes**. Attributes and classes are also referred to as schema **objects** or **metadata**.

❑ Attributes are defined separately from classes. Each attribute is defined only once and can be used in multiple classes. For example, the Description attribute is used in many classes, but is defined once in the schema, ensuring consistency.

❑ Classes, also referred to as object classes, describe the possible directory objects that can be created. Each class is a collection of attributes. When you create an object, the attributes store the information that describes the object. The User class, for example, is composed of many attributes, including Network Address, Home Directory, and so on. Every object in Active Directory is an instance of an object class.

A set of basic classes and attributes are supplied with Windows 2000 Server. Experienced developers and network administrators can dynamically extend the schema by defining new classes and new attributes for existing classes. Active Directory does not support deletion of schema objects; however, objects can be marked as deactivated, providing many of the benefits of deletion.

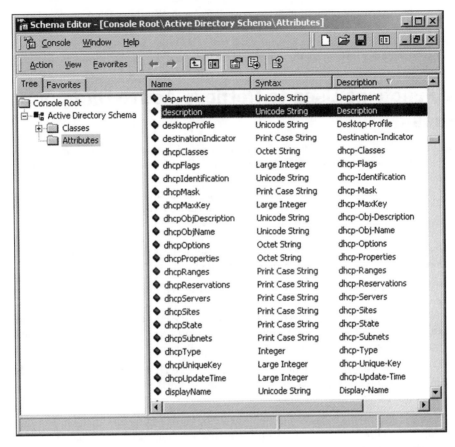

Because of the potentially disastrous ramifications of editing or extending the Active Directory Schema, the Active Directory Schema Editor is not installed by default, but can be installed by following the instructions included in a number of places, including the Active Directory Developers Reference Library available through Microsoft Press.

Programming the Directory Service

Now that you have covered all the fundamentals of Directory Services, let's write some code! A powerful and robust component that you will need for your Windows DNA application, should be able to search the Active Directory and be able to read from and write to the Active Directory. This component will most definitely need three public methods:

❑   Search the Active Directory for a user

❑   Read attributes from the Active Directory

❑   Write attributes to the Active Directory

The encapsulation of these three methods, which each access the Active Directory, into a middle-tier component will serve two purposes:

❑ Isolate the seemingly "rocket science" from your page-level developers

❑ Provide the reusable functionality you need for your Windows DNA application

The code for this component can be downloaded from the Wrox web site at http://www.wrox.com. I suggest you download it now so that it will be easier to follow the explanation.

Private Functions Used to Retrieve Active Directory Properties

First, there are five properties that you will need to access the Active Directory programmatically. All three of the public methods on this COM component will need some or all of these properties in order to function. I have chosen to persist these values in the registry and read them from that location with internal, private functions, but you could just as easily change the interface to pass them in as optional parameters. Obviously, I could have hard-coded these values in the component itself, but that would necessitate a code change in the component for each installation. These values are:

❑ strServerName – the name of the server hosting the Active Directory. The private function that retrieves its value from the registry is called GetServer.

❑ strPortNumber – the port number on which the Windows 2000 LDAP server is listening to service requests to the Active Directory. By default the Active Directory is serviced on port 389 and that cannot be changed, but other directory services, like Site Server 3.0 Membership, allow their LDAP servers to live on any TCP/IP port that's available. The private function that retrieves its value from the registry is called GetPort.

❑ strAdminName – the name of the user in the Active Directory that will be used to securely bind to the Directory Service. The private function that retrieves its value from the registry is called GetUser.

❑ strPassword – the password of the user in the Active Directory that will be used to securely bind to the Directory Service. The private function that retrieves its value from the registry is called GetPassword.

❑ strDN – the fully qualified **Distinguished Name (DN)** of the user in the Active Directory that will be used to securely bind to the Directory Service. An example of a DN is: CN=Administrator,CN=Users,DC=TimHuck,DC=com. Every entity in Active Directory has a fully qualified DN that follows the structure of the schema. Take special notice ofthe screen shot opposite. It is the ADSI Edit tool that shows the Active Directory in a "Tree Control" view. It does a good job in displaying how the DNs are formed:

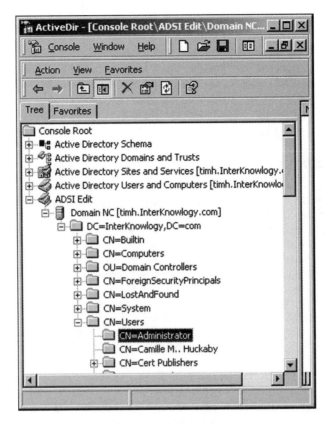

The private function that retrieves its value from the registry is called GetDN.

The format of these private functions is simple. I have included a Visual Basic module in my project called modRegAccess.bas which includes three internal functions to read values from the registry. I simply call the GetRegKey function with the Registry Key and String Value Name of the value I want returned. Here is the format of the GetServer private function:

```
Private Function GetServer() As Variant

   GetServer = GetRegKey("SOFTWARE\InterKnowlogy\Directory Services\Active @ _
                        & "Directory", "server")

End Function
```

In a chapter on the Active Directory it is, of course, out of scope to explain the code behind "digging the registry". I could have compiled the modRegAccess functions into their own standalone COM+ component. This would provide the ability to reuse that registry access functionality in other COM+ components and Active Server Pages that we write. This would be the "right" way to do it. If I had a standalone registry reader component, I could simply "wrap" its functionality in the Active Directory COM+ component (or any other component that needs registry read access). But, for the sake of explanation and so that you can get up and running quickly and easily, without having a dependency on another COM+ component, I have included the code within the Active Directory component project.

Private Functions Used to Connect to the Active Directory

There are two internal, private functions (which use the parameters retrieved from the registry as described above) that connect to the Windows 2000 Active Directory. These private functions are used in the three public methods (which search, read, and write to and from the Active Directory). They are:

- ❑ GetRootObjectName
- ❑ GetRootDomainNamingContext

GetRootObjectName

GetRootObjectName derives the DNS Host name of the Active Directory that you connect to. I have a notebook computer with Windows 2000 Advanced Server installed that I use for demonstrations, testing, development, etc. It hosts an Active Directory. I do not expose it to the Internet, so I have "made up" an Internet domain called "TimHuck.com". Windows 2000's internal DNS server resolves "TimHuck.com" to the static IP address that I have given to my notebook computer. On my notebook computer, the private function GetRootObjectName returns the variant (which is cast to a string) "timhucknotebook.TimHuck.com". I also have a user account on the Microsoft Corporate LAN. When I authenticate in the Microsoft Corporate Active Directory, I am authenticating on the DNS Host "NorthAmerica.Microsoft.Com". One of the great features of Active Directory is the tight integration with the operating system. Windows 2000 can resolve DNS names to the Active Directory. In other Directory Services, like Site Server 3.0 Membership or the Netscape Directory Service, the root object name has the x.500 syntax which starts with "o=". In other words "o=Microsoft".

The interface for GetRootObjectName is:

```
Private Function GetRootObjectName(ByVal strServerName As String, _
                                   ByVal strPortNumber As String) As String
```

You can see that GetRootObjectName takes two parameters, the name of the server that the Active Directory is hosted on and the port number of the LDAP Server, which is serving the Active Directory requests.

First, I dimension the variables that I will need in the GetRootObjectName private function. Of note are the two objects objADsBase and objADs. Windows 2000 Active Directory has exposed the IADs interface of ADSI. ADSI has other interfaces, which need not be explained here. I have included a reference to the Active DS Type Library in my Visual Basic project, which makes the IADs interface available. I have dimensioned these two objects of the type IADs. The IADs ADSI programming interface allows me to treat objects in the Active Directory as containers.

```
   Dim objADsBase, objADs As ActiveDs.IADs
   Dim strADsPath As String
   Dim strPassword As String        ' DS Administrator User Password
   Dim strDN As String              ' Distinguished Name of the DS Admin User
```

Next I dig the registry for the password and Distinguished Name because I will need them later in the function to securely bind to the directory service. I also set up some error handling to catch exceptions:

```
   strPassword = GetPassword()
   strDN = GetDN()

   On Error GoTo ExitGetRootObjectName
```

The next three lines of code (not counting the comments) are the heart of the function.

First I build an AdsPath to the "rootDSE" of the Active Directory. The root of the directory tree is called `rootDSE`, or directory root. `rootDSE` is an "imaginary" object that has no hierarchical name or schema class, but it does have a set of attributes that identify the contents of a given domain controller (that is `dnsHostname`). Thus, `rootDSE` constitutes the root of the directory tree from the perspective of the domain controller to which you are connected. In the case of the Active Directory running on my notebook computer, the `strADsPath` resolves to: "LDAP://timhucknotebook:389/rootDSE".

```
' build the ADS Path string
strADsPath = "LDAP://" & strServerName & ":" & strPortNumber & "/rootDSE"
```

Secondly, I call "`GetObject`" on the LDAP Server. This gives me a context on the base object of the LDAP Server to which I am going to connect.

```
' get base object
Set objADsBase = GetObject("LDAP:")
```

Thirdly, I use the base object to securely bind to the Active Directory with the ADSI `OpenDSObject` method.

```
' securely open the DS object
Set objADs = objADsBase.OpenDSObject (strADsPath, strDN, strPassword, 0)
```

> It is important to note that the **OpenDSObject** method is <u>not</u> a method that I have written and included in my Visual Basic project. It is a standard method provided by ADSI and available because I have included a reference to the Active DS Type Library in my Visual Basic project. This is the same syntax that you would use to bind securely to any directory service including those that are not Microsoft Directory Services. LDAP, the universal translator, handles the slight nuances seamlessly for you so that the same code base can access a number of disparate directory services.

I send the `OpenDSObject` method 4 parameters:

❑ `strADsPath` – the ADsPath to the rootDSE as described above (that is `LDAP://timhucknotebook:389/rootDSE`).

❑ `strDN` – the fully qualified domain name of the user that I want to bind to the Active Directory with (that is `CN=Administrator,CN=Users,DC=TimHuck,DC=com`).

❑ `strPassword` – the password of the user that I am using for binding to the Active Directory.

❑ The fourth parameter specifies the authentication options used in ADSI for binding to directory service objects. The code below shows the authentication options enumerated:

```
typedef enum {
    ADS_SECURE_AUTHENTICATION   = 0x1,
    ADS_USE_ENCRYPTION          = 0x2,
    ADS_USE_SSL                 = 0x2,
    ADS_READONLY_SERVER         = 0x4,
```

```
ADS_PROMPT_CREDENTIALS       = 0x8,
ADS_NO_AUTHENTICATION        = 0x10,
ADS_FAST_BIND                = 0x20,
ADS_USE_SIGNING              = 0x40,
ADS_USE_SEALING              = 0x80
} ADS_AUTHENTICATION_ENUM;
```

Where:

ADS_SECURE_AUTHENTICATION - Requests secure authentication. From the MSDN documentation: When this flag is set, Active Directory will use Kerberos, and possibly NTLM, to authenticate the client. When the user name and password are NULL, ADSI binds to the object using the security context of the calling thread, which is either the security context of the user account under which the application is running or of the client user account that the calling thread is impersonating.

ADS_USE_ENCRYPTION – Forces ADSI to use encryption for data exchange over the network.

ADS_USE_SSL – Encrypts the channel with SSL. Data will be encrypted using SSL. Active Directory requires that the Certificate Server be installed to support SSL encryption.

ADS_READONLY_SERVER – For Active Directory, this flag indicates that a "writeable" server is not required for a serverless binding.

ADS_PROMPT_CREDENTIALS – User credentials are prompted when the authentication is initiated, if the selected **Security Support Provider Interface** (**SSPI**) provides a user interface to do so.

ADS_NO_AUTHENTICATION – Request no authentication. Active Directory establishes a connection between the client and the targeted object, but will not perform any authentication. Setting this flag amounts to requesting an anonymous binding, which means "Everyone" as the security context.

ADS_FAST_BIND – When this flag is set, ADSI will not attempt to query the `objectClass` property and thus will only expose the base interfaces supported by all ADSI objects instead of the full object support. A user can use this option to boost the performance in a series of object manipulations that involve only methods of the base interfaces. However, ADSI will not verify if any of the request objects actually exist on the server.

ADS_USE_SIGNING – Verifies data integrity to ensure that the data received is the same as the data sent. The ADS_SECURE_AUTHENTICATION flag must be set also in order to use the signing.

ADS_USE_SEALING – Encrypts data using Kerberos. The `ADS_SECURE_AUTHENTICATION` flag must be set also in order to use the sealing.

Now that I have securely bound to the Active Directory I can retrieve the `dnsHostName` by doing a simple ADSI "Get" method. I assign the value of the `dnsHostName` to the function so that it will be returned properly, destroy my objects, and get out:

```
' get the DNS host name from the Active Directory
GetRootObjectName = objADs.Get("dnsHostName")

' destroy the objects
Set objADs = Nothing
Set objADsBase = Nothing

Exit Function
```

GetRootDomainNamingContext

`GetRootDomainNamingContext` derives the Organization name of the Active Directory that you connect to by doing an ADSI "Get" on the "`defaultNamingContext`" of the Active Directory. The syntax and functionality are identical to the previous private function, `GetRootObjectName`, as described above so I won't go into details on the secure binding and format of the function.

On my notebook computer, the private function `GetRootDomainNamingContext` returns the variant (which is cast to a string) "`DC=TimHuck,DC=com`".

The interface for `GetRootDomainNamingContext` is:

```
Private Function GetRootDomainNamingContext(ByVal strServerName As String, _
                          ByVal strPortNumber As String) As String
```

You can see that `GetRootObjectName` takes two parameters, the name of the server that the Active Directory is hosted on and the port number of the **LDAP Server**, which is serving the Active Directory requests.

Upon securely binding to the Active Directory, as described above, I can retrieve the `defaultNamingContext` by doing a simple ADSI "Get" method. I assign the value of the `defaultNamingContext` to the function so that it will be returned properly, destroy my objects and get out:

```
' get the organization name from the Active Directory
GetRootDomainNamingContext = objADs.Get("defaultNamingContext")   'this is AD

' destroy the objects
Set objADs = Nothing
Set objADsBase = Nothing

Exit Function
```

The Public Functions

Now let's get to the "meat" of the code where all the functionality lives. Reading and writing from the Active Directory requires knowing the fully qualified domain name of the object (or container) in which a user lives. Before you can read or write properties in the Active Directory you need to derive, build, or search for the user container. An example of a fully qualified user object is:

```
LDAP://timhucknotebook.TimHuck.com/CN=Tim Huckaby,CN=Users,DC=TimHuck,DC=com
```

Now, you see the reason for the `GetRootObjectName` and `GetRootDomainNamingContext` private functions. They help in building the fully qualified user object string.

Thankfully, ADO 2.5 (Active Data Objects) has a provider for searching the Active Directory. It makes searching the Active Directory quite a bit easier than manually having to iterate though each container looking for objects that match your search criteria.

Each of the three public methods (`ADOSearch`, `GetAttribute`, and `SetAttribute`) is dissected and explained in detail below.

ADOSearch

The purpose of the public function `ADOSearch` is to use the ADO provider for directory services to return the results of a search in the Active Directory in the form of an ADO recordset or a stream of Attribute Normal XML.

> **There is a weakness in using the ADO 2.6 provider for Directory Services to search the Active Directory. The interface is unable to deal with multi-valued attributes. This is a major weakness that hopefully will be rectified in the next version of ADO. For now, if you want to return multi-valued attributes from this function, you will have to hard-code some form of solution. There is an OLEBD provider which supports searching the directory service in T-SQL like syntax. It supports multi-valued attributes nicely, but doesn't allow you the quick conversion from a recordset to an XML stream.**

The interface for `ADOSearch` is:

```
Public Function ADOSearch(Optional ByVal FieldList As String, _
                          Optional ByVal strWhere As String, _
                          Optional ByVal strXML As String = "") As Variant
```

You can see that `ADOSearch` takes three optional parameters:

❑ `FieldList` – a list of attributes to return from the Active Directory. This is not the display name of the attribute, but the actual attribute name, (in other words "cn, sn, name, distinguishedName").

❑ `strWhere` – the SQL equivalent to building a filter or defining criteria for searching the Active Directory. For example, to limit or filter the search to objects in the Active Directory who's user name begins with "T" and are of the object class "user" and object category "person" you would use the filter syntax:
`(&(objectCategory=person)(objectClass=user)(cn=T*))`

❑ strXML – a flag used to control whether a stream of XML is returned from the function or an ADO recordset (which is the default).

First, I dimension the variables that I will need in the ADOSearch public function. Of note are the ADO objects that I will use to utilize the ADO provider for Directory Services. For the majority of you who are familiar with using ADO to access Microsoft SQL Server, the Connection, Command, and Recordset objects will look very familiar.

```
Dim ObjCon As New ADODB.Connection
Dim ocommand As New ADODB.Command
Dim rs As New ADODB.Recordset
```

After setting up some error handling to catch exceptions, I dig the registry for the server name and port number. I will need them later to build the LDAP server string, which is the basis for the search.

```
On Error GoTo ExitADOSearch

'dig the registry for the server vars
strServerName = GetServer()
strPortNumber = GetPort()
```

Next, I call the internal private function GetRootDomainNamingContext, which derives the Organization name of the Active Directory that I am searching (in this case "DC=TimHuck,DC=com"). Upon deriving the Organization name I simply wrap the string with "<LDAP://   >", which is the syntax for the ADO provider that I am using.

```
strRootDomainNamingContext = GetRootDomainNamingContext(strServerName,_
   strPortNumber)

' build the local LDAP server and ADS Path prefix strings
strLDAPServer = "<" & "LDAP://" & strRootDomainNamingContext & ">"
```

Now, I create the ADO Connection and Command objects. Take notice of the syntax of the ADO provider for the Active Directory. It is different, of course, from the provider for SQL Server.

```
'Create ADO connection object for Active Directory
Set ObjCon = CreateObject("ADODB.Connection")
ObjCon.Provider = "ADsDSOObject"
ObjCon.CursorLocation = adUseClient
ObjCon.Open "Active Directory Provider"

'Create ADO command object for the connection.
Set ocommand = CreateObject("ADODB.Command")
ocommand.ActiveConnection = ObjCon
```

Now that I have my ADO Connection and Command objects defined, I can start building the command string that I will use to execute the query with the ADO Execute method of the Command object. The command string has a strange syntax that does not resemble ADSI, or anything else that I have seen, for that matter. When I'm done building the string in code it will look something like this:

```
<LDAP://DC=TimHuck,DC=com>;(&(objectCategory=person)(objectClass=user)(cn=T*));cn,
sn, name, distinguishedName;subTree
```

If you stare closely at the syntax, you can see that there are four parameters separated by semicolons.

1. The root level domain controller hosting the Active Directory
(`<LDAP://DC=TimHuck,DC=com>`)

2. The types of active directory classes that contain a description of what is to be searched
for (`((objectCategory=person)(objectClass=user)(cn=T*))`)

3. The attributes you want returned in the results (`cn`, `sn`, `name`, `distinguishedName`)

4. The depth of the search you want to perform, as described below (`subTree`)

First I will build the filter element or search criteria. Notice that if I do not send the optional parameter, `strWhere`, then by default the filter will search the Active Directory for objects with a category of Person and a class of User. Examples of what I might send in this parameter are `cn=*` (which means give me everybody) or `st=*` (which means give me everybody who has the state attribute populated).

```
'Build the filter element of the commandtext
If (strWhere = "") Then
   sFilter = "(&(objectCategory=person)(objectClass=user))"
Else
   sFilter = "(&(objectCategory=person)(objectClass=user)(" & strWhere & "))"
End If
```

Next, I populate the list of attributes that I want returned in my search of the Active Directory. If I choose not to specify attributes by not sending the optional field list parameter to the function, then by default I get the `cn`, `ADsPath`, and `distinguishedName` in my result set.

```
' If no fields sent, return the cn, distinguishedName and the ADsPath
If Len(FieldList) = 0 Then
   FieldList = "cn, ADsPath, distinguishedName"
End If
```

Next, I build the depth element of the command text. With this ADO provider I can specify the depth or scope that I want to search the Active Directory. The choices for the depth element are:

❑ A "subtree" search (or a deep search) includes all the objects excluding the base object. This search may generate referrals to other servers. This search has the greatest scope and may return a very large result set.

❑ A "base" search limits the search to only the base object. The maximum number of objects returned is always one. This search is useful to verify the existence of an object for retrieving group membership.

❑ A "one-level" search is restricted to the immediate children of a base object, but excludes the base object itself. This setting can perform a targeted search for immediate child objects of a parent object. For example, if you have an object's distinguished name, and you need to verify the object's existence based on the path, you can use a one-level search.

I have not chosen to use the other scope options, "base" and "one-level" in my component, but that might be a nice feature to add.

```
'Build the depth element of the command text.
sDepth = "subTree"
```

Next, I assemble all the elements of the command text, execute the ADO query, and persist its results in an ADO recordset:

```
'Assemble the command text.
ocommand.CommandText = strLDAPServer & ";" & sFilter & ";" & FieldList & ";" _
  & sDepth

'Execute the query.
Set rs = ocommand.Execute
```

Now, that I have successfully executed a search and have a recordset of the results, I can use a really incredible feature of ADO 2.5. I define a `Stream` object (which is like allocating RAM) and use the `Save` method to painlessly convert the recordset to XML! I include this feature because we, at InterKnowlogy, have written some really incredible web applications, which facilitate easy search, read, and write capabilities for the Active Directory. When I return my result set as XML, I can do some fancy things on the client side like sorting on any attribute without having to round trip back to the server.

```
If (strXML = "XML") Then
  Dim s As Stream
  Set s = New Stream
  rs.Save s, adPersistXML
End If
```

Lastly, I disconnect the recordset, do some cleaning up, and then determine what format to return (an ADO recordset or XML):

```
'disconnect the recordset
Set rs.ActiveConnection = Nothing
ObjCon.Close
Set ObjCon = Nothing

If (strXML = "XML") Then
  ADOSearch = s.ReadText(adReadAll)
Else
  Set ADOSearch = rs
End If
```

I build a small test container (a project that uses the COM component), which allows me to quickly, and efficiently test the ADO search method. Here is a screenshot of the results when choosing to return a recordset from an ADO search:

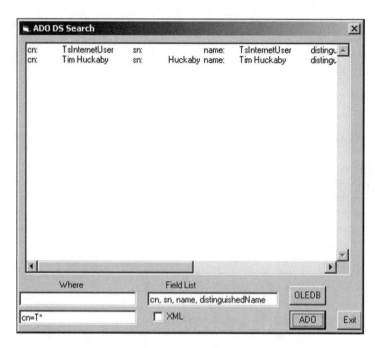

And here is a screen shot of the results when choosing to return XML:

GetAttribute

The purpose of the public function GetAttribute is to return a value of an attribute from a Directory Service class in the Active Directory as described by the ADsPath parameter. GetAttribute returns a variant or variant array containing the attribute value(s); Null if the attribute doesn't exist.

The interface for GetAttribute is:

```
Public Function GetAttribute(ByVal strADsPath As String, _
                             ByVal strAttributeName As String) As Variant
```

You can see that GetAttribute takes two parameters:

❑ strADsPath – the partial ADsPath to the class without the prefix, (in other words CN=Tim Huckaby,CN=Users,). Notice the trailing comma.

❑ strAttributeName – the attribute name, not the display name of the attribute being searched (that is cn or l).

First, I dimension the variables that I will need in the GetAttribute public function. Of note are the two objects, objADsBase and objADs. Like in the GetRootObjectName private function, I have dimensioned these two objects of the type IADs. The IADs ADSI programming interface allows me to treat objects in the Active Directory as containers.

```
Dim objADsBase, objADs As ActiveDs.IADs
```

Next, I declare a constant for the error number returned when I try to retrieve an attribute from the Active Directory that is not persisted. Then, I set up some error handling to catch exceptions. Then, I dig the registry for:

❑ The name of the server that hosts the Active Directory

❑ The TCP/IP port that the LDAP server is listening on

❑ The administrative user that I want to bind with

❑ The password of the administrative user that I want to bind with

I will need these later in the function to securely bind to the directory service.

```
Const E_ADS_PROPERTY_NOT_FOUND = &H8000500D

On Error GoTo ExitGetAttribute

'dig the registry for the server vars
strServerName = GetServer()
strPortNumber = GetPort()
strAdminName = GetUser()
strPassword = GetPassword()
```

Next, I call the internal private function GetRootObjectName which derives the DNS Host name of the Active Directory that I want to connect to, (in this case "timhucknotebook.TimHuck.com").

Next, I call the internal private function `GetRootDomainNamingContext`, which derives the Organization name of the Active Directory that I am searching (`"DC=TimHuck,DC=com"`). Upon deriving the Organization name I can use the IADs interface to get the schema container object. The call would be something like this:

```
Set objADs = GetObject("LDAP://HUCKABY.tim.com/CN=Tim
Huckaby,CN=Users,DC=tim,DC=com")

  strRootObjectName = GetRootObjectName(strServerName, strPortNumber)
  strRootDomainNamingContext = GetRootDomainNamingContext(strServerName,_
    strPortNumber)

  ' build the local LDAP server and ADS Path prefix strings
  strLDAPServer = "LDAP://" & strRootObjectName & "/"

  ' get schema container object
  Set objADs = GetObject(strLDAPServer & strADsPath & strRootDomainNamingContext)
```

Upon successfully getting an instance of the schema container object, I can use the ADSI `"Get"` method to retrieve the value of the attribute in the Active Directory. If the attribute is not persisted, hence does not exist, I set the value returned to `Null`. If it's a real error I process accordingly, otherwise the value of the attribute returned from the Active Directory is set to the function and returned.

```
  ' I'll handle the property not found error
  On Error Resume Next

  ' return the value
  GetAttribute = objADs.Get(strAttributeName)
  If Err.Number > 0 Then
    If Err.Number = E_ADS_PROPERTY_NOT_FOUND Then
      Err.Clear

      ' destroy the object
      Set objADs = Nothing
      Set objADsBase = Nothing

      GetAttribute = Null
      Exit Function
    Else
      ' it's a real error
      GoTo ExitGetAttribute:
    End If
  End If
```

I turn the error processing back on, then I do some cleanup by setting my objects to `Nothing` and return control to the calling program, page or component.

```
  On Error GoTo ExitGetAttribute

  ' destroy the object
  Set objADs = Nothing
  Set objADsBase = Nothing

  Exit Function
```

I wrote a small Active Server Page that uses the `GetAttribute` method on the COM component to retrieve data from the Active Directory. Here is the ASP code:

```
<%@ Language=VBScript %>
<%
Response.Expires = 0
%>
<HTML>
<BODY>


<%
  Dim objDSAD
  Dim str_attrib

  ' create the object
  Set objDSAD = Server.CreateObject("DSObjsAD.IADSI")

  str_attrib = objDSAD.GetAttribute("CN=Tim Huckaby,CN=Users,", "CN")
  Response.write("CN:" & str_attrib & "<BR>")

  str_attrib = objDSAD.GetAttribute("CN=Tim Huckaby,CN=Users,", "givenName")
  Response.write("Given Name:" & str_attrib & "<BR>")

  str_attrib = objDSAD.GetAttribute("CN=Tim Huckaby,CN=Users,",
"distinguishedName")
  Response.write("distinguishedName:" & str_attrib & "<BR>")

  Set objDSAD = Nothing

%>

</BODY>
</HTML>
```

And here is a screenshot of the results:

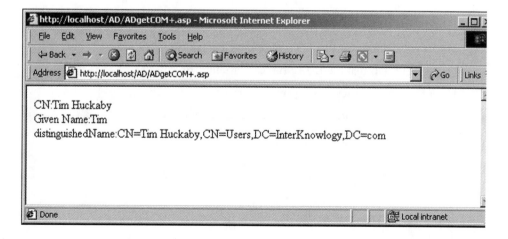

SetAttribute

The purpose of the public function SetAttribute is to set or remove the value of an attribute from a Directory Service class in the Active Directory as described by the ADsPath parameter. SetAttribute returns a variant containing True or False which determines its success or failure.

The interface for SetAttribute is:

```
Public Function SetAttribute(ByVal strADsPath As String, _
                    ByVal strAttributeName As String, _
                    ByVal varAttributeValue As Variant, _
                    Optional ByVal intPutexType As Integer = 3) As Variant
```

You can see that SetAttribute takes four parameters:

❑ strADsPath – the partial ADsPath to the class without the prefix (CN=Tim Huckaby,CN=Users,). Notice the trailing comma.

❑ strAttributeName – the attribute name, not the display name of the attribute being searched (cn or l).

❑ varAttributeValue – the value to set the attribute to.

❑ intPutexType – this multi-valued attribute is the ADSI PutEx flag where:

    ❑ 1 = Erase the contents and remove the attribute(s)

    ❑ 2 = Update the contents (replace what's already there)

    ❑ 3 = Append values to the existing attributes

First, I dimension the variables that I will need in the SetAttribute public function. Of note are the two objects, objADsBase and objADs. Like in the GetRootObjectName private function, I have dimensioned these two objects of the type IADs. The IADs ADSI programming interface allows me to treat objects in the Active Directory as containers.

```
Dim objADsBase, objADs As ActiveDs.IADs
```

Next, I set up some error handling to catch exceptions. Then, I dig the registry for:

❑ The name of the server that hosts the Active Directory

❑ The TCP/IP port that the LDAP server is listening on

❑ The administrative user that I want to bind with

❑ The password of the administrative user that I want to bind with

I will need them later in the function to securely bind to the directory service.

```
On Error GoTo ExitGetAttribute

'dig the registry for the server vars
strServerName = GetServer()
strPortNumber = GetPort()
strAdminName = GetUser()
strPassword = GetPassword()
```

Next, I call the internal private function GetRootObjectName, which derives the DNS Host name of the Active Directory that I want to connect to ("timhucknotebook.TimHuck.com").

Next, I call the internal private function GetRootDomainNamingContext, which derives the Organization name of the Active Directory that I am searching ("DC=TimHuck,DC=com"). Upon deriving the Organization name I can use the IADs interface to get the schema container object. The call would be something like this:

```
  Set objADs = GetObject("LDAP://HUCKABY.tim.com/CN=Tim
Huckaby,CN=Users,DC=tim,DC=com")

  strRootObjectName = GetRootObjectName(strServerName, strPortNumber)
  strRootDomainNamingContext = GetRootDomainNamingContext(strServerName,_
    strPortNumber)

  ' build the local LDAP server and ADS Path prefix strings
  strLDAPServer = "LDAP://" & strRootObjectName & "/"

  ' get schema container object
  Set objADs = GetObject(strLDAPServer & strADsPath & strRootDomainNamingContext)
```

Upon successfully getting an instance of the schema container object, I can use the ADSI "Put" and "PutEx" methods to set the value of the attribute in the Active Directory. I use the ADSI "PutEx" method to persist multi-valued attributes and to delete an attribute value. I use an ADSI "Put" method to persist a single-valued attribute.

```
  ' set the value
  strAttributeValue = varAttributeValue
  If IsArray(strAttributeValue) Then
    Call objADs.PutEx(intPutexType, strAttributeName, strAttributeValue)
  Else
    If intPutexType = 1 Then                    'remove the attribute
      Call objADs.PutEx(intPutexType, strAttributeName, "")
    Else
      Call objADs.Put(strAttributeName, strAttributeValue)
    End If
  End If
```

The values changed by the "Put" and "PutEx" ADSI methods live in cache until they are flushed to disk with the ADSI "SetInfo" method:

```
  ' commit the value
  Call objADs.SetInfo
```

I do some cleanup by setting my objects to Nothing, assign "True" to the function to signify success, and return control to the calling program, page or component:

```
  ' destroy the object
  Set objADs = Nothing
  Set objADsBase = Nothing

  SetAttribute = True

  Exit Function
```

481

Summary

The basis of this chapter was to help "get you smart" on Directory Services, specifically the Windows 2000 Active Directory. You learned about the purpose of directory services and why we need them. You learned about the authentication and authorization features of the directory service. You learned about the different types of Directory Services and how we have a unified programming model called ADSI to code to directory services. Also, and very importantly, you learned that we, as software developers, don't have to worry about the slight nuances between different directory services – LDAP handles that seamlessly and automatically for us.

Next, I covered some of the basic tools you will need that will help you in your programming of Directory Services. Lastly, I stepped you through a middle-tier COM component that manages access (search, read, and write) to the Active Directory. (You can download that code from the Wrox web site at http://www.wrox.com/.)

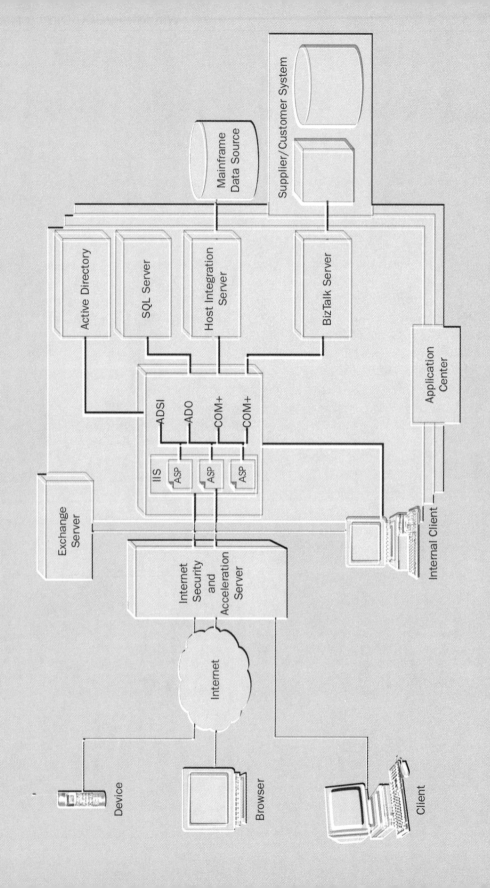

16

How Rich are Your Clients?

Overview

The Windows DNA architecture is designed to support a wide variety of possible client hardware and user presentation technologies. At the high end, Windows DNA supports the actual Windows environment, with client software created using sophisticated technologies such as Microsoft Office, Visual Basic, or C++ with MFC (Microsoft Foundation Classes). At the other end of the spectrum, Windows DNA supports presentations on microbrowsers, cell phones and other highly specialized, limited environments.

There are three main areas we need to consider when choosing or designing the client and presentation for an application:

❑   The presentation may be rich or basic

❑   The presentation may have wide or limited reach

❑   The difficulty of deployment

This spectrum of presentation, or client, technologies is often described in terms of **richness**. Richness is the measure of responsiveness or interactivity with the user. A rich client is one where the user is provided with a highly interactive, responsive experience – typically due to the sophisticated capabilities of the client device or environment. A client that is not rich is one where the user is provided with a basic experience with little interactivity and low responsiveness.

Another very important consideration is the **reach** of our application. How many people do we want to use our application? If the application is to be used by anyone, anywhere, running any operating system and (if a web app) using any browser, then we want wide reach. On the other hand, if we restrict users to always use the same browser on various operating systems then the application's reach is narrower. If we go so far as to say that users must use a specific client application or browser on a specific operating system then our reach may be quite narrow – users on other operating systems or with other browsers may not have access to the application.

The final facet of client design is that of **deployment**. Some presentation technologies have minimal requirements for the client device – there is little to no effort involved in deploying our application to these devices. A basic HTML browser, for example, has very limited capabilities and can merely display HTML. Our only deployment concern in this case is to get the browser itself installed on the client device.

> *I am specifically avoiding discussions of thick and thin clients. These terms are so vague as to be useless in this chapter. 'Thin' HTML user interfaces require a 35 MB runtime in the form of a browser. 'Thick' or 'fat' VB applications, in comparison, require a mere 4 MB runtime. Which was thinner again?*

Other presentation technologies require more sophisticated and complex client support – increasing the complexity involved in deploying the application's presentation. If we use a rich display technology like Shockwave then we're making deployment more complex – the user must install Shockwave before they can use the application. Beyond that, if the application's UI is built based on Microsoft Office or other robust client technologies, then that requires the installation and maintenance of those packages in order to work.

With today's technologies, it is difficult to create a rich client with broad reach that is easily deployed. We are constantly faced with choosing which facet of the presentation is most important – often compromising the other facets to meet our requirements.

There is often a link between reach and deployment. The technologies that provide broad reach typically have minimal deployment requirements. Usually broad reach applications rely on basic HTML support – meaning that the only deployment concern is the installation of an HTML browser on the client device.

There is also a link between richness and deployment. Technologies that enable rich user interaction must be deployed to the client device. Typically, a richer presentation will have more deployment requirements – often increasing the complexity of the client device.

The relationship between richness and reach is the opposite. Technologies that provide a rich user experience almost always limit the reach of an application.

> **In short, a rich client is typically hard to deploy and has limited reach. A client with broad reach is typically easy to deploy, but has limited interaction with the user.**

In this chapter we'll discuss the ramifications on an application's design that come along with a decision to support a rich client, to support a basic client, or to support various types of client. Additionally we'll touch briefly on the disconnected client – an environment quite familiar to laptop users, and increasingly to wireless users.

Spectrum of Clients

The choice between having a rich client and a basic client often comes down to the choice between reaching a wide audience and considerations of deployment complexity.

Let's consider client richness, deployment, and reach by taking a brief, highly simplified, stroll down memory lane.

Over the history of computing there have been many types of user display and provisions for user input. We're not going to cover all of them here, but it is beneficial to get a quick grasp of the dominant approaches over time.

3270 Terminal

Years ago, the most common way to interact with applications was through a terminal. One of the most common types of terminal was the IBM 3270. In fact this terminal and style of presentation is quite common even today – it is not uncommon to watch someone enter some data and press the Transmit key to send the contents of the screen to the actual computer that does the work.

Typically the computer behind the scenes is a mainframe or AS/400, and the application itself is probably written in COBOL or RPG – but the user doesn't see or care. They just interact with the terminal itself, oblivious to what lies behind it.

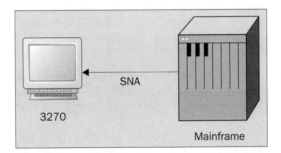

This style of user experience can be described as **batch-oriented** or **block-mode**, because the user enters their data into the terminal, then sends it all to the computer in a batch by pressing the Transmit key. The advantage to this approach is that it helps minimize some of the load on the mainframe. While the user is reading what's on the screen and entering in new data, there is minimal interaction with the host computer.

The drawback to this approach is that the terminal's ability to interact with the user is extremely limited. Basically the terminal knows where to display data and where to allow the user to input data, but has no capability of applying logic to the display or the input. This means that validation, calculations or any other operations must wait until the user presses that Transmit key – thus sending the data to the actual computer where that work can be done.

Obviously the reach of this technology is pretty limited. Only users that have the right kind of terminal can use applications. Anyone else is just out of luck.

While this technology doesn't provide a very rich user experience, there are minimal deployment issues involved. As long as the user has a terminal, they can use applications – that's all there is to it. Since the terminal is not capable of performing complex activities, there's no worry about installing add-on components or anything like that.

Telnet and VT Series Terminals

Another relatively old terminal-based technology came in the form of teletype, Telnet, ANSI and the VT series of terminals. The communication model used by these terminals is one where the host computer (often a Unix or OpenVMS machine) receives each character typed by the user – one by one.

Contrast this with the 3270 terminals we were just discussing and they are quite different. Where the 3270 had the intelligence to buffer the user's input and send it to the host computer in a single batch of data, these other terminals sent each character entered by the user to the host immediately.

This model offers a unique set of capabilities. Unlike the 3270 model, in this model the application – though running on a host computer – can immediately react to user activity. This means that the application can provide immediate validation of user input and can provide the user with feedback (via screen updates or a simple beep sound) at any point.

As with the 3270 terminals, the reach of this technology is limited to only those users with the right kind of terminal. On the other hand, this type of terminal is incredibly widespread, and emulators exist for Windows and pretty much all other popular client computers.

The user experience with this type of terminal is fairly limited. While it is more interactive and responsive than the 3270 style of terminal, the display is basically limited to text – possibly with color or special fonts. Additionally, all the processing for the application occurs on the host computer – including handling all the I/O resulting from each key pressed by the user – meaning that large computers (or clusters of smaller computers) are required to handle even relatively small numbers (tens or hundreds) of users.

XWindows Terminals

The IBM 3270 and Telnet/VT style terminals are text based. Another type of terminal is the XWindows terminal – which is different in that it provides the user with a graphical interface. Typically the host computer in this case will be a Unix machine, though certainly other host computers support XWindows as well.

XWindows is not entirely dissimilar to the Telnet/VT terminal model in that any action taken by the user such as a key press or mouse movement is reported back to the host application. The host application in turn can interact with the user by requesting that the terminal alter its display as required.

The XWindows model is actually quite interesting. The terminal in this case is considered to be a server, while the application running on the host computer is the client. This reverse terminology is quite important, in that unlike the previous terminal models, the XWindows terminal can actually be communicating with more than one application at a time – and those applications may be running on separate host computers. Each application is displayed within its own window.

The XWindows terminal is a server, because it is providing display services for the application. The application is a client of those services – requesting various display options or input from the user.

Regardless, the user experience tends to be the graphical equivalent of a Telnet session or a VT series terminal. As the user interacts with the presentation, the application is notified and can respond as needed. This can include immediate validation of user input, as well as performing business processing and calculations.

Just like the previous types of terminal, the reach of an XWindows application is limited to only those users with an XWindows terminal or an emulator.

The user experience with XWindows is quite a bit superior to the previous terminal types, primarily because of the graphical capabilities of the terminal. Additionally, the XWindows terminal takes care of a great deal of the display complexity – offloading much of that work from the host computer. Couple that with the ability to interact with multiple host-based applications at the same time and XWindows provides decent scalability and flexibility.

PC-based GUI

The limitations of the terminal-based user environment were a contributing factor to the rise of the PC-based graphical user interface (GUI) over the past decade or so. The GUI experience is quite a lot different, since the user is no longer interacting with a mere terminal, but rather with an actual computer. Because the UI is being provided by a computer, developers were able to run code right there at the point of interaction between the application and the user.

In the typical GUI experience, users expect to get instant validation of the data they are entering, customized displays for their data based on various criteria, and often some level of calculation. A GUI point of sale system would be expected to prevent the user from typing invalid data into any field, and probably also would have a running total for the sale in one corner of the screen. The client device itself handles this code – giving the user a much more immediate reaction than the terminal-based model.

As with terminal technology, PC-based clients have somewhat limited reach, since only users with a PC and the application itself can make use of applications. Of course the counter to this point is that some 90% of the computers used by people around the world are PC's running the Windows operating system. So while this technology does have 'limited reach', it is limited to a very large pool of users!

Perhaps the bigger consideration with a PC-based GUI client is that of deployment. The typical GUI client is an actual application in its own right, often relying on various components such as ActiveX controls, data access components and so forth. These must all be installed and maintained on the client PC for the application to function – obviously creating some deployment issues and concerns.

HTML Forms

More recently the World-Wide Web and browser technology have emerged. There are many different technologies in this space, but the first (and still most common) is HTML forms. HTML forms are, in almost every meaningful respect, comparable to the IBM 3270 terminal. In this case the browser acts as the terminal, knowing how to display data and knowing where to allow the user to enter information. When the user clicks the Submit button (like the Transmit key of old), the user's entries are sent to the host computer for processing.

> *Of course HTML browsers are capable of displaying graphics, different fonts, various colors and so forth. From an aesthetic perspective there's a huge difference between the 3270 terminal and a browser. However, from a pure application functionality perspective – how the user interacts with the application – the two technologies are incredibly similar.*

In this case the host computer is probably not a mainframe, but rather is likely to be a Unix or Windows computer, and instead of COBOL the code is probably written using ASP (JavaScript or VBScript) – or maybe Perl, Java, C, C++ or a wide range of other languages.

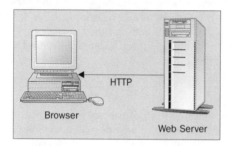

The key point is that the programming model and user experience is quite comparable between the IBM 3270 terminal and basic HTML forms.

Deployment is largely a non-issue for HTML forms, since the only requirement is that the client device have an HTML browser installed. Given a browser, regardless of pretty much any other factor, a user can access any HTML-based application.

Perhaps the biggest single advantage to the HTML approach is that we can reach a very broad audience. Given that the only client requirement is a basic HTML browser, and that most client computers (PCs, Macs, Unix machines, etc.) have browsers, an HTML application can reach almost anyone.

Dynamic HTML

Of course browser technologies have evolved to compensate for the limitations of pure HTML presentation. One of the most common technologies is dynamic HTML (DHTML), which takes the basic HTML model and extends it through scripting code and an object model by which the script code can interact with the display.

DHTML provides developers with some basic tools they can use to run code within the context of the browser – essentially lending some intelligence to the browser, and elevating it beyond the level of a mere terminal.

With DHTML it is quite possible to include script code in an HTML page that can validate user input and perform calculations such as maintaining a display of the total on a sales order as the user enters line items.

DHTML can still be quite limited in capability as compared to a full-blown GUI client, but at the same time it is far more capable than simple HTML forms. Additionally, DHTML is more demanding of the browser – somewhat reducing the reach of the application.

Wireless and Microbrowsers

Even more recently we're confronted with another set of presentation technologies – handheld, wireless devices such as cell phones or devices with microbrowsers. If HTML forms were limited in capability, these new form factors take it to the next level, with ultra-simplistic presentations and very limited capabilities for user input, much less any form of client-side validation or processing.

There are some competing technologies in this space, including the Wireless Access Protocol (WAP), Wireless HTML (WHTML) and possibly others. None of these technologies is terribly consistent at this point. Taking the time to quickly read through the web sites of WAP vendors, for instance, we can find various different implementations that all adhere to the same vague scheme – each with its own unique twist.

All the application code for this newer class of devices runs on the host computers – typically a web server to generate the content, and a gateway server to handle communications with the wireless device.

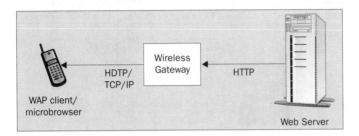

The wireless gateway server can almost be viewed as a proxy browser. From the web server's perspective, the gateway *is* the browser after all. This means that the programming model for our application (basically still running on a web server) is the same as with the IBM 3270 or HTML forms.

The capabilities of wireless gateways vary greatly from vendor to vendor. Some merely provide validation of the content to ensure it can be displayed on the user's device. Others translate HTML so it can be displayed within the limits of the wireless device, while still others provide complex emulation of browser capabilities such as cookies – tricking the web server into thinking the wireless device has capabilities that aren't directly supported.

Wireless devices communicate with the gateway using various technologies. Some connect fairly directly, using Remote Access Server technology to establish a TCP/IP connection. Others use HDTP – a variation on HTTP better suited to the needs of a wireless client.

There's even less of a deployment issue in these environments than with HTML applications. For HTML applications the user may have to install a browser on their client machine – but the devices we're talking about here typically come with the microbrowser built directly into the device. Given how new this technology is, there is a lot of variation as to how completely each device implements the emerging standards, and as to how each vendor interprets the way the standards are to work.

On the other hand, if we construct an application to specifically target these devices today we'll be limiting our reach. This area of technology is changing very rapidly, with various competing standards – none of which is totally compatible with more broadly used concepts like HTML. This means that, by choosing a given 'standard' today, we won't be supporting devices that follow other 'standards', nor will we be supporting the bulk of non-wireless devices such as PCs.

Disconnected Clients

To complicate matters however, there is yet another class of mobile client device – the disconnected client. This category of client spans several types of device, ranging from PC laptops to handheld devices such as the PocketPC. To some degree this even includes home computer users, who might only dial into the Internet from time to time.

The distinction with this type of client is that the client device is not always connected to any form of network. The laptop user may be on a plane doing some work. The device is not connected to any other computers, but the user wants to be productive – and wants the results of their work to be integrated into the network database when the device *is* connected to the network later.

Likewise, a user may be using a PocketPC or Palm Pilot, working with an application as they walk into a wireless dead zone such as an elevator. Rather than having their work disrupted, the user should seamlessly continue to do their work – secure in the knowledge that the application will resync as soon as they leave the dead zone and the PocketPC can reestablish its wireless connection.

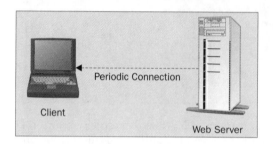

This environment imposes some limits on the technologies we have at our disposal. It is not practical to build applications based on server-side processing. This precludes typical HTML or browser-based presentation technologies, since these rely on the web server to do all the actual work of the application.

We're left with two main approaches.

1. The client can be written using GUI-style presentation technologies – essentially creating an application that runs on the client device, designed such that it synchronizes with the network when possible. This is the most common solution, since it uses well-known client-side programming techniques and the only main obstacle is dealing with the issue of synchronizing with the network-based portions of the application.

2. The other approach is to install a web server directly on the client device. The user can then use a browser-based presentation, running against the local web server. The design of the application running on the disconnected client remains mainstream, since it is designed to run against a web server that is always available.

Where this second approach gets complex is in the design of the 'server-side' components. These components aren't *really* server-side at all – they are running in the web server on the client device. If the network-based portion of the overall application is available, these 'server-side' components need to include logic to synchronize the client and the *real* server.

It is a rare case where this second approach is implemented. We typically want to avoid complexity on the client – and adding a web server and all the 'server-side' components of our application to the client certainly increases its complexity.

In either case, the complexity of a disconnected client is typically higher than that of a connected client. At a minimum the client device will need some form of data store so the client application can manage its data while disconnected. The device will also need some form of synchronization software to update data in both the client and server data stores.

While disconnected clients offer a great set of benefits, the underlying technologies are in flux and tend to be fairly immature – except for the laptop platform, where we typically have access to the full Windows environment.

Applications designed for disconnected clients are typically built for a specific type of device and environment. This means that the reach of such applications tends to be pretty limited.

> *There is an expectation that 'always-on' wireless will soon be widespread to the point where disconnected clients are obsolete. Personally I question this 'wisdom'. I frequently travel into very rural areas where even analog signals are rare. I also frequently use elevators, where digital signals often fail. I also go to a lot of conventions, where wireless providers become entirely overloaded and cell phones become barely usable. I also fly a lot on airplanes where wireless services are not available. I think it will be a long time before the disconnected client scenario falls by the wayside.*

Because all the software required to run the application must reside on the client device (so it is available when the device is disconnected from the network), our applications must be deployed directly to the device. It also means that supporting software, such as a database engine, must be deployed to the client as well, so deployment is an issue we need to consider carefully.

The richness of a disconnected client varies greatly based on the nature of the device and the technique we use to implement the application. Some devices have very limited display or input capabilities, limiting the level of interactivity we can provide to the user. Other devices, such as laptops, provide all the capabilities of Windows and so our client can be highly interactive.

Terminal Services Clients

The final type of client that we'll discuss is another form of terminal. Microsoft Terminal Services or other competing products such as the Citrix server offer a Windows-based environment presented to the user via a terminal device.

This newer breed of terminal is quite unlike the text-based terminals of old, however, because they provide a full GUI experience to the user. At the same time, at a basic level these GUI terminals are very similar to the old mainframe terminals – in that all they do is provide a display for the user, and pass the user's input or other actions back to the host computer for processing.

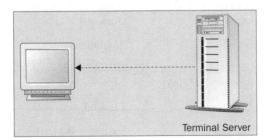

Terminal Server

From a development perspective, creating software for a terminal services client is no different than building software for a full-blown Windows client. The only real difference between the two is that a traditional Windows application interacts with the user directly, while a terminal services application interacts with the user via a remote terminal. Our application doesn't know there's any difference whatsoever – the underlying technology takes care of that for us.

The primary design implication to be aware of is that anything that is 'displayed' on the screen must be relayed across the network to the terminal device for actual display. This means that animations or other non-static types of display can be problematic. All those changes must be continually transferred across the network – increasing network bandwidth requirements and reducing the responsiveness of our application.

There are other more technical issues to consider as well. Each terminal in use corresponds to a 'virtual' computer running within our server machine. Some lower-level technologies (such as older data access technologies, or other shared DLLs) can get confused or fail outright when used by several virtual machines at once.

This problem has become less common over time, as software tools vendors have changed to accommodate this environment. However, we always need to carefully test software in the terminal server environment before knowing for sure it will operate effectively.

This environment allows us to create very rich, interactive client applications. Essentially we have the full capabilities of the Windows GUI environment to work with.

Deployment issues are fairly minimal. As with the simple HTML scenario, where we need to install a browser, the terminal services scenario simply requires that we install a terminal client. Once this client is installed, we can run any application that is installed on the terminal server itself, since it is the server that runs all our applications – with the client merely acting as a terminal.

Terminal services applications have fairly good reach, though not nearly as wide as a basic HTML client. There are terminal services clients available for all the Windows platforms as well as for MS-DOS. This means we can run a full-blown Windows 2000 based application from a client running merely MS-DOS. Pretty impressive!

The following table summarizes the richness, reach and deployment for each type of client supported by Windows DNA:

Client type	Richness	Reach	Deployment
HTML	Low	High	Easy
	(batch-oriented experience)	(cross platform, cross browser)	(must install browser)
DHTML	Good	Medium	Easy
	(client-side programmability)	(requires advanced browser)	(must install browser)
PC-based GUI	High	Limited	Complex
	(full client programmability)	(requires Windows client)	(must install app and supporting software)
Wireless	Low	Good	Easy
	(devices are limited or rely on batch-oriented model)	(emerging standards lean toward cross-platform)	(rely on native support by device)

Client type	Richness	Reach	Deployment
Disconnected	Varies	Low	Complex
	(laptops: high, handhelds: limited)	(apps targeted at specific devices)	(must install app and supporting software)
Windows terminal	High	Medium	Easy
	(full GUI experience)	(fairly wide support for client software)	(must install terminal client)

Ultimately we find that richness comes at the cost of reach and deployment complexity. If we can settle for a less interactive user experience, we can typically increase reach and simplify deployment issues.

Windows DNA and Clients

As a platform, Windows DNA supports many of the models we've just reviewed in our stroll through memory lane. Windows DNA is often discussed only in terms of browser-based clients, but that is inaccurate: it certainly covers browser-based clients, but it is intended to also support full Windows GUI clients, microbrowser clients and even internet-enabled cell phones. The challenge we face is that the typical diagrams used to describe the Windows DNA architecture are either quite vague or are targeted at fairly basic browser-based scenarios.

Many of the technologies we just discussed are directly supported by Windows DNA, including the PC-based GUI, HTML forms, Dynamic HTML, wireless, disconnected clients and Terminal Server. The model used by terminals like the IBM 3270 is supported via HTML forms, but there's no direct analog for the Telnet and VT series terminals in Windows DNA. XWindows functionality is not directly supported either, but is approximated by Terminal Server.

Regardless of the model, there is one key tenent of Windows DNA that must never be compromised – the separation of business logic from the user interface. If designed correctly, a Windows DNA application can be converted from one client model to another – say from a PC-based GUI to HTML forms – by merely replacing the interface code. The business logic and backoffice processing should remain consistent. This topic is covered thoroughly in Chapter 11.

> **The most common technical reason Windows DNA projects fail is because business logic is written in the UI code rather than being kept separate.**

All of the application models within Windows DNA follow this model of separation. Unfortunately there's nothing to *enforce* it, and so many developers find business logic (validation, rules checking, etc.) creeping into their ASP code or GUI forms.

What follows now is a set of diagrams illustrating some practical approaches that support each major category of Windows DNA client. Keep in mind that there are many other potential scenarios and ways to apply all the technologies at our disposal. These diagrams simply reflect the most commonly used and successful applications of the technologies.

PC-based GUI

The richest, most interactive user experience can be provided through the use of a full-blown Windows client application. That being said, this type of client is often overlooked when designing Windows DNA applications.

Obviously there are a wide variety of options when building a rich client. We might build the client using Visual Basic, Microsoft Excel or any other Windows tool or development environment. The following diagram shows generally how such a rich client fits into Windows DNA.

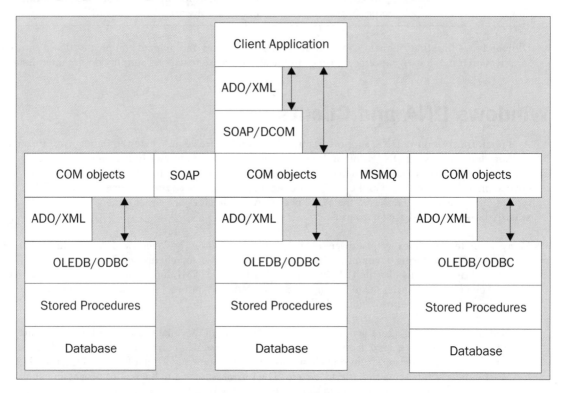

The client application, be it written in VB, VC, MS Office or some other tool, interacts with one or more servers to do its work. In many cases the client application will be written to work with disconnected ADO Recordset objects. Sometimes client applications are written to directly interact with server-side components without the use of ADO.

In any case, the client application relies on server-side components to do work – at least to interact with the database, but often to interact with other backoffice systems. In many cases the server-side components will be running in COM+ Applications on a Windows 2000 server. These components use ADO and/or OLEDB or ODBC to interact with the database. Ideally the data interaction is handled via stored procedures to increase performance, though direct database access is certainly possible.

To interact with the server-side components, the client may use SOAP – thus being able to make method calls over the Internet, through firewalls and to our server. If the clients are connected to the same network (LAN or WAN) as the server, then DCOM is commonly used.

SOAP is attractive because it is a standards-based technology that allows a client to invoke services (often methods of objects) on a server – regardless of the type of server or technology used to create the service itself. SOAP is cross-platform, cross-language, virtually cross-everything. And it typically utilizes the HTTP protocol for communications, meaning that all its communications use TCP/IP on port 80. Since most firewalls have port 80 open to allow web server traffic, SOAP tends to bypass most firewall security issues. If this statement concerns you (and it should) then turn to Chapter 12 for a more complete study of SOAP.

> *Of course at this point SOAP is still an emerging technology, and so its use is limited. However, Microsoft has indicated that SOAP is central to its future technology strategy and both IBM and Sun have voiced support for the standard, so it should be considered in any Windows DNA architectural planning.*

DCOM is also attractive, though for different reasons. DCOM is a much more mature, time-tested technology that offers a rich set of functionality. DCOM provides strong support for security and is a connection-based technology – meaning that a client can cause an instance of an object to be created on the server and maintain a connection to that object over time. That is something SOAP is not designed to support.

On the left-hand part of the diagram we can see that server-side components may interact with other server-side components via SOAP (or maybe DCOM). While the diagram shows these other server components in a Microsoft technology set, there's really no limit to the type of servers that can be used via SOAP. Thus, these other server components may be written in and running in some totally different technology such as CORBA or Java.

Likewise, on the right-hand side of the diagram the server-side components may interact with other server-side components via message queuing (MSMQ). This is also a powerful concept, since queued messaging is usually asynchronous and is not connection-based at all. Asynchronous calls are useful if the client makes a request that will require substantial time to complete. Rather than making the user wait all that time, we may choose to send a message to some other server-side component and have it do the work asynchronously – allowing the user to continue on to work on other tasks.

If the server that we're trying to invoke is temporarily down, or the network to reach that server is down – no problem. MSMQ queues all the messages and will deliver them when the remote server or network becomes available. This is often a highly desirable design trait, especially when interacting with backend systems over which we have little to no control.

MSMQ tends to be more Microsoft-centric than SOAP, so it makes sense that the server configuration on the right-hand side of the diagram is based on Microsoft technologies. However, gateways do exist to allow MSMQ to communicate with IBM MQSeries queues and other platforms, so the servers on the right *could* be IBM mainframes in such a case.

For all that this diagram illustrates a rich, highly interactive client based on the Windows platform, most of the effort is spent describing the server-side components and architecture. This is a general truth about Windows DNA – the server-side components are the stable, reliable part of the architecture. On top of that foundation we are able to build rich GUI clients as shown here, as well as the clients we'll see going forward.

Next let's take a look at a basic HTML browser client.

HTML Forms

The HTML browser client relies entirely on the server-side components to handle all processing. The browser acts as a simple terminal device, presenting information to the user and gathering user input for relay back to the servers.

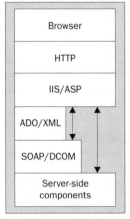

To simplify the diagram, the server-side components from the previous diagram have been consolidated into a single box. What we want to focus on here is the change in the way the client interacts with the server-side technologies. Between the browser and the other server-side components is a new component – the web server running IIS and ASP.

In this type of application, a web server should be viewed as a *UI proxy*. Our business logic is not really used by the UI (the browser), it is used by the UI code running on the web server – making that UI code effectively a proxy for the 'real' UI shown to the user. Whatever code we would historically have written to run in the UI on the client workstation in a GUI setting is now written to run on the web server. Even though the user interacts with the application via the browser, it is the code on the web server that actually comprises the UI.

Since the browser runs no code, all the processing to generate the UI and to accept user input is handled by the web server. However, and this is important, the code running on the web server should be UI code – not all the business logic. As with the PC-based GUI client, the business logic should reside in the server-side components reached via SOAP or DCOM.

The difference between the PC-based GUI diagram and this diagram is subtle. And if our applications are properly designed, switching from one type of user presentation to the other should be a matter of merely rebuilding the UI code. All the business logic and complexity should be unaffected by the specific presentation we choose for our user.

Of course that's pretty idealistic – but is a great goal to keep in mind while designing Windows DNA applications.

Dynamic HTML

Things get a bit more interesting with the introduction of 'smart' browser environments based on DHTML. While still browser-based, this type of client also can make use of the processing power on the user's local device – often a Windows workstation.

> *To be fair, there are more technologies than just DHTML that enable this type of architecture. ActiveX controls, COM components, client-side scripting and other client enhancement technologies that run within the browser are examples. Each of these types of technology enables the basic architecture described here.*

What we end up with is kind of a hybrid between a PC-based GUI client and a basic HTML browser client.

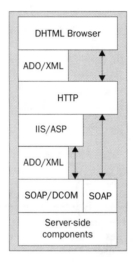

The DHTML browser client is much like the simpler HTML browser client, in that it often relies on a web server running IIS and ASP to provide UI processing and interaction with the other server-side components. However, the DHTML pages may contain code – code that runs on the client device.

The code running in a DHTML page may make use of disconnected ADO Recordset objects or XML data streams. This data may be provided from the web server, but may also be provided directly by server-side components via SOAP. Likewise, the code running on the client workstation may make direct method calls to server-side components rather than relying on the ASP code in the web server.

Since DHTML allows a developer to write code that directly alters the user's display without round trips to the web server we are able to provide an interface that *feels* more interactive to the user. By directly invoking server-side components and using data directly within the browser we can *really* increase the level of interactivity available to the user.

With no round trips to the web server, a DHTML page can retrieve, add, update, or remove data from server-side data stores. While the user remains on the same page, DHTML code can retrieve data to update a list box or immediately validate a user's selection.

In many ways this hybrid between HTML and GUI technologies offers the best of both worlds – easy deployment, but a pretty rich, interactive user experience.

Wireless and Microbrowsers

Increasingly users are presented with options for small wireless devices that interact with server-side applications. Typically these devices don't provide the functionality of a full HTML browser due to limited display and input capabilities. However, in many ways the application architecture to support these clients is the same as a basic HTML browser scenario.

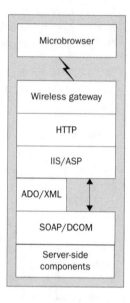

The microbrowser acts as a browser – typically interacting with a wireless gateway machine. This gateway in turn interacts with a web server to retrieve content for display. Any user input is relayed to the web server, and the client device relies on the web server to handle any processing and return results via the gateway for display to the user.

Between the microbrowser and the wireless gateway itself is the wireless network. Some wireless devices communicate with the gateway via Remote Access Services (RAS), others via standards such as WHTP. The wireless network providers basically extend the existing Internet network into the wireless world – effectively hooking the wireless device into the larger world of the Internet.

The thing to keep in mind with this technology is that the applications we serve up are totally unavailable to the user if they are not in an area covered by their wireless provider. To overcome this limitation we need to look at disconnected clients, which we'll discuss next.

Disconnected Clients

Disconnected clients cover a wide spectrum of possible client devices – ranging from laptops running Windows 2000 to hand-held Windows CE and PocketPC devices. These devices are almost always more feature-rich than the pure wireless devices from the previous section – and they need to be.

A disconnected client needs to be totally self-contained and able to operate without interaction with server-side components. This is critical because the device may be operated when the servers are physically unavailable, yet the user wants to continue to be productive.

Because of the wide variety of possible disconnected client devices, it is difficult to create a descriptive diagram to cover all of them. There are three consistent client-side components however – the client application, a client-side database and synchronization software.

The client application must provide the user with all the features and functionality they need to be productive – without any server-side interaction. In other words, the application must stand-alone and have everything it needs right there on the client device to take care of the user.

Applications almost always require data. The user may view data, update data, add data, or remove data. The application may require peripheral data for validation or display purposes even if the user doesn't directly interact with that data. To take care of these requirements, the client device must have some form of data store – typically a simple database.

When the client device eventually becomes physically connected to the network (by serial cable, USB, Ethernet, wireless, or some other means), the data on the client device must be synchronized with the data on the host network. Beyond merely synchronizing data, we may need to invoke some application code during or after the synchronization to make sure the overall application functions properly.

On a fairly basic device, such as a Windows CE 2.1 device, the application may be written in C++, using the built-in CEDB database for a data store. ActiveSync 3.0 is likely to be the underlying synchronization technology used to keep the client and server devices coordinated.

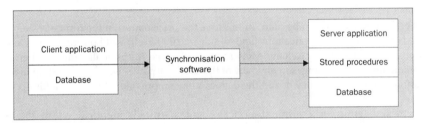

A more sophisticated client device, such as a laptop running Windows, can enable the use of a more complex architecture. The client-side application may make use of more technologies, including not only a database, but also queuing and other services.

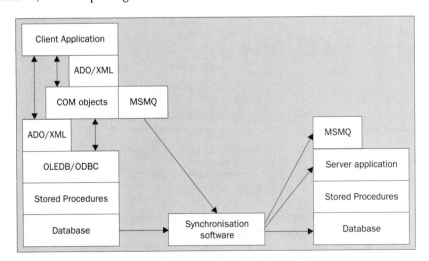

Both approaches are fundamentally the same. In each case, the client application interacts primarily with a client-side database, and perhaps other services or components. At some point the user will connect their device to the network, allowing some synchronization software to move queued messages, data from the database, files, or other information between the client device and the servers on the network.

In most cases there will be a server application, or at least some server-side components, that runs during or after the synchronization process. Most synchronization software is concerned with merely moving data between the client device and the network server – not in actually enforcing business rules or handling business processing. Thus we need to build server-side components to take care of these custom requirements.

Terminal Services Clients

The terminal services client relies on a graphical terminal to display the full Windows GUI to the user – providing the user with the illusion that they are interacting with a regular Windows computer. In reality the user is interacting with a 'virtual' computer that is running within a server somewhere across the network.

The beauty of this arrangement, from a developer's perspective, is that we can just build regular Windows-based client applications and users can use them via these terminals. No extra effort on our part required.

Of course there's always a price to be paid. In this case the price comes in the form of expensive servers and network bandwidth. Since the applications (and Windows 2000 itself) will be running on the server computer, it takes a pretty substantial server to handle any number of users. Additionally, the data being passed across the network contains all the changes to any part of the user's display – which can add up to a lot of data. The communication protocol is optimized, and the data can be compressed – but it still adds up.

The architectural diagram for a terminal services client is virtually identical to that of a regular PC-based GUI client.

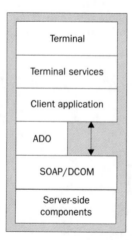

Again we've collapsed all the complexity of the server-side components and options into a single box – but they all remain as shown earlier in the diagram for PC-based GUI clients. The only real addition to this diagram is that the user interacts with a terminal, which relies on Windows Terminal Services (or a comparable technology such as Citrix) to interact with the client application.

For more information on Windows Terminal Services go to http://www.microsoft.com/windows2000.

The client application itself is running within a Windows environment – in a virtual machine on a server. From there it can interact with databases, server-side components, MSMQ queues, or anything else that our application requires.

Summary

In this chapter we explored the delicate balance between providing a highly interactive user experience, providing broad access or reach, and dealing with the resulting deployment issues that surround those issues. There is a definite tradeoff between richness, reach, and deployment:

- ❑ Richer clients tend to limit the reach of our application
- ❑ Richer clients tend to be harder to deploy
- ❑ Clients with broad reach have limited user interaction or richness
- ❑ Clients with broad reach tend to be easily deployed
- ❑ Minimal deployment tends to mean limited richness

With Windows DNA we can implement clients with broad reach and minimal deployment requirements, or we can choose to implement a full Windows-based client, making use of all the rich capabilities of that environment.

With careful design we can do one better – supporting multiple types of client device and presentation style. This can be done with little to no changes required to our business logic and server-side components and design.

Windows DNA is a very flexible and powerful architecture that can support virtually any type of client we require.

Online diagram at http://.../eOr.www.com

17

Building Win32 Clients – ActiveX Controls

In previous chapters we learned how to build COM components that handled most of our business logic. However, most of these components had no user interface associated with them – they only provided us with services. These services can be invoked from any COM-enabled application, such as Visual Basic, or even a scripting language, such as VBScript. In this chapter, we'll build Win32 user interfaces (UIs) that can interact with a COM server.

The type of user interface that we're going to be looking at here is an **ActiveX control**. Using Visual Basic 6, we can create our own custom built ActiveX controls as easily as we can create a Standard EXE project. Building ActiveX controls is fairly straightforward, with similarities to building a VB form (which you can also use as a type of rich Win32 client – but in this chapter, we're assuming that you've already had enough experience of VB to know how to do that).

There are several benefits to developing user interfaces as ActiveX controls. These include the ability to create multiple styles of rich clients, such as a desktop client, or a Web client that demands rich functionality. And because ActiveX controls are COM objects you get all the advantages that you usually get with COM – like the ability to reuse your code.

After reading this chapter, you should understand:

- ❑ What ActiveX controls are
- ❑ The difference between bound and unbound controls
- ❑ How to use properties, methods, and events
- ❑ How to create an ActiveX control
- ❑ How PropertyBags provide persistence for controls

ActiveX Controls – A First Look

Developing ActiveX controls in VB is easier than you think. However, you do need to watch out for some details, which is what we are going to walk through in this chapter.

What are ActiveX Controls?

> **An ActiveX control is a special type of in-process COM object – one with a user interface. In Visual Basic terms, an ActiveX control can be thought of as an ActiveX DLL with support for an additional set of well-defined interfaces.**

If you use Windows operating systems, you can't fail to come across ActiveX controls on a regular basis. The Visual Basic 6 toolbox itself provides several controls that we can use in our applications to avoid having to code that functionality from scratch.

ActiveX controls are similar to ActiveX components in that they have properties, methods, and events. The main difference is that ActiveX controls require a **container** – they can't run in their own process space. The framework that VB provides for creating ActiveX controls is called the **UserControl**.

Creating an ActiveX Project

We can start a new VB project of type ActiveX Control, simply by selecting the option in the New Project dialog:

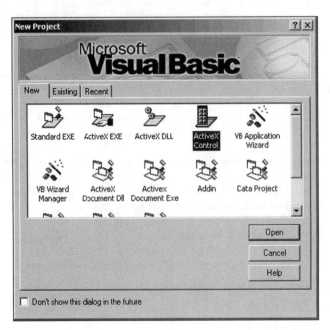

When we start a new ActiveX Control, we get a new control wrapper called UserControl1:

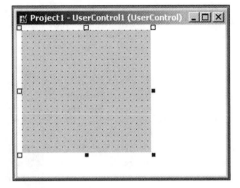

We can build and code this control in pretty much the same way as you would a VB Form.

From this point we can go in multiple directions and create several variations on ActiveX controls. We'll discuss some of these control types next.

Types of Controls

Shortly, we'll see how we can build our ActiveX control by placing additional controls on the UserControl. These controls are referred to as **constituent controls**. When starting with a new UserControl, we can choose to place as many constituent controls on it as required, depending on the richness of our user interface. These can be pre-existing and registered controls, or new ones.

There are generally two categories that any of these controls can fall under:

❏ Databound controls

❏ Unbound controls

We'll see how to create each of these types of controls later. For now let's define what they are in more detail.

Databound Controls

You can develop an ActiveX control in VB that is bound to a data provider. The data provider can be linked to the ActiveX control, either at the time that you're designing your control, or at run-time.

> When we talk about run-time in this context, we're referring to the environment that the control will be developed in: for VB, this will be when our control is being used in another project. Run-time for our control is design-time for the developer using our control.

If you choose to bind your control at run-time, the developer can then decide on how the control will be bound to a data source. Choices include an ADO control or the **ActiveX Data Environment Designer** (**DED**). We'll explore the two different styles of databound controls later in this chapter.

Unbound Controls

Unbound controls are controls that do not get their contents or data directly from a data provider (such as a data control), but rather expose properties and methods for other COM components to populate their fields.

Unbound controls can come in two flavors:

❑   **Owner-draw** – a control that we create from scratch

❑   **Subclassing** – a pre-existing control that we customize for our own purposes

For example, imagine we wanted to create our own TextBox control with special formatting, designed specifically to accept US Social Security numbers. It would accept 3 numbers, then a dash, then 2 numbers, and so on. We can accomplish this in two ways: by coding an owner-draw control or subclassing an existing control.

Using Owner-Draw Controls

Owner-draw controls are controls that we build from scratch using Windows APIs. In the case of our social security control, we'd have to create a control that looks like a TextBox control by coding all the 3D effects and the borders, providing back color support, and formatting the contents of the control.

This is a lot of work just to develop one control – especially since someone has already written all that code to create a TextBox control in VB that's very similar to what we want. Owner-draw controls are good solutions if you want to develop something simple, or if the control you need is unlike anything that's already to hand. However, in this case, a better solution is to subclass an existing control.

So What is Subclassing?

Subclassing means taking an existing control and customizing it. Since there's already a TextBox control provided by VB, all we need to do is take that control and subclass it. In other words we can reuse the functionality that we need and override the functionality we don't want, by creating procedures that handle the messages to this control.

We can use the textbox control look and feel, and add to it our special formatting requirements. Once we're done, the user will not notice the difference in behavior – all they'll see is the new enhanced functionality that we added.

For example, if we want to be able to resize our new control, we can do so just by adding the following line of code to the UserControl resize event:

```
Text1.Move UserControl.ScaleLeft, UserControl.ScaleTop, _
        UserControl.ScaleWidth, UserControl.ScaleHeight
```

Bound or Unbound – Which to Use

So how do we decide whether to use bound or unbound controls? Consider, for example, a control that will display customer information. It needs to display all typical customer information fields that are stored in a database. We have two choices:

❑   We can develop our control as an unbound control and expose some properties that receive the data, then populate our control.

❑   We can develop our control as a databound control and connect it directly to a data source provider.

In this chapter we'll develop both styles of controls, to show you how this works. The decision about whether to develop bound or unbound controls is exclusively an architectural one. From the point of view of the flexibility of the design, it's much more effective to create unbound controls. This gives us control of the source of the data, without limiting ourselves to a specific database or table. Databound controls, on the other hand, have a predetermined data source and data access mechanism.

So without more ado, let's take a look at our first ActiveX control.

An Unbound ActiveX Control

The best way to understand the theory behind ActiveX controls is to actually look at one. We've supplied a project with the code download for the book that will help you to do just that. The FirstControl project illustrates the concepts we'll explain below.

You can recreate the ActiveX control from this project by doing the following:

❑ Create a new **ActiveX Control** project from the **New Project** dialog in VB.

❑ In the **Properties** window, rename **Project1** to **FirstControl**.

❑ Add four TextBox controls and four Label controls to **UserControl1**, leaving their names as the default values, and their captions as follows:

Coding the Unbound Control

Our project will have two public methods:

❑ ClearAllText, to clear all the text in the control names

❑ MatchTextColor, to match the background color property of all the constituent controls

Finally, we'll program an event that is raised when one of the TextBoxes is clicked.

> *The FirstControl project provided in the code download has other features, including a property page that accepts a Social Security number. We'll discuss property pages later in the chapter.*

For now, just take a look at the code we added behind this control:

```
Event txt1Click()

Private mvarSocialsec As String

Public Property Let SocialSec(sSocialSec As String)

    mvarSocialsec = SocialSec

End Property


Public Property Get SocialSec() As String

    SocialSec = mvarSocialsec

End Property

Private Sub Text1_Click()

    RaiseEvent txt1Click

End Sub

Private Sub UserControl_Resize()

'Text1.Move UserControl.ScaleLeft, UserControl.ScaleTop, _
          UserControl.ScaleWidth, UserControl.ScaleHeight

End Sub

Public Property Get TextBackColor() As OLE_COLOR

    TextBackColor = UserControl.BackColor

End Property

' Use Property Set for object properties.
Public Property Let TextBackColor(ByVal NewColor As OLE_COLOR)

    UserControl.BackColor = NewColor
    MatchTextColor
    PropertyChanged "TextBackColor"

End Property

Private Sub MatchTextColor()

    Dim Ctrl As Object
    For Each Ctrl In Controls
        If TypeOf Ctrl Is TextBox Then
            Ctrl.BackColor = UserControl.BackColor
        End If
        If TypeOf Ctrl Is Label Then
            Ctrl.BackColor = UserControl.BackColor
        End If
    Next

End Sub
```

```
Public Sub ClearAllText()
' Clears all the text properties of the Textbox Controls

    Dim Ctrl As Control

    For Each Ctrl In UserControl

        If TypeOf Ctrl Is TextBox Then
            Ctrl.Text = ""
        End If
    Next

End Sub
```

```
Private Sub UserControl_InitProperties()

    MatchTextColor

End Sub
```

```
Private Sub UserControl_ReadProperties(PropBag As PropertyBag)

    On Error Resume Next
    TextBackColor = PropBag.ReadProperty("TextBackColor")

End Sub
```

```
Private Sub UserControl_WriteProperties(PropBag As PropertyBag)

    PropBag.WriteProperty "TextBackColor", TextBackColor

End Sub
```

Don't worry if this doesn't make much sense at the moment – we'll be looking at what this code means in more detail throughout the rest of the chapter.

To finish, save the project, and on the File menu click Make FirstControl.ocx. .ocx is theVisual Basic file extension for ActiveX Controls. We can now use this control in our other Visual Basic projects, by referencing it in the Components dialog (Project | Components).

ActiveX Control Behavior

Whatever type of control we are developing, that control will need to expose an interface – properties, methods, and sometimes events – in order to become functional. It's through these interfaces that a control of a rich client will be able to send and receive messages and data.

Regardless of the Windows DNA design you are going to adopt in your project, you'll need to create flexible interfaces that capture the functionality provided by the user interface.

Exposing Control Properties

Properties are one of the most important attributes of your control. There are two types of properties:

❑ The first are properties that are defined by your control. These properties can be created to manipulate visual elements of your control, such as shape or border, or they can manipulate internal data dependencies used for business logic processing.

❑ The second are ambient properties, which we'll look at shortly. These are read-only properties that suggest behavior to our controls.

We can create the first type of properties either as a simple variable declaration, or in the form of a procedure.

If you declare a variable in your UserControl with the `Public` keyword, this variable will be exposed as a property for your control. For example, let's say we want to create a property that holds a social security number (`SocialSec`). We can do so by simply creating the following variable:

```
Public SocialSec as String
```

Alternatively, we can create properties via property procedures with `Get/Let` and `Set` attributes. We can rewrite the previous code by creating property `Get` and `Let` in the following manner. This is exactly what we did in our `FirstControl` project:

```
Private mvarSocialsec As String

Public Property Let SocialSec(sSocialSec As String)

    mvarSocialsec = SocialSec

End Property

Public Property Get SocialSec() As String

    SocialSec = mvarSocialsec

End Property
```

Creating `Get/Let` pairs is not mandatory: for example, we can create a property `Get` without a companion `Let`, which will make our property read-only. This works best if you want the users to retrieve calculated properties, for example a customer credit balance. We'll discuss the different property configuration settings later in the chapter.

Ambient Properties

Ambient properties are properties suggested by a control container to the hosted controls (of course, in the case of a Visual Basic control, the control container is the UserControl). For example, a container uses the `ForeColor` property to suggest the foreground color of a control, and the `LocaleID` property is used to indicate the locale of the environment that a control is running under – that is, the language and country of the user.

Ambient properties are read-only, and not every container provides the same properties. Therefore, if you can't guarantee that a particular property is going to be present in the container (say, if your control is going to be used in multiple containers), it's up to you to handle the properties.

We can access ambient properties using the AmbientProperties object: the properties of this object are the ambient properties of the container. The AmbientProperties object is available only when the InitProperties event or ReadProperties event of a control are raised.

> *The InitProperties event occurs only when a new instance of an object is being created, so we can use this event to initialize properties for a new instance of a UserControl (the AmbientProperties object is not available from the Initialize event).*

> *The ReadProperties event occurs when loading an old instance of an object that has a saved state.*

AmbientProperty Changes

If a control's appearance or behavior is affected by changes to any of the properties of the AmbientProperties object, you can place code to handle the change in the UserControl_AmbientChanged event procedure.

For example, if our control is for international use, we might want to use the AmbientChanged event to check for changes to the LocaleID property. That way, the labels in our control will always reflect the current locale, based on values returned by the LocaleID property value. We simply need to pass a string containing the name of the property that changed (in this case LocaleID) as the argument of the AmbientChanged event procedure:

```
Private Sub UserControl_AmbientChanged(PropertyName As String)

    Select Case PropertyName

    Case "LocaleID"
         ' Write control localization code here.

    End Select

End Sub
```

Exposing Control Methods

Methods are the brains for the ActiveX controls: they provide rich functionality exposed by the control. The code you place in your method will have access to all the UserControl properties, as well as constituent controls.

Constituent Control Properties

We now need to determine how we combine the individual properties, methods, and events of all the constituent controls with that of the UserControl, to produce a single set of interfaces that represents that ActiveX control. We also have to resolve how we delegate calls to a specific constituent control interface via the UserControl.

Exposing Constituent Control Properties

Exposing properties and methods of constituent controls is more of a design practice than a programmatic process. It's very easy to expose every single constituent control as an object, thereby making all of these objects' interfaces available to the programmer of the UserControl.

However, the danger in doing that is that users attempting to program your UserControl will be lost in a sea of interfaces, and will have to sift through all the names of the interfaces before they can determine the correct interface to code. What's more, the controls you use are a private implementation issue, and control consumers shouldn't need this level of interaction if the control's purpose is properly thought-out.

Property and Method Delegation

As we're not going to expose our constituent control objects as a whole, we need to determine how we are going to develop the interfaces of our control. The process of defining UserControl interfaces that represent constituent objects is done via something called **delegation**.

> **Delegation is a process that allows us to define general properties and methods (properties and methods in the UserControl), and then use the implementation code for these properties and methods to send the work to the contained controls. In other words, the code in the UserControl simply passes responsibility for the work to be performed on to the constituent controls.**

Let's say that we build a UserControl with a constituent control, `txtSocSec` – this constituent control is a textbox that represents a social security number. In the UserControl, we can create a property and call it `SocialSec`, using a property `Let` and `Get` as follows:

```
Public Property Get SocialSec() As String
    SocialSec = txtSocSec.Text
End Property
```

```
Public Property Let SocialSec(sSocialSec As String)
    txtSocSec.Text = SocialSec
End Property
```

The `SocialSec` property delegates the `Get` and `Let` calls for reading and writing to `txtSocSec`. You can also store the values in a member variable.

The code described above shows a one-to-one relationship between a property and a delegation to another property in a constituent control. We can take this a step further and create a single property that delegates to multiple properties in multiple constituent controls.

For example, in our `FirstControl` project we want to set the background color of all the TextBoxes on the constituent controls all at the same time, without having to create an individual property for each TextBox. We can do that by creating a property or a method that delegates the call to all the controls:

```
Private Sub MatchTextColor()

    Dim Ctrl As Object
    For Each Ctrl In Controls
        If TypeOf Ctrl Is TextBox Then
            Ctrl.BackColor = UserControl.BackColor
        End If
        If TypeOf Ctrl Is Label Then
            Ctrl.BackColor = UserControl.BackColor
        End If
    Next
End Sub
```

Avoid using property names that could conflict with the UserControl standard property names, such as Width *and* Left. *If you choose property names that are the same, the new property that you created will act as the default property when called, unless you explicitly call the UserControl name prior to invoking the property. You can see a list of these standard properties in the Properties window in VB, if you click on your control.*

Just like properties, methods can delegate calls to constituent controls. We just have to create a public method in the UserControl, which in turn delegates the call to a specific constituent control method.

For example, in our `FirstControl` project, we provide a method that clears all the text entries on a UserControl:

```
Public Sub ClearAllText()

    ' Clears all the text properties of the Textbox Controls
    Dim ctrl As Control

    For Each ctrl In UserControl

        If TypeOf ctrl Is TextBox Then
            ctrl.Text = ""
        End If
    Next

End Sub
```

Exposing Control Events

Events can be one of the trickiest aspects in programming components. Events in ActiveX controls allow you to manipulate other control actions through delegation. For example, imagine you have built an ActiveX control that has several constituent controls, and you want the user to have access to the events of a particular control.

This can be accomplished by following the easy three-step approach to coding events that we utilized in our `FirstControl` project. Our `txtClick` event fires when the first TextBox in our UserControl is clicked.

First - Declare

To declare an event we need to go to the General Declaration section of the UserControl, and declare a variable as the event:

```
Event txt1Click()
```

Second - Raise

The second step is to raise the event inside the control that we are interested in. So, as the control that we want the user to code against is Text1, we go into the Click event of that control and include the following code:

```
Private Sub Text1_Click()

    RaiseEvent txt1Click

End Sub
```

Third - Invoke

Finally, if we add the UserControl to a form, we'll find a new event added to the control's existing events:

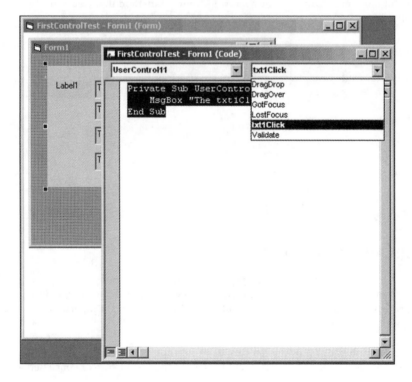

This is where we would write our code, as if we were writing it behind the original control itself. The code might be something like the following:

```
Private Sub UserControl11_txt1Click()

    MsgBox "The txt1Click event was raised"

End Sub
```

Using the ActiveX Control Interface Wizard

When you have a large number of constituent controls, or even one constituent control with many properties you wish to expose, the **ActiveX Control Interface Wizard** can significantly reduce the amount of work required to expose constituent control properties.

The ActiveX Control Interface Wizard helps you define and expose standard properties that are part of the control container, as well as create new properties, methods, and events and map them to constituent controls.

However, the Interface Wizard will not create the user interface part of the control for you. It assumes that you have already defined your user interface and know what you need to expose and map out.

To use the Wizard, open up your control in Visual Basic, and from the Add-Ins menu select Add-In Manager. Then choose VB 6 ActiveX Ctrl Interface Wizard from the list of Available Add-ins, and check the Loaded/Unloaded and Load on Startup checkboxes:

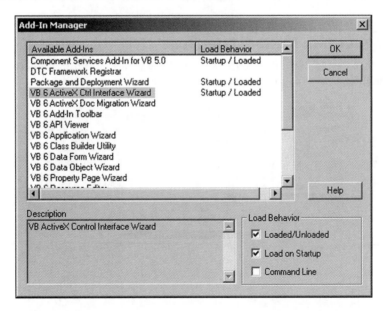

Click OK, and the ActiveX Control Interface Wizard option should be added to your Add-Ins menu.

Using the following four steps of the Wizard, you can quickly code your control interfaces.

Step 1 – Select Standard Interfaces

In this stage you can select which of the available public properties, methods, and events (the **Standard** interfaces) you wish to expose as part of your control:

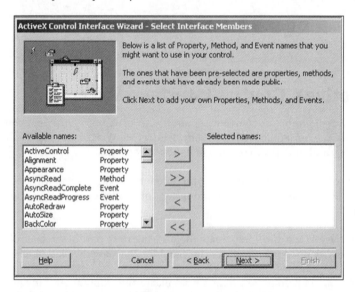

You should not include all the items available in this list: you should think carefully about which ones you would like to allow the user or developer access to, so that you're not compromising the integrity of your control.

Step 2 – Add Your Own Custom Interfaces

In most cases when developing a new ActiveX control you create your own properties, methods, and events (**Custom** interfaces). Any pre-existing interfaces will show up in this dialog:

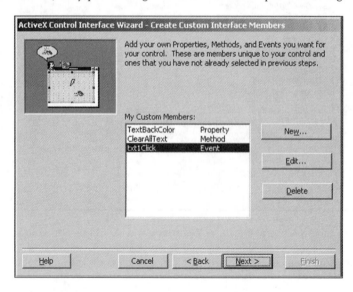

However, you do have the chance to edit these interfaces, delete them, or create new ones.

Step 3 – Map Properties, Methods, and Events to Constituent Controls

At this point you can map these interfaces (Standard and Custom) to members of your constituent controls:

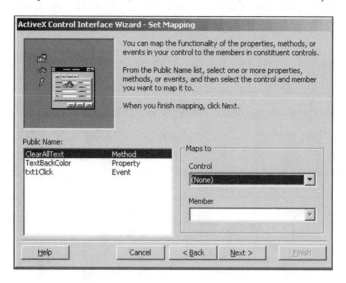

You can map individual interfaces to each control's member, or you can map multiple controls at a time to an individual constituent control.

Step 4 – Set the Properties, Methods, and Events Attributes

Finally, you can set individual interface attributes:

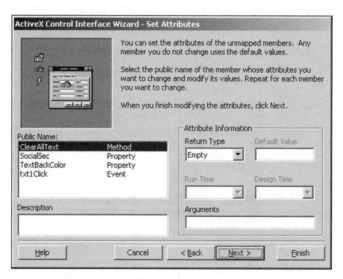

This step has the same effect as using the Procedure Attribute dialog to set the values, as we discussed earlier.

So, we've seen an example of unbound data control. Now let's move on to take a look a some databound controls.

Creating a Run-time Databound ActiveX Control

VB provides a Data Object Wizard that helps you create controls. However, we're going to design a data-aware ActiveX control without using the Wizard, so that you can see what is involved in creating a databound control.

To set up the new project:

❑   Create a new ActiveX Control project.

❑   In the Properties window, rename Project1 to prjAXCustomers.

❑   In the Properties window, rename UserControl1 to ctlCustomersInfo.

❑   Add six TextBox controls, seven Label controls, and one ComboBox control to the form, and set their properties as shown in the following table:

Object	Property	Setting
Text1	Name	TxtCustID
Text2	Name	TxtCustName
Text3	Name	TxtAddress1
Text4	Name	TxtAddress2
Text5	Name	TxtCity
Text6	Name	TxtZipCode
Combo1	Name	CboState
Label1	Caption	CustomerID
Label2	Caption	Customer Name
Label3	Caption	Customer Address 1
Label4	Caption	Customer Address 2
Label5	Caption	City
Label6	Caption	Zip Code
Label7	Caption	State

The control should look like this:

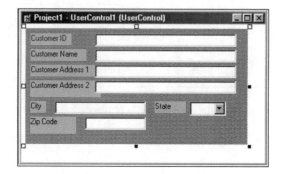

□ On the File menu click **Save Project**. Save the project using the names provided in the dialog boxes.

□ On the File menu click **Make ProductsCtl.ocx** to save the `.ocx` file.

So far we've created an ActiveX UserControl that we can use in other Visual Basic projects. Notice that we didn't even write any code – so it's about time that we did.

Coding Our Control

Now, the fun part begins. Let's write some code and make our control data aware. All we need to do is expose the fields that we placed on the UserControl as properties with `Get` and `Let`, then mark them as data aware.

Place the following code in the UserControl:

```
Public Property Get CustomerID() As String
    CustomerID = txtCustID.Text
End Property
```

```
Public Property Let CustomerID(ByVal newCustID As String)
    txtCustID.Text = newCustID
End Property
```

```
Public Property Get CustomerName() As String
    CustomerName = txtCustName.Text
End Property
```

```
Public Property Let CustomerName(ByVal newCustName As String)
    txtCustName.Text = newCustName
End Property
```

```
Public Property Get CustomerAddress1() As String
    CustomerAddress1 = txtAddress1.Text
End Property
```

```
Public Property Let CustomerAddress1(ByVal newAddress1 As String)
    txtAddress1.Text = newAddress1
End Property
```

```
Public Property Get CustomerAddress2() As String
    CustomerAddress2 = txtAddress2.Text
End Property
```

```
Public Property Let CustomerAddress2(ByVal newAddress2 As String)
    txtAddress2.Text = newAddress2
End Property
```

```
Public Property Get CustomerCity() As String
    CustomerCity = txtCity.Text
End Property
```

```
Public Property Let CustomerCity(ByVal newCity As String)
    txtCity.Text = newCity
End Property

Public Property Get CustomerState() As String
    CustomerState = cboState.Text
End Property

Public Property Let CustomerState(ByVal newState As String)
    cboState.Text = newState
End Property

Public Property Get CustomerZipCode() As String
    CustomerZip = txtZipCode.Text
End Property

Public Property Let CustomerZipCode(ByVal newZipCode As String)
    txtZipCode.Text = newZipCode
End Property
```

This code simply creates all our properties. The next thing to do is to bind these properties to fields in our database.

Property to Field Binding

When a control has properties that are data bound, the control is said to be a **data-aware control**. In order to make our control data-aware, we're going to use properties of an object called the `Extender` object.

> **The Extender object holds the properties of the control that are provided at run-time by the container. The difference between the properties supplied by the `Extender` object and the ambient properties is that ambient properties are for use by the control's author, while extended properties are only used by someone developing with a control.**

In particular, we're concerned with the `DataBindings`, `DataField`, and `DataSource` properties of the `Extender` object.

The `DataBindings` collection is a property that allows us to access the list of properties that are set as bindable in our control. If the control has multiple bindable properties, one property must be set as binding to the `Extender` object's `DataField` property. Otherwise, the `Extender` object will not provide a `DataSource` property.

Making Properties Data Bound at Design Time

Once we've added properties to our ActiveX control, there are several configurations that we need to set using the **Procedure Attribute** dialog. This is accessed from the Tools menu. We need to click the Advanced>> button in order to display all settings:

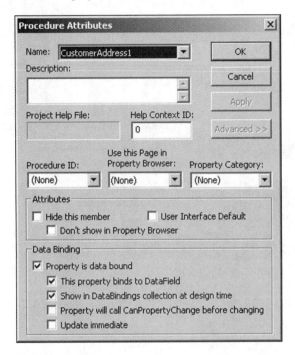

The Procedure Attribute dialog shows all the options we can choose in order to allow the control to be data aware. This allows us to map data bound properties with any field in a data source, by just setting the DataSource and DataField properties.

You can select one (and only one) property of your control to be bound to the DataField property. Typically, this is the most important piece of data your control holds.

To do this, we need check the Property is data bound box. We also need to check two additional check boxes:

❑   This property binds to DataField – allows us to bind the control to the specific data fields inside a data source.

❑   Show as DataBindings collection at design time – allows the control's bindable properties to be available when we start using the control in a new project.

Binding Properties at Run-time

Although you can mark only one field as bound to the field specified in the DataField property, you can mark additional properties of your ActiveX control as bindable at run-time. Developers can use the DataBindings collection to bind these additional bindable properties to data fields.

If you're using your control on a form, you can view the Data Bindings dialog by selecting the DataBindings property in the Properties window for the control. Click on the button marked ..., and the dialog will appear:

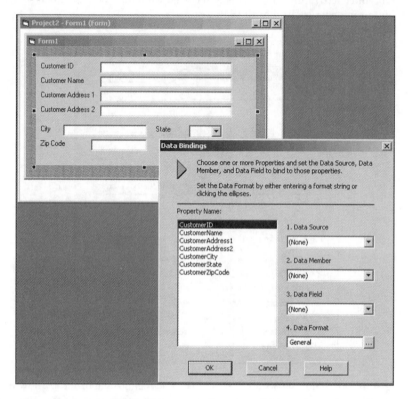

You can then start mapping the fields of the control to data fields.

Dealing with Updated Properties

One additional item to take care of is to mark the property as changed in the TextBox's Change event, as shown in the following code, because the user can change the value of the property while the TextBox displays it:

```
Private Sub txtCustID_Change()
    PropertyChanged "CustomerID"
End Sub

Private Sub txtCustName_Change()
    PropertyChanged "CustomerName"
End Sub

Private Sub txtAddress1_Change()
    PropertyChanged "CustomerAddress1"
End Sub

Private Sub txtAddress2_Change()
    PropertyChanged "CustomerAddress2"
End Sub
```

```
Private Sub txtCity_Change()
    PropertyChanged "CustomerCity"
End Sub

Private Sub txtZipCode_Change()
    PropertyChanged "CustomerZipCode"
End Sub
```

And now we're finished – well almost. In order for the new value to be written back to the data source, we must call the `PropertyChanged` method. If we don't call `PropertyChanged`, our control is not bound for updating. In other words, although all of the changes you made to the data will seem to have been made, if you check the database, you'll notice that the changes were never written, and that the control raises errors to warn you about this behavior.

To fix this, we need to call `CanPropertyChange` before changing the value of a property that is data-aware. If the control always calls `CanPropertyChange`, then we need to check the option called **Property will call CanPropertyChange before changing** in the **Procedure Attributes** dialog box. Currently, `CanPropertyChange` always returns `True`, so we'll need to test for it and inform that user of the change.

At run-time, we can create a data source and bind the fields of the data source to the bindable properties of the UserControl using the following code:

```
UserControl11.DataBindings("CustomerID").DataField = "CustomerID"
```

Finally, we have a control that is ready for use and re-use in different projects. You can simply drop the control on a new form and add an ADO data control, bind both of them together, and you are ready to run.

You'll find an example project using this control in the code download available from the Wrox Web site.

However, there are several ways to create different types of controls. Next, we'll see a different flavor of databound ActiveX controls.

Creating a Design Time Databound ActiveX Control

The second databound control that we'll look at is an `AccountView` control.

The `AccountView` control will use a VB tool called the Data Environment Designer, and the SQL Server `Northwind` database. This method presents a viable alternative way to build databound ActiveX controls.

Account View Design

The `AccountView` control's responsibility is to retrieve customers and orders from the database.

We'll build this databound control using the **Data Environment Designer** (**DED**). Although the DED is commonly used to build form-based UIs, it can work very well in building ActiveX controls-based UI. The objective is to use the existing table design and retrieve all customer information from the database.

> *The Data Environment Designer is a very powerful tool if it's used correctly. Our objective in using it is not to promote building Windows DNA applications with it, but rather to show how to build a databound control.*

Exploring the Data Environment Designer

The Data Environment Designer will map out the flow of your application or control, but it does require you to think about the behavior of your application or control before you code it.

Let's think for a minute about what elements of our SQL Server database elements are. We have tables, views, stored procedures, synonyms, and SQL statements. If a database is *normalized*, we have established relationships between tables.

The `AccountView` control gathers information from two different tables. So, we'll need to determine the hierarchy of the relationships of these tables. We'll then model this relationship in the Data Environment Designer.

Our control will use the `Customers` table and the `Orders` table.

Start up a new ActiveX Control Visual Basic project, and call it AccountView. From the Project menu choose Add Data Environment:

In the Data Environment Designer, we need to first establish a connection to the database. Right-click on Connection1 and select Properties. Choose Microsoft OLE DB Provider for SQL Server, and click Next:

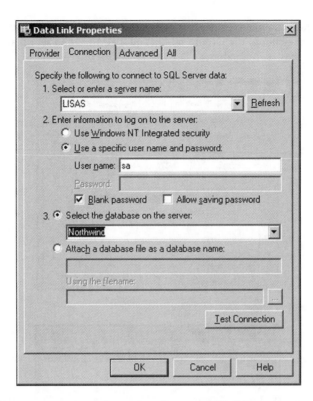

Then supply the relevant connection information for your SQL Server Northwind database, click OK, and refresh the DataEnvironment window to establish the connection.

Next we need to select the tables we're going to work with. Add a new Command object to the Data Environment Designer by right-clicking on Connection1 and selecting Add Command. Call up the Properties dialog for Command1, and select the Customers table from your database:

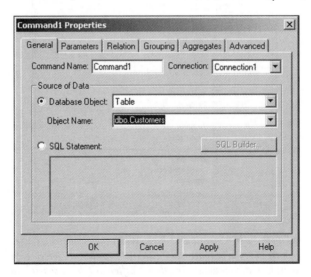

We'll then create a child command to the first command: right-click on **Command1**, select **Add Child Command**, and this time choose the **Orders** table. You'll also have to set up a relation between the CustomerID fields on these two databases:

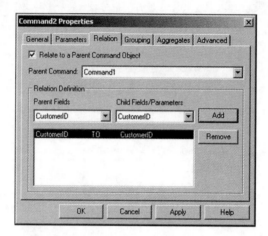

That's all there is to it:

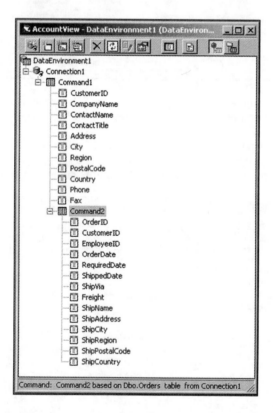

There's one more trick that's worth mentioning here. When the form creates a set of controls and a grid, Visual Basic chooses the type of controls to display the data in. However, you have control over the selection of the controls that you want. To select a different type of control, just pick the field out from the Data Environment and select Properties.

Building the Account View Control

To build the Account view control all we need to do is drag over the Command1 object from the Data Environment Designer onto the UserControl. The control UI will be automatically created and the links to the database will be established:

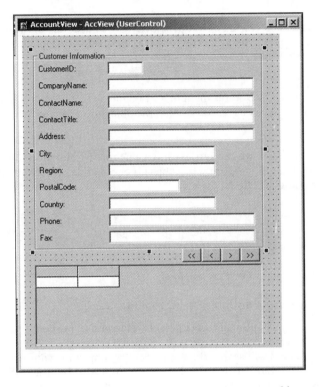

You can customize this as you like – here we've added some navigational buttons to scroll the Command1 Recordset object. The code for this functionality is trivial:

```
Private Sub Command1_Click()
    DataEnvironment1.rsCommand1.MoveLast
End Sub
```

```
Private Sub Command2_Click()
    DataEnvironment1.rsCommand1.MoveNext
End Sub
```

```
Private Sub Command3_Click()
    DataEnvironment1.rsCommand1.MovePrevious
End Sub
```

```
Private Sub Command4_Click()
DataEnvironment1.rsCommand1.MoveFirst
End Sub
```

You'll find a project that includes this control in the code download for this book, available from the Wrox Web site.

Persistence and Property Bags

PropertyBags were introduced with Visual Basic 5 as a methodology by which any of your control's properties can be stored.

> The `PropertyBag` object is an object provided by the UserControl, which enables an ActiveX Control to persist its properties – that is, save information about the state of the control at design-time.

When you use PropertyBags, VB stores them in a `.frm` file, with any binary information being stored in a `.frx` file. When we use and set a `PropertyBag`, the object is passed to our control using the `ReadProperties` and `WriteProperties` events.

When our control is initialized, we can retrieve any value that we stored in the bag using the `ReadProperty` method of the `PropertyBag` object. For example, if we wanted to retrieve the foreground color, we could use the following:

```
Private Sub UserControl_ReadProperties(PropBag As PropertyBag)
    txtSocialSec.ForeColor = PropBag.ReadProperty("ForeColor", &H80000008)
End Sub
```

The `ReadProperty` method has two parameters:

❑ The first is the name of the property we want to retrieve

❑ The second (which is optional) is the default value of that property

The `ReadProperty` method will search the `PropertyBag` object for your property. If it finds it, the value stored will be returned; otherwise, the default we supplied is returned. If neither a return value nor a default value was found, then the result is ignored, and you must provide some error trap to handle this case.

The `WriteProperties` method is fired when a control needs to save its properties to the `.frm` file. This method takes three parameters:

❑ The name of the property you want to store

❑ The property value to persist

❑ An optional default value for the property if the second parameter is empty

The following code save the `ForeColor` property value:

```
Private Sub UserControl_WriteProperties(PropBag As PropertyBag)
    Call PropBag.WriteProperty("ForeColor", txtSocialSec.ForeColor, _
                        &H80000008)
End Sub
```

Property Pages

Property pages are a good way to group individual related properties and present them to the user in a dialog where they can be set. These can be properties that need to be set together, and information to be validated or changed at the time it is being entered. The Windows user interface is littered with property pages, and we've already seen several in this chapter:

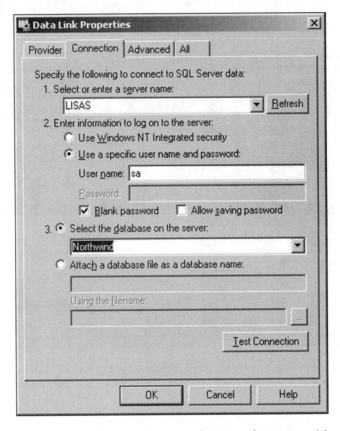

We can create property pages just like these to display (or change) our controls' properties.

It's a common practice not to include these properties as part of the Property Browser window. We can accomplish this by selecting the Don't Show in Browser flag in the Procedure Attribute dialog.

We can write validation code behind any of the controls on a property page, in much the same way as we develop our ActiveX control.

Once we create the property page, a new property will be created for our UserControl, called Custom. At VB design time, we can display the property page by clicking on the button associated with this property. We can then set the values of all the properties of that page and dismiss the dialog.

VB makes creating property pages easy for us, by providing the Property Page Wizard to do all our work for us.

The Property Page Wizard

The Property Page Wizard is a quick and convenient wizard that maps existing properties and creates the page for you automatically, including all the user interface elements.

To access the Wizard, either click Project | Add Property Page and select VB Property Page Wizard, or include it in the Add-Ins menu using the Add-In Manager. Then all you have to do is run the wizard, either Add a new property page or choose an existing one, and then select which properties you want to go on your chosen page:

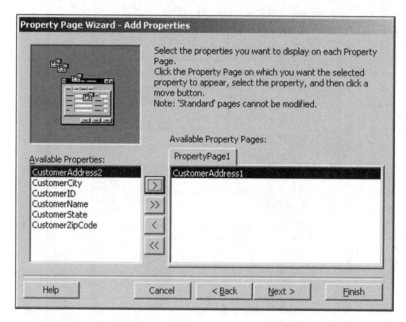

You can then organize the visual look and feel of your page, change the captions for the label controls to something more presentable to the user, instead of the default property name caption, and so forth:

Licensing Our Control

The final stage in all our hard work is to compile, package, and deploy our control. Many of the project settings when creating an ActiveX control are identical in behavior to the ones we set when building a VB COM server component. However, there is one setting that does not apply to our COM servers – in fact, it's disabled for an ActiveX DLL – which we can set in an ActiveX control. This is the Require License Key setting:

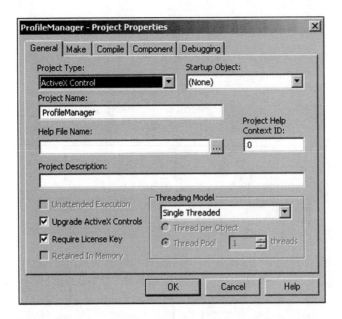

A license is a registry key that allows a developer to use a control in the design-time environment. This means that even if someone has got hold of your .ocx file and registered it for use, they won't be able to use it because they don't have the license key.

If we select to generate a license file, a Visual Basic license file (.vbl) will be created when we build the project. The .vbl file must be registered on the user's machine for the components to be used in the design environment.

The Package and Deployment Wizard will build a setup program that properly registers the information in the .vbl file on the end user's machine when that setup program is run. That's all you need to do if you want to generate a license file for your control. From this point on, all compatibility and interface versioning rules that we discussed earlier in the book should still be enforced here as well.

Summary

Windows DNA is a very rich platform of tools and technologies. It provides the developer with a long list of choices. Although the Internet has taken development by storm, the need to build rich Win32-based user interfaces is still in high demand, especially for those applications that possess very complicated UI requirements.

In this chapter we explored building these user interfaces as an ActiveX control. We have chosen Visual Basic to demonstrate this because it's the most popular language for developing UIs, and it's easy to migrate your existing form-building skills to creating ActiveX controls.

We have been building on the knowledge we gained in previous chapters of how to create servers, access databases, and retrieve data. We discussed using the most appropriate technology for your application, and bringing this data to the client. Once the data is at the client you can build your ActiveX control and bind it to the data.

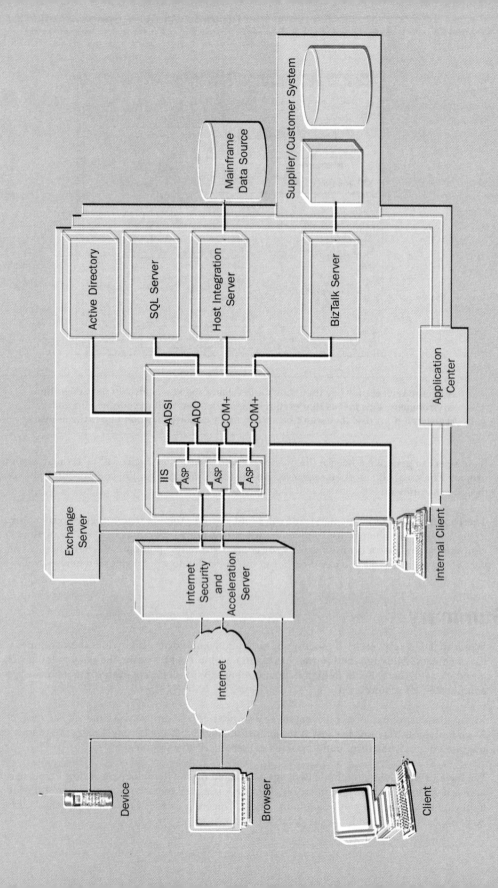

18

Developing Office-Based User Services

Microsoft Office has grown to be one of the world's favorite development tools for the small office environment, for many good reasons. With the growth and ease of use of **Visual Basic for Applications** (**VBA**), many computer users can perform such tasks as automating their work, or customizing a mailing list. They can even use the built-in data tools available to get at data stores that live on other data-hosting platforms, such as Oracle, SQL Server, MSDE, or an XML document. With the growing number of users wanting to get at data and functionality that lives on other platforms, COM naturally leads programmers into being able to make this functionality available to users, with very little end-user training. As we will see in this chapter, some standard functionality can be built into COM components and utilized by an Office application in order to quickly get a user the data they need without compromising data validation and security measures.

Microsoft Office fits into the DNA picture in two ways, by providing developers with alternative front-end development tools:

❑ To enhance an existing DNA application

❑ To create a pure Office-based application, using COM objects specifically developed for that application

The Office suite of applications uses **VBA modules**, and references to COM DLLs within those modules, to integrate into the DNA programming infrastructure. VBA is not a great departure from VB, but is an enhanced subset of VB in which the programmer can take advantage of the object models contained in each of the Office applications.

In this chapter we'll outline some examples that will give you an idea of:

❑   How to integrate Office applications (Excel, Access, Outlook, Word) as the front-end in a distributed network architecture

❑   How to call a COM object within a VBA application

❑   Examples of some business situations where Office should be considered as an alternative development tool to more standard options such as VB or web-based user interfaces

Why Use Office-Based User Interfaces?

Let's look at an example of how we can integrate Office into an application that already has a web or VB front-end. Suppose there is an existing application, a Sales and Marketing package in this case, that is used by perhaps 100 or so telephone marketing agents, and that has a good front-end but poor reporting capabilities. This application has COM objects that expose the data, so we can take advantage of these by utilizing other front-ends. As shown in the diagram below, we have our Marketing application taking advantage of the COM objects, and we also have our COM objects being used by several other front-ends:

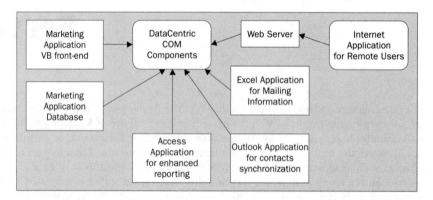

A standard web front-end for remote sales agents might be integrated into such an application, as shown, and we can also build:

❑   An Excel front-end that would pull mailing information from the COM components to create customized mailing lists

❑   An Outlook application to synchronize contacts information

❑   An Access application to enhance our reporting capabilities and integrate other valuable data in with our marketing and sales information

With many software packages the original code is not modifiable, but in this scenario we can use the available COM objects to make our enhancements, and customize the front-end to meet our requirements. In this way we can exploit the users' familiarity with common tools, such as those available in the Office suite.

Considerations When Using Office

Each development tool in the market has its own merits, and this is true of the Office suite as well. The Office suite provides us with the most flexibility in report presentation and the widest variety of interfaces that users are already familiar with. While VB is a great tool and makes attractive front-ends, there are times when using Access to do reporting, as opposed to other reporting tool add-ins that work with VB, is simply a better choice. For instance, sometimes there are proprietary data formats we need to develop special reports against, such as pre-packaged accounting software. Access with ADO can be used to get to any ODBC-compliant format and can further be used to extract specific information to combine into reports. This can actually be faster and more reliable than using a tool such as Crystal or FRX to simply "hook into" the existing data structures, due to the proprietary indexes that exist in these pre-packaged systems.

Reuse of Existing Objects

Another example of the flexibility we gain from Office products is that Outlook can be integrated into an existing application, instead of having to try to integrate a custom e-mail front-end into an application we are designing. In this chapter the examples we look at include some code for a new COM component, however the goal of this chapter is to outline how we can use the Office suite of products to access *existing* COM components that already work with an Office front-end. A programmer usually doesn't need to write any custom COM components specifically to include the Office suite in an application's set of interfaces. The most important aspect of designing an application where the programmer knows that there will be multiple front-ends is to take any common functions and create COM object libraries that can be accessed by all the front-ends.

Familiarity with Language

A few other considerations are necessary when using Office as a front-end environment. VBA is based on the VB language, so VB programmers already know the basics of the language. I won't pretend that you can just copy and paste code from a VB screen into a VBA module, but Microsoft is making the syntax cross over more in each release of VBA.

The data structures that other front-end tools use are the same as those used by Office. Office can interface with arrays, disconnected recordsets, scripting host dictionaries, XML streams and many of the other commonly used data structures. VBA does a few things differently, such as handling enumeration, and the methods of an ADO recordset are more limited currently than a DAO recordset.

The biggest limitation in VBA is that, other than when using COM components, the VBA code is directly linked to a worksheet, document or database and is not accessible outside of that resource. This is usually not a problem because we are directly affecting the resource we are running against. It is, however, a primary consideration that we need to always be aware of when deciding which code to extract to our own COM components in order to minimize redundancy.

Programming Standards

The use of subroutines versus functions is also an issue when programming in Office. If a routine is not going to be expected to give a return value or require a parameter, a subroutine is a good way to go, otherwise a function will be necessary. While working with VBA in an Office environment you can choose to run, or execute, a subroutine at any point by choosing Run from the menu, while a parameterized function requires a calling routine. For testing purposes it is best to use subroutines so you can execute the routine independently of the overall application menu or command structure.

Other considerations regarding programming standards do come into play, such as just in time activation of our objects. The goal when using COM within an Office application should always be to initialize objects as late in the application as possible and release them as early as possible. With the way COM+ handles object pooling and connection pooling the application will show no degradation in speed by initializing the COM component multiple times. This minimizes the number of components that are active at once, thus optimizing the use of our server resources. (Refer back to Chapter 6 for more details on how COM+ operates.)

The VBA modules we create in Office use references to other objects in a similar way to how a VB application would. Therefore, we also need to keep in mind that when we use other references in our projects in Office, such as integrating a calendar control in a form by installing an OCX, we have to include these additions as well in the rollout of the application. In planning for rolling out applications as Office documents, we will need to make specific plans on what to include in our rollout and do quite a bit of testing on different platforms to ensure it will all work smoothly.

We also need to keep in mind that Access databases have a tendency to grow in size as we work with them, so we need to compact them frequently. The worst instance I ever saw regarding Access' tendency to bloat was when a 9MB database had grown to 1GB due to some tables being imported then deleted without the compacting tool being used.

Using Schemas

Another programming technique that is available in the Office application suite is the use of schemas in our programs. In the past, not every object exposed its structure so that a programmer could gain access to its information store and know what pieces of information it contained. We want to take advantage of **schemas** to gain information that has become available that previously would have only been accessible if it was stored separately and then made available in a database. A schema is a structure definition that relates to an object, for example a database, network security. For instance, a database schema contains many things including the column list of a table, the list of tables within a database, and the list of indexes and to which tables the indexes belong. A network security schema would include the list of users, and their attributes, such as full name, groups belonged to, and what resources they have access to. The Office suite can also access XML schemas that provide the structure for data stored in XML streams. There is an example at the end of this chapter of how we can take an existing COM component and enhance it to include field names by accessing the schema tables of a SQL Server database. Further information on XML and schemas can be found in *Beginning XML* from Wrox Press (ISBN 1-861003-41-2.)

Benefits of Using COM Functionality in an Office Program

There are several benefits of using COM functionality in an Office program. A COM object makes available common elements of data across applications – information such as name and address from a payroll database, top customer information for a mailing located in a sales database, etc. In small and medium sized organizations different departments want to track different things about individuals – such as their medical and emergency contact information for personnel, phone list information, salary information. The core data for them all could be in a core information store somewhere, but the likelihood of it being complete with all possible pieces of information is low. Many departments resort to customizing a small application to track the information themselves, often at the expense of data integrity and security. A central COM component can expose data to individuals without these sacrifices so they can utilize or enhance the data with their own set of data, while the data can still be accessible to all other departments.

One of the other things end-users like is the way that Office can help them to present information attractively for ease of reading and use. Many other programs print out hard-to-read reports, which get re-typed and re-worked into easy-to-read consolidated information. COM can help automate these tasks as well by presenting a standard way to get to the data, while not sacrificing the capabilities built into the Office environment. This gives users the ability to customize the presentation of the data.

Many of the administration concerns have surrounded the topics of security and data integrity. As outlined in Chapter 20, the security behind COM can verify who gets access to the data store that the COM object has access to. As long as a data store is centralized, we can build COM components that expose the data in this data store to allow end-users to add to the data for their own needs, yet be guaranteed that the data is the most accurate in the organization.

The other main concern for programmers these days is the ability to re-use code. As stated throughout this book and many others, a well-designed COM component exploits the re-use of code by being available for use in any front-end application that can utilize COM functionality.

Developing the Office-Based Front Ends

In this chapter several examples are presented to demonstrate using the Office suite as an alternative front-end programming environment, in order to make available the specific functionality that Office provides. As illustrated in the diagrams and explanations in this section, each member of the suite has its own merits and common uses.

Firstly, we will develop a simple COM component that exposes mailing list and accounting data in a database, and performs validations. The purpose of the COM example is not to go over VB COM programming in detail, but just to give an example of a simple COM object that exposes and/or validates data against a SQL Server database. (Chapters 3 to 11 covered the details of designing and creating COM components.)

Once we've created the COM object we can move on to the front-end application examples from Excel, Access, Outlook and Word, which all use the COM component for data retrieval and validation. The first front-end example, done in Excel, exploits Excel's capabilities for a user to present data in a custom way for a mail-merge application. The Access example gives an idea of how Access can be used to enhance the data that is available through our COM component by adding information that might be tracked in another system. Our Outlook application utilizes the data-centric functionality of the COM component to synchronize a contacts folder. Finally we use Word to create customized documents using selected information from the database. There is also an example at the end of this chapter that describes how to take advantage of the schemas that are built in to SQL Server.

In all of the front-end examples, we have created the VBA macros through the Tools | Macros | Visual Basic Editor choice from the menu. All of our front-end examples include a reference to our COM object, which is named DNA2000.DNAMod and some have a reference to MSXML. All of the code is available in the download file from the Wrox web site.

SQL Server Database

The database is called COM Repository, and it has tables called MailingList, Departments, Divisions, GLAccounts and ValidCombinations. After creating a new database called COM Repository, the COMRepository.sql script file in the code download can be used to set up and populate the tables.

The COM Component

The COM component will be used later to hook into from Excel, Access, Outlook and Word. There is just one class, created in a VB6 project and then compiled into a DLL. In keeping with the idea of being able to utilize a single component for many front-ends and minimizing redundancy in code, our COM component is used in many ways. Our first piece of functionality serves the purpose of connecting to a SQL database via OLEDB, querying a table of mailing information, and then returning the results in an XML stream. This is implemented in a single function, which will be used to retrieve information for a mailing list, feed information to an Access data entry form and also synchronize a contact list in Outlook.

Our second piece of functionality serves the purpose of validating user input sent to it. It is made up of three functions that can be called individually to validate different pieces of information, and it also has one function that uses the other individual functions to validate a whole group of information. This validation functionality will validate a budget spreadsheet and will be used for approval of expense items in Access. I've added comments into the code to help explain what is going on in each function.

You will need to carry out a global search for "NTWKS", replacing it with the name of your SQL Server.

The Data-Centric Functionality

The DNAMailingListXML function in the COM component can be called upon to return an XML stream of information regarding a list of people. This function will be called to feed data into Excel for a mailing list, into Access for a data entry form, and to synchronize a contact list in Outlook. The function connects to a SQL Server database, parses the information from a recordset into an XML stream, and returns the data as an XML stream:

```
Function DNAMailingListXML(ByVal XMLDoc As msxml.DOMDocument) As msxml.DOMDocument

   Dim mConn As New ADODB.Connection
   Dim mRS As New ADODB.Recordset
   Dim XMLDoc As New MSXML.DOMDocument

 'Connect to SQL server database via OLEDB
   mConn.ConnectionString = "Provider=SQLOLEDB;UserID=RandomUser;" & _
                            "Persist Security Info=False;Initial Catalog=COM
 Repository;" & _
                            "Data Source=NTWKS"
   mConn.Open mConn.ConnectionString, "RandomUser"

 'Open data that we want to work with
   mRS.CursorLocation = adUseClient
   mRS.Open "SELECT Name, Address1, Address2, City," & _
            "State, Zip FROM MailingList", mConn, adOpenForwardOnly
   mRS.Save XMLDoc, adPersistXML

 'Close data connections
   mRS.Close
   mConn.Close
   Set mRS = Nothing
   Set mConn = Nothing

 End Function
```

Looking at the code there are a few things to note. First, I used the ADODB reference because this is something that must be done for Office, otherwise our reference is to a DAO recordset. In any case it's a good habit to get into so that the code is clear, even though it is redundant from a VB point of view:

```
Dim mRs As New ADODB.Recordset
```

The connection string includes a reference to the SQL Server OLEDB provider, which is specific, so we don't use the OLEDB provider for ODBC. The database is called COM Repository on the SQL Server NTWKS and there is a user of RandomUser. These would normally be variables passed in from the registry or a login function of some sort.

```
mConn.ConnectionString = "Provider=SQLOLEDB;UserID=RandomUser;" & _
                         "Persist Security Info=False;Initial Catalog=COM
Repository;" & _
                         "Data Source=NTWKS"
mConn.Open mConn.ConnectionString, "RandomUser"
```

Next our function loads an XML stream with data from our recordset, which will later be returned to our front-end application:

```
mRS.Save XMLDoc, adPersistXML
```

The Validation Functionality

One of the other common uses for COM objects is for validation. This type of COM object validates information passed to it, and indicates whether the information passed is valid or not. It is very useful in systems such as the one in this example, where data is being fed into an accounting system. In this example, this functionality is implemented by a set of functions within the COM component that can be called upon to validate a set of accounting information. These functions will be called to validate an Excel budget spreadsheet, and in Access for a data entry form. The example connects to the SQL Server database, validates the information, and returns feedback to the calling application in a variety of ways. The accounting information that is being validated is an account number, a company division (or organizational unit) number, and a department number. Our database table diagram looks like this:

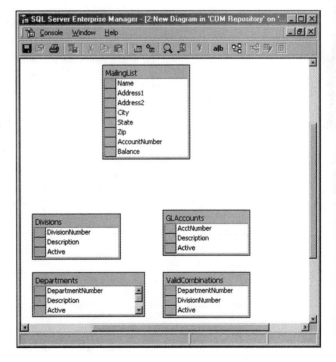

In our accounting example there is the ability for an account, department or division to either be active or inactive. In a real business a company division, for instance the North American division, might not use all of the department codes. If the North American division were a manufacturing division only, then it would not need the department codes for marketing or sales, just administration and accounting. Thus we not only want to be able to validate whether the division is a valid code, but that the code used in conjunction with the department code is acceptable, so we need to have our `ValidCombinations` table to link our valid department and division combinations.

Since we are trying to accommodate many different front-end applications that might want to validate individual pieces of information, our COM component contains four validation functions. We can go to each of three individual functions to validate the specific piece data or we can use the `AccountCombos` function to validate the account, division and department information all at once.

In the diagram below we see that, in order to use the function, a front-end application would need to supply our function with information and would receive return codes and text information regarding whether the information passed was valid. In this example, we use the `AccountCombos` function, which validates the account, department and division information individually and further validates the department and division combination:

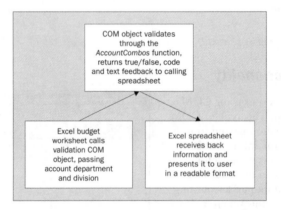

Let's look at the validation functionality in individual pieces. In accounting systems different pieces of information are valid during different time frames, so the information can be invalid, valid, valid and active, or valid but inactive, as you will see reflected in the return codes. Below I have the section of the COM component that sets up our return codes, which makes the rest of the COM component code easier to read. The code sets up the values for valid items, valid but inactive items, and invalid items by enumerating constants that relate to our numeric codes. This is placed in the general declarations section of the class module in our COM component:

```
Public Enum Results
    dnaInvalidItem = 0
    dnaValidInactive = 1
    dnaValidItem = 2
End Enum
```

Three of our four validating functions are identical to each other regarding the code used in the function, each validating against the appropriate table. We will look at the `Glacct` function which deals with a piece of General Ledger Account information. The `Dept` and `Division` functions use the same methodology but against the `Departments` and `Divisions` tables instead, so we won't study them here.

When thinking about departments keep in mind that they are often used to categorize the functional areas of a company. A department might not use all of the GL Accounts, for instance the sales department wouldn't use a GL Account for Advertising Expense, and not all departments would be located in all divisions because some things, such as accounting, are a centralized "overhead" function of a business.

```
Public Function Glacct(vAcct As Variant, sResult As Variant, sTxtResult As Variant)
As Variant
   On Error GoTo ReadError
   Dim mConn As New ADODB.Connection
   Dim mRS As New ADODB.Recordset
   mConn.ConnectionString = "Provider=SQLOLEDB;UserID=RandomUser;" & _
                            "Persist Security Info=False;" & _
                            "Initial Catalog=COM Repository;Data Source=NTWKS"

   mConn.Open mConn.ConnectionString, "RandomUser"

   mRS.Open "SELECT * FROM GLAccounts WHERE AcctNumber = '" & vAcct & "'", mConn, _
            adOpenForwardOnly

   sResult = dnaInvalidItem
   sTxtResult = vAcct & " Is Not A Valid GLAcct"

'********validate record

   If mRS.EOF Then
     sResult = dnaInvalidItem
     BuildResult vAcct, sResult, sTxtResult, "GlAcct"
   Else
     Do While Not mRS.EOF
       If mRS.Fields("Active").Value <> True Then
         sResult = dnaValidInactive
         Glacct = False
       Else
         sResult = dnaValidItem
         Glacct = True
       End If
       mRS.MoveNext
     Loop

'*********end validate record

     BuildResult vAcct, sResult, sTxtResult, "GlAcct"
   End If
   mRS.Close
   mConn.Close
   Set mRS = Nothing
   Set mConn = Nothing

   Exit Function

ReadError:
   mRS.Close
   mConn.Close
   Set mRS = Nothing
   Set mConn = Nothing
   GLAcct = False

End Function
```

After connecting to the database, the COM component connects to the database and queries the
GLAccounts table for the account number passed in:

```
mRS.Open "SELECT * FROM GLAccounts WHERE AcctNumber = '" & vAcct & "'", mConn, _
         adOpenForwardOnly
```

If the recordset comes up empty, then the account number passed in is not a valid account. If we get a
record in our recordset we then have to check the Active field to set up the return code for whether
our valid account is active or inactive. This is accomplished in this code:

```
Do While Not mRS.EOF
    If mRS.Fields("Active").Value <> True Then
        sResult = dnaValidInactive
        Glacct = False
    Else
        sResult = dnaValidItem
        Glacct = True
    End If
    mRS.MoveNext
```

Based on this result we set up our code and text results with a generic function (BuildResult) used
throughout the application, that is called by this code:

```
BuildResult vAcct, sResult, sTxtResult, "GlAcct"
```

The BuildResult function shown below sets up the text string that describes whether the information
returned is valid. This string is then returned to the application:

```
Function BuildResult(ByVal vItem As Variant, & _
         sResult As Variant, sTxtResult As Variant, & _
         ByVal sType As String) As Variant

   If sResult = dnaValidItem Then
     sTxtResult = "Valid, Active for " & sType & " "
   End If

   If sResult = dnaValidInactive Then
     sTxtResult = vItem & " Is Not an Active " & sType & " "
   End If

   If sResult = dnaInvalidItem Then
     sTxtResult = vItem & " Is Not a Valid " & sType & " "
   End If

End Function
```

In this example we return a true/false for the function, a numeric return code, and a text return code. The
true/false can be used if the front-end application simply wants to know if the validation succeeded or
failed completely. If the front-end application is more discerning about how much of the validation
succeeded or failed, it can use the numeric return codes to make decisions about what to do next. If the
front-end application wants to display text to inform a user about what portions failed or succeeded, our
text return code will accommodate that need. When programming a validation function it is important to
keep in mind the various front-end applications and how they might use the information returned to them.

Our fourth function consolidates the other functions just in case someone is trying to validate a GLAccount, Division, and Department combination. In our sample database not all departments function in all divisions. This function runs the other individual validations then looks to see if the combination of department and division is valid:

```
Public Function AccountCombos(vAcct As Variant, vDept As Variant, _
                vDivision As Variant, sResult As Variant, sTxtResult As Variant)
  On Error GoTo ReadError
  Dim mConn As New ADODB.Connection
  Dim mRS As New Recordset
  Dim bWorkRes As Boolean
  Dim sWorkRes As String

  mConn.ConnectionString = "Provider=SQLOLEDB;UserID=RandomUser;" &_
                    "Persist Security Info=False;Initial Catalog=COM
Repository;" &_
                    "Data Source=NTWKS"
  sResult = dnaValidItem

'*************** Validate GLAcct
  bRes = Glacct(vAcct, sResult, sTxtResult)
  sWorktxt = sTxtResult
  If sResult <> dnaValidItem Then
    AccountCombos = False
  Else
    AccountCombos = True
  End If
'*************** end GLAcct validation

  bWorkRes = AccountCombos
  sWorkRes = sResult

'*************** Validate Dept
  bRes = Dept(vDept, sResult, sTxtResult)
  sWorktxt = sTxtResult & sWorktxt
  If sResult <> dnaValidItem Then
    AccountCombos = False
  Else
    AccountCombos = True
  End If
  If bWorkRes = True And AccountCombos = True Then
    bWorkRes = bRes
  Else
    AccountCombos = False
  End If
'*************** end Dept validation

  bWorkRes = AccountCombos
  sWorkRes = sResult

'***************Validate Division
  bRes = Division(vDivision, sResult, sTxtResult)
  If bWorkRes = True And bRes = True Then AccountCombos = True
  sWorktxt = sTxtResult & sWorktxt
'*************** end Dept validation
```

```
'************* if all above is value, check combination
  If AccountCombos = True Then
    mConn.Open mConn.ConnectionString, "RandomUser"
    mRS.Open "SELECT * FROM ValidCombinations WHERE" & _
             "DivisionNumber = '" & vDivision & "' and" & _
             "DepartmentNumber = '" & vDept & "'", & _
             mConn, adOpenForwardOnly
    If mRS.EOF Then
        sWorkRes = dnaValidInactive
        sWorktxt = "Invalid Department, Division" & _
                   "combination" & "; " & sWorktxt
        AccountCombos = False
    ElseIf mRS("Active") = "N" Then
        sWorkRes = dnaValidItem
        sWorktxt = "Inactive Department, Division" & _
                   "combination" & "; " & sWorktxt
    Else
        sWorktxt = "Valid Combination" & "; " & sWorktxt
    End If
    sResult = sWorkRes
    sTxtResult = sWorktxt
    mRS.Close
    mConn.Close

    Set mRS = Nothing
    Set mConn = Nothing
    Exit Function
    Else
      sResult = sWorkRes
      sTxtResult = sWorktxt
      Set mRS = Nothing
      Set mConn = Nothing
    Exit Function
  End If
'************* end Valid combination checking

  Exit Function

  ReadError:
    mRS.Close
    mConn.Close
    Set mRS = Nothing
    Set mConn = Nothing
End Function
```

In this combination function we use our other three functions to validate the individual pieces, setting up a cascading result for the whole combination of values. The code lines similar to the one shown below are the ones which call the other three functions:

```
bRes = Glacct(vAcct, sResult, sTxtResult)
```

After each of the three other functions we determine whether the three functions as a whole were successful:

```
sWorktxt = sTxtResult
If sResult <> dnaValidItem Then
    AccountCombos = False
Else
    AccountCombos = True
End If
```

Given that all three pieces of information are valid we then connect to the `ValidCombinations` table...

```
mRS.Open "SELECT * FROM ValidCombinations WHERE" & _
    "DivisionNumber = '" & vDivision & "' and" & _
    "DepartmentNumber = '" & vDept & "'", & _
                    mConn, adOpenForwardOnly
```

... And check the department/division combination using the same logic we did in the individual functions. We then, by the same manner as for our other three functions, give the front-end application feedback as to whether or not the combination of values is valid:

```
If mRS.EOF Then
        sWorkRes = dnaValidInactive
        sWorktxt = "Invalid Department, Division" & _
                    "combination" & "; " & sWorktxt
        AccountCombos = False
    ElseIf mRS("Active") = "N" Then
        sWorkRes = dnaValidItem
        sWorktxt = "Inactive Department, Division" & _
                    "combination" & "; " & sWorktxt
    Else
        sWorktxt = "Valid Combination" & "; " & sWorktxt
    End If
```

In summary, the COM component discussed above is used for retrieval of data and for validation of data. The first function retrieves data, and returns it as an XML stream for use later by a variety of front-end applications. The second part of the component takes data from a variety of front-end applications and returns information that could be used in several ways to give feedback to the user whether the information input is valid.

The Use of Excel with COM Components

As programmers we can empower users through the use of Excel as a COM front-end. As mentioned earlier, Excel is an everyday tool for many computer users. For quite a while, Excel users have had programmers automating their spreadsheets in order to save time. For example, we can put a button on a spreadsheet that organizes data, enters defaults based on other entry items, or creates a different layout on another worksheet for a more attractive presentation of the data on the original spreadsheet. It is now easy to integrate COM into our automation scenarios so that users can gain access to data outside their worksheets, which cuts down on retyping data and ensures better data validation.

As programmers, we know that many users are familiar with how to use functions like Sum, Min, Max, Left, and Right and understand the basics of providing a function with information in order to get a required result. This end-user knowledge makes it very easy to teach an Excel user, who understands modules, how to use a COM function. For those users who aren't macro and module savvy we can automate their worksheets or databases by adding code to buttons on their worksheet or on a startup form. I have made simple COM objects available for use in an Excel application with great success due to the ease of use of functions.

When working with Excel, you can get into the VBA area of any workbook by selecting Macro from the Tools menu, then selecting Visual Basic Editor in the sub-menu. This opens up a Visual Basic Editor session. At this point you would add a module by selecting Module from the Insert menu.

VBA in Word, Excel 97, Access 2000 and Outlook 2000 opens up the VBA session as a completely separate process instead of within the current application process, which is a change over previous versions where the VBA editor appeared to be a more integral part of the application.

Once you have an opened module you can use the References section to add a reference to a registered COM object. This makes the object available to any module within the spreadsheet.

The Excel Object Model

The Excel object model includes functions that allow a programmer to manipulate everything that a user can do from the Excel menus. The object model is complete and inclusive of properties and events for major classes within Excel, like the `Application`, `Workbook`, `Worksheet`, and `Range` objects. A diagram of the four major objects in the object model and some common properties and functions specific to Excel is shown below:

Application Object	Workbbok Object	Worksheet Object	Range Object
Properties	**Properties**	**Properties**	**Properties**
ActiveWorkbook	Name	Cells	Cells
ActiveSheet	Activesheet	Rows	Address
ActiveCell	Sheets	Columns	Columnwidth
Name	Saved	Name	Rowheight
		Visible	Value
Methods	**Methods**	**Methods**	**Methods**
FindFile	Activate	Activate	Clear
GoTo	Close	Copy	Offset
Onkey	Save	Move	Filldown
Quit	SaveAs	Printout	Insert
			Delete

Excel Example Using the Data-Centric Functionality of the COM Object

Earlier we built a data-centric COM component that, when called, returns an XML stream of mailing information. This type of COM object is quite useful in Excel – it can be used with the mailing list information in order to present the information in a custom format, or used in a Word MailMerge to form a list of mailing labels or a batch of custom letters. The purpose of the macro below is to unpack the XML stream returned by the COM object into a spreadsheet, which is laid out in a format for a Word MailMerge. The macro has some code in it to help illustrate some of the properties and methods shown in the diagram above.

Let's now look at our example code from the Excel macro (the code is available in the `getdata` macro in the Excel spreadsheet file `mailinglistxml.xls`). We first dimension our variables, including our COM object, which is referenced by `DNA2000.DNAMod`. We then create the object reference and call the object that sets `mData` to our returned XML stream:

```
Sub getdata()

Dim mData As New MSXML.DOMDocument
Dim mObject As DNA2000.DNAMod
Dim x As Integer
Dim child
Dim currnode
Dim childnode
Dim item

x = 0
'Create object reference
Set mObject = CreateObject("DNA2000.DNAMod")

'Call object, setting mData to the result of our function, an XML Stream
mObject.DNAMailingListXML mData

'Destroy object once results are received
Set mObject = Nothing
```

We then traverse our XML tree to get to where our data resides:

```
'Set up XML Document element and childnodes
Set child = mData.documentElement
Set currnode = mData.documentElement.childNodes.item(1)
```

We then move to cell A1, and populate the worksheet by setting the values of cells equal to our XML schema contents:

```
Application.Goto reference:=Worksheets(1).Range("A1")
For Each item In currnode.childNodes
    Set childnode = currnode.childNodes.item(x)
    Selection.Value = childnode.getAttribute("Name")
    Selection.Offset(0, 1).Select
    Selection.Value = childnode.getAttribute("Address1")
    Selection.Offset(0, 1).Select
    Selection.Value = childnode.getAttribute("Address2")
    Selection.Offset(0, 1).Select
    Selection.Value = childnode.getAttribute("City")
    Selection.Offset(0, 1).Select
    Selection.Value = childnode.getAttribute("State")
    Selection.Offset(0, 1).Select
    Selection.Value = childnode.getAttribute("Zip")
    Selection.Offset(0, 1).Select
    x = x + 1
    Selection.Offset(1, -6).Select
Next

End Sub
```

The results of our macro would look something like this:

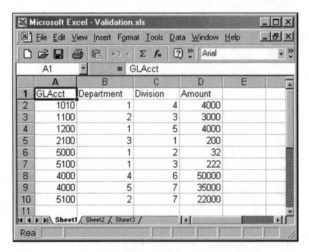

Excel Example Using the Validation Functionality of the COM Object

We also built validation functionality into the COM component that, when called, returns a result Boolean, code, and a text string of information. This type of COM object is quite useful in Excel to validate input against a database of known good items or values. The purpose of the macro below is to take some data entry from an Excel budget-style worksheet and send it to our COM object for validation. The macro then receives the information back about any errors that occurred, and displays an easy to understand error message for the user. Below is a sample worksheet that would be used to run against our validation object. The purpose is to ensure that our combination of Account, Department and Division is valid to be imported into our Accounting Budget System:

Let's look at the code in our macro (available in the `validate` macro in `validation.xls`):

```
Sub Validate()

Dim sResult As Variant
Dim sTxtResult As Variant
Dim mObject As DNA2000.DNAMod
Dim x As Integer
Dim vAcct As Variant
Dim vDivision As Variant
Dim vDept As Variant
```

After dimensioning our variables we pick up the values for Account, Division and Department from their appropriate cells on the worksheet:

```
Application.Goto reference:=Worksheets(1).Range("A2")

Do While Selection.Value > 0
    'Store worksheet values to pass to object
    vAcct = Selection.Value
    Selection.Offset(0, 1).Select
    vDept = Selection.Value
    Selection.Offset(0, 1).Select
    vDivision = Selection.Value
```

We then create the object reference and call our object that sets `mData` to the Boolean return value:

```
    'Create object reference
    Set mObject = CreateObject("DNA2000.DNAMod")

    'Call object, setting mData to the result of our function
     mData = mObject.AccountCombos(vAcct, vDept, vDivision, sResult, sTxtResult)

    'Destroy object once results are received
    Set mObject = Nothing
```

We then populate the last column with the text string return message so the user can fix any errors and revalidate the data:

```
    'Populate worksheet with return message
    Selection.Offset(0, 2).Select
    Selection.Value = sTxtResult
    Selection.Offset(1, -4).Select
Loop
End Sub
```

The results of running our worksheet above is illustrated below. As you can see, the user would be able to act on the result listed in the right-hand column and resubmit the worksheet for validation again after the errors were fixed:

	A	B	C	D	E
1	GLAcct	Department	Division	Amount	
2	1010	1	4	4000	Valid Combination; Valid, Active for Division Valid, Active for Department Valid, Active for GlAcct
3	1100	2	3	3000	Valid, Active for Division Valid, Active for Department 1100 Is Not a Valid GlAcct
4	1200	1	5	4000	Valid Combination; Valid, Active for Division Valid, Active for Department Valid, Active for GlAcct
5	2100	3	1	200	Valid Combination; Valid, Active for Division Valid, Active for Department Valid, Active for GlAcct
6	5000	1	2	32	Valid Combination; 2 Is Not an Active Division Valid, Active for Department Valid, Active for GlAcct
7	5100	1	3	222	Valid Combination; Valid, Active for Division Valid, Active for Department Valid, Active for GlAcct
8	4000	4	6	50000	Invalid Department, Division combination; Valid, Active for Division Valid, Active for Department Valid, Active for GlAcct
9	4000	5	7	35000	7 Is Not a Valid Division 5 Is Not a Valid Department Valid, Active for GlAcct
10	5100	2	7	22000	Invalid Department, Division combination; 7 Is Not a Valid Division Valid, Active for Department Valid, Active for GlAcct
11					

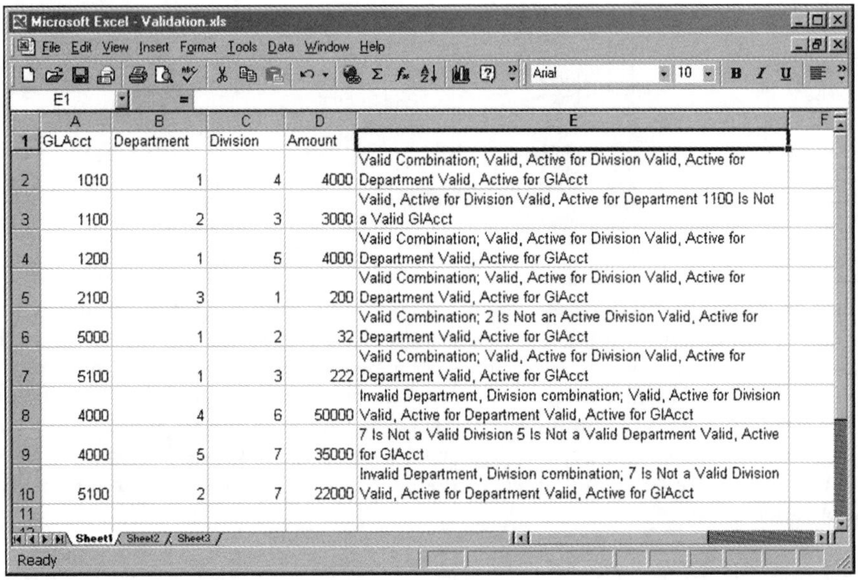

The Use of Access with COM Components

Access has become well known as a desktop database solution. Many users are familiar with how to utilize its strong reporting and querying capabilities. Everyday users are more familiar with it than other tools that might be add-ins to a front-end application written in Visual Basic. Access has many form features to allow users to also have their own custom data integrated with valid data from another database. An example would be the adding of contact management information to customer information, updated via a COM object linked to an accounting package. Another example would be tracking returns on items, the reasons and response times, with returns information supplied by the accounting package and reasons and response times being custom.

The Access Object Model

The Access object model includes all of the functions relating to an Access project, including forms, reports, and the objects such as text boxes, option groups, labels, listboxes, comboboxes and command buttons. A programmer can dynamically change the appearance of a user form or report, make command buttons appear and disappear, and even change the purpose of a command button in code on the fly. Access modules are often written as functions to feed back information to calling forms or command buttons. Since Access is a database there is another level of functionality – that of the DAO database object model for backward compatibility with older versions of Access and the Jet 4.0 database object model for the Access 2000 release. These database object models are available for caching data locally for manipulation and use in reporting or forms. The ability to access localized database tables without having to retrieve information externally is a feature of using Access forms that isn't available to other front-end development tools such as VB. Reporting capabilities that are inherent to Access are very powerful and provide another good reason to use Access as a development tool. One example of a difference between VB and Access is that while VB has direct access to the Common Dialog boxes, Access needs to have a reference to comctl32.ocx to gain the same functionality.

The major objects, and some of their properties and functions, are shown below:

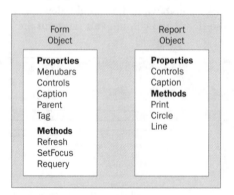

Generally, in an Access database that has been set up for end-users, we set up an option which opens a form, with command buttons leading to other forms and reports, so the user doesn't have to interface with the Access main menu. When the database is opened the user has a simple menu of things to choose from. This is set up under the Tools, Startup Menu choice. The form we have set up for our example has simple command buttons on it that lead the user to the forms and reports available in our database. This is the basic concept behind the switchboard wizard Access provides. There is also a multi-level menu structure command object available if you wish to design custom menus for the users of your application.

In Access, a programmer can either place the code behind an individual object residing on a form or report or centralize the code in a single module that is called by the event properties of the form or report. Both methods are done through the properties of the form. On the form's Properties, Events tab you can point to an event that is coded behind the form, or type in the name of a valid function residing in an Access module. Centralizing the code in Access modules makes it easier for other programmers to locate code, and also makes it clearer as to which events in a form or report cause code to get executed. We've used centralized code in our examples, under the open events.

Access Example Using the Data-Centric Functionality of the COM Object

Let's now look at an example using our previously explained data-centric functionality. In this example we will be using the returned XML stream to bring up information in an Access form. We have used the same COM object that we did in our earlier Excel example that created a mailing list, illustrating one of the primary reasons for using COM components – code re-use.

In this Access example (customer.mdb) we have a simple data entry form that is to be utilized for rapid entry of returned items. This business example illustrates how a certain group within an organization might want to track information outside of other software systems. This example would interface with a main database, where data is stored and maintained for its name and address information, but where information regarding product returns is only stored locally.

We have used a menu with two buttons on it to work as a main menu for our application, as shown below:

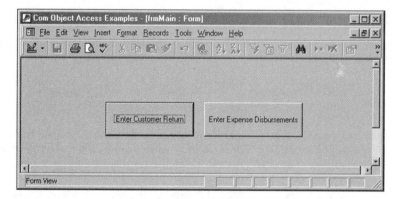

Once the user selects the left-hand button we go into our data entry screen, used to track additional information regarding the return of products in our example. We'll step through the code for this next.

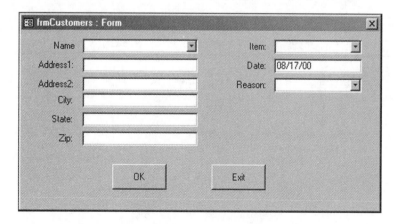

Let's look at the code that interfaces with our COM object. This runs when we hit the "Enter Customer Return" button on our menu:

```
Function frmCustomerReturn() As Boolean

    Dim mData As New MSXML.DOMDocument
    Dim x As Integer
    Dim i As Integer
    Dim mObject As DNA2000.DNAMod
    Dim child
    Dim currnode
    Dim childnode
    Dim item
```

Before our customer form opens we use our COM object to locally cache the data for our form. We call our COM object that returns our populated XML stream:

```
'set up to call COM Object
Set db = CurrentDb()
Set mObject = CreateObject("DNA2000.DNAMod")

'Get data from database
mObject.DNAMailingListXML mData
Set mObject = Nothing
```

We then use the `SysCmd` command to display a message to the user along the bottom left-hand corner of the Access screen:

```
'Cache data locally in Access, letting user know what's going on
SysCmd acSysCmdSetStatus, "Creating Table for Customers"
```

We cache the data by clearing a local table and caching the information received from our COM object. This method always keeps the customer information synchronized with the main database. Note the setting of the two variables, `child` and `currnode` which sets up the ability to traverse our XML tree:

```
db.Execute "DELETE * FROM Customers", dbFailOnError
Set mRst = db.OpenRecordset("Customers", dbOpenTable)

Set child = mData.documentElement
Set currnode = mData.documentElement.childNodes.item(1)

For Each item In currnode.childNodes
    Set childnode = currnode.childNodes.item(x)
    mRst.AddNew
    mRst(0) = childnode.getAttribute("Name")
    mRst(1) = childnode.getAttribute("Address1")
    mRst(2) = childnode.getAttribute("Address2")
    mRst(3) = childnode.getAttribute("City")
    mRst(4) = childnode.getAttribute("State")
    mRst(5) = childnode.getAttribute("Zip")
    x = x + 1
    mRst.Update
Next
mRst.Close
```

After the data is cached we use the DoCmd command to open our form, whose open event fires another piece of code, as we'll explain next:

```
    DoCmd.OpenForm FormName:="frmCustomers", WindowMode:=acDialog,
DataMode:=acFormEdit

    Set mFrm = Nothing

End Function
```

For ease of tracking what events occur in our form, we have centralized the code for our form in a module called frmCustomer_Events. As you can see from the form's **Property Event** tab shown below, the **On Open** event goes to our code and passes the parameter of the OpenForm event:

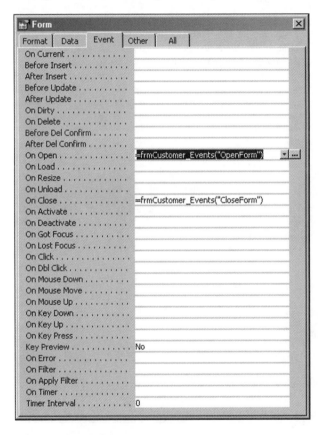

Let's look at the code that runs behind the events that fire on our form:

```
Function frmCustomer_Events(cEvent As String)
    Dim mRstUpdate As Recordset
    Set mFrm = Forms!frmCustomers
    Set db = CurrentDb()
    Set mRst = db.OpenRecordset("Customers", dbOpenDynaset)
    Set mRstUpdate = db.OpenRecordset("CustomerReturnNotes")
```

```
Select Case cEvent

   Case "OpenForm"
     SysCmd acSysCmdSetStatus, "Ready"
     mFrm.cmbname.SetFocus

   Case "NameChange"
     mRst.FindFirst ("Name = '" & mFrm.cmbname & "'")
     mFrm.txtAddress1 = mRst("Address1")
     mFrm.txtAddress2 = mRst("Address2")
     mFrm.txtCity = mRst("City")
     mFrm.txtState = mRst("State")
     mFrm.txtZip = mRst("Zip")

   Case "cmdOK_Click"
     mRstUpdate.AddNew
     mRstUpdate("Name") = mFrm!cmbname.Value
     mRstUpdate("Item Returned") = mFrm!cmbItem.Value
     mRstUpdate("Date Returned") = mFrm!txtdate.Value
     mRstUpdate("Reason Returned") = mFrm!cmbReason.Value
     mRstUpdate.Update
     SysCmd acSysCmdSetStatus, "Record Saved, Enter next record or Exit"
     mFrm.cmbname = ""
     mFrm.txtAddress1 = ""
     mFrm.txtAddress2 = ""
     mFrm.txtCity = ""
     mFrm.txtState = ""
     mFrm.txtZip = ""
     mFrm.cmbItem = ""
     mFrm.txtdate = Format(Now(), "mm/dd/yy")
     mFrm.cmbReason = ""
     mFrm.cmbname.SetFocus

   Case "cmdCancel_Click"
     DoCmd.Close acForm, mFrm.Name, acSaveNo
     SysCmd acSysCmdSetStatus, "Ready"

   Case "CloseForm"
     Set mFrm = Nothing
     mRst.Close
   End Select

End Function
```

Now, looking at the events that fire behind our form, we can see that our OpenForm event sets the focus on our form to the **Name** combobox:

```
SysCmd acSysCmdSetStatus, "Ready"
mFrm.cmbname.SetFocus
```

The user would then choose the customer name, and that would fire the NameChange event in our event handling code. Once the screen is updated with the particular information for that customer, the user would enter the item returned, date, and reason, and press **OK** to move onto the next item returned. The pressing of the **OK** button on our form executes more code, shown below, that updates a local database and prompts the user to go onto the next item:

```
Case "cmdOK_Click"
    mRstUpdate.AddNew
    mRstUpdate("Name") = mFrm!cmbname.Value
    mRstUpdate("Item Returned") = mFrm!cmbItem.Value
    mRstUpdate("Date Returned") = mFrm!txtdate.Value
    mRstUpdate("Reason Returned") = mFrm!cmbReason.Value
    mRstUpdate.Update
    SysCmd acSysCmdSetStatus, "Record Saved, " & _
    "Enter next record or Exit"
    mFrm.cmbname = ""
    mFrm.txtAddress1 = ""
    mFrm.txtAddress2 = ""
    mFrm.txtCity = ""
    mFrm.txtState = ""
    mFrm.txtZip = ""
    mFrm.cmbItem = ""
    mFrm.txtdate = Format(Now(), "mm/dd/yy")
    mFrm.cmbReason = ""
    mFrm.cmbname.SetFocus
```

Some simple techniques have been applied in the database, such as comboboxes to control entry to valid items, and pre-population of fields for improved data entry speed.

Access Example Using the Validation Functionality of the COM Object

In this example we will be taking data from a form and sending it to the same object we used for our Excel validation project above. The form is opened by code similar to that used in the data-centric example above, and the code that holds the events for this form is again centralized into a frmExpense_Events module. The data entry form, accessed when a user clicks on the Enter Expense Disbursements button in the menu, is shown below:

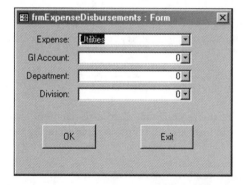

The idea behind this form is that it queries a local database for outstanding expense items that don't have disbursement information included in the record, and brings up those records for a user to complete the disbursement information. The user would choose the disbursement information and then click OK. Let's examine the code:

```
Function frmExpense_Events(cEvent As String)
    Dim mObject As DNA2000.DNAMod
    Dim bresult As Boolean
    Dim sResult As Integer
    Dim sTxtResult As String
    Set mFrm = Forms!frmExpenseDisbursements

    Select Case cEvent
```

557

Now, looking at the events that fire behind our form, we can see that our OpenForm event looks at the data and sets up the form to rotate through any expenses that don't have any account, department and division information. It also sets the rowsources of the comboboxes so the user has a valid set of items to choose from, making data validation more controlled:

```
Case "OpenForm"
  SysCmd acSysCmdSetStatus, "Ready"
  mFrm.RecordSource = "SELECT * FROM Expenses where GLAcct = 0"
  mFrm.cmbGlAcct.RowSource = "SELECT * FROM GlAccounts"
  mFrm.cmbDepartment.RowSource = "SELECT * FROM Departments"
  mFrm.cmbDivision.RowSource = "SELECT * FROM Divisions"
  mFrm.cmbExpense.SetFocus
```

The user would then choose the customer name that would fire the NameChange event in our event handling code. Once the screen is updated with the particular information for that customer, the user would enter the item returned, date, and reason, and press OK to move onto the next item returned. Once the user enters the data and clicks the OK button, the data on the form is sent to our COM object for validation:

```
Case "cmdOK_Click"
  Set mObject = CreateObject("DNA2000.DNAMod")
  bResult = mObject.AccountCombos(mFrm.cmbGlAcct.Value, mFrm.cmbDepartment.Value, _
          mFrm.cmbDivision.Value, sResult, sTxtResult)
  Set mObject = Nothing
```

The object returns any error information which is then placed on the lower left corner of the Access status bar:

```
If bResult = False Then
  SysCmd acSysCmdSetStatus, sTxtResult
  mFrm.cmbGlAcct.SetFocus
Else
  DoCmd.SelectObject acForm, mFrm.Name
  DoCmd.GoToRecord Record:=acNext
```

The form checks for the end of the records that need disbursement information in them by looking for the newrecord indicator of the form's recordsource, and ending the user's data entry session:

```
  If mFrm.NewRecord Then
      DoCmd.Close acForm, mFrm.Name, acSaveNo
      SysCmd acSysCmdSetStatus, "Record Saved, End of Entry"
    Else
      SysCmd acSysCmdSetStatus, "Record Saved, Enter Next Record or Exit"
    End If
  End If

Case "cmdCancel_Click"
  DoCmd.Close acForm, mFrm.Name, acSaveNo
  SysCmd acSysCmdSetStatus, "Ready"

Case "CloseForm"
  Set mFrm = Nothing
End Select

End Function
```

In our Access examples we looked at how we could use the data-centric and validation functionality of our COM object to retrieve and validate information that was entered and maintained in a local Access database. We used many properties and methods from our Access object model for illustration.

The Use of Outlook with COM Components

Microsoft Outlook is quickly becoming a desktop standard for e-mail front-end applications, competing against ISP-based mail services. Many companies are also using it in-house in preference to Exchange and other mail servers that are available today. Outlook 2000 added the capabilities to have a VBA module available within an Outlook session. This gave programmers the same capabilities that we have had in the other products within the Microsoft product suite to utilize VBA modules to access our COM functions.

Digital Dashboards

Outlook also has the ability to have **Digital Dashboards** written for users. A Digital Dashboard is a centralized location where users can see important information that has many diverse sources. For example, these sources could include the e-mail inbox, a stock quote web page, a spreadsheet, a things-to-do list, and a global message updated daily to company employees. Digital Dashboards can also be integrated with data sources that are relational or OLAP-based.

The fundamental reasoning behind the use of a Digital Dashboard is to provide users with consolidated views of their critical information with little to no training. A Digital Dashboard application uses the familiar web-browser style controls for friendly user interaction. A Digital Dashboard is easily deployed throughout an organization and has low administrative overhead.

There is a Digital Dashboard Resource Kit downloadable from the MSDN download subscription site. The most recent version of the resource kit was designed with end-users in mind, and has greater flexibility and increased ease of management.

The Outlook Object Model

The Outlook object model for VBA mainly consists of interaction with user-customized forms, or with generating contacts, e-mails, appointments and notes. You can also access the object model from other front-ends, such as Access, and schedule appointments or update contacts from another front-end. The Outlook object model is illustrated below:

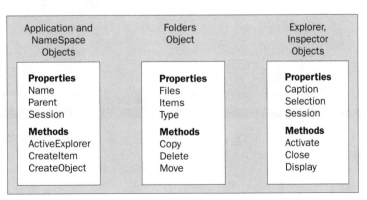

We can now use this VBA functionality in similar ways to how we did in our other examples in this chapter. Adding a module in Outlook is similar to the way we do it in Excel. In the example which follows we have a customized Contact form that is using the standard address fields for Home Address Street, Home Address City, Home Address State and Home Address Postal Code and populating/updating those fields against our mailing list database. This example will speed input and allow users to be certain that this data is correct within their contacts area of Outlook at all times.

Outlook Example Using the Data-Centric Functionality of the COM Object

By using a customized Contact form, as shown below, we can access more address and other types of fields than we could on a standard form. We are again going to access our COM object in order to keep our contact information synchronized with our main data store of customer information. Using this customized form we can use a VBA module to keep the address information updated without having the user do any additional typing. The macro should be added to the standard toolbar in Outlook to make it available to users. This example could be further enhanced to add any contacts to the contact list that were added to the database:

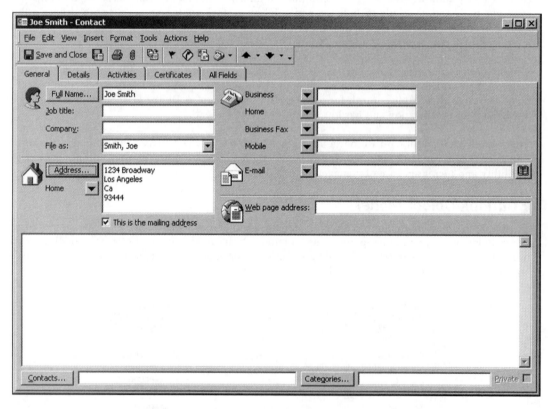

Let's look at the code entered in our VBA module that synchronizes our contacts. This code is available in Outlook.txt:

```
Sub getdata()

    Dim mObject As DNA2000.DNAMod
    Dim mData As Variant
```

We have dimensioned several Outlook variables to gain access to our Contacts folder and items which are in that folder:

```
Dim mAppl As Outlook.Application
Dim mItem As Outlook.ContactItem
Dim objContactsFolder As Outlook.MAPIFolder
Dim objContacts As Outlook.Items
Dim objContact As Object
Dim i As Integer
Dim x As Integer
Set mObject = CreateObject("DNA2000.DNAMod")
```

We firstly call the COM object and retrieve the latest contact information from the database:

```
'Call object, setting mData to the result of our function, an XML Stream
mData = mObject.DNAMailingList
Set mObject = Nothing

' Specify which contact folder to work with
Set objContactsFolder = Session.GetDefaultFolder(olFolderContacts)
Set objContacts = objContactsFolder.Items
```

We then go item by item through our Contacts folder, updating those contacts that exist. At the end we display a message for the user, telling them how many contacts were updated:

```
i = 0
x = 0

Do While x < UBound(mData, 1)
    ' Process the changes
    For Each objContact In objContacts
        If TypeName(objContact) = "ContactItem" Then
            If objContact.FullName = mData(x, 0) Then
                objContact.HomeAddressStreet = mData(x, 1)
                objContact.HomeAddressCity = mData(x, 3)
                objContact.HomeAddressState = mData(x, 4)
                objContact.HomeAddressPostalCode = mData(x, 5)
                objContact.Save
                i = i + 1
            End If
        End If
    Next
    x = x + 1
Loop

MsgBox "Number of contacts updated:" & Str$(i)

Set objContact = Nothing
Set objContacts = Nothing
Set objContactsFolder = Nothing

End Sub
```

In our Outlook example we used a VBA module to interact with our COM object's data-centric behavior so that our contacts would stay up-to-date. We would add items to the toolbar in Outlook to make our VBA macros available to other users.

The Use of Word with COM Components

Word has become the absolute standard for word processing. It accommodates everything from short letters to book-length documents. It works well with other Windows programs to incorporate objects such as spreadsheets, charts, and pictures into its documents. We have the ability to utilize the VBA modules within Word, much like we do in Excel, to gain access to data that lives on other platforms. Many times we want to integrate data into documents such as mailing lists, mail-merge letters, and envelopes. In the past we really used the Mail Merge feature, either with an Excel-based list or a table within a Word document, to generate these documents.

The Word Object Model

The Word object model allows a programmer to work with objects such as documents, tables, styles, find and replace, MailMerge and envelopes, to name just a few. It allows you to type directly into a document, copy and paste OLE objects, and apply formats to existing documents. The Word object model's most popular elements are:

Document Object	Paragraph Object	MailMerge Object	Tables Object
Properties	**Properties**	**Properties**	**Properties**
Application	Alignment	Datasource	Borders
Count	Borders	Fields	Columns
Creator	Format	Destination	Rows
Parent			Parent
Methods	**Methods**	**Methods**	**Methods**
Add	Add	Check	Select
Open	Next	EditDataSource	Delete
Save	Previous		Split
	Delete		

Word Example Using the Data-Centric Functionality of the COM Object

The example below illustrates some of the uses of our object model. This code is available in the `getdata` macro in `samplewordoc.doc`. In the example we are using our COM object to provide the data to build a letter with appropriate address information, as supplied from our data store of customer information. The code is very simple. We dimension our variables for our XML stream and our object, call our COM object, and store the results in our XML stream, `mData`:

```
Sub getdata()

    Dim mObject As DNA2000.DNAMod
    Dim mData As New MSXML.DOMDocument
    Dim x As Integer
    Dim child
    Dim currnode
    Dim childnode
    Dim item
    Dim addresstext As String

    Set mObject = CreateObject("DNA2000.DNAMod")
    mObject.DNAMailingListXML mData
    Set mObject = Nothing
    Set child = mData.documentElement
    Set currnode = mData.documentElement.childNodes.item(1)
    x = 0
    Set childnode = currnode.childNodes.item(1)
```

We then build our Word document by adding paragraphs and populating the paragraphs with text and the results of our COM object:

```
Application.ActiveDocument.Paragraphs(1).Range.Text = "Hi There,"
Application.ActiveDocument.Paragraphs.Add
Application.ActiveDocument.Paragraphs.Add
Application.ActiveDocument.Paragraphs(3).Range.Text = _
            "This is an example of a letter made" & _
            "with the information supplied from a COM Object."
Application.ActiveDocument.Paragraphs.Add
Application.ActiveDocument.Paragraphs.Add
Application.ActiveDocument.Paragraphs(5).Range.Text = _
            "The address we have on file for you is:"
Application.ActiveDocument.Paragraphs.Add
Application.ActiveDocument.Paragraphs(6).Range.Text =
childnode.getAttribute("Name")
Application.ActiveDocument.Paragraphs.Add
Application.ActiveDocument.Paragraphs(7).Range.Text =
childnode.getAttribute("Address1")
Application.ActiveDocument.Paragraphs.Add
If Not IsNull(childnode.getAttribute("Address2")) Then
    Application.ActiveDocument.Paragraphs(8).Range.Text = _
            childnode.getAttribute("Address2")
End If
Application.ActiveDocument.Paragraphs.Add
addresstext = childnode.getAttribute("City") _
            & ", " & childnode.getAttribute("State") & " " _
            & childnode.getAttribute("Zip")
Application.ActiveDocument.Paragraphs(9).Range.Text = addresstext
Set mData = Nothing

End Sub
```

This produces a personalized Word document – with a bit of further development this could be turned into a useful mail-merge facility. As illustrated by our example here, automating projects which would otherwise involve intensive typing can be a very worthwhile pursuit.

Utilizing Schemas in Office-Based Programs

A schema is basically a description of the structure which any object has. For example, a table in a database has the possibility of having all or some of the following: columns, indexes, constraints and referential constraints. Without knowing the information, such as column names, within a table it is impossible to construct a specific query for a table and return useful information to a user. For our examples in this section we will be using SQL Server database schemas, however there are many other schemas that we can take advantage of. Some examples could be the Active Directory schema in Windows 2000, application schemas for forms within Windows programs like Outlook, or a schema that defines an XML stream.

Why Should Programmers Care About Schemas?

Programmers should care about schemas because they will help create more generic pieces of code. This cuts down on maintenance due to changes in the schema the code works with. In the case of a SQL Server database we have tables in each database that are accessible and which hold information such as the column names for a given table. We can use this information to construct more generic code that works against multiple tables and returns a given result. Programmers should want to do this specifically to avoid having to change code when a table structure changes. For example, if we want to construct a generic COM object that returns an XML stream of the column names of a table and a given set of records from the table, we would only need to be supplied with a table name. By using the `Information_Schema.Columns` table in our SQL Server database we could get the columns names and follow that with a query that would return data to our front-end application. Reviewing our Excel example which used the data-centricity of the COM object for retrieving data for a mailing list, we wouldn't be able to dynamically accommodate another column because we wouldn't know what its contents were about. We might be querying many tables from many sources that have slightly different schema, so being able to retrieve the structure of a table will help the user or program know what data is available.

A COM Object that Utilizes a Database Schema

In this example we will simply take the `DNAMailingList` function from our COM object and modify it somewhat to incorporate the table schema, as retrieved from the schema tables in our SQL Server database. We will set up two XML streams to hold our schema and data respectively. On our Excel front-end macro all that we need to change is the call to the COM object and the passing of the parameter that indicates which table we want to access.

Our COM object is similar to the one we explained earlier for our mailing list example, with one extra section. The new section begins with the comment `"open the schema for the given table"`. This code looks at the `Information_Schema.Columns` table for the passed in `TableName` parameter, and returns the column names for the given table:

```
Function DNASchemaXML(TableName As String, ByVal XMLSchema As msxml.DOMDocument, _
        ByVal XMLData As msxml.DOMDocument) As msxml.DOMDocument

    Dim mConn As New ADODB.Connection
    Dim mRS As New ADODB.Recordset
    Dim x As Integer

    x = 0
    'Connect to SQL server database via OLEDB
    mConn.ConnectionString = "Provider=SQLOLEDB;UserID=RandomUser;" &_
                        "Persist Security Info=False;Initial Catalog=COM
Repository;" &_
                        "Data Source=NTWKS"
    mConn.Open mConn.ConnectionString, "RandomUser"

    'Get the Data we want to work with
    mRS.CursorLocation = adUseClient
    mRS.Open "Select * from MailingList", mConn, adOpenForwardOnly
    mRS.save XMLData, adPersistXML
    mRS.Close
```

```
    'Open the schema for the given table
    mRS.CursorLocation = adUseClient
    mRS.Open "SELECT Column_Name FROM Information_Schema.Columns WHERE Table_Name =
'" &
            TableName & "'", mConn, adOpenForwardOnly
    mRS.Save XMLSchema, adPersistXML
    mRS.Close

    'Close data connections
    mConn.Close


End Function
```

The database schema for our table columns can be retrieved from the `Information.Schema` table called `Columns`. This table holds all of the column names in a given database. As illustrated above, the use of the schema of a SQL Server database gives the flexibility to retrieve the data element names, thus giving our COM component a more generic functionality. The more generic our functions become, the less functions we will need, and the more efficient our code libraries will be.

On the Excel side not much changed from our earlier example (that used the COM object to retrieve a mailing list to populate a spreadsheet). This time we have simply added the column names to row 1 of our spreadsheet, which gives us a better definition of the data we are looking at. This code is in the `getdata` macro in `MailingListSchema.xls`:

```
Sub getdata()

    Dim mData As New MSXML.DOMDocument
    Dim mSchema As New MSXML.DOMDocument
    Dim mObject As DNA2000.DNAMod
    Dim x As Integer
    Dim child
    Dim currnode
    Dim childnode
    Dim item

    'Create object reference
    Set mObject = CreateObject("DNA2000.DNAMod")

    'Call object, setting mData to the result of our function, an XML Schema
    mObject.DNASchemaXML "MailingList", mSchema, mData

    'Destroy object once results are received
    Set mObject = Nothing
    Set child = mSchema.documentElement
    Set currnode = mSchema.documentElement.childNodes.item(1)
    X = 0
    Application.Goto reference:=Worksheets(1).Range("A1")

    For Each item In currnode.childNodes
      Set childnode = currnode.childNodes.item(x)
      Selection.Value = childnode.getAttribute("Column_Name")
      Selection.Offset(0, 1).Select
      x = x + 1
    Next
```

```
        Application.Goto reference:=Worksheets(1).Range("a2")
      Set child = mData.documentElement
      Set currnode = mData.documentElement.childNodes.item(1)
      x = 0
      For Each item In currnode.childNodes
         Set childnode = currnode.childNodes.item(x)
         Selection.Value = childnode.getAttribute("Name")
         Selection.Offset(0, 1).Select
         Selection.Value = childnode.getAttribute("Address1")
         Selection.Offset(0, 1).Select
         Selection.Value = childnode.getAttribute("Address2")
         Selection.Offset(0, 1).Select
         Selection.Value = childnode.getAttribute("City")
         Selection.Offset(0, 1).Select
         Selection.Value = childnode.getAttribute("State")
         Selection.Offset(0, 1).Select
         Selection.Value = childnode.getAttribute("Zip")
         Selection.Offset(0, 1).Select
         x = x + 1
         Selection.Offset(1, -6).Select
      Next

   End Sub
```

We added the section repeated below to get our column names into the spreadsheet. We have an additional XML stream that holds our column names, that we have accessed here to place the information in row 1:

```
   Set child = mSchema.documentElement
   Set currnode = mSchema.documentElement.childNodes.item(1)
   x = 0

   Application.Goto reference:=Worksheets(1).Range("A1")

   For Each item In currnode.childNodes
      Set childnode = currnode.childNodes.item(x)
      Selection.Value = childnode.getAttribute("Column_Name")
      Selection.Offset(0, 1).Select
      x = x + 1
   Next
```

To summarize, this section outlined a simple example of how to access the schema for a SQL Server database in order to determine additional properties of the columns in a table. Schemas are going to become most prevalent for use in programming as the use of XML grows. Schema-based programming shines brightest in the context of Word, because of all the applications in the Office suite, Word produces the most semi-structured data. All the other applications can get by with tabular ADO data, but Word documents can't – they need XML.

Summary

In summary, we have reviewed some details about Microsoft Office and its interaction with COM objects. We stated that Microsoft Office has grown to be one of the world's favorite development tools for the business office environment. We gave some specific examples utilizing the Office suite and illustrated how easy it can be for a more advanced programmer to make available a library of functions that retrieve and validate data for a developer of an Office based front-end application. We illustrated that Office is an effective alternative front-end development tool to use to interact with COM objects. We also talked about what schemas are and how they can facilitate the retrieval of data when structural change can occur dynamically.

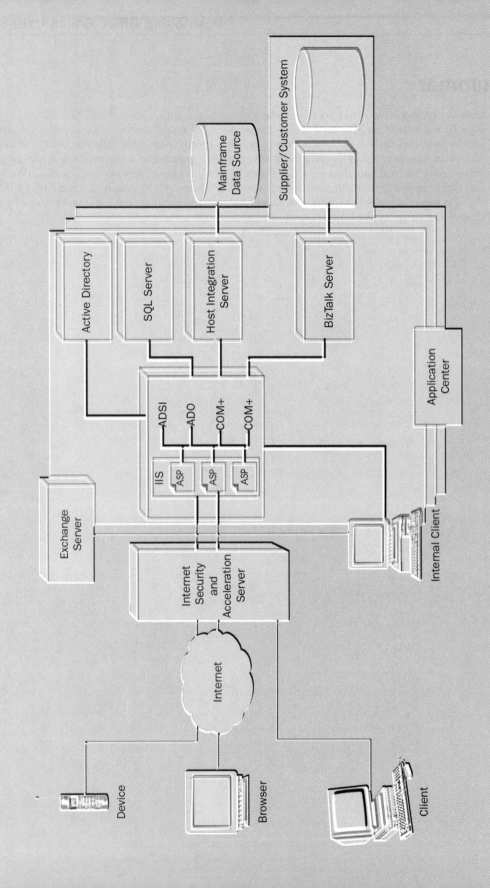

19

Improving Scalability and Availability of DNA Applications

Scalability and availability take on a whole new meaning with today's DNA applications, especially if your application is accessible via the Internet. If a Web application becomes popular, it may receive requests from millions of users, and if scalability wasn't taken into account during the design phase, it may fail under the extreme load.

Creating applications that scale well is by no means trivial – many consider it an art form. In this chapter, we'll talk about the different methods you can use for scaling Web applications. We'll also talk about the specific technologies available that you can deploy to scale your application.

In the first half of the chapter, we'll give you an overview of the issues involved. Then we'll move on to a more practical demonstration of how to actually implement some of the technologies involved.

After reading this chapter, you should understand:

❑ Why we need to be concerned with the scalability and availability of our DNA applications

❑ The difference between vertical and horizontal scalability

❑ What partitioning is, and how it can help with scalability

❑ What load balancing is, and how it can improve both the scalability and availability of your applications

❑ How server clusters can help with availability

❑ How to create and configure Network Load Balancing (NLB)

But we'll start by considering why scalability and availability are so important – isn't the performance of our application what we should be most concerned about?

Performance Isn't Everything

Well, if you strictly focus on maximizing performance, you run the risk of losing perspective of the "big picture". Let's face it, the application that would achieve the best possible performance would be a monolithic application written in assembly language. This would give the developer ultimate control, allowing the application to most efficiently utilize the hardware it runs on.

However, when we're designing applications in the real world, there are a few tradeoffs. In addition to performance, a couple of things to keep in mind are:

❑   Is time to market important?

❑   Is the application maintainable?

❑   Does the application scale well enough to meet your business needs?

❑   Is the application (and underlying infrastructure) designed for high availability?

Let's consider each of these in turn.

Time to Market

We could argue that commercial software development is driven by the need to solve business problems. We could also argue that the first company to provide a solution to a particular business problem has a significant competitive advantage over its rivals. So, in the commercial world, time is very definitely of the essence.

In fact, whoever you're designing software for, chances are you're only going to have a limited amount of time in which to do so. In short, software developers are motivated to deliver solutions that meet the needs of their customers as soon as possible.

Maintainability

In order to stay competitive, an application must evolve to better meet the needs of the customer. New functionality needs to be released at an ever increasing rate – both to serve your customers' changing needs, and for maintenance reasons (bug fixes).

Applications that allow developers to adapt and upgrade functionality easily are said to be **maintainable**.

Scalability

> Scalability is the ability of an application to cope with increases in usage without experiencing any significant loss of performance.

The best performing solution is not necessarily the most scalable.

For example, many highly scalable systems being built today place much of the business and data logic into COM objects, when that logic could just as easily have gone into stored procedures. In many cases, business logic represented in TSQL and compiled as a stored procedure offers better performance than it's COM counterpart, so on the face of it, using stored procedures should offer the best performance.

However, as the load on the application grows, your scalability options will more than likely be limited to either buying a larger database server, or splitting your database across multiple servers (**partitioning**). The former solution is often quite costly, and the latter solution is quite difficult to implement.

On the other hand, an application server that houses business logic encapsulated in COM objects comprises a very scalable unit. COM components provide advantages like resource sharing (such as database connections) and easy distribution of the encapsulated logic to multiple locations. As the load on the application increases, additional application servers can be easily added without having to deal with the complexities of partitioning data. The requests can then be distributed across the application servers using a **load balancing** mechanism.

We'll discuss partitioning and load balancing in more detail later in the chapter.

Availability

> **Availability is the ability of an application to always keep running, even in the event of abnormal conditions such as hardware failures or significant surges in network traffic.**

Ensuring that mission-critical applications provide high availability has been an important goal since the first computer went on line, and high availability is just as important for today's popular web sites.

For example, eBay experienced a series of outages in 1999. According to Reuters, one of the outages – which lasted less than a day in June of 1999 – cost the company 3.9 million dollars in lost revenue.

The rest of this chapter is going to be concentrating on just the last two of these important considerations: scalability and availability.

Scalability

Scalability is as important for scaling backend services as it is for scaling front-end Web servers. Two of the most common paradigms for scaling applications are vertical and horizontal scalability.

Vertical Scalability

Vertical scalability involves hosting applications on bigger, faster, more powerful machines, in order to accommodate increased workloads or increased business complexity.

While vertical scalability does have its place, this type of scalability has some practical limitations. In today's market, larger computers typically sell at premium prices. Cost per transaction is often higher than their commodity counterpart, especially when redundant servers are needed to meet availability requirements.

Horizontal Scalability

Horizontal scalability involves distributing the load of an application across many computers. As the number of requests increase, additional computers are added to accommodate the additional load. You can often achieve near linear scalability as additional computers are added. Therefore, the cost per transaction remains relatively constant as the infrastructure is scaled.

For example, say you have a COM+ component called Math. The component is responsible for performing a complex calculation, and does not utilize resources located on other servers. We have a DNA application that utilizes the Math component, which must support 5000 simultaneous users.

After performing stress testing on the component, it is determined that the server hosting this component can process 100 requests per minute. If each user accesses the Math component on average once every 10 minutes, then the infrastructure for the Math component must handle an average of 500 requests per minute. After looking at the distribution pattern of the requests, we estimate a maximum peak load of 1000 requests per minute. Therefore, in order for our DNA application to support 5000 simultaneous users, we must install 10 application servers to host the Math component. When the number of simultaneous users grows beyond 5000, we can simply add more Math application servers to accommodate the additional load.

There are a couple of techniques we need to discuss when thinking about horizontal scalability:

❑ Partitioning

❑ Load balancing

Let's see what these involve.

Partitioning

> **Partitioning is the act of dividing up a particular resource across multiple servers.**

For example, say we have one database server that handles all client requests. As the load increases, we can split the data contained in the database across two or more servers.

Exchange 2000 is an example of achieving scalability through partitioning. Messaging applications lend themselves well to partitioning, since each user tends to have their own discrete set of data: their own inbox, calendar, etc. This scenario means that the application can be easily scaled, by dividing the user base across multiple servers.

One of the toughest challenges is devising a way to partition a resource so that the workload is evenly distributed across all of the servers. In general, it's easier to partition a resource when you have a small number of clients, who need access to a particular subset of the data that needs to be partitioned. Partitioning becomes more challenging when you have a large number of clients needing access to the same set of data. The problem becomes even more difficult when those large numbers of clients do not follow a consistent pattern when accessing the data.

In general, there is a high administrative cost associated with partitioning. Without support from the application, partitioning is usually a very manual and time-intensive process. Not only do you have to create and then implement a partitioning scheme, but you also have to administer it. Operations have to constantly monitor the workload of each partition, and repartition when necessary, which can exponentially increase the administrative costs.

SQL Server 2000 ships with features that can simplify partitioning data contained in a particular table across multiple servers. However, administering backups and performing disaster recovery is not a trivial task. Backups need to be synchronized across the multiple servers in order to ensure that referential integrity is maintained when the data is restored. In general, you should avoid partitioning your database across multiple servers, and instead consider vertically scaling the database.

Load Balancing

> The concept behind load balancing is to distribute client requests across a cluster of servers, where any one node (server) is capable of handling a given request.

When we talk about a **cluster** in this context, we mean two or more independent servers that are addressed and managed as a single system.

Load balancing can be used to achieve horizontal scalability, and it is most often associated with **web farms**. A web farm is a group of servers that that looks like a single unit to the client.

For example, in the diagram below, the client's request can be handled by any of the nodes in the cluster:

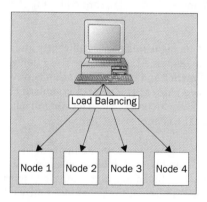

Load balancing is an equally viable solution for back-end services, such as component application servers, read-only file shares, etc.

Two examples of load balancing in Windows DNA are **NLB** (**Network Load Balancing**), which ships with Windows 2000, and **CLB** (**Component Load Balancing**), which ships with AppCenter Server.

> *AppCenter Server will include management, monitoring, and replication features suitable for working with Web server clusters built with Network Load Balancing. We will be discussing NLB in detail later in this chapter.*

Load balancing systems typically have the following characteristics:

❑ Independent nodes

❑ Support for small-grained requests

❑ Even distribution of load

❑ When a node is incapable of handling requests, the load balancing system will automatically remove the node from the cluster

Let's see what's important about these characteristics.

Independent Nodes

It's ideal to have a load-balanced cluster made up of independent nodes. Each node should be capable of handling the client's request, and should not be reliant on any other node in the cluster. That's because, at any time, the node handling the client's request could fail, and another node might need to be enlisted to complete the request.

What's more, if the cluster is composed of independent nodes, then nodes can be easily added or removed allowing the cluster to be scaled up or down as demand changes.

One example of a situation where a node is not independent is if it has data stored locally that is required to complete the client's request. If the node failed, then no other node in the cluster would be capable of completing the job.

Granularity

The granularity of a load-balancing system is determined by the unit size of a user's request that can be effectively load balanced.

The granularity of a load-balancing algorithm can significantly affect the scalability and availability of the load balanced resource. Course-grained units of work can be hard to evenly distribute among the various load-balanced servers. Smaller and more constant units of work are often easier to evenly distribute across the load-balanced cluster. The level of granularity provided by the load-balancing scheme also determines the level at which the load-balancing mechanism can facilitate application availability that is transparent to the client.

The granularity of the load-balancing system may be impacted by the way the load-balanced resource is used. For example, later in the chapter we will look at instances where NLB has the ability to apply a smaller level of granularity to its load-balancing algorithm (the algorithm used to determine how load balancing occurs) for a particular resource, if the developer utilizes the resource in a given way.

Even Distribution of Load

A load-balancing system should route requests so that load is evenly distributed across all nodes in the cluster. How this is achieved is often determined by the granularity of the requests.

A load-balancing system that handles larger-grained requests is typically more proactive in monitoring statistics on each node, such as CPU utilization, the size of a node's request queue, etc. It can therefore route requests to the least utilized node.

This type of monitoring may involve too much overhead for finer-grained requests. Typically a hash algorithm or a simple round robin algorithm is used to evenly distribute fine grain requests across the nodes in the cluster.

Dead Node Detection

A load-balancing system should be able to detect when a node is no longer capable of handling requests, and effectively remove the node from the cluster, or otherwise ensure that requests are no longer routed to it. If a load-balancing system does not have a mechanism for detecting dead nodes, then when a node does go down, a certain percentage of your clients' requests will fail. This is only likely to be acceptable if the percentage of failures is low and retries are hidden from the user.

The HTTPMon utility that ships in the Windows 2000 Resource Kit is an example of dead node detection. HTTPMon will monitor Web servers within an NLB cluster, and automatically remove a node if it is no longer responding to HTTP requests.

Dynamic load-balancing algorithms are usually not a substitution for dead node detection. On the contrary, dynamic loadbalancing will often increase the need for dead node detection, since it may increase the overall number of failures experienced by clients when a node in the cluster fails.

For example, say we deploy a load-balancing system for our web farm that routes requests to the web server with the lowest CPU utilization. While CPU utilization may be an effective gage for server utilization, it's not an effective method for identifying dead nodes. What if the HTTP service stops on one of the nodes? Its CPU utilization drops significantly, since the server is no longer processing requests. As a result, our load-balancing system starts routing most, if not all, of the requests to the disabled web server, since it has very low CPU utilization compared to the other nodes in the cluster.

Dynamic load balancing without some form of dead node detection is inadequate for determining the node best capable of handling the request.

Say we deploy a new load-balancing system that not only monitors CPU utilization, but also monitors the HTTP service on each server. Soon after, one of the nodes looses its connection to the database. Requests that would have been fairly CPU intensive return a response to the user very quickly. In this case the load-balancing system will once again be routing the majority of requests to the node that is least capable of handling them.

As this example demonstrates, dead node detection mechanisms usually need to be very specific to the resource that is being load balanced. Implementing dead node detection is not trivial and involves careful planning.

A Quick Word on Replication

With all of the benefits of load balancing, we might be inclined to consider using **replication** to horizontally scale resources that should have otherwise been scaled vertically. Replication involves creating and synchronizing replicas of resources in separate locations, and it's often used successfully for read-only content. For example, web content, such as HTML, ASP, and images, is often replicated across the servers in a web farm. However, some problems arise when modifiable data is replicated across load-balanced servers.

One of the difficulties with replication is dealing with data coherency. Since multiple copies of the same data living on different servers are available to the user, we need to ensure that the infrastructure exists to keep all copies of the data in sync. This infrastructure has to deal with conflicts that arise when two users modify the same data on two different servers. The problem can be simplified if a single machine handles all writes, but obviously this scenario is only practical if the data is read more often then written, since all writes are bottlenecked to one server. There are some issues with this scenario.

575

Most replication technologies (including SQL Server merge replication and Exchange 2000) have a lag time associated with how often the data is replicated. This lag time may be an issue for your application. For example, consider an application where each read and write request may be routed to different servers. Say a user edits their profile, and data is written to one server. If the user then chooses to view their edited profile before replication has occurred, and a different server handles the read request, their profile will not display the results of their changes.

SQL Server 2000 offers transactional replication to address this problem. When a user adds, modifies, or deletes a record, the changes are made to all database replicas or are not made at all. Since replication occurs synchronously, a row will not be inserted into the database until it is successfully inserted into all corresponding databases. As you can imagine, modifications made to replicated data will take longer to complete as more servers are added to the cluster.

That concludes our discussion of scalability for the time being. Let's now turn our attention to the other subject we're looking at in this chapter – availability.

Availability

As we've already said, today's mission critical DNA applications should not only scale well – they must offer high availability. System availability is often communicated as **percentage uptime**. For example, if a system has 99.9% availability, that means it only experienced 0.1% unexpected downtime over a given period of time. However, some companies may allow for scheduled downtime.

There are many different ways to compute the percentage uptime, so this number only has meaning if it is accompanied by a description of how it was obtained. For example, a system that must be operational 7x24 and requires 99.999% uptime only allows for 5.3 minutes of downtime per year.

Computing uptime, establishing availability goals, and putting processes in place to attain availability goals is beyond the scope of this book. Instead, we'll focus on the solutions that can be leveraged to reach a company's uptime goals, and the impact they have on the overall architecture of the application.

Availability Solutions

One advantage of load balancing is that in addition to addressing scalability, it can help increase the overall availability of your application. If a node in the cluster fails, the load balancing system is responsible for routing future requests to the remaining operational nodes. Operations simply need to deploy enough nodes in the cluster to handle the capacity when a failure occurs. As more nodes are added to the cluster, the impact of a single node failure is reduced proportionally.

As we have learned, some resources are not well suited for load balancing, and these resources are typically scaled vertically or by partitioning. Unfortunately, scaling resources in this manner does not inherently increase the overall availability of the resource.

Two popular solutions for increasing the availability of those resources not suited to load balancing are hot standby servers and server clusters.

Hot Standby Servers

A **hot standby** is a server that can be brought online at a moment's notice to take the place of a down production server. Hot standby servers are generally kept in sync with their production server counterparts via one-way replication. When the production server goes down, replication is terminated and the hot standby is brought online.

The primary advantage of a hot standby is that it offers complete redundancy. If any part of the production server fails – hard drive, memory, motherboard, etc. – the standby is able to take over. Sometimes, hot standbys are located in a different geographic location to the production server, connected with a dedicated connection. If the production server is destroyed by a natural disaster, such as fire or flood, the standby is not taken down as well.

Server Clusters

Server clusters – such as **MSCS** (**Microsoft Cluster Server**) – provide another high availability option. As we've seen, a cluster is composed of two or more independent nodes that are addressed and managed as a single system. Cluster software is responsible for maintaining a heartbeat between these servers. In the event that the primary server no longer produces a heartbeat, the cluster software is responsible for bringing another node in the cluster online.

We can categorize clusters as shared-resource clusters or shared-nothing clusters:

❑ In a **shared-resource cluster**, any node on the cluster can access a resource. This requires a distributed lock management system that coordinates access to shared resources by the nodes of the cluster.

❑ In the **shared-nothing cluster**, resources are not shared between nodes of a cluster. If one of the nodes fails, then another node in the cluster must obtain ownership of the resource before bringing the resource back online. This process is commonly referred to as resource **failover**.

These two categories are illustrated by the following figure:

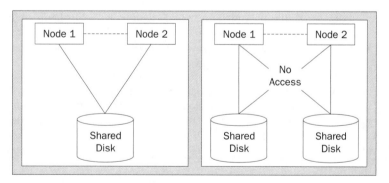

In both categories of clusters, the disk subsystems are still a single point of failure. In this case, redundancy is most often provided with **RAID** (**Redundant Array of Inexpensive Disks**) configurations.

Rolling Upgrades

One advantage cluster technology offers is the ability to perform **rolling upgrades**. A rolling upgrade is a method of upgrading a particular resource without clients incurring system downtime. Rolling upgrades can be performed on both load balancing clusters and server clusters.

An example of a rolling upgrade is the need to upgrade a COM+ object that is dynamically load balanced across multiple servers. We can perform a rolling upgrade on the object by removing servers one at a time from the cluster, and upgrading the particular COM object until we have upgraded half of the servers. Once half of our servers have been upgraded, we can then swap the remaining servers in the cluster with the servers that are hosting the upgraded component. After testing our application, we would then proceed with upgrading the remaining servers and adding them to the cluster. If the upgrade was not successful, we could immediately switch back to the servers hosting the original component.

To ensure that clients experience uninterrupted service, the upgraded resource must support the same interfaces that were supported by the original resource. For example, our upgraded COM+ object must support all the interfaces exposed by the original COM+ object. In the case of NLB, the upgraded network resource must support the same protocol as the original network resource.

We'll take a detailed look at Network Load Balancing shortly. First, we'll take a brief look at Component Load Balancing (CLB).

Component Load Balancing Service

The Component Load Balancing (CLB) service gives the developer the ability to distribute their COM+ components across multiple servers. CLB was originally scheduled to release with COM+ 1.0. However, CLB was removed from Windows 2000 RC2 and instead was folded into Microsoft Application Center. Even though the CLB is no longer an "out-of-the-box" COM+ service, it is a very important component for building COM+ based applications that offer high scalability and availability.

CLB has component level granularity, which means that load balancing is handled at the component level. Once a component has been configured to be load balanced, client requests to create an object are handled by CLB. The CLB is responsible for forwarding the request to a server that CLB has determined is most capable of handling the request.

The level of granularity provided by the load-balancing scheme also determines the level in which the load-balancing mechanism can facilitate application availability that is transparent to the client. CLB will allow your applications to survive failures at the component level. If CLB passes a request to create an object to server and that request fails, the CLB will reroute that request to the next appropriate server. CLB has a special hook into COM+ where failure to create a particular object on a particular server will be reported back to CLB.

Applications will not survive server failures at a smaller level of granularity than the class. Once you receive a reference to a requested object, CLB is no longer involved. For example, if you are holding a reference to an object that resides in a CLB cluster and that server fails, all future methods to that object will fail. Surviving application failure at a smaller granularity that is supported by the CLB load-balancing scheme requires implementation on the developer's side. Once a method call fails, the developer can opt to create a new instance of the class, restore the object to its previous state, and then call the method that originally failed.

In short, CLB allows you to load-balance your business logic, just as NLB lets you scale your Web server and other network resources. Unfortunately, since CLB is not a part of Windows 2000, we won't go into any more detail about it here. You'll have to look into AppCenter Server 2000 for more information on CLB.

Network Load Balancing (NLB)

The scalability and availability of a distributed application is only as good as its weakest link. Most, if not all, distributed applications depend on network-based resources.

NLB ships with Windows 2000 Advanced or DataCenter Server. Resources that can be addressed by NLB include, but are not limited to:

❑ Web service

❑ FTP service

❑ Networked file shares

❑ Printer resources

Network Load Balancing can dramatically increase the scalability of a DNA application – for example, using a web farm.

An NLB cluster is made up of a number of standalone servers – there is no central server responsible for receiving and then routing network requests. All servers in the cluster receive the packet. The servers then use the same static statistical algorithm, which uses the IP address, the requested port, and other information, to determine whether or not to process the packet. For example, when a packet is received that is a part of an HTTP request, each NLB node uses the data contained within the packet to determine whether to forward it on to its local web server.

The servers within the cluster communicate with each other of regular intervals. If one of the servers does not respond within a predetermined number of intervals, the other servers in the cluster will redistribute the load between the remaining servers. Likewise, if a server is added to the cluster, it will send a message to all servers within the cluster. All servers will then exchange messages to determine the new state of the cluster, and redistribute the load amongst themselves. The process of redistributing the load when a server is either added or removed from the cluster is called **convergence**.

> *It takes a certain number of missed messages (heartbeats) to initiate convergence – by default, the number is 5, but as we'll see later in the chapter, this value can be adjusted using the AliveMsgTolerance registry parameter.*

Note that convergence occurs when NLB on a particular server either starts or stops exchanging messages with the cluster. NLB does not monitor the actual service that it is load balancing. Therefore, its possible for the service that is being load balanced to fail. However, since NLB is still functioning properly on the server, convergence will not occur even though a portion the cluster's clients cannot access the load-balanced service.

One solution is to create a program responsible for monitoring the service and if the service goes down, deactivate NLB on that server. The following code will stop NLB on the local host if the default web site is no longer running:

```
Const IIS_STATUS_RUNNING = 2
Dim objIISDefaultWeb As Object

Set objIISDefaultWeb = GetObject("IIS://LocalHost/W3SVC/1")
If (objIISDefaultWeb.Status <> IIS_STATUS_RUNNING) Then
  Shell "wlbs drainstop"
```

Another option is to use the HTTPMon utility that ships with the resource kit. HTTPMon will send HTTP requests to each node in the cluster. When a response is not received, the node will be removed from the cluster. Application Center 2000 further refines this concept, and allows ultimate control over what is monitored and the actions that are taken when a certain event occurs.

Most developers, myself included, are motivated to get the infrastructure up and running as quickly as possible so they can get to the fun part – writing code that takes advantage of the new infrastructure. Therefore, we'll first present a basic recipe for creating an NLB cluster for commonly used resources. In a later section we'll explore some of the configuration parameters we see here in more detail. This later section can serve as a reference for fine-tuning the NLB cluster as needed.

Creating a Basic NLB Server Cluster

We'll explore the steps necessary for creating an NLB cluster. At the end of this section you should have a basic working NLB cluster. The steps we'll take to create our NLB cluster are:

❑ Preparation

❑ Configuring the servers in the NLB cluster

❑ Verifying the configuration of the cluster

Preparation

Some preparation is required before we set up our NLB cluster. First and foremost, you must have either Windows 2000 Advanced or DataCenter Server installed on the servers that will participate in the cluster. Each server must have a network card and be assigned a dedicated IP address.

The cluster itself must be assigned its own virtual address. Clients will use this virtual IP address when accessing network resources hosted on the cluster. The IP addresses for the cluster and each individual server must reside within the same subnet.

Verify Primary IP Address and Subnet Mask

First, on each server, verify that the primary IP address and subnet mask is setup correctly:

1. Right-click on the My Network Places icon located on the desktop, and select Properties.

2. Right-click on the network icon where NLB will be installed. If you have more than one NIC installed on the server, this is usually your primary NIC. Select Properties:

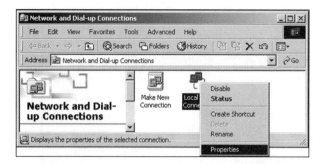

3. This displays the Local Area Connection Properties dialog box. In the list of network components, highlight Internet Protocol (TCP/IP):

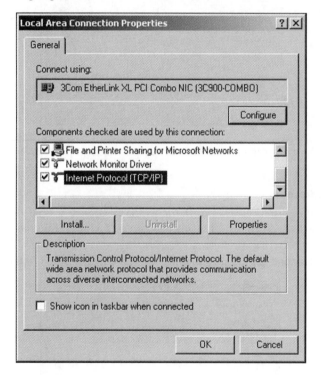

Then click the Properties button.

4. Ensure that the Use the following IP address is selected and verify that the IP address, Subnet mask, and Default gateway are correctly set:

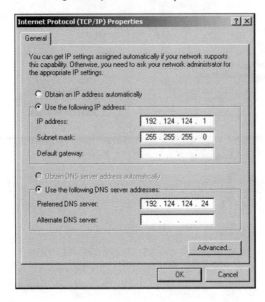

5. Leave the Internet Protocol (TCP/IP) Properties dialog box open for the next step.

Add the Cluster IP Address

Since each server in the cluster receives all IP traffic, the IP address for the cluster must also be added to each server's IP stack. Perform the following tasks on all servers within the cluster:

1. Press the Advanced... button to display the Advanced TCP/IP Settings dialog box:

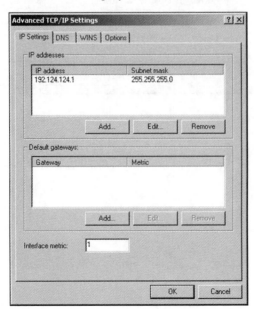

2. In the IP addresses section, click the Add... button.

3. Enter the IP address and Subnet mask of the cluster and click the Add button:

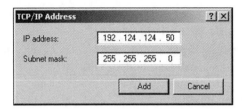

4. Press the OK button on all open dialog boxes.

5. If prompted, reboot the machine for the changes to take effect.

Installing NLB

We will now install NLB on the servers that will participate in the cluster. To do so, perform the following tasks:

1. Right-click on the My Network Places icon located on the desktop, and select Properties.

2. Right-click on the network icon where NLB will be installed, and select Properties to display the Local Area Connection Properties dialog box:

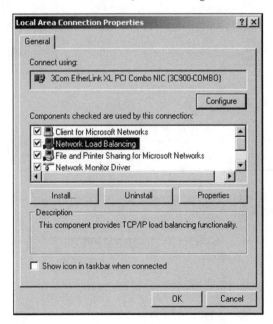

3. Select the General tab.

4. In the list of network components, check Network Load Balancing.

5. Leave the property dialog box open for the next step.

Configuring the Servers in the Cluster

We'll now configure the NLB properties for each of the servers within the cluster. We'll look at exactly what these settings mean in more detail later in the chapter.

Setting the Cluster Parameters

We'll start with some cluster parameters. Perform the following steps for each server in the cluster.

1. Push the Properties button to display the Network Load Balancing Properties dialog box:

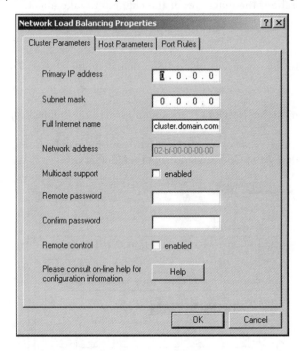

2. Enter the static IP address and subnet mask assigned to the cluster (virtual server) in the Primary IP address and Subnet mask text boxes.

3. Optionally, enter the domain name that DNS will resolve to the cluster's IP address in the Full Internet name text box.

4. Leave the Multicast support check box unchecked.

5. Optionally, check the Remote control check box and enter a password in the Remote password and Confirm password text boxes to enable remote administration.

6. Leave the property dialog box open for the next step.

Prioritizing Servers Within the Cluster

Next, we'll assign priorities to our servers. The priority must be unique for each node in the cluster, and is used by NLB for more advanced cluster configurations. We'll discuss the configuration parameters, including priority, later in the chapter.

If the servers have different hardware configurations, perform the following steps starting with your most robust server (based on CPU speed, physical memory, fastest hard drives, etc.):

1. Select the Host Parameters tab:

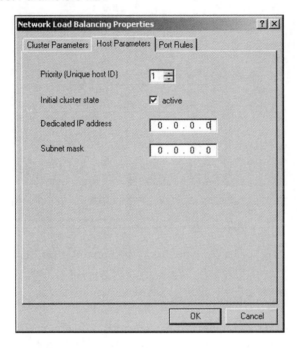

2. Select the default Priority (Unique host ID) for the first server, and increment the Priority for each subsequent server.

3. Leave the Initial cluster state set to active.

4. Enter the static IP address and subnet mask assigned to the server in the Primary IP address and Subnet mask text boxes.

5. Leave the property dialog box open for the next step.

Setting Port Rules

We'll now adjust the default port rule, so that it is set to a reasonably conservative client affinity setting.

Port rules determine how network traffic gets routed within the cluster. The client affinity settings determine whether or not multiple requests from the same client will be routed to the same node in the cluster. We'll discuss the client affinity configuration parameter when we look at port rules in more detail later in the chapter.

585

1. Select the Port Rules tab:

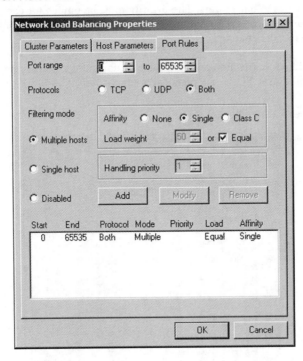

2. Select the default port rule from the list at the bottom of the dialog box. In the above screen shot, this is the port rule where the starting port is 0 and the ending port is 65535.

3. Change Affinity from Single to Class C.

   This will ensure that all requests from clients within the same class C address will be routed to the same node in the cluster. Network packets received from clients accessing the network resource through a proxy server will have the source address set to the proxy server as apposed to the client.

   Some large corporations load balance their clients across multiple proxy servers. Since the proxy servers typically reside within the same class C address, setting the client affinity to Class C will ensure that the same node in the cluster will service users accessing the network resource via a proxy server.

4. Press the Modify button, and verify that default port rule has been changed in the list.

5. Click the OK button on all open dialog boxes.

Verify the Configuration

If we did everything correctly, we should have a working cluster. We'll check the Event Log to verify this:

1. Navigate to Start | Programs | Administrative tools, and finally select Event Viewer.

2. In the left tree view, select the System Log.

3. Double-click on the top log entry that lists WLBS as its source.

4. If the server successfully joined the NLB cluster, then the Event Properties dialog box should look similar to the screenshot below:

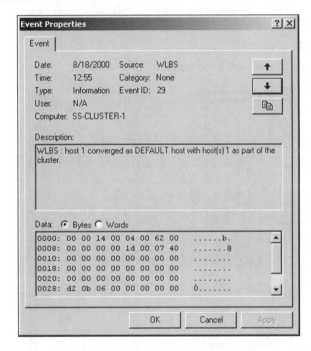

You may now access network resources using the IP address for the cluster. Access to network resources within the cluster is usually limited to read-only. If you make modifications to a network resource hosted on individual servers within the cluster, ensure that appropriate mechanisms are in place to replicate the change to the other servers within the cluster.

Configuring an NLB Cluster

As we've seen, most of the configuration parameters for NLB can be modified within the Network Load Balancing Properties dialog box.

Note that a majority of the configuration parameters must be configured the same on each server within the cluster. This includes the IP address and subnet mask for the cluster, the port rules, the multicast setting, and the convergence parameters. We'll discuss all of these parameters shortly.

As we've seen, we can display the dialog box by doing the following:

1. Right-click on the My Network Places icon located on the desktop, and select Properties.

2. Right-click on the network icon where NLB is installed, and select Properties to display the Local Area Connection Properties dialog box.

3. Select the Networking tab, and in the list of network components, highlight Network Load Balancing.

4. Click the Properties button to open the Network Load Balancing Properties dialog box.

We'll now review the properties in each of the tabs in the Network Load Balancing Properties dialog box.

Cluster Parameters

The Cluster Parameters tab contains the parameters that can be set for the cluster itself:

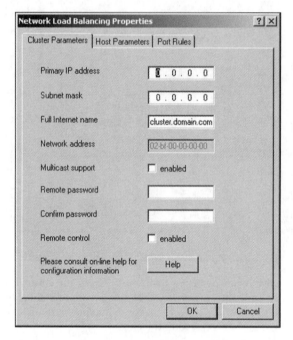

The Primary IP address, Subnet mask, and the Full internet name text boxes should contain the information for the cluster's virtual server. The virtual server is the entity that represents the cluster.

Multicasting

Recall that the servers within the cluster communicate with each other at predetermined intervals. This "heartbeat" can be **multicasted**, which means that instead of sending separate messages to each client, the server can send just one message and all clients within the cluster will receive that message. More importantly, messages from the client are multicasted to each server within the cluster.

NLB offers multicast support. Multicasting can significantly increase the performance of your cluster, especially if each of your servers only has only one NIC.

To enable multicasting, check the Multicast support check box. If clients are accessing the clustered network resource through a router, in order to support multicasting, the router must support the use of a multicast Media Access Control (MAC) address.

If multicast support is not enabled, it's highly recommended that you install more than one NIC for each server within the cluster. If you only have one NIC installed on each server, and multicast support is not enabled, you won't be able to access individual machines within the cluster. Therefore, you will not be able to remotely administer the machines or push content to them. Furthermore, adding an additional NIC to each server within the cluster will help increase throughput, especially if the servers within the cluster are accessing backend network resources, such as a database server.

Remote Configuration

The NLB server can be remotely administered using WLBS.exe. To allow the NLB server to be remotely administered, enter a password of your choosing into the Remote password and Confirm password text boxes. Then check the Remote control enabled check box. If remote administration is enabled, it's highly recommended that the ports responsible for receiving the remote control commands be secured by the firewall.

By default, UDP ports 1717 and 2504 for the cluster's (virtual server's) IP address are used for receiving remote control commands. Modifying the value in the RemoteControlUDPPort registry value – found under the HKEY_LOCAL_MACHINE\System\CurrentControlSet\Services\WLBS\Parameters registry key – can alter Port 2504.

Host Parameters

The Host Parameters tab contains parameters for the particular server in the cluster:

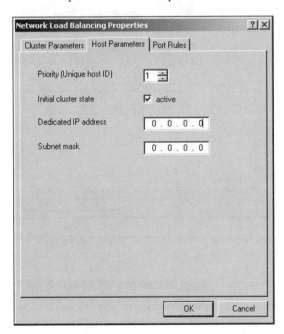

The Dedicated IP address and the Subnet mask text boxes contain the information for the server itself. These values must be the same as the static IP address and subnet mask settings for the NIC.

Priority

Each server within the cluster must be assigned a unique host ID in the Priority text box. A server will not be allowed to join the cluster if its priority matches the priority of a server already in the cluster.

The host with the highest priority (lowest numerical value) is responsible for handling network traffic for TCP and UDP ports that are not otherwise specified in a port rule (described below). Substantial network traffic that falls into this category may influence sizing of servers within your cluster. So, if your cluster is composed of non-homogenous server hardware, give the servers with the most powerful hardware the lowest value, or highest priority.

Initial Cluster State

The Initial cluster state check box will determine whether or not the server will attempt to join the cluster once the OK button has been pressed in the Network Load Balancing Properties dialog box. One of the uses for this setting is for performing rolling upgrades, as we discussed in the Availability section.

Port Rules

The Port Rules tab is used to define what network resources will and will not be load balanced, and also to define how the resource will be load balanced:

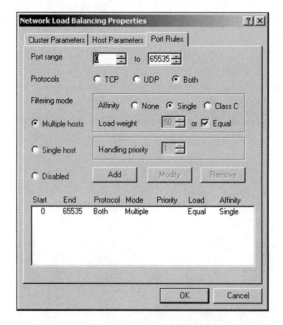

This is done by creating one or more port rules. The list of active port rules is located at the bottom of the Port Rules tab, and you may add, modify, or remove port rules from this list.

- ❏ To add a port rule, set the appropriate parameters and click the Add button.

- ❏ To modify a port rule, select the port rule you wish to modify from the list, change the parameters, and click the Modify button. Note that if you click the OK button without clicking the Modify button, your changes will not be saved.

- ❏ To remove a port rule, select the port rule you wish to delete from the list and click the Remove button.

> **Port rules must be the same on all servers within the cluster.**

The following settings make up a port rule:

❑ Port range

❑ Protocols

❑ Filtering mode

❑ Load weight

❑ Affinity

Port Range and Protocol

The **port range** and the **protocol** specify the set of ports that the port rule applies to. You may not have two port rules with overlapping sets of ports of a particular protocol. The valid range of ports is 0 to 65,535, and NLB will only work in conjunction with the TCP or UDP protocols.

The table below presents a list of the most commonly load-balanced network resources and their corresponding ports and protocols:

Resource	Protocol	Port
HTTP	TCP	80
HTTPS	TCP	443
FTP	TCP	21, 20, 1024-65,535
Windows File Share	UDP (Single)	139, 1024-65,535
Windows Terminal Server	TCP	3389
SQL Server	TCP	1433

NetBIOS over TCP/IP (NBT) is the session-layer network service that performs name-to-IP address mapping for name resolution. NBT makes it possible for NLB to provide load-balancing support for Windows file shares. However, there is one primary limitation. The cluster will not advertise the cluster's NetBIOS name, but the servers within the cluster will respond to requests that are made to the cluster. Therefore you must add the cluster's static IP address to WINS, DNS, or the client's hosts file. Or you may simply reference the share by its IP address (for example \\127.0.0.1\myshare).

Filtering Mode

The **filtering mode** determines how the network load for a given port range is distributed across the cluster. The default is the **multiple hosts filtering mode**.

Multiple servers within the cluster will process network packets within the specified port range and protocol type. The multiple hosts filtering mode provides scalability and availability for clients of a particular network resource. Scalability is achieved because client requests are distributed across all active servers in the cluster. Availability is achieved because if one server fails in the cluster, then client requests are redistributed across the remaining servers.

The **single host filtering mode** will ensure that a single host processes the network packets within the specified port range and protocol type. If you select the single host filtering mode then you must give each server within the cluster a unique **handling priority**.

The single host filtering mode offers your network resource availability. It also can improve the scalability of the network resource if the cluster is hosting more than one network resource. Since you can specify different handling priorities for each network resource (defined within a port rule), each network resource could be partitioned to a different server within the cluster.

The **disabled filtering mode** can be used to block unwanted access to the server. It's usually a good practice to block network traffic to all unused ports for both the TCP and UDP protocol, especially if the cluster is exposed to the Internet.

If you specify the multiple hosts filtering mode, you must also specify affinity and load weight. Affinity determines the granularity of the load balancing performed and load weight determines the distribution of the load across the servers within the cluster.

Affinity

NLB supports three types of **affinity**:

❑ None

❑ Single

❑ Class C

None offers the smallest granularity and thus the best scalability for a given network resource. None specifies that any server within the cluster can handle a new request, either a UDP packet or a TCP connection.

> **It is important to note that the individual packets that make up a TCP connection are not distributed across the cluster.**

However, some network resources require affinity between the client and the server. The most common example of this is web-based 3-tier applications, where the user tier is implemented in ASP and maintains state in the ASP `Session` object. Setting affinity to **single** will ensure that all requests from a single IP address that are within the specified port range and protocol will be processed by the same server.

Sometimes user affinity cannot be assured by associating them with their IP. Many corporations and large ISPs have multiple load balanced proxy servers to provide Web access for their users. This would not be a problem if affinity were maintained between the user and the proxy server. However, this is usually not the case. Therefore, each user request could be handled by a different proxy server, and thus be associated with a different IP address. Specifying **class C** affinity addresses this situation, since more than likely all proxy servers will reside within the same class C address. Class C affinity will ensure that the same server within the cluster will service all requests originating from IP addresses residing in the same class C address.

Load Weight

Load weight specifies the amount of the load the particular server within the cluster will handle. You may specify a number between 0 and 100. This number is not a percentage, so the sum of the load weight of all of the servers in the cluster does not have to add up to 100. The *percentage* of the load handled by a given server can be determined by dividing the total of the load weights of all servers within the cluster by the load weight of the individual server.

Convergence Parameters

The parameters for modifying the length of time between intra-server communications and the number of intervals that need to pass before NLB initiates convergence can be found under the HKEY_LOCAL_MACHINE\System\CurrentControlSet\Services\WLBS\Parameters registry key.

The AliveMsgPeriod registry value determines the period of time in milliseconds between sending messages to the other servers within the cluster. The AliveMsgTolerance registry value determines the number of periods to wait for a message from one of the servers in the cluster before initiating convergence.

Take care when modifying these parameters. Under most circumstances, each host in the cluster should have AliveMsgPeriod and AliveMsgTolerance set to the same value.

Microsoft Clustering Service (MSCS)

Microsoft Clustering Service (MSCS) is Microsoft's cluster offering based on the shared-nothing clustering model. MSCS manages automatic failover when a node in the cluster is no longer capable of servicing client requests. MSCS is composed of two parts: the Cluster Service and the Resource Monitor.

The **Cluster Service** runs on each node within the cluster, and is composed of six components:

❑ The **Database Manager** is responsible for maintaining the database containing information about the cluster, such as the cluster name, resource types, groups, etc.

❑ The **Event Processor** is responsible for the initialization process, and any cleanup required when a node exits the cluster

❑ The **Node Manager** is responsible for monitoring the status of other nodes within the cluster

❑ The **Communications Manager** is responsible for managing the underlying message delivery system used by all other MSCS components

❑ The **Global Update Manager** is responsible for providing notification to the other nodes in the cluster for initiating and managing updates to the state of the cluster

❑ The **Resource Manager** is responsible for controlling all interaction with the resources, such as bringing a resource online, taking a resource offline, performing failovers, etc.

The **Resource Monitor** is responsible for enabling communication between the Cluster Service and a particular resource hosted on the cluster. In the event that the Cluster Service fails, the Resource Monitor is responsible for bringing all of the resources and resource groups hosted on the node offline.

Windows 2000 Advanced Server ships with MSCS, and supports two-node clustering. Windows 2000 Datacenter Server is expected to ship with support for four-node clustering.

The easiest way to get MSCS up and running in a development environment is to install SCSI adapters in two servers running Windows 2000 Advanced Server, and connect them to an external SCSI disk drive. Once you get MSCS installed and running, you can install any number of MSCS resources. Some resources that ship with Advanced Server include MSMQ, Print Spooler, and network file shares to name a few. Other software packages that support MSCS, including SQL Server, can also be installed as a resource.

> *In order to host a resource in an MSCS controlled cluster, the application that manages the resource must be MSCS aware. However, writing MSCS aware applications is beyond the scope of this chapter. For additional information, please refer to the documentation in the Microsoft Platform SDK or reference books dedicated to this subject.*

Programming Considerations

One of the benefits of clustering technology is that very little, if any, change is required for the client to take advantage of the clustered resource. To the client, the clustered resource – whether it's a load balancing cluster or a server cluster – looks like a single server. Therefore, clients continue to use the same APIs, connection strings, etc. to access the clustered resource as if it was hosted on a single server.

However, there are a couple of things a developer should do to maximize the advantages offered by the clustered resource. When leveraging cluster technology within DNA applications, we should take the following into account:

❑ Consider the time it takes for the cluster to recover from a server failure.

❑ Ensure that any state maintained on the failed server is re-hydrated on the new server.

❑ If possible, design the application so that the fine-grained load-balancing capabilities can be exploited for the particular load-balanced resource.

❑ Maintain consistent state across all networked resources within the cluster. Limit access to data stored on a clustered resource to read-only. Otherwise, ensure that replication occurs to maintain consistent state across all networked resources within the cluster.

If the request for a clustered resource fails, retry your request. When retrying the request, be aware of the time it takes for the cluster to recover from a server failure. For example, if a server fails in an NLB cluster, the default values of the parameters specify that it will take at least five seconds for the other servers in the cluster to start the convergence process to recover from the failure. If the application simply performs a single retry without regard to time, the application will fail and therefore not exploit the availability the cluster offers.

If a server in the cluster failed while the client was in the middle of a session with a resource that maintains state, the programmer must take into account state that might have been lost when recovering from the failure. For example, if the server that is hosting the COM+ object fails, the programmer must ask the CLB router for a new instance of the COM+ object, re-hydrate the state of the previous COM+ object, and then continue processing the client's requests. Of course, another alternative would be to design the COM+ object so that it maintains its state in a persistent manner.

Whenever possible, design your load-balanced resource so that it can take advantage of the fine-grained load-balancing capabilities of the particular load-balancing technology. For example, if the web front end of your DNA application does not maintain state on the web server, then a different server within the cluster can service each request from the client.

Ensure that state is consistent across all nodes within a load-balanced cluster. If state is maintained on individual nodes within the cluster, ensure that clients are not exposed to inconsistencies between the state across all resources in the cluster. Access to network resources within a load-balanced cluster is usually limited to read only. If you allow modifications to a resource hosted on individual servers within the load-balanced cluster, ensure that appropriate mechanisms are in place to replicate the changes to the other servers within the cluster.

For example, you may wish to load balance a number of SQL Servers. The databases within the cluster can expose read-only views of the data to its clients without issue. However, if clients were allowed to add, modify, or delete records in the databases, the use of replication would be required to maintain consistent state across all databases within the cluster. See the section *A Quick Word About Replication* for more information.

Summary

Scalability and availability are important design goals when creating mission critical DNA applications, but fortunately, there are quite a few technologies that can be leveraged to achieve the desired level of scalability and availability. The type of technology used is heavily determined by the resource.

When applicable, load-balancing clusters offer excellent scalability and improved availability.

Otherwise, vertically scale your resource by running the application on faster hardware, or horizontally scale your resource through partitioning. Vertically scaled resources, or horizontally scaled resources via partitioning, that require high availability should leverage server cluster technology such as MSCS.

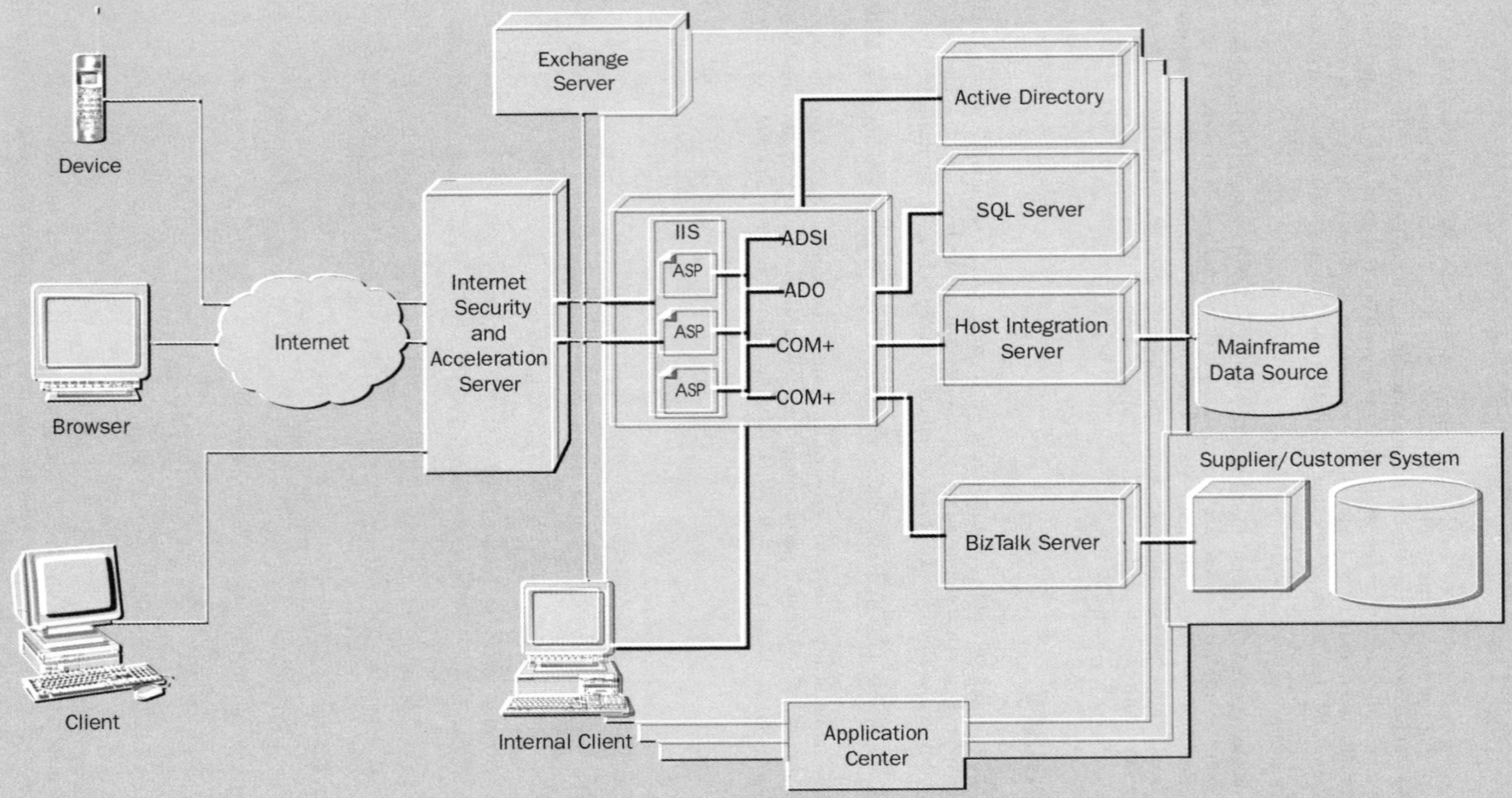
Device
Browser
Client
Internet
Internet Security and Acceleration Server
Exchange Server
IIS
ASP
ASP
ASP
ADSI
ADO
COM+
COM+
Active Directory
SQL Server
Host Integration Server
BizTalk Server
Mainframe Data Source
Supplier/Customer System
Internal Client
Application Center

20

An Overview of Windows DNA Security

Introduction

Security was once a topic that many people paid little attention to – after all, there were far more interesting things to be devoting your time to, weren't there? Nowadays, amid scare stories of viruses, invasion of personal privacy, electronic commerce and banking fraud, and attacks on Internet services and corporate web sites, the implementation of security within your DNA application ought to be one of the major factors in determining its design and development.

In making the assumption that many of you reading this book will have little or no knowledge of security, this chapter will give you an overview of the basic concepts and terminology you will need to understand. We will explain to you what is meant by **authentication**, **authorization**, **permissions** and **privileges**, and **auditing**, and how they can be implemented. One of the most important security improvements Windows 2000 has introduced is the use of Active Directory to plan, configure, and administer security over your distributed network; though we cover the security aspects of Active Directory here, be sure to read Chapter 15 for more complete coverage of the subject.

After that, we're going to take a peek under the hood of the Windows 2000 architecture, and show you how the security system fits into the operating system, and contrast it to how things worked in NT4. You will learn about how to protect the integrity of your data, through the use of technologies such as **CryptoAPI**, **Encryption File System** and **Certificate Server**. This part will only be a short introduction, since the whole of Chapter 21 is devoted to Certificate Services and Certificate Server.

At this point you need to be warned that since these systems are based on a variety of protocols, you are going to find yourself inundated with a whole new set of buzzwords and acronyms – but fear not! We'll attempt to walk you through this minefield of information, and explain to you what is going on at each step, and the impact it will have on you as a developer. Suffice to say, you won't need to have a detailed knowledge of how each of these protocols work, but to be forewarned is to be forearmed as they say.

Once we have these basics out of the way, we will then show you the really interesting stuff regarding how to implement security on your COM+ components in the business tier. Stopping briefly to reveal to you what Microsoft's Internet Security and Acceleration Server can offer you, we will finish up with four handy developer checklists, giving you useful tips to secure Windows 2000 and NT4.0, SQL Server 6.5/7.0, COM+, and IIS5.0.

Since there is an awful lot of ground to cover, which is nearly impossible to do within a single chapter, we provide you with a rich list of further resources in Appendix A that you can turn to for further information. So, without further ado, let's have a look at what is in the Windows 2000 security system, and explain to you the fundamentals of system security.

What's in the Windows 2000 Security System?

In general, the fundamental areas of security within a distributed application are tied to the operating system it runs on. Up until now, Windows NT has provided a foundation for integrated security for the Microsoft BackOffice family of application services. The Windows NT security model provides a solid framework for deploying client/server applications for the enterprise. Today, however, enterprises have opened up to the Internet. Businesses now need to interact with partners, suppliers, and customers using Internet-based technologies. Security is essential for controlling access to the resources in an enterprise network, on intranets, and on Internet-based servers.

The Internet and intranets are quickly becoming the most effective way to share information for many different business relationships. Creating user accounts controls access to non-public business information by outside parties. Partnerships help define the trust relationships that once applied only to employees who used corporate assets, but that now include many more people such as customers, vendors, suppliers etc.

With Windows 2000, Microsoft has made significant enhancements to the security-related features in the NT operating system. To fully comprehend the strengths and benefits incorporated in the Windows 2000 security features, one needs a little background on the concepts and terminology that NT security was based around. We will then discuss some of the shortcomings Windows NT 4.0, and then look at how these have been addressed in Windows 2000.

Windows NT Shortcomings

Windows NT 4.0 laid a solid foundation for security, but as system administrators and developers pressed NT into enterprise service, several inadequacies surfaced:

❑ With Windows NT 4.0, the ability to assign limited administrative privileges for a limited set of accounts to another user or delegation was woefully inadequate. For instance, you couldn't give Help Desk personnel the right to reset passwords on user accounts without making them full administrators. You couldn't properly model your organizational hierarchy and administrative structure with flat NT domains. In truth, this matter is still not completely resolved in Windows 2000 – for example, you cannot assign a user in the domain the right to set quotas unless they are added to the Admin group – however, it is still a step in the right direction.

❑ Windows NT 4.0 had several scalability problems, such as the number of users that a domain could manage. Windows NT 4.0 didn't scale well for large organizations because it limited domains to approximately 40,000 users, and the **Primary Domain Controllers** (**PDCs**) and **Backup Domain Controllers** (**BDCs**) used one-to-many replication.

❑ Windows NT 4.0 provided no place to put application-specific information about user accounts. Although much of NT 4.0 was extensible, the directory wasn't. NT 4.0 required developers to handle application-specific user properties and the location of application services in some application-specific databases. The functionality of NT's public key infrastructure (PKI) – the method by which users were authenticated in an electronic transaction – was rudimentary at best. It was limited to web environments, and provided limited support for Microsoft Exchange Server-based communications.

❑ Windows NT 4.0 lacked a distributed single sign-on. One had to resort to a cumbersome add-on product.

Security Improvements in Windows 2000

With all these shortcomings in mind, Windows 2000 security has undergone major improvements to support the Internet-based enterprise or a large organization for mission critical applications. Many of NT's security holes stemmed from backward compatibility with **NT LAN Manager** (**NTLM**), which in turn was inherited from Windows for Workgroups. Windows 2000 has 'replaced' NTLM network authentication with **Kerberos** to address NTLM vulnerabilities. However, Kerberos supports both methods of authentication – NTLM when either the client or the server is running a previous version of Windows, and Kerberos for Windows 2000 servers and clients.

Physical access to hard disks by tools available on other operating systems has been a growing problem. In response, the new **Encrypting File System** (**EFS**) in Windows 2000 provides the core encryption technology to store NTFS files encrypted on the disk.

Standards-based Security

Windows 2000 relies heavily on industry standards and protocols, such as:

❑ **Lightweight Directory Access Protocol** (**LDAP**)

❑ **Kerberos**

❑ **Public Key Cryptography Standards** (**PKCS**)

❑ **PC and smart card integration** (**PC/SC**)

❑ **X.500**

❑ **DNS**

❑ **IP Security** (**IPSec**)

Many of these have replaced Microsoft proprietary technologies such as NTLM, the Security Access Monitor (SAM), Windows Internet Naming Service (WINS), and Point-to-Point Tunneling Protocol (PPTP) – which Windows 2000 will support for backward compatibility. Windows 2000's use of standards automatically makes it more interoperable and lets you replace Microsoft-specific (cross vendor) components with best-of-breed solutions as necessary.

Windows 2000 provides a platform that reduces application development and maintenance costs. Windows NT 4.0 was an initial attempt to provide such capability with the **Security Support Provider Interface (SSPI)** and the **CryptoAPI**. Windows 2000's APIs let developers re-use services (for example, cryptographic services, which are explained in more detail in the following chapter) that the operating system provides. Abstracting applications from the provider also protects the applications from obsolescence. You can update and enhance provider components as technology progresses without affecting the application. For example, an application that uses the cryptographic services can quickly take advantage of the next standard encryption algorithm.

Windows 2000 users have easy-to-use tools and common interface dialogs for managing the private/public-key pairs and the certificates that they use to access Internet-based resources. Storage of personal security credentials, which uses secure disk-based storage, is easily transported with the proposed industry-standard protocol, **Personal Information Exchange**. Windows 2000 also supports the optional use of smart cards for interactive logon, in addition to passwords. Smart cards support cryptography and secure storage for private keys and certificates, enabling strong authentication from the desktop to the domain.

Declarative Security Using Active Directory

The Active Directory (AD) stores domain security policy information such as domain-wide password restrictions and system access privileges that have direct bearing on the use of the system. Security-related objects in the directory must be securely managed to avoid unauthorized changes that affect overall system security. The Windows 2000 operating system implements an object-based security model and access control for all objects in the Active Directory. Every object in the Active Directory has a unique **security descriptor** that defines access permissions that are required to read or update the object properties.

The need for crude NT 4.0 domain models (for example "complete trust" and "master domain") is obsolete. The Active Directory supports a hierarchical name space for user, group, and computer account information. Organizational units, rather than the flat domain account namespace provided by earlier versions of Windows NT can use group accounts.

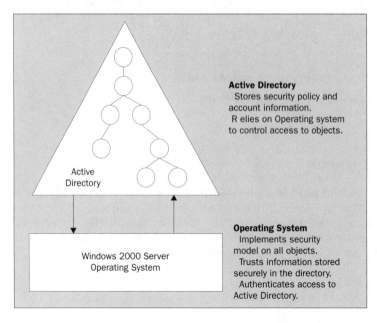

Active Directory
Stores security policy and account information.
R elies on Operating system to control access to objects.

Active Directory

Operating System
Implements security model on all objects.
Trusts information stored securely in the directory.
Authenticates access to Active Directory.

Windows 2000 Server Operating System

With AD, developers can add new objects and new properties to existing objects, instead of maintaining a separate application directory. Note that AD isn't appropriate for storing data that changes often. AD does NOT replace the traditional database that one would use for storing application-related data. AD lets you publish resources such as shared folders in such a way that users don't need to know the physical location of the server. What does this mean to you as a DNA developer? Less maintenance and deployment issues! Any changes on the servers are transparent to the users and you don't have to walk around your users' workstation updating all the client executables.

Active Directory replication allows account updates at any domain controller, not just the primary domain controller (PDC). Multiple master replicas of the Active Directory at other domain controllers, which used to be known as backup domain controllers (BDCs), are updated and synchronized automatically.

NT 4.0's problematic WINS and broadcast name resolution NetBIOS is replaced with dynamic DNS in Windows 2000. You can store the DNS database in Active Directory (AD) and base it on the AD domain hierarchy. The DNS dynamic protocol allows client computers to update DNS name servers, so that the resource records can be updated without the intervention of system administrators.

> *See Chapter 13 (Windows 2000 Directory Services) in this book for details regarding programming the directory services.*

Security Concepts and Terminology

OK, your brain is probably fizzing over with all the jargon and terminology we've just presented. Let's now take a step back and explain what these terms actually mean.

Microsoft has developed a **Distributed Security Model**, the three basic concepts of which are:

1. Authentication – confirmation of user identity

2. Access control authorization – restricting and enabling access

3. Data protection – data integrity and privacy

Authentication is the main mechanism of identifying a client to the server, and then allowing or denying access to the system based on credentials provided by the client, such as user name, domain name and password.

Once the system has determined who the client is, the system's **access control** security will determine which system resources – be they files, components or other services – will be made available (or unavailable) to that particular user. This works hand in hand with authentication, but it is important that you are aware of the difference between the two. The Distributed Security Model supports two different approaches to implementing these security concepts: **declarative** security and **programmatic** security. Declarative security is taken care of through administrative settings and configurations; we will show you shortly how Active Directory takes care of this in Windows 2000. Programmatic security is implemented in the code you write when developing you applications.

I don't think the concept of data protection needs particular explanation at this point. We will come on to that in good time, and show you the multitude of technologies and protocols that are available to you. Right now, let's dig a little deeper into Authentication and Authorization.

Authentication

Authentication is the method of verifying a user's credentials. The Windows 2000 **Distributed Security Services** include integration with Windows 2000 **Active Directory Services** to provide scalable, flexible account management for large domains. The default authentication security protocol used is Kerberos 5. Also, authentication can be validated through public-key certificates and secure channels.

In order to create a meaningful policy, client authentication is required. For COM+ applications, authentication can be managed declaratively with the Component Services administrative tools. The COM+ library application can be configured so it may or may not participate in authentication. In this case the client will be always be authenticated. We will be looking at COM+ application authentication in more detail later on in the chapter.

For the server application several levels of authentication can be set, providing different degrees of security, and they may include encryption for each method call. Such a security system will affect the application's performance, but it's up to developers to decide what should take priority – security or performance.

Kerberos

Kerberos is a network-authentication protocol. It is designed to provide strong authentication for client/server applications by using secret-key cryptography. In Greek mythology, Kerberos is the name of the three-headed dog that guards Hades, which makes it an apt name for a security service. The Kerberos protocol was created by Massachusetts Institute of Technology (MIT) as a solution to network security problems. A free implementation of this protocol is available from the MIT web site (`http://web.mit.edu/`) under a copyright permission notice.

Many of the protocols used on the Internet do not provide any security. Tools to "sniff" passwords off the network are in common use by systems crackers. Thus, applications that send an unencrypted password over the network are extremely vulnerable. Worse yet, other client/server applications rely on the client program to be "honest" about the identity of the user. Other applications rely on the client to restrict its activities to those that it is allowed to do, with no other enforcement by the server.

Some sites attempt to use firewalls alone to solve their network security problems. Unfortunately, firewalls assume that "the bad guys" are on the outside, which is often an incorrect assumption. Insiders carry out most of the really damaging incidents of computer crime. Firewalls also have a significant disadvantage in that they restrict how your users can use the Internet. After all, firewalls are simply a less extreme example of the dictum that "there is nothing more secure than a computer which is not connected to the network – and powered off"! In many places, these restrictions are simply unrealistic and unacceptable.

The Kerberos protocol works across machine boundaries and has the following objects and services:

❑ A packet of encrypted client information that allows a client to access server resources when decrypted – called **Ticket**

❑ **TGT** (Ticket-granting ticket) – temporary tickets from the ticket-granting service for each authentication

❑ **KDC** (Key distribution center) – a service that runs as part of Active Directory and administers a ticket-granting ticket

❑ **TGS** (Ticket-granting service) – a service that is accessed by a client with a ticket-granting ticket and that administers tickets for the network resources

TGS allows a user to access different resources without the need to log on for each request. A client has to use a password to identify himself to the KDC only once. The KDC issues a TGT to the client. When network resources are accessed by the client, the TGS sends the TGT as proof of identity. After a ticket is authenticated the network resources are released for client decryption. Both client and server machines must be on the same Windows 2000 domain with a trust relationship between those domains.

The Kerberos protocol relies on temporary **tickets** and a complex system of encoding keys using other keys so that unencrypted passwords don't need to be transmitted across the network. After a client and server have used Kerberos to prove their identity, they can also encrypt all of their communications to assure privacy and data integrity as they go about their business.

The current version, Kerberos version 5, has been published by the **IETF** (Internet Engineering Task Force) as RFC 1510 (`http://www.ietf.org/rfc/rfc1510.txt`), and Windows 2000 implements Kerberos as described in this standard. The Kerberos authentication protocol enhances the underlying security features of Windows 2000 and provides the following features:

❑ Faster server authentication performance during initial connection establishment. The application server does not have to connect to the domain controller to authenticate the client. This allows applications' servers to scale better when handling large numbers of client connection requests.

❑ In Windows NT, what was formerly called Windows NT Challenge/Response, or (NTLM), is now **Integrated Windows Authentication**. Integrated Windows Authentication supports both the Kerberos version 5 and its own challenge/response protocol. With Kerberos, the client browser exchanges a hash of the user's credentials with the Web server to prove identity. NTLM also exchanges a hash. So what's so special about Kerberos? **Delegation**. Delegation allows IIS to use a client's credentials to connect to remote machines; we will be explaining it in more detail in the next few pages.

For Kerberos to work, the client and server machines must both be running Windows 2000, and both machines must be in Windows 2000 domains that have a trust relationship. A note here is that Kerberos supports **cloaking**. Cloaking determines the identity used during impersonation on the server.

❑ Transitive trust relationships for inter-domain authentication. Users can authenticate to domains anywhere in the domain tree because of the authentication services (KDCs) in each domain trust ticket issued by other KDCs in the tree. Transitive trust simplifies domain management for large networks with multiple domains.

Kerberos credentials consist of the domain and user name (which could be in the form of Internet friendly names, such as `joness@widgets.com`), and the Kerberos-style encrypted password. When the user signs on to the system, Windows 2000 obtains one or more Kerberos tickets to connect to network services. The Kerberos tickets represent a user's network credentials in Kerberos-based authentication.

Windows 2000 automatically manages the Kerberos ticket cache for connections to all network services. Tickets have an expiration time and occasionally need to be renewed. Ticket expiration and renewal are handled by the Kerberos security provider and associated application services. Most services, such as the file system Redirector, automatically keep session tickets up-to-date. Regular ticket renewal gives added session security by changing the session keys periodically.

Details on how Kerberos works are beyond the scope of discussion in this book. Check the references in the additional resources (in Appendix A) for more information on Kerberos.

Secure Sockets Layer (SSL)

SSL is used to encrypt authentication and data transmission for HTTP and NNTP transmission using public-key cryptography between client and server. Client and server do not have to be on the same domain and SSL works only across machines, but the server name must be resolved. SSL does not support anonymous server. SSL is usually used between a web browser and a web server to ensure the security of the transactions.

Client and server must be authenticated before sending encrypted data over a network:

❑   The client requests a secure channel connection

❑   In response, the server creates a public-key certificate and requests mutual authentication

❑   The client verifies the server certificate and, if requested by the server, sends the client's certificate, which is verified by the server

❑   The client creates an encrypted session key and sends it to the server with the server certificate

❑   The server sends encrypted data back to the client with a session key

❑   Windows 2000 Server stores information about it in the following registry key:
    HKey_Local_Machine\System\CurrentControlSet\Control\
    SecurityProviders\SCHANNEL\Protocols\

Secure Socket Layer supports only the impersonate level of impersonation. If a call made with any other impersonation level, the call will fail. So what's impersonation then?

Impersonation and Delegation

Impersonation is the process of performing a task on behalf of a client's identity. In other words, impersonation is the ability of a thread to execute under a different identity. Client credentials are presented to the server as an access token. By using this token the server can perform the task on behalf of the client at the client's security authorization level. The user's group policies will determine the user's access rights and what can be done under the client impersonation.

Windows 2000 supports the following impersonation levels: *Identity*, *Impersonate*, and *Delegate*.

❑   The Identity level is the default server method to identify the caller and allow client to do Access Control List (ACL) checks.

❑   The Impersonate level allows the server to impersonate the client's security context while acting on behalf of the client.

❑   The Delegate level is new to Windows 2000 and the most powerful impersonation level. At this level the server can impersonate the client's security context while acting on behalf of the client, and the client's credentials can be accessed by any number of local or network machines.

A client's impersonation can be configured administratively in the Default Properties tab of DCOMCNFG.EXE (which can be found at %systemroot%\system32\DCOMCNFG.EXE), and must be supported in the code of the application. The impersonation is the agreement between the client and the server. A client must identify itself in order for the server to act on the client's behalf – this act is called **delegation.** Delegation is the impersonation of clients over the network.

When a server is acting as a client it hides its identity and **cloaking** is enabled to make calls to other COM components under the client's identity. To effectively use both, the client and server user accounts must be properly configured in the Active Directory Service, and the server identity must be set to "Trusted for delegation". The client identity must not be set to "Account is sensitive and cannot be delegated" in the Active Directory Service. With this type of configuration, the domain administrator gains a high degree of control over delegation.

Access Control

Windows 2000 supports Win32 security automatically for all Win32-based applications without programmatic security adjustments. The Windows 2000 Security Model controls access to all Win32 objects with minimal impact on security functions and performance. The Win32 security supports the following access control features:

❑ Restricted access to secured objects (files, directories, threads, registry, services)

❑ Access rights

❑ Audit and access logging

There are two basic components to access control: **Access control tokens** and **Security descriptors**. Before we take a look at these, I need to introduce to you Access Control Lists, Access Control Entries, Security Identifiers, and Privileges.

Access Control Lists and Entries

An **Access Control List** (**ACL**) is a list of security protections that applies to an object, and consists of multiple **Access Control Entries** (**ACE**). Each ACE can specify the corresponding security principal that is to be allowed or denied access. There are two types of access-control list:

❑ A **discretionary** access-control list (**DACL**) recognizes the callers that are allowed or denied access to a securable object. When a process is accessing a securable object the discretionary access control list is checked. If it is valid, then access is granted to the object. Note that if the object does not have a DACL then it is wide open for all users to have full access. If it does then access is restricted by ACE.

❑ A **system** access-control list (**SACL**) allows administrators to keep track of all attempts to access a secure object in the security event log. For any failed or successful attempts an audit report can be generated.

Security Identifiers (SIDs) and Privileges

A **security identifier** (**SID**) is a unique number to identify user account, group account, or logon session to which an ACE applies. Each access control entry in an access control list has one security identifier that identifies the user or group account, or logon session. All methods of the ISecurityProperty interface work with SIDs, but don't have the flexibility of the role-based security, because SIDs specifically identifies only one unique user or group. SIDs can be used in functions of the Win32 API to increase the complexity of the Windows security.

A security identifier is used in the following security elements:

❑ Security description – to identify the primary group and an object's owner

❑ Access tokens – to identify the user and his group

❑ Access control entries – to identify the trustee access rights

In addition to the SIDs there are well-known SIDs, which identify generic groups and generic users. Those well-known, universal SIDs are recognized by all security systems using the security model. Win32 API contains a set of constants that can be used to create well-known SIDs, and a number of functions to modify SIDs.

The system uses an access token not only to identify the user, but also to inform the system what kind of access rights a user has. The access token contains information about account rights or privileges.

A **privilege** is the account's rights to perform various systems-related operations. Windows 2000 stores all accounts' privileges for all users and groups in an account database. When the user logs on to the system an access token is created with all necessary information about a user's rights. The user rights are defined with privilege constants, which are part of the `WINNT.H` file. Here are a few examples of privileges:

❑ Back up files and directories

❑ Create a token object

❑ Debug programs

❑ Load and unload device drivers

❑ Take file ownership

❑ Act as part of the operating system

Access Control Tokens

Access control tokens provide the main source of information about a logged on user. The token is created only if user log on was successful. An access token is present in all processes executed on behalf of the logged on user. The token contains the information about the user and a list of the privileges they hold. The access token contains the following information:

❑ **SID** – the security identifier for the user's account, the unique identifier for a trustee

❑ A logon session SID

❑ **Privileges** held by the user

❑ The SID for the primary group

❑ The access token source

❑ Token type

❑ Impersonation levels

By default, the system uses a primary token when the process interacts with a securable object. The client's impersonation thread contains both primary and impersonation tokens.

Security Descriptors

A security descriptor contains the following security information about a securable object:

- ❑ SID for the owner and primary group of an object
- ❑ A discretionary access-control list that specifies the access rights
- ❑ A system access control list for audit purposes

The security descriptor should not be modified manually to ensure that SIDs, ACLs remain syntactically correct. The setting should be set with functions provided by the Win32 API, such as `SetSecurityDescriptorGroup`, `SetSecurityDescriptorOwner`, `SetSecurityDescriptorSacl`.

Auditing

The Windows 2000 Security Model provides a mechanism that enables the tracking of all security information on all callers and on all calls made by those callers to components. The audit log can provide the following information on caller and component calls:

- ❑ Number of callers
- ❑ Caller's identity
- ❑ Caller's account name
- ❑ Least security authentication level
- ❑ Authentication service used
- ❑ If it was a direct call
- ❑ Level of client's impersonation

Before setting objects security tracking, the Audit Policy must be set in the Local Computer Settings:

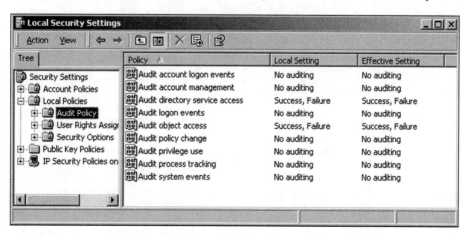

To enable an object for auditing:

- ❏ Right-click on the object in Windows Explorer and choose **Properties**.

- ❏ Click on the **Advanced** button in the **Security** tab

- ❏ On the **Auditing** tab click **Add** button

- ❏ Type or select the Name from the Names list

- ❏ From the Access list select whether successful access, failed access, or both types of access are audited:

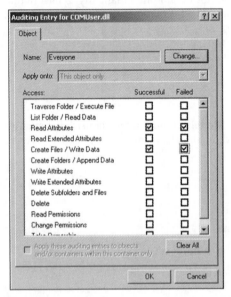

The Audit logs can be viewed from the Event Viewer under Security by the system Administrator:

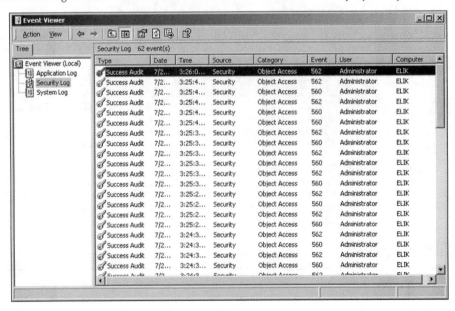

Protecting Data Integrity

So far we've talked about determining **who** is trying to access **what** in our system, and we've thought about allowing them access to **this** particular resource, but not **that** one. It's great being in control, isn't it! Now let's move on. We're going to look at some really complex stuff here – but thankfully most of this complexity is hidden from us. In fact, 'hidden' is a very apt word, since we're now going to look at how we can hide our data away from prying eyes. Encryption is the name of the game, and we're going to introduce you to some of the players in town.

Encryption File System (EFS)

A standard safety measure on a personal computer system is to attempt to boot from a floppy disk before trying to boot from the hard disk. This guards users against hard drive-failures and corrupted boot partitions. It also adds the convenience of booting different operating systems. Unfortunately, this can mean someone with physical access to a system can bypass the built-in security features of the Windows 2000 operating system file system access control by using a tool to read Windows NTFS on-disk structures. Many hardware configurations provide features like a boot password to restrict this kind of access. Such features are not in widespread use, and in a typical environment where multiple users are sharing a workstation, they do not work very well. Even if these features were universal, the protection provided by a password is not very strong.

Data encryption is the only solution to this problem. With the **Encryption File System** (EFS), data in NTFS files is encrypted on disk. The encryption technology used is public key-based and runs as an integrated system service, making it easy to manage, difficult to attack, and transparent to the user. If a user attempting to access an encrypted NTFS file has the private key to that file, the user is able to open the file and work with it transparently as a normal document. A user without the private key to the file is denied access.

EFS integrates with Windows 2000's PKI and has support for data recovery in case the user's private key is lost or unavailable. EFS will be a nice enhancement for laptop users because these systems are vulnerable to theft.

Certificate Server

The **Microsoft Certificate Server**, which is included with Windows 2000 and IIS 4.0, provides customizable services for issuing and managing certificates for applications using public-key cryptography. The Certificate Server can perform a central role in managing systems to provide secure communications across the Internet, corporate intranets, and other non-secure networks. The Certificate Server is customizable to support the application requirements of different organizations. That's all we're going to say on this topic right now, since the whole of the following chapter is devoted to it.

CryptoAPI

The CryptoAPI has been around since Windows NT 4.0, but Windows 2000 benefits from the introduction of **CryptoAPI Certificate Management** to support public-key security. Windows 2000 included some major new features of CryptoAPI, such as:

❑   Digital signature and verification, and data encryption support using higher-level functions available to applications in Visual Basic, Visual Basic Scripting Edition (VBScript), Java, and C/C++

❑   Support for PKCS #10 certificate requests and PKCS #7 for signed and enveloped data

❑   Support for X.509 version 3 certificates and X.509 version 2.0 CRLs through common encoding/decoding functions, certificate parse, and verification

❑   Adding and retrieving certificates and CRLs from certificate stores, locating certificates by attributes and associating private keys

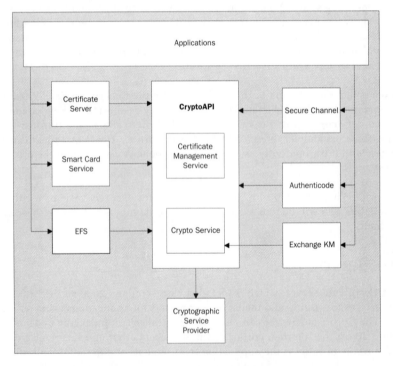

CryptoAPI brings a lot of benefits to application developers:

❑   Programmers/developers need not write their own proprietary cryptographic code.

❑   Developers can concentrate on the business rules and interfaces in their application without having to worry about the different cryptographic standards and protocols.

❑   Abstracting applications from the provider protects the applications from obsolescence. That is, developers need not worry about any redesign or redeployment issues with changes in the underlying encryption logic.

❑   Developers cannot request and publish certificates and **certificate revocation lists** (CRLs) and build certification paths when a server application needs to know whether a certificate is valid.

IP Security

The Internet Engineering Task Force's **IP Security Protocol** (IPSec) is included in Windows 2000. It lies below the transport level so its security services are transparently inherited by applications. A DNA developer doesn't have to worry about changing the existing applications or training the end users.

Windows 2000 makes full use of powerful, industry-standard cryptographic algorithms and authentication techniques. These include:

❑ Diffie-Hellman Technique to agree upon a shared key

❑ Hash message authentication code (HMAC) and variations, to provide integrity and anti-replay

❑ Data Encryption Standard Cipher block chaining for confidentiality

See the references in Appendix A for more details on these.

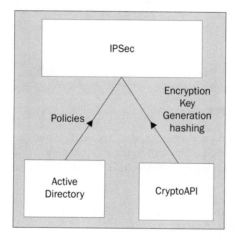

Proxies

To enable client PCs access to the Internet from a corporate network, one would have to run phone lines directly to the each user's desktop or set up a few PCs with Internet access and have several people share it. Both these solutions are not viable. A proxy server lets multiple clients access the Internet in a manner that is not only safe, but also secure.

The term proxy means: "to act on someone's behalf". Proxy in terms of networks and systems means that the machine would do something on someone else's behalf. Here, all the network clients in a secure environment can access content from the Internet or an intranet via the proxy server. A proxy provides multiple client PCs a secure gateway to the Internet.

A proxy makes the interaction between the client PC and Internet transparent to both parties. The client PC is unaware of the presence of a proxy (except in the case where the user is trying to access a site/content filtered by the administrator). The web site on the Internet interprets the requests from proxy server as if it was from one client the proxy server here shields each individual's information while acting on behalf of the client.

The proxy server should be setup as 'dual-homed', which means that the proxy server machine has two network cards. One network card connects to the outside world or the Internet and the second one connects to your network:

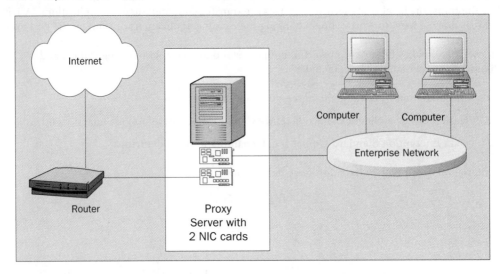

Microsoft ISA Server

In the construction of a building architecture, the "fire wall" is built to protect our assets from fire. Similarly, in a network we'd build a fire wall to protect our network from outside fire. Firewall is a system or collection of systems that enforces policies by which multiple networks can communicate with each other.

Microsoft's ISA Server 2000 (Internet Security and Acceleration Server) combines firewall protection with web caching for Windows 2000 servers.

The firewall features of the software include packet, circuit, and application level screening, allowing administrators to control Internet access by user, group, application, content type, schedule, and destination. Additionally, "smart application filters" have the ability to recognize and control Internet traffic based on the content of the traffic itself; in other words content can be recognized as e-mail or streaming media, for example, and access and trafficking rules can be applied based on that content. Dynamic packet filtering provides the safeguarding of opening data access ports only when they are needed.

ISA services consist of several technologies:

- The firewall service
- The w3proxy web proxy service
- Secure network address translation (SecureNAT)
- Advanced caching capabilities, including RAM caching and use of the Cache Array Routing Protocol
- Bandwidth control
- Static and dynamic Internet Protocol (IP) packet filtering
- Alerting

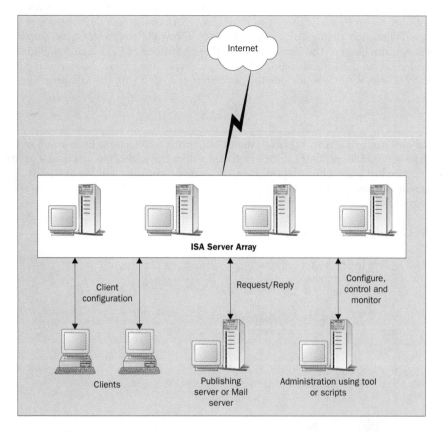

ISA Server is typically configured on a device with two network interfaces. One network interface connects directly to the private network, while the other interface connects to the public Internet. The interfaces can be any type that permits protocol bindings. On a local area network (LAN), for example, Ethernet, token ring network, or Attached Resource Computer Network (ARCnet) is commonly bound to Transmission Control Protocol/Internet Protocol (TCP/IP) or NetBIOS Enhanced User Interface (NetBEUI). An Internet connection might utilize a modem, Integrated Services Digital Network (ISDN), or network interface that connects to a router that connects to the Internet.

The administrator can also manage clients from a remote location, using either the ISA Server administration tool or scripting. For a DNA developer, the scripting aspect of this is of particular significance here.

ISA Administration Object Model

The ISA administration object model gives developers a mechanism to extend ISA functionality. Scripting allows you to use the ISA administration COM objects to access and control any ISA array within an organization. The administration objects allow for automation of everything done using the ISA administration tool. This capability allows administrators to create scripts to automate repetitive tasks requiring the use of the administration tool; these scripts can then be included in batch files. By programming with the same administration objects that ISA itself uses, developers can provide persistent and configurable data storage for their programs, and can have the ISA Server notify programs when the configuration data has changed.

Let's look at a programming example of using the ISA administration to automate a task such as assigning Internet access to a new user. You must have ISA installed for the procedures to work. From Visual Basic's 'Reference' dialog box, select "Microsoft Firewall Proxy and Cache Administration Library" to access the library. The library is defined in msfpccom.dll, which is a file included with ISA. This will make all the administration COM objects available to you. To start using the administration objects with C++, include the file msfpccom.dll with the following line of code:

```
#import "msfpccom.dll"
```

You can add new users to ISA by means of the FPCAccounts collection. Each group of FPCAccount objects holds a set of accounts that can be associated with a site and content rule or a protocol rule. The FPCSiteAndContentRule object represents a site and content rule, and the FPCProtocolRule object represents a protocol rule. You use protocol rules and site and content rules to restrict Internet access for a group of ISA accounts.

The following function adds a new ISA account that represents a new user:

```
Function AssignInternetAcess(ByVal strAccount As String)
    ' Add new user account
    'Input : strAccount is the format DOMAIN\ACCOUNT for example : SALES\BSMITH

    Dim objFPC              As New FPCLib.FPC
    Dim objMyFPCAccounts    As FPCAccounts
    Dim objMyNewFPCAccount   As FPCAccount

    Set objMyFPCAccounts =
    objFPC.Arrays.CurrentArray.ArrayPolicy.SiteAndContentRules(1). _
        AppliesToAccounts

    ' add new user account to collection
    Set objMyNewFPCAccount = objMyFPCAccounts.Add(strAccount, fpcInclude)

    Set objFPC = Nothing
End Function
```

An ISA user's Internet access is governed by protocol rules, site and content rules, and schedules. To enable the user to have appropriate levels of Internet access, appropriate rules must apply to this ISA account.

For more information on ISA or to download the SDK visit Microsoft's web site at http://www.microsoft.com/ISAServer

Routing IP addresses

IP forwarding is a TCP/IP routing feature of a web server. If you are using Microsoft Proxy Server, it will forward all IP connection requests received on any of the server network port if the IP forwarding feature is enabled. You must disable the default forwarding of all IP requests.

With the IP forwarding disabled, Proxy server sets network barriers and controls IP traffic between the two servers' network ports. It is extremely important to protect routers from the security standpoint as they handle most if not all the network traffic. A router whose security is compromised can change the routes and gateways, sniff traffic and could potential make your network vulnerable.

Some of the security measures you can take to are:

❑ Make sure the password for the router is very hard to guess.

❑ Make use of packet filtering routers that will enable you to filter incoming packets based on the address or port number in the packet. This should be skillfully combined with proxy servers and firewalls.

❑ If the Router Internet Protocol (RIP) is used, make sure it's properly controlled.

❑ Block all incoming traffic to port 137, 138 and 139 on the routers that are connected to the Internet. It will prevent the NBTStat command from being against your network.

❑ Make sure Simple Network Management Protocol (SNMP) is either disabled or secured properly. Block UDP ports 161 and 162 at the routers to stop any SNMP eavesdroppers on your network.

❑ Use the NetStat command to find out which TCP/IP ports are in the listening state. It lists all the incoming and outgoing connections on the server.

❑ Do not leave the Route command exposed to the Internet. This command can be used to clear routing tables, change the existing route. This command can be used to re-route the attacker's malicious IP address to a dummy IP address from your unused address pool.

Use of Network Monitors, Packet Sniffers and TCP/IP Port scanners are nifty utilities that every network administrator should possess.

Security for the Business Tier

In this part of the chapter, we are going to be looking at how you can enable security on the business tier of your DNA application. By design, COM+ applications are usually middle-tier applications and represent the business logic or data access logic layers. When deciding where to implement security, consideration should be given to minimizing the impact on application performance. In some cases, security validation can be shifted to the 'back end', at the database itself, or may be implemented in each tier and have different access priorities for each logical layer. No matter where you set your security validation, it should not impact on the durability of your application.

In today's environment, databases such as SQL Server provide reasonable security, but security validation at this level can be very expensive. Additionally, business rule COM+ objects will lose their main aspects of validating the right logical or decision call. Use of security validation at the database level is not as flexible and scalable as multi-tier COM+ objects. By applying security verification in COM your application can benefit in the following ways:

❑ Connection pooling

❑ Application scaling

❑ Flexibility through the use of declarative security and role-based security

With COM+ security authorization the database can create a trusted connection with a middle-tier object and provide audit logging for all application users. COM+ components will be able to decide who can perform what task based on application business rules and security access level. Even though COM+ applications are generally trusted, the database will be protected from unauthorized access from outside the COM+ application.

In the case of impersonation, the database will authenticate the user and the COM+ application impersonates the client while accessing the database on a per-call basis and connection cannot be reused. This scenario is used with small or very specific groups of users with restricted data access.

COM+ Access Control

The COM+ security model allows the control of four levels of access:

❑   Single component

❑   Specific interface of a component

❑   Methods of a component

❑   Package – an entire collection of components

A new feature in the COM+ security model is that, not only can application and class level objects be separately secured, but security can also be specified for a single method. Interface and method security was not supported by declarative security in previous versions of MTS – the only way to get to this level was by using programmatic security. In Windows 2000 it is possible to drill down to the specific method and set appropriate method security declaratively.

COM+ also supports the approach of defining users and user groups and then giving access permissions for a file or object. It is up to the developers of a specific project as to how to build the security system for that application. Declarative security can be combined with programmatic security in components prior to deployment.

Application Identity

An **application identity** is the unique account under which an application can be executed. The application identity can be set via DCOMCNFG.EXE in the application properties tab:

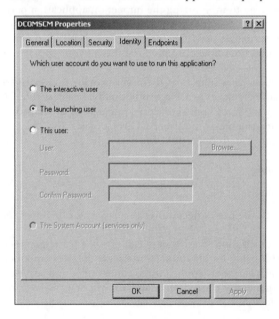

There are four types of application identity:

❏ Launching user – the most secure setting for the application identity, because of the separate server instances, which is run with an impersonation token. This is the default setting for the application. In this case each user gets a new instance of the server. The user will see no GUI interface of the application.

❏ Interactive user – the applications that use a graphical user interface (GUI) must have their identity set in the registry to run with interactive users. The interactive user is the user that is logged on to the system where the application is running. The application with settings for interactive users will not run if no users are logged on.

❏ Specific user – this type of application interface is more secure than an interactive user interface and also allows remote resource access. Specific user is identified by the user's password. In this scenario no logged users are required on the server and all clients can talk to the same server interface if the server is set for multi-use. The user will not see the GUI in the application.

❏ Service – if the application identity is set as a service the application will run as a service.

Security Boundaries

If the application calls one component from another component in the same application no security check is required. However, when two different applications share the same process and one application calls another application's component, security will be checked at the application boundaries. When two applications share one process, at least one of them must be a library application. COM+ library applications are hosted by other processes. In this case there is a security boundary between the hosting process and the library application. In order to have constant security checking between component calls, these should be placed in separate COM+ applications.

In COM+ server applications, access checking can be performed at the component level or at the process level. When component-level access validation is selected the security property will be included on the object context. With component-level security checking programmatic role-based security can be used, to assign roles to components, interfaces and methods.

With process-level checking, security-call context information is not available nor is the security property, and programmatic security cannot be implemented. Process level access checks apply only to the application boundary so do component level checks.

Security Needs

It is worth looking at a few common scenarios to determine how to set up your security.

Default COM+ Security

One of the easiest methods to use is default COM+ security settings. In this case you just lay back and relax and let COM+ manage all your needs. We will examine this shortly.

617

Restricted Application Access

Another scenario is to provide restricted access to specified components or applications. To restrict access to your application from a remote location, DCOM between remote machines can be disabled. For both legacy and new applications, security can be set process-wide in the registry by using DCOMGNFG.EXE. Another way is to use the security default for the whole process, but modify only certain interfaces in the process at the proxy-interface level. Those settings can be implemented by using the IClientSecurity interface, which allows the client to change the security settings associated with calls to a particular interface by controlling the security settings at the interface-proxy level.

Full Programmatic Restrictions

If it is not enough for your application to just use the default security settings, then all settings can be triggered programmatically. In this case automatic authentication must be disabled and security settings will be set on a per-interface basis.

No Security

In some cases, for example during development, process security can be completely turned off in order to enable security to be set individually.

COM+ Default Security

COM+ has its own default security settings that support role-based security. After proper configuration, those settings will be enforced by security policies and can also be modified to fulfill the needs of the application. COM+ default role-based security will cover most of your security needs without the need for specifying registry settings or using special security function calls. It will initialize and provide security management for your application. Default security will specify access settings for all components running on a local machine. When a user logs on to Windows 2000 the system validates the user through his user name and password. If these parameters are valid then the system creates a unique identification token, which is used by the security system.

Default Authentication Settings

The default Authentication Level setting specifies the base authentication level for the caller. The default Impersonation Level setting specifies the base impersonation level the caller runs on the system and can be set in the Default tab of the DCOMCNFG.EXE.

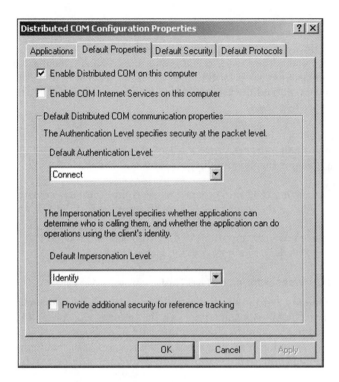

Role-Based Declarative Security

Roles are the key to a centralized declarative security system for COM+ objects, and we'll be seeing shortly how to design and implement roles. For now you just need to know that a system administrator, developer or component creator can create security roles. Each role can have different access rights and can include a variety of **users**. The same user can belong to different **groups**, which themselves are assigned to the different roles. In this way a user will have various access rights depending on which role he is using to access the application's components. A user must be assigned to the appropriate role in order to be allowed access to the data. A role can contain groups of users or single user accounts.

The MMC is the easiest way to manage declarative security. This type of declarative security does not require any component programming and can be modified at any time (either before application deployment or during the application lifetime) in a COM+ catalog external to the components. Role-based security does not require developers to use a low-level operating system security API.

When an application uses role-based security, a caller's role membership is checked on every call into the application – if the call is made from outside the boundaries. For example, when two applications share the same process and a component in the first application calls a component in the second application, a security check is done because an application boundary is crossed. In the case of package security settings, when the call does not cross the boundaries, there are no additional checks needed because the caller is already granted access to the package.

Creating Roles

The best and preferred way of creating roles and assigning users is to create user groups. This is similar to creating user groups and adding users to that group in NT. First, a local group must be created by using Local Users and Groups tool (a local user or group is an account that can be granted permissions and rights from local system) and the user must be added to this group. After that those groups can be assigned to the appropriate roles.

Filling roles using the MMC and groups makes life much easer in an enterprise environment, where the number of users can grow significantly. Also it is easier to manage groups of users who share relatively similar activity than it is to manage individual accounts and rights.

Before creating and managing roles and groups it is very important to understand how each group of users should behave. What is the security policy for this group of users? Is it an administrative group, just regular users, or perhaps someone in between? In order to make it easier for future changes in the user groups to take place it is very important to describe what the role policy is. The MMC allows comments to be added in a description field at the group level.

Using the Component Services Administrative Tool

To create, delete, or modify a group in a security role we can use the **Component Services** administrative tool in the MMC. Under COM+ Applications, open the Roles folder for the required application and find the role you would like to modify. You can then add or delete user accounts, or you can delete the entire role with all groups and user accounts in it. If the role is not in that folder it must first be created (if it doesn't exist at all) and added to the application before any user or group accounts can be assigned to the role:

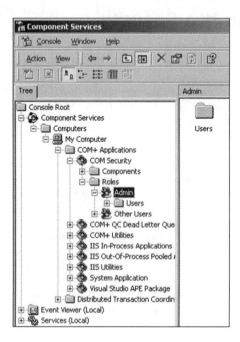

Creating a New Role

To create a new role right-click on the Roles folder, point to New, and then click Role. Create the desired role by typing the appropriate role name. After the role is created go to the role properties and add your comments in the role description, for future reference.

Adding a User or Group Account to a Role

A similar procedure is used to create a new user account, just right-click on the Users folder for the required role, point to New, and then click User. In the Select Users or Groups box type the fully qualified name (//domain/user_name) of the user or group you want to add. You can also make this selection by clicking on the user or group in the Name box. If a user or group is not in the specified domain you can change the domain and repeat the search in the Name box. Click OK when you have finished adding user accounts and groups to the role. Each user or group will have an icon in the User folder. To activate a new membership the application must be restarted. To restart application just right-click on the selected package and select Shut down and Start commands.

If in the future you need to change which roles a user or group account belongs to, you need to first delete the user or group account from the existing role and then add the account to the new role. Adding and removing users from groups is far easier than maintaining particular access permissions for many users.

The access rights will depend only on the role group policy. This may give you some flexibility in granting permissions to multiple users at once and differentiating which group of users can perform which task, but it may also introduce new problems in development process, increase level of complicity to track all permissions and secured object access based on assigned role.

Group Policy Management

Group Policy requires a different snap-in from the Role-based security we have just been looking at. When adding Group Policy to the MMC, in the Select Group Policy object dialog box, click Local Computer to edit the local Group Policy object, or browse to find the Group Policy object you want.

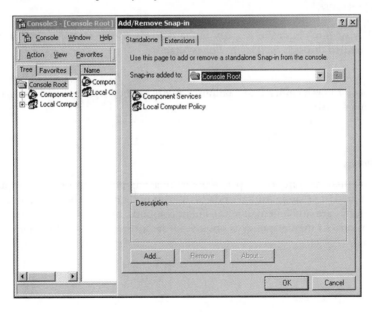

Group policy settings determine the various components of a particular user's environment that a system needs to manage. All specified group-policy settings are contained in a group policy object. The policy is applied when an existing system user logs on. If the user logs on interactively, for example, via the Internet or a network, the system finds and loads the user's profile first and then applies the group policy settings. The group policy object contains not only user configurations that are specific for the user, but also computer configurations that affect the computer's settings. The figure below shows the two available 'nodes' for administering these configurations.

Group policy information is located in the file that contains specific registry settings for the user or local machine and is written to the registry under HKEY_CURRENT_USER. Computer-specific settings are written under HKEY_LOCAL_MACHINE. The policy data is generally stored in the registry file system or the Active Directory.

The Group Policy snap-in obtains its registry-based policy settings from an administrative template file, which can be modified through the Group Policy snap-in.

> It is important to remember that Computer-related policy settings override User-related policy settings.

Applying Group Policy

In Windows 2000 there are only two types of object in group policy: users and computers. User policy is obtained from the User Configuration node (as shown in the figure above) when a user logs on. Most Group Policy settings are implemented at the client computer by DLLs on the client, which are called client-side extensions. Computer policy is obtained from a computer's configuration at boot time.

Policy Events

How should we control the policy if multiple applications can make policy changes at the same time? One of the following methods can be used to monitor policy changes for an application:

❑ Snap-in extension or service – the system can notify the application with a message if the policy has been changed using WM_SETTINGCHANGE. If such a window is not available to receive messages then the application can use the RegisterGPNotification function to receive notification of the change in policy.

❑ The way events are handled in the application depends on the policy data type. If this is the registry-driven policy all settings should be read and set on application start.

❑ To ensure that the policy is not updated in the registry by other applications, call the EnterCriticalPolicySection function to obtain ownership of the policy section. The next step would be to call the LeaveCriticalPolicySection function to release ownership so other applications can modify the policy.

❑ If the application is using file-based policy settings, then the ProcessGroupPolicyProc callback function is used. This system calls all registered callback functions when applying a policy. In order to register the callback function, a new key should be added to the registry under the following path:

HKEY_LOCAL_MACHINE\SOFTWARE\Microsoft\Windows NT\CurrentVersion\Winlogon\
GPExtensions\\{GUID}

This new key must be a GUID. In this case the services policy settings must be read on service start and the call to GetGPOList should be made to get a list of all GPOs.

Levels of Security

An entire application or process can be secured with different levels such as Activation or Lunch permission, Authentication, Impersonation and Delegation. That security can be set in the registry in two ways. If the client application creates a GUID, however, client applications do not normally appear in DCOMCNFG.EXE, then the registry can be modified with the DCOMCNFG.EXE simple UI. Security values can be set in the registry under AppID for the application. Also security can be implemented programmatically at a low-level. Access control provides a number of functions to create a security descriptor as well as functions to initialize.

Programmatic Security

A developer can programmatically define a component's security, thus allowing it identify a client's privilege to execute requested operations within that component. This is known as programmatic security, and it allows validated role membership to determine whether a particular part of code is executed. Security information can also be accessed using the security call context object.

The following are the key interfaces and functions used to implement programmatic security:

- ❑ ISecurityCallContext
- ❑ CoInitializeSecurity
- ❑ CoSetProxyBlanket
- ❑ IObjectContext
- ❑ IsCallerInRole
- ❑ IsSecurityEnabled
- ❑ IServerSecurity
- ❑ CoGetCallContext
- ❑ QueryBlanket

These interfaces and functions do not provide the ability to control activation or identity security because the settings must be verified *before* the component is invoked. On the other hand, programmatic security allows us to set features which would be impossible to set declaratively, for example when you need to use the client's identity to access a secured object protected by a security descriptor, or propagating the client's identity through to a database – you can perform impersonation programmatically. Programmatic security allows you to define roles for a single method. Let's take a look at some examples.

Examples of Programmatic Security

This sample shows how to validate if the caller is in the Administrators role. To be able to execute this code, references to the COM+ 1.0 Service Type Library (comsvcs.dll) must be set:

```
Public Function IsAdministrator() As Boolean
    On Error GoTo EH
    Dim oObjCon As ObjectContext
    Set oObjCon = GetObjectContext()
        If oObjCon.IsCallerInRole("Administrators") Then
            IsAdministrator = True
        Else
            ' Deny access and return failure
            IsAdministrator = False
        End If

Exit_Function:
        Set oObjCon = Nothing
    Exit Function
EH:
        Err.Raise vbObjectError + 1000, "IsAdministrator", Err.Description
        IsAdministrator = False
        GoTo Exit_Function
End Function
```

If the component is in-process, role checking would be disabled. In this case, `IsCallerInRole` always returns `TRUE`, which means the direct caller would always pass the authorization check. `IsSecurityEnabled` returns `FALSE` when the object runs in-process. When objects are not running in a secure environment the method IsSecurityEnabled can be used to disable a non-secure transaction. In this case you need to validate if role-based security is enabled:

```
Public Function IsSecure() As Boolean
    On Error GoTo EH
    Dim oObjCon As ObjectContext
    Set oObjCon = GetObjectContext()
        If oObjCon.IsSecurityEnabled Then
            IsSecure = True
        Else
            ' Deny access and return failure
            IsSecure = False
        End If

Exit_Function:
        Set oObjCon = Nothing
        Exit Function
EH:
        Err.Raise vbObjectError + 1000, "IsSecure", Err.Description
        IsSecure = False
        GoTo Exit_Function
End Function
```

The following example shows how to add a member to a security role, and get the security catalog programmatically. To be able to execute this code, references to the COM+ 1.0 Admin Type Library (`comadmin.dll`) must be set:

```
Public Function AddMemberToRole (sCatalog As String, sPackage As String, &_
                sRole As String, sNewMember As String) As Boolean
On Error GoTo EH
Dim oCatalog As COMAdmin.COMAdminCatalog
Dim oPackages As COMAdmin.COMAdminCatalogCollection
Dim oPackage As COMAdmin.COMAdminCatalogObject
Dim bFoundPackage As Boolean

Set oCatalog = New COMAdmin.COMAdminCatalog
'Open Catalog Connection
oCatalog.Connect sCatalog
Set oPackages = oCatalog.GetCollection("Packages")
oPackages.Populate

For Each oPackage In oPackages
    If oPackage.Name = sPackage Then
        bFoundPackage = True
        Dim oRoles As COMAdminCatalogCollection
        Dim oRole As COMAdminCatalogObject
        Dim bFoundRole As Boolean

        Set oRoles = oPackages.GetCollection("RolesInPackage", oPackage.Key)
        oRoles.Populate
```

```
                For Each oRole In oRoles
                    If oRole.Name = sRole Then
                        Dim oUsersInRole As COMAdmin.COMAdminCatalogCollection
                        Dim oNewMember As COMAdminCatalogObject
                        bFoundRole = True
                        Set oUsersInRole = oRoles.GetCollection("UsersInRole" _
                            , oRole.Key)
                        Set oNewMember = oUsersInRole.Add
                        oNewMember.Value("User") = CStr(sNewMember)
                        oUsersInRole.SaveChanges
                        Set oUsersInRole = Nothing
                        Set oNewMember = Nothing
                        Exit For
                    End If
                Next
                If Not bFoundRole Then Err.Raise vbObjectError + 1001, _
                    "AddMemberToRole", "Role '" & sRole & "' of package '" _
                    & sPackage & "' was not found in '" & sCatalog & "'"
                    Set oRoles = Nothing
                    Exit For
                End If
            Next
    If Not bFoundPackage Then
        Err.Raise vbObjectError + 1000, "AddMemberToRole", "Package '" _
            sPackage "' was not found in '" & sCatalog & "'"
        AddMemberToRole = False
    Else
        AddMemberToRole = True
    End If
ExitFunction:
    Set oPackages = Nothing
    Set oCatalog = Nothing
Exit Function
EH:
    Err.Raise vbObjectError + 1000, "AddMemberToRole", Err.Description
    AddMemberToRole = False
    GoTo ExitFunction
End Function
```

SecurityCallContext and SecurityIdentity Objects

In the Windows 2000 environment accessibility to the caller's security information is provided with the SecurityCallContext object's properties collection, which comprises:

❑ Callers

❑ DirectCaller

❑ OriginalCaller

❑ NumberOfCallers

❑ MinimumAuthenticationLevel

The `SecurityCallContext` properties collection provides information in the chain of calls to the component. All properties are read-only. The `SecurityCallContext` object can be accessed only by an application that is using role-based security. To use the `SecurityCallContext` object in your code, a reference to the COM+ Service Type Library (`COMSVCS.dll`) must be set. The reference to the `SecurityCallContext` object is provided by the `GetSecurityCallContext` function if role-based security is used.

```
Public Function GetCaller(sName as String) as Variant
   Dim objCaller as SecurityIdentity
   Set objCaller = GetSecurityCallContext("DirectCaller")
   GetCaller = objCaller(sName)
   Set objCaller = Nothing
End Function
```

The `SecurityIdentity` object is a collection that provides the information about a particular caller. The DirectCaller and OriginalCaller items of the SecurityCallContext collection are Security Identity objects. SecurityCallContext has the properties `Count and Item`.

The `Count` is the number of items in the `SecurityCallContext` collection. The Item property is an indexed property that allows you to retrieve a specific item in the security identity collection. The index is a string specifying returned items from a collection. The `SecurityIdentity` object has the following collection of items:

❑   SID

❑   Account Name

❑   Authentication Service

❑   Impersonation Level

❑   Authentication Level

The default access permission defines the access permission list for the machine in the registry under AppID for the Access Control List (ACL) if it cannot access classes for which there are no Access Permission settings. Default access permissions are used only for the applications that don't call the `CoInitializeSecurity` method. VB programmers can use SecurityCallContext instead to validate default access permissions. While the server impersonating the caller ACL checked if the caller has permissions to access the object that has been called, if successful access is allowed, if not the connection is aborted. By default, this named-value has no entries in it. In this case ACL grants permissions only to the systems to make a call to the server.

Access permissions in the registry entry are set under:

HKEY_LOCAL_MACHINE\SOFTWARE\Classes\APPID\{AppID_value}\AccessPermission = ACL

The registry value contains data describing ACL of the principals that can access instances of this class. Upon receiving a request to connect to an existing object of this class, the ACL is checked by the application being called while impersonating the caller. If the access-check fails the connection is disallowed.

VBA Security

Depending on the needs of your application, security can be implemented to restrict access to the sensitive information on your system. If you are developing a VBA application, additional access security will be very valuable for your application. Microsoft Office security can be provided in three ways:

❑   Password protection

❑   File-system access-control

❑   Programmatic security

You don't need to perform any programming to protect Word or Excel documents with a password. The **Save As** dialog box provides the option to protect a document with two kinds of passwords – one to open a document and another to modify the document after it has been opened.

The "Open document" password can be set programmatically using the SaveAs method of the Active Document:

```
ActiveDocument.SaveAs FileName:= "your file name", Password:= "password", _
    WritePassword:= "write password"
ActiveDocument.Close
```

After protecting a document with a password, to open it with code the same (case-sensitive) password must be applied to the Open.PasswordDocument or Open.WritePasswordDocument method:

```
Documents.Open FileName:= "your file name", PasswordDocument:= _
    "password", WritePasswordDocument:="write password"
```

If a user password is not desirable for your application then file-system access control can be used. This is basically the same as applying role-based security where the securable object is your document. This is the preferred document protection method in web-site management, which is supported by Microsoft IIS and FrontPage. Access permissions can be defined for an individual file or folder. If access permissions are defined for the folder, all documents in the folder will inherit those security settings.

Digital Certificates in Microsoft Office

Microsoft Office 2000 uses Microsoft Authentication technology to allow digital signing of VBA applications. To digitally sign your VBA application, a Digital Certificate must be obtained and installed on your machine. A Digital Certificate contains information about yourself, submitted to the public body called a certification authority, such as VeriSign, Inc. The certification authority validates your information and issues your Digital Certificate, which usually expires one year from the time it was issued. When a Digital Certificate is used, its ID information is stored with the signed item. This information can be displayed to a user to establish a trust relationship. The Digital Certificate identifies the developer as a trusted source. Microsoft Office and Microsoft Internet Explorer allow users to identify code created by the trusted sources and validate that the source code hasn't been changed.

Office 2000 provides only the ability to sign VBA *projects* containing a document, but not the document itself. However, Outlook 2000 provides the ability to sign and encrypt the content of messages.

Developer Security Checklists

In the previous sections of this chapter we have talked about the different technologies within Windows 2000 that one can use to secure an application. As a developer you need to enforce security at the various levels such as the operating system, the database server, middle/business tier, web server and so on. Listed below is a set of basic checklists that you can use to confirm the security of the application at various levels. Please be aware the these are security recommendations, but you should make your own judgment as to whether they are suitable within your application.

Windows NT 4.0/Windows 2000 Settings

Define your organizations security policy.

It's imperative to have a sound security policy. Document this policy and enforce it to the letter. Make sure every team member (be it the developer, database administrator, systems support engineer) is aware of this policy and procedures. The documentation should include items such as:

❑   Server and workstation configuration

❑   Communications, cabling and internetworking plan

❑   Periodic back policy

❑   Disaster recovery policy

❑   Server access and permission list for the users/applications/services

❑   Auditing and notification process for a breach in security

Check the additional resource listed in Appendix A for resources pertaining to security policy information.

Use the Security Template hisecweb.inf

Use the security template provided by Microsoft. It lets your configure some of the system-wide settings without having to manually modify/change the registry. Some of the registry modifications listed in this list are applicable to sites/applications hosted on a Windows NT 4.0 system. hisecweb.inf can be downloaded from: http://download.microsoft.com/download/win2000srv/SCM/1.0 /NT5/EN-US/hisecweb.exe.

Keep up with the latest Service Pack and Hot-fixes applied

Review all Microsoft Security Bulletins and then check for hot-fixes – Windows NT/2000, IIS, SQL Server, Certificate Server and other BackOffice products. Also review the latest Microsoft Security News (URL: http://www.microsoft.com/security). Also keep abreast on the latest NT hacker exploits and bugs by subscribing to the various newsgroups listed in the additional resources.

Use NTFS formatted hard disk(s)

Because NTFS supports Access Control Lists you can set security policy in Windows NT rather than spread around applications. If you are using FAT you can convert to NTFS using the convert.exe tool.

Turn off NTFS 8.3 Name Generation

NTFS can auto-generate 8.3 names for backward compatibility with 16-bit applications. Typically 16-bit apps are not be used on a secure web server so the 8.3 name generation can be safely turned off. There is, of course, the added performance benefit to turning this off. To turn off 8.3 name generation set the following registry entry:

Hive: HKEY_LOCAL_MACHINE\SYSTEM
Key: \CurrentControlSet\Control\FileSystem
Name: NtfsDisable8dot3NameCreation
Type: REG_DWORD
Value: 1

Set Domain Controller Type

Generally you should set the IIS server to be a standalone server, as this will minimize any possible exposure of domain user accounts. The same applies for other servers that you'll use to host databases or your middle-layer with COM+ components.

Remove All Net Shares

Run Net Share from the command-line and make sure you delete all of them using Net Share /d. The shares ending with the dollar sign are not visible from DOS or Windows when you browse the network. You should also prevent all administrative shares (C$, D$, ADMIN$) by setting the following in the Registry:

Hive: HKEY_LOCAL_MACHINE\SYSTEM
Key: CurrentControlSet\Services\LanmanServer\Parameters
Name: AutoShareServer
Type: REG_DWORD
Value: 0

Audit all Success/Failed Logon/Logoff

It's a good idea to audit all login and logoffs – successful or not. Periodically monitor the log for to check for anything out of the ordinary. Also check for the patterns to fine-tune your security policy.

Set Overwrite Interval for Audit Log

Open Event Viewer | Log | Log Settings, and set a maximum size and "Overwrite Events Older than" for all three logs. This does come with a performance penalty. If you are going to overwrite logs after only a few days and your log maximum size is small then you need to check the logs more frequently.

Tighten passwords for all accounts

Set all passwords to at least nine characters. This makes it much harder to guess than eight characters or less owing to the way Windows NT creates the hash of the password. Also, use numeric, punctuation and other non-alphabetic characters in the first 7 characters. Enforce password expirations. At a minimum, make all network users change their passwords once every quarter.

Remove or disable Guest account

The Guest Account is supposed to have limited access to resources on the server box. It's a good idea to remove or disable this account from your web and database server unless you absolutely need it.

Rename Administrator account

Add a 'fake' administrator to help detect account attacks. Give this 'Administrator' no rights and carefully audit its use. This is an example of "security through obscurity". It's an extra step a hacker must make to determine the Admin account.

Set network-only lockout for Administrator account

Normally, the Administrator account cannot be locked out if an attacker attempts to guess the password. However, a tool in the Windows NT Resource Kit called PASSPROP supports this option. If you run the following command the Administrator account will be locked out if an attacker attempts a brute force or dictionary attack but the administrator can still logon locally at the server:

```
passprop /adminlockout
```

Check user accounts, group membership and privileges

Minimize the number of users and groups on the server and keep group membership small. There should be only the most trusted accounts listed in the Administrators and Domain Admins groups. Also, be wary of the privileges given to users and groups beyond the default.

Set unnecessary services to start up manually or disable them

Shut off any services that you know you don't need. This will maximize your resources available to IIS/SQL Server or COM+ components/applications. If you're not using FTP Publishing Service or SMTP Mail services, set it to a manual start.

Restrict Anonymous Network Access

Windows NT has a feature that allows non-authenticated users to enumerate users on a Windows NT domain. If you do not want this functionality, set the following in the Registry:

Hive: HKEY_LOCAL_MACHINE\SYSTEM
Key: CurrentControlSet\Control\LSA
Name: RestrictAnonymous
Type: REG_DWORD
Value: 1

Prevent unauthenticated access to the registry

Using the Registry Editor, it is possible to modify or change the contents of the Registry via a remote access. You can prevent remote changes (even by the administrators) by creating the Registry key:

Hive: HKEY_LOCAL_MACHINE\SYSTEM
Key: \CurrentControlSet\Control\SecurePipeServers
Name: \winreg

Change "Access this computer from the network" from Everyone to Authenticated Users

This only allows users having an account in the domain or on the machine to access shares on the server. You can perform this by opening User Manager | Policies | User Rights, then choosing "Access this computer from network", remove Everyone from the list and add Authenticated Users to the list.

Limit access to removable drives.

Unauthorized users can use removable 3.5" disk and/or CD-ROM drives to boot alternative OSs that let them circumvent network security and gain unauthorized access to system data. You can also prevent attacks by setting the BIOS boot order option to boot from the hard disk first and boot from the 3.5" disk or CD-ROM drive second. This configuration also helps protect the server from boot sector viruses in the event a user leaves a boot sector virus-infected disk in the server's 3.5" drive.

Unbind NetBIOS from TCP/IP

Using tools like NBSTAT, one can access server information. Unbinding NetBIOS from TCP/IP is a good way of preventing this access.

Configure TCP/IP Filtering

Configure TCP/IP filtering by specifying which ports are allowable on each network card. Go to Control Panel | Network | Protocols | TCP/IP | Advanced | Enable Security | Configure. Now set the following options:

❑ Permit only TCP ports 80 and 443 (if you have SSL)

❑ Permit no UDP ports

❑ Permit only IP Protocol 6 (TCP)

Disable IP Routing

You run the risk of passing data between the intranet and Internet if routing is enabled. To disable routing, open the Control Panel | Network | Protocols | TCP/IP Protocol | Properties | Routing and clear the Enable IP Forwarding check box.

Move and ACL critical files

Place all commonly used administrative tools in a special directory out of %systemroot% and ACL them so that only administrators have full access to these files. For example create a directory called \CommonTools and place the following files in there:

arp.exe	ipconfig.exe	regedt32.exe
at.exe	nbtstat.exe	rexec.exe
atsvc.exe	net.exe	route.exe
cacls.exe	netstat.exe	rsh.exe
cmd.exe	nslookup.exe	runonce.exe
cscript.exe	ping.exe	secfixup.exe
debug.exe	posix.exe	syskey.exe
edit.com	qbasic.exe	telnet.exe
edlin.exe	rcp.exe	tracert.exe
finger.exe	rdisk.exe	wscript.exe
ftp.exe	regedit.exe	xcopy.exe

Synchronize Times

If you have multiple web servers/mail servers/ database servers you should make sure the times are synchronized. This will aid you when you need to evaluate multiple audit logs in the case of any intrusion detection. You also need to do it so that date and time stamps across the different tiers of your application are in sync. The simplest way is to use the NET TIME command and nominate one server as having the base time.

Configure IPSec Policy

It's a good idea to block all TCP/IP protocols other than those you explicitly support. It applies for the ports you want to open – enable only the ones you want to use. With Windows 2000, set the Internet Protocol Security (IPSec) packet-filtering policy on every web server in your web-farm. This policy provides an added level of protection should your firewall be compromised. Make use of the `IPSec` administration tool or the `IPSecPol` command line tool to deploy IPSec policy.

Securing SQL Server 6.5 or SQL Server 7.0

Change the 'sa' password periodically

Always have a password for the sa login. Periodically keep changing it and make sure it's documented. Remove the Guest user from databases to keep unauthenticated users out.

Change the default database and remove sample databases

The default database for the SQL Server installation is the master database. Change this to some other database. For SQL Server '*pubs*' database is the sample database that's installed with the default SQL Server installation. Remove this from your production database server. You don't need this database to be used as a launching pad for Trojan-horse type malicious programs or objects to access your database.

Use the LocalSystem account for SQL Server

This account has no rights on other systems and should help contain an attack to the server in case of a break-in. Note that is not totally foolproof. In some scenarios you won't be able to use this account, especially if you are using remote procedure calls, replication, or SQLMail.

Create well-defined groups

Create well-defined groups depending on your business/application needs and grant/revoke permissions on the different database objects based on these groups.

Avoid TCP/IP protocol

Avoid the use of TCP/IP protocol for your web server to access database server. Use named pipes instead.

Use NTFS partitions for all your SQL Server data and system files

Should someone gain access to the operating system or the directory, make sure that the necessary permissions are in place to prevent unauthorized access.

Use stored procedures for data access

Use stored procedures to access data. It's easier to enforce security through the use of stored procedure than allowing your users or applications go directly against the tables. Use the following query to periodically query which procedures have public access:

```
USE master
GO
SELECT sysobjects.name FROM sysobjects, sysprotects WHERE
    sysprotects.uid = 0
AND XTYPE IN ('X','P') AND sysobjects.id = sysprotects.id ORDER BY name
```

(Use "type" instead of "xtype" for SQL 6.5)

Remove all Select-Insert-Update-Delete permissions from all groups

Create a SQL script that removes all the direct select-insert-update and delete permissions from the tables. Create stored procedures that implement the same and assign the execute permissions to the correct user groups.

Use Views to mask underlying table structure

You can hide the underlying database objects or tables by the use of views. Consider a table, which has columns col1, col2, col3 and so on. Typically access to this table is done by a simple SELECT statement, which is:

```
SELECT col1, col2, col3 FROM table1 or SELECT * FROM table1.
```

Get around this by creating a view and exposing only the view to the user/application accessing the database. To create a view:

```
CREATE VIEW vwTbl1 AS
    SELECT NewCol1 = Col1, NewCol2 = Col2, NewCol3 = Col3 FROM Table1
```

Your user/application or web pages would access data as:

```
SELECT * FROM vwTbl1
```

Restrict access to developers and QA testers

Developers and QA testers' access to the production database should be restricted. An easy way of managing this is through the use of groups in each of the development-testing-production environments. If the developers need access to the production data, use the production database dump to create a pseudo-production database and restrict access to the developers/testers for a small window of time for the explicit purposes of debugging or troubleshooting.

Use SQL scripts to implement security periodically

Create a SQL script that manages the entire security for the database(s) specific to your application. Use systems stored procedures like **sp_addlogin**, **sp_addgroup** or SQL statements like **REVOKE** or **GRANT SELECT** to handle access permission on the various database objects like table, stored procedures, tables etc. Periodically run this script within your database to enforce security especially whenever there's modifications or change made to the database.

Disable xp_cmdShell extended stored procedure

A compromised SQL Server database could allow a hacker access to the entire network via the use of the extended stored procedure. The four simple lines of code displayed below allows a hacker to add a Windows NT account called 'meHacker' with a password 'secret' and then add 'meHacker' to the 'Administrators' group:

```
xp_cmdshell 'net user meHacker secret/ADD'
go
xp_cmdshell 'net localgroup /ADD Administrator meHacker'
go
```

Now if this SQL Server was a domain controller, the entire network is vulnerable.

Drop OLE automation and registry access stored procedures

Most of the application database objects such as stored procedures or triggers do not use the registry access and OLE automation. Drop them if you don't use it. Note: You'll lose some of the Enterprise Manager features if you drop these stored procedures. Make sure you check the documentation before doing so. The stored procedures are:

```
Sp_OACreate              Xp_regaddmultistring
Sp_OADestroy             Xp_regdeletekey
Sp_OAGetErrorInfo        Xp_regdeletevalue
Sp_OAGetProperty         Xp_regenumvalues
Sp_OAMethod              Xp_regread
Sp_OASetProperty         Xp_regremovemultistring
Sp_OAStop                Xp_regwrite
```

Disable any interactive access to the SQL Server.

Once a user can interactively log into a server, there are myriad privilege escalation attacks that can be used to obtain Administrative access.

Physical access to the SQL Server

Of course you need to prevent physical access to the server. Lock it behind a door and lock away the key while you're at it. This also applies to all production servers – Windows 2000 servers hosting the web pages, applications, COM+ components, mail servers etc.

Securing COM+

Use Roles and Groups to define access

A role is a logical group of users or groups and has been defined for the purpose of determining application access permissions. User has various access rights depending on which role he/she is using to access the application's components. A role can contain groups of users or single user accounts. Adding a user to a group with the Microsoft Management Console is the same as selecting the user or user group from the Windows 2000 users group.

Change the Default security for COM+

Default security for COM+ specifies access settings for all components running on a local machine. Make sure you change this to suit the needs of your application.

What's more important – security or performance?

For the server application, several levels of authentication can be set providing different degrees of security, and they may include encryption for each method call. Such a security system will affect the application's performance, but it's up to developers to decide what should take priority – security or performance.

Use of programmatic security versus declarative security

Programmatic security allows you to configure roles for a single method or in some select cases within a method. Make use of the interfaces provided by COM+ to implement programmatic security as it allows us to set features which would be impossible to set declaratively.

Use Active Directory Service for delegation and impersonation

When a server is acting as a client it hides its identity and cloaking is enabled to make calls to other COM components under the client's identity. To effectively use both, the client and server user accounts must be properly configured in the Active Directory Service, and the server identity must be set to "Trusted for delegation".

Clearly define and document security boundaries

In COM+ server applications, access checking can be performed at the component level or at the process level. Some of common COM+ components (such as data access layers or some utility functions) could be shared across multiple applications. Clearly defining the security access and boundaries between what's shared and what's not at a very early stage of development could save a lot troubleshooting efforts. Maintaining good documentation regarding the same will help you in the upgrade or future development efforts.

Securing IIS 5.0

Set appropriate IIS log file ACLs

Make sure the ACLs on the IIS-generated log files (`%systemroot%\system32\LogFiles`) are:

❑   Administrators (Full Control)

❑   System (Full Control)

This prevents a hacker or malicious user from deleting the files to cover his/her tracks.

Enable Logging

Logging is vital when you want to see if your server is being attacked. You should use W3C Extended Logging format by Loading the IIS MMC tool | Right-click on site in question, then select Properties | Web Site | Enable Logging (W3C Extended Log), then set the following properties:

Client IP Address
User Name
Method
URI Stem
HTTP Status
User Agent
Win32 Status
Server IP Address
Server Port

Set DNS Address/IP Address restrictions

If you wish to restrict your Web sites to certain users then this is one option. Note, if you enter DNS names then IIS has to do a lookup, which can be affect the site's performance.

Executable content validated for trustworthiness

It is difficult to know whether executable content can be trusted or not. One small test is use the DumpBin tool to see if the executable calls certain APIs. For example, use the following syntax if you wish to see if a file called MyFile.DLL calls RevertToSelf() or LoadLibrary:

```
dumpbin /imports MyFile.DLL | find "RevertToSelf" or
dumpbin /imports MyFile.DLL | find "LoadLibrary"
```

DumpBin is included with many Win32 developer tools.

Set appropriate virtual directory permissions and partition Web application space

This is application-dependant, but the following rules-of-thumb apply:

File Type	Access Control List
CGI etc .EXE, .DLL, .CMD, .PL	Everyone (Execute) Administrators (Full Control) System (Full Control)
Script Files, .ASP etc	Everyone (Execute) Administrators (Full Control) System (Full Control)
Include Files .INC, .SHTML, .SHTM	Everyone (Execute) Administrators (Full Control) System (Full Control)
Static Content .HTML, .GIF, .JPEG	Everyone (Read) Administrators (Full Control) System (Full Control)

Rather than setting ACLs on each file, you are better off setting new directories for each type of file and setting ACLs on the dir and allow the ACLs to inherit to the files. For example a directory structure may look like this:

```
c:\inetpub\wwwroot\myserver\static (.html)
c:\inetpub\wwwroot\myserver\include (.inc)
c:\inetpub\wwwroot\myserver\script (.asp)
c:\inetpub\wwwroot\myserver\executable (.dll)
c:\inetpub\wwwroot\myserver\images (.gif, .jpeg)
```

Remember, if write-access is specified for the folder, along with Scripts and Executables, the security of your site could be compromised. It could allow an unauthorized user to upload executable files or scripts to the server and cause damage.

Set up Secure Sockets Layer

SSL/TLS can be used to secure data as it's transferred from the client to the web server. SSL/TLS is used mainly when passwords or credit cards are to be transferred across the Internet. However, using SSL/TLS is slow, especially during the initial handshake, so keep pages that use SSL/TLS to a minimum and keep the content minimal.

Remove the IISADMPWD virtual directory

This directory, designed primarily for intranet scenarios, allows you to reset Windows NT passwords. Unless absolutely required, remove it. Refer to Microsoft Knowledgebase article Q184619 (http://support.microsoft.com/support/kb/articles/q184/6/19.asp) for more info about this functionality.

Remove Used Script Mappings

By default, IIS is configured to support files extensions such as .ASP and .SHTM. If you don't use some of these extensions or functionality, you should remove the mappings by opening Internet Services Manager, then right-clicking the web server | Properties | Master Properties | WWW Service | Edit | HomeDirectory | Configuration and remove these references:

If you don't use	Remove this entry
Web-based Password Reset	.htr
Internet Database Connector	.idc
Server-side includes	.shtm, .stm, .shtml

Remove all sample applications

Samples are just that, samples; they are not installed by default and should never be installed on a production server. This includes documentation, SDK, Admin Scripts etc. Here are the default locations for some of the samples:

Technology	Location
IIS	c:\inetpub\iissamples
IIS SDK	c:\inetpub\iissamples\sdk
IIS Documentation	c:\winnt\help\iishelp
Admin Scripts	c:\inetpub\AdminScripts
Data access	c:\Program Files\Common Files\System\msadc\Samples

Disable or remove unneeded COM Components

Unregister or remove some COM components that are not required by using the regsvr32 utility. For example, to unregister a component called myfile.dll, use the command line:

```
regsvr32 /u myfile.dll
```

Before you do so, make sure that the component you are removing is not being shared with other objects or applications on the machine that are vital.

Disable calling the command shell with #exec

The command can be used to call arbitrary commands at the Web server from within an HTML or ASP page. Within IIS this is disabled by default. Double-check this by making sure the following Registry hive/key is set to zero, or is removed:

Hive:	HKEY_LOCAL_MACHINE\SYSTEM
Key:	CurrentControlSet\Services\W3SVC\Parameters
Name:	SSIEnableCmdDirective
Type:	REG_DWORD
Value:	0

Disable IP Address in Content-Location

The Content-Location header may expose Internal IP addresses that are masked behind a Network Address Translation (NAT) Firewall or proxy server. Refer to Microsoft Knowledgebase article Q218180 (`http://support.microsoft.com/support/kb/articles/q218/1/80.asp`) for further information about disabling this option.

Disable 'Parent Paths'

Parent Paths allow you to use '..' in calls to MapPath and the like. By default this option is enabled and should be disabled.

Include File Security Based on the Security Credentials of Physical Path

In IIS 5.0, ASP enforces the security credentials of the physical path when processing server-side includes. Be aware of this major change between IIS 5.0 and IIS 4.0 where include files in virtual roots did not use the security credentials of the physical paths. Knowing this detail can help you properly set your permissions and save a lot of time troubleshooting.

Client-side scripting

Remember that any web client can view the client scripting code (VB Script/JavaScript) on your web page – all that is required is to view the HTML source in the browser. Also, if you are using RDS' (Remote Data Scripting) RDC control, the entire connect string (with the userid, password and database objects) is exposed in the HTML source. That being the case, remember to architect your application properly so that your vital server code/components/objects is not exposed in the browser. Do not forget to clean up your debug-code before it ends up your client's browser.

Disable RDS support

When incorrectly configured Remote Data Services can make a server vulnerable to denial of service and arbitrary code execution attacks. You should either remove the capability or restrict its usage using ACLs. Also, check your IIS logs regularly for signs of attack, the signature to look for is something like:

```
2000-08-19 12:34:56 - POST /msadc/msadcs.dll ...
```

You can automate the searching process by using command:

```
find /i "msadcs" logfile.log
```

Index Server only indexing documentation

If you are using the Index Server features on your web site, check what documents you are indexing. Indexing confidential source code isn't a good idea.

Pool Web applications with Medium Isolation

The different isolation levels in IIS 5.0 are High (Isolated), Medium (Pooled) and Low (IIS Process). Use **Medium** isolation in most scenarios. In this case, pooling means that every web application set to **Medium** will share the same instance of `Dllhost.exe`. **Medium** isolation offers a nice tradeoff between performance and reliability, and is great for trusted web applications.

Monitor Event Log when using IISReset.EXE

By default, IIS 5.0 uses a new utility, `IISReset`, to restart IIS services automatically if they fail. The downside is you may not notice problems with the server so easily so be sure to monitor the Event Log regularly. If you have to restart the web service, `IISReset` makes it easier by allowing you to stop and restart IIS services and out-of-process web applications with one command.

Web and Exchange Security Considerations

When a web application is accessing Exchange, IIS and Exchange can provide a number of ways for security to be enforced. There are three different security types in IIS and Exchange:

❑ Anonymous – a default IIS account. When an Anonymous account is used IIS provides access to the web for all users. In this case account `IUSR_MachineName` is used.

❑ NT LAN Manager – Windows 2000 still supports NTLM protocol, which is used to identify a domain user account. Before allowing the user access to the system resources, the user must be authenticated. If the security tokens match, then the user is granted access to the resource.

❑ Basic authentication – also known as 'Clear Text', basic authentication is used to send the user's name and password to the IIS. To be able to log onto Exchange the user must enter a domain name, user name and password.

For web applications, user authentication and validation could be done programmatically. The validation code could be handled in `Application_OnStart` or in `Session_OnStart` events, in `global.asa`. Also user validation code can be created in an include file. The include file with authentication validation can be used on any other page where user validation is required.

Summary

Security is a journey and not the destination. It should be an ongoing process instead of a one-off blitz only after your system has been compromised. This philosophy has not yet been fully embraced by the developer community. It's too important an issue to be left with your system administrator or database administrator. For a developer the goal should be to build security into your entire architecture at every level starting from the server access to the various data transmission, storage and access mechanisms.

The goal of the chapter has been to highlight the strengths offered by Windows 2000 operating system to understand the environment around which you can build a secure application so that you don't reinvent the wheel building proprietary APIs, which will fade with the changes in the industry. Too much security could drain your resources forcing you to spend a lot of time and CPU power managing and processing security. Integrated security between Windows 2000, COM+, IIS, ISA Server and SQL Server gives you more power over the system and makes security implementation easier. The developer checklist for Windows 2000, COM+, SQL server and IIS is just a starting point for a developer to adopt sound security principles in the tools and technologies listed.

Time and space restrict the amount of depth we can go into in this subject. Various books and URLs listed in the additional resources section (Appendix A) should help you dig deeper and keep up with the latest developments in this arena.

It is difficult to cover all areas of security implemented in Windows 2000, especially because its combine a lot of features from previous versions of NT, MTS, MSMQ and LAN. I believe that Windows 2000 default security defines an ideal access control policy and security settings. It is well balanced between security needs and application performance. A default access control setting provides a standard secure environment that is easily configurable and testable. Any details can be simply added on the top of any component or application declaratively by system administrator or programmatically by developer if desired. Windows 2000 Server allows organizations securely conduct their businesses over the Internet and intranet with greater control over authorization, access controls and confidentiality requirements.

Online discussion at http://p2p.wrox.com

21

Certificate Services

Security has become one of the hottest issues in today's distributed world. State-of-the-art web sites are selling more products, employees are transmitting more sensitive information, and servers are communicating or transmitting information with an increasing number of remote servers. At the same time, the technologies used to break into systems or impersonate users are becoming more efficient and more dangerous. As applications continue to become more and more distributed, the need to verify the identity of individual users or servers is critical to success. Microsoft's **Certificate Services** platform plays an important role in providing a level of security to applications through services used to manage, issue, revoke, and renew digital certificates.

While the added security provided by Certificate Services does play an important role in the overall Windows DNA architecture, the security of any distributed environment involves many key components including firewalls, secure code, secure databases, as well as other items, many of which are covered throughout this book. In the previous chapter we had an overview of many different approaches to security – in this chapter we will cover some basic concepts regarding keys, cryptography and digital signatures before moving on to look at how to make the most of Certificate Services in your applications.

Certificate Basics

Information sent across the wire using the basic HTTP protocol is not protected or secured, as you're probably well aware. Applications requiring sensitive information, for example credit card numbers, must use the available security features such as **Secure Socket Layers** (**SSL**) and server certificates to avoid exposing sensitive information to those who might desire access to it. Unfortunately, many people placing orders using unsecured applications are not aware of what is happening. They assume that they have a one-way communications pipeline to the company they are communicating with and that no one else can intercept the data. Things become even worse when the owner of the application isn't aware of the implications associated with allowing customers to transmit sensitive information to them. In both of these cases, the individuals involved are not aware of routers, hubs, and the variety of other pass-through mechanisms that exist in a distributed network like the Internet. They're not aware, and possibly not even interested, that there are standards available that rely on cryptography and keys to help secure data.

Keys and Cryptography

To prevent sensitive information from being accessed by prying eyes while in transit to a remote destination, various **encryption** techniques have been developed over the years. We'll steer away from the mathematical concepts and algorithms involved (which are highly complex) and concentrate on the practical *use* of encryption. Encryption takes data and transforms it into a form that is unrecognizable and completely unusable to anyone viewing it without knowledge of how to break the encryption code. These techniques involve one or more **keys** that contain specifics on how the information should be "encrypted" and how it should be "decrypted".

A Brief History of Cryptography and Keys

The concept and use of cryptography existed well before the Internet came into prominence. While it may seem that encryption is a fairly new process, it's actually been around for a long time. Those of you who consider yourselves to be history buffs will note that encryption techniques (however simplistic) have been used in wars throughout history to exchange messages between different troops. During these times, a message was encrypted using a written key or code machine and was decrypted on the other end with the same type of key or machine. This type of encrypted message exchange normally required that each side had the same "secret" key. If the key was captured, the information could be decrypted and read by the opposing side.

In 1976, Whitfield Diffie and Martin Hellman published their ideas on exchanging sensitive data without having to exchange secret keys between parties. The idea was groundbreaking, as only **public keys** were exchanged while each party's **private key** was kept safe. This concept became a reality in 1977 when MIT professors Ronald Rivest, Adi Shamir, and Len Adleman invented the **RSA Public Key Cryptosystem**. This system allows encrypted data to be exchanged by using a public and private key set. Data can be encrypted using the private key, for instance, and then decrypted by the receiving party with the public key. While this process will be discussed in more detail in the following section, it's important to know that this encryption/decryption process is done without ever exposing the private key to the general public.

How Do Keys Work?

You can think of a single cryptography key just like you would any key you use to get into your car or home on a daily basis. Without the key you have no way to open the door (unless you're really strong, of course). Encryption uses keys in a similar manner to allow authorized viewing of data, but the encryption/decryption process can also utilize two keys if necessary. An encryption process accepts plain text and uses **cryptography interfaces** (**Crypto APIs**) along with a special key to encrypt the data. The decryption process uses either the same key that was used during encryption (just like using a key to get into a house), or a different key to take the jumbled up data (called **ciphertext**) and transform it back into a usable format. The illustration below shows this process:

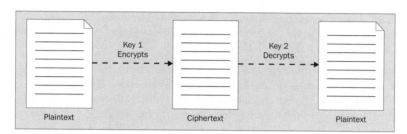

This entire encryption/decryption process is considered to be **symmetric** if the same key is used for both encryption and decryption. It is considered **asymmetric** (or **public-key**) encryption if one key is used for encryption while a different but related key is used for decryption. To illustrate how the symmetric and asymmetric processes work, let's cover a simple example.

Symmetric Encryption

Suppose that a company named ABC Widgets would like to exchange information securely with XYZ Tech. ABC Widgets will initiate all communications but XYZ Tech will issue the necessary key or keys. Using the symmetric method, company XYZ Tech would generate a single key using an API such as Microsoft's Crypto API and share this key with ABC Widgets. This key would be used to encrypt and decrypt data sent between the two companies. While this will work correctly and allow for encrypted communications, both companies run the risk of having the secret key discovered by an outside party. At that point, a new key would need to be generated and shared.

Asymmetric Encryption

Now let's suppose that XYZ Tech creates an asymmetric public-key cryptography set, meaning they create a public key and a private key that are related to each other. This relationship guarantees that data encrypted with the public key can only be decrypted using the private key that only XYZ Tech has access to. ABC Widgets can now send a message to XYZ Tech knowing that XYZ Tech is the only company holding the private key that will decrypt the message. This asymmetric method means that XYZ Tech can now keep their private key but can send out their public key to ABC Widget (or other interested parties) so that they can send information to each other securely.

The RSA cryptosystem allows for the key roles to be reversed as well. So, the public key can decrypt the data and the private key can encrypt the data. You may wonder what this accomplishes since anyone possessing the public key can now decrypt the data! By reversing the key roles, ABC Widgets can now verify that a message supposedly sent by XYZ Tech was truly sent by XYZ Tech since only data encrypted by XYZ Tech's private key can be decrypted with the public key that ABC Widgets (and possibly other parties) holds. While this doesn't secure the data sent by XYZ Tech, since anyone having the public key can decrypt the data, it does allow the identity of the sender (XYZ Tech in this case) to be positively confirmed. We'll talk more about why this identification is so important in just a moment. First let's discuss keys in greater detail.

Key Length and Cryptographic Providers

Thus far we've seen that a key is a secret code used to convert regular text into ciphertext and back. The previous examples showed how single or multiple keys can be used in the encryption/decryption process. Before going further into our discussion of cryptography and keys, it's important that we discuss how secure keys are and which cryptographic providers should be used to generate them. If the key used to create ciphertext is easily broken by someone skilled at cryptanalysis, then the encryption won't accomplish much as anyone can read it if they are able to generate the correct key. For example, an individual attempting to break the key could use brute force to try all possible keys in sequence. To prevent this from happening a few things can be done proactively.

❏ First of all, a **"salt"** value (random text) can be added to the end of encrypted data. Although this value is known by the attacker, it makes the brute force attack more difficult as a salt value must be appended to each brute force attack.

❏ While adding a salt value can act as a deterrent, the most effective way to prevent attackers from breaking a key involves the key's length. **Key lengths** can be made bigger and bigger to make the encryption harder and harder to break. MSDN documentation provides the following look at how increased key lengths can further secure the cryptography process:

Longer key lengths decrease the possibility of successful attacks by increasing the number of combinations that are possible. For example, for a 40-bit key, there are 2^{40} possible values. By using a personal computer that can try 1 million keys per second, an attacker can try all possible keys in about 13 days. However, an 128-bit key has 2^{128} possible values. If you could use a computer that would allow you to try 100 billion keys a second and you used 10 million of these computers, it would take about 10^{13} years to try every possible 128-bit key value. This is nearly 1000 times longer than the estimated age of the universe (15 billion to 20 billion years). Therefore, the longer the key, the more protection you have from attacks.

After reading this, your first impression may be to make keys as big as possible so that the encrypted data is unbreakable. While larger and larger keys provide additional security, the increased key length results in more and more complex algorithms as mentioned above. These algorithms take time to evaluate so that data can move through the encryption/decryption process. This of course translates to more CPU cycles and places a potential burden on the computer doing the encryption or decryption. A symmetric key used to encrypt or decrypt data is orders of magnitude faster than an asymmetric key set, since the two keys in the asymmetric (public-key set) are mathematically related to one another. This of course adds an extra layer of processing which can lead to more CPU cycles. This is an important point to consider when choosing to work with large amounts of encrypted data.

So how long can a key be? The answer to this depends upon which **cryptographic provider** is used to create the key.

Cryptographic Providers

A cryptographic provider exposes a set of application programming interfaces (APIs) that allows for the generation of keys. Although there are many types of providers available, Microsoft provides interfaces that can generate both short and long keys as appropriate. The table below shows two possible providers (**base** and **enhanced**) that are provided by Microsoft and what key lengths can be generated using specific algorithms available to these providers. This list is by no means complete, but it will give you a feel for key lengths:

Algorithm	Base Provider	Enhanced Provider
RSA public-key signature algorithm	Key length: 512 bits	Key length: 1,024 bits
RSA public-key exchange algorithm	Key length: 512 bits	Key length: 1,024 bits
RC2 block encryption algorithm	Key length: 40 bits	Key length: 128 bits Salt length: settable
RC4 stream encryption algorithm	Key length: 40 bit	Key length: 128 bits Salt length: settable
DES	Not supported	Key length: 56 bits
Triple DES (2 key)	Not supported	Key length: 112 bits
Triple DES (3 key)	Not supported	Key length: 168 bits

These cryptographic providers (and several others) can be chosen when setting up Certificate Services. This process will be covered later in the chapter.

Going back to our previous example involving two companies, to make processing of large chunks of encrypted data faster and less CPU-intensive, ABC Widgets could generate a symmetric key, encrypt it with XYZ Tech's public key, and then send this "**key blob**" to XYZ Tech. Since no one can use ABC Widgets' symmetric key without having XYZ Tech's private key to decrypt it, the key is safe during the transfer. After this exchange, ABC Widgets can now encrypt data using their own symmetric key and XYZ Tech can decrypt the data using the key they received earlier. As mentioned, this process will be much faster compared to an asymmetric process, especially if large amounts of data are being exchanged. The aforementioned process can be a little confusing, so a step-by-step breakdown is shown below:

❑ ABC Widgets generates a symmetric key

❑ This key is encrypted using XYZ Tech's public key

❑ The encrypted key (called a key blob) is then sent to XYZ Tech

❑ XYZ Tech uses the private key that matches up with the appropriate public key to decrypt the symmetric key

❑ Both parties now have a copy of ABC Widgets' symmetric key (secret key) and can more efficiently exchange larger amounts of encrypted data with each other

While all of this sounds rather complex, the entire process is handled behind the scenes by tools built into Certificate Services and many web servers and browsers available today. Many of these tools rely on certificates to exchange keys during the encryption/decryption process. To better understand the role of a digital certificate in the encryption process, let's cover what a certificate is and why it's useful.

What's a Digital Signature or Certificate?

Exchanging keys between parties is a big step towards allowing for secure communications, but the exchange process is still difficult. Those involved with cryptography development realized that a vehicle needed to be created to exchange keys and verify that the keys were actually issued from a valid source. If you receive a public key, how can you ensure that the key was generated by the organization you expected, and not by someone who hi-jacked the key or is posing as someone else? On the flip side of this problem, if you receive data encrypted with a company's public key, how can you know that the company you trusted to send the data actually initiated the transfer? To help solve this problem, **digital certificates** and **digital signatures** have come into existence.

Digital Signatures

Before jumping into certificate specifics, it's important to understand what digital signatures are and why they are important. A digital signature is similar to a normal written signature found on a paper-based document in that it specifies who signed or originated the document. However, while a written signature can be forged, a digital signature cannot – unless the appropriate key is stolen from the creator of the digital signature. Continuing with a digital document as an example, an individual desiring to digitally sign the document and send it to someone else can use a private key to encrypt the document's "digital fingerprint". Individuals receiving the document can verify or authenticate the person that sent the document by decrypting the signature using the document creator's public key. If the "digital fingerprint" contained within the received document cannot be decrypted properly then the document has been tampered with and may not be valid. While this example involves only a document, a digital signature helps in the authentication of other things such as a person or computer, through its association with a certificate.

A digital signature is composed of a **message digest** (a single string of digits) along with other information about the signer. Information such as a timestamp could be appended to the message digest. This "signature" is then encrypted using a one-way **hash function** (an algorithm used to generate fixed string lengths that cannot be unencrypted). The overall process is accomplished by using a private key. Upon receipt of a digital signature, the receiver can use a public key to verify the hash value and ensure that it has not been tampered with. This process is referred to as a "hashcheck".

Certificates

A certificate performs the simple but important task of binding a public key to an individual or organization through using a digital signature obtained from a trusted **certificate authority (CA)**. The certificate contains the public key, information about the organization, name of the certifying authority, an expiration date, and a serial number. By having an expiration date that is associated with the certificate, cryptanalytic attacks on the certificate's key can be made less threatening as the certificate will expire before the attacker has time to finish analysis of the certificate key. The length of the expiration date period depends upon the length of the key used in the certificate and is based on cryptanalytic formulas that determine how long an attacker's complete analysis of a key will take. A shorter key will likely be associated with a shorter expiration period while a longer key will be much harder to analyze and will therefore be associated with a longer expiration date.

What makes certificates useful is the inclusion of the certificate issuer's digital signature. This signature normally comes from a trustworthy source or points to another certificate issued by a trustworthy source, as in a **certificate hierarchy**. To understand certificate hierarchies better, consider the following example. A trusted department (or even individual) from within your company may apply to obtain a certificate from a trusted root certificate authority such as Verisign (http://www.verisign.com). This department or individual may in turn issue you a certificate to be used in helping to secure a computer or other item. Anyone receiving your certificate knows that it is valid because the certificate's hierarchy originates from a trusted CA (Verisign in this case). Having this chain of trust prevents anyone who wants to generate a certificate from impersonating another company because the imposter certificate will not have a valid root certificate authority signature in it. This is due to the fact that the imposter company will be thoroughly examined by the certificate authority before a certificate with its accompanying signature will be issued. For web-based applications, most browsers specify which root certificate authorities are trusted, as you'll see in a moment.

The digital signature embedded within the certificate is signed by the issuer's private key. Because the public key of the issuer is accessible by the public, this signature can be validated. To see a few public root certification authorities' certificates, open up Internet Explorer 5 and click Tools | Internet Options. Next click on the Content tab followed by the Certificates button. Finally, click the Trusted Root Certification Authorities tab. After doing this you should see the following screen, which contains root certification authority certificates and their associated public keys:

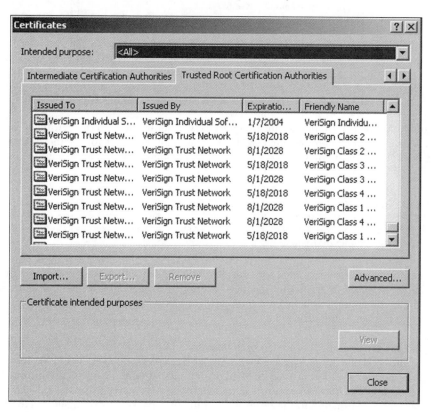

By double-clicking on one of the certificates listed, you can view all of its associated information, as shown below:

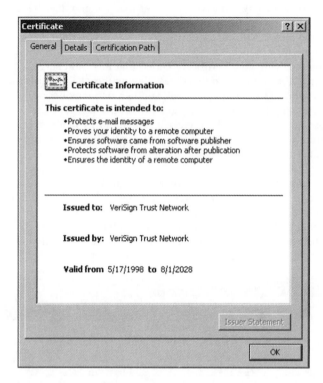

Clicking on the Details tab of the certificate interface will show you who the certificate was issued by, when it was issued, when it expires, the certificate serial number, and a lot of other information including the public key. If you've never seen a public key before, here's an example:

```
3081 8902 8181 00AA D0BA BE16 2DB8 83D4 CAD2 0FBC 7631 CA94 D81D 938C 5602 BCD9
6F1A 6F52 366E 7556 0A55 D3DF 4387 2111 658A 7E8F BD21 DE6B 323F 1B84 3495 059D
4135 EB92 EB96 DDAA 593F 0153 6D99 4FED E5E2 2A5A 90C1 B9C4 A615 CFC8 45EB A65D
8E9C 3EF0 6424 76A5 CDAB 1A6F B6D8 7B51 616E A67F 87C8 E2B7 E534 DC41 88EA 0940
BE73 923D 6BE7 7502 0301 0001
```

Any changes to the certificate's digital signature by a third party will make the digital signature invalid since the public key used to verify the signature will not work correctly. Remember that once something (such as a digital signature) has been encrypted using a private key, it can only be decrypted using the public key that has ties to the private key.

Using public-key cryptography allows an organization to build a secure infrastructure based on digital certificates. These certificates can be used with Secure Sockets Layer (SSL/HTTPS), Secure Multipurpose Internet Mail Extensions (S/MIME), and others, to allow for secure information transmission. Using HTTPS as an example, a user hitting a web server using the HTTPS protocol can transmit encrypted information to the server so that the data packets traveling across the Internet are useable and readable only by the receiving server containing the appropriate key. Since the server presents a certificate to the user's browser that is digitally signed by a trusted authority, the user can rest assured that their encrypted data is going to the proper place and that it cannot be decrypted by an imposter during the transmission process.

Going back to our example using ABC Widgets and XYZ Tech, there is one big problem that wasn't addressed. Even though the two companies could exchange messages securely after ABC Widgets received XYZ Tech's public key, what would happen if the key was intercepted by a third party on its way to ABC Widgets? During the interception, the culprit could substitute their own public key in place of XYZ Tech's. Assuming the culprit can also intercept ABC Widgets' encrypted messages intended for XYZ Tech, they could now decrypt them using the private key that matches up with the public key they sneakily put into the initial message to ABC Widgets.

To help solve this problem, RSA's flexibility in reversing key roles can be used. Since exchanging keys directly may not be possible, especially if the two are located on different continents, XYZ Tech could send a certificate signed by a trusted certificate authority to ABC Widgets. As mentioned earlier, the authority would use a private key to create the signature and they would then place it into the certificate. Then, ABC Widgets could use the certificate authority's public key to verify the signature. Once the signature is verified, XYZ Tech's public key can be used by ABC Widgets with confidence, as the digital signature included in XYZ Tech's certificate has now been authenticated and validated.

Types of Certificate

As far as certificates go, there are many different types. Here's a list of the most commonly used certificates and their purpose:

- ❑ Client Authentication Certificate – can be used by a client to validate their identity with an application, computer, or other individual.

- ❑ e-Mail Protection Certificate – serves the purpose of protecting e-mail data transmissions through validating the sender of the e-mail and encrypting the transmission.

- ❑ Server Authentication Certificate – allows clients (a browser for instance) to verify that the server receiving data from the browser is the correct server and not an imposter.

- ❑ Code Signing Certificate – used to sign applications (an ActiveX control for example) so the client can rest assured that the code has not been altered and will therefore be safe to execute. It obviously does not ensure that the code is well-written, only that it comes from the correct source.

Before going into more specifics concerning certificate services as a whole, let's take a brief look at the standard that certificates follow.

X.509 Certificate Standard

Certificates issued by certifying authorities comply with a standard referred to as **X.509**. The X.509 messaging-handling standard is an ITU (International Telecommunication Union – http://www.itu.int) recommendation used on an international basis for authenticating and encrypting messages. Version 1 of the standard was first published in 1988 with the second version coming in 1993. The latest version (version 3) was published in 1995 and built on version 2 by adding in **extensions**. Extensions increase flexibility in issuing certificates through allowing for additional information such as key usage restrictions and certification policy information.

The X.509 standard allows for certificate extensions that are defined as standard or private extensions. Allowing flexibility in extensions means that SSL (client and server), S/MIME, PKCS #10, SET, and X.509 version 1 and 3 certificates can be issued.

An X.509-compliant certificate consists of the following fields:

❑ version

❑ serial number

❑ signature algorithm ID

❑ issuer name

❑ validity period

❑ subject (user) name

❑ subject public key information

❑ issuer unique identifier (version 2 and 3 only)

❑ subject unique identifier (version 2 and 3 only)

❑ extensions (version 3 only)

❑ signature on the above fields

By following the X.509 standard, certificates issued between organizations and certificate authorities can be used in a variety of software packages including web servers and browsers. For more information on the X.509 standard visit http://www.ietf.org/html.charters/pkix-charter.html.

The Certificate Authority (CA)

As we saw earlier, a certificate authority (CA) is essential in the process of creating and issuing a valid certificate. As the name implies, the certificate authority is the organization that is ultimately trusted to issue valid certificates. The CA is willing to vouch for the existence and validity of a particular organization or individual, so that public keys sent out by the organization or individual are known to be legitimate. This validation is done through a variety of means including background checks, physical calls, identification (driver's license, passport, etc.), checking the business' DUNS number, or checking business activity.

Certificate authorities can be divided into hierarchies, with the **root certificate authority** being the parent of the hierarchy. Examples of third-party certificate authorities include Verisign, Thawte, and RSA Security.

To obtain a digital certificate digitally signed by a CA, a specific process is followed as shown below. These instructions involve the ABC Widgets company discussed earlier:

❑ ABC Widgets generates a public and private key and sends the public key to a certificate authority along with identifying information.

❑ After performing background checks, making sure they received the correct public key, and verifying information supplied by ABC Widgets, the authority issues a certificate back to ABC Widgets. The certificate authority's name is included in the certificate as well as its digital signature. The certificate will likely contain a hierarchy of certificates that verify the CA's public key. This hierarchy will ultimately go up to the root certificate authority (the authority at the top of the hierarchy).

❑ ABC Widgets can now use this certificate in exchanging information with other organizations. How the certificate is used depends upon what type of certificate request ABC Widgets made to the certificate authority.

Because the process of issuing a certificate requires individuals or organizations to be identified, many organizations will act as a CA for their own employees and departments. Doing this means that the public key used to digitally sign any certificates must be made available to the organization. It also means that each certificate issued will contain a hierarchy of certificates verifying the organization's public key. Doing this allows for lower costs relative to certificate requests made to third parties (such as Verisign or Thawte) and allows for tighter control over which individuals within an organization can receive a certificate. For example, imagine if every department went out and obtained their own certificate from a certificate authority. Not only would the company as a whole be spending more money to obtain the certificates, but control over which departments have valid certificates may possibly become an issue.

Certificate Server in Windows 2000 has built-in capabilities to act as a subordinate CA in a CA hierarchy, or even act as the root CA. A CA acting as the root authority within an organization would be similar to the role Verisign plays in issuing certificates to different organizations throughout the world. These different roles are shown in the following diagram:

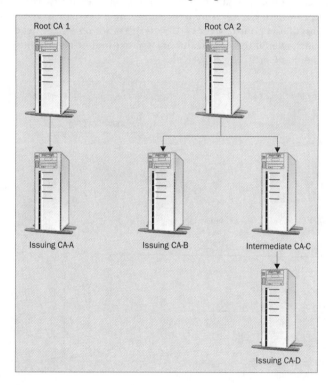

In cases where a Windows 2000 server acts as the root authority, a public key is first generated. This key is then placed in a certificate and digitally signed. If the server that the root authority is being installed onto has access to **Active Directory**, certificates generated by the root authority will be placed automatically in all domain users' **Trusted Root Certification Authorities certificate store**. This store can be local to the user's machine or within Active Directory so that all users or computers within a Windows domain can access and share the certificates. This process allows trust throughout the domain to be established for the root certificate authority. The root authority in an organization will normally only generate certificates for other CA's in the organization, called **subordinate CAs**.

Looking at the previous diagram, a subordinate CA issues certificates that relate hierarchically to a root certificate issued by the root CA. A subordinate CA (also referred to as an intermediate or issuing CA depending on their position in the hierarchy) will therefore issue certificates that include the root CA's public keys rather than generating a new key. In the case of a corporation, the root CA may be run by the top-level Information Technology department who generates the public and private key and issues an initial certificate. Each subordinate IT department within the corporation may potentially act as a subordinate CA and issue certificates to members of the department that tie to the root CA's certificate. Because the root CA is trusted within the corporation, subordinate CAs that issue certificates based on the root CA's certificate can be trusted and used within the corporation's applications.

Certificate Server's Role

Certificate Server plays in important role in maintaining security within an infrastructure through managing, issuing, renewing, or revoking certificates. It provides the capability to centrally distribute certificates through Active Directory and maintain and update **certificate revocation lists** (**CRLs**). A CRL acts as a repository where CA's within an organization can check to see which certificates are valid and which are not. This allows control over certificates that are no longer needed due to application upgrades or other events, even if the certificates are not expired or compromised. The following diagram shows the role that Certificate Server plays:

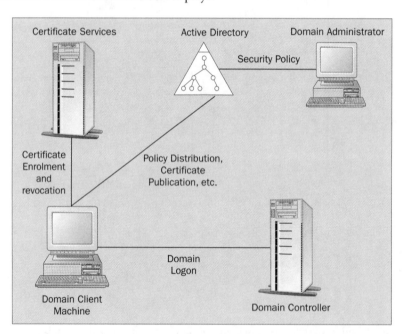

As this diagram shows, Certificate Services provides certificates to a user, computer, or service. These certificates can be held by the client or managed in a central location such as Active Directory. Because Certificate Services maintains control of the issue, renewal, and revocation of certificates, complete control over certificates is provided. This means that compromised certificates can quickly be revoked and added to the CRL while valid but expiring certificates can be renewed. Applications, computers, or individuals receiving a certificate can check the CRL to see whether or not a particular certificate is valid. If it is valid, the identity of the computer, application, or individual can then be verified. Some examples of the importance of this in a Windows DNA environment are discussed in the new few sections.

High Security

Because Certificate Server can issue client and server certificates while integrating with Active Directory, security is increased and efficiently controlled. Requiring certificate verification in an application ensures that the client is who they say they are. Also, from the client's perspective, a certificate sent by a web server allows the client to know that they are communicating with the appropriate server and that information passed to it will be handled appropriately. For e-mail, certificates allow for the encryption and positive identification of messages sent between departments or even between companies. This positive identification between individuals or between client and server allows for the highest level of security. For cases where authentication needs to be performed over an insecure network, certificates allow for validation of an individual without forcing users to send user IDs and passwords across the wire.

Secure Controls

Certificates can also be used to sign controls used within applications. **Software Publisher Certificates** (**SPCs**) can be issued to developers needing to sign their controls. Like the other certificates discussed already, this certificate embeds a public key that can be used for verification purposes. This prevents malicious material from making its way onto user machines and allows auto-updates of software to occur seamlessly and securely. For more details on this process search MSDN using the words "Signing and Checking Code with Authenticode".

Customization

Certificate Server supports the creation of custom **policy modules**. We'll discuss these later, but essentially these modules control what certificates can be issued and can be as strict or loose as desired. When policy modules are used, certificate requests must meet specific guidelines in order to be issued. This allows some departments within an organization to require personal appearances to receive highly secured certificates while other departments may allow applications for certificates to come in through the company intranet. More details on custom policy modules can be found in the "*Certificate Services Architecture*" section of the chapter.

Less Complexity

Aside from the aforementioned security benefits brought about by having positive identification between client and server and policy modules, Certificate Server makes managing certificates within an organization less complex. This support allows for structured certificate authorities to be created within an organization, as mentioned earlier, so that certificates that are issued, renewed, or revoked are tightly controlled within the hierarchy. Plus, Certificate Server allows for publishing certificates throughout infrastructure hierarchies, making maintenance easier and applications more scalable.

Single Log On

One of the most annoying calls received by a help desk worker or network administrator is the "I forgot my password" call. The increased security measures being implemented throughout organizations world-wide can often require users to remember too many passwords. Using Certificate Server and its ability to generate the appropriate certificate type, the requirement to logon to a particular application can be reduced through the issue of **client certificates**. Doing this allows the certificate to be installed on the client machine. In cases where multiple profiles exist on the same machine, Windows presents the certificate or certificates associated with each profile as appropriate. This of course means the user's identity can be confirmed without having to logon each time they access an application, since their certificate information can be sent with each request so that their identity can be validated as needed. After the first successful logon, the client certificate can be presented to any other applications that the user may need access to. The end result is less calls to the help desk or Network Administrator and higher client satisfaction.

Certificate Services Architecture

At the simplest level, a complete certificate system can be broken into three parts:

❑ Certificate consumers

❑ Intermediaries

❑ The certificate server

The consumer (or client) is the entity in need of a certificate, and it is responsible for initiating the certificate transaction. It interfaces with an intermediate system, which in turn can access the certificate server. The certificate server verifies a certificate request and returns the appropriate certificate to the consumer:

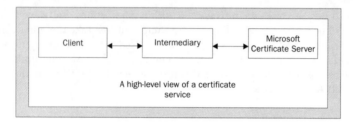

A high-level view of a certificate service

Certificate Consumers

The **certificate consumer** (client) gets the certificate service in motion by issuing a request for a certificate. The consumer can be a person, a machine, an application, or any single entity. For example, a certificate-enabled web browser will often act as a certificate consumer – it needs a certificate to carry out secure communication with a web server. By the same token, a web server needs a certificate to carry out secure communication with a web browser. Other examples might be e-mail clients, or online purchasing systems.

When a consumer submits a request, it must include certain information. It is this information, in fact, that is actually being certified. If you wanted a certificate, for example, that would provide positive proof of your identity (such as name, company name, and address), you would need to submit this identity information to a certificate authority, which would in turn issue a certificate back to you.

Intermediaries

The **intermediary** is responsible for receiving requests from a certificate consumer in a language that the consumer speaks, like HTTP. It translates and formats the request so the certificate server can understand it. Just as the consumer is often a web *browser*, the intermediary is often a web *server*, such as Microsoft Internet Information Server. The intermediary may also act as the vehicle through which the certificate is delivered to the consumer, by displaying the certificate in the web browser and allowing the user to cut and paste the certificate manually, or by allowing the user to download the certificate through HTTP.

In the case of Microsoft Certificate Server, the intermediary (usually IIS) will communicate with the server through a set of COM interfaces that are exposed by the certificate server expressly for that purpose. These objects provide all of the functionality necessary for submitting a request and retrieving a response, the specifics of which will be discussed later in this chapter.

The Certificate Server

The **certificate server** is perhaps the most complex part of our certificate system. The server is responsible for receiving certificate requests, granting or denying certificates in response to requests, revoking certificates, and publishing certificates (as well as lists of certificates that have been revoked). This functionality is distributed across sub-modules within the server:

❏ Entry module

❏ Policy module

❏ Exit module

❏ The certificate server database

At a very high level, entry modules handle server input, policy modules evaluate and carry out operations within the server, and exit modules handle server output. The certificate server database stores certificates, certificate lists, and revocation lists:

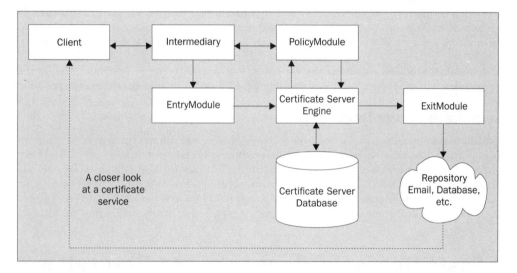

Entry Module

Entry modules are the certificate server's front door. Any request that comes to the certificate server is handled by the entry module. The entry module receives a request for the intermediary (in a language that the intermediary speaks), translates it into a language the server speaks, and passes it along to the 'guts' of the certificate server, namely the certificate authority, in a language that the CA speaks.

Like the other modules that are part of Microsoft Certificate Server, the entry module is fully customizable, since you can write your own! Certificate Server ships with a perfectly good entry module, but, should needs dictate, a custom entry module can be written using the COM libraries that Certificate Server provides. A full description of these libraries can be found later in this chapter, in the section called "*Development for Certificate Server*".

Policy Module

The **policy module** is the decision maker of the certificate service. The policy module is ultimately responsible for evaluating the request and then granting or denying a certificate. It evaluates the information that was provided with the request and verifies it. It can go as far as checking external data sources to verify request information. It can even send an alert to an external party (like a system administrator) if manual verification is necessary.

If a certificate is granted, the policy module is also responsible for packaging the certificate. It can also package additional information with the certificate, such as extra parameters or restrictions that may apply.

Certificate Server includes a functioning policy module. If necessary, of course, the policy module can be home-grown using the COM interfaces that Certificate Server provides.

Exit Module

The **exit module** packages a certificate response for export to the necessary parties, such as the consumer or a database. For example, it might send a certificate back to a web server via TCP/IP, it may e-mail a certificate to someone, and it usually stores it in the certificate server's database. The server may actually incorporate multiple exit modules, in case a certificate needs to go to multiple recipients (like storing it in some external database, as well as sending it to back to the client).

As with the other modules, Certificate Server comes with a functioning exit module. And, as with the other modules, exit modules can be written using COM if custom modules are necessary.

The Certificate Server Database

The **database** is fairly transparent to the user or administrator, and will not be covered in detail. Its primary purpose is to store copies of all certificates that have been issued. It also stores a list of certificates that have been revoked, known as the **revocation list** (the revocation list, and the need for one, will be discussed in more detail later). Finally, the certificate server database stores a log of the server's activities. Additionally, the database provides queuing functionality. After a new request is handled by the entry module, it is stored in a queue in the database before it is picked up by the policy module.

Certificate Requests, Renewals, and Revocation

The life cycle of a certificate begins with a request. If the request is rejected by the server to which it was submitted, the life cycle ends quite abruptly. If it is approved, the certificate will be assigned an expiration date. If it is not revoked in the meantime, the certificate will function until its expiration date, at which point it will need to be renewed if it is to remain valid.

Certificate Requests

The genesis of a request really comes when someone (or something) desires an authoritative certificate. Like most cases in life, however, desire is not quite enough to get a certificate. It is, of course, necessary to submit a request. Certificate requests frequently occur across mediums such as the Internet, where the certificate consumer and the server may or may not be on the same platform, and probably are not even aware of the other's platform. As a result, it was necessary to develop a standard language that certificate requests could be formulated in.

The standard certificate request language is encapsulated in the **PKCS #10 standard** (PKCS stands for **Public-Key Cryptography Standards**). Microsoft Certificate Server supports the PKCS #10 standard, as do the interfaces provided for formulating requests. Basically, a PKCS #10 certificate request contains version information, the owner's public key, some additional information about the owner, information about the signature (such as the algorithm used to generate it) and the signature itself. The standard itself is quite complex, and is outside of the scope of this book. If you want more information, the specification can be found at http://www.rsasecurity.com/rsalabs/pkcs/pkcs-10/index.html.

The properties associated with a request can contain a great deal of information. Examples include common name, given name, e-mail address, street address, county of origin, or device serial numbers. Of course, any information that is supposed to be certified must be included in the request.

Certificate Renewals

Any issued certificate always has an expiration date associated with it. This expiration date is actually embedded within the certificate and should be verified (checked against the current date) when a certificate is evaluated. Just like a driver's license, when a certificate expires, it must be renewed if it is to still be used.

The certificate renewal process is fairly simple. The underlying assumption is that the entity requesting renewal is not seeking to certify new or different information than was certified before. The server can therefore handle the process much quicker, since the information does not need to be re-verified. Essentially, the server will verify that the certificate is not on its revocation list, and issue a new certificate. The new certificate is identical to the old certificate in every aspect, except that the expiration date will be updated. If any certified information needs to be changed, a certificate cannot be renewed – a new certificate must be obtained.

Certificate Revocation

There are some circumstances under which a certificate must be revoked. A good example might be the case of a terminating employee who has a certificate installed on a home machine which allows access to the corporate network. Naturally, the employee no longer has cause or authority to access the network. In this case it is necessary to revoke the certificate (rather than raiding the employee's home and destroying the certificate on the hard drive).

Microsoft Certificate Server allows for the manual revocation of certificates. For example, the certificate server administrator can revoke a certificate through the administration client. In addition, it can be configured to accept revocation requests from an end user or someone using a custom administration tool. Once a certificate has been revoked, it is added to the **certificate revocation list** (**CRL**). This list is published on a regular basis to other interested parties, such as other certificate servers in the cluster or hierarchy.

The catch to keep in mind with certificate revocation is that the certificate itself is not affected. The certificate remains untouched, intact, and in its original state. As a result, an application generally consults the CRL anytime a certificate is verified, in order to ensure that the certificate has not been revoked.

Installing Certificate Services

The installation process for Certificate Server is fairly straightforward and simple. However, before you start installing you must know what type of CA you want to install. Will your CA be the enterprise root CA within a Windows domain, or will it be a subordinate CA in a hierarchy? These questions must be answered and planned for appropriately to prevent multiple CAs from entering a domain when existing CAs are already available to service certificate requests. While every possible installation scenario cannot be covered here, the next few sections give some guidelines to help in deciding which CA to install.

Stand-alone Root CAs

For root CAs that are not within a particular Windows domain but that will service the general Internet, you'll want to install a **stand-alone root CA** if users receiving the certificate trust you. An example of this would be Verisign.

The stand-alone root CA is the top-level in a certification hierarchy. Because it is a stand-alone server, it is not required to participate in a domain and does not require Active Directory to function. If Active Directory does exist, a stand-alone root CA can leverage its features. Due to not relying on Active Directory, the stand-alone root CA machine can be disconnected from the network and placed in a secure area. This can be useful in times where you need to create a secure offline root CA.

Stand-alone root CAs are intended primarily for extranets or for the Internet. Because of this, stand-alone root CAs require that the requestor of a certificate submit all information about themself. Once this information is received, all certificates are placed in pending status until the administrator can verify the information provided for the certificate and either accept or deny the certificate. This differs from an enterprise CA where a user's identify can be verified using Active Directory. Also, for obvious security reasons, the administrator of the stand-alone CA must distribute an approved certificate to the user's domain certificate store themselves or the user must check back using the web interface to verify the certificate's status and then install the certificate.

Stand-alone Subordinate CAs

If you'll be issuing certificates to the general Internet that are based on a certificate generated by a root CA, consider setting up a **stand-alone subordinate CA**. For example, you may receive a root certificate from Verisign and then use this certificate to issue other certificates to users on the Internet.

A stand-alone subordinate CA (like all subordinates) must receive its certificate from another CA. Because it is a stand-alone, it does not need to participate in a domain and therefore does not require Active Directory. However, it can use Active Directory if it exists.

Enterprise Root CAs

If no **enterprise root CA** exists within your company and you want to be able to secure applications that are in use throughout the company, you should consider installing one. This type of CA generates its own public-key set and generally distributes certificates to subordinate CAs rather than directly to individuals.

An enterprise root CA is the top-level in a certification hierarchy. Because it's at the top of the hierarchy, it signs its own CA certificate and then publishes that certificate to the Trusted Root Certification Authorities store of every Windows 2000 server or workstation within the domain. When you select the enterprise root CA during installation of Certificate Server, the host computer must be a member of a Windows domain and must use Active Directory. Because of this, the administrator installing the enterprise CA must be allowed to write to the Active Directory.

An example of this could be the head Information Technology department within an organization, such as the Office of the CIO who is ultimately responsible for issuing certificates either directly or to other subordinate CAs.

Enterprise Subordinate CAs

If an enterprise root CA already exists and your department or company organization wants to issue certificates to individuals directly, then an **enterprise subordinate CA** is likely to be appropriate. This cannot create its own certificate and therefore must receive it from another CA. This could be the root CA, but this depends upon the subordinate's place in the domain hierarchy. When you select the enterprise subordinate CA during installation of Certificate Server, Active Directory must be available.

An example of an enterprise subordinate CA could be a department that would like to issue certificates within the department but is not necessarily trusted throughout the entire organization. By setting up a subordinate CA within the department, tight control over which individuals or computers receive certificates (within the department) can be maintained and these certificates will be trusted since they have ties to the organization's root CA.

Setup and Configuration of a Standalone Root CA

This chapter cannot possibly cover each installation option as it relates to your organization, due to Active Directory configuration issues and the overall purpose that the certificate server will perform within your organization. For large organizations, careful planning needs to occur across the company so that the proper certificate servers are set up.

Once you have decided which type of CA to install, the installation is very quick. The following example will show the steps necessary to install a standalone root CA on a local machine. The installation instructions will assume that IIS is installed on the machine on which you are installing Certificate Server. Once the installation section is completed, we'll demonstrate how easy the Certificate Server web interface is to use by making a simple certificate request through the browser.

The following installation example will install a stand-alone root CA. This example was chosen due to its simplicity and ease of access. For the other enterprise installs, the host computer must be a member of a Windows domain and the administrator must have domain administration rights. Also, the enterprise installations require that Active Directory is up and running. Since many users may not have domain administrator rights or be on a domain using Active Directory yet, the stand-alone root CA installation was chosen for this example.

Once Windows 2000 Server or Advanced Server has been installed on a host machine, the Certificate Server installation wizard can be accessed from Settings | Control Panel | Add/Remove Programs | Add/Remove Windows Components.

The Add/Remove Windows Components screen will appear and the Certificate Services checkbox should be unchecked. If it is checked, Certificate Services have already been installed on the machine. Clicking the checkbox will pop-up the following message box:

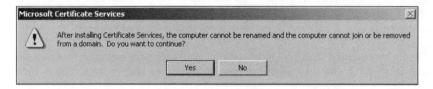

This box appears because of how CAs generate certificates. If a CA (root or other) changes computer names or is removed from a domain, certificates associated with that CA will no longer be valid as the issuer no longer exists. Once you understand these implications, you may click Yes and then click the Next button. The Certificate Services installation wizard will now appear as shown below:

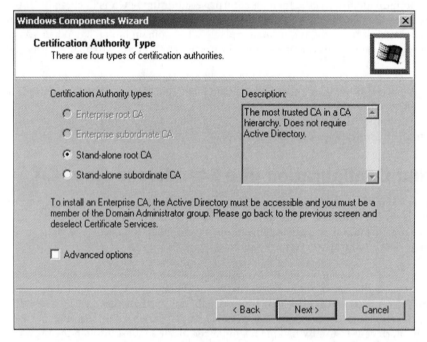

From this screen you can choose what type of certificate authority you would like to install according to your needs. For information about the different installation options, see the descriptions above. As mentioned, this example will install a stand-alone root CA. As the above screen shows, both enterprise CA installation options will be disabled if you are not a domain administrator, if the computer is not within a domain, or the domain the computer is in does not have access to Active Directory. Continuing with the stand-alone root CA installation, you'll notice a checkbox next to Advanced options. Clicking this box, followed by the Next button, will display the following screen:

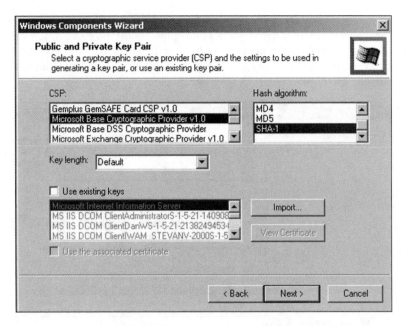

This screen allows you to select the **cryptographic service provider** (CSP) that will generate public/private key sets to be used for certificate generation and other cryptographic operations. The default selection is the **Microsoft Base Cryptographic Provider v1.0**. Depending upon what key lengths you want to generate, picking the appropriate provider will be important. If you will encrypt data that isn't considered "top secret" then the default base provider will be sufficient. However, if you plan on generating long keys you'll want to use a provider such as the enhanced provider. Once this has been chosen, the public key's length can be set by choosing a value from the dropdown box. The longer the key, the more secure it is. However, a longer key will require a longer generation time during the setup procedure and at run-time.

If you would like to use keys that already exist, click the **Use existing keys** checkbox and select the appropriate key. If the keys do not exist in the listbox, click the **Import...** button to locate the keys. This can be useful if you are restoring a CA that was previously online. After this has been accomplished, one final choice involving the **Hash algorithm** (used in digital signature generation) can be chosen. The default value is **SHA-1** (Secure Hash Algorithm) which will generate a 160-bit hash value. This algorithm was published by the United States Government and the official standard can be found at http://www.itl.nist.gov/fipspubs/fip180-1.htm.

> *The MD5 (Message Digest Algorithm 5) algorithm is intended for use on 32-bit machines and is considered to be safer than the MD4 algorithm which has already been broken. MD5 takes a byte string and converts it into a 128-bit hash value. The MD algorithms were developed by RSA Data Security.*

For this installation the default selections were used. This doesn't infer that these selections are the best ones to use as the base provider clearly is not the most powerful of the cryptographic providers. The settings you choose will depend upon the security level of data that will be encrypted or decrypted with the appropriate key or keys. To continue with the installation process, click the **Next** button. This screen allows for CA identifying information to be entered:

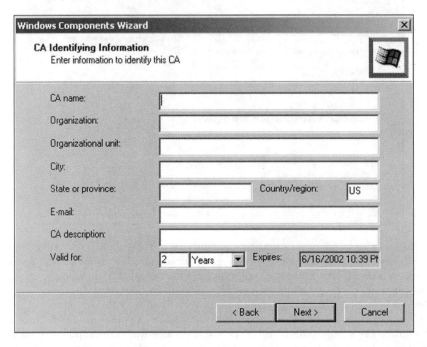

It's important to note that none of the information listed on this screen can be changed without uninstalling and then reinstalling Certificate Services. As a result, understanding the purpose of each of these fields is crucial to a successful installation. Descriptions of each field are listed below:

❑ CA Name: the name you want to give the CA. While most characters are acceptable, for situations where special characters occur in the name, a "sanitized" CA name will be used when operations are not able to work with the unmodified name. So, special characters such as the "*" character will be removed when it is not appropriate in a particular operation and replaced with a "!xxxx" format. For example, if you enter a name of *RootCA then the sanitized version of the name will look like !002aRootCA. Special characters are considered to be non-ASCII characters as well as many ASCII punctuation characters. The following table shows what characters will be converted to the "!xxxx" format:

Character	Value in !xxxx format
<	!003c
>	!003e
"	!0022
/	!002f

Character	Value in !xxxx format
\	!005c
:	!003a
|	!007c
?	!003f
*	!002a
#	!0023
,	!002c
+	!002b
;	!003b
!	!0021

❑ **Organization:** the legal name of your organization as it is registered with the state, country/region, or city authority. So if your organization's legal name is ABC Widgets, then that's what should be entered here. No checks are made to ensure that a legal name is being entered so in reality any organization name can be entered, although to ensure that certificates issued by the authority are trusted by end users, a legal name is obviously recommended.

❑ **Organizational Unit:** used to enter a department name or other ID that exists within an organization.

❑ **City:** the city your organization resides in.

❑ **State or Province:** the physical location of your organization.

❑ **Country/Region:** this field accepts a two-character country or region code. The characters must comply with the X.500 Naming Scheme standard (http://www.itu.int/itudoc/itu-t/rec/x/x500up/index.html).

❑ **E-mail:** an e-mail address associated with the CA or CA administrator.

❑ **CA Description:** this is simply a general description of the CA.

❑ **Valid For:** specifies for how long the CA will be valid.

Upon completion of this screen, hit the Next button and you will be taken to the Data Storage Location screen in the wizard:

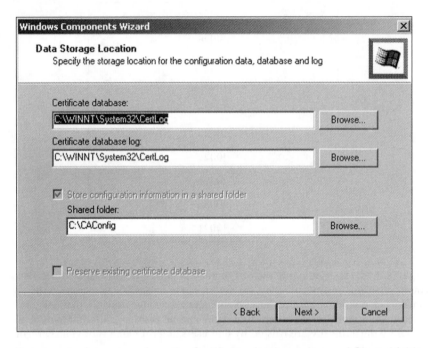

This page allows you to determine where the Certificate database, log, and Shared folder will reside. This database is used to store information about certificates that have been renewed, issued, revoked, etc. The shared folder is useful only with stand-alone CAs and can be used by computer users to find information about certification authorities.

After choosing the various file locations, hitting Next again will result in a message box stating "Internet Information Services is running on this computer. You must stop this service before proceeding. Do you want to stop the service now?" This message will appear if Internet Information Services (IIS) is running on the host machine. Click OK to continue and the installation program will automatically stop IIS temporarily while it installs the Certificate Services web interface. Once IIS has been stopped, the installation of Certificate Server files will begin. Depending upon how Windows 2000 was installed, you may be prompted for your Windows 2000 CD so that additional files can be installed.

Upon completion of a successful Certificate Services installation click the Finish button to complete the installation process. So what has this process accomplished? First of all, the files necessary to make the Certificate Server functional were installed along with any necessary supporting files. If IIS was located on the machine where the install occurred, a virtual directory named certsvc was created and several .asp files, used to allow end users to create certificates, were also created. The different services offered and web pages available to the end user are discussed a little later.

Subordinate CA Setup Features

For subordinate CAs (enterprise or stand-alone) that do not have the ability to generate their own certificate, they must submit a request to a parent CA in a CA hierarchy. The process to obtain the certificate depends upon how accessible the parent CA is and how the distribution of certificates from parent to subordinate CAs is handled. The following information details the process of obtaining a certificate from a parent CA for both online and offline CAs. An online CA is one that is able to connect to a parent CA through the network while an offline CA typically has no connection available to use to connect to the parent CA.

Getting a Certificate from an Online Parent CA

After choosing the storage location for a CA, the installation will show a button titled Send the request directly to a CA already on the network. Click this button and then fill in the Computer Name field with the name of the computer on which the parent CA is installed and running. In the Parent CA field, click the name of the parent CA. This process will send a request across the network and allow the parent CA to issue a certificate to the subordinate CA.

Getting a Certificate from an Offline Parent CA

Obtaining a certificate for a subordinate CA from an offline parent CA is slightly more complicated and involves the following steps:

1. Click the Save the request to a file button.

2. Enter the path and file name for the file that will store the request in the Request file field.

3. Obtain the certificate for the subordinate CA from the parent CA.

Depending on how the parent CA is set up and administered, this process can vary. The parent CA should be able to provide a file containing the newly issued certificate and the full certification path up to the root CA.

Requests that do not come back with a certification path require that a valid CA chain be installed on the subordinate CA. To start, the parent CA's certificate must be stored in the Intermediate Certification Authorities certificate store of the subordinate CA computer. Any other intermediaries in the chain should also be stored in this location. Once the path's root CA is reached, its certificate should be placed in the subordinate CA computer's Trusted Root Certificate Authorities store. The previously mentioned certificates in the CA hierarchy chain should be installed in the appropriate certificate store prior to installing the subordinate CA's certificate.

4. After the certificate has been obtained from the parent CA, open up the Certification Authority console by going to Start | Programs | Administration Tools | Certification Authority.

5. On the console tree that appears, click the name of the CA.

6. Now go to the Action menu and select All Tasks. From the menu that appears, click Install CA Certificate.

7. Locate the certificate file that was received from the parent CA, click the file, and then click Open.

Certificate Services Administration

Starting and stopping the Certificate Services server is almost as easy as doing the same with IIS. To access the console, go to Start | Programs | Administration Tools | Certification Authority. Click on the CA name and then click the appropriate start or stop button located on the console. Alternatively, you can right-click the CA name, select All Tasks, and then select to start or stop the service, as shown below:

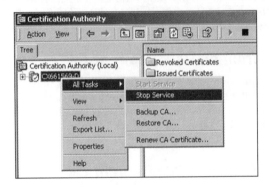

Other tasks can be carried out from this administration console. Open up the CA's folders and you'll see folders named Revoked Certificates, Issued Certificates, Pending Requests, and Failed Requests. To see how to use the console folders to approve, deny, or revoke certificates, let's run through an example that generates a certificate request from the Web to our stand-alone root CA server installed earlier.

Assuming IIS is set up on the same computer where Certificate Services was installed, users can access the services to request certificates and check on the status of certificate requests in progress. To access the services, they simply navigate to http://CAServerName/certsrv. Upon successfully connecting to the server, they should see a screen similar to the following:

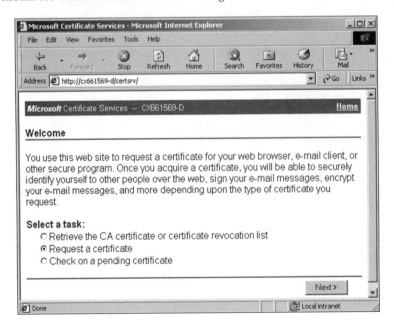

Upon selecting **Request a Certificate** and clicking the **Next** button, they will be taken to a page that allows them to choose a **Web Browser Certificate** or an **Email Protection Certificate**. Another option allows for the creation of a more advanced certificate. If they select the more advanced certificate they will be allowed to request a certificate from the CA, submit a certificate request using a base64 encoded PKCS #10 file or a renewal request using a base64 encoded PKCS #7 file, or request a certificate for a smart card. Assuming they select the first option (submit a request to the CA using a form), they will then see an enrollment page containing several fields:

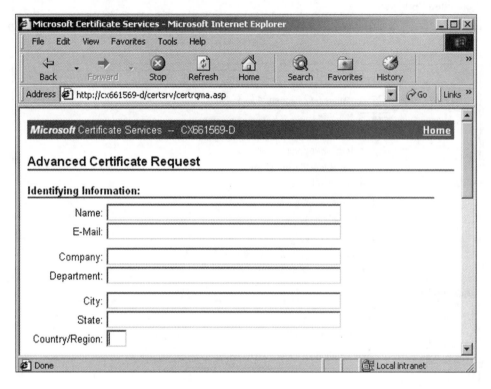

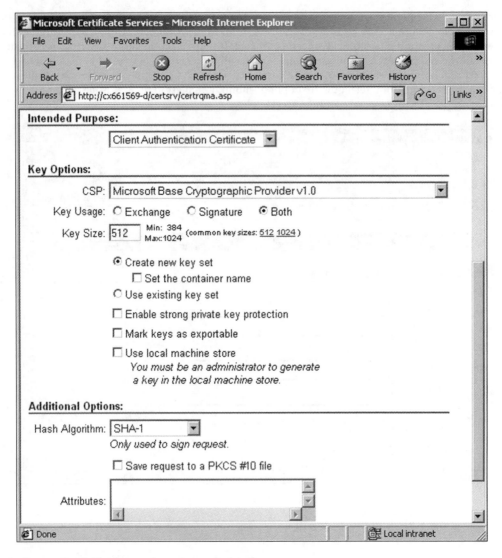

Let's discuss the fields shown above in more detail:

❑ **Identifying Information**: this allows the end user to enter their personal information.

❑ **Intended Purpose**: the end user can select from the following options:

    ❑ Client Authentication Certificate

    ❑ E-Mail Protection Certificate

    ❑ Server Authentication Certificate

    ❑ Code Signing Certificate

    ❑ Time Stamp Signing Certificate

    ❑ IPSec Certificate

    ❑ Other

❑ **Key Options**: this section allows the user to select the cryptographic service provider (CSP) used to generate the keys, the key usage type, key size, and other selections relating to generating new keys or using existing keys.

❑ **Additional Options**: this section allows the user to choose which hash algorithm they would like to use, and select if the request should be saved to a PKCS #10 file.

After completing all of the available options, the user can submit the form. They will then receive a message saying that they should check back within two days to monitor the progress of the certificate request. This time span is specified because the stand-alone CA must verify the validity of the user. With an enterprise CA, requests can be approved or denied automatically based on user permissions in the Active Directory.

Now that the user request has been submitted, the CA administrator can go into the **Certificate Services** console to view certificate requests. After opening the **Pending Request** folder of the CA, they should see the certificate request made by the user:

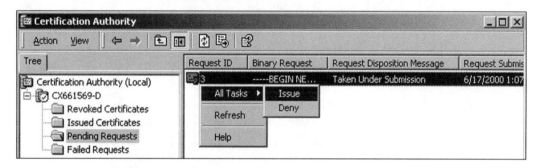

If the user's request is valid and follows policy rules, the certificate can be **Issued**. Otherwise the administrator can **Deny** the request.

Assuming the certificate request is validated and the certificate is issued, the user requesting the certificate can go back to the web page they were at earlier, choose the **Check on a pending certificate** option, and then download and install the certificate. If the administrator had issued the certificate in error, the certificate can be revoked by going to the "**Issued Certificates**" folder, choosing **All Tasks**, and then choosing **Revoke Certificate**. A message box will pop-up to ask for the reason the certificate is being revoked.

Revoking the certificate will cause the certificate to be invalid and will add it to the certificate revocation list (CRL) the next time it is published. Only certificates that have been revoked and given a reason code of "Certificate Hold" can be un-revoked. This allows the administrator flexibility in placing questionable certificates on hold while more research is performed. To un-revoke the certificate, the administrator must use the `certutil.exe` command line utility. This utility identifies the certificate to "un-revoke" through the certificate's serial number as shown below (ignore spaces):

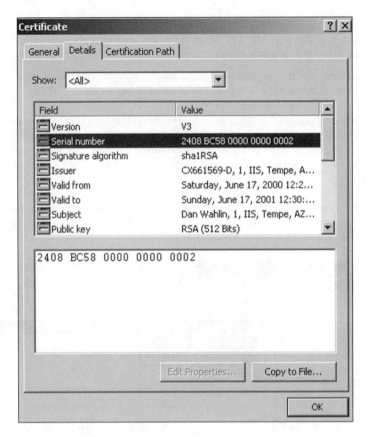

This utility must be run on the computer that Certificate Server was installed on. For example, they could type:

```
certutil -revoke 2408bc58000000000002 unrevoke
```

If it is decided to permanently revoke the certificate, the administrator can run `certutil.exe` as shown above but substitute the appropriate revocation code in place of `unrevoke`. The following list contains the revocation codes and their associated command line code:

Revocation code	Command line code
Unspecified	certutil -revoke certificateserialnumber 0
Key Compromise	certutil -revoke certificateserialnumber 1
CA Compromise	certutil -revoke certificateserialnumber 2
Affiliation Changed	certutil -revoke certificateserialnumber 3
Superseded	certutil -revoke certificateserialnumber 4
Cessation of Operation	certutil -revoke certificateserialnumber 5

For additional management features associated with the Certificate Services console, consult the Windows 2000 online help section, searching for "Certificate Services".

Development for Certificate Server

Microsoft Certificate Server incorporates a comprehensive COM library (included with Certificate Server) for development purposes. We will not discuss every interface here, but we will cover the major ones. The following interfaces are exposed by the server engine itself:

❑ ICertAdmin

❑ ICertServerPolicy

❑ ICertServerExit

❑ ICertConfig

❑ ICertView

❑ ICertRequest

Furthermore, a policy module will expose:

❑ ICertPolicy

❑ ICertManageModule

And an exit module exposes:

❑ ICertExit

❑ ICertManageModule

If you're *really* into diagrams, the figure below is all you need to start writing clients and modules for your certificate service. The rest of us might benefit from a little explanation, which follows after the diagram:

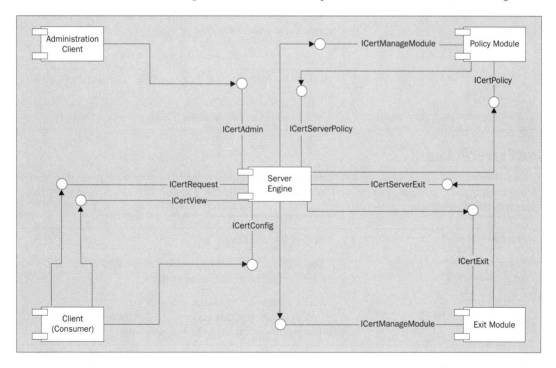

Server Interfaces

The interfaces exposed by the server provide the functionality necessary to request certificates, administer the server, receive granted certificates, and gather general information about the server. They are used by certificate consumers, administration tools, and the various server modules. This section is not intended to be a substitute to the MSDN Library, where you will find detailed information about each interface and method. Rather, it is an overview of the functionality each provides, and the methods that are implemented. For more detailed information, as well as some sample code, refer to the MSDN: http://msdn.microsoft.com/library/default.asp?URL=/library/psdk/certsrv/crtsv_int1_157y.htm.

ICertAdmin

The ICertAdmin interface provides functionality to manually grant or deny a certificate request, revoke certificates, verify certificates, or retrieve the certificate revocation list. It implements the following methods:

DenyRequest	Forces a specific request to be denied
GetCRL	Retrieves the certificate revocation list
GetRevocationReason	Used to determine why a specific certificate was revoked
ImportCertificate	Imports a previously issued certificate into the database, which would be especially useful if the database were lost or corrupted, for instance
IsValidCertificate	Validates the certificate in question
PublishCRL	Forces the server to publish a new CRL
ResubmitRequest	Sends a previously submitted request back to the policy module for another review
RevokeCertificate	Revokes a certificate as of a specified date
SetCertificateExtension	Adds extra information, known as an extension, to a given certificate
SetRequestAttributes	Used to build attribute name/value pairs in a request

ICertServerPolicy

ICertServerPolicy is used by the policy module to access information about a request. It can also be used to change certain parameters, and to manipulate certificate extensions. ICertServerPolicy implements the following methods:

EnumerateAttributes	Used to list attributes
EnumerateAttributesClose	Cleans up memory and resources associated with an EnumerateAttributes operation
EnumerateAttributesSetup	Initializes resources associated with an EnumerateAttributes operation, and sets the enumeration pointer to the first attribute

EnumerateExtensions	Lists extensions associated with a certificate
Enumerate ExtensionsClose	Cleans up memory and resources associated with an EnumerateExtensions operation
Enumerate ExtensionsSetup	Initializes resources associated with an EnumerateExtensions operation, and sets the enumeration pointer to the first extension
GetCertificateExtension	Retrieves a specified certificate extension
GetCertificate ExtensionFlags	Gets the flags associated with the extension retrieved by the most recent call to GetCertificateExtension
GetCertificateProperty	Gets a property associated with a certificate
GetRequestAttribute	Gets an attribute associated with a request
GetRequestProperty	Gets a property associated with a request
SetCertificateExtension	Adds a new extension to the certificate
SetCertificateProperty	Adds a new property to a certificate
SetContext	Sets the request that operations will be performed on

ICertServerExit

This interface is used by the exit modules to gather information about requests and certificates. All operations of ICertServerExit are read-only. It implements exactly the same methods as ICertServerPolicy, except that it omits the functionality to add extensions and properties:

EnumerateAttributes	Used to list attributes
EnumerateAttributesClose	Cleans up memory and resources associated with an EnumerateAttributes operation
EnumerateAttributesSetup	Initializes resources associated with an EnumerateAttributes operation, and sets the enumeration pointer to the first attribute
EnumerateExtensions	Lists extensions associated with a certificate
EnumerateExtensionsClose	Cleans up memory and resources associated with an EnumerateExtensions operation
EnumerateExtensionsSetup	Initializes resources associated with an EnumerateExtensions operation, and sets the enumeration pointer to the first extension
GetCertificateExtension	Retrieves a certificate extension
GetCertificateExtensionFlags	Gets the flags associated with the extension retrieved by the most recent call to GetCertificateExtension

Table continued on following page

GetCertificateProperty	Gets a property associated with a certificate
GetRequestAttribute	Gets an attribute associated with a request
GetRequestProperty	Gets a property associated with a request
SetContext	Sets the request that operations will be performed on

ICertConfig

This interface is typically used to gather information about the Certificate Services environment. It can be used to determine which servers are present, how they are configured, and which server acts as the default. ICertConfig implements the following methods:

GetConfig	Retrieves the configuration string, which consists of the server name and the CA name
GetField	Gets a named field from the configuration database
Next	Moves the pointer to the next server configuration in the configuration database
Reset	Sets the configuration database query state to a specified point

ICertView

ICertView allows clients to view the certificate database. The clients, of course, must be properly authorized. The client can retrieve a custom view of the database, or the entire database. ICertView implements the following methods:

EnumCertViewColumn	Retrieves a pointer to a column view for schema enumeration
GetColumnCount	Returns a count of the columns in the view
GetColumnIndex	Returns the zero-based index of the specified column
OpenConnection	Opens a connection to the server
OpenView	Opens a view in the database
SetRestriction	Specifies sorting and filtering of parameters on a column
SetResultColumn	Specifies a column to be used in a view
SetResultColumnCount	Specifies the number of columns to be used in a view's result set

ICertRequest

This interface is used to submit requests, check the status on a request, and get the results of a request (including any certificate that was issued). It can also be used to retrieve the certificate server's CA certificate. ICertRequest implements the following methods:

GetCACertificate	Gets the server's CA certificate
GetCertificate	Gets the certificate that was the result of a successful request
GetDispositionMessage	Gets the status of a request in plain-text
GetLastStatus	Retrieves the most recent return code associated with a request
GetRequestId	Gets the ID of the request (useful for referencing a request in another interface, for instance)
RetrievePending	If a request was determined to be in an intermediate status in an earlier operation, RetrievePending can be used to get the certificate that may have eventually been issued
Submit	Sends a request to the server

Module Interfaces

The server modules (specifically the policy and exit modules) expose COM interfaces for use by the server. These interfaces are used to gather information about a request, check requests, and gather general information about the individual modules.

ICertExit

ICertExit is exposed by an exit module for use by the server. The server uses it to either send a granted certificate, or to revoke a certificate. It implements the following methods:

GetDescription	Gets a plain-text description of the module and its functionality
Initialize	Called during server initialization, so that the exit module can perform any necessary initialization
Notify	Used to notify the exit module of certain events

ICertPolicy

This interface is exposed by the policy module. It is used by the server to notify the policy module of certain events, such as a new certificate request arriving for consideration, and to verify requests. ICertPolicy implements the following methods:

GetDescription	Gets a plain-text description of the module and its functionality
Initialize	Called during server initialization, so that the policy module can perform any necessary initialization
Shutdown	Called by the server during shutdown, so that the policy module can perform any necessary cleanup tasks
VerifyRequest	Used to submit a new request to the policy module for review

ICertManageModule

The ICertManageModule is exposed by both the exit module and the policy module. It allows the setting and getting of module properties, and exposes an interface that allows the module's graphical configuration interface to be opened. ICertManageModule implements the following methods:

Configure	Opens the module's graphical configuration interface
GetProperty	Gets the value of a module property
SetProperty	Sets the value of a module property

Putting It All Together

To finish off this discussion of Certificate Services, let's take a look at a couple of practical examples.

A Client Certificate

The first is a start-to-finish example of a digital certificate request utilizing Microsoft Certificate Server. Let's assume that you, an IT worker, would like to connect to your network remotely using a laptop computer. Your network administrator is fully aware that a username/password combination can be compromised through human error, or through foul play if it is not properly encrypted. Any remote access, therefore, requires a client certificate so that the identity of the computer accessing the network can be guaranteed.

You network administrator has provided a web interface (an intermediary) through which you can request and obtain a certificate. This screen could be similar to the one shown earlier in the chapter:

Using your laptop connected to the LAN, you access this page. You enter your name, title, e-mail address, and some other basic information. You then click submit, which generates a certificate request, which is in turn sent to an entry module. The entry module packages the request, along with other information (such as where the request came from, network permissions, and user credentials) and sends it to the policy module.

It is now up to the policy module to evaluate the request. If it determines that all criteria have been met (for example, the request came from the local network and had the proper login credentials) it will grant a certificate. The certificate will then be packaged by the exit module. If the certificate installation process is automated, it may be automatically installed onto your laptop. In a manual process, the actual text of the certificate may be displayed in your browser, and you would be given instructions on pasting it into a file and installing it on your laptop.

A Web Server Certificate

Your boss has asked you to create an application that will gather benefit enrollment information (healthcare, dental, life insurance, etc.) over the web. You're told that the system will run on the company Internet so that employees can enroll from home and that it's important that SSL be utilized since personal identification numbers and other sensitive information will be transmitted across the wire. While setting up SSL on the web server does require a little bit of work on your part, it's a straightforward process once you know where to start.

First, go to Internet Services Manager, select the web site containing the enrollment application, right-click on the web site and click **Properties**. On the web site properties screen that appears select the **Directory Security** tab at the top. You should see the following screen:

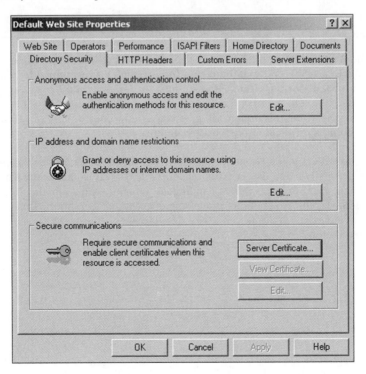

From this screen, click the **Server Certificate** button. Clicking this will take you to a web server certificate wizard. On this screen hit the **Next** button and you will see the following screen that will allow you to create a new certificate, use an existing certificate, or restore a certificate stored in a Key Manager backup file:

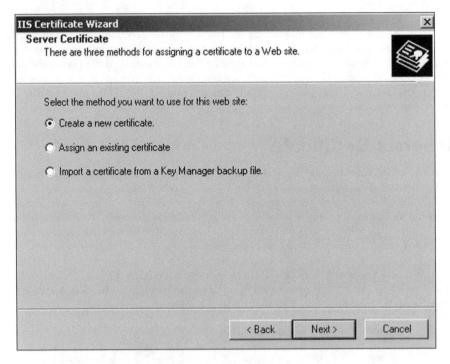

Select the **Create a new certificate** option and click the **Next** button once again to continue. Since you've been asked to use SSL on the intranet and Internet site, it's recommended that you obtain a certificate from a trusted root certificate authority such as Verisign (http://www.verisign.com) or Thawte (http://www.thawte.com). On the next screen in the wizard, select the **Prepare the request now, but send it later** option. Selecting this option will give you a better idea of how certificates work and what is involved in generating a certificate from a trusted authority.

Next you will be asked to enter a **Name** for the certificate and a **Bit length** for the encryption key. The name should be a friendly name that is easily recognizable. In this example, the name "Open Enrollment" is being used. As far as the bit length goes, remember that a higher length will lead to the generation of a more secure key, but that processing encryption/decryption requests will take longer and place more of a burden on the server as key sizes grow. For this example, select the **512** bit option and click the **Next** button:

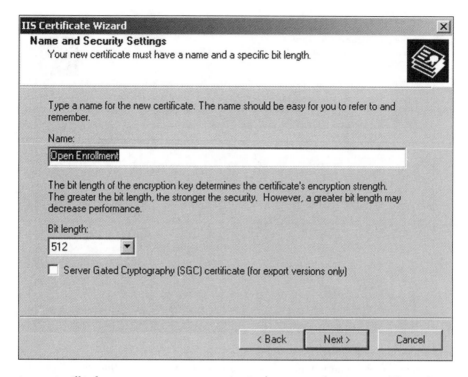

The next screen will ask you to enter your organization's name and unit name. This information will show up in the subject field of the certificate, as shown below:

OU = Information Technology
O = ABC Widgets

The O field serves the obvious task of describing the organization's name while the OU field describes the organization unit's name. Clicking the Next button yet again will result in a screen that asks you for the common name that will show on the certificate. Since the generated certificate will be used on an Internet web server, enter the fully qualified domain name (a valid DNS name) for the web site. This name will show up in the certificate's "subject" and "issued to" fields as CN=valid_DNS_Name where CN represents the common name. Clicking the Next button once again, you'll be prompted to enter the Country/Region, State/Province, and City/Locality of your organization. Certificate Authorities require that the State/Province is spelled out rather than abbreviated. So, instead of entering "AZ" you should enter "Arizona". This screen is quite self-explanatory, click Next again to see the following:

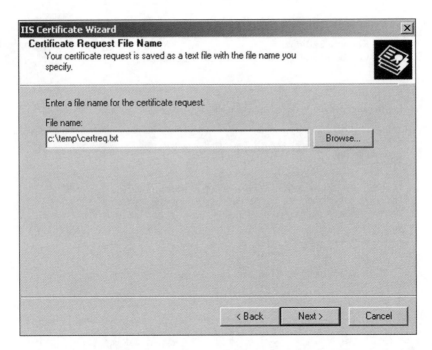

This screen allows you to enter the path to the ASCII file that will store your certificate request. You'll need to remember the path that you enter, as the information written to the file will be used when the official certificate request is made to the Certificate Authority. The next screen in the wizard will present you with all of the information you've entered up to this point and allow you to verify that it is correct. Once you click the Next button again, the **Certificate Signing Request** (**CSR**) file will be generated that contains the necessary key to be sent to the Certificate Authority. To see this request, navigate to the path you specified above and open up the file in Notepad. You should see text similar to the following:

```
-----BEGIN NEW CERTIFICATE REQUEST-----
MIIChDCCAi4CAQAwdDESMBAGA1UEAxMJYWJjd2lkZ2V0MR8wHQYDVQQLExZJbmZv
cm1hdGlvbiBUZWNNobm9sb2d5MRMwEQYDVQQKEwpBQkMMgV2lkZ2V0MQ4wDAYDVQQH
EwVUZW1wZTELMAkGA1UECBMCQVoxCzAJBgNVBAYTAIVTMFwwDQYJKoZIhvcNAQEB
BQADSwAwSAJBANiePzXpla5hsR/qXONl7qkHnosAuHeF51dmAhez5t+eWPbBG4Ob
6GvNUzysi1tlyUSf7WChmfw3Ts9yNHXaa1sCAwEAAaCCAVMwGgYKKwYBBAGCNw0C
AzEMFgo1LjAuMjE5NS4yMDUGCisGAQQBgjcCAQ4xJzAlMA4GA1UdDwEB/wQEAwIE
8DATBgNVHSUEDDAKBggrBgEFBQcDATCB/QYKKwYBBAGCNw0CAjGB7jCB6wIBAR5a
AE0AaQBjAHIAbwBzAG8AZgB0ACAAUgBTAEEAIABTAEMAaABhAG4AbgBlAGwAIABD
AHIAeQBwAHQAbwBnAHIAYQBwAGgAaQBjACAAUAByAG8AdgBpAGQAZQByACAAdjGJAF8T
bgM+oHAWmVHXn/FkNjwK6CjFvLKa3Cr+0A9np3M+v1nLfQ2eQpBspyxstH/i33+1
YkgyasWFmievHXaoF8gKiIpRet5Irz04gussS2jV+ub93JyhceFK1Kxl2bbm+zO/
zbsUoqTltFb+8gh4Gp8qcQ8kc6eiIbpRJy+ADxB+AAAAAAAAAAwDQYJKoZIhvcN
AQEFBQADQQAh+ePMZxgo0k+ET/SA46l/PZ6DX1mTLCvtj7jiCJkikLQOBz1tjvLK
SwNchgvsdNx7sgq+8T0G0n6FOMWU780n
-----END NEW CERTIFICATE REQUEST-----
```

Now that you have the certificate request available, you are ready to make the request for a certificate to a trusted certificate authority such as Verisign or Thawte. To make this request, go to the web site of whichever one of these authorities you'd like to obtain a certificate from (or another trusted root authority if desired).

Both Verisign and Thawte sites make it easy to obtain a web server SSL certificate. For Verisign, select the "Web Server Certificates" link on the homepage and for Thawte select the "SSL Certificates" link. Enrolling for a certificate is as simple as pasting in the entire CSR text into a submit box, selecting your server software, and hitting the submit button. Assuming the CA approves your certificate request, the certificate can be sent to you via e-mail or you can download it from the CA's web site.

Once you've received the certificate, open up the Internet Service Manager again, select the web site properties, and select the Directory Security tab. Click the Server Certificate button to see the following screen:

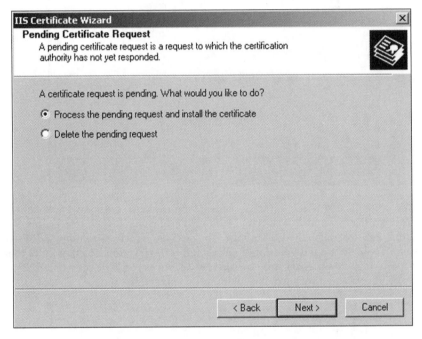

Select the first option (Process the pending request and install the certificate) and hit the Next button. If you decide against installing this certificate you can always select the Delete the pending request option. Assuming the first option is selected, the next screen will prompt you to enter the path to a .cer file. This will be the file that you received back from the Certificate Authority. Upon entering the file's path, hitting the Next button will result in a screen that displays all of the certificate information that you entered when you first used the certificate wizard to create the CSR file. After viewing this information, click the Finish button.

Once this process is completed, the certificate has been installed on the web server and can now be used to enable SSL either for the entire server or for one or more virtual directories. Since using SSL can result in a slower site, it is recommended that you only enable virtual directories that must secure data transmissions to and from the client. Doing this ensures that CPU cycles are not wasted for client requests that are not in need of encryption.

Enabling SSL for a virtual directory is as simple as right-clicking on the virtual name, choosing Properties, and then selecting the Directory Security tab. Since a certificate has been installed on the web server, you should see the following screen options:

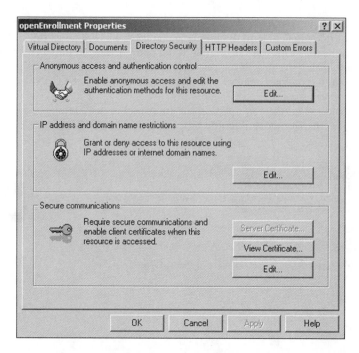

In the Secure communications section of the screen, you can click the View Certificate button to see all of the various fields that have been associated with the certificate. However, to enable SSL for this particular virtual directory click the Edit button. The next screen will allow you to SSL-enable the virtual directory and determine if you want to force 128-bit encryption. It's important to note that due to export restrictions, the 128-bit encryption option is available only within the United States and Canada. This policy is being evaluated by lawmakers and may change in the future.

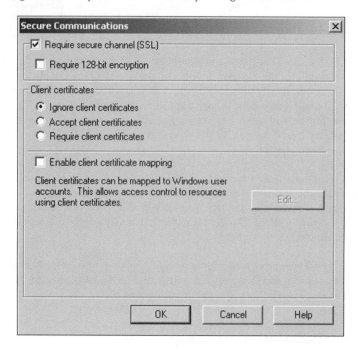

The next set of options allows you to determine whether or not client certificates are required. Choosing the Ignore option results in all client certificates going unnoticed by the web server. In applications that rely on identifying end users through the use of certificates, the Require or Accept options may be selected. Once the client certificate aspect has been decided upon, the client certificate mapping option can be evoked if desired. This option allows you to configure the web server to authenticate a user based on their client certificate. Clients with valid certificates can be matched up against a Windows user account in order to be able to inherit certain rights needed to use an application. By checking this option and then clicking the Edit button, you will see the following screen that allows for matching of a single certificate to a single user account, or multiple matching fields within the certificate to a single user account:

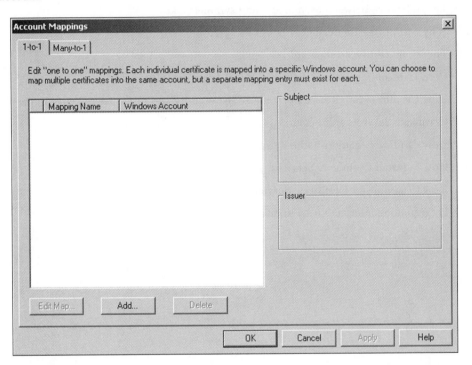

While account mappings will not be discussed in detail here, they do present an interesting alternative to user IDs and passwords and make a user's interaction with a server or application more seamless.

Although we've covered several different steps, you can see that enabling SSL on a web server is a rather trivial task once a few key points of the process are understood. Before ending this discussion, you may be wondering how this all integrates with Certificate Services. Although this example used an outside root CA to generate the certificate, the certificate generation could have been performed by a CA within the company. Why wasn't this done in the above scenario? The answer revolves around the trust and accessibility of the internal CA's certificate/public key. Employees using the Open Enrollment system from home may not have access to the certificate and public key created by a CA from within the company since this certificate will likely be used on an internal basis only. Because the Internet is involved in this application, it makes more sense to obtain a certificate from a trusted root CA like Verisign or Thawte since the CA's certificate (which includes the public key) is found in most popular browsers. If it was decided that the application should only be offered over the company intranet then the web-server certificate could be generated by an enterprise CA internal to the company, since the certificate containing the public-key for the CA would most likely be available throughout the company.

Summary

Certificate Services offers a robust set of features used to manage, issue, revoke, and renew digital certificates in the Windows DNA framework. Through using the services provided, the identities of clients and servers can be positively identified making the exchange of sensitive data safer and more secure.

In this chapter we learned about the following Certificate Services features:

❑ Public-key cryptosystems

❑ The difference between asymmetric and symmetric keys

❑ Why certificates are needed

❑ The X.509 certificate standard

❑ Certificate authorities and their role in certificate management

❑ How Certificate Services can provide added security and minimize reliance on passwords

❑ Certificate Services architecture

❑ How certificate requests and renewals work

❑ How to install Certificate Services

❑ How to administer Certificate Services

❑ Programming interfaces used to interact with Certificate Services

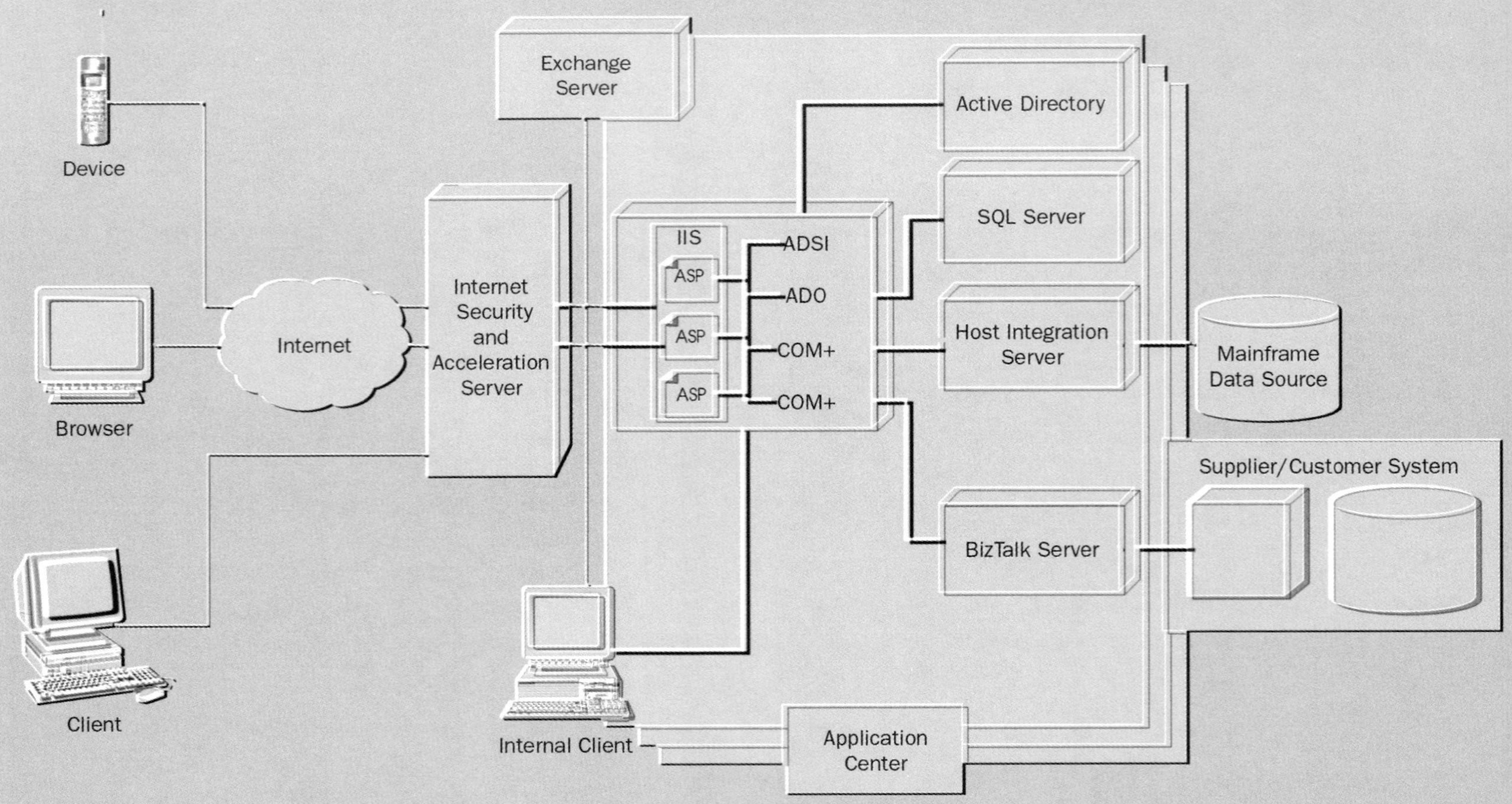
Device
Browser
Client
Internet
Internet Security and Acceleration Server
Exchange Server
IIS
ASP
ASP
ASP
ADSI
ADO
COM+
COM+
Active Directory
SQL Server
Host Integration Server
BizTalk Server
Mainframe Data Source
Supplier/Customer System
Internal Client
Application Center

22
Debugging DNA Applications

DNA applications can be very challenging to debug. This is especially true when a problem occurs in production that can't be reproduced in the development environment or in the QA environment. We often don't have access to the same set of tools we would have in the development environment.

In this chapter, we'll not only examine the development tools available for debugging our Windows DNA applications, but we'll also take a look at how to debug certain scenarios and the tools we can use to do that.

In particular, we'll be looking at:

❑ Debugging COM+ components in Visual Basic

❑ Debugging COM+ components in Visual C++

❑ Using symbol files

❑ Windows 2000 debugging tools

And we'll be discussing how to go about tracking down:

❑ Memory leaks

❑ Access violations

❑ Memory corruption

❑ High CPU utilization

But we'll start with some general guidelines that you should always bear in mind.

The Four Simple Rules

John Robbins, the author of Debugging Applications and of the BugSlayer column in MSDN Magazine, described his four simple rules for effectively debugging applications in his Bugslayer column in the April 1998 issue of MSJ:

- ❑ **Always build both release and debug executables with full program database (PDB) debug symbols.** As you'll see, debug symbols are almost mandatory for debugging difficult problems, especially when they only occur in production. We'll discuss how to create PDB files for Visual Basic and Visual C++ projects later in the chapter.

- ❑ **Always save a copy of all binaries and their PDB files that leave your desktop.** The binaries that are released to QA and/or the end user are just as important as the source code itself. Get into the habit of checking the binaries and their matching PDB files into a source code repository in conjunction with the source code.

- ❑ **Always rebase DLLs and OCXs so they load in unique address spaces.** If two DLLs that have the same base address are loaded in the same process space, the operating system loads one into a different place in memory, and recalculates addresses used to access another portion of the code. If the relocated DLL crashes, there is virtually no way to tell which DLL crashed. We'll discuss how to determine and set the base address for a DLL later in the chapter.

- ❑ **Always try to obtain the maximum amount of information about the crash.** Data surrounding the crash is often the best source of information for isolating the root cause of the crash. Some potential sources of information are the Event Log, error information (error number, description, and source), what the user was doing at the time of the crash, etc.

In this chapter, we'll demonstrate how to use certain tools and techniques for debugging Windows DNA applications. In the first section, we'll review the use of the Visual Basic and Visual C++ debuggers. If using these debuggers is old hat, please feel free to skip these sections. We'll then explore some specialized tools that can be used in addition to the debugger.

Debugging COM+ Components in Visual Basic 6.0

Visual Basic offers the ability to host the component within the debugger.

The debugger is launched by selecting Run | Start from the menu bar, or by pressing the Start button on the toolbar. Once the debugger is running, a client can create an instance of the component.

We can optionally specify the particular client to be launched when the debugger is started from the Debugging tab of the Project Properties dialog box:

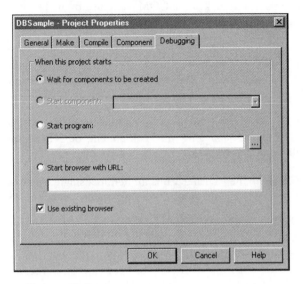

which gives us the following options:

❑ If Wait for component to be created is selected, the debugger will wait for a client to be launched

❑ If you want an executable to be launched whenever the debugger is started, select Start program, and enter the executable to be launched in the text box

❑ If you want a Web page to be launched when the debugger is started, select Start browser with URL, and enter the URL of the page to be launched in the text box

When the debugger is launched, VB modifies the registry settings for the component. If the component has not yet been registered, then VB will register the component's ProgID(s) and map the ProgID(s) to corresponding CLSID(s). For each CLSID entry, VB will add the appropriate registry settings so that the InProcServer32 parameter is set to point to the VB debug proxy (VB6DEBUG.DLL) – this is generally located in the \Microsoft Visual Studio\VB98\ directory.

When the client requests a new instance of the component, the VB debug proxy will communicate with the VB debugger for the actual implementation of the component.

Debugging COM+ Applications in VB

The VB debugger also has the capability to debug components that execute within the context of a valid COM+ Object Context. This allows developers to debug VB components that require the services provided by COM+, such as transactional support, COM+ Events, etc.

You can configure a VB class to run under a COM+ Object Context by either setting the MTSTransactionMode property to something other than 0 – NotAnMTSObject, or by compiling the project and installing the component into a COM+ application before invoking the debugger (see Chapter 8 for more information about the MTSTransactionMode property).

If the component is not installed in a COM+ application, then it will receive transactional support as specified by the MTSTransactionMode property. However, if the COM+ component is installed in a COM+ application, then the properties of the COM+ application will be used to configure the component's Object Context.

For example, if the VB class being debugged had its MTSTransactionMode property set to 1 – NoTransactions, but the class was configured in COM+ to require transactions, the MTSTransactionMode property would be ignored, and the component would get created in the context of a transaction.

Support for debugging VB components within a valid Object Context has been available since MTS 2.0 running on NT 4.0 SP4. If you're debugging MTS components on NT 4.0, there are some limitations that have since been eliminated in COM+:

❑   Debugging MTS components using VB is limited to a single client calling a single component. In COM+, a client can call any number of components contained within a VB Group project.

❑   You should not set breakpoints in an MTS component's Class_Initialize and Class_Terminate events. This is no longer a limitation in COM+.

❑   If your MTS component implements IObjectControl, you cannot put breakpoints into the IObjectControl_Activate, IObjectControl_Deactivate, and IObjectControl_CanBePooled methods. This is no longer a limitation in COM+.

For additional information, see article Q170156, INFO: VB 6.0 Readme Part 12: Transaction Server (MTS) Issues *at* http://support.microsoft.com/support/kb/articles/ Q170/1/56.ASP, *and* COM+ Visual Basic Debugging Support Contrasted with MTS *in MSDN, at* http://msdn.microsoft.com/library/psdk/cossdk/ pgwritingcomponents_debugging_38mr.htm.

Limitations of the VB Debugger

There are some limitations when debugging components within the VB debugger. We'll discuss what these limitations are, and then we'll discuss one possible way to overcome them.

First, the VB debugger resides within the same process as the component that is being debugged. If the component crashes, then the debugger crashes as well.

Second, the VB debugger is only capable of debugging the P-Code (packed code) representation of the executable. Since most developers compile their components to native code, there is no way of debugging the actual image that will eventually run in production with the VB debugger.

Since VB 5.0, compiled executables can be generated from VB. However, VB 6.0 still does not offer a way to debug compiled executables within VB. The VB debugger is limited to debugging the interpreted P-Code (packed code) representation of the executable. Without the ability to debug executable code within VB, you cannot truly debug the executables actually being run in production.

The VB debugger can only debug COM+ components within the context of a Library application. Therefore, if a component resides within a COM+ Server application, and is configured with attributes that are not supported by Library applications, you won't be able to debug the component with the VB debugger.

For example, if you attempt to debug a component residing within a Server application configured to run under an identity other than the interactive user, you'll receive the following error message when you try to run the debugger:

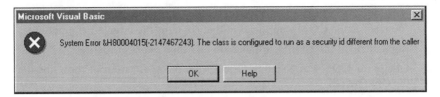

In these instances, we can use another debugger to debug the compiled VB component – as we'll see later in this chapter in the Debugging Components Compiled with Other Languages section.

Debugging COM+ Components within Visual C++ 6.0

Debugging COM+ components written in VC++ is fairly straightforward if the component resides within a COM+ Server application.

In the Project Settings, we need to configure the debugger to start an instance of the COM+ application, and then attach the debugger to the process. This can be done by performing the following steps:

❑   Open the VC++ project containing the component.

❑   Open the Project Settings dialog box by selecting the Project menu bar option, and then Settings.

❑   Under the Debug tab, enter the full path to the dllhost.exe file residing in the system32 directory into the Executable for debug session text box:

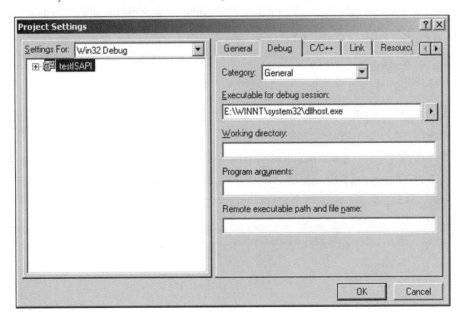

❑ Enter /*ProcessID*:{*AppID*} (without the double quotes) into the **Program arguments** text box and press **OK**. The *AppID* is the GUID of the COM+ application obtained from the Component Services MMC. You can find this through the following steps:

    ❑ Open the Component Services MMC.

    ❑ Navigate to the COM+ application that contains the targeted component.

    ❑ Right-click on the COM+ application and then select properties.

    ❑ Obtain the COM+ application GUID from the application's **Properties** dialog box, under the **General** tab.

❑ Set the appropriate breakpoints within the VC++ project.

❑ Ensure that the COM+ application is not running, by right-clicking on the COM+ application in the Component Services MMC, and selecting **Shut Down**.

❑ Start the VC++ debugger by pressing *F5*.

When debugging a C++ component that resides in a Library application, either manually attach the C++ debugger to the client process, or have the debugger launch the client process and then automatically attach to it.

You can manually attach the C++ debugger to the client process by selecting the **Build** menu bar option, then **Start Debug | Attach to Process**, and finally choosing the client's process from the dialog box.

Once the debug session is invoked, the VC++ debugger will launch the dll host for the COM+ application and attach the debugger to it.

Debugging Components Compiled by Other Languages

The VC++ debugger can also be used to debug components compiled by other languages, such as VB. Earlier in the chapter, we discussed situations where this technique would come in handy. The one requirement is that the component DLL must have a corresponding debug symbols file (more on these in a moment). For best results, the component DLL should be compiled without optimization.

Perform the following steps to debug a compiled COM+ component DLL:

❑ Open VC++.

❑ Select **File | Open Workspace**.

❑ In the **Open Workspace** dialog box, select **All Files (*.*)** in the **Files of type** drop down box.

❑ Select the targeted DLL and then click the **Open** button.

❑ Open the corresponding source code files by selecting **File | Open**.

❑ Follow the instructions in the previous section depending on whether the component resides in a COM+ Library or Server application.

Symbol Files

At the very minimum, every executable that leaves a developer's workstation should be accompanied by its corresponding **symbol file**. Symbol files provide a mapping between functions and their space in memory. They also provide variable names. Symbol files play an important role when debugging your application.

The two most common file types for symbol files are PDB and DBG:

❑ **PDB** (**program database**) is the de facto format for Visual Studio compilers. Both the Visual Basic compiler and the Visual C++ compiler generate PDB files by default. The debug information contained within a PDB file is in a binary format that is proprietary to Microsoft.

❑ On the other hand, the **DBG** (**debug**) format is a container for various types of debug information.

We'll look at each of these in more detail.

PDB Format

The PDB file format is a proprietary format developed by Microsoft that was first introduced with Visual C++ version 1.0. One of the advantages of the PDB format is that it allows incremental linking of debug versions of programs. One of the disadvantages is that Microsoft enhances the format quite often – there's no guarantee that today's debug tools will work with PDB files generated by a previous version of the compiler.

Generating PDB Files from Visual C++

Two steps are required in order to generate a PDB file for a Visual C++ project: have the compiler put debug information into the OBJ files, and have the linker generate the PDB file. In order to accomplish this, you'll need to modify two project settings.

First, open up the Project Settings dialog and select Win32 Release. Select the C/C++ tab, and set Debug Info to Program Databases. This setting will add the /Zi switch to the compiler options:

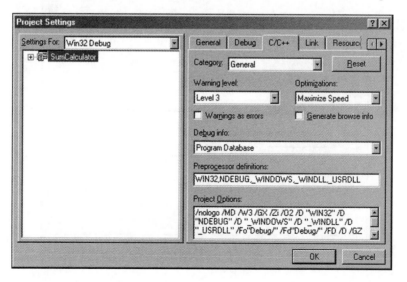

Next, select the Link tab and check the Generate debug info option. This setting will add the /DEBUG switch to the linker options:

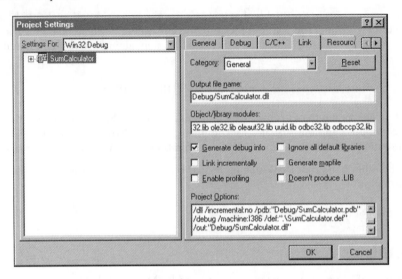

Finally, it's recommended that you manually add the /OPT:REF switch to the linker options. The /DEBUG switch instructs the linker to include all functions within the executable, whether they are needed or not. This will result in executables that are larger than necessary. The /OPT:REF switch reverses this side effect, by instructing the linker to include only the functions that are directly called by your program.

Generating PDB Files from Visual Basic

A PDB file can be generated for Visual Basic projects by opening up the Project Properties dialog box, and checking the Create Symbolic Debug Info option in the Compile options tab:

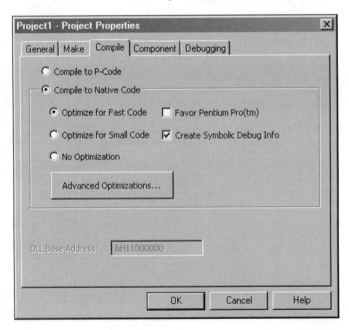

DBG Format

The DBG format is not a format for debugging information – it's a binary specification for a container that holds debugging information. DBG files often contain more than one type of debug information.

Some of the more common types of information they contain include COFF, FPO, and CodeView. The COFF format originated from Unix System V, whereas Microsoft created the CodeView format, so it should be no surprise that most Microsoft tools, such as Visual Studio and WinDBG, consume the CodeView information contained in the DBG files.

For more information on the COFF format, refer to the technical specification (`http://msdn.microsoft.com/library/specs/msdn_pecoff.htm`).

The WinDBG debugger is a graphical tool that we can use to debug Win32-based applications – we'll discuss it in more detail later in the chapter. The WinDBG files are installed with the developer tools included with the Platform SDK, and the latest version is also available for download on `http://msdn.microsoft.com/developer/sdk/windbg.asp`.

You can verify which debug formats are supported by a particular DBG file by running the following command:

```
dumpbin /headers [DBG filename]
```

The `dumpbin.exe` file is located in the `\Microsoft Visual Studio\ VC98\Bin` directory – you may need to specify the full path name to `dumpbin`.

As well as having VC++ installed, you'll need the VC++ environmental variables set. Either check the relevant checkbox at install time, or run the `\Microsoft Visual Studio\VC98\Bin\VCVARS32.BAT` batch file in the same command window you execute `dumpbin` from.

For example, running the command above against `\MSSQL7\Binn\ums.dbg` will give output including the following. Notice that the COFF, FPO, and CodeView (cv) formats are contained within the DBG file:

Type	Size	RVA	Pointer	
cv	44	00000000	E80	Format: NB10, 364bed47, 10, c:\mssql7\binn\ums.pdb
Fpo	20	00000000	EC4	
Misc	110	00000000	EE4	Image Name: \\xbuild016\sql70b1\sphinx \ums\dll\x86\lego\ums.dll
Fixup	2148	00000000	FF4	
-> src	1BE8	00000000		

Generating DBG Files from VC++

Some debuggers, such as the Console Debugger (CDB), cannot read PDB files, in which case, it's necessary to create DBG files for your executables. A DBG file can optionally be generated from Visual C++.

First, open the Project Settings dialog box for the project you wish to create a DBG file for. Select the configuration you wish to create the DBG file for from the Settings For drop down box. Then select the C/C++ tab and set Debug info to Program Database:

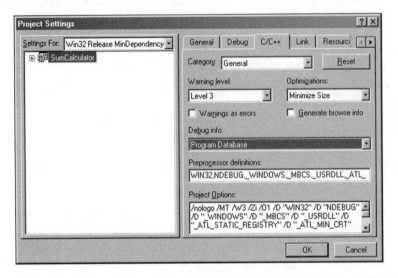

Next, select the Link tab. Select Debug from the Category drop down list, check the Debug info option, and select either the Both formats or COFF format radio buttons. This will add either the /debugtype:both or the /debugtype:coff switch to the linker options:

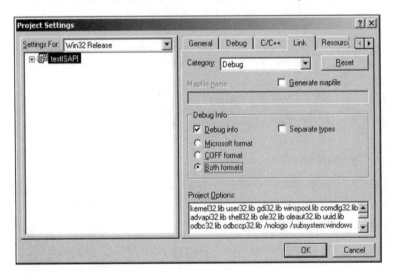

To create a DBG file for your application, follow the instructions above to configure the project to produce a PDB file. If you're only interested in producing a DBG file, modify the /PDB:"file name" switch to read /PDB:NONE before the project is compiled. Then select the Customize category, and uncheck the Use program database option:

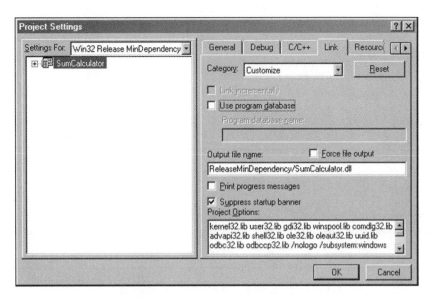

Next, build the executable file with debug information embedded in it. Open a command window and navigate to the directory containing the executable, ensuring that the Visual C++ environmental variables are set (if not, run `vcvars32.bat`). Then we need to attempt to obtain the images base address by executing the following command:

```
dumpbin /headers executable file name
```

The image base address can be found in the OPTIONAL HEADER VALUES section of the output, labeled image base. The default image base value for an executable is 0x400000 and for a DLL is 0x10000000. After obtaining the image base address, run the following command to strip the debug symbols from the executable and place them in a DBG file:

```
Rebase -b image base address -x . executable file name
```

For more information, see article Q216356 – INFO: Visual C++ Project Settings and .DBG File Creation *in MSDN at* `http://support.microsoft.com/support/kb /articles/Q216/3/56.ASP`.

Installing Windows 2000 Symbols

In addition to the symbol files for your Windows DNA application, it's often very helpful to install the symbol files for Windows 2000.

The symbol files for Windows 2000 are located on CD 2 labeled Windows 2000 Customer Support Diagnostics Tools. Insert the CD into the target machine and follow the instructions within the browser window launched by auto run.

The full set of symbol files can consume over 450 megs of hard drive space. If you're short on disk space, just copy symbols\dll and the idw directories. If disk space is real tight, then copy the symbol files for the following DLLs:

- ❑ kernel32
- ❑ ntdll
- ❑ rpcrt4
- ❑ advapi32
- ❑ user32
- ❑ netapi32

The symbol files for Windows 2000, as well as earlier versions of NT and commonly used component object modes, can also be downloaded from Microsoft. The following lists the URLs where the most commonly used symbol files may be obtained:

Windows 2000	http://www.microsoft.com/Windows2000/downloads/otherdownloads/symbols/download.asp
Windows NT 4 Service Pack 6a (40-bit)	http://www.microsoft.com/ntserver/nts/downloads/recommended/SP6/debug/x86DLType.asp (~54 mb)
Service Pack 6a (128-bit):	http://www.microsoft.com/ntserver/nts/downloads/recommended/SP6/debug/128bitx86/download.asp (~54 mb)
Windows NT 4 Service Pack 5 (40-bit)	http://www.microsoft.com/ntserver/nts/downloads/recommended/sp5/debug/x86Lang.asp (~54 mb)
Windows NT 4 Service Pack 5 (128-bit)	http://www.microsoft.com/ntserver/nts/downloads/recommended/sp5/debug/128bitx86 (~54 mb)
Windows NT 4 Service Pack 4 (40-bit)	http://download.microsoft.com/msdownload/sp4/x86/en/Sp4symi.exe (~33 mb)
Windows NT 4 Service Pack 4 (128-bit)	http://support.microsoft.com/support/ntserver/content/servicepacks/128SP4.asp
Windows NT 4 Service Pack 3 (40-bit)	ftp://ftp.microsoft.com/bussys/winnt/winnt-public/fixes/usa/nt40/ussp3/i386/Nt4sym3i.exe (~20 mb)
Windows NT 4 Service Pack 3 (128-bit)	http://support.microsoft.com/support/ntserver/content/servicepacks/SP3.asp

NT Option Pack	ftp://ftp.microsoft.com/bussys/IIS/iis-public/iis40/symbols/x86/symbols.cab (~64 MB)
	ftp://ftp.microsoft.com/bussys/IIS/iis-public/iis40/symbols/x86/install.inf
	ftp://ftp.microsoft.com/bussys/IIS/iis-public/iis40/symbols/x86/install.exe
NT Option QFE Update	ftp://ftp.microsoft.com/bussys/IIS/iis-public/fixes/usa/IISUPD/SYMBOLS/x86/IISUpdis.exe
MDAC 2.1 SP2	ftp://ftp.Microsoft.com/developr/mdac/unsup-ed/da212syi.exe
MDAC 2.1 SP1	ftp://ftp.Microsoft.com/developr/mdac/unsup-ed/da211syi.exe

Please refer to the following articles for additional information:

Q221191 – How to Install/Extract Symbols for Windows NT 4.0,
http://support.microsoft.com/support/kb/articles/Q221/1/91.ASP

Q148659 – How to Set Up Windows NT Debug Symbols,
http://support.microsoft.com/support/kb/articles/Q148/6/59.ASP

Rebasing In-Process Components

All in-process components, such as DLLs and OCXs, are compiled for a particular base address. If the address space is not available, the operating system will load the component in a virtual memory location that is free – the components will be **rebased**. The problem is, if the rebased component crashes, it's virtually impossible to tell which component crashed.

There are other reasons for ensuring that each in-process component is loaded at its base address. One reason is that rebasing can significantly slow the process of loading the in-process component. The operating system must read through the relocation section of the component, and modify the offset for any addresses that reference other parts of the component. Another reason is that rebased components cannot be shared across multiple processes. Whereas, code pages for in-process components that are loaded at their base address can be shared among multiple processes.

We'll discuss two different ways to set the base address of your components.

The first is with the Rebase tool, which ships with the Platform SDK and Visual Studio. The following command sets the base address of TestComponent.dll to 0x68000000.

```
rebase -b 0x68000000 TestComponent.dll
```

The other option is to set the base address at link time:

❑ For C++, add the /BASE linker option to the Project Options located on the Link tab in the Project Settings dialog box.

❑ For VB projects, set the base address in the Project Properties dialog box, on the Compile tab:

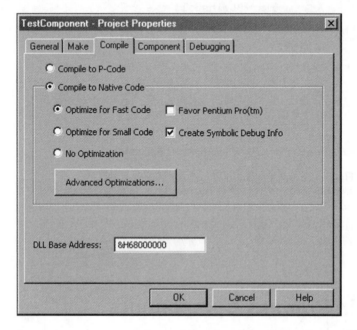

The rebase documentation suggests using a base address based on the first letter of the component name, as follows:

First Letter	Base Address
A – C	0x60000000
D – F	0x61000000
G – I	0x62000000
J – L	0x63000000
M – O	0x64000000
P – R	0x65000000
S – U	0x66000000
V – X	0x67000000
Y – Z	0x68000000

Choosing an address in the range 0x60000000 to 0x68000000 ensures that you avoid the clashes with the system DLLs.

Windows 2000 Debugging Tools

Windows 2000 ships with a variety of debugging tools that can be utilized to diagnose problems with DNA applications. The debugging tools can be installed from the Windows 2000 CD 2, labeled Windows 2000 Customer Support Diagnostics Tools.

The installation program will install a whole host of tools, but we'll be focusing on the following subset:

❑   Exception Monitor

❑   Windows Debugger (WinDBG)

❑   Dump Heap (DH)

To demonstrate how you might want to use these tools, we'll look at some common scenarios. First, memory leaks.

Memory Leaks

> **A memory leak occurs when memory is allocated by the system and is never freed, leading to loss of performance.**

The memory will be freed when a process ends, so this is really only a problem for processes that run for a long time, gradually eating more and more memory. Memory leaks are not normally a problem in VB – since you don't manage your memory manually in VB.

Memory leaks are often very difficult to track down, especially in DNA applications that are made up of many different components – COM+ components, ASP, MDAC, IIS, etc.

We're going to proceed through an example scenario on how to isolate the source of a memory leak. By no means are we presenting a failsafe process for detecting memory leaks. We're merely suggesting one scenario where the root cause of the memory leak is discovered, and discussing some tools that may help.

The process we're going to follow is to:

❑   Identify the process where the memory leak is occurring

❑   Minimize the code that is executing within the process

❑   Identify the cause of the memory leak within the isolated code

We need a culprit, so we'll create a COM object that exposes a method that has a deliberate memory leak. The following code snippet shows the LeakMemory method of the TestDebug2.CMisbehave class:

```
STDMETHODIMP CMisbehave::LeakMemory(long lSizeInK)
{
   malloc(lSizeInK * 1024);

   return S_OK;
}
```

We'll call the `LeakMemory` method from an ASP, `LeakMemory.asp`, and then display a message to the browser when we've done so:

```
<%
Set objX = CreateObject("TestDebug2.CMisbehave")

objX.LeakMemory 10000
%>

Just leaked 10000k of memory ...
```

Step 1 – Identify the Offending Process

When a memory leak is detected, it's important to isolate the process where the memory leak is occurring. This is not necessarily the process that reports an out-of-memory error.

One tool that can be leveraged to help determine the process where the memory leak is occurring is Performance Monitor.

Performance Monitor

Performance Monitor (PerfMon) is an MMC snap-in that can be used to monitor performance counters exposed by the operating system, applications, services, etc. PerfMon is installed by default on Windows 2000, and is launched by clicking Start | Programs | Administrative Tools | Performance (or via the Control Panel in Windows 2000 Professional).

In this section, we're going to walk through an example where we use PerfMon to find the offending process by monitoring the memory that has been allocated to each process.

First, we install the `LeakMemory.asp` file in an IIS virtual directory called `Debugging`, and register the `TestDebug2` component as an ordinary COM object using `regsvr32`. Since the default configuration for a virtual directory is to run in a shared surrogate process (`dllhost.exe`), we need to execute an ASP on the default web site in order to have IIS create the instance of `dllhost.exe` that contains the shared ASP worker thread pool.

The next step is to configure PerfMon to monitor the virtual memory that has been allocated for each process. First, we need to modify the chart's scale. To do that, press the Properties button (in the far right on the right-hand pane) to open the System Monitor Properties dialog box, and then select the Graph tab. Set the maximum vertical scale to 1000 and then press the OK button:

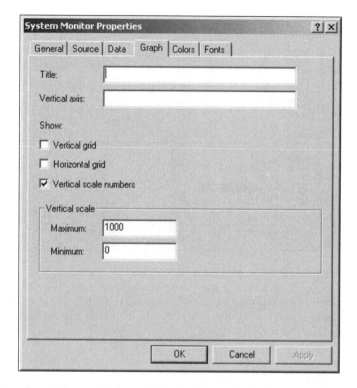

We can also optionally set the update interval in the General tab. Increasing the update interval is very useful for graphing longer trends:

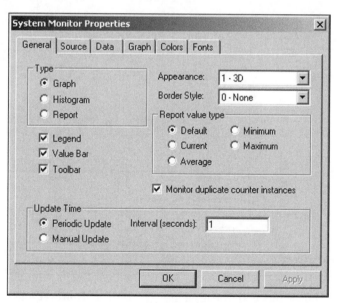

Next, we'll add the virtual memory counters for all processes to the graph. In the PerfMon MMC, click the plus sign button to add counters to the graph. For the Performance object, select Process, then select the Virtual Bytes counter. Finally, select the All instances radio button:

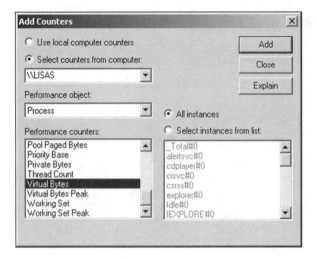

Unfortunately only one counter per executable name is added. Therefore, you'll have to open the **Add Counters** dialog box again and manually add the remaining processes. The processes created from the same image name will be appended with a pound sign and then a number. For example if there were two processes running `dllhost.exe`, you would have to manually add the virtual memory counter for the `dllhost#1` process.

Now that we have PerfMon set up, we'll load the `LeakMemory.asp` and hit refresh a couple of times to simulate user load. This produces the following result:

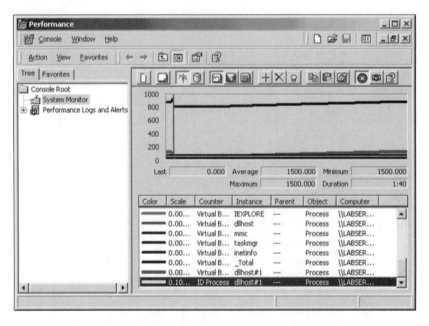

The line at the top of the graph corresponds to the **_Total** value. However, there's also one process that stands out above the rest at the bottom of the graph, so in this case, it's clear what process contains the memory leak – `dllhost#1`.

Unfortunately since there are multiple `dllhost.exe` processes running, we need to figure out the process ID for the one that's actually creating the memory leak. One way of accomplishing this is to add the process' ID Process counter to the graph. As we can see in the screen shot above, the process ID is 1500 (as listed in the Average, Maximum, and Minimum boxes).

> *For additional information see article* Q130926 – Using Performance Monitor To Identify A Pool Leak, `http://support.microsoft.com/support/kb/articles/Q130/9/26.ASP`.

Next, we need to identify the owner and purpose of a `dllhost.exe` process. In general, we should be able to do this by navigating through its open handles.

HandleEx

HandleEx is a very handy utility available for free from SysInternals (`http://www.sysinternals.com`). HandleEx shows the handles that are open in a process.

The following screen shot shows us that in the case of process ID 1500, it's an ASP worker thread pool process, since it has an open file handle to the `asp.dll` and the Debugging web application's virtual directory (`C:\Debugging\ASP`). We can also see that the process has the `TestDebug2` component loaded as well, which should be no surprise:

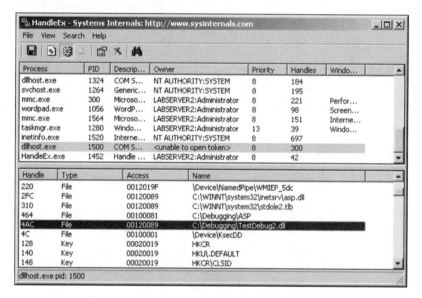

Step 2 – Minimize Code Executing in Offending Process

Now that we've identified the offending process, we need to narrow the source of the memory leak down to a particular object. This is especially true since the process we identified is the shared ASP thread pool for all Web applications residing under the default Web site. We now need to identify which application contains this component.

We can leverage the process isolation features of IIS to identify the problem application. IIS 5.0 offers three different process isolation levels for web applications – low, medium, and high:

❑   Low means that the ASPs execute within the same process space as IIS

❑   The default setting, medium means that all ASPs execute within a separate process from IIS, which is shared among all other web applications that are set at medium

❑   High means that the ASPs for that particular Web application will execute in their own process space

In order to identify the web application that has the memory leak, we should configure the process isolation level for all web applications in the default web site to high. We can then execute step 1 and monitor each one of the `dllhost.exe` files for each web application.

Now that we've narrowed the memory leak down to the `Debugging` web application, we need to identify the component that is causing the memory leak. In general, you should suspect components that are written in C/C++, VB components that load DLLs using the `Declare` statement, and third-party components.

Utilize the process isolation features of COM+ to narrow down memory leaks occurring in COM/COM+ components. We can install each COM/COM+ component utilized within the web application into its own COM+ Server application. Then we can monitor the `dllhost.exe` process for the web application and the `dllhost.exe` processes for each of the COM+ applications.

Step 3 – Identify the Root Cause

Once we've isolated the component that's causing the memory leak, we need to identify the root cause of the leak within the component. One utility that we can use to do this is Dump Heap (DH)

Dump Heap (DH)

DH is used to obtain stack traces of memory that has been allocated to a process but has not yet been freed. DHCMP is used to report the differences in memory allocations between two DH outputs. Both `DH.exe` and `DHCMP.exe` can be obtained from `diag.cab` file on the Windows 2000 Resource Kit CD.

Before DH can be used, we must set a couple of global flags. The easiest way to set these flags is to use the Global Flags (`gflags.exe`) utility that installs with the debugging tools.

Launch the utility by clicking Start | Programs | Debugging Tools | Global Flags. Check the Create user mode stack trace DB and the Enable debugging of Win32 Subsystem options as shown below:

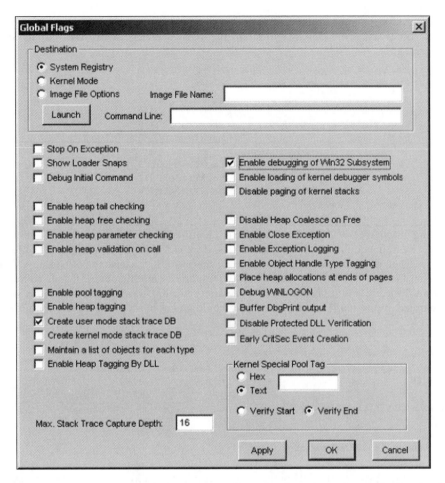

Once the changes have been applied, the system will need to be rebooted in order for the changes to take affect.

In addition, you should make sure you have the correct symbol files installed. The correct operating symbol files should be installed in the %systemroot%\symbols directory, or the _NT_SYMBOL_PATH environment variable should be set to point to the location where the correct symbol files are installed (see the Symbol Files section for more information). You should also install the symbol files for the application's executable, and all supporting DLLs. In the case of a web application hosted in IIS, this includes all COM/COM+ DLLs and ISAPI DLLs that are used by the web application.

Once the system is configured, you can run DH periodically against the targeted process to identify memory that has been allocated but not yet been freed. You can then run DHCMP against two of the DH output files to report the differences between the two.

Going back to our example, we can use HandleEx to identify the dllhost.exe process that is hosting our TestDebug2 component, and then run DH against it using the following command line:

```
DH -p [Targeted PID} -f 1.txt
```

After pressing refresh on our `LeakMemory.asp` a couple of times, we run DH again, outputting the results to `2.txt`. Finally, run DHCMP to report the deltas between the two DH outputs, saving the output to `cmp.txt`:

```
DHCMP -d 1.txt 2.txt > cmp.txt

The resulting output:
+ 20488480 ( 41238272 - 20749792)     BackTrace00000
+      152 (     152 -       0)        BackTrace00010

-      152 (       0 -     152)        BackTrace00008
-      176 (      88 -     264)        BackTrace36651
-      288 (     696 -     984)        BackTrace16554
Total increase == 20488016
```

The resulting output clearly shows a memory leak identified by `BackTrace00000`. The next step is to open up `2.txt` and examine the stack traces to see if we can identify the root cause. Unfortunately, `BackTrace00000` does not have stack traces associated with it, because the offending COM+ object has gone out of scope. To solve this issue, we can temporarily modify our ASP code so that all objects created from the `TestDebug2` component are session scoped. Unfortunately, this effort would be in vain if the object supported JIT, since the object would go out of scope after each method call:

```
<%
  If(IsEmpty(Session("objX"))) Then
    Set Session("objX") = CreateObject("TestDebug2.CMisbehave")
  End If

Session("objX").LeakMemory 10000
%>

Just leaked 10000k of memory ...
```

We then repeat the process: run DH outputting the results to `3.txt`, refresh `LeakMemory.asp` a couple of times, run DH again outputting the results to 4.txt, and finally run DHCMP against both DH outputs. The partial output of DHCMP is shown below:

```
+ 10244096 ( 20491088 - 10246992)     BackTrace44036
+      168 (  370368 -  370200)        BackTrace99999
+      120 (     120 -       0)        BackTrace03158

-       64 (   10616 -   10680)        BackTrace27462
-      288 (     288 -     576)        BackTrace06541
-      816 (  346464 -  347280)        BackTrace00000
Total increase == 10243216
```

As you can see, the memory leak is associated with `BackTrace44036` as opposed to `BackTrace00000`. We can now open `4.txt` and search for stack traces.

When searching the stack traces for memory leaks, it's often better to search the file from the bottom up, since there may be quite a few valid memory allocations that occurred when the executable was first invoked. For instance, COM+ will perform valid memory allocations when it creates the object's environment. This includes initializing marshalling, security, loading the actual component DLL, etc.

Tracking down the source of the memory leak in our "loaded example" was rather easy. Below is the very last entry in 4.txt:

```
0138a000 bytes in 0002 allocations (@ 9c5000) by: BackTrace44036
        MSVCRT!_heap_alloc+0xed
        MSVCRT!_nh_malloc+0x10
        ntdll!LdrpRunInitializeRoutines+0x1df
        ntdll!LdrpLoadDll+0x2dd
        ntdll!LdrLoadDll+0x17
        ole32!CClassCache__CDllPathEntry__LoadDll+0x6a
        ole32!CClassCache__CDllPathEntry__Create_rl+0x35
        ole32!CClassCache__CClassEntry__CreateDllClassEntry_rl+0xbe
        ole32!CClassCache__GetClassObjectActivator+0x18c
        ole32!CClassCache__GetClassObject+0x21
        ole32!CCGetClassObject+0x17
        ole32!CStdMarshal__GetPSFactory+0xbe
        ole32!CStdMarshal__CreateStub+0x95
        ole32!CStdMarshal__ConnectSrvIPIDEntry+0x24
        ole32!CStdMarshal__MarshalIPID+0x7b
        ole32!CStdMarshal__MarshalObjRef+0xb4
        ole32!CStdMarshal__MarshalInterface+0x80
        ole32!StdMarshalObject+0x66
        ole32!CDestObjectWrapper__MarshalInterface+0x140
        COMSVCS!CCtxtCntrlMarshal__MarshalInterface+0x63
        ole32!ActivationPropertiesOut__OutSerializer__GetSize+0x10f
        ole32!ActivationProperties__GetSize+0x9c
        ole32!ActivationProperties__GetMarshalSizeMax+0xa3
        ole32!CDestObjectWrapper__MarshalInterface+0xa3
        COMSVCS!CCtxtCntrlMarshal__MarshalInterface+0x63
        ole32!DoServerContextCCI+0x3b
        ole32!EnterForCallback+0x6d
        ole32!SwitchForCallback+0xe8
        ole32!PerformCallback+0x50
```

A large block of memory was allocated via malloc(). This discovery should prompt us to search through our code and look for calls to malloc() that do not have an associated call to free().

As you can see, the stack trace does not give us any obvious clues as to where in the method call the memory leak occurred, let alone the parameters that were passed. Therefore, if your component's code base is large, you might want to consider using some of the third-party tools available on the market that can aid in this. These include NuMega's BoundsChecker (www.numega.com) and Purify from Rational (http://www.rational.com). However, discussion of the use of these utilities is outside the scope of this book.

711

Access Violations

> **An access violation occurs when you attempt to read from or write to a protected place in memory.**

One of the more common times an access violation occurs is when an invalid pointer is referenced. For this reason, Windows 2000 intentionally does not give developers access to the lower and upper portions of memory, in an effort to trap invalid pointer references.

For a 2 GB user process address space, the protected areas of virtual memory are 0x00000000 through 0x0000FFFF, and 0x7FFE1000 through 0x7FFFFFFF. Any attempts to access these regions of memory will result in an access violation. A memory access violation will also occur if any other page in virtual memory is protected.

An access violation will typically throw an exception, and if that exception is not trapped, then the application will fault.

For example, the VB code below:

```
Public Sub CauseAV()

    Dim strTemp As String
    GetProfileString strTemp, strTemp, strTemp, strTemp, 2

End Sub
```

creates a memory access violation similar to the following:

The instruction at "0x77e873dc" referenced memory at "0x00000000". The memory could not be "written".

In `CauseAV`, we are calling `GetProfileString` – a Win32 API function – and are passing it an invalid parameter. The declaration for `GetProfileString` is as follows:

```
Public Declare Function GetProfileString Lib "kernel32" _
        Alias "GetProfileStringA" (ByVal lpAppName As String, _
                            ByVal lpKeyName As String, _
                            ByVal lpDefault As String, _
                            ByVal lpReturnedString As String, _
                            ByVal nSize As Long) As Long
```

When a memory access violation occurs, examine the thread's call stack to locate the offending call. It's relatively trivial to obtain the call stack when using the VC++ debugger in the development environment. However, debugging access violations in the VB debugger presents a problem, since the debugger and the target application reside in the same process. When the access violation occurs, the process containing the VB debugger is terminated, because it resides in the same process as that in which the access violation occurs. That's why you should consider debugging both your VB and C++ components with the VC++ debugger.

However, other tools may be more appropriate if the problem needs to be debugged in the production environment.

Exception Monitor

The Exception Monitor is a very powerful diagnostic utility that can be used to debug complex problems. The Exception Monitor automates the use of WinDBG to obtain information on an exception that was thrown by the application, and provides a user-friendly interface to output results produced by WinDBG.

The Exception Monitor was originally called the IIS Exception Monitor, and was developed by Microsoft Product Support Services (PSS) to provide an easy-to-use means for technical support to debug IIS crashes. Version 7.0, which ships with Windows 2000, has been dramatically enhanced, and can be used for considerably more than trouble shooting IIS, hence the name change to Exception Monitor.

Exception Monitor automates the steps required to attach to a process and trap exceptions that occur on that process. The Exception Monitor can also be used to debug problems on servers running NT 4.0.

Step 1 – Preparation

We can use the Exception Monitor to identify the source of the memory access violation within the web application that calls our `TestDebug.CauseAV` method.

To get the most usable information from the Exception Monitor, you must install the debug symbols for the components that make up your DNA application. You should also install the symbols files for the targeted operating system. See the *Symbol Files* section of this chapter for more information.

We'll create a web application with its Application Protection property set to Medium (Pooled). Within the Web application, we'll create an ASP named `CauseAV.asp` that contains the following code:

```
<%
Set objX = CreateObject("TestDebug.CMisbehave")

objX.CauseAV
%>

Just caused AV ...
```

The first step is to ensure that the offending web application is running, and then to identify its process ID (we saw how to do this in the Identifying the Offending Process section earlier in the chapter). With process ID in hand, we're ready to fire up the Exception Monitor by pressing Start | Programs | Debugging Tools | Exception Monitor, and then the Exception Monitor icon.

Step 2 – Log Exception

The Exception Monitor presents us with a very simple Wizard UI. After pressing Next on the welcome screen to the Select Application State screen, we have the option to attach to a running application or service, or start a service. The Start Service that is not Currently Started option is invaluable if a service is failing during initialization.

See the Exception Monitor help file for more information about debugging a service.

Since we are debugging a web application, we'll select Attach to a Running Service/Application and press Next.

The Process Options screen allows you to select what type of service or application you would like to monitor:

❑ Select the Service radio button for debugging services, Web applications, and COM+ server applications

❑ Select the Other Application radio button to debug other types of applications, including those using in-process components such as COM objects or COM+ library applications

Since we are interested in debugging a web application, we'll select the Service radio button:

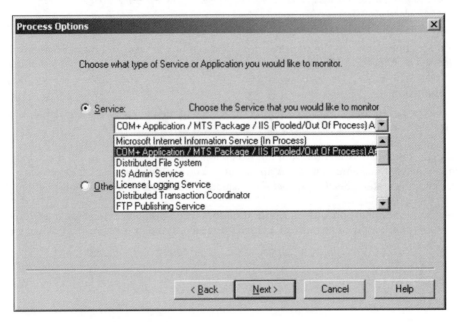

This gives us several more options:

❑ If the web application's Application Protection setting is set at Low, select Microsoft Internet Information Service (In Process) in the drop down box

❑ If the setting is either Medium or High, select COM+ Application / MTS Package / IIS (Pooled/Out Of Process) Applications

Since we set our targeted Web application Process Isolation setting to Medium (Pooled), we'll select COM+ Application / MTS Package / IIS (Pooled/Out Of Process) Applications: Then press the Next button to advance to the Select Out Of Process Application screen. Select the correct web application – based on the process ID we obtained during step 1 – and then press the Next button.

The Session Options screen allows you to configure how the debugging session will behave. Unless you're working with a Microsoft Support Engineer, you'll almost always select the Automatic radio button.

The Enable Recursive Mode checkbox is enabled only if a service is being debugged. Checking it instructs the Exception Monitor to restart the monitoring process once the service has been restarted.

We can also optionally select the Notify Admin option. This option will send remote notification when an exception is caught. The Exception Monitor can provide this notification via a NET SEND command or an e-mail:

❑ To enable notification via NET SEND, replace COMPUTER NAME with the name of the computer you wish to receive notification from.

❑ If the SMTP service is configured on the server, you can configure Exception Monitor to send an e-mail when an exception occurs with the debug log file (DBL) attached. Just replace COMPUTER NAME with the SMTP e-mail address of the recipient.

Finally, press Next to go to the Start Monitoring screen. Besides the Wizard navigation buttons, this screen has a single button labeled Run This Monitoring Session. Pressing it will launch the Exception Monitor VBScript file (em.vbs), which launches WinDBG, attaches to the targeted process, and performs a series of debug commands when an exception is caught.

Pressing Next moves us to the Session Status screen, which presents a list of Exception Monitor sessions and their current status. Our current WinDBG session will show an end time of Running.

We can then attempt to access CauseAV.asp. When the access violation is trapped by WinDBG, various information about the current state of the process will be caught, as well as information about your system. Once WinDBG terminates, hit the Refresh Status button to update the status of the current session.

Step 3 – Analyze the Log File

The Exception Monitor Log File Analyzer is used to analyze the log files that are generated from the Exception Monitor. The Exception Monitor Log File Analyzer can be accessed from either the Welcome screen, or the Session Status screen of the Exception Monitor. It can also be accessed by pressing Start | Programs | Debugging Tools | Exception Monitor and then the Exception Monitor Log File Analyzer icon.

Once the log file is loaded, we can click on the Fault Stack button to view the state of the application's stack when the crash occurred:

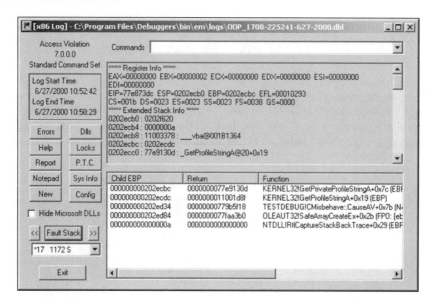

As you can see, the source of the problem is very apparent. The `CMisbehave.CauseAV` method called `GetProfileStringA` (the ANSI version of `GetProfileString`), which in turn called `GetPrivateProfileStringA`.

Memory Corruption

> **Memory corruption occurs when a program writes to memory other than what is owned by the targeted data structure.**

Unless caught at the time of the corruption, memory corruption bugs are very difficult to locate, since it may take some time before the corrupted memory causes a problem for the application.

For example, a corruption could occur during initialization of a COM object, but may not affect the object until many method calls later, when the data structure that was inadvertently overwritten is accessed. Memory corruption almost always results in a general protection fault. However, the code that generates the general protection fault is often far removed from the code that caused the memory corruption

The most common cause of memory corruption occurs when a program overwrites or underwrites the boundaries of a memory allocation. Let's take a look at a simple example. The following C++ code attempts to initialize an array, but loops one too many times, corrupting memory:

```
STDMETHODIMP CMisbehave::CorruptHeap()
{
    int *pArray;
    int nIndex;

    // Initialize.
    // Memory corruption will occur the 11th time the program
    // iterates through the loop.
    pArray = new int[10];
    for(nIndex=0; nIndex <= 10; nIndex++)
    {
     pArray[nIndex] = 0;
    }

    return S_OK;
}
```

In an effort to initialize an array of integers, we first allocate memory on the heap by calling the new operator. Then we iterate through the array, initializing all of its values to zero. Unfortunately, we iterate through our loop eleven times for an array that only contains ten integers. Therefore on the eleventh iteration, we overwrite memory that does not belong to the array. We'll use the `CorruptHeap.asp` page shown below to create an instance of the `CMisbehave` class, and then call its `CorruptHeap` method:

```
<%
Set objX = CreateObject("TestDebug2.CMisbehave")

objX.CorruptHeap
%>

Just corrupted heap ...
```

The chances are very high that the above code will execute without causing an immediate error, even though we overwrote memory that we were not supposed to. If the corrupted memory is not accessed by other code, and if the program terminates, we would never know there was a problem. However Murphy's Law will ensure that the memory corruption will cause a problem in the production environment.

Unfortunately, once the program fails due to a memory corruption, it's next to impossible to identify where the corruption occurred. The problem is that the source of the corruption is usually far removed from where the error was encountered. This is precisely why heap corruption is so difficult to track down. We need a means to identify memory corruption when it occurs.

PageHeap

The PageHeap utility is an invaluable tool for identifying the source of common memory corruption bugs. For example, PageHeap will help identify attempts to write off the end of data structures allocated on the heap, and attempts to write to memory on the heap that has already been freed.

Prior to Windows 2000, you were required to install a modified version of the `ntdll.dll` to utilize PageHeap. As of Windows 2000 SP1, PageHeap is now integrated with the operating system.

When enabled, PageHeap intercepts calls made to the heap management functions exported by `ntdll.dll`, such as `RtlAllocateHeap`, `RtlReAllocateHeap`, etc. This includes all heap related functions exported by the Visual C++ run-time (`new`, `malloc`, `realloc`, etc.) and the heap related Win32 functions exported by `kernel32.dll` (`HeapAlloc`, `HeapReAlloc`, `GlobalAlloc`, `LocalAlloc`, etc.).

When memory is allocated on the heap, PageHeap surrounds each allocation with a page of memory that is read/write protected. When memory allocated on the heap is freed, PageHeap will read/write protect the pages of memory that have recently been freed. When an executable attempts to access the protected pages, an access violation will be generated. The result is that an access violation occurs at the point in time where the offending executable attempts to write to one of the protected blocks of memory.

One of the side-effects of PageHeap is that your applications will consume more memory than normal, which can pose a problem when working with memory-intensive applications. To help with this issue, PageHeap offers an array of configuration options.

PageHeap supports two modes: Normal and Full. The primary difference between the two modes is when memory corruption problems are identified:

❑ Full will trap a wide array of memory corruption errors at the moment in which they occurred.

❑ Normal will trap all of the errors that are trapped by Full. However, some of the errors that would be immediately trapped by Full, are instead trapped when the memory block is freed.

Obviously, trapping errors when they occur allows the source of the error to be more easily identified. However, running PageHeap in Normal mode consumes considerably less memory than Full. Therefore, Normal mode is typically used to debug programs that consume large amounts of memory, where making use of Full is impractical.

Normal mode may also be used to isolate the program that is experiencing memory corruption errors. Once the program has been isolated, you can configure PageHeap to run the targeted program in Full mode.

PageHeap can be enabled for every process running on the system, a single executable, or a single DLL running within a particular executable. This can be configured using `pageheap.exe` or `gflags.exe`. Both of these utilities ship with Windows 2000 Application Compatibility Toolkit, which can be obtained from the Microsoft web site at `http://msdn.microsoft.com/compatibility`.

The following table lists some of the most common commands used to configure PageHeap:

`Gflags -r +hpa`	Enables PageHeap system wide. Requires a reboot before taking effect.
`Gflags -r -hpa`	Disables PageHeap system wide. Requires a reboot before taking effect.
`Pageheap [Program]`	Returns whether or not PageHeap is enabled for a particular program.
`Pageheap /enable [Program] /full`	Enables Full PageHeap for a particular program.
`Pageheap /enable [Program] /dlls [DLL1 DLL2 ...] /full`	Enables Full PageHeap only for the executables contained within the specified DLLs.
`Pageheap /disable [Program]`	Disables PageHeap for a particular executable.

PageHeap settings survive a reboot, therefore it's important to remember to disable the PageHeap settings once testing has concluded.

> *For more information on the command syntax type* `gflags /?` *and* `pageheap /?`.

Recall that when we called `CorruptHeap.asp`, an error was not produced. Since `CorruptHeap.asp` resides within a web application with its process isolation setting configured for Medium, the ASP and the `TestDebug2` component is executed within an instance of `dllhost.exe`. Therefore, we need to execute the following command to enable PageHeap for our web application:

```
pageheap /enable dllhost /full
```

We could alternatively target the component by executing the following command:

```
pageheap /enable dllhost /dlls TestDebug2.dll /full
```

PageHeap settings only take effect after the targeted program is loaded into memory. Therefore, we need to unload our Web application, which releases the targeted instance of `dllhost.exe` from memory.

Once PageHeap has been enabled, we can access `CorruptHeap.asp`. Now when the `CMisbehave.CorruptHeap` method is called, it produces an access violation, and an error message identifying `CorruptHeap` as the culprit is displayed within the web browser:

```
Microsoft VBScript runtime (0x800A01FB)
An exception occurred: 'objX.CorruptHeap'
/Debugging/CorruptHeap.asp, line 4
```

As you can see, PageHeap allowed us to easily locate the source of a memory corruption bug that could have otherwise been very difficult to track down.

It's worth considering leveraging PageHeap during all phases of testing in your Windows DNA applications.

High CPU Utilization

Bugs that cause abnormally high CPU utilization can quickly bring a DNA application to its knees. One of the most common causes of this type of bug is when application code enters into an endless loop.

For example, the following VB code will generate high CPU utilization:

```
Public Sub EndlessLoop()
    Do While True
        ' Do nothing.
    Loop
End Sub
```

`EndlessLoop` is a method exposed by our `TestDebug.CMisbehave` component. It will be called from an ASP page, `EndlessLoop.asp`, as follows:

```
Entering an endless loop ...
<%
Response.Flush

Set objX = CreateObject("TestDebug.CMisbehave")

objX.EndlessLoop
%>
```

Step 1 – Identify the Offending Process

The first step is to identify the process that is spiking the CPU utilization. We'll use Task Manager to accomplish this.

Open Task Manager by pressing *Ctrl*, *Alt*, *Delete* and then pressing the **Task Manager** button. Next select the **Processes** tab and click **CPU** to sort the processes by current CPU utilization. The Task Manager dialog box should look similar to the one below with the offending process at the top of the list:

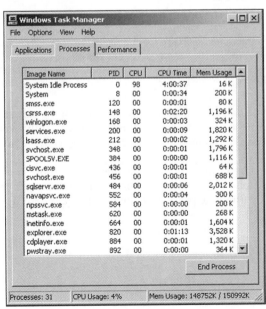

The offending process in our case will be the instance of DLLHOST executing our EndlessLoop.asp web page. We need to record the image name and the process id for use in step 2.

Step 2 – Identify Root Cause

In an effort to identify the root cause, we need to examine the stack traces for each of the threads within the offending process. Even though this can be accomplished using the Exception Monitor, it's more straightforward to use WinDBG directly.

In order to obtain current stack traces for each of the threads in the current process, we will attach WinDBG to the process. Open WinDBG by clicking the Start | Programs | Debugging Tools, and finally click the WinDBG Debugging icon. Attach to the offending process by selecting Debug on the menu bar, and then selecting Attach to a Process ... You will be presented with a dialog box listing the processes that are currently running, and their corresponding process ids in hex.

If there are multiple processes running with the same image name (which is generally the case when attaching to DLLHOST), then it's necessary to convert the process id obtained in step one to hexadecimal. One way to accomplish this is to use the calculator installed by default with Windows 2000. To launch the calculator, click Start | Programs | Accessories | Calculator. Set the View to Scientific, then enter the process id obtained in step one, and select the Hex radio button to convert the decimal process id to hex.

Once you have successfully attached to the offending process, you can display the call stack for each thread by entering ~*kb at the WinDBG command prompt. Obtain multiple stack traces over a period of time and look for threads that appear to be stuck executing the same method call.

In the case of EndlessLoop.asp, every time we outputted the stack trace for the threads, thread 20 was always the same. The stack trace for thread 20 is shown below:

```
20   1792 Running  9 0x7ffa6000
FramePtr          RetAddr          Param1            Param2
    Param3        Function Name
0000000001e2ed34  00000000779b5f18  00000000000bd9e8  0000000000000000
    000000000000000a  TESTDEBUG!CMisbehave::EndlessLoop+0x40
0000000001e2ed80  0000000077a7d2aa  0000000077b324fc  0000000001e2ed90
    0000000000000000  OLEAUT32!SafeArrayCreateEx+0x2b
0000000000000004  0000000000000000  0000000000000000  0000000000000000
    0000000000000000  OLE32!+0x4a
```

As long as the proper debug info is available, the last column in the call stack contains the function names currently being executed. As you can see, thread 20 is currently executing the EndlessLoop method of the CMisbehave class contained in the TestDebug component.

The technique we just described can also be used to identify the root cause for processes that are hung. In either case, it may be helpful when trying to identify the root cause, to minimize the code executing in the offending process, by using the process isolation techniques described in the Memory Leaks section.

Summary

The complexity of today's Windows DNA applications presents challenges when debugging. However, Visual Studio provides a powerful tool for debugging issues within the development environment, and there's a rich set of features provided by the individual debug environments within Visual Studio, including advanced breakpoints, watches, and call stack window.

Unfortunately, it's not always possible to reproduce bugs in the development environment that users are experiencing in the production environment. Therefore, it's sometimes necessary to isolate bugs within the production environment. However, this can be challenging, since operations typically don't allow development tools to be installed on production servers. We can overcome this limitation with a battery of tools specifically designed to be used in the production environment.

The tools we discussed here include:

- WinDBG
- Exception Monitor
- Dump Heap
- PageHeap

In this chapter, we discussed the use of these tools in the context of common debugging scenarios.

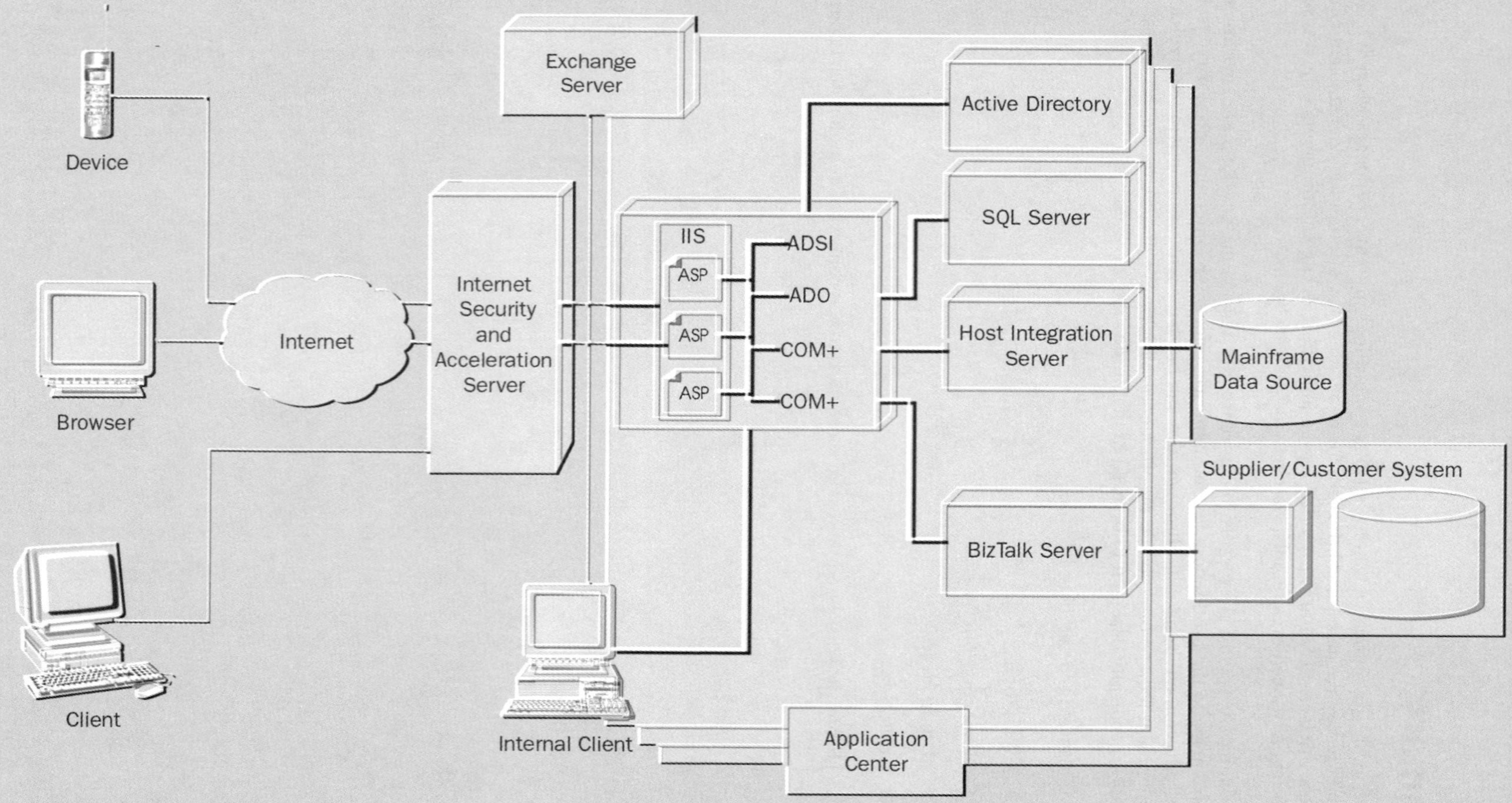
Device
Browser
Client
Internet
Internet Security and Acceleration Server
Exchange Server
IIS
ASP
ASP
ASP
ADSI
ADO
COM+
COM+
Active Directory
SQL Server
Host Integration Server
BizTalk Server
Mainframe Data Source
Supplier/Customer System
Internal Client
Application Center

23

A Sample DNA Application

In this book we've covered all the key parts of a successful Windows DNA application. While there's a lot to be said for covering each part in detail, it is also important to show how they all come together to create a great application. That's what this chapter is all about.

We're going to walk through the creation of a basic Windows DNA application. We will be building an n-tier application, and for this we will use the component that we created in chapter 6. Our n-tier application will demonstrate all the parts of an n-tier application:

❑ User presentation

❑ User interface processing

❑ Encapsulated business logic

❑ Encapsulated data access

❑ Data handling

The overall architecture and design of this application will follow good Windows DNA principles.

The presentation will be browser neutral, providing for the widest possible audience for the application. Our user interface code will run within IIS, and will be built using the Active Server Pages environment and VBScript.

All business logic, including validation, rule enforcement, and business processing, will be encapsulated within the set of COM objects created in chapter 6. These were written using Visual Basic.

> *At first glance it will appear that our COM business objects are stateful, since they have properties as well as methods. However, they are no more stateful than an ADO recordset – in that they'll maintain a set of data only for the duration of a page. Any long-term state must be managed by other means – cookies, the ASP* `Session` *object, a database, etc.*

Those same business objects will encapsulate our data access code as well. Data access technologies are constantly changing, so minimizing the amount of code that would be affected if ADO was to go the way of DAO or RDO is a good practice. Even if ADO is with us forever, there might well be changes in future versions that will affect your code – anyone who's had to make painful coding modifications due to changes in each previous release of ADO is not likely to forget that. Likewise, it's always advisable to minimize the impact of changing the underlying database – such as a change from a simple JET database to SQL Server or Oracle – or the impact of underlying data structure changes.

In our case, the data access technology will be ADO and OLE DB (version 2.5), with the database itself being SQL Server 7. This combination is very widely used and accessible, and can be easily adapted to different environments if required.

All the data processing, including creating, reading, updating, and deleting data, will be handled by stored procedures in the database. The use of stored procedures is important for performance, since stored procedures are precompiled and optimized within the database – as compared to dynamic SQL from our middle-tier code, which would have to be evaluated by the database server each time it is used.

It's worth noting that heavy use of stored procedures can reduce an application's portability – since if we change the underlying database, we're required to rewrite all the stored procedures. However, in this application we'll avoid putting complex logic into the stored procedures – instead we'll use them to optimize retrieving and updating data. It's in this capacity that stored procedures provide us with optimum performance gains, while minimizing the impact of database changes by avoiding complex SQL coding.

In this chapter, we'll put together a very basic Windows DNA application, avoiding the use of more technologies such as queuing, BizTalk, and so on.

Let's take a look at this application in more detail.

Sample Application Overview

Building an entire application within a single chapter, and making it illustrate all the critical components of the Windows DNA architecture, is challenging. To achieve this goal, our application will be quite straightforward, avoiding some complex issues such as using a separate application server from the web server, using XML for backend data access, queued messaging, etc. These topics are covered later in this book as appropriate.

The application will be a basic contact management system. We'll allow the user to list, view, add, edit and remove contacts. While this is nothing fancy, it's complex enough that we'll be able to create a series of pages for presentation, some UI logic for navigation, and some simple business logic and data validation.

This application should provide a good model on which more complex applications can be built. The focus of our effort is to illustrate the creation of a highly scalable, easily maintainable Windows DNA application.

User Interface and Presentation

Windows DNA applications support many different forms of presentation. These range from specialized devices such as cell phones, through hand-held devices, browsers, and the rich Windows operating system itself.

A large part of the reason Windows DNA can support so many forms of presentation is that the user interface (UI) code is viewed as a separate thing from the presentation itself. The UI code typically runs on a web server, not even on the same machine or device that is handling the presentation.

Note that we are distinguishing here between *presentation* and *UI code*. These are often viewed as the same thing – and they often are the same thing in a traditional client-server environment. In the Windows DNA environment, however, it's valuable to view them as separate concepts:

❑   The **presentation** is the actual display that is presented to the user and collects the user's input. In many cases there is little or no code or processing present on the device that handles presentation – such as a basic HTML browser.

❑   The **UI code** actually generates the data sent to the presentation device. It is the UI code that actually acts on the data input by the user.

In a traditional VB forms-based interface, the presentation and UI code tend to be blurred together within a VB form. When dealing with an HTML browser, or a cell phone device, the separation is much more clear. The device used merely handles presentation – all actual UI processing is performed on a server somewhere across the network.

Presentation

Most Windows DNA applications today are targeted at the browser for presentation, and so that's what we'll focus on in this sample application.

When targeting the browser we have to make a choice between providing a broad reach across many types of browser, and providing a rich, interactive user experience by targeting a narrower set of browsers. This is discussed in more depth in Chapter 16. Our sample contact manager will be designed for reach – meaning that it will use basic HTML with no client-side scripting, and won't make use of other features that are not available in most browsers. The fanciest feature it will use are tables – and those are almost universally supported.

Additionally, so we can remain focused on the application architecture, the presentation will be pretty rudimentary. The application will provide the user with a simple set of pages to allow the following functionality:

❑   Home page

❑   List contacts

❑   Add a contact

❑   Edit a contact

❑   Remove a contact

Each page will have a header to indicate to the user the purpose of the page. Beyond that, the page will just provide a basic display or HTML form so the user can interact with the presentation as appropriate.

The navigational structure of the pages is illustrated by the following diagram:

All the logic to generate the presentation and to react to the user's input or requests will be handled by the UI code on the web server.

User Interface

The user interface code will be written within Active Server Pages (ASP) and will run on the web server. The code will be written in VBScript, though it could be written in any language supported by the ASP environment. Typically this means another scripting language such as JavaScript or Perl. With some extra effort it is possible to use more advanced languages such as Visual Basic or C++, but that is far less common.

The UI code is responsible for generating the HTML that will be sent to the browser and presented to the user. It's also responsible for fielding requests from the user, including the handling of data provided from HTML forms that the user has posted back to our ASP pages.

In fact, the UI manages the user's overall experience. The most obvious manifestation of this is that the UI must provide meaningful and useful means of navigation as it generates each page for display.

Business Objects and Data Access

Of course any code within an ASP page is script. This provides a set of advantages and disadvantages. On the upside, we can simply update the code, save the file, and the changes are live – no compilation required. On the downside, the code is interpreted, has no real data types, and employs late binding when talking to COM objects – all of which contributes to applications that are slower and harder to maintain.

To minimize this impact, we'll take care of most business logic and data access within COM objects written in Visual Basic. This code is compiled, so it's a bit more difficult to update than simple script code. On the other hand, VB code has access to a wide range of data types, is compiled for better performance, and employs visable binding for talking to COM objects – all contributing to fast, scalable, and easily maintained applications.

It's worth noting that this approach may not be acceptable for some Application Service Provider (ASP) environments. Many ASPs allow running ASP pages, but prohibit the use of COM components on their servers. In such a case we'd be forced to move our business logic and data access out of the compiled COM components and into the interpreted ASP script pages.

We will be using the `contactobjects` component, which was created in Chapter 7. Because our sample application's scope is small, this component was created with only two business objects, Contact and ContactList. Refer to Chapter 7 for information about the component, and instructions on how to build it.

Database Design and Data Services

Scalable solutions require scalable databases. For this application we'll use SQL Server 7, providing access to all required data services via a set of stored procedures.

Database Design

Our database structure will be fairly basic, but effective. Obviously we'll have a table to store our basic contact data. Each contact will have simple name and address data. However, each contact may also have multiple phone numbers and e-mail addresses, so we'll have tables to store that data as well. This provides an extensible data model, but also illustrates how we can encapsulate a number of tables within a single business object.

Contact table

The `Contact` table will have the following structure:

Column	Type
ID	uniqueidentifier
LastName	VarChar(50)
FirstName	VarChar(50)
Address1	VarChar(50)
Address2	VarChar(50)
City	VarChar(30)
State	VarChar(20)
ZipCode	VarChar(10)

The `ID` column is designated as the primary key for the table. It is marked as a uniqueidentifier data type – which means that it can store a GUID (globally unique identifier) value. When we actually build this table in the database, we'll need to set it so that the GUID value is automatically generated as a new row is added to the table by checking the **IsRowGuid** box in the far right column of the designer.

We'll also want to uncheck all of the Allow Nulls checkboxes, to disallow NULL values. (See the Adding the Tables sub-section of the Building the Sample Application section below for more details.)

Phone table

Each contact may have many phone numbers. We'll design this so a contact can have one of each type of phone number:

- ❏ Home
- ❏ Work
- ❏ Cell

The Phone table will have the following structure:

Column	Type
ContactID	uniqueidentifier
PhoneType	Integer * 4
Phone	VarChar(30)

The ContactID and PhoneType columns combine to form the primary key for the table.

Again, all of these columns should be set to disallow NULL values.

EMail table

The EMail table will have the following structure:

Column	Type
ContactID	uniqueidentifier
EMailType	Integer * 4
EMail	VarChar(100)

The ContactID and EMailType columns combine to form the primary key for the table, and, as usual, we want to disallow NULLs.

Data Services

While it is certainly possible to have our middle-tier code interact directly with the tables in the database, it is often preferable to make use of stored procedures instead. Stored procedures provide a more abstract view of the database, allowing us to encapsulate data implementation details within the database itself. The programmer using the database can then just make use of a clearly defined set of services provided by the database developer.

For the contact application the database will need to expose a set of basic services to allow the retrieval, addition, update and removal of contact data:

Stored procedure	Description
addContact	Add a contact to the database. This procedure will generate a primary key value for the new contact, and will return it to the calling code.
deleteContact	Remove a contact from the database.
getContact	Retrieve all information for a contact. The results will be returned via three resultsets (contact, phone, e-mail).
getContacts	Retrieve basic contact information for all contacts on file. No phone or e-mail data is returned.
updateContact	Update an existing contact's data in the database.

This set of services will allow the Contact and ContactList business objects to perform any data-related operation that they require.

Now that we've reviewed the high-level design for the application, we can set out to build it.

The Database

To set up the database, tables and stored procedures in SQL Server 7 we'll use the SQL Server Enterprise Manager tool. Typically this can be found under Programs | Microsoft SQL Server on the Start menu.

Creating the Database

Bring up the Enterprise Manager and expand the tree on the left so it displays the details for the SQL Server we'll be using. To add a database, right-click on the Databases entry in the tree and select the New Database... option. This will bring up a dialog to allow us to set up the database:

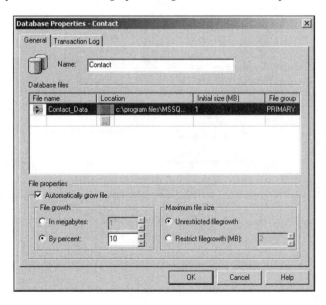

For a simple application, SQL Server 7 makes this process very easy. All we need to do is type Contact as the name of the database and click OK. By default, the database is set up such that it will automatically grow if needed.

When creating a real-world application there are more factors to be considered when creating a database. We need to think about what goes on different disks, anticipated data size and growth, and so forth. These issues are beyond the scope of this chapter.

For more information on working with SQL databases, try Professional SQL Server 7.0 Programming, ISBN 1861002-31-9, *from Wrox.*

Once we click OK on this dialog, SQL Server will create the database. To see the database, expand the Databases entry in the tree on the left, and highlight the Contact database:

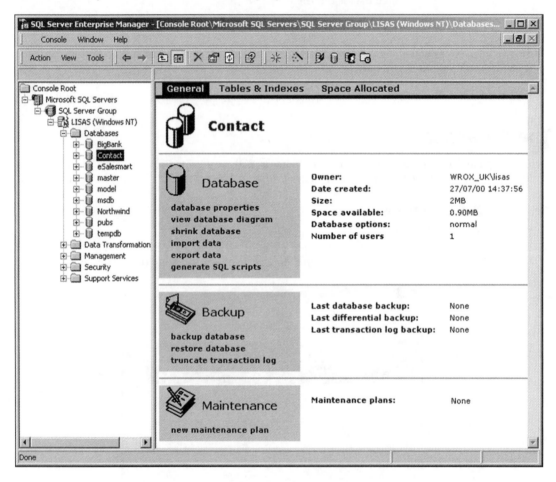

Enterprise Manager displays details about the selected database in the panel on the right.

Adding the Tables

In the tree on the left, we can expand the Contact database entry to show the various elements contained within the database. To start with, our new database has only a few system tables – we need to add our own tables to store the data for the contact application.

We'll use the same process to create each of the three tables we need to add – Contact, Phone and Email – based on the column definitions we covered earlier in the chapter. Let's walk through creating one of the smaller tables to see how it works.

To add a table, right-click on the Tables entry and choose New Table… from the menu. This will bring up a dialog asking for the table's name:

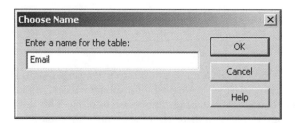

Enter EMail for the table name and click OK. We're then presented with a dialog where we can enter in the definitions for all of our columns, and specify our primary key and other indexes. The following diagram illustrates the dialog with the entries for the EMail table:

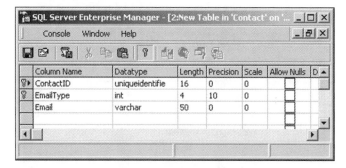

Notice that the column names, data types and lengths are set in the dialog, and that you'll need to uncheck all the Allow Nulls checkboxes, so that there must be an entry in each column of the record. The ContactID and EMailType columns are specified as the primary key (noted by the key icon on the left). You can do this by highlighting both columns at once (click on the gray area to the left of the column and hold down the Ctrl key) and clicking on the primary key icon in the toolbar.

Finally, click on the disk icon in the toolbar to save the changes to the table, and we're all set.

You'll need to repeat this process for the other two tables we defined earlier, Contact and Phone.

Adding a Login

Before our middle-tier code can access, the database we'll need to provide a login ID. There are various schools of thought around login IDs and security for a database and application. We might choose to have a database login ID for each physical user of our application, or we might choose to have a single login ID for the application – handling security some other way.

If we choose to utilize the database security by providing each physical user with a SQL Server login ID things can get messy fast. The first drawback is that this scheme pretty much entirely defeats any use of database connection pooling. Also, if our application becomes popular, we may end up adding thousands or millions of login IDs into our server. It may not be entirely desirable to have random people around the world with login access to our database.

> *Database connection pooling pools all connections with the same connection string (or property list). The login ID and password are part of the data that is compared, so connections using different login IDs are not pooled together.*

The better choice for a Windows DNA application is to use a single login ID for an application. The middle-tier code can consistently use this login ID for all data access, meaning that all users of our application will gain the benefits of database connection pooling. This does mean that we need to implement security for our application through some means other than database login IDs, but that is typically a fair trade.

To add a login ID for our database, expand the Security entry on the tree on the left of Enterprise Manager. Under Security is an entry for Logins. Right-click on Logins and choose the New login... menu option. This will bring up a dialog allowing us to add a login:

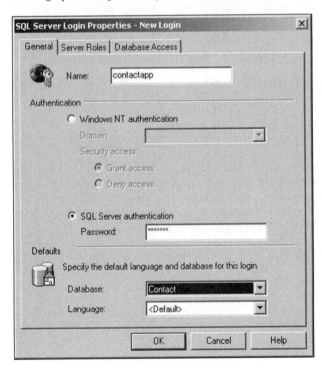

In the **Name** field enter the login ID for our application. In this case we've entered contactapp as the login ID for the contact application.

Then select the appropriate security model. The easiest model for an application login ID is to use **SQL Server authentication**, and just enter a password directly into this dialog. This option works well, since it's unlikely that our application will need a login ID for the Windows 2000 domain or server – just for SQL Server itself. In this case enter the password as contact (it will be displayed as *******).

Then select the **Database** so the default is **Contact**.

While we're done with this tab, we're not done with the dialog just yet. Click on the **Database Access** tab, which will allow us to specify the databases this new login ID can access:

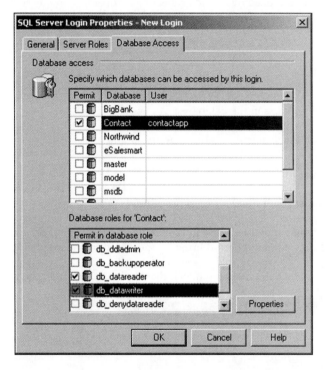

By default the new login has no access to tables. Click the box by the **Contact** entry to enable access to that database.

In the lower section of the dialog we can specify the roles this user can play within the Contact database. The **db_Public** role is selected by default, but provides no real access. Scroll down and select the **db_user, db_datareader** and **db_datawriter** entries. These will allow the login to read and write to tables in the database – exactly what we need for our application.

Click **OK** to close the dialog and save our new login ID. At this point we have our tables set up and a login ID created so we can access them. Next we need to create the stored procedures that will be called by our middle-tier objects.

Creating the Stored Procedures

Stored procedures can be created directly from within the Enterprise Manager tool. In the left-hand panel expand the Databases tree and the Contact database tree itself. This is what we did to create our tables earlier. Notice that there are several options listed besides the Tables entry – including one for Stored Procedures.

If we left-click on the Stored Procedures entry, the right-hand pane will display a list of all the stored procedures that exist for our database. The initial list we see here are stored procedures created by SQL Server itself when the database was created. Once we've added our new procedures they'll be listed here as well.

We'll create several stored procedures – each reflecting an operation required by the Contact and ContactList business objects. The procedures to be created were listed earlier in the chapter in the section on design.

getContacts

Perhaps the simplest of the stored procedures we need to create is the one to be used by the ContactList object. The purpose of the ContactList object is to retrieve a list of the basic contact information for all the contacts in the database.

The SQL to retrieve all the data from a table is pretty simple:

```
SELECT * FROM Contact;
```

Given that SQL statement, let's build a stored procedure.

Right-click on the Stored Procedure entry in the left-hand pane of the Enterprise Manager. Select the New Stored Procedure… menu option to bring up the stored procedure dialog.

Change the template code in the dialog to match that shown in the screenshot:

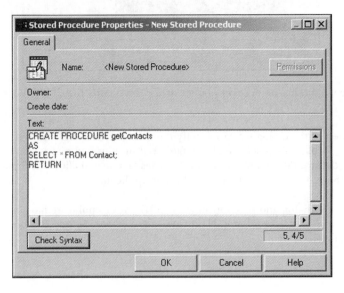

Notice that the original SELECT statement is there. First though, there is some code to create the stored procedure itself – giving it the name getContacts. Also, once the stored procedure is done there is a RETURN statement to complete the process.

To do a syntax check of the code, click the **Check Syntax** button. In this case there should be no problems with the syntax, so just click **OK** to add the stored procedure to the database.

Alternately, we could use a Transact-SQL script to create the stored procedure:

> *Transact-SQL is SQL Server's own flavor of the Structured Query Language. It's a complex language, and covering it in detail is beyond the scope of this book. For more information on SQL and T-SQL, refer to* Professional SQL Server 7.0 Programming, *ISBN 1861002-31-9, from Wrox.*

Our script would look like this:

```
if exists (select * from sysobjects where
           id = object_id(N'[dbo].[getContacts]')
           and OBJECTPROPERTY(id, N'IsProcedure') = 1)
drop procedure [dbo].[getContacts]
GO

SET QUOTED_IDENTIFIER  ON     SET ANSI_NULLS  ON
GO

CREATE PROCEDURE getContacts
AS
SELECT * FROM CONTACT;
RETURN
GO
SET QUOTED_IDENTIFIER  OFF    SET ANSI_NULLS  ON
GO
```

To use the script, first enter the code into a text editor and save it in a file named getContacts.sql. Then use the **Query Analyzer** tool (select **Tools | SQL Server Query Analyzer** from the Enterprise Manager). Click the **Load SQL Script** icon on the tool bar to load the script file you just created, and – making sure that you have **Contact** selected in the **DB** drop down box – click the green arrow to run it and create the stored procedure. In this chapter we'll stick with the use of the Enterprise Manager tool, since it's the easier approach.

getContact

The process to create each stored procedure is the same as that used for the getContacts stored procedure we just added. Right-click on **Stored Procedures** to add a new stored procedure, and enter the following code:

```
CREATE PROCEDURE getContact @id uniqueidentifier
AS
SELECT ID, LastName, FirstName, Address1, Address2, City, State, ZipCode
  FROM Contact
  WHERE ID = @id;
SELECT PhoneType, Phone
  FROM Phone
```

```
        WHERE ContactID= @id;
SELECT EMailType, EMail
   FROM EMail
      WHERE ContactID= @id;
 RETURN
```

This stored procedure is a bit more complex, since it accepts a parameter, @id, which is an integer. The @ in SQL signifies a local variable: global variables are signified by @@. This value indicates the specific contact that is to be retrieved, and it's used in the WHERE clauses of the SELECT statements.

To make things even more interesting, this stored procedure has three SELECT statements – thus it returns three separate data sets. This is really nice, since with one call to the database we'll be able to retrieve all the data pertaining to a given contact. Typically this would be done with three separate queries to the database.

We'll take a look at the ADO code needed to work with this multiple data set return when we build the Contact object later in the chapter.

addContact

The addContact procedure is added using the same process as the previous two stored procedures. Since this procedure needs to add records to the Contact, Phone, and EMail tables, as well as generate a unique primary key for the contact, it's quite a bit more complex than the simple SELECT procedures we've seen so far.

The code for this procedure is as follows:

```
CREATE PROCEDURE addContact
    @id uniqueidentifier output, @lname varchar(50),
    @fname varchar(50), @add1 varchar(50), @add2 varchar(50),
    @city varchar (30), @state varchar(30), @zip varchar(20),
    @phome varchar(30), @pwork varchar(30), @pcell varchar(30),
    @emhome varchar(100), @emwork varchar(30)
AS

Set @id = NewID();

INSERT INTO Contact
    (ID, lastname, firstname, address1, address2, city, state, zipcode)
    VALUES
    (@id, @lname, @fname, @add1, @add2, @city, @state, @zip);

IF (Len(@phome) > 0) BEGIN
    INSERT INTO Phone
        (ContactID, PhoneType, Phone)
        VALUES
        (@id, 0, @phome);
END

IF (Len(@pwork) > 0) BEGIN
    INSERT INTO Phone
        (ContactID, PhoneType, Phone)
        VALUES
```

```
            (@id, 1, @pwork);
    END

    IF (Len(@pcell) > 0) BEGIN
        INSERT INTO Phone
            (ContactID, PhoneType, Phone)
            VALUES
            (@id, 2, @pcell);
    END

    IF (Len(@emhome) > 0) BEGIN
        INSERT INTO EMail
            (ContactID, EMailType, EMail)
            VALUES
            (@id, 0, @emhome);
    END

    IF (Len(@emwork) > 0) BEGIN
        INSERT INTO EMail
            (ContactID, EMailType, EMail)
            VALUES
            (@id, 1, @emwork)
    END

    RETURN
```

The procedure accepts all the data fields required to define a contact, including the data for the Phone and EMail tables. Notice that the @id parameter is marked as an output parameter.

```
CREATE PROCEDURE addContact
    @id int output, @lname varchar(50),
```

This means that the value of @id will be returned to the calling code when the procedure is complete. Since we'll be generating a new primary key value for the contact, this will be used to return that new value to our Visual Basic Contact object for its use.

The first thing this procedure does is generate a unique primary key value for the new contact. This is done by using the T-SQL NewID function, which creates a unique value of type uniqueidentifier:

```
Set @id = NewID();
```

The @id parameter now contains the new primary key value for this contact. We'll use this value throughout the remainder of the procedure, and since @id is an output parameter, this value will also be returned through ADO to the code that called this procedure.

Next, the procedure simply adds a new entry to the Contact table for this contact using an INSERT INTO statement. This is easy, since there'll always be an entry for the contact itself:

```
INSERT INTO Contact
    (ID, lastname, firstname, address1, address2, city, state, zipcode)
    VALUES
    (@id, @lname, @fname, @add1, @add2, @city, @state, @zip);
```

More interesting is the code for the `Phone` data. We only want to add an entry to the `Phone` table for each phone number provided as a parameter. Some phone number parameters could be empty if the user didn't provide that type of phone number.

To take care of this, prior to each `INSERT INTO` statement for a phone number, we'll check to make sure that we were provided with a value to store:

```
IF (Len(@phome) > 0) BEGIN
    INSERT INTO Phone
        (ContactID, PhoneType, Phone)
        VALUES
        (@id, 0, @phome);
END
```

Thus, if the length of the `@phome` parameter is greater than 0, we'll run the associated `INSERT INTO` statement to add a corresponding entry into the table. Notice that we need to use a `BEGIN..END` block to mark the start and end of the code that is affected by the `IF` statement.

The `PhoneType` and `EMailType` values are the numeric values corresponding to the `Enum` data types we'll define in Visual Basic. Unfortunately, the `Enum` data type doesn't extend from Visual Basic into the stored procedures, so here we're stuck with cryptic numeric values:

0	home
1	work
2	cell

This same technique is repeated for each phone and e-mail parameter.

updateContact

Updating data is very similar to adding data, so this procedure will be quite similar to the `addContact` procedure we just created. In many cases, these two procedures (`addContact` and `updateContact`) can be merged into a single stored procedure – minimizing the code to be maintained. They are separate in this chapter for the purpose of clarity:

```
CREATE PROCEDURE updateContact
    @id uniqueidentifier, @lname varchar(50), @fname varchar(50),
    @add1 varchar(50), @add2 varchar(50), @city varchar (30),
    @state varchar(30), @zip varchar(20),
    @phome varchar(30), @pwork varchar(30), @pcell varchar(30),
    @emhome varchar(100), @emwork varchar(30)
AS

UPDATE Contact
    SET lastname=@lname, firstname=@fname,
        address1=@add1, address2=@add2, city=@city, state=@state, zipcode=@zip
    WHERE ID = @id;

DELETE FROM Phone
    WHERE ContactID = @id;
```

```
IF (Len(@phome) > 0) BEGIN
    INSERT INTO Phone
        (ContactID, PhoneType, Phone)
        VALUES
        (@id, 0, @phome);
END

IF (Len(@pwork) > 0) BEGIN
    INSERT INTO Phone
        (ContactID, PhoneType, Phone)
        VALUES
        (@id, 1, @pwork);
END

IF (Len(@pcell) > 0) BEGIN
    INSERT INTO Phone
        (ContactID, PhoneType, Phone)
        VALUES
        (@id, 2, @pcell);
END

DELETE FROM EMail
    WHERE ContactID = @id;

IF (Len(@emhome) > 0) BEGIN
    INSERT INTO EMail
        (ContactID, EMailType, EMail)
        VALUES
        (@id, 0, @emhome);
END

IF (Len(@emwork) > 0) BEGIN
    INSERT INTO EMail
        (ContactID, EMailType, EMail)
        VALUES
        (@id, 1, @emwork);
END
```

Since this procedure is updating, not adding, we don't need to generate a new primary key value. This means that the @id parameter is used for input rather than output in this case.

The procedure goes directly to the process of using the UPDATE statement to update the data in the Contact table.

The Phone and EMail data is a bit trickier. We could try to come up with some matching algorithm to determine which entries are new, which need to be updated, and which deleted. However, it's much simpler to just remove all Phone and EMail entries, then add those provided through the parameters. This is the approach taken here.

Before updating any Phone data, all the previously existing data is removed.

```
DELETE FROM Phone
    WHERE ContactID = @id;
```

Then INSERT INTO statements are used to add the current Phone entries to the table. This code is exactly the same as in the addContact procedure.

deleteContact

The last procedure we need to create is fairly straightforward:

```
CREATE PROCEDURE deleteContact @id uniqueidentifier
AS
DELETE FROM Contact WHERE ID=@id;
DELETE FROM Phone WHERE ContactID=@id;
DELETE FROM EMail WHERE ContactID=@id;
RETURN
```

This procedure accepts a parameter to indicate which contact is to be removed. That value is used in the WHERE clause of each DELETE statement.

With this stored procedure added, we now have the ability to retrieve, add, update and remove contact information using a very clear and simple set of procedure calls. Now let's create the business objects that will interact with the database.

The User Interface

We'll use the Visual Interdev tool to create the user interface code. The UI will consist of a single HTML file and a series of ASP files to create the interface described earlier in the chapter.

Of course, if you prefer, you can just create the HTML and ASP pages in a text editor, such as Notepad, and install them in a virtual directory on your web server.

Obviously, the presentation can be as complex as needed or desired. However, in this case we'll keep the presentation very basic, so we can remain focused on the creation of basic navigation and the code that interacts with our business objects.

Open Visual Interdev and choose to create a new project. Name the project Contact and put it in a virtual site on the web server.

Default.htm

The first page is Default.htm, a simple HTML page that provides a starting point for the user.

Right-click on the *webserver* | Contact entry in the Project Explorer window (the *webserver* entry will be specific to your environment). Choose the Add | New Item... menu option. Name the new item Default.htm and make sure that the item type selected is HTML Page, then click Open.

Either use the WYSIWYG editor or click on the Source tab, and enter the following code:

```
<HTML>
<HEAD>
<Meta NAME="GENERATOR" Content="Microsoft Visual Studio 6.0">
<TITLE></TITLE>
</HEAD>

<BODY>
```

```
<H1><IMG ALIGN="middle" SRC="images/wroxlogo.gif" WIDTH="56" HEIGHT="56">
 Contact System</H1>
<P>
<HR>
</P>
<P>What would you like to do?</P>
<MENU>
    <LI><A HREF="contactlist.asp">List the contacts</A></LI>
    <LI><A HREF="contactedit.asp">Add a new contact</A></LI>
</MENU>
<P> </P>

</BODY>
</HTML>
```

This creates a very basic page. The important parts are the two links to `contactlist.asp` and `contactedit.asp`. The former will provide the user with a list of contacts in the database, while the latter page will bring up an edit dialog, so the user can add a new contact.

contactlist.asp

The ability to list all the contacts on file is a major part of the user experience. From here, the user can choose to view details of the contact, edit the contact, or remove the contact from the database. Since we've already created the `ContactList` object, this page is relatively easy to build.

Right-click on *webserver* | Contact in the Project Explorer, and choose Add | New Item.... Name the new file `contactlist.asp`, and make sure the ASP Page option is selected, then click Open.

Enter the following code:

```
<%@ Language=VBScript %>
<%Option Explicit%>
<HTML>

<HEAD>
<meta NAME="GENERATOR" Content="Microsoft Visual Studio 6.0">
</HEAD>

<BODY>
<H1><IMG ALIGN="middle" SRC="images/wroxlogo.gif" WIDTH="56" HEIGHT="56">
 Contacts</H1>
<HR>
<%
    Dim objContactList
    Dim strName
    Dim arData
    Dim lngIndex

    Set objContactList = Server.CreateObject("ContactObjects.ContactList")
    arData = objContactList.GetContacts
%>
```

```
<TABLE BORDER="1">
<TBODY>
<TR><TD><B>Name</B></TD><TD><B>City</B></TD><TD></TD></TR>
<%
    For lngIndex = 0 to UBound(arData,2)
%>
<TR><TD>
<%
        strName = Server.HTMLEncode(arData(1, lngIndex) & ", " & _
                                    arData(2, lngIndex))
        Response.Write "<A HREF=contactdetail.asp?id=" & _
                        arData(0, lngIndex) & ">" & _
                        strName & "</A>"
%>
</TD>
<TD>
<%
        Response.Write Server.HTMLEncode(arData(5, lngIndex) & ", " & _
                                         arData(6, lngIndex))
%>
</TD>
<TD>

<P><FONT SIZE=2>
  
<A HREF="contactedit.asp?id=<% = arData(0, lngIndex) %>">Edit</A>
  
<A HREF="contactdelete.asp?id=<% = arData(0, lngIndex) %>">Remove</A>
  
</FONT></P>

</TD></TR>
<%
    Next
%>
</TBODY>
</TABLE>

<P><FONT SIZE=2>
<A HREF="contactedit.asp">Add a new contact</A>
  
<A HREF="Default.htm">Home</A>
</FONT></P>

</BODY>
</HTML>
```

The first thing we need to do is use the `ContactList` object to retrieve the list of contact data for display:

```
<%
    Dim objContactList
    Dim strName
    Dim arData
    Dim lngIndex

    Set objContactList = Server.CreateObject("ContactObjects.ContactList")
    arData = objContactList.GetContacts
%>
```

As compared to the 'traditional' approach of creating the `Recordset` object directly from within ASP and then converting it to a `Variant` array, this is much simpler code. The COM component totally encapsulates all the complexity, retrieving the `Recordset` and converting it to an array.

The rest of the code just uses the array to generate an HTML table to display the results. This includes creating links for each contact so the user can choose to edit or remove the contact. These links go to the `contactedit.asp` and `contactdelete.asp` pages respectively. In either case, the contact's ID value is passed as a URL parameter to the target page.

To wrap up, the page also has links to add a new contact or to return to the home page.

If the user clicks on a contact they are taken to a detail page to view that contact's details.

contactdetail.asp

As with the previous page, add a new ASP page to the project and name it `contactdetail.asp`. This page will display the details about a contact. The contact to be displayed is identified by the ID value in the URL. Enter the following code:

```
<%@ Language=VBScript %>
<%Option Explicit%>
<HTML>

<HEAD>
<Meta NAME="GENERATOR" Content="Microsoft Visual Studio 6.0">
</HEAD>

<BODY>

<H1><IMG ALIGN="middle" src="images/wroxlogo.gif" WIDTH="56" HEIGHT="56">
 Contact detail</h1>
<HR>

<%
    Dim strContactID
    Dim objContact

    strContactID = Request.QueryString("ID")
    Set objContact = Server.CreateObject("ContactObjects.Contact")
    objContact.Load CStr(strContactID)
%>

<TABLE>
    <TBODY>
    <TR><TD vAlign=top><b>Name</b></TD><TD>
<%
        Response.Write Server.HTMLEncode(objContact.LastName & ", " & _
                                        objContact.FirstName)
%>
    </TD></TR>
    <TR><TD vAlign=top><b>Address</b></TD><TD>
<%
```

```
        If Len(objContact.Address1)>0 Then _
           Response.Write Server.HTMLEncode(objContact.Address1) & "<BR>"
        If Len(objContact.Address2)>0 Then _
           Response.Write Server.HTMLEncode(objContact.Address2) & "<BR>"
        If Len(objContact.City & objContact.State & objContact.ZipCode)>0 _
           Then _
           Response.Write Server.HTMLEncode(objContact.City & ", " & _
           objContact.State & " " & objContact.ZipCode)
%>
    </TD></TR>
    <TR><TD vAlign=top><b>Phone</b></TD><TD>
<%
        If Len(objContact.Phone(1))>0 Then _
           Response.Write Server.HTMLEncode(objContact.Phone(1)) & _
                                        " (work)<BR>"
        If Len(objContact.Phone(2))>0 Then _
           Response.Write Server.HTMLEncode(objContact.Phone(2)) & _
                                        " (cell)<BR>"
        If Len(objContact.Phone(0))>0 Then _
           Response.Write Server.HTMLEncode(objContact.Phone(0)) & _
                                        " (home)<BR>"
%>
    </TD></TR>
    <TR><TD vAlign=top><b>EMail</b></TD><TD>
<%
        If Len(objContact.EMail(1))>0 Then _
           Response.Write "<a href=mailto:" & objContact.EMail(1) & ">" & _
           Server.HTMLEncode(objContact.EMail(1)) & "</a> (work)<BR>"
        If Len(objContact.EMail(0))>0 Then _
           Response.Write "<a href=mailto:" & objContact.EMail(0) & ">" & _
           Server.HTMLEncode(objContact.EMail(0)) & "</a> (home)<BR>"
%>
    </TD></TR>
    </TBODY>
</TABLE>

<P><FONT SIZE=2>
<A HREF="contactedit.asp?id=<% =CStr(objContact.ID) %>">
Edit this contact</A>
  
<A HREF="contactlist.asp">List the contacts</A>
  
<A HREF="contactedit.asp">Add a new contact</A>
  
<A HREF="Default.htm">Home</A></P>
<P>
<A HREF="contactdelete.asp?id=<% =CStr(objContact.ID) %>">
Remove this contact</A>
</FONT></P>

</BODY>
</HTML>
```

The code creates a new Contact object and calls its Load method to retrieve the data from the database:

```
<%
    Dim strContactID
    Dim objContact

    strContactID = Request.QueryString("ID")
    Set objContact = Server.CreateObject("ContactObjects.Contact")
    objContact.Load CStr(strContactID)
%>
```

Using the loaded Contact object, we're then able to build a nice display showing all the data for the selected contact.

At the bottom we simply insert some basic navigational links that the user can use to move around our application.

Whether from the contact list or the contact detail page, if the user chooses to edit the contact, they are taken to the contactedit.asp page.

contactedit.asp

Add a new ASP page to the project and name it contactedit.asp.

This page will serve two functions – the addition and editing of a contact. If the page is passed an ID value as a parameter, it will edit the contact, otherwise it will assume we are adding a new contact.

In addition, this page is recursive. The page will start out displaying a form with fields so the user can enter or edit contact information. When that form is posted back to the web server, this page is run again – this time to process the data from the user, and to generate a page indicating that the update took place.

Enter the following code:

```
<%@ Language=VBScript %>
<%Option Explicit%>
<HTML>

<HEAD>
<Meta NAME="GENERATOR" Content="Microsoft Visual Studio 6.0">
</HEAD>

<BODY>

<%
    Dim objContact
    Dim strID

    Set objContact = Server.CreateObject("ContactObjects.Contact")
```

```asp
    If Request.Form("hdnID") = Empty Then
        strID = CStr(Request.QueryString("ID"))
        If Len(strID) > 0 Then
            objContact.Load CStr(strID)
%>
<H1><IMG ALIGN="middle" SRC="images/wroxlogo.gif" WIDTH="56" HEIGHT="56">
 Edit Contact</H1>
<%
    Else
%>
<H1><IMG ALIGN="middle" SRC="images/wroxlogo.gif" WIDTH="56" HEIGHT="56">
 Add Contact</H1>
<%
    End if
%>
<HR>
<FORM ACTION="contactedit.asp" METHOD="POST" id=form1 name=form1>
    <% If Len(objContact.ID) > 0 Then %>
        <INPUT TYPE="hidden" ID="hdnID" NAME="hdnID"
               VALUE="<% =objContact.ID %>">
    <% Else %>
        <INPUT TYPE="hidden" ID="hdnID" NAME="hdnID"
               VALUE="new">
    <% End If %>

    <TABLE>
        <TBODY>
        <TR>
        <TD VALIGN="top">Name</TD>
        <TD VALIGN="top">Last</TD>
        <TD><INPUT ID="txtLastName" NAME="txtLastName"
                   VALUE="<% =objContact.LastName %>"></TD>
        </TR>

        <TR>
        <TD VALIGN="top"></TD>
        <TD VALIGN="top">First</TD>
        <TD><INPUT ID="txtFirstName" NAME="txtFirstName"
                   VALUE="<% =objContact.FirstName %>"><BR></TD>
        </TR>

        <TR>
        <TD ALIGN="top">Address</TD>
        <TD VALIGN="top"></TD>
        <TD>
        <INPUT ID="txtAddress1" NAME="txtAddress1"
               VALUE="<% =objContact.Address1 %>"><BR>
        <INPUT ID="txtAddress2" NAME="txtAddress2"
               VALUE="<% =objContact.Address2 %>">
        </TD></TR>

        <TR>
        <TD VALIGN="top"></TD>
        <TD VALIGN="top">City</TD>
        <TD>
```

```
            <INPUT ID="txtCity" NAME="txtCity"
                VALUE="<% =objContact.City %>"></TD></TR>

            <TR>
            <TD VALIGN="top"></TD>
            <TD VALIGN="top">State</TD>
            <TD>
            <INPUT ID="txtState" NAME="txtState"
                VALUE="<% =objContact.State %>"></TD></TR>

            <TR>
            <TD VALIGN="top"></TD>
            <TD VALIGN="top">Zip</TD>
            <TD>
            <INPUT ID="txtZipCode" NAME="txtZipCode"
                VALUE="<% =objContact.ZipCode %>"><BR></TD></TR>

            <TR>
            <TD VALIGN="top">Phone</TD>
            <TD VALIGN="top">Work</TD>
            <TD> <INPUT ID="txtPhoneWork" NAME="txtPhoneWork"
                    VALUE="<% =objContact.Phone(1) %>">
            </TD></TD>

            <TR>
            <TD VALIGN="top"></TD>
            <TD VALIGN="top">Cell</TD>
            <TD> <INPUT ID="txtPhoneCell" NAME="txtPhoneCell"
                    VALUE="<% =objContact.Phone(2) %>">
            </TD></TR>

            <TR>
            <TD VALIGN="top"></TD>
            <TD VALIGN="top">Home</TD>
            <TD> <INPUT ID="txtPhoneHome" NAME="txtPhoneHome"
                    VALUE="<% =objContact.Phone(0) %>">
            <BR></TD></TR>

            <TR>
            <TD VALIGN="top">EMail</TD>
            <TD VALIGN="top">Work</TD>
            <TD> <INPUT ID="txtEMailWork" NAME="txtEMailWork"
                    VALUE="<% =objContact.EMail(1) %>">
            </TD></TR>

            <TR>
            <TD VALIGN="top"></TD>
            <TD VALIGN="top">Home</TD>
            <TD> <INPUT ID="txtEMailHome" NAME="txtEMailHome"
                    VALUE="<% =objContact.EMail(0) %>">
            </TD></TR></TABLE>

<P><INPUT ID="submit1" NAME="submit1" TYPE="submit" VALUE="Submit"> 
<INPUT ID="reset1" NAME="reset1" TYPE="reset" VALUE="Reset"></P>
```

```
            </TBODY>
        </TABLE>
    </FORM>

    <P><FONT SIZE=2>
    <A HREF="contactlist.asp">List the contacts</A>
      
    <A HREF="contactedit.asp">Add a new contact</A>
      
    <A HREF="Default.htm">Home</A></P>
    <P>
    <% If Len(objContact.ID) > 0 Then %>
      <A HREF="contactdelete.asp?id= <% =CStr(objContact.ID) %>">
      Remove this contact
      </A>
    <% End If %>
    </FONT></P>

    <%
        Else
            strID = Request.Form("hdnID")
            If strID <> "new" Then
                objContact.Load CStr(strID)
            End If
            objContact.LastName=Request.Form("txtLastName")
            objContact.FirstName=Request.Form("txtFirstName")

            objContact.Address1=Request.Form("txtAddress1")
            objContact.Address2=Request.Form("txtAddress2")
            objContact.City=Request.Form("txtCity")
            objContact.State=Request.Form("txtState")
            objContact.ZipCode=Request.Form("txtZipCode")

            objContact.Phone(1)=Request.Form("txtPhoneWork")
            objContact.Phone(2)=Request.Form("txtPhoneCell")
            objContact.Phone(0)=Request.Form("txtPhoneHome")

            objContact.EMail(1)=Request.Form("txtEMailWork")
            objContact.EMail(0)=Request.Form("txtEMailHome")
            objContact.Save
    %>
    <H1><IMG ALIGN="middle" SRC="images/wroxlogo.gif" WIDTH="56" HEIGHT="56">
     Contact Updated</H1>
    <P>The contact information you submitted as been updated.</P>

    <%
        strID = objContact.ID
    %>

        <TABLE>
            <TBODY>
            <TR><TD vAlign=top><b>Name</b></TD><TD>
    <%
        Response.Write Server.HTMLEncode(objContact.LastName & ", " & _
                                        objContact.FirstName)
    %>
```

```
        </TD></TR>
        <TR><TD vAlign=top><b>Address</b></TD><TD>
<%
      If Len(objContact.Address1)>0 Then _
         Response.Write Server.HTMLEncode(objContact.Address1) & "<BR>"
      If Len(objContact.Address2)>0 Then _
         Response.Write Server.HTMLEncode(objContact.Address2) & "<BR>"
      If Len(objContact.City & objContact.State & objContact.ZipCode)>0 _
         Then _
         Response.Write Server.HTMLEncode(objContact.City & ", " & _
         objContact.State & " " & objContact.ZipCode)
%>
        </TD></TR>
        <TR><TD vAlign=top><b>Phone</b></TD><TD>
<%
      If Len(objContact.Phone(1))>0 Then _
         Response.Write Server.HTMLEncode(objContact.Phone(1)) & _
                                     " (work)<BR>"
      If Len(objContact.Phone(2))>0 Then _
         Response.Write Server.HTMLEncode(objContact.Phone(2)) & _
                                     " (cell)<BR>"
      If Len(objContact.Phone(0))>0 Then _
            Response.Write Server.HTMLEncode(objContact.Phone(0)) & _
                                        " (home)<BR>"
%>
        </TD></TR>
        <TR><TD vAlign=top><b>EMail</b></TD><TD>
<%
      If Len(objContact.EMail(1))>0 then _
         Response.Write "<a href=mailto:" & objContact.EMail(1) & ">" & _
         Server.HTMLEncode(objContact.EMail(1)) & "</a> (work)<BR>"
      If Len(objContact.EMail(0))>0 then _
         Response.Write "<a href=mailto:" & objContact.EMail(0) & ">" & _
         Server.HTMLEncode(objContact.EMail(0)) & "</a> (home)<BR>"
%>
        </TD></TR>
        </TBODY>
   </TABLE>

<P><FONT SIZE=2>
<A HREF="contactedit.asp?id=<% =CStr(objContact.ID) %>">
Edit this contact</A>
  
<A HREF="contactlist.asp">List the contacts</A>
  
<A HREF="contactedit.asp">Add a new contact</A>
  
<A HREF="Default.htm">Home</A></P>
<P>
<A HREF="contactdelete.asp?id=<% =CStr(objContact.ID) %>">
Remove this contact</A>
</FONT></P>

<%
   End If
%>
</BODY>
</HTML>
```

The code at the start of the page performs several vital functions. First, it creates a Contact object for use throughout the remainder of the page:

```
<%
    Dim objContact
    Dim strID

    Set objContact = Server.CreateObject("ContactObjects.Contact")
```

It then determines if the page is calling itself or if it is being called directly. We can detect this by examining the hdnID field – a hidden field within the input form. If the page is called directly this field will always be empty, but if the page is calling itself we'll ensure that the field contains a value:

```
    If Request.Form("hdnID") = Empty Then
```

Adding/Editing a Contact

Assuming the page is being called directly, we need to decide if we're creating a new contact or editing an existing one.

```
        strID = CStr(Request.QueryString("ID"))
        If Len(strID) > 0 Then
            objContact.Load CStr(strID)
%>
```

The Request.QueryString method allows us to retrieve URL parameter values – in this case the ID parameter. If that value is greater than zero then we know that we're editing an existing contact, so the Contact object's Load method is called to load the data.

The next major section of the page creates a form so the user can edit or enter contact information. One key element of the form is the definition of the hdnID field.

```
        <% If Len(objContact.ID) > 0 Then %>
            <INPUT TYPE="hidden" ID="hdnID" NAME="hdnID"
                VALUE="<% =objContact.ID %>">
        <% Else %>
            <INPUT TYPE="hidden" ID="hdnID" NAME="hdnID"
                VALUE="new">
        <% End If %>
```

By ensuring that this field has some value – even if it is a zero – we are enabling the recursive call back to the same page.

The form also includes Submit and Reset buttons. If the Submit button is clicked, the form will be posted back to the contactedit.asp page – but this time though the hdnID field will not be empty.

Updating the Database

If we determine that the page is calling itself by posting the form, then we'll run some different code. Instead of generating a form for the user to enter or edit data, we'll take the data from the posted form and put it into the database.

The code first determines if hdnID contains a value other than new. If it does, then we're editing an existing contact so that data needs to be loaded:

```
strID = Request.Form("hdnID")
If strID <> "new" Then
    objContact.Load CStr(strID)
End If
```

Then we set the object's properties based on the values supplied by the user (via the Request object's Form collection). Once those values are loaded into the object we can simply call the Save method to update the database:

```
objContact.Save
```

Again, the ASP code is very simple and easy to read because most of the complexity of the application is encapsulated within our Contact object.

contactdelete.asp

The only feature remaining to implement is the ability to remove a contact. This function is invoked from several pages in the application, including the contactlist.asp and contactdetail.asp pages. In each case, the contactdelete.asp page is called, passing the appropriate ID value as a parameter in the URL.

Add a contactdelete.asp page to the project and enter the following code:

```
<%@ Language=VBScript %>
<%Option Explicit%>
<HTML>

<HEAD>
<Meta NAME="GENERATOR" Content="Microsoft Visual Studio 6.0">
</HEAD>

<BODY>

<%
    Dim objContact
    Dim strID

    Set objContact = Server.CreateObject("ContactObjects.Contact")

    If Request.Form("hdnID") = Empty Then
        strID = CStr(Request.QueryString("ID"))
        objContact.Load Cstr(strID)
%>
<H1><IMG ALIGN="middle" SRC="images/wroxlogo.gif" WIDTH="56" HEIGHT="56">
 Remove Contact</H1>
<HR>

<TABLE>
    <TBODY>
```

```
      <TR><TD vAlign=top><b>Name</b></TD><TD>
<%
      Response.Write Server.HTMLEncode(objContact.LastName & ", " & _
                                      objContact.FirstName)
%>
   </TD></TR>
   <TR><TD vAlign=top><b>Address</b></TD><TD>
<%
      If Len(objContact.Address1)>0 Then _
         Response.Write Server.HTMLEncode(objContact.Address1) & "<BR>"
      If Len(objContact.Address2)>0 Then _
         Response.Write Server.HTMLEncode(objContact.Address2) & "<BR>"
      If Len(objContact.City & objContact.State & objContact.ZipCode)>0 _
         Then _
         Response.Write Server.HTMLEncode(objContact.City & ", " & _
         objContact.State & " " & objContact.ZipCode)
%>
   </TD></TR>
   <TR><TD vAlign=top><b>Phone</b></TD><TD>
<%
      If Len(objContact.Phone(1))>0 Then _
         Response.Write Server.HTMLEncode(objContact.Phone(1)) & _
                                      " (work)<BR>"
      If Len(objContact.Phone(2))>0 Then _
         Response.Write Server.HTMLEncode(objContact.Phone(2)) & _
                                      " (cell)<BR>"
      If Len(objContact.Phone(0))>0 Then _
         Response.Write Server.HTMLEncode(objContact.Phone(0)) & _
                                      " (home)<BR>"
%>
   </TD></TR>
   <TR><TD vAlign=top><b>EMail</b></TD><TD>
<%
      If Len(objContact.EMail(1))>0 Then _
         Response.Write "<a href=mailto:" & objContact.EMail(1) & ">" & _
         Server.HTMLEncode(objContact.EMail(1)) & "</a> (work)<BR>"
      If Len(objContact.EMail(0))>0 Then _
         Response.Write "<a href=mailto:" & objContact.EMail(0) & ">" & _
         Server.HTMLEncode(objContact.EMail(0)) & "</a> (home)<BR>"
%>
   </TD></TR>
   </TBODY>
</TABLE>

<FORM ACTION="contactdelete.asp" METHOD="POST" id="form1" NAME="form1">
   <INPUT TYPE="hidden" ID="hdnID" NAME="hdnID"
          VALUE="<% =objContact.ID %>">
   <P><INPUT ID="submit1" NAME="submit1" TYPE="submit"
          VALUE="Remove contact"> </P>
</FORM>

<P><FONT SIZE="2">
<A HREF="contactlist.asp">List the contacts</A>
  
<A HREF="contactedit.asp">Add a new contact</A>
  
```

```
     <A HREF="Default.htm">Home</A>
     </FONT></P>
     <%
        Else
            objContact.DeleteContact CStr(Request.Form("hdnID"))
     %>
     <H1><IMG ALIGN="middle" SRC="images/wroxlogo.gif" WIDTH="56" HEIGHT="56">
      Contact Removed</H1>
     <P>The contact has been removed from the list.</P>

     <P><FONT SIZE="2">
     <A HREF="contactlist.asp">List the contacts</A>
       
     <A HREF="contactedit.asp">Add a new contact</A>
       
     <A HREF="Default.htm">Home</A>
     </FONT></P>

     <%
        End If
     %>

     </BODY>
     </HTML>
```

As with the contactedit.asp page, this page is recursive. If called directly it asks the user to confirm the deletion of the chosen contact. If the user clicks the Submit button, the form is posted back to the contactdelete.asp page and the contact is deleted.

The first thing the page does is to determine whether it's being called directly.

```
<%
    Dim objContact
    Dim strID

    Set objContact = Server.CreateObject("ContactObjects.Contact")

    If Request.Form("hdnID") = Empty Then
```

Confirming the Delete

If the page was called directly, the ID value is pulled from the URL by using the QueryString method of the Request object and is used to load a Contact object:

```
    If Request.Form("hdnID") = Empty Then
        strID = CStr(Request.QueryString("ID"))
        objContact.Load Cstr(strID)
%>
```

That object is then used to display the contact's details.

A hidden field in the form is loaded with the contact ID value as well, enabling the recursive feature of this page:

```
<INPUT TYPE="hidden" ID="hdnID" NAME="hdnID"
       VALUE="<% =objContact.ID %>">
```

If the user clicks the **Submit** button, the form will be posted back to the same page, but this time the `hdnID` field will contain a value – indicating that the delete operation should take place.

Deleting the Contact

When the delete operation is confirmed, the page will run the code to delete the `Contact` object from the database:

```
<%
    Else
        objContact.DeleteContact CStr(Request.Form("hdnID"))
%>
```

In this case we're making use of the `DeleteContact` method – passing the ID value as a parameter. By using this method we can avoid loading the contact data from the database just to turn around and request that it be deleted.

Global.asa

The `Global.asa` file for this application is trivial:

```
<SCRIPT LANGUAGE=VBScript RUNAT=Server>

</SCRIPT>
```

Our application is now ready to run. We should be able to load the `Default.htm` page:

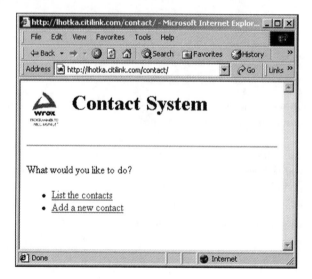

and navigate from there to list, view, add, edit and remove contacts from the database:

Summary

In this chapter, we've built a complete Windows DNA application. While fairly basic, this application illustrates all the key parts of the Windows DNA architecture, and can act as a good basis for building more complex applications.

The application is composed of four main tiers:

❑ Presentation

❑ User interface

❑ Business logic

❑ Data services

The theory behind the design and implementation of each of these tiers is covered throughout the rest of the book, while in this chapter we tied it all together to create an application.

As applications grow in complexity and scalability requirements, the model used in this chapter may not be sufficient. More sophisticated techniques and technologies are covered in Chapter 11.

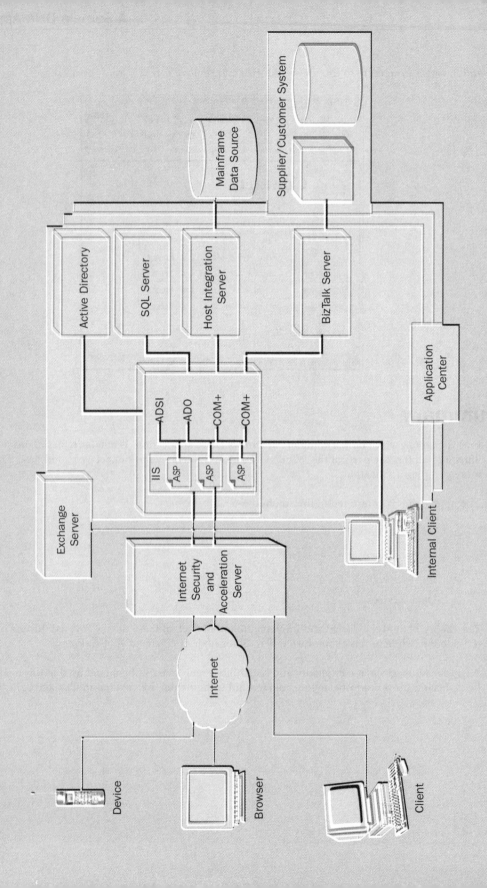

24

Case Study: Airline Booking System

This is the second of our three case studies that are designed to put together the principles you've learned in this book and show you how they might be applied to a real DNA application.

The reason that there is more than one case study is because even if you follow the guidelines for writing great Windows DNA applications, you will still find that any two DNA applications may differ substantially in their implementation. There are two main reasons for this:

❑   There is always a lot of room for individual style in how you decide to design your architecture. For example, programmers will each have different preferences for precisely when some functionality should be left inline, moved to functions in an ASP include file, or shifted to a component. To some extent there is also a compromise between the requirements of scalability, performance, platform-independence and maintainability; although DNA architecture should, in theory, give you all of these benefits, there are cases in which the requirements to some extent conflict and some tradeoff needs to be made. As an example, efficient database access will generally mean you use stored procedures for your database operations. However, if you want your application to be portable to a different database, you'd generally find it easier to just pass standard SQL queries to the database instead. In these sorts of cases you will need to make design decisions based on the likely needs of your own particular requirements.

❑ When you get into the real world you will find it's not just a question of which technology or technique is the best, but which ones you are allowed or skilled enough to use. Factors such as the requirement to meet tight deadlines, the particular prejudices of your managers, or the skills you know your company developers have, come into play. For example, good design might say that certain business rules should be implemented by separate components, but if your support developers don't know anything about COM or how to code or maintain components, then you may end up compromising that principle for the sake of getting something out the door that works and can be easily supported in the department. You may also find that if you are running a medium-sized organization rather than a large enterprise, and you have your web site hosted by an ISP rather than running the servers entirely in-house, then your ISP may not allow you to run certain software – a common example is of ISPs allowing ASP pages but refusing to allow components to be installed, because of the security problems. (A badly written or even a deliberately harmful component can potentially do a lot more damage to a server than an ASP page can). Obviously this last point will not apply to intranets or to large organizations that maintain their own servers.

What this is leading up to is that although two applications can both be following reasonably good DNA principles, be scalable, efficient and maintainable, they can still look very different in style when you look at the details of the coding, the languages, algorithms and data structures used, and at the details of the application architecture. Which is why in this book we've decided to present four different case studies, written by different authors, so you can compare the differences in style – each case study does follow the DNA principles we've covered throughout this book. Unlike a real application written for an organization, these case studies are specially prepared for the book, and therefore not restricted by the skill sets of the supporting developers or by managerial decisions – though they are restricted by the requirement to fit the complete case studies into a single chapter each. Although these examples are carefully designed to perform their tasks well, and you won't go far wrong if you design your applications along the same lines as these case studies, you won't see some of the more advanced subtle nuances or technologies here that you'd see in a full-scale enterprise application which could take advantage of advanced Enterprise Server capabilities and so on. We will point out places where these restrictions have influenced the coding.

So these case studies are designed to be approximate blueprints. Use them to see how we've chosen to apply the various technologies we've covered in this book. And also use them to see several different ways that a DNA application can be designed. It's then up to you to decide how you need to adapt these designs to fit in with the requirements of your own applications, and to fit in with any restrictions within the context of your own organization.

In this case study we've chosen to concentrate on looking at how you plan out and design the architecture of your project. That means we've been very selective about which bits of code we've actually presented here – only showing you the stuff that is relevant to the way we've set about designing the application. Needless to say, if you want the full code for the project, you can download it from the Wrox Press website. The second case study concentrates more on presenting the detailed code for the project.

Introducing NoseDive Airlines

The case study in this chapter is based around an airline booking system for the company *NoseDive Airlines Inc.* (*NDA*). It's a classic example of a system that's based around a database, and which is open for the public to make bookings on the Internet – in other words this type of system:

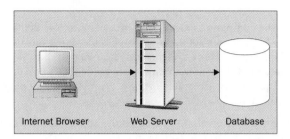

Internet Browser   Web Server   Database

Also typical of a system of this nature, there are two types of user we need to support:

❑ The customers, making bookings over the Internet

❑ The administrative staff, who need to maintain the database, and ensure it contains correct details of flights, and so on

We could also mention a third category – the sales staff who will be making bookings on behalf of customers who ring up or call in to the offices – but since this basically involves the same functionality as customers on the Internet, we'll let the sales staff use the Internet pages. This is our first example of a design decision caused by a restriction imposed on us – in this case the requirement to keep the application simple enough to fit into one chapter! In a real airline, the sales staff would probably have access to additional functionality, such as the ability to bring up and modify bookings for different customers, and would almost certainly have to log in to identify themselves to the system.

Let's take a look at the functionality required of our system. We'll start off with the customer pages. People should be able to visit the site on the Internet and:

❑ Search the database for flights between set destinations on a given date

❑ Check the prices of those flights

❑ Book seats on those flights, paying by credit card

While the administrators will need to:

❑ Input and modify details of flights and prices

❑ Check to see how booked up flights are

In a real airline, they'd also be doing things like preparing reports, but we won't bother with that here.

Application Requirements

What we've just gone through is a rough statement of what the problem we need to solve is. In practice you'd normally be given a rather more thorough specification for what your application needs to do. So to keep this realistic we're going to have one here. This is what NoseDive Airlines have stated they require of the system:

❏ It should run on the company's existing network of Windows 2000 machines. The backend database must be SQL Server 2000. As far as possible, however, the bookings system should be designed to be flexible. There are currently no plans to shift the database, for example, but it would be preferable if the system architecture made this a possibility in the future. However, performance and scalability are crucial. Any cross-platform independence should not come at the cost of performance.

❏ The software engineers who will be coding up the application are skilled in writing components, and are comfortable coding in C++, VB, or ASP – so it's OK to use whichever language is most appropriate.

❏ As stated earlier, the system is designed to allow booking of flights over the Internet. Customers should be able to query what flights are available between two given destinations, view the fares, and make bookings with their credit card. For our purposes we only need to take credit card details – we'll be buying in some standard commercial software to sort out the actual verification of the card.

❏ All flights will have two categories of seating: Business and Economy. Administration staff should be able to edit details of these two fares separately.

❏ While customers must be able to log in over the Internet, all the administration staff are based in the NDA main offices in the village of Wyre Piddle, Warwickshire. Hence these staff will have direct access to the company's main network and will not need to connect over the Internet to access the database. The staff should be able to edit, add and remove flights, and set the fares (though flights can only be edited when there are no current bookings).

❏ The number of Business and Economy seats for each flight depends on the aircraft flying – so the database will need to link the flight to the aircraft. Also, NDA tends to run flights on very regular schedules – every day or every week at the same time for example. So it would be best if the administration staff were allowed to enter flights by specifying, for example, from London Heathrow at 10.30 am every Monday between specific dates, rather than having to separately enter details of numerous nearly identical flights. The administration staff should also be able to view current take-up of bookings for any given flight.

That's our specifications outlined – admittedly still a bit more brief than you'd normally find in real life, but it'll do for our purposes. Now we need to look at how we are going to design something that meets our requirements.

Application Design

The first major bit of work we have to do is writing the application that is going to satisfy the specifications we've just outlined.

Planning

The first thing I want you to notice is the size of the 'application design' section of this chapter. Go on, flick ahead through the next few pages – see how much space I've devoted to discussing the architecture for this application. And not a single line of code anywhere in this section. That's so important that I'm going to repeat it. Not a single line of code anywhere in this section. Application design is important. It's so tempting to rush in and start coding, but if you do that before you've carefully worked out how your application is going to fit together, you're asking to have to do a lot of rewriting. And you're asking for missed deadlines and a lot more work than you'd bargained for.

Of course good application design doesn't mean you don't do any coding whatsoever. You might want to test out a couple of ideas just to make sure they are going to work. If there's any part of the design that will require skills you're not quite certain of then it probably will make sense to write a few bits of code to try out the ideas and make sure they aren't going to fail because you've misunderstood how some bit of technology will work. In practice I've noticed two approaches to coding:

❏ Firstly there's the one that most programmers seem to like. That involves jumping in and writing the first bits of code that come to your head. Of course a couple of months later you realize that the code you've written and the code that you actually needed to write are so completely different that basically you've just wasted quite a bit of time. There's also this strange assumption that someone else wil do the testing.

❏ On the other hand there's the approach that seems to be recommended by most theory books and academic work on how to write large projects. This involves planning out everything right down almost to the parameter specifications for all your function calls and estimating how long this is all going to take. That way you know you've got everything right and then for the last part of the project you can start coding and testing. All my experience is that this approach rarely works either.

The point is that in designing projects it's quite rare to get everything right the first time. There's always some feedback – you design something, then when you actually code it up something comes up and you realize that you need to make some improvements to your design. The different stages of any project aren't totally separate – the application design, coding, and testing all feed back into each other. And all stages are important. Trying to omit the boring stages will lead to a bad application, but in all probability so will keeping the stages too well separated.

If this all sounds like I've argued us back into doing some early coding, don't worry, I haven't. I said this section wasn't going to have a single line of code in it and I'm sticking to that. We need to accept that when we start coding and testing that will almost certainly throw up issues that will lead us to make some small design changes – but that's not the same thing as rewriting the entire design from scratch. So it's still important to make sure that we do have the design carefully thought out before we start coding – it's more a case of having the application architecture sufficiently well thought out that we know what we're doing when we code up, and at the same time being prepared to be flexible about the design if we need to be.

And like I said, at the design stage you may still want to do some programming in order to test out a few ideas. But just make sure this coding doesn't accidentally (or accidentally on purpose?) move from testing ideas into actually coding up a project that you haven't yet designed properly.

One thing that this all means is that, in reality, this case study is only a study of the first part of the project – we're going to go through a good design for our flights booking system and we'll do the first draft of code – enough to get it working. At that point we will have a working application, and the chapter will finish. In real life you'd get back to the customers (or your managers) to see if they like what you've done, do stress testing to check whether performance is good enough, and of course test that the thing works – and that will all lead to a few rounds of improvements and (hopefully minor) rewrites of some sections.

The Booking System Architecture

But with those caveats let's figure out some architecture. We can make out from the project specifications that we're looking at something like this:

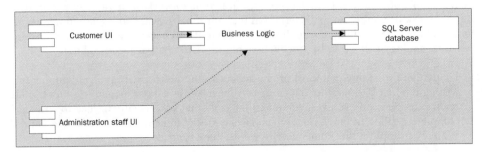

This is just the earlier diagram but with a few more details filled in. We've got a database at one end, two different user interfaces at the other end, and some kind of business logic in between. We'll look at the ends of the application first.

The Database

There are no real arguments here. We've actually been told in the design spec that it's going to be SQL Server 2000. Is SQL Server 2000 the best choice? Well, although it's true that many other database products such as SyBase or Oracle would server equally well, that's not really a relevant question – management have told us that's what the database is going to be – so unless we've got an incredibly good reason to go back and question their judgment... But seriously, SQL Server is a fine choice. It's scalable, has high performance, and does all we need. There's perhaps a slight question mark about using a new technology. Mightn't we want to wait a year or so until all the bugs have been ironed out of it? Should we use SQL Server 7 instead of SQL Server 2000 and upgrade in a few months? Since this is a book about DNA, there's not really a choice.

One question we need to address is how are we going to get the data out of the database? The options are stored procedures and plain SQL statements. Let's look at the advantages of each.

Stored Procedures

- ❏ Give greater performance.

- ❏ Give greater security protection against inappropriate database access, since we can set up security on the database to only allow the account the application will use to get to the data via the stored procedures. This will stop any SQL statements from being used to read or change the database in ways that don't conform to our business rules.

- ❏ Allow separation of the operations wanted from the underlying SQL.

Passing in SQL statements

- ❏ Makes it easier for us to swap to a different database if we later need to do so.

Looking again at the project specification, performance was given a high priority. Shifting to another database server is not something that looks likely to happen in the near future. So stored procedures win out easily here.

Now let's consider the user interfaces – both of them.

Customer User Inteface

This is going to be implemented as web pages. We do however need to decide how sophisticated they are going to be – where do we find the balance between reach and richness (as described in Chapter 16). Well it's customers over the Internet, so we've absolutely no control over the browser they are going to use. So we're really restricted to code that all the common browsers will understand (unless we implement some page that checks what the browser is and generates appropriate HTML). As a rough guide it would probably be sensible to make sure our web pages will work on Internet Explorer versions 3 onwards. That far back? Yes, as programmers some of us might be used to IE5.5 and Windows 2000, but I can think of a couple of friends of mine who are still running Windows 3.1. It works – it gives them Internet access and lets them write and print out Word documents. Why on earth should they upgrade just for the sake of upgrading? By the same reasoning we ought to go back to Netscape Navigator 3 onwards. And then there are those Linux people who keep going on about how great Lynx is for web browsing.

I don't want to start getting into complications like detecting browser type and matching web page richness to the browser here. That's getting a bit too far from the purpose of this case study. Which really means we're going to be confined to basic HTML. No fancy DHTML or JavaScript. In order to keep to some standards, I'm going to stick to strict HTML 4.0, but I won't use any features that might not be understood by earlier browsers. So tables are acceptable, for example – but not frames. And I'll make sure I test the web pages on several different browsers. (Given many common browsers only support HTML 3.2, you might wonder why I'm saying HTML 4.0. Well I'm not going to use any of the new HTML 4.0 features that are not supported by earlier browsers so this way I get a web page that is based on the newest standard but still has a good reach amongst browsers.)

Since we're dealing with the Web, by the way, we need to choose our web server. We are going to use ASP3.0/IIS5.0 because that is a good system to use on the Windows 2000 platform, and because this is specifically a book about Windows DNA. But in real life, it would be worth your while checking that alternative web servers (such as Apache) are not going to serve your needs better.

Administration User Interface

We've got a lot more choice here. The staff dealing with inputting the flight schedules etc. are all going to be based at the main offices, using the main network of workstations. They will be able to access the database from their own machines, so there's no real need to use web pages (though we might choose to). This gives us three main choices:

❑ Web pages

❑ Some custom application with its own UI

❑ MMC SnapIns

Let's examine the options in turn.

Web Pages

We're already writing web pages for the customers so we might be able to reuse some code, which will make development easier. We also know if we use web pages that if the company later decides to really go net-savvy and wants people to be able to do administration work from home, they'll be able to do it. On the other hand, web pages are slow. Interpreting scripts does put an overhead on the server, which is simply not necessary if people are only going to be logging in on the local network. Web pages also restrict the user interface a little. That could be seen as an advantage if it means staff will be using the kind of interface they are already used to – it reduces training time. But it does mean that unless we really go overboard on the client-side JavaScript we won't be able to get such a rich user interface as we could do.

MMC SnapIn

At first sight this looks like a good idea. MMC is, after all, the preferred Microsoft way of presenting administrative interfaces, so administrators should be very familiar with it. And it means we don't have to write much user interface code because the MMC console will handle most of that for us. However, before we get too excited, think again. 'Administrator' in the MMC context means systems administrator – someone who's an expert in the administration side of Windows. But what we've been talking about is company/flight administrators, in other words the people who work in scheduling flights etc. That's different – these people aren't necessarily going to be skilled in Windows or familiar with MMC. In short, this isn't really the type of application that MMC was designed for after all.

But it gets worse. To use MMC, we've got to be familiar with the MMC interfaces. How many of our staff have those skills? It certainly wasn't on the list of skills we were given in the project specification. Also, MMC presents the things to be managed in a hierarchical tree view. But we're dealing with a relational database. How easy is it going to be to map our relational structure into the hierarchical structure that MMC likes?

Custom User Interface

You'll probably have gathered from the discussions above that I've basically ruled out the previous two options, so this is the one we're going for. It's flexible, will give us a rich user interface, and not having the overhead of any scripting will mean we'll have relatively efficient, responsive code. For a user interface, efficiency isn't that important, but responsiveness is. We don't want the user to sit waiting for a couple of seconds while IIS processes our page, before the database even gets a look in, if we can help it.

Another advantage is ease of code development – we can code our user interface in VB, and thereby take advantage of debugging facilities far superior to those of ASP/VBScript. We may lose out on not being able to reuse some VBScript code that we wrote for our customer ASP pages, but we can minimize that to some extent by using COM components for business objects.

There is a disadvantage of using what comes down to a Win32 UI. It can be harder to deploy. Certainly on Windows NT4, it would have been necessary to make the executable available on all the machines from which it might be used, as well as registering any required COM components. These problems have eased considerably on Windows 2000, with the arrival of the Windows Installer. And in our case our application will only need to be used on the main NoseDive Airlines corporate network – so we'll accept this disadvantage for the sake of the other advantages gained.

Having said all that, we will make one concession to web pages. Just in case the company later decides it needs a web interface so its staff can do administrative tasks from other locations, we'll make sure all the middle-tier objects are designed in such a way that they would be able to talk to VBScript if necessary.

One thing I've put in here is the assumption that we'll be using VB. We could use C++, which would give us better performance, but that's not really an issue here. Unless we want to do something *really* fancy with our user interface, VB wins hands down for writing this part of the application, just on ease-of-coding grounds. Ditto for VB versus J++, another possible alternative for the front end.

I should mention before we move on that the issues we've covered here are correct for ASP and IIS up to version 5. ASP+ and the new Windows.NET platform will introduce many new features, which will have an impact on our choice of user interface and may shift the balance more in favor of a web-based architecture.

The Middle Tier

We've sorted out the ends of the architecture. Now it's time to look at what is going to go on in the middle – the business objects and all that.

Well, components are going to come in. The only real argument for not using them would be if our developers weren't sufficiently skilled and the deadlines didn't allow for getting them trained up. By implementing all the middle-tier administrative functionality that our user interfaces are going to call as components, we make it easy to swap to a different user interface if necessary.

So we're going to make the decision that all database access will be through components. This is starting to tie our architecture down a lot more. We now have something like this:

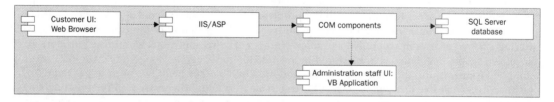

Notice that we now have a fairly distinct interface – in both senses of the word– at the point where our user interface talks to our business/data objects. So we now have a classic n-Tier architecture! There's absolutely no need for our user interface or ASP components to know anything about SQL or about the structure of the database. If we're careful about how this interface is designed, we'll be able to simply tell the components to do something like add a new booking or tell us what flights there are from Manchester to Mauritius on a certain day, and not have to worry about how that information is extracted from the database. The resultant ease of maintainability is an incredibly good reason for keeping *all* database access in the same set of components.

Earlier in the book, we saw why it's sometimes appropriate to add an extra tier of components, separating the business objects into data tier components that talk to the database, and business objects that handle the user interface issues. We're not going to do that in this project.

COM Interface Design

The biggest thing now that's going to affect our code maintainability is the design of the COM interface presented by the components to the user interface code – so it's worth some thought upfront about how we're going to set about it.

The first point is that we've already indicated these components should be useable from scripting languages. That basically means all their `ByRef` parameters ought to be variants or objects. There should be no making up parameters that are strings or integers unless they are passed by value. That will give us a small performance overhead for the VB clients, but not a particularly significant one. (VBScript doesn't recognize any data type except the Variant but when passing parameters by value to components we can use the conversion functions like CStr and CInt to get round this).

We should make sure this interface is simple to understand. This means that it should be consistent. In other words, let's say that the method to add a new booking is called `AddBooking`, it takes parameters that give all the information about the booking, and returns a value (a Variant) that will uniquely identify the booking for any future use. Given that, it would make an awful lot of sense if the method to add a new airport to the list of airports served is called `AddAirport` (and not `AddNewAirport` or `CreateAirport`), and also takes parameters that give all the required information about the new airport, and returns a value (a Variant) that will uniquely identify the airport for any future use.

When we come to code up the components, I'll say a bit more about the interfaces they are going to present, so you can see the consistency.

Scalability

It is a requirement, so it is important that we do whatever we can to make sure our architecture is scalable. You'll have gathered from previous chapters that the most important thing we can do for scalability is to make sure our components are *stateless*. Accordingly, each component that talks to the database will present methods that take all the information needed to do the job as parameters. There will be no properties exposed.

That's the components dealt with. It's worth thinking about making our ASP pages stateless as well as our components. There are a couple of points here. And there's a common fallacy in the developer community that in order to avoid scalability problems it's sufficient to avoid storing inappropriate components at session scope. Unfortunately, for true scalability that's not the case. We need to avoid storing *anything* at session scope. No variables. Nothing. The reason is that as soon as you store anything at session scope, that data has to be stored independently for every session. And if you have several thousand user sessions, that data can quickly add up. On the other hand, we need to get some perspective. What I've just said is correct for true scalability. But how many web sites routinely have tens of thousands of simultaneous sessions? In most cases it's more likely that you'll typically have a few tens or perhaps hundreds of simultaneous sessions – and in that case storing a few variables at session scope isn't really such an issue.

So if you are intending your site to be scalable to the point of coping with thousands or tens of thousands of serious users, you do need to give serious consideration to actually disabling the IIS session. This can be done quite easily in the Internet Services Manager. Right-click on the web site to bring up the Property sheet. Select the Home Directory tab and click on the Configuration button. This brings up a second tabbed dialog box, in which you need to select the AppOptions tab. You'll find a check box there that you can uncheck to disable the session state.

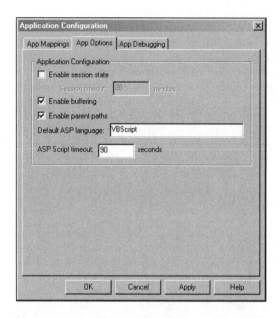

Disabling session state is the easy part, and by itself isn't normally a real problem. The reason I'm emphasizing it here is that it brings up another issue: We won't be able to use session cookies to remember users. You see, what can happen when a user logs on to a web site and starts doing things like filling a shopping basket is that the web server remembers the user between page requests by sending their browser a session cookie. At least that's what happens in a web site that's not been designed with this scalability in mind. It's tempting to do it because it's so easy. If the user hasn't specifically disabled sessions then IIS will by default send the browser the session cookie – which means you can write code that remembers sessions with virtually no effort on your part.

Unfortunately, using the session cookie is only possible if session state has been enabled, and it means your ASP pages are no longer stateless – so they won't scale as well. So we won't do that here. We need our web server to run by disabling sessions altogether, and rely entirely on information sent back with the HTTP form to identify the 'session'. This may mean more work in passing form data from page to page, but it will mean that at least in this regard the NoseDive Airlines site will be scalable. Going over the code for sessions is beyond the scope of this chapter. Suffice to say that if you go down that route, you will need to store some alternative session keys (some random sequence of letters and numbers!) in your database, and regularly purge them to ensure out-of-date ones are removed. The NoseDive Airlines site has been implemented in this way, and if you need to you can see how it's been done by downloading the code from the Wrox Press web site.

Don't confuse the (time-limited) session cookies with the cookies that are stored permanently on a client machine and automatically sent by the browser with every page request whenever it connects to a web site for which it has a relevant cookie available. These cookies are there to identify the user rather than the session. They don't stop the ASP pages from being stateless, and there are no problems with using them, at least as far as scalability is concerned.

Component Language

One final area we haven't touched on is what language we're going to use to code up our components. The choice is C++ or VB. And frankly, it's not a clear-cut decision. There are advantages to both. (We're not going to consider J++ because of the need to install the Java Virtual Machine in order to use it, as well as doubts about its future.)

When it comes to components, using C++ in conjunction with Microsoft's Active Template Library (ATL) is fairly quick. It depends a bit on your prior experience, but in general the learning curve to know how to write ATL components is far greater than for VB. However if you already have the relevant skills then that's not an issue. Once you know how to use ATL, all other things being equal, writing business objects using ATL is likely to be only slightly slower than if you were using VB. And in return for using ATL you get a bit more flexibility in the design of your components, and in all probability a bit better performance.

What slants the performance issue in favor of ATL here is that we are doing database access. If we write our business objects in VB, we will normally need to use ADO to talk to the database. ADO in turn is a wrapper round OLE DB – the ADO objects just call up underlying OLE DB objects, in the process theoretically making the coding easier for you, while also adding some performance overhead because of the extra layer involved. But if we use C++, we can just use OLE DB directly, knocking out ADO's performance overhead. Even better, ATL comes with OLE DB consumer templates, which in practice make writing code that accesses OLE DB pretty much as easy and quick as writing code that accesses ADO. Provided, of course, that you know how to use the consumer templates – but again once you've learned how that's not a problem. In terms of the existing skill set of the developers for this project, ATL/OLE DB is fine!

At this point I can see all the VB programmers reading this starting to panic about the prospect of having to plough through ATL code for this case study. But don't worry – there's one other factor which I decided firmly put the advantage back in VB's court for this particular application. And that's the fact that these components need to talk to scripting clients, and ideally need all their ByRef (that is, all the [out]) method parameters to be Variants. You see, ATL does have good support for Variants, but the OLE DB interfaces don't use them at all – preferring to rely on the more efficient native data types of C++. That means that if I go down the ATL/OLE DB path, I'm going to be responsible for all the data conversions between Variants and the data types OLE DB provides. That's not a trivial programming task, and is one that's likely to lead to me having to do a fair amount of debugging. If I go with VB/ADO then ADO will handle all those type conversions for me – and Microsoft's own developers have (hopefully) already done all the relevant debugging. That means that VB/ADO is going to lead to shorter development times. Of course, I could have gone with ATL/ADO but then I'd still have the performance overhead imposed by ADO as well as the slight extra complexity of coding using ATL.

So, in summary, we're going to write our components in VB.

> You might be thinking, 'so what? Isn't that the obvious choice anyway?' Well no, it was one of two choices. Perhaps I'd have still gone for VB if I'd had to make a snap decision, but in the end good application design is crucial – and that does mean you ought to carefully consider all the different options to decide what is best for your circumstances. That's why the preceding discussion was so important.

There is one other factor that I should mention: if we wanted to take advantage of the object pooling facilities available in COM+, then we would have to write our components using C++ in order for them to be able to use the free threading model (at least until Visual Studio7/.NET comes out, when VB should support this model). However, we don't need to worry about that here since we don't anticipate our components will put much performance overhead on initializing. The bottleneck here would have been setting up the database connection from each component when it initializes, but OLE DB will do connection pooling for that behind the scenes anyway.

The Database

The final thing before we start coding – we need to plan our database structure:

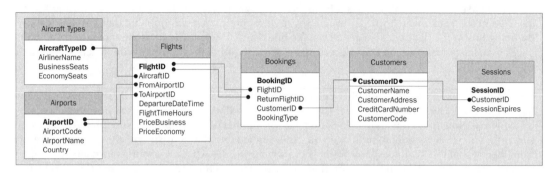

The centerpiece of the database is the `Flights` table which shows all the details of any individual flight. This is linked to the `AircraftTypes` table to get data on which type of aircraft is supposed to be running the flight (and hence how many seats there are), and to the `Airports` table to show where the flight is going from and to. The `Airports` table stores three bits of information about each airport – its name, country, and the code – that's the three-letter code that is often used to identify airports, for example MAN for Manchester, LGW for London Gatwick. Note that because this code is unique we could have made it the primary key of the `Airports` table. The reason I didn't is just for performance/storage. Since there are going to be a *lot* of entries in the `Flights` table, each one requiring two references to the primary key in the `Airports` table (the `From` and `To` airports) I decided it was best to keep the primary key as small and easy to deal with as possible – and hence to keep it as a number.

On the other side of the database are the customers. Each customer is represented by a row in the `Customers` table – and for simplicity we've kept the information in this table down to a minimum – name, address and credit card number (which in practice would be encoded). The customer code is there for use in customer cookies. These are the cookies stored on the customers' machines – not session cookies! Basically, regular customers will probably want a cookie on their machine to identify themselves automatically. The code is the string that will be stored in this cookie. It's a longish sequence of letters and numbers generated at random, though it has the customer ID incorporated into it to ensure it is unique. Why have we done this and not just used the customer ID? The answer is for security. If we used the ID, then almost any small number would be a valid ID – so it would be very easy for a customer to pretend to be any other customer, just by changing the ID in his cookie. By incorporating a long random sequence of letters in it, we can almost completely prevent this, since if our dishonest customer tries making up other cookies at random, it's extremely unlikely that the string he comes up with will actually be recognized by the database as a valid customer code. By the way, we're deliberately not using GUIDs for this purpose. Although GUIDs are guaranteed to be unique, they are not really designed for security. GUIDs are partly made up of information obtained from the computer's hardware address, which doesn't change when you generate further GUIDs – as well as information derived from the system time. The result is that when you generate successive GUIDs on the same machine, they often differ by a few digits – which would make it too easy for a dishonest customer to guess other customers' codes.

> *As an extra precaution, we would probably not allow tickets to be sent to anywhere other than the customer's registered address – a restriction that's getting quite common anyway. In a more realistic scenario, each customer would probably also have a password that they'd need to supply in order to change any of their details, but for this sample we won't be providing that functionality.*

The Sessions table is our way of getting round the requirement that the Session object is not used in ASP, for scalability reasons, and will be used for those customers who do not have a cookie on their machine. Instead of using the ASP session, we will create our own session key (a random string) and use hidden HTML form controls to pass it from page to page. Just as for IIS sessions, our session key will have a timeout value, which will always be set at 20 minutes after the time that that key was last used. By doing this in the database, we get all the facilities of ASP sessions, but at the same time our ASP pages remain stateless. Doing this process manually is slightly laborious but is important to maintain true scalability.

Finally, the Bookings table shouldn't need any comment. It simply links together the customer and the flight. The BookingType is an integer that contains the value 0 if the booking is Business class, or 1 if it is Economy. Note that all bookings include a return flight ID. For simplicity NoseDive Airlines won't currently accept one-way bookings. We will generally assume that tourists will always want to return from their holidays. (Well, perhaps 'want' is the wrong word – what they want is probably to elope with the new lover they've just picked up on that tropical island in the Indian Ocean, but they'll return home anyway.) The return fare is just twice the single fare, (though this doesn't really affect us since we're not dealing with the actual credit card transactions in this example).

The Code

If you're starting to wonder when we're ever going to start coding, we've finally got there.We're not going to go over all the code in this chapter – there's not really much point since apart from the actual fields used in the SQL statements, the stored procedure to add a new airport looks pretty much like the stored procedure to add a new aircraft type, which in turn looks basically like the stored procedure to add a new booking. And ditto for the corresponding functions in our data objects (the components). So we'll present just enough code to give you an idea of the principles we've used when coding, and leave you to download the entire code from the Wrox Press web site if you feel inclined to set up your own airline company and want a pre-written booking system for it.

If you do set up your own airline, we suggest that you don't call it NoseDive Airlines, since that name is the product of several million dollars worth of research into the name most likely to attract passengers, and so we'd be likely to sue you for breach of copyright.

We're going to start off with the COM interface design.

Interface Design

We are only going to need one component for our data object – a component that has a long list of methods that perform various actions against the database. To give you an idea of the interface design, here's the list of methods that deal with adding, modifying, and looking up airports:

```
Public Function AddAirport(ByVal sAirportCode As String, _
    ByVal sAirportName As String, ByVal sCountry As String _
    ) As Variant
End Function

Public Sub ModifyAirport(ByVal sAirportID As String, _
    ByVal sAirportCode As String, _
```

```
        ByVal sAirportName As String, ByVal sCountry As String _
        )
    End Sub

    Public Sub RemoveAirport(ByVal sAirportID As String)
    End Sub

    Public Function GetAirports() As Collection
    End Function
```

Since we're coding our project in VB, this is how the set of functions looks in VB, not what the IDL looks like. Basically, this is the class module before I've actually added any code to the functions. And these functions should hopefully illustrate what I mean by a well-designed, easy to use, interface. The idea is that you can understand exactly what all of those functions do and how to use them without much more explanation from me. The only point that may need clarifying is that the return value from the AddAirport function is the unique identifier that should be used in all client code to identify this airport in the future.

As it happens, this identifier is going to be the same as the primary key in the Airports *table, although this need not be the case – all we require is that that identifier is recognized by all the other relevant methods of the data object – the client code doesn't need to be concerned with how this identifier actually maps into the database.*

And to demonstrate what "consistency of the interface" means, here's a few more of the methods from it. These are the methods that let you do similar operations on the flights:

```
    Public Function AddAircraftType(ByVal vBusinessSeats As Variant, _
        ByVal vAircraftTypeName As Variant, ByVal vEconomySeats As Variant) As Variant
    End Function

    Public Sub RemoveAircraftType(ByVal vAircraftTypeID As Variant)
    End Sub

    Public Function AircraftTypes() As Collection
    End Function
```

The functions have an identical structure and scheme for naming them, except that there's no ModifyAircraftType function. (Think of the disruption it would cause if you suddenly came along and changed the number of seats available in an aircraft type that was already in use for lots of flights.) If NoseDive Airlines does some modifications to an airliner to change the seating arrangements in it, they'll have to add a new aircraft type to the database to describe it.

Returning Sets of Data: Collections

One point I've passed over without comment in the above definitions is the way we're choosing to return the results of queries against the database. In ADO these will be returned as *recordsets*. But I've defined these methods as returning *collections*. Why? Well it's really got to do with isolating technologies in order to better separate the functionality of different bits of the booking system to make it easier to replace different components.

This is an area in which many experienced developers hold diametrically opposed opinions. Almost whatever approach you take, someone is going to disagree with you. So I'll explain my reasoning for using collections here, and what some of the counter-arguments are, and leave you to judge what is best for you in your own applications.

It's true that returning a recordset is arguably going to be highly efficient, since we are going to use ADO internally, and ADO will give recordsets back to our component – so it would be the easiest thing in the world to simply pass those recordsets back to the client. Recordsets are easy to use as well.

However, that means that the clients are going to have to be aware of ADO. What happens if, in four years time, ADO is made obsolete by some whizzy new data-access technology and we all stop using recordsets? We're going to end up in a situation where the component will have to convert the data from the database into this now obsolete data structure, which the clients will have to use. Either that or the user interface client code will need to be updated to whatever the new data structures are. Not a pleasant prospect in either case.

Note here that I'm not saying that the application will break just because a new technology comes out – more that we want this application to have a long lifetime – and it's almost certain that we will gradually want to improve it, adding new features and updating it to reflect any new business activities NoseDive Airlines gets involved with. In a few years there might be something that is so much better than ADO available that there is an overwhelming case for swapping the database access to the new technology as part of the normal maintenance/upgrading of our software. If that is the case then we want our booking system to be architectured in such a way that we will be able to swap technologies with minimum disruption to the system. By separating the client layers from all the ADO code, we can achieve this. In essence we've achieved greater componentization and hopefully future maintainability at the expense of some performance.

Depending on the requirements of your own projects, you may feel happy to pass recordsets back to the client code – you might feel that the high performance gains through doing things this way makes it worthwhile. That's fair enough, though you should be aware you are completely tying your entire project down to use ADO indefinitely (or until you rewrite the entire booking system). Another argument that's sometimes presented is that we're already tying our project down to using VB, ASP and COM/COM+. What's so different about doing this from using ADO? After all, COM+ will eventually become obsolete. In all probability so will VB if we look far enough into the future. Well, dependence on some technology is unavoidable! The point of my trying to confine ADO recordsets to the components that talk to the database is that I'm minimizing the dependence of the project on particular technologies as far as possible, and maximizing our ability to replace individual parts of the system with minimal impact on the rest of the project.

> **So we've gone for completely insulating the client code from all the details of the database access. By returning collections – a standard VB structure – we know that we can, if we choose, replace ADO by some other technology to access the databases in our component, and the rest of our DNA application will still work fine without any modifications. The penalty of course is the performance overhead involved in converting a recordset to a collection – which isn't trivial.**

I should mention that if you want to insulate the client code from ADO, but are unhappy about using recordsets, then a good alternative would be to use XML – this would be relatively easy since ADO does now have good support for XML. Other possibilities are to pass some strings back that contain the data according to some agreed format.

So now we've got our collection, what's it going to be a collection of? Well, obviously we will need to define some new objects to represent the things that we need to return, and which can go in the collections. So we'll need an `Airport` object, an `AircraftType` object, a `Flight` object, etc. Here's the interface definition for the `Airport` object:

```
Public Property Get ID() As Variant
End Property

Public Property Let ID(ByVal vNewValue As Variant)
End Property

Public Property Get Code() As Variant
End Property

Public Property Let Code(ByVal vNewValue As Variant)
End Property

Public Property Get Name() As Variant
End Property

Public Property Let Name(ByVal vNewValue As Variant)
End Property


Public Property Get Country() As Variant
End Property

Public Property Let Country(ByVal vNewValue As Variant)
End Property
```

Again this should be self-explanatory. The `Airport` object just exposes properties from which the various items of information about the airport can be obtained.

At this point I imagine some readers raising two concerns about our use of this object:

❏ The first concern is the usage of properties. Doesn't this contradict everything we've said about scalability and making objects stateless? Well, yes it would do, but making things stateless isn't really something that applies here. The `Airport` object isn't a huge COM component that is going to be pooled or reused by different clients – so it's not something that will affect our scalability concerns. It's basically no more than a data structure used to group together some related bits of information. Our real data object is still stateless.

❏ The second point is that we've already got a substantial performance overhead in converting a recordset to a collection. Aren't we adding an extra performance overhead in calls to the COM runtime by creating objects to store in the collection? It looks at first sight that, in order to group these fields together into an `Airport` object, we're going to have to go back to the COM runtime to go through the (non-trivial) process of locating the DLL that hosts this object and instantiating an object, every time we want to get back some data. But in fact this is not the case. The `Airport` and similar objects are going to be hosted in the same DLL that hosts the main data object. Which means that whenever our data object needs to create an `Airport` object, it will be able to do so internally, without any calls to COM at all. VB will handle that for us automatically. The overhead of going to the COM runtime to instantiate these objects would be an issue if the `Airport` object were being created in the client code, which is hosted in separate ASP pages and executables. But if you look carefully at the interface definition for the data object, you'll see that the `Airport` object is only used in the `Airports` method, in which data is being returned to the client. We never use it as an [in] parameter to a method – for example, the `AddAirport` function just takes individual Variants that contain the required information about the airport. So the client code never needs to instantiate an `Airport` object – only the data component ever does this.

The Administration User Interface

As mentioned, the airline staff will use a VB user interface to modify flight details. The application looks like this:

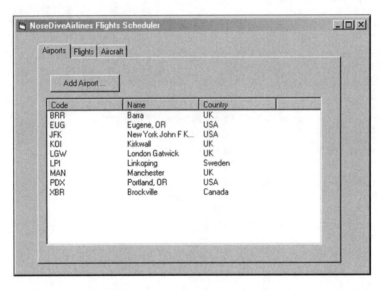

The main part of the window is devoted to a list box that shows details of – depending on which tab in the tab strip is selected – the Airports served, the Flights available, or the Aircraft types defined. The basic principle in the user interface is – as with all user interfaces – to try to ensure that the interface is as intuitive/self-explanatory as possible, and conforms to the Windows UI guidelines. Thus, for example, an item in the list box can be edited by double clicking on it – the normal behavior for list boxes. For example double-clicking on the KOI airport code yields this dialog:

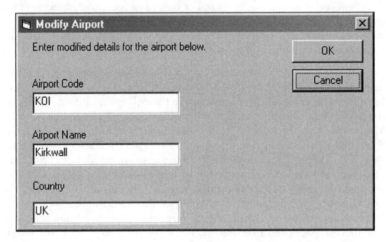

This invites the user to make any necessary modifications to the airport details.

Adding a new item is done by clicking on the Add button, while tabbing through the tab strip will cause the appropriate items to be displayed. For example, clicking on Aircraft gives this:

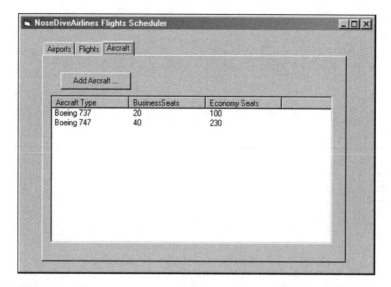

The user interface project is a standard VB executable. We'll quickly go through some of its more notable coding points – the full code for the project is available from the Wrox Press web site.

The tabstrip is called TabListViews, since it allows selection of various views of different data in the database. There is also an (effectively invisible, since they have no borders) collection of frame controls called FrameTab. Each frame control in the collection contains the controls that will be seen when one of the tabs in the tabstrip is selected. The list views have the obvious names – eg. LVAirports, LVAircraft, LVFlights. The corresponding buttons to add items are called CmdAddAirport etc.

Loading the Form and Displaying the List Views

We start off with the initial action taken on coding the form:

```
Option Explicit

Private Sub Form_Load()

    MoveControlsIntoPlace
    ShowAirports

End Sub
```

There's nothing too surprising going on here. MoveControlsIntoPlace is a function that ensures all the frame controls are correctly lined up with the tabstrip. ShowAirports is one of three functions, ShowAirports, ShowFlights, and ShowAircraftTypes, which are called in order to display the appropriate tab of the tabstrip. We start off by calling ShowAirports since we need to make sure that *something* is displayed when we start the application!

One point I will mention before we continue. We'll see that Hungarian notation is used where appropriate for the variables. Thus, for example, strings start with s, and globals start with g_. Whether you use Hungarian or not is a matter for personal preference – I know some programmers who swear by it and others who refuse to have anything to do with it because they think it makes the variable names more complex, making it harder rather than easier to figure out what's going on. The important thing is to be consistent in your choice throughout the project.

We'll have a look next at the sub, `MoveControlsIntoPlace`, which is called when the form is first loaded. Here it is:

```
Sub MoveControlsIntoPlace()

    Dim i As Integer
    For i = 0 To TabListViews.Tabs.Count - 1
        With FrameTab(i)
        .BorderStyle = 0
        .Move TabListViews.ClientLeft, _
        TabListViews.ClientTop, _
        TabListViews.ClientWidth, _
        TabListViews.ClientHeight
        End With
    Next i

End Sub
```

On loading the form, we next call the subroutine `ShowAirports`. This is the subroutine that ensures that only the Airports radio button is shown as clicked, and the airports are displayed in the list view. As mentioned earlier there are similar routines called `ShowAircraftTypes` and `ShowFlights`. They are also invoked by clicking the tab of the tab strip:

```
Private Sub TabListViews_Click()
    Select Case TabListViews.SelectedItem.Index
    Case 1:
        ShowAirports
    Case 2:
        ShowFlights
    Case 3:
        ShowAircraftTypes
    End Select
End Sub
```

We'll only go over `ShowAirports` here since the others work along the same lines. (I actually created them all by copying then doing a few text replacements on `ShowAirports` – cut and paste still reigns supreme when it comes to code reuse!)

We start by ensuring only the Airports frame and its accompanying controls are visible and clearing out the Airports list view:

```
Public Sub ShowAirports()

On Error GoTo ErrorHandler

    FrameTab(0).Visible = True
    FrameTab(1).Visible = False
    FrameTab(2).Visible = False

    LVAirports.ListItems.Clear
```

Then we actually instantiate an instance of our component that talks to the database, use it to retrieve a list of airports, populate the list view and clean up our objects:

```
Dim oNDA As NoseDiveAirlines.AirlineDBCalls
Set oNDA = New NoseDiveAirlines.AirlineDBCalls

Dim oAirports As Collection
Dim oAirport As NoseDiveAirlines.Airport
Set oAirports = oNDA.GetAirports
For Each oAirport In oAirports
    LVAirports.ListItems.Add , toKey(oAirport.ID), oAirport.Code
    With LVAirports.ListItems.Item(toKey(oAirport.ID))
        .SubItems(1) = oAirport.Name
        .SubItems(2) = oAirport.Country
    End With
Next

Set oAirport = Nothing
Set oAirports = Nothing
Set oNDA = Nothing
Exit Sub

ErrorHandler:
    LogError Err.Number, Err.Description

End Sub
```

We need to note one helper function, `toKey`. The point about this is that we would like to use the Airport ID as the key to identify each row in the list view – recall that ID is suited for this since it uniquely identifies the airport. However, I found in practice that the list view control isn't happy about accepting purely numeric keys, and raises an error if you try to use a string like "1" or "3" as the key. The `toKey` function just gets round this problem by prefixing the letter 'e' to the Airport ID, so it looks like a string! An equivalent function, `fromKey`, performs the reverse process:

```
Function toKey(ID As Variant) As String
    toKey = "e" & CStr(ID)
End Function

Function fromKey(Key As String) As Variant
    fromKey = Mid(Key, 2)
End Function
```

Error Handling

The sub we've just looked at to display the list view is the first case in which there is a direct access to the database, for which something might go wrong. We've adopted a fairly simple approach to error handling, as you can see from the `ShowAirports` sub. Any error detected will lead to a function, `LogError`, being detected. At present, `LogError` has a fairly simple implementation:

```
Sub LogError(Number As Integer, Description As String)

    MsgBox "Sorry, a problem occurred: " & vbCrLf & _
        "Error code is " & Number & vbCrLf & _
        "Full description of error is: " & Description

End Sub
```

In other words, it displays a message box with details of the error. This doesn't look at first sight adequate for a real application – in reality we'll want to be doing things like making sure that non-technical users get presented with a simple, descriptive message while support staff would get to see the full details of the error condition. We'd also probably want to log some errors to an application log, perhaps the Event Log, and try to recover from as many errors as possible without bothering the user. However, we're treating that as beyond the scope of this case study. The point here is that by modularizing the error handling into a separate function, we'll later be able to expand this function to do whatever else we want to. Most likely, we'll want to check some flag to see if the code is being run in an environment in which full diagnostic messages should be displayed, and if not generate some simple error message based on the error number.

Note that our LogError sub takes the error number and description as parameters. This is to guard against the possibility of the error object getting unexpectedly cleared - there are some known issues with this happening in some circumstances. It also gives us the chance to define our own custom errors and pass them in without having to actually raise our own exceptions, if we wish to do so.

Modifying a Record

This occurs when we double click on an item in the list view – and requires that we bring up a new dialog box (or VB form) asking the user to make the appropriate changes to the item. The event procedure for clicking an item in the list view is as follows – as before, we'll take the airports as an example:

We first identify the Airport ID that has been double clicked – this will simply be whichever item in the list view is selected, and we store the current data for that airport in a set of string variables:

```
Sub LVAircraft_DblClick()

    Dim iAircraftTypeIndex As Variant
    iAircraftTypeIndex = fromKey(LVAircraft.SelectedItem.Key)

    Dim sName As String, lBusinessSeats As Integer, lEconomySeats As Integer
    sName = LVAircraft.SelectedItem.Text
    lBusinessSeats = CInt(LVAircraft.SelectedItem.SubItems(1))
    lEconomySeats = CInt(LVAircraft.SelectedItem.SubItems(2))
```

Then we actually display the form – a form named DlgModifyAirport in our project. For this purpose, the form has a function, ShowDialog, which actually displays the form as a modal dialog, writes any new data to the variables sCode, sName and sCountry, and returns True or False depending on whether the user clicked **OK** or **Cancel**. If the result is True, we need to use an instance of the AirlineDBCalls component to actually make the modifications and redisplay the list view with the updated data. We'll look at the ShowDialog function soon.

```
    Dim bOK As Boolean
    bOK = DlgModifyAircraftType.ShowDialog(sName, lBusinessSeats, lEconomySeats)
    If (bOK) Then
        Dim oNDA As New NoseDiveAirlines.AirlineDBCalls
        oNDA.ModifyAircraftType iAircraftTypeIndex, sName, lBusinessSeats,
lEconomySeats
        ShowAircraftTypes
        Set oNDA = Nothing
    End If

End Sub
```

Note that this procedure doesn't do any error checking to see if two users are simultaneously updating the same data. Although the stored procedures that actually make the changes will each lock the database to prevent any data corruption due to the same data being accessed by two different processes, one of the user's modifications will be lost. This isn't really something we have to live with – we can't lock data in the database just because one user is viewing it with the admin tool and might decide to modify it!

Let's have a look at the dialog that invites the user to change the data. We've already seen the screenshot earlier. The code behind the dialog looks like this:

```
Option Explicit
Private m_bOK As Boolean
Private m_sCode As String, m_sName As String, m_sCountry As String

Public Function ShowDialog(sCode As String, _
    sName As String, sCountry As String) As Boolean

    m_bOK = False
    TextCode.Text = sCode
    TextName.Text = sName
    TextCountry.Text = sCountry
    Me.Show vbModal
    If (m_bOK) Then
        sCode = m_sCode
        sName = m_sName
        sCountry = m_sCountry
    End If
    ShowDialog = m_bOK

End Function

Private Sub CancelButton_Click()

    Me.Hide

End Sub

Private Sub OKButton_Click()
    m_bOK = True
    m_sCode = TextCode.Text
    m_sName = TextName.Text
    m_sCountry = TextCountry.Text
    Me.Hide
End Sub
```

There are essentially three procedures in this – one to display the dialog and two to remove it, depending on whether the user clicked on OK or Cancel. Note that these three procedures are not called sequentially. ShowDialog will be the first one that begins executing, when the main program form calls it. When the line:

```
    Me.Show vbModal
```

is reached, the procedure will be halted until the user has clicked on OK or Cancel, in which case either OKButton_Click or CancelButton_Click will be executed, then ShowDialog can resume.

Implementing the Components

We've now seen how the user interface works, and how it uses the various interface methods presented by the `NoseDiveAirlines.AirlineDBCalls` and related components, without actually looking at the implementation of the components. We'll cover that now. Again we'll concentrate on the methods to modify the `Airports` table of the database, since the methods that deal with the other tables are implemented in a parallel fashion.

Initialization and Data Validation

We'll start off with some basic member variables etc. for the DLL that hosts the components:

```
Option Explicit

' types of information stored in the DB - this can be used for data validation
etc.
' if needed in future
Private Enum String_Types
    NDA_ID
    NDA_AirportCode
    NDA_AirportName
    NDA_Country
    NDA_AircraftTypeName
    NDA_Seats
    ' others commented out for clarity
End Enum

Private Const g_sConnString As String = _
      "Provider=SQLOLEDB; data source=" & _
      "BIGGYBIGGY; Initial Catalog=NoseDive Airlines;  " & _
      "User Id=NDAUser; Password=tardis3413"
```

The connection string here is fairly obvious. Note though that the password contains digits as well as a word – to prevent dictionary-cracking attempts to break the password. More interesting are our set of class-module-global enumerated constants with names beginning `NDA_`. These are for data validation. We haven't yet discussed data validation and where that should go – client, component or database. Generally speaking, it's a good idea for the database to be able to verify that its own data follows the business rules satisfactorily. However, performing some data validation on the component does also have advantages: For a start it can save on needless calls to the database with invalid data. But also, it means the error messages generated by invalid data are much more under our control – since we are writing the entire component. It becomes easier for us to, for example, create user-friendly messages that identify in plain English what the problem is; (for example, *you've just tried to set an airport to have the same code as an existing airport*). Set against that is the problem of duplication of verification of the data if the database is doing some validation too – and the risk that the two validation routines will get out of sync, so that, for example, the component is checking that a string is no longer than 50 characters while in the database the corresponding field is defined as `varChar(60)` – meaning that the database will implicitly validate the length to be no more than 60 characters – clearly we want to avoid situations like that.

For this project I decided to allow some data validation on the component, but to separate this from the rest of the code, so that it could be easily maintained separately. I also wanted to consider at the same time the related problem of ensuring that any strings supplied are in a suitable format – for example, all leading and trailing spaces have been removed before submission to the database. Later we might want to extend this to e.g. remove invalid characters or any occurrences of multiple spaces.

The result is two general-purpose functions:

```
Private Function ValidateString(vString As Variant, iType As Integer) As Boolean

    vString = CorrectStringSyntax(vString, iType)
    ValidateString = True

End Function

Private Function CorrectStringSyntax(vString As Variant, iType As Integer) _
           As String

    CorrectStringSyntax = Trim(vString)

End Function
```

ValidateString returns True if the string supplied to it is fine, and in the process additionally performs any corrections needed to the string supplied to it to make sure its format is correct. CorrectStringSyntax is the lower level function that actually reformats the string. Both functions take two parameters – the string itself (actually a Variant for compatibility with ASP pages), and an integer that indicates the nature of the information contained within the string – for example, airport code, airport name, etc. And this is the reason why we defined the constants NDA_ID, NDA_AirportCode etc.

As you can see, these functions are pretty basic at the moment – ValidateString always returns True and CorrectStringSyntax doesn't do any more than remove leading and trailing spaces. I've left it that way because, to be honest, this is a case study about the principles of how you might go about writing a DNA application. So I don't think you need to be presented with tons of code that just shows how to check the length of a string or that a phone number doesn't contain any invalid characters – that's just basic string manipulation. But hopefully you can see that by shifting all data validation into these two functions we can very easily expand on this functionality later on. Moreover, we can ensure data validation is done in a consistent manner, at least within the component. Note that this means that CorrectStringSyntax doesn't at present use the second parameter supplied to it – but I've left it there because we probably will need it when we implement a more realistic version of this function.

Adding an Airport

We're now ready to look at the actual public functions. The code here is going to show some of the same functions and subs that we saw in the interface definition earlier – except that this time the procedures have their implementations filled in. We'll start off with adding an airport:

```
Public Function AddAirport(ByVal sAirportCode As String, _
    ByVal sAirportName As String, ByVal sCountry As String) As Variant

'   On Error GoTo ErrorHandler

    If (ValidateString(sAirportCode, NDA_AirportCode) = False) Then _
        Err.Raise ERR_INVALID_STRING, , "Incorrect Format for Airport Code"
    If (ValidateString(sAirportName, NDA_AirportName) = False) Then _
        Err.Raise ERR_INVALID_STRING, , "Incorrect Format for Airport Name"
    If (ValidateString(sCountry, NDA_Country) = False) Then _
        Err.Raise ERR_INVALID_STRING, , "Incorrect Format for Country"

    ' set up connection an command objects
    Dim oConnection As ADODB.Connection
    Set oConnection = New ADODB.Connection
    oConnection.Open g_sConnString
```

```
Dim oCommand As ADODB.Command
Set oCommand = New ADODB.Command
oCommand.ActiveConnection = oConnection
oCommand.CommandType = adCmdStoredProc
oCommand.CommandText = "AddAirport"
Dim oParam As ADODB.Parameter

' sort out parameters for the stored procedure
Set oParam = oCommand.CreateParameter( _
    "AirportCode", adWChar, adParamInput, 3, sAirportCode)
oCommand.Parameters.Append oParam

Set oParam = oCommand.CreateParameter( _
    "AirportName", adWChar, adParamInput, 50, sAirportName)
oCommand.Parameters.Append oParam

Set oParam = oCommand.CreateParameter( _
    "Country", adWChar, adParamInput, 20, sCountry)
oCommand.Parameters.Append oParam

Set oParam = oCommand.CreateParameter( _
    "AirportID", adInteger, adParamOutput)
oCommand.Parameters.Append oParam

' execute stored procedure
oCommand.Execute , , adExecuteNoRecords
oConnection.Close
Set oConnection = Nothing
Set oParam = Nothing

' return ID of new airport
AddAirport = CInt(oCommand.Parameters(3))
Set oCommand = Nothing
Exit Function

ErrorHandler:
    Err.Raise Err.Number, Err.Description

End Function
```

There shouldn't be anything too surprising here – we basically check the values of the strings supplied to us, then use a stored procedure in the database to add a new record with these values. Since we're using a stored procedure, the various parameters it requires are passed to it using the command object's parameters correction. Note that we trap any error that occurred in the database so we can raise it again for the client to handle it. Good programming practice would normally say we should define our own errors. For simplicity, I've only done that where we really are creating our own errors (eg. when validating strings fails) – if any errors are raised by COM then we will simply return those errors.

The stored procedure is AddAirport, it takes three input parameters – the code, name and country of the airport, and has one output parameter, into which the ID of the newly created airport is placed. The procedure looks like this:

```
CREATE PROCEDURE AddAirport
@AirportCode    VarChar(3),
@AirportName    nVarChar(50),
@Country     nVarChar(20),
@AirportID   int OUTPUT
AS
INSERT INTO Airports (AirportCode,AirportName,Country)
VALUES (@AirportCode,@AirportName,@Country)
SELECT @AirportID = @@Identity

GO
```

A fairly basic procedure – if we wanted to be clever we might start doing things like generating our own user-friendly error messages if anything goes wrong (like when we try to add a duplicate entry), but as you've probably realized by now – we're not up to writing an absolutely perfect application first time round. The point is rather to get all the different bits of functionality separated so we can easily improve on any one aspect without breaking other parts of the system.

This procedure, by the way, should give you an idea of the precise details of the fields in the `Airports` table – but just for the record they are shown below:

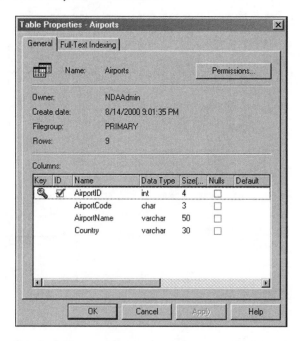

Note that `AirportID` is not only the primary key, but also serves as an identity field. (In other words, a field whose value is automatically computed by SQL Server to ensure a unique value.) `AirportCode` and `AirportName` are also specified as unique – no duplicate values are allowed. (Not allowing duplicate values is something that is set in the database, and which I specified when creating the table.)

Modifying an Airport

The process here is fairly similar to that for adding an airport:

```
Public Sub ModifyAirport(ByVal sAirportID As String, _
   ByVal sAirportCode As String, _
   ByVal sAirportName As String, ByVal sCountry As String)

   On Error GoTo ErrorHandler
   If (ValidateString(sAirportID, NDA_ID) = False) Then _
      Err.Raise ERR_INVALID_STRING, , "Incorrect Format for Airport ID"
   If (ValidateString(sAirportCode, NDA_AirportCode) = False) Then _
      Err.Raise ERR_INVALID_STRING, , "Incorrect Format for Airport Code"
   If (ValidateString(sAirportName, NDA_AirportName) = False) Then _
      Err.Raise ERR_INVALID_STRING, , "Incorrect Format for Airport Name"
   If (ValidateString(sCountry, NDA_Country) = False) Then _
      Err.Raise ERR_INVALID_STRING, , "Incorrect Format for Country"
```

```
        Dim oConnection As ADODB.Connection
        Set oConnection = New ADODB.Connection
        oConnection.Open g_sConnString

        Dim oCommand As ADODB.Command
        Set oCommand = New ADODB.Command
        oCommand.ActiveConnection = oConnection
        oCommand.CommandType = adCmdStoredProc
        oCommand.CommandText = "ModifyAirport"
        Dim oParam As ADODB.Parameter

        Set oParam = oCommand.CreateParameter( _
            "AirportID", adInteger, adParamInput, , sAirportID)
        oCommand.Parameters.Append oParam

        Set oParam = oCommand.CreateParameter( _
            "AirportCode", adWChar, adParamInput, 3, sAirportCode)
        oCommand.Parameters.Append oParam

        Set oParam = oCommand.CreateParameter( _
            "AirportName", adWChar, adParamInput, 50, sAirportName)
        oCommand.Parameters.Append oParam

        Set oParam = oCommand.CreateParameter( _
            "Country", adWChar, adParamInput, 20, sCountry)
        oCommand.Parameters.Append oParam

        oCommand.Execute , , adExecuteNoRecords

        oConnection.Close
        Set oConnection = Nothing
        Set oCommand = Nothing
        Set oParam = Nothing
        Exit Sub

ErrorHandler:
    Err.Raise Err.Number, Err.Description

End Sub
```

The main difference is that now the airport ID is an input rather than an output parameter. The corresponding stored procedure looks like this:

```
CREATE PROCEDURE ModifyAirport
    @AirportID   integer,
    @AirportCode     nchar(3),
    @AirportName         nvarchar(50),
    @Country     nvarchar(20)
AS
UPDATE Airports SET
AirportCode=@AirportCode,AirportName=@AirportName,Country=@Country
WHERE
AirportID = @AirportID

GO
```

Removing an Airport

Removing an airport is even easier since we don't need any parameters apart from the ID of the airport:

```
Public Sub RemoveAirport(ByVal sAirportID As String)

    On Error GoTo ErrorHandler

    If (ValidateString(sAirportID, NDA_ID) = False) Then _
        Err.Raise ERR_INVALID_STRING, , "Incorrect Format for Airport ID"

    Dim oConnection As ADODB.Connection
    Set oConnection = New ADODB.Connection
    oConnection.Open g_sConnString

    Dim oCommand As ADODB.Command
    Set oCommand = New ADODB.Command
    oCommand.ActiveConnection = oConnection
    oCommand.CommandType = adCmdStoredProc
    oCommand.CommandText = "RemoveAirport"

    Dim oParam As ADODB.Parameter

    Set oParam = oCommand.CreateParameter( _
        "AirportID", adInteger, adParamInput, , sAirportID)
    oCommand.Parameters.Append oParam

    oCommand.Execute , , adExecuteNoRecords

    oConnection.Close
    Set oConnection = Nothing
    Set oCommand = Nothing
    Exit Sub

ErrorHandler:
    Err.Raise Err.Number, Err.Description

End Sub
```

While the corresponding procedure is this:

```
CREATE PROCEDURE RemoveAirport
    @AirportID  Int
AS
DELETE FROM Airports WHERE AirportID=@AirportID

GO
```

Retrieving the Airports

This process is somewhat more complex as we need to convert the information from the recordset that ADO returns to us into the collection that we need to return to the client:

```
Public Function GetAirports() As Collection

    On Error GoTo ErrorHandler

    Dim oRS As New ADODB.Recordset

    Dim oConnection As ADODB.Connection
    Set oConnection = New ADODB.Connection
    oConnection.Open g_sConnString

    Dim oCommand As ADODB.Command
    Set oCommand = New ADODB.Command

    oCommand.ActiveConnection = oConnection
    oCommand.CommandType = adCmdStoredProc
    oCommand.CommandText = "GetAirports"
    Set oRS = oCommand.Execute
    Set oCommand = Nothing

    Dim collAirports As Collection
    Set collAirports = New Collection

    Dim oAirport As Airport
    Do While (Not oRS.EOF)
        Set oAirport = New Airport
        oAirport.ID = CorrectStringSyntax(CStr(oRS("AirportID")), NDA_ID)
        oAirport.Code = CorrectStringSyntax(CStr(oRS("AirportCode")),
NDA_AirportCode)
        oAirport.Name = CorrectStringSyntax(CStr(oRS("AirportName")),
NDA_AirportName)
        oAirport.Country = CorrectStringSyntax(CStr(oRS("Country")), NDA_Country)

        collAirports.Add oAirport
        oRS.MoveNext
    Loop

    Set oRS = Nothing
    oConnection.Close
    Set oConnection = Nothing
    Set oAirport = Nothing
    Set GetAirports = collAirports
    Set collAirports = Nothing
    Exit Function

ErrorHandler:
    Err.Raise Err.Number, Err.Description

End Function
```

Note that before adding the items to the collection, we call our `CorrectStringSyntax` function to make sure the syntax is appropriate. You could argue that this shouldn't be strictly necessary, since all the entries should have been through this process before they were written to the database in the first place. However, I did find in practice that SQL Server seemed to be padding strings out with spaces before returning them, so I inserted this check to make sure that the strings returned to the client are in exactly the form that we'd expect them to be stored in the database. Extra checks like this are useful – they may add a small performance overhead but can help to prevent problems later.

Finally, here is the stored procedure used to return the information about the airports:

```
CREATE PROCEDURE GetAirports
AS
SELECT * FROM Airports

GO
```

Customer Pages

We'll briefly go over the customer pages now. To be honest the code here doesn't really illustrate any new principles so we'll only show highlights from it, and leave you to download the full code from the Wrox Press web site if you need it.

First, the ASP page design. When a customer first logs on to the NoseDive Airlines site, this is what they'll see:

No frills here – these pages are very practical. The customer gets presented with a number of list boxes from which he can choose the airports he's flying between and the approximate outward and return dates of travel.

Incidentally, I've gone for approximate dates of travel because one of my particular bugbears is airline web sites that expect you to give exact dates upfront when what I really want to do is hunt around an approximate date to find day I can get the cheapest ticket or the most convenient time of day for the flight.

When the customer hits the continue button then assuming he's entered valid data (invalid data would be something like choosing 31st of February or a return date earlier than the departure date), he'll get to a page that lists the appropriate flights and asks him to select which one he wants:

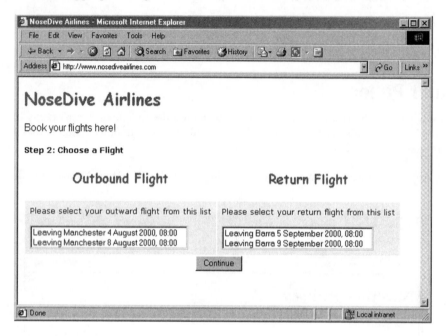

There are a couple more screens in the process – these simply confirm the purchase and so aren't as interesting. Since we want to concentrate on the design principles here, we'll leave the screenshots there.

The ASP Code

The main aspect of the ASP code is that I've gone for heavy modularization – almost any repeated action (like displaying a listbox) is done using functions – this will make it easy to make any changes to the user interface. At the same time, using ASP functions rather than COM components spares us the overhead of instantiating a component where we only want to execute a couple of lines of code.

Reusable Functions

These functions aren't particularly exciting, but we need to see them before we can look at the actual parts of the pages that do any work. They're also generic enough that you may want to produce functions that are extremely similar to these for use in your own web pages.

First a couple that make it easy for us to put double quotes round values of HTML tags, and encode the tags if necessary.

```
Function Quote(sText)
    Quote = Chr(34) & sText & Chr(34)
End Function

Function QuoteEncode(sText)
    QuoteEncode = Chr(34) & Server.HTMLEncode(sText) & Chr(34)
End Function
```

Now a couple of functions that deal with hidden form controls. The first writes a new hidden control. The second makes sure that some value passed in with the POST data is passed on to the next page called:

```
' write out a hidden control with given name and value
Sub HiddenControl(sName, sValue)
    Response.Write "<INPUT TYPE=hidden NAME=" & QuoteEncode(sName) & _
        " VALUE=" & QuoteEncode(sValue) & ">"
End Sub

' makes sure the value of a field is passed on to the next page
Sub PropagateFormInfo(sField)
    Response.Write "<INPUT TYPE=hidden NAME=" & Quote(sField) & _
        " VALUE=" & Quote(Request.Form(sField)) & ">" & vbCrLf
End Sub
```

And these are the functions that make it easy for us to write out list boxes:

```
Sub ListBoxStart(sName, lSize)
    Response.Write "<SELECT NAME=" & QuoteEncode(sName) &  _
        "SIZE=" & lSize & ">" & vbCrLf
End Sub

Sub ListBoxEnd()
    Response.Write "</SELECT>" & vbCrLf
End Sub

Sub ListOption(sName, sValue, sDefaultValue)
    Dim sText
    sText = sText & "    <OPTION VALUE=" & QuoteEncode(sValue)
    If (sDefaultValue = sValue) Then
        sText = sText & " SELECTED> "
    Else
        sText = sText & " >"
    End If
    sText = sText & Server.HTMLEncode(sName)
    Response.Write sText & vbCrLf
End Sub
```

ListBoxStart and ListBoxEnd should be pretty self-explanatory. ListOption adds an option to a list box for which the text displayed is sText, the value sent with the form data is sValue, and the value is selected at the start if it happens to be the default value, sDefaultValue.

You might question the value of a function like ListBoxEnd – it is so simple that why would we want the overhead of turning this into a function? The answer is that I'm very concerned about code maintainability – doing it this way does make it very easy if we subsequently want to change the way we are displaying list boxes right across our site. (E.g. we might decide that all list boxes should go in their own tables for layout reasons.)

Finally we'll end with a slightly more complex function – the one that displays the list boxes that allow the user to select dates.

```
' writes out three list boxes that between them allow the user to select a date
Sub DateListBoxes(sName, dDefaultDate)

    ' figure out day, month and year for the default date
    Dim lYear, lMonth, lDay, bOK
    lYear = Year(dDefaultDate)
    lMonth = Month(dDefaultDate)
    lDay = Day(dDefaultDate)

    ' do list box for the day
    Dim i
    ListBoxStart sName & "D", 1
    For i=1 To 31
        ListOption CStr(i), CStr(i), CStr(lDay)
    Next
    ListBoxEnd

    ' do list box for the month
    ListBoxStart sName & "M", 1
    For i=1 To 12
        ListOption MonthName(i), CStr(i), CStr(lMonth)
    Next
    ListBoxEnd

    ' do list box for the year
    ListBoxStart sName & "Y", 1
    For i=lYear To lYear+1
        ListOption CStr(i), CStr(i), CStr(lYear)
    Next
    ListBoxEnd

End Sub
```

Note that allowing the user to freely select the day and the month independently does mean we will have to validate that a valid date has actually been selected. It would be possible to avoid this problem using some client-side scripting but we've chosen not to allow ourselves that luxury so we can maximize compatibility with old browsers.

There are a few more functions to do things like start and end forms, but you probably get the idea of the programming style by now!

The Main Page

We're ready to have a look at the ASP file for the main page of the NoseDiveAirlines site. This is default.asp:

```asp
<%@ Language = VBScript %>
<% Option Explicit%>
<!-- #include virtual="/Step.asp"-->



<!DOCTYPE HTML PUBLIC "-//W3C//DTD HTML 4.0 Transitional//EN">
<HTML>
<HEAD>
<TITLE> NoseDive Airlines</TITLE>
<META NAME=Description CONTENT="Book your holiday or business flights here.
    NoseDive Airlines offers quick and efficient service">
<META NAME=Keywords CONTENT="NoseDive Airlines, NDA, Flights, Bookings, Holiday,
Travel">
<LINK REL=STYLESHEET TYPE="Text/css"HREF = "Style.css">
</HEAD>

<BODY>

<H1> NoseDive Airlines  </H1>

<%
Dim sStep
sStep = GetStep



Select Case sStep
   Case 1:
      Server.Execute "PlanJourney.asp"
   Case 2:
      Server.Execute "ChooseFlight.asp"
   Case 3:
      Server.Execute "ConfirmFlight.asp"
   Case 4:
      Server.Execute "UserDetails.asp"
   Case 5:
      Server.Execute "ConfirmBooking.asp"
   Case 6:
      Server.Execute "BookingDone.asp"
End Select
%>

</BODY>
</HTML>
```

The main thing you'll notice about this is the almost complete lack of any processing other than displaying basic HTML headers. That's because we've chosen to take advantage of the new `Server.Execute` method that was introduced with ASP 3.0 to deal with sorting out the individual pages the user sees as he books his ticket. What happens is that we call a function, GetStep (which is defined in the file `Step.asp`), which has responsibility for figuring out what stage we are at in the process. We're not going to go over the code for GetStep – it's basically a huge set of statements covering several pages, that test various conditions. We'll just explain that what it does is examine the POST data (if any) submitted with the page. At each step a hidden control with the value Step is used to indicate the number of the step in the booking process that we should have reached; (if this value is missing from the POST data then we know we are at the first step). However GetStep does a lot more than examine the Step value from the POST data – it also validates all the other data that has been submitted with the form controls. If GetStep finds any problems it writes the appropriate messages to the Response object asking the user to correct the data, and sets the step back to the previous page instead.

Once we've established which stage of the process we are at, we call the `Server.Execute` method. This executes the ASP page indicated – and at the end of that passes control back to the page from which it was called.

The PlanJourney Page

This is the first page the user encounters, the one that invites him to select the travel dates and the airports he wishes to travel between.

We first include a few files that contain other useful functions and display the headings:

```
<% Option Explicit %>

<!-- #include virtual="/Forms.asp"-->
<!-- #include virtual="/UserID.asp"-->

Book your flights here! <P>

<STRONG>Step 1: Plan Your Journey</STRONG><P>

<TABLE>
<THEAD>
<TH> <H3>Airports</H3></TH>
<TH> <H3> Departure Date </H3> </TH>
<TH> <H3> Return Date </H3> </TH>
</THEAD>

<TBODY>
<TR><TD CLASS=TableCell VALIGN=Top>Select where you are travelling from <BR>
```

Next we need to actually instantiate our component that can talk to the database, in order to retrieve the list of airports – which we display in the first list box:

```
<%
FormStart

Dim oNDA
Set oNDA = Server.CreateObject("NoseDiveAirlines.AirlineDBCalls")
Dim collAirports
Set collAirports = oNDA.GetAirports()
ListBoxStart "StartAirport", 1
Dim oAirport
```

```
For Each oAirport In collAirports
    ListOption oAirport.Name, oAirport.ID, ""
Next
ListBoxEnd

Response.Write "<P>"
Response.Write "Select your final destination<BR>"
ListBoxStart "DestAirport", 1
For Each oAirport In collAirports
    ListOption oAirport.Name, oAirport.ID, ""
Next
ListBoxEnd

%>
```

Then we do the same for the list boxes that display the dates:

```
</TD>
<TD CLASS=TableCell VALIGN=Top>
Select the approximate date for your outbound journey.
<P> All flights within 3 days of this date will be displayed.
<P>
<%   DateListBoxes "DepartureDate", Now %>
</TD>
<TD CLASS=TableCell VALIGN=Top>
Select the approximate date for your return journey.
<P> All flights within 3 days of this date will be displayed.
<P>
<%
DateListBoxes "ReturnDate", Now

%>
</TD>
</TR>


</TBODY>
</TABLE>
```

Finally we display the hidden control to indicate the next step is step 2. Note that SubmitButton is another function we've defined which simply displays a submit button:

```
<CENTER>
<%
HiddenControl "Step", "2"
SubmitButton "Continue"
FormEnd
%>
</CENTER>
```

That's as far as we're going to go with showing you the ASP pages. The successive ones become increasingly more complex as we need to deal with various error conditions, but are essentially written in the same style as the PlanJourney page.

Other Tasks

We're going to leave the detailed presentation of code here – since the aim of this chapter was always to go over the principles used in planning the case study rather than swamp you with code. I should mention that other stuff that needs to be done includes registering our components as COM+ components and setting the detailed security permissions on them. The case study in the following chapter goes over that process.

At this point we have a working application which appears to meet the functionality we needed – it lets customers book seats on flights over the Internet, while giving a separate user interface for the airline staff to enter details of flights, prices etc. This is where the case study for this chapter ends, but it's important to remember that if this were a real system we would only have completed the first stage. The next thing to do would be some extensive testing (including stress testing). And that doesn't just mean debugging – it also means things like trying out the user interfaces on real people. We think we've designed them in an intuitive, friendly, way, but have we? The real test is what the end users actually think. So we need feedback on how easy customers found it to go through the procedures of looking up flights and booking them, and how easy our administrative staff found it to work their way around the VB user interface. One way to do this is to get people to use the system and ask them for their opinions. Another way that's been used successfully by some organizations is simply to watch people using the applications, noting everything they do. Are they consistently making a certain mistake, for example going to the wrong menu to perform a particular operation? If people are having any sort of trouble understanding what to do then remember, the problem isn't with the people. It's a problem with the design of user interface. Well, you could just blame the people if you want, but they're your customers, and there's plenty of competition out there for their custom.

While the user interface is being sorted out, we'll also need to have a look at the backend of the application – the business logic, the data objects and the overall application architecture. Now we've actually had the experience of writing it, did we encounter any problems that could be removed with a few tweaks to the design? If we approached the design properly at the start, then any such tweaks should only be very minor ones. You might realize, for example, that a couple of extra methods implemented by your data objects would be very useful.

You'll probably also find out at this stage that some of the functionality of your application needs to be slightly modified. It might become apparent, for example, that your customers need the ability to pay using different currencies. You can guarantee there'll be something in the initial specifications that wasn't quite right, but which only became obvious when the first draft of the application was working. Then you'll need to do your stress testing to make sure it really does perform and scale well – and if it doesn't where are the bottlenecks?

At this point we could digress into a lot of abstract discussion about code design – but that isn't really what this book is about. The point I want to get across here is that you will need to go through these processes. But if you've designed your application well from the start and used the DNA principles explained in this book, you'll find that the process of going through these additional steps becomes a lot easier.

Summary

In this chapter we've gone through a case study designed to illustrate the principles of writing a DNA application. We've not gone through every detail of the code – that could be a complete book in itself if we did. Rather, we've focused on how DNA allows easy separation of the different parts of your code, enhancing maintainability, and also on how to ensure that your code is efficient and scalable – the key here being the use of stateless objects.

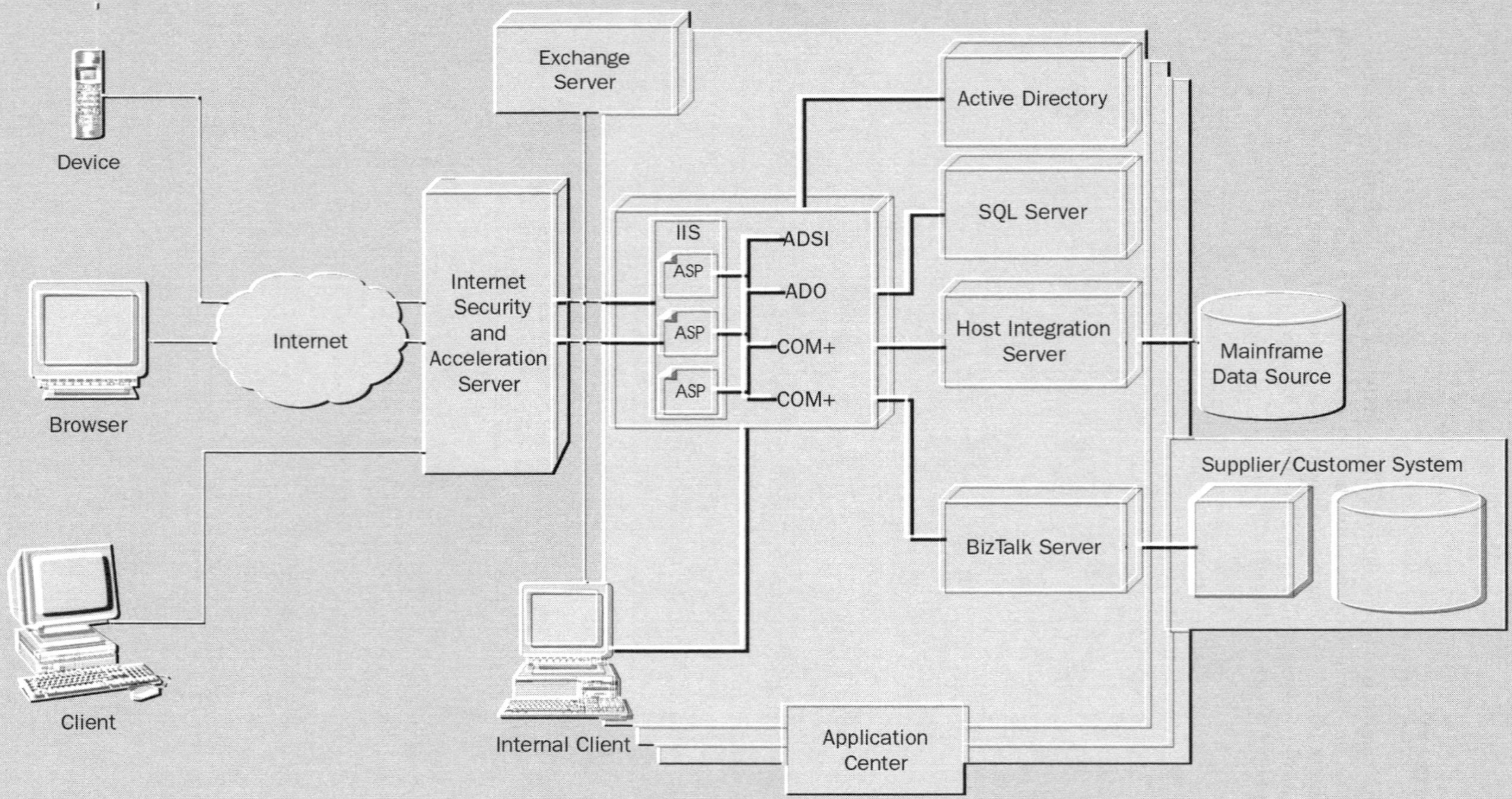

Active Directory

SQL Server

Host Integration Server

BizTalk Server

Mainframe Data Source

Supplier/Customer System

ADSI

ADO

COM+

COM+

IIS

ASP

ASP

ASP

Exchange Server

Internet Security and Acceleration Server

Internet

Internal Client

Application Center

Device

Browser

Client

25

Case Study: The Wrox Hire Shop

Now that we have covered the fundamental aspects of building DNA apps in Windows 2000, it is time to bring these concepts together into a real-world application. We will be discussing the core architecture that COM+ components require in order to support a business process.

The subject for our case study could have been literally one of hundreds of real-world scenarios. The key concept is that we want to sell products to our customers; therefore the principles apply regardless of the actual business process.

Introducing the Wrox Hire Shop

The core business of the **Wrox Hire Shop** is to offer building equipment for hire to its customers. The Hire Shop stocks various products, such as cement mixers, scaffolding and ladders, from different manufacturers. These items, when available, can be hired out to customers for any number of days. A typical scenario is one in which the customer hires a number of different products and returns each one as and when he has finished with them.

In order to invoice the customer, the system must store details of the products that have been hired along with the date that they were hired out (**on-hire**) and the date that they were returned (**off-hire**). To complicate matters somewhat, it is possible for a customer to hire out three sets of ladders on the same day, but then subsequently return one set after, say, five days and the others after nine days.

The number of products available gives us great scope to cover the **e-commerce** metaphor now very popular in web-based applications. We will demonstrate the use of a thin-client, browser-independent, **web-based** product search feature that allows users to explore the catalogue of products and to add or remove these items from their **shopping basket**.

As with all order processing systems there must be some way of administering our data. In the case of the Wrox Hire Shop, we need the ability to amend customer and order details. This will be achieved using a Win32 **desktop-application** – HireShopAdmin.

The use of these two distinct client applications allows us to explore the issues discussed in Chapter 16 covering client richness and separation of the presentation layer from the business and data services layers.

> **You can download the complete set of Visual Basic, ASP, and SQL Server source code for this case study from the Wrox web site at http://www.wrox.com. Follow these instructions to set up the Wrox Hire Shop Example on your computer:**

1. Create the HireShop Database

The file HireShop.bak contains a full SQL Server backup of the **HireShop** database. It has been backed up on a server with the following character set, sort order and collation properties:

Charset	1252/ISO Character Set (Default)
Sort Order	Dictionary order, case-insensitive, accent-insensitive
Unicode Collation	General Unicode
Case-insensitive	Yes
Accent-insensitive	Yes
Width-insensitive	Yes
Kana-insensitive	Yes

Your server must be running with these values otherwise SQL Server will not restore the backup. If any of these values are not the same and you could alter the settings using \MSSQL7\Binn\rebuildm.exe but **ONLY if it's OK to lose your other databases!**

Don't forget to add a login called HireShopUser before doing the database restore.

If you can't complete the database restore then you will have to create a database called HireShop then run each of the 12 SQL files in the SQL Server Query Analyser. This will create the database, its users, tables, stored procedures and finally populate all of the tables with data.

2. Registering DLLs

Each of the DLLs needs to be registered with Component Services.

Create a Component Services Application called Hire Shop Utils and register the wxHSDBUtils.dll there. Don't forget to set the construct string to a valid ADO connection string pointing to the HireShop database above.

Now you can create a separate Application for each of the components:

Hire Shop Customer should contain `wxHSCustomerDB.dll` and `wxHSCustomerBR.dll`.
Hire Shop Order should contain `wxHSOrderDB.dll` and `wxHSOrderBR.dll`.
Hire Shop Product should contain `wxHSProductDB.dll` and `wxHSProductBR.dll`.

Don't forget to set the **Transaction** properties to **Supported**.

3. The Wrox Hire Web Site

There's no need to do any special configuration. Just unzip the source files using the directory structure option so that it creates the `Includes` and `Pictures` directories.

Business Processes

We've just covered a short introduction into the core business processes of the Wrox Hire Shop. Now it's time for us to look at each area in detail so that we can decide on our physical database schema and the best manner in which to create our COM+ objects.

> *This book is aimed at COM+ development so we aren't going to cover the in-depth fundamentals of designing business objects. For a thorough examination of business components design check out "Visual Basic 6 Business Objects – Enterprise Design and Implementation" by Wrox Press (ISBN 1-861001–07-X). Chapter 5 of this book discusses business objects, and "Professional Active Server Pages 3.0" by Wrox Press (ISBN 1-861002-61-0) has a whole section on components.*

'The System Users

There are two primary users of the system: the end-users and the administrators that support them. Those customers that use the browser-based search and shopping basket features can be termed as our **end-users**. In the future, this could be extended to include product suppliers accessing our systems through an extranet site.

> *Extranets are fast becoming an essential part of business-to-business communications. Essentially, an extranet is an extended intranet site created by a company so that external companies, such as suppliers, can share data electronically in a controlled and secure fashion.*

Our **administrators** are the operations staff that update the product catalogue and track which products are issued to customers.

Application Environment

Before we launch into a discussion of the tasks involved, we'll note the environment that we need to be aware of when designing our applications.

Our end-users will be using a browser-based environment. We need to be mindful of their limited client-richness and of the **incompatibilities** between different Internet browser software. To this end we will not be using any fancy DHTML. We will also be keeping graphical content to a minimum for those users that connect via a dial-up line. The only images presented to the user are those of the actual products.

The use of web-based applications as a new sales channel brings lots of benefits to our business, but at a price. We need to remember that popular sites need to be **scalable**, in other words, does site performance scale upwards in response to escalating user requests?

Unfortunately Netscape Navigator does not, and will probably never provide native support for ActiveX controls or any of the other Microsoft Office components. So we must be careful not to alienate a fair percentage of users with Netscape Navigator. If you really must use ActiveX controls then there is a 'plug-in' available for Netscape Navigator called ScriptActive from NCompass Labs that must be installed in order to support ActiveX controls.

We have somewhat better control over the environment that our administrators will use to access our systems. We will be using a client-rich Win32 application that shares the same components as our web-based clients. This gives us the ability, as and when required, to leverage the power of other office applications such as spreadsheet applications for reporting, or ActiveX controls for enhanced functionality.

We aren't going to cover it just yet, but we also need to spare some thought to the servers that our components and applications are to be physically installed upon.

Functional Requirements

Now it's time to define the core functionality of the system. As with all business systems, there are many tasks and sub-tasks partitioned into groups of logical business functions. We don't want to bloat this case study by including those tasks that are not relevant to our example, so areas such as invoicing and bill payments (all very important to the cashflow of a company) and equipment purchase/damage will not be discussed.

The main high-level task or function that we are going to concentrate on is "Hire Equipment". The purpose of this can be decomposed into the following sub-tasks:

- ❏ Identify the user
- ❏ Search for a product
- ❏ Add or remove a product from the shopping basket
- ❏ Accept order
- ❏ Issue products
- ❏ Return products

Let's look at each of these in a little more detail.

Identify the User

Before we can take an order we need to verify the **identity** of the user. For existing users we will ask for their login name and password. This will be compared to the login name and password stored in the database. If the user is authorized, we will make a note of their customer number and give them access to the system.

New users must **register** with the system. They can enter any login name, such as their e-mail address, and password along with their address for billing purposes. We must, however, ensure that any new login name entered is unique and inform the user if they have entered a duplicate name.

Search for a Product

Once we have validated the user they will have full access to the product catalogue. We will give the user a number of ways of searching our database of products in order to make it more flexible. Typically the customer will know the kind of product they are looking for, but we can complement this by adding a category search, such as *Gardening Equipment*. For those customers that have more specific requirements we will also provide them with the ability to specify a particular manufacturer.

Add or Remove a Product from the Shopping Basket

Our search results page will list the products that match the user's search criteria. Once they have found the product required they can add it to their shopping basket. Essentially a shopping basket is synonymous with an order. The user will have the ability to add multiple products to their shopping basket until they take it to the **checkout** to be accepted. Conversely, the user will also have the ability to remove any item from their shopping basket.

If the user does not have a current order basket open then we will generate a new order number and that will be used until they close the browser or the order.

At any one time items may be coming in and out of our Hire Shop. This will be reflected in the Search Results page; we will tell the user how many items are available at present and give them a user-friendly message if they have requested more than the number currently available.

Accept Order

Once the user has filled their shopping basket with all of the products required, they must move to the checkout section where the order will be accepted. They can then create new orders if required.

Issue Products

The process of issuing hire products to a customer can be started once the order has been accepted. Unfortunately this can be rather complex because at the time of ordering there may not be the required number of products available.

Return Products

In order for us to calculate how much the customer owes, we need to track when each product item is returned back to us. The number of days between this date and the off-hire date multiplied by the daily rate defines how much is owed.

The issue and return of products is beyond the scope of our case study, but it would be a nice exercise to extend the components and the HireShopAdmin Win32 application to allow items to be physically booked out to a user, using a unique barcode/serial number for each item, and track when they are returned so that we can invoice the customer.

The Database Schema

Now that we've identified the primary areas we can move onto mapping out the physical database design that we plan to implement in order to support the required functionality.

With large applications it often becomes necessary to categorize groups of tables into their own individual entity relationship diagrams. In our case we can group them into three distinct areas, thus:

❑   Customer Data

❑   Product Data

❑   Order Data

Do these categories look vaguely familiar? You may have come across them in any standard **customer order processing** system. Now that we've established our categories, let's delve a little deeper to see which tables go where, and which attributes we need in order to support the hire process.

Customer Data

This is the simplest category; we only have one table, Customer, which stores the names, addresses and login details of all of our customers (or 'users' in the web site).

Customer			
Column Name	**Data Type**	**Nullable**	**Description**
CustomerID	Int Identity	N	The primary key. Used to identify customer in the related tables
CustomerName	Varchar	N	The name of the customer. Typically the trading name or the person's name
Address1	Varchar	N	Line 1 of the address
Address2 - Address5	Varchar	Y	Lines 2 to 5 of the address
ZipCode	Varchar	Y	Zip code or post code
LoginName	Varchar	N	Their login name for the web site
Password	Varchar	N	Their login password for the web site

You'll notice that the fields CustomerID (the primary key), CustomerName and Address1 are all required fields for obvious reasons. In our business model, we will use the customer's e-mail address as their login name as this tends to be unique and allows us a mechanism in which we can **push** information to them electronically.

Product Data

Our product data covers a few more entities than that of our customer data. We need to store categorized product details along with the manufacturer and hire charges.

Product

This table stores the actual catalogue of products available for the user to search for and hire.

Product			
Column Name	**Data Type**	**Nullable**	**Description**
ProductID	Int Identity	N	The primary key. Used to identify product in related tables
ManufacturerID	Int	N	Foreign key to the Manufacturer table
ProductTypeID	Int	N	Foreign key to the ProductType table
ProductName	Varchar	N	This is the name we look for in the product search screen
Description	Varchar	Y	A friendly description of the product
DailyHireCharge	Smallmoney	N	The amount that we charge for this item per day
WeeklyHireCharge	Smallmoney	N	The amount that we charge for this item per week
PictureFileName	Varchar	Y	The file name used to store the picture of this item. We don't use the database to store binary data

ProductType

This table allows us to group similar products together. For example, we may have a stepladder and a loft ladder that can be grouped together as types of 'Ladder'. This table also allows us to provide additional search functionality.

ProductType			
Column Name	**Data Type**	**Nullable**	**Description**
ProductTypeID	Int Identity	N	The primary key. Used to identify product type in Product table
CategoryID	Int	N	Foreign key to the Category table
ProductTypeName	Varchar	N	The name of the product type

Category

ProductTypes can be further grouped into specific areas, such as *Gardening* or *Welding* equipment. This also provides the user with additional searching criteria.

Category			
Column Name	**Data Type**	**Nullable**	**Description**
CategoryID	Int Identity	N	The primary key. Used to identify category in the ProductType table
CategoryName	Varchar	N	The name of the category, Gardening, for example.

ProductItem

Our business needs to track individual product item details, for example, we may stock two electric drills for hire in which case we would find two entries in ProductItem using each drill's serial number for physical identification. The date when each item is hired out and returned is tracked in the BasketContentsHire table detailed later.

ProductItem			
Column Name	**Data Type**	**Nullable**	**Description**
ProductItemID	Int Identity	N	The primary key. Used to identify product items in other tables
ProductID	Int	N	Foreign key to the Product table
SerialNumber	Varchar	N	A way to physically identify items
DatePurchased	Smalldatetime	Y	Allows us to build age and usage statistics for items
PurchasePrice	Smallmoney	Y	We can work out how much money has been made on each line

Product Data Entity Relationship Diagram

We can now put these tables together to see how they relate to one another:

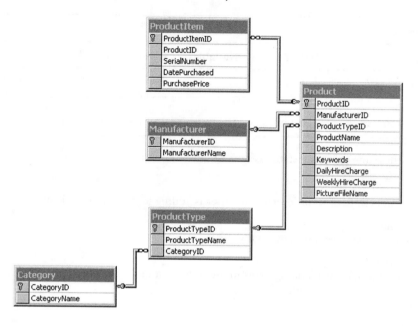

Order Data

Finally, we can define the tables that allow us to implement the shopping basket and the movement of individual product lines.

OrderBasket

This table forms the shopping basket itself. It doesn't actually store the products that have been selected. Its purpose is to group together items for a customer and track their overall status.

OrderBasket			
Column Name	**Data Type**	**Nullable**	**Description**
OrderID	Int Identity	N	The primary key. Used to identify order in other tables
CustomerID	Int	N	Foreign key to the Customer table to determine which customer this order belongs to
OrderDate	Smalldatetime	N	When the order was originally raised
OrderStatusID	Int	N	Foreign key to OrderStatus table. Determines the current state of the order, either New or Accepted

OrderStatus

A simple lookup table to store the status of each order.

OrderStatus			
Column Name	**Data Type**	**Nullable**	**Description**
OrderStatusID	Int Identity	N	The primary key. Used to identify the order status in the Order table
OrderStatusName	Varchar	N	The name of this status

An order can have the following status assigned to it:

❏ **New**
The initial state of an order when the user is adding to it from the web site.

❏ **Complete**
All items have been hired out and returned.

❏ **Accepted**
The user has finished adding items to the order and has proceeded to the 'checkout' and now wants to collect their items.

BasketContents

This table stores the items that a user adds to their order baskets.

BasketContents			
Column Name	**Data Type**	**Nullable**	**Description**
BasketContentsID	Int Identity	N	The primary key. Used to identify item in the BasketContentsHire table
OrderID	Int	N	Foreign key to OrderBasket table to determine which order this item relates to
ProductID	Int	N	Foreign key to Product table
QuantityRequired	Int	N	Stores the number of items that customer actually wants

BasketContentsHire

The final table, BasketContentsHire, stores the movement of an individual item of stock as it goes out "on-hire" and is then returned by the customer – "off-hire". We can use this table to determine how much to charge the customer by calculating the number of days between the date the item went out and the date it was returned.

BasketContentsHire			
Column Name	**Data Type**	**Nullable**	**Description**
HireID	Int Identity	N	The primary key
BasketContentsID	Int	N	Foreign key to BasketContents table to identify which product is moving.
ProductItemID	Int	N	Foreign key to ProductItem table to define the physical product
DateOnHire	Smalldatetime	N	For an item to appear in this table we must know when it was handed over to the customer
DateOffHire	Smalldatetime	Y	The date when the user returned the item to us

Order Data Entity Relationship Diagram

Our next entity relationship diagram brings together the order tracking tables, thus:

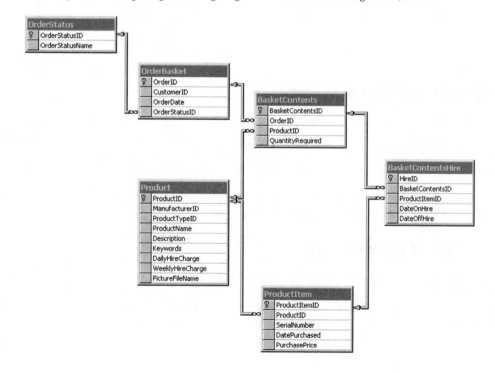

At this stage, it might be useful to see how all of the sections relate to one another with the use of a system entity relationship diagram before we move onto designing the application components:

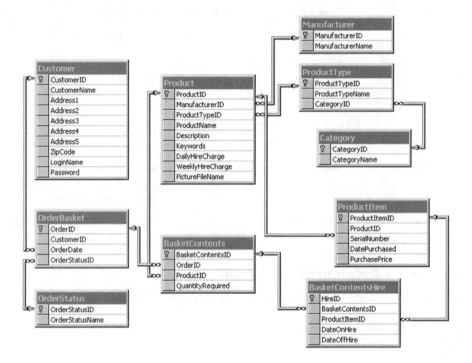

Application Components

One of DNA's primary aims is to provide client transparency, in that a calling application does not need to be concerned with how a component processes a request. To illustrate this point we will build two distinct client applications, a standard Visual Basic project compiled for Win32, and an ASP-based web application. Both clients will be calling the same collection of components to achieve their requirements.

Before we discuss the actual implementation of our components we will take some time out to cover the overall architecture of components from a COM+ perspective.

Application Architecture

When designing applications we have many choices to make that will affect its performance and usability. These decisions are also coupled with the need for on-going support and maintenance throughout the lifetime of the evolving application. With this in mind we need to make some design decisions up front which could have major implications later if we were to change them.

A colleague of mine, named Ian Stirk, once told me about his "First Principle of Software Design'. This principle states that a system may have two of the following desirable areas: Quality, Features and Cost, at detriment to the third.

For example, choosing to have a high quality application with great features will result in a higher cost. Alternatively, you could choose low cost with lots of features, but this will result in low quality!

I think this a great principle that I have always tried to follow.

N-Tier Implementation

The Wrox Hire Shop will be implemented using the n-tier paradigm described earlier. Just to recap, an n-tier application can be divided into the following tiers or layers:

❑ **Presentation Tier**
  The interface that we provide to users in order to manipulate our components.

❑ **Business Rules Tier**
  Provides validation of business rules for an object, such as those required to provide a life insurance quote.

❑ **Data Access Tier**
  The tier that communicates with a data store in order to persist data from our components.

These can be thought of as **logical** tiers that are grouped together conceptually. In reality they may be **physically** located on the same server.

The Presentation Tier

We will be providing an ASP-based web application to allow users to search for products, and a traditional Win32 HireShopAdmin program to allow administrators to edit customer and order details. These applications will never communicate directly with our database; rather they will call middle layer, business rule objects, that in turn will pass their parameters to separate data services objects.

The Business Rules Tier

Components within the middle tier provide validation and apply certain business rules. In the case of the Wrox Hire Shop there are not too many business rules that need to be implemented.

The Data Access Tier

Once the business rule component has successfully completed its rule validation it can marshal the component's properties over to the corresponding components in the data access tier. The data access tier is responsible for calling the correct SQL Server stored procedure in order to manipulate a record in a table.

Although we have listed three tiers, our components will be implemented in an n-tier architecture. So what makes it n-tier? In our case we are going to make use of a specialized sub-tier component within this data access tier to wrap and fine-tune ADO functionality.

The sequence of calls can be seen in the following diagram. This example shows a user pressing the Register button on our ASP script:

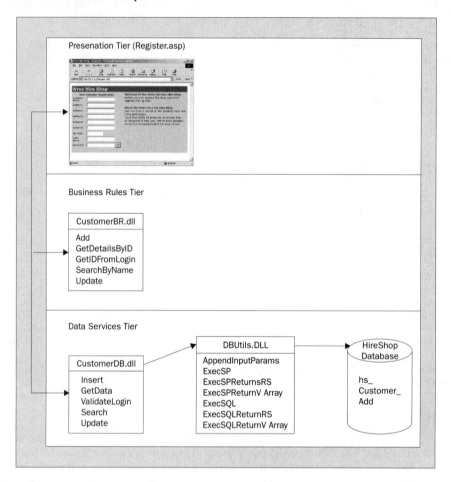

Every functional area of our system, customer, order and product, has a collection of business rules and a corresponding collection of data services.

Intercomponent Communications

Our next decision determines how we communicate between our components. How do we pass parameters to our method calls, and how do we get results back from them? We have a number of choices that can affect application performance; particularly that of distributed architectures.

We can define a list of arguments in a fine-grained approach for each of our method calls or we can bundle them up into a container type, such as a `Variant Array` or a disconnected RecordSet, that allows use to pass multiple values in a single call.

Each has its own pros and cons, so we are going to implement both approaches so that you can see how they work: our business rules will accept discrete parameters, whereas our generic data access layer will use `Variant Arrays`.

> Our business rules layer will be returning data as either a `Recordset` or a `Variant Array`. For those methods that return multiple records, such as a search, we will be returning data in a Recordset. Those methods that return a single row containing multiple columns of data will be using `Variant Arrays`.
>
> It is worth remembering that Microsoft has spent a great deal of time in writing high-performance ADO `Recordset` objects that are optimised for network packets travelling around the network. I believe that `RecordSets` should be evaluated in comparison to the overhead required in assembling and disassembling Variant Arrays between calls.

Error Handling

We know that our applications are going to be aimed at users with varied levels of skill. This will be particularly apparent with our web-based application where we have little control over what the user does or where they decide to navigate to. Therefore we have decided to display minimal runtime error messages to the end-users. What would we expect the average web-user to do when presented with the following SQL error message?

Server: Msg 515, Level 16, State 2, Line 1. Cannot insert the value NULL into column 'CustomerName', table 'HireShop.dbo.Customer'; column does not allow nulls. INSERT fails.

They would not be suitably impressed with this, even if they did know that they had left the `CustomerName` field blank. Also, we don't want to give any clues to potential hackers about the environment in which our application runs. To prevent these data errors, we will shift initial validation nearer to the cause of the problem: the client application. We will perform all data validation on the client before passing values to our business objects.

Any runtime errors that do occur are likely to be environmental or programming bugs so we will be logging them in the Windows Event Log for later analysis. So what do we tell the user? Well in the case of our web-users: "The Wrox Hire Shop is currently experiencing server problems. If this message persists then please try again later."

Database Access

Our business layer components will communicate directly with the data services components, which in turn will communicate with a specialized database utility class that essentially provides us with a wrapper for ADO.

Our database utility class will be optimized to handle data manipulation in a generic fashion. It will also use one of the new features of COM+, the **IObjectConstruct** interface to allow us to specify a different ADO connection string on different servers without having to recompile our applications as they move into production.

Database Utility Component

The Wrox Hire Shop Database Utility component (wxHSDBUtils.dll) forms all communication between our data services layer and the database. This component is relatively simple in that it contains just one class, cDatabase. We will be implementing a number of specific methods that our data access objects will call depending upon their requirements, in other words, do we want to execute a stored procedure or a native SQL statement and do we want to return data from it?

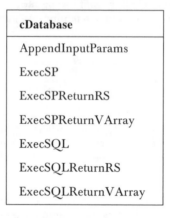

cDatabase
AppendInputParams
ExecSP
ExecSPReturnRS
ExecSPReturnVArray
ExecSQL
ExecSQLReturnRS
ExecSQLReturnVArray

We will be using Visual Basic to create all of our components, so first off, open Visual Basic and create a new ActiveX DLL project called wxHSDBUtils:

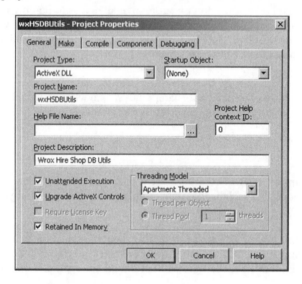

It is important to set the **Unattended Execution** option so that Visual Basic does not display any messages dialogs on the server, which will probably have no user sitting in front of it to respond. We also set **Retained in Memory** so that the DLL stays in memory until the calling process ends – that can save valuable instantiation time.

Before we dive into the `cDatabase` class we will cover the generic error logging procedure that is going to be shared among all of our components: `LogError`.

Add a new module called `modProcs`. When it comes to saving this file it is suggested that you save it in a directory called `Shared` above the code for this component. That way you will be able to share it easily with all other components.

`LogError` makes use of two other small procedures to get the application version and application path for logging purposes, so we'll add these simple procedures first:

```
Public Property Get AppVersion() As String
    On Error Resume Next
    With App
        AppVersion = .Major & "." & .Minor & "." & .Revision
    End With
End Property

Public Property Get AppPath() As String
    On Error Resume Next
    AppPath = App.Path
End Property
```

`LogError` itself is relatively simple, its only purpose is to retrieve as much information as possible and log it with the Windows Event Log:

```
Public Sub LogError(ByVal lngNumber As Long, _
                    ByVal strDescription As String, _
                    ByVal strProcName As String, _
                    ByVal strSource As String, _
                    Optional ByVal strAdditionalInfo As String = "")
```

We pass in various properties of the `Error` object along with any additional information that might be useful, in the case of the `DBUtils` object; this could be the SQL string to execute:

```
    Dim strErrorMessage As String

    strErrorMessage = "Runtime Error" & vbNewLine & _
                      "Number:" & lngNumber & vbNewLine & _
                      "Description:" & strDescription & vbNewLine & _
                      "ProcName:" & strProcName & vbNewLine & _
                      "Source:" & strSource & vbNewLine & _
                      "AppVersion:" & AppVersion & vbNewLine & _
                      "AppPath:" & AppPath

    If strAdditionalInfo <> "" Then
        strErrorMessage = strErrorMessage & vbNewLine & _
                          "Info:" & strAdditionalInfo
    End If

    App.LogEvent strErrorMessage, vbLogEventTypeError
```

We build up the message, add any additional information to the end, and then use the `App.LogEvent` method to log the error:

```
Err.Raise lngNumber, strSource, strDescription

End Sub
```

Finally we need to re-raise the error, so that it is passed back to the calling application, to indicate that something has gone wrong.

Now it's time to look at our first class, `cDataBase`: add a **Class Module** to the project and call it `cDatabase`. Before we add any code let's set the **Instancing** property to **5-MultiUse** and the **MTSTransactionMode** to **3-UsesTransaction** so that this component can participate in COM+ transactions:

We can now add some code to make use of the new `IObjectConstruct` interface. This interface contains a procedure `Construct` that is called each time the object is initialized by Component Services. It allows us to pass a string value to our component as set by a dialog in the Component Services Snap-In. In our case this is a great way to set the ADO connection string that our components are to use:

```
Option Explicit
Private Const m_cModuleName = "wxHSDBUtils.cDatabase."
Implements IObjectConstruct
Private m_strConnectionString As String
```

We need to store the connection string in a module level variable, `m_strConnectionString`, as the value will be lost as the `Construct` method closes:

```
Private Sub IObjectConstruct_Construct(ByVal pCtorObj As Object)

    On Error GoTo ProcError
    Const cProcName = m_cModuleName & "IObjectConstruct_Construct"
```

Note our standard error header declaration:

```
    Dim objConstructString As IObjectConstructString
    Dim strConstructString As String

    Set objConstructString = pCtorObj
    m_strConnectionString = objConstructString.ConstructString

    Set objConstructString = Nothing
    Exit Sub
```

We coerce the late-bound `pCtorObj` object into an `IObjectConstructString` to enable us to get at the `ConstructString` value:

```
ProcError:
    LogError Err.Number, Err.Description, cProcName, Err.Source, _
            "Construct=" & strConstructString

End Sub
```

Finally we can add our standard error handling code using the `LogError` procedure declared earlier, passing it the value of the constructor string for reference.

> *When it comes to registering our DLL with Component Services we mustn't forget to set the value of the connection string.*

Now that we have a flexible approach to retrieving connection strings we can look at our data manipulation procedures in detail. We have six procedures that allow us to execute SQL commands, and a private supporting procedure called `AppendInputParams`.

AppendInputParams

Each of our SQL execution procedures is passed a value identifying the SQL string to execute along with a `ParamArray` of input parameters for each call. This only applies to those calls that are stored procedure based.

Here we make use of the ADO `Command` object's `Parameters` collection to allow us to build up a list of input parameters in such a way that will not be effected should the position of certain arguments change with time, and also to provide support for `NULL` values:

```
Private Sub AppendInputParams(ByRef objCmd As ADODB.Command, _
                              ParamArray varInParams() As Variant)

    On Error GoTo ProcErr
    Const cProcName = m_cModuleName & "AppendInputParams"

    Const cValueElelement = 3

    Dim varParams As Variant
    Dim intCount As Integer
    Dim varValue As Variant

    varParams = varInParams(0)
```

varInParams is defined as a `ParamArray`, so if there were no parameters passed, `UBound` will return 0 so we will not need to continue.

Element 0 of `varInParams` contains the actual array of parameters passed in. We need to navigate through each of the parameters converting NULL values first:

```
For intCount = LBound(varParams) To UBound(varParams)

    Select Case TypeName(varParams(intCount)(cValueElelement))
        Case "String"
            If varParams(intCount)(cValueElelement) = "" Then
                varValue = Null
            Else
                varValue = varParams(intCount)(cValueElelement)
            End If

        Case "Boolean"
            varValue = varParams(intCount)(cValueElelement)

        Case Else
            If IsNumeric(varParams(intCount)(cValueElelement)) Then
                If varParams(intCount)(cValueElelement) < 0 Then
                    varValue = Null
                Else
                    varValue = varParams(intCount)(cValueElelement)
                End If
            Else
                varValue = varParams(intCount)(cValueElelement)
            End If
    End Select
```

Now that we've retrieved the value for each item we can simply add it to the `Parameters` collection using the `Append` method:

```
        objCmd.Parameters.Append _
            objCmd.CreateParameter(varParams(intCount)(0), _
                                   varParams(intCount)(1), _
                                   adParamInput, _
                                   varParams(intCount)(2), _
                                   varValue)

    Next intCount
    Exit Sub

ProcErr:
    LogError Err.Number, Err.Description, cProcName, Err.Source, _
    "Element=" & intCount

End Sub
```

All of our data manipulation procedures are essentially the same except that they set the `CommandType` property accordingly and pass the `adExecuteNoRecords` option to our `CommandObject's` Execute function when do not they need to return data.

ExecSP

This method allows us to execute a stored procedure that does not return any data. Typically it will be used in those stored procedures that update or delete records:

```
Public Sub ExecSP(ByVal strSQL As String, _
                  ParamArray varParams() As Variant)

    On Error GoTo ProcErr
    Const cProcName = m_cModuleName & "ExecSP"


    Dim objCmd As ADODB.Command

    Set objCmd = New ADODB.Command
    With objCmd
        .ActiveConnection = m_strConnectionString
        .CommandText = strSQL
        .CommandType = adCmdStoredProc
    End With
```

First of all, we create and initialize the Command object using the connection string passed in through the IObjectConstruct interface. We need to tell ADO this is going to be a stored procedure call so we set the CommandType:

```
    AppendInputParams objCmd, varParams
```

Now it's time to call AppendInputParams to transfer any arguments to the Parameters collection. Note that there may not actually be any items to add anyway:

```
    objCmd.Execute , , ADODB.adExecuteNoRecords
```

With the input parameters set we can attempt to execute the stored procedure being careful to tell ADO that we don't want any records returned back in order to save processing using the adExecuteNoRecords constant:

```
    Set objCmd.ActiveConnection = Nothing
    Set objCmd = Nothing

    Exit Sub

ProcErr:
    Set objCmd = Nothing
    LogError Err.Number, Err.Description, cProcName, Err.Source, _
            "SQL=" & strSQL

End Sub
```

With the stored procedure executed we can close the ActiveConnection and the Command object.

ExecSPReturnRS

This function is similar to ExecRS in that it executes a stored procedure but the difference is it returns a disconnected RecordSet object:

```
Public Function ExecSPReturnRS(ByVal strSQL As String, _
                        ParamArray varParams() As Variant) As Recordset

    On Error GoTo ProcErr
    Const cProcName = m_cModuleName & "ExecSPReturnRS"


    Dim objRS As ADODB.Recordset
    Dim objCmd As ADODB.Command
```

Additionally we declare a variable, objRS, to store the results of our RecordSet fetch:

```
    Set objCmd = New ADODB.Command
    With objCmd
        .ActiveConnection = m_strConnectionString
        .CommandText = strSQL
        .CommandType = adCmdStoredProc
    End With

    AppendInputParams objCmd, varParams

    Set objRS = New ADODB.Recordset
    With objRS
        .CursorLocation = adUseClient
        .Open objCmd, , adOpenForwardOnly, adLockReadOnly
    End With
```

This time we use the Open method to execute our stored procedure, return some data and close down the objects:

```
    Set objCmd.ActiveConnection = Nothing
    Set objCmd = Nothing

    If Not objRS.ActiveConnection Is Nothing Then _
        Set objRS.ActiveConnection = Nothing
    Set ExecSPReturnRS = objRS
    Exit Function

ProcErr:
    Set objCmd = Nothing
    Set objRS = Nothing
    LogError Err.Number, Err.Description, cProcName, Err.Source, _
            "SQL=" & strSQL

End Function
```

ExecSPReturnVArray

There may be times when returning a RecordSet could be overkill, such as when returning a single record with only two columns. In this instance, we have ExecSPReturnVArray, which will return a Variant Array of data:

```
Public Function ExecSPReturnVArray(ByVal strSQL As String, _
                                ParamArray varParams() As Variant) As Variant

    On Error GoTo ProcErr
    Const cProcName = m_cModuleName & "ExecSPReturnVArray"

    Dim objRS As ADODB.Recordset
    Dim objCmd As ADODB.Command

    Set objCmd = New ADODB.Command
    With objCmd
        .ActiveConnection = m_strConnectionString
        .CommandText = strSQL
        .CommandType = adCmdStoredProc
    End With
```

Again, we are using the standard method of transferring the connection string to our Command object:

```
    AppendInputParams objCmd, varParams
```

If there has been any arguments passed for use with the input parameters then we'll need to set them using AppendInputParams:

```
    Set objRS = New ADODB.Recordset
    With objRS
        .CursorLocation = adUseClient
        .Open objCmd, , adOpenForwardOnly, adLockReadOnly
    End With
```

Open up the RecordSet in the usual way:

```
    With objRS
        If Not .EOF And Not .BOF Then
            ExecSPReturnVArray = .GetRows()
        End If
    End With
```

If we managed to retrieve some records then the GetRows() function can be used to convert the data into a Variant Array:

```
    Set objCmd.ActiveConnection = Nothing
    Set objCmd = Nothing

    Set objRS.ActiveConnection = Nothing
    Set objRS = Nothing
    Exit Function

ProcErr:

    Set objCmd = Nothing
    Set objRS = Nothing
    LogError Err.Number, Err.Description, cProcName, Err.Source, _
            "SQL=" & strSQL

End Function
```

So far our DBUtils component allows us to execute stored procedures, with or without parameters, and to return a `RecordSet` object, a `Variant Array`, or nothing for those that perform data modifications. When developing DNA applications it is a good idea to perform all database access through the use of stored procedures for the following reasons:

❑ **Less network traffic**
Caused when sending long strings of SQL commands.

❑ **Faster server response**
Stored procedures are compiled on the server and do not need to be parsed by the server each time they are executed.

❑ **Secure**
We can effectively remove all permissions on all tables only allowing access through stored procedures.

❑ **Low coupling**
Typically we do not need to recompile our data services components if we make a change to the internal working of a stored procedure – unless the returned data changes.

There are three other procedures defined in DBUtils: `ExecSQL`, `ExecSQLReturnRS` and `ExecSQLReturnVArray`. These allow batches of SQL commands to be executed, such as a SELECT statement built up on the fly to support search criteria. We will not be covering these here, as they are not actually used by any of our data services components, and because they also work in a very similar way to the stored procedures. However, if you would like to see how they work, then all of the code for this case study can be downloaded from the Wrox web site at http://www.wrox.com.

With all the required code defined we can move to compiling the DLL and registering it with the Component Services snap-in. From the File menu choose Make wxHSDBUtils.dll to compile the component.

> Once you have compiled a DLL ready for registration with Component Services you must remember to set the **Version Compatibility** option to **Binary Compatibility** so that Visual Basic uses the same internal IDs (GUIDs) to represent each procedure and class.
>
> You might find it useful to copy the DLL to a new file and suffix it with 'BinComp' to indicate this is the base file to use for binary compatibility.
>
> With version 5 of Visual Basic it was recommended that you do not point the binary compatible DLL to be the same as the destination compiled DLL as this would result in accumulating unwanted interface identifiers. I haven't seen any reference to this in the version 6 documentation so hopefully it has been addressed.

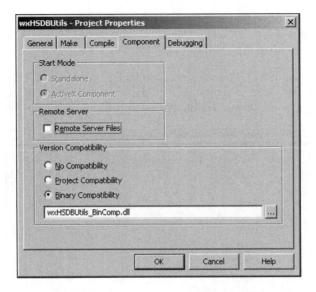

We only have two more steps left before we can move onto the actual components that use DBUtils; registration with Component Services and setting the construct string that represents our ADO connection string. If you don't already have Component Services running, then from the Start menu, select Programs | Administrative Tools | Component Services to start the snap-in.

We are going to create a separate package for each component, so in the case of DBUtils create a new application called Hire Shop 00 DB Utilities. The actual name used makes no difference to the performance of the component but it's a good idea to give them similar names for ease. Notice that we've included the string '00' as part of the name. The only reason for this is so that it appears before any other Hire Shop applications to indicate it is a dependency for the other applications that will follow.

We can leave the default settings for this application as they are.

> When it comes to releasing your components into a production environment it is a good idea to alter the account that this application is set to run as, to one created solely for COM+, because in reality there will not be an interactive user logged on to a production server.

Making sure that the Hire Shop 00 DB Utilities application is selected, right-click on the component and select New | Component. After choosing Install new component(s) from the Install Wizard dialog you'll be able to point to our newly compiled file wxHSDBUtils.dll.

From Visual Basic, we set the MTSTransactionMode for cDatabase to 3-UsesTransactions, so you should find that the Transaction support option on the Transactions tab of wxHSDBUtils.cDatabase is set to Supported. If it is not, then select Supported so that this object can participate in transactions.

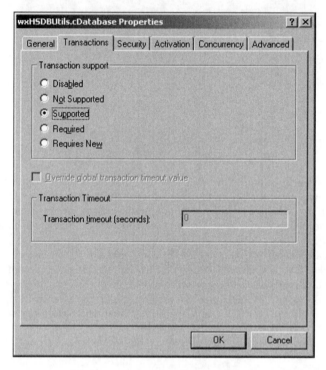

Finally, we have one more important property to set – the connection string passed to DBUtils in the Construct event of IObjectConstruct. Open the Properties dialog for our new component, DBUtils, choose the Activation tab and select the Enable object construction check box. This will enable the Object construction frame. Now we can add our connection string, in the example here the name of our SQL Server is HireShopDB so that should appear as the Data Source property, rename this to the name of your SQL Server. The Initial Catalog should be set to HireShop for the HireShop database. All stored procedures have execute permission granted to the HireShopUser user account:

```
Data Source=HireShopDB; User ID=HireShopUser; Password=HireShopUser; Initial
Catalog=HireShop; Provider=SQLOLEDB.1; Persist Security Info=False; Connect
Timeout=180
```

To recap, we have created a specialist data services support component that provides a utility wrapper around the ADO object to allow us to effectively and quickly execute stored procedures on our database server. We compiled and registered it as an Application with Component Services. Finally we set the construct string to a valid ADO connection string to allow us to move to different servers without having to recompile. Now it's time to use this component with our business and data services components.

Business and Data Services Components

The Wrox Hire Shop is built upon an n-tier architecture, as covered in earlier chapters, so each functional area has a single business layer that our website and administration programs interface, with which in turn have their own data services layer. Our requirements are grouped into three top-level areas:

- Customers
- Orders
- Products

As each area is covered, code will be introduced for each tier in a **bottom-up** approach:

> **Stored procedures   data services procedures   business rule procedures.**

Customer Components

The purpose of the Customer components is to register new users from the web site, allow administrators to update customer details, and to provide a method of validating the identity of web users.

Task	Business Rules	Data Services	Stored Procedures
Add new customer	Add	Insert, IsLoginNameUnique	hs_Customer_Add, hs_Customer_IsLoginNameUnique
Retrieve customer details	GetDetailsByID	GetData	hs_Customer_GetByKey
Login to web site	GetIDFromLogin	ValidateLogin	hs_Customer_ValidateLogin
Search for customers	SearchByName	Search	hs_Customer_Search
Update customer's details	Update	Update	hs_Customer_Update

For each task we will start at the lowest level by creating the stored procedures and and their associated data services procedures.

From Visual Basic, create a new ActiveX DLL project called wxHSCustomerDB. This will form our Customer data services component. With all of our components we will be using the same naming conventions; prefix the name with '**wxHS**' for Wrox Hire Shop, followed by the component group, '**Customer**', and '**DB**' to indicate the database services tier.

Do you remember the shared module to support error handling that we created for the DBUtils component? Now would be a good time to add it to our project using the **Project | Add File** menu option. In my case I called it modProcs.bas and saved it in a directory called wxHSShared:

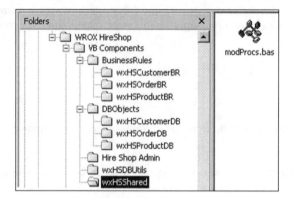

We need to add a number of references to our project:

❑ Wrox Hire Shop DB Utils (wxHSDBUtils.dll)
The component we created earlier as a wrapper for the ADO component.

❑ COM+ Service Type Library
For transactional support.

❑ ADO RecordSet 2.5 Library
A cut down version of ADO that supports just the Recordset object, as all other ADO functionality is encapsulated in the DBUtils component.

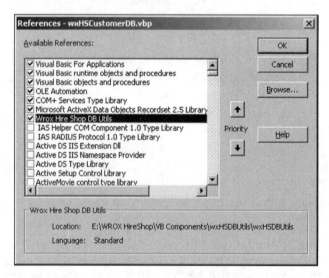

There will only be one class in the data services component, so add a new class module and call it cCustomer. We want this class to participate in transactions so set the **MTSTransactionMode** to **3-UsesTransactions**. Don't forget to make sure that the **Instancing** property is set to **5-MultiUse** so that one instance of the component can provide any number of objects.

Add Customer

From the Wrox Hire Shop web site, new users must register before they can access our database of products. The registration process uses the Add procedure within cCustomer to add a new customer's name and address and login details to the Customer table. So the first step is to create a new stored procedure in our HireShop database:

```
CREATE PROCEDURE hs_Customer_Add
  (
  @CustomerName   VARCHAR(30),
  @Address1       VARCHAR(50),  @Address2      VARCHAR(50),
  @Address3       VARCHAR(50),  @Address4      VARCHAR(50),
  @Address5       VARCHAR(50),  @ZipCode       VARCHAR(10),
  @LoginName      VARCHAR(50),  @Password      VARCHAR(50)
  )
AS
BEGIN

  SET NOCOUNT ON
```

We are going to use the same method throughout all of our stored procedures to add new records, we insert the record and return back to the client the @@Identity property. @@Identity returns the value for the identity column that was just created – in our case this will be the CustomerID column.

Notice the use of **SET NOCOUNT ON**. By default, SQL Server will return back a count of the number of records affected by each command that is executed. Unfortunately this behavior causes ADO to think that the records affected count is the actual value for the Recordset. If you attempt to read the Recordset or even navigate through it you will get runtime error number "3704 - Operation is not allowed when the object is closed." The use of SET NOCOUNT ON suppresses the records affected messages:

```
INSERT INTO Customer
  (CustomerName, Address1, Address2, Address3, Address4, Address5,
   ZipCode, LoginName, Password)
  VALUES
  (@CustomerName, @Address1, @Address2, @Address3, @Address4, @Address5,
   @ZipCode, @LoginName, @Password)
```

We simply insert a record into the Customer table using the parameters passed to the stored procedure:

```
SELECT @@Identity AS CustomerID

SET NOCOUNT OFF

END
```

Here we return the new CustomerID using the @@Identity property and switch back on the rows effected feature using SET NOCOUNT OFF. We could have added an OUTPUT parameter to the stored procedure to return back the new CustomerID. In our case we are using Recordsets to return data, as it is easier for our business rules to handle them in a generic and consistent fashion rather having to swap to output parameters every now and then.

Switch back to Visual Basic and add a new function called `Insert`:

```
Option Explicit
Private Const m_cModuleName = "wxHSCustomerDB.cCustomer."

Public Function Insert(ByVal CustomerName As String, _
                   ByVal Address1 As String, _
                   ByVal Address2 As String, _
                   ByVal Address3 As String, _
                   ByVal Address4 As String, _
                   ByVal Address5 As String, _
                   ByVal ZipCode As String, _
                   ByVal LoginName As String, _
                   ByVal Password As String) As Long

    On Error GoTo ErrorHandler
    Const cProcName = m_cModuleName & "Insert"

    Dim objDatabase As wxHSDBUtils.cDatabase
    Dim varData As Variant

    Insert = 0
    Set objDatabase = New wxHSDBUtils.cDatabase
```

We declare an object variable to hold an instance of the wcHSDBUtils component and set `Insert` to 0 as a default in case of failure; `Insert` returns back the new CustomerID if successful:

```
    varData = objDatabase.ExecSPReturnVArray("hs_Customer_Add", _
                Array("@CustomerName", adVarChar, 30, CustomerName), _
                Array("@Address1", adVarChar, 50, Address1), _
                Array("@Address2", adVarChar, 50, Address2), _
                Array("@Address3", adVarChar, 50, Address3), _
                Array("@Address4", adVarChar, 50, Address4), _
                Array("@Address5", adVarChar, 50, Address5), _
                Array("@ZipCode", adVarChar, 10, ZipCode), _
                Array("@LoginName", adVarChar, 50, LoginName), _
                Array("@Password", adVarChar, 50, Password))
```

We attempt to call the function `ExecSPReturnVArray` because we only want to return back a single value – the new CustomerID. You can see that the first parameter is a string representing the name of the stored procedure to execute - `hs_Customer_Add`. The remaining values are part of a ParamArray to describe each of the parameters for the stored procedure.

The `Insert` function needs to have explicit knowledge of the parameters for `hs_Customer_Add`. This allows `ExecSPReturnVArray` to call `AppendInputParams` generically without it having to know how `hs_Customer_Add` works. We always build up the parameters using the `Array` function to create the name of the parameter, its data type, maximum length, and the actual value so that `AppendInputParams` can perform any `null` conversions for us:

```
    If Not IsEmpty(varData) Then
        Insert = varData(0, 0)
    End If
```

If the call went well then `varData` will not be empty and element 0, 0 will contain the new CustomerID so we can set that as the return value:

```
    Set objDatabase = Nothing
    Exit Function

ErrorHandler:
    Set objDatabase = Nothing
    LogError Err.Number, Err.Description, cProcName, Err.Source

End Function
```

Finally we can close down our objects and exit the function.

Our business rule needs to ensure that each login name is unique so we need to add another stored procedure and Visual Basic function to support this. Add the following stored procedure:

```
CREATE PROCEDURE hs_Customer_IsLoginNameUnique
   (@LoginName  VARCHAR(30))
AS
BEGIN
   IF EXISTS( SELECT CustomerID
                FROM Customer
                WHERE Upper(LoginName) = Upper(@LoginName))
     BEGIN
       SELECT "N" AS Answer
     END
   ELSE
     BEGIN
       SELECT "Y" AS Answer
     END
END
```

We use the `EXISTS` command to see if there is already a record that has the specific login name. If there is we return `Y`, or `N` if not.

Add a new function to Visual Basic called `IsLoginNameUnique` to execute the stored procedure:

```
Public Function IsLoginNameUnique(ByVal LoginName As String) As Boolean

    On Error GoTo ErrorHandler
    Const cProcName = m_cModuleName & "IsLoginNameUnique"

    Dim objDatabase As wxHSDBUtils.cDatabase
    Dim varData As Variant

    Set objDatabase = New wxHSDBUtils.cDatabase

    IsLoginNameUnique = False
```

As ever, we'll be pessimistic and assume failure:

```
varData=objDatabase.ExecSPReturnVArray("hs_Customer_IsLoginNameUnique", _
                    Array("@LoginName", adVarChar, 50, LoginName))
If Not IsEmpty(varData) Then
    If varData(0, 0) = "Y" Then
        IsLoginNameUnique = True
    End If
End If
```

Execute `hs_Customer_IsLoginNameUnique` and if `varData` receives the value `Y` then it is a unique login name:

```
    Set objDatabase = Nothing

    Exit Function

ErrorHandler:
    Set objDatabase = Nothing
    LogError Err.Number, Err.Description, cProcName, Err.Source

End Function
```

> **We are using a standard set of error handling for all procedures within our components. So from now on we will not be showing the On Error Goto ErrorHandler and the ErrorHandler: label in order to concentrate on the fundamental pieces of code.**
>
> **If you are typing in the source code as we go don't forget to add the following lines at the top of each procedure:**
>
> ```
> On Error GoTo ErrorHandler
> Const cProcName = m_cModuleName & "procname"
> ```
>
> **Followed by the actual error handler code:**
>
> ```
> ErrorHandler:
>   Set objDatabase = Nothing
>   LogError Err.Number, Err.Description, cProcName, _
>           Err.Source
> ```
>
> **Of course in real life you must include error handling in your applications particularly with those for a mass market such as a web site.**

Also the DBUtils component is our standard component used to execute stored procedures so we will not be duplicating the variable declaration and initialization of this component any more. Again, you must include the following lines in your code:

```
Dim objDatabase As wxHSDBUtils.cDatabase
Dim varData As Variant

Set objDatabase = New wxHSDBUtils.cDatabase
```

Followed by:

```
 Set objDatabase = Nothing
```

before the procedure exits.

Retrieve Customer Details

We need some way of getting customer's address and contact details based on their CustomerID so add the following stored procedure to SQL Server:

```
CREATE PROCEDURE hs_Customer_GetByKey
   (@CustomerID        INT)
AS
BEGIN
  SELECT CustomerName,
         Address1, Address2, Address3, Address4, Address5, ZipCode,
         LoginName, Password
    FROM Customer
   WHERE CustomerID = @CustomerID
END
```

Back to Visual Basic and add a new function called GetData to wxHSCustomerDB.

```
Public Function GetData(ByVal CustomerID As Long) As Variant

...
Code for objDatabase omitted
...

   GetData = objDatabase.ExecSPReturnVArray("hs_Customer_GetByKey", _
                        Array("@CustomerID", adInteger, 4, CustomerID))
...
Code for error handling omitted
```

We use ExecSPReturnVArray to execute hs_Customer_GetByKey passing in one parameter, the CustomerID, which returns back a Variant Array containing all of the customer's details.

Login To Web Site

Before we allow users to access our database of products we need to verify who they are. This is achieved using the stored procedure hs_Customer_ValidateLogin:

```
CREATE PROCEDURE hs_Customer_ValidateLogin
  (@LoginName  VARCHAR(30), @Password     VARCHAR(30))
AS
BEGIN
  SELECT CustomerID
    FROM Customer
   WHERE Upper(LoginName) = Upper(@LoginName)
     AND Upper(Password) = Upper(@Password)
END
```

We simply return the CustomerID whose login name and password match those passed in. If the login name or password is incorrect then we will get an empty result.

Add a function to cCustomer called ValidateLogin:

```
Public Function ValidateLogin(ByVal LoginName As String, _
                              ByVal Password As String) As Long
  ...
     ValidateLogin = 0

     varData = objDatabase.ExecSPReturnVArray("hs_Customer_ValidateLogin", _
                    Array("@LoginName", adVarChar, 50, LoginName), _
                    Array("@Password", adVarChar, 50, Password))
```

We set ValidateLogin to a default value of 0 in case of failure and execute hs_Customer_ValidateLogin to return back the CustomerID:

```
     If Not IsEmpty(varData) Then
         ValidateLogin = varData(0, 0)
     End If
```

If the call was successful then element 0, 0 will contain the validated CustomerID.

Search for a Customer

Our HireShopAdmin program allows administrators to search for a customer record using their customer name. The stored procedure hs_Customer_Search uses the LIKE command to search the Customer table for matching customers and return summary information about them:

```
CREATE PROCEDURE hs_Customer_Search
  (@CustomerName  VARCHAR(30))
AS
BEGIN

  SELECT CustomerID,
         CustomerName,
         Address1,
         ZipCode,
```

```
(SELECT COUNT(OrderID)
    FROM OrderBasket ord
   WHERE ord.CustomerID = cust.CustomerID) AS OrderCount,
```

Get the total number of orders for this customer:

```
(SELECT ISNULL(SUM(BC.QuantityRequired), 0)
    FROM BasketContents BC,
         OrderBasket ord
   WHERE BC.OrderID = ord.OrderID
     AND ord.CustomerID = cust.CustomerID) AS TotalQuantity,
```

We use the SUM function to count how many items the customer has added to their Order Basket:

```
(SELECT COUNT(HireID)
    FROM BasketContentsHire BCH,
         BasketContents BC,
         OrderBasket ord
   WHERE BCH.BasketContentsID = BC.BasketContentsID
     AND BC.OrderID = ord.OrderID
     AND ord.CustomerID = cust.CustomerID
     AND DateOffHire IS NULL ) AS ItemsOut,
```

By examining the DateOffHire column we can see whether a customer has returned an item:

```
(SELECT COUNT(HireID)
    FROM BasketContentsHire BCH,
         BasketContents BC,
         OrderBasket ord
   WHERE BCH.BasketContentsID = BC.BasketContentsID
     AND BC.OrderID = ord.OrderID
     AND ord.CustomerID = cust.CustomerID
     AND DateOffHire IS NOT NULL) AS ItemsIn
```

Use the LIKE command to look for similar sounding customer names:

```
  FROM Customer cust
 WHERE CustomerName LIKE '%' + @CustomerName + '%'

END
```

We need to execute this stored procedure using a new function called Search to return a Recordset of matching customer details:

```
Public Function Search(ByVal CustomerName As String) As Recordset
  ...
    Set Search = objDatabase.ExecSPReturnRS("hs_Customer_Search", _
                    Array("@CustomerName", adVarChar, 30, CustomerName))
```

Updating a Customer

All we need now is the ability to update customer details using the stored procedure
hs_Customer_Update:

```
CREATE PROCEDURE hs_Customer_Update
  (@CustomerID INT, @CustomerName VARCHAR(30),
   @Address1 VARCHAR(50), @Address2 VARCHAR(50), @Address3 VARCHAR(50),
   @Address4 VARCHAR(50), @Address5 VARCHAR(50), @ZipCode VARCHAR(10),
   @LoginName VARCHAR(50), @Password VARCHAR(50))
AS
BEGIN

  UPDATE Customer
    SET CustomerName = @CustomerName,
        Address1 = @Address1, Address2 = @Address2, Address3 = @Address3,
        Address4 = @Address4, Address5 = @Address5, ZipCode = @ZipCode,
        LoginName = @LoginName, Password= @Password
  WHERE CustomerID = @CustomerID

END
```

Back to cCustomer and add a new procedure called Update to execute hs_Customer_Update:

```
Public Sub Update(ByVal CustomerID As Long, _
            ByVal CustomerName As String, _
            ByVal Address1 As String, ByVal Address2 As String, _
            ByVal Address3 As String, ByVal Address4 As String, _
            ByVal Address5 As String, ByVal ZipCode As String, _
            ByVal LoginName As String, ByVal Password As String)

...
    Call objDatabase.ExecSP("hs_Customer_Update", _
            Array("@CustomerID", adInteger, 4, CustomerID), _
            Array("@CustomerName", adVarChar, 30, CustomerName), _
            Array("@Address1", adVarChar, 50, Address1), _
            Array("@Address2", adVarChar, 50, Address2), _
            Array("@Address3", adVarChar, 50, Address3), _
            Array("@Address4", adVarChar, 50, Address4), _
            Array("@Address5", adVarChar, 50, Address5), _
            Array("@ZipCode", adVarChar, 10, ZipCode), _
            Array("@LoginName", adVarChar, 50, LoginName), _
            Array("@Password", adVarChar, 50, Password))
```

We use the ExecSP function, as Update doesn't return any data. That now completes our data services
component to support the Customer functions. All we need to do is compile and register it with
Component Services using the name wxHSCustomerDB.dll remembering to set Binary Compatibility
to point to a copy of this file afterwards.

Jump to Component Services to create a new package called Hire Shop Customer and add this new
component. We only need to check the Transaction support property on the Transactions tab to
ensure is it set to Supported.

Now we've created all of the code for `wxHSCustomerDB` we can move to a new Visual Basic component called `wxHSCustomerBR`. This is the business rules tier that our ASP and HireShopAdmin scripts communicate directly with.

Close the `wxHSCustomerDB` project and create a new ActiveX DLL project called `wxHSCustomerBR.dll`. We need to add references to COM+, ADO 2.5 Recordset and our Wrox Hire Shop Customer DB objects.

We will match the class name used in `wxHSCustomerDB`, so add a new class module called `cCustomer` and set the MTSTransactionMode to 3-UsesTransactions and Instancing to 5-MultiUse. Don't forget to add the shared error-handling file to this project.

We'll go through the list of tasks in the same order as we did with the Customer data services component.

Add Customer

The Customer business rule component provides the ability to add a new customer. It includes all data validation such as ensuring that the login name requested is unique. This is also the best place to put any validation code such as ensuring that required fields are not empty.

Add a new procedure to the `cCustomer` class called `Add`:

```
Option Explicit
Private Const m_cModuleName = "wxHSCustomerBR.cCustomer."

Public Sub Add(ByVal CustomerName As String, _
            ByVal Address1 As String, ByVal Address2 As String, _
            ByVal Address3 As String, ByVal Address4 As String, _
            ByVal Address5 As String, ByVal ZipCode As String, _
            ByVal LoginName As String, ByVal Password As String, _
            ByRef DuplicateLoginName As Variant, _
            ByRef CustomerID As Variant)

    On Error GoTo ErrorHandler
    Const cProcName = m_cModuleName & "Add"

    Dim objCustomerDB As wxHSCustomerDB.cCustomer
    Dim objContext As ObjectContext

    Set objContext = GetObjectContext()
    Set objCustomerDB = New wxHSCustomerDB.cCustomer
```

Now we are referring to our CustomerDB object. This is the component that takes our parameters and puts them together in a SQL call to update the database. Our business rule object is the component that votes on the success or failure of transactions so we need to create a reference to the COM+ `ObjectContext` in order to call `SetAbort` or `SetComplete` upon success or failure accordingly:

```
    DuplicateLoginName = False
    CustomerID = 0
```

We'll default to failure so set the `CustomerID` to 0:

```
If Not objCustomerDB.IsLoginNameUnique(LoginName) Then
    DuplicateLoginName = True
Else
```

The first call is to make sure the login name is unique as this is one rule for our component. If it is not unique then we set the `DuplicateLoginName` variable to `True` so that the calling application knows it has been duplicated:

```
CustomerID = objCustomerDB.Insert(CustomerName, _
                        Address1, Address2, Address3, _
                        Address4, Address5, ZipCode, _
                        LoginName, Password)

End If
```

We call the `Insert` function in the `CustomerDB` object, which will return back the new `CustomerID`:

```
Set objCustomerDB = Nothing
objContext.SetComplete
```

Finally we can clear down the Customer object and call `SetComplete` to indicate that the function executed successfully and that any transactions are safe to continue:

```
Exit Sub

ErrorHandler:
    Set objCustomerDB = Nothing
    objContext.SetAbort
```

If an error occurs our error handler will call SetAbort to indicate to COM+ and DTC that the result of this call was unsuccessful:

```
LogError Err.Number, Err.Description, cProcName, Err.Source

End Sub
```

As with all our components we will call the same standard error logging procedure, `LogError`, which in turn will re-raise the error back to our client, whether it is ASP or a VB program.

> As with our error handling and the DBUtils component we use the same **objContext** object to store the current object context from the GetObjectContext() function.
>
> Before the end of each successful procedure execution we make a call to **SetComplete** or **SetAbort** within the error handler to inform COM+ and DTC of the outcome of the procedure call.
>
> In order to save space we will not be duplicating this code again as it appears in much the same place through all of our procedures. This also applies to the **objCustomerDB** object as it is defined in the same manner between procedures.

> **If you are typing in the source code don't forget to include the following lines near the top of each procedure:**
>
> ```
> Dim objContext As ObjectContext
> Set objContext = GetObjectContext()
> ```
>
> **Followed by the SetComplete and SetAbort calls:**
>
> ```
> objContext.SetComplete
> Exit xxx
>
> ErrorHandler:
> Set objCustomerDB = Nothing
> objContext.SetAbort
> LogError Err.Number, Err.Description, cProcName, _
>          Err.Source
>
> End xxx
> ```

Retrieve Customer Details

In order to retrieve customer's name, address and order details we need to call `GetData` from the CustomerDB object. This is achieved using a new function called `GetDetailsByID`:

```
Public Function GetDetailsByID(ByVal CustomerID As Long) As Variant
...
Code for error handling, objContext and objCustomerDB omitted
...
    GetDetailsByID = objCustomerDB.GetData(CustomerID)
```

Call the `GetData` function and return a `Variant Array` back to the client.

Login To Web Site

The `CustomerDB` object has a function called `ValidateLogin` that will return back to us a valid `CustomerID` based on a login name and password. We will add a new function called `GetIDFromLogin` to call `ValidateLogin`.

```
Public Function GetIDFromLogin(ByVal LoginName As String, _
                               ByVal Password As String) As Long
...
    GetIDFromLogin = objCustomerDB.ValidateLogin(LoginName, Password)
```

When we call `GetIDFromLogin` we pass in the login name and password that were entered in our ASP script.

Search For Customers

The HireShopAdmin program allows administrators to search for customers based on their name so we need to create a function in the business rule object to call the CustomerDB object's `Search` function.

```
Public Function SearchByName(ByVal CustomerName As String) As Recordset
    ...
    Set SearchByName = objCustomerDB.Search(CustomerName)
```

Calling `Search` will return back a `RecordSet` object of all customers that meet the specified customer name.

Updating a Customer

Finally we need to add a procedure to allow our business rule to call the CustomerDB `Update` procedure.

```
Public Sub Update(ByVal CustomerID As Long, _
                  ByVal CustomerName As String, _
                  ByVal Address1 As String, ByVal Address2 As String, _
                  ByVal Address3 As String, ByVal Address4 As String, _
                  ByVal Address5 As String, ByVal ZipCode As String, _
                  ByVal LoginName As String, ByVal Password As String)
    ...
    Call objCustomerDB.Update(CustomerID, CustomerName, _
                      Address1, Address2, _
                      Address3, Address4, _
                      Address5, ZipCode, _
                      LoginName, Password)
```

We call the `Update` procedure passing in the `CustomerID` as the key and the remaining values. If this call fails for some reason, execution will be transferred to our error handler, which in turn will call the `SetAbort` procedure.

The issue of concurrency has not been covered here. How do we make sure that the user is not updating a record with old data that may have just been updated by another user whilst they were attempting to edit the record? This is a major point to consider when designing applications. One approach is to use the SQL function **TSEqual** in conjunction with a timestamp data type on the required table.

By selecting and storing this timestamp column each time you retrieve a record in preparation for updates, you can pass this back to the **Update** stored procedure, asking it to compare the old and current timestamps as part of the **WHERE** clause. Any differences will cause a server error to be raised and the record will not be updated. Information on TSEqual can be found in the SQL Server Books Online. An Example using TSEqual to check for concurrency can be found in Professional SQL Server 6.5 Admin - Wrox ISBN 1-874416-49-4.

Now we have completed all of the code for the customer business rule we can compile and register it with Component Services. As with the CustomerDB object compile the DLL, `wcHSCustomerBR.dll`, and set Binary Compatibility to point at a new copy of the DLL.

Jump to Component Services and add this component into the same COM+ Application that we added the `wxHSCustomerDB.dll` as it is often more convenient to group components together. Again, we earlier set the MTSTransactionMode to 3-UsesTransactions so Component Services should have set the Transaction support option to Supported. If not then you will need to set it manually:

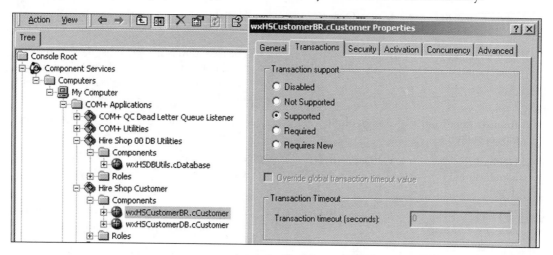

We have now created a separate Customer business rule and data services component that allows us to perform customer-related operations. We could now go ahead and create our Login and Registration ASP scripts for the Wrox Hire Shop web site. But we'll save that good stuff until we've compiled and registered all of our components. It's now time to look at the Order components that allows us to create and edit orders and add items to each order basket.

Order Components

The `Order` components are somewhat more complex than our `Customer` object. They contain classes to support the addition and amendment of an order and also allows us to implement the shopping basket approach whereby customers can **add** and **remove contents** in their shopping basket.

Task	Business Rules	Data Services	Stored Procedures
Create a new order basket	AddOrder	OrderBasket.Insert	hs_OrderBasket_Add
Get order details	GetDetailsByID	OrderBasket.GetData	hs_OrderBasket_GetByKey
Get a summary list of orders for a customer	GetSummaryDetails ByCustomerID	OrderBasket. GetDataSummary	hs_ OrderBasket_ GetByCustomerID

Table continued on following page

Task	Business Rules	Data Services	Stored Procedures
Get a list of valid Order Status values	GetOrderStatusList	OrderStatusDB. GetAll	hs_OrderStatus_ GetAll
Mark order as accepted	AcceptOrder	OrderBasket. AcceptOrder	hs_OrderBasket_ ProceedWithOrder
Update an order	UpdateOrder	Update	hs_OrderBasket_ Update
Add an item to basket contents	AddItem	cBasketContents. ProductExists, cBasketContents. Insert	hs_BasketContents_ ItemAlreadyExists, hs_BasketContents_ Add
Remove item from basket contents	RemoveItem	cBasketContents. Delete	hs_BasketContents_ Add
Get basket contents item details	GetDetailsByID	cBasketContents. GetData	hs_BasketContents_ GetByKey
Get basket contents summary by OrderID	GetDetailsByOrderID	cBasketContents. GetDataByOrderID	hs_BasketContents_ GetByOrderID

As with the Customer objects we'll start off by creating the stored procedures and data services component. Create a new Visual Basic ActiveX DLL project called wxHSOrderDB and add the COM+ Services Type Library, ADO 2.5 Recordset Library and the Wrox Hire Shop DB Utils component references.

We'll start with the order basket procedures, so add a new class module called cOrderBasket and set the MTSTransactionMode to 3-SupportsTransactions and Instancing to 5-MultiUse.

Creating a New Order

If a user of the Wrox Hire Shop web site wants to add items to their shopping basket then we will automatically create a new Order for them. The stored procedure hs_OrderBasket_Add allows us to add a new order record to the OrderBasket table:

```
CREATE PROCEDURE hs_OrderBasket_Add
  (@CustomerID INT, @OrderDate SMALLDATETIME, @OrderStatusID INT)
AS
BEGIN
  SET NOCOUNT ON

  INSERT INTO OrderBasket
    (CustomerID, OrderDate, OrderStatusID)
  VALUES(@CustomerID, @OrderDate, @OrderStatusID)

  SELECT @@Identity AS OrderID

  SET NOCOUNT OFF
END
```

Again we use the SET NOCOUNT ON and SET NOCOUNT OFF commands to ensure that ADO does not generate a runtime error when we try to retrieve the new OrderID using the @@Identity value.

Return to cOrderBasket in Visual Basic and add a new function called Insert to call hs_OrderBasket_Add:

```
Public Function Insert(ByVal CustomerID As Long, _
                       ByVal OrderDate As Date, _
                       ByVal OrderStatusID As Long) As Long

...

    varData = objDatabase.ExecSPReturnVArray("hs_OrderBasket_Add", _
                  Array("@CustomerID", adInteger, 4, CustomerID), _
                  Array("@OrderDate", adDate, 4, OrderDate), _
                  Array("@OrderStatusID", adInteger, 4, OrderStatusID))
```

Execute the stored procedure, hs_OrderBasket_Add, passing in the CustomerID, the order date, and OrderStatusID.

> **We could have defaulted the order date and status to a certain value within the stored procedure, but as they are effectively business rules they will be set from within the Order Basket business rule component described later.**

```
    If Not IsEmpty(varData) Then
        Insert = varData(0, 0)
    End If
```

If varData is not empty then element 0,0 will contain the new OrderID.

Retrieving the Order Details

In order to get the order date and current status we need to call the stored procedure hs_OrderBasket_GetByKey:

```
CREATE PROCEDURE hs_OrderBasket_GetByKey
  (@OrderID  INT)
AS
BEGIN

   SELECT ob.OrderDate, ob.OrderStatusID, os.OrderStatusName,
          cust.CustomerName
     FROM OrderBasket ob,
          OrderStatus os,
          Customer    cust
    WHERE ob.OrderID = @OrderID
      AND ob.OrderStatusID = os.OrderStatusID
      AND ob.CustomerID = cust.CustomerID

END
```

This stored procedure is called using the `GetData` function within cOrderBasket:

```
Public Function GetData(ByVal OrderID As Long) As Recordset
...
    Set GetData = objDatabase.ExecSPReturnRS("hs_OrderBasket_GetByKey", _
                              Array("@OrderID", adInteger, 4, OrderID))
```

`GetData` returns a `Recordset` from the `ExecSPReturnRS` function.

Retrieving an Order Summary List

The home page of the Wrox Hire Shop web site shows the user a summary of their orders to date, including the date, status and how many items have been added to each order. `hs_OrderBasket_GetByCustomerID` allows us to summarize this information:

```
CREATE PROCEDURE hs_OrderBasket_GetByCustomerID
   (@CustomerID  INT)
AS
BEGIN

   SELECT OrderID,
          OrderDate,
          OS.OrderStatusName,
          (SELECT ISNULL(SUM(BC.QuantityRequired), 0)
             FROM BasketContents BC
            WHERE BC.OrderID = OB.OrderID) AS TotalQuantity,
```

`TotalQuantity` returns the sum of the number of items required for each order:

```
          (SELECT COUNT(BC.OrderID)
             FROM BasketContents BC
            WHERE BC.OrderID = OB.OrderID) AS ContentCount,
```

`ContentCount` returns the total number of distinct products in the order basket:

```
          (SELECT COUNT(HireID)
             FROM BasketContentsHire BCH,
                  BasketContents BC
            WHERE BCH.BasketContentsID = BC.BasketContentsID
              AND BC.OrderID = OB.OrderID
              AND DateOffHire IS NULL) AS ItemsOut,
```

By looking at the `DateOffHire` we can see how many items have not yet been returned:

```
          (SELECT COUNT(HireID)
             FROM BasketContentsHire BCH,
                  BasketContents BC
            WHERE BCH.BasketContentsID = BC.BasketContentsID
              AND BC.OrderID = OB.OrderID
              AND DateOffHire IS NOT NULL) AS ItemsIn
```

If the `DateOffHire` is not a `NULL` value then this indicates that an item has been returned:

```
    FROM OrderBasket OB,
         OrderStatus OS

  WHERE CustomerID = @CustomerID
    AND OB.OrderStatusID = OS.OrderStatusID

  ORDER BY OrderID

END
```

We list all orders by their OrderID, which will turn out to be in chronological order. To execute this stored procedure, add a new Visual Basic function called `GetDataSummary`:

```
Public Function GetDataSummary(ByVal CustomerID As Long) As Recordset
...
    Set GetDataSummary = objDatabase.ExecSPReturnRS(_
                         "hs_OrderBasket_GetByCustomerID", _
                         Array("@CustomerID", adInteger, 4, CustomerID))
```

Updating an Order

The process of updating an order allows users of the HireShopAdmin program to change the order date and order status using the stored procedure hs_OrderBasket_Update:

```
CREATE PROCEDURE hs_OrderBasket_Update
  (@OrderID INT, @OrderDate SMALLDATETIME, @OrderStatusID INT)
AS
BEGIN

  UPDATE OrderBasket
         SET OrderDate = @OrderDate,
             OrderStatusID = @OrderStatusID
  WHERE OrderID =  @OrderID

END
```

cOrderBasket provides the `Update` function to call hs_OrderBasket_Update:

```
Public Function Update(ByVal OrderID As Long, ByVal OrderDate As Date, _
                       ByVal OrderStatusID As Long) As Boolean
...
    Call objDatabase.ExecSP("hs_OrderBasket_Update",
                     Array("@OrderID", adInteger, 4, OrderID),
                     Array("@OrderDate", adDate, 4, OrderDate),
                     Array("@OrderStatusID", adInteger, 4, OrderStatusID))
    Update = True
```

We execute the stored procedure using `ExecSP` and set `Update` to `True` to indicate success.

Accepting an Order

Users of the web site can continually add new items to their order basket but there comes a time when they need to proceed to the **Checkout** in order for us to accept their order and start the process of issuing the items they have added to it.

This is achieved using the simple stored procedure, hs_OrderBasket_ProceedWithOrder, to update the order status to Accepted.

```
CREATE PROCEDURE hs_OrderBasket_ProceedWithOrder
   (@OrderID INT)
AS
BEGIN

  UPDATE OrderBasket
    SET OrderStatusID = 5 --** Accepted
  WHERE OrderID =  @OrderID

END
```

AcceptOrder allows our OrderBasket data services component to execute hs_OrderBasket_ProceedWithOrder:

```
Public Function AcceptOrder(ByVal OrderID As Long) As Boolean
...
    Call objDatabase.ExecSP("hs_OrderBasket_ProceedWithOrder",
                         Array("@OrderID", adInteger, 4, OrderID))
    AcceptOrder = True
```

We call ExecSP to execute the stored procedure and set AcceptOrder to True if it is successful.

We've completed the code for our cOrderBasket class now we need to add a new class module called cOrderStatus whose only purpose is to return a list of valid order status items for the OrderStatus table. We have chosen to encapsulate this item in its own class to make future support easier by separating the task. When it comes to adding this call to the business rules component it will appear as a function call in the cOrderBasket class as that is a logical place to put it for those calling our objects from the presentation tier.

So add a new class module called cOrderStatus setting the MTSTransactionMode to 3-UseTransaction and Instancing to 5-MultiUse and create a new function called GetAll.

```
Public Function GetAll() As Recordset
...
    Set GetAll = objDatabase.ExecSPReturnRS("hs_OrderStatus_GetAll")
```

The stored procedure, hs_OrderStatus_GetAll, is simply a SELECT statement:

```
CREATE PROCEDURE hs_OrderStatus_GetAll AS
BEGIN
  SELECT OrderStatusID,
         OrderStatusName
    FROM OrderStatus
  ORDER BY OrderStatusName
END
```

Our last class module within the OrderDB component is cBasketContents that allows us to implement the shopping basket to add or remove selected items from the order basket. From Visual Basic add a new class module called cBasketContents and set the MTSTransactionMode and Instancing properties as before.

Adding an Item to the Basket Contents

The web site allows users to add any item to their order basket. The stored procedure hs_BasketContents_Add adds a record to the BasketContents table for the specified OrderID and ProductID.

```
CREATE PROCEDURE hs_BasketContents_Add
   (@OrderID INT, @ProductID INT, @QuantityRequired INT)
AS
BEGIN

   INSERT INTO BasketContents
      (OrderID, ProductID, QuantityRequired)
   VALUES
      (@OrderID, @ProductID, @QuantityRequired)

   SELECT @@Identity AS BasketContentsID

END
```

We execute hs_BasketContents_Add through a function called Insert that is passed the OrderID, ProductID and the quantity required.

```
Public Function Insert(ByVal OrderID As Long, _
                       ByVal ProductID As Long, _
                       ByVal QuantityRequired As Long) As Boolean
...
   Call objDatabase.ExecSP("hs_BasketContents_Add", _
                   Array("@OrderID", adInteger, 4, OrderID), _
                   Array("@ProductID", adInteger, 4, ProductID), _
                   Array("@QuantityRequired", adInteger, 4, _
                   QuantityRequired))
```

Removing an Item from the Basket Contents

It's all very well being able to add any number of items to an order basket, but users do make mistakes so we need to give them the ability to remove an item. The stored procedure hs_BasketContents_Delete deletes the specified item from the BasketContents table. Every item added to the BasketContents table is given a unique BasketContentsID to identify it:

```
CREATE PROCEDURE hs_BasketContents_Delete
   (@BasketContentsID  INT)
AS
BEGIN

   DELETE
      FROM BasketContents
   WHERE BasketContentsID = @BasketContentsID

END
```

We execute the stored procedure using a function called `Delete`:

```
Public Function Delete(ByVal BasketContentsID As Long) As Boolean
...
    Call objDatabase.ExecSP("hs_BasketContents_Delete", _
             Array("@BasketContentsID", adInteger, 4, BasketContentsID))
```

Retrieving Basket Contents Item Details

In order to show detailed information about each item in the `BasketContents` table we use the `hs_BasketContents_GetByKey` stored procedure:

```
CREATE PROCEDURE hs_BasketContents_GetByKey
  (@BasketContentsID  INT)
AS
BEGIN

  SELECT bc.ProductID,
         bc.QuantityRequired,
         prd.ProductName
    FROM BasketContents bc,
         Product prd
   WHERE bc.ProductID = prd.ProductID
         AND bc.BasketContentsID = @BasketContentsID

END
```

Our Visual Basic function `GetData` returns a `RecordSet` of data for the stored procedure:

```
Public Function GetData(ByVal BasketContentsID As Long) As Recordset
...
    Set GetData = objDatabase.ExecSPReturnRS("hs_BasketContents_GetByKey", _
             Array("@BasketContentsID", adInteger, 4, BasketContentsID))
```

Retrieving Basket Contents Summary Details

A number of pages on our web site show a summary of the number if items currently in the order basket. Typically this is the home page and the page following the addition or removal of items:

```
CREATE PROCEDURE hs_BasketContents_GetByOrderID
  (@OrderID  INT)
AS
BEGIN

  SELECT bc.BasketContentsID,
         bc.ProductID,
         bc.QuantityRequired,
         prd.ProductName,
         prd.DailyHireCharge,
         prd.WeeklyHireCharge,
         man.ManufacturerName,
         (SELECT COUNT(ProductID)
            FROM ProductItem prit
           WHERE prit.ProductID = prd.ProductID) AS ProductItemCount,
```

`ProductItemCount` returns the number of items that we stock:

```
(SELECT COUNT(HireID)
    FROM BasketContentsHire hire,
         ProductItem          prit
   WHERE prit.ProductID = prd.ProductID
     AND hire.ProductItemID = prit.ProductItemID
     AND hire.DateOffHire IS NULL) AS OnHireCount,
```

`OnHireCount` uses the DateOffHire column to count up the **overall** number of items that are still out on-hire:

```
(SELECT COUNT(HireID)
    FROM BasketContentsHire hire,
         ProductItem          prit
   WHERE prit.ProductID = prd.ProductID
     AND hire.ProductItemID = prit.ProductItemID
     AND hire.BasketContentsID = bc.BasketContentsID
     AND hire.DateOffHire IS NULL) AS BasketOnHireCount
```

`BasketOnHireCount` provides a count of the number of items on hire for each item in the basket:

```
    FROM BasketContents bc,
         Product prd,
         OrderBasket ord,
         Manufacturer man
   WHERE bc.ProductID        = prd.ProductID
     AND bc.OrderID          = ord.OrderID
     AND ord.OrderID         = @OrderID
     AND prd.ManufacturerID  = man.ManufacturerID
   ORDER BY prd.ProductName
END
```

We use the function `GetDataByOrderID` to return a RecordSet containing this data:

```
Public Function GetDataByOrderID(ByVal OrderID As Long) As Recordset
...
    Set GetDataByOrderID =
objDatabase.ExecSPReturnRS("hs_BasketContents_GetByOrderID", _
                    Array("@OrderID", adInteger, 4, OrderID))
```

Now that we have created the functions for our Order data services component we can compile the DLL and add it to Component Services in the same way that we have with the Customer objects. We will create a new COM+ Application called **Hire Shop Order** and install `wxHSOrderDB.dll` there. Again we need to check the `Transaction support` property is set to `Supported` after we add it.

Now we can close the Visual Basic project and create a new ActiveX DLL project called `wxHSOrderBR`. This is the component that our presentation tier is going to call to interact with the `wxHSOrderDB` component.

Don't forget to add the shared error-handling file to this project and references to the COM+ Services Type Library, ADO 2.5 Recordset Library and the Wrox Hire Shop Order DB component.

We can now go though our list of tasks and define the procedures that map to our **wxHSOrderDB** component. First of all, add a new class module called `cOrderBasket` and set its MTSTransactionMode and Instancing properties as usual.

Creating a New Order Basket

We create a new order basket by calling the `Insert` method from our `AddOrder` function. This business rule declares that all new orders must have an initial status of 1 for a **New** order and that the order date must be the current system time using the `Now()` function. `AddOrder` returns back to the client the new `OrderID` as set by `@@Identity` within the stored procedure.

We'll include the `ObjectContext` and error handling code as a quick refresher:

```
Public Function AddOrder(ByVal CustomerID As Long) As Long

    On Error GoTo ErrorHandler
    Const cProcName = m_cModuleName & "AddOrder"

    Const cNewOrderStatus = 1

    Dim objContext As ObjectContext
    Dim objOrderDB As wxHSOrderDB.cOrderBasket

    Set objContext = GetObjectContext()
    Set objOrderDB = New wxHSOrderDB.cOrderBasket
    AddOrder = objOrderDB.Insert(CustomerID, Now(), cNewOrderStatus)

    Set objOrderDB = Nothing
    Exit Function

ErrorHandler:
    Set objOrderDB = Nothing
    objContext.SetAbort
    LogError Err.Number, Err.Description, cProcName, Err.Source

End Function
```

Retrieving Order Details

We can retrieve the order date and status for a specific OrderID by calling the `GetData` function:

```
Public Function GetDetailsByID(ByVal OrderID As Long) As Recordset
...
    Set GetDetailsByID = objOrderDB.GetData(OrderID)
```

Retrieving Order Summary Details by CustomerID

To provide a summary of all orders for the customer we call the `GetDataSummary` function from `GetSummaryDetailsByCustomerID`:

```
Public Function GetSummaryDetailsByCustomerID(ByVal CustomerID As Long) _
            As Recordset
...
    Set GetSummaryDetailsByCustomerID = _
            objOrderDB.GetDataSummary(CustomerID)
```

Accepting an Order

When the user goes to the Checkout section of our web site we need to call the `AcceptOrder` function to accept the order ready for processing:

```
Public Function AcceptOrder(ByVal OrderID As Long) As Boolean
...
    AcceptOrder = objOrderDB.AcceptOrder(OrderID)
```

Updating an Order

The HireShopAdmin program can update the status and date of an order using the `UpdateOrder` function:

```
Public Function UpdateOrder(ByVal OrderID As Long, _
                            ByVal OrderDate As Date, _
                            ByVal OrderStatusID As Long) As Boolean
...
    UpdateOrder = objOrderDB.Update(OrderID, OrderDate, OrderStatusID)
```

Retrieving a List of Order Status Items

We created a separate class called `cOrderStatus` within the `OrderDB` component to handle the list of various Order Status items. At present it only contains a single function called `GetData` to retrieve the list of items. We will provide a function called `GetOrderStatusList` that creates the `cOrderStatus` item and returns a `RecordSet` of items:

```
Public Function GetOrderStatusList() As Recordset
...
    Dim objOrderStatusDB As wxHSOrderDB.cOrderStatus
...
    Set GetOrderStatusList = objOrderStatusDB.GetAll()
```

Adding an Item to The Order Basket

We can now move onto the cBasketContents class within wcHSOrderDB to manipulate the items that appear in the order basket for a particular order. Add a new class module called cBasketContents to wxHSOrderBR and set the **MTSTransactionMode** and **Instancing** properties to **3-UsesTransaction** and **5-MultiUse** respectively.

We need to add a new function called `AddItem` that will check to make sure that the Product has not already been added to this order basket before it calls the `Insert` function. `AddItem` will return `True` or `False` accordingly:

```
Public Function AddItem(ByVal OrderID As Long, _
                        ByVal ProductID As Long, _
                        ByVal QuantityRequired As Long) As Boolean
...
    Dim objOrderDB As wxHSOrderDB.cBasketContents
...
    If Not objOrderDB.ProductExists(OrderID, ProductID) Then
        AddItem = objOrderDB.Insert(OrderID, ProductID, QuantityRequired)
    End If
```

> The question of state arises here. Our users may be browsing through our catalogue, adding items as and when they feel like it. But how do we keep track of these items? We could have stored them in a container type such as an `Array` or a `Collection`.
>
> Instead we've decided to store them directly in the database, so that our components can add each item and then forget about them. Because all new orders are set to a status of `New`, we will know which ones have not been processed. If the customer decides not to bother with processing this order, it will stay as `New`. Over time our administrators could delete outdated orders.

Removing An Item from the Order Basket

To remove an item from the order basket we need to know the `BasketContentsID` used to identify this record. As with the `AddItem` function we will receive a `True` or `False` value to indicate success or failure:

```
Public Function RemoveItem(ByVal BasketContentsID As Long) As Boolean
...
    RemoveItem = objOrderDB.Delete(BasketContentsID)
```

Retrieving Basket Contents Item Details

`wxHSOrderBR` has a function called `GetDetailsByID` to retrieve details for the specified basket contents item:

```
Public Function GetDetailsByID(ByVal BasketContentsID As Long) As Recordset
...
    Set GetDetailsByID = objOrderDB.GetData(BasketContentsID)
```

Retrieving Basket Contents Summary Details

For a particular OrderID the web site shows a summary list of items in the order basket for that OrderID:

```
Public Function GetDetailsByOrderID(ByVal OrderID As Long) As Recordset
...
    Set GetDetailsByOrderID = objOrderDB.GetDataByOrderID(OrderID)
```

Now it's time to compile `wxHSOrderBR` and register it with Component Services. As with all of our components we set the **Binary Compatibility** project option to point to a copy of the compiled DLL. We will add `wxHSOrderBR` into the same COM+ Application as the `wxHSOrderDB` component – **Hire Shop Order**. We must also ensure that Component Services has set the **Transaction support** property to **Supported**.

Product Components

Our last two components are the data services and business rules to support the product search functionality. We are only interested in providing the search functionality within our components, but a future version could be created to support editing and creating new product details, but that is beyond the scope of this case study. We will be using the standard DBUtils component to execute our stored procedures in the same approach that we have used for the Customer and Order components.

Task	Business Rules	Data Services	Stored Procedures
Retrieving a list of manufacturers names	GetManufacturerList	cManufacturer.GetAll	hs_Manufacturer_GetAll
Retrieving a list of product types	GetProductTypeList	cProductType.GetAll	hs_ProductType_GetAll
Retrieving product details	GetDetailsByID	cProduct.GetData	hs_Product_GetByKey
Searching for a product	Search	cProduct.Search	hs_Product_Search

From Visual Basic, create a new ActiveX DLL project called wxHSProductDB and add the references to the COM+ Services Type Library, ADO 2.5 RecordSet library and our Wrox Hire Shop DB Utils component. We also need to add our standard error handling procedure, so from the Project menu select Add File and include modProcs.bas from a directory above.

Retrieving a list of Manufacturers Names

We'll start by adding a class module called cManufacturer to retrieve a list of manufacturers names. This is used in the Search.asp script to populate a drop-down select list of manufacturers for further search criteria. From the wxHSProductDB project, add a new class module called cManufacturer and set the MTSTransactionMode and Instancing properties as before.

We need to create a new stored procedure called hs_Manufacturer_GetAll:

```
CREATE PROCEDURE hs_Manufacturer_GetAll
AS
BEGIN

  SELECT ManufacturerID, ManufacturerName
    FROM Manufacturer
  ORDER BY ManufacturerName

END
```

We will execute this procedure using a function called GetAll. Once again we'll include the error-handling code and wxHSDBUtils creation as a reminder:

```
Public Function GetAll() As Recordset

    On Error GoTo ErrorHandler
    Const cProcName = m_cModuleName & "GetAll"

    Dim objDatabase As wxHSDBUtils.cDatabase

    Set objDatabase = New wxHSDBUtils.cDatabase
    Set GetAll = objDatabase.ExecSPReturnRS("hs_Category_GetAll")

    Set objDatabase = Nothing
    Exit Function

ErrorHandler:
    Set objDatabase = Nothing
    LogError Err.Number, Err.Description, cProcName, Err.Source

End Function
```

Retrieving a List of Product Types

In the same way as we retrieved a list of manufacturers we are going to provide a way to retrieve a list of product types, such as Lawnmowers, Timber Cutting, or Drills for use with the search page of our web site. Create another new class module called `cProductTypes` and set the **MTSTransactionMode** and **Instancing** properties.

From SQL Server create a new stored procedure to fetch the data:

```
CREATE PROCEDURE hs_ProductType_GetAll
AS
BEGIN

  SELECT ProductTypeID, ProductTypeName, CategoryID
    FROM ProductType
  ORDER BY ProductTypeName

END
```

Now we can add the `GetAll` function to Visual Basic in order to call `hs_ProductType_GetAll`:

```
Public Function GetAll() As Variant
...
    Set GetAll = objDatabase.ExecSPReturnRS("hs_ProductType_GetAll")
```

Searching for Products

Our web site allows users to see a variety of information about a product, such as the manufacturer, the hire rates and the number of items in stock. This is achieved using the `hs_Product_Search` stored procedure. This procedure accepts a `ManufacturerID` and `ProductTypeID`, either of which can be NULL, and a `ProductName` to search for. We use the SQL LIKE statement to search for products with a similar Product Name:

```
CREATE PROCEDURE hs_Product_Search
  (@ManufacturerID  INT, @ProductTypeID    INT,
   @ProductName      VARCHAR(1000))
AS
BEGIN

  IF @ProductName IS NULL
    BEGIN
      SELECT @ProductName = ''
    END

  IF @ManufacturerID <> 0 AND @ProductTypeID <> 0
    BEGIN
      SELECT prd.ProductID, prd.Description, prd.ProductName,
             prd.DailyHireCharge, prd.WeeklyHireCharge,
             ISNULL(prd.PictureFileName, '') AS PictureFileName,
             pt.ProductTypeName, man.ManufacturerName,
             (SELECT COUNT(ProductID)
                FROM ProductItem prit
               WHERE prit.ProductID = prd.ProductID) AS ProductItemCount,
```

ProductItemCount returns a count of the items of this type that we carry:

```
             (SELECT COUNT(HireID)
                FROM BasketContentsHire hire,
                     ProductItem        prit
               WHERE prit.ProductID = prd.ProductID
                 AND hire.ProductItemID = prit.ProductItemID
                 AND hire.DateOffHire IS NULL) AS OnHireCount
```

OnHireCount tells us how many of these products are currently on hire:

```
      FROM Product prd,
           ProductType pt,
           Manufacturer man

     WHERE prd.ProductTypeID = pt.ProductTypeID
       AND prd.ManufacturerID = man.ManufacturerID
       AND prd.ProductName LIKE '%' + @Description + '%'
       AND prd.ProductTypeID = @ProductTypeID
       AND prd.ManufacturerID = @ManufacturerID
     ORDER BY ProductName, ManufacturerName
    END
  ELSE
```

To save space we've omitted the code that does a search using either the ManufacturerID or ProductID as it returns exactly the same information:

```
    BEGIN
      SELECT prd.ProductID, prd.Description, prd.ProductName,
             prd.DailyHireCharge, prd.WeeklyHireCharge,
             ISNULL(prd.PictureFileName, '') AS PictureFileName,
             pt.ProductTypeName,
             man.ManufacturerName,
             (SELECT COUNT(ProductID)
                FROM ProductItem prit
               WHERE prit.ProductID = prd.ProductID) AS ProductItemCount,
             (SELECT COUNT(HireID)
```

```
                        FROM BasketContentsHire hire,
                             ProductItem          prit
                       WHERE prit.ProductID = prd.ProductID
                         AND hire.ProductItemID = prit.ProductItemID
                         AND hire.DateOffHire IS NULL) AS OnHireCount


            FROM Product prd,
                 ProductType pt,
                 Manufacturer man

           WHERE prd.ProductTypeID = pt.ProductTypeID
             AND prd.ManufacturerID = man.ManufacturerID
             AND prd.ProductName LIKE '%' + @ProductName+ '%'
         ORDER BY ProductName, ManufacturerName
       END

  END
```

We need to add a new class to wxHSProductDB, to call this Search stored procedure, so add a new class module and call it cProduct. We can now add a new function called Search that will return a RecordSet of matching products:

```
Public Function Search(ByVal ManufacturerID As Long, _
                       ByVal ProductTypeID As Long, _
                       ByVal ProductName As String) As Recordset
   ...
      ProductName = Trim$(ProductName)
      Set Search = objDatabase.ExecSPReturnRS("hs_Product_Search", _
                     Array("@ManufacturerID", adInteger, 4, ManufacturerID), _
                     Array("@ProductTypeID", adInteger, 4, ProductTypeID), _
                     Array("@ProductName", adVarChar, 1000, ProductName))
```

Retrieving Product Details

To give the user further information about a product such as the number of items available we call the stored procedure hs_Product_GetByKey:

```
CREATE PROCEDURE hs_Product_GetByKey
   (@ProductID  INT)
AS
BEGIN

  SELECT prd.Description,
         prd.ProductName,
         prd.DailyHireCharge,
         prd.WeeklyHireCharge,
         prd.PictureFileName,
         pt.ProductTypeName,
         man.ManufacturerName,
         (SELECT COUNT(ProductID)
            FROM ProductItem prit
           WHERE prit.ProductID = prd.ProductID) AS ProductItemCount,
```

`ProductItemCount` returns the number of products held by the Wrox Hire Shop:

```
        (SELECT COUNT(HireID)
            FROM BasketContentsHire hire,
                 ProductItem        prit
           WHERE prit.ProductID = prd.ProductID
             AND hire.ProductItemID = prit.ProductItemID
             AND hire.DateOffHire IS NULL) AS OnHireCount
```

`OnHireCount` checks the `DateOffHire` column to count all items that are currently still on-hire:

```
     FROM Product prd,
          ProductType pt,
          Manufacturer man

    WHERE prd.ProductTypeID = pt.ProductTypeID
      AND prd.ManufacturerID = man.ManufacturerID
      AND prd.ProductID = @ProductID
   END
```

Our last function, `GetData`, executes the `hs_Product_GetByKey` stored procedure:

```
    Public Function GetData(ByVal ProductID As Long) As Variant
    ...
        GetData = objDatabase.ExecSPReturnVArray("hs_Product_GetByKey", _
                        Array("@ProductID", adInteger, 4, ProductID))
```

Before we move onto the last component, `wxHSProductBR`, we need to compile this component as `wxHSProductDB.dll` and add it to a new Application in Component Services with the name **Hire Shop Products**. Again, don't forget to set the project's **Binary Compatibility** option and the COM+ component's **Transaction support** property.

Create a new ActiveX DLL project called `wxHSProductBR` and add a reference to the COM+ Services Type Library, ADO 2.5 RecordSet Library and Wrox Hire Shop Product DB. As usual we also include our shared error handling file `modProcs.bas`.

Now we can add the single class module to our project and call it `cProduct`. This class will encapsulate all of the classes in `wxHSProductDB` and provide an interface to all of the required procedures therein.

Retrieving a List of Manufacturers Names

Add a function called `GetManufacturerList` that returns a `RecordSet` of manufacturers names:

```
    Public Function GetManufacturerList() As Recordset

        On Error GoTo ErrorHandler
        Const cProcName = m_cModuleName & "GetManufacturerList"

        Dim objContext As ObjectContext
        Dim objManufacturerDB As wxHSProductDB.cManufacturer
```

```
    Set objContext = GetObjectContext()
    Set objManufacturerDB = New wxHSProductDB.cManufacturer

    Set GetManufacturerList = objManufacturerDB.GetAll()

    Set objManufacturerDB = Nothing
    objContext.SetComplete
    Exit Function


ErrorHandler:
    Set objManufacturerDB = Nothing
    objContext.SetAbort
    LogError Err.Number, Err.Description, cProcName, Err.Source

End Function
```

Retrieving a List of Product Types

The function GetProductTypeList is practically identical except that is calls the GetAll function in the cProductType class:

```
Public Function GetProductTypeList() As Recordset
...
    Dim objProductTypeDB As wxHSProductDB.cProductType
...
    Set objProductTypeDB = New wxHSProductDB.cProductType
    Set GetProductTypeList = objProductTypeDB.GetAll()
```

Retrieving Product Details

By calling the GetData function within the cProduct class we can return a RecordSet of product details:

```
Public Function GetDetailsByID(ByVal ProductID As Long) As Variant
...
    Dim objProductDB As wxHSProductDB.cProduct
...
    Set objProductDB = New wxHSProductDB.cProduct
    GetDetailsByID = objProductDB.GetData(ProductID)
```

Searching for a Product

Our very last function, Search, calls the wxHSProduct.cProduct.Search() function to return a RecordSet of products that meet the user's criteria:

```
Public Function Search(ByVal ManufacturerID As Long, _
                    ByVal ProductTypeID As Long, _
                    ByVal ProductName As String) As Recordset
...
    Dim objProductDB As wxHSProductDB.cProduct
...
    Set Search = objProductDB.Search(ManufacturerID, ProductTypeID, _
                                ProductName)
```

The stored procedure hs_Product_Search uses the SQL LIKE command to search for product details.

> We could have used SQL Server's free text search operators **FREETEXTTABLE** and **FREETEXT** to provide a more sophisticated search feature. This feature creates an index of the actual words found within a column and allows very powerful word searches to be specified much like that of an Internet Search Engine whereby different inflections of a word are matched and weighted. For further information check out the online SQL Server reference guide at **http://msdn.microsoft.com.**

We now have all of our components coded so we can compile this last one and add it to Components Services under the Hire Shop Product Application.

We have covered the major components of the Wrox Hire Shop, so we can take a look at how these are called from both of our presentation layers.

Bringing it All Together – The Presentation Layer

We've moved from defining our original business requirement, mapping out the database schema, and finally creating a whole set of COM+ components to support our business requirements. It's time to call these components from our front-end applications.

The Wrox Hire Shop Web Site

Our web site must perform the following functions:

- ❑ Allow new users to register with us
- ❑ Allow existing users to login
- ❑ Provide details of old and new orders
- ❑ Provide a shopping basket
- ❑ Allow users to search through our product catalogue
- ❑ Proceed with an order to the *Checkout*

In order to provide these features, we have 15 ASP script files that use our business rule objects to interact with the user. Before we detail how each of these scripts work, we'll just point out some initial design decisions that we have made.

Physical Architecture

Our web server runs on the same physical server, HireShopAdmin, as the Wrox Hire Shop components. The use of an n-tier architecture allows us, if need be, to split these two tiers into separate physical servers without any recompilation should that solution prove to be beneficial.

The actual SQL Server database runs on a different server, HireShopDB configured purely as a database server for best performance.

Server-Side Includes

We have made use of a number of server-side includes in our ASP scripts, particularly in the area of user validation. Rather than give our include files the standard .inc extension we have opted to give them an .asp extension as it is easier to edit them directly from Visual Studio.

User Security and Scalability

To make verification of access to the site easier, all pages that require a valid CustomerID contain a standard **include** file called /includes/CheckUser_inc.asp.

As we create the links around our site we will **not** be using any Session Variables to store the user's CustomerID or active OrderID as these tend to affect scalability of the server and may not be supported on those browsers where cookies are disabled. To counter this, we will add to all links an additional QueryString value that stores an encrypted version of the CustomerID. Also, where applicable, we will add the OrderID.

Each page that receives the QueryString CustID will have a local variable called varCustomerIDDecrypted. This variable will hold the **decrypted** version of the CustID QueryString.

By encrypting the CustID QueryString we can prevent malicious users from accessing other customer details by trying to guess another CustomerID. In the case of CustomerID number **1002**, the encrypted value passed around will be **3016340B45**.

The contents of the CheckUser_inc.asp is as follows:

```
<!-- #include virtual="/Includes/Encryption_inc.asp" -->
```

The file Encryption_inc.asp is our standard encryption include file as detailed later. Its purpose is to encrypt an ID into an obscure value:

```
<%
Dim varCustomerID
Dim varCustomerIDDecrypted
Dim varOrderID
```

Every page will now have three module level variables. varCustomerID is a cached version of the QueryString "CustID" that is passed around each page, varCustomerIDDecrypted is the decrypted CustomerID and varOrderID is the OrderID passed as part of the QueryString:

```
varCustomerID = Request.QueryString("CustID")
If varCustomerID <> "" Then
  varCustomerIDDecrypted = Encrypt(False, varCustomerID)
Else
  Server.Transfer "/Login.ASP"
End If
```

If for some reason the CustID QueryString is empty then the user may not be authorized so we simply make use of the new IIS5 Server.Transfer method to stop execution of the page and transfer it to the Login.asp script without having to tell the client to do a HTTP redirect.

So how does the CustomerID get set initially? We use the login page, `login.asp`, to get the correct CustomerID based on the login name and password. This then redirects to the home page and appends the CustomerID to the QueryString:

```
varOrderID = Request.QueryString("OrderID")
If varOrderID = "" Then varOrderID = 0
%>
```

To make life a little easier we also set the OrderID if it has been passed along._

The `encryption` include file simply takes the value and creates a random offset key which it XORs with a standard encryption key to each character in the value – `m_cEncryptionKey`. It might actually be a good idea for this encryption key to change on, perhaps, a daily basis to prevent users from book marking the URL and potentially bypassing our security:

```
<%
Private Const m_cEncryptionKey = "wroxhireshop2000"

Function Encrypt(ByVal EncryptFlag, _
                 ByVal SourceValue)

    On Error Resume Next

    Dim Count
    Dim EncryptionKeyPos, EncryptionKeyLen, SourceValueAsc
    Dim FinalValue, OffsetKey, TmpSourceValueAsc, SourceValuePos
    Dim FormattedItem

    EncryptionKeyLen = Len(m_cEncryptionKey)
```

If they passed in `True` for the `EncryptFlag` then they want to value to be encrypted:

```
    If EncryptFlag Then

        Randomize(Now())
        OffsetKey = Int((88 * Rnd) + 10)
```

We seed the random number generator and create an offset key ranging from 10 to 98:

```
        FinalValue = Hex(OffsetKey)
```

Convert the offset key into a hex number and store that in our `FinalValue` variable:

```
        For SourceValuePos = 1 To Len(SourceValue)
            SourceValueAsc = (Asc(Mid(SourceValue, SourceValuePos, 1)) + _
                              OffsetKey) Mod 255
```

Go through each character in the `SourceValue` and a convert each to a new ASCII value:

```
        If EncryptionKeyPos < EncryptionKeyLen Then
          EncryptionKeyPos = EncryptionKeyPos + 1
        Else
          EncryptionKeyPos = 1
        End If
        SourceValueAsc = SourceValueAsc Xor Asc(Mid(m_cEncryptionKey, _
                          EncryptionKeyPos, 1))
        FormattedItem = Hex(SourceValueAsc)
        If Len(FormattedItem) < 2 Then FormattedItem = "0" & _
                                      FormattedItem
        FinalValue = FinalValue & FormattedItem
        OffsetKey = SourceValueAsc
      Next

    Else
```

They must have passed in `False` so we'll decrypt the value:

```
    OffsetKey = Eval("&H" + Left(SourceValue, 2))
```

The first two characters represent the hex value of our offset key:

```
    For SourceValuePos = 3 To Len(SourceValue) Step 2
      SourceValueAsc = Eval("&H" + Trim(Mid(SourceValue, _
                        SourceValuePos, 2)))
```

Every two characters in the string represents a single hex value:

```
        If EncryptionKeyPos < EncryptionKeyLen Then EncryptionKeyPos= _
                  EncryptionKeyPos + 1 Else EncryptionKeyPos = 1
        TmpSourceValueAsc = SourceValueAsc Xor _
                        Asc(Mid(m_cEncryptionKey, _
                            EncryptionKeyPos, 1))

        If TmpSourceValueAsc <= OffsetKey Then
            TmpSourceValueAsc = 255 + TmpSourceValueAsc - OffsetKey
        Else
            TmpSourceValueAsc = TmpSourceValueAsc - OffsetKey
        End If
        FinalValue = FinalValue & Chr(TmpSourceValueAsc)
        OffsetKey = SourceValueAsc
      Next
    End If

    Encrypt = FinalValue

End Function
%>
```

Error Handling

All calls to our business objects should be followed by a quick look at the Error object to see if an error has occurred. If an error has happened, we will redirect to ServerBusy.asp and quit processing of the page.

In order for this to work we must ensure that that Response.Buffer = True has been set. Luckily for us, IIS5 now sets this by default so we do not need to set it explicitly ourselves:

```
""""On Error Resume Next
Set objRS = objHSBasketContents.GetDetailsByOrderID(varOrderID)
If Err.Number <> 0 Then
  Server.Transfer "ServerBusy.asp"
End If
On Error Goto 0
```

Object Creation

Rather than using the Server.CreateObject("ProgID") function to create our business objects, we will be using the HTML <OBJECT> tag. This offers greater efficiency because it allows the ASP script to determine when an object should be created and destroyed. It also gives us access to the new error-handling features in IIS5. It also works happily with Netscape Navigator!

Style

In order to provide a consistent look and feel to our web site we will be linking in a cascading style sheet file called main.css to all our presentation ASP scripts:

```
<STYLE>
BODY
{
    COLOR: black;
    FONT-FAMILY: Verdana, Arial;
    FONT-SIZE: 10pt
}
.PageTitle
{
    BACKGROUND-COLOR: red;
    COLOR: yellow;
    FONT-FAMILY: Verdana, Arial;
    FONT-SIZE: 16pt;
    FONT-WEIGHT: bolder
}
TD
{
    FONT-FAMILY: Verdana, Arial;
    FONT-SIZE: 10pt
}
.SmallText
{
    FONT-FAMILY: Verdana, Arial;
    FONT-SIZE: 8pt
}
.AreaTitle
{
```

```
        FONT-FAMILY: Verdana, Arial;
        FONT-WEIGHT: bolder
    }
    .InfoCell
    {
        BACKGROUND-COLOR: #eee8aa
    }
    </STYLE>
```

Form Submission

Each form submission will transfer to an ASP script with the same name as the source script file, except it will contain the suffix '_HND' to denote a handler, in other words, Register.asp submits to Register_HND.asp.

Site Navigation

Each of our ASP scripts uses a standard include file, LeftNav_inc.asp, to build up the navigation menu on the left-hand side. This allows us to easily alter the list of menu options for all pages without having to amend every page. If the user is viewing an order then we add a Checkout and Close Order link:

```
<CENTER>
<TABLE BORDER=0 cellPadding=2 cellSpacing=2 height=100%>
  <TR height=100%>
    <TD valign=top>
      <TABLE border=0 cellPadding=0 cellSpacing=0>
        <TR>
          <TD class=SmallText nowrap align="left">Customer Number:
           <B><%=varCustomerIDDecrypted%></B>
          </TD>
```

Tell the user their CustomerID – using the decrypted variable:

```
          </TR>
          <TR valign="top">
            <TD class=SmallText nowrap align="left">Order Number: <B>
             <%
             If varOrderID = 0 Then
               Response.Write "None"
             Else
               Response.Write varOrderID
             End If
             %>
```

If the user currently has an order number then tell them which one it is:

```
            </B>
           </TD>
        </TR>
        <TR><TD> </TD></TR>
        <TR valign="top">
          <TD>
```

```
<A HREF="/Default.asp?CustID=
  <%=varCustomerID%>&OrderID=<%=varOrderID%>">
  Home</A><BR>
```

Create a link to the home page but as usual we need to append the encrypted version of their CustomerID:

```
<A HREF="/Logout.asp">Logout</A><BR>
<A HREF="/ProductSearch.ASP?CustID=
  <%=varCustomerID%>&OrderID=<%=varOrderID%>">
    Product Search</A><BR>
<BR>
<%If varOrderID <> 0 Then%>
  <A HREF="/Checkout.ASP?CustID=
    <%=varCustomerID%>&OrderID=<%=varOrderID%>">
    The Checkout</A><BR>
  <A HREF="/Default.ASP?CustID=<%=varCustomerID%>">
    Close Order</A><BR>
  <BR>
<%End If%>
```

If they are looking at an order then we'll add the Checkout and Close Order links.

```
            </TD>
          </TR>
        </TABLE>
      </TD>
    </TR>
  </TABLE>
</CENTER>
```

Before we launch into the aspects of our web site it might be a good idea to alter one setting on your browser if you are using Internet Explorer version 5.

By default, IE5 enables the **Show friendly HTTP error messages** setting. This intercepts HTTP error 500 and shows a 'friendly' message saying that there was a problem with the web server.

This is a good idea for regular users, but developers really need to see the real error message that was generated, so it's a good idea to switch this setting off!

Verifying the User

We have four pages that cover user verification:

❑   `Register.asp` and `Register_HND.asp`

❑   `Login.asp` and `Login_HND.asp`

Register.asp

This page allows new users to **sign up** to our site. They must complete the standard customer profile questions such as their name and address, along with their unique login name and password. By pressing the **Register** button the form is submitted and they are transferred to the handler page, `Register_HND.asp`.

Both `Register.asp` and `Register_HND.asp` work together. If `Register_HND.asp` fails to register the new user then it transfers the contents of the form submission to the `QueryString` and sets `intRedraw` to 1 to indicate that `Register.asp` should redraw the form with the user's original data-entry values.

> *There is nothing more annoying than a web site that does not persist values between calls. Of course we don't append the password to the `QueryString` as someone else might catch sight of it.*

Unfortunately, there is no way of the customer knowing which login names have already been taken, so we will check for them and tell them if their choice has gone.

> *Many web sites offer suggested login names based on various combinations of the user's forename and surname. If these are all taken then the next step is to append an incremental number to the combination of their forename and surname until an available username is found:*

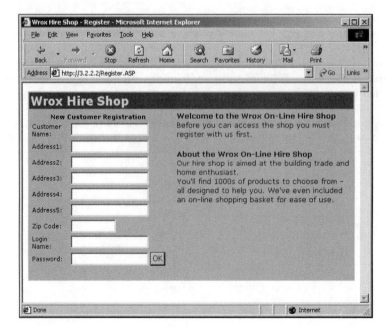

Let's take a look at the code behind this page:

```
<%Option Explicit

Dim blnDuplicatedLoginName, intRedraw
Dim txtCustomerName
Dim txtAddress1, txtAddress2, txtAddress3, txtAddress4, txtAddress5
Dim txtZipCode, txtLoginName, txtPassword

With Request
  blnDuplicatedLoginName = .QueryString("blnDuplicatedLoginName")
  intRedraw              = .QueryString("intRedraw")

  If intRedraw = 1 Then
    txtCustomerName = .QueryString("txtCustomerName")
    txtAddress1     = .QueryString("txtAddress1")
    txtAddress2     = .QueryString("txtAddress2")
    txtAddress3     = .QueryString("txtAddress3")
    txtAddress4     = .QueryString("txtAddress4")
    txtAddress5     = .QueryString("txtAddress5")
    txtZipCode      = .QueryString("txtZipCode")
    txtLoginName    = .QueryString("txtLoginName")
    txtPassword     = .QueryString("txtPassword")
  End If
End With
%>
```

If the registration failed then `Register_HND.asp` would have set the `intRedraw` QueryString to 1 to indicate a failure and that the page needs to be redrawn. We cache each of the fields into a local variable so that we can recreate them in the form again:

```
<!DOCTYPE html public "-//W3C//DTD HTML 3.2 Final//EN">
<HTML>
  <HEAD>
    <TITLE>Wrox Hire Shop - Register</TITLE>
    <LINK REL="stylesheet" TYPE="text/css" HREF="main.css">
  </HEAD>

<SCRIPT>
function submitForm()
  {
  if (document.frmRegister.txtCustomerName.value == '')
  {
  window.alert('Please enter your customer name.');
  document.frmRegister.txtCustomerName.focus();
  return false;
  }
...

  return true;
  }
</SCRIPT>
```

This JavaScript function, `submitForm()`, is called prior to our registration form being submitted to `Register_HND.asp` by setting the `ONSUBMIT` attribute. We use it to make sure the user has completed all fields before sending the page to our server. It looks at the `value` property of each required field, warns the user using `window.alert`, sets the focus to point to that control and returns the value `false` to indicate that the form should not be submitted. We have omitted some of the code validation to save space.

Of course this is not enough validation on its own, so our handler page can include some validation as well as the actual business rule component:

```
<CENTER>
<TABLE BORDER="0" CELLPADDING="2" CELLSPACING="2" WIDTH="600"
 BGCOLOR="silver">
 <TR>
   <TD COLSPAN="3" CLASS="PageTitle">
   Wrox Hire Shop
   </TD>
 <TR>
   <TD WIDTH="250" VALIGN="top">
      <!-- register form -->
         <FORM ACTION="Register_HND.ASP" ONSUBMIT="return submitForm();"
               METHOD="POST" ID="frmRegister" NAME="frmRegister">
```

Here we start off defining our form to collect the user's details. You can see the `ONSUBMIT` attribute that calls our JavaScript function `submitForm` and that the `Action` is set to `Register_HND.asp`.

HTML code to define form omitted to save space:

```
<%
If intRedraw Then
   Response.Write "<B>Sorry, your attempt to register failed.</B><BR>"
   If blnDuplicatedLoginName Then
      Response.Write "The login name entered is already in use. Please
try another."
      End If
   End If
%>
```

We check the `intRedraw` variable to see if this page is being redrawn. If it is set to `1` then the previous registration attempt failed so we'll tell them and if `blnDuplicatedLoginName` is set to `True` then the registration handler script was told that the login name already exists.

> We could have used the **OnTransactionAbort()** and **OnTransactionCommit()** methods to give a formatted message to the user stating that their registration failed.
>
> Unfortunately, in practice, this is not ideal as they would be the last events to get fired, and any messages outputted to the user through the **Response.Write** method would appear right at the bottom of the page. This may not be what we want in terms of look and feel.

Register_HND.asp

This page handles the submission of the registration page, Register.asp. It uses the cCustomer class within the wxHSCustomerBR object to attempt to register a new user. If registration is unsuccessful then the page redirects back to Register.asp so that the user can try again. Upon successful registration the user is redirected to the home page with their new CustomerID:

```
<%Option Explicit%>
<!DOCTYPE html public "-//W3C//DTD HTML 3.2 Final//EN">
<HTML>

  <HEAD>
    <OBJECT RUNAT="server" PROGID="wxHSCustomerBR.cCustomer"
           ID="objHSCustomer"></OBJECT>
  </HEAD>

  <BODY>
  <!-- #include virtual="/Includes/Encryption_inc.asp" -->
```

After the usual HTML tags we have used the OBJECT tag to hold an instance of our cCustomer component. We can refer to it throughout the script using its ID, in this case, objHSCustomer.

Notice that we have added the Encryption include file so that we can encrypt the new CustomerID before we redirect the user to the home page.

```
<%
Dim blnDuplicatedLoginName
Dim varCustomerID
Dim txtCustomerName, txtAddress1, txtAddress2, txtAddress3, txtAddress4
Dim txtAddress5, txtZipCode
Dim txtLoginName, txtPassword

With Request
  txtCustomerName = .Form("txtCustomerName")
  txtAddress1     = .Form("txtAddress1")
  txtAddress2     = .Form("txtAddress2")
  txtAddress3     = .Form("txtAddress3")
  txtAddress4     = .Form("txtAddress4")
  txtAddress5     = .Form("txtAddress5")
  txtZipCode      = .Form("txtZipCode")
  txtLoginName    = .Form("txtLoginName")
  txtPassword     = .Form("txtPassword")
End With
```

We transfer the values from the Form collection into local variables, for speed, as they are referred to more than once in our script:

```
Call objHSCustomer.Add(txtCustomerName, txtAddress1, txtAddress2, _
                   txtAddress3, txtAddress4, txtAddress5, txtZipCode, _
                   txtLoginName, txtPassword, _
                   blnDuplicatedLoginName, varCustomerID)
```

We call the Add method within our customer business rule to attempt to add the new user. blnDuplicatedLoginName will be set to True if the name already exists. If the registration is successful then this customer will have been added to the Customer table and varCustomerID will hold their new CustomerID:

```
If varCustomerID <> 0 Then
  Response.Redirect "Default.asp?CustID=" & Encrypt(True, varCustomerID)
Else
  Response.Redirect "Register.asp?intRedraw=1" & _
              "&txtCustomerName=" & Server.URLEncode(txtCustomerName) & _
              "&txtAddress1=" & Server.URLEncode(txtAddress1) & _
              "&txtAddress2=" & Server.URLEncode(txtAddress2) & _
              "&txtAddress3=" & Server.URLEncode(txtAddress3) & _
              "&txtAddress4=" & Server.URLEncode(txtAddress4) & _
              "&txtAddress5=" & Server.URLEncode(txtAddress5) & _
              "&txtZipCode=" & Server.URLEncode(txtZipCode) & _
              "&txtLoginName=" & Server.URLEncode(txtLoginName) & _
              "&blnDuplicatedLoginName=" & blnDuplicatedLoginName
End If
```

If varCustomerID is not 0 then we have a new customer so we can redirect them to the home page and add the encrypted version of their CustomerID to the URL. Otherwise we redirect them back to Register.asp and add their data-entry fields to the URL so that the original values can be recreated on the form.

Login.asp

This is the first page that the user sees each time they come to our web site. It allows existing users to enter their username and password, whereas new users can follow the link to Register.asp:

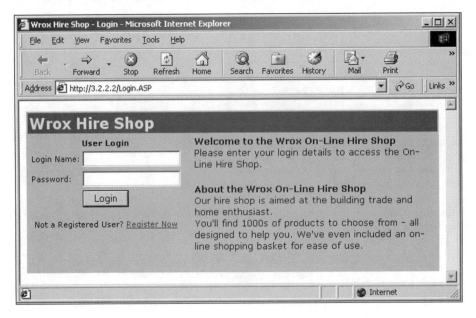

Rather than go through the entire HTML, we'll just cover the important aspects. The login form submits to the page `Login_HND.asp`. If there is a problem with the login attempt then `Login_HND.asp` will redirect back to this page and add the login name to the URL so that it can refill the login name field:

```
<%Option Explicit

Dim intRedraw
Dim txtLoginName

With Request
  intRedraw  = .QueryString("intRedraw")

  If intRedraw = 1 Then
    txtLoginName = .QueryString("txtLoginName")
  End If
End With
%>
```

HTML code omitted to save space:

```
<FORM ACTION="Login_Hnd.ASP" METHOD="POST" ID="frmLogin"
      NAME="frmLogin">
```

HTML code omitted to save space:

```
<%
If intRedraw = 1 Then
%>
  Incorrect username or password.<BR>
  Please try again.
<%
End If
%>
```

Login_HND.asp

This page takes the login form submission and attempts to log the user into the web site. An unsuccessful attempt will redirect the user back to the login page so that they can try again:

```
<%Option Explicit%>
<!DOCTYPE html public "-//W3C//DTD HTML 3.2 Final//EN">
<HTML>

  <HEAD>
    <TITLE>Wrox Hire Shop - Login</TITLE>
    <LINK REL="stylesheet" TYPE="text/css" HREF="main.css">
    <OBJECT RUNAT="server" PROGID="wxHSCustomerBR.cCustomer"
            ID="objHSCustomer"></OBJECT>
  </HEAD>

<BODY>
<!-- #include virtual="/Includes/Encryption_inc.asp" -->
```

Again we are using the OBJECT tag to hold a reference to the CustomerBR object and the Encryption include file is used to allow us to encrypt the validated CustomerID:

```
<%
Dim varCustomerID
Dim txtLoginName
Dim txtPassword

With Request
  txtLoginName = .Form("txtLoginName")
  txtPassword  = .Form("txtPassword")
End With
```

We adopt our usual manner of caching values that are used more than once, as it's faster:

```
varCustomerID = objHSCustomer.GetIDFromLogin(txtLoginName, txtPassword)
If varCustomerID <> 0 Then
  Response.Redirect "Default.asp?CustID=" & Encrypt(True, varCustomerID)
Else
  Response.Redirect "Login.asp?intRedraw=1&txtLoginName=" & txtLoginName
End if
%>
```

If the login attempt is successful then varCustomerID will hold a valid CustomerID so we can redirect to the home page, otherwise it's back to the login page to try again.

The Home Page

Our home page, default.asp, shows summary information about the user, such as the items in their current order basket and their order history. Every link to this page includes the encrypted CustomerID as mentioned earlier.

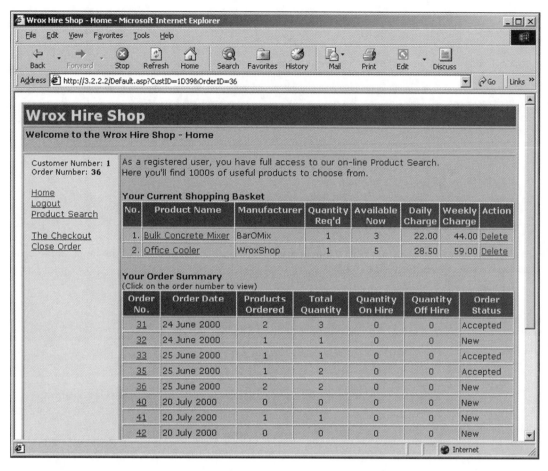

We use our standard include file CheckUser_inc.asp to make sure that any users accessing this page have already logged in. There isn't that much code to this page, so we'll go through the main areas section by section:

```
<OBJECT RUNAT="server" PROGID="wxHSOrderBR.cOrderBasket"
        ID="objHSOrderBasket"></OBJECT>
<OBJECT RUNAT="server" PROGID="wxHSOrderBR.cBasketContents"
        ID="objHSBasketContents"></OBJECT>

<!-- #include virtual="/Includes/CheckUser_inc.asp" -->
<!-- #include virtual="/Includes/BuildBasketContents_inc.asp" -->
```

We use the cOrderBakset and cBasketContents classes within the Order business rule to provide a summary of all orders for this customer and the current contents of the order basket.

There are a number of pages that provide a summary of the current order basket so this functionality has been moved into an include file called BuildBasketContents_inc.asp detailed below:

```
<OBJECT RUNAT="server" PROGID="wxHSOrderBR.cBasketContents"
        ID="objHSBasketContents"></OBJECT>
<%
Private Function GetBasketContentsSummary()

  Dim objRS, varReturnHTML
  Dim varAvailableCount, varRecordsExist, varCounter

  If varOrderID <> 0 Then

    On Error Resume Next
    Set objRS = objHSBasketContents.GetDetailsByOrderID(varOrderID)
    If Err.Number <> 0 Then
      Server.Transfer "ServerBusy.asp"
    End If
    On Error Goto 0
```

We call the GetDetailsByOrderID function to return back a RecordSet of the items in the order basket for the current OrderID:

```
    If Not objRS.EOF And Not objRS.BOF Then
        varRecordsExist = True
    End If
  End If

  If varRecordsExist Then
    varCounter = 1
    Do While Not objRS.EOF
      varAvailableCount = objRS("ProductItemCount") - objRS("OnHireCount")
```

How many items are there currently available?

```
      varReturnHTML = varReturnHTML & _
          "<TR>" & _
          "<TD align=right valign=center>" & varCounter & ".</TD>" & _
          "<TD><A HREF=ProductDetails.ASP?CustID="    & varCustomerID & _
                "&OrderID="    & varOrderID & _
                "&ProductID=" & objRS("ProductID") & ">" & _
            objRS("ProductName") & "</A></TD>" & _
```

Create a link to the ProductDetails.asp script so that users can see further information about the product:

```
          "<TD>" & objRS("ManufacturerName") & "</TD>" & _
          "<TD align=center>" & _
          objRS("QuantityRequired") & "</TD>" & _
          "<TD align=center>" & varAvailableCount & "</TD>" & _
```

Tell them the manufacturer, the quantity that they requested and the number currently available:

```
          "<TD align=right>" & _
          FormatNumber(objRS("DailyHireCharge"),2) & "</TD>" & _
          "<TD align=right>" & _
          FormatNumber(objRS("WeeklyHireCharge"),2) & "</TD>" & _
```

It's nice to know how much the item costs:

```
          "<TD><A HREF=javascript:deleteBasketItem(" & _
          objRS("BasketContentsID") & ")>Delete</A>" & _
          "</TD></TR>"
```

Add the **Delete** link so that they can remove this item from their basket:

```
    objRS.MoveNext
    varCounter = varCounter + 1
  Loop
  Set objRS = Nothing

  varReturnHTML = _
        "<TABLE WIDTH=100% BORDER=1 cellPadding=2 cellSpacing=0>" & _
            "<TR align=center valign=top class=PageTitle>" & _
            "<TD>No.</TD>" & _
            "<TD>Product Name</TD>" & _
            "<TD>Manufacturer</TD>" & _
            "<TD>Quantity<BR>Req'd</TD>" & _
            "<TD>Available<BR>Now</TD>" & _
            "<TD>Daily<BR>Charge</TD>" & _
            "<TD>Weekly<BR>Charge</TD>" & _
            "<TD>Action</TD></TR>" & _
            varReturnHTML & _
            "</TABLE>"
```

Create a nice header for the table:

```
  Else
    varReturnHTML = "You shopping basket is currently empty."
  End If

  GetBasketContentsSummary = varReturnHTML

End Function
%>
<SCRIPT>
  function deleteBasketItem(BasketContentsID)
    {
    if (window.confirm("Are you sure you want to delete this item from your
Shopping Basket?") == true)
      {
      window.location = "DeleteBasketItem.ASP?CustID=
              <%=varCustomerID%>&OrderID=
              <%=varOrderID%>&BasketContentsID=" + BasketContentsID;
      }
    }
</SCRIPT>
```

`deleteBasketItem` is a confirmation function that redirects to the `DeleteBasketItem.asp` script if
they click the **Delete** link.

So back to our home page where we also need to show a summary list of orders for the current `CustomerID`, so we use `GetSummaryDetailsByCustomerID` in `cOrderBasket` using the `GetOrderSummaryByCustomer` function:

```
<%
Private Function GetOrderSummaryByCustomer()

  Dim objRS, varReturnHTML

  On Error Resume Next
  Set objRS =
objHSOrderBasket.GetSummaryDetailsByCustomerID(varCustomerIDDecrypted)
  If Err.Number <> 0 Then
    Server.Transfer "ServerBusy.asp"
  End If
  On Error Goto 0
```

If an error occurred then transfer control over to the error page, `ServerBusy.asp`:

```
  If Not objRS.EOF And Not objRS.BOF Then

    varReturnHTML = "<SPAN class=SmallText>(Click on the order number to
view)</SPAN><BR>"
    Do While Not objRS.EOF
      varReturnHTML = varReturnHTML & _
        "<TR><TD align=center><A HREF=EditOrder.Asp?CustID=" & _
            varCustomerID & "&OrderID=" & _
            objRS("OrderID") & ">" & objRS("OrderID") & "</A></TD>" & _
```

Add a link to the `EditOrder.asp` script so that the user can see the items that make up their order:

```
      "     <TD align=left>" & _
      FormatDateTime(objRS("OrderDate"), vblongdate ) & "</TD>" & _
      "     <TD align=center>" & _
```

Tell them when the order was created:

```
      objRS("ContentCount") & "</TD>" & _
      "     <TD align=center>" & _
      objRS("TotalQuantity") & "</TD>" & _
      "     <TD align=center>" & _
      objRS("ItemsOut") & "</TD>" & _
      "     <TD align=center>" & _
      objRS("ItemsIn") & "</TD>" & _
      "     <TD>" & objRS("OrderStatusName") & "</TD>" & _
      "<TR>"
```

Finally how many items did they select and how many are available:

```
      objRS.MoveNext

    Loop

    varReturnHTML = "<TABLE WIDTH=100% BORDER=1 cellPadding=2 " & _
                " cellSpacing=0>" & _
```

```
                    "<TR valign=top align=center class=PageTitle>" & _
                    "<TD>Order<BR>No.</TD>" & _
                    "<TD>Order Date</TD>" & _
                    "<TD>Products<BR>Ordered</TD>" & _
                    "<TD>Total<BR>Quantity</TD>" & _
                    "<TD>Quantity<BR>On Hire</TD>" & _
                    "<TD>Quantity<BR>Off Hire</TD>" & _
                    "<TD>Order<BR>Status</TD>" & _
                    "</TR>" & vbNewLine & _
                    varReturnHTML & _
                    "</TABLE>"
        Set objRS = Nothing
        Else
           varReturnHTML = "You have no orders to date."
        End If

        GetOrderSummaryByCustomer = varReturnHTML

    End Function
%>
```

The function `GetOrderSummaryByCustomer` is called further down our page. Its purpose is to create a nicely formatted HTML table containing all of the customer's order details. After calling the `objHSOrderBasket.GetSummaryDetailsByCustomerID` function it loops through all of the records in the `Recordset`, `objRS`, to create a row for each order.

There isn't much more to the page so we'll just include the remaining sections that call our functions and include the standard navigation page:

```
<TR>
    <TD ROWSPAN="2" HEIGHT="100%" WIDTH="140" VALIGN="top"
        CLASS="InfoCell">
       <!-- #include virtual="/Includes/LeftNav_inc.asp" -->
    </TD>
```

This is our standard menu navigation page shown in the left-hand column:

```
<TD VALIGN="top">
    As a registered user, you have full access to our on-line Product
    Search.<BR>
    Here you'll find 1000s of useful products to choose from.
    <P><SPAN CLASS="AreaTitle">Your Current Shopping Basket</SPAN><BR>
       <%=GetBasketContentsSummary()%>
    <P><SPAN CLASS="AreaTitle">Your Order Summary</SPAN><BR>
       <%=GetOrderSummaryByCustomer()%>
    </TD>
</TR>
```

The Product Search Pages

From the home page the user can access our search page, `ProductSearch.asp`. As with the other form submission pages, it submits to a page with the _HND suffix, in this case, `ProductSearch_HND.asp`.

ProductSearch.asp

The user can select from the predetermined list of products and categories and specify the name of a product they are interested in:

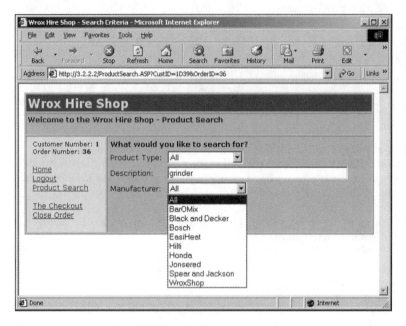

Again we'll only concentrate on the HTML code that creates this page:

```
<OBJECT RUNAT=server PROGID=wxHSProductBR.cProduct id=objHSProduct></OBJECT>
```

We use the `wxHSProductBR.cProduct` class to retrieve a list of manufacturers and product types:

```
<TR>
  <TD width=100 align="left">
    Product Type:
  </TD>
  <TD align="left">

    <SELECT NAME="ProductTypeID" SIZE="1">
      <OPTION VALUE=0>All</OPTION>
      <%
      Set m_objRS = objHSProduct.GetProductTypeList()
      If Not m_objRS Is Nothing Then
        Do While Not m_objRS.EOF
      %>
      <OPTION VALUE="<%=m_objRS("ProductTypeID")%>">
        <%=m_objRS("ProductTypeName")%>
      </OPTION>
```

```
<%
     m_objRS.MoveNext
    Loop
    m_objRS.close
  End If
  %>
  </SELECT>
  </TD>
</TR>
```

The code to populate the list of manufacturers is exactly the same except that it calls the
GetManufacturerList function to populate the m_objRS variable:

```
Set m_objRS = objHSProduct.GetManufacturerList()
```

ProductSearch_HND.ASP

By clicking the Search button on the ProductSearch.asp script the form will be submitted to our
handler page. This is the page that calls the product search function and creates a formatted table
containing their results:

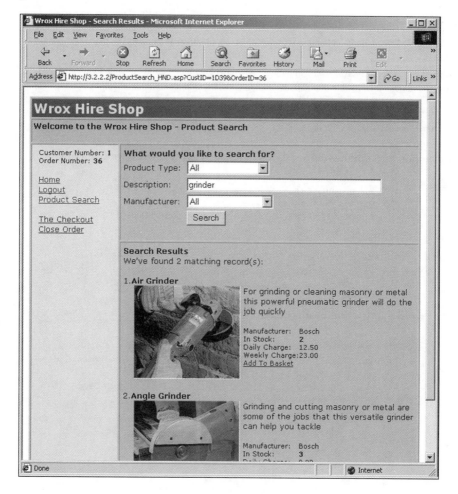

The search results page shows a picture of the item along with a description and additional information such as the manufacturer, the number in stock and the charge rates. We include a link **Add To Basket** that asks them to enter the number of items they would like before redirecting to AddToBasket.asp.

The search results are populated using a local ASP function called GetSearchResults that calls the Search function in our Product business rule component:

```
<OBJECT RUNAT=server PROGID=wxHSProductBR.cProduct id=objHSProduct></OBJECT>
```

HTML code to define form omitted to save space:

```
Private Function GetSearchResults()

   Dim varReturnHTML, varCounter
   Dim varPictureURL, varItemsAvailable

   varReturnHTML = "<DIV CLASS=AreaTitle>Search Results</DIV>"

   Set m_objRS = objHSProduct.Search(varFormManufacturerID, _
                                     varFormProductTypeID, _
                                     varFormDesciption )
```

Call the Search function to return a RecordSet of matching products:

```
   varReturnHTML = varReturnHTML & "We've found " & m_objRS.RecordCount & "
matching record(s):<br> "

   Do While Not m_objRS.EOF
     varCounter = varCounter + 1
```

Now we can loop through the RecordSet and create a row for each product found:

```
   varReturnHTML = varReturnHTML & _
       "<TR><TD>" & varCounter & ".</TD>" & _
       "    <TD COLSPAN=2><B>" & m_objRS("ProductName") & "</B></TD>" & _
       "</TR>"

   varReturnHTML = varReturnHTML & _
               "<TR><TD><!--blank col under number--></TD>" & _
               "    <TD align=center valign=top> "
```

Create the record number and product name:

```
   If m_objRS("PictureFileName") <> "" Then
       varReturnHTML = varReturnHTML & _
               "<IMG SRC=/Pictures/" & _
               CStr(m_objRS("PictureFileName")) & "> </TD>"
   Else
       varReturnHTML = varReturnHTML & _
               "</TD>"
   End If
```

If there is an image file name then we link to the image in our `Pictures` sub-directory:

```
       varItemsAvailable = Clng(m_objRS("ProductItemCount")) -
   Clng(m_objRS("OnHireCount"))
```

We calculate the number of items available so that we can tell the user if they are asking for more than the number currently in stock:

```
       varReturnHTML = varReturnHTML & _
                    "     <TD valign=top>" & vbNewLine & _
                        m_objRS("Description") & "<BR> "

     varReturnHTML = varReturnHTML & _
   "    <TABLE border=0 cellPadding=0 cellSpacing=0><TR><TD valign=top >" & _
   "      <TR><TD valign=top nowrap Class=SmallText>Manufacturer:</TD>"  & _
   "        <TD Class=SmallText>" & m_objRS("ManufacturerName") &  _
            "</TD></TR>" & _
   "      <TR><TD valign=top Class=SmallText>In Stock:</TD>" & _
   "       <TD Class=SmallText><B>" & varItemsAvailable & "<b></TD></TR>" &  _
   "      <TR><TD valign=top Class=SmallText>Daily Charge:</TD>"  & _
   "        <TD Class=SmallText>" & FormatNumber(m_objRS("DailyHireCharge"), _
              2 ) &  "</TD></TR>" &  _
   "      <TR><TD valign=top Class=SmallText>Weekly Charge:</TD>" & _
   "        <TD Class=SmallText>" & FormatNumber(m_objRS("WeeklyHireCharge"), _
              2) & "</TD></TR>"  &  _
```

Create a well-formatted daily and weekly hire charge:

```
   "      <TR><TD Class=SmallText COLSPAN=2 valign=top>" & _
   "        <A HREF=javascript:addToBasket(" & m_objRS("ProductID") & ")" & _
   "        >Add To Basket</A></TD></TR>" & _
```

The **Add To Basket** link allows the user to add an item to their order basket:

```
   "     </TABLE>" & _
   "</TD></TR>" & _
   "<TR><TD> </TD></TR>"

     m_objRS.MoveNext
   Loop

   If varCounter = 0 Then
     varReturnHTML = varReturnHTML & _
     "<BR>Sorry, we could not find any products that matched your criteria."
   Else
     varReturnHTML = "<TABLE WIDTH=100% BORDER=0 cellPadding=0 " & _
                     " cellSpacing=0>" & _
                     varReturnHTML & _
                     "</TABLE>"
   End If
   m_objRS.Close
   Set m_objRS = Nothing

   GetSearchResults = varReturnHTML

End Function
%>
```

Our final script is the `addToBasket` JavaScript function that displays a prompt for the user to enter the number of items that they require:

```
<SCRIPT>
  function addToBasket(ProductID)
    {
    var numberOfItems;
    numberOfItems = window.prompt("How many items would you like to add to your
shopping basket?","1");
      if (numberOfItems != null)
        {
        if (parseInt(numberOfItems) > 0)
          {
          window.location =
"AddToBasket.ASP?CustID=<%=varCustomerID%>&OrderID=<%=varOrderID%>&ProductID=" +
ProductID + "&Num=" + numberOfItems;
          }
        }
      }
</SCRIPT>
```

When the user presses the Add To Basket link and tells us how many products they want, we forward them to the `AddToBasket.asp` script that basically says thank you after it has created a new order number (if they haven't got one) and adds the item to their order basket.

Adding an Item to The Order Basket

The search results page has a link to `AddToBasket.asp` that calls our Order object to add a new item to the order basket. The URL includes the `CustomerID`, `OrderID`, `ProductID` and the number of items requested.

If there is no `OrderID` then we will create a new order for the user and add the item to it. If the item already exists then we will tell the user so. Because the user can request more items than those already in stock we display a well-formatted message saying they can take what we've got but they're going to have to wait for the remaining items:

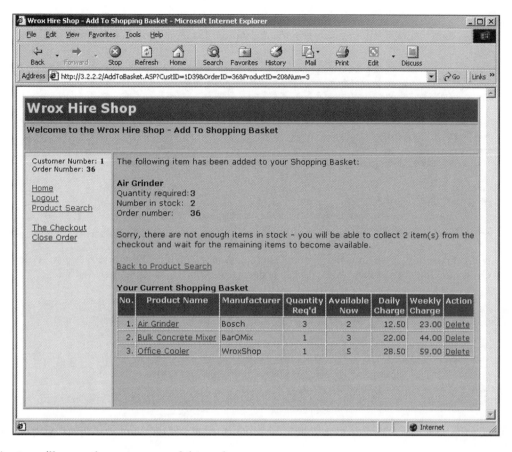

Again we'll cover the main areas of this code:

```
<OBJECT RUNAT="server" PROGID="wxHSOrderBR.cOrderBasket"
        ID="objOrderBasket"></OBJECT>
<OBJECT RUNAT="server" PROGID="wxHSOrderBR.cBasketContents"
        ID="objBasketContents"></OBJECT>
<OBJECT RUNAT="server" PROGID="wxHSProductBR.cProduct"
        ID="objProduct"></OBJECT>
```

We use the wxHSProductBR.cProduct component to get the product name and how many items are currently available. The wxHSOrderBR.cOrderBasket component is used to create a new Order if they haven't got one open and wxHSOrderBR.cBasketContents allows us to actually add the item to the order basket.

```
<!-- #include virtual="/Includes/CheckUser_inc.asp" -->
<!-- #include virtual="/Includes/BuildBasketContents_inc.asp" -->
```

The `CheckUser_inc.asp` include file is being used to validate the CustomerID along with `BuildBasketContents_inc.asp` to provide the standard summary of their order basket:

```
Const cProductNameElement = 1
Const cProductItemCountElement = 7
Const cOnHireCountElement = 8

Dim varItemsAvailable
Dim varProductNumber
Dim varProductName
Dim varNumRequired
Dim varData

If varOrderID = 0 Then
  varOrderID = objOrderBasket.AddOrder(varCustomerIDDecrypted)
End If
```

If they don't currently have an order open we'll create a new one by calling `AddOrder` to retrieve the new OrderID. Don't forget that `varOrderID` is declared in our CheckUser include file:

```
varProductNumber = Request.QueryString("ProductID")
varData = objProduct.GetDetailsByID(varProductNumber)

If Not IsEmpty(varData) Then
  varProductName = varData(cProductNameElement, 0)
  varItemsAvailable = CInt(varData(cProductItemCountElement, 0)) -
CInt(varData(cOnHireCountElement, 0))
End If
```

To make the screen user-friendlier we'll show the product name and the number of items available today:

```
varNumRequired = CInt(Request.QueryString("Num"))
%>
```

Cache the number required as passed to the ASP script. Now we can have a look at the code that attempts to add the item to the order basket:

```
  <%
 If objBasketContents.AddItem(varOrderID, varProductNumber, _
     varNumRequired) Then
   Response.Write "The following item has been added to your Shopping Basket:<P>"
& _
       "<TABLE CELLPADDING=0 CELLSPACING=0><TR><TD COLSPAN=2>" & _
       "<B>" & varProductName & "</B><BR>" & _
       "</TD></TR>" & _
       "</TR><TD>Quantity required:</TD><TD><B>" & varNumRequired & _
             "</B></TD></TR>" & _
       "</TR><TD>Number in stock:  </TD><TD><B>" & varItemsAvailable & _
             "</B></TD></TR>" & _
       "</TR><TD>Order number:     </TD><TD><B>" & varOrderID & _
             "</B></TD></TR>" & _
       "</TABLE><p>"
```

If the `AddItem` call was successful then we can create a little table to tell them how many items they asked for, how many are available and the order number that they were added to and a summary message:

```
If varItemsAvailable >= varNumRequired Then
    Response.Write "All items in stock - you will be able to collect your " & _
    varNumRequired & " item(s) from the checkout."
```

They haven't asked for too many items so tell them they can have all of the items:

```
Else
    If varNumRequired - varItemsAvailable> 0 Then
        Response.Write "Sorry, there are not enough items in stock - you will be
able to collect " & _
        varItemsAvailable & " item(s) from the checkout and wait for the
remaining items to become available."
```

This time, there are a few in-stock, but not enough so they will have to wait for the remainder to become available:

```
Else
        Response.Write "Sorry, there are not enough items in stock - you will
have to wait for the " & varNumRequired & " item(s) to become available."
    End If
```

Oh dear, we haven't got any in stock:

```
    End If
Else
    Response.Write "You Shopping Basket already contains the following item:" &
varProductName & "."
End If
%>
```

We don't allow the user to add exactly the same item to their order basket.

Deleting An Item from the Order Basket

Those pages that provide a summary of the order basket contents include a Delete link that allows any item to be deleted. After calling the confirmation JavaScript function `deleteBasketItem` the user is transferred to `DeleteBasketItem.asp`. This is a small script that calls the `RemoveItem` function in the `cBasketContents` class before redirecting the user back to the home page:

```
<OBJECT RUNAT="server" PROGID="wxHSOrderBR.cBasketContents"
    ID="objHSBasketContents"></OBJECT>
<!-- #include virtual="/Includes/CheckUser_inc.asp" -->
<%
Call objHSBasketContents.RemoveItem( _
                    Request.QueryString("BasketContentsID"))
Response.Redirect "/Default.ASP?CustID=" & _
                    varCustomerID & "&OrderID=" & varOrderID
%>
```

The Checkout

Our final area of functionality to the Wrox Hire Shop is The Checkout. We allow users to continually add and remove as many items to their order as they wish. During this time the order status will not change, for example, new orders will continue to have a New status.

Checkout.asp

Once a user has completed their 'shopping' they must move to the Checkout area. This simply updates the order status to be 'Accepted' which means they can, in principle, come to our Hire Shop in person to collect the items that they have requested:

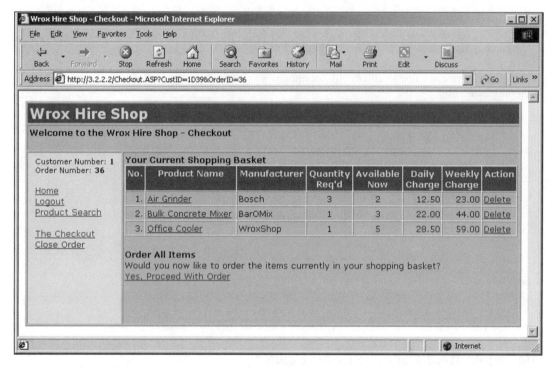

We use the standard `BuildBasketContents_inc.asp` include file to build the contents summary table. The link Yes, Proceed With Order redirects the user to `Checkout_HND.asp`.

Checkout_HND.asp

When the user clicks the Yes, Proceed With Order link above they are directed to this page that calls the `AcceptOrder` function:

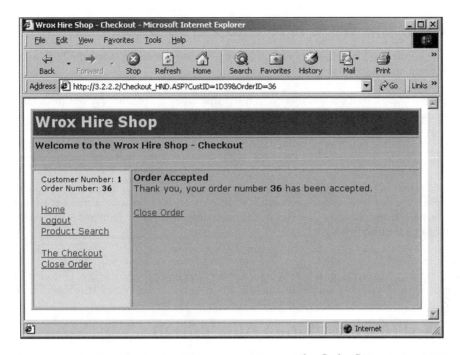

We use the `wxHSOrderBR.cOrderBasket` component to set the Order Status to `Accept`:

```
<OBJECT RUNAT=server PROGID=wxHSOrderBR.cOrderBasket id=objHSOrderBasket>
</OBJECT>
```

HTML code omitted to save space.

```
<%
If objHSOrderBasket.AcceptOrder(varOrderID) Then
%>
  <SPAN CLASS="AreaTitle">Order Accepted</SPAN><BR>
  Thank you, your order number <B><%=varOrderID%></B> has been
  accepted.<P>
  <A HREF="/Default.asp?CustID=<%=varCustomerID%>">Close Order</A>
<%
  varOrderID = 0
```

We call the `AcceptOrder` function and tell them it has been accepted. We also give them the chance to close this order now by linking to the home page without an OrderID included in the URL:

```
Else
%>
  <SPAN CLASS="AreaTitle">Order Rejected</SPAN><BR>
  Sorry, your order number <%=varOrderID%> has not been accepted.
<%
End If
%>
```

Summary of the Wrox Hire Shop Web Site

We've come a long way since identifying our business requirements, creating the SQL Server database to support them and the associated DNA components.

Our architecture was based around that of an n-tier implementation whereby our presentation tier called procedures from a business rules layer that in turn called its own data-services tier. Each procedure in the data-services tier knew which stored procedure to call in order to persist its state in our database, with the help of a specialized data-services utility class. This implementation allows us to effectively distribute each tier onto a separate physical server if required without any alteration.

We used a method called **QueryString Forwarding,** to maintain state between server requests, which should prove to be scalable, secure and cookie-independent. We also used a number of include files to encapsulate standard procedures across our web site, along with some standard error handling routines should things go horribly wrong.

Finally, we managed to use some of the new features in IIS version 5, namely the `Server.Transfer` command to save round-trips to the client before redirecting to a new ASP script. Our next exercise is to look at an alternative presentation tier to our ASP-based web site: the Win32 HireShopAdmin program.

The Wrox Hire Shop Admin Application

Our standard Win32 application, HireShopAdmin, uses the same components as our web site to provide the following functionality:

- ❑ Search for customers
- ❑ Edit and save customer details
- ❑ Edit and save customer orders

We have created a **Multiple Document Interface** that allows the user to open any number of Customer windows. As we stated earlier, we will be using the same set of components used by the Wrox Hire Shop web site, so from the Project | References menu we need to select the Wrox Hire Shop Customer and Order business rule components, and the ADO 2.5 RecordSet Library:

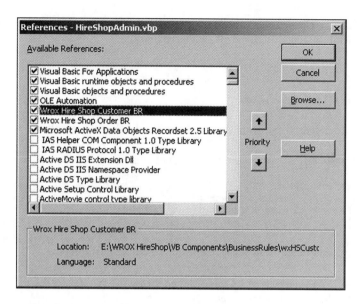

Selecting a Customer

As with all customer service applications, we need a way to find the customer's record. We implemented a `SearchByName` function in the `cCustomer` class of `wxHSCustomerBR`, so we'll use that:

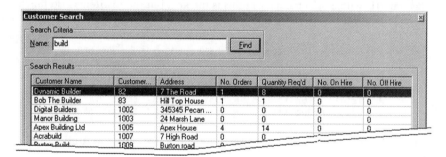

The VB form, `frmCustomerSearch`, lets the user type in the customer name they require. Pressing the Find button will take that customer name and pass it to our `Search` function, to return a list of customers whose name matches this criterion:

```
Private Sub cmdFind_Click()

    On Error GoTo ProcError
    Const cProcName = m_cModuleName & "cmdFind_Click"
```

Notice our standard error handling code. This time the `LogError` procedure is exclusive to this application – we'll cover that shortly:

```
    Dim objHSCustomer As wxHSCustomerBR.cCustomer
    Dim objRecordSet As RecordSet

    Dim objListItem As ListItem
    Dim strSearch As String
```

We use the `cCustomer` class to access our customer details. The `ListItem` is used to populate the ListView control with the matching records that were found:

```
cmdFind.Enabled = False

lvwResults.ListItems.Clear
```

Clear out any previous search results in the `lvwResults` ListView control:

```
Set objHSCustomer = New wxHSCustomerBR.cCustomer

strSearch = txtName.Text
If strSearch = "" Then strSearch = " "
Set objRecordSet = objHSCustomer.SearchByName(strSearch)
Set objHSCustomer = Nothing
```

Call the `SearchByName` function to retrieve a list of matching customers:

```
If Not objRecordSet.EOF And Not objRecordSet.BOF Then
    Do While Not objRecordSet.EOF
        Set objListItem = lvwResults.ListItems.Add(, "_" & _
            objRecordSet("CustomerID"), objRecordSet("CustomerName"))
```

For each item in the results we need to add a new item to the `ListItems` collection. Notice that we prefix the CustomerID with a "_" character as this is the key, but the ListItems `Add` function will interpret this as being a specific position into which it should add the item, if it looks like a number:

```
objListItem.SubItems(1) = objRecordSet("CustomerID")
objListItem.SubItems(2) = objRecordSet("Address1")
objListItem.SubItems(3) = objRecordSet("OrderCount")
objListItem.SubItems(4) = objRecordSet("TotalQuantity")
objListItem.SubItems(5) = objRecordSet("ItemsOut")
objListItem.SubItems(6) = objRecordSet("ItemsIn")
```

The `SubItems` collection refers to the collection of headings that form the Address and counter values shown on the control:

```
            objRecordSet.MoveNext
        Loop
    End If

    objRecordSet.Close
    Set objRecordSet = Nothing
    Set objListItem = Nothing
```

Clear down the remaining items:

```
    cmdFind.Enabled = True

    Exit Sub

ProcError:
    LogError Err.Number, Err.Description, cProcName, Err.Source

End Sub
```

`ProcError` is the standard error-handling procedure used throughout all of the procedures. As with our components it logs the error with the Windows Event Log using `App.LogEvent` but also displays the actual error message to the user:

```
Public Sub LogError(ByVal lngNumber As Long, _
                    ByVal strDescription As String, _
                    ByVal strProcName As String, _
                    ByVal strSource As String, _
                    Optional ByVal strAdditionalInfo As String = "")

    Dim strErrorMessage As String

    strErrorMessage = "Runtime Error" & vbNewLine & _
                    "Number:" & lngNumber & vbNewLine & _
                    "Description:" & strDescription & vbNewLine & _
                    "ProcName:" & strProcName & vbNewLine & _
                    "Source:" & strSource & vbNewLine & _
                    "AppVersion:" & AppVersion & vbNewLine & _
                    "AppPath:" & AppPath
```

Build up the error message to add to the event log:

```
    If strAdditionalInfo <> "" Then
        strErrorMessage = strErrorMessage & vbNewLine & _
                        "Info:" & strAdditionalInfo
    End If

    App.LogEvent strErrorMessage, vbLogEventTypeError
```

If there was any additional information passed that might be useful then add that to the end before calling the LogEvent method:

```
    MsgBox "The following error has occurred:" & vbNewLine & vbNewLine & _
            strDescription & vbNewLine & vbNewLine & _
            "Please contact your administrator", vbCritical

End Sub
```

Lastly, we can tell the user about the exact message. As they are internal users it is better that they see the real error message unlike that of our web site users.

Editing a Customer

Our user can edit any of the customer's details using frmCustomer:

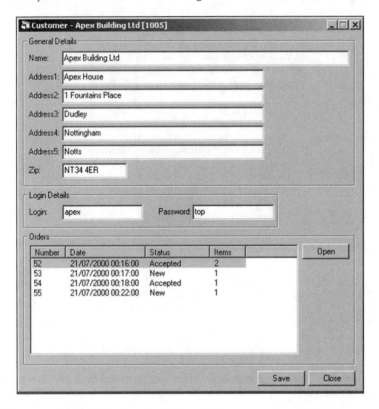

We have added a procedure called Display, into which we pass the selected CustomerID:

```
Public Sub Display(ByVal lngCustomerID As Long,
                   ByVal blnNewRecord As Boolean)

    On Error GoTo ProcError
    Const cProcName = m_cModuleName & "Display"

    Dim objHSCustomer As wxHSCustomerBR.cCustomer
    Dim objHSOrder As wxHSOrderBR.cOrderBasket

    Dim objRecordSet As Recordset
    Dim objListItem As ListItem
    Dim varData As Variant

    m_lngCustomerID = lngCustomerID
    m_blnNewRecord = blnNewRecord
```

We used two module level variables to store the CustomerID and the flag to indicate if this is a new Customer record – note that the current version of the Admin program does not allow users to create new Customer records:

```
If Not blnNewRecord Then
    Set objHSCustomer = New wxHSCustomerBR.cCustomer
    varData = objHSCustomer.GetDetailsByID(m_lngCustomerID)
```

Create the `wxHSCustomer.cCustomer` class and return back a `Variant Array` of the customer's details:

```
If Not IsEmpty(varData) Then
    Me.Caption = "Customer - " & varData(0, 0) & " [" & _
                 m_lngCustomerID & "]"
    txtName = "" & varData(0, 0)
    txtAddress1 = "" & varData(1, 0)
    txtAddress2 = "" & varData(2, 0)
    txtAddress3 = "" & varData(3, 0)
    txtAddress4 = "" & varData(4, 0)
    txtAddress5 = "" & varData(5, 0)
    txtZip = "" & varData(6, 0)

    txtLogin = "" & varData(7, 0)
    txtPassword = "" & varData(8, 0)
```

Notice that we prefix each of the controls with a "". This is to coerce any NULL fields into an empty string:

```
Set objHSOrder = New wxHSOrderBR.cOrderBasket
Set objRecordSet = objHSOrder.GetSummaryDetailsByCustomerID( _
                       m_lngCustomerID)
```

We call the `GetSummaryDetailsByCustomerID` function to return a `RecordSet` containing a summary of all of the customer's orders to date:

```
If Not objRecordSet.EOF And Not objRecordSet.BOF Then
    Do While Not objRecordSet.EOF
        Set objListItem = lvwOrders.ListItems.Add(, "_" & _
            objRecordSet("OrderID"), objRecordSet("OrderID"))
        objListItem.SubItems(1) = objRecordSet("OrderDate")
        objListItem.SubItems(2) = objRecordSet("OrderStatusName")
        objListItem.SubItems(3) = objRecordSet("ContentCount")

        objRecordSet.MoveNext
    Loop
```

As with the Customer Search screen we are using a ListView control to show a table of the customer's orders, so we must prefix the CustomerID column with a "_":

```
    lvwOrders.Enabled = True
    objRecordSet.Close
Else
    Set objListItem = lvwOrders.ListItems.Add(, "_0", _
                    "No orders")
    lvwOrders.Enabled = False
End If
```

If there are no orders, we'll just create an entry titled **No Orders** and disable the control:

```
        End If

        Set objRecordSet = Nothing
        Set objHSCustomer = Nothing
    Else
        Me.Caption = "New Customer"
    End If

    m_blnDataChanged = False
    Me.Show

Exit Sub

ProcError:
    LogError Err.Number, Err.Description, cProcName, Err.Source

End Sub
```

The administrator is free to make as many changes to the customer's details as necessary. Pressing the Save button will attempt to update the customer's record by calling the SaveRecord method declared on this form:

```
Private Sub SaveRecord(ByVal blnShowMessage As Boolean)
...
Error handling code omitted
...
    Dim objHSCustomer As wxHSCustomerBR.cCustomer
    Dim objRecordSet As Recordset

    If txtName = "" Then
        MsgBox "Please enter a customer name."
        txtName.SetFocus
        Exit Sub
    End If
...
```

This code looks very similar to the Register.asp form validation code. We need to make sure the user has entered all of the required fields before we attempt the Update call. The remaining code has been omitted to save space:

```
    Set objHSCustomer = New wxHSCustomerBR.cCustomer
    Call objHSCustomer.Update(m_lngCustomerID, txtName, _
                        txtAddress1, txtAddress2, txtAddress3, _
                        txtAddress4, txtAddress5, txtZip, _
                        txtLogin, txtPassword)
```

Attempt the `Update` call. If an error occurs we will be taken to the error handler:

```
        If blnShowMessage Then
            MsgBox "Customer record saved.", vbInformation
            m_blnDataChanged = False
        End If

        Set objHSCustomer = Nothing

        Exit Sub
    ...
    Error handling code omitted
    ...
    End Sub
```

The `Update` function will return `True` or `False` if it was successful or not, so we interpret this and display a `MsgBox` accordingly.

Order Details

From the Customer screen, the user can open any of the customer's orders. The form, `frmOrder`, is used to display details of the order:

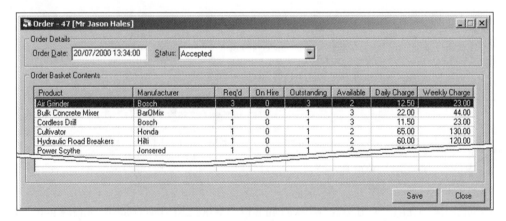

As with the customer form, we have a procedure called `Display` that is passed the required `OrderID`. We use three functions to retrieve information about this order:

❑ `wxHSOrderBR.cOrderBasket.GetDetailsByID()` to get details about the order, such as its date and status.

❑ `wxHSOrderBR.cOrderBasket.GetOrderStatusList()` for a list of valid order status items.

❑ `wxHSOrderBR.cBasketContents.GetDetailsByOrderID()` to get the contents of the order basket:

```
    Public Sub Display(ByVal lngCustomerID As Long, _
                       ByVal strCustomerName As String, _
                       ByVal lngOrderID As Long, _
                       ByVal blnNewRecord As Boolean)
```

```
        Dim objHSOrder As wxHSOrderBR.cOrderBasket
        Dim objHSBasketContents As wxHSOrderBR.cBasketContents

        Dim objRecordSet As Recordset
        Dim lngOrderStatusID As Long
        Dim objListItem As ListItem
...
        If Not m_blnNewRecord Then
            Set objHSOrder = New wxHSOrderBR.cOrderBasket
            Set objRecordSet = objHSOrder.GetDetailsByID(m_lngOrderID)

            If Not objRecordSet.EOF And Not objRecordSet.BOF Then
                txtOrderDate = Format$(objRecordSet("OrderDate"), _
                                       "general date")
                lngOrderStatusID = objRecordSet("OrderStatusID")

                Me.Caption = "Order - " & m_lngOrderID & " [" & _
                             objRecordSet("CustomerName") & "]"
            End If
```

We call the `GetDetailsByOrderID` function to return the order's current values:

```
Set objHSBasketContents = New wxHSOrderBR.cBasketContents
        Set objRecordSet = objHSBasketContents.GetDetailsByOrderID( _
                           lngOrderID)

        If Not objRecordSet Is Nothing Then
            Do While Not objRecordSet.EOF
                Set objListItem = lvwBasketContents.ListItems.Add(, "_" & _
                                  objRecordSet("BasketContentsID"), _
                                  objRecordSet("ProductName"))
                objListItem.SubItems(1) = objRecordSet("ManufacturerName")
                objListItem.SubItems(2) = objRecordSet("QuantityRequired")
                objListItem.SubItems(3) = objRecordSet("BasketOnHireCount")
...
```

After calling `GetDetailsByOrderID ()` we can populate the ListView control with the items that are in the order basket. We've omitted the trailing `SubItems` to save space:

```
                objRecordSet.MoveNext
            Loop
            objRecordSet.Close
            Set objRecordSet = Nothing
            Set objHSBasketContents = Nothing
        End If

        Set objRecordSet = objHSOrder.GetOrderStatusList()
        PopulateCombo cmbStatus, objRecordSet, "OrderStatusName", _
                "OrderStatusID", lngOrderStatusID
        Set objHSOrder = Nothing
```

Finally we call a general procedure, `PopulateCombo`, with the results of
`objHSOrder.GetOrderStatusList()`. This procedure simply populates a `ComboBox` with the
values that it finds in the `Recordset` passed to it. As it's a general procedure, we need to tell it which
columns are the name and value items and the current default value:

```
Public Sub PopulateCombo(cmbVictim As ComboBox, _
                    ByVal objData As ADODB.Recordset, _
                    ByVal strNameCol As String, _
                    ByVal strValueCol As String, _
                    ByVal lngDefaultValue As Long)

    Dim lngValue As Long

    If objData.EOF And objData.BOF Then Exit Sub
```

First off, we don't bother continuing if the RecordSet is empty:

```
Do While Not objData.EOF

    lngValue = CLng(objData(strValueCol))
    With cmbVictim
        .AddItem objData(strNameCol)
        .ItemData(.NewIndex) = lngValue
```

Each time you add a new item to a ListBox or ComboBox using `AddItem`, the `NewIndex` property
refers to the position into which that item was placed – useful for sorted controls where items may not
appear in the list in the order that they have been added. `ItemData` is an array of numeric values that
can be assigned to each item – typically a primary key number:

```
        If lngValue = lngDefaultValue Then
            .ListIndex = .NewIndex
        End If
```

If the value for this item matches our default value then automatically select it using the `ListIndex`
property:

```
    End With
    objData.MoveNext
    Loop
End Sub
```

Summary of the HireShopAdmin Program

Our Admin program showed that it is possible to use the same components as our Wrox Hire Shop web
site to manipulate the customer and order details without making any changes specific to the Win32
environment.

We used the Customer and Order business rules components, `wxHSCustomerBR.dll` and
`wxHSOrderBR.dll`, to search for customers, edit and save their details and edit and save their order details.

Summary

In this chapter, we worked through an example of a real-world business requirement – The Wrox Hire Shop. To recap what we achieved in this chapter:

❑ Identified the functional requirements of our case study.

❑ Designed the database schema to meet these requirements using SQL Server.

❑ Designed and deployed our business rules and data services COM+ components using Visual Basic 6.0 and ActiveX Data Objects 2.5 and the Component Services Snap-In.

❑ Created a web site complete with a shopping basket to allow verified users to search our database of products using the COM+ components with Internet Information Server version 5 and Active Server Pages.

❑ Created an administrator's Win32 desktop application using Visual Basic 6 to update customer and order data using our COM+ components.

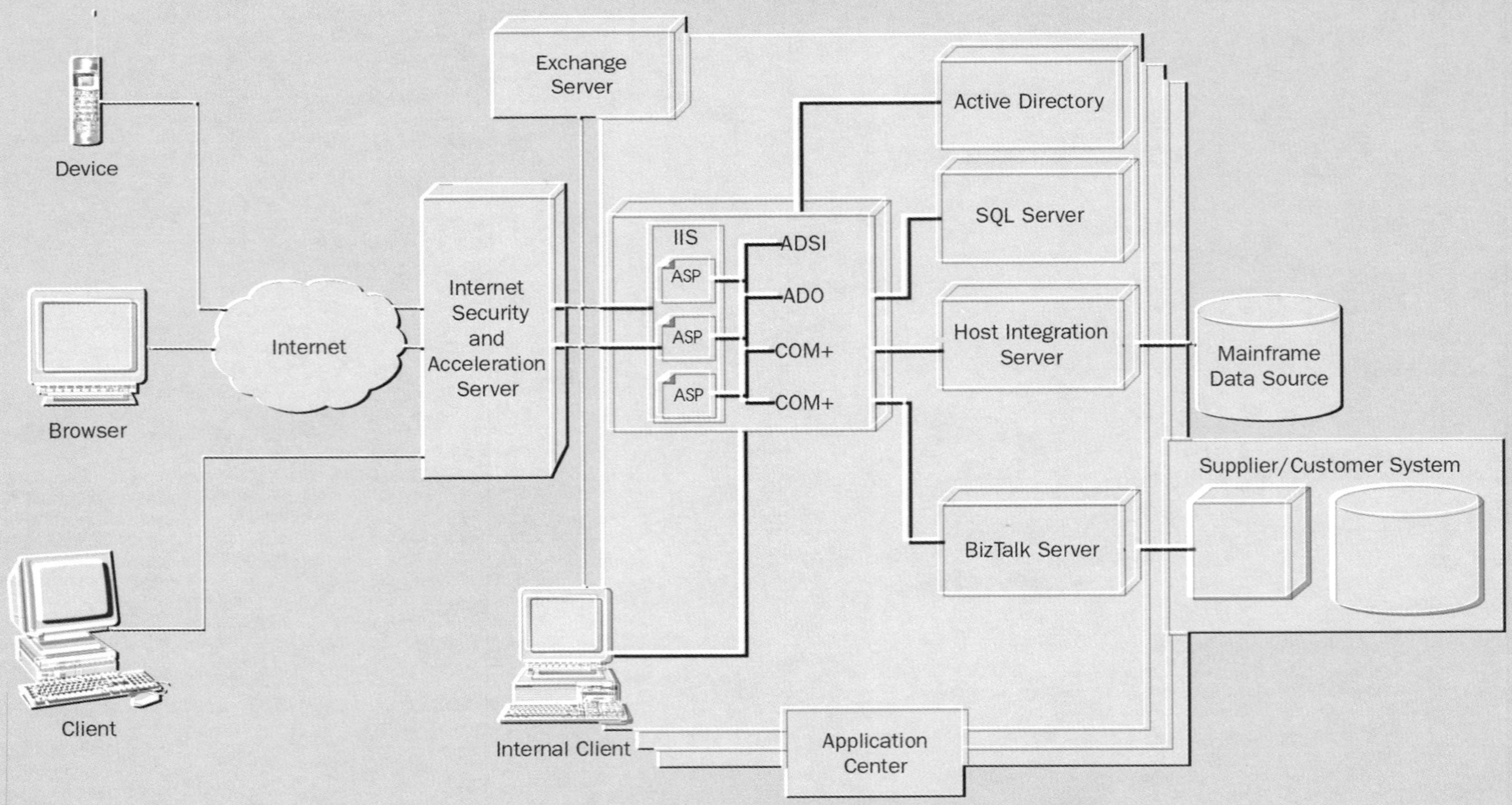
Device
Browser
Client
Internet
Internet Security and Acceleration Server
Exchange Server
IIS
ASP
ASP
ASP
ADSI
ADO
COM+
COM+
Active Directory
SQL Server
Host Integration Server
BizTalk Server
Mainframe Data Source
Supplier/Customer System
Internal Client
Application Center

26

Case Study: Distributed Application Message Monitor

As developers, we are increasingly living in a world of distributed applications. The days of the self-contained stand-alone application are drawing to a close. Two-tiered client-server applications are isolated islands that cannot be readily extended in the current environment of rapidly evolving technologies and business needs.

Modern applications of the present and near-term future will consist of loosely coupled pieces that work together through some sort of standardized communications protocol – such as SOAP, the Simple Object Access Protocol. SOAP-based Internet-enabled application components will provide and consume data via web services. Applications will span computers, trading partners, operating systems, and object models.

Debugging applications that rely on parts outside themselves to complete their tasks is an order of magnitude greater in difficulty than debugging standalone applications. If you string together five objects, perhaps in geographically different locations, or in different companies, or perhaps using different object models and operating systems, and something fails, how do you determine the point of failure? A link in the chain has failed, but which link?

In this case study, we'll show how a Windows DNA application can be used to implement a publish/subscribe mechanism to track messages generated by the component parts of a distributed application. We'll also see how we can implement error-handling techniques to help us track down problems within our system.

The Scenario

Let's say a fictitious company has three remote offices that participate in a business transaction:

❑ A sales office in San Diego

❑ A head office in London

❑ A manufacturing facility in Hong Kong

The premise is that when the sales office makes a sale, an order is submitted to head office. Head office would amalgamate orders, and then relay them on to manufacturing.

We'll not be building the application itself, as how the application works would not be relevant for our needs. Instead, we'll focus on how these separate parts of the application can communicate with a single point message pool using our publish/subscribe "message monitor".

Architectural Overview

This system is not by any means meant to be deployed in a high-volume production environment. One of the key reasons for this statement is that the system as presented uses an in-memory XML document for the message store, rather than persistent or database storage. With enhancements, it certainly could be made production-quality, but that's beyond the scope of this case study.

> **The system is intended as an example of a distributed Windows DNA application that uses SOAP to communicate between components, while at the same time providing a useful debugging aid for distributed applications.**

Our system consists of a central hub or message pool that receives and stores messages. This hub is implemented as a VB COM object. Applications communicate with the hub by posting SOAP-compliant messages to an ASP page.

Nomenclature used in this chapter is as follows:

❑ A **class** is a grouping/categorization mechanism for **messages**.

❑ **Messages** are pieces of text sent by a message poster, and they are received and distributed by the **Publisher**.

❑ The **Publisher** is the VB COM object, which takes messages posted to it and makes them available to anyone that has subscribed to a **message** of that **class**. This is also known as the **MessageMonitor**.

❑ **Subscribers** are entities that have registered for a certain **class** of **message**.

The entire system is implemented using XML, SOAP, and Windows DNA architecture. Thanks to this standard interface approach, as the following diagram illustrates, multiple types of processes can send a message to the SOAP listener:

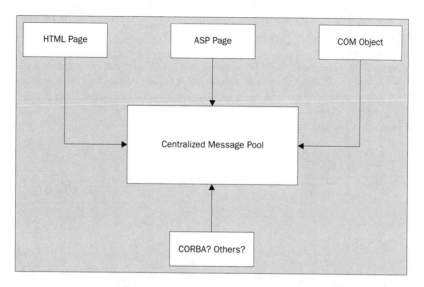

In normal usage, a subscriber would subscribe to a class of messages. Inside the COM object message pool, a <class> element would be created under the <subscriber> element for each class they subscribe to.

A typical message flow would be as follows:

❑ A **Message Poster** posts a message to the SOAP listener.

❑ The **SOAP listener** (in our case, an ASP called server.asp) instantiates the COM object and invokes its Publish method, passing through the SOAP request, which contains the class and the message itself.

❑ The Publish method creates a <message> element containing the message under each <class> element that matches the class of this message.

❑ An appropriate SOAP response is then created, which migrates back to the message poster that originated the request.

When a subscriber retrieves messages from the pool, it's a volatile read operation: the messages that have been read are removed from the pool upon retrieval.

Meet the Puzzle Pieces

In order to achieve our goals, we need to be able to access the centralized pool from many different types of processes, applications, and perhaps operating systems. We need to be completely language-agnostic, object model-agnostic, and operating-system agnostic.

> *For the purpose of this case study, we'll be examining the layers shown in the diagram below. However, given the flexibility of the system, there's nothing in the architecture that would prevent the addition of layers for other object models, operating systems, etc. This case study is not an end point – it's a functional piece of software that can be extended. Later in this chapter we'll discuss a few of those possible extensions.*

Our scenario consists of the following pieces:

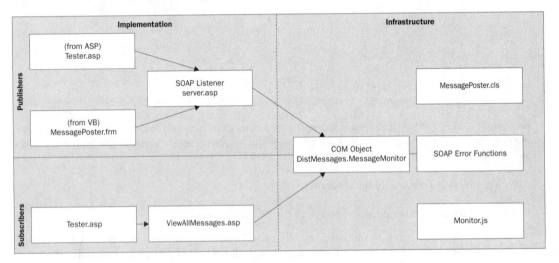

This diagram stratifies the pieces of our application into two groups:

- ❏ Above the horizontal line – entities that emit messages (post them to the publisher)
- ❏ Below the horizontal line – entities that retrieve them (the subscribers)

The diagram further categorizes:

- ❏ Implementation – to the left of the vertical line
- ❏ Infrastructure – to the right of the vertical line

The **infrastructure** provides the basic services required for the system to work. It encompasses the COM object, as well as support functions (a JavaScript file and a VB class to access the COM object, as well as error-handling functions).

The **implementation** pieces are more application-specific, such as a VB form that can post SOAP messages, or an ASP that enables a browser to do so. The implementation also includes the all-important `server.asp`, the SOAP listener that receives SOAP messages and relays them to the COM object.

The following is a breakdown of the different pieces and their descriptions:

Name	Description
`DistMessages.MessageMonitor`	Core "hub" of the system. This is the Publisher. It is the recipient of posted messages, and the module responsible for storing and redistributing them to subscribers. It manages the subscribers and messages.
`DistMessages.MessagePoster`	Visual Basic class that provides the functionality required to post messages. Used by either a VB application or DLL. This is the Visual Basic equivalent of `monitor.js`.
`MessagePoster.frm`	Visual Basic form that uses `DistMessages.MessagePoster` to post a SOAP message to `server.asp`.
`monitor.js`	JavaScript code that provides the functionality required to post messages to the `server.asp` SOAP listener, as well as retrieve them. This is the JavaScript equivalent of `DistMessages.MessagePoster`.
`server.asp`	This is the SOAP listener ASP. It is the recipient of message POSTs. Any conversation, between either a subscriber or a message poster will normally flow though here.
`SOAP_Errors_client.inc`	Include file that contains functionality required to examine a SOAP message looking for a `SOAP-ENV:Fault` element and advising the user of it.
`SOAP_Errors_server.inc`	Include file that contains functionality required to take an incoming XML document and error string, and put the error string inside a SOAP `Fault` message.
`tester.asp`	A test page capable of subscribing to messages and generating them. It also displays the current contents of the message pool by loading `ViewAllMessages` into an `IFrame`. This is the main test page.
`viewAllMessages.asp`	Retrieves all of the subscribers and messages in the system as an XML document. It's a useful "show me what's in there now" page.

Let's look at how these work in a little more detail.

The Listener

The VB COM object is the core piece of this system. It contains the functionality required to subscribe to and retrieve messages, and it keeps a list of current messages.

We can view the current messages with the ASP `viewAllMessages.asp`:

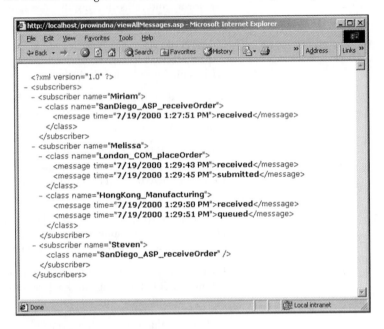

As you can see from the above structure:

❏   `<subscribers>` is the root element

❏   Each `<subscriber>` gets one and only one entry

❏   A `<subscriber>` may subscribe to several classes of message

❏   Messages of a given `<class>` appear inside that class

The labels are arbitrarily chosen text labels that are used to give some meaningful information as to the origin of the message.

For example, in the above screen shot, we can see that both Miriam and Steven subscribed to messages of the class `SanDiego_ASP_receiveOrder`, but we can deduce that Steven was not a subscriber when the `7/19/2000 1:27:51 PM` message was received. Melissa has also subscribed to messages of the `HongKong_Manufacturing` and `London_COM_placeOrder` classes.

There is no reason why a given process, say an ASP page, couldn't have several classes of messages within it, each representing a different step in the execution of that page.

The message time attribute is automatically filled in by the COM object, and represents the timestamp of when the message was received, based on the time at the server where the COM object is hosted. This means that all messages will share a common timeframe reference, regardless of the time zone of their points of origin.

The Test Programs

In order to reinforce the message architecture you've just seen, let's skip ahead to the ASP test program: tester.asp.

tester.asp was put together as a mechanism to allow us to "post" messages of different classes, and to see the messages that are currently in the COM object:

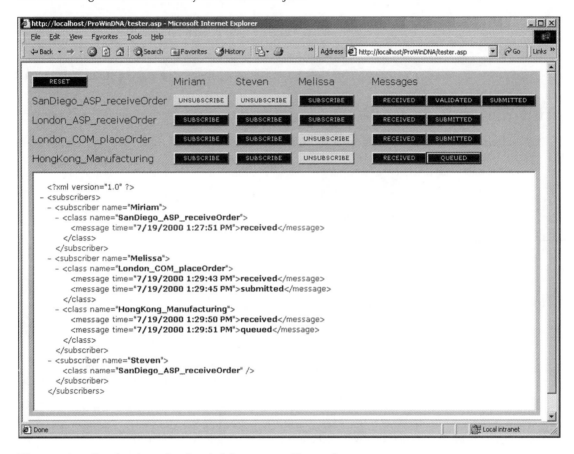

The user interface has been hard coded for our specific needs.

The left-most column shows us the names of the various classes in the system (for example, SanDiego_ASP_receiveOrder).

The first group of column headings going across the page show us the users in the system (for example, Miriam). The second group of column headings shows us the messages that this page can generate for a given class (for example, RECEIVED for SanDiego_ASP_receiveOrder or QUEUED for HongKong_Manufacturing).

The SUBSCRIBE and UNSUBSCRIBE buttons allow us to subscribe to a specific class of messages for a given user. To begin with, all users are unsubscribed and the buttons are blue. If a user subscribes to a message, the button becomes yellow as a visual indicator.

The XML document displayed below the buttons is actually being generated by viewAllMessages.asp, which we saw in the previous section. It's loaded into an <IFRAME>, and formatted for display by Internet Explorer's built-in default XSLT.

As you'll see later in this chapter when we look at the code for this page, we trigger a reload of this frame in the body onClick event, so that we can easily see an accurate view of the current contents of the message pool.

> Note that **tester.asp** uses client-side MSXML, and as such relies on IE5.x.

So now we have some idea how our application works, let's get down to looking at the code in detail.

The Server-Side Code

We'll start with the code we need installed on our server machine:

- ❑ The SOAP listener – server.asp
- ❑ The XML generator – viewAllMessages.asp
- ❑ An error-handling include file – SOAP_Errors_server.inc
- ❑ The DistMessages DLL

We'll start by taking a look at what goes on inside the SOAP listener.

The Listener – How It Works

As we've seen, the SOAP listener, server.asp, hosts the COM object that is the core of this system. We'll step through the code to see how it works.

The listener accepts an XML stream coming in via HTTP, and returns an XML stream. This is analogous to doing an HTML POST to an ASP. The XML streams received and returned by our listener are structured to be compliant with version 1.1 of the SOAP protocol.

It can at times be challenging to track down problem points in a SOAP listener. For this reason, we have code inside the listener that will execute when a debugging variable is set:

```
debugging = true
```

In debugging mode, various items are written out to a dump.log file. Among other things, the log records what comes in and what goes out of the listener.

To promote re-use, the SOAP Fault recording function has been moved into a separate file, SOAP_Errors_server.inc, which we include in server.asp:

```
<!-- #include file="SOAP_Errors_server.inc"-->
```

This file contains one function, `LogErrorDetails`, which we'll see shortly.

> Note that if you set up this code with **debugging = true**, you'll need to grant write permissions to the **IUSR_machinename** account for the folder where **server.asp** resides, or this step will fail.

Next we create an instance of the XMLDOM and load in the XML that was POSTed:

```
strMethodName = Request.ServerVariables("HTTP_SOAPACTION")

Set xmldoc = Server.CreateObject("Microsoft.XMLDOM")

xmldoc.async=false
xmldoc.load(Request)
```

Note the sequence in the code above. We need to retrieve the `Request.ServerVariables("HTTP_SOAPACTION")` variable prior to doing the binary read `xmldoc.load(Request)`, or an error will occur.

As we'll see in a moment, we'll add an HTTP header called SOAPAction on the client side. Here, we're looking for something called HTTP_SOAPACTION. This is because in ASP you get access to custom headers through the ServerVariables collection, and by prefixing the header name with HTTP_.

The SOAP protocol mandates that a `SOAPACTION` HTTP header be added when a SOAP message is sent via HTTP. This header allows non-XML capable systems, such as routers and firewalls, to recognize a SOAP message and dispatch it properly. To enforce compliance, we trap for the absence of the `SOAPACTION` header in the SOAP listener:

The next step is to ensure that the `SOAPAction` HTTP header is present and structured properly. In our case, the `SOAPAction` header contains a URI structured as `interface#methodcall`. We do error trapping to ensure this is the case:

```
'// Ensure there is a SOAPAction header...
If Trim(strMethodName)="" Then
  LogErrorDetails xmldoc, _
    "This SOAP listener expects to get a SOAPACTION header, and did not."
  Set objResponse = xmldoc
  Call EndPage()
End If

intIndex = InStrRev(strMethodName, "#")

'// Is the SOAPAction header the way we need it?
If intIndex=0 Then
  LogErrorDetails xmldoc, _
      "The SOAP did not get a properly structured SOAPACTION header."
  Set objResponse = xmldoc
  Call EndPage()
End If
```

```
'// Extract the ProgID name
strProgID = Left(strMethodName, intIndex - 1)

'// Extract the method name
strMethodName = Mid(strMethodName, intIndex + 1)
```

We need to store a reference to the `MessageMonitor` in an application variable. The first time this code is executed, the object is instantiated and a reference is stored in an application variable. Subsequent calls to this code will retrieve that reference:

```
If Not IsObject(Application("objMonitor")) Then
    '// if the monitor object has not been created yet, do so
    '// and give it an application scope
    Set objMonitor = Server.CreateObject(strProgID)

    Set Application("objMonitor") = objMonitor

    If debugging Then
        a.writeline("Assigned Application variable")
    End If
Else
    Set objMonitor = Application("objMonitor")
    If debugging Then
        a.writeline("Application variable already existed...")
    End If
End if

Set objMonitor = Application("objMonitor")
```

At this point, we've finally done all the checks needed, and we're ready to do the actual method call. All the work is done by the `Eval` function: it invokes the specified method, passing through the SOAP request we received as a parameter. As we'll see in the next section, all of the exposed methods in the COM object return a SOAP response. This response is in turn relayed from the ASP page back to the issuer of the SOAP request:

```
If IsObject(objMonitor) Then

    If debugging Then
        a.writeline("Invoking: objMonitor." & strMethodName & "(xmldoc)")
        a.writeline("xmldoc contains: ["& xmldoc.xml & "]")
    End If

    Set objResponse = Eval("objMonitor." & strMethodName & "(xmldoc)")

    If Not IsObject(objResponse) Then
        LogErrorDetails xmldoc, typename(objResponse) & _
                " *** Unexpected response received from, or unable to " & _
                "reach destination:" & strDestination
        Set objResponse = xmldoc
    End if

Else
```

```
'// Error condition: the object could not be created
LogErrorDetails xmldoc, "Unable to create class: " & strClass
Set objResponse = xmldoc

End if
```

All we need do then is clean up:

```
If debugging Then
    a.writeline("Result:" & objResponse.xml)
    a.writeline("--- Completed ---")
    a.Close()
End If

Call EndPage()

Function EndPage
    Response.Write objResponse.xml
    Response.End
End Function
%>
```

Fault Recording – The SOAP_Errors_server.inc File

The SOAP protocol mandates that any errors be structured in a strictly defined manner. This requirement makes a lot of sense, as any SOAP request originator needs to be capable of realizing they've received an error message.

Our SOAP Fault recording function, SOAP_Errors_server.inc, which we included in server.asp contains the following code:

```
<%
Sub LogErrorDetails(xmldoc, strError)

    '// This sub takes the passed xmldoc and replaces the elements below
    '// <SOAP:Body> with the <SOAP-ENV:Fault> message to tell the calling
    '// app about the problem

    Dim oFault, oBody
    Set oFault = xmldoc.createElement("SOAP-ENV:Fault")
    oFault.appendChild(xmldoc.createElement("faultcode")).text = "400"
    oFault.appendChild(xmldoc.createElement("faultstring")).text = _
                    "Application Error"
    oFault.appendChild(xmldoc.createElement("detail"))_
        .appendChild(xmldoc.createElement("message")).text = strError
    Set oBody = xmldoc.selectSingleNode("//SOAP-ENV:Body")
    oBody.replaceChild oFault, oBody.firstChild

End Sub
%>
```

As you can see, we take the incoming XML message, and simply replace the contents of the SOAP-ENV:Body with a SOAP Fault element.

viewAllMessages.asp

The last of our server-side ASPs, the `viewAllMessages.asp` page, will be called from the `tester.asp` page on the client. This page simply displays the current state of our message pool as an XML document.

The code to do this is quite trivial – because the `MessageMonitor` (`objMonitor`) object we created in `server.asp` has application scope, we can reference it here:

```
<?xml version="1.0" ?>
<%
If IsObject(Application("objMonitor")) Then
  Response.Write cstr(Application("objMonitor").xmlDoc.xml)
Else
  Response.Write "<error>Application(""objMonitor"") " & _
               "is not an object.</error>"
End If
%>
```

Inside the Message Pool – MessageMonitor

Now we'll take a look at the COM object that is the heart of this system – `DistMessages` – and its one class – `MessageMonitor`.

> At the time of writing, we were using the most current (July 2000) technology preview of the MSXML parser, which could be obtained by visiting **http://msdn.microsoft.com/xml**. Note that ProgIDs may change with future versions.
>
> If you're using this version, you'll need to set a reference to **Microsoft XML, v3.0 in** the **References** dialog for the **DistMessages** project.

Declarations and Initialization

The first thing we need to do in the `MessageMonitor` class is declare and initialize the `objSubscribers` private variable:

```
Private objSubscribers As MSXML2.DOMDocument30

Private Sub Class_Initialize()

  Dim objNode As Variant
  Set objSubscribers = New MSXML2.DOMDocument30
  Set objNode = objSubscribers.createElement("subscribers")
  objSubscribers.appendChild (objNode)

End Sub

Public Property Get xmlDoc() As MSXML2.DOMDocument30
  Set xmlDoc = objSubscribers
End Property
```

This instance of the XMLDOM is where we keep the XML tree that holds all the subscribers and messages. For convenience, we allow the outside world read-only access to it by creating the Public `xmlDoc` property.

Adding Subscribers

Before any messages get retained, we need subscribers. The following block of code is the method that allows entities to subscribe to messages of a given class:

```
Public Function subscribe(objXMLDoc As Variant) As Variant

    Dim strSubscriber As String, strClass As String
    Dim objNode As Variant, objClassNode As Variant

    strSubscriber = objXMLDoc.selectSingleNode("//m:subscriber").Text
    strClass = objXMLDoc.selectSingleNode("//m:class").Text
    Set objNode = _
        objSubscribers.selectSingleNode("/subscribers/subscriber[@name='" & _
        strSubscriber & "']")

    If TypeName(objNode) = "Nothing" Then
      '// subscriber has not been added yet, add 'em in...
      Set objNode = objSubscribers.createElement("subscriber")
      Call objNode.setAttribute("name", strSubscriber)
      objSubscribers.documentElement.appendChild (objNode)
    End If

    If TypeName(objNode.selectSingleNode("//class[@name='" & strClass & "' _
              and ../@name='" & strSubscriber & "']")) = "Nothing" Then
      '// subscriber is not registered for this class yet
      Set objClassNode = objSubscribers.createElement("class")
      Call objClassNode.setAttribute("name", strClass)
      objNode.appendChild (objClassNode)
    End If

    Set objNode = Nothing
    Set objClassNode = Nothing
    Set subscribe = createResponse(objXMLDoc, "Subscriber:[" & _
                strSubscriber & "] has been added for class:[" & _
                strClass & "]")

End Function
```

In this method, and most others in this class, we are receiving and returning a SOAP message – in this case, one that adds a new subscriber node into our XML.

Note that we're using a namespace, `m:` – as we'll see later, this is defined at the point of origin of the message.

The last thing we do in this method is call the `createResponse` function.

Creating the SOAP Response

Earlier, we used an include file to encapsulate adding a `SOAP-ENV:Fault` element, and we're going to use the same approach here. We have a single function in this class – `createResponse` – whose role it is to take a string and work it into a SOAP response:

```
Private Function createResponse(objXMLDoc As Variant, _
                                strMessage As String) As Variant

    Dim objNewNode As Variant, objBody As Variant

    Set objNewNode = objXMLDoc.createElement("m:result")
    objNewNode.Text = strMessage

    Set objBody = objXMLDoc.selectSingleNode("//SOAP-ENV:Body")
    objBody.replaceChild objNewNode, objBody.firstChild

    Set createResponse = objXMLDoc

End Function
```

All the remaining methods in our class use this function to create their SOAP responses.

Publishing Messages

Next we need a `Publish` method, which will look for all elements of a specified class in the XML document that contains our message pool. For each one that it finds, it will insert a new `<message>` element below it containing the message that was posted:

```
Public Function publish(objXMLDoc As Variant) As Variant

    Dim objNodeList As Variant, objMessage As Variant, ele As Variant
    Dim strMessage As String, strClass As String

    strMessage = objXMLDoc.selectSingleNode("//m:message").Text
    strClass = objXMLDoc.selectSingleNode("//m:class").Text

    Set objNodeList = objSubscribers.selectNodes("//class[@name='" & _
                    strClass & "']")

    For Each ele In objNodeList
      Set objMessage = objSubscribers.createElement("message")
      objMessage.Text = strMessage
      Call objMessage.setAttribute("time", Now)
      ele.appendChild (objMessage)
    Next

    Set objMessage = Nothing
    Set ele = Nothing

    Set publish = createResponse(objXMLDoc, "Published message to " & _
              objNodeList.length & " subscribers")

    Set objNodeList = Nothing

End Function
```

The textual contents of the new <message> element will be the same as the contents of the <message> in the SOAP request.

For example, the screen shot below shows what was in the message pool before and after the Publish method was called for the received message of the London_ASP_Receive_Order class:

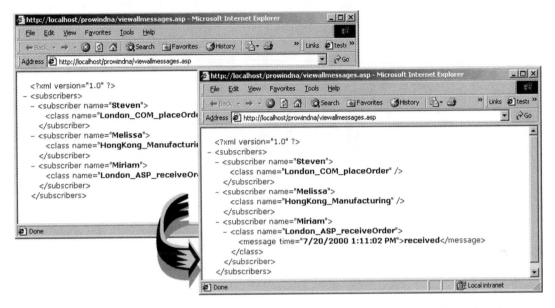

As you can see, as a result of the Publish method call, a new entry has appeared for subscriber Miriam.

Removing Subscribers

The counterpart to the Subscribe method is the Unsubscribe method, which allows the removal of the subscription to a specific class of messages. If a subscriber is un-subscribing from the only class that they are subscribed to, then the subscriber is also removed. This is a housekeeping task – because there's no point in keeping the subscriber if they aren't subscribed to anything:

```
Public Function unsubscribe(objXMLDoc As Variant) As Variant

    Dim strSubscriber As String, strClass As String
    Dim objSubscriber As Variant
    Dim objNode As Variant

    Set objSubscriber = objXMLDoc.selectSingleNode("//m:subscriber")
    strSubscriber = objSubscriber.Text
    strClass = objXMLDoc.selectSingleNode("//m:class").Text

    Set objNode = objSubscribers.selectSingleNode("//class[@name='" & _
                strClass & "' and ../@name='" & strSubscriber & "']")

    If TypeName(objNode) <> "Nothing" Then
```

```
      If objNode.parentNode.childNodes.length > 1 Then
        '// Subscriber is subscribed to more than one class,
        '// remove just this class.
         objNode.parentNode.removeChild (objNode)
      Else
        '// Subscriber is only subscribed to one class, remove the subscriber
         objNode.parentNode.parentNode.removeChild (objNode.parentNode)
      End If

    End If

    Set objNode = Nothing
    Set objSubscriber = Nothing

    Set unsubscribe = createResponse(objXMLDoc, "<result >Subscriber:[" & _
                  strSubscriber & "] has been unsubscribed for class:[" & _
                  strClass & "]</result>")

End Function
```

Retrieving Messages

Although it's not used directly by our `tester.asp` program, there is also a `GetMessages` method. The purpose of this method is to get all messages of a specified class for a specified subscriber. Once they've been retrieved, the messages are removed from the message pool:

```
Public Function getMessages(objXMLDoc As Variant) As Variant

    Dim strSubscriber As String, strClass As String, objNodeList As Variant
    Dim strMessages As String, ele

    strSubscriber = objXMLDoc.selectSingleNode("//m:subscriber").Text
    strClass = objXMLDoc.selectSingleNode("//m:class").Text

    Set objNodeList = objSubscribers.selectNodes("//message[../@name='" & _
                  strClass & "' and ../../@name='" & _
                  strSubscriber & "']")

    strMessages = "<messages>"

    For Each ele In objNodeList
      strMessages = strMessages & ele.xml
    Next

    strMessages = strMessages & "</messages>"

    For Each ele In objNodeList
         ele.parentNode.removeChild (ele)
    Next

    Set getMessages = createResponse(objXMLDoc, strMessages)

End Function
```

Resetting the Contents

And finally, the last method we have inside the COM object is used to reset the contents:

```
Public Function reset(objXMLDoc) As Variant

  Dim objSubscriberList As Variant
  Dim objRoot As Variant, objSubscriber As Variant

  Set objSubscriberList = objSubscribers.selectNodes("//subscriber")
  Set objRoot = objSubscribers.documentElement

  For Each objSubscriber In objSubscriberList
    objRoot.removeChild (objSubscriber)
  Next

  Set reset = createResponse(objXMLDoc, "Message Pool has been reset.")

End Function
```

This concludes (finally!) our look at what goes on inside the message pool. Next, we can move away from infrastructure and move on to the implementation level.

The Client-Side Code

So now we have the server side sorted, let's turn our attention to the client.

Putting It All Together – tester.asp

tester.asp is a multipurpose page – it's a message class subscriber, a message poster, and a portal into the message pool.

However, if you look at the code for tester.asp, you'll see very little there – which demonstrates the elegance of this kind of system. We have a relatively complex system under the hood, and yet it's easy to implement.

You'll find that most of the JavaScript code resides in a file called monitor.js, which we reference from tester.asp:

```
<script language="javascript" src="monitor.js"></script>
```

We'll take a look at the monitor.js file next, but first a brief look at tester.asp.

After some style declarations, we start by calling updateDisplay() from the BODY onclick event:

```
<BODY onclick = "updateDisplay();">
```

If we look at the code for the updateDisplay() function, you'll see that it loads the
viewAllMessges.asp page into an <IFRAME> that we've defined on this page:

```
<script language="javascript">

strViewAllMessages = strPublisher.substr(0,strPublisher.lastIndexOf("/") + _
                     1) + 'viewAllMessages.asp';

function updateDisplay(){
  updatewindow.location.href=strViewAllMessages;
}
```

```
td colspan=6><iframe name="updatewindow" id="updatewindow" _
                     style="{width:100%;height:400}"></iframe></td>
```

This is because the message pool is by definition shared, and messages can be added by other entities,
so as a convenience we have a quick way to refresh the display.

Next, we'll assign a variable the contents of an ASP include file (actually a pretty cool trick!). This is
done to simplify deployment of the code. When you set up the message posters and subscribers, all you
need to do is change the contents of the MessageMonitorLocation.inc file to reflect the machine
that is hosting the message pool:

```
strPublisher = '<!-- #include file="MessageMonitorLocation.inc"-->'
```

The include file contains a URL to the SOAP listener, for example:

```
http://brian1-notebook/ProWinDNA/server.asp
```

which means that in this particular case, the processed line of code would be executed as:

```
strPublisher = 'http://brian1-notebook/ProWinDNA/server.asp'
```

The next function in tester.asp is invoked from the buttons that let you subscribe or unsubscribe
users from messages of a specified class. The single function, toggleSubscribe, handles both tasks.
Note the calls to mm_subscribe and mm_unsubscribe – these functions are implemented in
monitor.js, as we'll see next. These are the calls that are really doing the work – everything else in
this function is purely to control the visual attributes of the buttons:

```
function toggleSubscribe(strPublisher, strSubscriber, strClass, oBtn){

  if (oBtn.value == "Unsubscribe"){

    mm_unsubscribe(strPublisher, strSubscriber, strClass);
    oBtn.style.backgroundColor="navy";
    oBtn.style.color="yellow";
    oBtn.value = "Subscribe";

  } else {
```

```
      mm_subscribe(strPublisher, strSubscriber, strClass);
      oBtn.style.backgroundColor="yellow";
      oBtn.style.color="navy";
      oBtn.value = "Unsubscribe";

   }
}
```

And the last function is the `resetAll` function, which is invoked from the RESET button. Again, the real work is being done by `mm_reset` in `monitor.js` – the rest of the code resets the buttons' visual state to the starting values:

```
function resetAll(){

   for(i=0; i<document.all.length; i++){

      if ((oBtn=document.all(i)).tagName=="BUTTON"){
         document.all(i).disabled = false;

         if (oBtn.value == "Unsubscribe"){
            oBtn.style.backgroundColor="navy";
            oBtn.style.color="yellow";
            oBtn.value = "Subscribe";
         }

      }
   }
   mm_reset();

}
```

The rest of the page is just an HTML table that holds the buttons that call this code:

```
<center>
<table width=80% bgcolor="lightsteelblue"
                 align="center" cellpadding=5>
  <tr>
    <td><button onclick='resetAll()'
               id=button1 name=button1>Reset</button></td>
    <td>Miriam</td>
    <td>Steven</td>
    <td>Melissa</td>
    <td> </td>
    <td>Messages</td>
  </tr>
  <tr>
    <td>SanDiego_ASP_receiveOrder</td>
    <td><button onclick='toggleSubscribe(strPublisher, "Miriam",
        "SanDiego_ASP_receiveOrder", this);'>Subscribe</button></td>
    <td><button onclick='toggleSubscribe(strPublisher, "Steven",
        "SanDiego_ASP_receiveOrder", this);'>Subscribe</button></td>
    <td><button onclick='toggleSubscribe(strPublisher, "Melissa",
        "SanDiego_ASP_receiveOrder", this);'>Subscribe</button></td>
    <td> </td>
```

```
    <td>
      <button onclick='mm_publish("received",
                    "SanDiego_ASP_receiveOrder");'>received</button>
      <button onclick='mm_publish("validated",
                    "SanDiego_ASP_receiveOrder");'>validated</button>
      <button onclick='mm_publish("submitted",
                    "SanDiego_ASP_receiveOrder");'>submitted</button>
    </td>
</tr>

<tr>
  <td>London_ASP_receiveOrder</td>
  <td><button onclick='toggleSubscribe(strPublisher, "Miriam",
            "London_ASP_receiveOrder", this);'>Subscribe</button></td>
  <td><button onclick='toggleSubscribe(strPublisher, "Steven",
            "London_ASP_receiveOrder", this);'>Subscribe</button></td>
  <td><button onclick='toggleSubscribe(strPublisher, "Melissa",
            "London_ASP_receiveOrder", this);'>Subscribe</button></td>
  <td> </td>
  <td>
    <button onclick='mm_publish("received",
                  "London_ASP_receiveOrder");'>received</button>
    <button onclick='mm_publish("submitted",
                  "London_ASP_receiveOrder");'>submitted</button>
  </td>
</tr>

<tr>
  <td>London_COM_placeOrder</td>
  <td><button onclick='toggleSubscribe(strPublisher, "Miriam",
            "London_COM_placeOrder", this);'>Subscribe</button></td>
  <td><button onclick='toggleSubscribe(strPublisher, "Steven",
            "London_COM_placeOrder", this);'>Subscribe</button></td>
  <td><button onclick='toggleSubscribe(strPublisher, "Melissa",
            "London_COM_placeOrder", this);'>Subscribe</button></td>
  <td> </td>
  <td>
    <button onclick='mm_publish("received",
          "London_COM_placeOrder");'>received</button>
    <button onclick='mm_publish("submitted",
          "London_COM_placeOrder");'>submitted</button>
  </td>
</tr>

<tr>
  <td>HongKong_Manufacturing</td>
  <td><button onclick='toggleSubscribe(strPublisher, "Miriam",
            "HongKong_Manufacturing", this);'>Subscribe</button></td>
  <td><button onclick='toggleSubscribe(strPublisher, "Steven",
            "HongKong_Manufacturing", this);'>Subscribe</button></td>
  <td><button onclick='toggleSubscribe(strPublisher, "Melissa",
            "HongKong_Manufacturing", this);'>Subscribe</button></td>
  <td> </td>
  <td>
```

```
        <button onclick='mm_publish("received",
                     "HongKong_Manufacturing");'>received</button>
        <button onclick='mm_publish("queued",
                     "HongKong_Manufacturing");'>queued</button>
    </td>
  </tr>

  <tr>
    <td colspan=6><iframe name="updatewindow" id="updatewindow"
                      style="{width:100%;height:400}"></iframe></td>
  </tr>

</table></center>

<hr>
Reporting to "<script>document.write(strPublisher)</script>",
          page generate at <%=now%>
```

JavaScript Client-Side Enablers

Thus far, we have covered the internal architecture of the message pool, we've seen pieces that can connect to the pool and display contents, and we've taken a look at the ASP test page.

When we were looking at `tester.asp` we saw a reference to an external JavaScript file – `monitor.js`, and we called several functions that this file includes. This series of JavaScript functions are essentially wrappers for functions that exist within the COM object. By including `monitor.js` in a client-side page, you gain all the functionality needed to post messages to the pool and to retrieve them.

Debugging

We include a `debugging` variable to determine whether or not to display the results of a SOAP method call:

```
debugging = false
```

It's used in conjunction with the `debugMessage` function:

```
function debugMessage(objHTTPReq){
  if (debugging){
    alert(objHTTPReq.responseText);
  }
}
```

As you'll see, `debugMessage` is called from almost every function in `monitor.js`. This provides us with a convenient way to turn debug feedback on or off.

Initialization

We use a global variable, `objMessage`, to hold an instance of the XMLDOM that contains a generic SOAP message:

```
var objMessage = mm_initMessage()
```

It is used as a "template": every function that needs it replaces the `<SOAP-ENV:Body>` element contents with what is required for that specific method call.

> *To reduce the risk of any possible name clashes with functions in the host page, all the Message Monitor support functions are prefixed with mm.*

The initialization function for `objMessage` looks like this:

```
function mm_initMessage(){
    var objTemp = new ActiveXObject('Microsoft.XMLDOM');
    var strXML

    strXML  = '<?xml version="1.0"?>';
    strXML += '<SOAP-ENV:Envelope ';
    strXML += '    xmlns:SOAP-ENV="urn:schemas.xmlsoap.org:soap/envelope" ';
    strXML +=   'xmlns:m="urn:stellcom.com/distMessages">';
    strXML +=   '<SOAP-ENV:Body>';
    strXML += '        <m:uninitialized></m:uninitialized>';
    strXML += '    </SOAP-ENV:Body>';
    strXML += '</SOAP-ENV:Envelope>';
    objTemp.loadXML(strXML);
    return objTemp;
}
```

Note that this is where we declare the `m:` namespace we saw earlier.

Client-Side Wrapper Functions

As we mentioned, the client-side functions are consistent with the functions in the COM object. In fact, you could conceptually think of the two parts as forming one function, with a break between the two halves. The SOAP message ties the two halves together.

These JavaScript functions are essentially wrappers for the remote COM object method calls, so we'll present the client-side functions in the same order as the COM object functions.

You'll notice that all of these functions are extremely similar. All of them take the predefined template SOAP message and substitute details of their method call as the contents of the `<SOAP-ENV:Body>` element. We'll step through the all-important `mm_subscribe` function in detail, but the same technique is used for all these JavaScript functions.

The mm_subscribe Function

The `mm_subscribe` function takes three parameters: the URL to the publisher, the label for the subscriber to add, and the name of the class they want to subscribe to.

We create an instance of `XMLHttpRequest`. This is part of MSXML, and is what allows us to "post" our message to the SOAP listener:

```
function mm_subscribe(strPublisher, strSubscriber, strClass){

    var objMethodCall, objBody
    var objHTTPReq = new ActiveXObject("Microsoft.XMLHTTP")

    objHTTPReq.open("POST", strPublisher, false);
```

Next we specify a `SOAPAction` HTTP header, as required by the SOAP V1.1 protocol. This HTTP header makes it possible for non-XML capable devices such as firewalls or routers to route the message, even though the message itself is meaningless to them:

```
// add the SOAPAction header
objHTTPReq.setRequestHeader("SOAPAction",
                            "DistMessages.MessageMonitor#subscribe");
```

Then we do some XML DOM manipulation. What we're doing here is creating an element called `<m:subscribe>`, which is our method invocation. It in turn has the child elements `<m:subscriber>`, to which we assign the string containing the subscriber's name, and `<m:class>`, to which we assign the string containing the name of the class we want to subscribe to:

```
objMethodCall = objMessage.createElement("m:subscribe");
objMethodCall.appendChild(objMessage.createElement("m:subscriber"))
             .text = strSubscriber;
objMethodCall.appendChild(objMessage.createElement("m:class"))
             .text = strClass;
```

Recall that the `m:` namespace is declared in the `mm_initMessage` function we saw above.

Next we get a reference to the `<SOAP-ENV:Body>` element, and replace its child with our method call:

```
objBody = objMessage.selectSingleNode("//SOAP-ENV:Body");
objBody.replaceChild(objMethodCall, objBody.firstChild);
```

And lastly, we actually send the message to the listener:

```
objHTTPReq.send(objMessage.xml);

debugMessage(objHTTPReq);
}
```

You'll notice that the `strPublisher` variable is undeclared and undefined. That's because this variable must be defined in the host file that is including these support functions. This dependency is required. The functions in this file need to know the SOAP end-point (the recipient of the SOAP messages), which, in this system, is contained in the `MessageMonitorLocation.inc` file (as we saw in the previous section on `tester.asp`).

As we stated, this next group of functions all share this same approach of plugging a method call into the body of a pre-defined message.

The mm_publish Function

Next we have the `mm_publish` function:

```
function mm_publish(strMessage, strClass){

  var objMethodCall, objBody
  var objHTTPReq = new ActiveXObject("Microsoft.XMLHTTP")
```

```
    objHTTPReq.open("POST", strPublisher, false);

    // add the SOAPAction header
    objHTTPReq.setRequestHeader("SOAPAction",
                            "DistMessages.MessageMonitor#publish");

    objMethodCall = objMessage.createElement("m:publish");
    objMethodCall.appendChild(objMessage.createElement("m:message"))
            .text = strMessage;
    objMethodCall.appendChild(objMessage.createElement("m:class"))
            .text = strClass;

    objBody = objMessage.selectSingleNode("//SOAP-ENV:Body");
    objBody.replaceChild(objMethodCall, objBody.firstChild);

    objHTTPReq.send(objMessage.xml);

    debugMessage(objHTTPReq);
}
```

The mm_unsubscribe Function

Then the mm_unsubscribe function:

```
function mm_unsubscribe(strPublisher, strSubscriber, strClass){

    var objMethodCall, objBody
    var objHTTPReq = new ActiveXObject("Microsoft.XMLHTTP")

    objHTTPReq.open("POST", strPublisher, false);

    // add the SOAPAction header
    objHTTPReq.setRequestHeader("SOAPAction",
                            "DistMessages.MessageMonitor#unsubscribe");

    objMethodCall = objMessage.createElement("m:unsubscribe");
    objMethodCall.appendChild(objMessage.createElement("m:subscriber"))
            .text = strSubscriber;
    objMethodCall.appendChild(objMessage.createElement("m:class"))
            .text = strClass;

    objBody = objMessage.selectSingleNode("//SOAP-ENV:Body");
    objBody.replaceChild(objMethodCall, objBody.firstChild);

    objHTTPReq.send(objMessage.xml);

    debugMessage(objHTTPReq);
}
```

The mm_getMessages Function

The mm_getMessages function looks like this:

```
function mm_getMessages(strPublisher, strSubscriber, strClass){

  var objMethodcall, objMethodCall, objBody
  var objHTTPReq = new ActiveXObject("Microsoft.XMLHTTP")

  objHTTPReq.open("POST", strPublisher, false);

  // add the SOAPAction header
  objHTTPReq.setRequestHeader("SOAPAction",
                            "DistMessages.MessageMonitor#getMessages");

  objMethodCall = objMessage.createElement("m:getMessages");
  objMethodCall.appendChild(objMessage.createElement("m:subscriber"))
            .text = strSubscriber;
  objMethodCall.appendChild(objMessage.createElement("m:class"))
            .text = strClass;

  objBody = objMessage.selectSingleNode("//SOAP-ENV:Body");
  objBody.replaceChild(objMethodCall, objBody.firstChild);

  objHTTPReq.send(objMessage.xml);

  debugMessage(objHTTPReq);
}
```

The mm_reset Function

Lastly, we have the mm_reset function:

```
function mm_reset(){

  var objHTTPReq = new ActiveXObject("Microsoft.XMLHTTP")
  objHTTPReq.open("POST", strPublisher, false);

  // add the SOAPAction header
  objHTTPReq.setRequestHeader("SOAPAction",
                            "DistMessages.MessageMonitor#reset");

  objHTTPReq.send(objMessage.xml);
}
```

Setting Up the Project

That's all the code we need to set up our application. To actually see it in action, you need to set it up as follows.

We'll assume you have a two-computer setup – a client and a server – although you can of course have as many clients as you wish. If you just want to see the application functioning, you can also set up the client and server code on the same machine.

First, we need to compile our component.

Compiling DistMessages.dll

When compiling the DistMessages project, ensure that:

❑ In the Project References dialog, you have a reference to Microsoft XML, v3.0 (for the July 2000 release version of MSXML – this may change for later versions)

❑ In the Project Properties dialog, you set the Threading Model to Single Threaded

Server-Side Installation Steps

You need to install the following files in a folder on your web server:

❑ server.asp

❑ viewAllMessages.asp

❑ SOAP_errors_server.inc

❑ DistMessages.dll

Then register the DLL on the server, and check security on the DLL to ensure that Everyone has execute privileges to it.

Finally, if you want to use the logging functionality (which is implemented by setting debugging=true) ensure the Everyone user has at least write rights to the folder. The default is to not log, so you'll only need to do this if you change the setting.

Client-Side Installation Steps

Next install the following files into a folder on the Web server on your client machine (this could be the same as where you put the server-side code, or on a separate machine):

❑ tester.asp

❑ MessageMonitorLocation.inc

❑ monitor.js

The only code you'll need to alter is the MessageMonitorLocation.inc – change the URL to point to the location where you have deployed the server-side code.

Testing the Installation

To test your installation, just point your browser at `tester.asp` on the web server where you deployed the client-side files. You should be able to add and remove subscribers and post messages as you wish:

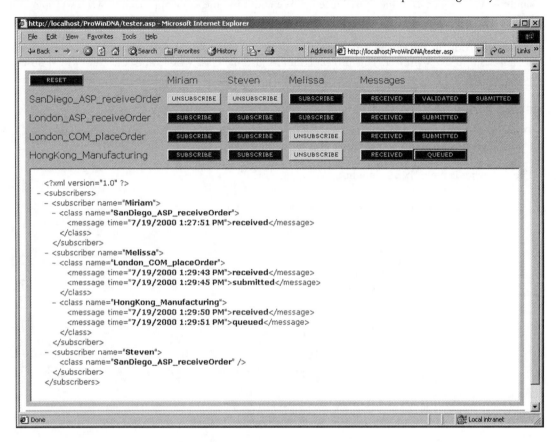

Security

If you followed the steps above, and the system doesn't work, it's probably a security issue.

If you're receiving a client-side "access denied" message – probably at the call to the Open method of `XMLHttpRequest` – then it's the security settings on your browser. Ease up the security level and this should go away. The easy solution is to **temporarily** change your browser security settings for the Internet zone (Tools | Internet Options | Security | Internet) to Low.

If you want to just get it running, then grant Everyone "full control" rights to the folder on the server. Otherwise, grant "write" rights for the folder (to enable logging), and "execute" rights to the DLL.

Visual Basic Client-side Enablers

In the previous section, we saw how JavaScript wrappers can interact with our remote COM object by sending SOAP requests to the SOAP listener. We could use the same approach to write wrappers for any scripting language or development language of our choice.

The source code for this chapter includes an example of how to do this using the DistMessagePoster Visual Basic ActiveX project. This project contains just one class – MessagePoster – which posts a simple message.

Posting Messages to the Pool

The MessagePoster class can easily be incorporated into a Visual Basic application or another COM object, giving it the ability to post messages to the message pool.

The following is the publish method:

```
Public Function publish(strPublisher As String, _
                        strMessage As String, strClass As String) As Variant

    Dim objMethodCall As Variant
    Dim objBody As Variant
    Dim objHTTPReq As Variant
    Dim objMessage As Variant

    Set objHTTPReq = New MSXML2.XMLHTTP30

    Set objMessage = createMessage()

    objHTTPReq.open "POST", strPublisher, False

    ' add the SOAP header
    objHTTPReq.setRequestHeader "SOAPAction", _
                        "DistMessages.MessageMonitor#publish"

    Set objMethodCall = objMessage.createElement("m:publish")
    objMethodCall.appendChild(objMessage.createElement("m:message"))_
            .Text = strMessage
    objMethodCall.appendChild(objMessage.createElement("m:class"))_
            .Text = strClass
    Set objBody = objMessage.selectSingleNode("//SOAP-ENV:Body")

    objBody.replaceChild objMethodCall, objBody.firstChild

    objHTTPReq.send objMessage.xml

    Set publish = objHTTPReq.responseXML

End Function
```

As you might expect, this is very similar to the publish function in our JavaScript enabler monitor.js.

At the top of the `publish` method, we call the `createMessage` function. This builds up our SOAP message in much the same way as `mm_initMessage` in `monitor.js`:

```
Private Function createMessage() As Variant

    Dim objTemp As New MSXML2.DOMDocument30
    Dim strXML As String

    strXML = "<?xml version=""1.0""?>"
    strXML = strXML & "<SOAP-ENV:Envelope " & _
            "xmlns:SOAP-ENV=""urn:schemas.xmlsoap.org:soap/envelope"" " & _
            "xmlns:m=""my-name-space"">"
    strXML = strXML & "    <SOAP-ENV:Body>"
    strXML = strXML & "        <m:uninitialized></m:uninitialized>"
    strXML = strXML & "    </SOAP-ENV:Body>"
    strXML = strXML & "</SOAP-ENV:Envelope>"

    objTemp.loadXML (strXML)
    Set createMessage = objTemp

End Function
```

Again, remember that you need to reference Microsoft XML, v3.0.

Testing the MessagePoster Class

The test form we've created for this class looks like this:

In the above form, the **End Point** is the URL of the SOAP listener we are posting to. When you click the **Post Message** button, the text of the response received from the listener is written to the **Result** window.

The following is **all** the source code required for the VB application (in this case the test form) to communicate with the message pool:

```
Option Explicit

Private Sub btnPost_Click()
```

```
    Dim objPoster As New DistMessagesPoster.MessagePoster
    txtResult.Text = objPoster.publish _
                    ("http://brian1-notebook/ProWinDNA/server.asp", _
                    "hello from cls", "SanDiego_ASP_receiveOrder").xml

End Sub
```

```
Private Sub btnCancel_Click()

  Unload MessagePosterTestForm
  End

End Sub
```

Remember to change the URL to point to the listener on your server machine.

This is an example of the level of complexity (that is, the lack of it) required in order to add support for the message pool to your VB project.

When the Post Message button is clicked, everyone that has subscribed to messages of the `SanDiego_ASP_receiveOrder` class will receive a `hello from cls` message.

Going further...

The system presented here is comprehensive and flexible, and it could easily be extended to accommodate other requirements. Some enhancement ideas you might want to try include:

❑ **Persistence**: in the architecture presented here, there is no persistence – the messages are kept in an XML document in memory. By enhancing the COM object, it could be made to persist to a data store, either a database such as SQL Server 2000, or in the file system as a `.xml` file.

❑ **Java**: a Java-based equivalent of the `MessagePoster` class, or wrapper functions in `monitor.js`, could be written so that Java applications would have an easy way to interact with the message pool.

❑ **Web Services**: at the time of writing, web Services are just hitting the radar of developers. Using a remote proxy approach and a modified SOAP listener, another layer could be added to interact with the message pool.

Summary

In this chapter, we have seen a way to implement a Windows DNA-based centralized message pool system. This message system allows different type of applications, spanning operating systems, object models, and development languages, to post and retrieve messages to and from a common message pool.

❑ We have used XML throughout the implementation of the system, and have used SOAP to facilitate interchanges with other systems

❑ We have examined the core infrastructure components of the system, as well as some test implementations that make use of them

❑ Most importantly, we have examined a useful technique that can help ease some of the complexities of developing a distributed application

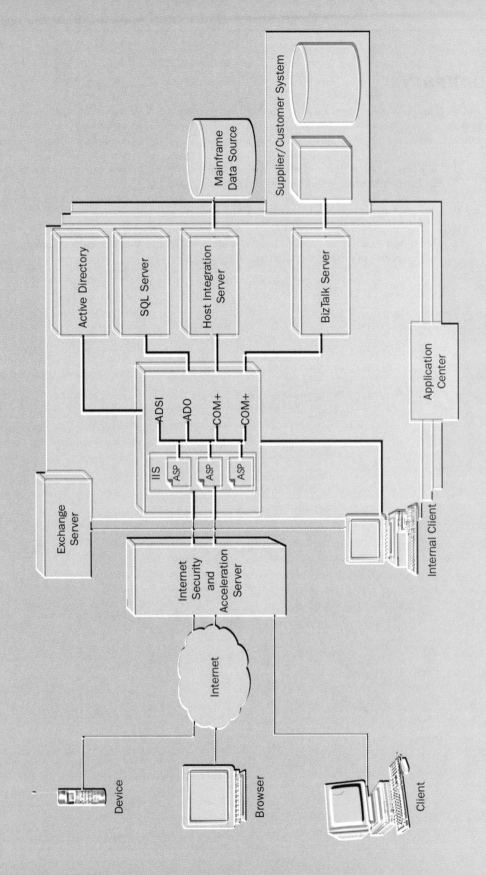

Online discussion at http://p2p.wrox.com

Further Reading and Resources

We've been saying all along that this book could never cover everything you need to know about all the subjects we've touched upon in this book. Instead, we've done some of the research for you and collected some links and books you could look at. If you liked the look of a subject and want to know more, try the following places first. Granted, there's probably more out there than we've presented here, but this should give you a pretty good start. We've divided the list up by technology area.

DNA

http://www.microsoft.com/dna – (Microsoft DNA Home)

http://www.microsoft.com/DCOM/dna/resources/resourceintro.asp
(Introductory Material Links)

http://msdn.microsoft.com/library/default.asp?URL=/library/techart
/dnablueprint.htm – (A Blueprint for Building Web Sites Using the Microsoft Windows DNA
Platform)

http://msdn.microsoft.com/library/default.asp?URL=/library/techart
/windnadesign_intro.htm – (Introduction to Designing and Building Windows DNA Applications)

http://msdn.microsoft.com/library/default.asp?URL=/library/techart
/windnadesign_guide.htm – (Guide to Designing and Building Windows DNA Applications)

http://msdn.microsoft.com/library/default.asp?URL=/library/techart
/windnamistakes.htm – (Top Windows DNA Performance Mistakes and How to Prevent Them)

http://msdn.microsoft.com/library/default.asp?URL=/library/techart
/dw1intro.htm – (Duwamish Sample DNA Application)

`http://www.devuniverse.com/dna` – (DevUniverse DNA Area)

`http://www.microsoft.com/Seminar/1033/19990120_DNA_COM/Seminar.htm`
(Online DNA and COM Seminar)

Programming Distributed Applications with COM+ and Microsoft Visual Basic 6.0,
Ted Pattison and Don Box, ISBN 0-735610-10-X, Microsoft Press

Programming Server-Side Applications for Microsoft Windows 2000,
Jeffrey Richter and Jason D. Clark, ISBN 0-735607-53-2, Microsoft Press

Designing for Scalability with Microsoft Windows DNA, Sten Sundblad and Per Sundblad,
ISBN 0-735609-68-3, Microsoft Press

COM and COM+

`http://msdn.microsoft.com/library/psdk/cossdk/complusportal_9o9x.htm`

`http://www.microsoft.com/com/tech/complus.asp`

`http://www.sql-zone.com` – (Development Exchange)

`http://www.oramag.com` – (Oracle Magazine)

`http://www.sqlmag.com` – (SQL-Server Magazine)

`http://www.developmentor.com` – (DevelopMentor)

`http://www.cetus-links.org` – (links to more sites)

Article Q170156, MSDN Library, INFO: VB 6.0 Readme Part 12: Transaction Server (MTS) Issues

COM+ Events, Platform SDK, MSDN Library: COM+ (Component Services)

COM+ and the Battle for the Middle Tier, Roger Sessions, ISBN 0-471317-17-9,
Wiley Computer Publishing

Programming Distributed Applications with COM and Microsoft Visual Basic 6.0, Ted Pattison,
ISBN 1-572319-61-5, MS Press

Designing Component-Based Applications, Mary Kitland, ISBN 0-735605-23-8, MS Press

Chapter 14: Transactions, MDAC 2.5 SDK – ODBC Programmer's Reference, ISBN 1-572315-16-4,
MS Press

Relational Database Design Clearly Explained, Jan L. Harrington, ISBN 0-123264-25-1,
Morgan Kaufmann

Beginning Visual Basic 6 Database Programming, John Connell, ISBN 1-861001-06-1, Wrox Press

Beginning Visual Basic 6 Objects, Peter Wright, ISBN 1-861001-05-3, Wrox Press

Professional Visual Basic 6.0 MTS Programming, Matt Bortniker, ISBN 1-861002-44-0, Wrox Press

Essential COM, Don Box, ISBN 0-201634-46-5, Addison-Wesley

Business Objects

VB6 UML Design and Development, Jake Sturm, ISBN 1-861002-51-3, Wrox Press

Instant UML, Pierre-Alain Muller, ISBN 1-861000-87-1, Wrox Press

Professional Visual Basic 6 Distributed Objects, Rockford Lhotka, ISBN 1-861002-07-6, Wrox Press

Visual Basic 6 Business Objects, Rockford Lhotka, ISBN 1-861001-07-X, Wrox Press

MSMQ

http://www.microsoft.com/msmq/

http://msdn.microsoft.com/library/default.asp?URL=/library/psdk/msmq/msmq_overview_4ilh.htm

http://msdn.microsoft.com/library/default.asp?URL=/library/psdk/cossdk/complusportal_9o9x.htm

http://msdn.microsoft.com/library/default.asp?URL=/library/psdk/cossdk/pgservices_queuedcomponents_2vhv.htm

Designing Distributed Applications with XML, ASP, IE5, LDAP and MSMQ, Stephen Mohr, ISBN 1-861002-27-0, Wrox Press

Professional MTS & MSMQ Programming with VB and ASP, Alex Homer and David Sussman, ISBN 1-861001-46-0, Wrox Press

Windows 2000

http://www.microsoft.com/windows2000 – (Windows 2000 Home)

http://msdn.microsoft.com/windows2000 – (MSDN Windows 2000 Home)

http://www.microsoft.com/windows2000/library – (Tech Library)

http://www.microsoft.com/technet/win2000 – (TechNet Windows 2000 Resources)

Understanding Microsoft Windows 2000 Distributed Services, David Chappell, ISBN 1- 572316-87-X, Microsoft Press

Enterprise Servers

http://www.microsoft.com/servers – (Microsoft Server Home)

http://www.microsoft.com/servers/Lineup.htm – (Overview)

http://www.microsoft.com/exchange – (Exchange Server)

http://www.microsoft.com/sql – (SQL Server)

http://www.microsoft.com/biztalkserver – (BizTalk Server)

http://www.microsoft.com/applicationcenter – (AppCenter Server)

http://www.microsoft.com/commerceserver – (Commerce Server)

http://www.microsoft.com/hostintserver – (Host Integration Server)

http://www.microsoft.com/isaserver – (Internet Security and Acceleration Server)

.NET

http://www.microsoft.com/net – (.NET Home)

http://www.microsoft.com/net/whitepaper – (.NET White Paper)

http://msdn.microsoft.com/net – (.NET on MSDN)

http://msdn.microsoft.com/vstudio/nextgen – (Visual Studio.NET)

A Preview of Active Server Pages+, Alex Homer et al, ISBN 1-861004-75-3, Wrox Press

SOAP and XML

http://msdn.microsoft.com/msdnmag/issues/0300/soap/soap.asp – (A Young Person's Guide to the Simple Object Access Protocol, Don Box, MSDN Magazine, March 2000)

http://msdn.microsoft.com/xml – (XML Manifesto, Don Box)

http://msdn.microsoft.com/xml/default.asp – (MSDN Web site in the XML area)

http://msdn.microsoft.com/xml/general/soap_firewall.asp (SOAP and Firewalls, David Chappell)

http://msdn.microsoft.com/library/periodic/period00/soap.htm (SOAP: The Simple Object Access Protocol, Aaron Skonnard)

SOAP specification at http://www.ietf.org/internet-drafts/

also MS SOAP specification at http://msdn.microsoft.com/xml/general/soapspec.asp.

Understanding SOAP, Kenn Scribner, ISBN 0672319225, SAMS

Beginning XML, David Hunter et al, ISBN 1-861003-41-2, Wrox Press

Professional XML, Richard Anderson et al, ISBN 1-861003-11-0, Wrox Press

UDA

You can download (for free!) Microsoft's latest MDAC components at:
http://www.microsoft.com/data/download2.htm

Microsoft white papers regarding UDA, OLE DB and ADO:

http://www.microsoft.com/data/ado/default.htm

http://www.microsoft.com/data/techmat.htm

Professional ADO 2.5, Ian Blackburn et al., ISBN 1-861002-75-0, Wrox Press. Both VB and C++ programmers can benefit from this book.

Professional Visual Basic 6 Databases, Charles Williams, ISBN 1-861002-02-5, Wrox Press

Directory Services

The Active Directory Overview is located at:
`http://www.microsoft.com/windows2000/guide/server/features/dirlist.asp`

"Exploring Directory Services":
`http://www.microsoft.com/windows2000/guide/server/features/activedirectory.asp`

Active Directory Developer's Reference Library, David Iseminger (Series Editor), ISBN: 0-7356-0992-6, MS Press

Site Server 3.0 Personalization and Membership, Robert Howard, ISBN: 1-861001-94-0, Wrox Press

Professional ADSI Programming, Simon Robinson, ISBN 1-861002-26-2, Wrox Press

ADSI ASP Programmer's Reference, Steven Hahn, ISBN 1-861001-69-X, Wrox Press

ASP

`http://www.asptoday.com` – (ASP Today)

`http://www.asp101.com` – (ASP 101)

`http://www.aspsite.com` – (SuperExpert)

`http://www.powerasp.com` – (PowerASP)

`http://www.aspin.com/` – (ASP Resource Index)

`http://www.aspfree.com/main.asp` – (ASPFree)

`http://aspwire.com/` (ASPWire)

`http://www.aspalliance.com` (ASP Alliance)

`http://www.aspzone.com` (ASP Zone)

`http://www.4guysfromrolla.com` (4 Guys From Rolla)

Beginning ASP 3.0, Brian Francis et al., ISBN 1-861003-38-2, Wrox Press

Professional ASP 3.0, Alex Homer et al., ISBN 1-861002-61-0, Wrox Press

A Preview of Active Server Pages+, Alex Homer et al, ISBN 1-861004-75-3, Wrox Press

Web Programming with ASP and COM, Matt Crouch, ISBN 0-201604-60-4, Addison-Wesley

Security

Windows 2000 and Windows NT Server info at `http://www.microsoft.com/ntserver` and the Windows NT Server Forum on the Microsoft Network (GO WORD: MSNTS).

Microsoft's security site: `http://www.microsoft.com/security`

For the latest IETF IPSec drafts: `http://www.ietf.org/html.charters/ipsec-charter.html`

The Microsoft Platform SDK contains info on Windows NT security architecture, Security Support Provider Interface, CryptoAPI, and Windows NT security APIs.

Online security magazines:
`http://www.icsa.net/`
`http://www.infosecuritymag.com/`
`http://www.lubrinco.com`, the Business Security e-Journal, lets you sign up for a free monthly newsletter on security.

Interesting articles on setting up security policies :
SANS Institute : `http://www.sans.org/newlook/home.htm`
Baseline Software, Inc : `http://www.baselinesoft.com`
Telstra's Security papers : `http://www.telstra.com.au/pub/docs/security`

`http://www.hackers.com` or `http://www.10pht.com`

Bugtraq Mailing List Archive : `http://www2.merton.ox.ac.uk/%7Esecurity`

Known NT Hacking Exploits : `http://www.iss.net/vd/bill_stout/ntexploits.htm`

Windows NT Exploits : `http://world.std.com/%7Eloki/security/nt-exploits/index.html`

Vulnerability Engine : `http://www.infilsec.com/cgi-infilsec`
`/if%3Faction=search%26amp;keywords=NT+WindowsNT`

Windows NT Systems Bugs : `http://161.53.42.3/%7Ecrv/security/bugs/NT/nt.html`

Windows NT Vulnerabilities : `http://www.txdirect.net/users/wall/winnt2.htm`

X-Force : `http://www.iss.net/cgi-bin/xforce/xforce_index.pl` X-Force is a searchable database of operating systems vulnerabillities and bugs.

Some sites on Windows NT Security & Administration:
`http://www.ntresearch.com`
`http://www.ntsecurity.com`
`http://www.ntinternals.com`

Configuring Windows 2000 Server Security, Thomas Schinder et al., ISBN 1-928994-02-4 Syngress Media Inc

Programming Windows Security, Keith Brown, ISBN 0-201604-42-6, Addison-Wesley

Windows 2000 Security: Little Black Book, Ian MacLean, ISBN 1-576103-87-0, Coriolis

Debugging

Article Q147931, MSDN Library: Entry Level Debugging Tutorial Using WinDBG/I386KD

Article Q148660, MSDN Library: How to Verify Windows NT Debug Symbols

Article Q121366, MSDN Library: INFO: PDB and DBG Files – What They Are and How They Work

Article Q170156, MSDN Library: INFO: VB 6.0 Readme Part 12: Transaction Server (MTS) Issues

MSDN Library: COM+ Visual Basic Debugging Support Contrasted with MTS

Article Q216356, MSDN Library: INFO: Visual C++ Project Settings and .DBG File Creation

Article Q221191, MSDN Library: How to Install/Extract Symbols for Windows NT 4.0,

Article Q148659, MSDN Library: How to Set Up Windows NT Debug Symbols

Article Q130926, MSDN Library: Using Performance Monitor To Identify A Pool Leak

Debugging Applications, John Robbins, ISBN 0-735608-86-5, MS Press

Office Programming

`http://www.microsoft.com/office` - (Microsoft Office Home)

`http://msdn.microsoft.com/officedev` (Microsoft Office Developer Home)

`http://msdn.microsoft.com/officedev/technical/articles/hottopics.asp` (Office Developer Hot Topics)

Professional Outlook 2000 Programming, Ken Slovak et al., ISBN 1-861003-31-5, Wrox Press

Excel 2000 VBA Programmers Reference, John Green, ISBN 1-861002-54-8, Wrox Press

Beginning Access 2000 VBA, Robert Smith and David Sussman, ISBN 1-861001-76-2, Wrox Press

Word 2000 VBA Programmers Reference, Duncan Mackenzie and Filipe Martins, ISBN 1-861002-55-6, Wrox Press

Microsoft Excel 2000 Power Programming with VBA, John Walkenbach, ISBN 0-764532-63-4, IDG Books Worldwide

Access 2000 VBA Handbook, Susann Novalis, ISBN 0-782123-24-4, Sybex

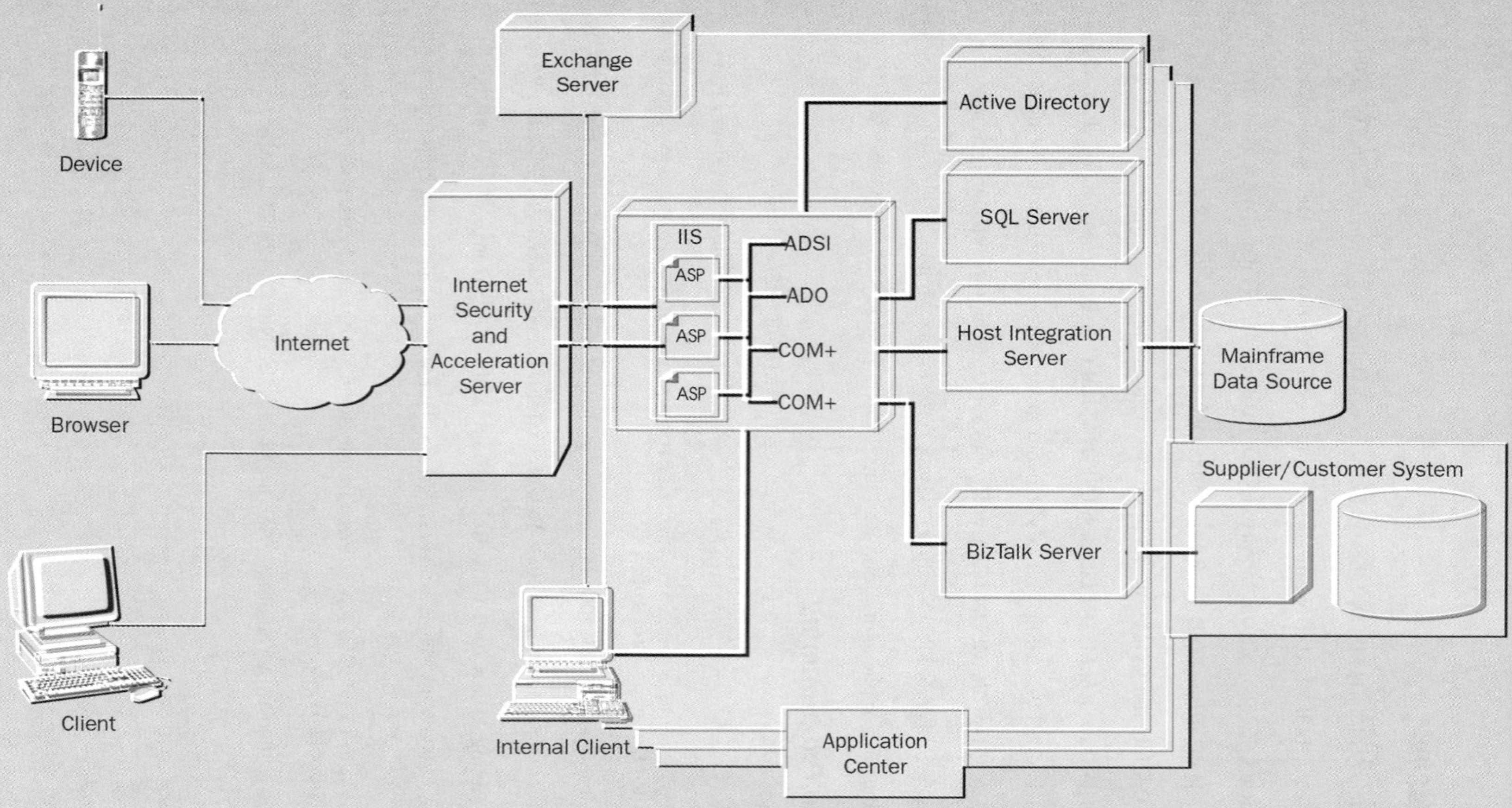
Device
Browser
Client
Internet
Internet Security and Acceleration Server
Exchange Server
IIS
ASP
ASP
ASP
ADSI
ADO
COM+
COM+
Active Directory
SQL Server
Host Integration Server
BizTalk Server
Mainframe Data Source
Supplier/Customer System
Internal Client
Application Center

Support, Errata and P2P.Wrox.Com

One of the most irritating things about any programming book is when you find that the bit of code you've just spent an hour typing simply doesn't work. You check it a hundred times to see if you've set it up correctly and then you notice the spelling mistake in the variable name on the book page. Of course, you can blame the authors for not taking enough care and testing the code, the editors for not doing their job properly, or the proofreaders for not being eagle-eyed enough, but this doesn't get around the fact that mistakes do happen.

We try hard to ensure no mistakes sneak out into the real world, but we can't promise that this book is 100% error free. What we can do is offer the next best thing, by providing you with immediate support and feedback from experts who have worked on the book, and try to ensure that future editions eliminate these gremlins. We are also now committed to support you not just while you read the book, but once you start developing applications as well through our online forums where you can put your questions to the authors, reviewers, and fellow industry professionals.

In this appendix we'll look at how to:

❏   Enroll in the peer to peer forums at p2p.wrox.com

❏   Post and check for errata on our main site, www.wrox.com

❏   e-mail technical support a query or feedback on our books in general

Between all three support procedures, you should get an answer to your problem in no time.

The Online Forums at P2P.Wrox.Com

Mailing lists exist for author and peer support. Lists which will be useful for Professional Windows DNA include Visual Basic, and SQL Server. There are lists created frequently, and if demand exists, a list may be created for Windows DNA. Our system provides **programmer to programmer™ support** on mailing lists, forums and newsgroups all in addition to our one-to-one e-mail system, which we'll look at in a minute. Be confident that your query is not just being examined by a support professional, but by the many Wrox authors and other industry experts present on our mailing lists. We will now see how to join the SQL Server mailing list.

How To Enroll For Support

Just follow this six-step system:

1. Go to p2p.wrox.com in your favorite browser.
   Here you'll find any current announcements concerning P2P – new lists created, any removed and so on:

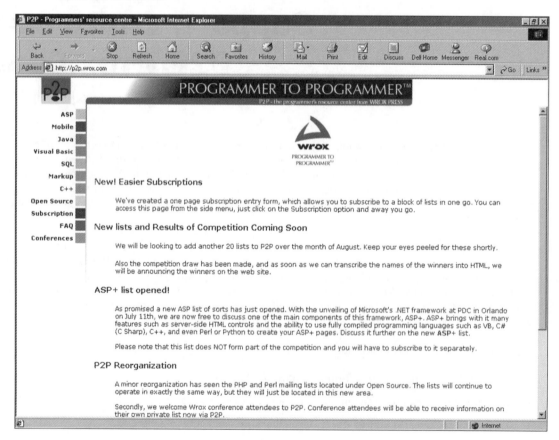

2. Click on the SQL button in the left-hand column.

3. Choose to access the SQL Server list.

4. If you are not a member of the list, you can choose to either view the list without joining it or create an account in the list, by hitting the respective buttons.

5. If you wish to join, you'll be presented with a form in which you'll need to fill in your e-mail address, name and a password (of at least 4 digits). Choose how you would like to receive the messages from the list and then hit Save.

6. Congratulations you're now a member of the SQL Server mailing list.

Why this system offers the best support

You can choose to join the mailing lists or you can receive them as a weekly digest. If you don't have the time or facility to receive the mailing list, then you can search our online archives. You'll find the ability to search on specific subject areas or keywords. As these lists are moderated, you can be confident of finding good, accurate information quickly. Mails can be edited or moved by the moderator into the correct place, making this a most efficient resource. Junk and spam mail are deleted, and your own e-mail address is protected by the unique Lyris system from web-bots that can automatically hoover up newsgroup mailing list addresses. Any queries about joining, leaving lists or any query about the list should be sent to: listsupport@wrox.com.

Checking The Errata Online at www.wrox.com

The following section will take you step by step through the process of posting errata to our web site to get that help. The sections that follow, therefore, are:

❑ Wrox Developers Membership

❑ Finding a list of existing errata on the web site

❑ Adding your own errata to the existing list

❑ What happens to your errata once you've posted it (why doesn't it appear immediately)?

There is also a section covering how to e-mail a question for technical support. This comprises:

❑ What your e-mail should include

❑ What happens to your e-mail once it has been received by us

So that you only need view information relevant to yourself, we ask that you register as a Wrox Developer Member. This is a quick and easy process, that will save you time in the long-run. If you are already a member, just update membership to include this book.

Wrox Developer's Membership

To get your FREE Wrox Developer's Membership click on Membership in the top navigation bar of our home site – http://www.wrox.com. This is shown in the following screenshot:

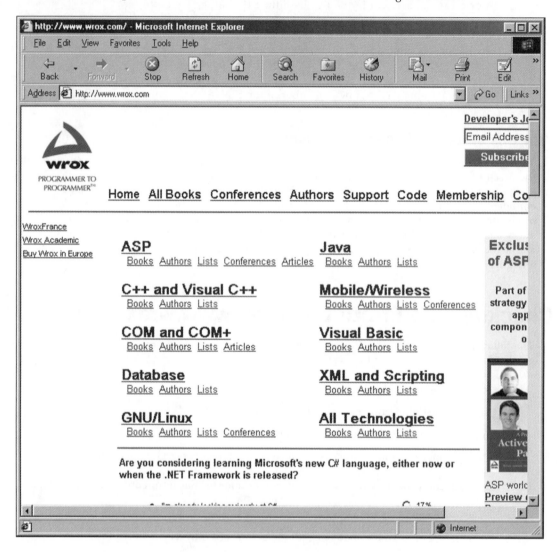

Then, on the following screen, shown below, click on New User. This will display a form. Fill in the details on the form and submit the details using the Register button at the bottom.

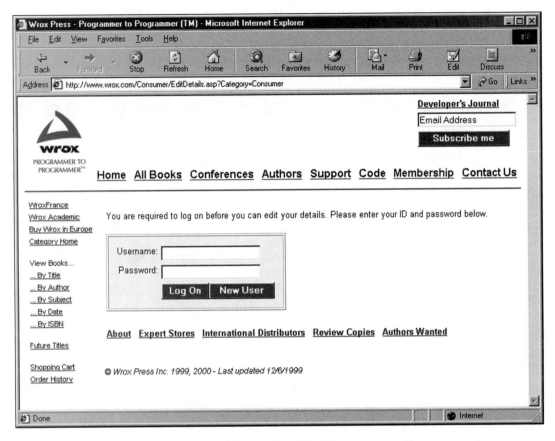

Type in your password once again and click Log On. The following page allows you to change your details if you need to, but now you're logged on, you have access to all the source code downloads and errata for the entire Wrox range of books.

Finding an Errata on the Web Site

Before you send in a query, you might be able to save time by finding the answer to your problem on our web site – http:\\www.wrox.com.

Each book we publish has its own page and its own errata sheet. You can get to any book's page by clicking on Support from the top navigation bar.

Halfway down the main support page is a drop-down box called Title Support. Simply scroll down the list until you see Book Errata. Select it and then hit Errata:

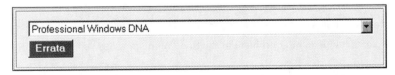

This will take you to the errata page for the book. Select the criteria by which you want to view the errata, and click the Apply criteria button. This will provide you with links to specific errata. For an initial search, you are advised to view the errata by page numbers. If you have looked for an error previously, then you may wish to limit your search using dates. We update these pages daily to ensure that you have the latest information on bugs and errors:

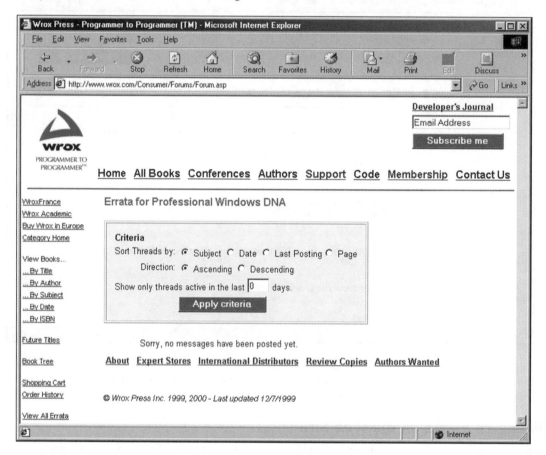

Add an Erratum: e-mail Support

If you wish to point out an erratum to put up on the web site or directly query a problem in the book page with an expert who knows the book in detail then e-mail support@wrox.com, with the title of the book and the last four numbers of the ISBN in the subject field of the e-mail. A typical e-mail should include the following things:

> The **name**, **last four digits of the ISBN** and **page number** of the problem in the Subject field.
>
> Your **name**, **contact info** and the **problem** in the body of the message.

We won't send you junk mail. We need the details to save your time and ours. If we need to replace a disk or CD we'll be able to get it to you straight away. When you send an e-mail it will go through the following chain of support:

Customer Support

Your message is delivered to one of our customer support staff who are the first people to read it. They have files on most frequently asked questions and will answer anything general immediately. They answer general questions about the book and the web site.

Editorial

Deeper queries are forwarded to the technical editor responsible for that book. They have experience with the programming language or particular product and are able to answer detailed technical questions on the subject. Once an issue has been resolved, the editor can post the errata to the web site.

The Authors

Finally, in the unlikely event that the editor can't answer your problem, s/he will forward the request to the author. We try to protect the author from any distractions from writing. However, we are quite happy to forward specific requests to them. All Wrox authors help with the support on their books. They'll mail the customer and the editor with their response, and again all readers should benefit.

What We Can't Answer

Obviously with an ever-growing range of books and an ever-changing technology base, there is an increasing volume of data requiring support. While we endeavor to answer all questions about the book, we can't answer bugs in your own programs that you've adapted from our code. So, while you might have loved the chapters on file handling, don't expect too much sympathy if you cripple your company with a routine which deletes the contents of your hard drive. But do tell us if you're especially pleased with the routine you developed with our help.

How to Tell Us Exactly What You Think

We understand that errors can destroy the enjoyment of a book and can cause many wasted and frustrated hours, so we seek to minimize the distress that they can cause.

You might just wish to tell us how much you liked or loathed the book in question. Or you might have ideas about how this whole process could be improved. In which case you should e-mail `feedback@wrox.com`. You'll always find a sympathetic ear, no matter what the problem is. Above all you should remember that we do care about what you have to say and we will do our utmost to act upon it.

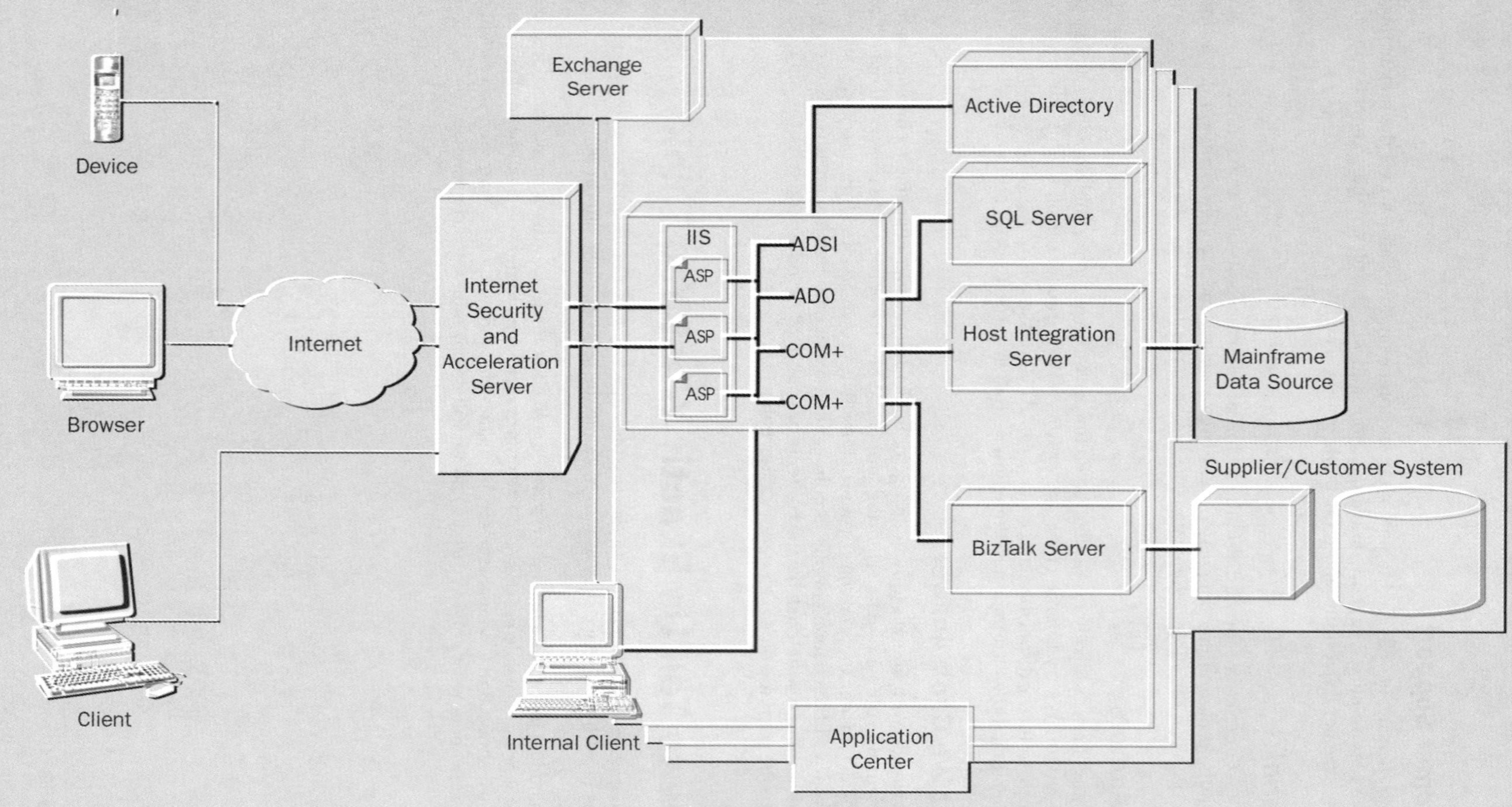
Device
Browser
Client
Internet
Internet Security and Acceleration Server
Exchange Server
IIS
ASP
ASP
ASP
ADSI
ADO
COM+
COM+
Active Directory
SQL Server
Host Integration Server
BizTalk Server
Mainframe Data Source
Supplier/Customer System
Internal Client
Application Center

Index

A Guide to the Index

The index is arranged hierarchically, in alphabetical order, with symbols preceding the letter A. Most second-level entries and many third-level entries also occur as first-level entries. This is to ensure that users will find the information they require however they choose to search for it.

A

Access
COM components, using, 552
access control, 605
access rights, 605
audit and access logging, 605
restricted access to secured objects, 605
Access Control List (ACL)
discretionary (DACL), 605
system (SACL), 605
made up of Access Control Entities (ACE), 605
access control tokens, 606
information contained, 606
Access COM object examples
data-centric functionality example, 553
validation functionality example, 557
Access object model, 552
diagram, 552
access violations, 712
invalid pointer is referenced, 712
memory access violation, 712
read or write from protected place in memory, 712
throws an exception, 712
Account view control
building, 529
ACID properties
atomic, 222
consistent, 222
durable, 222
isolated, 222
Activate() method
IObjectControl interface, 216
Active Directory, 444
access control, 446
security descriptors, 446
adding new objects, 601
ADSI, 444
attributes, 445, 446
can be included in global catalog, 447
can be indexed, 447
constraints, 447
organized into classes, 446
single or multi-valued, 446
synonymous with columns in database, 446

syntax, 446
Boolean, 446
integer, 446
numeric string, 446
authentication, 445
interactive logon, 445
network authentication, 446
COM+ security
delegation and impersonation, 636
containers representing organizations, 450
declaritive security, 600
definition, 445
diagram of relation with security services, 600
entities (objects) and containers diagram, 450
entities represent network resources, 450
extensibility, 454
global catalog, 447
group accounts, 446
hierarchy is flexible and configurable, 450
integration with DNS, 454
interoperability with other directory services, 454
nesting objects, 450
object orientated properties, inheritance, 450
objects have unique security descriptor, 600
policy-based administration, 454
replication, 454, 601
resource manager, does not have, 226
scalability, 454
security, fully integrated, 453
stores information about entities on a network, 445
types of objects stored
application information, 446
enterprise information, 446
user information, 446
Active Directory Schema
access control list, 449
class definitions
attributes present in instances of class, 449
mandatory attributes, 449
optional attributes, 449
structure rules determining parent class, 449
description of object, classes and attributes, 448
extensible, 449
can be updated dynamically, 449
Active Directory Schema Editor
adding attributes is non-reversible, 464
attributes and classes, 464

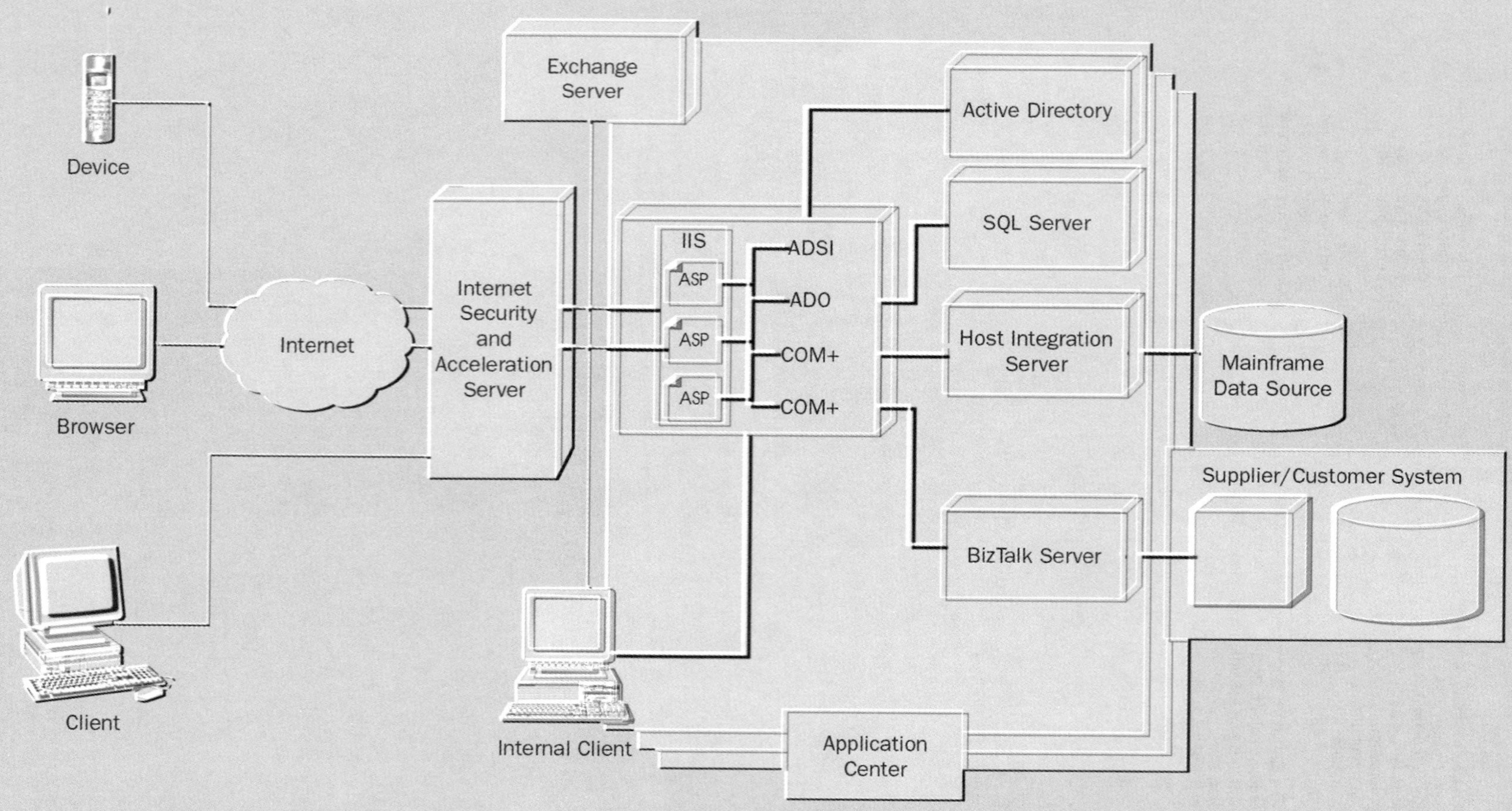
Device
Browser
Client
Internet
Internet Security and Acceleration Server
Exchange Server
IIS
ASP
ASP
ASP
ADSI
ADO
COM+
COM+
Active Directory
SQL Server
Host Integration Server
BizTalk Server
Mainframe Data Source
Supplier/Customer System
Internal Client
Application Center

Wrox Conferences provide timely, practical and code-heavy information for the programming community - true to the core values of Wrox Press. Focused on the latest technologies, our conferences all feature speakers who are authors, solution providers and industry professionals. They have one thing in common: they are all programmers. As such, they are able to share their knowledge with fellow programmers, teach their code, and offer practical solutions to today's developing needs.

What makes a Wrox Conference different?

● Wrox Conferences deliver Wrox-edited, code-heavy programming solutions, independent of commercial bias.

● Peer-to-Peer, the central ethic of Wrox, means that expert programmers share their knowledge and experience to enable delegates to build their skills and get ahead in programming.

Session details and registration information for Wrox Conferences can be found on:

http://www.wroxconferences.com

ASP and Web Development Tree

The Wrox ASP tree continues to offer an extensive ASP library for developers producing 	dynamic and interactive web pages, including those who wish to use ASP in conjunction with technologies such as ADO, COM+, XML and VB for the creation of scalable n-tier web solutions.

Most recently, Wrox published A Preview of ASP+, the very first title on Microsoft's latest version of the technology. An intrinsic part of the new .NET initiative, ASP+ is set to revolutionize the way

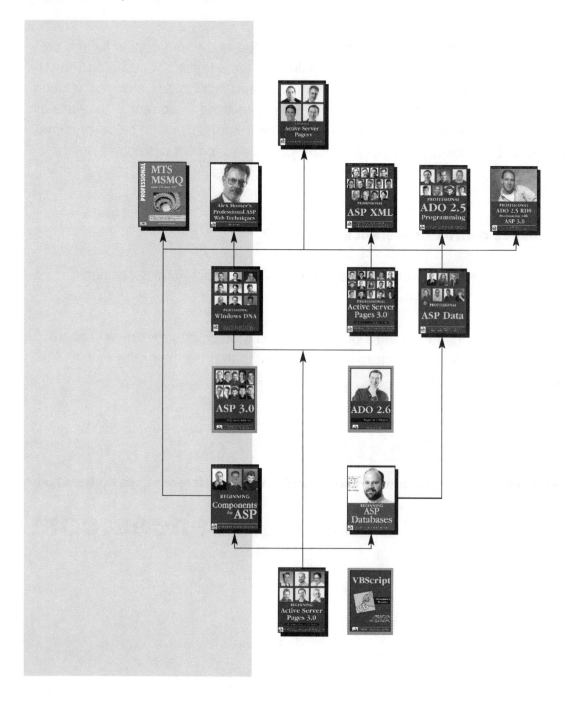

This is THE book in terms of teaching ASP and script-based programming from the ground up. It addresses all the fundamental questions including - what exactly ASP is, how to get up and running with ASP, how it actually works, and how ASP can be used to produce dynamic, interactive web applications. Beginning Active Server Pages 3.0 is for anyone with a grasp of HTML who wants to add more to their web pages. It also covers VBScript - a simple Internet programming language. This makes it the ideal first step for the aspiring web professional. It's also useful for more experienced programmers looking for a practical, no-non-sense introduction to ASP and programming for the web. If you're looking for a way to create attractive, intelligent web pages, or if you're just looking for a way to extend your HTML know-how, then ASP is an effective way to achieve your goals.

- A thorough grounding in the fundamentals of ASP
- Covers all the new developments that come with Windows 2000
- Shows how ASP integrates with the latest version of exciting new technologies such as ADO, COM+ and XML

David Buser
Jon Duckett
John Kauffman
Chris Ullman
Juan T. Llibre
David Sussman
Brian Francis.

1-861003-38-2

December 1999

US$ 39.99
C$ 59.95
£ 28.99

Summary of contents

ASP AND WEB DEVELOPMENT BOOKS

ASP 3.0 Programmer's Reference

Richard Anderson
Dan Denault
Brian Francis
Mathew Gibbs
Marco Gregorini
Alex Homer
Craig McQueen
Simon Robinson
John Schenken
Kevin Williams

1-861003-23-4

April 2000

US$ 34.99
C$ 52.95
£ 25.99

ASP is now the pivotal technology used by hundreds of thousands of web sites worldwide. Based upon the technique of combining HTML with server side scripting to create web pages dynamically, ASP along with IIS provides a significant amount of infrastructure and services that are needed to create simple or advanced intranet, Internet and extranet web applications with rich user interfaces and functionality. ASP 3.0 Programmer's Reference relates to ASP 3.0 as included with Windows 2000. However, because ASP is now a core part of so many Web-oriented features within Windows, this book covers a far wider area than just the ASP syntax, properties, methods and events. If you're writing an ASP application, this is a book you will refer to constantly.

Summary of Contents

IADO 2.6 Programmer's Reference provides a concise and comprehensive guide to the ways in which ADO 2.6 can be used in all kinds of applications. It demonstrates the use of ADO both in web applications written using ASP, and in compiled applications written using Visual Basic and other languages. It also includes a reference section for fast access to detailed lists of the properties, methods and events available in ADO. This book is a reference guide for the ADO programmer; it's primarily aimed at demonstrating and explaining the features of ADO 2.6 and the way that they can be used. As such, it isn't a beginner's guide - though if you have programmed any data-access applications in the past, you'll be able to use it to get up-to-speed with ADO.

- Explains ADO's continuing role at the heart of Windows DNA
- Covers the ADO 2.5 Record and Stream objects
- Describes the new features of ADO 2.6 and how you can use them with SQL Server 2000

David Sussman

1-861004-63-X

August 2000

US$ 29.99
C$ 44.95
£ 21.99

Summary of Contents

Richard Anderson
Alex Homer
Robert Howard
David Sussman

1-861004-75-3

July 2000

US$ 34.99
C$ 52.95
£ 25.99

This book comes complete with a supporting web site documenting new features, changes and updates to ASP+ through the product development lifecycle - **http://www.wrox.com/beta**

Online discussion of ASP+ is available at P2P - **http://p2p.wrox.com**

Microsoft's Active Server Pages technology is still a relatively new way to create dynamic web sites and applications. It has, however, evolved quickly to become the foremost tool in the Windows-oriented Web programmer's toolbox. Microsoft is currently working on the next generation of ASP, provisionally called ASP+ and part of the .NET strategy for web development. This is not just an update to ASP as we know it but instead an evolutionary leap in the whole concept of how ASP can provide a dynamic web development environment. This book covers a product that is still under development, and as such it is aimed at experienced ASP developers who are working at the leading edge, rather than the casual ASP developer or beginner. To make the most of this book, you should be experienced with ASP. You should also understand the general principles of using components, and have knowledge of Visual Basic (or VBScript).

This book was written as Microsoft was about to release the first preview version of ASP+. This release is almost feature complete, and stable enough for developers to begin learning about and using. While we can't guarantee that the final release version will be identical, you can be sure that almost all of the concepts, examples and explanations we provide are accurate within the timeframe of the first full version of ASP+.

- What ASP+ is, and how it makes building applications even easier
- Working with ASP+ pages and server-side controls
- Accessing data of all kinds in ASP+ pages, and an introduction to ADO+
- Using Web Services to provide asynchronous background services to applications
- An introduction to and demonstration of the ASP+ application framework
- Build and deploy custom ASP+ controls
- Combine the concepts discussed in the book into an ASP+ application
-

A Preview of Active Server Pages+ is the first in a series of books Wrox will publish covering the Microsoft.NET framework.

Professional Active Server Pages 3.0 is the next edition of the number one selling ASP book in the world; Professional Active Server Pages 2.0. This is a next edition covering all the new features that appear as part of Windows 2000 but it is also a completely new book in terms of content, recycling essentially nothing from the previous edition. Instead all the concepts are taken a step further for a more mature audience and ASP is considered in terms of an N-tier enterprise environment including extensive coverage of components, Index Server, ADO 2.5, XML, CDO, ADSI, and much more. This is your comprehensive guide to Active Server Pages 3.0 and the foundation for a whole new phase of web development.

- Changes in ASP 3.0, VBScript 5.0 and JScript 5.0
- Fundamentals of application development with ASP
- Securing your server and applications locally and globally

Summary of Contents

Richard Anderson
Chris Blexrud
Andrea Chiarelli
Dan Denault
Dino Esposito
Brian Francis
Mathew Gibbs
Alex Homer
Bill Kropog
Craig McQueen
George Reilly
Simon Robinson
John Schenken
Dean Sonderegger
David Sussman

1-861002-61-0

September 1999

US$ 59.99
C$ 89.95
£ 43.99

Alex Homer

1-861003-21-8

February 2000

US$ 49.99
C$ 74.95
£ 35.99

Getting started building a web site is simple enough - the hardware is cheap, the software is easy to install, and the market of potential visitors is huge. The problems come as your site starts to grow and mature. How do you maintain and keep control of a fast-growing and ever-changing site, while still keeping it informative, accurate, and error-free? The answer is automation; and the combination of Windows 2000 Server, Internet Information Server, a server-based data source, and Active Server Pages, makes it possible to design your site so that it's easy to manage and maintain. They even make it easier to add regular new content, and keep the site looking fresh.

- Real-world examples, taken from several busy public web sites
- Working code you can use directly, or modify to suit your own site
- Helps you add dynamic features to your web site quickly and painlessly

Summary of Contents

To build great web applications you need to drive your site with data, in whatever form it takes. This means data access and manipulation on the server to bring dynamic content to the end user. A well-constructed site will not only access data, but also manage it efficiently. Active Server Pages, together with ADO and OLEDB, can bring about this access to a myriad of data stores. Existing data access technologies have concentrated on relational databases, but ADO now brings the benefits of semi-structured data. So not only can you provide fast access to existing stores of data, but you can also access data in a less structured form, such as mail messages, web pages, XML and so on.

Professional ASP Data is aimed at those existing web programmers, perhaps just becoming familiar with ASP, who want to take the next step of driving their site from some form of data store; whether from a relational database, or from a less-structured form of data.

- Universal Data Access and ways of improving performance when accessing data
- OLEDB Providers and the various methods ADO allow to manipulate data
- Data access on the client and how data can be cached for quicker access

James De Carli
Richard Anderson
Simon Robinson
Martin Reid
Charles Fairchild
Rama Ramachandran
Joshua Parkin

1-861003-92-7

October 2000

US$ 49.99
C$ 74.95
£ 35.99

Programmer to Programmer

The support site from Wrox Press

Do you want to discuss ASP with programmers within your community? Is there a WAP query you need answered yesterday? Do you want access to "How To" and "Code Clinic" lists, moderated by experienced Wrox Technical Editors who are expert in the books you've consulted? P2P lists at http://p2p.wrox.com allow you to do just this. A free subscription service, with mailing lists ranging from ASP, Java, PHP, Perl, SQL, and VB, to the latest WAP and WML discussions, P2P will keep you current and in touch with your community and authors. You can choose to receive postings as they appear, in daily digests, or in weekly digests. For the solutions you need, just go to:

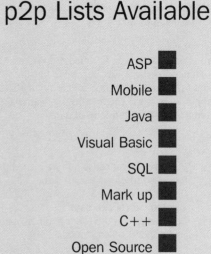

p2p Lists Available

ASP

Mobile

Java

Visual Basic

SQL

Mark up

C++

Open Source

http://p2p.wrox.com